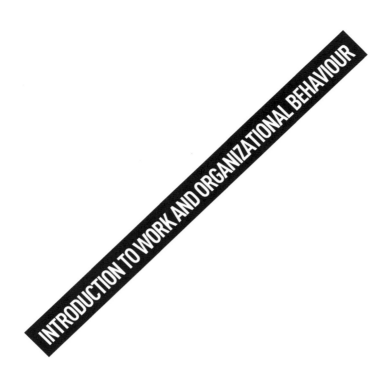

INTRODUCTION TO WORK AND ORGANIZATIONAL BEHAVIOUR

Message to students

Dear student,

Thank you for buying a copy of the popular and highly successful text *Introduction to Work and Organizational Behaviour*. This book is a new version rather than a third edition of what was published in 2010. Based upon extensive feedback from lecturers and students, we have: (1) updated the sources and information on all the topics discussed (with over 140 post-2010 references, more than 100 of which were published in 2013–15); (2) included a new chapter on organizational change; and (3) added new sections on research methods, personality and self, and managing conflict. In addition, there are 12 new **The Reality of Work** features and 12 new **Globalization and Organization Misbehaviour** features, as well as new **Links to Management** boxes that include videos of business professionals and academics discussing the connection between organizational behaviour and management practice in the workplace, with accompanying questions in the textbook. The new additions will ensure that *Introduction to Work and Organizational Behaviour* contains all the material and latest literature you need to pass your course with flying colours.

The book will provide you with an accessible but critical introduction to organizational behaviour. By 'critical' we mean that the text will help you reflect upon – and in your future professional life, perhaps act upon – how to make workplaces more effective given the challenges of global warming and resource depletion, and, we would add, more equitable as well. That is a tall order to say the least. But remember, change does not happen on its own, and a better understanding of the workplace is a vital starting point.

We have structured this third edition into four parts. Each chapter follows a similar structure in order to help you navigate the text easily. The **Key Concepts, Chapter Outlines** and **Chapter Learning Objectives** summarize the learning material that will be covered and the knowledge you will gain. The main text includes **Stop and Reflect** questions, which encourage you to think critically about key issues and the effects of human action and processes on people at work. Other features, such as **Globalization and Organization Misbehaviour** and **The Reality of Work**, help to illustrate current practices in organizational behaviour in the global economy. At the end of each chapter, you will find a **Summary** of the chapter content and **Chapter Review Questions** to help you reinforce and check your learning. There are also details for **Further Reading** to help you write an essay. The **Case Studies** are designed to provide useful illustrations of the concepts and issues raised in the chapter.

Looking for a higher mark? The digital resources accessible via the interactive ebook provide a rich array of multimedia content, including video interviews with managers, web assignments and critical insights to help you find out about the subject in more depth. There are also multiple choice questions and summary notes for each chapter to help you revise, a skill development guide to help you write essays, reports and presentations, and a glossary to help you check definitions of key terms. In addition, there are also OB in Film boxes which offer entertaining Insights into organizational behaviour through popular movies (accompanied by a film guide), and further examples of OB in the real world with OB in Focus boxes.

If you are not a native speaker of English, we have several features to help you get the best out of this book. The Online Resource Centre offers a feature entitled Vocab Checklist for English as a Second Language (ESL) Students that is a list of key terms to learn and check. It is designed primarily for non-native speakers of English, but all students may find it a useful reference point. You will also find some useful tips on learning from an ESL expert. You can access this website here: https://he.palgrave.com/companion/Bratton-Work-And-Organizational-Behaviour3/.

I would welcome any feedback on the book and any suggestions on how we can improve the next edition. Please contact me via my email address on the Online Resource Centre. Good luck with your studies.

John Bratton
Edinburgh

INTRODUCTION TO
WORK AND ORGANIZATIONAL BEHAVIOUR

THIRD EDITION

John Bratton

 macmillan education palgrave

This edition first published 2015 by
PALGRAVE

Palgrave in the UK is an imprint of Macmillan Publishers Limited, registered in England, company number 785998, of 4 Crinan Street, London, N1 9XW.

Palgrave Macmillan in the US is a division of St Martin's Press LLC, 175 Fifth Avenue, New York, NY 10010.

Palgrave is a global imprint of the above companies and is represented throughout the world.

Palgrave® and Macmillan® are registered trademarks in the United States, the United Kingdom, Europe and other countries.

ISBN: 978–1–137–40868–6

This book is printed on paper suitable for recycling and made from fully managed and sustained forest sources. Logging, pulping and manufacturing processes are expected to conform to the environmental regulations of the country of origin.

A catalogue record for this book is available from the British Library.

A catalog record for this book is available from the Library of Congress.

Library of Congress Cataloging-in-Publication Data

Bratton, John.
  Introduction to work and organizational behaviour / John Bratton. -- Third edition.
    pages cm
  ISBN 978-1-137-40868-6 (paperback)
  1. Organizational behavior. 2. Psychology, Industrial. I. Title.
  HD58.7.B73 2015
  302.3'5--dc23
                              2015014218

Typeset by Aardvark Editorial Limited, Metfield, Suffolk.

To my grandchildren, Owen and Colbie

Contents in brief

Contents

Figures and tables

Figures

Tables

About the author

John Bratton is Adjunct Professor at Athabasca University, Canada, and visiting professor at Edinburgh Napier University, UK. He was the first Director of the Workplace Learning Research Unit at the University of Calgary, and has served on the faculties of several other universities. His research interests span work and employment issues, and he was a member of the editorial board of the *Journal of Workplace Learning*, the *Canadian Journal for the Study of Adult Education* and *Leadership*. In addition to authoring this book, he is co-author (with Jeff Gold) of *Human Resource Management: Theory and Practice* (2012); co-author (with David Denham) of *Capitalism and Classical Social Theory* (2014); co-author (with Peter Sawchuk, J. Helms-Mills and T. Pyrch) of *Workplace Learning: A Critical Introduction* (2004); co-author (with Keith Grint and Debra Nelson) of *Organizational Leadership* (2005); and author of *Japanization of Work: Managerial Studies in the 1990s* (1992).

About the contributors

Bob Barnetson is an Associate Professor of Labour Relations at Athabasca University, Canada. His research interests centre on the political economy of workplace injury and vulnerable workers. He is the author of *The Political Economy of Workplace Injury in Canada* (2010) and various journal articles addressing agricultural workers, migrant workers and child labour in Canada.

David Denham is an Honorary Research Fellow at Wolverhampton University, UK, where he taught a variety of sociology courses over a career spanning 35 years. He has published articles on the sociology of law, criminology and the sociology of sport, and is co-author (with John Bratton) of *Capitalism and Classical Social Theory* (2014) and with Lorraine Wolhuter and Neil Olley of *Victimology: Victimization and Victims' Rights* (2008).

Karen Densky lectures in English as a second language and ESL teacher training at Thompson Rivers University, Kamloops, BC, Canada. Her research and teaching interests include curriculum and methodology for the ESL classroom. She has worked in teacher training programmes in Chile and Greenland. She is the author of *Creativity, Culture and Communicative Language Teaching* (2008).

Gretchen Fox completed Master's and PhD degrees in cultural anthropology at the University of North Carolina at Chapel Hill, USA. Her doctoral research focused on understanding cultural and economic approaches to natural resource use and management by Mi'kmaq First Nation people in Atlantic Canada. She is currently an Anthropologist and Impact Assessment Analyst at Fox Cultural Research.

David MacLennan teaches in the Department of Sociology and Anthropology at Thompson Rivers University, Canada. His main research interest is the sociology of learning. Current projects include research to promote environmental literacy and increase awareness of the cultural significance of local landscapes.

Lori Rilkoff holds the position of Human Resources Director at the City of Kamloops, BC, Canada, and is a former lecturer in HRM at Thompson Rivers University in Kamloops. She acquired her MSc in Training and HRM from the University of Leicester, Centre for Labour Market Studies. Lori's professional interest focuses on the practical application of HRM theory in the workplace.

Message to lecturers

Dear Lecturer,

Thank you for adopting the third edition of *Introduction to Work and Organizational Behaviour*, which we prepared in 2014 when it looked like Britain was emerging from the longest economic slump in a century. By the fourth quarter, however, there were pessimistic forecasts and warnings of a slowdown. This prompted the Bank of England's Chief Economist to describe Britain's recovery as 'jobs-rich, but pay-poor'. In the same month, it was reported that over 400,000 NHS staff in England were engaged in industrial action – the first action over pay in more than three decades.

We have tried to make connections between the economic recession and austerity economics and organizational behaviour in a way that we hope your students will find engaging and relevant. Although the book has been written to fulfil the needs of students completing an introductory undergraduate organizational behaviour module, it offers a counternarrative to mainstream organizational behaviour texts. Analytically, it privileges a concern with conflict-oriented discourse and how organizational behaviour serves, or neglects to serve, particular interests. In sharp contrast to many introductory texts, it encourages students to be sensitive to context, power and inequality in the contemporary workplace. Visit https://he.palgrave.com/companion/Bratton-Work-And-Organizational-Behaviour3/ for a video that explains this approach in more detail.

Palgrave subjected the manuscript to an extensive peer review process, and I am extremely grateful to the 20 reviewers from the UK, Denmark, Sweden, South Africa, Lebanon, New Zealand, USA and United Arab Emirates who made many valuable suggestions for revisions and additional material. The review process has created a new version rather than a third edition of the 2010 book. I have updated the information on all the topics discussed (with over 140 post-2010 references, more than 100 of which were published in 2013–15); included a new chapter on organizational change; and added new sections on research methods, personality and self, and managing conflict. There are 12 new **The Reality of Work** features, 12 new **Globalization and Organization Misbehaviour** features and, new to this edition, **Links to Management** boxes with online videos of business professionals and academics discussing the connection between organizational behaviour and management practice, with accompanying questions in the textbook. More detail on this is provided in the preface.

To add more value for your students I suggest you make reference to the book during your lectures, for instance identifying relevant sections of the chapter, referring to the various pedagogical features, as well as asking students to attempt the end-of-chapter case study in preparation for your seminar or in-class discussion. The interactive ebook includes a range of valuable multimedia resources, including videos and quizzes, that bring OB to life and help students engage with the subject.

As is inevitable, some high-quality articles and books may have inadvertently been omitted, so I would welcome suggestions of material to include and feedback to improve the next edition. Please contact me via email address on the book's website.

John Bratton
Edinburgh

Preface

Welcome *to Introduction to Work and Organizational Behaviour*. This book has been written specifically to fulfil the needs of introductory undergraduate courses for an engaging, accessible analysis of behaviour in work organizations, which draws on the two major human sciences of psychology and sociology. It assumes no previous knowledge of psychology or sociology by the student, practitioner or general reader.

In the era of globalized capitalism, textbooks on organizational behaviour date quickly. It is 5 years since we were writing the second edition of this book, but the synchronized global financial crisis, economic recession and, in the UK, austerity economics, as well as our own thoughts and the suggestions from users for improving the book, have already necessitated a major revision. The founding principles of the book remain unchanged – yet the socioeconomic context in which we all find ourselves has fundamentally shifted.

Context

As we argued in the first and second editions of this book, organizational behaviour is socially embedded and is profoundly influenced by contextual processes. As in the Great Depression of 1929–33, and the recessions of 1973–75, 1980–83 and 1990–93, the 2008–09 global economic meltdown and its aftermath continues to cause a psychological and social meltdown: people, whether employed or not, feel extremely vulnerable and afraid for their futures, and inequality is increasing. In 2014, the 85 richest people on the planet, about the same number that could ride on a double-decker bus, have, according to Oxfam, accumulated as much wealth, £1 trillion, between them as half of the world's poorest 3.5 billion people. As the rich have become richer, UK workers have suffered the longest and most severe decline in real earnings since the Victorian era, 1865–67 (Doward and Bissett, 2014). We make the case that understanding issues of inequality and equity across the major social divisions of society as it relates to work is a prerequisite for a deep understanding of organizational behaviour. For example, inequality affects employees' health, levels of trust and performance, and ultimately damages business (Dorling, 2014; Piketty, 2014; Stiglitz, 2013). In short, we live and work in an interconnected reality. Hence organizational behaviour in the twenty-first century is incomprehensible without understanding the effects of global capitalism and the response of nation states to the economic crisis.

The immediacy of the current events can easily distract us from the more persistent trends and features of organizational life. Work configurations and employment practices cannot be uncoupled from national and global contexts. Thus, although the monumental failure of management in a deregulated system has put management education in business schools (Currie et al., 2010) in general, and some aspects of organizational behaviour in particular, under critical scrutiny, the core attributes of work and how the employment relationship is managed remain unchanged. These attributes have been there since the era of globalization – the 1990s – and we examined them in the second edition of the book: the growth of non-standard or precarious employment, downsizing, the decline in trade union power and influence, deregulation, work intensification and consequential work-related stress.

We emphasized in 2010 that employers and managers operate within a wider institutional, cultural and social context, and that changing the way they behave requires a fundamental change in organizational context and culture. Following reports of white-collar crime and highly unethical and, in the case of US and UK bankers, reckless behaviour, we wrote then that the solution did not lie in removing 'a few bad apples' but in 'changing the way organizations are regulated by government, changing the way managers are compensated, and by changing the values that ultimately prevail in society'.

We believe that the solution to the problems caused by the Anglo-Saxon neo-liberal political economy lies in fundamental changes to the system. This is not to underestimate the management roots of the global crisis. North American and UK business schools are partly to blame for the global crisis. For the most part, they have been uncritical advocates and 'cheerleaders' of the 'neo-liberal' Anglo-Saxon model, and ultimately they have a responsibility for educating a new cadre of managers who can help to change the system. The new features of this third edition are set out below, but the broad aims remain the same as in the first: to encourage critical thinking and provide insight into and understanding of the sociology and psychology of work and the behaviour of people in work groups and organizations. We hope to make a modest contribution to developing critical pedagogy in business schools that will make organizations more effective in a variety of ways – more productive, more ecologically sustainable, more satisfying, more equitable – and perhaps even help to forge more democratic workplaces through increased employee voice in the future.

Critical approach

Our approach to explaining contemporary organizational behaviour is rather different. We cover the three levels of analysis – individual, group and organizational – found in traditional organizational behaviour textbooks, and examine the concepts and issues that comprise the core of an introductory course in the subject. However, we depart from 'mainstream' texts on organizational behaviour in three important respects.

First, we attempt to take the student of organizational behaviour into realms rarely explored in most undergraduate courses in management. We try to offer an intellectual journey that draws on familiar areas from workplace psychology, but also takes readers to unfamiliar paradigms and research from the realm of sociology, anthropology and politics. Our approach to studying organizational behaviour privileges the idea found in C. Wright Mills' (1959/2000) 'sociological imagination' and the importance it places upon locating human problems and management practices in context: that history and the interplay of people and society matter – that the work organization is embedded in the particularities of time and society, and in the dynamics of the local and the global. Our intention is to draw upon both mainstream *and* critical perspectives, as a requirement for generating a more eclectic interdisciplinary dialogue.

This is hardly an original orientation – but in adopting a more critical perspective, we believe this book embraces a more educative approach to studying organizational behaviour. It seeks to challenge students to question, to debate, to seek multicausality and to develop their own understanding of organizational behaviour. This is also an important element of our notion of a 'critical' approach, and is enhanced by the book's many teaching and learning features, discussed later in this Preface.

Second, we have brought together an eclectic selection of academic material and behaviour practices from the European Community, North America, Australia, New Zealand, the Middle East and parts of Asia. Thus, in an ever more globalized world in which managers and the managed are increasingly expected to be sensitive to cultural diversity, *Introduction to Work and Organizational Behaviour* offers students a more global appreciation of behaviour at work.

Third, this book emphasizes six core themes: competing standpoints, change in the workplace, the relationship between the self and the social, equality/equity, diversity and social power. In many ways, it is these core themes, and asking 'Cui bono' – To whom is the benefit? – that constitute and support what we understand as a 'critical' approach to work and organizational behaviour (Bratton and Gold, 2015).

Introduction to Work and Organizational Behaviour is political in the sense suggested by Karen Ashcroft and Brenda Allen (2003):

> As they orient students to the field and its defining areas of theory and research, textbooks perform a political function. That is, they advance narratives of collective identity, which invite students to internalize a particular *map* of central and marginal issues of legitimate and dubious projects. (p. 28)

As suggested above, knowledge is not neutral, shaping our understanding of it in particular ways. The 'map' we wish to lay out to students will, we hope, enable students to navigate through competing narratives and counternarratives on organizational behaviour. As such, we hope the reader will develop a more holistic and nuanced awareness of the forces and processes shaping the behaviour of people in the contemporary workplace. It is the commitment to educate, not simply to 'train' employable skills, that further differentiates *Introduction to Work and Organizational Behaviour* from mainstream textbooks.

New for this third edition

As we have already mentioned, the new edition was prepared during the longest economic slump facing Britain for a century. Wherever possible, we have tried to make connections between the global and national crises, labour market and employment trends and organizational behaviour in a way that we hope will be interesting and relevant for students. Users of the second edition of the book will notice that Bob Barnetson and David Denham have become contributors to the text. Bob's **Globalization and Organization Misbehaviour** and David's **The Reality of Work** vignettes are designed to stimulate interest, provide critical insight or act as a discussion point on the material. This third edition also includes new insights from current academic literature.

Suggestions from all the reviewers have been included in this third edition. Broadly speaking, the book retains the unique and successful approach of the previous editions – but this new edition has been supplemented with a range of new features:

- A new Chapter 18 on organizational change has been added, which draws on much of the material from the preceding chapters.
- 12 new **The Reality of Work** vignettes provide practical and thought-provoking examples of the interconnection between social context and organizational behaviour.
- 12 new **Globalization and Organization Misbehaviour** vignettes explore organizational behaviour outside the UK.
- New **Links to Management** online videos feature business professionals and academics discussing the connection between organizational behaviour theory and management practice in the workplace, with accompanying questions in the textbook.
- An extensively reworked Chapter 1, introducing contemporary organizational behaviour, provides an accessible entry into the field and emphasizes the value of studying organizational behaviour.
- The new Chapter 9 on diversity and people management demonstrates the practical relevance of organizational behaviour theory and research to the world of work, focusing on recruitment, rewards and training. It can also be used to provide an introduction to a more specialized module on human resource management.
- There are expanded or new sections on the following subjects: research methods (Chapter 1), the history of management thought (Chapter 3), the social construction

of the self (Chapter 4), emotion (Chapter 5), inequality (Chapter 8), reward practice (Chapter 9), programmed and non-programmed decisions (Chapter 13), the management of conflict (Chapter 14), boundaryless and virtual organizations (Chapter 15) and skills and technology (Chapter 16).

- The chapters have also been reordered and formed into a new four-part structure designed to create a better fit with organizational behaviour modules.
- An interactive ebook provides access to embedded mulitmedia content to enhance learning.

Content

Introduction to Work and Organizational Behaviour is divided into four major parts, based on the traditional division of behavioural studies. These parts are of course interconnected, but we believe that the division provides a convenient heuristic (teaching) device to guide the reader through the learning material. A brief outline of each part is given below.

Part 1 examines the nature of contemporary organizational behaviour, gives a summary of the historical dimensions of paid work, and presents concepts and theories. This provides a basis for evaluating the competing perspectives on what determines and influences the behaviour of people in organizations.

Part 2 turns its attention to how various individual differences affect individual behaviour in the workplace. Individuals have different personalities, perceptions and learning styles. The chapters here emphasize that the work experiences of women, visible minorities and the disabled may be different from those of white male employees.

Part 3 examines some of the important social processes that take place in the context of work groups and explores leadership, communication and decision-making processes. It also examines power, politics and conflict in the workplace.

Part 4 shifts the focus once again, this time to explore how organizational design, technology and culture influence social relations and the behaviour of people in organizations. A new chapter critically examines theories and the practice of organization change.

References

Ashcroft, K. and Allen, B. (2003) 'The radical foundation of organizational communication,' *Communication Theory*, 13, pp. 5–38.

Bratton, J. and Gold, J. (2015) 'Towards critical human resource management education (CHRME): a sociological imagination approach', *Work, Employment and Society*, doi: 10.1177/0950017014545266.

Currie, G., Knights, D. and Starkey, K. (2010) 'Introduction: a post-crisis critical reflection on business schools', *British Journal of Management*, 21, pp. S1–5.

Dorling, D. (2014) *Inequality and the 1%*, London: Verso.

Doward, J. and Bissett, G. (2014) 'Pay squeeze worst since Victorian age, study finds', *The Observer*, October 12, p. 6.

Piketty, T. (2014) *Capital in the Twenty-First Century*, Cambridge, MA: Belknap Press.

Stiglitz, J. (2013) *The Price of Inequality*, London: Penguin.

Treanor, J. and Farrell, S. (2014) 'London's super-rich dominate as UK leads G7 economies for inequality', *The Guardian*, October 15, p. 8.

Wright Mills, C. (1959/2000) *The Sociological Imagination* (40th anniv. edn), New York: Oxford University Press.

A tour of the book

For quick reference and revision ▶

Provide an overview of the chapter's content and aims

introduction

The mantra of mainstream contemporary management is 'Our employees are our most valuable resource' (Spencer and Kelly, 2013: 12). Since the late 1980s, human resource management scholarship has tended to emphasize the importance of investing in learning and in human resource development (Gold et al., 2013), primarily because it is regarded as a catalyst to the achievement of the organization's business objectives developed at the Tavistock Institute in London. The lessons of the Tavistock research were, however, disregarded in traditional bureaucratic organizations, with the majority of employees being given limited opportunity to learn on the job and to go on learning. Orthodox management wisdom viewed the factory or office as a place to work, not to learn. Learning was an activity carried out at school, college and university before

◀ Show you the relevance of each topic and how it links to the real world

Videos featuring business professionals talking about key concepts at work ▶

Elizabeth Douglas holds the position of Learning and Development Manager at an Edinburgh Care and Sheltered Housing Association, Scotland, and is a former Human Resource Manager with over 20 years' experience. She acquired her MA in Languages and Arts from the University of Aberdeen and, after postgraduate training, entered management with the Great Western Railway Company. Elizabeth's current project is designing and delivering a programme on diversity in the workplace.

In the ebook access the video to watch Elizabeth talking about recruitment and diversity at her organization, and then think about the following question:
- How do key adult learning principles guide the design of a training programme on diversity in the workplace?

stop...
When was the last time you felt that you had really learned something? Recall that occasion, reflect on it, and try to relate it step by step to the experiential learning model.
...and reflect

◀ Questions for you to think about

explicit knowledge: knowledge that is ordered and can be communicated between people

tacit knowledge: knowledge embedded in our actions and ways of thinking, and transmitted only through observation and experience

◀ Definitions of key terms

For you to explore further ▶

IN THE EBOOK ACCESS AN **OB IN FOCUS** BOX TO READ THE
OB IN FOCUS BOX 'THE LEARNING AGE: A RENAISSANCE FOR A NEW BRITAIN'.

Source: Image Source

Do internships lead to paid work?

For thousands of recent graduates, unpaid or low-paid work (internships) has become an obligatory stage between higher education and an entry-level job with a company, yet the rise in informal internships has occurred alongside rising unemployment among young people. Internships are concentrated in

majority (59 per cent) thought the system was exploitative, but they accepted it as necessary in order to get a job.

Interns saw work experience as providing benefits such as learning through performing particular tasks, gaining from hands-on experience, working alongside experienced staff and meeting 'the right people' who could get them a job. Both interns and stakeholders referred to the repetitive nature or the irrelevancy of tasks. Only 45 per cent of respondents with work experience found that it led to paid work. Trade unionists and student bodies thought that it was not just the lack of economic capital that prevented people from obtaining work experience, but also their lack of contact with social networks, leading to social exclusion.

Unpaid work, according to the trade unionists interviewed, led to redundancies and the replacement of temporary contracts wit…

Provide practical examples of the interconnection between organizational behaviour and society ◀

Give an insight into organizational behaviour issues across the world ▶

globalization & organization misbehaviour

Source: Stockbyte/Punchstock

Skills shortage and corporate (non) investment in training

Politicians and business leaders often claim that there is a skills shortage in the workforce. For example, Canadian Prime Minister Stephen Harper has repeatedly asserted that producing more skilled workers is 'the biggest challenge our country faces':

> For whatever reason, we know that peoples' choices, in terms of the education system, tend to lead us to … a

attitudes, capabilities and mobility of jobless workers. The question of whether there are any productive, decent jobs for those workers to fill is downplayed or ignored altogether. The problem is, in other words, not with unemployment. The problem is with the unemployed (Stanford, 2013).

Interestingly, employers' efforts to resolve the skills shortage are modest at best:

> Despite the skills shortage, half of employers said they make 'not much effort' to recruit from under-represented groups, such as aboriginal Canadians, visible minorities, and the disabled. … Asked about the high rate of youth unemployment, nearly one in five employers said the main cause is that young people are too demanding, while a slightly smaller number cited lack of experience. (Flavelle, 2014)

Chapter summary

- There has been a growing interest in learning in organizations, as contemporary management thinking and practice emphasize notions of knowledge work, flexibility, core competencies and sustainable competitive advantage through learning.

- Learning can be defined as a relatively permanent change in

- The third classical approach we examined related to social-learning theories. This suggests that individuals learn and develop through observational learning. That is, people learn by observing others – role models – whom they believe are credible and knowledgeable.

Help you to check and revise your learning ◀

Encourage discussion and debate ▶

Chapter review questions

1 What part do feedback and reinforcement play in the approaches to learning?
2 Why is workplace learning important for managers and workers?
3 What are the main differences between the cognitive and behaviourist perspectives on learning?

4 Why is a psychologically driven approach to workplace learning controversial?
5 What can managers do to encourage creativity and innovation?

Further reading

Billett, S. and Choy, S. (2012) 'Learning through work: emerging perspectives and new challenges', *Journal of Workplace Learning*, 25(4), pp. 264–76.
Collin, K. (2009) 'Work-related identity in individual and social learning at work', *Journal of Workplace Learning*, 21(1/2), pp. 23–35.

Gold, J. (2013) 'Workplace Learning and Knowledge Management', pp. 237–58 in J. Gold, R. Holden, J. Stewart, P. Iles and J. Beardwell (eds), *Human Resource Development: Theory and Practice* (2nd edn), Basingstoke: Palgrave Macmillan.
Guidice, R. M., Thompson Heames, J. and Wang, S. (2009) 'The

Help you read around the subject ◀

Illustrate some of the major concepts discussed ▶

Chapter case study: Learning to be green in New Zealand

The setting

In the twenty-first century, New Zealand is facing environmental issues similar to those of many countries: using water more sustainably, managing marine resources, reducing waste and improving energy efficiency. It is particularly concerned about the decline of its unique plants, animals and ecosystems. The country

Recently, the Ministry for the Environment announced the Sustainable Management Fund, which provides funding to support community groups, businesses and local government in taking practical actions that produce long-term environmental benefits, encourage proactive partnerships and promote commu-

Digital Resources

Interactive ebook

Included free with the print copy of this book is an interactive ebook.

The perfect companion to the print book, the ebook replicates the pages of the book and offers all the versatility you would expect, such as bookmarking and easy searching, but also offers added embedded multimedia content right at your fingertips, including:

- *Critical insight* boxes to demonstrate other perspectives on key topics
- *OB in focus* boxes to illustrate or supplement important issues explored in the textbook
- *OB in film* features to provide an entertaining illustration and exploration of organizational behaviour concepts and issues
- *Web-based assignments* to bring organizational behaviour to life

- *Vocab checklist for ESL students* to help non-native speakers of English get to grips with unfamiliar terminology, and guidance on getting the best out of the book for non-native speakers of English.
- A *glossary*.
- *Web links* and a *research guide* to aid further investigation
- *Multiple choice questions* to help check your progress and consolidate learning
- A *film guide* exploring organizational behaviour through popular film
- Video interviews with practitioners from private and public sector organizations discussing the links between organizational behaviour theory and management practice.

Elizabeth Douglas holds the position of Learning and Development Manager at an Edinburgh Care and Sheltered Housing Association, Scotland, and is a former Human Resource Manager with over 20 years' experience. She acquired her MA in Languages and Arts from the University of Aberdeen and, after postgraduate training, entered management with the Great Western Railway Company. Elizabeth's current project is designing and delivering a programme on diversity in the workplace.

In the ebook access the video to watch Elizabeth talking about recruitment and diversity at her organization, and then think about the following question:

- How do key adult learning principles guide the design of a training programme on diversity in the workplace?

Online Resource Centre

The Online Resource Centre (https://he.palgrave.com/companion/Bratton-Work-And-Organizational-Behaviour3/) hosts a number of additional resources to aid teaching and learning.

Teaching Resources

Lecturers who adopt the book on their course gain access to a selection of password protected resources to help plan and deliver their teaching:

- a *lecturer guide* including teaching ideas, guideline answers to Stop and Reflect questions and Chapter Review Questions, and case study debriefs
- *Chapter research questions* to set as homework
- *PowerPoint presentations* including figures and tables for every chapter

- a *testbank* including over 800 multiple choice questions
- a *sample course outline* and sample final exam paper
- *Lecturer notes on the film guide,* which explores organizational behaviour through popular movies
- guidance on using the book with English as a second language students.
- *additional case studies and vignettes*
- *chapter research questions*

Learning resources

For students a number of tools are provided to help you succeed in your OB course:

- a *Skills Development Guide* offering detailed guidance on completing assignment, including critical essays and oral presentations

- *Research Guide* offering tips on how to find information
- *Learning tips* for ESL students
- *chapter commentaries* for Chinese language speakers

Author's acknowledgements

To write and update a critical book on organizational behaviour is an audacious undertaking, since it is necessary to achieve a balance between respecting the classical canons covering organizational behaviour, labour process theory and critical management, and introducing new contemporary themes. This task is even more difficult when it involves taking over the responsibility for chapters written by friends and colleagues. Readers familiar with the two previous editions of this book will notice that Peter Sawchuk, Carolyn Forshaw, Militza Callinan and Martin Corbett are no longer co-authors. Their academic interests have gone in other directions. In writing this third edition, therefore, I am indebted to them for permitting me to take over the reins for their chapters. I have attempted to respect their considerable work and the perspective they bring to the field while at the same time updating, adding, deleting and rearranging material.

On behalf of the contributors to the book, I also wish to thank other people. First, to those who have reviewed and given considerable constructive feedback at various stages of the writing process. I wish to thank:

- Michael Allvin, Uppsala University, Sweden
- Omar Belkhodja, American University of Sharjah, United Arab Emirates
- Michelle Bligh, Claremont Graduate University, USA
- Anthony Boland, Newcastle University, UK
- Anne Bøllingtoft, Aarhus University, Denmark
- Chris Bond, University of Roehampton, UK
- John Chandler, University of East London, UK
- Carole Elliott, Durham University, UK
- Doug Engelbrecht, University of KwaZulu-Natal, South Africa
- Edward Granter, University of Manchester, UK
- Claire Hookham Williams, University of Hull, UK
- Ismail Hussein, Lebanese American University, Lebanon
- Shova Thapa Karki, University of Sussex, UK
- Orla McVicar, Glasgow Caledonian University, UK
- Sue Miller, Durham University, UK
- Helen Mortimore, Plymouth University, UK
- Joanne Murphy, Queen's University Belfast, UK
- Helen Nicholson, University of Auckland, New Zealand
- Mia Pranoto, King's College London, UK
- David Robotham, De Montfort University, UK

Second, this edition contains case studies, new features on The Reality of Work and Globalization and Organization Misbehaviour, and also online video vignettes of practitioners talking about their experience of management. The cases, features and video clips demonstrate how organizational behaviour is applied (or not applied) to the practice of management. Their contributions bring organizational behaviour to life. I wish to give my special thanks to:

- Chiara Amati, Keil Centre, UK
- Bob Barnetson, Athabasca University, Canada
- Andrew Brady, Union Solidarity International, UK
- David Denham, formerly University of Wolverhampton, UK
- Elizabeth Douglas, UK
- Gretchen Fox, Fox Cultural Research, Canada
- Dan Haley, Canada
- Len Hutt, Thompson Rivers University, Canada
- Alison Jones, Alison Jones Business Services, UK
- Ruth Law, UK
- David MacLennan, Thompson Rivers University, Canada
- Tony McGrory, UK
- David McGuire, Edinburgh Napier University, UK
- Gill Musson, University of Sheffield, UK
- Iain Nelson, UK
- Lori Rilkoff, City of Kamloops, Canada
- Ian Roper, University of Middlesex, UK
- Susanne Tietze, University of Bradford, UK
- John Wilson, UK

I would also like to thank my daughter, Amy, for assistance with the editing process, and my son, Andrew, for his help in researching online sources and for inspiring me to write about sustainability in the workplace. My greatest debt is to my partner, Carolyn Forshaw, who has given me unconditional support during the years over which this book and previous editions were written. Finally, I would like to acknowledge the support, creativity and hard work of the talented and dedicated editorial team at Palgrave, in particular my development manager, Amy Grant and my publisher, Ursula Gavin. Thanks, too, to Carrie Walker, who copy-edited the book, Alison Waggitt, who indexed it, Jim Weaver who designed it, and the team at Aardvark Editorial (Linda Norris for project management, Julie Lankester for artwork and Jo Booley for page layout).

John Bratton
Edinburgh

Publisher acknowledgements

The author and publishers are grateful to the following for permission to reproduce copyright material:

Ashgate Publishing for the adapted use of Figure 1.7 from © *Sociological Paradigms and Organisational Analysis*, by Gibson Burrell and Gareth Morgan, 1985, Ashgate.

Emerald Group Publishing for Figure 7.3 Three aspects of reciprocal learning from Bamber, D. and Castka, P. (2006) 'Personality, organizational orientations and self-reported learning outcomes', Journal of Workplace Learning, 18(1&2), pp. 73–92. © Emerald Group Publishing Limited.

Harvard Business Review for Figure 15.9 Divisional organizational structure based on strategic business units from Hamel, G. and Prahalad, C. K. (1994) *Competing for the Future*, Boston, Mass.: Harvard Business School Press, p. 279; and Table 5.2 Emotional Intelligence Domains and Competencies from D. Goleman, R. Boyatzis and A. McKee (2013) Primal Leadership, Unleashing the Power of Emotional Intelligence, p. 39. With permission from Harvard Business Review.

Penguin Books Ltd. for the adapted Figure 6.9 Three poles for the measurement of well-being from *Psychology at work*, 5th edition, edited by Peter Warr (Penguin Books, 2002), p. 3. Copyright © Peter B. Warr and contributors, 1996, 2002; and the adapted Figure 8.1 Income inequality in selective countries from *The Spirit Level: Why Equality is Better for Everyone*, by R. Wilkinson and K. Pickett (Penguin Books, 2010). Copyright © R. Wilkinson and K. Pickett, 2010. Reproduced by permission of Penguin Books Ltd.

Polity Press and University of California Press for Figure 14.1 Giddens' model of power from Giddens, A. (1985) *A Contemporary Critique of Historical Materialism, Volume 2: The Nation State and Violence*, Cambridge: Polity Press. UK and World rights granted by Polity Press, US, Canadian and dependencies rights granted by University of California Press.

SAGE publications for Fig 10.4: Five phases of group development, from Tuckman, B. and Jensen, M. (1977) 'Stages of small group development revisited', *Group and Organization Management*, 2, pp. 419–27. (Vol 2, No. 4). Reprinted by Permission of SAGE Publications; and Table 1.1 from Conger, J. A. and Kanungo, R. N. (1998) *Charismatic Leadership in Organizations*, Thousand Oaks, CA: Sage.

Taylor and Francis Ltd for the adapted Figure 9.7 Modelling the HRM–performance linkage from Paul, A. K. and Anantharaman, R. N. (2003) 'Impact of people management practices on organizational performance: analysis of a causal model', *International Journal of Human Resource Management*, 14(7), pp. 1246–66. Taylor and Francis. Reprinted by permission of the publisher (Taylor & Francis Ltd, http://www.tandfonline.com); and for Table 11.1: Selective communicating styles used by men and women, from *Impression Management in the Workplace*, DuBrin, A.J. (2011); permission conveyed through Copyright Clearance Center, Inc. Republished with permission of Taylor and Francis Group LLC Books.

University College London Special Collections for Figure 2.1 The panopticon building.

Wiley-Blackwell for Figure 14.2 Wrong on influence and power from Wrong, D. H. (1979) *Power: Its Forms, Bases, and Uses*, Oxford: Wiley-Blackwell.

part 1
Foundations of work and organizations

In this part of the book, we examine the nature of organizational behaviour, give a summary of the historical dimensions of paid work, and present concepts and theories. This provides a basis for evaluating the competing perspectives on what determines and influences the behaviour of people in organizations.

In Chapter 1, we explain that organizational behaviour is a multidisciplinary field of study. We emphasize that globalized capitalism has a significant impact on the way people work and behave. We explore the process of management through a three-dimensional model. As an introduction to what follows, we discuss how the social dynamics of class, gender, disability, race and ethnicity underpin contemporary organizational behaviour.

In Chapter 2, we explore the continuities as well as the discontinuities in paid work over time. We highlight diversity and equity issues in the workplace in order to counterbalance the conventional preference for male history. We explore different types of paid and unpaid work, emotional labour and the work–life boundary. Our interpretation of the past leads us to conclude that employment is inherently constructed, interpreted and organized through social relations and social discourse.

In Chapter 3, we explain how the three founders of the sociology of work – Marx, Durkheim and Weber – all continue to have contemporary supporters and detractors. Organizational theorists have used different theoretical approaches to exploring work organizations – technical, sociotechnical, contingency, culture, learning, social action, political, control, feminist, symbolic-interactionist and postmodernist perspectives.

1 Introducing contemporary organizational behaviour
2 The social nature of work
3 Studying work and organizations

2

chapter 1
Introducing contemporary organizational behaviour

Key concepts

- class
- constructivist approach
- employee misbehaviour
- employment relationship
- gender
- management
- managerial behaviour
- positivist approach
- psychological contract
- qualitative research
- quantitative research
- strategic choice
- *verstehen*

Chapter outline

- Introduction
- The meaning of organizational behaviour
- Why study organizational behaviour?
- A framework for studying organizational behaviour
- Managing work organizations
- The influence of class, gender, race, ethnicity and disability on organizational behaviour
- Researching organizational behaviour
- Summary and end-of-chapter features
- Chapter case study: Managing change at Eastern University

Chapter learning outcomes

After completing this chapter, you should be able to:

1 Explain the basic characteristics of work organizations and their connections to the wider social context
2 Define the term 'organizational behaviour'
3 Describe the contribution to the field of organizational behaviour of three disciplines: psychology, sociology and anthropology
4 Explain the nature and importance of the employment relationship and the psychological contract
5 Appreciate the meanings and complexities behind the words 'management' and 'organization'
6 Demonstrate an understanding of why behaviour may vary because of an organization's strategy, structure, technology and environment
7 Identify the key changes occurring in the world and the effect that they are likely to have on organizational behaviour
8 Describe the evolution of organizational behaviour as a field of research and learning, and explain an integrated framework for conceptualizing organizational behaviour
9 Describe the challenges of conducting research on organizational behaviour

introduction

The organization is the most obvious symbol of **capitalist modernity**. Most mornings, we leave our homes and set off to work in organizations such as banks, insurance offices, retail stores, garages, schools, universities, hospitals, sports centres, police stations, hotels and factories. In private and public organizations, people engage in a host of work-related activities, communicate and interact, and learn with and from each other. For example, members of an organization may operate a computer, serve customers, teach students, diagnose patients, coach athletes, apprehend and arrest criminals, cook meals for guests or build cars. People's behaviour in their workplaces – and indeed the way the workplaces and work processes themselves have been set up – are the result of myriad factors. Partly, they reflect individual preferences or psychologies among those in the workplace. But the full picture is more complex: people are exposed to a multitude of organizational processes and control systems that limit, influence or determine their behaviour in work organizations.

capitalist modernity: a term used to refer to the period in the history of social relations dating roughly from the 1780s that is characterized by the constant revolutionizing of production and culture

organizational behaviour: the systematic study of formal organizations and of what people think, feel and do in and around organizations

Organizations influence the fate of people, communities and national economies. The 2008 global financial crisis (GFC) has reminded us that the nature of bankers' behaviour is crucial to maintain employment, economic growth, living standards and welfare (Bakir, 2013). Since 2008, many people have been feeling far more insecure and experiencing acute anxiety at work (Noon et al., 2013), and the effects of economic austerity on employment and living standards have brought the fate of workers to the fore (Atzeni, 2014). Managers believe that managing people is the most important as well as the most demanding aspect of their job. As a result, an introduction to the fundamentals of work and **organizational behaviour** is considered to be central to understanding what constitutes 'effective' management.

The starting point for exploring organizational behaviour is to explain what is meant by an organization. This is a physical and legal structure within which people undertake paid work. And it is the people of course, rather than the organization, who undertake the relevant behaviours. Workers sell their mental or physical skills to organizations, and they also buy the goods or services that organizations provide. Our 'experience' of organizations, as employees, customers or stakeholders, may be good, bad or indifferent, and standard approaches to organizational behaviour explain this using a variety of individual, group or organizational processes. Theoretical accounts typically centre on how the behaviour of individuals evolves and adapts; how it is shaped by group dynamics; and how organizations are structured to establish the limits within which work behaviour can vary. It looks at why organizational controls occur in the way they do, and how organizational processes have an impact on societal and ecological stability or instability. The emphasis is on how theories of organizational behaviour underscore management practices as well as organizational efficiency and effectiveness.

Source: Matthew Benjamin Coleman

plate 1 Graffiti outside the Bank of England sums up public anger about MPs' expenses and bankers' bonuses as job losses and home foreclosures hit unusually high levels in 2009. Responses to the recession and the credit crunch may change the nature of capitalism, and ultimately the way work and people are organized and managed in organizations.

Critical workplace scholars take it as given that organizational behaviour can only be understood in the context of the wider sociocultural, political and economic factors that profoundly influence the organization and its members – as attested to by the extraordinary 2008 GFC. As with previous recessions, there is ample evidence that the economic and financial meltdown has caused a psychological meltdown, an emotional state in which people, whether employed or not, feel extremely vulnerable and afraid for their futures (Allen, 2014; Furness, 2008). We already know that the current situation of joblessness and precarious flexible working arrangements, such as zero-hours contracts, is – perhaps not surprisingly – having a damaging effect on the men and women, and their families, who experience it (Anderssen, 2009; Freedland, 2014; Helm, 2013). In concrete terms, it can mean underemployment or long-term unemployment, immense upheaval and dislocation, and poverty. In psychological terms, individuals may experience emotions of guilt, shame and fear, as well as problems related to mental health. Writing about the 1980–81 economic recession in Britain, this writer characterized its social effects as the 'fear syndrome', which was succinctly expressed by a trade union leader this way: 'We've got three million on the dole, and another 23 million scared to death' (R. Todd, quoted in Bratton, 1992: 70).

capitalism: an economic system characterized by private ownership of the **means of production**, from which personal profits can be derived through market competition and without government intervention

means of production: an analytical construct that contains the forces of production and the relations of production, which, when combined, define the socioeconomic character of a society

VISIT THE *ONLINE RESOURCE CENTRE* AT HTTPS://HE.PALGRAVE.COM/COMPANION/BRATTON-WORK-AND-ORGANIZATIONAL-BEHAVIOUR3/ THE FULL TEXT OF THE G20 COMMUNIQUÉ ON THE WORLD ECONOMY.

In this chapter, we emphasize that globalized **capitalism** has a significant impact on the way workers undertake paid work and behave in organizations. We explore the process of management using a three-dimensional model to help us understand that any social action by managers and other employees is not isolated from the rest of society but is deeply embedded in it. Furthermore, as an introduction to later chapters, we will discuss how the dynamics of class, gender, disability, race and ethnicity underpin contemporary organizational behaviour, and we will then examine the challenges of researching behaviour in workplaces.

The meaning of organizational behaviour

This book is about how people in capitalist societies are organized and managed in private and public organizations. Capitalism is a system for organizing economic activity. Although capitalist activities and institutions began to develop in Europe from the 1400s, modern capitalism has come to define the immense and largely unregulated expansion of commodity production, its related market and monetary networks and rule of law related to capitalism. The leitmotif of capitalism is the need to maximize profit from the 'rational' organization of work and the exchange of goods or the delivery of services (see Chapter 3), rather than to satisfy the material needs of the producers. Capitalist modernity gives rise to a kind of **work organization** and **society** that is qualitatively distinct from any of those that preceded it (Sayer, 1991).

work organization: a deliberately formed social group in which people, technology and resources are purposefully co-coordinated through formalized roles and relationships to achieve a division of labour designed to attain a set of objectives. It is also known as formal organization

society: a large social grouping that shares the same geographical territory and is subject to the same political authority and dominant cultural expectations

Theorizing about work organizations has deep historical roots. Well before the publication of any textbook on 'organizational behaviour', Adam Smith's *The Wealth of Nations* (1776) and Karl Marx's *Das Kapital* (1867) provided seminal accounts of how early factory owners organized and managed people. This current textbook has two broad goals. First, it aims to help readers understand how people living in this era of mature global capitalism undertake paid work, how they interact with each other in organizations, and how the decisions made by managers affect others. Second, it aims to help readers learn to influence the processes and shape events within organizations.

What are organizations?

So what is distinctive about work organizations? A work organization is a socially designed unit or collectivity that engages in activities to accomplish a goal or set of objectives that are centrally monitored; it has an identifiable boundary and is linked to the external society. It can be distinguished from other social entities or collectivities – such as a family, a clan or tribe, or a complex society – by five common characteristics.

Source: Nick Tutton

plate 2 Today, our lives revolve around diverse work organizations, universities, banks, hospitals and factories. Work organizations are structures and groups of people organized to achieve goals efficiently. For-profit organizations have financial goals, normally the maximization of profit. Non-profit work organizations, such as Friends of the Earth, organize their activities around raising public awareness and lobbying politicians and governments to, for example, protect the environment and wildlife, and to reduce greenhouse gas emissions.

First, when we state that an organization is 'a *socially designed* unit or collectivity', we mean that one essential property is the presence of a group of people who have something in common, and who deliberately and consciously design a structure and processes. We use the term 'social structure' to refer to those activities, interactions and relationships that take on a regular pattern.

Some form of hierarchy exists in organizations. There are standard methods of doing things and control techniques that are coordinated and repeated every day. Sociologists refer to this as the 'formal social structure'. Many aspects of the formal social structure are explicitly defined in organizational charts, job descriptions and appraisal documents. However, human activities emerge in the workplace that are not expressed in charts or written job descriptions. This covers an array of human behaviour including the communication of rumours – the 'grapevine' – misbehaviour such as the sabotaging of a computer by a disgruntled employee, and trade union action. These activities are referred to as the 'informal social structure'. The formal and informal social structures are the basic building blocks of an organization.

The second common characteristic of organizations is that human activity is directed towards accomplishing '*a goal or set of objectives*'. For-profit organizations have financial goals – specific targets towards which human action is oriented, normally those of profit maximization. For Bakan, the modern for-profit organization is a 'pathological institution' that strives for profit and power and primarily exists 'to pursue, relentlessly and without exception, its self-interest, regardless of the often harmful consequences it might cause to others' (2004: 1–2). This means that making money is the first priority for for-profit businesses. They survive by minimizing their costs in any way they can within the law. Global corporations with operations in a number of different countries escape overall surveillance by particular nation states and avoid paying taxes when possible; many also try to avoid spending on cleaning up the pollution they create, the cost being picked up by the governments in the countries where they operate (Benn et al., 2014; Monbiot, 2014; Stiglitz, 2006). Benevolent non-profit organizations have goals such as helping the destitute, educating students, caring for the sick or promoting the arts. In addition, most organizations have survival as a goal.

The third characteristic that distinguishes modern organizations is the '*centralized monitoring*' of the work activities they both permit and entail. As Giddens observed: 'Who says modernity says not just organizations, but organization – the regularised control of social relations across indefinite time-space distances' (1991: 15). The **neo-liberal** globalizing tendencies and technological innovations have altered previously established patterns of work (Atzeni, 2014), and call for a new conceptualization and understanding of monitoring processes and organizational behaviour.

The fourth characteristic of organizations is the existence of an '*identifiable boundary*' that establishes common membership, distinguishing between the people who are inside and outside the organization. Changes in the global **division of labour** and strategies to maximize flexibility have created new organizational configurations called 'boundaryless organizations' (Anand and Daft, 2007).

neo-liberalism: a theory of political economics that proposes free markets (laissez-faire), free trade, deregulation, privatization, shrinkage of the state, a hollowing out of social provision and low taxes to advance the role of private enterprise in **the economy**

the economy: the social institution that ensures the maintenance of society through the production, distribution and consumption of goods and services

division of labour: the allocation of work tasks to various groups or categories of employee

The fifth characteristic of organizations is the presence of the *'external society'*, which focuses on the connection between an organization's internal activities and the larger society. The 'societal effects' can be strong with regard to employment relations and institutions, influencing management behaviour within national and global organizations (Kornelakis, 2014).

corporation: a large-scale organization that has legal powers (such as the ability to enter into contracts and buy and sell property) separate from its individual owner or owners

However, big **corporations** can also strongly shape the macro-level processes, which we discuss in more detail below, to reinforce preferences for 'power over' workplace decisions (Dundon et al., 2014; Žižek, 2014). The impacts or 'outcomes' of organizations on society may include consumer satisfaction or dissatisfaction, political lobbying, pollution of the ecosystem and other by-products of the organization's activities. In Western capitalist economies, argues Stiglitz (2006), big corporations have used their economic muscle to protect themselves from bearing the full social consequences of their actions. Despite the rhetoric about organizations being 'socially responsible', the law 'compels executives to prioritize the interests of their companies and shareholders above all others and forbids them from being socially responsible – at least genuinely so' (Bakan, 2004: 35).

Types of organization

Organizations vary in their size, in the product or services they offer and in their purpose, ownership and management. An organization's size is normally defined in terms of the number of people employed. We are all familiar with very small organizations such as independent newsagents, grocery stores and hotels. Larger organizations include the Ford Motor Company, Lloyds Bank, Google and governments. Organizations can be grouped into four major categories according to their products:

- *food production and extraction* (for example, farms, forestry and mining)
- *manufacturing* (for example, apparel, cars and mobile phones)
- *services* (for example, tourism and train and air transportation)
- *information processing* (for example, market research).

The growth in the number of people employed in the service and information processing categories defines the ***post-industrial economy***.

Work organizations can also be categorized into those that operate for profit, and not-for-profit institutions, as described above. The purpose of for-profit organizations is to make money, and they are judged primarily by how much money is made or lost: the bottom line. Not-for-profit organizations, such as registered charities, art galleries and most hospitals, measure their success or failure not by profit but in some other way. A university, for example, might measure its success by the total number of students graduating or obtaining grants from research bodies.

The primary purpose of an organization is linked to who owns and manages the organization. An individual or a family may own and manage a small business, employing a few other people. Not all businesses are incorporated (that is, are companies), but also only a few individuals own many companies. It is estimated that just one-third of US Fortune 500 companies (the top 500 companies in the USA) are family controlled. Privately owned organizations are a large part of the British and North American economy. Private companies may have corporate shares (that is, they are part-owned by other companies), but these shares are typically not traded publicly on a stock market.

In contrast, publicly held organizations issue shares that are traded freely on a stock market and are owned by a large number of people. These organizations normally pay dividends – a proportion of their profits – to their shareholders. The owners are the organization's principals, and these individuals either manage the activities of the organization themselves or employ agents (the managers) to manage it on their behalf. Privately and publicly owned organizations have the rights, privileges and responsibilities of a 'person' in the eyes of the law. But because a company is not actually a 'person' as such, its director or directors are held responsible for its actions, and directors have been fined and even jailed for crimes committed by 'the organization'.

VISIT THE *ONLINE RESOURCE CENTRE* AT HTTPS://HE.PALGRAVE.COM/COMPANION/BRATTON-WORK-AND-ORGANIZATIONAL-BEHAVIOUR3/ FOR MORE INFORMATION ON ALTERNATIVE WAYS OF ORGANIZING AND MANAGING PEOPLE IN WORKPLACES, SUCH AS THE MONDRAGON MOVEMENT IN SPAIN.

Now we have reviewed the basic characteristics and types of work organizations, we can look more directly at the meaning and scope of organizational behaviour.

What is organizational behaviour?

As a field of study, organizational behaviour is not easy to define because it draws upon numerous disciplines, theoretical frameworks and research traditions. The task is not made easier by the use of different labels for similar fields: organizational behaviour and organization theory, for instance. Organizational behaviour is sometimes seen as the domain of psychologists and tends to focus on micro-level studies of individuals and groups in organizations. Organizational theory, on the other hand, is seen as the domain of sociologists and tends to focus on macro-level studies of groups and organizations following what is sometimes called the 'contingency' approach: the idea that organizations adapt to take into account situational or contextual factors, such as technological advances or the political landscape. Within both fields there is a collection of 'conversations' – from individuals with different standpoints on organizational theories – each offering a competing theory and interpretation of what goes on in an organization. Arguably, the existence of two terms is a matter of semantics since there is a consensus across the areas studied that this field embraces a wide range of issues and perspectives (Clegg et al., 2006).

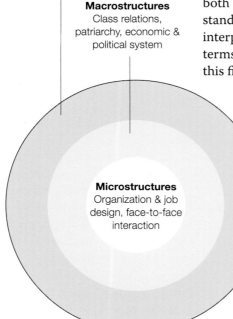

Global structures
International organizations, world trade, global inequality

Macrostructures
Class relations, patriarchy, economic & political system

Microstructures
Organization & job design, face-to-face interaction

Figure 1.1 The three levels of social structure surrounding the organization

This textbook follows convention by focusing in the earlier chapters on organizational behaviour and, in Parts 3 and 4, on organizational theory. We take the position that organizations are arenas of situated social behaviour (that is, places in which particular kinds of social behaviour take place), which are both explicitly organized by management theory and practices, and fashioned consciously and unconsciously by values, beliefs, a community of practices, gender, ethnicity and national employment relations systems and practices (Clegg and Hardy, 1999). Organizational behaviour is, in other words, embedded in the wider social, cultural and institutional fabric of society. It is best understood as a series of complex active processes in which people participate, both formally and informally, at several levels including the micro, macro and global (Figure 1.1), in ways that are shaped by organizational roles and power.

A wider, more inclusive definition would recognize the importance of 'social embeddedness' and the external as well as internal forces that affect the behaviour of people in organizations. We can define organizational behaviour as:

A multidisciplinary field of inquiry, concerned with the systematic study of formal organizations, the behaviour of people within organizations, and important features of the social context that structures all the activities occurring inside the organization.

As a field of inquiry, organizational behaviour is 'multidisciplinary'. It draws on a diverse array of social science disciplines, including psychology, sociology, anthropology, economics and political science.

Psychology literally means 'the science of the mind'. The research of industrial or work psychologists examines how individuals think, feel and behave, and connects directly to key concepts of perception, learning and motivation.

Sociology is the systematic study of the pattern of social relationships that develop between human beings, with a particular focus on the analysis of modernity. It connects most directly to understanding the concept of self-identity and the effects of macro- and global structures in buttressing or undermining organizational structures and processes.

Anthropology is the scientific study of the origin, and the social and cultural development, of human societies. It connects most directly to the concept of multiculturalism, focusing, for example, on concepts of **ethnocentrism**, **cultural relativism** and culture shock.

Politics is the study of individual and group behaviour within a political system. Politics contributes to understanding the key concept of power and how individuals and groups manipulate power for self-interest.

Economics examines the role of the state and the production and distribution of wealth, and directly connects to the inequality debate. Each of these social science disciplines produces a distinctive body of 'knowledge' for enquiring into and interpreting behaviour in organizations. This multidisciplinary framework and the major contributions to the study of organizational behaviour are shown in Table 1.1.

ethnocentrism: the tendency to regard one's own culture and group as the standard, and thus superior, whereas all other groups are seen as inferior

cultural relativism: the appreciation that all cultures have intrinsic worth and should be judged and understood on their own terms

Table 1.1 Towards a multidisciplinary approach to organizational behaviour

Social science	Contribution		Levels of analysis
Psychology	Personality	Communication	Individual
	Perception	Leadership	
	Learning	Group processes	
	Motivation		
Sociology	Class relations	Control processes	Group organization
	Power	Gendering of work	
	Bureaucracy	Technology processes	
	Conflict	Identity	
	Group interaction		
Anthropology	Comparative attitudes	Organizational environment	Group organization
	Comparative beliefs and values	Cross-cultural analysis	
	Organizational culture		
Political science	Conflict	Decision making	Organization
Economics	Power Rational choice Inequality	Decision making	Organization

Links to management

Chiara Amati

Chiara Amati is Lecturer in Human Resource Management at Edinburgh Napier University, UK. She is a Chartered Occupational Psychologist who joined Edinburgh Napier University Business School in 2010; she teaches on the MSc in HRM and on related undergraduate courses. Chiara's main area of expertise is the emotional experience of individuals and leaders at work, which includes an interest in aspects of job satisfaction, motivation, engagement and workplace stress. Chiara also works for the Keil Centre, a consultancy company that specializes in applying psychology and human factors expertise for organisational success.

In the ebook click on the play button to watch Chiara talking about the contribution of psychology and the medical model to the evidence-based approach in organizational behaviour.

conflict: the process in which one party perceives that its interests are being opposed or negatively affected by another party

microstructures: the patterns of relatively intimate social relations formed during face-to-face interaction

macrostructures: overarching patterns of social relations that lie outside and above a person's circle of intimates and acquaintances

Organizational behaviour is influenced – if not determined – by *microstructures* composed of, for example, job design, face-to-face communicating, ethical practice and leadership style. It also includes human thinking, feeling or perceiving, and values. In contrast to most North American and many British texts, we examine power struggles, alienation, bullying, racial, ethnic and gender discrimination, sabotage, **conflict** and resistance, and other forms of misbehaviour involving managers and workers.

In turn, the organization's microstructures can only be understood by reference to external contexts and developments. *Macrostructures*, composed of class relations, cultural, patriarchal, economic and political systems – the external environment – represent the 'macrocosm' or the immediate outer world that affects organizational life and behaviour. *Global structures* composed of international organizations, such as the World Bank, the International Monetary Fund and the International Labour Organization, and patterns of global communications, trade and travel also surround and permeate work organizations.

VISIT THE *ONLINE RESOURCE CENTRE* AT HTTPS://HE.PALGRAVE.COM/COMPANION/BRATTON-WORK-AND-ORGANIZATIONAL-BEHAVIOUR3/ FOR FURTHER INFORMATION AND RESOURCES RELATED TO INDUSTRIAL PSYCHOLOGY AND SOCIOLOGY.

Micro-, macro- and global structures surround people and influence organizational behaviour. These social structures are also interrelated: they are shaped by each other, and any action or change in one stimulates or affects actions in the others. Consider, for example, a change in the patterns of global trade and investment. In France, the change might cause the government to amend 'macro' public policy by increasing the length of the working week, with politicians claiming that this will improve labour productivity and increase France's international competitiveness. The change in the macrostructure might in turn generate action inside the organization, the microcosm zone, as workers stop work and take to the streets to protest against the government policy. We can think of these three levels of social structures – global, macro and micro – as concentric circles radiating out from people in the workplace, as shown in Figure 1.1.

Why study organizational behaviour?

At this point, the sceptical reader may be thinking 'I cannot see the practical use of organizational behaviour. I don't see how it helps the manager.' Organizational behaviour is more than just an intellectual exercise – it is an applied social science with practical, everyday management uses. Its practical use is to make the student and manager more attentive to unexamined common assumptions that may be influencing their decision making. It is best understood as a set of intellectual tools designed to help explain, predict and control organizational activities (Figure 1.2). These three goals of organizational behaviour represent increasing levels of sophistication. As with all the social sciences, students and managers often find that organizational behaviour draws attention to competing theories, conflicting evidence, ambiguities and paradoxes, issues we explore throughout the text.

The first goal of organizational behaviour is to *explain* and understand the behaviour of people in complex organizations. Social science often struggles to do this because, unlike the natural sciences, the subject under scrutiny – human behaviour – is highly changeable. People's perceptions change with experience, and behaviour is shaped by complex

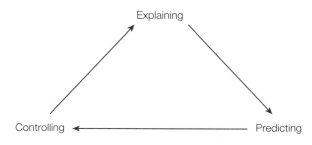

Figure 1.2 Reasons for studying organizational behaviour

social rules. For example, there are profound differences in social norms or 'rules' both between countries and across subcultures in the same country. There are different cultural mores and norms concerning mundane everyday behaviour, for instance how and when to shake hands, how much eye contact should be made and how close people should stand to each other in social settings. These observations affect how organizational behaviour theorists explain things, as well as set limits to our understanding. It would be unreasonable to discover universal laws governing human behaviour at work consistently across the cultures of Europe, North America and the Pacific Rim, for example.

The second goal of organizational behaviour is *prediction.* Both outside and inside the organization, predicting the behaviour of other people is an inherent requirement of everyday life. In other words, we want to be able to say that if X happens, then Y will occur. Our lives are made easier by our ability to predict when people will respond favourably to a request or when workers will respond favourably to a new reward system. So-called 'common-sense' predictions of human behaviour are often unreliable. Organizational behaviour theorists make generalizations from one setting to another about employee behaviour as systematically as possible in light of available research and theory.

Prediction and explanation are not the same. Accurate prediction usually precedes understanding and explanation. Through observation and experience, we are all capable of predicting the downward direction of an apple when it falls off a tree, but unless we have knowledge of the theory of gravity developed by Isaac Newton (1642–1727), we cannot fully explain *why* the apple falls to the ground. In the work context, organizational behaviour will help us explain (for instance) why individuals are less or more motivated when certain aspects of their job are redesigned, why various aspects of team processes cause misbehaviour and why networks and new forms of organization can have negative effects on performance.

The third goal of organizational behaviour is *control*, or the ability to manage change. As already noted, organizations can be characterized as 'structures of control', even though many regard the control or manipulation of human behaviour as unethical. There is an array of interventions inspired by organizational behaviour that are designed to control aspects of employees' behaviour. These include job design (Chapter 2), which attempts to control employees' commitment and motivation, groups and teams (Chapter 10), which aims to control the cohesion and performance of teams, and **organizational culture** (Chapter 17), which seeks to influence the values and beliefs shared by managers and workers. We will explore other interventions to control organizational behaviour in more detail in other chapters.

The ability to explain, predict and control organizational behaviour is a necessary prerequisite for making informed choices and for influencing management actions. According to Chris Grey, 'Theory is a weapon used to bludgeon others into accepting practice' (2005: 14). The key question is 'What is *really* happening in workplaces?' To address this question we need to analyse the values and priorities embedded in management behaviour, as well as investigate the effects of organizing and management action. As we have already explained, organizations are social structures, designed and created by people who have the capacity to shape and change them.

It can be argued that organizational behaviour theory is indispensable to students, managers and workers alike because it provides different concepts and

Source: Getty Images

plate 3 The ability to understand behaviour in the workplace is a necessary prerequisite for making informed choices and for influencing organizational action.

organizational culture: the basic pattern of shared assumptions, values and beliefs governing the way employees in an organization think about and act on problems and opportunities

theories for understanding the principles of organizational design and people management. It is a conceptual 'toolkit' with an array of alternative tools akin to a Swiss Army knife that we can use to at best understand and at worst justify social action in the workplace. It can also be characterized as a journey of self-enlightenment. In addition, we suggest that studying organizational behaviour is a requirement for active citizenship in advanced capitalist societies that are subject to periodic turbulence and change. To encourage a critical approach to studying organizational behaviour, we need to go to the root of the nature and tendencies of work organizations, and to use our sociological imaginations by presenting options for changing the way organizations function in society (Bratton and Gold, 2015).

> **stop...**
>
> What other reasons can you think of for studying organizational behaviour?
>
> **...and reflect**

A framework for studying organizational behaviour

The American sociologist C. Wright Mills (1916–62) argued that we can only gain a full understanding of human experience when we look beyond individual experiences and locate those experiences within the larger economic, political and social context that structures them. Mills wrote, the 'sociological imagination allows us to grasp the interplay of man [sic] and society, of biography and history, of self and world' (1959/2000: 4). We agree with Mills here, and suggest that the behaviour of managers, and the agency of individuals and work groups, cannot be fully understood without reference to the outer organizational context. While we focus here primarily on issues related to workplace behaviour in advanced capitalist economies, it is important to remind ourselves that 73 per cent of the world's workers live in developing economies (Ghose et al., 2008).

The workplaces employing the other 27 per cent of workers are arenas of competing social forces that mirror and generate paradox, tension, misbehaviour, conflict and change. This characterization of the organization as an 'arena' provides a theoretical framework for examining the behaviour of managers and other employees in relation to politics, gender, power and **ideology** (for early literature on this, see, for example, Clegg and Dunkerley, 1980; Esland and Salaman, 1980).

ideology: a term with multiple uses, but in particular referring to perceptions of reality as distorted by class interests, and the ideas, legal arrangements and culture that arise from class relations (a term taken from Marx)

agency: often used as a substitute for 'action', but with a wider meaning in sociology. Here, it emphasizes the undetermined nature of human action, as opposed to the alleged determinism of structural theories. This wider meaning highlights the psychological and socially constructed make-up of the actor, and the capacity for voluntary action

There are many valid ways of studying organizational behaviour, but by recognizing the interplay between the global, macrosocial and microsocial dimensions, we are led to acknowledge the dynamic linkages between external forces on the one hand, and internal management processes and individual and group **agency** on the other. These collectively control and shape how people and work are organized and managed. At the risk of oversimplification, we illustrate the multifaceted and interdisciplinary nature of organizational behaviour in Figure 1.3. This offers a simple integrative or 'open' model for studying organizational behaviour (Nadler and Tushman, 1997). It is divided into four major components:

- *global and macro-environmental* forces as inputs from the external context
- *processes* for converting the inputs into outputs in a managerial context
- an *evaluation* of the outputs
- a *feedback loop* that links the processes and external forces with feedback information on the organization's outcomes.

The external context: the STEPLE framework

STEPLE analysis framework: This categorizes the external context into six main types: Social, Technological, Economic, Political, Legal and Ecological

In examining the external context, we use three concepts in this section – key drivers, scenario planning and **STEPLE analysis** – to examine the wider global and macro-influences, the 'inputs' that are most crucial for studying people in work organizations. An analysis of the *key drivers* helps with focusing on what is most important to the organization, and on where to invest for the greatest effect; *scenario planning* builds on key drivers to identify one or more probable events or develop-

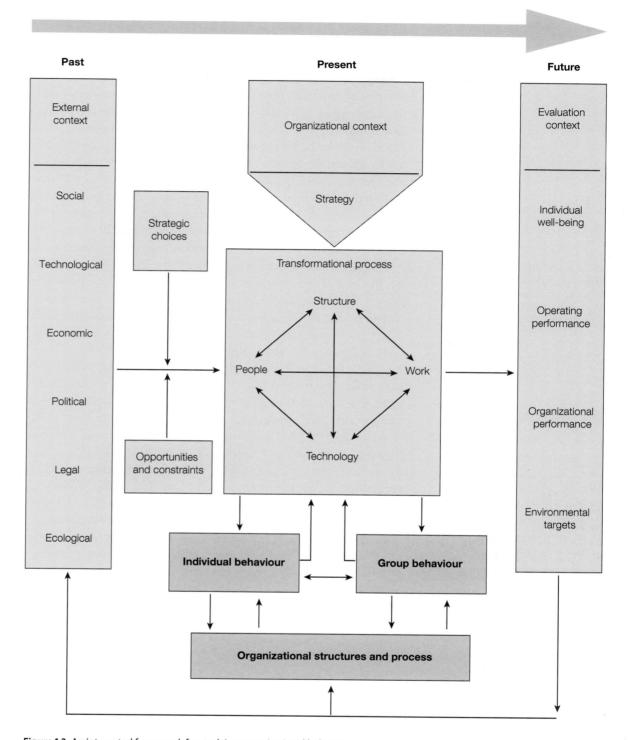

Figure 1.3 An integrated framework for studying organizational behaviour

ments and what their consequences or effects would be on the organization; and the STEPLE framework provides a wide-ranging audit of the organization's external context with the purpose of using this information to guide strategic decision making. Similar acronyms are PESTLE and PEST (Macintosh and Maclean, 2014; Morrison, 2013). STEPLE stands for Social, Technological, Economic, Political, Legal and Ecological. The following discussion is meant to be illustrative – rather than exhaustive – of how the external context affects organizational processes.

Social influences include cultural influences, changing values and demographics, for example the ageing populations in many Western societies. *Technological* influences refer to innovations such as the Internet, robotics and the rise of composite materials. For example, Epson's new inkjet cartridges used in home printing will, it is argued, turn its business model 'upside down', with profit coming from expensive printers rather than throw-away ink cartridges (Collinson, 2014). *Economic* refers to globalization and macro-economic factors such as the 2008 GFC, the Euro crisis and differential economic growth rates in the European Union and around the world. *Political* factors highlight the impact of government and global conflict such as the escalation of the Ukraine crisis in 2014 and Russian sanctions (Monaghan and Inman, 2014). *Legal* embraces legislative changes such as financial regulations, and finally *Ecological* refers specifically to 'green' or low-carbon issues such as land, sea and atmospheric pollution. For managers, it is important to analyse how these global and macro-factors are changing today and how they are likely to change in the future, identifying the opportunities, risks and implications for the organization.

globalization: when an organization extends its activities to other parts of the world, actively participates in other markets, and competes against organizations located in other countries

Globalization underscores the need to examine the organization within its totality, the embedded nature of organizational behaviour and the processes by which those with most power respond to the demands of the external context. However, globalization itself is a thoroughly contested concept, depending on whether it is viewed as primarily an economic, a political or a social phenomenon (Piketty, 2014; Saul, 2005; Scholte, 2005; Stiglitz, 2013).

The fact that we live in a globally interconnected world has become a cliché. As part of this interconnected world, the acceleration of the globalization of economic activity is one of the defining political economic paradigms of our time. In the early twenty-first century, globalization is arguably about the unfettered pursuit of profit (Hertz, 2002). The international management literature gives accounts of how higher profits can be realized by relocating production operations abroad, and by economies of scale. The STEPLE framework reminds us that organizations are embedded within their own social, economic, political and legal spheres, and that levels of corporate taxation, employment standards and other 'business-friendly' incentives can affect their profits. Since capital is portable (that is, it can be employed in different countries), it is possible for global corporations to indulge in an endlessly variable geometry of profit searching (Castells, 2000a). The logic of unfettered globalization means that any labour-intensive, value-added activity is likely to migrate from high-wage to low-wage economies – that is to say, from rich, developed countries like the USA and Western Europe to developing countries such as Brazil, Bangladesh, India and Vietnam.

stop...

What are the strengths and weaknesses of STEPLE analysis?

...and reflect

Iain Nelson has spent 27 years as a Principal Consultant and Manager with the International Training Service, and 4 years as an Internal Learning and Development Advisor with Petroleum Development Oman. As a freelance consultant, his clients include Unilever, Roche Products, Alcan, BP, Chevron, Lothian and Borders Police, British Council, ITF Nigeria, Total and Indian Railways.

Iain's core expertise is developing managers as learning specialists competent to design and deliver a company's corporate objectives and associated strategic business initiatives.

In the ebook click on the play button to watch Iain talking about using STEPLE analysis to scan an organization's environment, and then answer the following question:

• What data-gathering methods does Iain suggest that managers use to scan their organization's external environment to identify potential good and bad influences?

Since the 2008 GFC, the whole tide of economic thinking has begun to question this neo-liberal economic model, which has dominated the economic policies of governments in the European Union and North America for the last 36 years. In the past, economic thinking has been subject to critical scrutiny and democratic debate. In the 1930s, following the first Great Depression, modern economics was defined by the fierce arguments between Friedrich von Hayek (1899–1992) and John Maynard Keynes (1883–1946) over the merits of unfettered free markets and government intervention in the economy (Wapshott, 2011).

Today, arguments over 'light-touch' global capitalism (see, for example, Kwarteng et al., 2012) and the role of government in a progressive political economy (see, for example, Piketty, 2014; Sainsbury, 2013) rage as fiercely as they did 85 years ago. New conversations on political economy need to be based on a better understanding of the process of sustainable economic growth, one that better balances goals around profit, people, social justice and protection of the planet. One such model, drawn from policies and practices in the Nordic countries, is the 'Common Weal' programme. Developed by the Jimmy Reid Foundation, it calls for a new progressive economical economy based on high-quality, high-pay jobs, an active encouragement of employee ownership and involvement, social justice and a reversal of anti-trade union legislation (McAlpine, 2014).

A review of competing economic models is, of course, well beyond the scope of this text, but for our purpose, as politicians predict the end of the Great Recession, the primary issue is how economic globalization is affecting organizational behaviour and workers' well-being.

> **stop...**
>
> How have external environment factors impacted on work organizations that you, or members of your family or your friends, have been a part of? How did these external factors influence the behaviour of people in the organization?
>
> **...and reflect**

IN THE EBOOK ACCESS THE **CRITICAL INSIGHT** ON EMBEDDING ORGANIZATIONS IN A CAPITALIST SOCIETY.

The organizational context

The structure of the organization is formed from the interaction between individuals, groups and organizational controls. Organizational context describes the regular, patterned nature of work-related activities, technology and processes that is repeated day in and day out. There are at least six identifiable variables that impact on the active interplay of people within the structure of the organization: strategy, structure, work, technology, people and control processes.

strategy: the long-term planning and decision-making activities undertaken by managers that are related to meeting organizational goals

organizational structure: the formal reporting relationships, groups, departments and systems of the organization

bureaucracy: an organizational model characterized by a hierarchy of authority, a clear division of labour, explicit rules and procedures, and an impersonal approach to personnel matters

In an organizational context, *strategy* refers to what senior managers do over time to accomplish an organization's goals. *Structure* is defined as the manner in which an organization divides up its specific work activities, and coordinates and controls these activities. The structure of organizations can take many forms. Much debate on changing organizational forms has centred on the argument of whether organizations have shifted from **bureaucratic** forms with highly specialized tasks and a hierarchical authority, to post-bureaucratic forms with low specialization and 'flat' authority. Chapter 15 examines developments in organizational design.

VISIT THE *ONLINE RESOURCE CENTRE* AT HTTPS://HE.PALGRAVE.COM/COMPANION/BRATTON-WORK-AND-ORGANIZATIONAL-BEHAVIOUR3/ TO ACCESS ARTICLES ON STRATEGIC MANAGEMENT THAT OFFER AN ANALYSIS OF THE STRATEGIES OF VARIOUS ORGANIZATIONS.

Work refers to the physical and mental activities that are carried out to produce or achieve something of value. The way people interact within the organization will be strongly influenced by the way in which work activities are designed, for example how tasks are divided into various jobs, and the degree of autonomy employees have over their work. The names Frederick Taylor and Henry Ford have become synonymous with work design in today's organizations. Their ideas and others are critically examined in Chapter 2.

Source: Photoalto

The financial system: 'in every nook and cranny of society'

The term 'globalization' has become widely used in the analysis of capitalism in recent years, even if the definition of globalization has never been finally settled. Some writers, such as Lapavitsas (2011), concentrate instead on the term 'financialization' as it reflects the central place of the financial sector in modern capitalist economies. Lapavitsas points out that global flows of capital and the global spread of huge banks is in any case a major part of the phenomenon of globalization (Lapavitsas, 2011: Ch. 1). The financial system is ubiquitous and is found in 'every nook and cranny of society including housing, education, health and other areas of life that were previously relatively immune' (Lapavitsas, 2013).

The theorization of the financial sector has long been a concern among Marxist scholars, who have focused on explaining how the role of finance has changed in mature capitalism over the last 30 years. Lapavitsas (2011, 2013) argues that big businesses have become 'financialized'. They have sufficient profits to finance investment, are less reliant on loans and can engage in financial activities themselves, using their own funds. Large banks are less involved with business and find their profits by trading on international stock exchanges and from lending to households. As Lapavitsas (2013) puts it:

> Households have become 'financialized' too, as public provision in housing, education, health, pensions and other vital areas has been partly replaced by private provision, access to which is mediated by the financial system.

Households also possess financial assets such as savings and endowment policies so that they become dependent upon the services of the financial sector, and this stimulates an outlook or mentality that involves financial calculation and the **hegemony** of market rationality. As an example, Lapavitsas (2013) refers to the way in which people perceive house purchase not just in terms of the use of a house, but as an 'investment'.

The financial sector now obtains much of its profit from debtors who pay interest on their mortgages and credit cards. Those who are lucky enough to be creditors provide a source of income to the financial sector by paying fees and charges on pension funds and insurance.

The crash of 2007–09 showed how a financialized world is prone to bubbles and crises, and how it has contributed to the rise in inequality of income and wealth experienced in the advanced economies since the 1980s.

> Modern financial elites are prominent at the top of the income distribution, set trends in conspicuous consumption, shape the expensive end of the housing market, and transform the core of urban centres according to their own tastes. (Lapavitsas, 2013)

Lapavitsas (2013) has criticized the commitment of vast amounts of resources and talent to the creation of wealth through financial transactions, rather than productive activity. However, little has been done to control the powers of banks, which have become too big to fail and have had their existence guaranteed by governments, at great expense to tax payers.

Stop! Think about how you are already involved with financial institutions or may become so in the future. Do you think you may need to borrow money from a bank or building society to buy a house or to finance the lifestyle you aspire to? Have you considered pursuing a career in the financial sector, and is its high 'bonus culture' one of its attractive features?

Sources and further information
Lapavitsas, C. (2011) *Profiting Without Producing: How Finance Exploits Us All*, London: Verso.
Lapavitsas, C. (2013) 'Finance's hold on daily life must be broken', *The Guardian*, January 2.

Note: This feature was written by David Denham, Honorary Research Fellow in Sociology, Wolverhampton University, UK.

hegemony: a term derived from Karl Marx's historical materialism and his theory of social classes. According to Marx, each ruling class leads and dominates over others, which includes the dissemination of ideas

technology: the means by which organizations transform inputs into outputs, or rather the mediation of human action. This includes mediation by tools and machines as well as rules, social convention, ideologies and discourses

Technology affects the quality of work and the behaviour of individuals, groups and operating processes. Here we note that technology is a multidimensional concept. The key challenge for management within the approach being adopted in this textbook, which places the worker at the centre of the agenda, is to identify the circumstances in which technology can result in both high efficiency and higher levels of employee satisfaction and dignity. Chapter 16 examines the relationship between technology and behaviour.

In studying the fifth variable – *people* – critical scholars have long held that people entering the workplace are not isolated unique individuals, but the bearers of an objective structure of social relations shaped not only by psychology, but also by history and by culture (see, for example, Clegg and Dunkerley, 1980). This perspective means distinguishing between workers and employers or their agents, that is, managers. The formal relations between these two groups constitute the *employment relationship*. The nature of the employment relationship is an issue of central importance to understanding organizational behaviour. What, then, is the essence of the employment relationship?

There are two types of employment relationship in organizations: the *individual* employment relationship and a *collective* employment relationship (Farnham, 2015). The individual relationship is between the employer and the individual employee. This signifies the terms (wage or salary) and conditions (duties and obligations) of the relationship, which are normally determined by the employer. Collective employment relationships are between an employer and a group of employees or workers, where the terms and conditions of employment are determined *jointly* by collective bargaining between the employer and a trade union representing the employees – we examine the role of unions in Chapter 8.

The employment relationship is, first and foremost, an *economic relationship* between an employer and an employee – a *pay–effort bargain* – that places an obligation on both the employer and the employee. In exchange for a payment, the employee is obligated to carry out physical or intellectual duties and obligations, as directed by the employer or manager. Figure 1.4 shows that markets and the state may mediate the employment relationship.

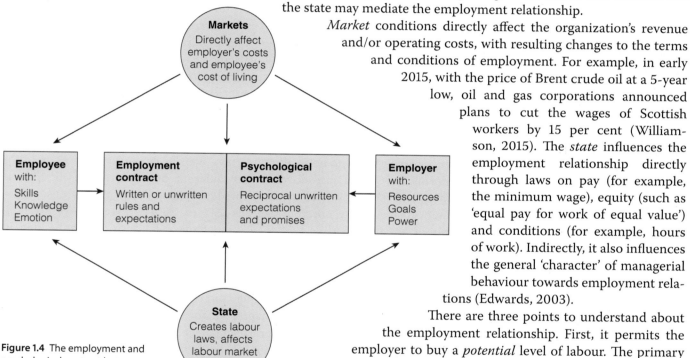

Figure 1.4 The employment and psychological contract between employee and employer

Market conditions directly affect the organization's revenue and/or operating costs, with resulting changes to the terms and conditions of employment. For example, in early 2015, with the price of Brent crude oil at a 5-year low, oil and gas corporations announced plans to cut the wages of Scottish workers by 15 per cent (Williamson, 2015). The *state* influences the employment relationship directly through laws on pay (for example, the minimum wage), equity (such as 'equal pay for work of equal value') and conditions (for example, hours of work). Indirectly, it also influences the general 'character' of managerial behaviour towards employment relations (Edwards, 2003).

There are three points to understand about the employment relationship. First, it permits the employer to buy a *potential* level of labour. The primary task of the employer or manager is to transform this potential into actual value-added labour in the most cost-effective way. Much of mainstream organizational behaviour theory is designed to help managers narrow the gap between employees' potential and their actual performance. Second, the employment relationship is based on employer or managerial *power* (see Chapter 14), and critical studies emphasize how the power imbalance is exercised (Burchill, 2014). Third, *conflict* is structured into the pay–effort 'bargain'. The 'pay' side of the bargain is a cost that, all things being equal, reduces profit and therefore, from the employer's perspective, needs to be minimized. As Brown (1988: 57) observes, 'Conflict is structured into employment relations' as the logic makes the pay to one group the cost to the other. The 'effort' element is also a potential source of conflict because it is inherently difficult to determine and is subject to disruptive change (see Chapter 18).

Sennett's (2012) research sheds light on the social dimension of the employment relationship. He suggests that workers forge informal bonds and friendships with co-workers including managers, and that although these do not transform work into a conflict-free Garden of Eden, they do help to make work less soulless and to create civility in the organization (2012: 148–9). We should further note that women and men enter organizations as the bearers of their own values, social norms, mores and history that help to shape their individual beliefs and values about work. These observations suggest that employment relations are deeply textured and profoundly sociological (Bratton and Denham, 2014). Figure 1.4 shows a second dimension of the employment relationship: a *psychological contract.* This concept is a metaphor that captures a wide variety of largely unwritten expectations and understandings of the employer and employee about their mutual obligations. Rousseau (1995: 9) defines it as 'individual beliefs, shaped by the organization, regarding terms of an exchange agreement between individuals and their organization'. In the context of the 'downsizing', transformative change and flexible, non-unionized work regimes that were seen in the 1990s, the psychological contract has become a fashionable framework for analysing the employment relationship (Saunders and Thornhill, 2006). We examine the psychological contract in more detail in Chapter 5.

stop...

What do you think of the concept of the psychological contract? Why does there appear to be more interest nowadays in managing it?

...and reflect

At the heart of the employment relationship are objectives related to efficiency, equity and voice (Budd, 2004). *Efficiency* is a standard of economic performance. *Equity* encompasses notions of 'fairness' and 'dignity' in employment and personal treatment. *Voice* is the ability of individuals and groups to have a meaningful input into work-related decisions. Efficiency is the objective of employers, whereas equity and voice are workers' objectives. The extent to which these three objectives are met will shape the employment contract and psychological contract, which act as a lever to increase the motivation and performance of both the individual and the group.

Analyses of the work regimes and changes imposed by management vary greatly between organizations and between countries. Over the last three decades, neo-liberal reforms have been introduced under different political regimes in diverse economies, and these have also been accepted or opposed by workers and societies in different forms and to different degrees (Atzeni, 2014). This diversity makes it more important to underline that the employment relationship is embedded in the fabric of society, which helps us to analyse the nature of individual, group and management behaviour and their differences.

Understanding the dynamics of the employment relationship and behaviour in the workplace is both complex and fascinating, and requires us to look at the concepts of personality and self-identity (see Chapter 4). The dynamics of both are shaped by perceptions and emotions (see Chapter 5). Employee misbehaviour – which can take the form of resistance, lying and stealing – tends to be under-reported, but these 'warts' constitute part of organizational reality (Ackroyd and Thompson, 1999). Critical narratives also emphasize that class, gender, race, ethnicity and disability also make an overwhelming difference to the organizational reality (Alvesson and Billing, 1997; Hearn et al., 1989; Wajcman, 1998; Wilson, 2003).

We therefore approach the study of 'people' in work organizations by viewing them not as atomized, unique individuals, but as the bearers of an objective structure of social relations shaped by life experiences, values, expectations and history. As others have observed:

> The time-honoured distinctions between three levels of analysis – the individual, the organization, and the environment – are clearly breaking down. The previous certainty of discrete, self-contained individuals, fully informed by their roles in organizations, has been shattered. (Clegg et al., 1999: 9)

We need to adopt a multidimensional approach to studying organizational behaviour. And, given the general nature of the divergence of interests between the managers and those who are managed, our reciprocal model contains *control* processes. Control systems enable managers to accomplish the organization's objectives and to deal with uncooperative and underperforming subordinates. Numerous studies suggest that formal organizations are, in essence, 'structures of control' (Clegg and Dunkerley, 1980; Salaman, 1979; Thompson and McHugh, 2009). If we accept this premise, the question is, how exactly is this control exercised and by whom, and why is control necessary anyway? Control may be exercised directly by technology or indirectly by peer pressure within groups, by the organizational culture, or by an array of management practices designed to make people's behaviour more predictable and controllable (Townley, 1994).

The evaluative context

An organization's processes are not an end in themselves but are explicitly related to the goals of the overarching organization. The evaluative context addresses the much-researched question 'Do certain behaviours actually lead to high-performance organizations?' Issues of individual, operating, financial and environmental performance are all involved. But although there is well-documented evidence that a combination of specific organizational behaviour variables is associated with positive performance outcomes, the association is by no means uncontested. Any serious analysis of the goals of management brings into focus the build-up of internal contradictions and the control of 'strategic tensions' (Boxall et al., 2008a). Among the most challenging are the tensions between maximizing profit or shareholder return and employee security and dignity, between profit and degradation of the environment, between organizational control and employees' motivation, and between managerial autonomy and social responsibility.

IN THE EBOOK ACCESS **OB IN FOCUS** BOX ON CLIMATE CHANGE - A CHALLENGE FOR US ALL.

Managing work organizations

The centralized monitoring of work activities that the modern organization both permits and entails is strongly influenced by what happens outside its boundaries, as well as by management decisions and actions within the organization. The term 'manager' refers to an occupational group that organizes, coordinates and makes decisions about what work is to be done, how it is to be done and by whom. Managers can adopt a wide array of means to accomplish their ends. These may range from communicating, motivating and coercing, to using complex technologies. Taken together, these constitute the manager's repertoire for 'getting things done through people', and each individual manager may be more or less skilled in or disposed towards using a particular process. This section aims to provide a short overview of the nature of management, and to consider how managerial behaviour affects the behaviour of other employees.

The meaning of management

The words 'manage' and 'manager' are derived from the Italian word *maneggiare* – to handle or train horses (Williams, 1983). In Peter Drucker's canonic text, *The Practice of Management*, management is seen as both a function and a social group. The emergence of management as a social group is seen as one of the most significant events in Western society (Drucker, 1954/1993: 4). Henri Fayol (1841–1925), a French businessman who is regarded as the 'father of modern management', identified management as a series of four key activities that managers must continually perform: planning, organizing, directing and controlling – the 'PDOC' tradition (Figure 1.5).

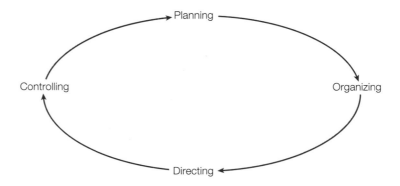

Figure 1.5 The classic Fayolian management cycle

The classic management cycle presents the job of the manager in a positive way, and to this day all mainstream management textbooks present management as having the four central functions outlined above. For Fayol, *planning* meant studying the future and drawing up a plan of action; *organizing* meant coordinating both the material and the people aspects of the organization; *directing* referred to ensuring that all efforts were focused on a common goal; and *controlling* meant that all workplace activities were to be carried out according to specific rules and orders.

The process of management

To study behaviour in workplaces, we need to address two related questions: 'What do managers do?' and 'Why do managers do what they do?' The nature of managerial work is an amorphous topic in the literature. Since the mid-twentieth century, studies have offered a comprehensive picture of what managers do. Many are in the Fayolian genre; that is, managerial behaviour is represented as a rational and politically neutral activity. Other studies offer a more complex account, emphasizing the politics of management (Braverman, 1974) or the building of reciprocal social networks (Mintzberg, 1973). Harry Braverman provides a critique on the degradation that traditional management ideas bring to modern work. We examine Braverman's critique in Chapter 16.

Henry Mintzberg's multifaceted model of managers' work identifies three sets of behaviours: interpersonal, informational and decisional (Mintzberg, 1989). He usefully distinguishes three different *interpersonal* roles – figurehead, leader and liaison – that arise directly from the manager's formal authority. By virtue of these interpersonal encounters with both other managers and non-managers, the manager acts as a 'nerve centre' for the dissemination of information.

The manager's three *informational* roles – monitor of information, disseminator of information and spokesperson – flow from the interpersonal roles. Finally, the manager performs four *decision-making* roles, those of entrepreneur, disturbance handler, resource allocator and negotiator. The extent to which managers perform these functions will depend on their position in the organization's hierarchy and their specific functional responsibilities. For example, we would expect human resource managers to give relatively more attention to the disturbance-handling and negotiating roles, given the nature of their work.

Unsurprisingly perhaps, studies have found that the relative importance of managerial work varies not only according to the individual's position in the management hierarchy, but also with the level of education of their co-workers. Interestingly, too, managerial work in 'creative milieus' may not follow the conventional activities. Evidence shows that, in research-intensive organizations, managers not only coordinate day-to-day work, but, as scientists, play a major role in scaffolding the research projects, so that 'conventional management practices and managerial concerns come, at best, second' (Sundgren and Styhre, 2006: 32). Despite claims to the contrary, surveys of managerial work exhibit striking parallels with the classic Fayolian management cycle (Table 1.2) (Hales, 1986).

Table 1.2 Summary of managerial work

Acting as the figurehead or leader of an organizational unit
Liaising with other managers
Monitoring, filtering and disseminating information
Allocating resources
Handling conflicts and maintaining workflows
Negotiating with other managers or representatives
Being creative and innovative
Planning
Controlling and directing subordinates

Source: Based on Hales (1986)

Much of the earlier research on management has an Anglo-American bias. Some more recent studies have, however, challenged the universality of managerial behaviour, and have emphasized the importance of factoring gender and cross-cultural considerations into the analysis (Alvesson and Willmott, 1996; Willmott, 1989). Others suggest that managerial behaviour is 'gendered', while others counterargue that the behaviour of male and female managers is largely determined by structural, control and market imperatives – in other words, there is no such thing as 'female' management behaviour (Wajcman, 1998).

An alternative, less flattering picture of managerial behaviour is indicated in studies on workplace bullying and sexual harassment (Bolton, 2005; Hoel and Beale, 2006). Bullying and harassment in workplaces is not a new phenomenon. Indeed, in the context of profit maximization and managerial control, bullying is part of the management repertoire of getting things done through people, and reflects the significance of the unequal balance of power in workplaces.

An integrated model of management

The different dimensions of managers' work are brought together in the three-dimensional model shown in Figure 1.6. The vertical axis lists activities that answer the first question we raised earlier – 'What do managers do?' The horizontal axis shows the contingencies, and relates to the second question, addressed later in this chapter, 'Why do managers do what they do?' The diagonal axis relates to the third question 'How do managers do what they do?' These are topics that are examined throughout this book.

The set of managerial activities is similar to those found in the classic Fayolian management cycle. The contingencies are those forces and events, both outside and inside the organization, that affect management behaviour, as shown in Figure 1.3. The third dimension, managerial behaviours, lists various means by which managers communicate ideas, gain acceptance for them and motivate others to change in order to implement these ideas. Managers use technical, cognitive and interpersonal processes and skills to accomplish their work. Power is included in the list because it is part of the influence process. Management involves a blend of processes, and individuals will vary in terms of their capacity or inclination to use them, but these processes are ultimately about human interaction and relationships.

The model suggests that management is a multidimensional integrating and controlling activity that permeates every facet of paid work experience and profoundly shapes employment relationships and human behaviour. It does not

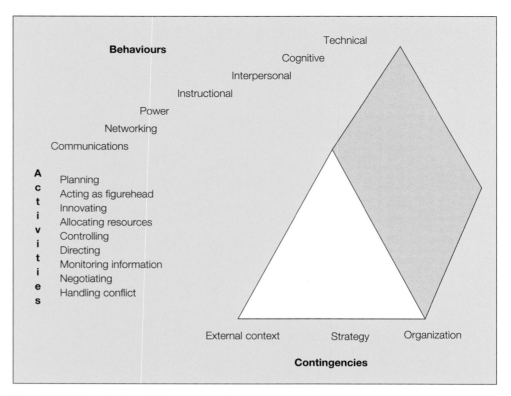

Figure 1.6 An integrated model of management

assign values to the relationships, and does not claim to be predictive. The model is, however, a useful device that helps us to explore how management functions are translated into means, such as leadership processes, and equally how various contingencies influence behaviour in workplaces.

The influence of class, gender, race, ethnicity and disability on organizational behaviour

Anyone who takes even a cursory look inside a contemporary organization will most likely see a diverse workforce. Although different groups may be segregated into specific jobs, the presence of women and visibly identifiable minority groups will be evident. Together, people of Afro-Caribbean, Bangladeshi, Pakistani, Asian, Chinese and East European origin account for an increasing proportion of the British workforce, and the same is true in many other European Union states and other countries that have expanded their populations through immigration, such as Australia and Canada. Studying diversity is not simply a matter of learning about other people's cultures; it also involves discovering how social class, gender, race and ethnicity and disability frame people's opportunities and work experiences. It may come as a surprise, therefore, to learn that academic journals and most mainstream textbooks in the organizational behaviour field show little interest in social class, gender, race/ethnicity and disability. Why is this? We address this serious question more fully in Chapter 8, but to frame our discussion at the outset, we suggest that class relationships, for example, are so deeply embedded in capitalist employment relations as to become all but invisible.

We focus on diversity and equity here not because they are an interesting yet benign fact of the modern workplace, but because we consider that social class, gender, race, ethnicity and disability underpin contemporary organizational behaviour.

A social *class* is defined as a large group of people in a given society who have a similar degree of access to a material resource such as income, wealth or property. The sociological analysis of social class has been important in allowing us to predict, explain and manage work-based conflict. *Gender* refers to the attitudes, feelings and behaviours members of a society typically associated with being male or female. It is a dimension of social organization, affecting how we interact with others, how we think about our identity, and what social behaviours and roles are expected of men and women both in general and in the workplace in particular. Gender is embedded in the modern organization. It is associated with hierarchy, because men and women tend to be found in different positions, as judged by their access to resources and power.

Although early theories of 'race science' and eugenics were thoroughly discredited scientifically, the notion of race remains a highly contested concept (Bratton and Denham, 2014: 12). 'Race' and ethnicity are complex sociological concepts to introduce into organizational behaviour. The notion of *race*, like gender, can be understood as a social and ideological construct. The notion of race as a social construct downplays the extent to which sections of the population may form a discrete ethnic group – that is, learn and share certain characteristics on the basis of common historical origins, patterns of social interaction and a sense of identity.

Whereas the concept of 'race' implies something biological and permanent, '*ethnicity*' is purely social in meaning (Giddens and Sutton, 2013; Tong, 1998). It refers to the shared cultural practices and heritage of a given category of people that set them apart from other members of society. Britain is a multiethnic society in which English is the official language, yet many people speak other languages at home, including Hindi, Punjabi and Mandarin. Ethnic differences are learned, and for many people ethnicity is central to their individual identity. The concepts of race and ethnicity are fundamental to an awareness of racism and discrimination in society and the workplace.

Although it is important to examine class, gender and ethno-racial issues in the workplace in order to generate a broad and critical view of organizational behaviour, here we wish to introduce another important under-researched area of inequality and disadvantage in the workplace: *disability*. Research on disability has been extremely limited as disability has tended to be analysed primarily within a 'medical model'. The common assumptions about disability focus on disabled people's lack of abilities. A critical perspective on disability draws to our attention how the capitalist mode of production is itself disabling for some people, and calls both for the 'normalization' of disabled individuals as socially valued members of society, and for an end to inequitable treatment in the workplace (Oliver, 1996).

To understand the significance of social class, gender, race, ethnicity and disability is to give emphasis to power imbalances, and to put the behaviour of individuals and groups in the organization into a wider social context. However, no book can contain everything: the material we have chosen inevitably not only reflects our personal bias, but is also highly selective. Although we draw mainly from the narrow field of workplace psychology and sociology, we cannot cover everything, even in a cursory fashion.

> ### stop...
> Have you experienced or observed discrimination in the workplace or at college or university based on class, gender, race or ethnicity, or disability? What form did it take? How did management handle the discrimination?
>
> ### ...and reflect

VISIT THE *ONLINE RESOURCE CENTRE* AT HTTPS://HE.PALGRAVE.COM/COMPANION/BRATTON-WORK-AND-ORGANIZATIONAL-BEHAVIOUR3/ FOR FURTHER INFORMATION AND RESOURCES ON RACE, ETHNICITY AND HUMAN RIGHTS IN THE WORKPLACE.

In our view, the various permutations of employment relationships stemming from the variables of class, gender, race, ethnicity and disability are necessary factors in explaining the social world of work and contemporary organizational behaviour. And while these variables are examined in far more detail in Chapter 8, we do not suggest that this book single-handedly redresses the imbalance in teaching and writing on these topics. Here we can do little more than skim the surface, but we hope that by adding these issues to the work behaviour equation, we can encourage more lecturers in organizational behaviour to give major coverage to these important issues, and support more students in asking serious questions about issues of diversity and equity.

globalization & organization misbehaviour

Source: Creatas

The appeal of 'temporary' workers

Historically, employers have adjusted how work is performed to maximize profitability. The replacement of cottage industries with factories, for example, was designed to increase employers' control over workers, and thus over the profits that could be wrung out of them (Marglin, 1974). Recent employer interest in using more temporary workers – often hired through a third-party agency – is simply another adjustment in organizational form in the pursuit of maximal profits.

Of course, temporary employment is not always bad. For example, actors Russell Crowe and Nicole Kidman are temporary workers – filming movies as it suits them. But most temporary workers are not independently wealthy. Indeed, temporary work is an important aspect of the broader concept of the precariousness of employment. Precarious employment can be defined as 'paid work characterized by limited social benefits and statutory entitlements, job insecurity, low wages and high risks of ill health' (Vosko, 2006: 4).

One reason employers find precarious employment so attractive is that it is often possible to arrange things so that workers are categorized as 'independent contractors' instead of 'employees'. Independent contractors frequently fall outside the ambit of protective employment legislation – laws that stipulate minimum wages, maximum hours of work and compensation for workplace injuries. When workers are contracted through a temporary work agency, it is often difficult to determine who is even the true employer – the agency or the employer who contracts with agency for the workers.

Australia's hotel industry, for example, frequently obtains staff via temporary work agencies. These temporary workers reduce the hotels' recruitment and wage costs, as well as accommodating seasonal (and sometimes daily) fluctuations in demand for cleaning and culinary staff. These temporary employees face significant instability in terms of pay, hours of work and duties, as well as few opportunities to increase their skills or seek permanent employment (Knox, 2010).

Permanent employees also report feeling pressured to work faster or harder for fear of being replaced. In effect, the presence of precarious workers disciplines permanent staff to work harder. And there is significant research linking precarious employment with negative health and safety outcomes. This includes a greater likelihood of experiencing a workplace injury, as well as poorer mental health and cardiovascular morbidity (McNamara et al., 2011).

Such precariousness of employment often overlaps with other forms of vulnerability. For example, international migrant workers often face this type of employment, but migrant workers' willingness to enforce the rights they do have may be further eroded due to their lack of citizenship. For example, David Gibney, an Irish worker who spent 2 years in Melbourne, notes that:

> Irish workers in Australia on a 457 visa are often exploited due to the fact their visa is tied to their employer and the withdrawal of their contract can often mean having a number of weeks to either find alternative sponsorship or to exit the country. (*Irish Times*, 2014)

Migrant workers from non-English-speaking countries may also face linguistic and social isolation, further reducing their willingness to rock the boat. Some governments are responding to the seemingly systemic exploitation of migrant workers with new legislation. For example, the New Zealand government is considering criminalizing the abuse of migrant workers. This follows reports that migrant workers hired to rebuild Christchurch in the wake of the 2013 earthquake were not paid for months and were often required to work on weekends for free (Su, 2014).

Stop! Do you think that temporary or agency work has any usefulness? If so, in what circumstances or under what restrictions? What balance should be struck between employers' rights to (re)organize work in the most profitable way and workers' rights to decent pay and safe workplaces? Do individuals who are not citizens of the country they are working in need and deserve additional protection in the workplace?

Sources and further information

Irish Times (2014) 'Know your rights as a temporary worker in Australia'. Available at: http://www.irishtimes.com/blogs/generationemigration/2014/02/05/know-your-rights-as-a-temporary-worker-in-australia/.

Knox, A. (2010) '"Lost in translation": an analysis of temporary work agency employment in hotels', *Work, Employment and Society*, 24(3), pp. 449–67.

Marglin, S. (1974) 'What do bosses do? The origins and functions of hierarchy in capitalist production', *Review of Radical Political Economy*, 6, pp. 60–112.

McNamara, M., Bohle, P. and Quinlain, M. (2011) 'Precarious employment, working hours, work-life-conflict and health in hotel work', *Applied Ergonomics*, 42, pp. 225–32.

Su, R. (2014) 'New Zealand migrant workers complain of exploitation; law proposed to make worker abuse a crime', *International Business Times*. Available at: http://au.ibtimes.com/articles/533030/20140106/new-zealand-christchurch-filipino-migrant-workers-worker.htm (accessed November 25, 2014).

Vosko, L. (2006) 'Precarious employment: towards an improved understanding of labour market insecurity', in L. Vosko (ed.), *Precarious Employment: Understanding Labour Market Insecurity in Canada*, Montreal: McGill-Queen's University Press.

Note: This feature was written by Bob Barnetson, Associate Professor of Labour Relations, Athabasca University, Canada.

Researching organizational behaviour

It has been said that what you see depends on where you stand, and this is especially true when studying organizational life. How researchers approach their study of work and organizations depends on their life experiences and a whole series of assumptions they make about people and society. Although this is acknowledged in most standard textbooks, accounts of organizational behaviour tend to be presented in a sanitized, matter-of-fact way, as an uncontested field of study devoid of controversy. Yet there are profound differences of opinion among academics about how work and organizations are designed, how people are managed and how they should be studied. Much of the controversy stems from competing theoretical perspectives, which we can define for our purposes as frameworks of interconnected beliefs, values and assumptions that guide our thinking and research on the nature of the social world. In organizational behaviour, these rival perspectives or ideologies tend to be reflected in different schools of thought, each of which disseminates its research findings through particular academic journals (Burrell and Morgan, 1979; Mills et al., 2005).

perspective: an overall approach to or viewpoint on some subject

When people ask, 'What's your perspective on this?', they might just as well be asking, 'What is your bias on this?' because each **perspective** reflects a particular bias based on our life experience, how we see an issue and our vested interests. Thus, perspectives are the theoretical 'lenses' or 'road maps' that we use to view the social world. When we refer to a perspective on organizational behaviour, we are therefore speaking of an interconnected set of beliefs, values and intentions that legitimize academic and organizational behaviours. Before we continue further with our educational journey in organizational behaviour, it is worth considering two fundamental questions: 'What major perspectives do academics adopt when studying behaviour in work organizations?', and 'To what extent can researchers construct a truly objective account of behaviour in work organizations?'

Major theoretical perspectives on organizational behaviour

Organizational behaviour theorists using one or more theoretical perspectives or 'lenses' offer many competing explanations to the question 'Why do people in organizations do what they do?' At the risk of glossing over a multiplicity of theoretical perspectives that academics identify with and defend with passion, it is possible to identify four competing ideological camps into which many, or most, academics fall. These are the managerialist, the **conflict**, the symbolic-interactionist and the feminist camps. These perspectives or **paradigms** will serve as useful points of reference for understanding the competing views discussed throughout the remainder of the book.

conflict perspective: the sociological approach that views groups in society as engaged in a continuous power struggle for the control of scarce resources

paradigm: a term used to describe a cluster of beliefs that dictates for researchers in a particular discipline what should be studied, how research should be conducted and how the results should be interpreted

The managerialist perspective

The managerialist perspective is also referred to as the *structural-functionalist* perspective in sociology, and is adhered to by most researchers studying organizations. Managerialists view organizations as complex systems whose parts work together to promote consensus and stability. They are interested in order, employee commitment and performance issues, with a partisan preference for managers rather than the managed. Although there are variations and tensions, functionalists make a number of core assumptions about the nature of organizational behaviour.

In their view, the question 'Why do managers do what they do?' is largely explained by the fact that managers serve as the 'agents' of owners and investors, and that, as agents, they strive to maximize efficiency and profits. Managers strive to be rational. That is, they systematically apply various techniques to accomplish some given goal. The organization itself is characterized as a paragon of rational decision making. Managers do what they do because of the imperatives of 'the market'. Those who do not manage in this way are deemed to be 'unsuccessful'. The managerialist perspective therefore becomes inseparable from the notion of efficiency and effectiveness. The focus of much of the research endeavour is on finding the 'winning formula' so that more managers can achieve prescribed goals by successfully shaping the behaviour of others.

Within the mainstream managerialist school, there are differences of view. The *contingency* literature focuses largely on the internal authority structure of the organization, and acknowledges that different technologies, depending upon their complexity, strongly explain managerial behaviour and impose different kinds of demands on people and organizations (Woodward, 1965). The *strategic choice* literature (see Figure 1.3) emphasizes that managerial behaviour is 'bounded' by such factors as cognitive capacity, imperfect information, organizational politics, strategic business decisions, workers' resistance and managers' beliefs, values and philosophies. Common to most variations of the managerialist paradigm is a failure to connect organizational behaviour to the larger dominant political economic paradigm of neo-liberalism.

The critical perspective

The critical management perspective views capitalism and organizations as a system that is both economically exploitative and socially alienating. The work organization is understood as an arena of inequality, exploitation and structured antagonism that generates conflict. Accordingly, understanding managerial behaviour is related to action to reduce the indeterminacy that results from the unspecified nature of the employment relationship. In turn, employees' misbehaviour and open conflict between employers and employees reflects some level of individual or collective discontent with the employment relationship. Critical theorists are interested in power, control, the degradation of work, inequality and conflict, with a partisan preference for the less powerful – the managed rather than the managers.

As is the case with the mainstream managerialist perspective, the critical management perspective is based on many theoretical ideas. Obviously, the starting point is criticism itself, that is, an identification of the limitations, paradoxes, contradictions and ideological functions of the orthodox standpoint (Thompson and McHugh, 2009).

plate 4 Information overload can lead to poor decisions and work-related stress.

Source: Getty Images

The symbolic-interactionist perspective

The behaviours of managers and other employees interacting in the workplace are the typical social behaviours that catch the attention of symbolic interactionists. Whereas managerialist and conflict theorists both analyse macro-level patterns of behaviour, the symbolic-interactionist perspective generalizes about everyday forms of individual-level social interaction in order to understand social behaviour. The symbolic-interactionist paradigm is captured in Karl Weick's notions of 'enactment' and 'sense-making' (Weick, 1995). It is argued that a sense of mission, goals and a language are constructed and communicated (or 'enacted') so that employees can make sense of what it is they do, and explain what it is they have accomplished.

The feminist perspective

feminism: the belief that all people – both women and men – are equal, and that they should be valued equally and have equal rights

The **feminist** perspective emerged out of criticisms of traditional research, which feminist scholars argue has been mainly concerned with research *on* men *by* men. The feminist perspective involves more than just criticizing the use of masculine pronouns and nouns (see Chapter 11). It is rooted in a critical analysis of society, and draws attention to aspects of organizational life that other perspectives neglect. We explore these different perspectives in more detail in Chapter 3.

Which of the four perspectives should a student use when studying workplaces? Each offers unique insights into the behaviour in organizations (Table 1.3). We do not aim to give preference to a singular perspective, but rather to provide a frame of reference against which readers can learn and develop their own understanding of organizational behaviour. Our view is that organizational behaviour cannot be understood without appreciating that organizations are places where those with power determine what work is done and how it is done, as well as the effects on people of getting work done in a certain way. We think these are really important issues that should be examined and debated in any study of organizational behaviour.

Table 1.3 Comparing major perspectives on organizational behaviour

Topic	Managerialist	Conflict	Symbolic-interactionist	Feminist
View of society	Stable Well integrated	Unstable Tension	Dynamic	Inequality
Key concepts	Functions Dysfunctions	Capitalism Power	Symbols Communications	Patriarchy
Primary focus	Management practices Performance	Conflict Control	Sense making	Gender equality
Prescriptions	Better practices Greater cooperation	Employee ownership and control	Create space Dialogue	Law reforms
Proponents	Emile Durkheim Talcott Parsons	Karl Marx Richard Hyman	George Mead Karl Weick	Mary Wollstonecraft Kate Millett

Organizational behaviour theorists as researchers

epistemology: a theory of knowledge particularly used to refer to a standpoint on what should pass as acceptable knowledge

ontology: a theory of whether social entities such as organizations can and should be considered as objective entities with a reality external to the individuals who form part of them, or as social constructions built up from the perceptions and behaviour of these individuals

objectivism: an *ontological* position which asserts that the meaning of social phenomena has an existence independent of individuals; compare this with **constructionism**

constructionism: the view that researchers actively construct reality on the basis of their understandings, which are mainly the result of a shared culture. It contrasts with realism (see below)

Organizational behaviour theorists do not merely approach their subject from different paradigms; they also make different assumptions about the way in which organizations should be investigated. In addition, they employ varied research methods to build and test organizational behaviour theory. The second question we asked – 'To what extent can academics construct a truly objective account of behaviour in work organizations?' – brings up issues of social ontology (which deals with the nature of being), **epistemology** (the theory of knowledge) and research methodology, which all affect the conduct of research into organizational behaviour. We have no wish to re-route our intellectual journey into an academic quagmire, but readers need some sense of these issues in order to appreciate some rather different aspects of the debate about organizational behaviour.

Social **ontology** issues are concerned with whether social entities, such as formal organizations, can and should be considered as objective entities with a reality that exists outside the individuals who work there, or whether they can and should be considered as no more than social constructions built up from the perceptions and actions of those individuals. These positions are referred to respectively as **objectivism** and **constructionism**. One simple way to think about this distinction is to look at the working of a hospital. In any hospital, there is a hierarchy of authority, a mission statement, a division of labour that assigns people to different jobs, and rules and regulations for doing those jobs. People learn the rules and follow the standardized procedures. The organization represents a social order in that it exerts pressure on its members to conform to the rules and regulations.

The 'objectivist' view is that the hospital (as an organization, not as a building) possesses a reality that is external to any individual who occupies it. Individuals come and go, but the organization persists, so it is something that is 'out there' in the social world, and not just something that exists in people's minds.

Constructionism is an ontological position which asserts that social entities such as work organizations are produced or constructed by individuals through their social interaction. The core of the 'constructivist' discourse is that organizational reality does not have an objective existence, but is constructed in the accounts of organizational researchers and others. The constructivist concept of a hospital, for example, is one of a 'social order'. The hospital does not just encompass the formal rules; it is concerned with informal rules and activities as well. For instance, the official rules may state that only a doctor can increase a patient's medication but, unofficially, nurses are routinely given the power to do this. Both these understandings become part of the researcher's construction of the hospital.

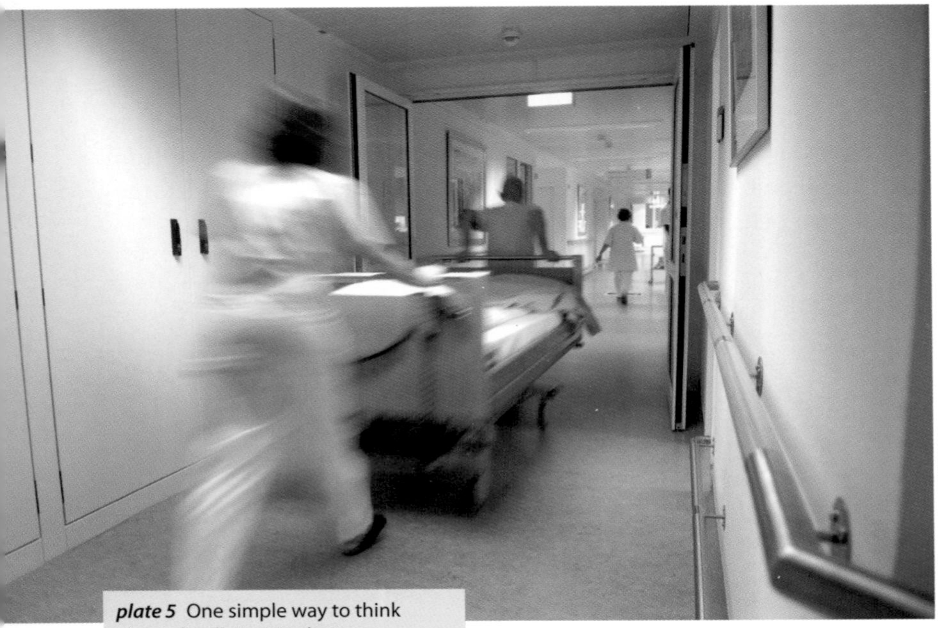

The social order of any work organization is characterized as an outcome of agreed-upon patterns of actions among the different social actors involved, and the social order is in a constant state of change because the informal agreements are constantly being established, revoked or revised (Palys and Atchison, 2013; Schwandt, 1994). The notion that knowledge and truth are created, rather than objectively discovered by researchers, means that constructionists are more inclined to challenge researchers to re-examine their perspectives, the research process itself and the whole process of producing knowledge.

An epistemological issue concerns the question of what is (or should be) regarded as acceptable knowledge in the social sciences, for example what forms of knowledge can be collected, and what is to be regarded as 'true' or 'false'. An important issue in this context is whether organizational behaviour can and should be investigated according to the same principles and methods as the physical sciences. The doctrine of **positivism** affirms the importance of modelling social science research on the physical sciences.

The French social theorists Auguste Comte (1798–1857) and Emile Durkheim (1858–1917) were early leaders in embracing positivist approaches to understanding human behaviour. There are five working assumptions that 'positivists' make in approaching their research. First, knowledge is arrived at through the gathering of social facts, which provide the basis for generalizations or laws by which human behaviour operates. Second, the purpose of theory is to generate hypotheses that can be tested, and this allows explanations of laws to be assessed. Third, only phenomena and regularities confirmed by the senses (that is, by, for example,

plate 5 One simple way to think about the distinction between the objectivist and constructivist positions is to look at the working of a hospital.

Source: © iStockphoto.com/thelinke

positivism: a view held in quantitative research in which reality exists independently of the perceptions and interpretations of people; a belief that the world can best be understood through scientific enquiry

sight or hearing) can genuinely be warranted as knowledge. Fourth, research can and must be conducted in a way that is value-free. And finally, social science must distinguish between 'scientific' statements and normative statements (Bryman, 2012). This means the social science deals with 'what is', not with what 'should be'.

It is a common mistake to equate positivism with 'scientific'. Many social scientists differ fundamentally over how best to characterize scientific practice. An alternative term to describe the nature of social 'science' practice is **realism** (Bhaskar, 1989; Sayer, 2000). This epistemological position shares two features with positivism: a belief that the social sciences can and should use the same approach to the collection of data and to its analysis, and a commitment to an external reality.

Two forms of realism can be identified. *Empirical realism* simply asserts that, using appropriate methods, social reality can be understood. *Critical realism* is a philosophy of and for the social sciences. It distinguishes between the social world and people's experience of it, as well as between the real, the actual and the empirical. It maintains that deeper social structures and generative processes lie beneath the surface of observable social structures and patterns. For empirical realists, a social scientist is only able to understand the social world – and so change it – if he or she is able to identify the structures at work that generate human activity.

An example of the application of both symbolic interactionism and critical realism is the work of Yrjö Engeström on informal workplace learning (discussed in Chapter 7). Individual and small group learning is understood as an observable social process – the 'tip of the iceberg' – but learning is also embedded in an interlocking human activity system – the 'submerged part of the iceberg' – consisting of a community of practice, rules and division of labour.

The doctrine of **interpretivism** is a contrasting epistemology to positivism. The interpretivists' preference is for an empathetic 'understanding' and interpretation of human behaviour. For them, it is important to examine how people define their situation, how they make sense of their lives, and how their sense of self develops in interaction with other people. The interpretive approach has its intellectual roots in Max Weber's concept of understanding, or *Verstehen* (*Verstehen* being a German word that can be translated as 'human understanding'). In Weber's view, the social scientist should try to imagine how a particular individual perceives social actions, and understand the meaning an individual attaches to a particular event. The symbolic-interactionist perspective attempts to provide an empathetic understanding of how individuals see and interpret the events of their everyday work experiences.

The purpose of this brief discussion of epistemological issues in social research is to point out that, over the last 30 years or so, some organizational theorists have abandoned the application of the canons of physical science – positivism – to the study of human enquiry. The ontological and epistemological issues we outlined above have direct implications for research methodology.

Research methods used by researchers

Researchers can choose a variety of research methods to study work and organizational behaviour. These methods can be broadly classified as either quantitative or qualitative methods. Each strategy reflects differences in ontological and epistemological considerations: differences in the types of question asked, the kinds of evidence considered appropriate for answering a question, the degree to which the analysis is carried out by converting observations to numerical or non-numerical data, and the methods used to process the data. It is therefore important to recognize that these methods are not simply a neutral toolkit; they are linked with the

---

realism: the idea that a reality exists out there independently of what and how researchers think about it. It contrasts with constructionism

critical realism: a realist epistemology which asserts that the study of human behaviour should be concerned with identifying the structures that generate that behaviour in order to change it

interpretivism: the view held in many qualitative studies that reality comes from shared meaning among people in that environment

ways in which researchers view and connect to different viewpoints. As Bryman explains, the method used by the researcher 'does not exist in a bubble, hermetically sealed off from the social sciences and the various intellectual allegiances that their practitioners hold ... methods of social research are closely tied to different versions of how social reality should be studied' (Bryman, 2012: 19). The seminal text by Weber (1949) examined this epistemological debate on the neutrality or bias of social science researchers.

Quantitative research can be defined as a research strategy that emphasizes numerical data and statistical analyses, and that involves a *deductive* approach to theorizing. It incorporates the practices and norms of positivism, is oriented towards aggregated data that compile responses from many respondents so that general patterns are visible (a process called nomothetic analysis), and embodies a view of social reality as a relatively constant, objective reality.

Qualitative research, on the other hand, can be defined as a research strategy that emphasizes non-numerical data, involves an *inductive* approach to theorizing, rejects positivism, is oriented towards case studies (a process called ideographic analysis), and embodies a view of social reality as the product of individual thought.

Figure 1.7 compares the differences between quantitative and qualitative, at least as they have historically been associated with different assumptions. At first glance, the quantitative/qualitative distinction seems to be about whether quantitative researchers employ more 'hard' measurements than qualitative researchers do, but there is in fact much more to it than that. These two approaches affect how social scientists do research and are fundamental to understanding any enquiry into organizational behaviour.

quantitative research: refers to research methods that emphasize numerical precision and deductive theorizing

qualitative research: refers to the gathering and sorting of information through a variety of techniques, including interviews, focus groups and observations, and inductive theorizing

deductive approach: research in which the investigator begins with a theory and then collects information and data to test the theory

inductive approach: the researcher begins with data collection and observations and then data are used to develop theory

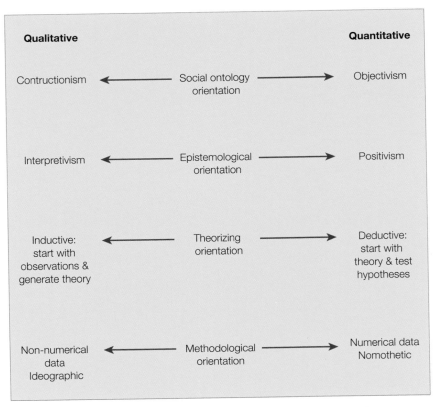

Figure 1.7 A scheme for comparing quantitative and qualitative research strategies

Source: Adapted from Figure 1.1 in *Sociological Paradigms and Organisational Analysis,* by Gibson Burrell and Gareth Morgan, 1985, Ashgate

In the ebook click on the play button to watch the author of this textbook talking about quantitative and qualitative research, and then answer the following questions:

- What is John's view on the influences impacting research?
- What does John mean when he suggests that politics play a role in research into organizational behaviour?

Links to management   John Bratton

Source: PhotoDisc/ Getty Images

Knowledge, evidence and propaganda

How do we produce knowledge about a phenomenon as complex as organizational behaviour? How do we find out what is true and what works in this particular area of human endeavour?

Philosopher Paul Boghossian (2006) offers us one way to think about these difficult questions. Using the subject of the first inhabitants of North America as an example, he offers the following perspective on how we arrive at rational beliefs:

> We may not know the facts [about North American's first inhabitants] … but, having formed an interest in the question, we seek to know. And we have a variety of techniques and methods – observation, logic, inference to the best explanation and so forth, but not tea-leaf reading or crystal ball gazing – that we take to be the only legitimate ways of forming rational beliefs about the subject. These methods – the methods characteristic of what we call 'science' but which also characterize ordinary modes of knowledge-seeking – have led us to the view that the first Americans came from Asia across the Bering Strait. This view may be false, of course, but it is the most reasonable one, given the evidence. (p. 4)

This perspective on knowledge is one version of what Boghossian calls the classical view of knowledge. This classical view typically includes the following set of assumptions:

- We should have evidence for believing something is true.
- We should look impartially at all the evidence, and not just the evidence that confirms what we already believe to be true. We should acknowledge that our beliefs are fallible.
- When confronted by new evidence, we should be willing to revise our beliefs about what is true or what works.

The classical view of knowledge offers a powerful way to think about how the knowledge on any given thing or process ought to be produced. It serves as an invaluable reference point for those who seek to understand how organizations work, and why people in organizations behave the way they do. So, for example, we could ask whether an organization is attaining its goals and, if it is not, what course of action might enable it to do so. Evidence

enters into this investigation at two key points: evidence supporting a claim that the organization's goals are not being met, and evidence supporting the claim that a particular course of action would enable it to attain its goals.

The classical model of knowledge, with its emphasis on evidence, is relevant here. But does it follow that the study of organizational behaviour is 'value-free' and is somehow insulated from politics and power? Not necessarily. Researchers need to recognize that an organization's goals may be contested and that the most obvious, official, versions of the organization's goals may not tell the whole story. Moreover, researchers have long recognized the existence of bureaucratic propaganda. Organizations may manipulate evidence to make it appear that official goals are being met.

So it makes sense for students of organizational behaviour to be aware of classical views of truth and evidence. The idea that we should use evidence to determine what is true and what works in the world of organizations is a useful starting point. But politics has a way of infiltrating the world of organizations and the knowledge we produce about organizations. Students should therefore be open to critical views of truth and should recognize that goal conflict, misinformation and manipulation of evidence are not uncommon in the world of organizations.

Stop! Debates over the role of Wal-Mart in society offer an interesting perspective on the issues of propaganda and counterpropaganda. Critics charge that Wal-Mart is guilty of discrimination and, more generally, that it contributes to 'reproletarianization' (a process that turns back the clock on the rights and protections that workers have won over the last century). Wal-Mart has fought back, pointing to the various benefits it has brought to the communities where it is located. Take a moment to assess critically the various positions in this debate, starting with the following resources:

- www.walmartwatch.com (for a critique of Wal-Mart)
- www.walmartfacts.com (for a defence of Wal-Mart).

If you were researching organizational behaviour in Wal-Mart, what biases might you yourself bring to the subject, and why?

Sources and further information

Boghossian, P. (2006) *Fear of Knowledge: Against Relativism and Constructivism*, Oxford: Oxford University Press.

Gereffi, G. and Christian, M. (2009) 'The impacts of Wal-Mart: the rise and consequences of the world's dominant retailer', *Annual Review of Sociology*, 35, pp. 573–91.

Note: This feature was written by David MacLennan, Assistant Professor, Thompson Rivers University, Canada.

Drawing on the elements in Figure 1.1, you should now be better able to account for researchers' misrepresentation of social reality. First, researchers make different ontological assumptions that affect how they attempt to investigate and obtain 'knowledge' about organizational behaviour. For example, if a researcher subscribes to the view that organizations are objective social entities that shape individual behaviour, the research endeavour is likely to focus upon an analysis of the formal properties and regularities between the various elements of the organization. Alternatively, if the researcher subscribes to a view that emphasizes the dynamic nature of organizational life, he or she will focus on the active participation of individuals in constructing reality.

Second, the epistemological assumptions that researchers make about the social world affect how they attempt to investigate and obtain 'knowledge' about organizational behaviour. As we have discussed, at the heart of epistemology lie questions such as 'What is the relation between seeing and knowing?' and 'Whose knowledge is produced in surveys and interviews?' For the positivists, the challenge is to discover the laws of human behaviour, and perhaps then predict future social action. The constructivists reject the notion that we can ever have an objective account of the phenomenon under investigation, because all such accounts are 'linguistic reconstructions'.

As we have seen, the constructivist approach recognizes that the researcher and those being researched create the data. Researchers' data do not discover social reality; rather, the 'discovery' arises from the interactive process (between the researcher and the organization) and the political, cultural and structural contexts. Traditionally, the interview, for example, is viewed as an opportunity for knowledge to be transmitted between, for instance, a manager and a researcher. Yet, through the interactional process, the viewed and the viewer are active *makers of meaning*, assembling and modifying their questions and answers in response to the dynamics of the interview. The researcher is not simply a conduit for information, but is in fact deeply implicated in the production of knowledge (Charmaz, 2005).

The constructivist approach suggests that what the manager and the situation actually are is a consequence of various accounts and interpretations. From this perspective, managers act as the 'practical authors' of their own identities. Furthermore, some interpretations are more equal than others. For example, one account of Tony Blair's leadership performance following the September 11, 2001 attack on the World Trade Center in New York might describe it as 'Churchillian eloquence'. Others could interpret his speeches as populist rhetoric. The point here is that if more powerful 'voices' (including the popular press and television news channels) support Blair, 'the Churchillian' view will prevail, and the negative voice will carry little weight. The constructivist conclusion in this case is that what is important is not what the leader (or the organization) is 'really' like, but the processes by which he or she (or it) is perceived and defined as a success or a failure. In terms of managerial behaviour, what constitutes a 'good' manager does not rest on an objective evaluation but on criteria generated by the social setting (Bratton et al., 2005; Grint, 1995).

This does not mean that constructing accurate knowledge is impossible. Rather, it means that the knowledge that is produced on what people in organizations allegedly do cannot be an objective narrative about their workplace activities. We must maintain a healthy scepticism as we read what researchers have to say about organizational behaviour.

Third, there are different research strategies, or general orientations for conducting an enquiry. The different research designs – such as questionnaire surveys, interviews and observational studies – may capture distortions of reality. For example, the mailed survey (a questionnaire sent out to employees or customers) is favoured

stop...

According to the constructivist approach to knowledge making, language does not transmit truth; instead, it produces what we come to regard as truth. What are your views of the positivist and constructivist models? University administrators are concerned that students experience difficulty in getting to speak to their tutors face to face. How would a positivist researcher approach this problem? How would a constructivist approach the problem? What are the implications of positivist and constructivist approaches for understanding research on organizational behaviour?

...and reflect

by quantitative researchers, but it can at best only provide a 'snapshot' of managerial and employee workplace activities. It cannot hope to provide an accurate picture of the subtleties and dynamics of employment relationships, or of how individuals perceive social actions. The sample size may vary considerably, and if small samples of organizational members were surveyed, one or more atypical participants could unduly influence the findings. Case studies and direct observational techniques, favoured by qualitative researchers, often provide 'rich' data on workplace activities but may not capture cognitive processes. For example, a manager who is captured sitting in his or her office staring through the window could be either reflecting on a long-term plan or simply admiring the spring blossom.

Finally, we should be aware that management is embedded in the social structure and is highly political. This means that it involves power relationships between managers and non-managers, and between managers and other managers. As a result, political issues will rarely be far removed from the research process (Easterby-Smith et al., 1991). Consequently, the data gathered by researchers might not provide a 'reality report' on what managers do inside the organization, but rather reflect the diversity of managers and their need for self-justification, perhaps in connection with complex internal power struggles.

To extend our discussion of the limitations of research methodology a little further, managerial behaviour is most often analysed using 'scientific' or positivist methods, but scholars of organizational behaviour sometimes quote managers' opinions to the exclusion of the opinions of other people who are affected by the managers' actions (not least, their subordinates). Interviewing people from a cross-section of the organization, including workers and trade union representatives in unionized establishments, is always likely to provide 'nuggets' of information that rarely surface in positivist research, and to suggest different lines of interpretation of human behaviour in the workplace (Bratton, 1992: 14).

Chapter summary

- In this introductory chapter, we have attempted to cover a wide range of complex issues. We introduced STEPLE analysis to emphasize that external contexts have a significant impact on the organization as well as on individuals and groups. The external context influences the structure and behaviour of work organizations, and in turn organizations influence the wider society. The linkage between the external contexts and the search for competitive advantage through employees' behaviour is complex.

- Organizational behaviour is a field of study with no agreed boundaries and draws from a variety of social science disciplines. We have defined it as a multidisciplinary field of inquiry concerned with the systematic study of formal organizations, the behaviour of people within organizations, and important features of their social context that structure all the activities that occur inside the organization.

- Studying organizational behaviour can help put people in a stronger position to influence and shape the workplace and their own future. Organizational behaviour provides a conceptual 'toolbox', a 'Swiss army knife', to help to explain, predict and control organizational actions.

- We have reviewed orthodox treatments of management – as a set of technical competencies, functionally necessary tasks and universal roles and processes that are found in any work organization. For the traditionalist, managerial work is regarded as rational, morally and politically neutral, and its history and legitimacy are taken for granted. Alternative accounts of management emphasize that managerial work is embedded in a politically charged arena of structured and contested power relationships.

- We have used a three-dimensional management model to help us deconstruct the many facets of organizational complexity. This encourages us to go beyond simply describing managerial behaviour, to provide an understanding of the contingencies that explain why managerial policies and behaviour vary in time and space. Managers are typically engaged in an assortment of frenetic, habitual, reactive, fragmented activities.

- We also focused on diversity because we consider that the social dynamics of class, gender, race and ethnicity underpin contemporary organizational behaviour. Understanding the significance of class, gender, race and ethnicity, and disability puts the behaviour of individuals and groups in the organization into a wider social context.

- We identified four major theoretical frameworks or paradigms used by organizational behaviour theorists to study of behaviour in organizations: the structural-functionalist perspective, the symbolic-interactionist perspective, the conflict perspective and the feminist perspective.

- Finally, we discussed two ontological orientations – objectivism and constructionism – and two epistemological orientations – positivism and interpretivism – and outlined how these influence decisions on research methodology. Depending on the researcher's perspective, which reflects a whole series of assumptions about the nature of the social world, organizational behaviour researchers will tend to lean towards either quantitative or qualitative research strategies.

IN THE EBOOK ACCESS **WEB BASED ASSIGNMENTS** TO APPLY YOUR LEARNING.

Chapter review questions

1 What is meant by 'organizations' and 'organizational behaviour'?
2 What are capitalism, management and globalization?
3 Give three reasons for studying organizational behaviour.
4 Some authors state that organizational behaviour relates to the process of a manager's job. What does this mean?
5 Which of the four sociological perspectives do you think best fits your own ideas about human behaviour in work organizations?

6 Why is it important to include gender, race and disability in the study of behaviour at work?
7 If you were asked to conduct research in organizational behaviour, which research approach would you use? Explain your preference.

Further reading

Atkinson, C. (2008) 'An exploration of small firm psychological contracts', *Work, Employment and Society*, 22(3), pp. 447–65.

Bakan, J. (2004) *The Corporation*, London: Penguin.

Bratton, J. and Gold, J. (2015) 'Towards critical human resource management education (CHRME): a sociological imagination approach', *Work, Employment and Society*, doi:10.1177/0950017014545266.

Bryman, A. (2012) *Social Science Methods* (4th edn), Oxford: Oxford University Press.

Cottrell, S. (2011) *Critical Thinking Skills: Developing Effective Analyst and Argument* (2nd edn), Basingstoke: Palgrave Macmillan.

Dundon, T., Dobbins, T., Cullinane, N., Hickland, E. and Donaghey, J. (2014) 'Employer occupation of regulatory space of the Employee Information and Consultation (I&C) Directive in liberal market economies', *Work, Employment and Society* (28), pp. 21–39.

Jacoby, S. (2005) *The Embedded Corporation*, Princeton, NJ: Princeton University Press.

Kornelakis, A. (2014) 'Liberalization, flexibility and industrial relations institutions: evidence from Italian and Greek banking', *Work, Employment and Society* (28), pp. 40–57.

McAlpine, R. (2014) *Common Weal: Practical Idealism for Scotland*, Glasgow: Jimmy Reid Foundation.

Morrison, M. (2013) 'PESTLE', pp. 110–52 in *Strategic Business Diagnostic Tools: Theory and Practice*, London: CreateSpace Independent Publishing.

Sainsbury, D. (2013) *Progressive Capitalism: How to Achieve Economic Growth, Liberty and Social Justice*, London: Biteback Publishing.

Weick, K. (2006) 'Faith, evidence, and action: better guesses in an unknowable world', *Organization Studies*, 27(11), pp. 1723–36.

Chapter case study: Managing change at Eastern University

The setting

In Canadian universities, it is evident that there is a need for positive change, including in how they manage and lead their employees. Various reports emphasize that they compete not only for government and sponsorship funding, but also for the market share of potential students in the increasingly competitive local, provincial and international arenas. In a university setting, key factors in facing these challenges successfully are cooperative and collaborative relationships between the administration and the unions representing the university's workers, including the support and faculty employees. Publicly funded universities are under increasing pressure to thrive in an atmosphere of reduced funding and increased competition. Working collaboratively in the same direction can produce a viable enduring future.

The problem

Eastern University College is located in Ontario, Canada, and has approximately 14,000 full-time and part-time students. It was recently granted full university status, enabling the institution to grant its own degrees. In addition, it was expanded to include a comprehensive distance learning programme as an alternative to traditional classroom learning. Resources for new research and developing postgraduate programmes are also planned for the near future. With these fresh opportunities, it was recognized that changes were needed in the institution's strategic direction, including in its management policies and practices.

The university's labour relations were a particular area of focus. Over the years, the university had developed an adversarial and confrontational relationship with the union representing the institution's 300 support workers. In a study undertaken by the administration to identify the drivers or resistors in creating a more positive alliance with the union, it was found that the university's hierarchical and bureaucratic organizational structure was one possible reason for the dysfunctional relationship. Agreements on issues became stalled as administrators were required to take items back to senior managers for their perusal. The union contributed to the delay of reaching resolutions as it referred back to its members for approval on any decisions to be made. In the process, each group sought to protect its own interests. The net result was loyalty to factions, departments, leaders and unions, rather than to the organization as a whole.

Lisa Chang, 28, was the new Assistant Human Resource Manager for Eastern University. Improving student services at the university was a high priority for Chang. Based on feedback from the students' union, one idea she had was to extend access to the computer labs so they would be available for student use 24 hours a day, 7 days a week, except when they were being used by lecturers for teaching.

Chang visited the websites of several universities and downloaded details of their student computer services. She met with the Manager of Facilities, Doug Brown, the Vice-president of Student Services, Dr Susan Allen, and the Head of Campus Security, Paul McGivern. Chang presented her proposal, which included the estimated cost, and was able to resolve the few questions the others had with examples and information acquired from other comparable universities. It was agreed that Chang would present her proposal to the next meeting of the Council of Deans.

The presentation to the deans went flawlessly. Chang was confident that the deans would agree to her proposal. But just as the meeting was to wrap up, the Dean of Arts said, 'Have the union agreed to this?' Alarm bells went off in Chang's head. 'Union?,' she thought. 'Why wouldn't they agree to the new service?' She told the Dean she would discuss it with her boss Peter Webster, Director of Human Resources.

At the next human resources management meeting to discuss the labour relations situation, administrators were reviewing the most recent grievances and potential arbitrations, and the generally poor relationship with the union representing the support staff. Peter Webster, a manager who had several years' experience in dealings with the union, sighed in frustration as he echoed a sentiment of many in the room. 'It seems to be impossible to work together collaboratively with this union. I think we may as well accept it.'

'It doesn't have to be this way,' said Chang, as she handed out copies of her proposed new student service. 'When I talked to one of the stewards last week, he actually expressed the same desire for a more cooperative relationship. That is a sign of positive change already.'

After some discussion on what could be done to build upon this progress, the group asked Lisa Chang to prepare a detailed report for the next meeting outlining the next steps.

The task

Working either alone or in a small group, prepare a report drawing on the material from this chapter that addresses the following:

- Thinking about the situation at Eastern University, how effective are Lisa Chang's and Peter Webster's performances in terms of each of Mintzberg's managerial roles?

- What recommendations would you make to the university's senior management? How would this help?

Sources and further information

Mintzberg, H. (1990) 'The manager's job: folklore and fact', *Harvard Business Review*, March/April, pp. 163–76.

Mintzberg, H. (2009) *Managing*, Harlow, UK: Financial Times Prentice Hall.

van Wanrooy, B., Bewley, H., Bryson, A., Forth, J., Freeth, S., Stokes, L. and Wood, S. (2013) *The 2011 Workplace Employment Relations Study*, London: HMSO.

Vie, O. (2011) 'Have post-bureaucratic changes occurred in managerial work?' *European Management Journal,* 28(3), pp. 182–94.

Note: This case study was written by Dan Haley, Director of Human Resources, School District No. 57, Prince George, Canada.

IN THE EBOOK ACCESS AN **OB IN FILM** BOX THAT USES *THE IMITATION GAME* (2014), STARRING BENEDICT CUMBERBATCH AND KEIRA KNIGHTLEY, AND *WORKING GIRL* (1988), STARRING MELANIE GRIFFITH AND SIGOURNEY WEAVER, TO ILLUSTRATE POWER, POLITICS AND GENDER ISSUES IN THE WORKPLACE AND TO ACCESS **AN INTERACTIVE QUIZ** TO TEST YOUR UNDERSTANDING.

chapter 2
The social nature of work

Chapter learning outcomes

After completing this chapter, you should be able to:

1. Explain the function and meaning of work
2. Explain the relationship between work and an individual's personal and social identity
3. Summarize the historical dimensions of work, pre-industry, the factory system, occupational changes and the emergence of knowledge work in the virtual worksite
4. Identify some key strategic issues involved in designing work
5. Discuss the debates around issues of emotional labour and work–life balance

introduction

The effects of the current global economic crisis on employment and living conditions have brought to the fore, once again, the changing nature of work and the quality of people's life at work. It is a paradox of life that its recognizable features are often the most difficult to understand, and this observation is highly relevant to the topic of work. Whether defined in conventional economic terms as 'paid work' or defined more inclusively as a broad range of activities beyond the boundaries of paid employment, work is, in many ways, at the centre of social life. It affects the nature of day-to-day interaction in the workplace and the most personal aspects of our experience in the family and the community. It can also have catastrophic outcomes, as shown by the death of 301 coal miners in Soma, western Turkey, in May 2014. Decisions about how paid work is organized and performed have created many different and contrasting types of work and patterns of social relations.

deindustrialization: a term to describe the decline of the manufacturing sector of the economy

occupation: a category of jobs that involve similar activities at different work sites

Since the Industrial Revolution, as factories have become more capital intensive, manual labour has undergone a transformation (Griffin, 2013). Most traditional 'trade' or 'craft' jobs based on tacit knowledge have disappeared or have been 'deskilled', lessening control by the craft workers who undertake them. Factory work has been increasingly influenced by the 'scientific management' principle of 'one best way' of organizing particular work tasks. As employment shifted from manufacturing to the service sector – the process of **deindustrialization** – the principles of scientific management became incorporated into clerical labour and professional work. Other trends throughout the twentieth century have been the growing presence of women in virtually all **occupations** and, especially since the 1990s, the global growth of flexible labour. Flexible labour is a plethora of employment contracts that are part time, fixed term, short term or seasonal and create what has become known as 'precarious' employment.

The essence of being human is to engage in waged labour, but most people have little influence over how their labour is designed and performed. Organizations can be regarded as the architects of waged work, as it is within organizations that work is structured, jobs are designed and the employment relationship is formed (Rubery, 2006). Paid work for most individuals and families is the primary source of income that determines their standard of living. But it is important for more than economic reasons. Bolton and Houlihan's (2009) book *Work Matters* juxtaposes both the bad and the good aspects of work. Waged work can be arduous, tedious, dirty, unhealthy and at times dangerous, but it can also bring connections and friendship, be a principal source of individuals' self-fulfilment and form part of their social identity. At the society level, how and where work is performed has consequences not only for the individuals who do it, but also for their families and for the communities they live in.

Writing about the 'transformation of work' might be described as a cottage industry for historians and sociologists. The historian E. P. Thompson, in *The Making of the English Working Class* (1963), gives a paradigm-setting account of the material losses and suffering that accompanied the transition to industrial work. Challenging this pessimist school of thought, Emma Griffin's book *Liberty's Dawn* (2013), while not denying the crushing poverty and degradation suffered by many individuals after the Industrial Revolution, offers an unromantic interpretation of rural work and living conditions, and argues that industrial work was characterized by regular employment, a vibrant labour market and some independence from the tyranny of rural employers.

Since the late 1970s, sociologists have offered both optimistic and pessimistic accounts of the effects of globalization and technological change on the nature of contemporary work. The optimistic scenario focuses on the potential liberating

stop...

Many predictions have been made about 'new' technology deskilling workers but, on the other hand, also liberating people from mundane work, and some even suggest that technology can create a 'leisure' society. What is your own view of the effects of information technology on work? Is it liberating or a curse?

...and reflect

effect of information technology. Andre Gorz, for example, predicted, under certain social conditions, 'the liberation of time and the abolition of work' (1982: 1). For more than a decade, Gorz set the trend for controversial 'future of work' books (Zuboff, 1988). In the optimist school, Jeremy Rifkin (1996) has argued that sophisticated 'Information Age' technologies are 'freeing up' the talent of men and women to create social capital in local communities. Similarly, Gates et al. (1996) have argued that computers allow us to increase the time we spend at leisure. Both Rifkin and Gates write very persuasively, and their material has reached a wide audience.

Critical scholarship offers strikingly different accounts of work found in the rhetoric of the Information Age and captures the realities of lower skilled work. Such accounts argue that the latest idiom of **flexibility** creates regimes that lead to the intensification of work, deskilling, tighter managerial control over work activities and work-based inequalities (Pahl, 1988; Wood, 1982). With a particular eye on the gendering of work, it is argued that 'Where the goal of most employers throughout the world is to get the work of one full-time male done for one part-time female at a fraction of the cost, talk of the new liberation from toil can sound offensive' (Pahl, 1988: 752). There is a growing consensus that there is currently a shortage of 'decent' work, with 'good' work being the preserve of the new privileged 'labour aristocracy' that is found in the professional, high-tech and creative industries, who are loosely defined as 'knowledge workers' (Atzeni, 2014; Bolton and Houlihan, 2009; Noon and Blyton, 2013). The effect of a neo-liberal ideology on employment over the last few decades has been to neglect the *quality* of work-related life. The Cambridge economist Ha-Joon Chang (2013) observes that issues of the quality of work and the connection between work and well-being have been marginalized in public discourse: 'the crisis for British wage-earners is much more than the cost of living. It is a work crisis too', he states.

This chapter has a very bold objective: to explain the nature of work in globalized capitalist societies, why work is connected to human well-being and why the design of work is important to understanding behaviour in organizations. This requires us to trace the evolution of work from early capitalism to late modernity. We look at the historical dimension of work in the belief that the current problems associated with work are an outcome of the past, and that the problems of the future are embedded in the social relations of work designed in the present. The broader context of work provides an essential background for understanding the connection between work, identity, dignity and private life, behavioural decisions in the workplace, and the implications for managing the employment relationship.

flexibility: action in response to global competition, including employees performing a number of tasks (functional flexibility), the employment of part-time and contract workers (numerical flexibility) and performance-related pay (reward flexibility)

Work and non-work

'What kind of work do you do?' is such a classic question that it is repeatedly asked in social conversation. This question is significant because it underscores the fact that paid work – employment – is generally considered to be a central defining feature of our identity. It is also one important means by which we judge others. Adults with paid jobs usually name their occupation by way of an answer, but we can see this question in a wider sense too. It invites us to explore the nature of work in relation to time, space and **social structure**.

Consider this everyday scene in any Western town or city. It is 2 o'clock in the afternoon, and a neighbourhood park is busy with adults and children enjoying themselves. Some are walking quickly through the park, perhaps going back to their office or store after their lunch break. A city employee is pruning roses in one of the flower beds. Near the bandstand, three musicians are playing a saxophone, a clarinet and a violin. Two people are playing tennis. Others are watching young children

social structure: the stable pattern of social relationships that exist within a particular group or society

play. A man sitting on a bench is reading a book, a woman is using a mobile phone, and a teenager is completing a printed form. This scene draws attention to the blurred boundary between work and non-work activity. It gives us an entry point for answering the question 'What is work?'

If we try to define some of these individual activities as work, the confusion and ambiguity about the meaning of work will become apparent. For example, the people walking back to their offices or to the shops might prune the roses in their gardens at the weekend, but they are unlikely to see the task in the same way as the gardener who is employed to do tasks such as pruning. The three musicians might be playing for amusement, or they might be rehearsing for an evening performance for which they will be paid. An amateur who plays tennis for fun and fitness does not experience or think of the game in the same way as a professional tennis player. Similarly, a parent keeping an eye on a child playing does not experience child care in the same way as a professional nanny. The person using the mobile phone might be talking to a friend, but she could be, say, a financial adviser phoning a client. The person filling in the form might be applying for a student grant, or might be a clerical worker catching up with an overdue job during his lunch hour. We can see from these examples that work cannot be defined simply by the activities that are carried out.

So what exactly is work? 'Work' can be contrasted with 'labour'. According to Williams, labour has a 'strong medieval sense of pain and toil' (Williams, 1983: 335), and 'work' can be distinguished from 'occupation', which is derived from a Latin word meaning 'to occupy or to seize' (Christiansen and Townsend, 2004: 2). The terms 'work', 'occupation' and 'job' have become interchangeable: work is not just an activity, something one *does*, but something a person *has* (Gorz, 1982). Conventionally, to 'have worked' or to 'have a job' is to use a place (or space) and sell time.

A substantial number of people have an *instrumental* orientation to work. They work for economic rewards in order to do non-work or leisure activity that they 'really enjoy'. For these people, life begins when work ends. Different occupations provide different levels of pay, so those doing them have different life chances and opportunities in terms of health, education, leisure pursuits and quality of life. Among people who 'have work', it is not simply the case that people need to work in order to have enough money to live on. People do paid work to earn money to acquire 'consumer power'. Thus, paid work is for many a means to an end – the consumption of commodities (buying designer clothes, fast cars, mobile phones and so on) or social consumption (such as drinking, dining out and holidaying). The central differentiating feature between people 'out of work' and those 'in work' is that the latter have much higher levels of consumer power and more choice about their lifestyle.

However, pay is only part of the equation. Research suggests that many people do paid work not primarily for extrinsic rewards (such as pay), but for the intrinsic rewards that work can bring, such as self-esteem, friendship, enjoyment and the social purpose of work. Traditionally, people occupying higher positions in an organization's hierarchy obtain more prestige and self-esteem than those in lower positions, and most people get satisfaction from participating in activities that demonstrably contribute to human well-being (Noon and Blyton, 2013).

> **stop...**
>
> Write down your own definition of 'work'. To help you, consider a chef preparing a meal at a five-star hotel, and the same chef going home and preparing the family meal. Are both activities 'work'?
>
> **...and reflect**

Source: Getty Images

plate 6 Work in the service sector often requires workers to provide more than physical labour. Jobs such as flight attendants, shop assistants and waiting at tables require workers to manage their feelings in order to create a publicly observable facial display: what Hochschild calls 'emotional labour'.

We can begin to understand the complexity of work and its social ramifications by exploring the following definition:

> Work refers to physical and mental activity that is carried out to produce or achieve something of value at a particular place and time; it involves a degree of obligation and explicit or implicit instructions, in return for pay or reward.

This definition draws attention to some central features of work (Thomas, 1999). First, the most obvious purpose of work is an economic one. The notions of 'physical and mental' and 'value' suggest that the activities of both a construction worker and a computer systems analyst can be considered as work. The 'mental activity' also includes the commercialization of human feeling, or what is called 'emotional labour'. Second, work is structured spatially – how social life is organized and where it is conducted geographically shape work and management practices (Herod et al., 2007). Throughout most of the twentieth century, work was typically carried out away from home and at set periods of the day or night. Thus 'place and time' locates work within a social context. However, in advanced capitalist economies, there are new expectations of spatial mobility and temporal flexibility (Hardill and Green, 2003; Noon and Blyton, 2013; Stravrou et al., 2015). The mass timetable of the '8 to 5' factory world, of the '9 to 5' office world and of recreational Sundays has given way to a flexi-place, flexi-time world. The Internet means that working times in a number of time zones may shape the timing of the working day.

Third, work always involves social relations between people: between employer and employee, between co-workers, between management and trade unions, and between suppliers and customers. Social relations in the workplace can be cooperative or conflictual, hierarchical or egalitarian. When a parent cooks dinner for the family, he or she does tasks similar to those performed by a cook employed by a hospital to prepare meals for patients. However, the social relations involved are quite different. Hospital cooks have more in common (in this sense) with factory or office workers than with parents, because their activities are governed by rules and regulations. They accept 'instructions' from the employer or the employer's agent, a manager. Obviously, then, it is not the nature of the activity that determines whether it is considered 'work', but rather the nature of the social relations in which the activity is embedded. Thus, to be 'in work' is to have a definite relationship with some other who has control of the time, place and activity.

extrinsic rewards: a wide range of external outcomes or rewards to motivate employees

intrinsic rewards: inner satisfaction following some action (such as recognition by an employer or co-workers) or intrinsic pleasures derived from an activity (such as playing a musical instrument for pleasure)

Finally, work is remunerated (that is, there is a reward for it). There are two types of reward: **extrinsic rewards** and **intrinsic rewards**. The worker provides physical effort and/or mental application, and accepts fatigue and the loss of control over his or her time. In return, the extrinsic work rewards that he or she usually receives consist (primarily) of wages and bonuses. The intrinsic rewards workers might get from the job include status and recognition from their peers.

VISIT THE *ONLINE RESOURCE CENTRE* AT HTTPS://HE.PALGRAVE.COM/COMPANION/BRATTON-WORK-AND-ORGANIZATIONAL-BEHAVIOUR3/ FOR INFORMATION ON EMPLOYMENT TRENDS.

Although our definition helps us to identify the key features of work, it is too narrow and restrictive. First, not all work, either physical or mental, is remunerated. We cannot assume that there is a simple relationship in which 'work' means a paid employment or occupation, 'real' work that is remunerated. Our definition obscures as much as it reveals. Most people would agree that some activities that are unpaid count as work. This work can be exhilarating or exhausting. Some of it is household-based work – cooking, child rearing, cleaning and so on – and some of it is done voluntarily, for the good of society – for instance, working for the Citizen's Advice Bureau. The activities that are done in the course of this unpaid or 'hidden' work are identical to those in some paid jobs, such as working in a nursery or advising people on their legal rights. Is it fair to exclude it simply because it is not paid?

Furthermore, whether an activity is experienced as work or non-work or leisure is dependent on social relations, cultural conditions, social attitudes and how others perceive various activities. So, for example, 'an active woman, running a house and bringing up children, is distinguished from a woman who works: that is to say, takes paid employment' (Williams, 1983: 335). Historically, unpaid work is undertaken disproportionately by one-half of the population: women. This book concentrates on paid work, and as a consequence we largely omit the critically important area of women's unpaid work in the household, although that is not to suggest that we see it as inconsequential.

Second, the economic-technical system assigns each employee into a specialized niche, which narrowly delimits the area that the employee is expected to be occupied with at work. At the same time, human beings have multiple interests and development needs. As a young man, I was employed as a welder; the employer's only interest was that I kept on welding. It was of no importance that I liked to go rock climbing and pot holing and that I would have liked to learn German. The limiting and one-sidedness of the economic-technical system clash with the limitedness and many-sidedness of human capability and people's development needs (Karlsson, 2012). This dilemma is examined in Chapter 6, when we discuss motivation at work.

Third, our definition of paid work says little about how employment opportunities are shaped by gender, ethnicity, age and abilities or disabilities. For example, when women do have access to paid work, they tend to receive less pay than men doing similar work. Women are disproportionately represented in paid work that involves tasks similar to those they carry out in their domestic life – catering, nursing, teaching, clerical and retail employment. Ethnic and racially defined minorities experience chronic disadvantage in paid work because of racism in organizations and in terms of recruitment. The likelihood of participating in paid work varies with age and certain types of work. For example, young people are disproportionately represented in more physically demanding paid work. Disabled adults, especially disabled young adults, experience higher levels of unemployment and underemployment than those who are able bodied (Barnes, 1996).

Fourth, paid work can be dangerous and unhealthy, but the hazards are not distributed evenly. Manual workers face more work-related hazards, and have more accidents at work, than do (for example) office workers. It has been argued that this unequal distribution of work-related accidents is not only related to the risks the individuals face, but also influenced by **values** and economic pressures.

Our approach to understanding the issue of inequality surrounding work involves an analysis of the differential treatment of people based on class, gender and race. We need to look at who does what job, analysing the social and sexual division of labour. We need to consider what sort of occupations there are, and who exercises power or control over the social institutions.

Fifth, our definition obscures an important element of the employment relationship: the *psychological contract* (Guest and Conway, 2002; Rousseau, 1995). The 'psychological contract', as discussed in Chapter 1, is a metaphor that captures a wide variety of largely unwritten expectations and understandings of the two parties (employer and employee) about their mutual obligations. Denise Rousseau defines it as 'individual beliefs, shaped by the organization, regarding terms of an exchange agreement between individuals and their organization' (Rousseau, 1995: 9). Most commentators view the concept as a two-way exchange of perceived promises and obligations. The concept has been around since the early 1960s, but in recent years it has become a 'fashionable' framework to support the development

value: a collective idea about what is right or wrong, good or bad, and desirable or undesirable in a particular culture

values: stable, long-lasting beliefs about what is important in a variety of situations

stop...

Do you think that managers need to manage the employment relationship differently for knowledge workers and for manual industrial workers? Why and how?

...and reflect

of more nuanced understandings of the employment relationships in large and small organizations (Atkinson, 2008). In Chapter 5, we examine this contemporary concept in more depth. As we discuss more fully below and throughout the book, work shapes the employment relationship, the behaviour of all employees and the relations between men and women inside and outside the workplace, and it has a significant bearing on individuals' personal identity, fulfilment, health and social life (Ha-Joon Chang, 2013; Hodson and Sullivan, 2012; Sveiby, 1997).

The development of work

Industrial Revolution: the relatively rapid economic transformation that began in Britain in the 1780s. It involved a factory- and technology-driven shift from agriculture and small cottage-based manufacturing to manufacturing industries, and the consequences of that shift for virtually all human activities

The structure of the labour market and paid work is not static: it reflects patterns of substantial change in the ways in which work is organized in specific industrial sectors. This is the essence of industrialization and a new emerging form of life – modernity. In this section, we trace the emergence of new work forms, starting with what the British historian Arnold Toynbee called the **Industrial Revolution** (around 1780–1830), and finishing with a look at employment in what has been called 'post-industrial' work.

We provide this brief historical overview of work because, in our view, it provides a perspective on contemporary work issues and problems, which often result from decisions made in the past. In addition, when we look at how work forms have developed, it becomes apparent that most 'new' work forms have deep historical roots. Contemporary management gurus might claim to have 'discovered' the importance of informal work-related learning, but such a mode of learning was important in the apprenticeship system of pre-industrial Europe. Similarly, the fact that 'virtual' home-based work reduces the need for office space and costs was well understood by employers in the eighteenth century who operated the 'putting-out' system of home working discussed below. In effect, these claims of 'new' or 'innovative', when viewed through a historical lens, might be a rediscovery of past practices that had been forgotten or abandoned.

Before we retrace the organization of work in the economy, we need to take a moment to make some general observations and highlight some challenges that this task presents. The history of work emphasizes that work is a social activity, not an individual one. Even those who work alone do so within a socially constructed network of relations among people associated with the pursuit of economic activity. History tends to contradict the suggestion that divisions on the basis of class, gender and race are systematic features created by, and found solely in, industrial capitalism. The social inequality of work, however, long predates the rise of capitalism. The history of industrial capitalism fosters the image of work as a predominantly male activity, separate from, and unrelated to, the home. Again, this is historically atypical: 'home and the place of work have always been, and still are, intimately connected by a seamless web of social interdependence' (Grint, 1998: 46).

stop...

To what extent does a 'good' or 'bad' work design depend on which approach we use and which theorist we believe?

...and reflect

Studying work and organizational forms from a historical perspective is a challenge for a number of reasons. By its very nature, such an exercise involves a compression of time periods and of different ways of organizing work. As the late Eric Hobsbawm (1997) wrote, 'The past is a permanent dimension of the human consciousness, an inevitable component of institutions, values and other patterns of human society' (1997: 10). The problem for social theorists is to avoid presenting the emergence of new work forms as a coherent, orderly and inevitable process of change.

Looking back from the vantage point of the early twenty-first century, it might seem reasonable to talk of the emergence of the factory, or of new forms of management control. But, as others have pointed out, the development of new work forms and social relations took place piecemeal, sporadically and slowly – and they were frequently resisted. Many features of work in the pre-industrial economy (the period before 1780) survived until late into the nineteenth and twentieth centuries, and similarly many twentieth work forms survive in the early twenty-first century. When we outline general trends, this not only compresses wide variations and collapses time periods, but also attaches a coherent pattern to these changes, which they did not in reality show (Littler, 1982; Salaman, 1981).

With this caveat, the rest of this section examines pre-industrial work, the transition to factory forms of work, the significance of concentrated production, the rise of the trade unions and interventions by the state.

Pre-industrial work

In the middle of the eighteenth century, the most striking feature of the economy in Europe was the importance of agriculture as a basic human activity. Manufacturing operated on a small scale, employed labour-intensive methods and used little fixed capital. Agricultural and industrial work was characterized by low productivity. Population growth created an ever-growing class of landless labourers who were compelled to relocate to towns and sell their **labour power** to survive. The human movement to the new cities, creating an urban population whose sole source of income was a wage, was critical for industrial capitalism to develop. As Max Weber explained, 'only where ... workers under the compulsion of the whip of hunger, offer themselves to employers does capitalism develop' (Weber, 1927/2003: 277).

Before 1780, the English economy was characterized by regulation. The central government intervened in the economy. The Statute of Artificers of 1563, for example, set the level of wages and conditions of employment, regulated the mobility of labour (as the government did during the Second World War, 1939–45), and protected and promoted, by force if necessary, domestic manufacturing and trade. In the towns, craft guilds regulated all activities related to their trade, including the training of apprentices, wages and prices, and standards of work.

Away from the town-based guilds, the rural-based **putting-out system** was a feature of the pre-Industrial Revolution manufacturing of woollen garments and many branches of metal working. The putting-out system was a decentralized method of manufacturing that, in the case of producing woollen cloth for example, involved the various processes of combing, spinning and weaving the wool usually being performed by different workers in their cottages (hence the term 'cottage industry'). Such a form of work organization had profound consequences for the social organization of work and the nature of workers' reactions to the Industrial Revolution:

> It could not be used in industries requiring bulky plant and power-driven machinery. Neither was it suitable for crafts demanding a high degree of skill or which needed close supervision ... Even when technical conditions were favourable to the use of out-workers, high costs of distribution and losses arising from pilfering and fraud by the workers were serious weaknesses. (Clarkson, 1971: 102)

Thus, the putting-out system, a premodern variant of home working, contained considerable rigidities and inefficiencies, which were apparent when markets expanded and there was a need for large-scale manufacturing.

Gender-based patterns of work predate industrial capitalism. In the pre-industrial European family, both men and women produced goods for the household and were also engaged in paid work as part of the putting-out system; however, depending on local norms and customs, there were 'rather strict ideas about women's work and men's work within the specific community' (Alvesson and Billing, 1997: 55). Moreover, work was 'a social activity circumscribed by custom and traditions that went deeper than the cash nexus' (Grint, 1998: 52), and work and family life were not regarded as separate spheres.

labour power: the potential gap between a worker's capacity or potential to work and their actual work

putting-out system: a pre-industrial, home-based form of production in which the dispersed productive functions were coordinated by an entrepreneur

Factory-based work

factory system: a relatively large work unit that concentrated people and machines in one building, enabling the specialization of productive functions and, at the same time, a closer supervision of employees than did the pre-industrial putting-out system. Importantly, the factory system gave rise to the need for a new conception of time and organizational behaviour

division of labour: the allocation of work tasks to various groups or categories of employee

The traditional work rhythms and practices of pre-industrial society gave way to the specialization and discipline of the **factory system**. We can describe the Industrial Revolution as a fundamental change in the structure of the economy, in which the pursuit and accumulation of profit by the capitalists guided the mode of organizing work, harnessing technology and determining the social relations of work. The change was characterized by the rise of the factory, a combination of power technology and specialized machines with specialized occupations. The significance of the concentration of workers lay in the potential for extending the division of labour, installing machines, regulating the flow of raw materials, and controlling and moulding workers' behaviour to meet the specific needs of large-scale production.

Here, the focus is on the **division of labour** within the factory as organized by the owner. The factory offered the opportunity to improve each specialized task through the use of innovative technology, more than was possible with the decentralized putting-out system: 'The very division of labour … prepared the ground from which mechanical invention could eventually spring,' wrote one historian (Dobb, 1963: 145). The factory also enabled a tighter control of the work in process than was possible with the domestic system. With the putting-out system, it was difficult to control the behaviour of cottage-based workers because the employer had 'no way of compelling his workers to do a given number of hours of labour; the domestic weaver or craftsman was master of his time, starting and stopping when he desired' (Landes, 1969: 59). The factory system offered new opportunities for controlling the pace and quality of work by the 'discipline of mechanization' – the actual speed of the machine – and by a hierarchy of control over the work in process.

Over the decades, historians have debated the role of technology in factory work organization. For example, it is argued that the origins of management within capitalist production do not lie in the extended division of labour created by technical developments, but in the desire for social control on the part of capitalists, so that levels of exploitation could be increased (Marglin, 1982). Factories were not the inevitable results of technical change, nor were they the inexorable results of the search for simple efficiency. The architecture of the new factories had much in common with prisons. Jeremy Bentham coined the term 'panopticon' in 1816 to describe a circular building that could provide 'hierarchical observation' and 'normalizing judgement' (Figure 2.1). Observing Victorian architecture and Bentham's idea of a panopticon, the twentieth-century philosopher Michel Foucault asked, 'Is it surprising that prison resembles factories, schools, barracks, hospitals, which all resemble prisons?' (Foucault, 1977: 30). The suggestion is that the factory, with its specialization and logical flows of processes, provided capitalists with a formal role as managers or coordinators. An alternative interpretation for the new forms of organizing work emphasizes the inadequacy of the family-based putting-out system in the face of expanding markets (Kelly, 1985).

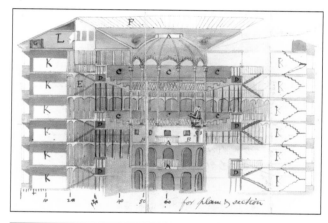

Figure 2.1 The panopticon building

Source: University College London Special Collections

plate 7 The First World War (1914–18) saw large numbers of women finding employment in the munitions and engineering factories.

Source: Nick Hedges

The new factory system transformed the social organization of work. Factories needed a disciplined workforce. In this lay another key development associated with factory-based work – the shaping of workers' behaviour based on new concepts of commitment and time. In the early period of industrialization, changing workers' behaviour had a number of aspects: in terms of both entering the factory itself, and the **work ethic**. Workers, particularly men, were reluctant to enter the factories, with their unaccustomed rules and discipline, because they 'lost their birthright, independence' (Hobsbawm, 1968: 51). The majority of workers were women and children, who were more pliant and easier to manage.

Once in the factory, the employers had to develop 'appropriate' and 'responsible' behaviour that met the needs of the new work regime. This involved the management instilling in workers attitudes of obedience to factory regulations and punctuality. What the employers required was a 'new breed of worker' whose behaviour reacted favourably to the inexorable demands of the pace-setting machine, factory rationality and the 'tyranny of the clock'. The process took several generations: 'by the division of labour; the supervision of labour; fines; bells and clocks; money incentives; preaching and schooling; the suppression of fairs and sports – new labour habits were formed, and a new time-discipline was imposed' (Thompson, E. P. 1967: 90). From the preoccupation with workers' work motivation and behaviour, there eventually emerged a specialized branch of management: personnel, or human resource management.

IN THE EBOOK ACCESS THE **OB IN FOCUS** BOX ON 'THE WORKING WEEK - A MATTER FOR THE LAW?'

Taylorism and Fordism

work ethic: a set of values that stresses the importance of work to the identity and sense of worth of the individual, and encourages an attitude of diligence in the mind of the people

In this section, we turn to what others call 'classical' work organization – Taylorism and Fordism. These are considered classical partly because they represent the earliest contributions to modern management theory, but also because they identify ideas and issues that keep occurring in contemporary organizational behaviour and management literature, although writers now tend to use a different vocabulary (Grey, 2013). We will now consider each of these in turn.

Taylorism

Taylorism: a process of determining the division of work into its smallest possible skill elements, and how the process of completing each task can be standardized to achieve maximum efficiency. Also referred to as scientific management

The American Frederick W. Taylor (1856–1915) pioneered the scientific management approach to work organization, hence the term **Taylorism**. Taylor developed his ideas on work organization while working as superintendent at the Midvale Steel Company in Pennsylvania, USA. Taylorism represents both a set of management practices and a system of ideological assumptions (Sveiby, 1997). The autonomy (freedom from control) of craft workers was potentially a threat to managerial control. For craft workers, the exercise of control over work practices was closely linked to their personality, as this description of 'craft pride', taken from the trade journal *Machinery* in 1915, suggests:

> [The craftsman] is engaged in tasks where the capacity for original thought is exercised: he has refined and critical perceptions of the things pertaining to his craft. His work creates a feeling of self-reliance … he lives a full and satisfying life. (Hinton, 1973: 97)

As a first-line manager, Taylor not surprisingly viewed the position of skilled shop-floor workers differently. He was appalled by what he regarded as inefficient working practices and the tendency of his subordinates not to put in a full day's work, what Taylor called 'natural soldiering'. He believed that workers who did manual work were motivated solely by money – the image of the 'greedy robot' – and were too stupid to develop the most efficient way of performing a task – the 'one best way'. The role of management was to analyse 'scientifically' all the tasks to be undertaken, and then to design jobs to eliminate time and motion waste.

Taylor's approach to work organization and employment relations was based on the following five principles:

- maximum job fragmentation
- separate planning and doing
- separate 'direct' and 'indirect' labour
- a minimization of skill requirements
- a minimization of handling component parts and material.

The centrepiece of scientific management is the separation of tasks into their simplest constituent elements – the 'routinization of work' (the first principle). Most manual workers were viewed as sinful and stupid, and therefore all decision-making functions had to be removed from their hands (the second principle). All preparation and servicing tasks were to be taken away from the skilled worker (direct labour) and, drawing on Charles Babbage's principle, performed by unskilled and cheaper labour (indirect labour, in the third principle). Minimizing the skill requirements to perform a task would reduce the worker's control over work activities or the labour process (the fourth principle). Finally, management should ensure that the layout of the machines on the factory floor would minimize the movement of people and materials to shorten the time taken (the fifth principle).

While the logic of work fragmentation and routinization is simple and compelling, the principles of Taylorism reflect the class antagonism that is found in employment relations. When Taylor's principles were applied to work organization, they led to the intensification of work: to 'speeding up', 'deskilling' and new techniques to control workers, as shown in Figure 2.2. And since gender, as we have discussed, is both a system of classification and a structure of power relations, it should not surprise us that Taylorism contributed to the shift in the gender composition of engineering firms. As millions of men were recruited into the armed forces for the First World War (1914–18), job fragmentation and the production of standardized items such as rifles, guns and munitions enabled women 'dilutees' to be employed in what had previously been skilled jobs reserved exclusively for men (Grey, 2013).

Figure 2.2 A craft union response to Taylorism

Some writers argue that Taylorism was a relatively short-lived phenomenon that died in the economic depression of the 1930s (Rose, 1988). However, others have argued that this view underestimates the spread and influence of Taylor's principles: 'the popular notion that Taylorism has been 'superseded' by later schools of 'human relations', that it 'failed' … represents a woeful misreading of the actual dynamics of the development of management' (Braverman, 1974: 56). Similarly, others have made

stop...

Can you think of jobs in the retail and service sector that would support the charge that work systems in the modern workplace continue to be affected by neo-Taylorism?

...and reflect

Fordism: a term used to describe mass production using assembly line technology that allowed for a greater division of labour and time and motion management, techniques pioneered by the American car manufacturer Henry Ford in the early twentieth century

a persuasive case that, 'In general the direct and indirect influence of Taylorism on factory jobs has been extensive, so that in Britain job design and technology design have become imbued with neo-Taylorism' (Littler and Salaman, 1984: 73).

Fordism

Henry Ford (1863–1947) applied the major principles of scientific management in his car plant, as well as installing specialized machines and adding a crucial innovation to Taylorism: the flow-line principle of assembly work. This kind of work organization has come to be called **Fordism**. The moving assembly line had a major impact on employment relations. It exerted greater control over how workers performed their tasks, and it involved the intensification of work and labour productivity through ever-greater job fragmentation and short task-cycle times. In 1922, Henry Ford stated his approach to managing shop-floor workers: 'The idea is that man ... must have every second necessary but not a single unnecessary second' (Beynon, 1984: 33).

The speed of work on the assembly line is determined by the technology itself rather than by a series of written instructions. Management's control of the work process was also enhanced by a detailed time and motion study inaugurated by Taylor. Work study engineers attempted to discover the shortest possible task-cycle time. Recording job times meant that managers could monitor more closely their subordinates' effort levels and performance. Task measurement therefore acted as the basis of a new structure of control.

Two other essential features also characterize Fordism. The first was the introduction of an interlinking system of conveyor lines that fed components to different work stations to be worked on, and the second was the standardization of commodities to gain economies of scale. Thus, Fordism established the long-term principle of the mass production of standardized commodities at a reduced cost.

Ford's production system was, however, not without its problems. Workers found the repetitive work boring and unchallenging, and their job dissatisfaction was expressed in high rates of absenteeism and turnover. In 1913, for example, the turnover of Ford workers was more than 50,000. The management techniques developed by Ford in response to these employment problems serve further to differentiate Fordism from Taylorism. Henry Ford introduced the 'five dollar day' – double the pay and shorter hours for those who qualified. Benefits depended on a factory worker's lifestyle being deemed satisfactory, which included abstaining from alcohol. Ford's style of paternalism attempted to inculcate new social habits, as well as new labour habits, that would facilitate job performance.

Taylorism and Fordism became the predominant approaches to job design in vehicle and electrical engineering – the large-batch production industries – in the USA and Britain (Littler and Salaman, 1984).

Post-Fordism

As a strategy of organizing work and people, Taylorism and Fordism had their limitations. First, work simplification led to boredom and dissatisfaction, and tended to encourage adversarial relations and conflict, including frequent work stoppages. Second, Taylor-style work involves control and coordination costs. As specialization increases, so do indirect labour costs as more production planners, supervisors and quality control inspectors are employed. The economies associated with the division of labour tend to be offset by the diseconomies of management control costs.

Third, Taylorism and Fordism affect what might be called 'cooperation costs'. As management's control over the quantity and quality of workers' performance increases, workers experience increased frustration and dissatisfaction, which leads to a withdrawal of their commitment to the organization. The relationship

Source: Bananastock

McDonaldization and McJobs

The terms 'McDonaldization' and 'McJobs' refer to the increasing rationalization of work organization in the late twentieth century pioneered by the McDonald's restaurant chain, which intensifies the alienation of employees and the dehumanization of workers and consumers. Unskilled, low paid jobs with little chance of career progression have come to be called McJobs as a result of George Ritzer's *The McDonaldization of Society*, which was first published in 1993. There have been several subsequent editions of this, but the theoretical basis of the study, which draws on Max Weber's discussion of rationalization and bureaucratization, has remained the same.

Ritzer identifies the McDonald's fast-food restaurant as the model of an organizational form that he believes is even more rationalized than the type of bureaucracy specified by Max Weber. He also claims it has spread to many organizations in other areas such as other restaurant chains, shopping malls, package holidays, higher education, healthcare, online dating, suburban housing and more. The reasons for the expansion of the McDonald's model, Ritzer contends, are as follows: its efficiency, for example the speed at which a restaurant chain can feed people; the quantification and calculation based on standardized servings that appear to give value for money; predictability based upon the uniformity of the product from any outlet; and control through the use of technology directly over the restaurant workers, and indirectly over the customers.

There are elements of a Marxist analysis of work in Ritzer's discussion of how workers are trained to perform a few simple tasks in the way described in the company's manual, and how technology removes skill and creativity by only allowing the worker to perform tasks in a standardized way, for example by measuring the amount of drinks served. McDonald's combines elements of bureaucracy, scientific management and the assembly line. Moreover, Ritzer's critical insight is to apply a Weberian analysis of how rational systems can be undermined by irrationalities that 'serve to deny the basic humanity, the human reason of the people who work within them or are served by them'. This is the main irrationality of McDonaldization – the work there is dehumanizing because it is routinized and deskilled, which leads to low morale and high labour turnover. The experience for customers is also dehumanizing and impersonal as they are offered eating on a 'conveyer belt' with very restricted interaction with staff, and are expected to eat and leave the restaurant quickly.

In Weber's writing on rationalization, there is tension between the benefits of rationalization and the attendant loss of control, human initiative and creativity that is experienced by employees, and this is also the basis of Ritzer's critique. If the process of rationalization cannot be reversed, the best that Ritzer can suggest is that those who are uneasy as consumers in such an environment should choose small independent businesses that stress the quality that comes from their skills, or disrupt the uniformity of their purchases by requesting a hamburger cooked rare!

> **Stop!** Why do you think that rational systems of organization, designed to reduce costs or gain other efficiencies, may lead to results that can be regarded as 'irrational'? In addition to the dehumanization of work, can you think of other ways in which McDonald's can be seen as 'irrational'?

Sources and further information

Bratton, J. and Denham, D. (2014) *Capitalism and Classical Social Theory* (2nd edn), Toronto: University of Toronto Press.

Ritzer, G. (2009) *McDonaldization: The Reader* (3rd edn), Thousand Oaks, CA: Sage.

Ritzer, G. (2012) *The McDonaldization of Society*, London: Sage.

Note: This feature was written by David Denham, Honorary Research Fellow, Wolverhampton University, UK.

---

between controller and controlled can deteriorate so much that it results in a further increase in management control. The principles of Taylorism and Fordism thus reveal a basic paradox, 'that the tighter the control of labour power, the more control is needed' (Littler and Salaman, 1984: 36–7). The adverse reactions to the extreme division of labour led to the development of new approaches to work organization that attempted to address these problems.

Elton Mayo (1880–1949)

Elton Mayo was an academic at Harvard University. In this post, he was responsible for directing the 5-year investigation of the Hawthorne works of the Western Electric Company in Chicago, USA. Elton Mayo has often been called the founder of the human relations movement (Pugh and Hickson, 1996: 157). The 'human relations' movement attempted to address the limitations of Taylorism and Fordism by shifting attention to the perceived psychological and social needs of workers. In the 1920s, Mayo set up an experiment in the relay assembly room at the Hawthorne Works, which was designed to test the effects on productivity of variations in working conditions (lighting, temperature and ventilation). The

Hawthorne research team found no clear relationship between any of these factors and productivity. However, the study led the researchers to develop concepts that might explain the factors affecting worker motivation. They concluded that more than just economic incentives and the work environment motivated workers: recognition and social cohesion were important too. The message for management was also quite clear: rather than depending on management controls and financial incentives, it needed to influence the work group by cultivating a culture that met the social needs of workers.

Mary Parker Follett (1868–1933)

Mary Parker Follett's pioneering ideas brought into prominence the view that managers and workers must first be understood not as 'machines' but as human beings with social needs. She introduced social psychology and human relations into management, and rejected the underlying assumptions about human behaviour on which Taylorism and Fordism had been built. Managers and workers – the human dimension of work organizations – were the key to improving overall performance. Her work infused a humanistic element into the management of people, and several modern management concepts are based on her ideas, including dynamism, leadership, empowerment and participation (Verstegen and Rutherford, 2000).

Follett's approach to managing people was based on the belief that formal organizations are complex systems of *dynamic* social relations. Individual managers and workers influence each other and react to each other. She emphasized that effective leadership entailed the communication of a vision rather than 'commanding'. There are two types of power, according to Follett. There is 'power-over', which is coercive, and there is 'power-with', which is jointly developed. She believed that employees had to be nurtured and given the opportunity to develop their power. The modern concept of *empowerment* draws on her pioneering ideas. Follett proposed new methods of management by proposing worker *participation*, which she described as the coordination of the contribution of each individual employee to create a cohesive working unit.

The human relations movement advocated various management techniques such as worker participation and non-authoritarian supervisors, which would, it was thought, promote a climate of good (neo)-human relations in which the quantity and quality needs of management could be met. This largely forgotten history, which examined concepts such as atmosphere, informal structures and organizational climate, reminds us that twenty-first-century cultural scholarship (see Chapter 17) is not a completely new development in the thinking about organizations (Parker, 2000a).

Criticisms of the human relations approach attributed this to managerial bias and the fact that advocates of the human relations approach tended to play down the basic economic conflict of interest between employer and employee. Critics pointed out that when the techniques were tested, it became apparent that workers did not inevitably respond as predicted. The human relations approach also neglects wider socioeconomic factors (see Thompson's 1989 text for an excellent critical analysis of this approach to work). Despite these criticisms, however, the human relations approach to job design began to have some impact on management practices in the post-Second World War environment of full employment.

In the 1970s, competitive pressures spawned new approaches to work design in the manufacturing and service sectors. New thinking stressed the principles of closure, whereby the scope of the job is such that it includes all the tasks to complete a product or process, and task variety, whereby the worker acquires a range of different skills so that job flexibility is possible and the worker can personally monitor the quantity and quality of the work. New techniques such as 'job enrichment' gave workers a wider range of tasks to perform and some discretion over how those tasks were done. For example, in the context of a fast-food outlet, an employee's job would, instead of being limited to grilling burgers, be enlarged to grilling the burgers, preparing the salad and inspecting the quality of the food on delivery.

Some theorists have been critical of these new work designs. An influential study argues that although job enrichment techniques may increase job satisfaction and commitment, the key focus remains managerial control. Although post-Fordist work design strategies gave individuals or work groups a wider measure of discretion over their work, or 'responsible autonomy', the strategy is a 'tool of self-discipline' and a means of maintaining or even intensifying managerial control.

With the growth of call centres over the past decade, critical research has drawn attention to 'new' forms of Taylorism. It is alleged that sophisticated electronic eavesdropping on salesperson–client conversations, and peer group scrutiny, have created 'computer-controlled autonomy' and 'electronic sweatshops', or a form of 'electronic Taylorism' (Bratton, 1992; Callaghan and Thompson, 2001; Sewell, 1998).

VISIT THE *ONLINE RESOURCE CENTRE* AT HTTPS://HE.PALGRAVE.COM/COMPANION/BRATTON-WORK-AND-ORGANIZATIONAL-BEHAVIOUR3/ FOR MORE INFORMATION ON TRENDS IN WORK ORGANIZATIONAL DESIGN.

Work teams and high-performance workplaces

The favoured work configuration over the last two decades has been teamworking. The focus on work teams has grown out of, drawn upon and sometimes reacted against Taylorism and Fordism (Grey, 2013). The centrepiece of teamworking is functional flexibility, with members undertaking a wide range of tasks with a high degree of autonomy.

In the 1980s, Japanese work and employment practices were held up as a model for the struggling UK and North American manufacturing sectors (Bratton 1992; Elger and Smith, 1994; Oliver and Wilkinson, 1992; Thompson and McHugh, 2009; Womack et al., 1990). The Japanese model has been a 'contested concept' in its description, interpretation and explanation (McCormick, 2007). Pioneering interpretations of the model identify three notable elements: flexibility, quality control and minimum waste.

Flexibility is achieved by arranging machinery in a group – what is known as 'cellular technology' – and by employing a multiskilled workforce. Thus, the work organization is the opposite of that of 'Taylorism': a generalized, skilled machinist with flexible job boundaries is a substitute for the specialized machinist operating one machine in one particular workstation. Higher quality standards are achieved by making quality every worker's responsibility. Minimum waste, the third element of the Japanese model, is achieved by just-in-time techniques. As the name suggests, this is a hand-to-mouth mode of manufacture that aims to produce no more than the necessary components, in the necessary quantities, of the necessary quality and at the necessary time. Teamworking has a cultural and social dimension. The practices aim to generate social cohesion and a 'moral commitment' to common organizational goals. We examine work teams in more detail in Chapter 10.

The managerial mantra of the 1990s was flexibility, although various terms were used to describe these fashions in work organization: flexible specialization or 'flexspec', 'lean production', 're-engineering' and 'high-performance work systems' are well established in the literature. In the late 1990s, Japan experienced slow economic growth, and thereafter the US model of work organization was again held up as the exemplar. The new debate focused on whether the high-performance workplace, comprising a combination of work and employment variables or 'bundles' of 'best' practices, can deliver a comparative advantage.

Post-industrial work

The 'Information Revolution', which we date from 1980 with the development of the silicon chip, marks, as does the Industrial Revolution 200 years earlier, a fundamental transformation of human activity. One theme running through this chapter has been the continuities as well as the discontinuities across time. There is no doubt that, for many people, paid work has changed profoundly during the Information Age, but these changes must be set in a historical context if we are to appreciate their significance and relevance.

IN THE EBOOK ACCESS THE **CRITICAL INSIGHT** ON 'GENDER AND WORK DESIGN'.

Knowledge work

knowledge work: paid work that is of an intellectual nature, is non-repetitive and results oriented, engages scientific and/or artistic knowledge, and demands continuous learning and creativity

The emergence of **knowledge work** – intellectual capital – and 'knowledge worker' – employees who carry knowledge as a powerful resource that they, rather than the organization, own – is closely associated with the contemporary, sophisticated, Internet-based information technologies. Defining the notions of knowledge work and knowledge worker has proven problematic. Following Horwitz et al., however, we can say that knowledge work is characterized as 'ambiguity intensive', and a knowledge worker is an individual with the ability to communicate and apply professional knowledge, as well as manage other employees (see Horwitz et al., 2003: 31).

The nature of knowledge work is said to be fundamentally different from what we have traditionally associated with the 'machine age' and mass production, and hence it requires a different order of employment relations. It should not be confused with routine clerical work. It requires knowledge workers to learn a broad range of skills and knowledge, often with a focus around problems or customers, and to work in small groups or project teams to co-create new insights. It is also said to require a different employment relationship, with a psychological contract that has implications for employee commitment and career trajectories.

These differences in the nature of traditional work and knowledge work are spelled out in Table 2.1. In the Information Age, when an organization's wealth and ability to compete may exist 'principally in the heads of its employees' and human competitiveness can effectively 'walk out the gates' every day, it is not surprising that organizations are concerned with 'better' human resource practices and 'knowledge management' (Boud and Garrick, 1999: 48). Information technology, new employment contracts and knowledge work have changed the 'spatiality' of work: some people do paid work at home, and others undertake more short-term work assignments as organizations reduce the number of their 'core' employees and contract work out (Hardill and Green, 2003). Critical accounts of contemporary work in advanced capitalist

Links to management Iain Nelson

Iain Nelson has spent 27 years as a Principal Consultant and Manager with the International Training Service, and 4 years as an internal Learning and Development Advisor with Petroleum Development Oman. As a freelance consultant, his clients include Unilever, Roche Products, Alcan, BP, Chevron, Lothian and Borders Police, the British Council, ITF Nigeria and Total.

Iain's core expertise is developing managers as learning specialists competent to design and deliver a company's corporate objectives and associated strategic business initiatives.

In the ebook click on the play button to watch Iain talking about managing people in organizations and then answer the following question:

• What potential dangers does Iain identify when managers treat employees differently?

Table 2.1 The nature of traditional work and knowledge work

	Traditional work	**Knowledge work**
Skill/knowledge sets	Narrow and often functional	Specialized and deep, but often with diffuse peripheral focuses
Locus of work	Around individuals	In groups and projects
Focus of work	Tasks, objectives, performance	Customers, problems, issues
Skill obsolescence	Gradual	Rapid
Activity/feedback cycles	Primary and of an immediate nature	Lengthy from a business perspective
Performance measures	Task deliverables Little (as planned), but regular and dependable	Process effectiveness Potentially great, but often erratic
Career formation	Internal to the organization through training, development, rules and prescriptive career schemes	External to the organization, through years of education and socialization
Employee's loyalty	To the organization and his or her career systems	To professions, networks and peers
Impact on company success	Many small contributions that support the master plan	A few major contributions of strategic and long-term importance

Source: Adapted from Despres and Hiltrop (1995) and Boud and Garrick (1999)

economies offer a counterweight to the bullish management perspectives on the knowledge economy, and provide data showing that the International Labour Organization's definition of 'decent work' remains elusive only for the privileged minority (Baldry et al., 2007; Karlsson, 2012). As European studies attest, there are too many businesses taking the 'low road' and striving for competitive advantage on the basis of a low-skill and low-pay workplace (Bolton and Houlihan, 2009).

Emotional labour

With the growth of routinized service work – such as fast food, tourism, hotels and call centres – with its demands of customer sovereignty, new kinds of social relationship and aspects of the self have developed and come under scrutiny. As the service sector has grown in importance, there has, not surprisingly, been a growing interest in embodied attributes and dispositions that are stereotypically feminine, such as patience, deference to the customer and a pleasant demeanour, associated with what sociologists call 'emotional labour'. Much has been written in recent years on how emotion is an important part of the effort–wage exchange, that workplaces in general have 'emotions' (Bolton, 2005; Fineman, 2003) and that 'strong' cultures strive to engender emotional energy, affection and even love for the organization (see Chapter 17).

VISIT THE *ONLINE RESOURCE CENTRE* AT HTTPS://HE.PALGRAVE.COM/COMPANION/BRATTON-WORK-AND-ORGANIZATIONAL-BEHAVIOUR3/ FOR MORE DEFINITIONS OF EMOTIONAL LABOUR.

alienation: a feeling of powerlessness and estrangement from other people and from oneself

Although the sociological analysis of workplace emotions is an expanding field of research, the classical sociological canons of Marx, Durkheim, Weber and Simmel do contain important ideas about emotions. For instance, **alienation** engendered feelings of anger, and sentimentality was eliminated in bureaucracies gripped in the 'iron cage' of rationality (see Chapter 3). Modern critical scholarship emphasizes the servility of routine work performed by service workers within the customer–employee interface (Warhurst and Nickson, 2007).

It was the pioneering work of Arlie Hochschild (2003) that drew attention to the significance of social interaction as a crucial element of service provision. She considered emotional labour as part of the employment contract when 'the emotional style of offering the service is part of the service itself'. Although servers in restaurants have always been trained to 'serve with a smile', there has been a growing recognition that emotional labour is far more significant for a larger proportion of service employees than this, as management theorists emphasize 'customer service' as a vital aspect of business competitiveness. Emotional labour exists when workers are required, as part of the wage–effort bargain, to show emotions with the specific aim of causing customers or clients to feel and respond in a particular way. They might do this by verbal means – 'Good morning, sir/madam' – or non-verbal means, for example by smiling. Thus, the recent interest in emotional labour is focused on how managers can harness emotion into the 'service' of the organization as an added dimension of the worker's 'self' (see Chapter 5) that the organization can appropriate, as has traditionally occurred with physical and mental labour (Noon and Blyton, 2013).

It is important to understand that emotional labour, like physical and intellectual labour, is bought by the employer for a wage. It requires a specific set of attributes and behaviours, and it can be a potential source of stress and alienation. Emotional labour 'carries the potential for individuals to become self-estranged – detached from their own "real" feelings – which in turn might threaten their sense of their own identity' (Noon and Blyton, 2013: 193). The embodied attributes and skills associated with emotional labour compromise a particular type of working-class masculine identity. Manual labour has traditionally been a key source of identity, self-esteem and power for many working-class men. Emotional labour, however, is antithetical to masculine identity. A study by Nixon in 2009 suggested that unskilled unemployed male workers were psychologically mismatched to the demands of customer sovereignty. He found that those men who had been employed in service jobs did not last long: 'I've got no patience with people basically. I can't put a smiley face on, that's not my sort of thing,' said one 24-year-old unskilled manual worker. Others said they disliked the pressure to 'chase customers', and found work at call centres involved 'Too much talking' (Nixon, 2009: 314–15). The seismic shifts associated with the 'new economy' appear to have eliminated not only particular types of jobs, but also a type of masculine identity.

Our brief history of work organization suggests that when an economy enjoys economic success, its work and management practices will often be regarded as a model by slower growing economies (Jacoby, 2005). Consistent with this prediction, European organizations adopted US management ideas for most of the twentieth century, and adopted the 'Japanese model' in the 1980s, including teamworking. Much of the literature on 'new' forms of work simplifies the analysis to a polar comparison between 'traditional' Fordism and new 'post-Fordism' work team characteristics. But although it looks elegant to draw up lists of opposite characteristics, this is not a good reflection of reality (Jaffee, 2001; Vallas, 1999). We can today still witness old 'boring' work forms existing alongside new 'decent' work configurations. Working life research shows that what qualifies as 'dignified work' requires 'that workers can feel self-worth and self-respect, as well as respect from others' (Karlsson, 2012: 6). Too much work in post-industrial capitalism, however, is still routinized in both the manufacturing and service sectors. In this brave new world of work, task variety is low, skill requirements are low, security and dignity are low, and managerial control, reminiscent of Frederick Taylor's philosophy of a century ago, remains rule bound. All this suggests that the nature of work remains largely unchanged for millions of workers, that the design of work is not a smooth transition from one model to another, and that contemporary work regimes are most likely to resemble a hybrid configuration, with elements from the old work design and parts of the new.

stop...

A major theme of this section has been the continuities as well as the discontinuities across time in paid work. Can you see any similarities between knowledge work in home-based locations and the putting-out system? Look at Plate 6 (page 40), showing a scene of customers and a server. What does the picture reveal about emotional labour? Have you ever been in a situation at work where you had to manage your feelings before customers? If so, what did it do to your sense of self?

...and reflect

VISIT THE *ONLINE RESOURCE CENTRE* AT HTTPS://HE.PALGRAVE.COM/COMPANION/BRATTON-WORK-AND-ORGANIZATIONAL-BEHAVIOUR3/ FOR MORE INFORMATION AND STATISTICS ON LABOUR MARKET TRENDS AND GENDER RELATIONS IN ORGANIZATIONS.

Work in organizations: an integration of ideas

In discussing post-Fordism, we emphasized competing claims over whether new forms of work lead to an enrichment of work or the degradation of work. Managerial optimists argue that new work structures empower employees, and celebrate the claim that managerial behaviour has shifted its focus from 'control' to 'commitment' (Walton, 1985). Critical analysts contend that some new work regimes are 'electronic sweatshops' and are basically a euphemism for work intensification. To capture the new realities of the modern workplace, critics often use the term 'McWorld' or **'McDonaldization'** (Ritzer, 2012), meaning that a vast amount of work experience, especially for young people, women and workers of colour, involves menial tasks, part-time contracts, close monitoring of performance and entrenched job insecurity (Sewell, 1998: 72–5).

In Figure 2.3, we draw together the developments in work and employment practices over the last 200 years by highlighting four paradigms or distinctive approaches: craft/artisan, Taylorism/Fordism, neo-Fordism and post-Fordism. Work is shown to vary along two dimensions: the *variety of work* – the extent to which employees have the opportunity to do a range of tasks using their various skills and knowledge – and the *autonomy in work* – the degree of initiative that employees can exercise over how their immediate work is performed.

Here, *craft/artisan* refers to the types of work organization that are based on craft-based skills and are often associated with a narrow range of specialized tasks, a high level of skill and a high degree of autonomy. *Taylorism/Fordism* means the adoption of basic scientific management principles and the assembly line methods pioneered by Henry Ford, and *neo-Fordism* refers to a work configuration that has modified the core principles of Fordism through flexible working practices so that it will fit contemporary operations. In contrast to the craft/artisan paradigm, the Taylorism/Fordism and neo-Fordism paradigms are often associated with a narrow variety of tasks, a low level of skill and a low degree of autonomy in work. *Post-Fordism* refers to organizations that do not rely on the principles of Taylorism or Fordism, and is often associated with 'high-performance work systems', with self-management and with a high degree of autonomy in work.

McDonaldization (also known as 'McWork' or 'McJobs'): a term used to symbolize the new realities of corporate-driven globalization that engulf young people in the twenty-first century, including simple work patterns, electronic controls, low pay and part-time and temporary employment

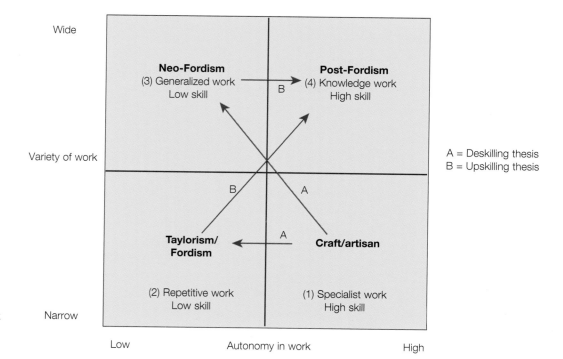

Figure 2.3 Development of work organization and employment relationships

As others have mentioned, the strength of this conceptual model is as a heuristic device – a teaching aid – to help us summarize the complex development of work organization and employment relations. The research on the trends in work design suggests that Taylorism and Fordism have dominated the managerial approaches to work organization.

In addition to the four broad classifications of work organization, the model shows two trends proposed by the proponents of the 'deskilling' and 'upskilling' theses. The deskilling thesis maintains that, in Western capitalist economies, there is a general trend in paid work towards a narrow variety of tasks and low autonomy; the arrows marked 'A' in Figure 2.3 represent this trend in the diagram. The upskilling thesis suggests an opposite trend towards a wide variety of tasks and high autonomy in work; the arrows marked 'B' represents this trend. It is important to understand that different regimes of work organization affect the nature of the employment relationship, whether or not this is explicitly acknowledged in the writings of organizational theorists. For example, if work is reorganized to deskill or upskill employees, this will change the degree of interdependency, and typically the power dynamics, between the employer and employee.

To sum up, some of the more recent empirically based literature offers a context-sensitive understanding of the development of work, and rejects a general tendency towards either deskilling or upskilling. The 'context-sensitive' view makes the point that new work structures do not have uniform outcomes, but are likely to be 'mixed' and contingent on a number of variables, such as business strategy, the nature of new technology, the degree of employee involvement in decision making, union involvement in the change process, and the extent to which 'bundles' of employment practices support the new work regime. In sum, the identification of potential benefits and costs for workers from new work configurations provides a more complex picture, one that strongly supports the **hypothesis** that changes in the nature of work can strengthen or threaten the 'psychological contract'.

hypothesis: in research studies, a tentative statement of the relationship between two or more concepts or variables

hypotheses: statements making empirically testable declarations that certain variables and their corresponding measures are related in a specific way proposed by theory

Gender and the sexual division of work

Figure 2.3 does not, however, show how gender ideologies shape work or the sexual division of work. To understand contemporary issues of gender – by which we mean the processes of gender roles, inequalities in society and women's subordination and exploitation – we need to look at the historical developments of gender–work patterns.

Gender-based patterns of work and gender inequality were universal in early industrial capitalism. In 1838, over 70 per cent of factory textile workers were adult women and children. Family labour, with women and their children working together, was a feature of employment relations in the new factory system. The factory owner did not accept direct responsibility for the conditions of employment or supervision of the workforce, but subcontracted these people-management functions to an intermediary. Factory owners negotiated with the heads of families for the whole family unit. There is evidence that the worst conditions of employment under industrial capitalism existed in these circumstances. Child labour began at the age of 4 in some cases in order to oblige the parents, but most child workers started between the ages of 7 and 10. An adult man entered the new textile factories with his family, and the 'fact that discipline was imposed on the children largely by their own parents made the harshness of the new disciplines socially tolerable' (Mathias, 1969: 202).

After 1850, with the exception of waged work in domestic service and textiles, industrial capitalism tended to create a clear distinction between the paid work opportunities of women (particularly married women) and of men. With the spread of the factory system, the need for cheap labour power provided opportunities for working-class women to do waged work in areas unrelated to their former work in the home. Large-scale food-processing factories – for example, bakeries – were dominated by women in the late nineteenth century. In working-class families, women often remained in the labour market to support the family income. When middle-class women married, they were primarily expected to withdraw from paid employment to take care of the house and children. Reinforcement of the belief that work and family life were two separate spheres – the stereotypes of men as strong and competitive and women as frail and nurturing – began to emerge: 'images that depicted men as naturally suited to the highly competitive nineteenth-century workplace and women as too delicate for the world of commerce' (Reskin and Padavic, 1994: 21).

Gender-based patterns of work changed when war broke out in Europe in 1914. The First World War was the first 'mass' war in the sense that it required the mobilization of massive quantities of products and people. Whereas Napoleon waged war against Prussia in 1806 using no more than 1500 rounds of artillery shells, in 1917 the French munitions industry had to produce 200,000 shells a day: 'Mass war required mass production' (Hobsbawm, 1994: 45). It also made it necessary to rethink the social organization of work. As Britain mobilized 12.5 per cent of its able-bodied men for the armed forces, the government encouraged women to enter the munitions and engineering factories, and this led to a revolution in waged work for women outside the household. It resulted in several occupations turning permanently into female preserves, including offices, hotels, shops, cinemas and to a lesser extent transport. In other occupations, such as engineering, men were reabsorbed in 1919 and women went back to pre-war patterns of paid or unpaid work.

Did industrial capitalism segregate the home from work, and allocate women to the former and men to the latter? Gender-based patterns of work and family-located sites of work are forms that predate capitalism: they are not the results of social changes induced by capitalism. Women's work tended to be concentrated around six human activities that predate capitalism: bearing children, feeding them and other members of the family, clothing the family, caring for the young and old when they were sick, educating children and taking care of the home (Berg, 1988). Explanations for why some work was men's and some was women's are almost as various as the patterns of wages that have existed. In the pre-Industrial Revolution period, there is some evidence that women did a much greater variety of jobs, but even then gender influenced the allocation and reward of work. A disproportionate number of women undertook the most menial, poorly paid and domestically related jobs.

Evidence about work-related gender relations before the nineteenth century is sparse. Contemporary accounts emphasize that the gender division of work is socially constructed, and that work tended to be labelled female or male on the basis of socially changeable expectations about how to view, judge and treat the two sexes. Part of the long historical process of gender inequality at work can be explained by the activities of the pre-industrial craft guilds and the **trade unions**. The town-based craft guilds, the forerunners of the trade unions, tended to be exclusively male oriented, with severe restrictions on women's membership. In the context of competitive pressure to reduce labour costs and the economic effect of female workers in terms of depressing wages, male-dominated trade unions worked hard to maintain or restore wage levels and traditional employment privileges (Bradley, 1986).

trade union: an organization whose purpose is to represent the collective interest of workers

VISIT THE *ONLINE RESOURCE CENTRE* AT HTTPS://HE.PALGRAVE.COM/COMPANION/BRATTON-WORK-AND-ORGANIZATIONAL-BEHAVIOUR3/ FOR FURTHER INFORMATION ON THE HISTORY OF TRADE UNIONS AND CURRENT STATISTICS ON TRADE UNION ORGANIZATION.

Trade union bargaining strategies developed gender-based occupational segregation. Describing the function of trade unions, Turner's (1962) seminal text quoted a union leader: the purpose of unions was 'to bring about a condition ... where wives and daughters would be in their proper sphere at home, instead of being dragged into competition for livelihood against the great and strong men of the world' (Turner, 1962: 185). Prior to 1858, women participated in medicine quite widely, but thereafter, as in other traditional professions, the work became a male preserve. With the exception of midwifery and nursing, a combination of government legislation and male tactics excluded middle-class women from all medical practices (Witz, 1986). Feminist critiques of the sociology of work have demonstrated in important ways the manner in which both the theory and practice of work and work behaviour have excluded women as subjects, as well as their experiences and voices (Sydie, 1994).

Married women were systematically removed from waged work after the initial phase of the Industrial Revolution. The new factory system proved beneficial to working-class women, particularly unmarried women, providing waged work outside the grossly exploitative decentralized putting-out system. Throughout the nineteenth century and well into the twentieth century, men managed to effectively exclude working-class and middle-class women from participating in many trade and professional occupations, by retaining old 'skills' or monopolizing new ones, using their professional privilege and power, using strategies of exclusion and demarcation, and encouraging the concepts of 'skill' and 'profession' to be seen as male property (Knights and Willmott, 1986a).

In the twenty-first century, although the realities of workplaces have changed, ideas about them have lagged far behind (Kimmel, 2004). Many Europeans and North Americans still believe in the 'traditional' male breadwinner/female home-keeper model, even though household lives and financial imperatives no longer reflect it. In Germany, for example, the traditional sense of family roles remains strong, and women who do paid work can be called *Rabenmutter*, meaning a raven mother. Commenting on German social values in 2006, Reiner Klingholz, head of the Berlin Institute for Population and Development, said, 'These old-fashioned ideas about the sexes aren't really part of mainstream German thought any more, but it's still embedded in the neurons of our brains that women have to stay home and take care of the children' (quoted in Kimmel, 2004).

VISIT THE *ONLINE RESOURCE CENTRE* AT HTTPS://HE.PALGRAVE.COM/COMPANION/BRATTON-WORK-AND-ORGANIZATIONAL-BEHAVIOUR3/ FOR FURTHER INFORMATION ON WOMEN EMPLOYED IN ADVANCED CAPITALIST SOCIETIES.

Work less, live better? Managing the work–life balance

work–life balance: the interplay between working life, the family and the community, in terms of both time and space

The interplay between working life, the family and the community, often expressed as the '**work–life balance**', is a 'hot' topic of debate and research that is receiving increasing attention from policy makers and managers (Greenhaus, 2008; Purcell et al., 2004; Sturges and Guest, 2004). The main message of the debate is that a balance between work and life is desirable, and that too much work has negative effects on private life – in effect, a more sophisticated version of the popular proverb 'All work and no play makes Jack a dull boy'. In spite of the spate of literature, for Warhurst and his colleagues, the current debate on work–life balance remains problematic both empirically and conceptually (Warhurst et al., 2008). Empirical research does indeed reveal a significant degree of interest in many organizations, but data show a mismatch between the work–life balance **discourse** and the reality in most workplaces.

discourse: a way of talking about and conceptualizing an issue, presented through concepts, ideas and vocabulary that recur in texts

This gap is illustrated by the findings from the Workplace Employment Relations Study 2006. The European Union Social Charter of 1961 obliged Member States to ensure 'reasonable and weekly working hours', yet research indicates that British workers work the longest hours in the then EU-15 Member States (European Trade

globalization & **organization misbehaviour**

Source: PhotoDisc/Getty Images

Upstairs, downstairs: the exploitation of migrant domestic workers

When we think of employment, the first images that often jump to mind are large workplaces, such as factories, offices and fast-food restaurants. Yet small and medium-sized businesses account for 59 per cent of all private sector employment in the UK (Federation of Small Businesses, 2014). Among the smallest workplaces are homes, where nannies and other domestic staff are employed in ones and twos. There are approximately 50 million domestic workers employed worldwide and most of them are women (Chowdhry, 2013).

In 2012, a new visa system for foreign nannies in the UK began prohibiting migrant domestic workers (MDWs) from changing employers. Not surprisingly, MDWs whose presence in the country is linked to their employment are experiencing twice the rate of mistreatment than MDWs did under the old visa system (Kalayann, 2014). 'UK: Migrant domestic workers face serious abuse' (Human Rights Watch, 2014) documents the confiscation of passports, confinement to the home, physical and psychological abuse, extremely long working hours with no rest days, and very low wages or non-payment of wages:

> 'Workers who are mistreated now face a horrendous choice: either endure the terrible abuse, or escape and become undocumented migrants, where of course they are much more vulnerable to further abuse and exploitation', said Leghtas. 'It's abhorrent that anyone should be tied into abuse in this way.'

It is somewhat disconcerting that workers providing one-on-one services in an employer's home – often caring for their employer's children – are treated so poorly. Yet this is hardly surprising. Employment occurs in the context of a capitalist economy (where employers seek to minimize costs) and the master-and-servant tradition of employment (where workers and employers have asymmetrical employment rights and obligations). In this way, employment is not just an (unequal) economic relationship, but also a social one: by accepting employment, workers are accepting managerial authority and agreeing to comply with managerial rules and direction (Godard, 2005). When given the chance, employers dominate the lives of workers far beyond what is necessary to obtain work. And government policy – in this case, immigration policy restricting the labour mobility among non-citizens – buttresses employers' power. Furthermore, the poor treatment of servants – particularly women from ethnic minorities – has a long pedigree in Western societies.

Yet when stories of abuse emerge, they often take a strange turn. For example, in late 2013, the Indian Deputy Consul in New York was arrested for lying on her nanny's immigration documents about the nanny's salary and paying her $573 a month for working up to 100 hours per week (Lakshmi, 2014). The diplomat's arrest and strip-search generated outrage and copious headlines. Not so much the diplomat's treatment of her nanny:

> 'The fact that the domestic worker's rights were violated was completely eclipsed by the shrill outcry by the government over the treatment of its diplomat', said Ananya Bhattacharjee, who heads a domestic workers' group called Gharelu Kaamgar Sangathan … . 'We had to try very hard to remind everybody that there are two Indian citizens involved in this case, not just one.'

Government indifference towards MDWs, in both their home and host countries, suggests that the organization of work is driven by a variety of economic, political and social factors. Ignoring these factors yields an incomplete understanding of how and why organizations act as they do.

> **Stop!** What motivates employers to overwork MDWs? In what ways are MDWs different from so-called regular workers? How does this impact upon their treatment in the workplace? Do gender and race affect the broad organization of work in society?

Sources and further information

Chowdhry, A. (2013) 'India–US diplomatic row puts spotlight on globe's domestic workers'. Available at: www.theglobeandmail.com/news/world/india-us-diplomat-row-puts-spotlight-on-globes-domestic-workers/article16069305/ (accessed December 13, 2014).

Federation of Small Businesses (2014) 'Small business statistics'. Available at: www.fsb.org.uk/stats (accessed December 2014).

Godard, J. (2005a) 'Contemporary management practices', pp. 112–48 in J. Godard *Industrial Relations, the Economy and Society* (3rd edn), Concord: Captus.

Human Rights Watch (2014) 'UK: Migrant domestic workers face serious abuse'. Available at: www.hrw.org/print/news/2014/03/31/uk-migrant-domestic-workers-face-serious-abuse?dm_i=LF4%2C2BRLI%2C86UIIE%2C8G06K%2C1 (accessed December 13, 2014).

Kalayann (2014) 'Still enslaved: the migrant domestic workers who are trapped by the immigration rules'. Available at: www.kalayaan.org.uk/documents/tied%20visa%202014.pdf (accessed December 13, 2014).

Lakshmi, R. (2014) 'Indian rights groups say Khobragade case shows callousness toward domestic workers'. *Washington Post.* Available at: www.washingtonpost.com/world/indian-rights-groups-say-khobragade-case-shows-callousness-toward-domestic-workers/2014/01/12/8ecb9f88-7ba9-11e3-97d3-b9925ce2c57b_story.html (accessed December 13, 2014).

Note: This feature was written by Bob Barnetson, Associate Professor of Labour Relations, Athabasca University, Canada.

Union Confederation, 2009). Not surprising, therefore, the UK labour market has been characterized as the 'long hours culture' (Bonney, 2005). Setting a limit on the number of hours an employee must work in a working day and week most directly affects the work–life balance.

VISIT THE *ONLINE RESOURCE CENTRE* AT HTTPS://HE.PALGRAVE.COM/COMPANION/BRATTON-WORK-AND-ORGANIZATIONAL-BEHAVIOUR3/ FOR FURTHER INFORMATION ON THE EUROPEAN UNION WORKING TIME DEVELOPMENTS.

Paid work	Life
Tasks	Child care
Projects	Housework
Deadlines	Elder care
Travel	Community activities
Meetings	Hobbies
Client demands	Holidays

Figure 2.4 The notion of the work–life balance

Source: Getty Images

plate 8 The interpenetration between work and life is most obvious in contemporary home-working, which allows professionals to engage in paid work and domestic activities in the same physical space, and perhaps even on occasion at the same time.

The boundary between work and private life is influenced by flexible working arrangements, such as 'home-working'. Women were more likely than men to have access to home-working arrangements, yet home-working was slightly more prevalent in workplaces where women were not in the majority (Kersley et al., 2006). There are a number of possible causes for this, including inadequate or high-cost child-care provision, non-standard or precarious employment and perhaps, in more recent years, a 'flight to work' in the age of austerity.

The concept at the centre of the work–life balance debate is problematic (Noon and Blyton, 2013). The notion of work–life balance has been defined as 'the relationship between the institutional and cultural times and spaces of work and non-work in societies where income is predominantly generated and distributed through labour markets' (Felstead et al., 2002: 56). Warhurst et al. (2008) argue that the concept of work–life *balance* is based on a traditional, large-scale workplace model which presumes that paid work and life constitute two distinct spheres, separated by time and space (Figure 2.4). This orthodox binary interpretation adopts a particular interpretation of labour under capitalism, viewing paid work as an encroachment on people's 'real' private life, particularly family life, and seeing it as something that therefore has to be contained. As the examples and case studies included throughout this book suggest, work can be boring and alienating – a 'blank patch' between morning and evening – unhealthy and at times dangerous. Yet work can also offer self-fulfilment and friendship, and people can potentially derive joy from it. Work brings structure to people's lives, dignity and satisfaction, and is an important source of identity (Karlsson, 2012).

Warhurst's et al. (2008) premise is that the work–life interface is not best articulated as one of 'balance' because 'interpenetration' occurs between the two spheres. This interpenetration between work and life is most obvious in contemporary home-working, which, through information and communication technology, allows professionals to engage in paid work and domestic activities in the same physical space and maybe at the same time. Thus, the concept of work–life balance, with its suggestions of a binary opposition between 'work' and 'life', does not indicate how the complex interplay of personal choice and constraints, competing interests and power relations, shapes the relationship between work and life.

People are what Anthony Giddens (1984) has called 'knowledgeable agents' – that is, they construct perceptions of work and life – and through their agency they produce social practices, which can be translated into what Warhurst et al. (2008) call 'work–life patterns'. These social patterns and practices that human beings construct relate to work, family activities, maintaining friendships and the pursuit of leisure activities. Naturally, depending on the individual's context, the way in which work–life patterns are experienced can vary markedly between individuals. The advocates of the work–life pattern approach identify four implications for researchers and discerning managers:

- The focus of praxis proposes an analysis of actual work practices and the impact that these have on work–life patterns. For example, if work takes place in a fixed and unmovable location (for example, assembly line work), work–life patterns are likely to exhibit a clear delineation between work and life.

- Employment analysts and practitioners need to understand the structural constraints (economic, social and cultural resources) that fashion work–life patterns. For example, economic capital can buy additional time for work (for example, hiring a nanny) or life (for instance, only part-time paid work); cultural (such as education) and social (for example, extended family) resources also affect job opportunities and work–life choices and opportunities.
- Lifestyles – values, beliefs and work-related perceptions – influence individual practices and work–life patterns. Max Weber first proposed a connection between lifestyle (religion and asceticism) and work–life patterns (Weber, 1905/2002). The lifestyle of artists, musicians or theatre actors, for example, might promote a fusing or 'amalgamation' of a work–life pattern. Thus, creative artists are more likely to regard 'work as life, and life as work' (Warhurst et al., 2008: 14). However, the notion of the fusing of a work–life pattern is not restricted to artistic labour. As Michelle Gillies, a recently unemployed professional who had been a promotion manager and producer in the Canadian broadcasting sector, said, 'My job was me. I spent 10 years so closely linked to what I did there that there were no lines separating the two' (Gillies, 2009). Examples of work–life amalgamation illustrate that the experience of work and life cannot be understood using a simple model that separates the two spheres and sets them into opposition.
- Work–life patterns are constructed following a range of logics, depending on the context. Whereas work centres on exchanges between effort and pay, life embraces a multitude of logics, such as unconditional love for family, the reciprocity of friendships and self-gratification through conspicuous consumption. These logics of work and life coexist, allowing individuals 'a fairly frictionless *alternation* between the two distinct spheres' (Warhurst et al., 2008: 15).

Work–life patterns are continually (re)constructed as employees' work and life cycles change. Examples of such changes might include:

- the shift from independent single person to mid-life with family dependants and so on
- a change in perceived economic insecurity
- government incentives and regulations to help individuals achieve their work–life goals (Kvande, 2009).

Although the idea of work–life 'balance' may appear complex and problematic, employers' strategies in this area can have important benefits for the organization. For example, work–life policies and practices might be important for attracting and motivating professionals and innovative behaviours (De Cieri et al., 2002) – and conversely, the failure to introduce such policies and practices can have a detrimental effect. Many law firms in North America, for example, retain 'a dominant male hierarchy and a suspicion of women who crave a balance between work and family', and the industry is losing talented professionals as a result. As one anonymous lawyer attests, 'A lot of male lawyers ... were extremely unhappy about losing these really high-calibre people' (Makin, 2009: 4).

However, the idea of achieving a work–life 'balance' still seems remote for millions of low-income families. As we have seen, the approach of the work–life pattern is more complex than the notion of a 'balance' between two separable spheres, and it is a perspective that has important implications for how work and people are managed in the workplace. In the next chapter, we move on to examine how developments in work have been conceptualized and theorized.

Chapter summary

- One of the major themes running through the study of paid work has been the continuities as well as the discontinuities across time. There is no doubt that changes occur all the time, but these must be adequately studied in context if we are to appreciate their relevance. Sociologists study the way work is actually experienced by individuals and groups as well as ideologies that constitute a work ethic. Thus, we can only really talk about the demise of the work ethic and a rise in instrumental attitudes (for example, the desire to maintain an income) to work if we know what previously existed.

- Trying to summarize the experience of work over several millennia is a difficult task. There is so much material to cover that no text of conventional size would be able to deal adequately with the complexities. However, this chapter has been written on the assumption that some knowledge is preferable to complete ignorance, especially if we have to situate the present against the past in order to understand it. The chapter has tended to highlight gender issues in the workplace to balance out the conventional preference for a male history.

- The complexity of the experience of work defies any simple assumptions about the significance of work. However, we can perhaps salvage from the past a conclusion that highlights the significance of the social. Work, like other institutions, is inherently socially constructed, interpreted and organized through social behaviour and social discourse.

- We have explained how, with the growth of routinized service work, new kinds of social relations and aspects of the self have developed and come under scrutiny. As the service workforce has grown in importance, we noted the growing interest in 'emotional labour', pioneered by Arlie Hochschild.

- The persistence of gender ideologies on work, discrimination and the sexual division of paid work have been discussed, as has the persistent belief in the 'traditional' male breadwinner/female home-keeper model, particularly in periods of economic recession.

- We have explored the concept of work–life balance and why this orthodox binary view is based on traditional large-scale work and life patterns separated by time and space. As such, paid work is regarded as an activity that is an encroachment on people's private lives. A more complex approach is represented by the notion of work–life patterns, which sees the activity of labour itself as an important source of identity and satisfaction.

IN THE EBOOK ACCESS **WEB BASED ASSIGNMENTS** TO APPLY YOUR LEARNING.

Chapter review questions

1 What is work?
2 What were the advantages and disadvantages of the putting-out system?
3 Why were men reluctant to enter the new factories during the Industrial Revolution?
4 Why were male trade unionists so hostile to women entering traditional occupations?

5 Explain the importance of 'control' in a factory system.
6 How does knowledge work different from traditional work?
7 How does emotional labour differ from traditional paid work?
8 What is the difference between work–life balance and work–life patterns? Why is it considered important for managers to understand these concepts?

Further reading

Atzeni, M. (ed.) (2014) *Workers and Labour in a Globalised Capitalism*, Basingstoke: Palgrave Macmillan.

Bolton, S. C. and Houlihan M. (2009) *Work Matters, Critical Reflections on Contemporary Work*, Basingstoke: Palgrave Macmillan.

Carter, B., Danford, A., Howcroft, D., Richardson, H., Smith, A. and Taylor, P. (2011) 'All they lack is a chain: lean and the new performance management in the British civil service', *New Technology, Work and Employment*, 26(2), pp. 83–97.

Edgell, S. (2006) *The Sociology of Work*, London: Sage.

Emslie, C. and Hunt, K. (2009) '"Live to work" or "work to live"? A qualitative study of gender and work–life balance among men and women in mid-life', *Gender, Work and Organization*, 16(1), pp. 151–72.

Frenkel, S. J. (2006) 'Service workers in search of decent work', pp. 356–75 in S. Ackroyd, R. Batt, P. Thompson and P. Tolbert (eds), *The Oxford Handbook of Work and Organization*, New York: Oxford University Press.

Kelan, E. (2008) 'Gender, risk and employment insecurity: the masculine breadwinner subtext', *Human Relations*, 61(9), pp. 1171–202.

Kvande, E. (2009) 'Work–life balance for fathers in globalized knowledge work. Some insights from the Norwegian context', *Gender, Work and Organization*, 16(1), pp. 58–72.

McCormick, K. (2007) 'Sociologists and "the Japanese model": a passing enthusiasm?', *Work, Employment and Society*, 21(4), pp. 751–71.

McIvor, A. (2001) *A History of Work in Britain, 1880–1950*, Basingstoke: Palgrave Macmillan.

McKinlay, A. and Smith, C. (2009) *Creative Labour*, Basingstoke: Palgrave Macmillan.

Noon, M. and Blyton, P. (2013) *The Realities of Work* (4th edn), Basingstoke: Palgrave Macmillan.

Standing, G. (2011) *The Precariat*, London: Bloomsbury.

Warhurst, C., Eikhof, D. R. and Haunschild, A. (2008) *Work Less, Live More?*, Basingstoke: Palgrave Macmillan.

Chapter case study: Service with a smile: McJobs in China

The setting

Although McDonald's is well known for its Fordist method of food production, China has had experience using an assembly line approach to feeding many people for over two centuries. As early as the nineteenth century, Chinese public dining halls had perfected breaking down the cooking process into basic procedures performed by a separate team of workers.

McDonald's brought its own brand of food production and management to China in 1990 when it opened its first restaurant in the city of Shenzhen. In 1992, the world's largest McDonald's was opened in Beijing, serving 40,000 customers on that first day. McDonald's now operates over 2000 restaurants in more than 190 Chinese cities, and opened 300 new outlets in China in 2014.

More than 70 per cent of McDonald's restaurants worldwide are owned and operated independently by local men and women. In recent years, McDonald's future growth strategy has focused on China's smaller urban areas, known as second- and third-tier cities. McDonald's is not alone as many multinational and domestic companies are now looking to expand outside the traditional economic bases in the larger Chinese centres. McDonald's faces particularly stiff competition from KFC, a fellow American fast-food restaurant chain, which dominates the Chinese market.

While Chinese fast food operators do not deal with the high turnover rates seen in American cities (sometimes as high as 300 per cent for non-managerial employees), the rapid expansion by multiple companies has resulted in competition for quality workers and rising wage costs in the new tighter labour markets.

The problem

Hai Yan is one of the new owners of a McDonald's franchise in an area several hours outside Beijing. As with other franchisees, Hai had relied on the McDonald's corporation to assist him with recruiting and training his new employees to bring them in line with the company's expectations.

Peter Bepple, a new Human Resources Manager assigned to the region, flew in from New York to help. Peter had never worked in China before and was looking forward to getting the new franchises up and running. He had been briefed on the recruiting issues and had been told that although the Chinese were hard workers who respected management authority and leadership, they also expected their managers to build supportive relationships with them.

Upon his arrival in Hai's area, Peter immediately set up recruitment advertising on the company website, interviewed applicants on the phone and made arrangements for selected candidates to come into Hai's restaurant for 3 days of work. Accompanied by a McDonald's employee, each candidate tried various roles from waiter to assistant manager in the restaurant. To Hai's dismay, 80 per cent of the candidates were not offered permanent employment. He became concerned that he would not find enough suitable workers to serve customers on his restaurant's opening day. Hai decided to approach Peter to find out why so many of the candidates had not been successful during the recruitment process.

Peter was sympathetic but explained to Hai that he had observed each failed candidate's reactions to the customers and was not impressed. 'The main challenge is to maintain a positive attitude and provide good service,' Peter told Hai. 'The most important characteristic is the willingness to communicate with others and that is best reflected with a smile. Those candidates simply did not smile enough.'

Hai was taken aback by the comment. 'Here in China customers are suspicious of workers who smile on the job,' he said to Peter.

Peter was surprised by this, but decided to check with his counterparts in other McDonald's locations in China to see if this was actually the case. They confirmed what Hai had said. 'Customers in China expect employees to be serious about their work,' he was told. 'The customers are more concerned about the efficiency, reliability and cleanliness of the restaurant than if the worker smiles at them.'

Before returning to New York, Peter's head office called and asked him to prepare a report on what he had learned on his first overseas assignment.

The task

Prepare a short report, incorporating answers to the following questions:

- How important is it for the McDonald's customer service strategy to insist on having its employees provide 'service with a smile'?
- What possible effects will forcing smiles have on the Chinese workers?
- How could Peter have better prepared himself for working in China?
- To what extent do you think the success of the US-based McDonald's corporation influences local Chinese companies to adopt its management practices, despite the cultural differences?

Sources and further information

Allan, C., Bamber, G. and Timo, N. (2006) 'Fast-food work: are McJobs satisfying?' *Employee Relations*, 28(5), pp. 402–20.

Deery, S. (2005) 'Customer service work, emotional labour and performance', Chapter 13 in S. Bach (ed.), *Managing Human Resources: Personnel Management in Transition*, Oxford: Blackwell.

Earnhardt, M. (2009) 'The successful expatriate leader in China', *Graziado Business Report*, 12(1). Available at: http://gbr.pepperdine.edu/091/expatriatesinchina.html (accessed December 13, 2014).

Gould, A. (2010) 'Working at McDonald's: some redeeming features of McJobs', *Work, Employment and Society*, 24(4), pp. 78–802.

Mujtaba, B. and Patel, B. (2007) 'McDonald's success strategy and global expansion through customer and brand loyalty', *Journal of Business Case Studies*, 3(3), pp. 55–66.

Watson, J. (2006) *Golden Arches East: McDonald's in East Asia*, Stanford: Stanford University Press.

Note: This case study was written by Lori Rilkoff, Human Resources Director, City of Kamloops, BC, Canada.

IN THE EBOOK ACCESS AN **OB IN FILM** BOX THAT USES THE CLASSIC *MODERN TIMES* (1936) STARRING CHARLIE CHAPLIN TO ILLUSTRATE THE MEANING OF TAYLORISM AND TO ACCESS **AN INTERACTIVE QUIZ** TO TEST YOUR UNDERSTANDING.

chapter 3
Studying work and organizations

Key concepts

- alienation
- androcentrism
- anomie
- ideal type
- labour power
- paradox of consequences
- rationality
- strategic choice
- symbolic interactionism

Chapter outline

- Introduction
- Classical approaches to studying work
- Contemporary theories of organizations
- The value of theory about contemporary organizational behaviour
- Summary and end-of-chapter features
- Chapter case study: Butting out smoking in Russia

Chapter learning outcomes

After completing this chapter, you should be able to:

1 Explain the classical approaches to studying work through the ideas of Marx, Durkheim, Weber and Simmel
2 Explain contemporary theories of work organizations and the importance of theory to understanding work and behaviour in the workplace

introduction

A historical perspective of the study of work and management helps in studying contemporary organizational behaviour. According to one management historian, we can better understand the here-and-now of contemporary management and its development by appreciating its past (Witzel, 2012). In the eighteenth and nineteenth centuries, the philosophers Adam Smith and Karl Marx pioneered organization studies. This chapter examines classical and contemporary approaches to studying work and work organizations. We begin by considering the classical social theories about paid work through the ideas of Marx, Weber, Durkheim and Simmel. These can be described as classical partly because they had their roots in European industrialization and culture – from about 1800 through to the early 1900s – and also because, in their response to industrial capitalism, the early social theorists set out a series of themes, concepts, assumptions, problems and ideas that continue to exercise an enormous influence over contemporary organizational theory. As pointed out elsewhere, the works of the classical theorists, and the characteristic focuses of those traditions, continue to dominate study of the sociology of work (Bratton and Denham, 2014).

As we discussed in Chapter 2, private and public organizations have over the last three decades fundamentally changed how they organize work and manage people. In Chapter 1, we not only observed that new concepts have been developed to help us understand these changes, but also explained that theory guides organizational behaviour research. One challenge that researchers face is producing relevant knowledge for practitioners (Radaelli et al., 2014). This chapter examines the theories of work that have influenced, and continue to influence, social scientists studying organizations and their management. In the 1970s, the orthodox view on organization theory focused on 'functionalism', which emphasized consensus and coherence rather than asymmetrical power relations and conflict (Clegg and Hardy, 1999). The key concept is that of the organization as a 'system' that functions effectively if it achieves explicit goals, which are formally defined through 'rational' decision making. Alternative theoretical approaches have, however, since challenged the supremacy of functionalism.

A multitude of contemporary theories of formal organizations exist, so we cannot hope to do justice to the complexities of such a wide-ranging debate. We therefore seek here to highlight the major distinguishing themes related to work and organizations. In this chapter, we review 11 competing theoretical perspectives in organization and management theory: the technical, social-technical, contingency, culture, learning, social action, political, control, feminist, symbolic-interactionist and postmodernist perspectives.

Classical approaches to studying work

Marx, Durkheim, Weber and Simmel each analysed the new work forms, but they also placed their analysis within a wider discourse on modern society. While Karl Marx focused on social conflict and social change, Emile Durkheim concerned himself with the nature of order, Max Weber developed his theory of rationality and bureaucracy, and Georg Simmel examined micro human interactions.

Karl Marx (1818–83)

Marx told an intriguing narrative about industrial capitalism. This story takes elements from the past, along with social factors in modern times, and predicts what will happen in society. By a detailed analysis of work, it tells us not only *why* but also *how* workers are exploited (Allan, 2013). Marx believed that industrialization was a necessary stage for the eventual triumph of human potential, but that

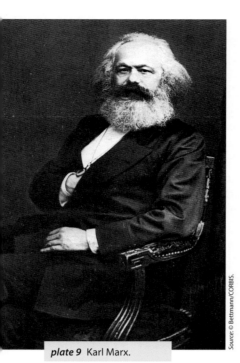

plate 9 Karl Marx.

objectification: Karl Marx's term to describe the action of human labour on resources to produce a commodity, which, under the control of the capitalist, remains divorced from and opposed to the direct producer

surplus value: the portion of the working day during which workers produce value that is appropriated by the capitalist

the mainspring of this social formation was capitalism, and not industrialism as such. It is only capitalism that carries within it the seeds of its own destruction. For Marx, the human species is different from all other animal species, not because of its consciousness, but because it alone produces its own means of subsistence.

Marx's argument is that what distinguishes humans from other animals is that our labour creates something in reality that previously existed only in our imagination:

> We presuppose labour in a form that stamps it as exclusively human … But what distinguishes the worst architect from the best bees is this, that the architect raises his structure in imagination before he erects it in reality.
> At the end of every labour process we get a result that existed in the *imagination* of the labourer at its commencement. He not only effects a change of form in the material on which he works, but he also realizes a purpose. (Marx, 1867/1970: 178, emphasis added)

Marx calls this process whereby humans create external objects from their internal thoughts **objectification**. This labour does not just transform raw materials or nature; it also transforms humans, including human nature, people's needs and their consciousness. We can begin to understand Marx's concept of objectification by thinking of the creative activity of an artist. The artist's labour is a representation of the imagination of the artist: 'the art work is an objectification of the artist' (Ritzer, 2010). In addition, through the labour process, the artist's ideas of the object change, or the experience may prompt a new vision or creativity that needs objectification. Labour, for Marx, provides the means through which humans can realize their true human powers and potential. By transforming raw materials, we transform ourselves, and we also transform society. Thus, according to Marx, the transformation of the individual through work and the transformation of society are inseparable.

Marx's discussion of work under capitalism focuses on the nature of employment relationships. Under capitalism, the aim is to buy labour at sufficiently low rates to make a profit. Marx is careful to distinguish between 'labour' and 'labour power'. Human labour is the actual physical or mental activity incorporated into the body of the worker. Labour power, on the other hand, refers to the *potential* of labour to add a use value to raw materials or commodities. This labour power is bought by the capitalist at a lower value than the value it creates. In purchasing the worker's potential or capacity to labour and add values to materials, all at a wage level less than the value created by the worker's labour, the capitalist is able to make a profit.

We can begin to appreciate the significance of Marx's use of the term 'labour power' when we think of it as a promise: it is therefore indeterminate, and there may be a gap between the potential or promise of labour and the actual labour. This distinction between 'labour' and 'labour power' allowed Marx to locate the precise mechanism that creates profit in capitalist societies. It also gives rise to the creation of two classes that are potentially, if not always in practice, in conflict with each other.

Capitalism involves the work relationship between the buyers and sellers of labour power. Marx's concept of **surplus value** is rooted in this social relationship. Surplus value is the value remaining when the worker's daily costs of subsistence have been subtracted from the value that she or he produces for the capitalist. As such, it is unpaid and 'goes to the heart of the exploitation of the worker' (Bratton and Denham, 2014: 143).

In the workplace, the primacy of profit and conflict relationships gives rise to three broad necessary features of activity and change. Each of these involves substantial shifts in the work performed. Most significant is the need for the capitalist to centralize the labour power that is purchased, and to discipline the interior of the factory by organizing space, time and the behaviour of workers whose commitment is unreliable. The aim is to close or minimize the gap between potential labour power and actual labour power. For Marx, the accumulation of profit is inevitably and irrevocably mediated by managerial control strategies. It is the inevitable outcome of capitalism: 'The directing motive, the end and aim of capitalist production, is to extract the greatest possible amount of surplus-value, and consequently to exploit labour-power to the fullest possible extent' (Marx, 1867/1970: 331).

The second broad plane of activity changing the nature of work is the **division of labour** (also discussed in Chapter 2). To increase control and surplus value for the capitalist, extensive division of labour takes place within the factory. According to Marx, 'Division of labour within the workshop implies the undisputed authority of the capitalist over men that are but parts of a mechanism that belong to him' (Marx, 1867/1970: 356). As an example, Marx described the manufacture of horse carriages. In pre-capitalist production, the manufacture of carriages involved the simple cooperation of various trades: coach construction, ironwork, upholstery and wheelwright work. Each of these trades was regulated by guilds in order to maintain their specialization and control over these operations. In capitalist production, simple cooperation gives way to what Marx described as 'complex cooperation', as individual trades lose their specialized skills, and workers perform operations that are disconnected and isolated from one another, and carried out alongside each other. According to Marx and his colleague Engels, this mode of production also creates a hierarchy of managers and supervisors:

> Modern industry has converted the little workshop of the patriarchal master into the great factory of the industrial capitalist. Masses of labourers, crowded into the factory, are organized like soldiers. As privates of the industrial army they are placed under the command of a perfect hierarchy of officers [managers] and sergeants [supervisors]. (Marx and Engels, 1848/1967: 227)

Marx examined the impact of technological change on employment relationships. He argued that machinery is used by the capitalist to increase surplus labour by cheapening labour, to deskill workers and thus to make it easier to recruit, control and discipline workers. Machinery, he argued, led to the progressive reduction of skills:

> On the automatic plan skilled labour gets progressively superseded. The effect of improvements in machinery [results] in substituting one description of human labour for another, the less skilled for the more skilled, juvenile for adult, female for male, [and] causes a fresh disturbance in the rate of wages. (Marx, 1867/1970: 433)

Machinery allows the capitalist to transfer the knowledge and skill involved in production from the worker to reliable agents of capital – that is, managers. Marx described the process like this: 'Intelligence in production expands in one direction, because it vanishes in many others. What is lost by the detail labourers is concentrated in the capital that employs them' (Marx, 1867/1970: 361). Machinery also increases the capitalist's control over the workers' work activities. In what Marx referred to as the despotism of the factory, machinery sets the pace of work and embodies powerful mechanisms of control: 'the technical subordination of the workman to the uniform motion of the instruments of labour [machinery] … gave rise to a barrack discipline'. He continued: 'To devise and administer a successful code of factory discipline, suited to the necessities of factory diligence, was the Herculean enterprise, the noble achievement of Arkwright!' (Marx, 1867/1970: 423–4).

These characteristics of work in industrial capitalism have two major consequences: the **alienation** of the workers, and conflict that ultimately results in social change. Whereas objectification embodies the worker's creativity, work under

division of labour: the allocation of work tasks to various groups or categories of employee

alienation: a feeling of powerlessness and estrangement from other people and from oneself

capitalism is devoid of the producer's own potential creativity and sensuousness. Because workers' labour is not their own, it no longer transforms them. Hence, the unique quality of human beings – their ability to control the forces of nature and produce their own means of existence, to realize their full creative capacity through work – is stultified by capitalism.

Alienation

Drawing on the 1807 work by Georg Hegel, *The Phenomenology of Mind*, Marx developed the theory of alienation. In essence, alienation ruptures the fundamental connection that human beings have to the self-defining aspect of their labouring activity (Bratton and Denham, 2014). Marx broke down the formulation of alienation into four conceptually discrete but related spheres.

First, workers are alienated (or separated) from the product of their labour. The product – its design, quality, quantity and how it is marketed and disposed of – is not determined by those whose labour is responsible for its manufacture.

Second, workers are alienated from productive activity. Marx emphasized the tendency for machinery to deskill work:

> Owing to the extensive use of machinery and to division of labour, the work of the proletarians has lost all individual character, and, consequently, all charm for the workman. He becomes an appendage of the machine, and it is only the most simple, most monotonous, and most easily acquired knack, that is required of him. (Marx and Engels, 1848/1967: 227)

Thus, work offers no intrinsic satisfaction. Workers only work for the money; workers only work because they have to. Marx called this the 'cash nexus'. Accordingly, work takes on an instrumental meaning: it is regarded simply as a means to an end.

The third type of alienation discussed by Marx is alienation from the human species. Marx contended that self-estrangement develops because of the 'cash nexus'. In order to be clear on Marx's meaning, we need to know that Marx believed that people were essentially creative and that individuals expressed their creativity through their work. Work, according to Marx, is the medium for self-expression and self-development. It is through work that people should be able to shape themselves and their communities in accordance with their own needs, interests and values. Under alienating conditions, however, work becomes not a social activity that personifies life, but simply a means for physical survival: people become detached from their true selves.

The fourth type of alienation discussed by Marx is alienation from fellow human beings and from the community. This results when the sole purpose of life is competition and all social relations are transformed into economic relations. Workers and managers are alienated from each other. This economic relationship – between those who are controlled and the controllers – is an antagonistic one. And this asymmetry of social relationships in the workplace creates the foundation for a class structure that necessitates sharp differences in power, income and life chances.

Marx's analysis of the social organization of work underscores the fact that people express themselves through their work, and in so far as their labour is merely a commodity to be paid for with a wage, they are alienated. Although Marx did not explicitly focus on the analysis of emotion in the workplace, he did acknowledge that the way in which industrial work was organized and managed did provoke in workers feelings of numbness, anger and resentment. Alienation is characteristic of a certain kind of organization of work – industrial capitalism – that is predicated on a set of socioeconomic conditions. In short, then, capitalism destroys the pleasure associated with labour, the distinctively human capacity to shape and reshape the world.

Social change

The second major consequence of work in capitalism, that relations between capitalists and workers are in constant conflict, is the engine of social change. In *The Communist Manifesto*, Marx and Friedrich Engels captured the idea of continuous change: 'Constant revolutionizing of production, uninterrupted disturbance of all social conditions, everlasting uncertainty ... all new-formed ones become antiquated before they can ossify. All that is solid melts into the air' (Marx and Engels, 1848/1967: 223). For Marx, the logic of capitalism, the accumulation of profit, demanded ceaseless change. In Volume 1 of *Capital*, he explains that technology had to be introduced into factories to secure ever-lower labour costs:

> The technical and social conditions of the labour process ... must be revolutionized ... Modern Industry, indeed, compels society, under penalty of death, to replace the detailed-worker of today ... by the fully developed individual. (Marx, 1867/1970: 315, 488)

Marx also identified falling or squeezed profits as a recurring phenomenon under free-market capitalism. Crises in profits, accordingly, generate workplace change as capital restructures to restore profit margins.

According to Marx these internal dynamics help the development of **class consciousness** among the workers or **proletariat**. The defining features of work – deskilling, intensification of work, constant pressure to lower the wages allocated to labour – encourage the development of **class conflict**. Marx and Engels explain the logic whereby capitalism develops and then destroys itself. In their search for profits, capitalists closely control and discipline workers (Bratton and Denham, 2014).

Capitalism creates new **contradictions**, such as the concentration of workers into factories. As workers are concentrated under one roof, they become aware of their common exploitation and circumstances. As a result, over time, workers begin to resist capitalist controls, initially as individuals, and then collectively as groups. Gradually, the workers become organized, through trade unions, and increasingly they become more combative and engage the ruling class in wider social struggles, which Marx believed would culminate in replacing the rule of the **bourgeoisie** and ridding society of capitalism: 'What the bourgeoisie therefore produces above all, is its own gravediggers. Its fall and the victory of the proletariat are equally inevitable' (Marx and Engels, 1848/1967: 233). Thus, those selling their labour power, the workers, are exposed to such exploitation and degradation that they begin to oppose the capitalists, in order to replace the system.

Marx provides a sophisticated theory of capitalism, with the working class as the embodiment of good, but his concentration on the extraction of surplus value in the labour process prevents him from considering managerial and government strategies that serve to develop consent and cooperation. The capitalist mode of production is not characterized solely by the conflict between employer and labour: it is also marked by competition between organizations and economies. To put it another way, profits are realized by gaining a competitive advantage, and the need to gain workers' cooperation undermines the contradictory laws that promote constant conflict and crises. Thus, Marx systematically underestimates the possibility that management may need to organize on the basis of consent as well as coercion.

The reconceptualization of management as being necessarily engaged in building consent also suggests that Marx's zero-sum theory of power is insufficient. Critics argue that although the interests of labour and capital do not coincide, the assumption that they are irreconcilably and utterly antagonistic is misleading. Therefore, the inadequacy of Marx's account lies at the level of analysis. Marx emphasized the irreconcilable interests of the social classes at the societal level, but this obscures

class consciousness: Karl Marx's term for the awareness of a common identity based on a person's position in the means of production

proletariat (or working class): Karl Marx's term for those who must sell their labour because they have no other means of earning a livelihood

class conflict: a term for the struggle between the capitalist class and the working class

contradictions: contradictions are said to occur within social systems when the various principles that underlie these social arrangements conflict with each other

bourgeoisie (or capitalist class): Karl Marx's term for the class comprising those who own and control the means of production

the very real way in which, in the workplace, the interests of employers and employees may be very closely intertwined.

Marx lacked the statistical data needed to refine his analysis of early industrial capitalism (Piketty, 2014: 10). Despite this major handicap and the strong criticisms of his prediction of an apocalyptic end to capitalism, his analysis remains relevant in several respects. For example, the way in which he illuminates the relationship between the accumulation of capital and ceaseless change (see Chapter 18) and his insight into the politics of work both encourage critical thinking about how organizations operate – the relationships of power and managerial strategies inside the workplace, and the relationship between big business and the distribution of power in society at large. Marxism therefore still informs contemporary analyses of work and the social relationships between employers and workers, as we shall see throughout this book.

VISIT THE *ONLINE RESOURCE CENTRE* AT HTTPS://HE.PALGRAVE.COM/COMPANION/BRATTON-WORK-AND-ORGANIZATIONAL-BEHAVIOUR3/ FOR FURTHER INFORMATION ON KARL MARX'S WORK.

Emile Durkheim (1858–1917)

Emile Durkheim's contribution to our understanding of work is essentially derived from his book *The Division of Labor in Society* (1893/1997), and its discussion of the relationship between individuals and society, and of the conditions for social cohesion. Durkheim was preoccupied with the issue of **social solidarity** and unity during a time when France was subject to the profound revolutionary changes that created modern society. The popular belief of the time was that the collapse of social life was imminent in response to the expansion of the division of labour, the ever-increasing industrialization and **urbanization**, and the declining significance of traditional moral beliefs. This was described as the transition from *Gemeinschaft* or 'community' forms of society, to *Gesellschaft* or 'social' forms, representing mere 'associations' where social solidarity was disintegrating. Durkheim suggested that such fears were not just exaggerated, but actually wrong. His thesis held that heightened feelings of group solidarity and order were being reconstructed in a different form. Durkheim's position was that the interdependence resulting from the progressive differentiation and specialization of labour gave rise to a new form of social solidarity, which is the bond that unites individuals when there is no societal **normative order** or consensus on the rules and shared expectations governing a particular social situation.

Durkheim's prime question was, if pre-industrial societies are held together by shared understandings, ideas, norms and values, what holds a complex industrial society together? He believed that the increasing division of labour has enormous implications for the structure of society. In pre-industrial society, social solidarity is derived from people's similarities and the rather suffocating effects of uniformity of experience and thought. Such societies are held together through the collective consciousness at the direct expense of individuality: 'individual personality is absorbed into the collective personality', as Durkheim put it (Durkheim, 1893/1997: 85). He called this form of social unity **mechanical solidarity**. In contrast, the increasing division of labour causes a diminution of collective consciousness, and 'this leaves much more room for the free play of our initiative' (Durkheim, 1893/1997: 85).

Complex industrial societies, with new work forms based on functional specialization, are held together by relations of exchange and people's reciprocal need for the services of many others. Durkheim called this symmetry of life **organic solidarity**. He believed that, in societies whose solidarity is organic, individuals are increasingly linked to each other rather than to society as a whole. The totality of

social solidarity: the state of having shared beliefs and values among members of a social group, along with intense and frequent interaction among group members

urbanization: the process by which an increasing proportion of a population lives in cities rather than in rural areas

normative order: a concept most often found in functionalist theory. It is any system of social rules and shared expectations governing a particular social situation

mechanical solidarity: a term to describe the social cohesion that exists in pre-industrial societies, in which there is a minimal division of labour and people feel united by shared values and common social bonds

organic solidarity: a term for the social cohesion that exists in industrial (and perhaps post-industrial) societies, in which people perform very specialized tasks and feel united by their mutual dependence

the nature of these social links compels individuals to remain in contact with one another, which in turn binds them to each other and to society. Thus, each of us becomes aware of our dependence on others and of the new cultural norms that shape and restrain our actions.

For Durkheim, only the division of labour could furnish social solidarity and ethical decision making on the part of individuals in society: 'Since the division of labour becomes the source of social solidarity, it becomes, at the same time, the foundation of moral order' (Durkheim, 1893/1997: 333). In summary, he argued that there was no necessary correlation between an increased division of labour and decreasing solidarity. On the contrary, it was a source not of disorder and conflict, but of order and social solidarity. The nature of moral solidarity in industrial society has not disappeared, but it has changed.

Of course, Durkheim was not oblivious to the reality of industrialization in Western Europe, which might have been argued to show the opposite. Not least, there were intense class conflicts and widespread labour strikes in France, often led by radical workers known as revolutionary syndicalists, in unions organized in the *Confédération Générale du Travail*. Durkheim explained the existence of instability and social fragmentation by analysing what he called 'abnormal' forms of the division of labour. These abnormal forms occur when the development of the division of labour is obstructed and distorted by various factors. He identified these as the anomie division of labour, the forced division of labour and the mismanagement of operations.

The first abnormal effects can arise because of the *'anomie'* condition of the division of labour. The word anomie comes from the Greek *anomia*, meaning 'without law'. For Durkheim, anomie results from a condition in which social norms and/or moral norms are confused or simply absent. Generally, Durkheim believed that anomie results from widespread business failure, or from rapid and uneven economic development that has expanded ahead of the necessary developments in social regulation. In such circumstances, he suggests, breaches occur in the social solidarity existing between specialized occupations, causing tensions in social relationships and eroding social cohesion.

Durkheim also considered anomie to be another 'pathology' of industrialization, but believed that such deviant behaviour could be 'cured' through the proper level of regulation. He argued that occupational associations centred within civil society are the most effective means of regulating anomie in modern society. Such collective institutions provide moral authority, which dominates the life of their members. They are also a method by which individualistic egotism can be harmoniously subordinated to the general interest.

Durkheim explained the importance of occupational groups like this: 'wherever a group is formed, a moral discipline is also formed.' He continued:

> A group is not only a moral authority regulating the life of its members, but also a source of life *sui generis*. From it there arises warmth that quickens or gives fresh life to each individual, which makes him disposed to empathise, causing selfishness to melt away. (Durkheim, 1893/1997: 111)

Durkheim also warned that the mere construction of consensually grounded goals without any associated provision of opportunities to achieve such goals would extend the form of social 'pathology' under which anomie prevailed.

The second factor causing abnormal development, according to Durkheim, is the *forced division of labour* (Durkheim, 1893/1997: 310). He emphasized that the division of labour is frequently not 'spontaneous' because of the class and inherited privilege that operate to limit a person's chances in life. Durkheim, then, is considered to be a supporter of meritocracy. The normal division of labour would occur if social inequalities mirrored what Durkheim took to be personal inequalities:

anomie: a state condition in which social control becomes ineffective as a result of the loss of shared values and sense of purpose in society

> The division of labour only produces solidarity if it is spontaneous, and to the degree that it is spontaneous. But spontaneity must mean not simply the absence of any deliberate, formal type of violence, but of anything that may hamper, even indirectly, the free unfolding of the social force each individual contains within himself … In short, labour only divides up spontaneously if society is constituted in such a way that social inequalities express precisely natural inequalities. (Durkheim, 1893/1997: 313–14)

Thus, Durkheim's 'normal' division of labour is a 'perfect meritocracy' produced by eradicating personal inheritance (Bratton and Denham, 2014). For the division of labour to give rise to solidarity, society must allocate functions based on ability rather than class or hereditary tendencies, so that 'The sole cause then determining how labour is divided up is the diversity of abilities' (Durkheim, 1893/1997: 313).

The third factor responsible for an 'abnormal' development of the division of labour is the *mismanagement of functions* or operations in society. Durkheim believed that when functions are faltering or are badly coordinated with one another, individuals are unaware of their mutual dependence, and this lessens social solidarity. Thus, if work is insufficient, as a result of mismanagement and organization, Durkheim argues that solidarity 'is itself naturally not only less than perfect, but may even be more or less completely missing' (Durkheim, 1893/1997: 326).

In addition, if class-based social inequalities are imposed on groups, this not only forces the division of labour, but also undermines social linkages. It means that individuals are mismatched to their functions and that linkages between individuals are disrupted, and this creates inequitable forms of exchange. In the absence of a centralized authority (either the state or the government) exerting some restraint over the situation, there is disequilibrium, which leads to instability and conflict. For Durkheim, most of the pathologies of the new industrial order were attributable to the prevalence of anomie.

In sum, while Marx's critique was directed at capitalism, Durkheim's critique was aimed not at the essence of capitalism, but at industrialism. Whereas Marx is against the fragmentation of work and for the reintegration of skills, Durkheim is for the expansion of specialization in line with individuals' 'natural' abilities. Although the concepts of alienation and anomie lead to a significantly different analysis and different political results, and are different too in their assumptions about human nature, sociologists have compared the two concepts. For Marx, alienation results from certain kinds of social control; on the other hand, according to Durkheim, anomie results from the absence of social control. While Marx's solution to the crisis of capitalism is dependent on the state or the government, Durkheim argues that centralized government is too far removed from the people's everyday experience to play this role. He believes that mediating organizations would form the primary mode of social organization. For Durkheim, the crisis of modern society is a moral one, caused by a lack of social unity. Socially regulated institutions coupled with an ever-widening division of labour therefore achieve the solution. He believed this would facilitate the development of individual potential and create a future Utopia. The process of social change was to be evolutionary, not revolutionary.

In this chapter, we cannot provide a thorough critique of Durkheim's theory of the relationship between the increasing differentiation and specialization of labour, and transformative social change. However, we must critically assess some of his assumptions, for example those about 'natural' inequalities. He regarded men as more intelligent than women, and industrial workers as more intelligent than farmers. Durkheim also assumed that the gender-based domestic division of labour was a good example of the social harmony generated when social inequalities were allowed to mirror 'natural' inequalities. His assumptions about gender relations provoked the beginnings of a critique of patriarchy (Bratton and Denham, 2014).

VISIT THE *ONLINE RESOURCE CENTRE* AT HTTPS://HE.PALGRAVE.COM/COMPANION/BRATTON-WORK-AND-ORGANIZATIONAL-BEHAVIOUR3/ FOR FURTHER INFORMATION ON DURKHEIM'S WORK.

Max Weber (1864–1920)

Max Weber's work is broad and wide-ranging, and has been much misrepresented. It is often assumed to be a dialogue with the ghost of Marx, but that does not do it justice. Weber wrote on a wide range of topics including art, architecture and music; he examined the role of ideology in social change; and he explored the emergence and nature of modernity. His contribution to the study of work and work organizations has been extensive. The main contributions he made are: first, his theory concerning the rise of capitalism; second, his arguments concerning rationality, the nature of bureaucracy and authority; third, his theory of social class and inequality; and fourth, his methodology and theory of knowledge.

The rise of capitalism and rationalization

Weber's interpretation of the rise of capitalism in the West is presented in his best-known work, *The Protestant Ethic and the 'Spirit' of Capitalism* (1905/2002) (written in 1905), which links the rise of modern capitalism to Protestant (or, more precisely, Calvinist) religious beliefs and practices. Briefly, Weber argued that a new attitude to work and the pursuit of wealth was linked to the rise of Calvinism. In this attitude, work became a means of demonstrating godliness, and Weber saw this cultural shift as being associated with the rise of 'rational' capitalism itself.

According to Weber, while Catholics believed they could secure their place in heaven through (among other things) 'good works' on behalf of the poor or by performing acts of faith on earth, Calvinism developed a set of beliefs around the concept of predestination, which broke the hold of tradition. It was believed by followers of Calvin that it was already decided by God ('predestined') whether they would go to heaven (as one of the 'elect') or hell after their death. They had no means of knowing their ultimate destination, and also no means of altering it. This uncertainty led Calvinists to search for signs from God, since naturally they were anxious to be among the elect. Wealth was taken as a manifestation that they were one of God's elect, and this encouraged the followers of Calvin to apply themselves rationally to acquiring wealth. They did this through their ascetic lifestyles and hard work.

The distinctive features of 'rational capitalism' that Weber identified – limits on consumption, especially luxury consumption, and a tendency to reinvest profits in order to systematically accumulate more wealth – had a clear similarity to the Calvinist lifestyle. Although Weber did not believe that Calvinism was the cause of the rise of industrial capitalism, he did believe that capitalism in part grew from Calvinism. Contrary to Marx, Weber argued that the development of rational capitalism could not be explained through wholly material and structural forces; the rise of modern Western society was embedded in the process of rationalization.

Rationalization

rationality: the process by which traditional methods of social organization, characterized by informality and spontaneity, are gradually replaced by efficiently administered formal rules and procedures – bureaucracy

Central to Weber's analysis of the rise of capitalism and new organizational forms is this concept of rationalization. But what did he mean by this term? Weber's use of the term **rationality** is complex and multifaceted. He used it to describe the overall historical process 'by which nature, society and individual action are increasingly mastered by an orientation to planning, technical procedure and rational action' (Morrison, 1995: 218). For Weber, all societies exhibited rationality, in that all people could explain the basis of their behaviour, but only in the West did a particular type of rationality, based on capitalization, bureaucracy and calculation, become dominant. The essence of the concept consisted of three facets: secularization, calculability and rational action.

Rationality means the decline of magical interpretations and explanations of the world. Scientific models of nature and human behaviour are good examples of this type of rationalization, which involves calculating maximum results at minimum cost. It means the replacement of 'traditional' action by 'rational' action. Rationalization depends on two types of activity: strategies of human action, and modification of the means and ends of action in the pursuit of goals. Rather than doing things for emotional reasons, people do things because they calculate that the benefits will outweigh the costs, or because they assess the action as being the most efficient way to achieve their goals. Human actions are also guided by the use of rational decision making in pursuit of unlimited profit. Rules are obeyed because they appear to be built upon rational principles and common sense. In the business sphere, for example, technical and managerial rules are obeyed because they result in efficiency and profits.

Rationalization is different from rationality. Rationalization, the principal process of modernity, refers to the overall process by which reality is increasingly mastered by calculation and rational action, while rationality refers to the capacity of human action to be subject to calculation about means and ends. Four types of rationality have been identified in Weber's work: practical, theoretical, formal and substantive:

- *Practical rationality* assumes that there are no external mystical causes affecting the outcome of human actions, and sees reality in terms of what is given.
- *Theoretical or technical rationality* involves a cognitive effort to master the world through causality, logical deduction and induction. This type of rationality allows individuals to understand the 'meaning of life' by means of abstract concepts and conceptual reasoning.
- *Formal rationality* refers to the accurate procedures of calculation that go into decisions, to ensure consistency of outcome and efficiency in attaining goals.
- *Substantive rationality* refers to the degree to which human action is guided or shaped by a value system, regardless of the outcome of the action. Accordingly, 'Where formal rationality involves a practical orientation of action regarding outcomes, substantive rationality involves an orientation to values' (Morrison, 1995: 222).

Although these four different rationalization processes can complement each other, they can also conflict. For example, the pursuit of efficiency and productivity by calculating the 'best' means to achieve a given end (formal rationality) sometimes conflicts with ethical behaviour (substantive rationality). When examined through a substantive lens, formal rationality is often irrational. In his book, The *McDonaldization of Society* (2012), George Ritzer makes a strong case that formal rationality, embodied in standardized fast-food products, undermines values of social responsibility and individualism in the pursuit of efficiency. In the early twenty-first century, rationalization is shaping the subjective experiences of peoples as they understand and evaluate climate change and global warming in terms of non-sustainable growth, maximization of profits and **corporate social responsibility**.

corporate social responsibility: an organization's moral obligation to its stakeholders

bureaucratization: a tendency towards a formal organization with a hierarchy of authority, a clear division of labour and an emphasis on written rules

Bureaucracy

According to Weber, **bureaucratization** is an inescapable development in modern society. Weber's analysis of the development of capitalism was similar to that of Marx, in that he believed that the rise of capitalism had been marked by the centralization of production, by increased specialization and mechanization, by workers' progressive loss of the means of production, and by an increase in the function and growth of management. With centralized production, all human activity gives way to a more systematic, rational and extensive use of resources, including labour, which is facilitated by calculable techniques such as accounting. Weber's contention was that 'Where capitalist acquisition is rationally pursued, the corresponding action is oriented towards the calculation of capital. In other words, such action takes place within a planned utilization of material or personal output' (Weber, 1922/1968: 359).

According to Weber, bureaucracies are goal-oriented organizations, administered by qualified specialists, and designed according to rational principles in order to attain the stated goals efficiently. He saw the development of bureaucracy as involving the exorcism of emotional or 'irrational' personal elements such as hate, love or sentiment. In his *Economy and Society*, written in 1921, Weber explained that 'Bureaucracy ... is fully developed in the private economy only in the most advanced institutions of capitalism' (Weber, 1922/1968: 956). He also noted that as the complexity of modern society increases, bureaucracies grow. He defined the bureaucratic 'ideal type' by these characteristics: business is continually conducted, there are stipulated rules, individual spheres of competence are structured in a hierarchy, offices (that is, positions at work) are not owned, selection and promotion is through proven ability, and the rewards are commensurate with people's qualifications, ability and performance.

formalization: the degree to which organizations standardize behaviour through rules, procedures, formal training and related mechanisms

Two core ideas underscore Weber's concept of bureaucracy: formal rationality and **formalized** decision making. Formal rationality operates on the principles of expert knowledge and calculability, whereas formalized decision making operates on the basis of set procedures. This means that decisions can be judged as correct or otherwise by reference to a body of rules.

It would, however, misrepresent Weber to assume that he was an avid supporter of bureaucracy. Weber was not unaware of the dysfunctions of any overformalized work form. Bureaucracy removes workers from the decision-making process. It consists of rational and established rules, and restricts individual activity. As a result, it can resemble an 'iron cage and it can mean that organizational behaviour becomes less and less regulated by ethical principles, as these are replaced by technical means and ends' (Morrison, 1995: 297). Weber's argument is that because bureaucratic work forms remove workers, including white-collar and managerial staff, from ownership of the means of production, there is a loss of democracy in the workplace, and a panoply of managerial control measures is then necessary to keep the workers in line (Weber, 1922/1968).

Types of authority

All systems of work require a minimum of 'voluntary compliance' and some mechanism of coordination and control over the activity. This compliance, which is defined as 'an interest in obedience' (Weber, 1922/1968: 212) of the subordinate who is being controlled (such as a worker) to the dominant controller (such as a manager), is based on the ulterior motives of the subordinate, which are governed by custom and a material calculation of personal advantage, as well as her or his perception of the employment relationship.

power: a term defined in multiple ways, involving cultural values, authority, influence and coercion as well as control over the distribution of symbolic and material resources. At its broadest, power is defined as a social system that imparts patterned meaning

Weber's analysis of authority relations provides another insight into the changing structure of work systems. Weber used the terms 'domination' and 'authority' interchangeably in *Economy and Society*. Both derive from the German term *Herrschaft*, which points to leadership, and Weber's theory of domination does have direct relevance to theories of organizational leadership (see Chapter 12). However, Weber did make a distinction between power and domination. He defined **power** as the ability to impose one's will on others in a given situation, even when the

plate 10 Rational-legal authority is derived from the rationality of the authority. For example, car drivers usually obey police officers imposing traffic laws (like this one in Paris) because their actions appear to make sense, not because police officers have some inherited authority or are charismatic.

Source: Nick Tutton.

stop...

Do contemporary organizational behaviour theorists have anything to learn from the classical sociologists such as Marx, Durkheim and Weber?

...and reflect

others resist. Domination, or authority, is the right of a controller to issue commands to others and expect them to be obeyed. Underscoring Weber's study of authority is his concern for 'legitimacy'. Essentially, he was interested in knowing on what basis subordinates actively acknowledge the validity of authority figures in an established order, and give obedience to them, and on what basis men and women claim authority over others.

Subordinates and those who are controlled obey dominant controllers by custom and for material advantage and reward, but a belief in legitimacy is also a prerequisite. Weber pointed out that each authority system varies 'According to the kind of legitimacy which is claimed, the type of obedience, the kind of administrative staff developed to guarantee it, and the mode of exercising authority' (Weber, 1922/1968: 213). He then went on to propose three types of legitimate authority: traditional, rational-legal and charismatic. All types of authority, however, require a managerial system characterized by efficiency and continuity.

Traditional authority is based on the sanctity of tradition and the legitimacy of those exercising authority under such regimes. It is usually acquired through inheritance: this, for example, is the kind of authority held by kings and queens in monarchies. Compliance rests on a framework of obligations that binds followers to leaders by personal loyalties.

Rational-legal authority is derived from the rationality of the authority. For example, car drivers usually obey traffic laws because they appear to make sense, and not because police officers have some inherited authority or are charismatic.

Charismatic authority refers to an attribute or exceptional quality possessed by an individual. In charismatic domination, the leader's claim to legitimacy originates from his or her followers' belief that the leader is to be obeyed because of his or her extraordinary attributes or powers of inspiration and communication.

Weber's typology of authority is important in understanding why individuals behave as they do in the workplace. He was one of the earliest social theorists who saw domination as being characteristic of the relationship between leaders and followers, rather than an attribute of the leader alone.

Social class, inequality and types of class struggle

Authority equates to possessing power, and a difference in the degree of power is one factor that gives rise to differentiated social classes. Weber's description of social class was similar to Marx's, in that he defined social classes in terms of property ownership and market relations. He stated that:

> a class is a number of people having in common a specific causal component of their life chances. This component is represented exclusively by economic interests in the possession of goods and opportunities for income, under the conditions of the commodity or labour markets. (Weber, 1922/1968: 927)

However, whereas Marx had proposed that individuals carry forward their class interests by virtue of dominant economic forces, Weber argued that the 'mere differentiation of property classes is not "dynamic", that is, it need not result in class struggles and revolutions' (Weber, 1922/1968: 303). He argued instead that the complex and multidimensional nature of social stratification in modern society necessarily inhibits people from acquiring the degree of class consciousness that is necessary for a revolution to occur.

In this argument, people who experience inequality and who have a degree of political consciousness are much more likely to form into rational associations (such as trade unions and social democratic political parties) that would thrust them to the forefront of political activity, than they are to start a revolution. Under these conditions, there are no class interests as such, only the 'average interests' of individuals in similar economic situations, and therefore the class struggle and revolution predicted by Marx are extremely unlikely to happen. Instead, the nature of class conflict changes in a modern society in two fundamental ways. First, there is a shift from direct confrontation between the owners of capital and the workers to mediated pay disputes, and second, conflicts between social classes are resolved through the courts and by legal means.

Weber's methodology

Between 1902 and 1903, Weber wrote two papers that were central to shaping his views about the nature of doing research in the social sciences, and which continue to influence contemporary enquiry into work and behaviour in the workplace. Let us look at two concepts he developed: ideal types and *Verstehen*.

ideal type: an abstract model that describes the recurring characteristics of some phenomenon

The **ideal type** is one of Weber's best-known contributions to contemporary organizational theory. At its most basic level, an ideal type is a theoretical abstraction constructed by a social scientist who draws out important characteristics and simultaneously suppresses less important characteristics. It can be viewed as a measuring rod or yardstick whose function is to compare **empirical** reality with preconceived ideas of a reality. Weber put it like this: 'It functions in formulating terminology, classifications, and hypotheses, in working out concrete causal explanation of individual events' (Weber, 1922/1968: 21). As a methodological construction, ideal types are neither ideal nor typical. That is, they are not ideal in any evaluative sense, nor are they typical because they do not represent any norm. They merely approximate reality. To put it differently, ideal types are heuristic devices (teaching aids) that are used to study slices of reality and enable us to compare empirical forms. Organizational theorists refer, for example, to an 'ideal type of bureaucracy' or 'ideal flexibility'.

empiricism: an approach to the study of social reality suggesting that only knowledge gained through experience and the senses is acceptable

We introduced the second concept, *Verstehen*, when we discussed research methods in Chapter 1. Weber believed that social scientists must look at individuals' actions and examine the meanings attached to these behaviours. His approach to understanding human behaviour suggests that observational language is never theoretically independent of the way in which the observer sees a phenomenon and the questions he or she asks about the action. As a consequence, an individual researcher's interpretation of human activity is an inherent aspect of knowledge about organizational behaviour. Weber's 'interpretative' methodology is based on *Verstehen*, meaning 'human understanding'. Human subjects, in contrast to the objects studied in the natural sciences, always rely on their 'understanding' of each other's behaviour and on the 'meanings' they assign to what they and others do.

Verstehen: a method of understanding human behaviour by situating it in the context of an individual's or actor's meaning

This interpretive approach to studying reality is best illustrated by distinguishing between someone walking in a park as a pleasurable leisure experience, and someone walking in a park in an aimless way to kill time because he or she is unemployed and bored. The outer behaviour is exactly the same, but the inner state of the two people is different. It is difficult for a researcher to understand and explain the fundamental distinction between the inner states of the (in this case) employed and unemployed people just by observing their outer states, or behaviour. We need an interpretive understanding in order to give a convincing analysis of what is seen.

Weber's theories have been challenged. For instance, it is argued that the earliest examples of rational capitalism are not restricted to Calvinist or even Protestant nations. Some Calvinist countries, such as Scotland, failed to 'take off' as capitalist industrialized nations, and some Catholic nations, such as Belgium, were among the market leaders.

VISIT THE *ONLINE RESOURCE CENTRE* AT HTTPS://HE.PALGRAVE.COM/COMPANION/BRATTON-WORK-AND-ORGANIZATIONAL-BEHAVIOUR3/ FOR FURTHER INFORMATION ON MAX WEBER.

Source: Image Source

The relevance of theory to work and organizational behaviour

Theory can often seem abstract and difficult, and at times it can be so. Consequently, students tend to find it unappealing. It is, however, very important, not least because everyone engages to some extent in theorizing about society. People theorize about their own social situation or that of people they know, for instance why they are unemployed or why some marriages end in divorce. This kind of everyday theorizing is ad hoc and pragmatic compared with social theories that attempt to be logically consistent and to describe and explain how different parts of society are interrelated.

Theories contain assumptions about the natural and the social world and how they work, and they define which facts are theoretically relevant. Natural science theories are expected to be abstract and different from everyday understanding. Kuhn understood theories or 'paradigms' as ways of viewing the natural world, and argued that most scientists are 'normal' scientists who work within a dominant paradigm. Occasionally, an exceptional scientist may develop a paradigm with superior explanatory power, ushering in a scientific revolution that establishes a new dominant paradigm.

Contemporary economics is dominated by a neo-liberal theory of markets, while sociology has retained a plurality of theories. Classical sociological theories, which attempted to come to terms with industrial capitalist society and the philosophy of the Enlightenment, still exert an influence on contemporary research. These theories include assumptions about human nature, how modern capitalism developed, the nature of social change and the relationship between economic and cultural institutions. The analysis of work in capitalist society was central to classical theory, and its

nature was understood as alienation, anomie or dehumanization within the theories of Marx, Durkheim and Weber, respectively. In addition, these theorists made their respective predictions about the future: the collapse of capitalism and its succession by socialism; an organic form of moral regulation; and a rational bureaucratic nightmare that would stifle creativity and leadership.

Theories make statements about what can be observed, but they sometimes refer to hidden processes such as Marx's discussion of the extraction of surplus value, or exploitation, which he described as being concealed behind the surface appearance of the free exchange of labour for a wage. In his theory of religion, Durkheim explained that when native Australian clans worshipped their totem, they were really celebrating the power of society.

Classical theories still influence the range of theories about work organizations, and contemporary theories highlight recent organizational changes. Some are concerned with managerial effectiveness and performance, while others adopt a critical stance towards organizations as systems of control and exploitation. But the dichotomy between managerial and critical theories points out that theories contain values and worldviews. No theory can be completely value-free as a theory is bound to contain, to some extent, the experiences and preferences of its creator.

> **Stop!** Consider the classical theories of work discussed so far in this chapter: Which theories, if any, do you think are most relevant to the analysis of work and organizations in the early twenty-first century? Would you say the theory or theories you have chosen have a 'managerialist' or a 'conflict' perspective?

Sources and further information

Bratton, J. and Denham, D. (2014) *Capitalism and Classical Social Theory* (2nd edn), Toronto: University of Toronto Press.

Craib, I. (1992) *Modern Social Theory: From Parsons to Habermas*, Hemel Hempstead: Harvester Wheatsheaf.

Kuhn, T. (2012) *The Structure of Scientific Revolutions: 50th Anniversary Edition*, London: University of Chicago Press.

Note: This feature was written by David Denham, Honorary Research Fellow, Wolverhampton University, UK.

Georg Simmel (1858–1918)

Born in Berlin, Georg Simmel was an intellectual contemporary of Weber. Simmel regarded society as a web of myriad complex interactions and social relations between individuals. Microscopic social details, rather than abstract generalizations, are given prime position in Simmel's work (Bratton and Denham, 2014). His sociology, which is multifaceted, is attentive to the seemingly unimportant minutiae of everyday urban life, such as linguistic practices, human interaction in small groups and the cultural implications of body language. The German philosophers Georg Hegel (1770–1831) and Friedrich Nietzsche (1844–1900) influenced

Simmel's sociology. An unorthodox sociologist, it is said that 'no sociologist before him had sought to capture the modes of experiencing modern life nor the fleeting moments of interaction' (Frisby, 1981: 103; also quoted in Bratton and Denham, 2014: 297). In this section, we review some of Simmel's central concepts as they relate to human behaviour in the workplace.

Social geometry and group size

Simmel described sociology as the geometry of social life. Central to his work are the concepts of form and reciprocity. *Form* refers to those aspects of human life that compel individuals into associations (sociation) with each other: people's needs, drives and goals. Social relationships always contain the capacity for creativity, innovation and change. Simmel's concept of *reciprocity* refers to human interaction or 'reciprocal effects': each social phenomenon has meaning only through its relationships with others.

For Simmel, the size of a group influences how the members interact with one another. Adding to the group alters the group dynamics, since the increased number of relationships results in different configurations of interactions. The dyad (a relationship of two people), the triad (a relationship among three) and the mass (a relationship among many) are examples of forms in which the group size affects the organization of the group and the kinds of relationship that are possible within it. For example, when a third member joins the dyad to form a triad, the dynamics change: the new member brings two new relationships, as in addition to the interaction between the two original individuals, there are now three (see Figure 10.3). In general, the larger the size of the group, the more its members can become dissimilar to each other, and the more independence and intellectual development can take place. This observation has influenced research on work teams (see Chapter 10).

The metropolis, money and personality

Urban life is intimately intertwined with the omnipresence of money in modern society. Simmel's most insightful observation concerns the effect of the cash nexus on individual personality. He begins by emphasizing that the individual is not an isolated observer of the physical world, but a participant in human society whose personality is formed through an affiliation to and interaction with many social groups. Simmel writes:

> Just as the essence of the physical organism lies in the fact that it creates the unity of the life process out of the multitude of material parts, so a man's inner personal unity is based upon the interaction and connection of many elements and determinants.

> Only the combination and fusion of several traits in one focal point forms a personality which then in its turn imparts to each individual trait a personal-subjective quality. It is not that it is this *or* that trait that makes a unique personality of man, but that he is this *and* that trait. The enigmatic unity of the soul cannot be grasped by the cognitive process directly, but only when it is broken down into a multitude of strands, the re-synthesis of which signifies the unique personality. (D. Frisby, quoted in Bratton and Denham, 2014: 310)

This idea gave rise to a social theory of the human self and the distinctively American symbolic-interactionist tradition. Charles Horton Cooley (1864–1929) and George Herbert Mead (1863–1931) developed Simmel's ideas. There are evident parallels, for example, between Simmel's *Philosophy of Money* (1900) and Charles Horton Cooley's (1902) *Human Nature and the Social Order*, and Simmel's account of the 'looking glass self' and George Herbert Mead's (1934) *Mind, Self and Society* and his theory of the social mind (see Chapter 4).

The more critical assessments of Georg Simmel's work expose his paradoxical thinking towards gender relationships in society. On the one hand, he championed the right of women to enter professions such as medicine where sensitivity, intuition, empathy and other feminine characteristics can be useful (Bratton and Denham, 2014: 312). On the other hand, however, he believed that specialization is more congruent with the 'nature' of the male than the female. The tragedy of women, he wrote, is that they 'live in a world of otherness'. Viewing themselves through the lens of the male culture, they come to see themselves as valued only as 'means for the man, for the home, for the child'. Simmel's work shifted the focus away from an exclusive concern with macro-issues, such as the domination of capital, specialization and centralized tendencies, towards individualism, differentiation and seemingly superficial moments of microsocial interaction. Importantly, his writings on the stranger influenced America's pre-eminent African American scholar, W. E. B. Du Bois (1868–1963) and social theory on race and identity.

As our review of the theories of work moves from the classical sociological theories – Marx, Durkheim, Weber and Simmel – to contemporary perspectives on organizations and management, we will be better equipped to see how these classical theories continue to inform contemporary theories of work, organizational design and managerial behaviour.

> *stop...*
>
> Can you think of any workplace studies that have based their findings on data gathered through observing people in the workplace? How should the interpretative method affect your evaluation of the studies?
>
> *...and reflect*

VISIT THE *ONLINE RESOURCE CENTRE* AT HTTPS://HE.PALGRAVE.COM/COMPANION/BRATTON-WORK-AND-ORGANIZATIONAL-BEHAVIOUR3/ FOR FURTHER INFORMATION ON GEORG SIMMEL.

Contemporary theories of organizations

Organizational studies constitute a discipline in themselves, with a plethora of alternative theoretical perspectives. In recent years, different theoretical approaches to studying work and organizations have forced organizational theorists to re-examine and be more reflexive about organizational 'knowledge'. Being reflexive, according to Antonacopoulou (2010), encourages a critique of prevailing theoretical perspectives, arguments and propositions, and also prevailing dominant assumptions and personal biases. With the changes that have occurred, as Clegg and Hardy put it, 'Gone is the certainty about what organizations are; gone, too, is the certainty about how they should be studied' (Clegg and Hardy, 1999: 3). In this chapter, we cannot hope to do justice to the complexities of the bewildering variety of perspectives, and we shall therefore seek to highlight what Clegg and Hardy call the major 'conversations' in organizational studies.

How we represent these conversations always involves a choice concerning what theories we wish to represent and how we represent them. To help, we have drawn on Keith Grint's (1998) work and produced a schema of organizational theories. The competing theories are plotted along two interlocking axes.

The *critical–managerial axis* represents the political left–right continuum (see Chapter 1). At one extreme, the managerial pole positions those perspectives which are essentially concerned with issues of organizational efficiency and performance. Thus, researchers adopting this approach have tended to develop theoretical frameworks and generate empirical data aimed at understanding organizational structures, work arrangements and social processes that can improve labour productivity and organizational effectiveness, or that can help solve people-related 'problems' in the workplace. As we explained in Chapter 1, this particular framework is often viewed as mainstream thinking in organizational behaviour texts. At the other extreme, the critical pole, lie critical explanations of work and organizational

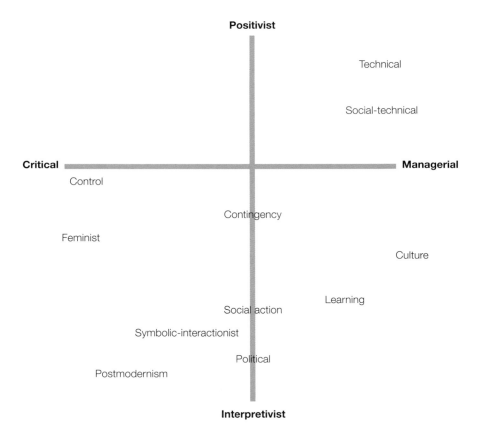

Figure 3.1 Contemporary theories of work organizations

behaviour that have traditionally been concerned with issues of exploitation and the alienating effects of dividing and routinizing paid work. Researchers adopting this perspective tend to conceptualize organizational structures and management behaviour as control mechanisms that function to fulfil economic imperatives.

The *positivist–interpretivist axis* affirms the importance of epistemological considerations when conducting research: what is (or should be) regarded as acceptable knowledge in organizational behaviour theory. The axis distinguishes between the doctrines of 'positivism' and 'interpretivism'. The positivist epistemological position is generally taken as involving the application of natural science research methods to the study of work organizations, as we saw in Chapter 1. It puts emphasis on the scientific and technical way in which organizational activities can be studied and assessed (using goals, efficiency ratios, rational decision making, productivity measures and so on). In contrast, the interpretivist position maintains that human behaviour is not fully controllable, and therefore a research strategy for organizational behaviour must respect the differences between people and inanimate objects. For interpretivists, the role of the social scientist is to grasp the subjective meaning of behaviour or social action. Researchers focus on the indeterminate and contingent nature of social reality, the unintended consequences of human action and the influence of interpretation.

Where the conversations or theories are plotted on the 'map' of Figure 3.1 is clearly a matter of interpretation and subject to dispute; here the map's function is to act as a heuristic device to review the history of organizational theory and management thought.

Technical

The 'technical' approach to studying work organizations is most closely associated with the work of Frederick Winslow Taylor (1865–1915). Taylor, an engineer at an

American steel mill, experimented with work arrangements to improve labour productivity. Taylor's work configuration rests upon the principle of the technical and social divisions of mental and manual labour. The technical division of labour generally refers to how a complex task is broken down into its component parts. Adam Smith's classic observations on pin manufacturing (Smith, 1776/1982) give us one of the first discussions of this in relation to potential increases in labour productivity.

The social division of labour refers to issues of which individuals occupy specific positions in the technical division of labour, how, why and for how long. In addition, **scientific management**, or Taylorism (as it became known), involved the following five principles: maximum job fragmentation, the separation of planning and doing, the separation of direct and indirect labour, minimum skill requirements and minimum material handling (see Chapter 2). These five job design principles gave to management 'the collective concept of control' (George, 1972: 97).

Other important theorists contributing to this organizational studies genre were Henry Gantt (1861–1919), a protégé of Taylor, who designed the Gantt chart, a straight-line chart to display and measure planned and completed work as time elapsed, Frank Gilbreth (1868–1924), who helped to improve labour productivity through the pioneering use of time and motion techniques, and Henry Ford (1863–1947), who perfected the application of the principles of scientific management to assembly line production, an approach others would later call 'Fordism'. For most of the twentieth century, the essential principles of Taylorism and Fordism represented a 'common-sense' management strategy in North America and Western Europe (Braverman, 1974; Littler and Salaman, 1984; Thompson and McHugh, 2009).

> **scientific management:** this involves systematically partitioning work into its smallest elements and standardizing tasks to achieve maximum efficiency

VISIT THE *ONLINE RESOURCE CENTRE* AT HTTPS://HE.PALGRAVE.COM/COMPANION/BRATTON-WORK-AND-ORGANIZATIONAL-BEHAVIOUR3/ TO READ MORE ABOUT TAYLORISM AND FORDISM.

Social-technical theory

Disenchantment with the technical approach to work and organizational design led to the development of the human aspects of work organization. Research at a US factory – subsequently known as the Hawthorne studies – suggested a positive association between employees' performance and management style. The phenomenon can be explained like this: 'The determinants of working behaviour are sought in the structure and culture of the group, which is spontaneously formed by the interaction of individuals working together' (Mouzelis, 1967: 99).

Elton Mayo (1880–1949) is most closely associated with the Hawthorne studies. Another pioneer in organizational theory and organizational behaviour, Mary Parker Follett (1868–1933) (see Chapter 2), is associated with the early **human relations** management movement. She contended that traditional authority as an act of subordination was offensive to an individual's emotions, and therefore could not serve as a good foundation for cooperative relations in the workplace. Instead, Follett proposed an authority function, whereby the individual has authority over her or his own job area (George, 1972).

> **human relations:** a school of management thought that emphasizes the importance of social processes in the organization

Despite the criticisms, the Hawthorne studies provided the impetus for a new 'common-sense' management strategy sometimes known as 'neo-human relations', which emphasized workers' social needs as the key to harmonious relations and better performance, albeit narrowly conceived because workers' needs were defined in terms of the employer's needs.

Prominent contributors to neo-human relations theory were Abraham Maslow (1908–70), with his idea of 'self-actualization' needs, and Douglas McGregor (1906–64), with his Theory X and Theory Y approach to work motivation (see Chapter 6).

In the UK, the most influential research on attaining a 'joint optimization' of both the technical and social systems was through the concept of social-technical theory associated with the work of the Tavistock Institute. Joan Woodward (1958, 1965) is an influential scholar of social-technical theory. Her research emphasizes that any technical system requires both a technological organization and a social relations system relating workers who perform the necessary tasks to each other: 'The technological demands place limits on the type of work possible, but a work organization has *social and psychological properties of its own independent of technology* (Woodward, 1958: 4, emphasis added). Within the social-technical school, Emery and Thorsrud (1976) identify workers' needs for work design to provide a minimum of variety of learning on the job and decision making that individuals can call their own. Social-technical theory lies within a theoretical framework of anti-Taylorism, believing that workers are not motivated simply by economic self-interest, but also have inherent social needs. Social-technical theory highlights the positive outcomes that occur when the worker's psychological aspirations are fulfilled. As Karlsson (2012: 7) observes, 'If one optimises the technical system at the expense of the social, the results will be suboptimal.' These contributions to organizational studies have promoted principles of 'good' work design that gives workers greater autonomy and provides for continuous work-based learning (Bratton et al., 2004).

The neo-human relations and social-technical movements have been criticized at both the technical and the political level. Technically, it has been contended that early researchers at the Hawthorne plant used a 'rudimentary' research design, and that their analysis of the data was faulty. At a political level, charges of managerial bias, insularity from wider socioeconomic factors, a neglect of workers' organization – trade unions – and workplace conflict were effectively levelled against the researchers. The critique included the charge that neo-human relations theorists conceptualized the 'normal' state of the work organization in 'romantic' and harmonious terms, and neglected workplace conflict because of their pro-management bias (Clegg and Dunkerley, 1980; Thompson, 1989).

Contingency theory

Contingency theory, sometimes also known as the 'rational' systems approach, focuses on the three-way relationship between structure, contingency and outcomes, and has proved to be one of the most influential of all organizational theories. Contingency, as it applies to work organizations, means that the effectiveness of a particular strategy, structure or managerial style depends on the presence or absence of other factors or forces. Accordingly, there are no absolutely 'one best' strategies, structures or styles. Instead, whether an action is 'best' must be gauged relative to the market, technology and the predictability of tasks or the other factors.

The most noted contingency research was conducted over 50 years ago. Joan Woodward (1958, 1965), for example, found that there was no best way of organizing production, but that a particular organizational design and managerial style of behaviour was most appropriate for each technological situation (for example, worker-oriented production as found in car assembly compared with process production as found in chemical plants). She reported that organizations differed not only in the general character of their structure and technology, but also in such detailed respects as managerial behaviour, methods of intermanagement communication and interactions. In some organizations studied, 'it was not always easy to distinguish between those who gave and those who took orders' (Woodward, 1965: 27).

The British writers Burns and Stalker (1961) suggested that organizational structures and managerial behaviours differed according to a range of environments differentiated by their degree of predictability and stability. Management styles would tend to be different in what they called 'mechanistic' or 'organic' systems. The American researchers Lawrence and Lorsch (1967) developed contingency analysis,

stop...

What contemporary jobs tend to incorporate social-technical principles into job design, and what kind of jobs seem to be imbued with neo-Taylorism?

...and reflect

by showing the importance of establishing integrative mechanisms to counter the centrifugal forces that differentiate and fragment managers and non-managers alike.

For the dominant controllers of organizations, the appeal of a contingency perspective is in part because the 'if–then' formula represents an explicit break with the simpler 'one best way' approach, which assumed that organizations operate unproblematically as more or less closed systems. Contingency theory also appealed because it offered a persuasive normative guideline for what leaders and managers should do to sustain organizational performance.

Where the contingency approach is most vulnerable to criticism is in its construction of independent variables. This is why it is open to the charge of 'determinism' in which the productive technique obeys a logic of its own and, as such, acts as the principal determinant of social relationships, which is why contingency theory is positioned close to the determinist line in Figure 3.1. The various studies argue that although some degree of contingency exists, in so far as controllers can choose between different forms of organizational structure, only those who choose the most 'appropriate' structure are likely to be successful. Others have noted the role of 'environmental determinism' and the removal of contingency by specifying the external conditions under which success can be determined: 'environments are not only given determinate power ... but they are literally reified through the language of environments acting on passive organizations' (Thompson and McHugh, 2009: 63).

Culture theory

The notion of applying 'cultural' thinking to organizational studies is derived from Durkheimian concerns for producing organizational solidarity through ideological consensus, and from Max Weber's pronouncements in *The Protestant Ethic* on the connections between a distinctive 'cultural phenomenon' and Western capitalist modernity. Organizational culture refers to artefacts, the shared beliefs and values and the core assumptions that exist in an organization. Typically, the approach tends to be normative: that is, it is intended to explain not so much what the contemporary culture of an organization is, but what it should be. Thus, it may well persuade managers to act as if the preferred cultural attributes already existed, so the acting-out of a cultural myth becomes the organizational reality (Lopez, 2003). A less manipulative approach to the significance of organizational cultures is provided by Gareth Morgan (2006). According to Morgan, culture is shared property and has a language and symbolism that can be decoded.

Morgan believes that how we define, understand and conceptualize organizations depends on our images or mental models of the essential shape, artefacts and features of organizations. He has argued that most definitions and theories of work organizations can be associated with a particular organizational metaphor. The most common metaphors view organizations as cultures, organisms, an iron cage, machines, networks or learning systems. These metaphors are embedded in various theories of organizational behaviour.

Charles Handy (1985) suggested that 'role cultures', which are typically found in large bureaucracies, exude rationality, specialization, routines and rule following. Generally speaking, in *Understanding Organizations* he suggests that the larger an organization, the more expensive its technology and the more routine its environment, the more likely it will be to adopt a role culture.

The cultural perspective converges with popular human resource management models, which highlight the importance of 'contextual relations' and organizational 'climate' for generating commitment from employees (Crow, 2005). Although the use of metaphor has entered popular culture, we need to be aware of the common error of treating metaphors as literal descriptions of social reality. See Chapter 17 for more discussion on organizational culture, and Chapter 11 for more on the use of metaphors in organization communications.

Learning theories

learning organization: an organization that facilitates its employees' learning as a strategy for continuous planned change

A 'learning organization' and 'workplace learning' are two popular, and relatively new, metaphors in organizational studies. Proponents equate the learning organization with organizational economic success (Pedler et al., 1988; Rowley, 1998). Typically, the learning organization's approach is interpretive because it is more closely related to the concept of organizational culture than to something tangible. The focus in a learning organization is on creating an environment that fosters learning through strategies that promote a 'growth-oriented workplace' (Bratton et al., 2004). Learning organizations are understood as places where individuals can be 'creative' and where people 'learn how to learn together'. We discuss workplace learning further in Chapter 7.

IN THE EBOOK ACCESS THE **CRITICAL INSIGHT** ON 'LEARNING ORGANIZATIONS AND ORGANIZATIONAL LEARNING'.

Social action theory

The most influential contributions to social action theory were those of Silverman (1970). He advocated a view of organizations as the product of individuals pursuing their own ends with the available means. He argued that social reality did not just happen, but had to be made to happen. The implication of this was that, through social interaction, people could modify and possibly even transform social meanings, and therefore any explanation of human activity had to take into account the meanings that those involved assigned to their actions. For example, whether failure to obey a manager's instruction is a sign of worker insubordination or militancy, or is caused by the beginnings of deafness, depends not on what managers or researchers observe to happen, but on what the worker involved means by her or his behaviour. This approach drew from Weber's work on the methodology and theory of knowledge action.

The social action approach involves examining six interrelated areas (Brown, 1992):

- the nature of the role system and pattern of interaction that has developed in the organization
- the nature of involvement of 'ideal-typical' actors and the characteristic hierarchy of the ends that they are pursuing
- the actors' present definitions of their situation within the organization, and their expectations of the likely behaviour of others
- the typical actions of different actors, and the meaning they attach to their actions
- the nature and source of the intended and unintended consequences of action
- any changes in the involvement and ends of the actors, and in the role system.

This method of analysing workplace behaviour is influenced by the symbolic-interactionist tradition (see p. 98).

IN THE EBOOK ACCESS THE **OB IN FOCUS** BOX ON 'DEVELOPING ORGANIZATIONAL LEARNING IN THE NATIONAL HEALTH SERVICE'.

Political theory

The political approach to understanding work organizations characterizes the workplace as a purposive miniature society, with politics pervading all managerial work. By politics we mean the power relationships between managers and other relevant people, and in turn the capacity of an individual manager to influence

Iain Nelson has spent 27 years as a Principal Consultant and Manager with the International Training Service, and 4 years as an internal Learning and Development Advisor with Petroleum Development Oman (PDO). As a freelance consultant, his clients include Unilever, Roche Products, Alcan, BP, Chevron, Lothian and Borders Police, the British Council, ITF Nigeria, Total and Indian Railway.

Iain's core expertise is developing managers as learning specialists competent to design and deliver a company's corporate objectives and associated strategic business initiatives.

In the ebook click on the play button to watch Iain talking about unintended consequences, and the answer the following question:

- What skills does Iain identify that can help to avoid the possibility of unintended consequences (sometimes referred to as the paradox of consequences)?

others who are in a state of dependence. It refers to those social processes which are not part of a manager's formal role, but which influence (perhaps not directly) the distribution of resources for the purpose of promoting personal objectives.

Politics in organizations is simply a fact of life. However, as others have observed, the political quality of management practice is 'denied' or 'trivialized' in many studies of work organizations. And although individual managers might privately question the moral value and integrity of their actions, 'Caught in the maelstrom of capitalist organization, managers are pressured to emulate and reward all kinds of manipulative and destructive behaviours' (Alvesson and Willmott, 1996: 39). This perspective on studying organizations offers an approach that examines individual managers as 'knowledgeable human agents' functioning within a dynamic arena where both organizational resources and outcomes can be substantially shaped by their actions. It also reinforces the theoretical and practical importance attached to building alliances and networks of cooperative relationships among organizational members. These negotiating processes shape, and in turn are shaped by, organizational dynamics (see Chapter 14).

An early study of management adopting a political perspective was undertaken by Dalton in 1959. Building on work by Fox (1971), Graeme Salaman stated the political approach most clearly. Power relations that reflect the social inequality prevailing in the wider society determine the structure of work organizations. Organizations are not independent bodies but are embedded in a wider (again political) environment. Furthermore, notions of identity and the part played by organizational life in the construction of both individual and group identity are important.

The political perspective has also drawn attention to the role of strategic choice (see Chapter 1) in shaping organizational structures and management behaviour (Child, 1972). The strategic choice approach emphasizes the importance of the political power of the dominant coalitions' capital (for example, manufacturing corporations and financial institutions) and ideological commitments in explaining variations in managerial policies and behaviour, and ultimately in explaining variations in managerial effectiveness and organizational outcomes. The political perspective has been criticized, however, for failing to offer little or no explanation of the asymmetrical nature of power, which is the essence of the 'radical' control perspective on management.

Control theories

At the critical pole of the managerial–critical continuum lie the 'control' theories. Much of this work has its roots in Marx's analysis of capitalism. This approach to work and management has come to be associated with the seminal work of Harry

labour process: the process whereby labour is applied to materials and technology to produce goods and services that can be sold in the market as commodities. The term is typically applied to the distinctive labour processes of capitalism in which owners/managers design, control and monitor work tasks so as to maximize the extraction of surplus value from the workers' labour activity

Braverman (1974). Organizational theorists approaching the study of work and organizations from this perspective stress the inherent source of tension in organizations that arises from technological rationality (Alvesson and Willmott, 1992). A related focus is the **labour process** approach, which conceptualizes organizational managers as controlling agents who serve the economic imperatives imposed by capitalist market relations. Managerial control is thus *the* central focus of management activity. According to this perspective, organizational structures and employment strategies are instruments and techniques to control the labour process in order to secure high levels of labour productivity and corresponding levels of profitability.

The control perspective views work organizations as hierarchical structures in which workers are deskilled by scientific management techniques and new technology. Managerial behaviour is classically characterized primarily as relations of control. Such an approach recognizes the existence of inconsistent organizational designs and management practices, and these paradoxical tendencies provide the source of further management strategies that attempt to eradicate the tensions they have caused. The most important of these paradoxes is considered to be the simultaneous desire for control over workers, and for cooperation and commitment from them.

The control perspective has also attracted much criticism from both critical and mainstream management theorists. For example, critiques of the deskilling and control thesis draw attention to moderating factors such as markets, worker resistance and batch size (Bratton, 1992; Wood, 1982).

Feminist theory

Despite recent reports that violence against women outside, and inside, the workplace is widespread in the European Union (FRA, 2014), studying the workplace using a 'feminist' approach had not been a major topic of enquiry until relatively recently. The organizational discourse is still, in the main, a masculine endeavour to shed light on organizational behaviour. For radical feminists, science is not sexless: on the contrary, 'the attributes of science are the attributes of males' (Sydie, 1994: 207). Research about work organizations tends to be both androcentric (focused on males) and ethnocentric (focused on the white Anglo-Saxon culture). One interpretation is that it has focused on the management agenda, and up to now this has consisted largely of 'important' white men in one field (academia) talking to, reflecting on and writing about 'important' white men in another field (organizations) (Townley, 1994).

Feminist theory emerged as a critique of Marx's analysis of capitalism (Federici, 2014). At the centre of the feminist critique is Marx's blindness to the significance of unpaid reproductive work, which, feminists argue, limits his understanding of the 'true extent of the capitalist exploitation of labour' (Federici, 2014: 85). Theoretically, one of the most important consequences of feminist analysis in organizational studies is its power to question research findings that segregate organizational behaviour from the larger structure of social and historical life. Accordingly, much of the recent work most directly related to the feminist approach requires us to look at the interface between the social context and work. It is argued that this shapes and reshapes the employment relationship. We need to look at gender divisions in the labour market, patriarchal power, issues of sexuality and inequality in society and at work, and the interface between home and work (the 'dual-role' syndrome). More importantly, however, incorporating gender development into the study of organizational studies will represent the life experience of both men and women in a more comprehensive and inclusive way.

VISIT THE *ONLINE RESOURCE CENTRE* AT HTTPS://HE.PALGRAVE.COM/COMPANION/ BRATTON-WORK-AND-ORGANIZATIONAL-BEHAVIOUR3/ TO READ THE EU REPORT 'VIOLENCE AGAINST WOMEN: AN EU-WIDE SURVEY'.

Symbolic-interactionist theory

Society consists of people interacting with one another. This benign observation is the essence of the symbolic-interactionist approach to studying people in work organizations. Symbolic interactionism offers a lens into the workplace by exploring the meaning (the symbolic element) of individuals' daily social interactions. Although other means are available – gesture, touch and dress, for example – a shared language is the principal medium by which humans exchange meaning. At the simplest level, and taking into account that we can each interpret symbols in different ways, this means that someone shouting at the top of her or his voice is angry and acting accordingly, or that someone wearing a dress in our society is female and acting on the basis of this decision. Language and culture allow humans to understand and interpret what other individuals *mean* by their social actions. Organizational study, therefore, involves notions of 'symbolic meaning' and 'sense making' so that individuals can make sense of what they do.

These characteristics distinctive to humans were emphasized in the work of Charles Horton Cooley and George Herbert Mead, who were discussed earlier in the chapter, and W. I. Thomas (1863–1947), three of the early American symbolic interactionists. They demonstrated that symbolic language, and the concepts and shared meanings embodied within the use of language, can only be learnt through *socialization*. There is a close connection between the learning process and the development of a thinking, reasoning self. This social self has an individual identity and an individual capacity for reflexive thought: individuals can reflect on their own actions and the way others respond to those actions. The work of American philosopher, sociologist and social psychologist George Herbert Mead emphasized the individuals' sociability and put the human experience of 'self' centre-stage. According to Mead, the self is constructed as we interact with others, and the social self allows us to take on social roles, reflect on ourselves and internalize social expectations.

Another important figure in the symbolic-interactionist tradition was the Canadian sociologist Erving Goffman (1922–1982), who coined the term 'impression management' in his book *The Presentation of Self in Everyday Life* (1959). This term refers to the ways in which people present themselves in specific roles and social situations. Goffman famously introduced the 'dramaturgical approach' to conducting social research as if everyday life were taking place on a theatrical stage. According to Goffman, when observing servers in a restaurant, they acted differently when they were 'front-stage', that is, in the public domain, compared with when they were 'back-stage' in the kitchen, away from the gaze of dining customers. The restaurant employees presented themselves differently depending on which stage they were on. It was Goffman's insights into the minutiae of workday life and the processes of interaction that informed Bolton's work on emotion in the workplace (2005).

To summarize, there are multiple versions of symbolic interactionism, but Hewitt and Shulman identify five major tenets underpinning this approach. First, symbolic interactionists theorize about human action. They believe that 'patterns and regularities cannot be fully grasped without understanding the social processes that create them' (Hewitt and Shulman, 2011: 26). Second, human behaviour depends on the creation and maintenance of *meaning*: 'conduct is predicated on meaning' (p. 26). Third, behaviour is self-referential, which suggests that individuals 'act toward themselves with purpose much as they act towards the external world with purpose. They take themselves – their feelings, their interests, their images of self – into account as they act' (p. 27). Fourth, humans form behaviour as they interact with one another. Individual behaviour 'is formed in real time as people form plans and purposes, take themselves into account, and interact with one another' (p. 28). Fifth, culture shapes and constrains human behaviour, but it

stop...

Apply Goffman's theory to airline flight attendants. Who makes up the 'front-stage' audience? Where is the 'back-stage'?

...and reflect

is also the product of human action. Thus, symbolic interactionism orients us to an environment of 'symbolic communities and contrasting definitions of reality' (p. 181), a perspective we will draw upon as we examine the human dimension of the workplace. Critics have stressed that the micro-level approach of symbolic interactionism does not give sufficient attention to the 'big picture' and the inherent conflict of interest between the key actors representing capital and labour.

Postmodernism

postmodernism: the sociological approach that attempts to explain social life in modern societies that are characterized by post-industrialization, consumerism and global communications

Since the early 1990s, **postmodernist** theory has been applied to the study of organizations and management behaviour (Boje et al., 1996; Hassard and Parker, 2000; Locke, 2003). While traditional writings on organizational theory tend to view work organizations as fine examples of human rationality, postmodernists such as Michel Foucault regard organizations as being more akin to defensive reactions against inherently destabilizing forces. The postmodernist perspective has its roots in the French intellectual tradition of post-structuralism, an approach to knowledge that puts the consideration of reflexivity and how language is used at the centre of the study of all aspects of human activity. Thus, postmodern perspectives question attempts to 'know' or 'discover' the genuine order of things (what is known as representation). Researchers must possess the ability to be critical of their own intellectual assumptions (that is, they must exercise reflexivity).

This approach plays down the notion of a disinterested observer and instead stresses the way in which people's notion of who and what they are – their agency, in other words – is shaped by the discourses that surround them. This is known as decentring the subject. Postmodernists also believe that researchers are materially involved in constructing the world they observe through language (by writing about it). Thus, where modernists perceive history as a grand narrative of human activity, rationality and progress, postmodernists reject the grand narrative and the notion of progressive intent. Clegg and Hardy frame the postmodern approach this way: 'They are histories, not history. Any pattern that is constituted can only be a series of assumptions framed in and by a historical context' (1999: 2).

Michel Foucault's relevance for organizational theory lies in several related spheres (1977, 1979). First, he argues that contemporary management controls human behaviour neither by consensus nor by coercion, but rather by systems of surveillance and human relations management techniques. Second, he suggests that although an organization is 'constructed by power', its members do not 'have' power. Power is not the property of any individual or group. While modernists see the direction of power flowing downwards against subordinates, and its essence as negative, Foucault argues that power should be configured as a relationship between subjects. It has 'capillary' qualities that enable it to be exercised '*within* the social body, rather than *above* it' (Sheridan, 1980: 39). Third, with the ever-increasing expansion of electronic surveillance in the workplace, Foucault offers his own image of an 'iron cage' in the form of the extended panopticon (see Chapter 2) – hidden surveillance.

Postmodernism is a useful way to study work organizations. In particular, the notion of power as a 'web' within which managers and non-managers are held has much to offer. However, some critics, for example Martin Parker (1993), have described postmodern epistemology as a reactionary intellectual trend, which amounts to a 'fatal distraction' from engaging in a rigorous analysis of the organizational changes located within late modernity.

The value of theory about contemporary organizational behaviour

In this chapter, we have reviewed the main themes and arguments of both classical and contemporary theories of work. As we explained, the classical theories are derived from the works of Karl Marx, Emile Durkheim, Max Weber and George Simmel, and are an intellectual response to the transformation of society caused by industrial capitalism. A legitimate question for students of organizational behaviour is, 'Why bother studying sociological classics – four "dead white men"?' We believe that an understanding of the classical accounts of work is important because, as others have also argued, the epistemological, theoretical and methodological difficulties that were identified and debated by the quartet of Marx, Durkheim, Weber and Simmel and other classical social theorists remain central to the conduct of contemporary research on organizational behaviour (Bratton and Denham, 2014). Those of us who study contemporary work organizations are informed by the 'canonical' writers and constantly return to them for ideas and inspiration.

In terms of understanding what goes on in the workplace, theory cannot be separated from management practice. It is used both to defend existing management practices and to validate new ways of organizing work, or *doing*. The nature of the employment relationship is clearly an issue of central importance to understanding human behaviour in work organizations. The classical sociologists developed a body of work that, directly or by inference, provides an account of the relations between employers and employees.

For Marx, conflict is structured into the employment relationship and is, for most of the time, asymmetrical. That is, the power of the employer or agent (manager) typically exceeds that of the workers. Durkheim's work influenced how theorists have studied organizations, and he reminds us that there are multiple ways in which society imposes itself upon us and shapes our behaviour.

A number of Weber's concepts also continue to have much relevance in the early twenty-first century. For example, his concept of charismatic domination is prominent in contemporary leadership theories. In addition, Weber's concepts of bureaucracy and rationalization have been applied to the fast-food sector, and have exposed the irrationality associated with the paradigm of McDonaldization. Weber's interpretive method, and in particular the researcher's capacity to assign different meanings to shared reality, gives a postmodern ring to his theory.

Simmel's sociology is relevant to modern theories of group dynamics and the social self. Finally, classical theories enter the contemporary debates on work organization and management practices by reinforcing the message that understanding the nature of the employment relationship necessarily involves considering organizational culture, societal values and norms as well as national institutions. It is through these that individuals acquire a self-identity and the mental, physical and social skills that shape their behaviour both outside and inside the work organization.

Links to management   John Bratton

In the ebook click on the play button to watch the author of this textbook talking about the connection between theory and workplace research, and then answer the following questions:

- What types of theory does John identify?
- According to John, how can theory guide the research process?

Chapter summary

- The four founders of the sociology of work all continue to have their contemporary adherents and detractors.

- Marx's fascination with class, conflict and the labour process formed the basis for the most popular new approach throughout much of industrial sociology, from the late 1960s to the 1980s. It spawned a complete school of thought in the labour process tradition, but its limitations became more evident as the approach attempted to explain all manner of social phenomena directly through the lens of class.

- Durkheim's moral concerns continue to pervade the market economy, and make predictions about human actions that are based on amoral, economically rational behaviour less than convincing. Perhaps where Durkheim has been most vigorously criticized has been in relation to the allegedly cohering effects of an extended division of labour. The mainstream of managerial theories does not support Durkheim on this point: dependency does not generate mutual solidarity.

- Weber's theories of rationalization and bureaucracy have never been far from the minds of those analysing the trend towards larger and larger organizations and the recent movement towards more flexible work organization patterns. Again, however, Weber's over-rationalized approach underestimates the significance of destabilizing and sectional forces within work organizations.

- Simmel's theories related to human relationships in groups and the connection between the social and the self, as well as his contribution to the symbolic-interactionist perspective on organizational behaviour, were also examined in this chapter. We noted that there are multiple versions of symbolic interactionism but five important dimensions were identified in the chapter: symbolic interactionism theorizes human action; human behaviour depends on the creation and maintenance of *meaning*; behaviour is self-referential; humans form behaviour as they interact with one another; and culture shapes and constrains human behaviour, but is also the product of human action. However, critics argue that symbolic interactionism does not give sufficient attention to the 'big picture'.

- This chapter has reviewed 11 theoretical approaches to studying organizations and management behaviour: the technical, social-technical, contingency, culture, learning, social action, political, control, feminist, symbolic-interactionist and postmodernist approaches. It has adopted a particular form of differentiating between the various theories through an organizational grid based on two axes: managerial–critical and determinist–interpretative. This is a heuristic way of structuring the various possibilities.

IN THE EBOOK ACCESS **WEB BASED ASSIGNMENTS** TO APPLY YOUR LEARNING.

Chapter review questions

1 To what extent has the decline of Communism undermined the utility of Marx's ideas?
2 Why was Weber so pessimistic about work, when Durkheim and Marx were so optimistic?
3 Do we need theory to explain the way organizations work?
4 What is the relevance of Weber's concept of *Verstehen* for organizational behaviour researchers?
5 What is meant by symbolic-interactionist theory and contingency theory? Why is it important to understand each of them?
6 What is meant by the suggestion that theory cannot be separated from management practice?

Further reading

Bratton, J. and Denham, D. (2014) *Capitalism and Classical Social Theory* (2nd edn), Toronto: University of Toronto Press.
Coupland, C., Brown, A. D., Daniels, K. and Humphreys, M. (2008) 'Saying it with feeling: analyzing speakable emotions', *Human Relations*, 61(3), pp. 327–53.
Heracleous, L. and Jacob, C. D. (2008) 'Understanding organizations through embodied metaphors', *Organization Studies*, 29(1), pp. 45–78.
Hewitt, J. P. and Shulman, D. (2011) *Self and Society* (11th edn), Boston, MA: Pearson Education.
Jaffee, D. (2001) *Organization Theory: Tension and Change*, Boston, MA: McGraw-Hill (see Chapters 1 and 2).
Manning, P. K. (2008) 'Goffman on organizations', *Organization Studies*, 29(5), pp. 677–99.
Parker, M. (2000) 'The sociology of organizations and the organization of sociology: some reflections on the making of a division of labour', *Sociological Review*, 4(1), pp. 124–46.
Reed, M. (1999) 'Organizational theorizing: a historically contested terrain', pp. 25–50 in S. R. Clegg and C. Hardy (eds), *Studying Organization: Theory and Method*, London: Sage.
Rowlinson, M. (2004) 'Challenging the foundations of organization theory', *Work, Employment and Society*, 18(3), pp. 607–20.
Tsoukas, H. (1992) 'Postmodernism, reflexive rationalism and organizational studies: a reply to Martin Parker', *Organizational Studies*, 13(4), pp. 643–9.
Verstegen, R. L. and Rutherford, M. A. (2000) 'Mary Parker Follett: individualist or collectivist? Or both?', *Journal of Management History*, 5, 207–23.
Witzel, M. (2012) *A History of Management Thought*, Abingdon, Oxon: Routledge.

Chapter case study: Butting out smoking in Russia

The setting

With the collapse of the Soviet Union, the privatization of Russia's tobacco industry began. In the new Russia, tobacco advertising is unavoidable. Smoking is promoted on half of all billboards in Moscow and on three-quarters of the plastic bags in the country. As a result of tobacco companies promoting smoking as part of a 'Western lifestyle' and striving to capitalize on the public's new disposable income, smoking rates have doubled. Russia is now the fourth heaviest smoking country in the world, with one in four boys under the age of 10 and 60 per cent of men over the age of 15 classified as smokers. While most of the Western world is experiencing a decrease in smoking rates, the number of Russian smokers continues to climb.

The government has proposed legislation banning smoking in workplaces and other public places, such as on aircraft, trains and municipal transport as well as in schools, hospitals, cultural institutions and government buildings. The legislation also requires specially designated smoking areas to be set up, and for restaurants and cafes to set up no-smoking areas. The changes will affect not only Russian companies, but also international firms looking to invest in the expanding privatization of the economy. The emerging middle class has produced a potential market of 150 million consumers that lures companies from all over the world hoping to tap into the vast natural resources, advanced technology and skilled workers that Russia has to offer.

The problem

Kendles & Smith is a global British pharmaceutical, medical devices and consumer packaged goods manufacturer, with 150 subsidiary companies operating in over 32 countries. It recently opened a new operation in Moscow as part of a strategy to make its mark on the new prosperous Russian economy.

The management at Kendles & Smith were versed in Russian history and understood that worker attitudes and behaviours had been shaped by 70 years of Communist dictatorship, a centrally planned economic system, and government bureaucracy that had ruled the people's lives. Like most international firms, management at Kendles & Smith found Russian workers to be cooperative and compliant, but not risk takers. Many of the supervisors hired from the local labour pool lacked confidence and drive. Although they followed corporate policies strictly, the employees in turn expected the new company to take care of them and their families.

With the UK having one of the lowest smoking rates in Europe, the management at Kendles & Smith were surprised at the number of the employees who were smokers – almost 65 per cent. As a company with a focus on health products, one of its first goals was to develop a voluntary tobacco reduction programme, including counselling and nicotine cessation aids, to improve the health of its new staff. Unfortunately, only a small group of workers took

advantage of the programme in its first year, and the majority of these were supervisors.

The next step was to implement a smoking ban in the Russian operations. Although it was made clear to all employees that the company president wanted to see the worksites smoke-free regardless of the government's legislation, only the supervisors were to be given an opportunity to express their positions on the matter. Jonathan Williams, one of the UK managers assigned to the Moscow operation, was given the task of doing the research. There were over 100 supervisors, and Jonathan was given only a short time frame within which to present his findings. Although Jonathan was free to speak to the supervisors, the company president stressed that he really just wanted to know whether or not the majority of the supervisors favoured the ban.

As Jonathan had not conducted workplace research before, he felt overwhelmed when he began reading about the various methods that could be used. He wanted the rich qualitative information that in-person interviews could give, but he thought that taking a more quantitative approach, such as using a questionnaire, would provide the anonymity that the supervisors might need to be honest with their answers.

The task

As Jonathan, ask yourself the following questions:
- What would be the disadvantages of using a questionnaire in this case?
- What might be missed by gathering only the supervisors' opinions?
- What qualities do the Russian workers exhibit that could influence the research results? Why?

Sources and further information

Allan, G. and Skinner, C. (eds.) (1991) *Handbook for Research Students in the Social Sciences*, London: Falmer Press.

Bryman, J. (ed.) (1988) *Doing Research in Organizations*, London: Routledge.

Elenkov, D. (1998) 'Can American management concepts work in Russia? A cross-cultural comparative study', *California Management Review*, 40(4), pp. 133–56.

Oppenheim, A. N. (1992) *Questionnaire Design, Interviewing and Attitude Measurement*, London: Pinter.

Visit www.ethics.gc.ca/eng/policy-politique/interpretations for an example of a research ethics policy.

Note: This case study was written by Lori Rilkoff, Human Resources Director, City of Kamloops, BC, Canada. Data on smoking in Russia in 2012 are available at: www.who.int/tobacco/surveillance/policy/country_profile.

IN THE EBOOK ACCESS AN **OB IN FILM** BOX THAT USES *ROGER & ME* (1989), DIRECTED BY MICHAEL MOORE, TO PROVIDE AN INSIGHT INTO CORPORATE RESTRUCTURING AND US DEINDUSTRIALIZATION. IT ALSO RAISES QUESTIONS ABOUT THE VALUE, POLITICS AND PRACTICAL CONSIDERATIONS OF DOING ORGANIZATIONAL BEHAVIOUR RESEARCH AND TO ACCESS **AN INTERACTIVE QUIZ** TO TEST YOUR UNDERSTANDING.

part 2
Individuals in the workplace

In this part of the book, we turn our attention to how various individual differences affect individual behaviour in the workplace. Individuals have different personalities, perceptions of the world around them and learning styles. The chapters here emphasize that the work experiences of women, visible minorities and disabled individuals may be different from those of white, male employees.

Chapter 4 examines personality, which we define as the distinctive and relatively enduring pattern of thinking, feeling and acting that characterizes a person's response to her or his environment, and self-identity, defined as the ongoing process of self-development through which we construct a unique sense of ourselves and our relationship to the world around us.

In Chapter 5, we examine perception and emotions. We learn that perception, like personality, is interdependent with socialization, and impacts on people's behaviour in the workplace in complex ways. Understanding perception is important because the fundamental nature of perceptual processes means that individuals usually interpret other people and situations differently; therefore they routinely hold different views of reality, which in turn strongly influence their attitudes and actions. Finally, we consider the concept of emotional intelligence and discuss its significance for understanding behaviour.

In Chapter 6, we explain that motivation is the driving force in individuals that affects their direction, intensity and persistence of work behaviour in the interest of achieving organizational goals. We go on to explore two competing approaches to understanding motivation: the needs-based and process theories of motivation.

4 Personality and self-identity
5 Perception and emotions
6 Motivation

In Chapter 7, we explore learning in the workplace. Here, we explain the growing interest in workplace learning, and how the learning experience may depend upon how the organization is structured, how work is designed and how individuals engage with, interact with and construct knowledge from their work situations.

We begin Chapter 8 with the claim that understanding issues of equity across the major social divisions of society is vital for a full understanding of organizational behaviour. We explore the general and specific tensions in organizations that make the issues of equity, inequity and justice relevant topics for learning and research. We also ask the following question 'If the vast majority of people in our society experience systematic inequities in relation to work, why is it so difficult to realize significant, positive change?'

Finally, in Chapter 9, we examine diversity in the workplace, compare it with equal opportunities and then go on to apply organizational behaviour theories to core practices of people management. In particular, we focus on workplace planning, recruitment and selection, reward, and training and development practices in organizations and how they can drive diversity. We conclude the chapter by exposing some internal paradoxes in people management.

7 Learning
8 Class, gender, race and equality
9 Diversity and people management

chapter **4**
Personality and self-identity

Key concepts

- extroversion
- Freudian iceberg
- idiographic
- introversion
- personality
- nomothetic
- personality traits
- personhood
- self-concept
- selfhood

Chapter outline

- Introduction
- What is personality?
- Trait theories of personality
- The psychodynamic theory of personality
- Sociocultural theories of personality
- Identity and personality
- Applying personality theories in the workplace
- Summary and end-of-chapter features
- Chapter case study: Identifying leaders in Nigeria

Chapter learning outcomes

After completing this chapter, you should be able to:

1 Define personality and identity and understand their importance in the workplace
2 Distinguish between the trait and psychodynamic theories of personality
3 Understand how cultural and lifelong social experience shapes personality
4 Critically assess how individual identity affects and is affected by the organization
5 Understand more of the main characteristics of your own personality and self-identity
6 Apply the key findings of personality and self-research to the workplace

introduction

At the morning coffee break, three nurses sat around a table in the hospital's cafeteria. Elizabeth spoke first. 'I'm really disappointed in Alan's behaviour. He became really excitable and loud again during the night shift when I asked him to assist in the emergency ward. He seems to become emotional and excitable whenever we have more than two or three critical cases in the ER. At the interview, he came over as so confident and experienced.' 'And he had a wonderful CV,' Eleanor added. 'Interviews and good reference letters can't tell you about a person's personality and how they will perform under stress,' said charge nurse Judy Finlay. 'Yet, you know, he can be totally different outside the ER. He's sociable and pleasant when we go to the pub or when things are quiet on the ward,' replied Elizabeth.

It is the office Christmas party. On past occasions you have gone alone, and always left alone, early. This year, you have someone to bring. There is a promotion coming up early next year, and you wonder what your colleagues, especially your boss, will think of your partner. As you walk through the reception and into the hotel bar, your sycophantic boss, Nathan, comes across, a glass of lager in his hand: 'Carolyn, good to see you.' He turns slightly, and pauses … You take a deep breath: 'Nathan, this is my partner, Alex.'

Source: © twilightproductions

plate 11 The first thing we do on meeting strangers is to use cues, such as embodiment, clothing and language, to identify them in our 'mind tapestry'.

The personality of a co-worker can matter enormously. In the case of Alan, why is he such a different person in different situations? Are certain personality types better adapted for certain job types? Should managers try to recruit all employees with similar personalities? How does the personality characteristic influence motivation at work? Why do some people find it difficult to work in a team, while others excel as 'team players'? What personality types make for a 'good' team player? Behaviour analysts have long been interested in the relationships between personality traits and job performance, and whether personality homogeneity (people having similar personalities) facilitates a high-performance workplace. Over the decades, researchers have attempted to understand how personality acts as an important factor shaping behaviour in the workplace.

Many of us, much of the time, are able to take identity for granted. But in situations such as those experienced by Carolyn, who we are, who we think we are, or who we are *seen* to be matters. Identity does not just involve brief social encounters, and it is not always a mundane or trivial matter (Jenkins, R., 2008). There are occasions when we may have to establish our identity, for example, at immigration control or at a bank when we apply for an account. Although what we mean by our identity always involves us as an individual, the social context and our life experience are crucially important. Identifying oneself, or others, is a matter of meaning, and the creation of meaning entails interaction with others, including co-workers. It is important to note here that identity is not some*thing* that simply *is*, but can only be understood as a social process of 'being' or 'becoming' (Jenkins, R., 2008: 17).

A person's identity and identities, single and plural, are never a settled matter. The essence of being human is to have a sense of who we are and a means of establishing who others are. The first thing we do on meeting strangers, for example, is to attempt to identify them on our 'mind tapestry'. The cues that we rely upon include embodiment, clothing, language and answers to questions such as 'Which school did you go to?' People's enduring patterns of behaviour generate identity boundaries and, related to this, it is argued that stereotypes are extremely condensed symbols of collective identification. Indeed, in work organizations, recruitment and promotion decisions, and the criteria that inform them, are based upon and reproduce a set of class, gender and race identifications (Jenkins, R., 2008). Transformative change is also particularly likely to provoke concerns about identity. In 2014 in the UK, the Referendum on Scottish Independence provoked debate on Scottish national identity and the question 'What does it mean to be Scottish?' (Leadbetter, 2014). Whichever way we look at it, a person's identity seems to matter, both in everyday life and in organizational behaviour.

Modern organizations in the context of global labour markets must not only accommodate their employees' diversity, but must also understand their employees' personalities and identities. Although personality theories go back to 400 years BME (Before Modern Era), some seminal theories go back to the late nineteenth century, such as those of Carl Gustav Jung (1875–1961), Isabel Briggs Myers (1897–1980) and Katharine Cook Briggs (1875–1968). Today, there are at least 24 academics or groups of researchers who have contributed to theories of personality. An established sociological literature on social 'self' or 'social identity' goes back to the classical theorists: Charles Horton Cooley (1864–1929), George Herbert Mead (1863–1931), Georg Simmel (1858–1918) and W. E. B. Du Bois (1868–1963) (see Chapters 2 and 3).

Therefore our coverage in this chapter has to be highly selective, and we can hope to provide only a glimpse of the complexity and scope of the theories. To help navigate through the literature, we can divide the study of individual differences into two broad approaches: **nomothetic** and **ideographic**.

> **nomothetic approach:** an approach to explanation in which we seek to identify relationships between variables across many cases
>
> **idiographic approach:** an approach to explanation in which we seek to explain the relationships among variables within a particular case or event; it contrasts with nomothetic analysis

The *nomothetic approach* is a specific and measurable perspective that assesses and compares individuals on the basis of a collection of observable traits and personality. The *ideographic approach* is a holistic and dynamic perspective that takes into account a 'whole' understanding of individual differences within a 'society' context. As such, the ideographic perspective goes beyond pure psychology theory to emphasize the development of the individual and the set of perceptions that individuals have about themselves – their self-concept.

VISIT THE *ONLINE RESOURCE CENTRE* AT HTTPS://HE.PALGRAVE.COM/COMPANION/BRATTON-WORK-AND-ORGANIZATIONAL-BEHAVIOUR3/ FOR INFORMATION ON PERSONALITY TESTING.

Figure 4.1 brings the two main approaches into a conceptual schema. The nomothetic focuses on *personality* (how we appear to others), and the ideographic emphasizes *self-concept* (how we perceive ourselves). *Selfhood* is the process of primary socialization and subsequent ongoing social interaction during which individuals define and redefine themselves and others throughout their lives (Jenkins, R., 2008). Selfhood is expressed through attitudes, values, styles, perceptions and emotions. We consider these expressions below and in more detail in Chapter 5. Each employee is therefore a unique and variable individual. This is a banal observation, of course, until one remembers that modernity and globalizing forces are radically altering the nature of day-to-day interactions in a constantly changing social milieu, which affects human experience and the perceptions we hold about who we are, who we think we are, how we see others and how others see us (Giddens, 1991). As a consequence, the connections between these perceptions are complex and problematic, but together they provide a foundation for a better understanding of the individual in the workplace.

The aim of this chapter is to provide a conceptual vocabulary for thinking about the nature of the interrelationship between personality and self-concept. Although we review the contribution of psychologists, this is primarily a work of sociology with a focus on the self and the social processes of self-identity, which are shaped by the social milieu in late modernity (see Chapter 3). The chapter concludes with a discussion of the connections between personality and aspects of job performance.

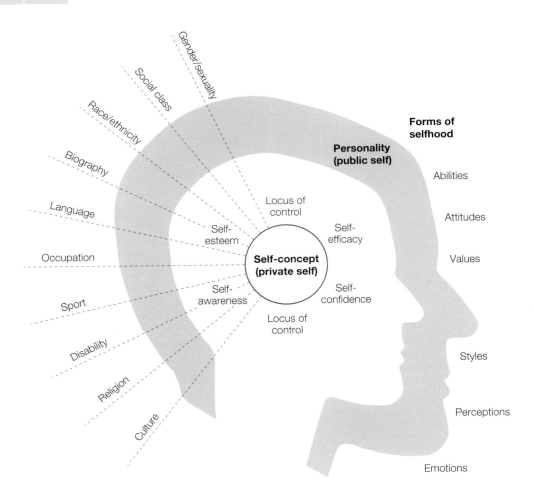

Figure 4.1 A conceptual schema for studying personality, self-concept and individual differences

What is personality?

The notion of personality permeates popular culture and discussion in the work-place. In Western cultures, the mass media – print, radio, television, films and other communication technologies – endlessly discuss 'cool' or 'nice' personalities. And like Alan in our opening vignette, we sometimes meet people at work who seem to have a personality that does not 'fit' with the job requirements or work group. We all use the term 'personality' quite often, and most people feel they understand it intuitively. But what exactly is personality? There is, unfortunately, no universally accepted definition. Cattell (1965: 117–18) explained it simply as 'that which permits a prediction of what a person will do in a given situation'. According to Child (1968: 83), personality consists of:

> The more or less stable, internal factors that make one person's behaviour consistent from one time to another, and different from the behaviour other people would manifest in comparable situations.

Four key words are worth noting in Child's definition:

- *Stable* – personality remains fairly constant over time.
- *Internal* – personality lies within each individual.
- *Consistent* – if personality remains constant over time, we would expect individuals to behave reasonably consistently.

- *Different* – when we refer to personality, we assume that there are individual differences (Eysenck, 2009).

Most definitions of personality conventionally exclude purely physical differences, such as height or strength or mental abilities, although these obviously have an effect (Cook, 2013: 2). We define **personality** here as a relatively enduring pattern of thinking, feeling and acting that characterizes a person's unique response to her or his environment.

Several aspects of these definitions need further explanation:

- The concept of personality refers to notions of *individuality*; people differ significantly from each other in how they routinely think, feel and act.
- Personality refers to an enduring or *stable* set of characteristics and tendencies that a person possesses. An individual's personality encapsulates her or his way of responding to their world. One important reason why psychologists study personality is in order to assess people (Cook, 2013). Personality rests on the observation that people seem to behave somewhat consistently over time and across different life situations. Thus, we would not characterize a person as having a shy personality if that individual tended to be dominantly shy and retiring only some of the time but on other occasions was frequently observed to be very sociable and outgoing.
- As Figure 4.1 suggests, individual differences in personality traits exist because they depend in large measure on each individual's experiences in life (Eysenck, 2009). Behaviour is influenced by social context. Individuals may be shy and retiring in a situation where they perceive the context to be unfavourable (such as meeting new people on the first day of employment), but outgoing when the situation is perceived as favourable. This perceived consistency can be classified as a trait that characterizes individuals' customary ways of responding to their environment. Research suggests that stability or consistency becomes greater as we enter adulthood, but even in adulthood there remains a capacity for meaningful personality change (Holt et al., 2012).
- Finally, our selective definitions of personality draw attention to the fact that, in studying personality, we are interested in the factors within people that cause them to behave as *consistently* as they do. Conley (1984) and other social psychologists have argued that it is 'situations' and not traits that determine individual behaviour. However, Colin Cooper (2010: 54) ripostes that 'if personality were determined purely by situations, personality traits simply would not exist and so measures of these traits would be unable to predict any aspects of behaviour'.

The patterns of thinking, feeling and acting that are viewed as reflecting a person's personality typically have three characteristics. First, they are seen as elements of identity that distinguish that individual from other people. Second, the individual's behaviours seem to 'interconnect' in a meaningful fashion, suggesting an inner element that shapes and directs behaviour. Third, but contestable, the behaviours are viewed as being caused primarily by 'internal' rather than contextual factors.

However, in studying personality, we need also to look at how social experience (external factors) structures or shapes it. People develop a personality by internalizing – or taking in – their social experiences or surroundings. Without social experience, personality cannot develop. Sociological research on the effects of social isolation on feral (meaning 'wild') children points to the crucial role of social experience in forming personality (Curtiss, 1977; Davis, 1940; Rymer, 1994). Sociologists suggest that, in the process of interacting with parents, siblings, relatives, teachers and others, people develop an individual identity. We shall examine identity later in this chapter, but we define it here as the core

personality: a relatively enduring pattern of thinking, feeling and acting that characterizes a person's unique response to her or his environment

stop...

What do you think of these typical observations of people that give rise to the concept of personality? Do they accurately reflect how you form an opinion of a person's personality?

...and reflect

understandings that human beings hold about who they are and what is meaningful to them. Figure 4.2 illustrates some perceived characteristics that are seen as reflecting an individual's personality.

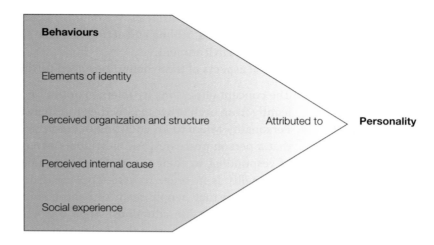

Figure 4.2 Perceived characteristics of behaviours that are seen as reflecting an individual's personality

In the next section, we will examine three approaches to the study of personality: the trait, psychodynamic and sociocultural approaches. These have guided the study of personality and provide very different conceptions of what personality is and how it functions. No doubt, as in other chapters of this book, you will find some of the theories more in accord than others with your own life views. Before we describe and evaluate each of the theories, we need to offer a few words of warning about personality in the workplace:

- As we have already said, the many studies that have been undertaken affirm that there is no 'one best' personality type. Some personality characteristics are useful in certain situations, and organizations need to appreciate the value of diversity. When all employees hold similar personality traits and have similar values, studies suggest that fewer rules are needed to get things done. For many managers, this may seem like a good thing, but in some circumstances this same homogeneity could hinder the organization's ability to adapt to change (Giberson et al., 2005).
- Although many organizations consider personality to be an important criterion for employment, personality tests are still considered to be a relatively poor instrument for selecting people for key positions, such as management roles.
- The excessive 'classification' of personality types may prevent others from appreciating a person's potential to contribute to an organization.
- If we draw attention to context and social experience, there is less likelihood of exaggerating the effect of personality on individual work-related behaviour. In highly structured situations – such as the armed forces – with clearly defined rules, roles and punishment contingencies, personality will have the least effect on work-related behaviour. In less structured situations – such as a volunteer community organization – personality will have the most effect on organizational behaviour (Adler and Weiss, 1988).

Trait theories of personality

Almost 2000 years ago, the ancient Greeks used the humoral theory to explain individual differences in personality (Martin et al., 2013). The body was thought

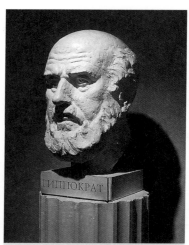

plate 12 The theory of personality or 'temperament' proposed by the Greek physician Hippocrates (469–399 BC) was based upon bodily 'humours', which produced four fundamental personality types: sanguine, choleric, melancholic and phlegmatic.

factor analysis: a statistical technique used for a large number of variables to explain the pattern of relationships in the data

plate 13 Observable traits, such as friendliness, are those traits that are obvious to others.

to contain four humours or fluids: black bile, blood, phlegm and yellow bile. Individuals' personalities were classified according to the disposition supposedly produced by the predominance of one of these humours in their bodies. Optimistic or sanguine people, who had a preponderance of blood (*sanguis*), were cheerful and passionate. Melancholic people, who had an excess of black bile, had a pessimistic temperament. Phlegmatic individuals, whose body systems contained an excessive proportion of phlegm, were calm and unexcitable. Choleric individuals, on the other hand, had an excess of yellow bile and were bad-tempered and irritable. Although subsequent research discredited the humoral theory, the notion that people can be classified into different personality types has persisted to this day.

If you were to describe the personality of a close friend or relative, you would probably make a number of descriptive statements, for example, 'He is a real extrovert. He likes to be the focus of attention, is abrasive in debate, but is also brilliant and charming. He works hard but he is generous with his time, and he is a truly caring person. He will always try to help if he can.' In other words, you would describe others by referring to the kind of people they are ('extrovert') and to their thoughts ('caring' and 'brilliant'), feelings ('attention') and actions ('works hard'). Together, these statements describe personality traits, enduring personal characteristics that reveal themselves in a particular pattern of human behaviour in different situations.

The English dictionary contains approximately 18,000 words that could be used to describe personal traits, and obviously it would be impractical, even if it were possible, to describe people in terms of where they fell on some vast scale. In order to understand and predict human behaviour, trait theorists therefore attempt to condense various descriptors into a manageable number of core personality traits that people display consistently over time.

Gordon Allport (1897–1967) pioneered research on personality traits. He believed that the set of words chosen to describe an individual reflects that person's central traits, personal characteristics that are apparent to others and that shape the individual's behaviour in a variety of environments. A central trait is equivalent to the descriptive terms used in a letter of reference (such as 'conscientious' or 'reliable'). Another aspect of what Allport called the 'building blocks' of personality is secondary traits, those which are more specific to certain situations and have less impact on behaviour. An example of a secondary trait is 'dislikes crowds' (Bernstein, 2015).

Psychologists have used the statistical tool of **factor analysis** to identify clusters of specific behaviours that are so highly correlated with one another that they can be viewed as reflecting basic personality traits. Different people fall into these different clusters. For example, you might find that most people who are shy and socially reserved stay away from parties and enjoy solitary activities such as reading. At the other end of the spectrum are people who are talkative and outward-going, like parties and dislike solitary activities such as reading. These behavioural patterns define a dimension that we might label introversion–extroversion. At one end of the dimension are highly introverted behaviours, while at the other end are highly extroverted behaviours. As we describe below, studies have found introversion–extroversion to be a major dimension of personality.

In 1965, Raymond Cattell, a British psychologist, built upon Allport's investigations to develop his theory of personality. Cattell used a process of factor analysis to identify clusters of traits that he believed represented a person's central traits. He analysed questionnaire responses from thousands of people, and also obtained ratings from people who knew the participants well, eventually identifying 16 basic behaviour clusters, or factors. He called these 16 traits 'source traits' because they were, in his view, the building blocks upon which personality is built. From his data, Cattell developed a personality test called the 16 Personality Factor Questionnaire (16PF) to measure individual differences on each of the dimensions, and to provide personality profiles for individuals and groups of people. Figure 4.3 compares the personality profiles of a hypothetical individual rated on Cattell's 16PF test.

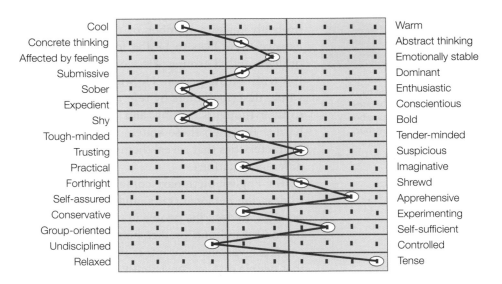

Figure 4.3 Two hypothetical personality profiles using Cattell's 16PF test

Source: Based on Cattell and Kline (1977), Table 4.1

Eysenck's three-factor model of personality

Hans J. Eysenck (1916–1997), another well-known British psychologist, also used factor analysis to devise his theory of personality. From his research, Eysenck concluded that normal personality can be understood in terms of three basic factors or dimensions: **introversion–extroversion**, stability–instability and psychoticism (Eysenck, 1970). These factors are bipolar dimensions. Introversion is the opposite of extroversion, stability is the opposite of instability (sometimes called neuroticism), and psychoticism is the opposite of self-control.

As mentioned above, introversion refers to a reserved nature and the pursuit of solitary activities. Introverts tend to be shy, thoughtful risk avoiders, and to shun social engagements. Extroversion refers to the opposites of these human characteristics. Extroverts tend to be sociable and spontaneous, thrive on change and be willing to take risks.

Psychoticism refers to an egocentric and antisocial nature. People high on psychoticism display such attributes as aggression, coldness and moodiness, are fraught with guilt and are unstable. People who score low on psychoticism do not show these attributes. Such people tend to be even-tempered and are characterized by emotional stability. Eysenck believed that the most important aspects of a person's personality can be captured by a two-dimensional model (Figure 4.4).

Figure 4.4 illustrates the effects of various combinations of the three dimensions of introversion–extroversion, stability–instability and psychoticism, and relates them to the four personality types described by the Greek physician Galen in the

introversion: a personality dimension that characterizes people who are territorial and solitary

extroversion: a personality dimension that characterizes people who are outgoing, talkative, sociable and assertive

second century AD. We should note that the two basic dimensions intersect at right angles (meaning that they are statistically uncorrelated or independent). There-fore, knowing how extrovert an individual is reveals little about a person's level of emotional stability – she or he could fall anywhere along the stability dimension. The secondary traits shown in the diagram reflect varying combinations of these two primary dimensions. Thus, we can see that the emotionally unstable (neurotic) extrovert is touchy, restless and aggressive. In contrast, the stable extrovert is a carefree, lively individual who tends to seek out leadership roles. The unstable introvert is moody, anxious and rigid, but the stable introvert tends to be calm, even-tempered and reliable.

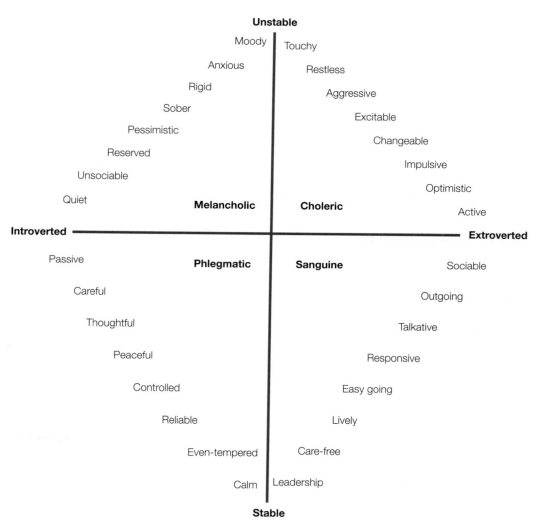

Figure 4.4 Eysenck's major personality dimensions
Source: Eysenck (1973)

Eysenck's research produced data to show that test scores measuring these two basic personality dimensions can predict people's key personality patterns, includ-ing specific behaviour tendencies or disorders. Leaders, for example, are likely to be in the 'sanguine' quadrant and tend to display outgoing, sociable behaviour. Criminals, on the other hand, are likely to be in the 'choleric' quadrant and tend to display aggressive and impulsive behaviour. Eysenck's trait theory of personality has received considerable support because the three dimensions have been replicated in factor analyses performed by many different researchers (Martin et al., 2013).

The five-factor model of personality

As we have seen, trait theorists tend to divide into those who suggest that personality is best captured by measuring a large number of basic traits, such as Gordon Allport and Raymond Cattell, and those who suggest that the basic structure of personality can be captured by grouping 'high-order' dimensions, such as Hans Eysenck. The 'Big Five' model of personality trait structure proposes that personality is organized around only five core dimensions: openness, conscientiousness, extroversion, agreeableness and neuroticism (Goldberg, 1990; McCrae and Costa, 1995). These Big Five personality dimensions, represented by the handy acronym 'OCEAN' (or 'CANOE' if the words are reconfigured), are shown in Table 4.1.

Table 4.1 The Big Five model of personality trait structure and the associated lower order traits

Dimensions	Lower order traits
Openness	Artistically sensitive, intellectual interests, reflective, insightful, curious, imaginative
Conscientiousness	Efficient, reliable, responsible, scrupulous, ethical, persevering, organized, self-disciplined
Extroversion	Talkative, outgoing, candid, adventurous, sociable, assertive, gregarious, energetic
Agreeableness	Good-natured, forgiving, generous, non-critical, warm, gentle, cooperative, trusting, compassionate
Neuroticism	Anxious, self-pitying, nervous, tense, hostile, excitable, emotionally unstable, impulsive

Source: Based on information from Bernstein (2015)

stop...

Where would you place yourself on the personality scales? What is your reaction to the models? Are personality traits such as these inherited, or do they arise from social experience? What are the predictive advantages of the broad general traits and the narrow specific traits?

...and reflect

Researchers using the Big Five model hold that when a person is placed at a specific point on each of these five core personality dimensions by means of a test or direct observations of behaviour, the essence of that person's personality is captured. These Big Five personality dimensions may be universal since they were found to be consistent in studies of women and men in diverse Asian, European and North American cultures (Dalton and Wilson, 2000; Paunonen, 1996).

The research also shows evidence that some personality dimensions tend to be more stable than others over time. For example, introversion–extroversion tends to be quite stable from childhood into adulthood and across the adult years. When it comes to stability of behaviour across situations, personality again shows both a degree of stability and some capacity for change. For example, regarding the higher order trait of 'conscientiousness', an employee might be highly conscientious in one situation (such as handing in class assignments on time to complete a college programme of studies) without being conscientious in another (such as coming to work on time).

Trait theorists have made an important contribution by focusing attention on the value of identifying, classifying and measuring stable and enduring personality characteristics. But this nomothetic approach to understanding personality has severe limitations. For example, it is argued elsewhere that, if we are to capture the true personality, researchers need to pay more attention to how traits interact with one another to affect various behaviours. There is a tendency for researchers to make predictions on the basis of a single measured personality trait without taking into account other personality factors that might also influence the action in question (Holt et al., 2012).

The psychodynamic theory of personality

Many social psychologists and organizational theorists believe that personality emerges from complex processes that are too dynamic to be captured by factor analysis. The Austrian physician Sigmund Freud (1856–1939) developed the influential psychoanalytic theory of personality, which claims that the dynamic interplay of inner psychological processes determines ways of thinking, feeling and acting. Freud's work introduced terms such as 'ego', 'fixation', 'libido', 'rationalization' and 'repression' into Western popular discourse, as well as having a profound effect on twentieth-century personality research. Sociologists have recognized the significance of psychoanalytic theories of socialization pioneered by Freud.

When working with the French neurologist Jean Charcot to treat patients, Freud became convinced that conversion hysteria, a disorder in which physical symptoms such as paralysis and blindness appeared suddenly and with no apparent physical cause, was connected to painful memories, which were often sexual or aggressive in nature, and seemed to have been repressed by the patient. When his patients were able to re-experience these traumatic memories, their physical symptoms often markedly improved or disappeared.

Freud experimented with various techniques, including hypnosis and dream analysis, to unearth the buried contents of the unconscious mind. His research convinced him that personality develops out of each person's struggle to meet her or his basic needs in a world that often frustrates those efforts. Freud suggested that an individual's personality is determined by conscious, preconscious and unconscious brain activity, with the unconscious part of the mind exerting a great influence on consciousness and behaviour. He proposed that most psychological events are located in what he termed the subconscious, a vast repository of traumatic events that a person can apparently no longer consciously recall without the use of hypnosis. The conscious mind, which consists of mental events of which people are presently aware, represents just the 'tip of the iceberg' (Figure 4.5).

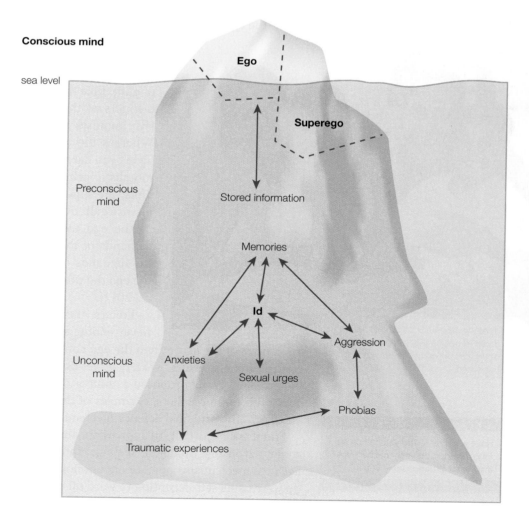

Figure 4.5 Freud's conception of the personality structure: 'the Freudian iceberg'

The structure of personality: id, ego and superego

According to Freud, personality is made up three separate but interacting parts: the id, the ego and the superego. In Figure 4.5, the pointed arrows inside the 'Freudian iceberg' are meant to show the connections and the dynamic nature of the structure of personality. Freud saw the **id** (the Latin word for 'it') as the unconscious portion of the personality, where the libido, which is the primary source of life instincts, resides. The id is the only structure present at birth, and it functions in a totally irrational manner. The id operates on the pleasure principle, seeking the immediate gratification of impulses produced by two innate drives: sex and aggression. For Freud, the id is:

> the dark, inaccessible part of our personality ... It is filled with energy reaching it from the instincts, but it has no organization, produces no collective will, but only a striving to bring about the satisfaction of the instinctual needs subject to the observance of the pleasure principle.
> (S. Freud, 1933, quoted in Carlson et al., 2005: 462)

The **ego** (Latin for 'I') is the thinking, organizing and protective self. It functions primarily at a conscious level, controls and integrates behaviour, and operates according to the reality principle. It negotiates a compromise between the pressures of the id and the demands of reality, deciding when and under what conditions the id can safely discharge its impulses and satisfy its needs. For example, the ego would seek sexual gratification within a consenting relationship rather than allow the pleasure principle to dictate an impulsive sexual assault.

The third component of personality is the **superego** (Latin meaning 'beyond' or 'above' the ego), which is subdivided into the conscience and the ego ideal, and tells us what we should and should not do. The superego, the moral arm of the personality, determines which actions are permissible and punishes wrongdoing with feelings of guilt. Like the ego, the superego strives to control the instincts of the id, particularly the sexual and aggressive impulses that are condemned by Western society. Whereas the id screams 'I want!', the superego replies, 'Don't you dare! That would be wicked!' For the superego, moralistic principles take precedence over realist ones. Thus, the superego might cause a person to experience intense guilt over sexual deviance.

The ego must achieve a compromise between the demands of the id, the constraints of the superego and the demands of reality. This mediating role has earned the ego the title the 'executive of the personality' (Holt et al., 2012).

Freud's theory of personality set the scene for a never-ending struggle between the id and the superego for control of the ego. When the ego confronts id drives that threaten to get out of control, anxiety results. Anxiety serves as a signal and motivates the ego to deal with the problem. Freud proposed a number of defence mechanisms to enable people to cope with these conflicts; examples of these defence mechanisms are described in Table 4.2. The principal defence mechanism is repression.

Freud believed that, in repression, the ego uses some of its energy to prevent anxiety-arousing thoughts, feelings and impulses from entering consciousness. Defence mechanisms operate unconsciously, so people are unusually unaware that they are using self-deception to ward off anxiety.

id: Sigmund Freud's term for the component of personality that includes all of the individual's basic biological drives and needs that demand immediate gratification

ego: according to Sigmund Freud, the rational, reality-oriented component of personality that imposes restrictions on the innate pleasure-seeking drives of the id

superego: Sigmund Freud's term for the human conscience, consisting of the moral and ethical aspects of personality

Source: Bananastock.

plate 14 Research into the genetic basis of personality suggests that traits such as extroversion may be inherited.

stop...

Have you ever found yourself using any of Freud's defence mechanisms? If so, what situation were you in?

...and reflect

Table 4.2 Psychoanalytic defence mechanisms

Defence mechanism	Description	Example
Repression	An active defensive process through which anxiety-arousing impulses or memories are pushed into the unconscious mind	A sports celebrity who was sexually abused in childhood develops amnesia for the event
Denial	A person refuses to acknowledge anxiety-arousing aspects of the environment. The denial may involve either the emotions connected with the event or the event itself	A young man who is told he has terminal cancer refuses to consider the possibility that he will not recover
Displacement	An unacceptable or dangerous impulse is repressed and then directed at a safer substitute target	A female employee who is harassed by her boss experiences no anger at work, but then goes home and abuses her husband and children
Rationalization	A person constructs a false but plausible explanation or excuse for an anxiety-arousing behaviour or event that has already occurred	An employee caught stealing justifies the act by pointing out that the company can afford the loss, and besides, other employees are stealing too

Source: Adapted from Passer, M., *Psychology: The Science of Mind and Behavior*, 2/e © 2004, McGraw-Hill Education. With permission

In Freud's theory, personality develops through seven psychosexual stages: oral, anal, phallic, Oedipus complex, Electra complex, latency and genital – which involve seeking pleasure from specific parts of the body called erogenous zones. A major shortcoming of psychoanalytic theory is that many of its concepts are ambiguous and difficult to define and measure operationally. A second major criticism is that Freud laid too much emphasis on the events of early childhood as determinants of adult personality.

VISIT THE *ONLINE RESOURCE CENTRE* AT HTTPS://HE.PALGRAVE.COM/COMPANION/BRATTON-WORK-AND-ORGANIZATIONAL-BEHAVIOUR3/ FOR MORE INFORMATION ON SIGMUND FREUD AND HIS WORK.

Sociocultural theories of personality

In this section, we present an introduction to the work of prominent social psychologists and sociologists who, in different ways, are interested in understanding personality from a sociocultural perspective. According to the trait and psychodynamic approaches, personality consists of traits that shape a person's thoughts, feelings and actions. In contrast, those taking a sociocultural approach understand personality to be fundamentally rooted in life experience, communities of practice, social relationships and the self-concept. As discussed in Chapter 1, the idiographic approach posits that personality is acquired through learning in an immediate social milieu – the social setting that is directly open to an individual's personal experience. In essence, its central tenet is that personality should not be located within typologies but should be understood as a complex social entity, closely related to self-image and social identity (Giddens, 1991).

Sociocultural researchers examine how personality is connected with social experience and the society in which people live: the culture, socialization and social dynamics of social interaction and situations. To illustrate this broad sociocultural perspective, we consider significant social-cognitive and **phenomenological** approaches to personality.

The social-cognitive approach, sometimes called the **social-learning approach**, emphasizes the development of personality through people interacting with a social environment that provides learning experiences. The phenomenological approach to personality suggests that the way people perceive and interpret social experience forms their personalities and influences their thoughts, feelings and actions.

The social-cognitive approach to personality

The most influential social-cognitive or social-learning theories are those of Julian Rotter (1966) and Albert Bandura (1978, 1997). These theorists have developed an

phenomenological approach: a philosophy concerned with how researchers make sense of the world around them. Adherents to this theory believe that the social researcher must 'get inside people's heads' to understand how they perceive and interpret the world

social-learning theory: a theory stating that much learning occurs by observing others and then modelling the behaviours that lead to favourable outcomes, and avoiding the behaviours that lead to punishing consequences

approach that views personality as the sum total of the cognitive habits and behaviours that develop as people learn through experience in their social setting.

Julian Rotter (pronounced like 'motor') argued that a person's decision to engage in a behaviour in a given situation is determined by two factors:

- what the person expects to happen following the action
- the value the person places on the outcome, which is called the reinforcement value.

expectancy theory: a motivation theory based on the idea that work effort is directed toward behaviours that people believe will lead to desired outcomes

Expectancy is our perception of how likely it is that certain consequences will occur if we engage in a particular behaviour within a specific situation. 'Reinforcement value' is basically how much we desire or dread the outcome that we expect the action to produce. For example, candidates for a particular position may spend a lot of money on new clothes to attend a job interview because past learning leads them to expect that doing so will help secure the job, and they place a high value on having the job.

locus of control: a personality trait referring to the extent to which people believe events are within their control

In Figure 4.1, **locus of control** is shown as part of the web of self-identity. This influential concept helps to explain the differences found between individuals in terms of how much personal responsibility they take for their behaviour and its consequences. Rotter argued that people learn general ways of thinking about their environment, in particular about how life's rewards and punishments are controlled. Differences in this generalized expectancy concerning the degree of personal control that individuals have in their lives produced Rotter's concept of the internal–external locus of control. People with an internal locus of control believe that life outcomes are largely under personal control and depend on their own efforts. In contrast, people with an external locus of control believe that the environment is largely beyond their control, and that their fate has less to do with their own efforts than with the influence of external factors, such as luck.

Research suggests that the locus of control that people develop has important implications for their personality in later life. For example, in the workplace, there is evidence that an internal locus of control is positively related to self-esteem, which refers to that part of the self-concept concerned with how we view our own self-worth based on an overall self-evaluation (Branden, 1998). Thus, an internal locus of control is positively correlated to perceptions of personal effectiveness. People who are internally focused are less likely to experience depression or anxiety, and tend to cope with stress in a more active and problem-focused manner than do those who are externally focused (Jennings, 1990, quoted in Passer et al., 2003: 565). One study has shown that because locus of control is fashioned by people's social experience, this aspect of personality can change (Frese, 1982). In the workplace, for example, experiencing participative decision-making arrangements may cause a shift towards an internal locus of control in managers and non-managers alike.

According to Albert Bandura, neither personal traits nor the social context alone determines personality. Instead, he argues that the environment, the person and the person's behaviour interact in a pattern of two-way causal links. In short, personality is determined by what Bandura calls *reciprocal determinism* (Figure 4.6).

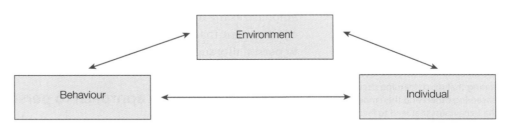

Figure 4.6 Bandura's model of reciprocal determinism

self-efficacy: the beliefs people have about their ability to perform specific situational task(s) successfully

For Bandura, the concept of self-efficacy (see Figure 4.1) is particularly important in this web of interaction and influence. **Self-efficacy** is that part of the self that is concerned with a person's beliefs about her or his ability to perform the actions needed to achieve the desired outcomes. People whose self-efficacy is high have confidence in their ability to do what it takes to overcome obstacles and achieve their goals.

Self-efficacy not only determines whether a person will engage in a particular behaviour, but also determines the extent to which he or she will sustain that behaviour in the face of adversity. For example, if you believe that you are qualified for a job at the BBC, you are likely to apply for an interview. Even if you are turned down for the job, you are apt to apply for an interview at another TV company because you are confident of your abilities. High self-efficacy can facilitate both the frequency and the quality of behaviour–environment interactions, and low self-efficacy can hamper both (Martin et al., 2013).

For Bandura, self-efficacy beliefs are always specific to particular situations. Thus, we may have high self-efficacy in some situations and low self-efficacy in others. For example, those who have mastered sophisticated computer software skills do not feel more generally capable in all areas of their life, despite their enhanced computer abilities. Efficacy beliefs are strong predictors of future performance and accomplishment. In short, they become a kind of self-fulfilling prophecy. We present more of Bandura's work in Chapter 7.

> ## stop...
> Which environmental factors do you feel may be more important for shaping personality? What kinds of personality difference between males and females have you observed? Are these differences genuine or a product of your culture? How do you know?
>
> *...and reflect*

Links to management · Alison Jones

Alison works with small and medium-sized enterprises and entrepreneurs to make them stand out from the competition and grow their businesses, clarifying strategy and creating effective content marketing, including print and ebooks. She also provides executive coaching and consulting services to the traditional publishing sector.

After an MA in English Language and Literature from Edinburgh University and an MBA from the Open University, Alison pioneered digital publishing over a 22-year career in publishing, most recently as Director of Innovation Strategy with Palgrave Macmillan. She set up Alison Jones Business Services and the Practical Inspiration Publishing imprint in 2014 to establish a new model: position, or brand, publishing. She is an associate lecturer with Oxford Brookes University, teaching on their MA in Publishing, and an affiliate lecturer with the University of Falmouth.

In the ebook click on the play button to watch Alison talking about self-esteem, and then answer the following question:

- What concrete steps can managers take to encourage talented women to take up leadership roles?

The phenomenological approach to personality

The most influential phenomenological theories, also known as humanistic theories, of personality are those of Abraham Maslow (1908–1970) and Carl Rogers (1902–1987). These theorists emphasize the positive, fulfilling experiences of life, and argue that how people perceive and interpret their social experiences forms their personality. Maslow believed that human motivation is based on a hierarchy of needs, and that understanding personality requires an understanding of this hierarchy of needs (Maslow, 1954). According to Maslow, personality is the expression of a basic human tendency towards growth and self-actualization. The innate drive for self-actualization – a person's realization of their true intellectual and emotional potential – is not specific to any particular culture. Maslow considered it to be a fundamental part of human nature: 'Man has a higher and transcendent nature, and this is part of his essence' (Maslow, 1964: xvi).

Like Maslow, Carl Rogers saw personality as the expression of a basic human tendency towards growth and self-actualization (Rogers, 1961). However, unlike Maslow, he did not view the development of personality in terms of satisfying a hierarchy of needs. Rogers argued that personality development centres on a person's self-concept, the part of social experience that a person identifies as 'I' or 'me'. He believed that people who accurately experience the self – with all its preferences, approval, love, respect and affection – are en route to self-actualization.

The key to forming a psychologically positive personality is to develop a positive self-concept or image of oneself. But how does a person do this? According to Rogers, people are happy if they feel that others are happy with them. Similarly, people are unhappy when others are dissatisfied or disappointed with them. People's feelings towards themselves depend significantly on what others think of them. From early childhood, we learn that there exist certain criteria or conditions that must be met before others give us positive regard. Rogers called these criteria 'conditions of worth'. In Rogers's view, rewards and punishment from others are important in personality development because they influence behaviour and shape self-perceptions. In short, personality is formed partly by the actualizing tendency and partly by others' evaluations (Bernstein, 2015).

The self and personality

In the conceptual framework shown in Figure 4.1, personality is the 'public face', that is, how the individual appears to others. As discussed briefly at the beginning of this chapter, the sociological concept of the self-concept or *self-identity* – how we view ourselves – offers an alternative explanation of individual differences in organizational behaviour. For sociologists, the processes of socialization and the environ of symbolic communities by which we identify ourselves or others (such as friendship groups or social clubs) has great relevance for understanding personality.

Anthony Giddens defines socialization as 'the process whereby the helpless infant becomes a self-aware, knowledge person, skilled in the way of the culture in which he or she is born' (Giddens, 2009: 284). Socialization is a very important part of early human development, but growing up also involves other processes. Gerald Handel (2006) argues that one of these processes is 'individuation' – 'the process of becoming an individual person' (p. 665). People are 'not carbon copies of their parents, nor are all members of society identical to one another' (p. 665). Individuation gives rise to another key sociological concept, that of 'self-identity'.

stop...

Before reading the next section, go back to Chapter 3 and read Simmel's contribution to symbolic interactionism. How does this sociological tradition help us to understand individual differences?

...and reflect

VISIT THE *ONLINE RESOURCE CENTRE* AT HTTPS://HE.PALGRAVE.COM/COMPANION/BRATTON-WORK-AND-ORGANIZATIONAL-BEHAVIOUR3/ FOR MAJOR IDEAS IN THE SOCIOLOGICAL STUDY OF SOCIALIZATION.

Since the self is a somewhat amorphous phenomenon, what do we mean when we talk about 'the self' and 'self-identity'? Richard Jenkins (2008: 49) defines 'the self' as:

> an individual's reflexive sense of her or his own particular identity, constituted vis-à-vis others in terms of similarity and difference, without which she or he wouldn't know who they are and hence wouldn't be able to act.

The importance of reflexive activities is also emphasized in Anthony Giddens' definition of 'self-identity'. He writes:

> The 'identity' of the self, in contrast to the self as a generic phenomenon, presumes reflexive awareness. It is what the individual is conscious 'of' in the term 'self-consciousness'. Self-identity ... is not something that is just given ... but something that has to be routinely created and sustained in the reflexive activities of the individual. (Giddens, 1991: 52)

Source: PhotoDisc/Getty Images

globalization & organization misbehaviour

Identity and instability in an uncertain economy

In Western cultures, when first getting to know someone, it is common practice to ask them what they do for work. Being able to connect a person to a particular profession can help us to identify that person in relation to the characteristics we associate with that line of work. For instance, we might imagine that someone working as a librarian might be shy or reserved, while a commodities broker might be assumed to be self-confident and assertive. Although such stereotypes often have little bearing on individuals' actual identities or personalities, we nonetheless persist in the notion that what someone does for work has something to say about who they are as a person. Likewise, many workers identify themselves in terms of the work they do and their social position in the workplace.

For workers in today's uncertain economy, the prospect of being made redundant generates stress not only about the lost income, but also about the threat of an unmooring of their personal identities. Psychologists specializing in organizational behaviour note that, for many workers, their sense of self is inseparable from the work they do and the social environment of the workplace. The inability to engage in those familiar practices can leave them feeling ungrounded and even depressed. In a *Financial Times* article (Jacobs, 2008) dealing with redundancy and depression, a former banker explains how an organizational culture that promotes hard work, high achievement and an 'alpha male' approach can position workers for a long fall should they be made redundant:

> Some think the world revolves around them, in good times and bad. When things are good they feel like masters of the universe, but when the bubble bursts they take it very hard. It can be devastating.

In such situations, workers can stake their sense of self almost entirely on their work and, more specifically, on their place within the structure of the organization. Being unseated from their position within the organization can be equated to losing the reference point from which they are able to make sense of the world and their place in it. According to London therapist Christine Martin, 'Redundancy demands existential questions alongside the financial worries' (Jacobs, 2008).

Anthropologist Dorothy Holland and her colleagues (Holland et al., 1998) describe identity as a sense of self that is actively and continually constructed, tested and refigured through daily social practices. They explain that these social practices take place in particular cultural realms that provide resources and structures which individuals can draw on to formulate personal identities that reproduce (or resist) those cultural realms. The importance of improvization, agency and creativity – within defined social worlds – is also central to the formation of identity.

Using Holland et al.'s approach to identity, we can consider workplace culture in the UK as a cultural realm that provides workers with a set of practices and social relations that they use to position themselves vis-à-vis their work tasks, relationships with colleagues and the world at large. Understanding the links between organizational culture, personal identity formation and economic stability (or instability) can help managers to provide appropriate support services to workers when redundancies are deemed necessary.

> **Stop!** Do you think it is a positive or a negative thing for workers to have identities closely entwined with – even dependent upon – their work? Would such close links between identity and work benefit or hinder the workplace? How might they benefit or hinder other areas of workers' lives?

Sources and further information

Holland, D., Lachicotte, W. Jr., Skinner, D. and Cain, C. (1998) *Identity and Agency in Cultural Worlds*, Cambridge, MA: Harvard University Press.

Jacobs, E. (2008) 'Redundancy and a depression', *Financial Times*, August 19. Available at: www.journalisted.com/article?id=763449 (accessed December 14, 2014).

Sheedy, B. (2005) 'All is not lost', *Management Today*, November/December. Available at: www.doningtongroup.com/UserFiles/Media/0905-allisnotlost-SB-AIMmag.pdf (accessed December 14, 2014).

Note: This feature was written by Gretchen Fox, Cultural Anthropologist and Impact Assessment Analyst, Fox Cultural Research, Canada.

---

looking-glass self: Cooley's term for the way in which a person's sense of self is derived from the perceptions of others

The classical social theorists identified the social processes that create, shape and sustain self-identity. A century ago, in 1902, sociologist Charles Horton Cooley, in his book *Human Nature and the Social Order*, introduced the term **looking-glass self** to mean a conception of self based largely on how we imagine we appear to others and imagined judgements likely to be made about that appearance.

Georg Simmel's most insightful observation in *The Philosophy of Money* (1900/2004) was that the individual is not an isolated observer of the physical world, but a participant in human society whose personality is formed through affiliation to and the interaction of many social groups: 'Just as the essence of the physical organism lies in the fact that it creates the unity of the life process out of the multitude of material parts, so a man's inner personal unity is based upon the interaction and connection of many elements and determinants' (1900/2004: 296).

Writing almost 30 years before the psychologist Carl Rogers, sociologist George Herbert Mead expounded a *process-relational theory* to explain how personality is formed through social interaction with other people. Mead believed that people form a personality by internalizing – or taking in – their locale. In Mead's theory, the self has two parts: the 'I' (the unsocialized self) and the 'me' (the socialized self). The 'I' is the spontaneous, incalculable, impulsive, unsocialized and creative aspect of the self. Mead emphasized the 'I' because it is a key source of creativity in the social process, an individual's values are located in the 'I', it holds something that all individuals seek – self-realization – and finally, as society develops, people become increasingly dominated by the 'I' and less by the 'me'.

Mead therefore rejected the notion that the self is inherited at birth and that personality is formed by biological inner impulses or drives, as argued by Sigmund Freud. According to Mead, the self develops only with social activity and social relationships, and if there is social isolation, as in the case of an isolated or feral child, the human body may develop but no self emerges.

Early formulations of the self have had an enduring influence on the sociology of the mind today. However, they are limited in that these Eurocentric self-theory scholars examined the phenomenon through their own cultural blindness. In contrast, W. E. B. Du Bois, America's pre-eminent African-American scholar, unmasked American racism and its effects on metropolitan black self-identity. In Du Bois' *The Souls of Black Folk* (1903/1994), the 'self' of African-American individuals is conceptualized as being divided – two souls, two thoughts, one body. This 'Two-ness' reflects the reality of dual lives and experiences: as an American, as a Negro, a 'double consciousness'. Du Bois' 'double self' is conceptually powerful: 'There is no universal self. There are only selves' (Bratton and Denham, 2014: 362). The metaphor 'different sides of the same coin' attempts to communicate the notion that, in each person, the internal (self) and external (person) cohabit in an ongoing process of self-identification (Jenkins, R., 2008).

The self is dialectically related to the human mind. The body is therefore not a self but only becomes a self when the mind has developed and engaged in reflexiveness. While Freud concentrated on the denial of the id's drives as the mechanism that generates the self's objective side, self-theorists drew attention to the source of the 'me' – how we become self-aware – by taking 'the role of the other'. People are interpretative creatures who must make sense of the world they live in. We learn to play different roles in this process. We are at different times children, students, friends, workers, parents and so on, and we do not behave in the same way in every situation. This process of role taking demonstrates that personality is a social product, and that 'group or collective action consists of aligning of individual actions, brought about by individuals' interpreting or taking into account each other's actions' (Tucker, 2002: 218).

Language is an important aspect of socialization and the development of the self. As children learn to understand words and later to use them, they simultaneously learn to categorize their experience and evaluate their own behaviour and that of others. For instance, the first words many English or German children say is 'No' or 'Nein'. The use of language is one way individuals emphatically gauge different cultural meanings in disparate social situations and act accordingly. The self is reflexive, in that a person can become the object of her or his thought and actions. Language is central to the development of individual identity, the self. Moreover, 'the dynamics of the self and others are open to complex layers of interpretation and reflexive distancing' (Ray, 1999: 160).

This reflexive process is invariably a social one, in which people form their sense of self in the context of family, peers and the mass media (Tucker, 2002). Thus, a person's personality will change across her or his life course as she or he participates in a community and interacts with different pervasive agents of socialization – family, school, peer group and mass media.

stop...

Make a list of the personality traits you think characterize you. Share your list with others who know you well, and ask what they think. To what extent, if at all, do you think your own personality originates from the interaction between you and your environment? Can you give examples?

...and reflect

Mead's concept of the 'I' and the 'me' should not be confused with Freud's concept of the id and superego. As others have pointed out, Freud believed that the id and superego were firmly embedded in the biological organism, whereas Mead rejected any biological element of the self. Furthermore, whereas the id and superego are locked in constant struggle, the 'I' and the 'me' work cooperatively.

interactionism: what people do when they are in one another's presence, for example in a work group or team

individualism: the extent to which a person values independence and personal uniqueness

Detractors argue that Mead's theory of personality is completely social, neglecting any biological element at all. Moreover, Mead's analysis of personality is rooted in the tradition of symbolic **interactionism**, a sociological perspective that focuses on the subjective meanings that people create through face-to-face communication in micro-level social settings. This was a perspective that resonated deeply in early US sociology and in the North American culture of **individualism**.

Source: © Royalty-Free/CORBIS

Why does she behave that way?

Many researchers who study work and personality stress the person–organization relationship. The assumption is that some personalities are a better 'fit' in particular organizational settings. Often, however, the question of person–organization fit is a complex one, and personality traits associated with highly skilled employees can sometimes be problematic.

One such personality trait is narcissism. A recent study suggests those with narcissistic personalities will have little to offer an organization:

> narcissists tend to lack empathy, engage in aggressive behavior and have self-serving motives ... narcissists should be especially unlikely to contribute positively to an organization's social and psychological climate by helping others, being courteous and a good sport, and going above and beyond the call of duty for the greater good. (Judge et al., 2006, p. 765)

Narcissism would appear to be a personality trait that employers would want to avoid at all costs. However, it is important to realize that personality is only one of several factors that contribute to an individual's behaviour. Consider the following scenario. Sharon Smith had recently been hired by a mid-sized hospital as a specialist nurse practitioner – a new role situated midway between the physician and the traditional nurse. Those employed in more traditional nursing roles at the hospital resented the fact Sharon had taken over some of the more interesting and challenging aspects of their work. Sharon showed little sympathy for their concerns: 'Nurses need to understand that their education does not prepare them to perform these kinds of procedure safely.' Sharon's interactions with physicians were also problematic. On one occasion, she clashed with Dr William Grant, a senior physician at the hospital. Dr Grant had questioned Sharon's recommendation that a particular patient could benefit from 'lifestyle changes'. Sharon responded without hesitation, 'There is no conclusive diagnosis for this patient, so why not proceed with the treatment the patient believes is best for him?' Later, in a conference with the ward manager, Sharon expressed her anger: 'Dr Grant has no right to question my judgement. In a

situation like this, lifestyle changes are a perfectly reasonable course of action.'

Clearly, the idea of personality could prove useful in this context. Recognizing that Sharon exhibited many of the characteristics of a narcissistic personality might help managers make sense of a situation that seems to be getting out of control. However, it is possible to view Sharon's behaviour in a more positive light. Perhaps Sharon's actions were the function of a conscientious rather than a narcissistic personality. Supporters of this more optimistic view might argue that Sharon was anxious to prove herself as an invaluable member of the healthcare team. But rather than working patiently to secure the trust and respect of her colleagues, she wanted immediate and unqualified validation. With the right 'coaching', however, Sharon could become aware of her personality traits, refine her social skills and make a genuine contribution to the hospital.

It is important to bear in mind that personalities are composed of a complex blend of 'traits' and, with appropriate mentoring, individuals may learn to manage various aspects of their personality. Issues of workplace design are also relevant here. When a new occupation is introduced into a well-established, hierarchical division of labour, conflicts are inevitable. Managers need to provide a clear rationale for change well in advance of the actual change. They must also create opportunities for dialogue among different members of the work team as the new occupation is integrated into established work roles and routines.

> **Stop!** What do you think? Is Sharon 'programmed' by her personality to be an endless source of conflict at the hospital? Are there steps that could be taken help her become a productive member of a relatively harmonious work team? What about the role of gender? Is the clash between Sharon and Dr Grant aggravated by the fact that healthcare workplaces have traditionally been dominated by men?

Sources and further information

Austin, E. and Deary, I. (2002) 'Personality dispositions', pp. 187–211 in R. Sternberg (ed.), *Why Smart People Can Be So Stupid*, New Haven, CT: Yale University Press.

Judge, T., LePine, J. and Rich, B. (2006) 'Loving yourself abundantly: relationship of the narcissistic personality to self- and other perceptions of workplace deviance, leadership and task and contextual performance', *Journal of Applied Psychology*, 91(4), pp. 762–76.

For more information on the nurse practitioner, see the *Journal for Nurse Practitioners*.

Note: This feature was written by David MacLennan, Assistant Professor, Thompson Rivers University, Canada.

Identity and personality

The term 'identity' is derived from the Latin root *idem,* implying sameness and continuity. Its precise meaning is contested, but here we first note that there are doubts about whether identity, in itself, actually *determines* human behaviour (Jenkins, R., 2008). As we have already said, identity can be viewed as a complex fusion of the interplay between the inner self and the outer communal culture and social interaction (Kellner, 1992; Mills and Tancred, 1992). For Peter Berger, identity is defined clearly to be 'socially bestowed, socially sustained and socially transformed' (1966: 98). The main sources of identity include social class, gender, disability, sexual orientation and race and ethnicity (see Figure 4.1). Like the concept of 'the self', identity is a complex multifaceted phenomenon. Richard Jenkins defines it in this way:

> Identity is the human capacity – rooted in language – to know 'who's who' (and hence 'what's what'). This involves knowing who we are, knowing who others are, them knowing who we are, us knowing who they think we are, and so on: a multidimensional classification or mapping of the human world and our place in it … It is a process – identification – not a 'thing'. It is not something that one can have, or not; it is something that one does. (Jenkins, 2008: 5)

Jenkins' central argument is that identity can only be understood as a process of 'being' or 'becoming'. The work of British postmodernist cultural theorist Stuart Hall offers a fluid, porous, multidimensional, post-colonial interpretation of this thesis:

> Identity is not only a story, a narrative which we tell ourselves about ourselves, it is stories which change with historical circumstances. And identity shifts with the way in which we think and hear them and experience them. Far from only coming from the still small point of truth inside us, identities actually come from outside, they are the way in which we are recognized and then come to step into the place of the recognitions which others give us. Without the others there is no self, there is no self-recognition. (Hall, 1995: 8)

personal identity: the ongoing process of self-development through which we construct a unique sense of ourselves and our relationship to the world around us

social identity: the perception of a 'sameness' or 'belongingness' to a human collective with common values, goals or experiences

According to Giddens and Sutton (2013) and Dickerson (2012), people can think of themselves in terms of **personal identity** (personal self) and **social identity** (collective self). Personal identity (or self-identity) refers to the ongoing process of self-development through which we construct a unique sense of ourselves and our relationship to the world around us. Identity is constructed through both social relations and discourses around, for example, gender (woman versus man), sexuality (straight versus gay) and race (black versus white). So, for example, ethnocultural factors may define identity. If I am Jewish, my religion may play a larger role in my identity than if I am agnostic, by virtue of the fact that Jewish people have been historically stigmatized. Identity theories draw upon the symbolic-interactionist tradition. But self-perception is highly fluid and context dependent (Dickerson, 2012).

The identity approach to understanding personality is located within a process-relational view of the subject or individual. According to this perspective, individuals are conceived as having emerging identities that are developed by, and also develop, the institutions and processes of modernity (Giddens, 1991). As children develop, they identify social roles, first within their family and later in the community. They also develop an understanding of status differences and the ways in which roles interact with class, gender, ethnicity and race to create complex patterns of social behaviour. This process of socialization is therefore affected by whether they are the son or daughter of a neurosurgeon or a hospital porter; whether they grow up in a two-parent or a single-parent household; whether they

plate 15 As children develop, they identify social roles, first within their family and later in the community. They also develop an understanding of status differences, and the ways in which roles interact with class, gender, ethnicity and race to create complex patterns of social behaviour.

Source: ©iStockphoto.com/bonnie jacobs.

grow up in London or Londonderry; whether they speak English or Hindi; and whether they worship at a mosque or a synagogue. As a result of socialization, most people acquire a set of attitudes, values, skills and behaviours that enable them to form and sustain relationships with others, work cooperatively with co-workers, avoid deviant behaviour and form a sense of self and identity.

The difference between personality and identity can be understood by answering the question 'Who am I?' You could respond to this question with a list of personality traits such as 'I am an introvert, thoughtful, and reliable in my work at the Body Shop, and I am a university student'. The second set of responses, unlike the first, makes no reference to personality traits, but portrays a sense of identity on the basis of how we are related to others (for example, partner, mother, employee or student), and as such is deeply contextualized within the multiple social relations within which we are embedded. Identity speaks to social relations, to a fluid process of 'becoming' rather than an end state of 'being'. Identity is not something we are born with: it is structured or shaped by, and also shapes, societal influences.

If self-identity sets people apart as distinct individuals, social identity is the perception of 'sameness' or 'belongingness', the ways in which individuals are the same or members of some human collective – signs that denote who, in a basic sense, that person *is* (Giddens and Sutton, 2013). Examples of social identities might include an occupation, for example, a lawyer, trade unionist, feminist, environmentalist, mother, Asian, disabled, Muslim and so forth. Social identities have a collective dimension and are based on a set of common values or goals or experiences. An individual can have multiple identities, some of which may be more dominant depending on a specific situation. What makes our identity dynamic, rather than static, is our capacity as self-conscious, self-reflexive human beings to constantly construct and reconstruct our identities.

Does identity matter? As noted, identity, per se, does not *determine* human behaviour in the workplace, but to identify someone implies evaluation and might be enough to influence how one worker treats another (Jenkins, R., 2008). The set of perceptions that we have about others and ourselves has the power to influence the employment relationship. The process of identification always lies within a web of relationships, whether between individuals or groups, which suggests that there are hierarchies of preference, of ambivalence, of hostility and of cooperation.

Individuals spend a significant amount of time in work organizations and, unsurprisingly, derive a sense of identity from their occupation or from the organization or a work team within the organization. When a person says, 'I love my work; I am my work', it connotes a sense of identity and its power to influence proactive behaviours. Each occupation, work group or organization will have a set of shared beliefs, values, norms and demands particular to that group. Organizational goals and processes, such as sustainable products and practices, job design or rewards, can shape the relative value that individuals attach to joining and retaining their membership of groups or organizations. Equally, the termination of the employment relationship can lead to a loss of identity.

The advocacy for a 'strong' organizational culture as a motivational strategy in a historical context of high-performance work systems underscores the importance of identity. Cultural control aims to have employees possess direct links to the values and goals of top managers in order to activate the emotion and create an identity that might elevate loyalty and commitment to the organization (see Chapter 17).

The power of social identity to define the status of an occupation or organization relative to others can pose significant challenges to managers. For example, individuals may avoid or disassociate from a low-status organization considered to be managed without due regard to social responsibility, environmental sustainability and ethical practices. Some new theories of motivation, such as self-concept theory and whole-self theory, have linked the psychological treatment of work motivation to the notion of identity or self (see Chapter 6). Studies suggest that an individual's coherent sense of identity or loss of identity is far more important than most traditional treatments of work motivation acknowledge (Fulop and Linstead, 2009; Herriot et al., 1998). The important concept of emotional intelligence (EI) and shared/distributed theories of leadership all highlight the importance of the self-concept and self-identity (see Chapters 5 and 12).

Applying personality theories in the workplace

While managers tend to think of diversity in terms of such factors as gender, ethnic origin and disability, the variety of personalities in the workplace is also important. The nomothetic view of personality dominates the management literature, partly because it enables management to render individuals 'knowable' and 'quantifiable' by identifying traits through personality testing (Townley, 1994). Personality attributes determine how people interact with other workers, whether they can work on their own without supervision, whether they are conscientious or just do the minimum to 'get by', how they respond to change, whether they behave ethically or unethically and much more (Lee and Klein, 2002). For these reasons and others, organizations have developed an array of human resource management techniques to identify personality differences and help them admit the 'right' people into the organization. Once staff have been selected, this knowledge will help to identify those with the personality traits said to be required of an effective leader (see Chapter 12).

John Holland (1985) best articulated the view that organizations should consider aligning the requirements of the job and the characteristics of the workplace with personality characteristics. In recent years, the awareness that organizations should focus on the degree of congruence between the individual and her or his work environment has expanded because of the need for workers to change and adapt to new work structures and employment relations. These include teamworking, individual-oriented performance-related compensation and the 'learning-oriented' organizational culture. Holland's personality–job fit model identifies six personality types – realistic, investigative, social, conventional, enterprising and artistic – each of which has a congruent occupational environment. Holland proposes that high congruence leads to satisfaction and the propensity to remain in that job or career. Table 4.3 defines these personality types and their personality attributes, and gives examples of congruent work environments.

Holland developed a model shaped like a hexagon that shows the relationships among occupational personality types, based on his Vocational Preference Inventory questionnaire, which contains 160 occupational titles. Respondents were asked to indicate which of the occupations they liked or disliked, and their answers were used to construct personality profiles. The closer two fields or orientations are in the hexagon, the more compatible they are. For example, the enterprising and social personality types are adjacent to each other in the hexagon model so, according to Holland's theory, individuals with both enterprising and social personalities have high compatibility (Figure 4.7).

Table 4.3 Holland's typology of personality and congruent work environments and occupations

Personality type	Traits	Workplace characteristics	Congruent occupations
Realistic	Practical, shy, persistent, conforming, stable	Prefers physical activities that require skill and coordination	Mechanical engineer, farmer
Investigative	Analytical, creative, independent, reserved	Work involves thinking and analysing	Mathematician, biologist, systems analyst
Social	Sociable, friendly, outgoing, cooperative	Work involves helping and developing others	Social worker, teacher, counsellor, nurse
Conventional	Dependable, orderly, self-disciplined	Work is unambiguous, rule-regulated, orderly	Accountant, banker, administrator
Enterprising	Confident, ambitious, assertive, energetic	Prefers leading others, verbal activities, result-oriented setting	Lawyer, entrepreneur, salesperson, financial planner/consultant
Artistic	Creative, disorderly, impulsive	Thrives on ambiguous and unstructured activities	Musician, architect, painter, designer

Source: Based on information from Holland (1985) and Greenhaus (1987)

There are three key points we should note about Holland's model:

- Intrinsic differences in personalities exist based on the restrictive Big Five personality model.
- Different types of occupation and work environment are better suited to certain personality types.
- Workers in workplaces and occupations congruent with their personality types should be more satisfied and more likely to remain with the organization than workers in incongruent occupations.

Research appears to strongly support the hexagonal model, but critics have pointed out that the model only incorporates the Big Five personality dimensions, and there are doubts whether the model can be generalized across cultures (Brown, 1987; Furnham, 1997; Young and Chen, 1999).

With the resurgent interest in recruiting the 'right' people for the 'new' work regimes, and the 'discovery' of the Big Five personality model, research examining the relationships between personality traits and job performance, personality and social integration, and the efficacy of personality measuring instruments, has flour-

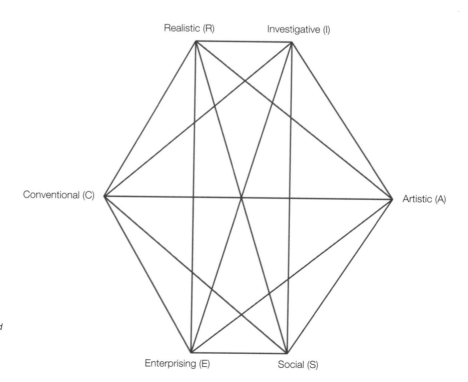

Figure 4.7 Holland's individual–occupation hexagonal model

Source: Holland, J. L., *Making Vocational Choices: A Theory of Vocational Personalities and Work Environments*, 2nd edition. © 1985. Reprinted by permission of Pearson Education, Inc., Upper Saddle River, NJ.

ished. According to Silvestor et al. (2014: 273), for example, a number of significant and 'logical' associations were identified between personality and self-rated performance. Underlying the research on the relationship between personality traits and job performance is the presumption that a proactive personality – defined as a disposition to take action to influence one's environment – promotes job performance (Thompson, 2005). This is achieved by building a network of social relationships within an organization in order to gain access to information, wield influence and effect positive change – a process referred to as **social capital**. In short, the social capital approach advocates a view that individual power within a work organization is predicated on developing a network of relationships, which in turn enhances job performance (Figure 4.8).

social capital: the value of relationships between people, embedded in network links that facilitate the trust and communication that are vital to overall organizational performance

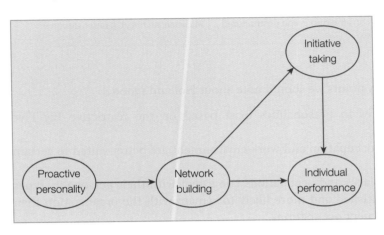

Figure 4.8 A model of proactive personality and individual job performance

What do proactive employees do? By definition, employees with a proactive personality are inclined to construct their own environment. Proactive individuals are likely to seek ways to build a network of contacts in the organization that is conducive to their own self-interest. Proactive types, therefore, tend to seek allies and build alliances with other co-workers to support personal initiatives, and actively strive to become friends with people who occupy positions of influence and power. Thompson's quantitative study found a direct positive relationship between a proactive personality, network building and individual performance, suggesting that 'network building may occupy a critical stage in the process by which proactive personality engenders performance' (Thompson, 2005: 1015).

Organizational behaviour theorists have long been interested in the connection between personality and innovative behaviours, and between personality and social integration. Henry Moon and his colleagues (2008) identified personality and procedural fairness within a work organization as antecedents to proactive behaviour or 'taking charge'. Interestingly, the results show that the antecedents to proactive behaviour are based more on concerns about others than on self-interest. This suggests that getting employees to take charge within the firm may be more about 'we' than it is about 'me'.

An important aspect of the current wave of interest in self-managed work teams is the cultural dimension. In addition to changing methods of job performance, work teams demand changes in workers' attitudes and behaviour (Procter and Mueller, 2000). Accordingly, organizational theorists are devoting increased attention to whether individuals with similar personalities make up more effective work teams.

The argument is that similar personalities might facilitate social integration among team members, increase the likelihood that co-workers will cooperate with each other, and foster trust between team leaders and members. Employment recruitment practices that create a homogeneous workforce of people with similar personalities and values may appear ideal in a team-based environment. As mentioned above, studies suggest that when employees hold similar personality characteristics, few rules, regulations and formal decision-making processes are needed to get work done. As a consequence, organizational leaders tend to choose people with personality traits similar to their own. The danger in top managers recruiting a workforce with similar personality traits is that homogeneity is a force potentially detrimental to change and long-term organizational survival in the face of external forces of change (Giberson et al., 2005).

stop...

If you were recruiting people to join you on an important work project, would you try to hire people with a personality profile similar to your own? If so, why? Can you think of any advantages and disadvantages of this approach?

...and reflect

Chapter summary

- Personality is the distinctive and relatively enduring pattern of thinking, feeling and acting that characterizes a person's response to her or his environment. In this chapter, we have examined a number of different approaches to personality. Each of these theories offers a view of how personality forms.

- Trait theorists try to identify and measure personality variables. However, they disagree concerning the number of traits needed to adequately describe personality. Raymond Cattell suggested a 16-factor model to capture personality dimensions, Eysenck offered a two-factor model, and McCrae and Costa suggested the Big Five factor model. Traits have not proved to be highly consistent across situations, and they also vary in consistency over time.

- We went on to examine Freud's psychoanalytic theory, which views personality as an energy system. He divided the personality into three structures: the id, the ego and the superego. According to Freud, the dynamics of personality involve a continuous struggle between the impulses of the id and the counterforces of the ego and superego.

- Sociocultural theorists emphasize the social context and the subjective experiences of the individual, and deal with perceptual and cognitive processes. We examined the theory of Albert Bandura, a leading social-cognitive theorist, who suggests that neither personal traits nor the social context alone determines personality. A key concept is reciprocal determinism, relating to two-way causal relations between personal characteristics, behaviour and the environment.

- Phenomenological theories, also known as humanistic theories, of personality were also examined. Influential humanist theorists such as Abraham Maslow and Carl Rogers emphasize the positive, fulfilling experiences of life, and argue that the way in which people perceive and interpret their social experiences forms their personality. Self-actualization is viewed as an innate positive force that leads people to realize their positive potential, if they are not thwarted by their social context.

- In addition, the chapter examined Mead's theory of personality and his key concept of the self. He argues that people develop a personality by internalizing – or taking in – their immediate environment. He rejected the notion that the self is inherited and that personality is the product of biological inner impulses or drives, as argued by Sigmund Freud. According to Mead, the self develops only with social activity and social relationships.

- Finally, the chapter has examined the role that an individual's self-identity (or identities) plays in influencing individual behaviour in the workplace. Whereas personality is based on a cluster of traits, some of which are believed to be genetic and evident from birth, self-identity is perceived as socially constructed: it is developed by, and also develops, the institutions and processes of modernity. Identity is fluid and multiple, and emerges through our relationships with others.

IN THE EBOOK ACCESS **WEB BASED ASSIGNMENTS** TO APPLY YOUR LEARNING.

Chapter review questions

1 What is personality, and why is the concept difficult to define?
2 What is meant by the trait theory of personality? Choose one trait theory, and explain the strengths and weaknesses of this approach to personality assessment.
3 Drawing on your knowledge of Freud's psychoanalytic theory, explain why the ego is sometimes referred to as the 'executive of the personality'. What do you understand by 'defence mechanism', and what relevance has this concept to understanding behaviour in the workplace?

4 Critically assess the importance of understanding the terms 'socialization' and 'self', and explain how attitudes and values are developed and changed.
5 How are the concepts of personality and self-identity different?
6 Why is it important for managers to understand the concept of self-concept?
7 Are the concepts of self-esteem and self-efficacy helpful in understanding self-limiting behaviour in women, for example, a low self-efficacy concerning leadership in organizations?

Further reading

Anderson, C., Spataro, S. and Flynn, F. (2008) 'Personality and organizational culture as determinants of influence', *Journal of Applied Psychology*, 93(3), pp. 702–10.

Bandura, A. (1997) *Self-efficacy: The Exercise of Control*, New York: Freeman.

Branden, N. (1998) *Self-esteem at Work: How Confident People Make Powerful Companies*, San Francisco, CA: Jossey-Bass.

Dickerson, A. and Taylor, M. A. (2000) 'Self-limiting behavior in women: self-esteem and self-efficacy as predictors', *Group and Organization Management*, June, pp. 191–210.

Giberson, T. R., Resick, C. and Dickson, M. (2005) 'Embedding leader characteristics: an examination of homogeneity of personality and values in organizations', *Journal of Applied Psychology*, 90(5), pp. 1002–10.

Hall, S. (1995) 'Negotiating Caribbean identities', *New Left Review*, January 1, pp. 3–14.

Institute of Personnel and Development (1997) *Key Facts: Psychological Testing*, London: IPD.

Jenkins, R. (2008) *Social Identity*, London: Routledge.

Moon, H., Kamdar, D., Mayer, D. and Takeuchi, R. (2008) 'Me or we? The role of personality and justice as other-centered antecedents to innovative citizenship behaviors within organizations', *Journal of Applied Psychology*, 93(1), pp. 84–94.

Onorato, R. S. and Turner, J. C. (2004) 'Fluidity in the self-concept:

the shift from personal to social identity', *European Journal of Social Psychology*, 34, pp. 257–78.

Silvestor, J., Wyatt, M., and Randell, R. (2014) 'Political personality, Machiavellianism, and political skill as predictors of performance', *Occupational and Organizational Psychology*, 87, pp. 258–79.

Sternberg, R. (1999) 'Survival of the fit test', *People Management*, 4(24), pp. 29–31.

Suff, R. (2012) Employers' use of psychometric testing in selection: 2012 XpertHR survey. *IRS Employment Review,* May 30.

Tucker, K. H. (2002) 'Freud, Simmel, and Mead: aesthetics, the unconscious, and the fluid self', pp. 193–227 in *Classical Social Theory*, Oxford: Blackwell.

Toplis, J., Dulewicz, V. and Fletcher, C. (2005) *Psychological Testing: A Manager's Guide*, (4th edn), London: Chartered Institute of Personnel and Development.

Wiggins, J. S. (ed.) (1996) *The Five-Factor Model of Personality: Theoretical Perspectives*, New York: Guilford Press.

Chapter case study: Identifying leaders in Nigeria

The setting

Nigeria is Africa's most populous country, with over 140 million people. In 2014, the United Nations Human Development Index, which measures a country's life expectancy, literacy, educational attainment and gross domestic product (GDP) per capita, ranked Nigeria 152 out of 187 countries. Devastating poverty affects 57 per cent of its population, and of the 57.2 million people who make up the labour force, over 10 per cent are unemployed. It struggles to cope with an inadequate infrastructure and underdeveloped human capital.

Nigeria's economy also has a detrimental overdependence on a capital-intensive oil sector. At the beginning of the twenty-first century, Nigeria's crude oil production was averaging around 2.2 million barrels per day and providing 20 per cent of GDP, 95 per cent of foreign exchange earnings and about 65 per cent of government revenues. Nigeria is Africa's top oil producer.

In recent years, with a new civilian government taking over from the former military rulers, there have been attempts to diversify the economy. The government has strived to attract foreign investors, citing locally available raw materials and the large national market as opportunities for long-term investments and joint ventures. However, these efforts have been stalled by foreign investors' fears of continued corruption, weak regulations, poor surveillance and inefficiencies.

For those willing to deal with such market impediments, investment advisors recommend that companies thoroughly educate themselves on local conditions and business practices, and establish a local presence. Researchers point out the importance of blending African work principles, such as an emphasis on work group activities and assigning leadership positions based on age (which is associated with experience and wisdom), into the workplace. Instead of front-line supervisors being held responsible for hiring, Nigerian workers expect and respect the involvement of senior managers in the process. Despite this knowledge, contrary foreign management methods still dominate human resource management practices in the multinational companies based in Nigeria. This has resulted in confusion, frustration and malaise among the Nigerian workforce.

The problem

A leading gas company in Europe, German-owned Lebenskraft is one of 200 multinational companies settled in Nigeria. In its over 80-year history, Lebenskraft has developed from a German regional distributor to an international gas company. As Germany has relatively few natural resources, it must import large quantities of energy, and the company has found ample supplies through its operations in Nigeria, where it first became established nearly a decade ago.

Since its arrival in Nigeria, Lebenskraft's middle- and upper-level positions have been filled by candidates who have been educated and have lived in Germany. As a way of broadening its choice of candidates, Lebenskraft's senior management has decided to consider employees from the Nigerian operations to fill a recent management vacancy.

The company has always used personality testing when assessing individuals for promotional opportunities as part of an overall succession plan. The test they normally use, Review, was developed in Germany and has been previously applied within that country with great success. For this latest management recruitment, it has been suggested that a previously used tailored job benchmark, identifying the desired characteristics for leadership roles, should be used. The test would then be applied to compare the abilities, interests and personality traits of multiple Nigerian candidates to the benchmark to identify the best candidate for the current vacancy.

The company has created the customized benchmark using the characteristics of assessed top performers in their German operations as well as current management input. They hope that by using their Nigerian employees' assessment results, in conjunction with the benchmark, they will successfully fill the management vacancy and perhaps create an effective local succession plan. However, since the personality testing has never been used outside Germany, the company is hesitant to rely on its results. The human resources department in the Nigerian operations has been given the task of making recommendations on the selection process before the local management are asked to proceed.

The task

As a member of the human resources department, prepare a short report including answers to the following questions:

- What advantages do you see in using the testing?

- What cultural aspects of Nigeria should be considered by the Lebenskraft management team when considering the use of the test's benchmark and in developing the selection process?

Sources and further information

Anakwe, U. P. (2002) 'Human resource management practices in Nigeria: challenges and insights', *International Journal of Human Resource Management*, 13(7), pp. 1042–59.

Cooper, D. and Robertson, I. (1995) 'Selection methods – psychometrics', Chapter 8 in *The Psychology of Personnel Selection*, London: Routledge.

Jackson, T. (2002) 'Reframing human resource management in Africa: a cross-cultural perspective', *International Journal of Human Resource Management*, 13(7), pp. 998–1018.

Note: This case study was written by Lori Rilkoff, Human Resources Director, City of Kamloops, BC, Canada.

IN THE EBOOK ACCESS AN **OB IN FILM** BOX THAT USES *AMERICAN BEAUTY* (1999) TO ILLUSTRATE HOW MULTIPLE FACTORS CAN IMPACT ON AN INDIVIDUAL'S BEHAVIOUR AND TO ACCESS **AN INTERACTIVE QUIZ** TO TEST YOUR UNDERSTANDING.

chapter 5
Perception and emotions

Chapter learning outcomes

After completing this chapter, you should be able to:

1 Understand the basic nature of human perception and its far-reaching influence on the nature of decision making, behaviour and relationships in organizations
2 Identify and define the elements of the process of perception, how they relate to each other, and why the sequence in which they occur affects how individuals view people and situations
3 Understand the nature of emotions and how our emotions affect, and are affected by, our perception of people and situations
4 Distinguish between positive and negative emotions and how they are judged
5 Define emotional intelligence and explain how it is relevant to organizational behaviour
6 Explain how perception is influenced by limitations on information-processing and by a person's existing knowledge and expectations, including those arising from their cultural background
7 Discuss how knowing about processes of perception can generate an insight into phenomena that are of particular significance in the workplace, such as human error, interpersonal conflict, stereotyping, performance expectations and intergroup relations

introduction

If one manager's idea of creativity (or enthusiasm, or intelligence) is their own personal view and different from another's, how can employees know for sure that their potential and performance at work are being assessed fairly? If it happened to be another manager making the judgment, would that person have viewed things differently and given a particular employee that job, or that promotion, rather than turning her or him down? If one manager's idea of a suitable candidate for a job is very particular to them and different from another's, how can applicants know for sure that they have not been rejected because of stereotyping? If candidate A is perceived to possess more emotional intelligence than candidate B, which person should be considered for a leadership position? It is these types of concern about the accuracy and consequences of individuals' perceptions that drive the use of systematic assessment procedures in many organizations.

Source: © Image Source

plate 16 How do you know if your own perception of these employees' enthusiasm is the same as someone else's? How can employees know their performance at work is being judged fairly in this case?

perception: the process of selecting, organizing and interpreting information in order to make sense of the world around us

Subjective, informal thought processes are used to make judgements about our own identity or that of others, and often much more, during the course of our day-to-day interactions. It is all those complicated thought processes that makes us human, rather than brilliant robots, capable of retaining vast amounts of information and making programmed decisions (Burkeman, 2015). Systematic, formal procedures are used to make judgements in personnel selection and performance appraisals, and structured systems are sometimes used to assess the strategic options and risks that organizations face. In order to minimize the reliance on what is 'in the head' of one individual when important decisions are made, formal procedures usually aim to include multiple viewpoints and to use concrete definitions of the criteria by which a person or situation is to be assessed (for instance, 'creativity is defined as the number of brand new ideas generated'). But why is it necessary to employ complicated assessment procedures? Can't we just train each individual manager to be more objective so that managers will all make the same judgements when faced with the same decision?

We show in this chapter how subjectivity in the way we perceive the world around us arises from the fundamental nature of the processes of human **perception**. It is not simply the result of lazy thinking; subjectivity is the normal state of affairs in human judgement because of the particular way our senses gather information from the world, and the way our brains go about making sense of that information.

This chapter aims to outline and discuss the psychological and sociological basis of perception: that is, what happens 'in the head' that leads us to perceive in particular ways who we are, singular *and* plural, who we are *seen* to be, and the situations in which we find ourselves. After introducing some examples of how individuals' perceptions can have unintended side-effects in organizational life, we explore the central features and processes of human perceptual systems that allow us to experience a seamless view of our world, through the use of cognitive efficiencies such as time- and energy-saving mental short cuts and the packaging of information for convenient retrieval.

In order to structure our discussion, the issues that arise from the workings of perception are grouped into two main themes: those relating to selective attention and those relating to the influence of existing knowledge. The discussion will emphasize the central importance of context, social interaction and the perceivers' background and characteristics in determining what is perceived.

The final three sections of the chapter each focus on an aspect of perception that has particular significance in the workplace. First, we shall see how perceptions have an important influence on individuals' future behaviour and motivation to pursue particular courses of action. We then look at the role of emotions in relation to perception and the concept of emotional intelligence (EI). Finally, the last section highlights the broader impact of individuals' perceptions on the social climate of organizations.

The topic of perception lies at the heart of the study of human experience and behaviour, whether it occurs inside or outside work organizations, because it is through our perception that we decide what the reality of the world is. The truth, however, is that perceptions, and therefore views of reality, are far more dependent on the perceiver than on what is actually 'out there'. The implication of this is that there is not one 'true' reality at any given moment waiting to be discovered, because what each of us believes to be the basic reality of the world around us is 'mostly convenient, internally generated fiction' (Ramachandran and Rogers-Ramachandran, 2005: 95). Based on our goals, experience and personal qualities, we each create and then act upon our own unique perceptual worlds. Crucially, this creative work is mostly automatic, so we tend to act confidently upon our perceptions while remaining blissfully unaware that there might be alternative ways of seeing things.

The topic of perception is particularly important in organizational behaviour because work organizations represent a real challenge to our perceptual abilities; to use Weick's words, they are inherently 'puzzling terrain' (Weick, 2001). So much of what occurs in organizations is both constantly changing and ambiguous, especially because workplaces are social settings, and interpreting other people's behaviour is rarely straightforward. Changing market conditions and competitors, workforce diversity, multiple communications in various media, organizational politics – all of these contribute to the complexity of what people must make sense out of when they go to work each day. Because *the way things are* in an organization is rarely indisputable, the particular perceptions formed by its members become important influences on the nature of individuals' behaviour and how they relate to each other, as well as on the nature and fate of the whole enterprise.

Take, for example, the role of employees' perceptions among a multigenerational workforce. Today's workplaces may house three generations – Baby Boomers, Generation X and Generation Y – and this diversity of perceptions can present a number of opportunities and challenges for managers. Mencl and Lester's (2014) research concerning the values that generations hold found that generations share more similarities than differences regarding the extent to which work factors are important. The main value differences related to career advancement opportunities, diversity and 'perceived' fulfilment by work (2014: 10).

Furthermore, the role of employees' perception is important in terms of the issue of fairness, as illustrated by a spate of so-called 'boss-nappings' in France in the Spring of 2009. As the downturn in the global economy took its toll on French businesses, French trade unions and workers reacted angrily to news of job losses at a time when they perceived that company executives were receiving large bonuses or generous early retirement packages. Employees at 3M, Scapa adhesives and Sony expressed their anger by taking the law into their own hands and holding senior company executives for ransom in their company offices overnight in an effort to force the companies to reconsider their positions. Large demonstrations were also held in the centre of Paris by employees of Total who were angry about the announcement of significant job losses just days after the company had announced the biggest annual profit in French corporate history (€13.9 billion).

These collective responses to perceived unfair treatment also serve to highlight the social dimension of human perception. Our perceptions do not just form in isolation and then remain in our heads. The way we view ourselves, others and the world around us shapes our behaviour, and our behaviour influences the perceptions and behaviour of others. Although this interdependence underlies many of our actions, the social dynamics of perception become more obvious in situations such as giving a presentation, conducting a negotiation or joining a new work team.

A good example of the social (and emotional) dynamics of perception is a lecturer giving a lecture to students. The lecturer may quickly lose confidence if he or she perceives signs from the audience that things are not going well. Now lacking confidence and feeling anxious, the lecturer becomes self-conscious, begins to speak far too quickly and forgets some of the key points. It is entirely possible that the lecturer has misread the earlier signs from the watching students – they may have been whispering to each other because they were actually very interested in the talk. But ironically, the lecturer's dive in confidence and collapse in performance may themselves create the negative audience perceptions the lecturer feared had occurred earlier. The point is that our perceptions are in part formed on the basis of information or cues picked up from the environment, to which we must then attach meaning. The way we interpret the situation will then shape what we do next, which will affect our environment and the cues we pick up after that, and so on and so on.

These examples all illustrate the significance of understanding the links between individuals' perceptions and their behaviour in the work context. The rest of the chapter will explore the nature and consequences of perception in detail.

The nature and process of perception

The basic features of perception

Before we explore the component processes involved in perception, it may be helpful to set the scene by highlighting some features that are inherent in the way we deal with the information that we receive from the world. These features seem to provide a good explanation for the phenomena highlighted in the introduction. Perception is selective, subjective and largely automatic rather than conscious.

To function in our day-to-day existence, we need to gain information about the world around us. This information is gained through our six bodily senses of sight, hearing, touch, smell, taste and proprioception (the sense of the position and movement of our own body). Having sensed something, we then endeavour to make sense of what we are seeing, hearing, touching, tasting, smelling and/or feeling. This process is not always simply a matter of information processing of the kind that is carried out by a computer, because we often experience an emotional reaction to the information we receive. This is most obvious when the primary information comes from our senses of smell or taste (certain odours and tastes provoking powerful feelings of disgust or nausea, for example), but, as our earlier example of 'boss-napping' illustrates, emotional feelings such as injustice and anger can also be triggered by information gained from any of our senses. We will return to the role of emotion in perception later in this chapter.

We usually feel very certain about what we experience, and this certainty is actually helpful and adaptive because it allows us to go about our daily lives without having to think about every single thing we encounter. Our surroundings often make perfect sense to us without any conscious effort. We seem to need this feeling of order, but we actually have to work hard to create it, because the environment is not nicely ordered and organized. For one thing, there is just too much information available from the external environment for our senses to take it all in, and, to make things more difficult, this information comes in the form of raw data such as light and sound waves. So the basic ingredients of our perceptions are highly ambiguous sensory stimuli, and it takes a lot of 'brain work' to sift, organize and interpret them.

It is only possible for us to deal with the continuous bombardment by sights and sounds, smells and sensations because we employ **selective attention**. An obvious example is being able to focus on a companion's conversation in a busy cafe despite

selective attention: the ability of someone to focus on only some of the sensory stimuli that are reaching them

a myriad of sensory distractions such as others talking and laughing, background music, clattering plates, icy draughts or an uncomfortable chair. But the target of attention is determined by factors inside the person as well as by what stands out in the immediate context or setting. Individuals' preoccupations, emotional states and motivations will cause them to focus their attention on specific aspects of people or situations. A professional salesperson meeting a client will probably be monitoring his or her speech and body language specifically for buying signals such as precise questions about the product. A manager who suspects an employee of time wasting may start particularly to notice whenever he or she is away from his or her desk, or talking to colleagues.

In this way, two perceivers can genuinely capture different aspects of the same situation through selective attention. We do not have unlimited capacity for taking in information, so focusing on some environmental cues necessarily means ignoring others. And because this process is automatic rather than conscious, we are usually not too aware that we have been selective. When it comes to perception, rather than acting as neutral receivers of signals, we select the part of the environment to which we want to attend by acting as 'motivated tacticians' (Fiske and Taylor, 1991). The motivation at any particular time may be to prioritize speed, such as when we scan information to 'get the gist of it'. We may perceive defensively, as when we 'block out' information that we do not want to receive, or we may be looking for specific types of information to support a particular theory, for example when we think someone is lying to us. The point is that our intentions and emotions colour our perceptions, playing a large part in determining what we draw from the environment.

Beyond selective attention, another central feature of perception is that the interpretation or meaning we attach to the external information we receive is strongly influenced by our existing knowledge: our ideas, experiences and backgrounds, including our ethnic and cultural origins. In other words, what we experience is subjective because others are unlikely to base their perceptions on exactly the same mix of motivations and prior knowledge. This principle applies to individuals who share cultural backgrounds, but culture-based assumptions will add an additional and powerful source of difference. So in the event that two individuals of a different nationality, for instance, did manage to attend to exactly the same aspects of a shared situation, their cultural differences would mean that they would probably still not share the same thoughts about the meaning and relevance of the information.

plate 17 It is estimated that 80 per cent of the information we perceive comes through our sense of sight. Even when someone is talking to us, we still rely heavily on a host of additional non-verbal, visual information when we attend to and interpret what is being said.

Source: © IStockphoto/Chris Schmidt

It is estimated that 80 per cent of the information we perceive comes through our sense of sight. Even when someone is talking to us, we still rely heavily on a host of additional non-verbal, visual information when we attend to and interpret what is being said. How we interpret much of this non-verbal communication is dependent on our cultural upbringing. Hand gestures offer a good example of this. Raising your hand and placing the tip of your index finger against the tip of your thumb so that the fingers form a circle is known as the 'ring gesture'. In English-speaking countries and in Indonesia, this gesture means 'everything is okay'. However, in France it can also mean zero or 'worthless', in Japan it can mean 'money', and in some Mediterranean countries it is used to infer that a man is homosexual. In Tunisia, the ring gesture means that the signaller feels extreme personal animosity towards you!

So existing knowledge, which includes culture-, gender-, race/ethnic- and age-related assumptions and expectations, as well as what we have learned and emotionally experienced in our lives, will influence how we interpret what we perceive. The key point is that existing factors specific to the perceiver will determine a large part of the picture that he or she creates from the available information. So individuals' perceptions are likely to differ in the meaning attached to the information, as well as in the information picked up from the environment in the first place.

IN THE EBOOK ACCESS THE CRITICAL INSIGHT ON 'THE DIFFERENT COMMUNICATION STYLES OF MANAGERS'.

The basic sequence of and key factors in perception that we have discussed so far are shown in Figure 5.1. Out of the bombardment of sensory stimuli, the perceiver selects some of the information for attention and processing. Based on their prior knowledge and current motivations, the perceiver then works out what the information means and responds accordingly. Once the person has responded in some way, her or his actions become part of the environment and so influence the person's own, and others', ongoing perceptions of what is happening.

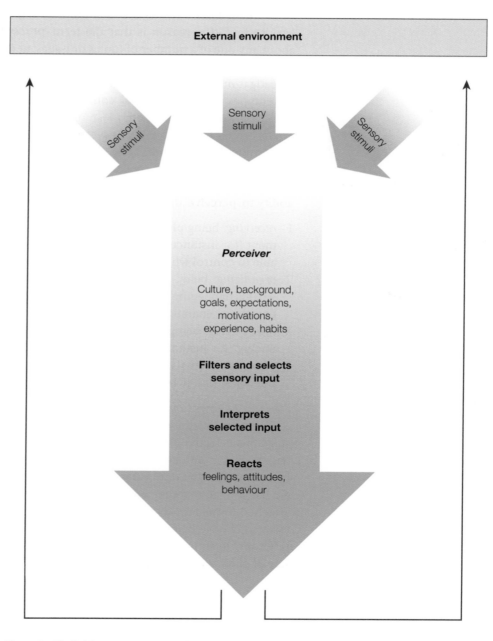

Figure 5.1 The link between perception, behaviour and the environment

In summary, human perception can be characterized as a process that is largely automatic, subjective and selective. Perception is not just something inside an individual: it has an emotional and a social dimension because perceptions affect our behaviour, which influences others. Our perceptions most certainly provide only a limited perspective, because there will almost always be another point of view – and, dangerously, we are often 'blind' to this simple fact. By understanding how perception works, we become more able to understand and effectively manage our own and others' behaviour in organizations. The next section will examine the nature of perceptual processes in more depth.

The process of perception

Perception is, then, a topic of significance in organizational behaviour because people's decision making and behaviour depend on how they interpret situations, and different interpretations are usually possible. But what exactly does the term 'perception' cover?

In truth, a definitive and comprehensive definition of human perception is not easy to find. The reason is that the term 'perception' may be used in discussions about any one of a number of topics or issues, at different levels of analysis, from the physiological to the social. Research studies about human perception range from investigations of the inner workings of the human eye, to the impact of individuals' stereotypes on cross-cultural communication. Nonetheless, it is still possible to identify a working definition.

According to the cognitive psychologists Eysenck and Keane, 'At the very least, perception depends upon basic physiological systems associated with each sensory modality, together with central brain processes which integrate and interpret the output from these physiological systems' (Eysenck and Keane, 2005: 43). So our ability to 'perceive' depends upon three things:

1 *receiving:* being physically able to attend to and receive signals from the environment (for instance, having intact sight, hearing, touch, taste and smell, and being able to control which of these we employ at a given moment)
2 *organizing:* being able to mentally organize and combine the signals (which is what is happening when we see and hear speech in perfect synchronization, or see objects as separate from their surroundings rather than as a mass of light patterns)
3 *interpreting:* being able to assign meaning or make sense of what we are experiencing (for instance, attaching personal significance to particular combinations of sensory signals, like knowing when we are in a conversation and we need to talk back, or a person is threatening us, or a bus is approaching).

Figure 5.2 shows how these three elements are connected to each other.

To return to the features of perception already introduced, it is at the *receiving* stage that selective attention 'happens', and at the *interpreting* stage that subjectivity has its major influence. The *organizing* stage of perception is perhaps the most mysterious, in that our brains somehow work out those combinations of signals that are likely to go together, and those which are just not feasible. In this way, speech is attached to the face that is making the right movements even when there are other faces to choose from. This is how we know when we are looking at an image that is 'wrong' in some way, such as when the perspective is manipulated so the relative size of objects is unusual.

The sequence of perception: top-down or bottom-up?

Although it is helpful to separate the three elements of perception from one another so that we may better understand them, in reality they do not occur separately or in sequence; instead, they overlap and sometimes even occur in parallel. In addition,

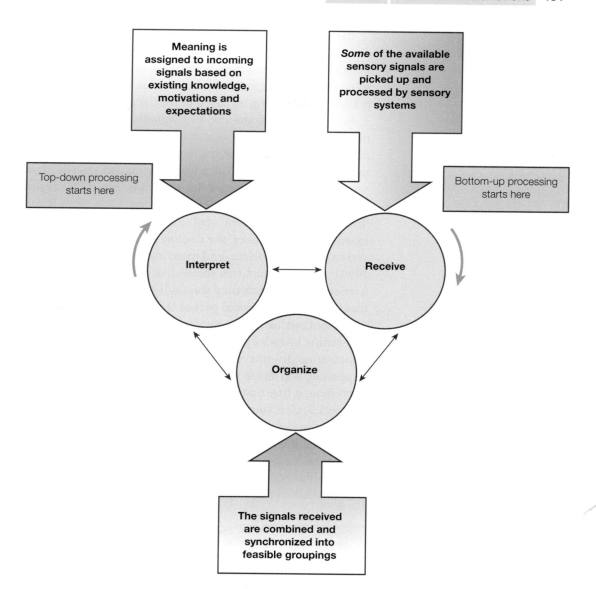

Figure 5.2 The elements and process of perception

all three stages can be, and often are, influenced by our emotional reactions and dispositions. As we have discussed, our perceptions are actually constructed in a process that combines external information with our existing ideas about the world. Rarely do we start from scratch by piecing together the external 'clues' one by one. While we are still receiving and organizing the external information, we are already attaching some meaning to what we are in the process of perceiving. That is how we 'know' what someone is about to do or say, and why we are frequently surprised. The weight of evidence suggests that we almost always engage these three processes simultaneously (Eysenck and Keane, 2005). Our relative reliance on external and existing information is, however, not fixed but will depend on the specific context.

When perception is led predominantly by gathering external sensory data and then working out what they mean, it is called 'bottom-up' or 'data-driven' information processing. When we think there may be consequences in getting it wrong, we are likely to rely more heavily on **bottom-up processing**. For instance, the requirement in most assessment centres that assessors explain and justify the ratings they award to candidates is thought to exert a 'press of accountability' (Tetlock, 1983). The need to justify their judgements publicly leads assessors to pay extra attention to all aspects of the candidates' behaviour.

bottom-up processing: perception led predominantly by gathering external sensory data and then working out what they mean

Rather than always ensuring accuracy, 'thinking too much' can actually hinder our attempts at sound judgement and decision making. If we try too hard to take in as much information as possible, it can interfere with our ability to focus on the most important aspects of the situation. If that happens, irrelevant pieces of information end up being included in the decision-making process.

Some studies of the use of magnetic resonance imaging (MRI) technology in medical diagnosis bear this out. MRI scanners offer doctors incredibly detailed images of the interior of the body. However, research suggests that these images may contain so much misleading information that the accuracy of a doctor's diagnosis can be badly affected. In one study, the spinal regions of 98 people with no back pain or back-related problems whatsoever were scanned by an MRI machine. The pictures were then sent to doctors without any other information. After examining the pictures, the doctors reported that two-thirds of the scans revealed serious spinal problems, and many recommended immediate surgery (Jensen et al., 1994). The MRI pictures showed so much information that the doctors found it harder to know what they should be looking at. In fact, the serious problems they diagnosed were a normal part of the ageing process.

In contrast to the 'bottom-up' approach, perception that is led predominantly by existing knowledge and expectations is called 'conceptually driven' or **top-down processing**. In this case, our working theory and expectations about what is happening will shape what we look for. We may fill in the scene from memory after perceiving a tiny number of cues that we think confirm our theory. Take a look at Figure 5.3. Can you see a black and white dog in this picture? If you can, you have just conformed to what psychologists called the 'law of closure', which states that if something is missing in an otherwise complete figure or object, we tend to try and complete it ('close the gaps') by adding additional information. In this case, our existing ideas of what a dog 'should' look like lead us to see a more complete picture of a dog than is actually there.

top-down processing: perception led predominantly by existing knowledge and expectations rather than by external sensory data

Figure 5.3 The law of closure

Researchers have found that we tend to rely on top-down processing in circumstances that are very familiar. For instance, Roth and Woods (1988) reported that novice operators in nuclear power plants relied heavily on feedback from monitoring the environment to guide their interventions – a bottom-up strategy. Experienced operators, by contrast, relied much more on their existing knowledge of the operating systems, making much less frequent checks of environmental information.

However, there is a danger of relying too much on existing knowledge. The danger is that changes in the environment that really require a response from us may simply go unnoticed. This can happen because we are focused on the picture of the situation that already exists in our heads, so we fail to perceive the signals telling us that the actual situation actually looks somewhat different from what we expected. When the cognitive task in question is making a judgement about someone or something, rather than maintaining a work system, we may never become aware of the failure to consider key bits of information. Sadly, there are no system alarms that go off when we judge people on their mistakes and forget about the things they did really well.

The dangers of 'thinking too little' (Highhouse, 2001) when making judgements have been well researched in the field of decision making (see Chapter 13). We have some **perceptual biases**, or automatic tendencies to attend to certain cues that do not necessarily support good judgements. The **primacy effect** is the term used to describe our tendency to pay too much attention to our first perceptions about someone. Although many people are aware of the power of first impressions, and try to avoid 'judging a book by its cover', it can be surprisingly difficult to change our initial perceptions. On the other hand, if we are not careful, we may be prone to the opposite bias, overemphasizing the last things we perceived about someone, which is called the '**recency effect**'.

Another general tendency in perceiving people is making broad-based assumptions about a person's qualities on the basis of one or a small number of observations, the so-called '**halo and horns effect**'. For instance, if an employee makes a mistake on one job task that is considered to be very important, it may bias a manager's overall perceptions, so that he or she assumes that the person is incompetent in every aspect of the job. It is always useful to guard against such biases in dealing with others, but it becomes particularly significant in the context of selection and appraisal interviewing, or indeed any situation at work where we are evaluating a person in order to make a decision with further consequences. It is for this reason that good design is so crucial in assessment procedures.

The key point about our use of perception strategies is that there is a trade-off or balance to be struck between avoiding the risk of holding inaccurate perceptions that comes with top-down processing, while at the same time minimizing the mental effort of perceiving everything from the bottom up.

Perceptual tricks, manipulations and illusions

The goal of human perception seems to be to make sense of the environment as quickly as possible, even if a bit of accuracy is sometimes lost along the way. As a result, it is quite easy to trick our brains to 'set off' these tendencies to seek meaning and certainty by using various common tricks and illusions. These tricks make it possible for us to get brief glimpses of some of the usually automatic, non-conscious, workings of our perceptual systems. Indeed, history suggests that having our senses duped endlessly amuses us. Magicians capitalize on our selective attention when they use sleight of hand in card tricks and disappearing acts. Ventriloquists amuse us because we cannot stop our brains organizing, or associating the ventriloquist's voice with the dummy's mouth movements, despite knowing

---

perceptual bias: an automatic tendency to attend to certain cues that do not necessarily support good judgements

primacy effect: a perceptual error in which we quickly form an opinion of people based on the first information we receive about them

recency effect: a perceptual error in which the most recent information dominates our perception of others

halo and horns effect: a perceptual error whereby our general impression of a person, usually based on one prominent characteristic, colours the perception of other characteristics of that person

---

stop...

Have you ever had a first impression of someone that was very different from how you think about them now?

...and reflect

Alison works with small and medium-sized enterprises and entrepreneurs to make them stand out from the competition and grow their businesses, clarifying strategy and creating effective content marketing, including print and ebooks. She also provides executive coaching and consulting services to the traditional publishing sector.

After an MA in English Language and Literature from Edinburgh University and an MBA from the Open University, Alison pioneered digital publishing over a 22-year career in publishing, most recently as Director of Innovation Strategy with Palgrave Macmillan. She set up Alison Jones Business Services and the Practical Inspiration Publishing imprint in 2014 to establish a new model: position, or brand, publishing. She is an associate lecturer with Oxford Brookes University, teaching on their MA in Publishing, and an affiliate lecturer with the University of Falmouth.

In the ebook click on the play button to watch Alison talking about perceptions in the workplace, and then answer the following question:

- What can managers do to counteract the influence of perceptions of personality on selection procedures?

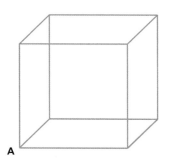

Figure 5.4 The Necker cube

the truth. There appears to be something pleasing for us about being perceptually confused, although – paradoxically – only for as long as we know it is happening.

Some 'serious' artists such as Salvador Dali and M. C. Escher have also produced work which plays with a feature of visual perception that means we can visually reverse the figure and the background of an image. So, in a painting such as *The Great Paranoiac* by Dali, it is possible to see the image as being made up of many small scenes, or to 'phase out' the detail and see one large image of a man's head, which is actually made up of the smaller images. The simplest demonstration of figure–ground reversal is the Necker cube (Figure 5.4). This is named after Louis Albert Necker, who discovered in 1832 that the perspective of the cube spontaneously changes if it is looked at continuously. So the front face becomes the back one, or, if you prefer, the corner marked A 'moves' from being at the front to being at the back of the cube. This is a demonstration of what is called 'multistability' in perception (Attneave, 1971). When there are multiple possible interpretations of something, and they are equally good or feasible, we will sometimes choose one, sometimes another, but never two at the same time.

VISIT THE *ONLINE RESOURCE CENTRE* AT HTTPS://HE.PALGRAVE.COM/COMPANION/BRATTON-WORK-AND-ORGANIZATIONAL-BEHAVIOUR3/ TO REVIEW A NUMBER OF CLASSIC VISUAL ILLUSIONS.

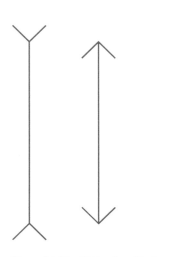

Figure 5.5 The Müller–Lyer illusion

Using the same principles as illusionists, perception researchers manipulate sensory inputs in a controlled way in order to explore how the elements of the perceptual process work and how they relate to each other. A simple and now classic experimental image, the Müller–Lyer illusion, is shown in Figure 5.5. The straight lines are actually the same length, but the placement of the arrowheads makes them appear to be different: the line on the left appears longer than the one on the right. Curiously, researchers have found that the Müller–Lyer illusion tricks our eyes but not our hands. There was no illusory effect when the lines were made into three-dimensional figures and people were asked to reach out and grab them between their thumb and index finger (Haart et al., 1999). In other words, in each case the study participants positioned their fingers at the right distance apart to grab the figures. The illusory effect also seems to depend to some extent on the perceiver's cultural background. When the illusion is depicted in the form of rectangular corners where walls intersect, people from cultures where the built environment does not include these angular features are less likely to perceive the lines as being of different lengths.

linguistic relativity: the theory that the language we speak has such a fundamental influence on the way we interpret the world that we think differently from those who speak a different language

plate 18 We know the fork is all in one piece, but our eyes deceive us.

perceptual set: describes what happens when we get stuck in a particular mode of perceiving and responding to things based on what has gone before

In fact, the exact relationship between culture, particularly language, and thought or cognition is the subject of much research and debate among psychologists. Followers of the theory of **linguistic relativity** argue that the language we speak has such a fundamental influence on the way we interpret the world that we actually think differently from those who speak a different language. There is a difference, for instance, between English and Nepalese speakers in the way that the relative position of two people or objects is described (Mishra et al., 2003). In English, the positions would be described egocentrically, in relation to one's own body (for example, *'He is on my left and she is on my right'*). In Nepalese, however, an environmentally centred description would be given instead (such as *'He is on the west side and she is on the east side'*).

The question that researchers have been trying to answer is whether such linguistic differences are linked to basic differences in the way in which people raised in different cultures select and interpret environmental information. The contrasting view to linguistic relativity is that language plays a much less fundamental role in perception and cognition. From this standpoint, it is our thoughts that come first, and we use the language available to us to express those thoughts. As is often the case in the social sciences, there seems to be good evidence to support both viewpoints. The 'compromise view', as explained by Bloom (2004), is that there are some universal perceptions and interpretations of the world that all people share, but that our native language, the symbolization of the conversation of gestures, shapes other distinctions in the meanings we attribute to what we experience (Jenkins, R., 2008).

The question of whether culture and language shape thought and perception clearly has important implications for our understanding of cross-cultural communication in organizations. Stated simply, the notion of linguistic relativity suggests that, for people attempting to live and work internationally, learning the language of the host country as an adult may not be enough to ensure that shared perceptions, understandings and ideas can be automatically developed with colleagues.

To focus on the context of organizational behaviour, not all of the perceptual tricks and illusions aimed at demonstrating the fundamental principles of perception, interesting as they are, can be applied directly to organizational life. One perceptual manipulation that has been used in a work context, however, is the old sales technique of the 'agreement staircase'. The technique involves making a series of requests to a customer that he or she is highly likely to agree to. The salesperson then immediately follows this with the main question – will the customer go ahead and buy? The idea is that the customer will instinctively say yes because he or she has fallen into the habit of doing so. Although this technique sounds a bit naive, it can work if executed subtly because we do develop what are known as **perceptual sets**.

A perceptual set describes what happens when we get stuck in a particular mode of perceiving and responding to things based on what has gone before. The same effect can occur if you read, for example, a list of French words followed by an English one. You will tend to pronounce the English word as if it were French – which can be stupidly amusing if it is a particularly unromantic word like 'cabbage'! These experiments and manipulations do raise an important point that needs to be included in our exploration of perception. They demonstrate the significant effect of context on how we interpret even apparently straightforward information that we receive from the environment. When that information becomes more complex, as in social encounters, that point becomes even more significant.

The processing limitations underlying selective attention

We have already established that we attend selectively to environmental information. One central reason for selective attention is that there are actually physiological limits on how much information we can take in at once, as well as on how much mental work or processing we can do in a given time frame. In other words, there are capacity constraints on two of the three elements of the perception process – receiving and organizing. Perception researchers have sought to understand how much of the different kinds of sensory information we can absorb, as well as what gets priority under different conditions.

An example of research in this area is the study of what is called 'dual-task interference', which is when the attentional demands of one perceptual task limit our ability to do another at the same time. Put very simply, it is easier for us to do two tasks simultaneously if they involve different kinds of information input and require different kinds of response. Doing two computer screen monitoring tasks, each requiring a key stroke response, is more difficult than doing one visual and one auditory monitoring task simultaneously, for instance. As an example of the practical significance of this kind of knowledge, consider the controversy about the use of mobile cell phones while driving. This issue is of very real practical concern to the large number of people whose work involves driving, as well as to their employers.

The legal case for prohibiting the use of mobile phones when driving is that the behaviour can cause road accidents because holding a phone and dialling numbers distracts motorists' attention and interferes with their ability to operate the vehicle's controls. In fact, two separate studies provide evidence that the interference with driving arises not from operating the phone, but rather from the amount of attention taken up by having a conversation. Whereas a passenger is aware of what is happening and will stop talking if the driver needs to act or concentrate, a person on the end of the phone cannot see what is happening in the car or on the road, so the conversation becomes more demanding for the driver. The findings reported in the studies included the statistic that drivers using mobile phones were four times more likely to be in an accident (Redelmeier and Tibshirani, 1997), had slower reactions and were two times more likely to miss traffic signals than those who were not on the phone (Strayer and Johnston, 2001).

VISIT THE *ONLINE RESOURCE CENTRE* AT HTTPS://HE.PALGRAVE.COM/COMPANION/BRATTON-WORK-AND-ORGANIZATIONAL-BEHAVIOUR3/ TO VIEW VIDEOS ABOUT INATTENTIONAL BLINDNESS AND CHANGE BLINDNESS.

Other kinds of research study concerned with the limitations of information processing have identified two perceptual phenomena called 'change blindness' and 'inattentional blindness'. In these experiments, researchers test the focus of people's attention during various 'realistic' encounters by either changing the situation in some way or introducing something unexpected and then finding out whether the manipulation has been spotted. Change blindness refers to the fact that we simply do not seem to notice even large or obvious changes to things if they are not central to our concerns. In one experiment, somewhat reminiscent of a comedy sketch, members of the public who were giving directions to a researcher failed to spot that they were talking to a different person after two men carrying a door had walked in between them (Simons and Levin, 1998)!

Another amusing experiment in the same vein, conducted by Simons and Chabris (1999), involved a man in a gorilla suit. Study participants were asked to watch a group of people passing a basketball between them and to count the number of passes that were made in a given time period. Amazingly, around 50 per cent of participants did not even see the man in the gorilla suit who walked among the ball players while they were counting the passes. This phenomenon has been termed 'inattentional blindness', because it seems we do not perceive even unusual or obvious things when we have focused our attention elsewhere. We appear to be very effective in automatically filtering out information that is not needed for the current task or goal. This propensity to reduce mental workload led to the characterization of human perceivers as 'cognitive misers' (Nisbett and Ross, 1980), using various short cuts to deal with limited processing capacity.

The influence of existing knowledge in perception

So far we have emphasized the idea of perceivers as 'cognitive misers', seeking the quickest, most energy-efficient route to decisive perceptions with the use of a bit of external information and a lot of expectation and existing knowledge. Because existing knowledge is so influential, questions about what we store and how we store it are important in understanding perception. How we store knowledge matters because it affects how quickly and how often we are able to bring specific thoughts to mind in a particular circumstance. Our brains have the same basic architecture, so all individuals will go through the same process of perception – receiving, organizing and interpreting information in some order. But similarities and differences in the content of the mental models held, and when they are used as a basis for perception, will help to determine the degree to which two or more people will form overlapping views of the same experience.

The reason we are able to bring information to mind so quickly is because our knowledge is organized into packages of related content. This means that it is necessary to stimulate only one piece of information for all the related knowledge that is held with it to come to mind. These knowledge packages are ready-made 'mental models' or simplified representations of the world, which provide the frameworks and theories against which we then 'test' and place incoming data. Cognitive psychologists call these mental models '**schemas**', or 'schemata' to be more accurate. A schema can be described as:

schema: a set of interrelated mental processes that enable us to make sense of something on the basis of limited information

> a set of interrelated cognitions (for example, thoughts, beliefs, attitudes) that allows us quickly to make sense of a person, situation, event, place and so forth on the basis of limited information. Certain cues activate a schema, which then fills in missing details. (Hogg and Vaughan, 2004: 48)

Individuals have a large number of schemata, each of which will contain more or less information depending on how much exposure they have had to the phenomenon in question. Our schemata will include those for people (such as a close friend or your mother), for situations (such as a job interview or eating at a restaurant) and for roles (like managing director or student). Schemata about people, roles and places we have not experienced may contain very general, simplified information. For instance, we may hold snapshot, idealized images of exotic countries we have not yet visited, and also associate those images with particular moods, feelings and personal goals. Even without having been there or read anything about it, a place like Zanzibar may, for someone from Northern Europe, conjure up images of golden beaches and sun-speckled blue seas that stimulate emotional feelings of warmth and relaxation, along with thoughts about winning the national lottery! By contrast, self-schemata, those which contain our thoughts and feelings about ourselves, will be both numerous and complex, and will include much more detailed information.

Schemata are based on our previous knowledge of and expectations about the world gained through the perceptual processes of receiving, organizing and interpreting information. Figure 5.6 shows how our schemata are activated and become progressively more accurate as they interact with the world. In the top-down processing mode, when perception begins with a clear theory or expectation, relevant schemata have already been activated and drive attention selectively towards external stimuli or cues that match or confirm the mental model in use. If I expect my boss to be angry, I will be selectively looking for signs of anger. So in the event that he or she smiles welcomingly at me, I might consider the possibility that I am

stop...

Can you map the mental associations that you make in relation to some familiar roles, situations and people, including yourself?

...and reflect

seeing sarcasm in action, and look for other signs of anger rather than assume that my theory was wrong.

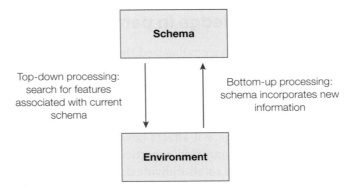

Figure 5.6 The schema activation process

When people perceive in bottom-up mode, it is, as the diagram indicates, the cues that are noticed in the environment which drive the process. If I am going to see my boss and have no idea what mood he or she is in, I will start with the smile I see and build a theory based on all the signals I am getting. We tend to use distinctive and easily detected features such as a person's physical appearance as the cues for choosing the right schemata (Hogg and Vaughan, 2004). The stimuli that grab our attention, those which are most salient, are received and organized, and these salient cues activate relevant schemata. The organizational element of this process includes the basic categorization of the object, person or situation in question into a class or type before any meaning is attached. As an example, some 'person' categories might be police woman, elderly foreign man or trendy young woman. This categorization process then determines which schema will be activated, and in turn how the perceiver will evaluate and respond to the encounter.

It is quite difficult to gain any mental control over the process of schema activation because it is so automatic. The associations between environmental cues, categories and schemata are not easily broken once they have been formed. In fact, you might have had personal experience of the research finding that trying to stop yourself having a particular thought actually has the opposite effect. It appears that we suffer 'post-suppression rebound' when we try to block thoughts from our heads (Macrae et al., 1994). The effect has been found in experiments where people were asked, and failed, to suppress thoughts of white bears, sex and past romantic relationships, among other things.

One explanation for this effect is that, in order to suppress thoughts, we first have to detect them and then replace them with an alternative. Whereas the 'ironic monitoring process' that scans our thoughts to check for 'forbidden' content is automatic, the replacement process is not automatic, and takes mental effort. So when we have a lot to think about and the amount of mental processing capacity available to us is diminished, the replacement process breaks down, but the monitoring process continues, making the unwanted thoughts more rather than less accessible to conscious awareness.

Like most aspects of perception, the activation of schemata is not a neutral process. For each person, some schemata are more easily accessible than others as a result of the individual's previous experiences, emotional state, personality characteristics and self-identity (see Chapter 4). These more accessible schemata will then be brought to mind and used more often, making them even more easily retrieved as time goes on. In this way, we develop habitual tendencies to perceive the world in particular ways. When an individual frequently uses certain schemata, these are said to be 'chronically accessible schemata'. An expatriate for instance, accustomed to living and working within different nations, may be prone to make sense of social misunderstandings in terms of cultural differences rather than the personality of the other person involved. An extrovert may interpret a wide range of situations as opportunities for social contact, as anyone cornered on a long journey with one will testify!

The use and misuse of perceptual cues

Differences in the accessibility and use of schemata also mean that some environmental cues will be routinely more salient for some people than others. This is because schemata drive the selectivity in our attention, and lead us to notice what we expect or hope to see. In the last section, we gave the example of physical appearance as a cue for activating schemata. However, there is evidence that some aspects of physical appearance can trigger the kinds of perceptual bias we discussed earlier in the chapter. For example, research has shown that taller people are often perceived as more authoritative and more physically attractive than people of below average height. Indeed, in 2007 a survey found that 58 per cent of all CEOs of the Fortune 500 companies were over 462 cm (6 feet 2 inches) tall, whereas only 4 per cent of adult US males are this tall (Gladwell, 2005). In addition, an analysis of 8590 people found a significant correlation between height and income (Judge and Cable, 2004). It would seem that people receive higher evaluations and higher pay even when the job involved has nothing whatsoever to do with height. This is a good example of the 'halo effect' in action.

The fact that people routinely make judgements about others based on such cues has motivated many people to attempt to manage the way they are perceived by others. Indeed, the research just described suggests that if you are of average height, your career prospects may be improved by the simple expedient of wearing shoes with higher heels. In fact, as individuals, we happen to be very good at influencing what others think of us, and seek to do so much of the time. **Impression management** (IM) is 'the process whereby people seek to control or influence the impressions that others form' (Rosenfeld et al., 2002). We are motivated to manage the way we are perceived in order to make real the image of ourselves we prefer, and to exert some control over how others respond to us.

Presenting the best possible picture of ourselves to others requires us to do two things: enhance our positive attributes, and minimize the attributes that might be perceived negatively. Self-promotion techniques such as describing our actions or qualities in a selective and favourable way, as well as non-verbal behaviour such as eye contact and walking and dressing in a certain style, can serve to enhance the positive in a given situation. Techniques such as providing excuses and justifications for less desirable facts about us serve to meet the goal of minimizing negative aspects. Further IM behaviours, such as flattery and agreement, are directed towards the other people involved, but these still serve to create a particular image of the actor.

Relating these techniques to what we know about perceptual processes, we can describe IM as the way in which individuals seek to actively direct others' selective attention towards the cues that will stimulate the desired interpretation. For example, by wearing a smart business suit and walking into an interview room assertively, we seek to stimulate a 'professional, confident applicant' schema in the mind of the interviewer. Actually, we are not always even aware we are managing our image, but when we know we are being evaluated, as in the case of a job interview, the process becomes more of a conscious effort.

The workplace presents many evaluative situations, both formal and informal, which makes IM an important concept in organizational behaviour. The significance of self-presentational techniques and their effects are perhaps most obvious in the formal setting of personnel selection and appraisal procedures. However,

impression management: the process of trying to control or influence the impressions of oneself that other people form

given that the point of paid work is to perform a specified role and set of tasks, workers' performance and behaviour will often be under a good deal of scrutiny from their peers, superiors and employees on an ongoing basis, which will motivate positive self-presentation.

One concern is that some people are just better at using IM techniques, so will be perceived more favourably than those with equal or greater talents who are less skilful or less motivated in their self-presentation. This is a key concern in relation to the accuracy and fairness of decisions about people at work and the opportunities that are, as a result, made available to them. In one study, women managers were less willing than male colleagues to use IM behaviours such as networking, self-promotion and ingratiation to get ahead in their organizations, preferring instead to rely on doing an excellent job (Singh et al., 2002). The difficulty with the women's approach is that promotion decisions are affected by seniors' *perceptions* of potential and promotability, as well as actual by performance. Because male managers tend to be more accepting of the need to 'play politics' to secure promotion, they are more willing to actively manage their image with their seniors, so may have an advantage over women when it comes to promotion.

IM is not restricted to individual behaviour. Organizations also try to influence the way in which people perceive them. Corporate advertisements in the mass media are an obvious example of this, but researchers have discovered that many companies employ IM techniques in their design of annual reports to shareholders, particularly in the design of graphs showing financial data. One of the most commonly used types of IM technique in financial graph design is called 'proportionality measurement distortion'. A basic principle of graph design is that the physical measurements of the graph should be in direct proportion to the numerical values displayed on the graph – for example, if sales have doubled in one year, the length of the bar representing current sales should be twice as long as the bar representing sales a year earlier. Unfortunately, not all company reports follow this principle, and empirical evidence reveals that annual reports of companies in the USA, Canada, the UK, France, Australia and Hong Kong frequently contain graphs that distort financial information in this way (Beattie and Jones, 2000). Researchers have found that such distortion in measurement tends to overemphasize the growth in sales and income, and to underemphasize losses. In other words, the data are presented in such a way that they reinforce a favourable impression of the company's annual performance. Such an IM technique can be effective, as experimental studies have revealed that people were significantly more likely to invest in companies with low growth rates when the graphs of their performance were inaccurately drawn in this way than when the graphs were accurately drawn (Arunachalam et al., 2002).

IN THE EBOOK ACCESS THE CRITICAL INSIGHT ON 'GLOBALIZATION, IDENTITY AND EMOTION'.

The studies discussed above serve to highlight the controversial and ambiguous nature of IM behaviour. The line between simply highlighting one's best points and 'false advertising' is very difficult to determine, and each of us will have a different view about how far it is acceptable to 'manage' others' perceptions. Such controversy also surrounds the IM behaviours that management stipulate as a contractual requirement of employees' behaviour. In some organizations, the desire to create a favourable impression leads management to require some employees, especially those who regularly engage in face-to-face contact with customers, to carefully manage their emotional behaviours. In Hochschild's (1983) influential sociological study, she calls this behaviour *emotional management* – the management of employees who are paid to adjust their emotions to the needs of the customer and the requirement of the work situation.

Source: Image Source/
Christopher Robbins

Smile to save the company

In the service sector, paid work involving direct contact with customers requires workers to provide more than just physical labour; it also requires them to manage their emotions in order to create a publicly observable facial display.

Faced with depleted profits, Air Canada (the country's largest carrier) vowed to restore competitive advantage by placing a renewed focus on customer service and by encouraging their cabin crew to display a smile. The aim was to follow the lead set by low-cost carrier WestJet, which had long prided itself on courteous staff. In an internal message to Air Canada staff, the company's CEO Montie Brewer wrote, 'While Air Canada has the lead in hard attributes, it's up to each and every one of us to work together to be sure that we're also out in front in the soft attributes such as a ready smile, eagerness to help customers and simply perform jobs well' (Brewer, 2008).

Arlie Hochschild (1983) has called this aspect of paid labour 'emotional labour'. Emotions are strong feelings that individuals express and experience, such as anger, love, joy and friendship. For front-line service workers, such as flight attendants, she argues that the emotion accompanying the service is part of the service itself. Moreover, this service must be delivered not only with a smile, but also, in an emergency, with reassurance. She quotes a flight attendant:

> Even though I'm a very honest person, I have learned not to allow my face to mirror my alarm or my fright. I feel very

protective of my passengers. Above all, I don't want them to be frightened. If we were going down, if we were going to make a ditching in the water, the chances of our survival are slim, even though we [the flight attendants] know exactly what to do. But I think I would probably – and I think I can say this for most of my fellow flight attendants – be able to keep them from being too worried about it. (p. 107)

For front-line service workers, the service cannot be separated from the mode of delivery. Hochschild's pioneering work emphasized that emotions are social and can be symbols that are widely recognized and form part of the way in which individuals manage and express themselves in social interaction. As social actors, workers' ability to manage emotions is based on their expectations of others and the expectations of others towards them. In understanding organizational behaviour, emotions become part of the social self and are one means that we use to interpret stimuli and develop an appropriate response.

Stop! Can you identify occupations where emotional labour might apply? How important is emotional labour in organizations?

Sources and further information
Ashforth, B. and Humphrey, R. (1993) 'Emotional labour and authenticity: views from service agents', pp. 184–203 in S. Fineman (ed.), *Emotion in Organizations* (2nd edn), London: Sage.
Brewer, M. (2008) *Globe and Mail*, November 11, p. B1.
Hochschild, A. (1983) *The Managed Heart: Commercialization of Human Feeling*, Berkeley, CA: University of California Press.
Morris, J. A. and Feldman, D. C. (1996) 'The dimensions, antecedents and consequences of emotional labour', *Academy of Management Review*, 21(4), pp. 986–1010.

Note: This feature was written by the author, John Bratton.

Hochschild conducted research to explore how attendants on board commercial passenger aircraft are trained to manage their 'real' emotions in order to present a pleasant, smiling demeanour to passengers regardless of how afraid, tired, irritated or angered they may actually feel. From the passengers' perspective, such a demeanour is perceived as pleasant and can enhance their enjoyment of the flight (and the likelihood of flying with that particular airline again). However, looking at it from the employees' perspective, Hochschild argued that such behaviour represents a distortion of their feelings of self-esteem and self-identity.

The stability of schemata

Schemata develop over time through learning and experience, and, once formed, can be remarkably resistant to significant change. Although we add complexity to our mental models as we experience new examples of a particular phenomenon, the wholesale revision of a schema is less likely. This is because a schema acts as a lens through which relevant new information is interpreted. Data that are inconsistent with what we 'know' to be the case are just reinterpreted so that they do not challenge our existing views. As numerous recent reality television shows demonstrate, if you strongly believe yourself to be a very promising singing talent, even the most uncompromising feedback to the contrary can be easily discounted and fully explained by the nasty personality of the judge.

Some failures to take on board feedback and change mental models do, however, have more serious consequences than wounded pride. A serious fire in 1949 in the USA called the Mann Gulch disaster claimed many lives despite the fact that skilled fire-fighters were in attendance (Weick, 2001). A central point to come from the analysis of the incident pointed to the failure of the fire crew to acknowledge quickly enough that this was not the type of fire they thought it was. As a result, the men did not respond appropriately to the situation they were actually in because they reinterpreted discrepant information about what they were experiencing and continued to respond according to the routine for the wrong type of fire. Tragically, some of the men could have kept their lives if they had listened seriously to one of their colleagues, who was engaging in bottom-up processing and understood the need for different behaviour.

Most of what happens inside organizations is not a life-and-death matter, of course, but it does nonetheless affect people's livelihoods and well-being. The consequences of senior managers failing to adjust their schemata about the organization's competition and strategy quickly enough in response to new information have been a topic of interest to researchers. For instance, Hodgkinson (1997) investigated UK estate agents' (realtors') perceptions of the competitive environment in the industry just before a recession hit the property market and again once the slump was established. The estate agents demonstrated 'cognitive inertia'. Their perceptions of the environment in which they were operating remained stable even though there was clear evidence of a downturn in the market. In other words, the estate agents were overly dependent on their schemata of the situation, failing to monitor and interpret environmental cues appropriately. As a consequence, their ability to respond effectively to the real threat to the organizations' viability that was posed by the downturn was seriously compromised.

Apart from demonstrating the stability of schemata, this study also illustrates that schemata are not always specific to an individual but can be shared between groups of people. In this case, the estate agents' shared perceptions were a result of similar work roles and industry context. Broad similarities between people, such as gender, ethnicity, national culture and educational background, can also increase the chances that there will be some similarity in their perceptions about some things. A study found that two people randomly paired are likely to share only about 10 per cent of their chronic mental constructs, that is, their stable knowledge (Bargh et al., 1988). However, people who live or work together are not random pairings; they will share some common roles, backgrounds or experiences. Stereotypes are a class of schema that appear to be shared between people, and are of particular consequence in organizational life because of their effects on perceptions of, and subsequent behaviour towards, individuals.

stereotyping: the process of assigning traits to people based on their membership of a social category

Sociologists view **stereotyping** as an important dimension of classification and identification (Jenkins, R., 2008). Social psychologists consider stereotypes to be a form of schema containing generalized ideas about the qualities and characteristics of individuals within particular groups (Hogg and Vaughan, 2004) – for example that people with financial worries make motivated salespeople, that stock market traders are usually privately educated men in their 20s and 30s, that Chinese men and women are the best mathematicians, and that taller people are more authoritative. These are all examples of stereotypical beliefs about groups of people because they make an assumption that the characteristics in question will be true of all or most of the individuals in the category. Not all stereotypes are negative or unflattering, of course. But when assumptions about certain groups are automatically applied to individuals in the work context, unfair, potentially discriminatory and probably ineffective judgements and decisions can result.

A case in point is the issue of age discrimination on the part of employers. In countries where this is prevalent, the exclusion of skilled and capable older workers from the workforce based on negative stereotypes of their potential to contribute is laying to waste a sizeable portion of that nation's available labour. As well as denying opportunities and income to the older workers, this exclusion of capable individuals based on non-performance-related characteristics is making it harder for organizations to recruit enough people, leading to reduced performance and profitability.

It is also known that people do not perform as well as they are able when they feel they are being stereotyped (Steele et al., 2003). So even when given an opportunity, a worker who is a member of a minority group in an organization may not be able to contribute fully if he or she feels that the group membership is uppermost in others' minds. Gender-based stereotypes are of particular concern in organizations, because women still do not get the same rewards for paid work as their male counterparts, and some occupations appear to be 'gendered', or occupied predominantly by one or other sex.

The phrase '*think manager, think male*' was coined by Virginia Schein (1973, 1975) to describe the effect of sex-role stereotypes on the perceptions of what it takes to be a successful manager. Many studies have shown that both men and women, and people of different nationalities, describe successful managers as having characteristics that they also associate more with men than women, such as competitiveness, decisiveness and ambition (Schein, 1996). As well as affecting women's motivation and expectations, such perceptions may create a bias in decision makers' evaluation of potential and existing managers if they are unaware of or unconcerned about the effect of gender-based stereotypes on their judgements.

As we have already discussed, it is actually very difficult to intervene in the automatic processes by which we associate people or situations with particular thoughts and feelings, even if we become aware of them. Trying to suppress stereotypical thoughts will probably result in 'thought rebound', bringing them even more to the forefront of our minds. We can, however, be vigilant about questioning and exploring our perceptions, reactions and decisions about people, in order to actively counter the inevitable biases and assumptions to which we would otherwise be prone.

It is hard to imagine a person who could not be stereotyped on some dimension, so we are all potentially at risk of being judged inaccurately at some point. Why then do we form stereotypes about people? We have already discussed the marvellous efficiency of schemata for making sense of the world quickly with minimum effort. Stereotypes allow us to size up people with the same efficiency, and apparently that includes ourselves. According to self-categorization theory, which is an extension of **social identity theory** (Tajfel and Turner, 1979), stereotyping people occurs from the same process we use to categorize and understand the kind of person we are in relation to others. The basis of these influential theories is that part of our self-concept is defined in terms of the series of social groups to which we belong. Such groups include demographic ones based on age, gender and socioeconomic status, as well as those we have some choice about, including student, work or sports groups, and more loosely defined groups such as 'clubbers' or classical music fans.

In order to decide whether an individual is a member of a particular group, we use as a basis what we consider to be the defining features or stereotypical attributes of the members of that group. The effect of this process is to simplify the picture by maximizing the distinction between groups and minimizing any differences between individuals within groups. We can then easily work out whether they, or we, have the key features necessary for membership. It has been suggested that one of two sources of motivation for this social comparison is to reduce uncertainty about the social world and how to behave in it, which, as we have discussed, is what our basic perceptual processes also appear to achieve (Hogg and Terry, 2000).

---

stop...

Have you ever become aware you were being stereotyped? How did you feel about it? How did it affect your behaviour?

...and reflect

social identity theory: the theory concerned with how we categorize and understand the kind of person we are in relation to others

in-groups: groups to which someone perceives he or she belongs, which he or she accordingly evaluates favourably

out-groups: groups to which someone perceives he or she does not belong, which he or she accordingly evaluates unfavourably

stop...

How would you define your social identity? Think about the types of people you identify positively with (your in-groups) and the types of people you are sure you are different from (your out-groups).

...and reflect

A second motivation for making these social distinctions concerns our need to maintain self-esteem, and this is crucial in relation to stereotyping. Although we categorize ourselves in the same way as others, this need to view ourselves positively means that we have an inherent tendency to evaluate the characteristics of the groups we belong to (**in-groups**) favourably, and those of other groups and their members (**out-groups**) negatively. So it is possible to see how perceptions of difference and negative stereotypes can form through basic social perception processes.

The ideas of self-categorization and social identity theories can be applied to trying to understand some troublesome issues in contemporary organizations (Haslam, 2001). For instance, the evidence from reports of mergers and acquisitions is that 'people issues' are cited as one of the most difficult aspects of integrating two previously distinct firms (Chartered Institute of Personnel and Development, 2000). From the perspective of social identity theory, the hostility and culture clashes that are a feature of such an integration can be explained by the tendency to favour our own groups and view others as both distinct or different, and less desirable. It is further suggested that events such as organizational restructuring may actually stimulate people to identify even more strongly with their in-groups as they seek to reduce the uncertainty that surrounds such events (Hogg and Terry, 2000). On the more positive side, the comparison groups we use are dynamic and flexible, so it may be possible to intervene in situations where there is unhelpful rivalry or hostility between work groups by trying to subtly change individuals' perceptions of their identity. Focusing the attention of all the groups on external competitors rather than each other is one example.

Perceiving causes

As well as perceiving and judging people and situations, we are also naturally inclined to form perceptions about what has caused the behaviour and events we encounter. From the pursuit of religion to the public's fascination with getting 'into the mind' of serial killers, it is a human tendency to assume that there must be some meaning in all things, and some motive behind all people's actions. Hence, we develop ideas and expectations about causes and effects, and general ideas about how things happen and relate to each other, based on experience.

Broadly speaking, we distinguish between stable causes for things and transitory or changeable ones, and between two sources of explanation: those which are about the person (internal), and those which are about the situation (external). The explanations an individual chooses to use, **causal attributions** as they are called, are important because they can have a significant influence on the person's expectations and behaviour. This applies to expectations about ourselves, as well as about other people.

causal attribution: the explanations an individual chooses to use, which are either internal (about the person) or external (about the situation), and either stable or transitory

Consider the experience of being shortlisted but then not selected for a prestigious and challenging job. Many people's reaction is to spend some time thinking about why they were not considered to be the most suitable candidate. If the rejected applicant puts the result down to a lack of preparation on his or her part – an attribution to an internal but changeable cause – he or she might well consider applying for a similar job in the future, but make changes in his or her preparation for the interview. If, on the other hand, the person perceives the main cause of the rejection to be a lack of the required level of intelligence – an internal, stable attribution – he or she will probably believe that such prestigious jobs are simply out of reach, and apply only for less challenging jobs in the future. Of course, the applicant might make an external attribution, deciding that the outcome was nothing to do with him or her at all, but was caused by, for example, the personal connections of the successful job seeker. In this case, the person's perceptions create no reason to reduce his or her ambitions based on this rejection, or indeed to make changes in approach.

This example demonstrates the way in which our perceptions about what causes things to happen can shape both the options for any action that we consider, and our beliefs about what will result from that action. **Perceived self-efficacy**, which is part of the self-concept (see Figure 4.1), is the term used to describe the 'beliefs in one's capabilities to organize and execute the courses of action required to produce given attainments' (Bandura, 1997: 3). Levels of self-efficacy for a specific activity or goal will determine what goals people actually attempt, how much effort they exert to achieve those goals, and how willing they are to persevere in the face of difficulty.

By definition, in order to develop high self-efficacy in an area, it is necessary to make at least some internal causal attributions for relevant outcomes, because efficacy requires us to believe in our ability to personally control what happens. The exception to this is the attribution of failures to stable, unchangeable personal qualities, which will naturally work to lower our expectations of success. Of course, efficacy-lowering attributions are sometimes accurate, and in that sense they are useful. Failing to recognize appropriately when we do not have the skills or qualities required for a certain pursuit can be damaging in that it causes us to direct our effort in unproductive ways. It is when individuals' low expectations are not based on a realistic assessment of their capabilities that they constrain their ability to reach their potential.

There is solid evidence that efficacy beliefs are an important factor in determining many performance outcomes over and above actual ability (Bandura, 1997). An important example is the early study choices made at school, because these choices work to constrain the career options available to students later on. The sex-role stereotyping of subjects and occupations appears to affect girls' and boys' interests and expectations early on, through the subtle feedback and encouragement for different pursuits that children get from their social environments. From a young age, girls tend to have lower perceived self-efficacy for male-typed subjects such as maths and quantitative skills, regardless of their actual capabilities. For this reason, girls are less likely at school to choose and continue to study maths, which means they are not then well equipped to enter occupations, such as science, for which continued exposure to maths is required.

The case of girls and study choices shows how individuals' expectations can become **self-fulfilling prophecies**. That is, if we think it is unlikely we can achieve a particular goal, we tend not to bother even trying, or tend to give up easily if we do try. This means we do not actually give ourselves the opportunity to succeed and so end up reinforcing our original expectation. Of course, this process can also work in a positive direction, where expectations of success can lead to an engagement with, and increased efforts to achieve, the goal in question. The implication of this information for organizational behaviour is that we cannot always assume that an individual's performance and attainment directly reflects her or his basic abilities. When setting goals, and when motivating and appraising performance, it may be helpful for individuals and their managers to examine causal beliefs and self-efficacy levels in order to identify potential barriers to achievement.

Given its practical significance, there is a good deal of theory and research that focuses on the ways in which we might come to make one type of causal attribution over another, but the ideas of Kelley are particularly influential here (Hogg and Vaughan, 2004). In his **co-variation model**, Kelley (1973) suggested that we use information about the co-occurrence of the person, the behaviour and the potential causes to work out an explanation. Specifically, three aspects of the occasion are considered:

- *Distinctiveness*: Does the person behave this way in other situations, or is the behaviour uncommon for them and specific to this situation?

(margin glossary)

perceived self-efficacy: a person's belief in his or her capacity to achieve something

self-fulfilling prophecy: an expectation about a situation that of itself causes what is anticipated to actually happen

co-variation model: Kelley's model that uses information about the co-occurrence of a person, a behaviour and potential causes to work out an explanation

- *Consistency*: Does the person always behave this way in this type of situation?
- *Consensus*: Does everyone behave this way in this type of situation, or is this person's behaviour different?

The pattern of answers to these three questions will rule out some potential causes and suggest others. Imagine that a colleague has just been very rude to you when passing on information. If this person is always rude to you (high consistency) but also rude to others (low distinctiveness), and everyone else in the organization is very friendly (low consensus), you will probably think that the person, and not

---

globalization & organization misbehaviour

Source: Getty

Abused and undervaluing: gender and emotional labour

Drunk customers. Angry patients. Abusive parents. Many workers have to cope with and manage unsettling displays of hostility in their jobs. This is called emotional labour and typically involves trying to produce a more desirable emotional state in a customer or a client by controlling one's own outward displays of emotion. Remember, smiles are free at McDonald's.

Consider the high-profile case of Jenny Lauren (Ralph Lauren's niece). In January 2014, Lauren was arrested in Ireland after a Delta Airlines flight from Barcelona to New York was forced to land at Shannon Airport. Allegedly high on alcohol and prescription medication, Lauren was found crying in her seat. When a flight attendant intervened:

> Lauren told stewardess Constance Topping to 'get the f*** out of my face' as she tried to help, and when told to calm down she became more abusive.

> The court heard Ms Topping went to brief her supervisor, Jennifer Simpson, at the top of the plane and Lauren, who was not a first class passenger, nevertheless followed her through first class and into the galley 'at speed' where she ranted, roared and shouted incoherently.

> ... 'She told the air hostess she was going to go ballistic and pushed the air hostess hard and she hit her back against the wall of the aircraft.'

> She revealed her frightening experience continued with Lauren calling her a '"f****** ugly, blonde b***h" and Ms Simpson a "fat, ugly, unhappy, blonde b***h". (Malm et al., 2014)

While Jenny Lauren's behaviour is perhaps an extreme case, anyone who has worked in the service industry has their own tales of rude and abusive customers. Workers who must meet hostility with good cheer and deference (so that the customer will continue to patronize the employer) frequently experience work-related stress arising from emotional dissonance. This dissonance stems from the difference between the worker's real and displayed emotions (Macdonald and Sirianni, 1996).

Long-term exposure to stress can lead to a wide range of potentially serious health effects. In this way, employers are externalizing an unpleasant side effect or cost of business (that is, placating unhappy customers) onto workers via mandating stressful

emotional labour (Andrews et al., 2008). Interestingly, however, deep acting – influencing one's emotions such that one actually feels the emotion one is expected to display – appears to reduce the stress associated with emotional labour (Phillip and Schupbach, 2010).

Women are disproportionately employed in occupations requiring emotional labour (for example, as waitresses, nurses and teachers) and may also be expected to undertake a greater degree of emotional labour than men in the same occupation (Soares, 2003). Not surprisingly, emotional labour does not tend to factor into job evaluation systems. Such work is often considered part of an occupation's 'calling'.

But have you noticed that employers in distinctly non-vocational areas of the economy often claim that the jobs they offer are 'callings' too? Starbucks' careers page says, 'We're dedicated to serving ethically sourced coffee, caring for the environment and giving back to the communities where we do business.'

In fact, the emotional engagement that front-line workers bring to callings is very much what companies demand from management, rather than employees. So the 'Pouring coffee is a calling' assertion is just part of an effort to make employees think and behave like management, although, of course, without the same level of pay (O'Connell, 2010).

> **Stop!** Think about a time when you've had to 'produce a desired emotional state' in a customer, or even a university colleague or friend. How did you know you were supposed to do this? Why were you required to do this and who benefited from your actions? What were the personal costs of doing so?

Sources and further information

Andrews, B., Karcz, S. and Rosenberg, B. (2008) 'Hooked on a feeling: emotional labor as an occupational hazard of the post-industrial age', *New Solutions: A Journal of Environmental and Occupational Health Policy*, 18(2), pp. 245–55.

Macdonald, C. L. and Sirianni, C. (1996) 'The service society and the changing experience of work', in C. L. Macdonald and C. Sirianni (eds), *Working in the Service Society*, Philadelphia: Temple University Press.

Malm, S., Reilly, J., Deegan, G., Bates, D., Thornhill, T and Gayle, D. (2014) '"I was not intoxicated": Ralph Lauren's niece insists she was real victim of air rage incident as she blames rude flight attendant', *Daily Mail*, January 14. Available at: www.dailymail.co.uk/news/article-2539092/I-not-intoxicated-Ralph-Laurens-niece-insists-real-victim-air-rage-incident-blames-rude-flight-attendant.html (accessed January 21, 2015).

O'Connell, A. (2010) 'Emotional labor doesn't pay', September 29. http://blogs.hbr.org/2010/09/why-is-it-that-we/ (accessed January 21, 2015).

Phillip, A. and Schupbach, H. (2010) 'Longitudinal effects of emotional labour on emotional exhaustion and dedication of teachers', *Journal of Occupational Health Psychology*, 15(4), pp. 494–504.

Soares, A. (2003) 'Tears at work: gender, interaction, and emotional labour', *Just Labour*, 2, pp. 36–44.

Note: This feature was written by Bob Barnetson, Associate Professor of Labour Relations, Athabasca University, Canada.

you, is the cause of the problem. In the event that there is a lack of consistency in the person's behaviour in the situation – in this case, he or she is sometimes rude and sometimes friendly – we tend to discount the immediate possibilities and assume that there must be some other explanation.

One of the issues with Kelley's (1973) model is that it does not make too much sense unless we have experienced the person and the situation more than once. If this is our only experience, we must use different criteria because we do not have the same information. In such cases, Kelley suggested that we use causal schemata as guiding frameworks for making attributions. There is supporting evidence for the co-variation model, but it is not actually clear whether we always or exclusively use this particular process to attribute causation. Nonetheless, the framework has proved a useful tool for understanding the implications of these perceptions.

As with the other aspects of perception discussed in this chapter, causal attribution is not a purely rational process free of selectivity and the workings of motivation. Just as we display biases towards perceiving some environmental cues over others, we are also subject to some general tendencies in the way we attribute causes to things. One bias that has been noted in our perception of causes is the **false consensus effect**, which is the tendency to overestimate the degree to which other people think and behave in the same way as we do. We also have a tendency to favour internal attributions for others' behaviour, but external ones to explain our own behaviour. So we are likely to assume that a colleague misses a deadline because she or he is unreliable or disorganized, whereas we miss our own deadlines because of unavoidable constraints. This is called the **fundamental attribution error**.

Actually, the error is not really fundamental in the sense of applying to all people. The extent to which people fall prey to this tendency appears to depend on their cultural background, because those from non-Western cultures are more likely to use external attributions (Morris and Peng, 1994). It is also the case, mirroring the phenomenon of the chronic accessibility of certain schemata discussed earlier, that individuals appear to adopt particular 'explanatory styles', or have a predisposition to employ some types of explanation over others.

Two familiar explanatory styles are optimism and pessimism. Most of us have met someone who is unfailingly optimistic about life regardless of the circumstances, and someone for whom every silver lining has a cloud. Although we often treat such differences light-heartedly, they do have serious consequences. Optimism has been linked to achievement across life domains as well as physical health and psychological well-being, whereas pessimism has been linked with depression and lack of success (Peterson, 2000). It has been suggested that optimists are those who habitually favour external, unstable and specific (only affecting one part of their life) explanations for bad events (Seligman, 1991). By contrast, pessimists attribute bad results to internal, stable and global (affecting all aspects of their life) causes.

false consensus effect: the tendency to overestimate the degree to which other people think and behave in the same way as we do

fundamental attribution error: the tendency to favour internal attributions for the behaviour of others but external ones to explain our own behaviour

VISIT THE *ONLINE RESOURCE CENTRE* AT HTTPS://HE.PALGRAVE.COM/COMPANION/BRATTON-WORK-AND-ORGANIZATIONAL-BEHAVIOUR3/ TO FIND OUT MORE ABOUT LEARNED OPTIMISM AND OTHER SIMILAR WORK, SUCH AS THE SUBJECTIVE HAPPINESS SCALE, WHICH YOU COULD USE FOR A RESEARCH PROJECT OF YOUR OWN.

Perception, emotions and emotional intelligence

Much has been written in recent years on the role that emotion plays in human perception, the formation of selfhood (see Chapter 4, especially Figure 4.1) and decision making. Like perception, emotions involve processes outside our conscious awareness, and research now shows that emotion plays a much bigger role in perception and thinking than was previously believed. Our schemata are not simply internal models of the world; they also contain emotional information and biases. Indeed, we have already seen in this chapter how feelings of anger, injustice, attractiveness, pessimism, wanting to belong and desire to make a good impression on others can all influence how we interpret and interact with the world. We will also see in later chapters how emotional factors are important in motivation (Chapter 6), teamworking (Chapter 10), communication (Chapter 11) and leadership (Chapter 12).

But it is not just our perception of other people that is coloured by our emotions. Take, for example, our perception of risk. Findings from neuroscientific research suggest that our emotions have a key part to play in the creation of a perceptual bias against risk taking (Montague, 2007). Our emotional brain would appear to be 'pre-programmed' to maximize feelings of pleasure and minimize feelings of pain. In modern societies, these feelings are commonly associated with the gain and loss of something we value. We have an aversion towards loss because of the negative emotions this generates. Such loss aversion can seriously affect how we perceive and evaluate the riskiness of a particular situation. As a consequence, our desire to avoid feeling a sense of loss or regret can sometimes lead us to make very poor decisions. This may explain why investors put money into government bonds rather than corporate stocks even though the latter have historically outperformed the former by quite some margin – bonds are perceived to be safer (Zweig, 2008). It may also help us to understand why people sometimes continue on a particular course of action (for example, a large investment in a new organizational information system) even when that action is clearly failing: we do not want to regret wasting our 'sunk costs' (the time and effort that have gone into achieving the goal) even if the longer term costs of continuing may end up being greater.

The neuroscientist Jonah Lehrer (2009) suggests that the emotional bias in our schemata to maximize pleasurable feelings lies at the heart of our irrational, impulsive decision making. He gives the example of the US subprime mortgage lending market (the collapse of which many economists blame for the onset of the 2008 global financial recession). The most common type of subprime mortgage is the 2/28 loan, which offers a very low fixed-interest rate for the first 2 years and a much higher variable rate for the next 28 years. This type of mortgage accounted for 20 per cent of all US mortgages before the housing market collapse in 2007. Clearly, for many people, the short-term benefits of these mortgages proved too tempting to resist. They were driven by the pleasurable feelings of getting a 'cheap deal' and overlooked the longer term risk of rising interest rates. Our emotional brain is impulsive and not well equipped to look into the future. This is why decision making based on emotion and intuition is fraught with danger, and why so much research has been conducted on how to enhance the rationality of the decision-making process (see Chapter 13).

Although a concern with people's emotions is present in much organizational behaviour, the myth of rationality – that employees pursue organizational goals in a logical manner – denied the existence of emotions and held back research on the importance of emotions in workplace decision making (Ashforth and Humphrey, 1995). Research on emotions is therefore a more recent area of interest and does not have the same research traditions as the enquiry into personality. The idea of emotion contains three interconnected terms and conceptualizations: emotions, moods and affect (Kelly and Barsade, 2001):

- *Emotions* are object specific, that is, they are usually feelings directed at someone or something. For example, a person may be angry at someone or happy about something.
- By contrast, *moods* are not object specific and are displayed less intensely.
- *Affect* describes the broad range of feelings that individuals experience, covering both emotions and moods.

The disciplines of psychology and sociology offer different models for analysing this area. One psychological model – the organismic model – suggests that feelings happen within the individual, are experienced physically and are then interpreted. Reflecting this perspective, Watson and Clark (1994: 89) define emotions as:

> Distinct, integrated psychological response systems ... An emotion contains three different systems: [1] a prototypic form of expression (typically facial), [2] a pattern of consistent autonomic changes, and [3] a subjective feeling state.

Richard Lazarus (1991) brings in a utilitarian aspect by defining emotions as 'complex, patterned, organismic reactions to how we think we are doing in our lifelong efforts to survive and flourish and to achieve what we wish for ourselves' (p. 6). Daniel Goleman (1996: 289) defines emotion as 'a feeling and its distinctive thoughts, psychological and biological states, and a range of propensities to act'. The words 'organismic' and 'biological' emphasize that emotions involve the whole person – they are psychological, biological and social.

The academic interest in harnessing and managing emotion (for example, Goleman, 1996) parallels the exponential growth of service labour and the increasing demand from employers for interpersonal skills. A sustained interest in the sociological study of emotions emerged only during the 1980s with the pioneering work in this field by Arlie Hochschild (1983). Several sociological models of analysis exist, one of which is the **constructionist model**. This maintains that feelings are socially constructed and that they do not apply to inner states, but are cultural meanings given to emotions. For example, happiness may be given very different meanings, such as something akin to pure joy or something that resembles mere contentment. Related to this, the **interactionist model** interprets emotions as an property that emerges from the interaction between the body and the environment (Scott and Marshall, 2009). Sharon Bolton (2005) presents an insightful multidimensional sociological approach to understanding emotional life in organizations. She writes:

> The social view of emotion ... involves the view of the actor as a purposive agent. [This] allows an understanding that, in negotiating between the feeling rules that are operative in *different situations*, actors are usually highly skilled from the point of the management of emotions ... in that the individual may *select* from sources of conflicting feeling rules and often creatively interpret and manipulate them. (p. 3, emphasis added)

Viewed in this way, emotions are lived interactional experience, and we can see this in different workplace situations when certain emotional conventions are regarded as being more important than others. For example, in a social group in and around work or in a project team, a typology of accepted norms and rules of emotion, such as a preference for seriousness or enthusiasm, may be observed.

Psychologists have quibbled over precisely which emotions can be considered 'primary' or 'core'. The discovery that the facial expressions for fear, anger, sadness and enjoyment are universally recognized is the basis of the thesis that there are just four core emotions (Goleman, 1996). Lazarus' definition is goal-driven and makes a distinction between 'positive' and 'negative' emotions (Table 5.1).

It is suggested that some emotions are triggered by achieving a goal. These would be called *positive emotions* and consistent with personal goals, which is known as goal-congruent. For example, students are likely to display the positive emotions of happiness, pride and relief on graduation. On the other hand, they are likely to experience the *negative emotions* of sadness, anxiety and guilt if they do not graduate in the same year as their peers. The emotions experienced in this situation are

constructionist model: maintains that feelings are socially constructed and do not apply to inner states, but are cultural meanings given to emotions

interactionist model: interprets emotions as an property that emerges from the interaction between the body and the environment

Table 5.1 Selective positive and negative emotions

Positive emotions	Negative emotions
Enjoyment/ happiness	Sadness
Love	Anger
Relief	Fear/anxiety
Pride	Shame

Source: Based on R. S. Lazarus (1991) *Emotion and Adaptation*, New York: OUP

emotional intelligence: the personal faculty of knowing and managing one's own emotions, perceiving and understanding emotions in others and handling relationships

negative because they are said to be goal-incongruent. There is a debate, however, over how to classify multiple emotions. For example, how should we categorize a mixture of jealousy and happiness, or a variant of anger that melts anxiety and fear (Goleman, 1996)? In social studies on emotions, there are several unresolved issues, including the exact nature of emotions, the relationship between cognition and emotions, and the degree to which emotions are neurologically 'hard-wired' or are socially constructed (Turner, 2009).

Emotional intelligence

The concept of **emotional intelligence** (EI) has become a very popular topic only in the last decade (Cooper, 2010). This can be partly explained by its links to contemporary theories of leadership (see Chapter 12). The intellectual roots of EI can be traced to Edward Thorndike's (1874–1949) work on the concept of 'social intelligence' in the 1920s. EI helps us to understand why some individuals are 'good with people'. This is because individuals with greater EI are able to identify and control their own emotions, be aware of others' emotional states and know what to say and do to demonstrate social sensitivity. According to Cooper (2010: 60): 'EI reflects how sensitive a person is to their own and other people's emotional states and their skill with dealing with other people'. Because of everyday social interaction in the workplace, EI is, according to Goleman (1996), more important in understanding individual differences than is general intelligence (measured in terms of IQ).

There are currently several models of EI, of which Goleman's model is the most well known. His model suggests that EI has four key domains: self-awareness, self-management, social awareness and relationship management. The first two domains are referred to as 'personal' competencies, while the other two are referred to as 'social' competencies (Table 5.2).

Table 5.2 Emotional intelligence domains and competencies

Personal competence	Social competence
Self-awareness	**Social-awareness**
Emotional self-awareness: Reading one's own emotions and recognizing their impact; using intuition to guide decisions	*Empathy:* Sensing others' emotions, understanding their perspectives and taking an active interest in their concerns
Accurate self-assessment: Knowing one's limits	*Organizational awareness:* Reading strengths and the currents, politics and decision networks at the organizational level
Self-confidence: A realistic sense of one's self-worth	*Service:* Recognizing and meeting capabilities; and the needs of management's followers and customers
Self-management	**Relationship-management**
Emotional self-control: Keeping disruptive impulses under control	*Inspirational leadership:* Guiding emotions and and motivating with a compelling vision
Transparency: Displaying honesty and integrity; trustworthiness	*Influence:* Using a range of persuasive tactics
Adaptability: Flexibility in adapting to new situations	*Developing others:* Improving others' abilities through mentoring
Achievement: The drive to improve performance and meet inner standards of excellence	*Change catalyst:* Initiating, managing and leading change
Initiative: Readiness to act and seize opportunities	*Conflict management:* Resolving disagreements
Optimism: Seeing the positive in events	*Building bonds:* Cultivating and maintaining a web of relationships
	Teamwork and collaboration: Cooperation and team building

Source: Adapted from D. Goleman, R. Boyatzis and A. McKee (2013) *Primal Leadership*, Boston, MA: Harvard Business School Press, p. 39.

VISIT THE *ONLINE RESOURCE CENTRE* AT HTTPS://HE.PALGRAVE.COM/COMPANION/BRATTON-WORK-AND-ORGANIZATIONAL-BEHAVIOUR3/ TO WATCH A VIDEO ON EMOTIONAL INTELLIGENCE.

Goleman posits that there is an association between greater EI and a greater effectiveness of individual leadership. However, Petrides and Furnham (2000), Woodruffe (2001) and others have critiqued this theory. Petrides and Furnham observe that EI is a cognitive skill – a mental ability – and therefore a personality trait, and Woodruffe argues that the concept 'emotional intelligence' is simply a rebranding of long-established competencies.

Perception, emotions and employee relations

There is one final topic that needs to be included in this discussion about perception and organizational behaviour, namely the role that perception plays in shaping the tone of the employee relations that exist in the workplace. Employee relations are more than simply a domain of organizational management. The dynamic relationship between employees and employers reflects changes in the nature of work and significantly affects key aspects of organizational life. The relevance here is that the differences in role expectations, motivations and rewards associated with being either an employer or an employee mean that individuals in these two groups are likely to perceive and emotionally respond to what happens in the organization somewhat differently. This is significant because there is evidence that the extent of the agreement between employers' and employees' perceptions about key aspects of work will have consequences for employees' work attitudes and performance.

Perceived unfair treatment can lead to misbehaviour and industrial disputes, such as those highlighted earlier involving workers from Sony and Total in France. More broadly, such perceptions have been found to predict employees' feelings of job satisfaction and trust in managers, as well as their willingness to engage in discretionary behaviour such as helping colleagues or staying to complete tasks beyond contracted hours (Gilliland and Chan, 2001). In fact, the notion of fairness or justice can be separated into two components: fairness of outcomes, or **distributive justice**, and fairness of procedures, or **procedural justice**. People tend to be concerned with the process by which decisions are made as well as with the decision itself, and may in fact be willing to accept a personally disappointing outcome if the procedures used are perceived to have been equitable.

The importance of employees' perceptions of fairness or social justice is not, however, restricted to how specific aspects of employment such as formal contract terms, for example pay, are viewed. The employment relationship is an ongoing, dynamic interaction between the parties made up of a sequence of exchanges over time, each of which will influence the thoughts and perceptions of those involved. The *psychological contract*, a concept we introduced in Chapter 1, has become important in understanding organizational behaviour and misbehaviour.

This concept is a metaphor that captures a wide variety of expectations and understandings of the two parties about their mutual obligations. In essence, it is an unwritten contract that exists between employees and their employer. It consists of employees' ideas about what they are expected to contribute to the organization and what they can expect to get back in return for their efforts. As we explained in Chapter 1, the contract is formed by the perceptions of the employer and employee with regard to the reciprocal promises and obligations that are implied in employment relationship. These expectations are formed during the recruitment process and once inside the organization, from what managers say and do, as well as from the communications and culture of the company. There is evidence that the psychological contract has important implications for the way in which people behave and are managed. Ineffective management practices may communicate different beliefs about these reciprocal promises and obligations (Guest and Conway, 2002).

plate 19 Our emotional brain is impulsive and not well equipped to look into the future. This is why decision making based on emotion and intuition is fraught with danger. What is your view on the safety or otherwise of 'tombstoning' (shown in the picture)? To what extent is that view based on emotions, and to what extent on rationality?

distributive justice: justice based on the principle of fairness of outcomes

procedural justice: justice based on the principle of fairness of the procedures employed to achieve the outcomes

Research has shown, for example, that 'downsizing' may impact negatively on those employees who have been categorized as 'survivors' of organizational restructuring, even when their employment contracts ostensibly remain largely unaffected (see, for example, Hendry and Jenkins, 1997; Saunders and Thornhill, 2006). Thus, the resulting decreases in the level of employment in an organization may communicate a change about unwritten notions of loyalty and commitment, and thereby affect the employment relationship (Hendry and Jenkins, 1997). In addition, the perceived psychological contract is context sensitive (Rousseau, 1995). In the post-2008 recession era, 'downsizing' has become a ubiquitous fact of organizational life (Datta et al., 2010), and against this backdrop it is more likely that the psychological contract will be violated if workers perceive that there is procedural 'unfairness' (Arshad and Sparrow, 2010: 1810).

For all the reasons we have discussed for why people's perceptions may differ, one person's ideas about what the organization has promised and expects may not be fully or even partly shared by managers or indeed other employees. Much potential exists, then, for organizations to fall short of employees' expectations and vice versa, leading to feelings that agreed promises have been broken. Perhaps unsurprisingly, the results from a number of studies suggest that violations of individuals' psychological contracts are linked to outcomes such as intentions to quit, reduced job performance and lower levels of commitment (see, for example, Lester et al., 2002; Taylor and Tekleab, 2004).

One final point in reflecting upon the nature of the employment relationship and potential violations of the psychological contract is that critical approaches to studying perception and emotions focus on patterns of inequality and relationships of domination and subordination. The dynamics of class, gender, race, disability and, increasingly, precarious underemployment and inequality of income alter the 'rules of the game' and affect how emotions are displayed and distributed. The hierarchical arena in which emotions at work are performed and managed ensures 'the continual and re-creation of social inequalities,' as Bolton (2005: 156) argues.

Chapter summary

- Perception is important in organizational behaviour because the fundamental nature of perceptual processes means that individuals usually interpret other people and situations differently, so routinely hold different views of reality, which in turn strongly influence their attitudes and actions. This means that avoiding conflict and ensuring that important workplace decisions are based on sound judgements is not a matter of training people how to see things as they 'really are', because multiple realities always exist. More can be gained from understanding how perception works, and from shaping organizational activity so that the possibilities for negative outcomes (both emotional and behavioural) are minimized.

- 'Perception' refers to the process by which our senses gather information from the environment and our brains make sense of that information. The perception process is characterized as inherently selective, subjective and largely automatic rather than conscious. It can be broken down into three steps or elements – receiving, organizing and interpreting – which represent the path by which we mentally transform sensory stimuli from the environment into meaningful information.

- The three elements of the perception process do not occur separately or in sequence, but overlap and sometimes occur in parallel. When perception proceeds from the sensory data received from the environment, it is called 'bottom-up' information processing. In contrast, when perception begins with existing knowledge that is used to interpret the incoming data, it is called 'top-down' processing. Whereas bottom-up processing requires a lot of mental effort, top-down processing carries the risk of assumptions and jumping to the wrong conclusions, so some degree of balance is required between the use of these two perception strategies.

- The processing limitations of our brains mean we can only experience the mass of sensory stimuli in the environment as orderly and meaningful because we employ selective attention. Our choice of what to attend to is driven by the environmental cues that are most salient, or by our own motivations, expectations, emotions and goals. This selectivity is highly resource efficient, but the downside is that we can miss crucial pieces of information and form misleading perceptions of what we are experiencing. If we then act on those perceptions, we may suffer serious consequences.

- Existing knowledge has a powerful effect on how we perceive new experiences. We store knowledge in the form of mental models, or schemata – packages of related content (for instance, thoughts, emotions and attitudes) about people, situations and roles. Schemata do develop over time, but they do not change much once formed because they act as lenses by which we view new information. New data that are inconsistent with what we 'know' are simply reinterpreted to fit. In perception, when one bit of information related to a schema is brought to mind, everything else in the package comes to mind as well, so we can very quickly make sense of something on the basis of a small bit of information. But these stable, automatic linkages between thoughts can be unhelpful, as in the case of stereotypes. Although we can choose not to act upon stereotypes, it may not be possible to stop them coming to mind in the first place.

- Two different types of emotion were identified: positive emotions, which are personal reactions to circumstances congruent to one's needs and goals, and negative emotions, which are reactions to circumstances incongruent with one's needs and goals. EI, the ability to manage one's own emotions and those of others in constructive ways, was discussed. EI has four key dimensions: self-awareness, self-management, social awareness and relationship management.

- Two specific classes of perception were identified that hold particular significance for organizations. The causes that people perceive (or attribute) for particular outcomes will significantly affect their future expectations and behaviour. If a person sees a failure to meet a goal as the result of stable, internal causes – such as intelligence – she or he is less likely to try again than if the cause of the failure is perceived to be more about his or her circumstances at the time. This knowledge is important for understanding individual performance and motivation. The second class of perception – employees' views of justice and fairness in the workplace – is significant because these impact on the employment relationship. If employees perceive that they are being treated unfairly by the organization, it will negatively influence their attitudes and motivation at work. The difficulty is that employees and employers are very likely to perceive things differently by virtue of their respective roles and experiences, so it is a particular challenge for organizations to ensure that employees feel fairly treated.

IN THE EBOOK ACCESS **WEB BASED ASSIGNMENTS** TO APPLY YOUR LEARNING.

Chapter review questions

1 Describe the basic features of human perception processes, and why these features explain the fact that people generally perceive the same situation differently.

2 Identify and explain two consequences of selective attention that can occur in the workplace.

3 Outline the pros and cons of the mental packaging of information into schemata.

4 What is causal attribution? Outline one scenario that might occur in an organization where a person's perceptions about the causes of things affect her or his motivation to achieve a goal.

5 What are your own experiences of positive emotions being negative, and of negative emotions being positive?

6 Consider your own experiences of group working. In what situations was EI important for group dynamics and for completing the assignment?

7 In what ways can individuals' perceptions affect other people, groups of people and the social climate of an organization?

Further reading

Ashforth, B. E. and Humphrey, R. H. (1995) 'Emotion in the workplace: a reappraisal', *Human Relations*, 48(2), pp. 97–125.

Bandura, A. (1997) *Self-efficacy: The Exercise of Control*, New York: Freeman.

Bolton, S. (2005) *Emotion Management in the Workplace*, Basingstoke: Palgrave Macmillan.

Eysenck, M. W. (2009) *Fundamentals of Psychology*, Hove: Psychology Press.

Hamermesh, D. S. (2011) *Beauty Pays: Why Attractive People Are More Successful*, Princeton: Princeton University Press.

Haslam, S. A. (2001) *Psychology in Organizations: The Social Identity Approach*, London: Sage.

Hendry, C. and Jenkins, R. (1997) 'Psychological contracts and new deals', *Human Resource Management Journal*, 7(1), pp. 38–44.

Hogg, M. A. and Vaughan, G. M. (2013) *Social Psychology: An Introduction* (7th edn), Hemel Hempstead: Prentice Hall.

Lehrer, J. (2009) *The Decisive Moment: How the Brain Makes up its Mind*, Edinburgh: Canongate.

Locke, E. A. (2005) 'Why emotional intelligence is an invalid concept', *Journal of Organizational Behavior*, 26, pp. 425–31.

Mencl, J. and Lester, S. W. (2014) 'More alike than different: what generations value and how the values affect employee workplace perceptions', *Journal of Leadership and Organizational Studies*, doi: 10.1177/1548051814529825.

Rosenfeld, P., Giacalone, R. and Riordan, C. A. (2002) *Impression Management: Building and Enhancing Reputation at Work*, London: Thomson Learning.

Saunders, M. N. K. and Thornhill, A. (2006) 'Forced employment contract change and the psychological contract', *Employee Relations*, 28(5), pp. 449–67.

Turner, J. H. (2009) 'The sociology of emotions: basic theoretical arguments', *Emotion Review*, 1(4), pp. 340–54.

Zeidner, M., Roberts, R. D. and Matthews, G. (2008) 'The science of emotional intelligence: current concerns and controversies', *European Psychologist*, 13(1), pp. 64–78.

Chapter case study: The blame game

The setting

This case is set in a medium-sized factory specializing in the manufacture of metal boxes and cases. The factory workers are semi-skilled but receive a good wage. Employee relations are generally good.

The problem

It began as a normal day on the shop floor in the metal working factory Chidi Manufacturing. By mid-morning, the manufacturing process was in full swing and Morenike, the factory manager, was able to take a short break to enjoy a well-earned cup of tea. However, just as she had sat down in her office, Daren (one of two line managers in the factory) came rather timidly into her office.

'I'm afraid we have a serious quality problem, boss,' he said apologetically. 'Edwin is turning out sub-standard work that is threatening to disrupt the whole production run'.

'Can't you sort this out, Daren?' Morenike replied. 'After all, this falls firmly within your remit as line manager.'

'That's true, but Edwin is adamant that he is not the cause of the problem, and he is getting quite angry about it,' Daren replied. 'I'd be grateful if you could help out.'

The two managers walked swiftly through the busy factory until they came to Workstation 42. Edwin stood by his machine, which appeared to be switched off despite the fact that the production run was in full flow all around him. A stockpile of work was building up by the side of his workstation.

'Okay, Edwin,' Morenike said quietly, 'would you like to tell me what is going on and why you're not working?'

'Good morning, boss' he replied. 'About an hour ago I realised that my workstation was beginning to produce material that was falling below quality standards. I told Daren and he just told me to "put things right" and maintain production speed. But it isn't my fault that the machine is faulty. I was working at Workstation 18 all last week, and there was never any problem with my work there. This Workstation 42 machine needs overhauling or something, so there's no point in carrying on using it if it's not up to the job.'

'Oh, I see,' Daren interjected, 'you're saying that it's the machine's fault and not yours. How do you explain the fact that Workstation 42 was working perfectly well on the night shift and then started misbehaving only once you came to work? A bad worker always blames his tools.'

'I don't see how you know how well the machine was working last night. You weren't here and neither was I!', Edwin replied angrily.

'Gentlemen, let's keep our tempers here,' Morenike insisted. 'Edwin, your job is to operate Workstation 42, and if your line manager tells you to keep working, then you darn well should. Please get back to work immediately or I'll be forced to enforce disciplinary procedures.'

Edwin shrugged his shoulders and muttered something under his breath. Nevertheless, he turned round and switched the machine back on. The two managers stayed for a few minutes to ensure that everything was working smoothly and then Morenike returned to her office. However, less than 10 minutes later, the line manager was back in her office complaining bitterly that Edwin had deliberately 'sabotaged' his workstation so that it now appeared incapable of functioning. 'Never mind disciplinary procedures. I want him sacked,' Daren declared. 'He's trying to undermine my authority and make me look as if I'm in the wrong and not him. I want your support on this matter.'

Tasks

- Which theory or theories of perception best help us understand the causes of the conflict described in the case?

- What should the factory manager do next?

Sources and further information

Hammermesh, D. S. (2011) *Beauty Pays: Why Attractive People Are More Successful,* Princeton: Princeton University Press.

Lester, S. W., Turnley, W. H., Bloodgood, J. M. and Bolino, M. (2002) 'Not seeing eye to eye: differences in supervisor and subordinate perceptions of and attributions for psychological contract breach', *Journal of Organizational Behavior*, 23, pp. 39–56.

Moisi, D. (2009) *The Geopolitics of Emotion: How Cultures of Fear, Humiliation, and Hope are Reshaping the World*, New York: Doubleday.

Note: This case study was written by Martin Corbett, Reader in Technology and Organizational Psychology, University of Leicester, UK.

IN THE EBOOK ACCESS AN **OB IN FILM** BOX THAT USES *THE FLYING SCOTSMAN* (2006) TO ILLUSTRATE HOW DIRECTORS CAN USE PERCEPTUAL TRICKS TO INFLUENCE AND MANIPULATE YOUR PERCEPTIONS OF KEY CHARACTERS AND TO ACCESS **AN INTERACTIVE QUIZ** TO TEST YOUR UNDERSTANDING.

chapter 6
Motivation

Key concepts

- alienation
- equity theory
- expectancy theory
- extrinsic motivator
- goal setting
- human needs
- instrumentality
- intrinsic motivator
- motivation
- organizational culture
- orientation to work
- self
- self-concept theory
- valence
- whole-self needs

Chapter outline

- Introduction
- The nature of work motivation
- Content theories of motivation: workers with needs
- Process theories of motivation: workers with choices
- The sociological analysis of motivation: alienation, culture and self-identity
- Integrating the approaches
- Applying motivation theories
- Summary and end-of-chapter features
- Chapter case study: Equity at FindIT

Chapter learning outcomes

After completing this chapter, you should be able to:

1 Define motivation and explain how motivation reflects the exchange embodied in the employment relationship
2 Compare and contrast needs-based theories of motivation at work
3 Describe the expectancy and equity theories of motivation
4 Discuss the managerial implications of process-based motivation theories
5 Understand the complexity of motivation at work through sociological insights, including those of alienation, culture and self-identity

introduction

In the post-2008 'age of austerity', there has been much public debate on the need to pay large executive bonuses to retain and motivate bankers. In a rare insight into the culture of the bonuses being paid to top bank employees, the chairman of the Royal Bank of Scotland, Sir Philip Hampton, described in 2013 how he felt like he was having an 'out of body experience' when a banker protested to him that his £4 million pay package was 'unfair'. And this was not an isolated case. The chairman of the bank RBS said he had been contacted 'quite a lot' by bankers wanting bigger pay deals (Treanor, 2013). Is a £4 million pay package enough to motivate a top banker? How much is enough? It's a question we all ask ourselves, especially if we are one of the 9 million people in private rented accommodation whose rent consumes nearly half of our disposable income. In 2015, top UK directors earn 120 times the average wage, up from 45 times in 1998. Britain's highest-paid director earned a year's worth of the living wage in less than an hour (O'Grady, 2015). Does increasing inequality disincentivize low- and middle-paid employees? Is money the key to understanding employee motivation? Common sense may tell us that money is a key determinant of work motivation – but then common sense told us that the world was flat, and that the Sun orbited the Earth. The motivation debates have provoked much research and debate in contemporary organizational behaviour, and, for managers, the task of discovering what motivates different categories of employee in different work settings is of the same magnitude as finding the Holy Grail.

motivation: the forces within a person that affect his or her direction, intensity and persistence of voluntary behaviour

organizational commitment: the employee's emotional attachment to, identification with and involvement in a particular organization

stop...

Before reading on, you may wish to ask yourself what motivates *you*. In doing your current or planned paid work, are you motivated primarily by money, or by something else? Does money make you happier? Go to the Online Resource Centre at www. palgrave.com/bratton-ob and click on the 'Motivation questionnaire'.

...and reflect

The observed differences in effect among people doing identical work reflect differences in individual knowledge, skills and abilities, or can reflect differences in the extent to which individuals are prepared to direct their energies. Work-related effort is thus contingent upon two different kinds of variable: the ability and skill of the individual, and his or her **motivation** to make use of personal endowments to perform paid work within a given social context. It is perhaps unsurprising, then, that organizational scholars have been interested in the role of motivation in the workplace and its relationship to performance and work-related goals (Myers et al., 2010).

The issue of motivating workers underscores the nature of the employment relationship. At its most basic, the employment contract represents the exchange of effort or knowledge for pay. This effort–pay contract is, however, typically indeterminate: whereas the contract specifies pay, benefits, hours to be worked and so on, a worker's capacity to work – in Marxist terminology, his or her labour power – is indefinable with regard to the amount of effort and **commitment** the employee will apply to the job. The contract implies that workers are 'free' to decide whether to accept the pay on offer, free to internalize about their work situation and develop positive or negative attitudes towards their employment, and free to seek employment elsewhere (Legge, 2005). In other words, employees have, as Peter Drucker once wrote, 'control over whether they work, how much and how well' (Drucker, 1954/1993: 14).

The indeterminate nature of the typical employment contract makes motivation (working harder) a running theme of management. Managers find themselves in positions of subordination as well as superordination and, as a result, they themselves also have to be motivated in order to be able to motivate others. Top managers are often mystified on a daily basis by what motivates middle managers and what motivates male and female knowledge workers; in turn, middle managers are frequently mystified by what motivates male and female front-line employees. Why do highly paid managers and knowledge workers resign or not perform as expected? Why do low-paid manual and front-line non-manual workers baulk at resigning even when they receive better job offers? Pritchard and Ashwood (2008) express the managerialist view on motivation that 'Management practices and systems are designed to *change* some aspects of behavior in order to improve effectiveness. To change behavior, *you must understand motivation*, the process that determines how people behave' (2008: 4, emphasis added).

The mainstream theories of work motivation that emerged in the twentieth century as part of the hoped-for movement towards employee commitment and enhanced effort focus on what are called *content theories* of motivation and *process theories* of motivation. We begin the chapter by discussing these two theories in detail. We then go on to explain how the 1990s witnessed what is called the 'motivation renaissance', a shift toward a situated approach and with a more pronounced relevance for learning (Dörnyei and Ushioda, 2013). Moreover, in the 2000s there has been a resurgence of interest in the role that emotions play in employee motivation (Ryan, 2007).

Next, we explain how two perspectives can be identified in social psychology – the *individualistic* and the *societal*. The individualistic perspective is most exploited in *social cognition theory*, whereas *social identity theory* is the most influential paradigm within the societal perspective. These two schools of thinking have divided social psychologists into two 'starkly separate camps' (Dörnyei and Ushioda, 2013: 7). Examining the relationship between the individual and her or his surrounding social context is also a defining feature of critical theories of motivation. However, critical scholars are more attentive to the contradictory nature of capitalist employment relations, to power relations, to the meanings that men and women attach to paid work and to the ways by which management practices are expressed and reproduced (Fox, 1974; Thompson, 1989). As a result, they tend to emphasize the need for a societal analysis of work motivation.

This chapter therefore has two broad aims. The first is to examine the mainstream theories of motivation. The second is to provide a more holistic understanding of work motivation by expanding beyond ideas of individual needs and cognitive processes, to incorporate an awareness of the effects of the complex, interconnecting contextual factors that stem from class, gender and race relations in society.

The nature of work motivation

After the Second World War, Western economies invested in education, and people experienced relatively full employment. In this social context, workers' fear of unemployment was no longer an individual or a collective motivation for work performance. If workers became dissatisfied with the effort levels expected by managers, or with another aspect of the job, they could find alternative employment relatively effortlessly. As management guru Peter Drucker wrote, 'fear no longer supplies the motivation for the worker in industrial society' (1954/1993: 303). This post-Second World War phenomenon led to an interest in the question 'What motivates workers to perform effectively?' 'Effectively' referred to closing the gap between the workers' potential to work and their willingness to maximize their efforts towards attaining their work objectives.

As explained in a preceding chapter, the indeterminacy of the employment relationship is interpreted by both managers and pro-management theorists as the problem of motivation. Management's concern with discovering the motivation elixir is a direct response to the constant pressure on management to employ people even more efficiently, thoroughly and rationally (Salaman, 1981). Much of the scholarship is primarily *normative*, directed at providing prescriptions for motivating workers. It tends to emphasize what it is that managers *should* do to ensure that subordinates close the gap between their potential and their actual performance.

What is motivation?

The word 'motivation' comes from the Latin *movere*, 'to move', and organizational psychologists have traditionally focused their attention on answering the question of what moves a worker to make certain choices, to engage in work-related behav-

goals: the immediate or ultimate objectives that employees are trying to accomplish from their work effort

iour, to expend effort and to persist in accomplishing organizational **goals.** This line of questioning lies at the heart of motivation theory and research, and it should come as no surprise that it has provoked considerable debate and generated many definitions and theoretical models, all of which has resulted in little consensus. So let us start our exploration by identifying some of the most important dimensions of motivation that most scholars agree upon. Psychologists agree that motivation is by definition concerned with direction, the choice of a particular action or behaviour, the intensity expended on it and the duration of effort or energy. All these dimensions can be found in the following definitions of motivation:

> A driving force or forces responsible for the initiation, *persistence, direction* and vigour of goal-directed behaviour. (Coleman, 2009: 480, emphasis added)

> Motivation can be defined as a choice about where to *direct* your energy, how *persistently,* and how much *effort* to put in to achieving a goal. (Myers et al., 2010: 543, emphasis added)

In other words, work motivation is responsible for why employees decide to do something, how much *effort* they are willing to put into it and how long they are going to sustain it.

The first element common in these definition is '*effort*', which is a measure of intensity that maximizes workers' potential capacity to work in a way that is appropriate to the job. The second characteristic of motivation is '*persistence*', which refers to the application of effort to work-related tasks that employees display over a time period. The third characteristic of motivation is '*direction*', which emphasizes that persistent high levels of work-related effort should be channelled in a way that benefits the organization. Whereas effort and persistence refer to the *quantity* of paid manual or knowledge work, direction refers to *quality* of work done.

Intrinsic versus extrinsic motivation

intrinsic motivator: a wide range of motivation interventions in the workplace, from inner satisfaction after following some action (such as recognition by an employer or co-workers) to intrinsic pleasures derived from an activity (such as playing a musical instrument for pleasure)

extrinsic motivator: a wide range of external outcomes or rewards to motivate employees, including bonuses or increases in pay

Theorists distinguish between **intrinsic** (inside) and **extrinsic** (outside) motivators. An intrinsic motivator stems from a person's 'internal' desire to do something, and is therefore usually self-applied. Outside the workplace, avid participation in hobbies or sports is typically intrinsically motivated. For example, we may be willing to exert a considerable amount of effort over many months with the aim of climbing a mountain, without any thought of financial reward, because we expect it to provide personal satisfaction: that is, we are intrinsically motivated. In the workplace, pure interest in a project and the sense of professional accomplishment or positive recognition by our peers are examples of intrinsic motivators. 'No single phenomenon,' Ryan and Deci (2000: 68) argue, 'reflects the positive potential of human nature as much as intrinsic motivation.' Intrinsically motivated people tend to seek out new challenges and explore new ways of doing things and learning. Extrinsic motivators, on the other hand, stem from outside the individual, and are generally applied by others higher in the organization's hierarchy. Extrinsic motivators include such tangible rewards as pay, bonuses and promotion (Figure 6.1).

	Intrinsic	Extrinsic
Individual-based	Feeling of self-accomplishment	Pay increase
Organization-based	Professional pride in being a member of a 'socially responsible' company	Profit sharing

Figure 6.1 Examples of intrinsic and extrinsic motivators

We should be aware that there is disagreement over these definitions and over the relationship between intrinsic and extrinsic motivators, and even more disagreement over whether organizations can categorize all work

globalization & organization misbehaviour

Source: © Stockbyte Royalty Free Photos

'It's clearly time to tighten the net on disability support pension scheme,' opines the January 14, 2014 editorial in the *Courier-Mail* (2014) in response to news that Australia's Disability Support Pension (DSP) program has a 4 per cent error rate in payments, while acknowledging that errors can be overpayments, underpayments or simply incorrect reporting. Never mind that, say the editors.

It also raises the question of whether the Australian government should consider the British government's recent decision to have all disability pensioners reapply and face tougher medical tests. Nearly 900,000 decided not to do so, and an additional 750,000 were found to have capacity for work (*Courier-Mail*, 2014).

Here we get to the nub of the issue. Across the globe, employers, governments and the media have largely bought into the notion that workers are prone to malingering. That is to say, workers will exaggerate (or even fabricate) reasons not to work. According to this line of thought, the spectre of secondary gain (for example, a disability pension) outweighs the secondary costs (for example, the stigma of being on the dole) and thus requires vigorous policing. This is not all that different from blaming workers for workplace injuries.

This approach to policing and reducing social benefits is part of a broader neo-liberal effort to 'recommodify' labour. In short, by reducing workers' access to the financial resources necessary to buy food and shelter, they can be pressurized to accept waged employment on whatever terms the employer wants to set (Broad and Hunter, 2010). This reduces the employer's wage costs and payroll taxes.

One implication of the belief that workers need discipline is that they must be 'motivated' to perform their jobs. Yet workers rarely have to be motivated to do things in their own lives. People buy reusable water bottles, care for their friends, clean up parks and volunteer for children's charities on their own initiative. So why must workers be explicitly motivated at work?

Bluntly, work often sucks. It can be tedious, demeaning and dangerous. And the rewards of work mostly go to the employer. While workers normally receive a wage for their time, employers endlessly seek to grind wages down. Jobs are reassigned as casual labour (to reduce benefit costs), and job duties are expanded (so there is less downtime) or just moved entirely offshore (where workers earn less). This reflects the employer's desire to maximize profitability but comes at the cost of alienating workers – who must then be 'motivated' to continue.

Employers' need to motivate their workers reflects a unique property of labour. Unlike petroleum, machinery or cardboard boxes, when labour is purchased, ownership of the workers does not pass to the employer. Instead, the employer has purchased the workers' capacity to work. Whether the workers will actually produce anything during this time and whether they will produce what the employer wants is uncertain. It is up to the employer to turn this capacity to work into actual work. If the employer creates a nice workplace, workers are likely to perform their jobs with little supervision (as, for example, school teachers). If the employer creates an unpleasant working environment, workers are likely to resist through diminished efforts.

What this suggests is that one way to look at employers' efforts to motivate workers is as a substitute for decent wages and working conditions. Emphasizing workers' alleged proclivity to malinger is simply a means by which to draw attention away from employer-determined structural factors that influence workers' behaviour.

Stop! Have you ever had a job where you sometimes slacked off? Why did you not work flat out all the time? And how did your employer respond? What does this tell you about the degree of alignment between your interests and your employer's interests in the workplace? If you have had little or no work experience, you might like to think about a time when you had to complete an important assignment but did not work particularly hard to get it finished.

Sources and further information

Broad, D. and Hunter, G. (2010) 'Work, welfare, and the new economy: the commodification of everything', pp. 21–42 in N. Pupo and M. Thomas (eds), *Interrogating the New Economy: Restructuring Work in the 21st century*, Toronto: University of Toronto.

Courier-Mail (2014) 'It's clearly time to tighten net on disability support pension scheme', *Courier-Mail*, January 14. Available at: www.couriermail.com.au/news/opinion/editorial-its-clearly-time-to-tighten-net-on-disability-support-pension-scheme/story-fnihsr9v-1226801005873 (accessed January 21, 2015).

Note: This feature was written by Bob Barnetson, Associate Professor of Labour Relations, Athabasca University, Canada.

motivators as precisely as these definitions suggest. For example, an employee might receive a promotion that also results in more interesting and satisfying work and additional pay. Thus, some potential motivators have both intrinsic and extrinsic qualities (Vallerand, 1997). It should also be apparent from these examples that intrinsic and extrinsic motivators are strongly influenced by the values, ways of thinking, behaviours and social factors typical of a society. North American and European theories of motivation are embedded in management practices, as such practices offer the means to render workers and their behaviour predictable and measurable (Townley, 1994).

VISIT THE *ONLINE RESOURCE CENTRE* AT HTTPS://HE.PALGRAVE.COM/COMPANION/BRATTON-WORK-AND-ORGANIZATIONAL-BEHAVIOUR3/ FOR INFORMATION ON THE ROLE OF STOCK OPTIONS IN MOTIVATING MANAGERS AND OTHER EMPLOYEES.

Motivation theories attempt to explain how employees' behaviour is initiated and shaped, as well as the different factors that contribute to directing and sustaining that goal-directed behaviour. Models show the variables believed to be important, but remember that these are a simplification of the phenomenon. Bearing in mind this caveat, there is no shortage of theorizing and modelling. Students of management should know that there are no quick solutions for releasing the motivation genie. We will now focus on theories that have been categorized in the literature as *content* and *process* theories of work motivation.

Content theories of motivation: workers with needs

needs: deficiencies that energize or trigger behaviours to satisfy those needs

Content theories of motivation assume that all workers possess a common set of basic 'needs'. Five of the better known need theories are (1) Maslow's (1954) hierarchy of needs, (2) McGregor's (1960) Theory X and Theory Y, (3) McClelland's (1961) 'three learned needs' theory, (4) Alderfer's (1972) ERG theory, and (5) Herzberg et al.'s (1959) 'two-factor' need theory.

Maslow's hierarchy of needs

needs hierarchy theory: Maslow's motivation theory of five instinctive needs arranged in a hierarchy, whereby people are motivated to fulfil a higher need as a lower one becomes gratified

In what is probably the most well known of the content theories, psychologist Abraham Maslow proposed that people have a built-in set of five basic needs, which can be arranged in a hierarchy.

The so-called lower level needs in the **needs hierarchy** (the physiological and safety needs) are at first predominant: people's behaviour is directed towards satisfying these needs until they are met, at which point the next higher order need comes to dominate, and so on. For example, only once an individual's physiological needs for the basic necessities of life – food, water and shelter – have been satisfied will that individual focus on the next higher need. Once lower order needs have been addressed, the theory assumes that people direct their behaviours towards satisfying their needs for companionship, love and positive social regard by other people. The progression ultimately leads to behavioural change motivated principally by people's need to realize their full potential, which Maslow termed the **self-actualization** need.

self-actualization: a term associated with Maslow's theory of motivation, referring to the desire for personal fulfilment, to become everything that one is capable of becoming

According to Maslow, the self-actualization need, which involves people directing their behaviour towards learning opportunities in the workplace, is the ultimate motivator, because unlike the other needs, it is insatiable. The second key aspect of Maslow's theory is that a satisfied or satiated need is not a motivator of behaviour. Once a person satisfies a need at one level in the hierarchy, that need ceases to motivate him or her. Only the need in the next level up the hierarchy will motivate the person and influence her or his behaviour.

Although it was not originally intended as an explanation of employee motivation, Maslow's needs hierarchy theory has been influential in mainstream management texts. It has been seen as offering predictions about what directs behaviour in different contexts. In a context of relatively high unemployment, when jobs are relatively scarce and people do not automatically feel secure about meeting their basic needs, workers are motivated strongly by the need to satisfy their lower level needs. In contrast, in a context of relatively full employment, when lower order needs are more easily satisfied, social, self-esteem and self-actualization needs become important motivators in the workplace.

One implication of Maslow's theory is that, if workers are to continue to be motivated once their social needs have been satisfied, managers have to find ways to offer them self-actualization, which implies a focus on the intrinsic aspects of paid work. This might mean reconfiguring work structures and processes to challenge both manual and knowledge workers and offer them a degree of autonomy. To apply Maslow's theory to the current management practices of organizational re-engineering and outsourcing, it might be feasible to motivate part-time or other

plate 20 Will a person really focus on satisfying physiological needs before safety needs? Is this construction worker likely to stop to eat or drink before checking that the swinging girder is secured?

Source: iStockphoto.com

'peripheral' workers by appealing to their lower order needs, while knowledge-based 'core' workers might be motivated by satisfying their higher order needs. The prescription offered by Maslow's theory is that managers need to know where their employees are located on the needs hierarchy, and ensure that their lower order needs are satisfied before appealing to their higher order needs.

Maslow's needs hierarchy appears to offer common-sense advice to managers, but how valid is this theory of work motivation? One of the major problems with Maslow's theory is that it is extremely difficult to identify which need is predominant at any given time. Without this information, managers cannot confidently redesign the workplace or emphasize work-based learning to appeal to their employees' self-esteem or self-actualization needs, for instance, as these might not in reality be their main motivators.

To take a simple example, is it really true that a person will focus on satisfying physiological needs such as hunger and thirst before he or she attends to matters that threaten his or her security or safety? Does a construction worker have a bite to eat before checking that the scaffolding she is standing on is safe?

The significance of Maslow's work might, it is suggested, lie in its rhetorical value. Tony Watson, for example, offers a scathing critique of Maslow's theory, arguing that it has little scientific validity and that its main role has been as 'a propaganda device: propaganda in a good and humanistic cause, but propaganda nonetheless' (1986: 110). Maslow's theory is still worth reviewing, however, because of its influence on the subsequent alternative motivation theories developed by Douglas McGregor, David McClelland and Clayton Alderfer.

McGregor's Theory X and Theory Y

Whereas Maslow focused on defining a hierarchy of needs that influence work-related behaviour, Douglas McGregor, a human psychologist, drew heavily from Maslow to argue that managers need a greater understanding of and attention to employees' needs. McGregor contrasts two opposite theories of employees and management: Theory X and Theory Y. According to McGregor (1957/1970), managers can be classified in terms of how they believe others (and perhaps themselves) behave towards paid work, and how managers approach the issue of work motivation is strongly influenced by their assumptions about human nature. The two extreme sets of propositions are shown in Table 6.1.

McGregor suggests that underpinning the Theory X propositions is the conventional Tayloristic belief that the average employee is indolent, lacks ambition, dislikes responsibility, is inherently self-centred and is not very bright. These basic assumptions, he suggestions, shape and become embedded in organizational structures, culture and practices. McGregor's Theory Y offers an alternative set of assumptions about the essence of human nature and work motivation.

Theory Y holds that the problem of motivation lies not in the subordinate, but in the beliefs and resulting behaviour of the manager. Theory Y supports Maslow's higher level needs by advocating a clear shift towards 'self-control and self-direction', and towards allowing self-esteem and self-actualization needs to be satisfied (Pitsis, 2008). Despite the fact that many managers publicly support Theory Y, there may be a significant gap between the rhetoric and the practice, especially during an economic downturn.

stop...

Can you think of managers or perhaps even university lecturers you have encountered who were influenced by these two sets of assumptions about your attitude to work and motives?

...and reflect

Table 6.1 McGregor's Theory X and Theory Y of motivation

Theory X	Theory Y
1. Management is responsible for organizing the elements of productive enterprise – money, materials, equipment, people – in the interest of economic ends	1. Management is responsible for organizing the elements of productive enterprise – money, materials, equipment, people – in the interest of economic ends
2. With respect to people, this is a process of directing their efforts, motivating them, controlling their actions and modifying their behaviour to fit the needs of the organization	2. People are *not* by nature passive or resistant to organizational needs. They have become so as a result of their experience in organizations
3. Without this active intervention by management, people would be passive – even resistant – to organizational needs. They must therefore be persuaded, rewarded, punished, controlled – their activities must be directed. This is management's task in managing subordinate managers or workers	3. The motivation, the potential for development, the capacity for assuming responsibility and the readiness to direct behaviour towards organizational goals are all present in people. Management does not put them there. It is a responsibility of management to make it possible for people to recognize and develop these human characteristics for themselves
	4. The essential task of management is to arrange organizational conditions and methods of operation so that people can achieve their own goals *best* by directing *their own* efforts toward organizational objectives

Source: McGregor, Douglas. Edited by Rob Roy McGregor, Martha McGregor and Gregory N. Colvard, *Leadership and Motivation: Essays of Douglas McGregor*, figure from essay 'The Human Side of Enterprise', © 1966 Massachusetts Institute of Technology, by permission of The MIT Press.

McClelland's theory of needs

According to David McClelland's (1961) learned needs theory, workers are motivated by the need to satisfy six basic human needs: achievement, power, affiliation, independence, self-esteem and security. In contrast to preceding theories, McClelland argued that these needs are not inherent but learned from national culture. Employees are said to accomplish the most when they have a high need for achievement. Employees with a strong need for achievement tend to set goals that are moderately difficult, to seek out feedback on their performance and to be generally preoccupied with accomplishment.

Unlike Maslow, McClelland did not become preoccupied with specifying a hierarchical relationship between needs. Instead, he argued that employees differ in the extent to which they experience needs for achievement, affiliation and power. McClelland and Burnham (1976) addressed the issue of power as the 'great motivator'. They argued that, in practice, managers with a need for power might be more effective motivators than those with a need for achievement. The work of Harrel and Strahl (1981) suggests that assessing the strength of these learned needs can be helpful in identifying employees who will respond positively to different types of work context. The advice that follows from this alleged insight is that it might be important for managers to consider the extent to which employees possess these needs, and to design motivational strategies that permit workers to satisfy those needs which are strongest for each individual.

Alderfer's ERG theory

ERG theory: Alderfer's motivation theory suggests that more than one need may motivate simultaneously, and, contrary to Maslow's theory, that when a higher order need is obstructed, the desire to satisfy a lower need increases

growth needs: a person's needs for self-esteem through personal achievement, as well as for self-actualization

Clayton Alderfer's (1972) **ERG theory** is closely related to Maslow's work. Based upon an alternative set of assumptions, it conflates Maslow's five dimensions to three, thus suggesting that employee needs can be divided into three basic categories: Existence (E), Relatedness (R) and Growth (G). Existence needs include nutritional, safety and material requirements. Relatedness needs involve an individual's relationships with family and friends, and colleagues at work. **Growth needs** reflect an intrinsic desire for personal development.

As can be seen in Figure 6.2, Alderfer's ERG theory is not a major departure from Maslow's theory. However, ERG theory does not assume a progression up a hierarchy. Alderfer suggests that all three levels might be important at the same time, and he believes that it is better to think in terms of a continuum, from existence needs to growth needs, with workers moving along it in either direction. Consequently, if, for example, growth needs are not satisfied, an inner state of regression caused by

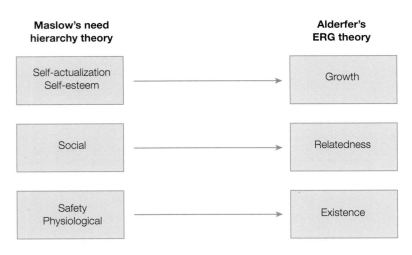

Maslow's need hierarchy theory

Alderfer's ERG theory

Self-actualization
Self-esteem

→

Growth

Social

→

Relatedness

Safety
Physiological

→

Existence

Figure 6.2 Comparison of Maslow's needs hierarchy and Alderfer's ERG theory

frustration occurs, causing the person to focus on fulfilling her or his relatedness needs. Or a supervisor unable to satisfy his or her higher order growth need by accepting greater responsibility might respond by demanding an increase in pay, thereby satisfying his or her lower order existence need. Therefore, unsatisfied needs become less rather than more important. This is the opposite of what Maslow assumed.

Furthermore, ERG theory emphasizes the importance to employees of satisfied needs. Alderfer's work suggests that growth needs are actually more important when satisfied, whereas Maslow argued that, when it is fulfilled, a need becomes less important to an individual. One implication of Alderfer's work is that work designs that satisfy workers' relatedness needs can continue to motivate workers, and that these are not necessarily superseded by growth needs. If this theory is correct, it would make it easier for managers to motivate their employees.

VISIT THE *ONLINE RESOURCE CENTRE* AT HTTPS://HE.PALGRAVE.COM/COMPANION/BRATTON-WORK-AND-ORGANIZATIONAL-BEHAVIOUR3/ FOR INFORMATION ON AND LINKS TO MOTIVATION THEORIES.

A study by Arnolds and Boshoff (2002) provided data to support a key hypothesis associated with Alderfer's ERG model. Unlike many conventional studies, Arnolds and Boshoff's research incorporated personality (see Chapter 4) into the motivation conundrum, and is sensitive to social factors that will potentially affect motivation at work. The study investigated to what extent a personality trait (self-esteem) impacts on the relationship between the satisfactions of needs – as modelled by Alderfer – and the performance effort or intentions of senior managers and white-collar 'front-line' employees in the banking, legal and retail sectors.

Arnolds and Boshoff hypothesize that employees' need for satisfaction, based upon Alderfer's theory, exerts a positive influence on their self-esteem, which in turn exerts a positive influence on their work behaviour in the form of job performance intentions. The authors argue that their data show that self-esteem significantly influences the performance intentions of senior managers, and conclude that 'top managers are primarily motivated by growth needs, in other words, higher order needs' (2002: 712). The empirical results suggest that front-line white-collar workers are primarily motivated by the satisfaction of their relatedness needs by their relationships with their co-workers, by satisfaction of their existence needs and particularly by monetary reward.

Interestingly, and in contrast to Maslow's belief that growth needs do not motivate lower level workers, Arnolds and Boshoff's sophisticated study suggests that higher order needs such as growth needs *can* motivate front-line workers through increasing their self-esteem, 'provided that the motivation strategies directed at these higher order needs are correctly implemented' (2002: 713). The importance of this study is that it provides a plausible explanation, with supporting empirical data, of the relationship between needs satisfaction, an individual personality trait (self-esteem) and job performance intentions. More generally, by differentiating between different categories of employee, the analysis affirms the importance of avoiding the common tendency to generalize about managers' interventions to improve motivation.

Although Maslow's, McClelland's and Alderfer's needs theories of work motivation have been popularized in mainstream organizational behaviour texts, their detractors have identified several important limitations. It is posited that these less than robust theories are conceptually flawed; they do not provide managers with a clear, unambiguous basis for predicting specific workers' behaviour to satisfy a particular need. Recent critics have also pointed out that the needs theories are strongly informed by the Anglo-American cultural paradigm of individualism – other societal cultures might have different hierarchies of needs. Finally, there is an assumption that needs motivate individuals regardless of the age, sex or ethnicity of those involved. As a result, it can be argued that these theories are androcentric and reflect the values of a hierarchical social order (Cullen, 1994; Gordon and Whelan, 1998; Wajcman, 1998).

> **stop...**
>
> How helpful are Maslow's and Alderfer's theories in explaining why chief executives and car assembly workers might be predisposed to respond to different ways of motivating them to work?
>
> **...and reflect**

IN THE EBOOK ACCESS THE **OB IN FOCUS** BOX 'MONEY IS THE KEY INCENTIVE TO WORK MOTIVATION'.

Herzberg's motivator–hygiene theory

Frederick Herzberg's motivation research (Herzberg, 2003) was designed to test the concept that a worker has two different needs: the need stemming from a human being's nature to avoid pain from the environment, and the need thought to stem from an individual's unique characteristic of growing psychologically. Samples of workers were asked to describe events that resulted in either a significant increase or a significant decrease in their job satisfaction. After analysing the data, Herzberg found that the factors identified as sources of job satisfaction – called 'satisfiers', and later 'motivators' – were different from those identified as sources of dissatisfaction (called 'dissatisfiers' or 'hygiene' factors). The strong *motivators* were achievement, recognition, work itself, responsibility and advancement. The strong *hygiene* factors causing work dissatisfaction were company policy and administration, supervision, salary, interpersonal relations and working conditions.

Herzberg's well-known research predicts that managers can motivate subordinates if they are aware of and incorporate 'motivators' into job design. His motivator–hygiene theory has clear parallels with other content theories of motivation. For example, Herzberg's motivators are similar to Maslow's higher order needs and Alderfer's growth needs, and his hygiene factors resemble Maslow's lower order needs, as well as Alderfer's existence and relatedness needs. Empirical studies on the motivator–hygiene theory have had mixed results, but they are credited with stimulating research on the association between job design and performance, including the later work of Hackman and Oldham (see Chapter 10).

Process theories of motivation: workers with choices

Early theories of motivation focused on the role of deep inner unconscious drives, emotions and instincts in guiding human action, and were influenced in particular by the Austrian neurologist Sigmund Freud (1856–1939) (Dörnyei and Ushioda, 2013). Since the 1970s, work psychologists have shifted the focus of research from unconscious to conscious motivational processes (for example, the interpretation of events, goals and expectations, and self-efficacy) in the shaping of employee behaviour.

In this stream of thinking, process theories of motivation focus on how employees make conscious choices that lead to a specific work behaviour; they emphasize the role of the individual's cognitive processes in determining her or his level of work motivation. Organizational leaders using process theories to motivate employees do so by clarifying the link between effort and reward. The three process theories of work motivation examined here are equity theory, expectancy theory and goal-setting theory.

Equity theory

Equity theory is one of the most influential process theories and is best known because of a series of studies by J. Stacey Adams (1965). Arguably, in the post-2008 age of austerity and escalating inequality, equity theory has contemporary resonance. Its basic premise is that there is one important cognitive process that involves employees comparing their own experience with the effort that other employees are putting into their work and the rewards that they are receiving. This process of 'social comparison' results in feelings of equity or inequity, and leads employees to form judgements on the value or 'valence' of a reward or outcome. According to equity theory, employees perceive effort and reward not in absolute but in relative terms, in the form of a ratio (Adams, 1965):

$$\frac{\text{Outcome (self)}}{\text{Inputs (self)}} : \frac{\text{Outcome (other)}}{\text{Inputs (other)}}$$

Employees experience equity when they perceive that others are receiving a similar ratio of inputs (such as hours worked, time studying for qualifications and relevant work experience) to outcomes (such as pay, status and promotion) as they are receiving themselves. When workers perceive an input–outcome ratio that favours other workers in the organization (underpayment) or relevant others (such as workers in a similar company) or themselves (overpayment), they experience inequity, which is assumed to be a sufficiently unpleasant experience to motivate changes in their behaviour.

One practical application of equity theory is in the area of *reward management*. Managers must be careful to avoid setting pay rates that cause employees to feel underpaid relative to others either in the same workplace (internal equity) or in comparison groups outside the organization (external inequity). It should be noted that the reward system is part of a diverse range of interlocking control techniques that contain internal tensions and inconsistencies. For instance, a performance-related reward system might become discredited in the eyes of employees because of perceived 'procedural injustices' caused by subjective and inconsistent appraisals by managers who did not have the skills needed to judge performance fairly. As a result, the employees would experience internal inequity, and instead of the reward system motivating them, their commitment would be weakened (Bratton and Gold, 2012). The nature of the internal inequity can generate negative feelings such as anger, which results in reduced employee commitment or even in acts of sabotage in the workplace. Collectively, if the perception of external inequity is strong and is shared by a sufficient number of workers, unionization and strike action can occur. Most recent studies are most conclusive about perceived negative inequity and 'relative deprivation' in conditions of underpayment (Feldman et al., 2002).

But how might self-identity, perceived inequality and dignity influence motivation in the workplace? Alex Haslam (2004) has applied the concept of self-identity to equity theory. He argues that employees' motivation is based on positive self-identity rather than on notions of fairness. For example, an employee passionate about wildlife who identifies with 'green' issues such as reducing greenhouse gases may well be motivated to work in an organization committed to reducing its level of carbon emissions. This interesting observation resonates with the notion that preserving human dignity *at* and *in* work might be a prime influence on employee motivation (Bolton, 2007).

A classic study by Baldamus (1961) of the 'wage–effort exchange' is still relevant to understanding misbehaviour in the workplace, because it links the notion of external inequity to inherent tensions and workplace conflict. A fuller understanding of this relationship between effort levels or inputs, and rewards or outcomes, is provided by the expectancy theory of motivation.

Expectancy theory

expectancy theory: a motivation theory based on the idea that work effort is directed towards behaviours that people believe will lead to desired outcomes

The role of the employee's perception of the link between effort or performance levels and desirable reward is further reinforced in the **expectancy theory** of work motivation. This theory assumes a rational model of decision making whereby employees assess the costs and benefits of alternative courses of inputs and outcomes, and choose the course with the highest reward.

The first formulations of expectancy theory can be found in the work of Kurt Lewin in 1935. The theory was popularized, however, by the work of Vroom, and further developed by Porter and Lawler (1968) and Lawler (1971, 1973). Psychologist Victor Vroom (1964) proposed that work motivation is contingent upon the perception of a link between levels of effort and reward. Perceiving this link is a cognitive process in which employees assess:

- whether there is a connection between their effort and their performance, labelled *expectancy*
- the perceived probability that their performance (such as higher productivity) will lead to valued outcomes (such as higher pay), which is labelled *instrumentality*
- the expected net value of the outcomes that flow from their effort, labelled *valence*.

Expectancy theory, therefore, has three basic parts:

effort-performance (E→P) expectancy: the individual's perceived probability that his or her effort will result in a particular level of performance

performance–outcome (P→O) expectancy: the perceived probability that a specific behaviour or performance level will lead to specific outcomes

valence: the anticipated satisfaction or dissatisfaction that an individual feels towards an outcome

1 the **effort–performance expectancy** (E→P)
2 the **performance–outcome expectancy** (P→O)
3 the attractiveness or **valence** of the outcomes (V).

According to expectancy theory, work motivation can be calculated if the expectancy, instrumentality and valence values are known. The formula for this calculation is:

$$Effort = E \, \Sigma \, I \times V$$

where *Effort* is the motivation of the employee to exert effort in her or his paid work, *E* is expectancy, *I* is the instrumentality of job performance, and *V* is the valence of an outcome(s). Σ (a capital sigma, the summation sign) indicates that effort is affected by a range of possible work and non-work outcomes that might result from job performance.

instrumentality: a term associated with process theories of motivation that refers to an individual's perceived probability that good performance will result in valued outcomes or rewards, measured on a scale from 0 (no chance) to 1 (certainty)

Expectancies are probabilities, ranging from 0 to 1, that effort will result in performance. An expectancy of 0.5 means that the person perceives only a 50 per cent probability that an increased effort will lead to an increased performance. The value for **instrumentality** can range from 0 to 1 (certainty). An instrumentality of 1 means that performance is certain to lead to the desired outcome. For example, an insurance agent selling a home insurance policy is certain to receive a commission. The instrumentality between the two events is therefore 1. **Valence** is defined as the perceived preference or value an employee has for a particular outcome, and it can be positive (+10), neutral (0) or negative (−10). A high anticipated satisfaction (a high positive valence) and a high anticipated dissatisfaction (a high negative valence) will, when multiplied by the associated instrumentalities and performance expectancy, have a large effect on work motivation.

As an example of the operation of expectancy theory, consider an employee – let's call him Joe – who perceives important work-related outcomes to be an increase in pay, promotion, a longer vacation time and less job-related stress. Figure 6.3 shows his expectancy theory calculations. Joe has ranked these four outcomes

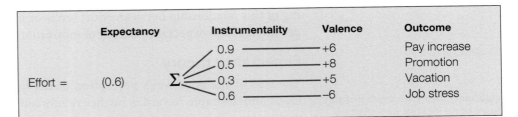

Figure 6.3 Sample expectancy theory calculations

on a +10 to −10 scale for valence, and has estimated the probability of an increased effort producing each of these outcomes. He sees both positive and negative expected outcomes from increased job effort. He reckons that there is only a 60 per cent chance that any increased effort on his part will lead to increased performance. The motivational force of the job – the effort an individual is willing to expend on it – is calculated by multiplying the expectancy value (0.6) by the products of the instrumentality and valence estimates. Thus:

$$\text{Effort} = (0.6) \times [(0.9)\,(+6) + (0.5)\,(+8) + (0.3)\,(+5) + (0.6)\,(-6)] = 4.38$$

Summing the expectancy theory variables, the overall motivation to exert an increased job effort is positive. Therefore, for Joe in this case, the rewards of putting in an increased effort outweigh the costs.

To use expectancy theory in an attempt to increase each employee's job efforts, a manager can focus on each element of expectancy theory. For example, a manager can aim to increase the employee's perception that her or his expenditure of effort will result in successful completion of the task. The effort–performance expectancy (E→P) for Joe, for instance, could increase from 60 per cent to 80 per cent, perhaps through additional training. In addition, a manager can help the employee to re-evaluate the performance–outcome expectancy (P→O). For example, the chances of promotion might be higher than anticipated by the employee. To go back to the example of Joe, his manager might use other employees' experiences to persuade Joe to increase his estimated probability of promotion if he does the job successfully from 50 per cent to 90 per cent. Finally, a manager can attempt to increase the attractiveness of the outcome, the valence (V). Thus, in our example, Joe could perhaps be persuaded that the outcome of exerting an additional effort (a pay increase, a promotion, a longer vacation) would be more important or have more value to him than he had previously thought.

A development of the expectancy theory of work behaviour is to be found in research by Porter and Lawler (1968). In their models, the determinants of each element are incorporated to provide a more comprehensive explanation of both the *what* and the *how* of the work motivation process. Effort–performance expectancy is, for example, moderated by past experiences of similar situations and communications from other people. The assumption here is that what employees learn from their past experiences contributes significantly to their effort–performance expectancies. If employees have had a series of past successes at similar work tasks, they will have a strengthened belief in their ability to perform those tasks, and to that extent their effort–performance expectancies will be high. But the informal learning – learning that is embedded in work activities – need not be only from personal past experiences. Employees can and do learn from their observations of relevant others in similar situations, and from others communicating their past experiences to their peers. If I see Sally, for instance, succeed at a work task, and she has qualifications and work experience similar to mine, I am more likely to calculate that I too will succeed at that task. This informal learning operates at an individual and a group level, as well as in the opposite direction.

plate 21 Expectancy theory can be used to better understand student motivation. It would predict that studying for an examination (effort) is conditioned by a result of correctly answering exam questions.

The performance–outcome expectancy link is contingent upon past experiences, communications from others and the attractiveness of the outcomes. The past experiences determinant refers to the individual's experience in relation to outcomes. Suppose, for example, that a manager introduces a reward system that is performance based, and that her appraisal ratings of her staff are known to be arbitrary. With knowledge of this past experience, it is unlikely that her subordinates will believe that the reward system will in practice be truly performance based. Thus, employees' past experience will influence their performance–outcome expectancies for the system. This assessment is, however, considerably affected by another determinant – communications from others – which represents an array of social interactions between employees, and between the supervised (employees) and their supervisors (managers), on a variety of outcomes, both positive and negative.

The valence of the outcomes (V) is moderated by the perceived *instrumentality* of the outcome to satisfy the individual's needs, and the perceived fairness or equity of the outcome. An outcome that is instrumental in satisfying an important need would have greater valence. But which outcome will an employee use to satisfy which need? Expectancy theorists suggest that it depends on the way the person has been socialized. Research suggests that, for Anglo-American employees at least, pay is most instrumental for satisfying physiological, security and ego-status needs, and not at all instrumental in satisfying social and self-actualization needs (Lawler, 1971).

The findings also explain why pay is important to both low-paid and high-paid employees. To the former, pay is instrumental in satisfying their physiological needs; to the latter, a high monthly pay cheque is instrumental in satisfying their ego-status needs (Kanungo and Mendonca, 1997). The value of the outcome is also determined by the perceived equity of the reward. As we discussed earlier, employees compare their own input–reward ratio with the input–reward ratio of relevant others. If the two ratios are perceived to be equal, equity exists and the reward's valence increases. Thus, the valence of an outcome is affected by employees' perception of its equity, considering their overall effort level relative to the effort levels and rewards of their co-workers.

By recognizing the importance of informal workplace learning and social comparisons, Lawler's model provides an insightful refinement of expectancy theory. The model enables managers to better understand the complexity of managing people and, in particular, how the elements of work motivation relate to one another in the motivation process.

Source: Getty Images

stop...

Based on your understanding of process theories, why are some managers more effective than others at motivating people?

...and reflect

goal setting: the process of motivating employees and clarifying their **role perceptions** by establishing performance objectives

role perceptions: a person's beliefs about what behaviours are appropriate or necessary in a particular situation, including the specific tasks that make up the job, their relative importance and the preferred behaviours to accomplish those tasks

Goal-setting theory

Another process theory of motivation is goal-setting theory, developed by Edwin Locke (1968). The theory proposes that participatory **goal setting** and the communication of accurate information on work performance can be positive motivators for employees. One version of this theory of motivation contains four major assumptions:

1 *Challenging* goals will produce a higher performance than less challenging goals.
2 *Specific* challenging goals will produce a higher performance than no goals or only vague or general goals, such as 'do your best'.
3 Goal-setting with *feedback* on goal attainment will produce higher performances than goal-setting alone.
4 *Employee participation* in goal-setting will produce higher performances than no participation.

management by objectives: a participative goal-setting process in which organizational objectives are cascaded down to work units and individual employees

Research conducted in several countries has been consistent in demonstrating that goal-setting techniques do have a positive influence on work motivation (Latham and Locke, 1990; Tubbs, 1986). The technique of **management by objectives** is one of the best-known applications of goal-setting theory and has been extensively used by Anglo-American management. In non-unionized workplaces, management by objectives also provides a mechanism for appraising pay awards based on employees' performance.

The most potent criticism of process theories is the insufficient attention they give to the relationship between the individual and the surrounding social context. Employees are social beings, and human behaviour is always embedded in a range of physical, psychological sociocultural contexts that considerably affect an employee's cognition, emotions, behaviour and achievements (Dörnyei and Ushioda, 2013). We can date the genesis of recent thinking on social context and motivation back to classical sociological studies on human alienation and orientation to work.

VISIT THE *ONLINE RESOURCE CENTRE* AT HTTPS://HE.PALGRAVE.COM/COMPANION/BRATTON-WORK-AND-ORGANIZATIONAL-BEHAVIOUR3/ FOR FURTHER INFORMATION ON MANAGEMENT BY OBJECTIVES.

The sociological analysis of motivation: alienation, culture and self-identity

Sociologists have developed a very different approach to understanding motivation in the workplace. Using concepts such as alienation, culture, orientation to work and the 'self', they challenge the adequacy of mainstream psychological theories of work motivation. This stream of intellectual thinking remind us of the complex connection between the patterns of people's lives shaped by the societal configuration of class, gender and race that lie *outside* the workplace environment, and the patterns of social relations with others *inside* the work organization. This analysis of motivation also incorporates what critical theorists call the 'antagonisms' or 'contradictions' inherent in capitalist employment relations.

Alienation

The problem of alienation as a condition of capitalist modernity is found in many novels. Witness Dr Robyn Penrose, a central character in David Lodge's novel *Nice Work*, set in the early 1980s, condemning the mindless, repetitive work and brutalizing conditions in Vic Wilcox's factory. As we discussed in Chapter 3, Karl Marx developed the concept of alienation. For most sociologists today, alienation is seen as residing in the social structure of the capitalist labour process rather than in personality traits. In other words, its causes are rooted in capitalist employment relations, and are *social* rather than psychological (Mandel and Novack, 1970; Noon and Blyton, 2013; Rinehart, 2006).

When we refer to alienation in this book, we mean a phenomenon in which people have little or no control over the products or services they produce or offer, the organization of work or the immediate work process itself. As James Rinehart writes:

> alienation is objective or structural in the sense that it is built into human relationships at the workplace and exists independent of how individuals perceive and evaluate this condition. Alienations can be viewed broadly as a condition of objective powerlessness. (Rinehart, 2006: 14)

Much of the psychology-based research on work motivation appears entirely indifferent to, and possibly even ignorant of, the concept of alienation (Salaman, 1981). For sociologists, a major source of alienated labour is division of labour or specialization (see Chapter 2). Critical analysts have argued that workers are alienated because the nature of the work progressively wears away their self-esteem, and

stop...

What do you think of this explanation of work motivation? To what extent, if at all, can work be designed to reduce alienation in the workplace?

...and reflect

consequently their commitment to work and the organization (Rinehart, 2006). Consistent with need and expectancy theories of motivation, alienating work obstructs higher level needs and valent outcomes (instrumentalities), causing low commitment and low work motivation.

IN THE EBOOK ACCESS THE **CRITICAL INSIGHT** ON 'THE IMPACT OF PERSONALITY TRAITS AND AGE, GENDER AND CULTURAL BACKGROUND ON MOTIVATION MODELS'.

Culture

The concept of culture refers to the tangible and intangible aspects of human society including material objects, technology, language, beliefs and values that are learned, rather than inherited, and shared from person to person and from one generation to the next. How does culture determine work motivation? We look at national and organizational culture in detail in Chapter 17, but here we can note that a national culture can shape individual work values and patterns of behaviour in the workplace. The recent focus on the role of emotions in work motivation seems to have emerged from a number of parallel developments, including cross-cultural psychology exploring culturally specific motives, emotions and values, and the rise of **positive psychology** (Ryan, 2007). Organizational culture, which draws upon concepts from anthropology and sociology, can act as a form of managerial control, prescribing and prohibiting certain activities to shape and reshape workers' behaviour in a way that is consistent with the expectations of top management (Roddick, 1991; Tichy and Sherman, 1993). A perceptual analysis, however, should remind us that a 'strong' culture that motivates one employee will not necessarily motivate another (Hofstede et al., 2010).

positive psychology: a branch of psychology that focuses on the positive, including positive state, strengths and happiness in an individual's personal or working life

Work orientation

Work orientation refers to the meaning that individuals give to paid work and the relative importance they assign to work within their lives as a whole. This perspective on understanding workplace behaviour encourages a greater awareness of the connections between work attitudes, values and behaviour patterns, and the structure and culture of society. As mentioned above, people's working and non-working lives are shaped by the societal configuration of class, gender and race that lies outside the workplace, as well as by the behaviour of managers and non-managers inside the organization. An interest in individual differences to work orientation has led some researchers to investigate the connection between work motivation and social factors. These social factors include, but are not limited to, class, gender and race (Mottaz, 1985).

work orientation: an attitude towards work that constitutes a broad disposition towards certain kinds of paid work

A classic British study by Goldthorpe et al. (1968) focused on the relationship between work orientation and social class. The researchers argued that if individuals enter an impoverished work situation in the full knowledge that intrinsic rewards are not available, their work motivation is not likely to be significantly influenced by the absence of such rewards. In essence, Goldthorpe et al. suggested that, for a majority of the workers in their study, extrinsic rewards – such as pay or what they called the 'cash nexus' – were much more important than intrinsic rewards. The majority of workers, they explained, had decided 'to give more weight to the instrumental at the expense of the expressive aspects of work' (Goldthorpe et al., 1968: 33).

Numerous studies have investigated possible gender-related differences in work orientation and the determinants of work satisfaction (Cullen, 1994; Hodson, 1999; Mottaz, 1986). Testing the hypothesis that men and women have different expectations from paid work, the results show that although women are more likely to enter an impoverished work situation than men, they have lower expectations and hence are as satisfied with their paid employment as men are. When men and

plate 22 The task of discovering what motivates different categories of employee in different work settings is of the same magnitude as finding the Holy Grail. For example, what factors motivate each of these men at work?

women in management positions are compared, it has been found that both have very similar orientations to work (Mottaz, 1986). One possible explanation for a gender-related work orientation is differences in sex-role socialization. In support of this argument, there is well-documented evidence that women are socialized to pursue occupations reflecting their stereotyped sex roles, regardless of their individual abilities and talent. Studies affirm that the aspirations and choices that women have with regard to employment are frequently far lower than the aspirations of men with a comparable ability (Wilson, 2003).

The work orientation approach was seen as an alternative to needs theories of work motivation. It adds support to *expectancy theory* in that it emphasizes the need to focus on the expectations that individuals bring to the workplace in order to understand their behaviour *inside* the workplace. It can also add support to *social cognition theory*, an individualistic perspective, which examines how the social context is reflected in a person's mental processes and in the attitudes, beliefs and values that result (Dörnyei and Ushioda, 2013). As others insist, the conundrum of how to motivate workers cannot usefully be considered until we know their needs and expectations relative to their employment (Goldthorpe et al., 1968). Although the orientation to work thesis is a useful corrective to the psychological universalism of needs and process motivation theories, it is important not to be drawn into a determinism about the possibilities for work motivation (Watson, 1986). More importantly perhaps, orientations to work are ever changing and can alter with the particular circumstances in which they become relevant to shaping behaviour. Examples of major change include attitudes to work–life balance, job insecurity arising from the global economic recession or precarious employment relationships, and employers' coercion of employees (Daniel, 1973; Kelly, 2005; Rousseau, 1995; Standing, 2011; Vosko, 2000). The notion of 'dynamic orientations' suggests that factors that will motivate the individual can be seen to be embedded in both the social context and the individual's psychological contract with the employing organization.

The 'self' at work

The sociological concept of the 'self' informs new theories of work motivation. As we discussed in Chapter 4, through life experiences we develop a sense of *self*, the perceptual picture we have of ourselves, our view of what kind of person we are.

The *self-concept theory* of motivation is derived from the concept of the self-identity as an underlying force that motivates non-calculative-based behaviour in the workplace. The self-concept theory connects individuals' self-identity with their motivation in the workplace (Haslam, 2004; Leonard et al., 1999). Social identity theory and self theory assume that employees are motivated to maintain a positive self-image and self-esteem (Myers et al., 2010). When individuals categorize themselves at a personal level, they are motivated to undertake activities that promote their personal identity, but when they categorize themselves at a social level, they become motivated to do activities that promote group membership (Haslam, 2004).

The self-identity theory of motivation is based on a number of assumptions about human nature: (1) people are motivated to retain and enhance their self-esteem and self-worth; (2) individuals are not only goal oriented but also self-expressive; (3) they are driven to maintain and increase their sense of self-consistency; (4) self-concepts are composed, in part, of social identities; and (5) self-concept behaviours are not necessarily related to specific calculative instrumental goals. So, for example, an individual may volunteer to do unpaid work at a shelter for homeless people out of a sense of self-esteem and responsibility. And a young person may choose to enter the family business or to enter a profession because it has since early childhood always been expected of her by significant others and has become an important part of her social identity.

A variant theory is the *whole-self theory* of motivation, which posits an association between an individual's needs for spirituality and for work. It assumes that human beings are motivated by more than financial rewards – by spiritual needs. According to this theory, people are looking for their work to provide deeper significance and self-meaning. So, as one advocate of the theory explained, 'the pressure many of us feel to recognize and respond to the sacred in us must find outlet in the secular workplace' (Fairholm, 1996). The whole-self theory is a variant of Maslow's higher order self-actualization need. The self-concept theory and whole-self theory of motivation imply that employee motivation is less susceptible to managerial initiatives and control. It seems intuitively plausible that there are significant individual differences based on self-concept that strongly influence motivation in the workplace. However, research is needed to support the hypothesis and establish a direct link between self-concept and workplace behaviour.

Integrating the approaches

Motivation theories attempt to explain nothing less than why people think and behave as they do, and it is doubtful that the complexity of this phenomenon can be comprehensively accounted for by a single theory (Dörnyei and Ushioda, 2013). With this in mind, the purpose of the model shown in Figure 6.4 is heuristic; it aims to convey to the reader that the intellectual thinking on work motivation is a complex, rich, interrelated set of accumulated multidisciplinary knowledge and ideas drawn from cognition (expectancy theory) and a person's emotional and self-identity dimensions.

The model suggests that individual behaviour and work performance are based on the three expectancies – effort–performance, instrumentalities and valence – as well as by individual abilities and personality traits (Box 1), by self-perceptions and the psychological contract (Box 2), by emotions (Box 3), by self-identity (Box 4), by

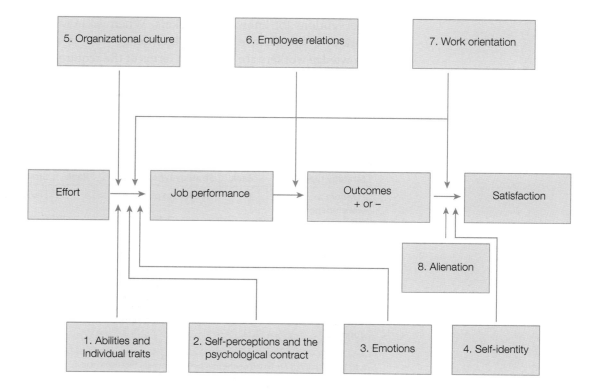

Figure 6.4 Integrating cognitive and sociological approaches to work motivation

organizational culture (Box 5), by employee relations (Box 6), by work orientation (Box 7) and by the alienating aspects of work (Box 8) all of which interact with each other, set in motion by past and present work life experiences. This integrated framework, inspired by Amabile and Kramer's (2007) 'inner work life' model, has several advantages. It is informed by the work of psychologists and sociologists, incorporates expectancy theories, and emphasizes the importance of complex social processes in shaping individual and group behaviour. It suggests that employees are motivated when their work experiences in the workplace include favourable perceptions of the work, the work group and the management, positive emotions, a stronger personal and social identity, and an experience of dignity at and in work. For an alternative integrated theory model, see the work of Klein (1989).

Applying motivation theories

Implementing motivational theory successfully in the workplace is challenging, and managers cannot simply transplant one of the theories discussed in this chapter and apply it in its 'pure' form. All individuals are unique and will respond differently to attempts to motivate them. What factors motivate a 56-year-old computer engineer? What factors motivate working mothers with young children? What factors motivate Muslim women at work? Managers need to be sensitive to the differences in individual needs and values among the people they manage. They need to avoid viewing their 'employees' as a homogeneous group. People are different in what they need and what they value, and in how they perceive and judge their work situation. For this reason, managers' interventions to increase motivation must take into account the occupation (for example, managers, knowledge workers or first-level employees) and the employees' age, gender, race, ethnicity and disabilities (if any). This is only possible when managers know their employees.

People engage in paid work for many reasons besides the weekly or monthly pay cheque. They work so that they can be with others, gain respect, form an identity and realize their human potential. As an illustration, consider possible motivation interventions for knowledge workers. When we examined the changing nature of work in Chapter 2, we said that knowledge work is 'ambiguity intensive' and that knowledge workers are defined in terms of the requirement to share and apply their professional knowledge with others in the organization. Drawing on a study by Horwitz and his colleagues (2003), Table 6.2 shows the most popular, highly effective and least effective motivation interventions for managing knowledge workers.

Table 6.2 Most popular, highly effective and least effective motivation strategies for knowledge workers

Most popular		Highly effective		Least effective	
Strategy type	Rank	Strategy type	Rank	Strategy type	Rank
Freedom to plan and work independently	1	Freedom to plan work	1	Flexible work practices	1
Regular contact with senior executives	2	Challenging work	2	Large cluster of knowledge workers	2
Incentive bonuses	3	Access to state-of-the-art technology and products	3	Generous funding for conferences	3
Challenging work	4	Top management support	4	Cash awards for innovations	4
Top management support	5	Ensure fulfilling work	5	Recruitment of people who fit the organizational culture	5

Note: These rankings are based on the number of responses that were marked as the five most frequently used motivation interventions, and the five most highly effective and ineffective in motivating knowledge workers.

Source: Adapted from Horwitz et al. (2003), pp. 31–2

As column 2 indicates, the most highly effective interventions to increase the motivation of knowledge workers included employment practices that allowed them the freedom to plan their work independently (in other words, to have autonomy). Although an important limitation of the research data is that they are based on employers' perceptions of effectiveness rather than on knowledge workers' views of what motivates them, the results are consistent with other studies surveying knowledge workers themselves (Horwitz et al., 2003). There is a sizeable literature indicating that work motivation strategies need carefully to consider appropriate rewards and job design.

Reward design and motivation

In the context of mobilizing employees' motivation in order to achieve the organization's objectives, rewards emphasize a core facet of the employment relationship: it constitutes an economic exchange or relationship. The reward is typically a package made up of pay, extended health plans, pension plans, vacation time and so on. Since the early 1980s, a 'new pay' agenda has been imported into UK workplaces moving from pay for time – show up and get paid – to pay for individual or team outputs – show up and perform to a satisfactory standard and get paid, perform to a highly satisfactory standard and cooperate with co-workers and receive more pay (Corby et al., 2009). This individualized performance model is undoubtedly associated with the decline of trade union influence, neo-liberal economics and market deregulation, topics too large to examine in detail here. Table 6.3 classifies types of reward and the behaviour objectives of the new pay paradigm.

Table 6.3 New rewards and behaviour objectives

Type of reward	Examples	Behaviour
Individual rewards	Pay Overtime Performance standard Commission Bonuses Merit Paid leave Benefits	Time: maintain work attendance Outputs: perform assigned tasks Competence: complete tasks without error
Team rewards	Team bonuses	Cooperation with co-workers, sharing information and knowledge
Organizational rewards	Profit sharing Share ownership	Commitment to culture and goals

Here we will be concerned with pay – money paid for work done – as an essential factor in work motivation. The motivational characteristics of pay are controversial, not least because of the fundamental tension between the economic, sociological and psychological theoretical frameworks or perspectives. Orthodox economic theory takes as its starting point the free labour market, which is based on the assumption that individuals are rational economic maximizers. Thus, other things being equal, higher pay will increase the number of people willing to work for the organization, and pay incentives will generate superior performance. Organizational scholars informed by sociological thinking emphasize that power relationships (see Chapter 14) can be of central importance in determining motivation at work. Furthermore, as previously discussed, sociology proposes that gender differences, culture and social inequality have a major influence on work motivation. The major psychological theories focus on the individual employee's perceptions, needs and expectations.

We began this book by noting the effects of the global recession on the *psychological climate*. The analysis of the motivational characteristics of pay cannot ignore a whole range of important contextual variables such as the economic recession, culture and pay inequality. Evidence from international studies indicates that the perceived importance of pay as a motivator is bound up in the 'cultural clothes of masculinity' (Hofstede, 1998a, 2001; Van de Vliert et al., 2008). On one important aspect of social inequality – economic inequity – the statistics are truly breathtaking (see Chapter 8). Over the last 25 years in both Britain and North America, neo-liberal capitalism has widened the gap between the pay levels of executives and the rest (Piketty, 2014).

Organizational psychology uses a distinctive range of concepts, and emphasizes individual employees' perceptions, needs and expectations. Pay is considered to be one of the most noticeable employment practices through which the psychological contract can be established, changed or violated (Rousseau and Ho, 2000). Pay shapes the psychological contract by signalling to employees the behaviour that the organization values. A violation refers to the feelings of anger, fear, helplessness and betrayal that are experienced when the employee perceives that a breach of contract has occurred. This may occur when a promise on the nature of the contract turns out to be less favourable (for example, lower payment) than the employee expected, or as a result of job loss when the employee expected long-term security. The nature of the psychological contract means that every employee will put a somewhat different valuation on the pay provided and on the value of their contribution depending on their individual traits and situational circumstances.

The motivational characteristics of pay are multifaceted as a result of the conflict between intrinsic and extrinsic motivators. According to Maslow's and Alderfer's need theories, pay addresses lower level needs as it can be exchanged for the basic necessities of life. Adam's equity theory posits that pay is an important motivator because workers compare their performance and pay with their peers. Pay should also prove motivational to the extent that it is highly valent and is clearly tied to performance, according to Vroom's expectancy theory.

So is pay an effective tool to motivate workers? Motivation is the nexus of character and circumstance. This observation takes account of both human perceptions, needs and expectations in terms of motivation, and the fact that human behaviour always happens within a particular time and situation. Empirical research has found that pay is not always an effective motivator as it will motivate only some people at some points in time, whereas with other people and at other times, it will actually demotivate them.

Research by Horwitz et al. (2003) highlights the contradictions and controversies surrounding pay–performance systems. In this case, pay being contingent upon performance had a detrimental effect on highly paid knowledge workers because, arguably, these individuals considered additional extrinsic rewards to be less important than intrinsic motivators. A study by Benabou and Tirole (2003) suggests that, in the short term, an emphasis on pay may act as a stimulus for effort, but in the long term, money may have a detrimental effect by reducing intrinsic motivation.

Finally, we can note in this discussion on motivation the role that reward has played in the recent global economic recession. A key contributor to the crisis leading to the pandemic criticism of executive bankers is that, in a 'culture of easy reward', they engaged in excessive risk-taking behaviour in their quest for huge bonuses (Perkins, 2009).

Empowerment and job satisfaction

Employment is a social activity, and for many people it is not regarded simply as a means to an end. Jobs are central to the lives of most people in that they provide identity, status and experienced meaningfulness. The motivation theories discussed in this chapter suggest that the design of work can be the most effective motivator for many employees (see Table 6.2).

Source: Image Source

Cut benefits to motivate 'skivers' versus pay bonus to motivate 'strivers'

The unemployed and the bankers, who occupy the lowest and highest extremes in terms of income, have one thing in common: their income has been capped. In 2013, the British government introduced a range of caps to the total of benefits and tax credits that limited the maximum to £500 for a couple or a lone parent and £350 for a single adult. The policy is intended to (1) produce savings for the Exchequer; (2) 'promote fairness by ensuring that workless households cannot receive more in benefit payments than the median average income of a working household' (House of Commons, 2013, p. 1); and (3) encourage people into at least 16 hours of employment per week.

The European Parliament has limited bankers' bonuses from 2015 to 100 per cent of their salaries, which can only be increased to 200 per cent with shareholder approval. This will reduce the income of bankers whose bonuses have far exceeded their salaries. For example, in 2013 Barclays paid more than £1 million in bonuses to 428 of its bankers. The banks have opposed the European Union directive limiting bonuses and defend high compensation in order to retain staff and to compete in global markets for talent. 'If we are to act in the best interests of our shareholders we have to make sure we have the best people in the firm,' the head of Barclays, Antony Jenkins has said (Treanor, 2014a).

The level of income is central in both these cases: for the unemployed it must be kept low in order to provide an incentive to work, and for bankers it must be high to attract and retain talented individuals to work on behalf of the bank's shareholders. To some extent, the emphasis on rewards is consistent with the psychological approaches outlined in this chapter, such as equity theory, according to which people develop perceptions of fairness in relation to the balance between effort and reward, and expectancy theory, in which employees are said to choose behaviours that are perceived as most likely to secure the highest reward. Goldthorpe et al. (1968) found, in their survey of workers at three firms in Luton, UK, that the majority of workers had

an instrumental orientation to work and had made a rational choice to prioritize high pay (extrinsic rewards) over any intrinsic satisfaction that work might provide. Their commitment to their employment was based on a 'cash nexus' so that they could to support a good family life and leisure status away from work.

The weakness in emphasizing the economic dimension of motivation to work is that this ignores other factors. Maslow's theory of needs and the sociological whole-self theory suggest that people may wish to find intrinsic satisfaction and meaning in work. It also ignores other material or cultural factors that influence decisions to seek work, such as the number of job vacancies. In the UK, there are four claimants per vacancy, with much higher competition in some areas such as the Isle of Wight, where in March 2014 there were 17.9 Jobseeker's Allowance claimants per job centre vacancy.

Stop! What obstacles do you think might prevent unemployed people from applying for work? Several chief executives of British banks have justified giving exceptionally high bonuses and share allowances in order to recruit and retain the best staff. Imagine that you occupy a highly rewarded position in a bank in London. Would you relocate to another part of the world for a higher reward, or would non-financial factors influence your decision to stay in your current position?

Sources and further information

Goldthorpe, J. H., Lockwood, D., Bechhofer, F. and Platt, J. (1968) *The Affluent Worker: Industrial Attitudes and Behaviour*, Cambridge: Cambridge University Press.

House of Commons (2013) 'The role of Jobcentre Plus in the reformed welfare system', *Work and Pensions Committee*. Available at: www.publications.parliament.uk/pa/cm201314/cmcelect/cmworpen/479/47909... (accessed March 24, 2014).

Office for National Statistics (2014a) 'Claimant count and vacancies'. Available at: www.ons.gov.uk/rel/lms/labour-market-statistics/march-2014/dataset-claimant-count-and-vacancies.html (accessed March 24, 2014).

Office for National Statistics (2014b) 'Nomis official labour market statistics'. Available at: www.ons.gov.uk/ons/rel/lms/labour-market-statistics/march2014/dataset-claimant-count-and-vacancies.html (accessed March 25, 2014).

Treanor, J. (2014a) 'Barclays condemned over £2.4bn bonuses', *The Guardian*, February 11. Available at: www.theguardian.com/business/2014/feb/11/barclays-hikes-bonuses-profits-slide (accessed March 25, 2014).

Note: This feature was written by David Denham, Honorary Research Fellow in Sociology, University of Wolverhampton, UK.

---

creativity: the capacity to develop an original product, service or idea that makes a socially recognized contribution

self-efficacy: the beliefs people have about their ability to perform specific situational task(s) successfully

Job design (see also Chapter 10) refers to the process of assigning tasks to a job, including the interdependency of those tasks with other jobs. Redesigning work to enlarge the number of tasks performed and allow greater decision making can be effective in motivating individual employees to superior performance and an enhanced sense of achievement and self-worth. The concept of *empowerment* is one term used to describe motivational job design practices designed to allow employees some 'voice' in group or/and organizational decision making, either in their day-to-day work or through formal managerially driven mechanisms that enlist workers' skills, experience and **creativity** (Marchington, 2008). Empowering job design initiatives are predicated on the social psychology theory that individuals have a cognitive need for self-actualization and self-determination and, as such, can heighten their **self-efficacy** (see Chapter 4). The cognitive concept of self-efficacy or a 'can-do' mentality refers to the beliefs that people have about their ability to perform specific situational task(s) successfully.

Contrary to the principles of Theory X, higher level growth needs have been shown to have a significant influence on the self-esteem of first-level employees as well as of higher level employees (see Figure 6.2). As Arnolds and Boshoff (2002: 715) put it, 'front-line employees ... also like to make one or more important decisions every day, use a wide range of their abilities and have the opportunity to do challenging things at work'.

However, research emphasizes that the relationship between job design and intrinsic motivation stresses the highly subjective nature of the motivation process. A recent study has posited that because the relationship between need satisfaction and autonomous motivation results from the situation, 'managers can influence the level of employees' intrinsic motivation in two ways: first, by changing the job design and working conditions in a way that fulfil employees' needs; and second, by changing the appraisals of the work regime by communicating about it (Vandercammen et al., 2014: 74).

Furthermore, although the motivation strategy behind job design focuses on notions of self-fulfilment, identity and employee perceptions of the task's characteristics, the way in which two employees view a particular job and perceive an identical task may be quite different depending on such factors as their age, personality and orientation to work, so achieving this is not straightforward.

Gender, for example, influences identity formation among women. Josselson (1987: 8), in her work on identity, found that 'in comparison to men, women orient themselves in more complicated ways, balancing many involvements and aspirations, with connections to others paramount; their identities are thus compounded and more difficult to articulate'. Following on from this and the requirement for a differentiation between occupational groups, it is insufficient to make objective changes in skill variety, autonomy or other job dimensions. Managers need to also appreciate and monitor how those objective changes influence the perceptions of different employees (see Chapter 5).

Herzberg's motivator–hygiene theory supports motivator empowerment strategies to increase job satisfaction. Hackman and Oldham's (1980) job characteristic theory identifies five core job characteristics – **skill variety**, **task identity**, **task significance**, autonomy and feedback – as critical factors to produce high job satisfaction (see Figure 10.8). Overall job satisfaction refers to a collection of feelings or emotions that an employee has about her or his job as a whole.

Peter Warr's (2002) three-dimensional model (Figure 6.5) portrays the range of emotional responses to paid work. Central to this model is the horizontal pole illustrating emotions of high or low pleasure. In research on job-related well-being, this horizontal pole is traditionally indexed as job satisfaction. The second pole runs between anxiety and comfort. In the top left quadrant, feelings of anxiety combine high mental arousal with low pleasure. The third pole runs from depression to enthusiasm. In the top right quadrant, feelings of positive motivation combine high mental arousal with high pleasure. An employee's location on each of the three poles can be determined using a standard questionnaire. This model has been extended with a fourth pole describing feelings of fatigue versus vigour (Daniels, 2000).

That job satisfaction is essentially an affective rather than a cognitive response means that the concept is integral to the wider context of emotional labour, job-related stress and psychological well-being. It is important to bear in mind that job satisfaction is not a totally individualistic notion. The accounts of their job satisfaction that employees give to researchers will be influenced by their life experiences and orientation to paid work. Finally, research on job satisfaction has proved

skill variety: the extent to which employees must use different skills and talents to perform tasks in their job

task identity: the degree to which a job requires the completion of a whole or an identifiable piece of work

task significance: the degree to which the job has a substantial impact on the organization and/or larger society

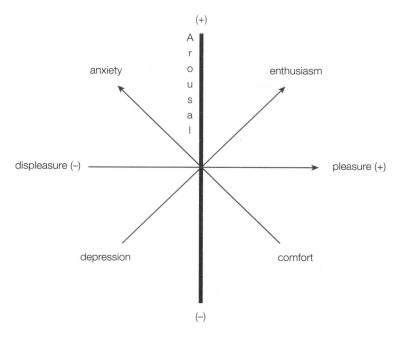

Figure 6.5 Three poles for the measurement of well-being

Source: Adapted from *Psychology at Work* (5th edn), edited by Peter Warr (Penguin Books, 2002), p. 3. Copyright © Peter B. Warr and contributors, 1996; 2002. Reproduced by permission of Penguin Books Ltd.

mixed results on the correlation between job satisfaction and workplace behaviour (Patterson and West, 1998; Somers, 2001).

Job satisfaction seems a crude measure for the almost infinitely complex array of social disparities in work-related stress and psychological well-being. A growing consensus points to wider life experiences, in particular the quality of people's social relationships in society. In some workplaces, employment relationships are supportive, helping individuals to deal with life's challenges. In other workplaces, these relationships are toxic, putting health-damaging stresses on workers. Here we have identified a number of factors influencing whether employment relationships are supportive or toxic. For example, Warr's research highlights the importance of job designs that foster a sense of autonomy and trust rather than powerlessness and distrust. Recent research by Wilkinson and Pickett (2010), by contrast, suggests that people's health depends on the quality of their social relationships, and that the most important determinant of the quality of relationships is the level of inequality. This is not a new idea, but if it is true, the effects of income inequality extend well beyond individual motivation and the work domain.

IN THE EBOOK ACCESS THE **OB IN FOCUS** BOX ON 'ANXIETY AND STRESS IN THE WORKPLACE'.

Chapter summary

- This chapter has emphasized the centrality of motivation in the employment relationship. Motivation is the driving force within individuals that affects the direction, intensity and persistence of their work behaviour in the interest of achieving organizational goals.

- We discussed Maslow's famous needs hierarchy. This assumes that when a person's need is not satisfied, that person experiences internal tension or states of deficiency, and this motivates the person to change their behaviour to satisfy that need (Kanter, 1990). All the need theories tend to be heavily prescriptive in nature.

- We explained how process theories of work motivation place emphasis on the actual psychological process of motivation. According to the equity theory, perceptions of equity or inequity lead employees to form judgements on the value (or valence) of a reward or outcome. When an employee perceives a reward item to be inequitable, the individual will be dissatisfied, which will result in the individual not finding the outcome attractive; thus, reward will not be an effective motivator.

- Expectancy theory is based on the idea that motivation results from deliberate choices to engage in certain behaviours in order to achieve worthwhile outcomes. Its most important elements are the perception that effort will result in a particular level of performance (E→P), the perception that a specific behaviour will lead to specific outcomes (P→O), and the perceived value of those outcomes, the valences. The attractiveness of work activities (their valence) depends on an employee's individual differences, cultural factors and orientation to work.

- This chapter also suggested that if we are to understand what motivates people, we must go beyond psychological notions of individual needs and cognitive processes. Scholars examining the relationship between the individual and the social context have adopted two perspectives: first, the individualistic perspective represented by the social cognition theory; and second, the societal perspective, which focuses on social processes and macro factors to explain motivation. We need to incorporate into any analysis the psychological climate, the culture, the dynamics of employment relations, orientation to work, social identity and the effects of complex interconnecting levels of domination, which stem from the class and gender relations in society.

IN THE EBOOK ACCESS **WEB BASED ASSIGNMENTS** TO APPLY YOUR LEARNING.

Chapter review questions

1 To what extent is motivating workers increasingly more or less challenging for managers in an era of escalating inequality? Explain your answer.

2 Compare and contrast Maslow's needs hierarchy theory and Alderfer's ERG theory. How are they similar? How are they different? What do the two theories imply for managerial practice?

3 Identify two different types of expectancy referred to in the discussion of expectancy theory and work motivation. What can a manager do to influence these expectations?

4 What are the limitations of expectancy theory in predicting an employee's work behaviour and performance?

5 What is the connection to the concept of self-concept, self-identity and motivation?

Further reading

Amabile, T. M. and Kramer, S. J. (2007) 'Inner work life: understanding the subtext of business performance', *Harvard Business Review*, 85(5) pp. 72–83.

Corby, S., Palmer, S. and Lindop, E. (2009) *Rethinking Reward*, Basingstoke: Palgrave Macmillan.

Horwitz, F. M., Chan Teng Heng and Quazi, H. A. (2003) 'Finders, keepers? Attracting, motivating and retaining knowledge workers', *Human Resource Management Journal*, 13(4), pp. 23–44 (see p. 33).

Latham, G. P. and Pinder, C. (2005) 'Work motivation theory and research at the dawn of the twenty-first century', *Annual Review of Psychology*, 56, pp. 485–516.

Pfeffer, J. (1998) *The Human Equation: Building Profits by Putting People First*, Boston, MA: Harvard Business School Press.

Pritchard, R. D. and Ashwood, E. L. (2008) *Managing Motivation*, New York: Routledge.

Schreurs, B., Guenter, H., Hetty van Emmerik, I. J., Notelaers, G. and Schumacher, D. (2015) 'Pay level satisfaction and employee outcomes: the moderating effect of autonomy and support climates', *International Journal of Human Resource Management*, 26(12) pp. 1523–46.

Van de Vliert, E., Van Yperen, N. W. and Thierry, H. (2008) 'Are wages more important for employees in poorer countries with harsher climates?', *Journal of Organizational Behavior*, 29, pp. 79–94.

Vandercammen, L., Hofman, J. and Theuns, P. (2014) 'The mediating role of affect in the relationship between need satisfaction and autonomous motivation', *Journal of Occupational and Organizational Psychology*, 87, pp. 62–79.

Chapter case study: Equity at FindIT

The setting

FindIT is a US-based company, founded in 1989. In 2014, it became the leader in publishing print and online directories for local and regional markets in the country. With the realization that their customers were looking to diversify their advertising outside the traditional channel of print, the company recently announced an expansion into the digital media market, including online and mobile platforms. At the same time, senior management began planning to introduce a new job evaluation scheme to simplify the pay structure.

To understand how management's plans affect people's experience of work, it is necessary to recognize the core features of job evaluation. First practised in the 1920s and 1930s, job evaluation is a systematic approach to establishing pay rates. Although variations have existed since its development, one popular method, the point system, attempts to create a more equitable process by ranking jobs based on a number of key factors (each assigned a number of points), such as required education, working conditions and supervision of others. Comparable jobs are grouped into different pay levels, creating a 'hierarchy of jobs': higher rated jobs are paid at the higher pay rates on the hierarchy. Although the actual pay rates are determined by comparing key jobs to the external market, the process of measuring jobs relative to each other within the organization creates a system focused on internal equity.

This approach was suited to the narrow and tightly structured jobs and job descriptions favoured by the classical organizations and unions of the first part of the twentieth century. Later, emerging human relations firms also embraced the method, believing that it established fairness and equity in a pay system. Job evaluation was perceived to minimize subjectivity, favouritism and management bias in the distribution of pay. Despite changing approaches to how work is organized and the increasing complexity of work since then, job evaluation as a means of determining base pay is still widely practised in unionized and government organizations in North America.

With the change in focus, many of FindIT's 600 employees whose work duties had been routine now argued that their jobs had become more complex. Several approached management and asked to have their jobs evaluated under the new system. The company agreed to first evaluate those jobs most directly impacted by the digital media initiative. A small group consisting of management and selected employees helped to gather the job information through worker questionnaires and conducted the evaluations.

The problem

The evaluations took 6 months to complete. When the results were released with the revised job descriptions, a number of employees were shocked to discover that their jobs had been overgraded under the old system, and they would not receive any salary increases, despite the new responsibilities and skills now required in their jobs. Of these employees, 25 per cent left the company, stating that their contributions or personal performances were not being recognized. For the rest, there was a distinct drop in their productivity and a rise in absenteeism. Interpersonal conflicts became more common as employees began to argue over the value of their jobs relative to others. On the shop floor, employees began to share notes on how to influence the evaluation results through the questionnaires they were asked to fill out.

The task

Working either alone or in a small group, prepare a report for FindIT's senior management on the employees' reaction to the new job evaluation scheme. Your report should address the following questions:

- How do equity theory and expectancy theory help to explain the reaction of the employees to the evaluation results?

- What role should managers play in ensuring the acceptance of a job evaluation system by the organization's employees?
- What would be the challenges in using job evaluation for today's more complex jobs, such as in research or information technology?

Sources and further information

Bassett-Jones, N. and Lloyd, G. C. (2005) 'Does Herzberg's motivation theory have staying power?', *Journal of Management Development*, 24(10), pp. 929–43.

Bratton, J. and Gold, J. (2012) 'Job evaluation', pp. 383–90 in *Human Resource Management: Theory and Practice* (5th edn), Basingstoke: Palgrave Macmillan.

Ulrich, D. and Ulrich, W. (2010) *The Why of Work*, New York: McGraw-Hill.

Note: This case study was written by Lori Rilkoff, Human Resources Director, City of Kamloops, BC, Canada.

IN THE EBOOK ACCESS AN **OB IN FILM** BOX THAT USES *DANGEROUS MINDS* (1995), STARRING MICHELLE PFEIFFER, TO EXAMINE WORK MOTIVATION AND TO ACCESS **AN INTERACTIVE QUIZ** TO TEST YOUR UNDERSTANDING.

chapter 7
Learning

Key concepts

- andragogy
- behaviourist approach
- cognitive approach
- creativity
- innovation
- learning process
- negative reinforcement
- Pavlovian conditioning
- positive reinforcement
- self-directed learning

Chapter outline

- Introduction
- The nature of workplace learning
- Classical learning theories
- Contemporary learning theories
- Critical adult learning theories
- Learning in a global economy
- Summary and end-of-chapter features
- Chapter case study: Learning to be green in New Zealand

Chapter learning outcomes

After completing this chapter, you should be able to:

1 Explain the importance of learning in organizations
2 Define learning and discuss the difference between formal, non-formal and informal learning
3 Discuss the contested nature of behavioural, cognitive and social learning theories
4 Articulate how adult learning theories add to our understanding of learning processes
5 Identify the effects of social class, ethnicity and gender on learning and training opportunities in the organization
6 Critically assess the strategic relevance and value of learning in the globalized economy

introduction

The mantra of mainstream contemporary management is 'Our employees are our most valuable resource' (Spencer and Kelly, 2013: 12). Since the late 1980s, human resource management scholarship has tended to emphasize the importance of investing in learning and in human resource development (Gold et al., 2013), primarily because it is regarded as a catalyst to the achievement of the organization's business objectives (Chartered Institute of Personnel and Development, 2010). The theoretical roots behind the practice of developing human capital are to be found in the social-technical theory that was developed at the Tavistock Institute in London. The lessons of the Tavistock research were, however, disregarded in traditional bureaucratic organizations, with the majority of employees being given limited opportunity to learn on the job and to go on learning. Orthodox management wisdom viewed the factory or office as a place to work, not to learn. Learning was an activity carried out at school, college and university before people joined the organization, or as part of a hybrid system of on-the-job and off-the-job apprenticeship training.

knowledge management: the capture of the individual's and group's tacit knowledge and learning, and its conversion into explicit knowledge so that it can be shared with, and built on by, others in the organization

> ## stop...
>
> The notion that education should serve business and the economy has been fiercely debated among adult educators. See Bruce Spencer and Jennifer Kelly's *Work and Learning* (2013) for an introduction to the debate. Look at the two opening quotes in their book. Is it reasonable to assume that education should serve business? What are your views on this?
>
> *...and reflect*

As notions of 'knowledge work', core competencies and sustainability have entered the contemporary management discourse, there has been a growing interest in the 'learning organization', 'workplace learning' and learning and talent development (Becker, 2001; Billett, 2001; Bratton et al., 2004; Foley 2001). The reliance on intellectual capital has led to the realization that corporate leaders need to foster learning-rich environments (Dochy, 2012; Senge, 1990; Watkins and Cervero, 2000). Advocates have asserted that there is no place for managers who do not appreciate their own vital role in providing rich learning experiences and workplaces (Becker, 2001; Boud and Garrick, 1999). The most successful organizations are, it is argued, those which capture the knowledge and expertise of talented knowledge workers and professionals, and disseminate it selectively throughout the organization. This is the essence of **knowledge management**, which has been heralded as 'essential to efforts to improve competitiveness and innovation' (Newell et al., 2009: 2).

In this chapter, we emphasize that an inclusive understanding of learning and employee development needs to acknowledge the general nature of capitalist employment relations, the way in which organizational control systems generate and express internal contradictions, and the tension between managerial control and learning. We begin by explaining the importance of work-related learning, and then proceed to examine competing classical theories of learning and contemporary approaches to adult learning. The final section discusses some practical applications of adult learning theories.

The nature of workplace learning

If you have worked in a paid job, can you recall how you felt on your first day? Like many young workers, you might have been nervous, even bewildered, as an environment filled with new faces and names, new tasks and new rules replaced the familiarity of school or college. But like most young workers, you probably adjusted to this new environment within a few days or weeks. This adjustment, or adaptation, to paid work can take many forms. Some are simple, such as responding to buzzers that sound to permit morning and lunch breaks from work.

New employees acquire explicit knowledge about the organization and working conditions in orientation workshops. The new information and skills needed for various aspects of the work are acquired from manuals, training workshops and co-workers. New employees also develop a knowledge about which aspects of their work behaviour are likely to be punished and which are likely to be rewarded. Some behaviours are appropriate only at certain times and in certain circumstances, and those circumstances must be identified and differentiated. Critical questioning, for example, might not be as acceptable at work as at school or college, but working collaboratively and sharing information – something perhaps forbidden by college academic rules – might be rewarded at work.

Learning in workplaces is laden with interest and can be contested (Jrvensivu and Koski, 2012). Workers learn to break rules in order to cope with work intensification, and they learn how to prevent unwanted consequences resulting from management actions. Karlsson (2012) observed that employees doing very dull work learnt to 'make time' by extending their tea breaks. In an industrial setting, because the wall clocks showed slightly different times, it was possible for workers to start a break by a fast clock and return by a slow clock, and thus gain a few minutes (p. 110). Workers can also learn *not* to learn because of perceived negative outcomes. For example, an individual employee or workers collectively may be reluctant to embrace learning and self-development because the resultant changes might undermine their collective interests (Bratton, 2001).

We can define **learning** as a relatively permanent change in behaviour or human capabilities resulting from processing new knowledge, practice or experience. These capabilities are related to specific learning outcomes, including cognitive skills, motor skills, attitudes and verbal information (Gagne and Medsker, 1996). Learning plays a central role in most aspects of individual and collective behaviour in the workplace, from the knowledge and skills that workers need to perform work tasks and the communication skills that managers use to motivate their subordinates, to clarifying the expectations, aspirations and understandings that managers and others have of each other (the psychological contract). Learning is people's primary mode of adaptation to ongoing social change (Jabri, 2012). People learn in organizations and other different settings: in educational institutions, in families, through community activities, from recreational events, through union activities and through political campaigns and action.

The quality of the learning experience in the workplace will depend on a range of situational factors. The way the work is designed – giving workers high or low autonomy – and the number of management levels in the organization affect work-related learning (Bratton, 2005). Working-life research emphasizes that engagement in work-related learning is one important dimension of the dignity *in* work model (Bolton, 2007). Research shows that a high, repetitive workload drives out an employee's experience of learning (Van Ruysseveldt and van Dijke, 2011). Clearly, different work regimes will affect how individuals engage, interact and construct knowledge from work situations. In this context, learning can take different forms:

- *Formal learning* is associated with college and university studies or professional programmes (such as study for accountancy qualifications).
- *Non-formal learning* involves some form of systematic instruction but takes place in a one-off situation (for example, a workshop on workplace violence) and typically does not lead to any formal qualifications.
- *Informal learning* occurs when people consciously try to learn from their context and everyday life experiences. It does not involve formal instruction, but does involve individual or collective (for instance, by a work team or trade union) critical reflection on experience. Over the last few decades, the conceptualization of informal learning in the workplace has undermined the supremacy of formal instruction and learning organized by educational institutions (Sawchuk, 2008).
- *Informal* and *incidental learning* are interconnected but are not necessarily the same (Marsick and Watkins, 1990). Incidental learning occurs through an activity or as a result of trial and error, and is seen as a by-product of direct experi-

learning: the process of the construction and ongoing reinforcement of new knowledge

explicit knowledge: knowledge that is ordered and can be communicated between people

tacit knowledge: knowledge embedded in our actions and ways of thinking, and transmitted only through observation and experience

learning organization: a metaphor representing an ideal of whole-organization learning on the part of all employees, and the use of learning to create value and transform the organization

organizational learning: a metaphor representing an organizational culture in which learning is continuous and embedded in what and how employees work, and in the systems that connect the parts together

intellectual capital: the sum of an organization's human capital, structural capital and relationship capital

reflexive learning: a view of adult learning that emphasizes learning through self-reflection

lifelong learning: the belief that adults should be encouraged, and given the opportunity, to learn either formally in education institutions or informally on or off the job

ence. Whereas people acquire **explicit knowledge** through formal, non-formal and informal learning processes, **tacit knowledge** is acquired through incidental learning.

Explicit knowledge is ordered and can be communicated between people. Tacit knowledge, on the other hand, refers to information that cannot easily be captured, measured or codified and communicated from one individual to another individual or group; it is therefore more subtle. The notion of tacit knowledge, at least in its emphasis on individual beliefs and taken-for-granted assumptions, comes close to what is called the social construction of reality (Salaman, 2007).

'**Learning organization**' and '**organizational learning**' are broad terms that are used to describe various learning principles as a means of coping with global competitiveness and budget constraints. In these learning paradigms, two types of learning are generally accepted:

- *Single-loop learning* – this involves employees improving their work processes through their daily work experiences.
- *Double-loop learning* – this entails employees questioning the underlying norms, assumptions and habits of workplace behaviour (Argyris and Schön, 1978; Matthews, 1999).

From a managerial perspective, it is suggested that an organization's investment in training and learning acts as a powerful signal of its intentions to develop its **intellectual capital**. This can help to develop employees' commitment to the organization rather than simply their compliance. With the wave of interest in flexible 'high-performance work systems' in the 1990s, it is not surprising that some academics and management gurus claimed that **reflexive learning** was a means to promote flexibility and achieve competitive advantage over an organization's rivals (Spencer and Kelly, 2013). Those subscribing to this view on sustainable competitive advantage advised companies to gain 'mutual commitment' by investing in training talented employees and encouraging **lifelong learning** (Kochan and Osterman, 1994). This belief in the efficacy of continuous work-related learning is linked to a broader debate about 'transformative' or 'progressive' human resource management, in which it is argued that work-related learning should be encouraged in order to enhance the performance of both the employees and the organization (Bratton and Gold, 2012).

Research has focused on evaluating the effectiveness of particular managerial or leadership styles in specific contexts, for achieving specific learning outcomes. The classic work of Peter Senge (1990) seeks to yield an understanding of how leadership practices can help bring about change and renew organizations through learning. He advocated that organizational leaders play the roles of teachers, designers and stewards in order to facilitate employee learning. Senge argued that 'leaders are responsible for building organizations where followers continually expand their capabilities to understand complexity, clarify vision, and improve shared mental models – that is, they are responsible for learning' (1990: 340).

A case study of 'leadership activity' that promoted work-related informal learning found evidence of leaders exhibiting the three roles Senge outlined: designer, steward and teacher. The followers' perception of their leaders highlighted the role of gender and power (Agashae and Bratton, 2001; Driver, 2002). For the most part, however, mainstream studies of leadership have paid little attention to how leadership activity actually encourages individual or group learning (Knights and Willmott, 1992).

The emergence of critical workplace learning studies has certainly added to the debate on the role of lifelong learning. Contributions to the debate have emphasized that 'cultural control' can be reinforced through learning (Legge, 2005). Critical accounts have exposed the potential of competency training to make work more 'visible' in order to make it more manageable (Townley, 1994). Others have criticized popular accounts of work-related learning for adopting a conflict-free managerialist perspective, in which it is assumed that the goals of managers and workers are shared, and inherent tensions in the employment relationship are largely ignored (Coopey, 1996).

Critical organizational theorists share a deep scepticism for popular prescriptive publications such as Senge's *The Fifth Discipline*, which discount the influence of power and political activity on workplace learning. For critical theorists, the likely effect of new learning regimes is to reshape organizational culture and strengthen the power of the managers over the managed. In fact, if learning is synonymous with change, attempts to manage a culture of learning, through either formal or informal processes or 'unlearning' the ways of thinking that worked in the past (Lei et al., 1999), can be regarded as a management strategy to promote a change in structures, attitudes and behaviour. It is argued that, in adopting a 'learning strategy', managers therefore hope to unfreeze traditional attitudes and work practices and foster creative thinking and new ways of doing, or innovation (see Chapter 18). Neglecting these wider socioeconomic dynamics, tensions and contested aspects of learning might mean that learning practices become a managerial tool for work intensification and control in the workplace (Spencer, 2001; Thompson and McHugh, 2009).

Despite the increasing diversity and feminization of the paid workforce in most economies of the Organisation for Economic Co-operation and Development, another notable feature of the contemporary learning discourse is the tendency for the academic research to be blind to race, ethnicity and gender issues. Some writers have focused critically on gender issues in workplace learning (for example, Davidson and Burke, 2011; Probert, 1999). The emergence of feminist accounts of workplace learning adds depth to our understanding of how sexuality, gender relations and the metaphorical 'glass ceiling' in organizations can shape – if not determine – access to learning for women managers. As these writers point out, the recent explosion of workplace learning practices still privileges men, and 'it is worth recognizing the continuities in women's unequal access to and benefit from workplace learning' (Probert, 1999: 112).

It should be apparent from this introduction that, as a field of study, learning can be explored and interpreted from different perspectives. Now that we have examined *why* learning is important to people and organizations, we go on to address two central questions: *how* do individuals learn, and *how* is work-related individual learning interconnected to collective learning in the organization?

IN THE EBOOK ACCESS THE **OB IN FOCUS** BOX ON 'THE LEARNING AGE: A RENAISSANCE FOR A NEW BRITAIN'.

Classical learning theories

Explicit and tacit knowledge are acquired in many different ways. The rest of this chapter gives an overview of both psychologically driven and socioculturally driven perspectives of learning. We begin by examining what can be called the 'classical' theories of learning. As in other areas of the discipline, these are considered classical partly because they represent the early contributions to our understanding of how children and adults learn, and also because some of the ideas recur in contemporary adult learning theories. It should be noted, however, that the explanations found in these different approaches are contested, and that no one theory

globalization & organization misbehaviour

Source: Stockbyte/Punchstock

Skills shortage and corporate (non) investment in training

Politicians and business leaders often claim that there is a skills shortage in the workforce. For example, Canadian Prime Minister Stephen Harper has repeatedly asserted that producing more skilled workers is 'the biggest challenge our country faces':

> For whatever reason, we know that peoples' choices, in terms of the education system, tend to lead us to ... a chronic shortage of certain skills. They are skilled trades, scientists and engineers,' he noted. (Morgan, 2014)

But is this analysis correct? 'No,' says Canada's Parliamentary Budget Office:

> '(In) the past couple of years, and certainly since the (mid-February federal) budget, there's been an assumption that we face a huge labour shortage and a skills mismatch,' said Mostafa Askari, assistant parliamentary budget officer. 'We just don't see that in the data.' (Wright, 2014)

There is certainly some level of skills mismatch in any economy. For example, young workers with medium to high literacy skills may hold jobs requiring medium to low literacy, and technological change may render some skills obsolete. For their part, employers have historically done a poor job of predicting skill demands; many new jobs require few skills and, of course, workers make choices about training and education for reasons other than satisfying the demands of employers (Livingstone and Scholtz, 2007).

Yet the most striking mismatch appears to be between the rhetoric of a skills shortage and its (un)reality. What explains this gap? It is possible that employers and politicians are simply misinformed. But ignorance does not explain why they continue to promulgate the skills gap narrative when faced with clear evidence that it does not exist.

Manufacturing a skills crisis allows employers to seek further government subsidies for training. For example, in 2014, Canada's federal government began rolling out the Canada Jobs Grant, which funds skills training for Canadians. Employers pay for one-third of the cost of training while the federal and provincial government cover the other two-thirds. Employers determine who receives what training. Behind the scenes, this programme appears to redirect government funding that was previously spent on training jobless Canadians to subsidize the employers' 'upskilling' of workers who are already employed.

Politicians may go along with such a demonstrably false narrative for political gain. According to union economist Jim Stanford, blaming workers for the skills gap obscures the broader issue of sluggish economic growth. According to this worldview, the biggest challenge facing our labour market is adjusting the attitudes, capabilities and mobility of jobless workers. The question of whether there are any productive, decent jobs for those workers to fill is downplayed or ignored altogether. The problem is, in other words, not with unemployment. The problem is with the unemployed (Stanford, 2013).

Interestingly, employers' efforts to resolve the skills shortage are modest at best:

> Despite the skills shortage, half of employers said they make 'not much effort' to recruit from under-represented groups, such as aboriginal Canadians, visible minorities, and the disabled. ... Asked about the high rate of youth unemployment, nearly one in five employers said the main cause is that young people are too demanding, while a slightly smaller number cited lack of experience. (Flavelle, 2014)

What this analysis suggests is that workplace learning is embedded in a broader political economy, and that ideas and explanations – such as skills shortages – need to be evaluated with an eye to who benefits from them. As Bouchard (1998) points out, convincing workers that training is the answer provides the illusion that prosperity is just around the corner (if people could only get 'enough' of the 'right' skills) and the responsibility for failure lies with the individual workers.

> **Stop!** Do you believe there is a skills shortage among workers? If so, what evidence supports your position? And how do you explain persistently high levels of unemployment? Would more training result in higher levels of unemployment? Why or why not?

Sources and further information

Bouchard, P. (1998) 'Training and work: some myths about human capital theory', pp. 128–39 in S. M. Scott, B. Spencer and A. M. Thomas (eds), *Learning for Life: Canadian Readings in Adult Education*, Toronto: Thompson Educational.

Flavelle, D. (2014) 'Skills shortage top concern, employers say', *Toronto Star*, June 2. Available at: www.thestar.com/business/2014/01/21/skills_shortage_top_concern_employers_say.html (accessed January 20, 2015).

Livingstone, D. and Scholtz, A. (2007) 'Contradictions of labour processes and workers' use of skills in advanced capitalist economies', pp. 131–62 in V. Shalla and W. Clement (eds), *Work in Tumultuous Times: Critical Perspectives*, Montreal: McGill-Queens University.

Morgan, G. (2014) 'Rising to the challenge of Canada's skills shortage', *Globe and Mail*, April 6. Available at: www.theglobeandmail.com/report-on-business/economy/rising-to-the-challenge-of-canadas-skills-shortage/article17850271/ (accessed January 20, 2015).

Stanford, J. (2013) 'Canada's sluggish labour market and the myth of the skills shortage', *Academic Matters: The Journal of Higher Education*, November. Available at: www.academicmatters.ca/2013/11/canadas-sluggish-labour-market-and-the-myth-of-the-skills-shortage/#sthash.Ym5HvUfe.dpuf (accessed January 20, 2015).

Wright, L. (2014) 'Labour, skills shortage in Canada? Budget watchdog says no', *Saskatoon Star-Phoenix*, March 25. Available at: www.thestar.com/business/2014/03/25/labour_skills_shortage_in_canada_budget_watchdog_says_no.html (accessed January 20, 2015).

Note: This feature was written by Bob Barnetson, Associate Professor of Labour Relations, Athabasca University, Canada.

– classic or contemporary – offers a 'correct' account of the learning process in the workplace. We would also suggest that the theories outlined here, and the organizational practices that derive from them, are not appropriate to all forms of adult learning in all situations.

classical conditioning: a view of 'instrumental' learning whose adherents assert that the reinforcement is non-contingent on the animal's behaviour, that is, it is delivered without regard to the animal's behaviour. By contrast, in instrumental conditioning, the delivery of the reinforcement is contingent – dependent – on what the animal does

The classical behavioural approach: learning through reinforcement

What factors stimulate or inhibit the learning process, and what types of learning do people engage in? Our working definition of learning – that it is a relatively permanent change in behaviour or human capabilities – emphasizes the importance of experience and reinforcement. The best-known *behaviourist* psychologists, Ivan Pavlov (1849–1936) and B. F. Skinner (1904–90), explained learning in terms of the interaction of the human being with his or her environment. They discounted the significance of internal cognitive or mental activities – characterized by behaviourist psychologists as 'black box' activity – in the learning process. They argued that since it was impossible to measure such mental activities objectively, they had no place in the science of psychology.

The Russian Ivan Pavlov is often referred to as the 'father of behaviourism'. Pavlov and his colleagues held that all kinds of learning, human and animal, could be explained by the phenomenon of **classical conditioning** (Chance, 2009). Working with dogs as his experimental subjects, Pavlov trained them to salivate in response to a variety of stimuli, such as the sound of a bell. This was achieved by continually pairing the sound of the bell or other stimulus, which originally produced no increase in saliva, with food. Salivation was the normal physiological response to food near or in the dog's mouth, and the repeated pairing of the bell with the food caused the dog to salivate simply upon hearing the bell, even when food was not available. Pavlov described the food as the 'unconditional stimulus' (UCS) and the sound of the bell as the 'conditional stimulus' (CS). Similarly, he described the dog's salivation when given food as the 'unconditional response' (UCR), and its salivation at the sound of the bell as a 'conditional response' (CR) (Figure 7.1). One way to distinguish between these two types of stimulus and response is to remember that 'unconditioned' means 'unlearned' and 'conditioned' means 'learned'.

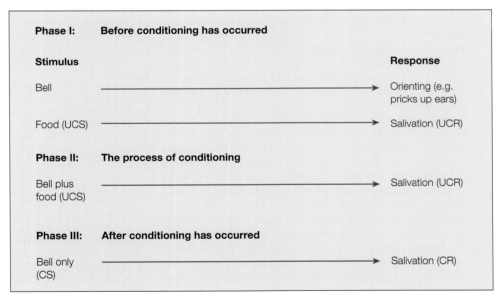

Figure 7.1 Classical or Pavlovian conditioning

VISIT THE *ONLINE RESOURCE CENTRE* AT HTTPS://HE.PALGRAVE.COM/COMPANION/BRATTON-WORK-AND-ORGANIZATIONAL-BEHAVIOUR3/ FOR FURTHER INFORMATION ON PAVLOVIAN CONDITIONING AND OTHER THEORIES OF LEARNING.

For Pavlov, learning was nothing more than 'a long chain of conditioned reflexes' (Walker, 1996: 20). The thought of using his findings in work situations, and dangling stimuli or rewards to elicit employee salivation, may seem offensive, but there are several reasons that Pavlov's research is considered important to learning in organizations. His research illustrates how internal mental events such as learning might be measured and studied. The American John Watson (1878–1958) developed Pavlov's work to demonstrate how the relationships between two variables – the environment and human behaviour – could be built into an objective and testable general theory of learning.

The American Burrhus Skinner is another well-known advocate of behavioural psychology who has made an important contribution to our understanding of the learning process (Bernstein et al., 2000). Skinner explained human behaviour in terms of the phenomenon of instrumental or **operant conditioning**, and he believed that reinforcement was a necessary part of this process (Skinner, 1954).

An operant is a response that has some effect on the situation or environment. For example, when an animal pulls a lever and food pellets are delivered, the animal has made an operant response that influences when the food will appear. Over time, the animal acquires the lever-pulling response as a means of obtaining food. In other words, the animal learns to pull the lever. Similarly, when a child cries and is then fed, the child has made an operant response that influences when food will be served. This kind of learning is called operant learning, because the subject learns to operate on the environment to achieve certain outcomes. Figure 7.2 illustrates operant or instrumental conditioning.

operant conditioning: a technique for associating a response or behaviour with a consequence

> ### stop...
>
> Can there be any negative effects of learning in the workplace?
>
> *...and reflect*

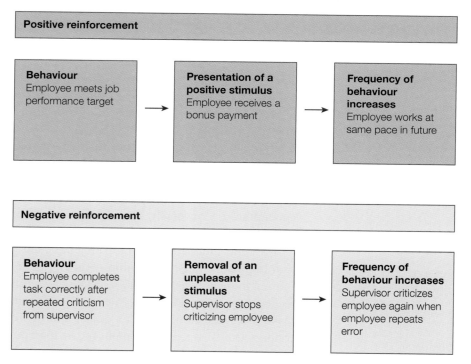

Figure 7.2 Examples of positive and negative reinforcement

A reinforcer increases the probability that an operant response will reoccur. Skinner believed that reinforcement operates either positively or negatively. **Positive reinforcement** is an event that strengthens an operant response if it is experienced after that response occurs. Positive reinforcers are therefore a form of reward. In the context of a work organization, money, recognition, praise from a manager and promotion can all act as positive reinforcers, since they all increase the likelihood of the preceding response being repeated. Negative reinforcers are unpleasant stimuli, such as a disapproving frown, a verbal reprimand or a threat, which strengthen a response if they are withdrawn after the response occurs. For

positive reinforcement: occurs when the introduction of a consequence increases or maintains the frequency or future probability of a behaviour

negative reinforcement: occurs when the removal or avoidance of a consequence increases or maintains the frequency or future probability of a behaviour

Source: John Bratton

plate 23 Russian Ivan Pavlov is famous for his experiments with dogs, and is often referred to as the 'father of behaviourism'. Working with dogs as his experimental subjects, Pavlov trained them to salivate in response to a variety of stimuli, such as the sound of a bell.

example, a manager applies **negative reinforcement** when he or she stops criticizing an employee whose substandard job performance has improved. Reinforcements shape behaviour, and intermittent reinforcements also maintain established behaviours (Nye, 2000).

Skinner also investigated the effect of punishment in shaping human behaviour, defining punishment as either the presence of an unpleasant stimulus or unpleasant outcome, or the removal of a pleasant one. Threatening an employee with disciplinary action or dismissal for verbally abusing another co-worker is an example of an unpleasant stimulus. When an employee is forced to forfeit a company car because of a poor annual appraisal, this is punishment by removing a pleasant stimulus.

Most behavioural psychologists would agree with Skinner that punishment is a less powerful means of shaping behaviour than positive reinforcement or reward. Punishment only indicates what response an individual should suppress; it cannot guide an individual towards the desired behaviour. Moreover, punishment can cause anxiety and resentment, and might impact negatively on the psychological contract. Reward, on the other hand, has the virtue of indicating what desirable behaviour is required.

Skinner believed that learning in the organization was also influenced by what he called 'schedules of reinforcement'. The simplest schedule is *continuous reinforcement*: that is, every desired response behaviour is followed by a reward. A more complex schedule involves *intermittent reinforcement*, which involves applying the reinforcer after fixed or variable time intervals. For example, an employee is not rewarded each time he or she performs a desired behaviour, such as servicing a car, but the employee experiences the fixed-interval reinforcement schedule when he or she receives his or her weekly pay cheque. Likewise, when a supervisor is promoted to manager for outstanding performance, he or she experiences a variable interval reinforcement schedule, because promotion only occurs at relatively long time intervals.

The American psychologist Edward Thorndike (1874–1949) did much of the groundwork for Skinner's observations of the effects on learning of different reinforcement schedules. Thorndike developed the 'law of effect' (Thorndike, 1913), which states that if a response made in the presence of a particular stimulus is accompanied or closely followed by a satisfying state of affairs (such as a pay cheque), that response is more likely to be made the next time the stimulus is encountered. Conversely, responses that produce unpleasant experiences are less likely to be repeated (Walker, 1996).

The behaviourist theory of learning has been applied extensively in education and training institutions. For example, they often use learning objectives or outcomes framed in behavioural language, acknowledge the significance of giving immediate feedback on learners' achievements, use 'chaining' (the linking together of simpler tasks to create more complex ones), and appreciate the value for educators and trainers of positive reinforcement rather than punishment (Tennant, 1997).

Examples of operant conditioning pervade all formal organizations. Any manager who either explicitly or implicitly suggests that rewards (reinforcements) are dependent on some behaviour on your part is applying operant learning theory. However, the behaviourist approach to learning has been widely criticized for neglecting the individual's 'internal' mental states, for assuming that on occasion no learning occurs because others cannot 'observe' any change in behaviour, and for ignoring cognitive processes.

The cognitive approach: learning through feedback

An alternative theory of learning is the *cognitive approach*. Cognitive theorists believe that cognitive processes – how individuals perceive information, evaluate feedback, and represent, store and use information – play an important role in learning. Cognitive psychologists explicitly attempt to develop an understanding of the internal mental state – the 'black box' – of the learner.

The origins of the cognitive approach to learning can be traced back to research by three prominent European psychologists, Max Wertheimer (1880–1943), Wolfgang Köhler (1887–1967) and Kurt Lewin (1890–1947). At the University of Berlin's Psychological Institute, Wertheimer and Köhler became known as the **Gestalt** theorists, proposing that human consciousness cannot be adequately investigated by unscrambling its component parts, but only by investigating its overall shape or pattern.

There are many variants of cognitive learning theory; the aim here is to provide readers with an introduction to the work of the Gestalt psychologist Wolfgang Köhler. His work with chimpanzees made a significant contribution to the understanding of the learning process through his explanation of the phenomenon of *insightful learning.* In contrast to the behaviourist psychologist Edward Thorndike, who believed that animals learn gradually through the consequences of trial and error, Köhler argued that animals' problem solving does not have to develop incrementally through stimulus–response associations.

Köhler supported his assertion with three observations. The first observation was that once a chimpanzee had solved a problem, it would immediately repeat the action in a similar situation. In other words, 'it acted as if it understood the problem' (Bernstein et al., 2000: 201). The second observation was that chimpanzees rarely tried a solution that did not work. Finally, Köhler observed that they often solved the problem quite suddenly. Through these observations, Köhler concluded that learning involves insight into the problem as a whole, occurs suddenly, is retained and is transferred readily to new situations.

More recent interpretations, however, suggest that insight might not occur as suddenly as Köhler assumed. Insightful learning might only occur after a mental 'trial and error' process in which individuals envisage a course of action, mentally evaluate its results, compare it with logical alternatives, and choose the option that is most likely to aid **decision making** (Bernstein et al., 2000) The notion that learning involves a mental processing of **feedback** has led others to compare cognitive-driven learning processes to cybernetics and information-processing theories (Wiener, 1954).

The main differences between the behaviourialist and cognitive theories of learning are summarized in Table 7.1.

Gestalt: a German word that means form or organization. Gestalt psychology emphasizes organizational processes in learning. The Gestalt slogan 'The whole is greater than the sum of the parts' draws attention to relationships between the parts

decision making: a conscious process of making choices between one or more alternatives with the intention of moving towards some desired state of affairs

feedback: any information that people receive about the consequences of their behaviour

Table 7.1 Approaches to learning theory

Behaviourist approach to learning	Cognitive approach to learning
Learning in terms of responses to stimuli, 'automatic' learning	Feedback must be processed
Pavlovian (respondent) conditioning	Thinking, discovering, understanding, observing practices, relationships and meaning, dialoguing
Skinnerian (operant or instrumental) conditioning, negative or positive reinforcement	Reframing of previously learned concepts and principles
Schedules of reinforcement	Insightful learning

Source: Adapted from Bratton and Gold (2003), p. 343. Reproduced with permission of Palgrave Macmillan

The social-learning approach: learning through observation

This section examines a number of social-learning theories. Following the work of Albert Bandura, social-learning theorists explain human development as the interaction between internal processes and the external social context. Learning is characterized as a reciprocal process that happens through indirect observation and modelling (Figure 7.3). Individuals learn by observing others whom they believe

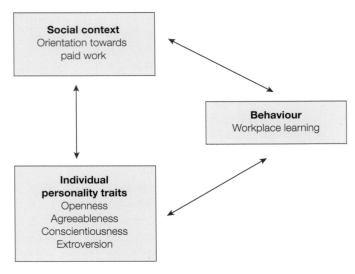

Figure 7.3 Three aspects of reciprocal learning
Source: Bamber and Castka (2006), p. 75

are credible and knowledgeable (so they can act as 'models'). What the observer acquires are symbolic representations of the model's actions. What is learned is then encoded into memory to serve as a guide for later behaviour. Observational learning involves four interrelated processes: attention, memory, motor activity and motivation (Bandura, 1977).

plate 24 Social-learning theory suggests that when an individual observes a 'model' performing a particular behaviour, this leads them to expect that if they perform the same behaviour, there will be a favourable result. For example, if a child observes their mother or father performing a task successfully, they will expect the same outcome when they perform the task.

Before an individual can learn much from a more knowledgeable person (a model), she or he must actively attend to the other person. Attention is affected by characteristics of both the observer and the model. Memory is an important element because we may learn how to perform a behaviour, but then forget what we have learned. A motor process is another component of social learning. The observer may need to practise one or more of the motor actions required in order to perform the behaviour. Remember learning to ride a bike or a snowboard? These behaviours were learned by observing others, but they needed to be perfected through practice – hence the importance of hands-on experience.

The fourth component of observational learning is motivation. Social-learning theorists believe that whether or not an individual performs a behaviour depends on whether she or he expects to be reinforced or punished for doing so. Observational learning suggests that learning new knowledge and skills comes from:

- actively attending to the behaviour of the relevant other (the 'expert')
- remembering the observed behaviour
- practising the observed behaviour and directly experiencing the consequences of using the knowledge or skills.

Finally, social-learning theorists believe that adult learning is influenced by a person's 'self-efficacy', that is, a person's judgement about whether he or she can successfully learn new knowledge and skills. It is also influenced by verbal persuasion from relevant others who encourage a person to believe that she or he can accomplish a behaviour, hence the importance of the social relations between the expert and learner (Bandura, 1977).

Contemporary learning theories

The two contemporary theories that we have chosen to focus on here – cultural-historical theory and communities of practice – draw upon social-learning theory and are a reaction against the classical psychologically driven theories of learning. They have been chosen because both approaches have informed much of the research and scholarly enquiry on workplace learning during the last 15 years.

The cultural-historical approach: learning through social exchange

The cultural-historical activity approach to learning was first developed by the Russian social psychologist Lev Vygotsky in the 1920s and early 1930s (Vygotsky, 1978). A colleague and protégé of Vygotsky's, Alexei Leontiev, further developed the theory (Leontiev, 1978, 1981). Vygotsky's sociocultural theory of learning emphasized the importance of social interaction in the learning process. Learning is not just about what happens internally, but is rather a product of interactions from the social to the individual.

semiotics: the systematic study of the signs and symbols used in communications

According to Vygotsky, learning occurs through a dynamic social exchange between a mature practitioner or expert (a more capable and knowledgeable individual) and the learner (novice) in the learning community. The relationship is not passive but dynamic, and is defined by the needs of the learner, by the forms of social practice that 'relate' the learner (novice) to the objective context, and by what that context means for the learner. Such a 'relational' view also focuses on '**semiotic** mechanisms', including diagrams, cultural tools (such as language), mnemonic techniques (such as multiple choice questions), works of art and writing, which are used to mediate the learning process and shape thinking. The acquisition of cultural tools enables knowledge to be transmitted. These semiotic mechanisms will vary across different activity contexts and cultures.

Another aspect of Vygotsky's theory is the importance of identifying the learner's lower and upper limits of ability. The learner's optimal performance level, called the zone of proximal development, is achievable only with support or 'scaffolding' (Wood et al., 1976). The concept of the zone of proximal development exemplifies Vygotsky's concern with the role of assistance, assessment and feedback. With support, the mature practitioner bridges gaps so that the novice can act 'as if she or he is already able to complete the given task' (Hung, 1999; Rogoff, 1990). The 'scaffold' allows learners to perform at a level beyond what they would be capable of on their own.

Vygotsky's approach to learning is, however, still a psychological model, since it focuses on the process of *internalization*. The psychological nature of his model is apparent in the clear boundary between self and social implied by Vygotsky's notion of internalization, and by the way in which sociocultural phenomena become psychological phenomena as they cross that boundary.

The community of practice approach: learning through socially embedded activity

communities of practice: informal groups bound together by shared expertise and a passion for a particular activity or interest

situated learning: an approach that views adult learning as a process of enculturation, in which people consciously and subconsciously construct new knowledge from the actions, processes, behaviour and context in which they find themselves

The concept of a **communities of practice** has antecedents in the work of Vygotsky and in social-learning theory. The approach has been articulated in the work of Lave and Wenger (1991), and Rogoff (1990). Whereas classical psychologically driven theories of learning developed primarily either in the laboratory or in classroom settings, **situated learning** theories have emerged from studies of learning in workplace settings. Jean Lave (1993), for example, used the term 'situated learning' to focus attention onto the development of knowledge and expertise through activity, and onto the context and culture in which learning occurs (that is, within which it is situated). Situated learning places a greater emphasis on people learning in context, and as such has expanded key notions of the sociopsychological paradigm. Participation in work activities that offer wide-ranging learning experiences has become increasingly a matter for research and for application in formal higher education programmes; it is also seen as legitimate means of addressing individuals' learning across all phases of their working careers (Dochy, 2012). For example, students on professional programmes, such as nursing, increasingly spend a large proportion of their learning in a 'practicum' – actually in a hospital – in the same way that many business and management students spend a 'year in industry'. A critical constituent of situated learning is social interaction and the concept of a community of practice.

Wenger (1998) further developed the notion that learning is a process of participation in a community of practice. A community of practice can be defined as 'a unique combination of three fundamental elements: a domain of knowledge, which defines a set of issues; a community of people who care about this domain; and the shared practice that they are developing to be effective in their domain' (Wenger et al., 2002: 27). The domain creates a sense of common identity for the members, the community creates the social fabric for the learning, and the practice is a set of ideas, information, stories, documents and tools that the community members share. All communities of practice share this three-dimensional structure, and a set of relations among the members is central to the process. Moreover, the concept of communities of practice is an intrinsic condition for learning, 'not least because it provides the interpretative support necessary for making sense of its heritage' (Lave and Wenger, 1991: 98).

Examples of communities of practice include systems of apprenticeships in manual trades (such as carpentry, plumbing and mechanics). As the novice moves from the periphery of the community to its centre, he or she becomes more engaged within the culture, eventually assuming the role of 'master' or 'expert'. The apprenticeship system includes instances of formal and informal learning in various situated work activities.

Lave and Wenger's central concept in explaining the process and the path individuals take as they progress from 'apprentice' or novice to 'master' or expert is what they call legitimate peripheral participation. The authors explain the process like this:

> By this we mean to draw attention to the point that learners inevitably participate in communities of practitioners and that the mastery of knowledge and skill requires newcomers to move toward full participation in the sociocultural practices of a community. 'Legitimate peripheral participation' provides a way to speak about the relations between newcomers and old-timers, and about activities, identities, artifacts, and communities of knowledge and practice. It concerns the process by which newcomers become part of a community of practice. (Lave and Wenger, 1991: 29)

In developing their argument, Lave and Wenger emphasize the need for taking a holistic view of learning involving the whole person, and for activity in and with the world rather than 'receiving' a body of knowledge. Other theorists have built upon the situated learning model by the notion of 'cognitive apprenticeships', which focuses on how the learner acquires, develops and uses cognitive tools in authentic work settings (Brown et al., 1989; Tynjälä, 2008). For example, architects, lawyers and physicians complete cognitive apprenticeships or internships. Physicians, for instance, acquire the situated experience and knowledge on which they build their practice in their internships and residencies in hospitals (Wilson, 1993).

As a model for understanding how employees learn in the workplace, the community of practice approach has been the subject of some debate in the adult learning literature. An extreme position would be that there is little need for formal classroom-based learning because effective learning only occurs through the engagement of community membership. Thus, it is suggested, the learner (the new employee) is a valued member of the community, and is expected to make contributions, as he or she 'learns the ropes'. The role of the participants (novice and master or expert) evolves over time, as new levels of mastery are achieved.

Feedback from expert members of the community (for example, managers) is formative and non-evaluative, is supportive and encourages risk taking. The 'scaffolding' provided by the expert may involve a modification of the task so that learning and success are possible. Another aspect is that the interaction between members of the community reflects the style of discourse appropriate for the context and the environment. The notion of movement across contexts becomes a key concept when the theory of situated learning is applied to complex work organizations (Østerlund, 1997). Moreover, occupations are increasingly understood to be shaped by the requirements of the particular organizational setting and the kinds of business goals it achieves, hence 'one key curriculum task is to identify sequencing and organization of learning experiences suited to specific occupational practices' (Billett and Choy, 2013: 273).

For individual employees, the perspective highlights the importance of finding the dynamic set of communities they should belong to and receive support from, and of fashioning a meaningful pathway of experience through these communities over time (Wenger, 2000). In terms of support within the community, an insightful Finnish study found that self-efficacy is positively related to vocational students' development of professional skills and also, importantly, to the fact that 'co-workers considered them professional' (Metso and Kianto, 2014: 141). Finally, situated learning assumes that the learner (novice worker) is motivated to learn, and that she or he develops and achieves the knowledge, expertise and value system that make up the community of practice.

plate 25 Informal learning can occur – sometimes unconsciously – from an everyday situation or workplace experience.

Source: © iStockphoto.com/STAMIK.

The work of Engeström and Rogoff has built on Lave and Wenger's situated learning model (Rogoff, 1995). Whereas Lave and Wenger downplay the importance of formal training and learning, Engeström emphasizes its necessity and value. While recognizing the central nature of social interaction in the mediation of adult learning, Engeström also emphasizes the value of structured instruction in developing knowledge and expertise. He argues that day-to-day learning consists of 'conditioning, imitation, and trial and error', but that instruction is necessary to reach the higher plane of 'investigative' and 'expansive' learning (Engeström, 1994). For Engeström, teacher-centred training practices complement, rather than negate, learner-centred approaches to individual development.

Barbara Rogoff's (1984, 1995) early laboratory research emphasized the importance of the social milieu in which learning is embedded, arguing that 'context is an integral aspect of cognitive events, not a nuisance variable' (1984: 3). In later work, she extended Lave and Wenger's theoretical approach by identifying two interrelated social processes, in addition to apprenticeships, that are important to learning – participatory appropriation and guided participation.

Participatory appropriation refers to the way individuals change through their involvement in apprenticeship activities. Rogoff believes that appropriation is different from Vygotsky's concept of internalization. Whereas 'internalization' implies static entities involved in the 'acquisition' of knowledge and skills, participatory appropriation treats learning as a series of active processes derived from the unfolding activity in which individuals participate. The nature of social relations required to support the apprenticeship system is captured by Rogoff's notion of *guided participation*, which includes direct communication about the behaviours involved, and communication, within the work setting, of the organizational culture through shared language and talk – such as folktales, language, legends, myths, sagas and stories (Beyer and Trice, 1987). The act of storytelling, for instance, helps individuals make sense of the situation they inhabit (Jabri, 2012).

Apprenticeship, participatory appropriation and guided participation activities all include processes such as 'scaffolding'. Guided participation, however, does not take place only between the master and novice, but also engages other members of the wider community of practice. In contrast to the behaviourist and cognitive approaches, the social theorists reject the transmission model of instruction, in which the learner is simply a passive recipient of information, arguing that learning can never be context-free.

A Dutch case study has used the concept of **activity theory** (Vygotsky and Engeström) and the community of practice theory (Wenger) to analyse how work-related learning is interconnected between individual and group, and group and organization. In this case, the two sides of innovation – creation and exploitation – are located at different levels in the organization (Figure 7.4). Using four key concepts – knowledge creation, an activity system, scripts and routines – the community of practice arranges the connection between the individual and the organization or collective (Hoeve and Nieuwenhuis, 2006).

activity theory: a view of adult learning that envisions learning as a social process whereby individual and group agency and learning occurs through interlocking human activity systems shaped by social norms and a community of practice

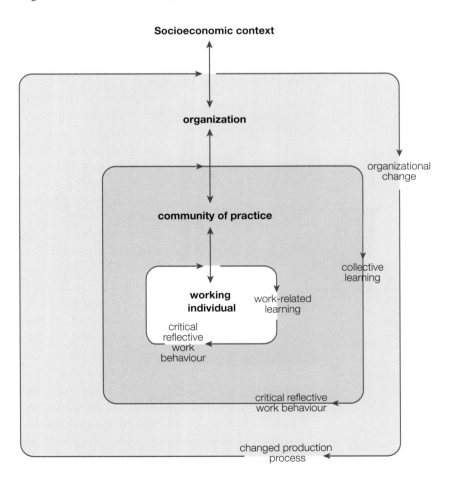

Figure 7.4 A model of work-related learning

Source: Hoeve and Nieuwenhuis (2006),58 p. 175. With permission of Emerald Group Publishing

The first concept of *knowledge creation* is a process whereby employees and work groups share tacit and explicit knowledge through intensive social interaction. The second concept of an *activity system* focuses on the dialectical relation between employees and objects. The third concept of *scripts* is a structure that describes appropriate sequences of events in a particular context or organization. The fourth concept used by the researchers, that of *routines*, is built around the notion of recurrent or repetitive patterns of work behaviour. A domain of knowledge and the routines specific to the organization are central to the change processes. It is argued that 'Simultaneously, routines link the collective to the larger organization, as organizations are a set of interlocking routines' (Hoeve and Nieuwenhuis, 2006: 184). The evidence suggests that, in innovative situations, individual, group and collective learning are a combination of grounded cognitive (Barsalou, 2008), emotional and relational processes.

Detractors of situated learning and the community of practice model point to problems for learning within the organizational context. Hiring practices and workplace inequalities can hamper the workplace discourse that transmits knowledge, attitudes and skills. Employees on zero-hours or part-time employment contracts may be removed or isolated from the community discourse simply because they are not there as often as other employees. This precarious class of workers (Standing, 2011) often tend to be aged between 18 to 26, women and members of minority groups, and this perpetuates their marginalization. If there are language barriers, workers may struggle to participate in the community of practice. Gender and racial bias, language barriers, zero-hours part-time schedules and isolating power structures create barriers to effective workplace learning. Would-be learners within the community of practice find that equal status and the opportunity to participate are withheld. Furthermore, the 'cultural tools' of the organization are not readily accessible, and limit the acquisition and creation of knowledge.

Critical adult learning theories

During most of the twentieth century, the behavioural approach dominated the learning discourse. The orthodox wisdom, much of it based on research conducted in artificial settings such as laboratories, assumed that learning was the objective perception of the world as it is, unmediated by personal interpretation or distortion. In the final quarter of the twentieth century, however, this dependence on psychologically driven learning theories began to give way to learning theories that articulated the unique characteristics of adult learning (Merriam, 1993). In this section, we examine four perspectives that attempt to understand adult learning in general, and adult learning in a work context in particular: the andragogy, self-directed, transformational and sociocultural perspectives.

VISIT THE *ONLINE RESOURCE CENTRE* AT HTTPS://HE.PALGRAVE.COM/COMPANION/BRATTON-WORK-AND-ORGANIZATIONAL-BEHAVIOUR3/ FOR FURTHER INFORMATION ON ADULT LEARNING AND LIFELONG LEARNING.

Andragogy

andragogy: the processes associated with the organization and practice of teaching adults; more specifically, various kinds of interaction in facilitating learning situations

A German teacher, Alexander Kapp, originally used the term **andragogy** in 1833 to describe the educational theory of Plato (Jarvis, 1985). But it was Malcolm Knowles (Knowles, 1975, 1980) who, over 40 years ago, popularized the concept of andragogy, 'the art and science of helping adults learn', which he contrasted with pedagogy, the art and science of helping children learn (Knowles, 1980). Knowles took the view that knowledge is activity constructed by the learner, and learning is the construction of meaning through experience. In his early work, Knowles characterized adult learners as:

- independent and 'self-directing'
- mature and experienced
- motivated by 'what they need to know'
- problem centred
- internally motivated.

In his seminal book, *The Modern Practice of Adult Education: From Pedagogy to Andragogy*, Knowles focuses upon and portrays the two forms of education as polar opposites. The four key assumptions of andragogy are summarized in Table 7.2. As can be seen from this table, andragogy as it is conceived is an amalgam of description and prescription. It describes the motivation and assumption of adult learners in these terms: 'As a person grows and matures his self-concept moves from one of total dependency (as is the reality of the infant) to one of increasing self-directedness' (Knowles, 1973: 45). It follows logically from this assumption that adult learning practitioners should embrace methodological techniques that focus on an adult's needs and life experiences, facilitation and internally driven motivation to learn.

Table 7.2 A comparison of the assumptions of pedagogy and andragogy

	Pedagogy	Andragogy
The learner	The role of the learner is a dependent one. The teacher directs what, when and how a subject is learned	The learner moves from dependency towards increasing self-directedness. The teacher encourages and nurtures this movement
The learner's experience	Of little worth. Hence learners will gain most from the teacher, textbooks, assigned readings and audiovisual presentations	A rich resource for learning. Hence teaching methods include discussion, problem solving and simulation exercises
Readiness to learn	Learners learn what society expects them to, so the curriculum is standardized	Learners learn what they 'need to know', so learning activities are designed around application to life
Orientation to learning	Learners see education as a process of acquiring subject matter organized by content	Learners see education as a process of developing increased competence in the curriculum to achieve their full potential in life. Learners want to be able to apply new knowledge and skills. Hence learning activities are centred around categories of developing competencies

Source: Based on Jarvis (1985, 1991)

Criticism from other adult educators caused Knowles to revise his original position that andragogy characterizes only adult learning. Many school teachers were using 'learner-centred' pedagogy that advocated problem-centred and 'discovery' learning strategies. In his later work, Knowles contended that pedagogy and andragogy represent a continuum ranging from teacher-directed to learner-directed learning, and that both approaches are appropriate with children and adults, depending on the situation (Merriam, 1993). It has been suggested elsewhere that self-directed learning principles became the vogue among professional adult educators because, in the mid-1960s, the philosophy underlying andragogy mirrored the 'expressive revolution' and the social and political climate of the time (Jarvis, 1985). Since then, the methodology of self-directed learning has been uncritically adopted as a technology of adult instruction (Pratt, 1993) and incorporated into mainstream formal adult education settings, from basic adult literacy through to professional development (Collins, 1991).

The detractors of andragogy maintain that self-directed learning as it is conceived, and deployed, in formal work organizations justifies an individualized and psychological approach to adult learning that is based exclusively on the perceived individual needs of the learner, and downplays the importance of social purpose and context. Furthermore, it is argued, Knowles's conception of andragogy is not so much an explanatory theory about the process of adult learning as a philosophical position with regard to the relationship of the individual to society. Drawing on Daniel Pratt's *Five Perspectives on Teaching in Adult and Higher Education* (1998), it is apparent that the language of andragogy is that of individual triumphalism.

Individuals are unique, they desire self-improvement, they have the power to achieve self-fulfilment in the face of social, political, cultural and historical forces, they are at the centre of adult education and their private goals dominate over collective goals. In addition, they are autonomous and capable of directing their own learning, and this self-direction and self-reliance is the true mark of mature adulthood within society. In the interests of achieving private ends, each individual must take responsibility, become self-directed, for his or her own idiosyncratic education and learning. Parallels may be drawn here with the business axiom 'The customer is always right'. In this case, the adult learner is always right. The values underpinning andragogy echo the influence of the white middle-class American belief system. The concept, it is argued, 'is saturated with the ideals of individualism and entrepreneurial democracy' (Spencer, 1998).

Paulo Freire's (1972) classic book, *Pedagogy of the Oppressed*, continues to influence critical perspectives on adult learning. Liberatory adult educators are concerned that the social purpose and context of adult education might be relegated to the periphery (Pratt, 1993). Because it describes the individual in psychological terms, separate from social, political, economic, cultural and historical contexts, andragogy does not acknowledge the vast influence of these social structures on the formation of the individual's identity and ways of interpreting the world, much of which is received and accepted without conscious consideration or reflection. The learner is portrayed simply 'as an uncritical and unwitting member of institutions and structures that generate rules about meaning, dominance, and judgment in society' (Pratt, 1993: 18). Nonetheless, the notion of self-directed learning continues to play an important role in adult learning in higher education and in the workplace. Education and training programmes continue to assume that adults continually learn from their experience through reflection, and that the adult learner prefers to identify her or his own learning needs, and prefers to join other learners to address real-life problems as laboratories of learning (see, for example, Brooks and Watkins, 1994; Mezirow, 1991).

The self-directed approach

The literature on self-directed learning has helped to define the unique characteristics of adult learning. Three main ideas are incorporated into the 'cult-like' concept of self-directed learning:

- a self-initiated process of learning that emphasizes the need for and ability of individuals to control and manage their own learning
- individual empowerment as far as learning is concerned
- a way of organizing instruction that allows for greater learner autonomy and control over the individual's learning (Rogers, 1983).

The individual learner is expected to assume primary responsibility for his or her own learning, and the learning process focuses on the individual and self-development. Carl Rogers, an influential writer on adult learning theory, believed that empowerment through a process of 'self-directed' learning was important for personal growth. The learner's life experience is central to the learning process, which critically assumes that learning is pragmatic in nature (Caffarella, 1993). Parallels can be drawn with the humanistic psychology of Maslow (1954) and with the North American philosophical orientation of individualism (see Chapter 6).

In terms of practice, the practitioner emphasizes the importance of specifying learning objectives, facilitating as opposed to 'teaching', negotiating the content of what is learned, empowering learners, and encouraging learners to develop plans for personal growth, often in the form of **learning contracts**. Others, linking adult learning to incremental social change, emphasize the need for learners to reflect on conceptions of knowledge, and question commonly held assumptions about the world in which they live and work. This internal change of consciousness occurs when process and reflection are jointed in the individual's pursuit of meaning.

This mode of adult learning represents the most complete form of self-directiveness: 'one in which critical reflection on the contingent aspects of reality, the exploration of alternative perspectives and meaning systems, and the alteration of personal and social circumstances are all present' (Caffarella, 1993: 26). Proponents of the learning organization emphasize reflective thinking as a key part of lifelong learning in professions, including management, medicine and architecture, learning in work teams, and small-group problem-solving activity in a learning organization (Watkins and Marsick, 1993). They assume (or hope) that reflective processes will enable workers to jettison their dysfunctional and taken-for-granted assumptions, and thus enhance their work performance in an unproblematic manner.

> **learning contract:** a learning plan that links an organization's competitive strategy with an individual's key learning objectives. It enumerates the learning and/or competencies that are expected to be demonstrated at some point in the future

Links to management
Elizabeth Douglas

Elizabeth Douglas holds the position of Learning and Development Manager at an Edinburgh Care and Sheltered Housing Association, Scotland, and is a former Human Resource Manager with over 20 years' experience. She acquired her MA in Languages and Arts from the University of Aberdeen and, after postgraduate training, entered management with the Great Western Railway Company. Elizabeth's current project is designing and delivering a programme on diversity in the workplace.

In the ebook access the video to watch Elizabeth talking about recruitment and diversity at her organization, and then think about the following question:

- How do key adult learning principles guide the design of a training programme on diversity in the workplace?

Critical scholars of workplace learning contend that learning is bounded by capitalist employment relations (Sawchuk, 2008). The voice of the architects building the learning organization nurtures only superficial critical reflection that improves the organization's financial bottom line. Thus, from a critical perspective, 'The objects for critical focus are carefully delineated to exclude the fundamental structures of capitalism … employees' minds are expected to remain colonized and loyal to the imperial presence of their employing organization' (Fenwick, 1998: 149). Critical reflection does not extend to questioning the power structures and the more dysfunctional aspects of top-down corporate governance.

The transformational approach

> **transformational learning:** a view that adult learning involving self-reflection can lead to a transformation of consciousness, new visions and new courses of action

The theory of **transformational learning** is another perspective that attempts to articulate what is unique about learning in the workplace. Various theorists in adult education use the term 'transformational' to describe a learning process that is said to shape people by producing far-reaching changes in the learner. The individual learner is different after the experience, and the learner and others can recognize these differences. These changes have a significant impact on the learner's subsequent experiences. The transformational learning process can be sudden or incremental, and it can occur in a structured training and development situation or informally through experience in a workplace (Clarke, 1993).

Learning in the sense being used here is most often associated with the work of Jack Mezirow (1981, 1990). His view of transformational learning emphasizes the 'psychocultural' and cognitive restructuring of the self. Thus, the concept of perspective transformation is defined as:

> The emancipatory process of becoming critically aware of how and why the structure of psycho-cultural assumptions has come to constrain the way we see ourselves and our relationships, reconstituting this structure to permit a more inclusive and discriminating integration of experience and acting upon these new understandings. (1981: 6)

A set of core beliefs underscores Mezirow's conceptualization of transformational learning: philosophical assumptions about the nature of human beings, beliefs about knowledge, and ideas about the relationship between the individual and society. Each of the three core beliefs of transformational learning has its own function. At the centre of Mezirow's theory is the concept of the autonomous, responsible and rational adult. Although social forces might limit individual choices, Mezirow believed that the goal of transformational learning is to gain 'a crucial sense of agency over ourselves and our lives' (1981: 20). In the workplace, this core assumption is often associated with individuals reflecting on a dysfunctional operational system or company policy, and taking action to change it.

A second core belief of transformational learning relates to knowledge creation. Mezirow's theory of knowing is *constructivist*. In this view, reality is a subjective construction by individuals rather than an objective fact. In other words, human beings are active participants in the process of making meaning and are the creators of knowledge. Through this process, individuals in the organization engage in critical reflection, through which the underlying premises of ideas are assessed and critiqued. A number of conditions are required for critical reflection to take place, including full information, the ability to objectively evaluate arguments, and freedom from self-deception or coercion.

The third main belief of Mezirow's transformational learning has relevance to social theory, which facilitates explanations of social order, conflict and change, and the relationship between the individual and society. For Mezirow, society is made up of autonomous, responsible individuals who can act to bring about incremental change to their world. He assumes that the individual learner is free to act upon any new understanding he or she may have gained. Most of the critical attention that Mezirow has received is in this area (Scott, 1998; Spencer, 1998). He puts forward a vision of society in which individuals are responsible for their collective futures. Critical theorists, however, point out that class divisions and power relations in both society at large, and the work organization in particular, may severely limit the capacity of the individual learner to change his or her world. As they comment, 'the lower in the social hierarchy learners may be the more inhibiting they may find the social structures, if they seek to be socially mobile' (Jarvis, 1985: 103).

What contribution does this specific type of learning make to our understanding of learning in the workplace? According to Clarke (1993), the work of Mezirow expands the definition of adult learning, and emphasizes the importance of sense making, and of going beyond notions of learning as behavioural change. The approach focuses on the mechanism of internalization, highlighting the changes in consciousness within the learner, and this, it is argued, adds a new dimension to the definition of adult learning and 'carries theory to a new level' (Clarke, 1993: 53). Transformational learning also makes a contribution to our understanding of learning by construing learning in terms of making sense of life experience: 'No need is more fundamentally human than our need to understand the meaning of our experience' (Mezirow, 1990: 11). Learning through an engagement of life experience means that adult learning can be conceptualized as the vehicle of individual development.

Transformational learning also encourages a more multidimensional approach to learning. The notions of reflection and changes in consciousness mean that the learning process cannot be understood solely in behavioural terms: it challenges researchers and practitioners 'to attend to multiple psychological factors' (Clarke, 1993: 53). While some theorists consider Mezirow's contribution to learning theory invaluable, others find that it is incomplete. For instance, the issue of how exactly the social context, and in particular gender, race and ethnicity, affect the learning process would seem to require elaboration.

Class, ethnicity, gender and learning

In Chapter 1, we emphasized the importance of understanding the effect of societal factors such as social class, ethnicity and gender on human behaviour in the work organization. The same is true with learning at work. In a multicultural and unequal society like that of the UK, we need to understand that social class, ethnicity, gender and power relations affect access to learning opportunities. While it seems we live in a 'post-feminist' society, gender is still the easiest predictor of talent development and who engages in learning in the workplace. Critical sociocultural perspectives of adult learning shift us from focusing on individual cognitive processes to an acknowledgment of the importance of social forces (Farmer, 1997; Hayes and Flannery, 2000; Probert, 1999).

Over the last half century, one focus of UK educational sociology has been on demonstrating the effects of class on educational attainment, and explaining the conscious and unconscious mechanisms by which these effects occur, particularly in the field of secondary education, where public policy aims to promote equality of opportunity (Douglas et al., 1968). Since the global financial crisis that began in 2008, and in the age of austerity, class has come to play a greater, not lesser, role in determining access to high-quality education and life chances (Bratton and Denham, 2014). The children and young people of upper middle-class parents have consolidated their historical advantage over pupils from the manual working class. In addition to finance, including the ability to buy private education and pay university tuition fees, studies have revealed a number of social mechanisms that serve to reproduce class differentials, including the effect of teachers' expectations on students' performance.

The stereotypes of the society in which teachers and trainers work influence their professional work (Becker, 1984). Many teachers tend to have a preconceived idea of what constitutes the 'ideal' student in terms of appearance, ability and conduct. Those students who fit this ideal image tend to come from 'middle' and 'upper' class groupings, and those outside this ideal image tend to come from 'lower' class groupings. They can be perceived by educators as being uninterested in learning. The underachievement of many students from working-class or 'blue-collar' social groups may be explained by how students' performances are affected by teachers' expectations. The effects of social class on educational achievement, career and life experience have been vividly captured in the epic television documentary *56 Up* (2012). Other social mechanisms that function to promote inequality of opportunity and reproduce social class differentials include differences in the types of language – referred to as 'linguistic codes' – used by middle-class and working-class students and their teachers, and differences in the patterns of socialization between middle-class and working-class families (Bernstein, 1971).

These same social mechanisms operate in the workplace. For example, managers and trainers may perceive that workers falling into the 'blue-collar' class are not trainable for certain tasks or jobs, or are less interested in developing their learning skills. In addition, those students who perform well at secondary school and experience university education enter the professional occupations, where the opportunities for career and work-related learning are greatest. It has become expected in some occupational fields such as the media, fashion, journalism, the arts, advertising, law, publishing and charities that prior 'work experience' through internships is a requirement to gain entry to permanent paid work. As parents often pay the interns' living costs and, in growing numbers, a fee for the privilege of an internship, the system amounts to a significant advantage to internees whose parents can meet these internship costs (Bratton and Denham, 2014: 393).

Source: Image Source

Do internships lead to paid work?

For thousands of recent graduates, unpaid or low-paid work (internships) has become an obligatory stage between higher education and an entry-level job with a company, yet the rise in informal internships has occurred alongside rising unemployment among young people. Internships are concentrated in popular sectors where earnings are above average, such as the law, politics, the creative industries and the media, which have traditionally recruited people from middle-class backgrounds (Hope and Figiel, 2012).

In this context, it is not surprising that graduates seek internships as the route into work in the industries such as these. People are motivated to undertake unpaid work in order to acquire social capital and employment. Social capital can be understood as (1) the 'obligations, expectations and trustworthiness of structures', (2) the provision of information held by members of the employment network and (3) the generation of effective norms that contribute to a sense of trust among those members (Siebert and Wilson, 2013: 713). In other words, interns hope to gain access to social networks within an organization in order to gain information and an advantage in the organization's recruitment process. Seibert and Wilson argue that there is a dearth of studies on the acquisition of social capital through internships, as well as a lack of information on the experiences of those who work with unpaid interns. They surveyed a sample of 71 interns and interviewed 22 'stakeholders' such as past interns, careers officers, representatives of student bodies and trade unions for the sector. Stakeholders referred to the exploitative nature of unpaid internships and the exclusion of those who could not afford to work for free from opportunities to acquire social capital. Among the interns, the

majority (59 per cent) thought the system was exploitative, but they accepted it as necessary in order to get a job.

Interns saw work experience as providing benefits such as learning through performing particular tasks, gaining from hands-on experience, working alongside experienced staff and meeting 'the right people' who could get them a job. Both interns and stakeholders referred to the repetitive nature or the irrelevancy of tasks. Only 45 per cent of respondents with work experience found that it led to paid work. Trade unionists and student bodies thought that it was not just the lack of economic capital that prevented people from obtaining work experience, but also their lack of contact with social networks, leading to social exclusion.

Unpaid work, according to the trade unionists interviewed, led to redundancies and the replacement of temporary contracts with unpaid labour. If it prevents people from getting the proper rate, it undermines trust in the workplace; and when staff are not properly trained, it produces poor quality work. Some of the interns referred to 'tensions arising from less than friendly attitudes of staff, a lack of interest in their learning and unwillingness to engage them in meaningful work.' The study shows a weakness in the social capital thesis as a rationale for unpaid work as an entry route into employment because it excludes from work some individuals who lack social capital, and also creates a lack of trust in the organization.

Stop! Search the Internet for internships in your preferred field of employment. What factors would influence your decision of whether or not to apply for one of the internships on offer? What are the benefits and costs of internships for (1) the individual, (2) the firm, (3) other employees, and (4) society?

Sources and further information
Hope, S. and Figiel, J. (2012) *Intern Culture: A Literature Review of Internship Reports, Guidelines and Toolkits from 2009–11*, London: Artquest.
Siebert, S. and Wilson, F. (2013) 'All work and no pay: consequences of unpaid work in creative industries', *Work, Employment and Society*, 27(4), pp. 711–21.

Note: This feature was written by David Denham, Honorary Research Fellow in Sociology, Wolverhampton University, UK.

In most industrialized societies, differential access to education and workplace learning is influenced by gender and ethnicity. Social 'exclusionary' or discriminatory mechanisms that produce differences in access to learning opportunities for women and ethnic groups are thought to operate to a greater or lesser extent in both developed and developing societies. Research data provide evidence of variations based on gender and ethnicity, but the differences are not always in the same direction for employees and students from different ethnic groups, suggesting that the social mechanisms promoting underachievement in education and training are

product or process that is new to an organization. As such, innovation is a major driver of organizational change. Of particular relevance to the learning–innovation debate is that certain *people* practices increase the creative agency and the organization's ability to innovate. The assumption is that prospective innovators possess certain psychological attributes, including an irreverence for the status quo – thus having a great need to achieve and to take risks. Idea generators 'often come from outcast groups or are newcomers to the company; they are less satisfied with the way things are and have less to lose if there's a change' (Galbraith, 1996: 176). The notion of innovative personality traits has its roots in Weberian sociology. Weber gave recognition to the role of intangibles – beliefs, values, aspirations – in business development (Weber, 1905/2002). A similar argument revolving around personality traits and innovation can be found in recent leadership studies (Bratton et al., 2005; Sotarauta, 2005). There is evidence that artists 'embedded' in an organization can produce innovative outcomes (Rasminsky, 2001). The central premise is straightforward: a rich learning environment provides fertile conditions for creative ideas or, to use the old cliché, 'out-of-the-box' thinking, for fostering innovation. The overriding task for managers is to be able to enlist employees' creativity to improve performance or the product or service, rather than having employees using their creativity to subvert management rules (Karlsson, 2012).

stop...

When was the last time you felt that you had really learned something? Recall that occasion, reflect on it, and try to relate it step by step to the experiential learning model.

...and reflect

Links to management **John Wilson**

John Wilson has a PhD in educational psychology and worked in teacher education and training in Scotland before becoming Foundation Professor of Education at Victoria University, Australia in 1992. He worked in human resource development in the education and training sectors in several countries including Bangladesh, Botswana, Canada, Laos and Thailand. In 2014, he was Asian Development Bank consultant on a project planning assistance in secondary education for the government of Kyrgyzstan.

In the ebook click on the play button and watch John talking about learning, and then answer the following question:

- What can managers do to encourage learning and creativity?

Chapter summary

- There has been a growing interest in learning in organizations, as contemporary management thinking and practice emphasize notions of knowledge work, flexibility, core competencies and sustainable competitive advantage through learning.

- Learning can be defined as a relatively permanent change in behaviour or human capabilities resulting from processing new knowledge, practice or experience. In organizations, the quality of this learning experience may depend on how the organization is structured, how the work is designed, how individuals engage, interact and construct knowledge from these paid work situations, and how managers lead their subordinates. Learning in organizations can take any one of the following four forms: formal, non-formal, informal and incidental.

- We examined classical approaches to learning that focused on how internal mental events such as learning might be measured and studied through Pavlovian conditioning, and the importance of reinforcement in the learning process.

- The cognitive approach to learning was also examined. The Gestalt theorists, as they were known, proposed that human consciousness could not be investigated adequately by unscrambling its component parts, but only by investigating its overall shape or pattern. Proponents of this school of thought believe that cognitive processes – how individuals perceive, evaluate feedback, represent, store and use information – play an important role in learning.

- The third classical approach we examined related to social-learning theories. This suggests that individuals learn and develop through observational learning. That is, people learn by observing others – role models – whom they believe are credible and knowledgeable.

- We examined some contemporary approaches to learning – activity theory and community of practice – and explained that social-learning theory underpins the concept of a community of practice, which has been the subject of some debate in the adult learning literature. For example, an extreme position is that there is little need for formal classroom-based learning because effective learning occurs only through the engagement of community membership.

- We also discussed how psychologically driven learning theories began to give way to learning theories that articulated the unique characteristics of adult learning, and we examined four perspectives that attempt to understand adult learning in general and adult learning in work: the andragogy, self-directed, transformational and sociocultural approaches.

- Finally, we defined creativity as the development of ideas about services, products or processes that can potentially increase individual and organizational performance. Innovation is the *creation* of any new service, product or process that is new to an organization.

IN THE EBOOK ACCESS **WEB BASED ASSIGNMENTS** TO APPLY YOUR LEARNING.

Chapter review questions

1 What part do feedback and reinforcement play in the approaches to learning?

2 Why is workplace learning important for managers and workers?

3 What are the main differences between the cognitive and behaviourist perspectives on learning?

4 Why is a psychologically driven approach to workplace learning controversial?

5 What can managers do to encourage creativity and innovation?

Further reading

Billett, S. and Choy, S. (2012) 'Learning through work: emerging perspectives and new challenges', *Journal of Workplace Learning*, 25(4), pp. 264–76.

Collin, K. (2009) 'Work-related identity in individual and social learning at work', *Journal of Workplace Learning*, 21(1/2), pp. 23–35.

Edmondson, A. C. (2010) *Teaming: How Organizations Learn, Innovate, and Compete in the Knowledge Economy*, San Francisco, CA: Jossey-Bass.

Evans, K., Hodkinson, P. and Unwin, L. (eds) (2002) *Working to Learn: Transforming Learning in the Workplace*, London: Routledge.

Fulop, L., Marechal, G. and Rifkin, W. (2009) 'Managing knowledge and learning', pp. 35–88 in S. Linstead, L. Fulop and S. Lilley (eds), *Management and Organization: A Critical Text* (2nd edn), Basingstoke: Palgrave Macmillan.

Gold, J. (2013) 'Workplace Learning and Knowledge Management', pp. 237–58 in J. Gold, R. Holden, J. Stewart, P. Iles and J. Beardwell (eds), *Human Resource Development: Theory and Practice* (2nd edn), Basingstoke: Palgrave Macmillan.

Guidice, R. M., Thompson Heames, J. and Wang, S. (2009) 'The indirect relationship between organizational-level knowledge worker turnover and innovation', *The Learning Organization*, 16(2), pp. 143–67.

Jrvensivu, A. and Koski, P. (2012) 'Combating learning', *Journal of Workplace Learning*, 24(1), pp. 5–18.

Ramstad, E. (2009) 'Developmental evaluation framework for innovation and learning networks', *Journal of Workplace Learning*, 21(3), pp. 181–97.

Chapter case study: Learning to be green in New Zealand

The setting

In the twenty-first century, New Zealand is facing environmental issues similar to those of many countries: using water more sustainably, managing marine resources, reducing waste and improving energy efficiency. It is particularly concerned about the decline of its unique plants, animals and ecosystems. The country is striving to build a positive image of New Zealand through exporting sustainable products and maintaining a reputation for being sustainable at home and abroad. The government has recognized that there is a need to increase reporting on sustainable practices among New Zealand businesses to raise the profile of the country globally on this important issue.

Recently, the Ministry for the Environment announced the Sustainable Management Fund, which provides funding to support community groups, businesses and local government in taking practical actions that produce long-term environmental benefits, encourage proactive partnerships and promote community action. Eligible environmental projects are considered for a minimum of $10,000 and up to a maximum of $200,000 of funding per financial year.

The problem

Capital Health Hospital, located near the city of Auckland, provides a wide range of complex medical, surgical and mental health services, and is not only one of New Zealand's largest healthcare centres, but its oldest. The hospital has a poor reputation in terms of its human resource management and struggles with adversarial union relations. Workers are given low autonomy in their jobs, and the organizational structure contains several layers of management.

The hospital's administration recently became aware of the funding provided by the government's sustainability initiative. Subsequently, in a public meeting, Chief Executive Officer Heath Nicol announced the creation of a Sustainability Innovation Committee, comprising staff members chosen from the various hospital departments: 'Environmental stewardship is a key component of our hospital's strategic and operational planning, and through this new committee we will be contributing to our

organization's and the country's goals to become more sustainable.' The committee would, he said, recommend and develop projects that would meet the funding criteria outlined by the government.

This new and revolutionary approach by the hospital administration took most of the staff by surprise. While many were eager to learn about the environmental issues and contribute their ideas through this experience, others were suspicious of management's motives in involving staff members when they had never previously been asked to participate in such a public initiative.

Shortly before the initial meeting of the selected group, the Human Resources Department received an angry call from the union executive questioning why they had not been asked to sit on the committee. The union demanded a meeting with management to discuss how workloads and jobs would be impacted by the employees' involvement.

The task

In small groups, discuss the following:

- How does the work of the critical organizational theorists explain the situation that the hospital administration now faces?

- What do you think is really the union's concern about the initiative?

Sources and further information

Billet, S. (2001) *Learning in the Workplace: Strategies for Effective Practice*, Sydney: Allen & Unwin.

Davenport, T. H. (2005) *Thinking for a Living: How to Get Better Performance and Results from Knowledge* Workers, Boston, MA: Harvard Business School Press.

Steiner, L. (1998) 'Organizational dilemmas as barriers to learning', *The Learning Organization*, 5(4), pp. 193–201.

For more on New Zealand's Sustainable Management Fund and its other environmental initiatives, go to www.mfe.govt.nz

Note: This case study was written by Lori Rilkoff, Human Resources Director, City of Kamloops, BC, Canada.

IN THE EBOOK ACCESS AN **OB IN FILM** BOX THAT USES *ERIN BROCKOVICH* (2000) TO RAISE QUESTIONS AROUND CORPORATE CRIME, THE EDUCATION AND TRAINING OF LAWYERS, AND ACCESS TO UNIVERSITY EDUCATION GENERALLY AND TO ACCESS **AN INTERACTIVE QUIZ** TO TEST YOUR UNDERSTANDING.

chapter 8
Class, gender, race and equality

Key concepts

- disability
- discrimination
- diversity
- equality/inequality
- ethnicity
- femininities/masculinities
- gender
- institutional racism
- intersectional analysis
- labour market segmentation
- patriarchy
- race
- sexual division of labour
- sexuality
- social class
- social exclusion

Chapter outline

- Introduction
- Equality and equity
- Social class and inequality
- Gender, inequality and discrimination
- Race and ethnicity
- Disability and work: an emerging focus for research?
- Summary and end-of-chapter features
- Chapter case study: Equity challenges in South African police service organizations

Chapter learning outcomes

After completing this chapter, you should be able to:

1 Understand and explain how patterns of inequality affect organizations
2 Describe some of the principal means by which equity issues are handled in organizational practices
3 Compare and contrast the current status of policy relating to gender, race/ethnicity, disability and class in organizational life in major English-speaking countries
4 Outline relevant areas where further investigation is needed in the many areas relating to equity in the workplace

introduction

In 2015, the 80 richest individuals on the planet, about the same number who could ride on a double-decker bus, have, according to Oxfam, accumulated as much wealth – £1 trillion – between them as half of the world's poorest 3.5 billion people. Top of the list is Carlos Slim Helú, the Mexican telecommunications mogul, whose family's net wealth is estimated at £45 billion. The world's richest woman, Liliane Bettencourt, has an estimated fortune of £18 billion derived from L'Oréal, the cosmetics company (Milne, 2015; Morris, 2014). Another woman made the news recently, although for a very different reason – Patience Molokwu, a planning engineer employed at the Aberdeen engineering firm PD&MS Energy. Ms Molokwo was awarded £27,000 in compensation after her employer dismissed her for being pregnant (Anonymous, *The Herald*, 2014).

Understanding issues of **equity and inequality** across the major social divisions of society as it relates to the labour market and work is vital for a deep understanding of organizational behaviour. Inequalities exist in all aspects of life – economic inequality, problems of access to education and healthcare, inequalities in the legal system and political power, and the exploitation of natural resources – not just business (Morrison, 2015). Here the interest is to understand the patterns of inequality that exist in Western societies, as well as how inequality affects employees' health, level of trust in the workplace and performance. Over the last 35 years, significant changes have occurred in Western Europe and North America. This century, Britain, for example, is the only country in the G7 group of leading economies where inequality has increased (Treanor and Farrell, 2014). As the rich have become richer, UK workers have suffered the longest and severest decline in real earnings since 1865–67, during the Victorian era (Doward and Bissett, 2014). And research by the Institute for Fiscal Studies found that the wages of British workers were 1 per cent lower in real terms in late 2014 than in the same period in 2001 (Stewart, 2015a). Unregulated capitalism has transferred more and more wealth into the hands of the richest 1 per cent of society and, moreover, there is a compelling case that such a concentration of wealth damages economies (Dorling, 2014; Piketty, 2014; Stiglitz, 2013).

However, we have also witnessed a movement of women from unpaid domestic work into paid work, especially managerial and professional, in greater and greater numbers. Furthermore, increased global migration has created more and more diverse workplaces. Civil rights movements and legislation have affected how all people think about the status of visible minorities. And, more recently, people with disabilities have been more effectively demanding full rights to participate in paid work.

employment equity: a strategy to eliminate the effects of discrimination and to make employment opportunities available to groups who have been excluded

stop...

Before getting started, take a moment to ask yourself how you understand the terms 'equality' and 'equity' now? After you have considered this, explore the web for sites devoted to equity across different countries. Three sites you might like to compare and contrast are: www.unicef.org/pon00; www.mtholyoke.edu/offices/comm/csj/040700/gender.html; www.gov.uk/equality-act-2010-guidance.

...and reflect

These broad social changes help to set the stage for our discussion, one that is not often addressed in textbooks on organizational behaviour. This relates to the role of social class, gender, race and ethnicity, and disability. We focus on these important issues here not because they are an interesting yet benign fact of the modern workplace, but because we consider that the social dynamics of social class, gender, sexuality, race and ethnicity, and disability underpin contemporary issues of inequality, equity and organizational behaviour. To understand their significance is to give an emphasis to power imbalances, and to put the behaviour of individuals and groups in the organization into a wider social context. However, no book can contain everything: the material we have chosen inevitably not only reflects our personal bias, but is also highly selective. We do not suggest that this book single-handedly redresses the imbalance in teaching and writing on these topics, and here we can do little more than skim the surface, but we hope that by adding social class, gender, race and ethnicity, and disability to the work behaviour equation, we can encourage more lecturers in organizational behaviour to give major coverage to these important issues, and support more students in asking serious questions about issues of inequality and equity.

Outside the academic field of organizational behaviour, a large proportion of literature up until the 1970s on work and inequities focused exclusively on issues of social class. Over more than three decades, however, studies of inequality have shifted away from examining social class to exploring other inequalities of gender, ethnicity, sexuality and disability (Giddens and Sutton, 2013). This, of course, should not be understood as making a case for the irrelevance of social class: clearly, social class is a major factor that shapes the work experience. Rather, it means that people's general understanding, as well as academic analyses, of paid work must become more sophisticated and nuanced to bring to light the relationships between social class and issues of gender, race and ethnicity, and disability.

In general terms, this chapter provides a systematic exploration of several of the key areas of inequality and equitable/inequitable practices in organizational behaviour, as well as more broadly in the institution of work, including labour markets. We begin with a general section on the concept of equality and the subfield of 'organizational justice', which has been developing for almost a quarter of a century.

Equality and equity

equality: the state of being equal, especially in status, rights or opportunities

The concept of 'social **equality**' will serve as the starting point for this chapter because, although we explore a variety of other forms of research literature, this provides the foundation for concepts derived from equity and organizational justice that firmly connect us to areas such as organizational behaviour and organizational psychology. In other words, this discussion is essential, although not sufficient, for the full development of a broad and useful theory of equity in the context of organizational behaviour.

Social equality

The principle of and our belief in social equality are rooted in a body of intellectual thought that we associate with the Enlightenment and social unrest in Europe and North America in the eighteenth century. The American and French revolutions both affirmed the equality of rights as an absolute principle. The United States Declaration of Independence (1776) proclaims that every citizen has an equal right to the pursuit of happiness and embodies the principle of universal justice, even though it took over a century to get there. The ideology of the French Revolution, found in the famous Declaration of the Rights of Man and the Citizen (1789), proclaims that 'men are born free and remain free and equal in rights' and goes on to state that 'social distinctions can be based only on common utility' (Piketty, 2014: 479). Although the first statement asserts the principle of absolute equality, the second sentence alludes to the existence of very real inequalities.

At a theoretical level, there is a consensus concerning the abstract principles of social justice. But, as Piketty observes, as with any rights-based approach, how far do equal rights extend in practice? The writers of the French Declaration were thinking mainly of the abolition of the privileges held by the aristocratic regime and the right for citizens to enter into free contracts, which at the time was 'quite revolutionary'. In the twentieth century, most states extended equal rights to education, health provision and pensions. But should equal rights be extended to housing and to a paid job? The second statement of the Declaration formulates a kind of answer to this question by reversing the burden of proof: 'equality is the norm, and inequality is acceptable only if based on "common utility"' (Piketty, 2014: 480).

The term 'common utility' can be interpreted in different ways. One broad interpretation is that social equalities are acceptable only if they are in the interest of all and in particular of the most disadvantaged social groups. Thus, human rights and material advantages must be extended in so far as is possible to all citizens, providing it is in the interest of those who have the fewest rights, opportunities and life chances to do so (Rawls, 1971). Since 1945, in Western Europe at least, political discourse on the redistribution of wealth within society has been based around a logic of human rights and a principle of equal access to certain resources that are deemed to be fundamental: education, health and retirement (Piketty, 2014). The precise extent of the social rights that can be granted to all cannot be answered by abstract principles but will be decided through democratic debate, confrontation and the relative power of different social groups.

Equity and justice in work organizations

This brief introduction to the principle of equality provides a starting point or a narrower and introductory exploration of equity law, specifically organizational justice, in the research literature on organizational behaviour. But first it is perhaps relevant to look briefly at the general issues of pay and employment equity, a subfield of legal and social studies of work that is well established but stands quite separate from the literature on organizational justice.

Pay and employment equity legislation is defined as those laws which are intended to eliminate established inequalities in the pay received by women and (often specifically identified) members of minority groups working for a given employer (Godard, 2005b). Different forms of this type of legislation exist across many countries. For example, the Equality Act 2010 enumerates the existing UK legislation and seeks to adopt a single approach to equality by introducing common definitions. In social democratic countries such as those of northern Europe, it is linked with legislation relating to the general work environment. In countries without these types of centralized legislative framework, such as the USA, Canada and the UK, it appears in stand-alone legal frameworks where litigation (as opposed to collective bargaining) is central. In such countries, pay and employment equity laws do not, as such, focus on the broader experiences of workers and inequity, even though employers found to be in violation of the legislation are often required to identify and eliminate many of the factors that have produced the violation. Instead, the focus is on comparisons based on the principle of equal pay for work of equal value. Establishing this value is, of course, not easy, and it reveals the many presumptions that infuse the world of work, which most of us take for granted. Generally speaking, however, such legislation has been shown to increase equity in the workplace in comparison to forms of self-regulation. For a good example of this type of policy research analysis, see Peetza et al. (2008), whose work focuses on Australia but can be used to reflect on such issues elsewhere.

stop...

Take a moment to come up with a list of key factors that could be used to compare different jobs for their relative 'value'. Now, using your set of factors, analyse some occupations. How did your system of comparison measure up? Do you think it produced a fair outcome?

...and reflect

human rights: the conditions and treatment expected for all human beings

A broader set of concerns, both in the work-based literature and in practice, revolves around **human rights** legislation. Here, the concern is again discrimination, but the focus is much broader than that seen in legislation on pay and employment equity. First, more personal characteristics are taken into account (that is, more than just gender and visible minority status), including disability, sexual orientation, age and even political or religious beliefs. Any analysis of human rights violation necessarily explores the full range of forms of discrimination and the factors involved, including those examined in the context of pay and employment equity. Here, we might look at issues relating to conditions of employment, harassment, mental duress, legal expenses (as well as pay) and so on. Employers found to be in violation of the legislation are often required by law to make employees 'whole' by restoring them to the circumstance they would have been in had the discrimination not occurred.

Equity law provides a lead-in for an introduction to the issue of equity, specifically organizational justice, in the research literature on organizational behaviour. Indeed, as we shall see, the two basic legal frameworks outlined above offer examples of the many different forms of organizational justice. First, however, we must ask what is known about how the issue of justice and the perceptions that surround it affect the actual behaviour of and within organizations.

Valuable work has recently been completed on these issues, in the form of general reviews of research and theory (Cohen-Charash and Spector, 2001; Colquitt et al., 2001; Cropanzano and Greenberg, 1997; Johnson et al., 2006; Sawyer et al., 2006). This research comes in a variety of forms: field research, experimental research and 'action' (or 'proactive') research. Each form and method has made important claims about the relations between different types of justice and variables such as job satis-faction, employee commitment and the evaluation of authority.

We can identify three basic lines of enquiry in the area of organizational justice: the distributive, procedural and interactional approaches. (Some researchers iden-tify four or more approaches, for instance distributive, procedural, interpersonal and informational, but here we use a model with three categories.) Briefly, the types can be roughly defined as follows:

- *Distributive justice* refers to the outcomes and allocations emerging from processes.
- *Procedural justice* refers to the procedures set in place to produce the perception of fairness.
- *Interactional justice* refers to the interpersonal treatment of people using these procedures.

In general, it is important to note that 'justice' is understood to be socially constructed in this field of research. It concerns practices and organizational structures, and the policies and procedures that shape them. Note too that justice is typically understood to be subjective, in the sense that 'fairness' is what the major-ity perceives it to be (Colquitt et al., 2001). However, justice can also be understood in more objective terms – involving proportional shares of resources, outputs and so on – and we use this understanding in this discussion. We feel it is necessary to include both the subjective and objective dimensions of justice at work because, when the focus is on subjective formulations of justice – what people think is just – it is easy to sidestep many contentious issues regarding rights, responsibilities and social justice in a broader, more politicized sense. Some of the research that has been carried out certainly sheds light on behaviour in work organizations. As in most sciences, the researchers tend to be preoccupied with how powerful the effects they identify are, and which specific theories are the most powerful predictors. Interested readers can look at the primary sources, but, for our purposes, we can say that organizational justice (or at least perceptions of it) correlates highly with positive outcomes and experiences of work as follows. We see not only that certain dimensions of personality shape organizational justice (Colquitt et al., 2006; Roberson, 2006), but also that increased organizational justice is found to be correlated with several outcomes: higher job satisfaction (McFarlin and Sweeney, 1992), higher organizational commitment (Tyler, 1990), more positive evaluations of managers (Ball et al., 1993), enhanced citizenship behaviour within the organization (Organ, 1990), lower turnover and absenteeism (Masterson et al., 2000), lower levels of workplace sabotage and revenge (Ambrose et al., 2002; Aquino and Douglas, 2003), and, as with societal equality, higher levels of trust between employers, managers and employees (Folger and Cropanzano, 1998). The literature on work performance is mixed, but overall it shows a positive correlation between forms of justice and better work outputs (Masterson et al., 2000).

plate 27 Women continue to be over-represented in the care-giving professions.

Source: © IStockphoto.com/nano

For our purposes, perhaps the most important point to be taken from all this is that the concept of 'justice', and with it 'equity', emerges and takes on personal relevance only when systematic injustices and inequities exist. That is, it occurs in a system of tension and conflict. Work, in other words, is contentious; and it is this fact that makes it reasonable for any of us to notice or care about justice and equity in this context. What makes work contentious is, of course, the subject of whole bodies of literature across a wide range of disciplines from political economy to industrial relations, including women's studies, sociology and so on (see Chapter 14). For this chapter, however, we can say that this system of conflict and tension can be understood in two major dimensions, horizontal and vertical, which bear directly and distinctly on each of the social variables of gender, race and ethnicity, disability and class that we examine later in the chapter.

The tension in the employer–employee relationship should not be confused with tension in the relationships between groups and individuals. Although in reality they coexist, analytically they represent two relatively distinct sets of dynamics, structures and determinants. This distinction is essential if we are to understand the different dynamics of justice and equity across different social groups that feature a mix of characteristics. Tensions that emerge from individual participation in work team or organizational contexts are related to human individuality, the burdens of negotiating scarce resources, and conflicts arising from interdependency within work structures and processes. Organizational theorists call these **horizontal tensions**. They tend to emerge from the relationship between the individual and the group or organization, where individual agency meets forms of collective need and social structure. Strictly speaking, these tensions can emerge in any form of collective activity, both in and beyond the workplace (such as in social movements, community groups, families, non-profit work and trade unions).

horizontal tensions: tensions and contradictions that emerge in terms of people's participation in group endeavours irrespective of hierarchical institutional relationships

vertical tensions: tensions and contradictions that emerge in terms of hierarchical institutional relationships

The tensions that arise in the context of employer–employee (or capital–labour) relationships necessarily involve these tensions, which are inherent in individual and group/organizational relationships, but there is a distinct set of further tensions that are more or less unique to economic life under capitalism. These tensions revolve around a specific class-based form of what could be called **vertical tensions**, which appear both within specific work organizations and in society generally. This set of relationships and tensions is rooted in the processes of **appropriation**. By this is meant the process by which the capital accumulation that defines the success of a business firm requires control to be placed in private ownership, in ways that are shaped by market exchanges, technological development and, ultimately, intercapitalist competition in the last instance.

appropriation: the process through which, in capitalist workplaces, a proportion of the value produced in work activities – above investment in raw materials, equipment, health benefits, facilities and so on – is retained under the private control of owners, ownership groups and/or investors. A more critical perception of this process sees it as an 'exploitation' of the organization's collective activities for private use

It is true that the vast majority of decisions taken by firms in capitalist economies revolve around the satisfaction of projected, rather than direct, human needs. This may or may not be a problem, depending on your viewpoint, but what is generally not disputed is that the employer–employee relationship that emerges is full of vertical tensions and contradictions. These and other distinctions draw our attention to the essence of the central contradiction and lines of tension that define the employer–employee relationship under capitalism. The distinction between vertical and horizontal tensions also provides a foundation for understanding some of the more specific discussions about equality and equity across different social groups. We present these below, beginning with the issue of social class.

IN THE EBOOK ACCESS THE **OB IN FOCUS** BOX ON 'EXAMINING DISCRIMINATION IN THE WORKPLACE'.

Social class and inequality

It is often suggested that social class is an obsolete concept, much like typewriters, fax machines or video players. 'The class war is over,' declared 'New Labour' Prime Minister Tony Blair (1999). However, class is an enduring phenomenon that enters the public discourse, as shown by three recent examples: the photo-tweet from Emily Thornberry MP of a white van and St George's cross during the Rochdale by-election; Andrew Mitchell's defeat in his 'plebgate' libel suit; and MP Chris Bryant's observation that the performing arts is becoming increasingly dominated by affluent, public school-educated performers such as James Blunt,

Benedict Cumberbatch and Oscar winner Eddie Redmayne (Anthony, 2014). Of course, in academic sociological analysis and research, class never went away. So should issues of social class be included in a discussion of equality, equity and organizational behaviour? Should we bother to resuscitate the term 'class society' from the apparently bygone industrial era? And (even if our answers are 'yes' and 'yes', respectively), what are the links between social class, social equality and other dimensions of equity, and why does this topic warrant a position so early in the chapter?

We would suggest that class is indeed highly relevant. In fact, we place this section near the beginning of the chapter to emphasize two points: first, the analytical development of sociological studies of inequality; and second, the fact that although each of the dimensions we discuss below involves substantial proportions of the population, relationships of social class underpin the most damaging effects of each of them.

In every society, inequalities exist between individuals and groups, with some people having more money, wealth, schooling and power than others. Sociologists use the term 'social stratification' to refer to the system by which each society ranks people in a hierarchy. One type of stratification is the class system. A **social class** is defined as a large group of people in a given society who have a similar degree of access to a material resource such as income, wealth or property. The sociological analysis of social class has been strongly influenced by the work of Karl Marx and Max Weber (see Chapter 3). In Marx's view, class is rooted in people's relationship to the means of production – the means by which they gain an economic livelihood. From this perspective, it can be understood in terms of 'owner/capitalist' or 'wage earner/proletariat'.

social class: the relative location of a person or group within a larger society, based on wealth, power, prestige or other valued resources

life chances: Weber's term for the extent to which people have access to important scarce resources such as food, clothing, shelter, education and employment

Weber expanded upon Marx's theory of class by arguing that there are internal divisions within each group, based on status, social prestige and power. For Weber, people's position in the class hierarchy derives not only from their ability (or inability) to control the means of production, but also from their 'market position', which is determined by their possession of skills and qualifications. Weber's more complex, multidimensional view of social class also led him to believe that a person's market position strongly influences her or his overall **life chances**. The American sociologist Erik Olin Wright (1997) combined elements from the perspectives of both Marx and Weber to show that the two classical perspectives on social class are not necessarily opposing views (Giddens and Sutton, 2013).

In the contemporary workplace, class translates into the employment relationship between the employer or agent (manager) and the workers. The analysis of this relationship in class terms has been important in allowing us to understand, explain and manage work-based conflict. There is an excellent, concise and accessible discussion in Milner's *Class* (1999), and an accessible summary of Marx's and Weber's theory of social class in Bratton and Denham's *Capitalism and Classical Social Theory* (2014). In summary, social class involves hierarchy, the means of generation of this hierarchy, and the resulting different life experiences and different levels of power, control, resources, sensibilities, behaviours and forms of practice.

Source: Image Source

plate 28 In male (main) stream organizational behaviour, the interests and ideas of women, racial minorities and people with disability are largely neglected or marginalized.

As pointed out above, modern redistribution is built around the logic of rights and the principle of equal access to a number of resources that are deemed to be fundamental to people's quality of life. Typically, the inequality of income is entrenched in class and life experiences. In this chapter, our focus is on those who find themselves at a disadvantage (such as women in our discussions of gender, and minority groups in our discussions of race and ethnicity), so here we deal primarily with those who are subordinated by class processes – that is, the working classes. It should be emphasized that class issues interrelate with other issues of discrimination, so those at a disadvantage because of their gender, disability, race or ethnic origin find themselves doubly (triply, quadruply) disadvantaged if they are waged workers.

We can introduce our discussion of how class hierarchies work under a capitalist system by looking at income differences between and within societies. Income inequality has been a universal feature of capitalist societies, even if the degree of inequality has varied enormously. However, before reviewing some relevant research, we should note here that for this section we draw heavily on Richard Wilkinson and Kate Pickett's work *The Spirit Level* (2010).

There are a number of ways of measuring income inequality. One measure is to compare the ratio of household income – after taxes and benefits, and adjusted for the number of people in each household – that is received by the top and the bottom 20 per cent of the population. Typically, the richest half of the population receive approximately 75 or 80 per cent of all income and the poorest half get the remaining 25 or 20 per cent. Figure 8.1 shows the size of income inequalities across selective capitalist countries. At the top are the most equal countries and at the bottom are the most unequal. For the highest ranked countries of Finland, Norway and Sweden, the richest 20 per cent are less than four times as rich as the poorest 20 per cent. In Singapore, the USA, Portugal and the UK, at the bottom of the chart, the richest 20 per cent get about nine times as much as the poorest.

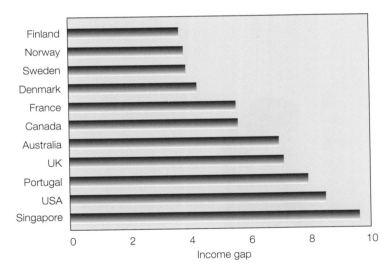

Figure 8.1 Income inequality in selective countries

Source: Adapted from *The Spirit Level: Why Equality is Better for Everyone*, by R. Wilkinson and K. Pickett (Penguin Books, 2010), p. 17. Copyright © R. Wilkinson and K. Pickett, 2010. Reproduced by permission of Penguin Books Ltd.

An alternative method for measuring income inequality is the Gini coefficient. This measures income inequality across a whole society rather than just comparing its extremes. The Gini coefficient would be equal to 100 if one person received all the income and everyone else received nothing (maximum inequality). The Gini coefficient would equal 0 if everyone received exactly the same amount of income (perfect equality). Figure 8.2 shows the rate of income inequality in selective European Union (EU) countries.

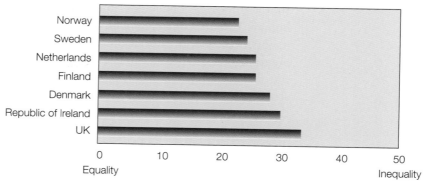

Figure 8.2 Rate of income inequality in selective EU countries
Source: Eurostat

A third measure of income inequality is to compare the pay rates of corporate CEOs and the average workers in the same organization. The ratio of the total pay received by the chief executives of Britain's FTSE 100 companies to the pay of the average UK employee increased from 45:1 in 1998 to 120:1 in 2010. According to the *New York Times*, the average CEO of a major corporation in the USA in 2002 received US$10.8 million in total compensation. That was 400 times as much as the average worker in those corporations, a proportion that has grown from a relatively modest 42 times in 1980. In Canada, a similar trend has been recorded over the last three decades. Earnings data also reveal this class-based income inequality. For example, 99 per cent of Canadians working full time throughout 2010 earned an average of $44,366. But, by around 10:33 a.m. on January 2, 2010, the top 100 CEOs whose companies are listed on the TSX index had already been paid that amount. The available statistics suggest that the rate of income inequality is greater in those countries that most closely embrace the neo-liberal troika of deregulation, privatization and flexible labour markets (Bratton and Denham, 2014: 155). Whichever measurement of income inequality is used produces similar results. Thomas Piketty's economic tome offers detailed evidence on the structured pattern of income inequality with a focus on the USA, the UK and France. He observes:

> Since the 1970s, income inequality has increased significantly in the rich countries, especially the United States, where the concentration of income in the first decade of the twenty-first century regained – indeed, slightly exceeded – the level attained in the second decade of the previous century. (2014: 15)

Arguably, the most significant insight of Piketty's work is that it shows that, if unregulated, capitalism can be expected to produce rates of return on investment that are so much higher than overall rates of economic growth that the only possible outcome is an even greater inequality in income (Graeber, 2014).

When a survey attitude company asked the public in 2014 which issue they considered the most important in Britain, inequality/poverty had its strongest showing ever, ranking above healthcare, crime and housing. In another comparative study, when respondents were asked whether 'large differences in income and wealth [are] bad for society', 67 per cent of Britons agreed – a larger proportion than in Sweden (Chakrabortty, 2014a: 5). Following the cataclysm that befell many EU economies, especially Britain in 2008, inequality in income has featured prominently in public debate. But what is the relevance of income inequality to the study of organizational behaviour? Research shows that inequality of income is found to be strongly correlated with ill-health, higher levels of social trust and a greater sense of public responsibility in environmental matters (Wilkinson and Pickett, 2010).

If we look at the major international journals on organizational behaviour, human resource management and human resource development, or at most major textbooks in each of these fields, we discover something interesting, as we mentioned in Chapter 1: there is little mention in them of social class as such. Given the wide-ranging research presented by Wilkinson and Pickett and others, why should *this* be the case? As we suggested earlier, it is perhaps because class relationships are so fundamental to the institution of work under capitalism that they have effectively become invisible. However, class is discussed in a wide range of indirect ways – perhaps most prevalently in discussing the role of trade unions.

IN THE EBOOK ACCESS THE **CRITICAL INSIGHT** ON THE WORK OF RICHARD WILKINSON AND KATE PICKETT ON WHY EQUALITY MATTERS, AND G.S. LEVENTHAL'S WORK ON 'ORGANIZATIONAL JUSTICE'.

Trade unions can be seen as an institutional expression of the class interests of subordinate groups. They operate on the principle that workers need to act collectively to balance the playing field of negotiation with their employers. Robust trade unions act as a 'countervailing power' against corporate power, an observation made over 60 years ago by the eminent American economist John Kenneth Galbraith (Chakrabortty, 2014a). It is hardly controversial to acknowledge that trade unions, like society more broadly, show fairly consistent patterns of inequity and hierarchy in relation to gender, race and ethnicity, and disability, although these organizations have in the recent past shown an enormous capacity to face up to these challenges (Burke et al., 2003). It can be said then that unions pursue generalized class interests, but until recently they had not been very effective vehicles for supporting the interests of specific disadvantaged groups. For all their inadequacies, however, unions remain for the average worker perhaps the only consistent vehicles for bettering conditions and increasing their say, or 'democracy', in the realm of work. As such, they are valuable institutions for addressing inequities in the context of organizational life.

In the 1970s, many women, ethno-racial minorities and progressives held out great hopes that equity and antidiscrimination legislation would improve equity in the workplace. As the statistics and the chapter vignette bear out, their hopes have, however, been only marginally satisfied. Although small shifts have taken place, minorities continue to experience widespread and multiple forms of discrimination, and the fortunes of women are not much different. For both groups, it has become increasingly clear that labour unions are an important means of helping the majority of low-paid men and women and people of colour to address income inequality and to overcome barriers in the workplace (see, for example, Bronfenbrenner, 2003). Perhaps disability advocates will soon realize this too.

While racism and sexism are seen in trade unions, the unions have increasingly actively addressed these issues, for the sake of both social justice and their own survival. Some have done so with considerable success. In general, we believe that unions are vital for alleviating some of the major difficulties that it seems neither legislation nor corporate antidiscrimination programmes can adequately address. According to the US Bureau of Labor Statistics, for example, unions continue to play the most significant role in closing the gender wage gap. Unionized women earn an average of 31 per cent more than non-unionized women. Wage inequality in Canada is much lower than in the USA, but in Canada, according to the national statistics service, unionized women earned 38 per cent more than non-unionized women in 2002. When race and ethnicity are factored in, the 'union advantage' drops only marginally, to 34 per cent.

In general terms, in the USA, the UK and Canada, where there is greater working-class representation (through unionization), there is a less ethno-racial and gender pay inequity. According to an Organisation for Economic Co-operation and Development (OECD) report in 1996, in the social democratic countries of Scandinavia, in countries with related 'social market' policies such as Germany and the Netherlands, and in France and Italy, where unionization coverage is high (50–90 per cent), the same basic correlation holds true. However, we can usefully ask how exactly unionization, equity in the workplace and economic activity are related in broader terms.

Most mainstream economists see unions as almost exclusively concerned with raising the wages of their members. This, we are told, is a bad thing that 'distorts' the 'proper' functioning of labour markets and the economy (see, for example Kwasi Kwarteng's et al., *Britannia Unchained*, 2012) for a Conservative view of neo-liberalism). In this mainstream approach, the gains of unionized workers come at the expense of other workers, and perhaps even of society as a whole. However, this mainstream view is false. While there are any number of ways of alleviating class inequities, the most developed economic literature recognizes that unions may in fact increase overall wage levels (across all workers, both unionized and non-unionized) without detrimental effects on the economy. At the same time, unions provide a host of other mechanisms for challenging ethno-racial and gender inequities, giving a greater democratic say to employees, and providing a portion of human dignity at work.

It is sometimes claimed that unionization is detrimental to economic success, but this too is not borne out by the facts. For example, a large-scale study by the World Bank (itself no union partisan) showed no relationship between levels of unionization and a country's economic or employment performance (Aidt and Tzannatos, 2003). Likewise, in 1996, the OECD (looking at the 1980s and 90s) found no valid statistical proof that unionization was related to the greater or poorer economic/employment performance of industrialized countries. The International Labour Organization similarly demonstrated in 2001 that high unionization is quite compatible with good economic and employment performance. In terms of income inequality, David Card's international research showed a link between falling rates of unionization in the USA, the UK and Canada since the 1980s and wage inequality (Card et al., 2003a).

Equality and equity are as compatible with a flourishing economy as they are with a fair and just society, and this is true in class terms as well as for ethno-racial minorities, women and those who are disabled.

In the early twenty-first century, social class, gender and ethnicity shape the life experiences of all people in the UK, other EU states and the USA. This fact has been widely documented in social research, and to some extent explains why studies of inequality have shifted away from a focus on social class to explore other social dimensions of inequality related to gender, ethnicity, sexuality and disability.

One influential approach to investigating inequality in European and North American societies has been via the concept of 'intersectionality' (Giddens and Sutton, 2013: 489). Intersectional analysis attests to an analytical dissatisfaction with the interpretation of inequality that highlights only one social group (Bratton and Denham, 2014). As McLeod and Yates (2008: 348) posit, 'To only analyse class (or gender or race) is now understood as a political and analytical act of exclusion.' We would also add disability to the social equation. Intersectional social research aims to unmask the different types of disadvantage and discrimination that occur as a consequence of one or a combination of two or more identities at different moments in time, for example Black Caribbean women, Muslim women, gay men, working class women, disabled women and so on. Intersectionality highlights the need to understand inequality 'in plural, across gender, race, disability, sexual orientation, religion or belief, and age' (Bagilhole, 2009: 3). By that, we mean that each informs the other, and that, when combined, they produce life experiences that are sometimes privileged and advantaged and sometimes oppressed and disadvantaged, depending on the social context (Smooth, 2010). In the following sections, we explore the connections between gender, race and ethnicity, and disability in what has been called the 'age of austerity'.

Links to management   Andrew Brady

Andrew Brady is Director of Union Solidarity International. He has also worked with the UK's largest trade union, Unite, in the Political and the Research and Policy Departments. He is currently writing up a PhD at the University of Strathclyde, UK. He acquired a Master of Science in Economic Management and Planning and a Post Graduate Certificate in Research Methodology in Business and Management from the University of Strathclyde. Andrew's current position involves organising, negotiating and campaigning around precarious forms of employment involving young workers.

In the ebook click on the play button to watch Andrew talking about the role of unions in pay bargaining in the workplace, and then answer the following questions:

- How can trade unions help to reduce inequality of income?

- Is there a connection between evidence of widening inequality in society and weaker trade unions?

Gender, inequality and discrimination

gender bias: behaviour that shows favouritism towards one gender over the other

gender identity: a person's perception of the self as female or male

gender role: attitudes, behaviour and activities that are socially defined as appropriate for each sex and are learned through the socialization process

gender socialization: the aspect of socialization that contains specific messages and practices concerning the nature of being female or male in a specific group or society

patriarchy: a hierarchical system of social organization in which cultural, political and economic structures are controlled by men

Traditionally, studies of organizational behaviour have devoted little attention to the question of **gender**. Gender refers to the attitudes, feelings and behaviours of members of a society that are typically associated with being male or female. Gender is a dimension of social organization, affecting how we interact with others, how we think about our identity, and what social behaviours and roles are expected of men and women in society in general, and the workplace in particular. Gender involves hierarchy, because men and women tend to be found in different social positions, as judged by their access to resources and power.

The feminist movement has produced a body of literature that offers various explanations for gender inequality. Radical feminism, for example, looks for explanations of gender inequality through the analysis of **patriarchy**: the systematic domination of women by men. From this perspective, men's power characterizes all the relationships between the sexes, including those in the public world of organizational activity, and is sustained by the whole of our culture (Bryson, 2003; Millett, 1985; Wilson, 2003). Comparative cross-sectional data covering selective EU states illustrate 'gender conflicts' between attitudes and perceptions of societal conventions. For example, O'Reilly et al. (2014: 17) found that conventions underpinning 'a "male breadwinner" gender contract are being compromised, but they are also being reinforced' in Spain, Poland and to an extent in the UK.

Gender is embedded in the modern workplace. Organizational structures and hierarchies are characterized by gender segregation, in which women predominantly occupy jobs that are part time, low skilled and low paid, whereas men occupy full-time, high-skilled, high-pay positions and are allowed to climb the corporate ladder to senior management. A career in management is typically viewed as a 'male career'. Some feminists emphasize that a patriarchal society confuses sex and gender, deeming appropriate for women only those occupations associated with the feminine personality. So in Western societies, for example, young women are encouraged to enter child care, nursing and elementary school teaching, and discouraged, or even barred, from entering such 'masculine' jobs as mining or working on oil rigs.

The gendering of work and organizations in 'malestream' organizational behaviour textbooks is usually discussed – if at all – in the context of the benefits to the organization (in economic terms) of a 'diverse' workforce. As Fiona Wilson correctly argues, 'women and issues about their work have been considered by many as less important than that of men' (Wilson, 2003: 3). In our view, one of the most important consequences of acknowledging the crucial role of gender analysis in organizational behaviour studies is its power to question research findings on organizational behaviour and analysis that segregates studies of work behaviour from occupational gender segregation, 'dual-role' work–family issues, the consideration of patriarchal power and issues of gender inequality.

To understand organizational behaviour and the various aspects of gender, we must take time to understand the aggregated results of organizational behaviours from the specific standpoint of women. Over the last 30 years, women have come to account for approximately half the labour force in most core capitalist countries (such as the G10 countries). At the same time, however, the wage gaps between men and women have hardly narrowed. Indeed, research by the World Economic Forum as recently as 2013 has shown the degree to which wage inequality exists in all countries. In Britain, for example, wage inequality for similar work is 68 per cent. Furthermore, the data show that the UK has failed to improve its standing for economic gender equality, being positioned at 35th. As in 2012, northern Europe dominated the table, with Iceland first, Finland second, Norway third and Sweden fourth (Elliott, 2013a). In fact, economies displaying the largest gap are also the same countries displaying among the highest rates of economic growth (United Nations, 2007). It is clear when we look at the available statistics that differential wages as well as differential occupational distributions persist.

Two phrases seem to best describe the status of women in the workplace. One is '**glass ceiling**', the concept that, despite their equal or greater educational training and performance, women remain systematically excluded from top corporate jobs. The other is the idea of the '**sticky floor**' on which women workers appear to be disproportionately glued. In other words, while women participate in paid work in numbers equal to men, they appear to be excluded from the top jobs, while vast numbers are clustered in low-paying, low-prestige jobs with little or no opportunity for advancement (Hirsch and MacPherson, 2003; Kim, 2002). This appears to happen through a combination of outright discrimination along with educational and occupational segregation; the mechanisms that produce these persisting inequities can together be referred to as patriarchy.

A significant amount of research over the last decade has looked at the dynamics of gender and management. 'Good news' stories are occasionally seen in the media about the burgeoning number of business and governmental leaders who are women. However, these are not necessarily representative of contemporary reality. According to Seabright's (2012) *The War of the Sexes*, 50 per cent of companies in Britain still have an all-male board of directors, and 19 out of 20 CEOs are men. And, as we have already noted, wage inequality exists. Women with equal qualifications have to work 6 hours to receive what a man will earn in 5, and in addition to this they run a much greater risk of losing their jobs.

Finally, gender-based **harassment** has recently been shown to be much more enduring and broad than had originally been thought. This harassment undermines efforts to develop career progression and decent working conditions for women (Glomb et al., 1997). In Denmark, for example, a Nordic country often viewed as an exemplar of progressive employment rights for women, the number of dismissals of women who are pregnant or on maternity leave has spiked in recent years. In 2012, 13 per cent of Danish female engineers reported they had been asked the unlawful question, 'Are you planning to have children?' at a job interview (Russell, 2013).

---

glass ceiling: the pattern of employment opportunities that disproportionately limits the achievement of top administrative posts by certain social groups

sticky floor: the pattern of employment opportunities that disproportionately concentrates certain social groups at lower-level jobs

sexual harassment: the unwelcome conduct of a sexual nature that detrimentally affects the work environment or leads to adverse job-related consequences for its victims

And it is not just a matter of fairness. Gender inequities in the workplace have recently been shown to have important, and under-researched, effects on women's health and access to healthcare. One researcher who has examined this issue explicitly shows that, at both the macro (large-scale) and the micro (individual) levels, there is a close correlation between gender inequality at work, itself shaped by the organizational practices, legal infrastructures and cultures of specific countries, and women's overall mental and physical health (Moss, 2002). Similarly, Merzel's (2000) study found that working-class women receive less consistent primary healthcare. In terms of life and employment experiences, 50 years after the publication of Betty Friedan's *Feminine Mystique*, gender still matters when interpreting social oppression and disadvantage.

Source: PhotoDisc/Getty Images

Gendered occupations and pay inequality

Understanding the relation between pay and gender begins with the segregated nature of work performed by men and women. The concentration of men and women in different sectors of the economy such as manufacturing, retail or finance is known as horizontal gender segregation, while working at different levels of an organization is referred to as vertical gender segregation.

In *Working Patterns in Wales: Gender, Occupations and Pay* (2014), Parken et al. argue that the uneven distribution of jobs and working hours is more important than gender pay discrimination in creating gender pay differences (p. vi). They found that 64 per cent of full-time jobs were held by men, while 80 per cent of part-time jobs were performed by women. Most occupations are also gendered, with only professional (jobs requiring a degree, possibly a postgraduate qualification and/or a formal period of experience-related training), associate professional/technical and elementary jobs having a gender balance. Within the professions, however, men comprise more than 90 per cent of those which are scientific and technical, while women comprise between 80 and 90 per cent of all primary, nursery and special needs teachers, social workers and librarians. Moreover, senior managers and officials are largely men, and skilled trades and process plant and machinery work are dominated by men, with men comprising 64, 91 and 86 per cent of employees, respectively, while women dominate administration (78 per cent), personal services (83 per cent) and sales (69 per cent). Professional women in Wales are concentrated in education, health, social care and public administration (84 per cent), whereas male professionals are more evenly distributed across the economic sectors. Some associate professional and technical occupations, for example medical and dental technicians, are gender balanced, but women comprise over 90 per cent of dental nurses, nursery nurses, child minders, hairdressers and beauticians. Parken et al. also found

that gender-segregated jobs were the norm for three quarters of employed people (p. ix).

Parken et al. describe 'masculinised and feminised working environments', and indicate the existence of vertical segregation even within areas of work that are balanced overall – so that men are more likely to work as managers, professionals or associate professionals. The earnings difference in terms of gross hourly median pay for all employees in Wales is 18 per cent higher for men than women, and for full-time workers the gender gap in favour of men is 12 per cent. The study concludes that 'working patterns matter in creating and reducing gender pay disparities' (p. xii).

The authors of the Welsh report are sceptical that the law can achieve much while jobs are still segregated. It is hard to find male comparators in sectors dominated by women, and the valuation of jobs is influenced by the gender of the people doing them (p vi). Nevertheless, Birmingham City Council has been found to be liable to recompense thousands of female staff such as cleaners, cooks and carers who should have been paid the same as equivalent grades of male workers. Compensation and legal fees have pushed the council's equal pay bill to over £1 billion, forcing the council to contemplate selling valuable assets such as the National Exhibition Centre, the National Indoor Arena and its share in the local airport (Elkes, 2013).

> **Stop!** Why has it been thought necessary to compare male jobs of equivalent value to those done by women in order to advance the parity in pay between men and women? Consider Parken et al.'s view that 'the gender of people doing it (a particular job) can have an impact on how jobs are valued'.

Sources and further information

Parken, A., Pocher, E. and Davies, R. (2014) *Working Patterns in Wales: Gender, Occupations and Pay*, Cardiff: University of Cardiff. Available at: www.wavewales.co.uk/uploads/STRAND1/Working_Patterns_In_Wales.pdf (accessed March 6, 2014).

Elkes, N. (2013) 'NEC sale on cards as council's equal pay bill hits £1bn: city's "crown jewels" will have to be sold to repay massive claims following workers' legal action', *Birmingham Post*, November 14, p. 5. Available at: http://search.proquest.com/uknews/docview/1457105708/14338E169C5711F6E53/16... (accessed January 27, 2014).

Note: This feature was written by David Denham, Honorary Research Fellow in Sociology, Wolverhampton University, UK.

Some studies have effectively conceptualized gender effects in small-group behaviour (Colarelli et al., 2006), and a variety of key researchers have linked general changes in work to a critical discussion of the emergence of new leadership styles that, on the surface, might seem to favour women (Meyerson and Fletcher,

2000; Rubenstein, 2003; Wajcman, 1998). Chapter 12 provides more discussion on male versus female leadership styles. Of course, as Wajcman points out, we need to consider to what degree these claims are based on gender stereotypes that may or may not be warranted:

> Traditionally, men have been seen as better suited than women to executive positions. The qualities usually associated with being a successful manager are 'masculine' traits such as drive, objectivity and an authoritative manner. Women have been seen as different from men, as lacking the necessary personal characteristics and skills to make good managers. The entry of women into senior levels within organizations over the last decade or so has brought such stereotypes into question. (1998: 55)

At the same time, of course, denying the essential validity of stereotypes does not prevent stereotypes from having real material effects in people's lives (see, for example, Yoder, 2002, on 'gender tokensim'). In the majority of workplaces, these stereotypes flourish, and through this and other factors, major barriers to female advancement are constructed.

But is there a really a 'male' and a 'female' style of management? According to Wajcman's careful studies, the answer is no. Perceptions of difference persist, for example in the area of 'risk preferences' (Siegrist et al., 2002), and certainly some variation is to be expected (Walters et al., 1998), but assessments of managerial practices show that there are far more similarities between female and male managers than there are differences, particularly in the areas that are seen as the most definitive of managerial work.

Wajcman's conclusions are not particularly hopeful, but there are some positive proposals in Meyerson and Fletcher's (2000) 'A modest manifesto for shattering the glass ceiling'. Although these authors do not question the basic principles of the capitalist model, which may very well be an important source of this and many other forms of inequity, they nevertheless build on the type of argument that Wajcman (1998) provides by seriously questioning both the efficacy of the current legislative structures and the reality behind the apparently increased 'sensitivity' towards gender equality of corporate oligarchs. Meyerson and Fletcher are particularly harsh critics of attempts merely to change attitudes. They prefer to change the very way in which work organizations operate, while arguing for an incremental approach of what they call 'small wins' within firms.

In Canada, authors like Falkenberg and Boland (1997) offer a slightly different prescription. Their careful research of employment equity programmes in workplaces reveals that negative stereotypes are strongly persistent. They go on to show that employment equity programmes have probably created a significant backlash, which is led by males targeting, in particular, those women who have successfully overcome the barriers. For Falkenberg and Boland, the solution is to be found not in a regulation of the workplace, but rather in government-led education programmes. The research by Wajcman and Meyerson et al., however, calls these conclusions seriously into question.

There is also a very clear business case against gender inequity, and this makes the reasons for the persistence of discrimination even more complex. Several researchers highlight the tendency for team decision-making processes to be male dominated, and argue that it is highly ineffective for men to dominate team-based work (LePine et al., 2002). Others outline the negative effects of gender stereotypes on mixed-gender negotiations at the bargaining table. They draw on fascinating experimental work that builds on the general theories of 'stereotype threat' (Kray et al., 2002).

An article by Ngo et al. (2003) reports, among other things, on the way in which such inequity leads to a decline in morale and performance levels, which ultimately

stop...

Does success for women in leadership mean becoming 'more like a man'? Should it? Do feminist critiques such as Wajcman's offer a threat to 'male identity' that undermines reforms? Why or why not? And is this a significant barrier to equitable changes to the workplace?

...and reflect

globalization & organization misbehaviour

Source: Image Source/Gary Houlder

Glass ceiling? Gender equity in the boardroom

Fifteen per cent lower wages. Fewer and slower promotions. Exclusion from executive positions (Bisom-Rapp and Sargeant, 2014; *The Guardian*, 2013). Although women have made major strides towards equality in society, sexism remains an endemic feature of the workplace, particularly in the ranks of senior management and on boards of directors. Recently, several countries – including Norway, Italy, France and even Dubai – have legislated quotas on female participation in the boardroom. In 2013, Germany's government agreed to follow suit as part of a deal to maintain power, but many employers were sceptical. The bosses of the country's four biggest car manufacturers – Volkswagen, BMW, Daimler and Opel – threatened to move production out of Germany if they were forced to introduce the quota (Oltermann and Neate, 2013).

Instead of legislation, employers suggest addressing structural barriers to female participation. Wolfgang Schmitz of the employers' association said that 'a quota merely treats the symptoms, not the causes of the low representation of women in leading roles', and 'It should be up to the state, not businesses, to create the right conditions. Instead of wading in with statutory requirements, the government should concentrate on improving infrastructures: more nursery places and all-day schools. We need chances, not quotas' (Oltermann and Neate, 2013).

Schmitz correctly notes that the task of social reproduction (which includes bearing and raising the next generation) is one that is disproportionately borne by women, even when women are engaged in paid employment. Over time, states have attempted to address this in various ways – from encouraging a 'family wage' for a male breadwinner (a wage that is sufficient to raise a family) to the provision of various social benefits designed to reduce the disadvantage faced by women.

Yet Schmitz's emphasis on addressing structural barriers to female participation in the workforce (which, coincidentally, shifts the costs from the employers to the state) ignores the fact that Germany does not face an 'either/or' choice. Indeed, Germany could both impose quotas and facilitate structural changes in the distribution of social reproductive tasks. In effect, employers are disinclined to accept remediation strategies that require them to change their employment practices despite the moral and legal obligations they face to eradicate systemic discrimination.

Not surprisingly, progress in gender equality has been slow across the EU. In the UK, women account for 20.7 per cent of board positions in the FTSE 100 companies. While this is up from 12.5 per cent in 2011, equal representation is a long way off. The numbers in other EU countries and the USA are similar, but they are still leaps and bounds ahead of Canada, Brazil, China, Russia, India and Japan (European Commission, 2013). Many of these jurisdictions have either voluntary requirements in relation to gender equity on boards, or no legal requirements at all.

Explanations for the slow increase in female membership on

boards vary. For example, Ann Francke, chief executive of the Chartered Management Institute, asserted:

> The real issue we need to confront is the lack of women in the talent pipeline. Too many talented women opt out before they fulfil their potential, because business culture puts them off. (Goodley, 2014)

Interestingly, any discussion of direct and indirect discrimination – good old sexism – in appointments is rare. Indeed, there has recently been an upswing in concern about declining opportunities for men (so-called reverse sexism) based upon research into boys' relatively poor classroom performance compared with girls'. Many critics of sexism find such assertions to be a distraction. If the economy really were a pull-yourself-up-by-the-bootstraps meritocracy – rather than one in which women did not even get boots –the 'boy crisis' handwringers might have a point. Academic rigor, ambition and self-control *should* be paths to financial success for both men and women. But the economic playing field is not just tilted toward men: it's pockmarked with pitfalls for women that they might not even be able to see coming (Covert, 2014).

One wonders if the inability even to acknowledge sexism as the root cause of female under-representation in executive positions isn't good evidence of deeply embedded sexism in Western society.

> **Stop!** Have you experienced or witnessed direct or indirect gender discrimination in the workplace? If you have not had a job, consider your experience in university or in social clubs. What appeared to be the motive for this behaviour? In what ways (if any) might the person who is doing the discriminating benefit from such discrimination, particularly in a workplace?

Sources and further information

Bisom-Rapp, S. and Sargeant, M. (2014) 'It's complicated: age, gender and life-time discrimination against working women: the US and the UK as examples', *Elder Law Journal*, 22(1), pp. 1–110.

Covert, B. (2014) 'Enough mansplaining the "boy crisis" – sexism still holds back women at work', *The Guardian*, May 20. Available at: www.theguardian.com/commentisfree/2014/may/20/boy-crisis-sexism-women-at-work (accessed January 23, 2015).

European Commission (2013) 'Women on boards – factsheet 2. Gender equality in the Member States'. Available at: http://ec.europa.eu/justice/gender-equality/files/womenonboards/factsheet-general-2_en.pdf (accessed January 23, 2015).

Goodley, S. (2014) 'Government warned it may miss target for women in FTSE 100 boardrooms', *The Guardian*, March 26. Available at: www.theguardian.com/business/2014/mar/26/government-warned-may-miss-target-on-women-in-ftse-100-boardrooms (accessed January 23, 2015).

Guardian, The (2013) 'Gender pay gap stands at 15%', *The Guardian*, November 7. Available at: www.theguardian.com/money/2013/nov/07/gender-pay-gap-official-figures-disparity (accessed January 23, 2015).

Oltermann, P. and Neate, R. (2013), Germany to vote in favour of more women in the boardroom', *The Guardian*, November 18. Available at: www.theguardian.com/world/2013/nov/18/germany-vote-more-women-in-boardroom (accessed January 23, 2015).

Note: This feature was written by Bob Barnetson, Associate Professor of Labour Relations, Athabasca University, Canada.

erodes the capacity of firms to retain top women (and, in some cases, top men too). On the surface, this would seem to be an issue in which the very principles of 'market competition' would bear progressive fruit, but this is not the case; that is, the market does not seem to be very effective at 'weeding out' weak firms on this basis. Ngo and colleagues provide a review of the literature, and also a case study suggesting that changes in organizational structures, rather than individual attitudes, are most important for addressing the perceived inequities.

Although the glass ceiling issue is clearly important, the greater problem of gender inequity – at least in terms of the pure number of workers affected – is in many ways experienced by women who are stuck to the 'sticky floor'. They range from Chinese garment workers in Canada and the USA, to women across the world who labour in sweatshops (Bao, 1991; Brooks, 2002; Hanson, 2003). Few surfaces are stickier than those to which domestic workers are fixed, and a recent study by Parrenas (2001) sheds light on just why this is. Her focus is on Filipino women, labouring across more than 130 countries, who represent one of the largest and widest flows of female migrant labourers on the contemporary scene. Parrenas shows the incredible difficulties these particular women face. They appear to be unable to take advantage of what legislation there is to prevent discrimination.

In many ways, Parrenas's study resonates with Smooth's (2010) analysis and highlights the difficulties in separating out different types of discrimination. Gender, race, disability and class issues are generally highly interwoven in an interactive complex of effects. How, we might ask, can we approach the issue of gender inequities and work in such as way as to encompass the fantastically diverse experiences of both those on the floor *and* those pushing against the ceiling?

Race and ethnicity

In autumn 1998, a fascinating article in *The Guardian* newspaper in the UK reported a pronounced pessimism about the future of race relations (Ward, 1998). It outlined how most young people in the UK (in this context, those aged 18–24) felt that race relations would worsen rather than improve over the coming years. As recently as 2012, *The Guardian* reported on a secret Metropolitan police report warning police chiefs that they needed to take tougher action 'to stop officers discriminating against black people' (Dodd, 2012). The classical work of the pre-eminent African American scholar, W. E. B. Du Bois (see 'W.E.B. Du Bois on race' in Bratton and Denham, 2014: 343–70), as well as excellent historical texts, adds depth to our understanding of the landscape of ethno-racial inequities and work (Galabuzi, 2006; Linden, 1995). As there seems to be an incredible persistence of a wide range of ethno-racial injustices in the context of work, it is appropriate to start by asking ourselves several important questions. What are we to make of this suggestion that young people in the UK see a growing, rather than narrowing, schism between ethno-racial groups? Is this pessimism well founded? And how does it involve the workplace?

General research over the last three decades has confirmed that, although some progress has been made in achieving greater equity for ethno-racial minority groups, it is relatively minor and the results are mixed internationally. In 2002, for example, black and Hispanic individuals in the USA held just 13 per cent of all managerial and professional positions (US Bureau of Labor Statistics, 2002). In a parallel with women's experience, studies of hiring practices in the USA have found that black workers are more likely to be employed in firms that are owned or managed by other black people.

In the UK, Labour Force Surveys show that, during the 1980s and 90s, there was some upward mobility among ethno-racial minorities (Jones, 1993). Figure 8.3

compares the levels of income enjoyed by different ethno-racial groups in the UK, again in the 1990s.

According to some researchers, ethno-racial minorities are greatly under-represented in the highest positions in UK workplaces, and over-represented in the lowest ones (Modood et al., 1997). Modood et al. note how there are also significant differences between minority ethno-racial groups. For example, in the UK, the earnings of Chinese men are on a par with those of white men, while Caribbean and South-East Asian immigrants are the worst off. According to the most recent UK Labour Force Survey, the unemployment rate in 2001 for people of Bangladeshi origin was 24.6 per cent and for Pakistanis it was 16 per cent, compared with 5.4 per cent for white people. Since these latter groups have now been in the UK in significant numbers for generations, this too suggests that if conditions *are* changing, they are changing very slowly indeed. For a more expansive discussion and more recent statistical information in Britain, see Modood (2007).

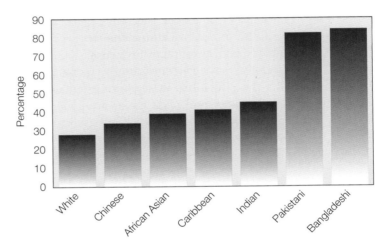

Figure 8.3 The proportion of people living in households in the UK with less than half the national average income, 1994
Source: Modood et al. (1997)

As we have begun to suggest, there are differences in the experiences of different non-white groups, and there are also systematic distinctions between groups with the same skin colour. Phillips and Loyd, for example, have shown that there is not always a clear match between race and ethnicity, and attitudes, opinion and values. They go on to show that diversity in general seems to promote more effective decision making, and in particular encourages the voicing of dissent in organizations (Phillips and Loyd, 2006).

In general, any exploration of different ethno-racial work experiences needs to bear in mind the cultural backgrounds involved. This includes both the history and culture of a group's country of origin, and the relationship between that country and the country where the group is now resident. We need to consider the effects of colonialism and imperialism, and how these continue to affect migrants from formerly colonized countries. Different groups have different varieties of diaspora (patterns of dispersion of émigré communities), and different cultural and material resources available to them. These same issues help to illuminate the processes by which stereotypes are produced, for example of African-Americans, Caribbean-Canadians and South-Asian British groups.

Another leading researcher on these types of question, Robinson, brings into play a range of other possible factors with the potential to deeply inform the types of inequity that occur in and through specific forms of organizational behaviour

plate 29 Gender inequality is in many ways felt most strongly by women workers who are stuck to the 'sticky floor', from Chinese garment workers in Canada and the USA, to women across the world who labour in sweatshops.

Source: Impactt Limited

(Robinson, 1990). For example, we can look at the degree of general social integration or marginalization of specific ethno-racial minority communities and at their 'desire for social mobility'. We need to consider whether these groups are excluded generally from all forms of mobility, or whether they are 'segmented' into and isolated in specific industries where they may experience some partial upward mobility. The difference often pivots on groups' differential success in schooling and their English language skills, but economic isolation is a factor that is not completely explained by these factors alone.

Modood et al. (1997) go beyond the concepts of exclusion and segmentation to explore how ethno-racial groups experience work differently. They look at aspects of communities such as how 'tightly knit' they are, the degree of hierarchy in communities and between families, and the strength of their connections to their country of origin, which have grown immensely with advanced telecommunications. All this makes it clear that we cannot ignore the background of home and community life when we try to assess equity in the context of work.

Much empirical research provides us with details of practices within organizations. There are obvious inequities associated with segmentation, exclusion, promotion and earnings, but there is also recent evidence explaining the processes that reproduce inequity across virtually every element of the workplace experience, from hiring practices to the labour process. There are some fascinating and highly instructive case studies that look at the ethno-racial dimensions of paid work – see, for example, Dombrowski (2002) reporting on aboriginal workers in the lumber industry of Alaska, Davis (2002) and Nelson (2001) on black longshoremen, and Bao (2002) on Chinese garment workers. In searching for an organizational perspective on issues of inequity, we can begin with the research of Brief et al. (2000), which looks at the experience of black job applicants. Drawing on an interesting experimental methodology, Brief et al. highlight the complex web of relationships between managerial justifications, ethno-racial prejudice and decisions to employ individuals. They show convincingly that the concentration of authority in firms is a key factor in inequitable hiring.

VISIT THE *ONLINE RESOURCE CENTRE* AT HTTPS://HE.PALGRAVE.COM/COMPANION/BRATTON-WORK-AND-ORGANIZATIONAL-BEHAVIOUR3/ FOR MORE INFORMATION ON ETHNO-RACIAL ISSUES.

Other researchers have provided a solid analysis of how African-Americans are systematically excluded and 'tokenized' in public services such as firefighting, and some of them focus specifically on women ethnic minority workers (Yoder and Berendsen, 2001). Participation in training programmes is obviously key for workers who want to obtain promotion and greater earnings. Some researchers have shown how non-English-speaking immigrants typically experience great difficulties in getting access to this kind of training (Vanden Heuvel and Wooden, 1997).

Recent studies in the USA have confirmed that, through the last decade, black and Hispanic individuals have typically earned 22 and 32 per cent less, respectively, than white workers; when combined with the findings reported in the previous section on gender, this illustrates the effects of power given that women in the USA also earn approximately 25 per cent less than men. See, for example, Bielby (2000) and more recently Penner (2008) for more on this. Penner goes on to make invaluable additional points regarding not merely the distribution of income, but also how the pooling of racialized groups in particular occupations explains a significant proportion of these wage disparities. For other countries where we find similar dynamics, the reader is referred to other sources such as Galabuzi in Canada (2006), Smyth in Australia (2008), and Modood (2007) in Britain.

Disability and work: an emerging focus for research?

UK Equality Act 2010: protects people against discrimination based on – age, disability, gender reassignment, race, religion or belief, sex, sexual orientation, marriage and civil partnership and pregnancy and maternity

It is vital to assess gender and ethno-racial issues in the workplace in order to generate an inclusive and critical view of organizational behaviour and its context in contemporary society. Here, we explore an important, understudied, although perhaps emerging area of inequality studies in the workplace: disability.

The **UK Equality Act 2010** includes a new concept of discrimination arising from disability, but the category of disability is broad and diverse. By convention, disability is divided into five subgroupings: sensory disability (such as blindness), physical disability, mental and psychiatric problems (such as depression), intellectual and developmental problems (like those experienced by individuals with Down syndrome) and learning difficulties (such as dyslexia). Beyond these categories, Kevin McLaughlin, in a recent committee session of the United Nations on disability, put forward this definition for consideration:

Impairment + Disenabling factor = Disability

Disability is defined differently across countries, but the available statistics confirm that, in general terms, a large number of people experience some form of disability, and that many of these people experience difficulty in obtaining and retaining paid work. In the USA, for example (where the American Disability Act [ADA] is a key piece of legislation), some researchers estimate that 31 per cent of non-institutionalized citizens aged between 18 and 64 who are considered to have a disability are employed. In other words, there is a 60–69 per cent unemployment rate among people with disabilities (Houtenville, 2003). In the UK (where the Disability Discrimination Act is in force), the Labour Force Survey longitudinal database in 2003 reported there were more than 2.4 million people in the UK who were disabled, out of work and wanting to work. Since Lehman Brothers' implosion in 2008 and the UK austerity measures, the level of poverty among disabled individuals has increased. In 2014, data suggested that UK government restrictions on incapacity payments were responsible for a sharp rise in poverty for disabled people (Clark, 2014).

stop...

The World Health Organization's International Classification of Functioning, Disability and Health website (www.who.int/features/2005/disability/en) features a photo contest entitled 'Images of health and disability'. Go to the website and examine the images you find there. There are several entries that deal with work. What kinds of question do they raise for you? How does this relate to issues of equity?

...and reflect

Recent research suggests that people who are disabled have difficulty finding work in which they can effectively apply their skills and talents. They also find difficulty in keeping paid employment, which research suggests is largely because of stereotyping and discrimination (Loprest and Maag, 2001). Once employed, workers with disabilities report a range of other difficulties, including issues of getting to and from work, movement within the workplace, a lack of adaptation of workstations, low flexibility in work arrangements, a lack of job coaches and a lack of Braille or other forms of text translation assistance.

Bruyere (2000) has carried out further research into employers' work practices, and reported that the most important challenges disabled workers faced involved the attitudes of the supervisors and employees in the firms they sampled. Specifically, it was reported that changing co-workers' and supervisors' attitudes remained the primary barrier to making a positive change in the workplace with regard to disability. Ranked as slightly less important were things like 'modifying return to work policy', 'creating flexibility in performance management systems' and 'change in leave policy'. Interestingly, Bruyere's research also allows us to see that there are inconsistent differences when comparing the private with the public sector regard-

stop...

Do you think that disability is more about a disabling environment than a physical impairment? Why have employers largely ignored the legislation aimed at securing equal employment rights for disabled people? A leading activist in Canada (David Lepofsky) frames these issues in terms of challenging our ideas about the meaning of legitimate workplace 'accommodation': (as a lawyer who is blind) he remarks, 'lights are an accommodation for people who see'.

...and reflect

ing the importance given to these concerns. While a concern for changing attitudes is roughly equal in these terms, return to work policies would seem to be more of a problem in the private sector, whereas additional issues such as 'ensuring equal pay and benefits' appear to be a greater concern in the public sector.

Importantly, these statistics point towards a view of disability that moves away from the (unfortunately still prevalent) view that 'disability' is a problem that an individual *has* (that is, he or she is a 'disabled person'), and towards the view that disability is a problem that individuals face *in society*. In other words, it is a problem of how we organize society, including workplaces. This is exemplified by a statement by the Society for Disability Studies (1993), that its field 'examines the policies and practices of all societies to understand the social, rather than the physical or psychological, determinants of the experience of disability'. This is a crucial shift in how people, including academic researchers, can best understand the phenomenon of disability.

Various overviews are available of international disability policies, including comparative employment policies (Thornton and Lunt, 1997). The journal *Disability and Society* is perhaps the most accessible English-language source of information on research in this area. However, its discussions of work and employment tend to focus on policy issues – see, for example, Shang on recent changes in China (2000), and Kitchin et al. (1998) on the experience of workers with disabilities in Ireland. The issue that is of greatest interest in an organizational behaviour context is the dynamics of behaviour towards those with disabilities, but there is comparatively little literature on this.

MacGillivray et al. (2003) provide a look at managerial perspectives and practice on discrimination claims, including a comparative look at the USA and the UK, although they do not focus on disability alone. In addition, an article by Premeaux (2001) provides a provocative discussion of the hiring process for applicants with disabilities (in particular, mental disabilities). An important determinant of equitable access to jobs and promotion is access to training, and Tharenou's (1997) study on organizational development reported significant barriers in this context.

An interesting case that raises complex questions for organizations can be found in the recent work of Reed (2003), who looks at litigation under the ADA over the last 30 years in the USA, and notes that the consideration of personal risk through employment is something that can now legitimately be taken into account. However well intentioned this legislation, it in effect provides grounds for discrimination. The duty to provide a safe work environment opens the door to important questions for human resource departments. Reed asks whether employer 'paternalism' should take precedence over the rights of a person with disability, as established under the ADA. A related question is how the kind of social definition of disability offered by the Society for Disability Studies relates to these legal structures, but Reed does not specifically consider this point.

VISIT THE *ONLINE RESOURCE CENTRE* AT HTTPS://HE.PALGRAVE.COM/COMPANION/BRATTON-WORK-AND-ORGANIZATIONAL-BEHAVIOUR3/ FOR MORE INFORMATION ON THE UK EQUALITY ACT 2010

Chapter summary

- We began this chapter with the claim that understanding issues of equality across the major social divisions of society – class, gender, race and ethnicity, and disability – is vital for a full understanding of organizational behaviour. We explored the general and specific tensions in organizations that make the issues of equality and inequality, equity and inequity, and justice a relevant topic for learning and research. Vertical and horizontal conflicts were shown to help us understand the complex forms of power that play out across organizations.

- We examined patterns of inequality within and across countries, mainly focusing on the EU, the USA and Canada. The chapter gave a brief exploration of the issue of stratification, in particular stratification according to social class, gender and race and ethnicity. It then went on to present material on class and gender inequality according to income, but noted the impact of discrimination in the workplace.

- Some suggest that the institution of work, including practices in work organizations, divisions in pay and related issues such as access to training and employment, has become fundamentally more equitable over the years. We argue that this is only partially correct. There is still much to be done.

- We suggest that the issue of inequality is absolutely central for organizational behaviour, not only because of the moral and power implications, but also because of the crucial role of equality in organizational life: levels of employee well-being, levels of social trust and sustainable behaviour are closely connected to the issue of equality and, in turn, to individual, group and organizational performance.

- Women, people from ethno-racial minorities, those who are disabled and members of the working class (and all combinations of these categories) continue to face major difficulties in gaining just and equitable treatment in relation to paid work. Students and scholars of organizational behaviour will benefit from a broader appreciation of these dynamics to inform the direction of future learning and research. When these are taken together, the vast majority of people in our society are subject to some form of discrimination. This begs the question of why, if the vast majority of people experience systematic inequities in relation to work, it is so difficult to realize significant, positive change. Some of the answers to this question lie within the realm of existing organizational behaviour research, but many others have not yet been addressed. To address these questions of equity, it is necessary to take a fundamental look at how work and society are organized. Through some of the interdisciplinary dimensions of this chapter, we hope readers will start on that journey of further exploration.

IN THE EBOOK ACCESS **WEB BASED ASSIGNMENTS** TO APPLY YOUR LEARNING.

Chapter review questions

1 What is the meaning of the concept of equality and how does it differ from equity?
2 What are the meaning and value of 'equitable practices' in organizations?
3 Is social class relevant to understanding the behaviour of individuals in organizations? What is the connection between social class, income inequality and organizational behaviour?

4 What is the relationship between the different dimensions of organizational justice and the specific social differences we explored in this chapter?
5 What do the terms 'sticky floor' and 'glass ceiling' have to do with gender, as well as with other forms of social difference?
6 How do these forms of social difference relate to one another to intensify or reduce inequities in organizations?

Further reading

Brief, A., Dietz, J., Cohen, R., Pugh, S. D. and Vaslow J. (2000) 'Just doing business: modern racism and obedience to authority as explanations for employment discrimination', *Organizational Behavior and Human Decision Processes*, 81(1), pp. 72–97.

Dorling, D. (2014) *Inequality and the 1%*, London: Verso.

Folger, R. and Cropanzano, R. (1998) *Organizational Justice and Human Resource Management*, Thousand Oaks, CA: Sage.

Jackson, A. (2000) *The Myth of the Equity–Efficiency Trade-off*, Ottawa: Canadian Council on Social Development.

Loprest, P. and Maag, E. (2001) *Barriers and Supports for Work among Adults with Disabilities: Results from the NHIS-D*, Washington, DC: Urban Institute.

O'Reilly, J., Nazio, T. and Roche Manuel, J. (2014) 'Compromising conventions: attitudes of dissonance and indifference towards full-time maternal employment in Denmark, Spain, Poland and the UK', *Work, Employment and Society*, 28(2), pp. 168–88.

Piketty, T. (2014) *Capital in the Twenty-first Century*, Cambridge, MA: Belknap Press.

Smooth, W. G. (2010) 'Intersectionalities of race and gender and leadership', pp. 31–40 in K. O'Conner (ed.), *Gender and Women's Leadership: A Reference Handbook*, Volume 1, London: Sage.

Stiglitz, J. (2013) *The Price of Inequality*, London: Penguin

Wilkinson, R. and Pickett, K. (2010) *The Spirit Level: Why Equality is Better for Everyone*, London: Penguin.

Wright, E. O. (1997) *Class Counts: Comparative Studies in Class Analysis*, Cambridge: Cambridge University Press.

Chapter case study: Equity challenges in South African police service organizations

The setting

Dramatic events transformed South African society with the end of apartheid and the democratic changes of 1994. The new government officially proclaimed goals of representativeness, including plans to eventually have workplace organizations become representative of the population as a whole from top to bottom. Informed by principles of organizational justice as well as democracy, employment and human rights legislation was developed and put into initial practice across a majority of economic sectors. One such sector was the police services in South Africa. Historically, these services remained dominated largely by white males with black male and black female officers (as a significant portion) only to be found in the lower third-class ranks, and the majority of women generally located in administrative work. Since the implementation of a range of laws and organizational policies, the police services in South Africa have shown slow progress.

The problem

Lawrence Cooper, a white South African man and 10-year veteran of the Public Order Police (POP) Service of South Africa (renamed as of 1995) had carefully cultivated a deep working understanding of what needed to be known and done in order to police effectively in Durban, the POP in Durban, which included over 800 employees.

Although the purposes and goals of the police services had been radically changed since the election of the African National Congress government in 1994, Officer Cooper knew for instance that cohesion among police officers was vital. He also knew that every effective police officer needed to have a vast working knowledge of the people, the places and the events. While some now said that these forms of knowledge were tinged with stereotypes – gendered and racial and highly linked to a long history of politics as well – and Officer Cooper knew that there was some truth in this, he also felt that they were part of the skills of effective police work. In fact, officers from all races used stereotypes for their work, and he felt there was importance to knowing how the various groups behaved in different circumstances – the whites (indigenous European descent), Indians (indigenous Asian descent), Africans (indigenous African descent) and Coloured people (of mixed racial descent), both Africans and Coloured people being generally referred to as black.

Moreover, the physical side of much police work, Officer Cooper believed, generally made it 'unsuitable' for women; they were emotionally fragile and he, felt, were prone to leave the service to care for a family before they could develop the necessary skills and advance in ability and status. And in any case, he knew of few women who wanted to do this type of work. These matters were deeply intertwined in the quality of his work. In some cases, his life literally depended on these forms of what could be called the informal 'cultural knowledge' of his job. These were things that were hard and important to learn, and he felt proud of his ability to do his assigned tasks well. On a personal level, he had developed a particular understanding of his role, learned it well and developed status as an excellent officer.

By 2001, Officer Cooper had seen important changes in the Durban POP. It had an African man as its unit commander, for example, although as far as he knew there was not, nor had there ever been, a requirement for the commander (or middle management for that matter) to be trained or have specialized skills in race relations within the force, which Officer Cooper thought was strange, especially given this new political environment and new policies. There were two high-ranking African women in operational management. What was clear, however, was that these appointments had a trickle-down effect: at the very least, officers in general complained less openly about the equity or affirmative action changes. In fact, reading a report from 2001, Officer Cooper already knew that over 50 per cent of officers were Africans and a third were Indian, while the proportion of white officers had dwindled to about 1 in 10.

At the same time, Officer Cooper also saw that many other things were much slower to change. Although not an official policy (the official policy in fact being to racially integrate the units), units in the Durban POP remained as racially segregated as they had traditionally been, but, importantly, the changes had, in his view, 'fragmented' the force in many ways. Non-white officers, for example, were now much more likely to complain of specialized treatment for the largely white-only units. Black officers had even formed their own 'POP Empowerment Committee' (a committee that nevertheless included only a very small number of black women officers), which was in Cooper's view an example of how changes were happening not just from the top down, but from the bottom up.

Officer Cooper knew that, separate from the citizens he dealt with as a police officer, matters of race and gender were part of working with other officers. His years prior to 1994 in policing had been built on a long tradition in which the black officers had for decades not only been limited in terms of whom they could arrest, and where and what they could police, but also frequently could not read or write, although this had changed quite a bit. Officer Cooper blamed 'affirmative action' for moving too quickly to bring both women and black individuals into key positions throughout the organization. The working skills and principles he had cultivated so carefully were under threat, and he resented it. In particular, the principle of cohesion, in Cooper's understanding so vital to the police services, had declined, and the quality of his work, if not the unit as a whole, was in jeopardy. For cohesion, officers needed to know their place and role. For effectiveness, he felt that policing needed to have the right person with the right abilities in the right position.

The task

In cases of equity in organizational behaviour, it is essential to consider organizational justice, equity and human rights policy and law, politics, history and social differences – as well as how each of these factors shapes and is given life in the course of the daily lives and working knowledge found within organizations. Such matters are particularly pronounced in the case described here, but they are just as likely to be found in various forms and types in other sectors and national settings. Begin working on this case study by noting factors related to policy, politics and history that are affecting the events summarized in the case above. Then create a list of important everyday organizational practices and forms of knowledge that have played a role. Finally, note that, over the last decade and a half, inequities have proven difficult to dislodge. Now turn to the following questions:

- What were the organizational structures that held back the creation of greater equity in the police services in this case study?

- How did organizational behaviour in everyday life (forms of informal 'cultural knowledge') play a role in here?
- Specifically, what is the role of forms of cultural knowledge in organizations in relationship to equity/inequity?
- What theories of organizational justice are most applicable to this case?

Following your work on this task, be sure to explore the expanded description of this case in the source documents listed below.

Sources and further information

Marks, M. (2005) *Transforming the Robocops: Changing Police in South Africa*, Durban: University of KwaZulu-Natal Press.

Marks, M. (2008) 'Looking different, acting different: struggles for equality within the South African Police Service', *Public Administration*, 86(3), pp. 643–58.

Wilkinson, R. and Pickett, K. (2010) *The Spirit Level: Why Equality is Better for Everyone*, London: Penguin.

Note: This case study was written by Peter Sawchuk, Professor, University of Toronto, Canada.

IN THE EBOOK ACCESS AN **OB IN FILM** BOX THAT USES *DIRTY PRETTY THINGS* (2002) TO PORTRAY THE MULTIPLE FORMS OF INEQUITY AND SOCIAL DIFFERENCE IN RELATION TO THE LOWER-TIER SERVICE ECONOMY THAT IS GROWING IN ALL G8 COUNTRIES AND TO ACCESS **AN INTERACTIVE QUIZ** TO TEST YOUR UNDERSTANDING.

chapter 9
Diversity and people management

Key concepts

- appraisal
- collective bargaining
- diversity
- diversity management
- diversity training
- equal opportunities
- human resource management
- recruitment
- rewards
- selection
- trade unions
- training
- workforce planning

Chapter outline

- Introduction
- Human resource management: management behaviour in action
- Theorizing people management
- Diversity in the workplace
- Functions of human resource management
- Outcomes and paradoxes in people management
- Summary and end-of-chapter features
- Chapter case study: Working but poor: organizing women in India

Chapter learning outcomes

After completing this chapter, you should be able to:

1　Explain the nature of and theoretical issues surrounding people management
2　Explain how management policies and practices help to prevent discriminatory behaviour and are drivers of diversity in the workplace
3　Explain the process of workforce planning and the requirements of diversity management
4　Explain the importance of recruitment and selection in the formation of the employment relationship
5　Understand the connection between learning theories, training and employee development
6　Explain the connection between motivation theories and reward management, and assess the various approaches to reward
7　Understand the purpose of performance management and assess different techniques for it

introduction

The chapters so far have covered a wide range of theories and research on individual employees to provide an understanding of work and behaviour in workplaces. We have highlighted how organizational behaviour is the result of complex processes involving how employees perceive, act in and respond to their lived experiences and interventions by management. We have also discussed how the workplace and society more generally are becoming more diverse. At the 2012 London Olympics, for example, around 21 per cent of Team GB's gold metals were won by immigrants or those with immigrant parents. A report entitled *A Portrait of Modern Britain* argues that there are clear and meaningful differences between the largest minority groups – Indian, Pakistani, Bangladeshi, Black African and Black Caribbean – which need to be fully understood by policy makers. But although we have made direct reference to the employment relationship, there has been little discussion of the employment practices developed by management. Recently, the outcomes of core employment practices have come under scrutiny and criticism. There are several examples of this: employment selection tests, which the ill-qualified Reverend Paul Flowers, alleged 'crystal Methodist', and the Co-operative Bank chief both passed (Rawnsley, 2013); the growth of zero-hours contracts (Chakrabortty, 2015); graduate interns being paid 50 per cent of the UK national minimum wage (Boffey, 2015); the discrepancies in pay for jobs of equal value (Davies and Butler, 2014); the unintended behavioural effects attributed to performance-related pay (PRP) (Bregn, 2013); and the fact that only 8 per cent of Scottish employers feel they are engaging with the education and training system (Latham, 2014).

These reported cases relate directly or indirectly to the policies used to select and manage people in organizations. People management or, to use the more popular term, human resource management (HRM) – the function responsible for developing integrated employment policies to support the organization's business strategy – analytically uses research findings on organizational behaviour to inform policies and practices, what is called evidence-based management. It is widely acknowledged, however, that there is a mismatch between social science research and management practice, which led to Karen Legge's memorable phrase of 'HRM rhetoric and reality'. It is not difficult to explain the gap. Few hard-pressed managers read the academic journals that publish organizational behaviour research, and management 'fads' are often 'a wonderful substitute for thinking' (Pfeffer and Sutton, 2006: 219).

Organizational behaviour and HRM have traditionally been taught in separate modules as they have their own traditions and methods, but there is a strong case for analytical HRM to incorporate organizational behaviour issues that are often neglected in the HRM canon, such as power, conflicts of interest, leadership and microsocial interactions in the organization (Bratton and Gold, 2012; Grint, 2005; Purcell and Kinnie, 2008).

This chapter aims to discuss just how important HRM policies and practices are in helping us to understand organizational behaviour and employment relations. We address a number of questions, some of which are essential to our understanding of how people behave in the contemporary workplace and the role of HRM therein. How do HRM techniques shape behaviour? How do managers manage diversity? Do organizations adopting different business strategies adopt different human resource strategies? Does HRM make a difference to the 'bottom line'? The debate brings out an important point: that there are fundamental structural constraints that emphasize the complexity of implementing different models of people management.

Human resource management: management behaviour in action

The term 'human resource management' has been the subject of considerable debate. However, given the nature of the employment relationship and the ongoing

Source: Image Source/Innocenti & Lee CM

Plate 30 Structured interviews and personality tests help to 'match' the right candidate to the right job.

debate since the 2008 financial and economic implosion on the need to infuse 'criticality' into management education (see, for example, Delbridge and Keenoy, 2010; Watson, 2010), we define HRM as:

> A strategic approach to managing employment relations which emphasizes that leveraging people's capabilities and commitment is critical to achieving sustainable competitive advantage or superior services, this being accomplished through a distinctive set of integrated employment policies, programmes and practices that are embedded in an organizational and societal context.

Following on from this definition, critical HRM underscores the importance of *people*: only the 'human factor' or labour can provide talent to generate value. With this in mind, it goes without saying that any adequate analytical conception of HRM should draw attention to the notion of *indeterminacy*, which derives from the employment relationship, and the fact that human knowledge and skills are a *strategic resource* that needs investment and adroit management. Moreover, motivated by the growing concern for protecting ecosystems, HRM practices have a role in promoting pro-environmental behaviour and improving an organization's *sustainable* performance (Bratton and Bratton, 2015). The notion of *integration* focuses on the need for a cluster of policies and practices to be integrated into corporate strategy.

It is plausible to argue that if people are so critical for sustainable performance and societal well-being, HRM is too important to be left solely to human resource specialists, but should be the responsibility of *all* managers. Moreover, human dignity *in* and *at* work is, or *ought* to be, at the heart of contemporary management (Bolton, 2007). The dignity at work dimension provides support for a reconceptualized HRM model of empowered, engaged and developed employees, in other words, the 'missing "human" in HRM' (Bolton and Houlihan, 2007: ix). The conception of HRM put forward here resonates with 'critical' approaches holding that HRM can only be fully understood in the context of wider cultural, political and economic factors that shape or direct those practices. In a phrase: *context* counts.

That said, the theory and practice of HRM continue to draw primarily on psychologically driven research in organizational behaviour, and are still viewed as a possible solution to such perennial problems as low worker commitment, low worker productivity and worker resistance. Table 9.1 displays the organizational behaviour topics covered in this text in terms of core HRM practices.

Table 9.1 Organizational behaviour theories and HRM practices

Organizational behaviour theories	HRM functions	HRM practices
Personality analysis Individual perception Race and ethnicity	Recruitment and selection	Structured interviews and personality tests to 'match' the right person to the right job
Adult learning Organizational design Technological change Leadership styles	Training and development	Designing orientation and training workshops for new employees, job redesign and leadership to encourage informal learning and change
Motivation Alienation	Rewards management	Pay systems, bonuses and benefit packages to maximize individual performance
Motivation Communication Psychological contract Group dynamics	Performance appraisal	Interview appraisal, pay policy, training policy, disciplinary policy
Conflict Workplace resistance Groupthink	Employee relations	Handling individual and group grievances, communication of policies, negotiating with unions

As we have discussed in the preceding chapters, one set of perspectives, drawing on psychology, suggests that human behaviour in the workplace is a function of at least four variables – ability, motivation, opportunity and role perception – and of situational contingencies. Another set of perspectives, drawing on sociology, emphasizes the problematic nature of employment relations – contradictions and tensions, and the interrelated problems of control and commitment.

It should be evident by now that human capital (employees) differs from other organizational resources for several reasons: partly because individuals are endowed with varying levels of ability (including in their aptitudes, skills and know-ledge), personality traits, self-identity, emotions and role perceptions (see Chapters 4 and 5); partly as a result of differences in their motivation and commitment (see Chapter 6); and partly because of differences in employees' lived experience as shaped by social class, gender, ethnicity and disability (see Chapter 8). In other words, people differ from other resources because of their ability to evaluate and to question management's actions, and their commitment and cooperation always has to be won. In addition, employees have the capacity to organize into trade unions to defend or further their interests (Bratton and Gold, 2012).

Theorizing people management

> Practice without theory is blind. (Hyman, 1989: xiv)

So far, we have focused on the meaning of HRM and the connection between organizational behaviour research and theory and HRM practices. We now turn to an important part of the HRM discourse, the search for its defining features, which allegedly demonstrate analytically the qualitative differences between traditional personnel management and HRM. Over the past 30 or so years, academics have given us something resembling Weberian ideal-type models that emphasize the allegedly unique features of HRM and HRM's strategic importance to the organization.

Readers may ask, why bother looking at theoretical models? Models fulfil at least four important intellectual functions for those studying the links between HRM and organizational behaviour. First, they provide an analytical framework for studying HRM (for example, contextual factors and strategic choice, and the organizational behaviour theories that underpin HRM practices). Second, they provide a characterization of HRM that establishes a cluster of variables as well as the relationships between the dependent and independent variables that are to be researched. For example, will 'high-commitment' HR practices (*independent* variables) enhance productivity, product or service quality and improve employee well-being (*dependent* variables)? Third, models legitimize HRM, by which we mean that, for those advocating investment in people, models help to demonstrate to sceptics the rationale and the effectiveness of HRM. Fourth, they serve as a heuristic device for explaining the nature and significance of key human resource practices.

Academics in the USA and the UK have offered several different HRM models. The early US models developed by Fombrun et al. (1984) and by Beer et al. (1984) reflect an individualistically oriented culture, different management styles and a general absence of trade union organization in the workplace. The widely cited UK models developed by Hendry and Pettigrew (1990) and Storey (1992) are more complex models that pay explicit attention to the wider 'outer' and 'inner' contexts in which human resource practices are designed and executed. In the following section, we examine two derivative models.

HRM cycle: an analytical framework that diagrammatically connects human resource selection, appraisal, development and rewards to organizational performance

The early HRM model developed by Fombrun et al. emphasizes the 'HRM cycle'. HRM activities aim to support an organization's corporate strategy (Bratton and Gold, 2012). The model shown in Figure 9.1 is derived from Fombrun et al. and

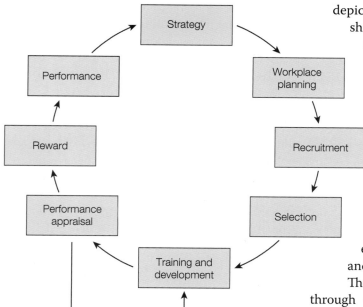

Figure 9.1 The human resource management cycle

depicts the link between strategy and HRM activities. It also shows the key stages an employee usually encounters on entering the workplace: recruitment, selection, training and development, performance appraisal and reward. The overall aim of these human resource activities is to increase organizational performance.

The HRM cycle serves as a heuristic framework for explaining the nature and significance of core people management practices. Indeed, it is used below to examine key practices for promoting diversity and improving organizational performance. Its weakness, however, is its prescriptive nature, with its focus on organizational performance. It also ignores different stakeholder interests, employee involvement and unions, contextual factors and the notion of management's strategic choice.

The model shown in Figure 9.2 focuses on the *processes* through which choices relating to HRM policies are shaped by both external and internal factors and, in turn, shape employees' behaviour and performance. This model is derived from the US-based Harvard model (Beer et al., 1984), the UK-based Warwick model (Hendry and Pettigrew, 1990) and the Bath people and performance model developed by John Purcell and his colleagues (Purcell et al., 2003). The resulting model takes account of several factors: external and internal factors influencing the choice of human resource policy, business strategy and human resource practices; assumptions about the links between human resource policies and practices and employees' behaviour; and predictions for long-term performance outcomes. It consists of six complex components:

- external factors (assessed by STEPLE analysis – see Chapters 1 and 18)
- internal factors
- HRM policy choices
- behaviour outcomes
- long-term performance outcomes
- a feedback loop through which the outputs flow directly into the organization.

The internal factors incorporate the business strategy, workforce characteristics, leadership and management philosophy, and unionization, which influence management's choice of human resource policies and practices. HRM policy

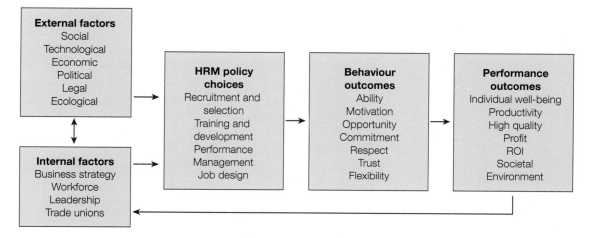

Figure 9.2 A model of HRM, behaviour and performance

choices emphasize that management's decisions and actions in terms of HRM can be fully appreciated only if it is recognized that they result from contingencies both outside and inside the organization and from an interaction between opportunities and constraints and strategic choices (see Figures 1.3 and 1.6). Employees' behavioural outcomes emphasize the requirements of ability (*how to*), motivation (to *do it*) and opportunity (to be *able to*), employees' commitment to organizational goals, trust and flexibility.

The underlying assumptions here are that humans are social beings, and that human behaviour is always embedded in a number of physical, psychological and cultural contexts, which considerably affect a worker's thinking, behaviour and motivation. Furthermore, workers have abilities that are often not fully utilized, and they show a desire to experience dignity in and at work. Thus, the model takes the view that employment relations should be managed on the basis of the assumptions inherent in McGregor's approach to people-related issues, which he labelled 'Theory Y' (see Chapter 6) – the theory that people work because they want to and not because they have to (McGregor, 1960).

The long-term outcomes distinguish between three levels: individual, organizational and societal. At the level of the individual employee, the long-term outputs comprise the physical and psychological well-being that workers should receive in exchange for their effort. At the organizational level, increased effectiveness, profit and a return on investment ensure the survival of the organization. At the societal level, some of society's goals (for example, sustainable growth, environmental protection and social justice) are attained as a result of fully utilizing people's skills and creativity, and by human resource practices that promote pro-environmental behaviours in the workplace.

The sixth component of the model is a feedback loop. As we have discussed, the internal factors influence HRM policy and choices. Conversely, long-term outcomes might influence the internal factors, including shareholders. The feedback loop reflects this two-way relationship.

This model serves as a heuristic device for explaining the nature and significance of key people management practices. Like the Harvard model, it contains elements that are analytical – that is, internal factors and strategic choice levels – and elements that are prescriptive, that is, notions of commitment, competence and so on (Boxall, 1992).

stop...

Reviewing the two models, what beliefs and assumptions do you find implied in them? What is the message for managers? What organizational behaviour theories do you see in each model? What is missing?

...and reflect

Diversity in the workplace

The degree of gender, ethnic, racial and age diversity in the workplace is on a steep upwards trajectory, and successfully managing diversity is seen as a strategic imperative in private and public organizations (Leslie, 2014). Research highlights the positive effects of management practices that promote diversity and inclusion for promoting trust, employee engagement and cooperation (Downey et al., 2015). In this context, people management policies and practices help to prevent discriminatory behaviour, are drivers of diversity and are central to managing diversity in organizations. We begin this section with examining the meaning of diversity.

Diversity

Diversity defines European modernity. In Britain, social surveys show that 8 million people, or 14 per cent of the UK population, are currently from ethno-racial minorities. By 2051, the size of the visible minority population is estimated to double to 16 million, and make up 20 per cent of the population. The presence of visible minorities, however, began well before the migration to Britain of Black Caribbean workers in the 1950s. The sugar and slave trade were the most lucrative industries in the British Empire and inevitably involved the movements of thousands of black people back and forth between Britain, Africa and the Caribbean. Stuart (2014: 38) observes that if the history of Britain were made into a film, 'black people would be in virtually every scene', from Roman times to the Tudor court, and from the Georgian era, when it was estimated that there were more than 15,000 black individuals in London alone, a proportion almost equal to that of today, up to the present day. In Chapter 8 (see Figure 8.1), we compared the levels of income received by the largest visible minority groups in the UK and noted that they tend to be over-represented in the lowest positions and under-represented in the upper hierarchy in organizations (Modood et al., 1997).

As we have previously discussed, there are differences in the experiences of non-white groups. Research shows that, for many workers from ethno-racial minorities, ethnicity shapes their experience: 'To imagine it doesn't is to imagine the earth is flat. I've lived that experience and I know it's real', writes King (2012). Two other social trends over the last 30 years also highlight diversity in the workplace: the growth in the number of women entering paid work and, partly due to demographic factors, health improvements and changes in pension legislation, the increasing numbers of older workers who are delaying retirement and remaining in employment.

Social interaction is a natural feature of behaviour in workplaces, and group- and teamworking are a major feature of organizational life. Diversity challenges many traditional stereotypes (see Chapter 5). As we suggested, social stereotypes are a form of schema containing generalized ideas about the characteristics or attributes of a group (Judd and Park, 1993). For example, we may say that Japanese men and women are better at mathematics than creative thinking, that differing traits and abilities make women particularly well suited to nursing occupations, and that older workers are less likely to accept change than their younger co-workers. These are all examples of stereotypical beliefs about groups of people that are related to ethno-racial factors, gender and age because they make assumptions that the characteristics in question will be true of all or most of the individuals in these categories.

Source: PhotoDisc/Getty Images

Plate 31 Research by Noon and Hoque (2001) found that women and men from visible minority groups received less favourable treatment on a range of measures related to pay, job performance and promotion opportunities.

The research evidence demonstrates that these stereotypical beliefs still exist, particularly with regard to gender differences (Allen, 1995; Bosseley, 1999; Schein et al., 1996) and age (Mencl and Lester, 2014; Powell, 1998). Although research shows that countries with greater social equality – Sweden, Norway, Finland and Denmark – are the most tolerant towards immigrants, ethno-racial minorities experience their own 'glass ceiling' and report more negative work experiences than their white co-workers (Cox and Finley, 1995; Modood et al., 1997). Noon and Hoque's (2001) study compared the work experiences of white and ethno-racial minority employees. They found that women and men from visible minority groups received less favourable treatment on a range of measures related to pay, job performance and promotion opportunities.

Diversity management

An important trend that can potentially counter these negative work experiences has been an interest in planning for a diverse workforce, known as 'diversity management' (Tatli et al., 2007). Many of the organizational behaviour theories we have examined so far affirm that human beings are not homogeneous. Diversity focuses on the facets that make each of us unique as individuals. Thus, individual differences are the essence of diversity:

The concept of diversity encompasses any sort of difference between individuals. These could be differences in ethnic origin, age, gender, disability, family status, education, social or cultural background, personality or attributes – in fact, anything that may affect workplace relationships and achievements. (Chartered Management Institute, 2008)

A common mistake is to believe that equal opportunities and diversity are synonymous. *Equal opportunities* is concerned with achieving equality of opportunity in the workplace regardless of gender, race, ethnicity, sexual orientation, disability, age or any other social categorization, so that 'individuals are enabled freely and equally to compete for social rewards' (Jewson and Mason, 1986: 307). European Union, Australian, Canadian and US laws mandate equal opportunities. The concept of *diversity* is, however, a more sophisticated extension of equal opportunities that was developed in the 1970s. It is based upon intersectional analysis, a concept we introduced in Chapter 8, which highlights the important reality of the different experiences of disadvantage that can occur between and even within social groups (Bagilhole, 2009). For example, experiences of racism and racial discrimination differ in important ways for Black Caribbean women and Black Caribbean men. Equal opportunities and diversity focus attention on 'multiple disadvantage', so that ensuring different treatment for different groups and managing equal opportunity and diversity are not alternatives, but are interdependent (Bagilhole, 2009; Chartered Institute of Personnel and Development [CIPD], 2010).

There is a growing consensus that diversity is necessary for effective organizational performance. However, there are conflicting narratives regarding the 'business case' for diversity (Leslie, 2014). On the one hand, a diverse workforce can be a valuable asset, provide a competitive advantage and improve the quality of decision making in the organization (Downey et al., 2015; Pilch, 2006: Schneider, 2001; Singh, 2002). Downey et al.'s (2015) study, for example, went so far as to conclude that 'diversity practices with employee engagement, [are] a vital ingredient in overall workplace well-being' (Downey et al., 2015: 35). From this perspective, there appears to be a positive association between a diverse workforce and performance. The benefits include the following:

Plate 32 Research suggests organizations with a diverse senior management team, including women and people from different ethno-racial groups, show an increased growth and market share.

Source: Image Source

- *Superior recruiting efforts* – attracting and retaining talented employees and promoting less 'obvious candidates' (Confederation of British Industry/Trades Union Congress, 2008) provides a competitive advantage.
- *Effective working relationships* – there is 'a high trust workplace including increased employee performance and well-being' (Downey et al., 2015: 42).
- *Enhanced creativity and innovation* – 'Great ideas come from differences' (Mishra and Jhunjhunwala, 2013: 5).
- *Increased sales and market share* – consumer diversity and workforce diversity define Western contemporary society. Research suggest that organizations with a diverse team, including women and people from different ethno-racial groups, experience sales growth (Thompson, 1999).
- *Improved problem solving and decision making* – 'diversity in board composition is necessary for effective board performance' (Mishra and Jhunjhunwala, 2013: 5). In organizations with a multigenerational workforce consisting of Baby Boomer,

stop...

The message throughout this section is that diversity is extremely beneficial for organizations. How can it be, then, that many organizations seem unable to plan for a diverse workforce?

...and reflect

Generation X and Generation Y members, this diversity of perspectives can help bring about 'well-thought decisions' (Mencl and Lester, 2014: 1).

On the other hand, it is posited that ethnic and racial diversity can undermine group and work team cohesion and social networking, and negatively affect performance. This is because group members may display a critical attitude towards, ostracize or even exclude people from outside the group. But inconsistent research findings on these two perspectives has led scholars to shift away from a focus on *whether* ethnic diversity affects performance to a focus on *when* ethnic diversity impacts performance. For example, one study found that:

> The presence of two ethnic subgroups that are separated by large differences in status within a work unit is negatively related to work unit cohesion, and in turn performance, but only in communities also characterized by ethnic subgroups. (Leslie, 2014: 20)

Leslie's research illustrates the need to avoid generalizations and to be sensitive to context.

Employment legislation provides an important statement on the values of society, a 'floor of rights', and can help to shape behaviour. But the law, albeit necessary, is insufficient to change attitudes, which underpin behaviours (CIPD, 2010). The management of diversity can, however, help to change workplace behaviour. Managing diversity involves the implementation of strategies through which a network of varied individuals is integrated into a dynamic workforce (CIPD, 2010).

So what can organizations do to effectively manage diversity? This will entail significant individual and organizational change, and human resource policies and practices can help in achieving diversity goals. Such policies can include:

- a targeted recruitment of professional and non-professionals to identify and recruit women, disabled people and individuals from visible minorities
- 'branding' the employer as a progressive organization, with public exposure relating to diversity practices
- diversity training to increase the awareness and value of diversity
- coaching and development practices to prepare employees from minority and traditionally excluded employee groups for greater responsibility and career advancement
- performance appraisal and reward systems that reinforce managers' need to manage diversity effectively.

A number of criticisms have been levelled at mainstream diversity management. It is argued, for example, that diversity management should not be mistaken for legal compliance in terms of equal opportunities (Chartered Management Institute, 2008), that diversity management gives too little focus to the ethical and moral argument for diversity (Nordström and Ridderstråle, 2001), and that the 'business case' should be broadened to include issues relating to social justice (Kirton and Greene, 2000). That said, engaging in diversity and intercultural management strategies speaks to how we globally interact with one another (Robinson-Easley, 2014).

Research over the last three decades has confirmed that some progress has been made in tackling stereotypical beliefs on gender, ethno-racial aspects and age, and in achieving greater diversity in the workplace. However, it also reports that this has been relatively minor, that results are mixed across the European Union, and that organizations need to devote more resources and time to meeting the challenges and opportunities associated with diversity and demographic changes.

stop...

How would you respond to a claim that diversity management is just another form of 'political correctness' and that, even if it isn't, in an age of austerity it is a cost that organizations cannot afford?

...and reflect

Elizabeth Douglas holds the position of Learning and Development Manager at an Edinburgh Care and Sheltered Housing Association, Scotland, and is a former Human Resource Manager with over 20 years' experience. She acquired her MA in Languages and Arts from the University of Aberdeen and, after postgraduate training, entered management with the Great Western Railway Company. Elizabeth's current project is designing and delivering a programme on diversity in the workplace.

In the ebook click on the play button to watch Elizabeth talking about recruitment and diversity at her organization, and then answer the following question:

- How can recruitment and selection practices help to create a more diverse workforce?

Links to management   Elizabeth Douglas

Functions of human resource management

As discussed above, HRM policies and practices shape the nature of work and regulate the behaviour between the employer and the workers – the employment relationship. It can also contribute to addressing the issue of gender, ethno-racial, disability or age stereotypes.

Drawing on employment relations research, we can identify several key HRM functions (CIPD, 2010; Green, 2004; Kersley et al., 2006; Morrison, 1992; Tatli et al., 2007). These are policies and practices designed in response to the organization's strategic goals and in order to manage diversity in organizations. Each function contains alternatives from which managers can choose. The core functions in the HRM cycle – workforce planning, recruitment and selection, training and development, rewards and performance appraisal, as well as employee relations – are examined in greater detail in this section.

Workforce planning

Effective management now more than ever demands an understanding of, and response, to diversity. Professional institutions emphasize the importance of managing diversity as a strategic priority (CIPD, 2007). The global financial crisis of 2008 and the consequent 'Great Recession', however, illustrate the challenges of predicting business and workforce changes. The decisions involved in making workforce plans rely on decisions based around the organization's corporate strategy and around available data on the future of the labour market. There are forecasts relating to the demand for labour, based on meeting the requirements of the strategic business plan. There are also forecasts for the supply of labour that will match the demand for it. The turbulence of the late 2000s is a further reminder for workforce planning to adopt analytical techniques to aid predictability, as well as a creative process for coping with the known 'unknowns'.

The theoretical roots of workforce planning can be found in the 'manpower' planning and human resource planning (HRP) techniques that were developed in the twentieth century. In 1974, the UK's Department of Employment defined *manpower planning* as 'a strategy for the acquisition, utilization, improvement and preservation of an organization's human resources'. The key stages of the manpower planning process are shown in Figure 9.3. The notion of achieving a 'balance' between demand and supply reflects the intellectual influence of labour economists, in which movement towards an 'equilibrium' is a normative ideal. The manpower planning process has four stages:

- an evaluation of the existing human resources
- an assessment of the proportion of currently employed human resources that are likely to be present in the organization by the forecast date
- a forecast of the human resource requirements that are needed for the organization to achieve its strategic goals by the forecast date
- decisions to ensure that the necessary human resources are available as and when required – the manpower plan.

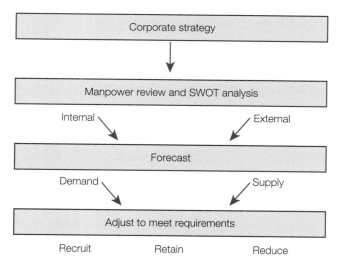

Figure 9.3 Balancing the demand and supply of labour. SWOT, Strengths, Weaknesses, Opportunities, Threats

The first two stages of the manpower planning process represent the supply side of human resources, and stage 3 represents the derived demand for labour. Stage 4 involves an analysis of the supply and demand forecasts so that employees' skills are utilized and developed. Owing to the complexity of the planning process, manpower planning incorporated operational research and behavioural models. The focus on sophisticated statistical models meant that manpower planning was not, however, 'user-friendly' and fully integrated into strategic management (Cowling and Walters, 1990).

During the 1990s, as the HRM model became established, academics began to use the gender-neutral term '*human resource planning*'. HRP was, however, more than just a matter of semantics. Research focused on the importance of HRP activities in developing a plan that integrated core human resource practices to meet both the performance needs of the organization and the growth needs of employees, in other words a human resource strategy that emphasized people as the key source of competitive advantage (Pfeffer, 1994). HRP therefore signalled the intent to link together business strategy, structure and people. In addition, a human resource plan had to involve coordinating the implementation of a 'bundle' of human resource practices that would complement each other (Hoque, 1999) and be context sensitive (Bowen and Ostroff, 2004). For example, a plan to introduce diversity training on its own would be far less effective without considering recruitment and selection, performance appraisal, career pathways, the organizational culture and everyday meanings surrounding work.

In this context, there was much debate about using HRP to meet the needs of a 'high-road' HRM strategy (high skills, high pay, high commitment) versus a 'low-road' HRM strategy (low skills, low pay, low commitment). In the UK, the emergence of the 'ownerless corporation' with an overriding concern for maximizing short-term profits made for a business environment that was largely incompatible with high-road HRM (Cooke, 2000). In reality, employers focused on people as 'numbers' and a 'cost' rather than an asset, and HRP became a process to accommodate 'pragmatic and opportunistic' management (Storey, 1995).

More recently, academics and organizations have used the term *workforce planning* to refer to a process that combines aspects of both 'manpower' planning and HRP. Workforce planning seeks to forecast the supply and demand for skills against the requirements of future services or production delivery in a global economic context of uncertainty and rapid change. It covers two broad activities: the use of statistical modelling found in manpower planning, such as estimating employee turnover, and the diagnostic and strategic understanding and nuances associated with HRP (Curson et al., 2010). Despite the use of sophisticated human resource infrastructure systems that enable the creation of various forecasts and scenarios related to future possibilities and unexpected shocks (Hurley-Hanson and Giannantonio, 2008), workforce planning has been viewed both as a 'science and an art' (Parsons, 2010), and as analogous to 'crystal-ball gazing' (Curson, 2006).

Recruitment and selection

Recruitment and selection processes must, it is suggested, recognize that people from different ethnic groups are motivated by different benefits. For example, compared with other ethnic groups, managers from Black Caribbean and Black African minority groups are more likely to cite good career progression opportunities, whereas white and black female managers are more likely to mention work–life balance (Chartered Management Institute, 2008).

Informed by the workforce plan, recruitment and selection activities are important for attracting a large pool of top talent and, as such, are a source of competitive advantage for an organization (Hinojosa et al., 2015). Traditional recruitment activities aim to select a candidate based on the criteria in the job description and on personnel specifications. In recent years, the idea of the 'employer brand' (Knox and Freeman, 2006) and the design and information contained on the employer's website (Hinojosa et al., 2015) has informed recruitment strategies. Candidates are selected using a variety of techniques including application forms, CVs, interviews, competency testing and psychometric testing. Figure 9.4 shows an overall view of the recruitment and selection process, and the link to workforce planning.

A job description, usually derived from a job analysis, provides a description of the tasks and responsibilities that make up the job. A personnel specification attempts to profile the 'ideal' person to fill the job position. Both job descriptions and personnel specifications have been key instruments in the traditional repertoire of managers (Bratton and Gold, 2012). The main means of attracting applicants include advertising, websites, professional agencies, walk-ins and employee referrals (stage 2 in the recruitment and selection process).

The selection methods chosen to select candidates in UK organizations will depend on a number of factors, such as the characteristics of the work, the level of responsibility and the level of pay (stage 3 of the process) (Wilk and Cappelli, 2003). Of the 'classic trio' – the application form, letters of reference and the interview – the face-to-face interview is the oldest and most widely used (Cook, 1994) of the traditional methods. The selection technique needs to be consistent in what it is measuring over repeated use: this is the *reliability* criterion. In addition, the selection technique must actually measure what it sets out to measure: the *validity* criterion. The selection interview has been the subject of much research, and Ulrich and Trumbo (1965) have found it to be deficient in terms of both reliability and validity.

Competency-based interviewing

Research by Barclay (2001) reported on developments in behavioural interviewing techniques to improve reliability and validity. For example, competency-based interviewing is used to align an organization's objectives on diversity and provide a basis for more consistency in its assessment practices. Table 9.2 shows an example of the identifiable competencies that a financial services organization may use to achieve its business strategy. Each competency is described by a range of indicators that, once analysed, seeks to identify behavioural dimensions that are associated with the effective behaviour needed to achieve the organization's strategy.

Competency-based interviewing, however, has its detractors. Competency-based questions are based on past behaviour, and assume that behaviour is consistent over time. Furthermore, using information and examples taken from the Internet, applicants can prepare their answers in advance to create a 'fake' but desirable impression (Levashina and Campion, 2006).

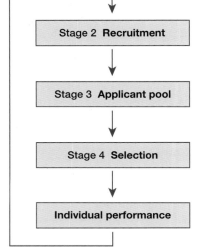

Figure 9.4 The stages of the recruitment and selection process

Table 9.2 Competencies in a financial services organization

Personal focus	Self-control Emotional intelligence Positive approach
Customer focus	Creating customer service Delivering customer service Continuous improvement
Future focus	Communicating the vision Creativity and change
Business focus	Delivering results Providing solutions Holistic thinking Attention to detail
People focus	Coaching people Resolving interpersonal conflict Influencing Being a change 'champion'

Source: Adapted from Bratton and Gold (2012: 218). Reproduced with permission of Palgrave Macmillan

Personality testing

The increased focus on identifying psychological factors through tests, and on to what degree such factors predict future job performance, has led to the expanded use of general mental ability tests for selecting candidates in UK organizations (Bertua et al., 2005). Personality testing provides organizations with insights into people's thoughts, feelings and behaviour. In other words, it makes aspects of personality quantifiable, and this allows the inner feelings of workers to be transmitted into measurements, from which management decisions can be made.

In the area of personality, there has, over the past three decades, been growing interest in the predictive validity of the 'Big Five' personality model (see Chapter 4). Studies have examined the five-factor model as an explanation of performance–personality linkages (Salgado, 1997). The research concluded that conscientiousness and emotional stability were positively correlated with job performance.

The major methods that organizations use to assess personality and predict work behaviour are shown in Figure 9.5. These consist of the interview, inventories, behaviour assessment, personality tests and e-assessment.

stop...

Re-read the section on the 'Big Five' personality model. If you were a manager and had the task of writing a complete personality description of an applicant you did not know for an important position in your organization, what would you do? What questions related to the Big Five model would you ask?

...and reflect

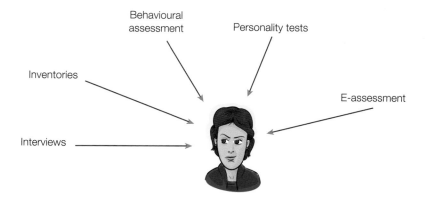

Figure 9.5 Measurement approaches used to assess personality

Myers–Briggs Type Indicator: a personality test that measures personality traits

One of the most widely used personality tests in North America is the **Myers–Briggs Type Indicator**. This contains 100 questions about how participants usually feel or act in certain situations. This personality test then labels participants as introverted or extroverted (I or E), intuitive or sensing (N or S), feeling or thinking (F or T) and perceiving or judging (P or J). Whether the use of Myers–Briggs Type

Indicator personality tests in fact accurately predicts future work performance is problematic (Dalen et al., 2001; Robertson et al., 2000). It has been argued, for example, that broad traits such as Eysenck's 'Big Two' and the Big Five may be useful instruments for predicting behaviour across a whole range of work situations, much as a wide-beamed floodlight illuminates a large area. However, like a narrowly focused and intense spotlight, an analysis of specific traits such as Cattell's 16PF may be a better instrument in specific situations that call for the behaviours measured by the narrower traits.

Another approach to personnel selection involves online personality testing, a technique known as e-assessment. This form of assessment provides managers with the ability to conduct personality tests at any time and any place in the world, with the added advantage of the rapid processing of applicants.

IN THE EBOOK ACCESS THE **OB IN FOCUS** BOX ON 'PSYCHOMETRIC TESTING: ENSURING THE RIGHT FIT'.

Some critical organizational theorists argue that psychometric testing measures what is effectively a stereotype of an 'ideal' employee. It provides management with new ways of 'knowing' and managing managers and non-managers alike. It also represents a shift in management practices from the coercion of bodies through, for instance, time and motion and other Tayloristic techniques, to the attempted construction of self-regulated minds (Hollway, 1991; Rose, 1990; Townley, 1994). It is argued, for example, that 'The minutiae of the human soul – human interactions, feelings, and thoughts, the psychological relations of the individual to the group – [have] emerged as a new domain for management' (Rose, 1990: 72).

Finally, personality assessment based on limited information can be damaging to the organization. For example, the overemphasis on traits to identify 'ideal' personality types in which employees 'fit' into the workplace potentially reinforces the notion that workplace problems are embedded only in the personality characteristics of people, rather than being embedded in the organization at large and the inner tensions associated with managing the employment relationship.

> *stop...*
>
> For some Muslim women, wearing a niqab is a symbol of emancipation and a commitment to their faith; for others, it represents patriarchal pressure. What issues does the wearing of a niqab raise for recruitment and selection practices in the workplace?
>
> *...and reflect*

Training and development

Training and development activities can contribute to creating a work culture that that respects individual differences and treats all employees with dignity and mutual respect. The effective management of diversity will entail a training and development programme that:

- develops the understanding and value of diversity
- educates employees about the culture and values of the members of a diverse workforce
- addresses prejudices and common stereotypes
- develops skills to communicate effectively with all employees, suppliers and customers.

In addition to diversity training, *human resource development* (HRD) can develop skills and competencies, help to shape the organizational culture, build employees' commitment, develop current and future leaders for the organization and develop low-carbon environmental behaviours.

Training and development can range from informal on-the-job learning to formal or planned learning on an MBA programme. In many large organizations, the training and development of managers is seen as part of a strategy involving long-term planning and individual professional development. Human resource development aims, first, to improve employees' performance, and second, to help individuals learn, develop and grow, within a specified period of time (Gold et al., 2013). Although performance appraisal is a contentious issue and is sometimes resisted by trade unions, it can help to identify employees' key skills and 'competencies', and plan for individual career development and training needs related to diversity. Crucially, for HRD to be effective, it requires both support from senior management, which needs to be communicated throughout the organization, and a supportive learning climate (Gold et al., 2013).

Understanding adult learning

The quality of the learning experience, and with it the concomitant potential for developing reflexive behaviour that will harness 'creative capital', will necessarily depend upon, not least, how the learning experience is designed. Throughout the twentieth century, a body of ideas concerning adult learning has developed (see Beckett and Hager, 2002; Bratton et al., 2004). There has been an interest in learning theories that focus on the interaction of adult learners with their context, often referred to as *experiential learning*. In this context, the notion of a **learning cycle** is popular within the formal learning canon, possibly because it contains elements of cognitive, behaviourist and andragogical concepts that can potentially encourage innovation (Kolb, 1984). The learning model depicts learning as a circular process with no start or finish (Figure 9.6). The Kolb learning model emphasizes the centrality of experience in the learning process, the role of individual needs and goals in determining the type of experience sought, and the importance of completing all the stages of learning before learning can occur.

learning cycle: a view of adult learning that emphasizes learning as a continuous process

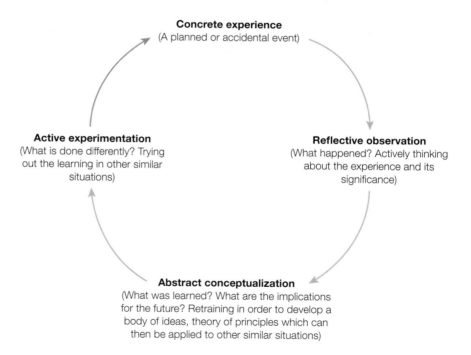

Figure 9.6 Kolb et al.'s experiential cycle of learning

KOLB, DAVID A., EXPERIENTIAL LEARNING: EXPERIENCE AS A SOURCE OF LEARNING & DEVELOPMENT, 1st Edition,©1984. Printed and Electronically reproduced by permission of Pearson Education, Inc., Upper Saddle River, New Jersey

The experiential learning cycle should be viewed as a holistic perspective that seeks to integrate behaviour, cognition, perception and authentic experience. Accordingly, the process of learning is both concrete and abstract, active and passive. Others have plausibly argued that the four moments in the learning cycle may not be totally discrete. In addition, experiences in the circumstances of work and learning shaped through these experiences (Billett and Choy, 2013) should not be viewed in isolation, reflection contextualizes the learning, and any action arising from the 'testing' may be contrary to power relations.

The 'good practices' and recommendations outlined in Table 9.3 can be traced to the learning theories examined in Chapter 7. Conflict theories of work, however, remind us that the application of learning theories in work organizations is never straightforward given the nature of the employment relationship, the network of power and control, and the persistence of inherent tensions in the management of learning and innovation.

Table 9.3 Applying learning theory in the organization

Social learning and adult learning concepts	Recommendations
Zone of proximal development	Expose learners to authentic tasks
Scaffolding	Encourage learners to interact with others
Communities of practice	Design work to allow knowledge to be applied
Participatory appropriation	Provide space and time for reflectivity
Guided participation	Develop the mentoring skills of managers/experts
Andragogy	Develop communities of practice through partnerships
Self-direction	Encourage learners to move towards self-directedness
Transformation	Draw on learners' life experiences
	Encourage critical thinking
	Design learning activities around learners' needs

Source: Based on Mezirow (1981), Knowles (1980) and Fuller and Unwin (1998)

stop...

Based on your own work experience, or on your studies of organizations, do you think that continuous learning in the workplace is more or less important for some organizations than others? If so, why?

...and reflect

Iain Nelson has spent 27 years as a Principal Consultant and Manager with the International Training Service, and 4 years as an internal Learning and Development Advisor with Petroleum Development Oman. As a freelance consultant, his clients include Unilever, Roche Products, Alcan, BP, Chevron, Lothian and Borders Police, the British Council, ITF Nigeria and Total.

Iain's core expertise is developing managers as learning specialists competent to design and deliver a company's corporate objectives and associated strategic business initiatives.

In the ebook click on the play button to watch Iain talking about the appraisal interview, and then answer the following questions:

- Why does Iain consider the appraisal interview to be a critical management competence?

- What skills does he identify as lying at the core of this competence?

Rewards

Pay always matters. It is the centrepiece of the employment relationship as it underscores the fact that the relationship constitutes an economic exchange (Arrowsmith et al., 2010). That is, an employee engages in work-related physical and/or mental activities that benefit the employer, in return for some payment or reward. But the nature of the pay, motivation and performance relation has provoked debate among scholars. A controversial issue in workplace rewards is the process of and extent to which extrinsic rewards influence employees' attitudes such as commitment (or employee engagement) and their behaviour, particularly their performance (or productivity). The concept of the psychological contract suggests that any 'incongruence' of expectations concerning the rewards employees receive when they join the organization can lead to a perceived violation of the contract (see, for example, Rousseau and Ho, 2000).

The design of pay systems is informed by evidence-based organizational behaviour research on motivation. Reward management entails judging the effectiveness of different types of performance-related reward, profit sharing and a range of benefits such as company pensions. These may be determined unilaterally by the employer or, depending on the level of union organization in the workplace, by joint negotiation with trade union representatives.

The 'new pay' agenda in Britain, which focuses on the employee's market worth, flexibility and performance (Corby et al., 2009), has been fuelled by neo-liberal ideology (Heery, 2000), and has dominated human resource practices and research for three decades. Reward systems are also shaped by the prevailing societal values and norms, which research suggests are strongly gendered (see, for example, Grimshaw and Rubery, 2010). In addition, pay stokes the incendiary debate over executive pay packages, the 'bonus culture', notions of 'fairness' and social inequality (see, for instance, Dawber, 2010).

Source: Getty

'Would top earners work less hard if they were paid less?'

Rowlingson and Connor (2011) turned round a long-standing debate concerning the grounds for providing state benefits to the working poor, and looked instead at whether 'the rich' need to be incentivized by large rewards to create wealth. This topic, they pointed out, has international significance because income inequality and the pay gap between senior managers and average workers has grown in many countries since the early 1990s (p. 438). The authors identified two work-related criteria for judging the 'deservingness' of the rich: (1) as a reward for merit or hard work, and (2) as an incentive to encourage people to create wealth.

The first criterion assumes that people have created their own wealth by working hard. However, the authors cite evidence that much of the wealth of the rich has come from inheritance. The children of the rich also benefit from social capital (because they are embedded in prestigious social networks) and cultural capital (in the sense that they receive knowledge and cultural attributes that give them an advantage) that they have inherited from their parents, so fare better economically than the offspring of poorer parents (p. 441).

Rowlingson and Connor point out that 'hard work' is difficult to conceptualize and to measure. Is it the hours worked, the effort put into work or its productivity? How is productivity to be measured when people work in a team? They quote research suggesting that management and senior professionals work slightly longer hours, but it is doubtful that a few extra hours at work can justify salaries that are double those of other workers (p. 442). The idea that more 'important' or 'skilled' work should be paid more comes up against the difficulties of assessing these aspects of work. Another view is that high rewards might be given to compensate for the unpleasantness or danger of a job. But manual jobs that are more unpleasant, risky or stressful receive the lowest rewards compared with stimulating, creative and flexible work (p. 443).

The second criterion also links rewards and merit, but argues that people need incentives to encourage hard work. Rowlingson

and Connor ask, 'would top earners work less hard it they were paid less?' (p. 444). They argue that once a certain threshold has been reached, other reasons may motivate people to work, including those quite separate from pay, such as 'intrinsic enjoyment' or 'status'. The authors cite research showing that 'Japanese CEOs earn less than a fifth of their US peers and have higher marginal tax rates, but there is no evidence that Japanese CEOs work less hard or less profitably than American ones' (p. 444). Indeed, incentives may have a negative role. The authors quote the House of Commons Treasury Select Committee, which, in 2009, following the financial collapse, concluded that 'bonus-driven remuneration structures created reckless and excessive risk-taking and that the design of bonus schemes was not aligned with the interests of shareholders and the long-term sustainability of the banks' (p. 445).

It could be argued that the market decides excessive rewards, and that talented key workers receive high rewards because they are in short supply. But it is remuneration committees within organizations that decide the rewards for senior executives, and these have been 'cosy clubs' comprising people in similar positions who lack an objective assessment of performance and contribution in the setting of pay.

Stop! Rowlingson and Connor conclude that incentive arguments for high salaried executives are at best spurious. The results of public opinion surveys, which they quote, show that the current ratios between the top earners and those with average wages are widely regarded as unjust. Consider the views for and against the use of taxing people more and more as they earn more money, in order to reduce income inequality. Could income and wealth be reduced at source by devices such as limiting the ratio of executive pay to average wages to, say, 20:1?

Sources and further information
Rowlingson, K. and Connor, S. (2011) 'The "Deserving" Rich? Inequality, morality and social policy', *Journal of Social Policy*, 40(3), pp. 437–52.
Treanor, J. (2014) 'Osborne under pressure as bonuses surge to £35m at bailed-out banks', *The Guardian*, March 7. Available at: www.theguardian.com/business/2014/mar/07/bailed-banks-rbs-lloyds-management-team-bosses-bonus-payouts-35m/ (accessed February 3, 2015)

Note: This feature was written by David Denham, Honorary Research Fellow in Sociology, Wolverhampton University, UK.

An organization can provide two broad types of reward: *extrinsic* and *intrinsic*. Extrinsic rewards satisfy an employee's basic needs for survival, security and recognition, and include financial payments. Intrinsic rewards refer to psychological 'enjoyment' and the satisfaction of 'challenge', sometimes called 'psychic income', that a worker derives from her or his paid work. The mix of extrinsic and intrinsic rewards provided by the employer is termed the *reward* system. We can define reward as:

> A package of monetary, non-monetary and psychological payments that an organization provides for its employees in exchange for a bundle of valued work-related behaviours. (Bratton and Gold, 2012: 364)

But can money change work behaviours? The differing answers to this question reflect a fundamental tension between economic theories and social psychological theories of motivation. Economics thinking emphasizes that pay incentives can achieve performance goals either by paying above the market rate or, possibly additionally, by offering selective employees large bonuses to spur extra effort on the part of all employees (tournament theory). In pre-crisis banking, for example, the bonus culture changed behaviours. As the Treasury Committee's report deftly observed, there was 'A culture of easy reward, illustrated by risky lending of credit and capital' (House of Commons, 2009: 14).

As we discussed in Chapter 6, the primacy of money as a key motivator of worker behaviour is challenged by social psychological and sociological theories. Psychologists have emphasized that all employees possess a common 'hierarchy of needs' (see, for example, Herzberg et al., 1959; Maslow, 1954), 'process' theories emphasize the role of an employee's cognitive processes (Adams, 1965; Locke, 1968; Vroom, 1964), and 'self-concept' theory posits that an inner source of energy motivates 'non-calculative-based' behaviour in the workplace (Fairholm, 1996; Leonard et al., 1999).

VISIT THE *ONLINE RESOURCE CENTRE* AT HTTPS://HE.PALGRAVE.COM/COMPANION/BRATTON-WORK-AND-ORGANIZATIONAL-BEHAVIOUR3/ FOR INFORMATION ON TEAM-BASED PAY AND PROFIT-SHARING REWARDS.

The nature of the relationship between pay and behaviour is complex, and reward research is replete with confusion and contradiction. It is not surprising therefore to find over decades a profound disagreement among academics over the effectiveness of the reward–performance link. On the one hand, Locke et al. (1980) argue that 'money is the crucial incentive' (pp. 379–81). On the other hand, Pfeffer (1998: 112) asserts that 'people do work for money – but they work even more for meaning in their lives'. The received wisdom is that a pay system that rewards workers 'fairly according to efforts expended and results produced creates a motivating work environment' (Caruth and Handlogten, 2001: 4). Researchers have also observed that creating dignity *at* work may improve workers' performance more than changing the pay system does (Blinder, 1990; Bolton, 2007), and that a wage reduction is likely to be perceived as a psychological contraction violation, with employees responding with negative behaviors (Chambel and Fortuna, 2015).

Table 9.4 shows three broad types of pay: individual, team and organizational. In broad terms, *individual* pay is paid directly to individual employees, and is based on a commitment of time, energy or a combination of both. Individual pay systems based on a job description are considered to reinforce bureaucratic hierarchical structures and be less compatible with team-based rewards (Guthrie, 2008). *Team* or *group* pay systems have become more prevalent in Europe and North America with the popularity of self-managed teams. *Organizational* pay, such as profit sharing, has also grown in popularity as a way of motivating workers (Kersley et al., 2006). Profit sharing is as a way of increasing organizational performance through employees' involvement in decision making (Marchington, 2008; Marchington and Kynighou, 2012) and their stronger identification with the business (Long, 2000).

stop...

Think about the reward system at your most recent job. How, if at all, did it influence your behaviour or that of your co-workers?

...and reflect

Table 9.4 Types of employee pay

Type of reward	Examples	Type of behaviour
Individual rewards	Basic wage Overtime Performance Commission Bonuses Merit Paid leave Benefits	*Time:* maintaining work attendance *Energy:* performing tasks *Competence*
Team rewards	Team bonuses Gain sharing	*Cooperation:* with co-workers
Organizational rewards	Profit sharing Share ownership Gain sharing	*Commitment* to strategic goals

stop...

If you are an employer, paying employees only when the desired performance takes place sounds like 'common sense'. Can you think of any circumstances in which individual-based performance pay would be advantageous or disadvantageous for a particular organization?

...and reflect

In 1980, 70 per cent of workplaces in the United Kingdom had their pay determined by collective bargaining between employers and trade unions representing employee groups (Brown, 2010). In 2012, collective bargaining coverage had decreased to 35 per cent (Farnham, 2015). Parallel with the decrease in collective bargaining coverage, a 'new pay agenda' developed, particularly in the major Anglophone states, which aligns rewards to strategic goals and focuses on individual performance-based pay systems (Corby et al., 2009). Pfeffer (1998: 99) explains the notion of pay-strategic alignment:

> The idea of alignment, that is, that an organization does specific things to manage the employment relationship and these practices need to be first, internally consistent ... and second, externally consistent, in the sense [that practices] produce behaviours ... required for it to compete successfully ... in that marketplace.

The strategic approach has been used for explaining the shift towards pay-for-performance, pay-for-knowledge and profit sharing. As Corby and her colleagues (2009: 7) note, one major objective of the 'new pay' paradigm is the 'individualization of reward packages, an objective that fits with a wider social decline in collectivism'. Much of the mainstream research has emphasized the need for organizations to adopt 'good' reward practices that encourage a constellation of attitudes and behaviours that meet the perceived needs of 'post-Fordist' work systems.

A notable feature of recent employment relations research is the growth of variable pay schemes in UK workplaces (Arrowsmith and Marginson, 2011). Data show that the most common form of variable reward is PRP schemes, also known as incentive pay schemes, which are present in 40 per cent of UK workplaces. PRP schemes were more prevalent in the private sector (44 per cent) compared with public sector workplaces (19 per cent). Recent survey data show marked differences in reward practices within sectors by size of organization, by occupation and between the private and public sectors (CIPD, 2010; Corby et al., 2009; Kersley et al., 2006). The CIPD reported that individual performance was the criterion used to manage pay progression in 68 per cent of organizations (CIPD, 2010). In British retail banking, for example, various forms of performance bonuses are now 'strongly embedded' as tools to motivate and control employees through pay (Arrowsmith and Marginson, 2011).

The growth of interest in variable pay arrangements can best be understood in terms of the dominance of neo-liberal ideology, particularly in North America and Britain. In the 1980s, this took the form of a concerted ideological campaign against unionization in general, and automatic annual pay increases in UK public sector pay in particular. One of Prime Minister Margaret Thatcher's major accomplishments lay in the deunionizing of the workplace. According to confidential government papers released in 2013, Thatcher instructed her head of policy in 1983 that the government should 'neglect no opportunity to erode trade union membership' (Chakrabortty, 2014b: 30) It was the policy of deunionization, privatization and deregulation that encouraged a movement towards performance-based pay (Grimshaw and Rubery, 2010).

Wage data show the effect of the decline in unionization in the workplace. The international research by David Card and his colleagues on the connection between unionization and wage inequality in the USA, the UK and Canada suggests that up to 29 per cent of all wage inequality between British men over the last three decades can be explained by deunionization (Card et al., 2003a). The new pay paradigm also raises concerns for both inequality and organizational performance. Individualized pay is less likely to address problems of inequality and indignity at work. It is also plausible that organizations will be disadvantaged by not hearing the collective employees' 'voice', which might contribute to innovations in the workplace (Grimshaw and Rubery, 2010).

As discussed in the preceding chapter, empirical research shows that, despite the economic recession, the median total remuneration for top executives in Britain's FTSE 100 companies was almost £3 million in 2010, up 19 per cent from 2009 (Dawber, 2010). Pay inequality still remains a legitimate concern for people and society (Wilkinson and Pickett, 2010).

VISIT THE *ONLINE RESOURCE CENTRE* AT HTTPS://HE.PALGRAVE.COM/COMPANION/BRATTON-WORK-AND-ORGANIZATIONAL-BEHAVIOUR3/ FOR DETAILS ON EMPLOYMENT STANDARDS LEGISLATION RELATING TO REWARDS AND WEBSITES PROVIDING DATA AND INFORMATION ON MEN'S AND WOMEN'S PAY LEVELS.

Let us finish our discussion of reward management by examining some of the tensions and contradictions inherent in pay systems, and some of the ethical issues. At both the practical and the theoretical level, reward management involves an interlocking set of tensions and paradoxes. For employers, reward is a cost, but for employees, it is typically their only source of income. Thus, conflict is structured into the management of pay. Furthermore, reward exhibits the 'overarching tension' between neoclassical economic theories and social psychological theories with regard to the management conundrum of employee motivation (Corby et al., 2009: 10). This tension is documented in research reporting that PRP does not match performance (Hutton, 2014), leads to risky behaviour (Bakir, 2013) and can undermine the effectiveness of work teams (Guthrie, 2008).

In the banking sector, a US bank incentivized employees to lend to small business and increased lending by 47 per cent, but defaults increased sharply too. Indeed, risky behaviour fuelled by 'inappropriate incentives' has been cited as a cause of the financial crisis that began in 2008 (Treanor 2014b). Heery's (2000) criticism of the new pay paradigm is based on its 'ethical deficiencies' because the practice increases employee risk and, simultaneously, diminishes collective representation in pay systems. Employee risk increases as a larger proportion of pay is contingent on individual performance, which, along with the growth of zero-hours contracts, means that earnings are far less predictable. The absence of a strong trade union voice in the new pay paradigm is arguably unjust as it affords little scope for democratic input in a key area of the employment relationship.

Performance appraisal

Most readers of this textbook will have experienced a periodic assessment of their academic work. The assessment of your capabilities may have taken the form of assignments, group activities, examinations and so on. The results of an assessment will more than likely have significant outcomes. As in a university, paid work is

globalization & organization misbehaviour

Source: Image Source/ EMMERICHWEBB CM

The worker–CEO pay gap

Over the past 30 years, increases in CEOs' pay have, throughout the developed world, far outstripped the earnings gains made by other workers. CEO compensation packages that are 200 (or more) times greater than those earned by entry-level workers have become commonplace in Europe and North America. For example, Canada's 100 top-paid CEOs each pocketed $47,000 (£26,000) by 01:11 pm on their first day of work in 2014. This is roughly what an average full-time worker makes in a year (McKenzie, 2014). In the UK in 2013, the average compensation for a CEO in a FTSE 100 firm was £4.25 million, while the average British worker earned £27,174 (Salmon, 2013).

The conventional argument for generous pay for CEOs is that high pay is necessary to motivate them to perform well. Yet research does not support this assertion. For example, a 2010 French study found no robust relationship between any firm performance variable and CEO's compensation (Baptista, 2010). In fact, the growth in CEOs' pay appears to be driven by bull markets, that is, upward-moving markets with generally rising prices. CEOs' compensation is often in the form of shares. During a bull market, CEOs benefit from both rising share values and a lack of concern among investors about CEOs' salaries (Bebchuk and Grinstein, 2005).

Such growing inequality in income throughout Western societies and increasing employment precarity for workers have contributed to a rising chorus of criticism over CEOs' compensation. Some critics ask whether such a vast inequality in income is socially desirable. Critics suggest that great wealth may give a small group of people undue levels of influence over social and economic policy – influence they will use to further their own interests.

Other critics suggest that increases in CEOs' pay in the context of heightened employment precarity – such as low wages, insecure employment and little access to employment or statutory benefits – will negatively impact employees' morale, effort and loyalty. This perceived injustice may even damage a company's brand. Consider former JC Penney CEO Ron Johnson, who grossed $53 million (£32.3 million) in 2011. By paying Johnson roughly 1,795 times the average wage and benefits of his US department-store workers (20,000 of whom were laid off during the final year of his tenure), JC Penney opened itself up to significant public criticism (Thompson, 2013).

Several European countries are taking steps to address the growing gap between compensation for workers and for CEOs. In late 2013, France's top court approved a proposal for companies to pay 75 per cent tax on annual salaries exceeding €1 million. French President Hollande had said the idea was 'not to punish', but added that he hoped it would spur companies to lower executive pay at a time when the economy was suffering, unemployment was soaring and workers were being asked to accept wage cuts (*Industry Weekly*, 2013).

At the same time, Swiss voters defeated a referendum proposing capping a company's executive pay at 12 times that of the lowest paid worker. This proposal grew from anger that some Swiss CEOs were paid up to 200 times what their employees earned (BBC, 2013).

> **Stop!** Do you think that compensating CEOs at hundreds of times the rate of regular workers is warranted? What are the potential consequences of such a decision in the workplace? Could employers face additional legislative intervention as a result of this policy? Could they face a potential loss of market share due to consumer distaste?

Sources and further information

Baptista, M. (2010) 'CEO compensation and firm performance in France', Unpublished MSc thesis, HEC, Paris.

BBC (2013) 'Swiss vote no to capping bosses' pay at 12 times lowest paid', November 24. Available at: www.bbc.co.uk/news/business-25076879 (accessed February 3, 2015).

Bebchuk, L. and Grinstein, Y. (2005) *The Growth of Executive Pay*. Working Paper No. 11443, Cambridge: National Bureau of Economic Research.

Industry Weekly (2013) '75% company tax on high salaries approved by French Court', December 30. Available at: www.industryweek.com/finance/75-company-tax-high-salaries-approved-french-court (accessed February 3, 2015).

McKenzie, H. (2014) *All in a Day's Work? CEO Pay in Canada*, Ottawa: Canadian Centre for Policy Alternatives.

Salmon, J. (2013) 'Top business leader' pay packets rise by 10%: bosses of top companies now enjoy £4.3million in pay and perks', *Daily Mail* Online, June 10. Available at: www.dailymail.co.uk/news/article-2338697/Top-business-leaders-pay-packets-rise-10--Bosses-companies-enjoy-4-3million-pay-perks.html (accessed February 3, 2015).

Thompson, D. (2013) 'What's behind the huge (and growing) CEO-worker pay gap?', April 30. Available at: www.theatlantic.com/business/archive/2013/04/whats-behind-the-huge-and-growing-ceo-worker-pay-gap/275435/ (accessed February 3, 2015).

Note: This feature was written by Bob Barnetson, Associate Professor of Labour Relations, Athabasca University, Alberta, Canada.

increasingly linked to performance in which appraisal is an important activity that has significant outcomes for, among other things, pay and training and development. Performance management is a set of interconnected practices designed to ensure that an employee's overall capabilities and potential are appraised, so that relevant monetary and non-monetary rewards and HRD goals can be set and met.

Job performance is at the centre of performance management. The process assumes that the principal dimensions of an employee's work can be defined precisely in performance terms, and can be measured over specific periods of time that take into account constraints within the performance situation (Furnham, 2004). Quantifying work performance yields data that become information, allowing decision making that can be used for performance appraisals, for feedback to individual objective-setting, an employee's development needs and monetary rewards (CIPD, 2009). A myriad of variables under the headings of internal business, financial measures, customer factors, learning and leadership – a 'balanced scorecard' (Kaplan and Norton, 2000) – can be used as measurements, and these can be aligned with strategy. It is argued that measurement is an important determinant of an organization's strategic thinking and culture (Pun and White, 2005).

The practice of performance management and appraisal in UK organizations has come under much critical scrutiny in recent years. Research on work psychology shows that a reliance on 'subjective global ratings' for measuring employees' performance is 'notoriously subject to individual supervisory biases and political decisions' (Kepes et al., 2009: 525); therefore, to eradicate the corrosive effects of politics, organizations need to design performance appraisal processes systematically and comprehensively. Critical scholars argue that the appraisal process is designed to make employees 'known' to managers (Townley, 1994); that it is 'inextricably linked to the contested terrain of control' (Newton and Findlay, 1996: 56); that it provides a 'disciplinary matrix' with which to communicate and reinforce the organization's values and inculcate employees' loyalty, commitment and dependency (Legge, 2005); and that the imposition of 'targets' is based on results rather than on the service delivered (Carter et al., 2011). As such, it is posited that performance management and appraisal is an important instrument that is used to engineer 'shared meaning' and change organizational culture, and that, as happens so often, it has unintended consequences in terms of behaviour and organizational outcomes.

VISIT THE *ONLINE RESOURCE CENTRE* AT HTTPS://HE.PALGRAVE.COM/COMPANION/BRATTON-WORK-AND-ORGANIZATIONAL-BEHAVIOUR3/ FOR DETAILS OF TRADE UNIONS IN BRITAIN, FOR COMPARATIVE INFORMATION BETWEEN COUNTRIES AND FOR INFORMATION ON COLLECTIVE BARGAINING.

Employee relations

A range of employee involvement/participation schemes in non-union or unionized workplaces may fall under the heading of managing employee relations. In workplaces where a trade union is recognized for collective bargaining purposes, it includes negotiating the substantive (pay and hours) and procedural (such as grievances, sabbatical leave and redundancy) issues of employment contracts, and administrating collective agreements at the industrial, organizational and workplace levels. With the developments in European employment law, many managers are seen as a source of knowledge on employment law matters, and act as guides to line managers. A study of workplaces found that handling disciplinary matters, grievance procedures and the employee consultation were some of the most common job responsibilities of managers who were primarily responsible for people management matters (Table 9.5).

Surveys have shown some difference in the number of tasks performed by generalists and specialists responsible for people management matters, as well as some variation in the tasks performed by managers depending on whether they are employed in the private or the public sector. Managers in public sector workplaces are less likely to be responsible for rates of pay, working hours and holiday and pension entitlements. In smaller organizations, generalists, or if present human resource managers, are more likely than their counterparts in larger organizations to do all the tasks listed.

stop...

Think back to the Fayolian management cycle (p. 20). Are these HRM tasks different from or similar to the ones shown there?

...and reflect

IN THE EBOOK ACCESS THE **OB IN FOCUS** BOX ON 'RAISING THE PROFILE OF THE HR AGENDA'.

Workforce planning, recruitment and selection, training and development activities are important for creating a diverse workplace and are a source of superior services or competitive advantage. However, the key people management practices discussed above and the main management activities listed in Table 9.5 give little indication of how power struggles inside the organization dictate the relative importance of HRM compared with other management functions. Within most organizations, there are power struggles over which functional area of management – finance, marketing, production, HRM – will dominate and fashion executive decisions. These disputes are partly the result of individual self-interest and power contests inside the management team, but they also represent differences in how best to compete in the marketplace – whether to emphasize market share and product price, or high-quality 'branding' and employees' skills. The role of HRM, how it is organized and how much power it has relative to other management functions is affected both by internal factors unique to the organization (such as product or service range, and organizational culture) and by external contexts – such as labour shortages and national employment legal regimes (see Jacoby, 2005).

Table 9.5 Work responsibilities of human resource managers

	All workplaces	Type of manager	
	(%)	Generalist (%)	Specialist (%)
Handling disciplinary matters	96	96	95
Handling grievances	95	95	95
Recruitment	94	94	93
Staffing plans	90	93	82
Employee consultation	90	91	89
Training	89	90	86
Performance appraisal	88	90	85
Health and safety	88	93	76
Equal opportunities	84	86	83
Working hours	80	80	80
Rates of pay	68	69	63
Holiday entitlements	62	60	65
Pension entitlements	37	37	37
Responsibility for all areas	27	29	22
Average number of areas of responsibility	10.6	10.8	10.4

Source: Adapted from Kersley et al. (2006, p. 48)

IN THE EBOOK ACCESS THE **CRITICAL INSIGHT** ON 'HRM BEST PRACTICES: CHIMERA OR CUL-DE-SAC?'

Outcomes and paradoxes in people management

Much research in recent years has tried to measure HRM outcomes. However, given the research on the mediating effects of employee perceptions and emotion and workplace behaviours, assessing outcomes increasingly examines the extent to which employee, organizational and societal outcomes are mutually fulfilling, and thus more sustainable (Boxall et al., 2008b). The questions 'for whom' and 'how well' in terms of measuring outcomes for HRM is more than a debating point. Evidence that better people management practices can indeed improve employee well-being and lead to superior organizational performance while meeting environmental targets has fundamental implications, not least for whether or not an organization should invest in human resource interventions. It has not been lost on either academics or practitioners that evidence of the effectiveness of human resource interventions enhances the status of the academic discipline of HRM, as well as the authority and self-importance of human resource specialists in the workplace.

Demonstrating that there is indeed a positive link between particular clusters or 'bundles' of human resource practices and business performance has become 'the dominant research issue' for over three decades (see, for example, Edwards and Sengupta, 2010; Guest, 1997; Ichniowski et al., 1996; Purcell et al., 2009).

The suggested process mediating the causal linkage between HRM practices and the organization's performance is presented in Figure 9.7. In this genre, a number of studies have found that bundles of human resource practices are positively associated with superior organizational performance (Hutchinson et al., 2000; Ichniowski et al., 1996; Paauwe, 2004; Paul and Anantharaman, 2003; Pfeffer, 1998). Two researchers concluded, however, that although no single human resource practice affects financial performance, 'every HRM practice influences financial outcomes indirectly through one or more intervening variables (for example, employee competence, teamwork, employee commitment to the employer, stronger customer orientation) and operational performance dimensions' (Paul and Anantharaman, 2003: 1261). Such claims of a positive linkage between sets of human resource practices and performance are particularly associated with **high-performance work systems** (see Chapter 2), which, in certain contexts, can result in mutual or 'win–win' outcomes (Boxall and Macky, 2009).

high-performance working environment: describes efforts to manage employment relations and work operations using a set of distinctive 'better' human resource practices. These are intended to improve outcomes such as employee commitment, flexibility and cooperation, which in turn enhance the organization's competitive advantage

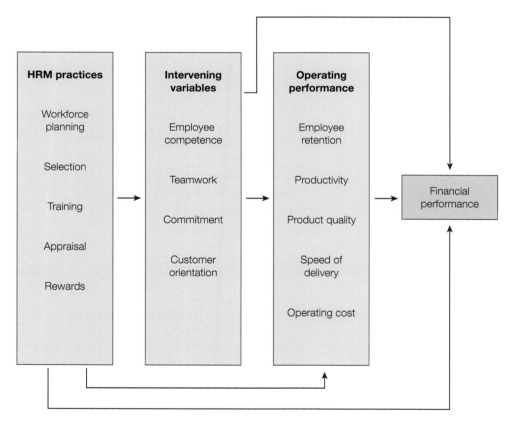

Figure 9.7 Modelling the HRM–performance linkage
Source: Adapted from Paul and Anantharaman (2003, p. 1249)

Some doubts remain both empirically and in the modelling of HRM–performance linkages. In terms of evidence, if there has been a 'breakthrough', any knowledge of the HRM–performance relationship seems to have fallen on the deaf ears of managers, as indicated by surveys reporting a mixed take-up of high-commitment employment practices, especially among smaller organizations (e.g. Kersley et al., 2005) and, more recently, by the rise of non-standard working arrangements such as zero-hours contracts (Stavrou et al., 2015).

In addition, modelling is a challenge because researchers have to estimate the effect size of human resource–performance linkages and draw causal inferences on them (Gerhart, 2008). It is argued that there is a need for multiple measures of performance to match the variety of goals and interests involved (Paauwe and Boselie, 2005). And where some studies do report positive associations between human resources and performance, others suggest that the data do not meet 'strict tests' in terms of the theory of causality (Purcell and Kinnie, 2008). So, for example, even when a positive link is established, there can be no certainty of the direction of causality (Legge, 2005; Thompson and McHugh, 2006). A cluster of HRM practices might be introduced as the *result* of favourable profits.

This chapter has already illustrated contradictions in work and people management activities. The more critical evaluations of HRM models expose internal paradoxes. Paradox involves ambiguity and inconsistency – two or more positions that each sound reasonable yet conflict or even contradict each other. Paradox is inherent in HRM. It results when, in pursuit of a specific organizational goal or goals, managers call for or carry out actions that are in opposition to the very goal(s) the organization is attempting to accomplish.

Critics of the HRM model have drawn upon the Weberian notion of a 'paradox of consequences' arising from policies and practices in HRM (Weber, 1922/1968). For example, new organizational designs have been introduced to improve productivity and employee autonomy. On the other hand, the productivity benefits arising from the new organizational forms are accompanied by a number of negative effects on the 'psychological contract', which have the effect of undermining other goals such as retaining employees' loyalty and commitment. More broadly, there is ambiguity over whether the main role of the HRM function is a 'caring' one, or a 'controlling' or 'manipulative' one.

An incisive critique of the HRM phenomenon identifies further ambiguities in the 'soft' and 'hard' schools of HRM (Legge, 2005). There is a huge difference between the 'rhetoric' and 'reality' of HRM. Whereas, for example, the rhetoric asserts that 'we are all managers now' as a result of 'empowerment', it conceals the legitimate question of whether a social group holding privileges (senior management) and material returns can hold on to power. Similarly, the inclusion of the human resource director in the strategic management team, the act of 'giving away human resource management' to line managers and the outsourcing of more specialized human resource activities might ultimately lead to the end of the human resource professional: the 'big hat, no cattle' syndrome (Caldwell, 2001; Fernie et al., 1994) The tendency in UK companies to be ruled by short-term accounting controls might well undermine long-term human resource goals oriented to the development of employees (Armstrong, 1989).

One notable feature of much of the HRM literature is the tendency for the research and debate on the HRM model to be gender blind. More recently, however, there has been more interest in the gender implications of HRM models (Dickens, 1994, 1998; Healy et al., 2006). The HRM model might be at odds with the promotion of equal opportunities, and pronouncements on the value of diversity and individual learning are often part of the rhetoric rather than the reality.

Chapter summary

- In this chapter, we examined the nature of HRM and some models of how people are managed in the contemporary workplace. In particular, we examined six core HRM functions – workforce planning, recruitment and selection, training and development, rewards, performance appraisal and managing employee relations. HRM is a product of its times, linked to the ascendancy of a new political and economic ideology called neo-liberalism, and to the changed conditions of national and global capitalism.

- We examined two HRM models derived from US academics, Fombrun et al. and Beer et al., and European academics Hendry and Pettigrew. The framework enables us to connect the outer (wider environment) and inner (organizational) contexts, and to explore how HRM adapts to changes in the context.

- After examining the concept of diversity, we discussed the apparent growing interest in managing diversity at work. Diversity is a means of creating heterogeneity in the organization's workforce, a variety of lived experiences, backgrounds and networks enhancing the ability to improve problem solving,

enhanced creativity and innovation. Managing diversity needs to be seen as part of a culture change in the workplace.

- The chapter examined core HRM activities that can increase diversity in the organization and influence the employment relationship. The human resource practices include workforce planning, recruitment and selection, training and development, rewards, performance appraisal and managing employee relations.

- As part of the review of the links between organizational behaviour research and HRM theory and practices, we examined the debate on the HRM–performance relationship before highlighting tensions and paradoxes in HRM.

- Finally, we should note that despite the economic and political pressures of globalization, a divergence of human resource practices still remains. This is influenced and shaped by national and organizational cultures in the developed and the developing world, and by variations in national regulatory systems, labour markets and business-related national institutions.

IN THE EBOOK ACCESS **WEB BASED ASSIGNMENTS** TO APPLY YOUR LEARNING.

Chapter review questions

1 What role do the concepts and theory relating to organizational behaviour and social science play in developing HRM practices?
2 Is it possible to adopt a Theory Y philosophy in HRM?
3 What is meant by diversity management? What are the obstacles to diversity and how can HRM practices create a diverse workforce?
4 Is there a 'business case' for diversity management?

5 Explain the difference between equal opportunities and the effective management of diversity in the workplace?
6 What evidence is there that HRM practices generate superior organizational performance?
7 When critical management scholars proclaim that there are 'tensions between control and consent' arising from people management practices, what do they mean?

Further reading

Arrowsmith, J. and Marginson, P. (2011) 'Variable pay and collective bargaining in British retail banking', *British Journal of Industrial Relations*, 49(1), pp. 54–79.

Bagilhole, B. (2009) *Understanding Equal Opportunities and Diversity: The Social Differentiations and Intersections of Inequality*, Bristol: Policy Press.

Bratton, J. and Gold, J. (2012) *Human Resource Management: Theory and Practice* (5th edn), Basingstoke: Palgrave Macmillan.

Bregn, K. (2013) 'Detrimental effects of performance-related pay in the public sector? On the need for a broader theoretical perspective', *Public Organization Review*, 13(1), pp. 21–35.

Carter, B., Danford, A., Howcroft, D., Richardson, H., Smith, A. and Taylor, P. (2011) 'All they lack is a chain: lean and the new performance management in the British Civil Service', *New Technology Work and Employment*, 26(2), pp. 83–97.

Chartered Institute of Personnel and Development (2010) *Sustainable Organizational Performance,* London: CIPD.

Corby, S. Palmer, S. and Lindop, E. (eds) (2009) *Rethinking Reward*, Basingstoke: Palgrave Macmillan (see pp. 102–19).

Downey, S. N., van der Werff, L., Thomas, K. M., and Plaut, V. (2015) 'The role of diversity practices and inclusion in promoting trust and employee engagement', *Journal of Applied Social Psychology*, 45(1), pp. 35–44.

Gold, J. Holden, R., Stewart, J., Iles, P. and Beardwell, J. (eds) (2013) *Human Resource Development: Theory and Practice,* Basingstoke: Palgrave Macmillan.

Legge, K. (2006) 'Human resource management', pp. 220–41 in S. Ackroyd, R. Batt, P. Thompson and P. Tolbert (eds), *The Oxford Handbook of Work and Organization*, New York: Oxford University Press.

Leslie, L. M. (2014) 'A status-based multi-level model of ethnic diversity and work performance', *Journal of Management*, 20(1), pp. 1–29.

Noon, M. (2007) 'The fatal flaw of diversity and the business case for ethnic minorities', *Work, Employment and Society*, 21(4), pp. 773–84.

Sambrook, S. (2008) 'Critical HRD: a conceptual analysis', *Personnel Review*, 38(1), pp. 61–73.

Chapter case study: Working but poor: organizing women in India

The setting

Since the early 1860s, easy access to raw materials and cheap labour has made India an attractive location for British investment. Today, the rapid expansion of industry and the growth of the working class has set the stage for unions to flourish in the Indian workplace. In 2010, the official number of registered unions in India was approximately 50,000, although it is suspected there are actually more than double that number in existence. The overwhelming majority of trade union members are male. The most striking exception is in the garment industry, where women can make up as high as 70 per cent of the total number of members. For the last two decades, garment manufacturing has played a major role in Indian export activities.

The problem

Several garment manufacturers have recently opened factories in the city of Hyderabad in Andhra Pradesh and its surrounding area. Deepa Haidu, a 20-year-old local woman, had watched with interest as many of her female friends acquired jobs at the factories. Deepa's family was financially unable to provide her with education, and she needed to work close to home as her father was ill and her mother needed help with his care, both physically and financially. Deepa was concerned that her only options were to find work as a cook or a nanny, which were the jobs primarily available for women in her area and did not pay enough to support her family.

Her cousin Sumati, who worked in the tailoring section at one of the new factories, told her that the factory management preferred to hire young women, saying that women were more efficient and disciplined than men. Sumati managed to get Deepa an interview with the supervisor of the factory she worked for.

At the interview, the supervisor talked to Deepa about job responsibilities and salary, and then ended the meeting by saying that she should not get involved in any kind of unionism. 'It's unproductive,' he said. 'You must pay attention only to your work.' Deepa nodded and was happy to learn that she was hired for the job, although the money she would earn would still not be enough to pay for all of her father's medical bills.

On her first day on the job, Deepa noticed that although there were a few men on the factory floor, the vast majority of her co-workers were women. The work was routine and the hours were long, but Deepa was appreciative of the opportunity the factory management had given her.

Several months after she began at the factory, Deepa's father's condition worsened and he needed more medical care. The family's financial situation began to reach a crisis point. Shortly after, Kavi, who had been hired at the same time as Deepa, approached her when they began their shift. He told her that he had contacted a trade union leader to start the process of unionizing the workers and asked for her support. 'The union can help improve our working conditions and get us an increment in pay,' he said.

Kavi stressed that he needed the women in the factory to get involved as there were far more of them than men. 'We will never get unionized unless the women come forward,' he said. 'It's for their benefit too.' He asked Deepa to meet him the next day to work out a strategy to get the other women to support the idea.

When Deepa told Sumati what Kavi had said, Sumati warned Deepa about talking to Kavi any further about unions. 'We cannot take this risk as it is the best work option we have. The men are always trying to bring in the union because it is easier for them to find work elsewhere if the factory lets us go. The other women will not cooperate with the men in trying to unionize our workplace.'

Deepa spent that night worrying about how she was going to continue to support her family and wondered if helping Kavi bring in the union was the right thing to do.

The task

In small groups, discuss the following:

- How does India's patriarchal society play a role in Deepa's situation and in that of Indian women in general?
- Looking back at Chapter 1, what would be the feminist perspective on the hiring practices of the factory management?
- If you were Deepa, would you help Kavi bring in the union? Why or why not?

Sources and further information

Chakravarty, D. (2007) '"Docile oriental women" and organised labour: a case study of the Indian garment manufacturing industry', *Indian Journal of Gender Studies*, 14, pp. 439–60.

Gani, A. (1996) 'Who joins the unions and why?: evidence from India', *International Journal of Manpower*, 17(6–7), p. 54.

Mohanty, M. (ed.) (2004) *Class, Caste, Gender: Readings in Indian Government and Politics*, New Dehli: Sage.

Ratnam, C. (2002) 'Women in trade unions in India', *International Journal of Manpower*, 23(3), pp. 277–92.

Note: This case study was written by Lori Rilkoff, Human Resources Director, City of Kamloops, BC, Canada. It is based on research by D. Chakravarty (2007).

IN THE EBOOK ACCESS AN **OB IN FILM** BOX THAT USES *MADE IN DAGENHAM* (2010) TO ILLUSTRATE DETAILS OF HOW EQUAL PAY FOR WOMEN WAS WON, AND *NORMA RAE* (1979) TO RAISE ISSUES AROUND EMPLOYMENT RELATIONS IN THE WORKPLACE AND TO ACCESS **AN INTERACTIVE QUIZ** TO TEST YOUR UNDERSTANDING.

part 3
Group dynamics and management processes

In this part of the book, we examine some of the important social processes that take place in the context of work groups.

In Chapter 10, we explore the development, nature and behavioural implications of work groups and teams. The nature of work groups is analysed through the concepts of size, norms, cohesiveness, group learning and groupthink. We suggest that self-managed teams shift the focus away from hierarchical, bureaucratic control structures, to structures with a culture of self-control.

In Chapter 11, we explore how the communication process in the workplace reflects the management style, the degree of employee empowerment and the culture. We emphasize that people engage with their world through symbols (verbal, non-verbal and written language). Language helps to define the culture of an organization and give form to notions of control, delegation and rationality.

In Chapter 12, we explain that leadership is a dialectic process in which an individual persuades others to do things they would not otherwise do. We explain that the terms 'leadership' and 'management' are not interchangeable. Management is associated with certain activities, whereas leadership produces change.

In Chapter 13, we examine the different models of decision making. We explain that, in reality, decision makers must suffer from bounded rationality. We go on to discuss ethics in decision making and explain the meaning of corporate social responsibility.

In Chapter 14, we explore the abstract concept of power and, drawing on the work of Gramsci and Foucault, examine the deep social roots of power systems. We go on to explore the causes of conflict in organizations before explaining how conflict is managed.

10 Groups and teams
11 Communication
12 Leadership
13 Decision making, ethics and social responsibility
14 Power, politics and conflict

chapter 10
Groups and teams

Key concepts

- group dynamics
- group processes
- group structure
- groupthink
- Hawthorne effect
- job characteristic model
- peer pressure
- psychic prison
- work group
- work team

Chapter outline

- Introduction
- Work groups and work teams
- Group dynamics
- Work teams and management theory
- Work teams: ending bureaucracy and extending employee empowerment?
- Paradox in team-based work systems
- Summary and end-of-chapter features
- Chapter case study: Building cars in Brazil

Chapter learning outcomes

After completing this chapter, you should be able to:

1 Distinguish between informal and formal work groups
2 Explain the current popularity of teams in work organizations
3 Articulate how group norms and cohesiveness exert an influence on individual and group behaviour
4 Describe and critically evaluate the theories of team development
5 Explain the meaning of 'groupthink' and how it impacts group decision making
6 Identify the different theoretical perspectives and paradoxes related to work teams

introduction

Without doubt, everyone will at some point in their life be a member of a group. You have probably already experienced group membership through participating in a sports team or climbing or caving club, undertaking jury service, attending church or joining a political party or study group. In many organizations, people are called upon to work in groups, and many claim to be 'team' oriented. Work groups influence the behaviour of their members, often enhancing job satisfaction, promoting learning, increasing individual and unit productivity and bringing about more effective decision making. The group can exert an influence over its members and act as a medium of change. What then are the factors that help people working in teams to fulfil their potential? What are the major determinants of team or group efficacy? What are the main threats to effective group work?

stop...

Consider your own experience of groups. You might have experienced working in a study group at university. What specific behaviours exhibited during the group sessions were helpful to the group and which were detrimental? How, for instance, did the group deal with a member who was constantly late for meetings?

...and reflect

Work groups, it is argued, increase individual and organizational performance as long as they are characterized by high-quality group processes. There is also a fit between a number of individual and organizational processes, which constantly adapt to one another (Xenikou and Furnham, 2013), including work variables, technology factors and a concomitant system of rules and rewards that is inevitably dynamic (see Figure 1.3). Work teams became part of management speak in the 1990s, but they are not something invented by management consultants. History shows that they have been part of human social development since ancient times. For thousands of years, membership in groups was inevitable and universal; men and women lived in small hunting and gathering groups, and later in small farming or fishing groups. It has only been in the last 200 years, with the advent of industrial capitalism, that small groups have become the exception rather than the rule (Johnson and Johnson, 2014). The factory system ushered in a minute division of labour and close direct supervision, which substantially improved labour productivity and profits. By the late twentieth century, however, extensive specialization and hierarchical forms of work organization were identified as a 'problem' (see Chapters 2 and 15).

A host of mainstream management literature promoted the notion that traditional work organization was an obstacle to innovation and competitiveness (Katzenbach and Smith, 2005; Kline, 1999; Mintzberg, 2009; Orsburn and Moran, 2000; Procter and Mueller, 2000). Teamwork as a system of paid work is intended to transcend the alleged problems of inflexibility, poor quality, low employee commitment and motivation that are associated with traditional work structures. The increased prevalence of teamwork in Europe and North America is a recognition by employers that competitive advantage comes from so-called lean organizations, the full utilization of their human capital and a set or 'bundle' of 'soft' human resource management practices that form part of an integrated high-performance workplace (HPW) (Stewart and Danford, 2008). In the critical literature, teamwork and HPW initiatives are a means of increasing work intensification, obtaining higher productivity, increasing workplace stress and controlling workers indirectly through a culture of self-control (Sewell, 1998; Sinclair, 1992; Wells, 1993).

If you paused and thought about the questions we asked in the 'Stop and reflect' box above, you should appreciate that understanding groups and teams in work organizations is important for several reasons. Teamwork has become a significant feature of organizational life. Individuals behave differently in a work group from how they do when they work independently. Team synergy can potentially transform moribund productivity and improve organizational performance. Finally, understanding group dynamics is seen to be an important aspect of managing (controlling) people more effectively.

control: the collection and analysis of information about all aspects of the work organization and the use of comparisons that are either historical and/or based on benchmarking against another business unit

This chapter introduces the complex phenomenon of work groups and work teams in organizations. It begins by examining the background, nature and behavioural implications of work groups. We also explore the nature of work groups through the concepts of group norms, cohesiveness and learning. Finally, we go beyond management rhetoric, and present arguments and evidence to suggest that self-managed teams shift the focus away from the hierarchy and direct and bureaucratic **control** processes, to a culture of self-control.

Work groups and work teams

What are work groups?

work group: two or more employees in face-to-face interaction, each aware of their positive interdependence as they endeavour to achieve mutual work-related goals

The term 'group' can be used to describe a cluster of individuals watching a hockey game or queuing at the bank. When studying the behaviour of groups, it is important to distinguish between a mere cluster of individuals and what organizational theorists call a 'psychological group'. This term is used to describe individuals who perceive themselves to be in a group, who have a shared sense of collective identity, and who relate to each other in a meaningful way. We can define a **work group** as two or more people who are in face-to-face interaction, each aware of their membership in the group, and striving to accomplish assigned work tasks.

The first part of this definition suggests that there must be an opportunity for people to interact socially with each other, that is, to communicate with each other, to behave in certain ways in each other's presence, and to be affected by the other's behaviour. Over time, group members who regularly interact socially become aware of each other's values, feelings and goals, which then influence their behaviour. Although a work group can theoretically range from two members to an unspecified upper limit, the need to interact limits the size of the group.

The second part of the definition refers to group members' perceptions of the group itself. Members of the group are able to distinguish who is and who is not in the group, and are aware that an action affecting one member is likely to affect all of them. This part of the definition helps us to exclude mere clusters of people who are simply individuals who happen to be assembled at the same location at a particular time (such as football fans, bank customers or airline travellers). These individuals do not consider themselves to be a part of any identifiable unit, nor do they relate to one another in any meaningful fashion, despite their close proximity.

On the other hand, a football team, an airline crew or a project team at the Bank of Scotland would fulfil the criteria for a work group. In a situation of extreme danger – such as the hijacking of an airline – an aggregate of passengers could be transformed into a group. For example, several passengers on US United Airlines Flight 93, which crashed on September 11, 2001, apparently formed a group that stormed the cockpit to prevent the hijackers from carrying out any further terrorist acts.

The third part of the definition implies that group members have common goals that they work collectively to accomplish. Six individuals drinking coffee in the company rest area at the same time would not necessarily be considered a group. They do not have common goals, nor are they dependent on the outcome of each other's actions. However, six union shop stewards drinking coffee together regularly to discuss health and safety issues or grievances *would* be considered a work group.

Groups in organizations can be formal or informal. Organizational decision makers create formal work groups to permit collective action on assigned task(s). In this sense, the rationale for creating work groups can be linked to an organization's competitive strategy. A manufacturing strategy that emphasizes flexibility can result in tasks and responsibilities being reassigned from individual employees and supervisors to a group of employees. This process of dividing up the tasks, assign-

job design: the process of assigning tasks to a job, including the interdependency of those tasks with other jobs

ing responsibility and so on, is called **job design**, and it is through the restructuring of work that formal work groups are created and consciously designed. Managers are interested in ensuring that the behaviour of the formal group is directed toward organizational goals. Not surprisingly, therefore, much of mainstream organizational behaviour research focuses on the dynamics of formal work groups.

informal group: two or more people who form a unifying relationship around personal rather than organizational goals

In addition to formal work groups, organizations also contain **informal work groups**. Managers do not specifically establish these work-based groups; they emerge from the social interaction of the workers. An organization employs people for their intellectual capital, but, unlike the situation with other forms of capital, the organization gets the whole person. People bring their personal needs to the workplace. Organizational behaviour theorists suggest that informal work groups are formed as an outcome of psychological processes: by the perception of a shared social identity and to fulfil social needs for affiliation and supportive relationships. A cluster of employees can become an informal work group when members influence others' behaviour and contribute to a satisfaction of needs. Informal work groups are important in that they can help to shape communication flows in the organization.

What are work teams?

teams: groups of two or more people who interact and influence each other, are mutually accountable for achieving common objectives, and perceive themselves as a social entity within an organization

The words 'group' and 'team' are often used as substitutes. In the management literature, the word '**team**' is more likely to be used in a normative sense as a special type of group with positive traits (Hertog and Tolner, 1998). Like a football team, it has connotations of collaboration, mutual support and shared skill and decision making (Buchanan, 2000). The observation and implied criticism that 'He is not a team player' or 'This group is not a team' expresses the difference in meaning between 'group' and 'team' in the management lexicon. A mainstream text defines a team as 'a set of interpersonal interactions structured to achieve established goals' (Johnson and Johnson, 2014: 539), and two popular writers define a team as 'a small number of people with complementary skills who are committed to a common purpose, performance goals, and approach for which they hold themselves mutually accountable' (Katzenbach and Smith, 2005: 45).

self-managed work teams: cross-functional work groups organized around work processes that complete an entire piece of work requiring several interdependent tasks, and that have substantial autonomy over the execution of those tasks

Another variant of 'teams' has become part of current managerial rhetoric – these are '**self-managed work teams**' (SMWTs). An SMWT, which suggests a new way of organizing work, is not the same as a 'work group': an SMWT is 'a group of employees who are responsible for managing and performing technical tasks that result in a product or service being delivered to an internal or external customer' (Yeatts and Hyten, 1998: xiii). The difference between work groups and SMWTs is explained in terms of the degree of interdependency and accountability. The interdependence among SMWT members is typically high, and the accountability for the work focuses primarily on the team as a whole rather than on any individual group member. Another distinguishing feature of SMWTs is their longevity: SMWTs are typically an integral part of a redesigned organizational structure, brought together for long-term performance goals.

plate 33 A self-managed work team allows employees in the core work unit to have sufficient autonomy to manage the work process.

Source: Getty Images

Work teams can be classified according to their position in the organization's hierarchy and their assigned tasks. Figure 10.1 shows the three types of work team most commonly found in organizations. Teams that plan and run things are positioned in the top echelon (senior level) of the organization, teams that monitor things occupy the middle levels, and teams that make things are found in the lower levels of the organization. It is important to emphasize, however, that the nature of teams varies considerably among organizations, depending on whether they are engaged in value-added activities in small batches or large batches, or whether they provide financial or other services.

The formal definitions of work teams are not so different from the definition of a formal work group, which might explain why both words are used interchangeably in the organizational behaviour literature. However, the conscious use of the word 'team' is not simply a question of semantics. As we discuss in Chapter 11, mainstream management rhetoric is awash with what Bendix (1956) called 'a vocabulary of motivation'. In this instance, communication emphasizes the 'team' (with phrases like 'We must all pull together') and the 'family' (suggesting that employees are brothers and sisters, and customers are family guests), using these metaphors to mask the power differentials and conflicting interests between management and workers. Whether employees are organized into a 'work group' or a 'work team', the effectiveness of the work configuration will be the outcome of complex group behaviours and processes, which is the focus of the next section.

VISIT THE *ONLINE RESOURCE CENTRE* AT HTTPS://HE.PALGRAVE.COM/COMPANION/BRATTON-WORK-AND-ORGANIZATIONAL-BEHAVIOUR3/ TO READ MORE ON TEAMS AND ON 'VIRTUAL GROUPS' WORK.

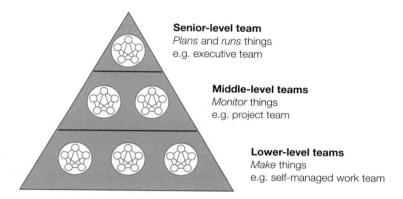

Figure 10.1 Classification of work teams

Group dynamics

group dynamics: the systematic study of human behaviour in groups, including the nature of groups, group development, and the interrelations between individuals and groups, other groups and other elements of formal organizations

Group dynamics refers to 'all the psychological processes that take place in groups' (Xenikou and Furnham, 2013: 4); in other words, it is the study of human behaviour in groups (Johnson and Johnson, 2014). The field studies the nature of groups, group development and the interrelations between individuals and groups. Group dynamics or processes emphasize changes in the pattern of activities, the subjective perceptions of individual group members and their active involvement in group life. Studies on group dynamics by mainstream researchers draw attention to two sets of process that underlie group processes: task-oriented activities and maintenance-oriented activities. Task-oriented activities undertaken by the group are aimed at accomplishing goals or 'getting the job done'. Maintenance-oriented activities, on the other hand, point to the subjective perceptions of group members and their active involvement in keeping acceptable standards of behaviour and a general state of well-being within the group. Conventional wisdom argues that the two processes constantly seek to coexist, and an overemphasis on one realm at the expense of the other leads to discontent and withdrawal. An effective group or team is one that creates a reasonable compromise between both realms.

Some of the major factors influencing group dynamics are shown in Figure 10.2. The framework does not attempt to offer a theory of group dynamics, nor does it necessarily follow that all elements of the model must, or can, be applied to every work group. We offer it here as a useful heuristic for understanding the complexities of group dynamics. Four major elements are graphically depicted in the model: a context, a team structure and processes, group effectiveness, and a feedback loop that links the outcomes back to the other main components. We look at each of the first three elements over the next few pages.

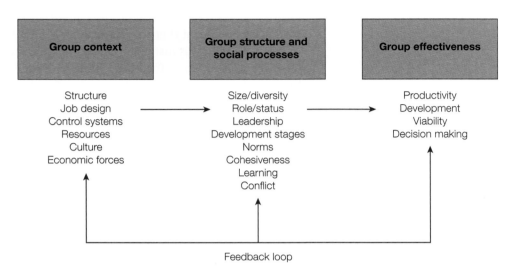

Figure 10.2 A model of group dynamics

Group context

Although the work group or team is a structure in itself, it is also a subset of a larger structure, the organization. Thus, the work group is constrained to operate within the structure of the organization, and **group context** refers to organizational and job design, organizational control systems, resources and the external political economy and economic forces.

The implementation of team-based working requires organizational restructuring, by which we mean changing the core dimensions of the organization: its centralization, complexity and formality (see Chapter 15). Tasks and responsibilities must be designated within and between teams. Task interdependence, which refers to the level of the relationship among members in the work activities, can affect the group structure, processes and outcomes. Alternative work configurations are typically followed by alternative control systems. For example, when work groups are introduced, the direct supervisory control of the employees is typically replaced by a computer-based control of group performance. The adoption of teamwork is normally contingent on management installing a computerized system to control the redesigned work process (Bratton, 1992).

Resources are another contextual factor affecting group structure and processes. The amount of resources that management is willing to commit to teams is directly related to the organizational context. Specifically, the policies and procedures of the organization must provide for sufficient physical (such as computer software), financial and human resources to enable the team to function and complete the task. Inadequate resources, it is argued, will delay group development and have a negative impact on group outcomes (Kline, 1999).

Group structure

Work groups and teams have a structure that influences the way in which members relate to and interact with one another, and makes it possible to explain individual behaviour within the group. Have you ever noticed that when people come together in a new group, some listen while others talk? Such differences between group

group context: refers to anything from the specific task a work group is engaged in, to the broad environmental forces that are present in the minds of group members and may influence them

members serve as a basis for the formation of the group structure. As differentiation takes place, social relations are formed between members. The stable pattern of relationships among the differentiated elements in the group is called **group structure**.

The group can be differentiated by a number of variables including size, roles, status and leadership. The size of the group plays a critical role in how group members interact with one another. The German sociologist Georg Simmel pointed out that increasing the size alters the group's dynamics, since the increased number of relationships results in different interactions (Bratton and Denham, 2014). Figure 10.3 shows the incremental impact of group size on relationships. Two individuals form a single relationship; adding a third person results in three relations; a group of seven, however, has 21 relationships. According to Simmel, as groups grow beyond three people, the personal attachments between individuals become looser, and coalitions emerge in which some group members align themselves against other group members. Thus, the more impersonal relationships need additional formal rules and regulations. At the same time, the group's growth allows it to become more stable, because the intensity of the interactions is reduced, and because it becomes better able to withstand the loss of some of its members.

group structure: a stable pattern of social interaction among work group members created by a role structure and group norms

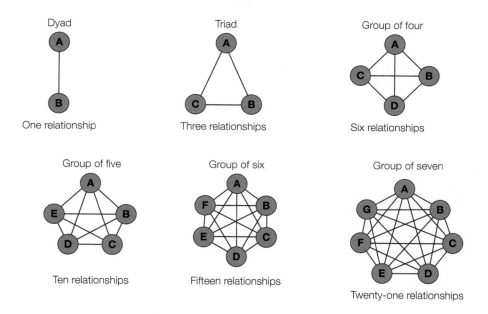

Figure 10.3 The incremental effects of group size on relationships

The *composition* or diversity of work groups is another key variable that influences individual behaviour in a group setting. Work group composition can be diverse in terms of gender, ethnicity, age, hierarchical status, performance levels and educational background. Research suggests that a group's composition is a predictor of its members' creative behaviour and of the quality of decision making. Diversity in terms of gender and hierarchical status tend to decrease a member's creative behaviour, and this negative effect appears to be particularly strong for women members in a minority and 'low-power' group situation. The group's composition may also impede the shared exchange, discussion and integration of information, with negative effects on the quality of decisions (Choi, 2007).

All group members are expected to carry out certain functions. The set of expected behaviours associated with a position within the group constitutes the **role** of the occupant of that position. The role concept helps us to understand how a member's behaviour is structured by the prescriptive dictates of the group and/or organization. A team-based culture will influence the roles individuals play

role: a set of behaviours that people are expected to perform because they hold certain positions in a team and organization

within the organization. With HPW forms of organization, a premium is placed on values such as cooperative behaviour with team members, sharing information and expertise with others, and more generally on promoting a social network necessary for the team's effective performance. Role definition is often used as a diagnostic tool by management consultants to determine causes of poor team performance. Problems of **role ambiguity** – uncertainty on the group member's part about what exactly he or she is supposed to do – and **role conflict** – conflicting requests from more than one source – allegedly have far-reaching negative outcomes on group performance (Kline, 1999). Role ambiguity and role conflict also affect the socialization of new employees into existing work groups (Slaughter and Zicker, 2006).

role ambiguity: uncertainty about job duties, performance expectations, levels of authority and other job conditions

role conflict: conflict that occurs when people face competing demands

---

globalization & organization misbehaviour

Source: Stockbyte

Power and culture in work team relations

The globalization of work has opened new opportunities for workers from different cultural backgrounds to work closely with each other – both in person and remotely. Diverse work teams can have positive effects on productivity and problem solving by generating a greater number of innovative ideas and approaches (Earley and Gibson, 2002). Many organizations with overseas operations have, however, also encountered challenges in managing multicultural work teams. These challenges are primarily related to team members' different cultural understandings about their role in the team (and within the larger organization) and how the work should be accomplished.

In an insightful study, Mutabazi and Derr (2003) explored the cultural and historical roots of a breakdown in work team relationships at a Franco-Senegalese organization the authors called Socometal, whose work teams were made up of French expatriates and local Senegalese workers. Mutabazi and Derr concluded that inefficiencies and misunderstandings in these multicultural work teams were, to a great extent, connected with the enduring legacy of colonialism. They explain:

> the problem associated with multiculturalism [on work teams] comes from preexisting attitudes about relations between Africa and the West. This is a deeply-rooted relationship with perceptions distorted by historical consternation. On one side, the West as the dominant partner overemphasizes its own culture, ideals and conceptions of the world ... the resulting tendency is to impose this cultural determination upon the party that is considered inferior ... [and] this characteristic of multiculturalism becomes embedded in the relationship creating a vicious cycle of misunderstanding. (p. 3)

At Socometal, French managers and work team members did not understand the Senegalese community-based approach to teamwork, which relies on the circulation of people, goods, services and information through local social and economic networks. Likewise, the Senegalese workers did not understand the approaches of the French expatriate managers and workers, mistaking their focus on top-down decision making and individual competition

as an assertion of superiority. The result was the reproduction of colonial power relationships between French and Senegalese workers, and work teams that were 'characterized by indifference toward the values and perspectives of fellow team members ... The professional and personal difficulties that [ensued led] to a breakdown of operations' (Mutabazi and Derr, 2003: 4).

This case highlights the centrality of power and culture in organizational behaviour. Gibson and Zellmer-Bruhn (2001) remind us that workplaces are culturally situated, and that relationships within organizations are shaped by culturally and historically embedded power relationships. Misunderstandings about work team relationships and responsibilities can be exacerbated in situations where team members make assumptions about their colleagues' capabilities and motivations based on preconceived notions. The potential of multicultural work teams to excel will remain untapped as long as they are managed according to a single cultural paradigm. Effective management approaches in these situations must address cultural misunderstandings and power imbalances head on, and provide enough flexibility to incorporate multiple approaches to teamwork and decision making into the organization.

> **Stop!** Have you ever worked on a project or a work team with members from different cultural backgrounds? Discuss any culturally based misunderstandings or 'disconnects' that you or your colleagues might have encountered while working on the project. How did you address your differences? Can you think of any other examples of how historical relationships between nations or cultures could affect organizational behaviour if members of those groups were assigned to the same work team?

Sources and further information
Earley, P. C. and Gibson, C. B. (2002) *Multinational Work Teams: A New Perspective*, Mahwah, NJ: Lawrence Erlbaum Associates.
Gibson, C. B. and Zellmer-Bruhn, M. E. (2001) 'Metaphors and meaning: an intercultural analysis of the concept of teamwork', *Administrative Science Quarterly*, 46(2), pp. 274–303.
Mutabazi, E. and Derr, C. B. (2003) 'The management of multicultural teams: the experience of Afro-Occidental teams', Research Paper 13, *European Entrepreneurial Learning*. Available at: www.em-lyon.com/%5 Cressources%5Cge%5Cdocuments%5Cpublications%5Cwp%5C2003-13.pdf; http://cat.inist.fr/?aModele=afficheN&cpsidt=18098760 (accessed September 22, 2009).

Note: This feature was written by Gretchen Fox, Cultural Anthropologist and Impact Assessment Analyst, Fox Cultural Research, Canada.

status: the social ranking of people; the position an individual occupies in society or in a social group or work organization

Status is the relative ranking that a member holds and indicates the value of that member as perceived by the group. Status is important because it motivates individuals and has consequences for their behaviour. Almost every work group has either a formal or an informal leader who can influence communications, decision making, learning and similar processes, thereby playing an important part in the group's outcomes.

It is necessary, but not sufficient for team efficacy, to have an organizational design strategy that incorporates adequate resources, effective control systems, role clarity and leadership. To be effective, managers and group members must learn to work in the new work structure. The group processes responsible for group development, norms, cohesiveness and learning are extremely important.

VISIT THE *ONLINE RESOURCE CENTRE* AT HTTPS://HE.PALGRAVE.COM/COMPANION/BRATTON-WORK-AND-ORGANIZATIONAL-BEHAVIOUR3/ TO READ MORE ON DIVERSITY IN TEAMS AND TO COMPLETE AN ACTIVITY ON TEAM ROLES.

Group social processes

group processes: refers to group members' actions, communications and decision making

The term '**group social processes**' refers to the manner in which various aspects of group behaviour are constructed on a continuing basis, and the behaviour that serves to encourage or discourage group learning and to ameliorate or exacerbate group conflict. Understanding group social processes is important in so far as they are often considered to be key predictors of group effectiveness.

Group development

Organizational behaviour theorists typically highlight the importance of understanding the developmental stages that a group must pass through: groups are born, they mature and they die. It is suggested that a group must reach the mature stage before it achieves maximum performance. Of course, it is also acknowledged that not all groups pass through all these stages, and some groups can become fixed in the early stage and remain ineffective and inefficient. A good example of the life cycle metaphor is Tuckman and Jensen's (1977) five-stage cycle of group development model: forming, storming, norming, performing and adjourning (Figure 10.4).

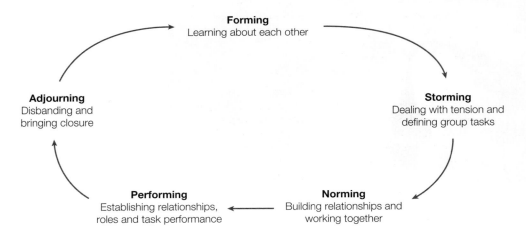

Forming
Learning about each other

Storming
Dealing with tension and defining group tasks

Norming
Building relationships and working together

Performing
Establishing relationships, roles and task performance

Adjourning
Disbanding and bringing closure

Figure 10.4 Five phases of group development
Source: Tuckman and Jensen (1977)

In the *forming* stage, individuals are brought together and there tends to be ambiguity about roles and tasks. Group members are polite as they learn about each other and attempt to establish 'ground rules' for accomplishing the assigned task(s). Dependency on the group leader is said to be high at this stage.

In the *storming* stage, individual members become more proactive by taking on specific roles and responsibilities. Members frequently compete for positions in the group, conflict occurs between individuals and/or alliances are formed between members. The group leader must be able to facilitate dialogue and handle conflict at this stage.

When the group members begin to accept differences of opinion, conform to their roles and cooperate (for instance, by sharing information), the group has reached what is called the *norming* stage. As a consensus forms around the group's goals and means of attainment, group cohesion grows.

High performance levels are typically achieved at the *performing* stage of group development. A high level of trust in each group member is prevalent at this phase, and there is 'consensual validation' in the sense that members are positively valued for their specific attributes and qualities.

A work group does not exist infinitely. The *adjourning* stage refers to individuals leaving the group and being replaced by others, or to the group's disbandment. Social rituals, such as having a party, often accompany group disbandment.

Tuckman and Jensen's model is based on the premise that a group must go through each stage before being able to move on to the next, and every transition holds the potential risk of regression to an earlier stage. Organizational behaviour theorists taking a managerialist perspective have tended to interpret the five-stage model in terms of levels of performance, with group productivity being higher after the second stage. While this assumption may be correct, what makes a work group effective is more complex than this model acknowledges. Although the model has become entrenched in mainstream organizational behaviour texts and in management training, it has more recently been shown 'to be of little or no assistance in getting teams to perform better' (Kline, 1999: 34).

plate 34 Organizations send their employees to outdoor corporate training centres where they learn to work as teams.

Source: ©iStockphoto.com/bedo

An earlier critique of Tuckman and Jensen's five-stage model found the phenomenon of 'punctuated equilibrium' to be a more useful concept for explaining group development (Gersick, 1988). Specifically, a team does not accomplish a great deal up to about the halfway point to completion (this midpoint occurring regardless of the time-frame involved). At the midpoint, there is an acceleration of activity by members to accomplish their assigned work. In essence, the 'punctuated equilibrium' model characterizes work groups as exhibiting long periods of inertia interspersed with shorter bursts of activity, initiated primarily by their members' awareness of the impending completion deadline. This would suggest, therefore, that not all groups develop in a universal linear fashion.

The research on group development has drawn criticism because much of it has tended to be laboratory-based rather than workplace-based research. For example, old favourites like Tuckman and Jensen's model were developed from work with therapy, laboratory or training groups, not 'real teams in real contexts'. Group development models that predict linear sequential phases have particularly been criticized. As Kline graphically points out:

> Imagine the following situation. The cockpit crew of a 747 boards the plane twenty minutes before take-off. You are seated in seat 117B, and as the airplane rushes down runway nine you hope like hell that this team is past the storming stage of group development. (Kline, 1999: 5)

Kline argues that there is something, personalities aside, about the aircrew that enables them to fly the aircraft safely, even when they have just met one another. These 'contextual variables', she asserts, are powerful tools for understanding group dynamics and group performance.

Although alternative research suggests that every group does not go through all the development stages, Tuckman and Jensen's model can be a useful heuristic for understanding group dynamics and why some groups fail to perform. A group might be ineffective and inefficient because individuals are pulling in different directions, since the goals of the group have not been agreed. Alternatively, individuals might have a tendency to dismiss or ridicule others' thoughts, ideas and feelings, which leads to low trust among the group. For all these reasons, effective group functioning and learning might be hindered. The main conclusion drawn from the group development models presented here is that a team-based organizational structure does not imply an effective and efficient organization. Top managers introducing team-based work structures need to attend to the development of group interactions.

Group norms

Have you ever noticed that professors do not normally criticize other professors? Why? The answer is 'norms'. Groups significantly influence their members' behaviour through the operation of norms. Social norms are a set of expected patterns of behaviour that are established and shared by the group's members. Norms inform members on what they ought and ought not to do in certain situations. A group's norms do not occur in a vacuum: they represent the interaction of historical, social and psychological processes. In the workplace, for example, a new employee joining a group will assess the norms for work effort from how most individuals in the group behave. In turn, members of the group will observe the extent to which the new member's behaviour matches the group's norms. Norms develop in work groups around work activities (the means and speed), around attitudes and opinions that should be held by group members regarding the workplace, and around communications, concerning appropriate language.

The classic Hawthorne studies (Mayo, 1946) highlighted the importance of **group norms** to management theorists. The Hawthorne effect identified three important norms: no 'rate-busting' (working too hard), no 'chiselling' (working too little) and no 'squealing' (telling the supervisor anything that could undermine the group). Group members who significantly deviated from these norms were subjected to either ridicule or physical punishment. Groups typically enforce norms that:

- facilitate the group's survival
- allow members to express the central values of the group
- reduce embarrassing interpersonal problems for group members – for instance, by a ban on discussing religion or politics at work (Feldman, 1984).

Norms are communicated to new employees through a process called 'group socialization', whereby the new member learns the group's principal values and how these values are articulated through norms. Emergent group leaders differ from their peers in that they make more attempts to influence the group and play a role in forming team norms (Taggar and Ellis, 2007).

Group cohesiveness

The term **cohesiveness** refers to the complex forces that give rise to members' perceptions of group identity and the attractiveness of group membership. The cohesiveness of a group has a major effect on the behaviour of its members, because higher cohesion amplifies the potency of group norms. A series of experiments conducted by Solomon Asch in 1952 and Stanley Milgram in 1963 suggested that

group norms: the unwritten rules and expectations that specify or shape appropriate human behaviour in a work group or team

stop...

Sociologists maintain that relationships formed in groups shape members' behaviour. Think about your own experience of working in a group. What norms and values did the group exhibit? Did any particular members challenge a particular group norm? If so, how did the other group members respond to the challenge? If they did not, why not?

...and reflect

cohesiveness: refers to all the positive and negative forces or social pressures that cause individuals to maintain their membership in specific groups

group membership can engender conformity, and also that members are likely to follow the directions of group authority figures, even when it means inflicting pain on another individual. These psychological experiments can be used to help explain the brutalizing acts inflicted on prisoners by both male and female US guards at Abu Ghraib prison (Zimbardo, 2008).

VISIT THE *ONLINE RESOURCE CENTRE* AT HTTPS://HE.PALGRAVE.COM/COMPANION/BRATTON-WORK-AND-ORGANIZATIONAL-BEHAVIOUR3/ FOR MORE INFORMATION ON MILGRAM'S CLASSIC PSYCHOLOGICAL PRISON EXPERIMENT.

A cohesive group can develop norms that can be a great asset to the organization, for example a norm that prescribes voluntary overtime working when required. Equally, a cohesive group can undermine organizational goals, for example by enforcing conformity to a work effort below what is considered acceptable by managers. Not surprisingly, therefore, sources of group cohesiveness are of considerable interest to mainstream organizational behaviour theorists and managers. For example, one study has contended that humour can have a positive effect on a variety of group or team processes, including group cohesiveness and the management of emotion (Romero and Pescosolido, 2008).

The attractiveness of a group is partly determined by its composition. Members of the group need to get along with each other, which might be difficult if the members have very different values, attitudes towards work or interests. Research suggests that behaviour in work groups is shaped by a sex difference in terms of aggressiveness, with male members engaging in more dominating behaviour than female members. Studies have found that, in groups, men talk more frequently, interrupt others and express anger more than women (Wilson, 2003: 181–3). As a result, more men than women are chosen as group leaders. In institutions of learning, the experiences of work groups by women and faculty members from racial and ethnic minorities tend to differ significantly from the experiences of white male group members (Smith and Calasanti, 2005).

Ensuring diversity in a work group or team is not only a matter of equity – a lack of diversity might also inhibit some of the performance benefits of group working. As previously explained, there are, however, conflicting narratives regarding the potential effects of ethnic and racial diversity on performance (Leslie, 2014) An early study suggests that moderate heterogeneity in a work group balances the requirements of cohesion and performance (Hackman and Oldham, 1980). As we will examine in the next section, one notable disadvantage of groups that are *too* cohesive is that their decision-making ability can be impaired by what Janis termed '**groupthink**' (Janis, 1972). He defined this group phenomenon as a psychological drive for consensus at any cost, which suppresses dissent and the evaluation of alternatives in cohesive decision-making groups.

groupthink: the tendency of highly cohesive groups to value consensus at the price of decision quality

VISIT THE *ONLINE RESOURCE CENTRE* AT HTTPS://HE.PALGRAVE.COM/COMPANION/BRATTON-WORK-AND-ORGANIZATIONAL-BEHAVIOUR3/ FOR MORE INFORMATION ON HOW 'GROUPTHINK' CAN INFLUENCE DECISION MAKING.

Group learning

We turn now to another aspect of social interaction within groups and teams: work-based learning. It will be apparent from this review of team theory and practice that expanding workers' skill sets and **empowering** workers to make prescribed decisions has significant implications for learning in the workplace. Rather than learning a narrow set of skills, the need for functional flexibility and interchangeability demands that workers acquire new knowledge and technical skills to perform the new repertoire of tasks. In addition, the experience of 'lived reality' – decision making, trial and

empowerment: a psychological concept in which people experience more self-determination, meaning, competence and impact regarding their role in the organization

error experimentation – and the social relations associated with teams create their own dynamic environment for enhancing informal work-based learning.

If the group or team is going to make its own decisions, control quality and control its own behaviour, its members must engage in learning and intergroup learning. Gold et al. (2013) emphasize the importance of intergroup learning that enables information sharing and collaboration across boundaries, both within and between organizations. Adult educators and human resource development theorists have suggested that, in order for a group or team to learn, individual members of the unit must be able to learn: that is, to experiment, reflect on previous action, engage in dialogue, and share and build on their individual knowledge (O'Brien and Buono, 1996). As we pointed out in Chapter 7, adopting a culture of learning in the workplace impacts on innovation, employment relations and leadership style.

Group conflict

Work groups do not exist in isolation: they are located within capitalist workplace dynamics and linked by a network of relationships with other groups. Unsurprisingly, with the proliferation of teams in organizations, there is more research on behaviours that serve to ameliorate or exacerbate the effect that group conflict has on their effectiveness. In critical studies, analysts have highlighted the inevitable tensions between the team-based HPW rhetoric and the reality of work intensification and job insecurity (Jenkins, J., 2008). Mainstream research on group conflict is, however, generally limited to investigating how dysfunctional behaviour at individual or group level affects the variance in groups' performance generally. There are many definitions of the term *conflict*. A broad definition describes conflict as 'that behaviour by organization members which is expended in opposition to other members' (Thompson, 1960, cited in Robbins, 1990: 411).

Researchers widely recognize that group conflict comprises two dimensions: task conflict and emotional conflict (Varela et al., 2008). *Task conflict* refers to disputes over group members' tasks, the extent to which members disagree on the utilization of resources or the realistic questioning of members' opinions and ideas related to group tasks. There is empirical evidence showing that task conflict can, under certain conditions, enhance group performance. As Xenikou and Furnham, 2013: 51) observe, task conflict can improve group performance by 'increasing the cognitive understanding of group tasks, the careful evaluation of alternatives as well as constructive criticism of processes'. *Emotional conflict*, which is also known as relational conflict, is more personal and involves personality clashes within groups and incompatibilities among team members, or the extent to which tension or verbal or non-verbal friction characterizes members' interactions within the group. Exemplars of specific types of behaviour associated with task and emotional conflict are shown in Table 10.1.

Table 10.1 Task-related and emotion-related behaviours in groups

Task-related behaviours	Emotion-related behaviours
Goal setting	Criticizing
Integrating	Judging
Utilizing resources	Violence
Calculating	Bullying
Compromising	Favouritism
Decision making	Teasing
Evaluating	Sexual harassment

Source: Based on Proctor et al. (2009)

Psychological studies confirm the idea that individuals' personalities are part of the contributions that group members make to work groups, and moreover that a mix of these individuals' personalities plays a key role in how intragroup conflict unfolds. It is well documented how many occupations regard teamwork and support from team members as 'lifelines' in coping with the various demands of their work. For example, nurses and air cabin crew are known to rely upon support from fellow co-workers to help them deal with work-related emotion and difficult situations (Bolton, 2005). Studies of the consequences of members' emotions on team performance show that the team members' shared negative emotion, or what is called 'negative affective tone', is inversely related to team performance (Cole et al., 2008). A conceptual framework for linking dysfunctional group behaviour and group effectiveness is shown in Figure 10.5.

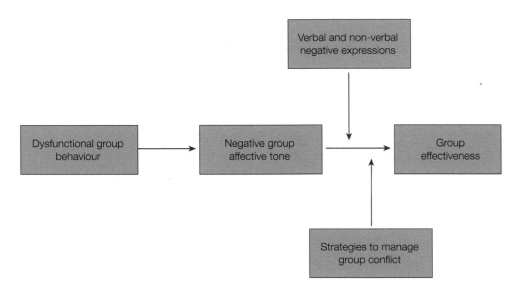

Figure 10.5 A conceptual framework for examining intragroup conflict
Source: Adapted from Cole et al. (2008), p. 946, itself based on Brown et al. (2005), p. 793

The proposed sequence of incidents depicted in the model begins with dysfunctional group behaviour causing an increase in what is labelled groups' 'negative affective tone' – their collective shared experience of negative emotions. In turn, it is hypothesized that that greater levels of negative group affective tone tend to reduce group effectiveness. It also proposes that 'display rules' capable of adjusting or varying the expression of negative emotions through verbal and non-verbal (for example, facial or bodily) cues is critical to groups' goal-directed behaviour and effectiveness. A study by Dunlop and Lee (2004) found that dysfunctional behaviour predicted 24 per cent of the variance in groups' performance. With this assertion in mind, the model further proposes that emotion management strategies will mediate the effect of a negative group affective tone (Cole et al., 2008).

Research findings suggest that how well conflict resolution strategies address a group-level balance between task and emotion management is what yields superior group productivity and viability (Behfar et al., 2008). On the basis of the reported results, it seems that work groups that can withhold displays of negative emotionality are better able to control the detrimental performance implications of dysfunctional behaviour (Cole et al., 2008).

Intergroup conflict might also occur. One explanation for intergroup conflict is that when a group is successful, members' self-esteem increases, and conversely when group members' self-esteem is threatened, they are more prone to disparaging members of other groups (Miller and Brewer, 1984). An alternative explanation contends that intergroup conflict is the result of one group perceiving another group as a threat to its goal attainment (Sherif et al., 1961).

The traditional managerial perspective tends to hold that conflicts between individuals and groups, and between workers and management, are a bad thing. An alternative perspective, the *interactionist theory*, holds that conflicts in work groups are productive and can increase rather than decrease job performance (De Dreu and Van de Vliert, 1997). This view holds that group leaders should encourage an ongoing 'optimum' level of conflict, which allows the group to be self-critical, creative and viable. It is important to note that the link between task conflict and group performance is far from proven (Xenikou and Furnham, 2013). Nevertheless, notions of 'win–lose' scenarios do complicate estimates of what constitutes an 'optimal level' of conflict. It has been suggested, for instance, that the more the intergroup conflict is defined as a 'win–lose' situation, the more predictable are the effects of the conflict on the social relationships within the group and on the relationships between work groups (Johnson and Johnson, 2014).

Links to management   Ruth Law

Ruth Law is the Practice Manager of a health centre in Edinburgh, Scotland. She has worked in practice management for more than 5 years, including 2 years running a general practice in central London. She previously spent more than 18 years in a variety of roles with an international executive recruitment company, and has worked as a volunteer Management Support Officer at the Ghana Education Service. She has an MA in German and Psychology from the University of Dundee and an MBA from the Open University.

In the ebook click on the play button to watch Ruth talking about group dynamics in the workplace, and then think about the following questions:

- Which work group characteristics seem to matter most in achieving high performance in a small office context?

- Do diverse work groups make better decisions?

Group performance

Since the widespread proliferation of teamwork, much research has been occupied with investigating the link between work teams and performance. The research has often drawn upon Hackman's normative theory of group effectiveness, in which effectiveness consists of (1) productivity, (2) employee development, or the opportunity of the individual team member to learn from her or his experiences within the team as well as from other team members, and (3) team viability, or the degree to which members of the team are able to continue working together in the future (Hackman, 1986). Early research on group dynamics was also concerned with the group as a medium of change and how a group is able to exert influence over its members (Hayes, 2014). In the 1990s, work group performance research attempted to show that a combination of high-level cohesion and norms, consistent with organizational objectives, will have a positive effect on team performance (Banker et al., 1996; Campion et al., 1996; Cohen and Bailey, 1997). Most of the group-performance models were built on an input–process–output analysis that is the dominant theoretical perspective on the relationship between the team and its performance (Xenikou and Furnham, 2013). Figure 10.6 illustrates the relationship between group cohesiveness and group performance norms. The improved performance of employees in SMWTs is said to stem from the fact that the interrelationship between the configuration of job design and employment practices inevitably leads to more intrinsic **job satisfaction**, higher commitment on the part of team members and a greater mobilization of discretionary effort from employees (Stewart and Danford, 2008). The evidence on group–performance links is, however, far from conclusive (Bratton and Gold, 2012). Xenikou and Furnham (2013) are critical

job satisfaction: a person's attitude regarding his or her job and work content

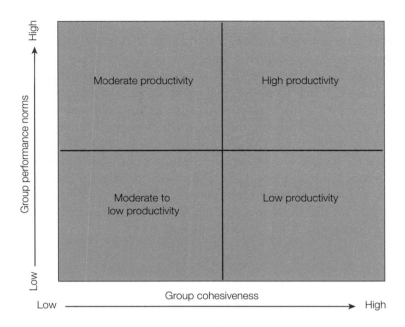

Figure 10.6 Cohesiveness, norms and group performance

of work group effectiveness models because 'they conceive group processes much more as another stable group characteristic rather than a dynamic psychological phenomenon' (p. 35).

Groupthink

Group theory has also examined group performance or outcomes in terms of the quality of decision making. In theory, one advantage of groups is that by combining member's unique expertise and knowledge, the quality of decisions is improved (Buyl et al., 2014; Harford, 2014). In mathematical logic, this phenomenon of groups, called synergy, suggests that 2 + 2 is greater than 4. The concept is used extensively in mainstream texts to understand group processes and to justify the implementation of work teams. The general assumption is that moderately cohesive work teams, together with better communications and 'enlightened' leadership, are best able to encourage the sharing of information and group learning – which results in superior decision-making outcomes. Research on group decision making has, however, shown that work groups often tend 'to polarize group members' initial preferences' (Xenikou and Furnham, 2013: 30). Decision-making issues are discussed at length in Chapter 13. In terms of group decision making, we examine here some important concepts and empirical research on the decision-making performance of groups.

An important concept that might cause groups not to live up to their decision-making potential is *conformity*, as people often change their behaviour to fit the norms of a group or team. It may make sense to follow others' behaviour or judgement when you are inexperienced or when the situation is ambiguous, but just how strongly do group norms influence individual behaviour and decision making when the situation is unmistakable?

Early research on group behaviour by Solomon Asch (1951) and Stanley Milgram (1973) cast some light on this question. Asch recruited several groups of students, allegedly to study visual perception. Before the experiment began, he explained to all the students, apart from one student in each group, that the real purpose was to put pressure on the one selected student. Each group of students was asked to estimate the lengths of lines presented on a card. A sample line was shown at the left, and the group was to choose which of the three lines on the right matched it (Figure 10.7). Group members were seated so that the subject answered last. Group pressure did not affect the subjects' perception, but it did affect their behaviour. Initially, as planned, the group members made the correct matches (line B on Card 2). When, however, Asch's accomplices made incorrect responses, the uninformed subject became uncomfortable, and 76 per cent of these subjects chose to conform by answering incorrectly on at least one trial. The study shows how strong the tendency to conform can be, even when the pressure comes from people we do not know.

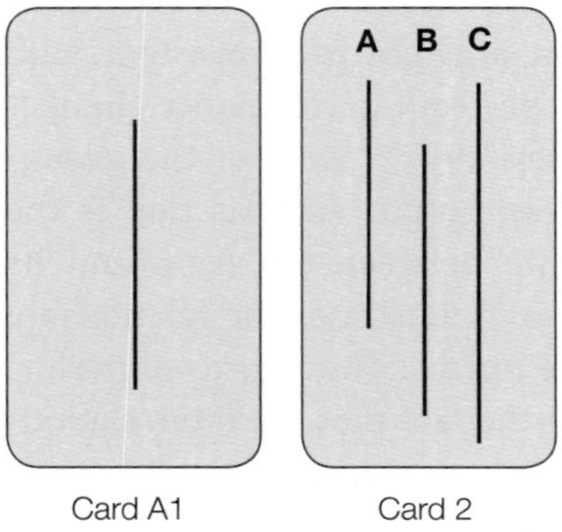

In Milgram's controversial study, a researcher explained to male recruits that they would be participating in an experiment on how physical punishment affects adult learning. The learner, actually an accomplice of Milgram's, was seated in a fake electric chair, with electrodes fastened to the wrist and secured by leather straps. In an adjoining room, the subject, playing the role of educator, was seated in front of a replica 'shock generator' with the capacity to administer an electric

Figure 10.7 An example of the cards used in Asch's experiment in group conformity

'shock' of between 15 and 315 'volts' to the learner. The educator was directed to read aloud pairs of words, and the learner was asked to recall the second word. Whenever the adult learner failed to answer correctly, the educator was instructed to apply an electric shock. Although the educator heard moans and then screams as the level of voltage increased, none of the subjects questioned the experiment. Milgram's research suggests that people are likely to follow the directions of 'legitimate authority figures', even when it means inflicting pain on another individual. To learn about how this classic experiment by Milgram has been related to contemporary events, see Russell and Gregory (2005).

As previously mentioned, Irving Janis's (1972) study illustrates how 'experts' can succumb to group pressure. Interestingly, to illustrate the concept of groupthink, Janis analysed the ill-fated attempt by President Kennedy's administrative team to invade Cuba in 1961. He argues that the executive group advising the US President displayed all the symptoms of groupthink: they were convinced of their invulnerability, and 'self-censorship' prevented members from expressing alternative views even when intelligence information did not align with the group's beliefs. There was, according to Janis, an illusion of unanimity, with silence being interpreted as consent. In other words, the pressures for conformity that can arise in a highly cohesive group can cloud members' judgement and the decision-making process. Table 10.2 outlines some symptoms of groupthink.

Table 10.2 Symptoms of groupthink

Symptom	Description
Illusion of invulnerability	Group members are arrogant and ignore obvious danger signals
Illusion of morality	Groups decision(s) are perceived not only as sensible, but also as morally correct
Rationalization	Counterarguments are rationalized away
Stereotypes of outsiders	Members construct unfavourable stereotypes for those outside the group who are the targets of their decisions
Self-censorship	Members perceive that unanimous support exists for their decisions and action
Mindguard	Individual(s) within the group shield the group from information that goes against its decisions

Groupthink obviously results in low-quality decisions. More seriously, it has been implicated in the decision processes that led to NASA's fatal launch of the space shuttle Challenger in 2003, the US and UK invasion of Iraq in 2003, the Bank of England's mishandling of the financial crisis and the collapse of the Royal Bank of Scotland in 2008. Prior to the invasion, the US official position was that Iraq illegally possessed weapons of mass destruction in violation of UN Security Council Resolution 1441 and had to be disarmed by force. The decision to embark on the Iraq invasion, termed 'Operation Iraqi Freedom', was made by President George W. Bush and a small group of military and intelligence advisers. After investigating the events, which continue to shape the course of twenty-first century history as we write, a US Senate Committee found that the Central Intelligence Agency had dismissed alternative reports, and that the intelligence community as a whole suffered from 'collective group think' (Koring, 2004).

Groupthink was a factor explaining the Bank of England's mishandling of the banking crisis in 2007. Secret documents released by the governor of the Bank of England, Mark Carney, who replaced Mervyn King in July 2013, provide insight into the behaviour of the Bank's executive team during the 'exceptional' period and the policies implemented to mitigate the banking crisis. Moreover, the documents, according to Andrew Tyrie MP, the chairman of the Treasury select committee, showed that 'the Bank appears to have been a very hierarchical organization, *with clear signs of "groupthink" among its leadership'* (quoted in Elliott and Treanor, 2015: 27, emphasis added). Groupthink was also one factor causing the epic implosion of the Royal Bank of Scotland. Martin's (2014) behind-the-scenes account of the bank's executive team reveals that most were too timid to challenge the high-risk behaviour and judgements of the CEO Fred Goodwin. There were plenty of opportunities to challenge Goodwin, writes Martin, and while excessive rewards had quite a lot to do with it, groupthink was a contributing factor. As one female employee put it: 'Grown men saying they were too scared of Fred to give him bad news? Isn't that a bit pathetic?' (Martin, 2014: 307).

Source: Image Source/David Jakle

Making it work

With the emergence of the idea of 'positive psychology', there has been a pronounced effort to shift research attention away from its traditional focus on abnormal or problematic patterns of human functioning, and towards the study of optimal functioning and human flourishing. This shift in attention away from the problematic and towards the optimal is evident in many fields of study – from organizational behaviour research to studies of marriage. For example, in a pioneering analysis of marriage dynamics, Frank Fincham and his colleagues argue (2007) that the traditional preoccupation with conflict in marriage must be corrected. Their article focuses on 'naturally occurring marital self-repair processes' (p. 282) and seeks to understand the mechanisms that enable some couples to bounce back from conflict while others separate or continue to live together unhappily.

Does this research on marriages have anything to tell us about group dynamics? Obviously, the differences between small work groups and marriages are fundamental, and there is no need to review those differences here. The question is, however, are there enough similarities between work groups and marriages to derive some insights into group dynamics from recent research on marriages? You be the judge. Consider the following synopsis of the work of Fincham and his colleagues.

Inspired by the move toward positive psychology, Fincham and his co-investigators set out to identify what distinguishes marriages that endure (or 'bounce back' after trouble) from marriages that fall apart. They found that couples who stay together do not necessarily experience conflict-free relationships. What distinguishes these resilient couples from couples who separate are mechanisms that work to defuse conflict, often without the help of external interventions. One might say that spouses in these resilient couples exhibit capacities for 'self-regulation' and the couples themselves are capable of 'self-repair'.

To understand how this works, Fincham and his colleagues suggest we consider how conflicts unfold in time. An initial disagreement or problematic event will often escalate over time as couples become locked into cyclical patterns of 'tit-for-tat' responding. Resilient couples seem to be able to avoid this pattern. They do so by engaging in two kinds of regulation: they regulate both 'the degree to which a negative partner behaviour elicits a correspondingly negative response' and 'the extent to

which negative partner behavior produces a change in the overall view of the relationship' (2007: 283). With regard to this second kind of regulation, one can imagine a wife (or husband) coming to the realization: this marriage is not worth saving. Spouses in resilient couples seem to be able to avoid these profound and irreversible changes of heart.

The two kinds of regulation associated with resilient couples are clearly relevant to work groups. Work groups experience internal conflict, and people in work groups become locked into cyclical patterns of 'tit-for-tat' responding. As with couples, the likelihood that members of work groups can resolve their conflicts without resorting to external mediation will depend on their capacity to engage in the kinds of regulation identified by Fincham and his colleagues.

Readers may feel comfortable with the analogy between marriages and work groups so far. But consider the proposed explanation of why some couples are more able than others to engage in effective self-regulation. Fincham and his colleagues offer the following list of factors that they believe enhance a couple's capacity for self-regulation and repair:

> Without methods for changing negative processes over time, or for changing direction once negative interactions begin, even the best marital skills for dealing with conflict may provide couples with insufficient basis for long-term marital satisfaction. The framework [described in this article has] … the potential to help us understand the impact [on self-regulatory processes] of forgiveness … commitment … valuing sacrifice … and sanctification. (p. 287)

Stop! Fincham and his colleagues associate this list of qualities – forgiveness, commitment, valuing sacrifice and sanctification – with couples who engage in effective self-regulation. Would these same qualities be associated with the optimal functioning of work groups? How would each of the four qualities contribute to higher levels of self-regulation among work group members? Given its links to organized religion, the idea of sanctification may seem irrelevant to many work groups. Is there a secular version of sanctification that might be relevant to a broader range of work groups?

Sources and further information
Bakkle, A. and Schaufeli, W. (2008) 'Positive organizational behavior: engaged employees in flourishing organizations', *Journal of Organizational Behavior*, 29, pp. 147–54.

Fincham, F., Stanley, S. and Beach, S. (2007) 'Transformative processes in marriage: an analysis of emerging trends', *Journal of Marriage and the Family*, 69, pp. 275–92.

Note: This feature was written by David MacLennan, Assistant Professor, Thompson Rivers University, Canada.

The research by Asch, Milgram and Janis tells us that groups influence the behaviour of their members, altering perceptions of reality and often promoting conformity, which can lead to imperfect and even catastrophic decisions. Weick points to the phenomenon of groupthink as an example of the dysfunctional consequences when a single, self-reinforcing mental model dominates group members' behaviour:

> Having become true believers of a specific schema, group members direct their attention towards an environment and sample it in such a way that the true belief becomes self-validating and the group becomes even more fervent in its attachment to the schema. What is underestimated is the degree to which the direction and sampling are becoming increasingly narrow under the influence of growing consensus and enthusiasm for the restricted set of belief. (Weick, C. E., 1979: 52)

The phenomenon of groupthink therefore has the potential to undermine the group's mental efficiency, reality testing, moral judgement and ability to appraise alternative communities of practice, which can be a barrier to organizational change (Hayes, 2014).

Another phenomenon that has the potential to adversely affect decision making is group polarization. This refers to the tendency of groups to make more extreme decisions than managers and employees working alone. For example, suppose that a board of governors of a college meets to make a decision on the future of a new sports complex for the college. Individual board members might come to the meeting with various degrees of support or opposition to the project. However, by the end of the board meeting, it is highly possible that the board of governors will agree on a more ambitious (that is, a higher financial cost) plan than the average individual had when the board meeting began.

One reason for the more ambitious preference is that individual board members feel less personally responsible for the decision's consequences because the entire board of governors makes the decision. Another reason is that board members become comfortable with more extreme positions when they realize that co-members also support the same position. Persuasive arguments favouring the dominant position convince doubtful members and help to form a consensus around the most ambitious or extreme option. So persuasion, group support and shifting responsibility explain why groups make more extreme decisions.

Research on decision making in groups has repeatedly demonstrated that group decision making is not always superior. In reality, groups sometimes do perform better than the average group member, but they rarely do better than the best member (Hayes, 2014; Winquist and Franz, 2008; Xenikou and Furnham, 2013). One explanation is that even relatively homogeneous groups often fail to show an exchange their members' unique resources. One key assumption underpinning the enthusiasm for group-based decision making is the expectation of benefiting from group members' distributed experiences and informational resources. This point is particularly important with regard to group diversity enhancing the quality of group decisions. Diversity is increasingly an organizational fact of life, and many work groups are diverse in terms of the characteristics of their membership, bringing together members who may differ in gender, ethnicity, age, disability, hierarchical status, educational background and so forth.

Research on diversity in work teams has shown mixed results regarding the effects of group diversity on team decision making. On the one hand, the processing of decision-relevant information may benefit from a wider pool, variety of perspectives and life experiences in more diverse groups. On the other hand, diversity may actually impede the exchange, discussion and integration of decision-relevant information, with consequential negative effects on decision quality (Kooij-de Bode et al., 2008). Others suggest that increasing diversity can have both positive and negative effects on group information processing and decision making that are contingent on 'individuals' beliefs about diversity' (van Dick and et al., 2008). Thus, educating employees in diverse organizations to value diversity can improve the quality of decisions. Furthermore, the positive effects of diversity might be propagated through several structured group processes that are designed to improve the exchange of group members' unique information, and therefore the quality of decisions. These structured group decision-making processes include brainstorming, the nominal group technique and the stepladder technique, which are discussed in Chapter 13.

Clearly, group social processes are complex and contentious, and are strongly influenced by the individual characteristics of team members and by dominant gender, race and power patterns. The wealth of research and interest in work teams over the last decade is related to the changing fashion in US and European management theory on how to compete in conditions of globalized capitalism.

VISIT THE *ONLINE RESOURCE CENTRE* AT HTTPS://HE.PALGRAVE.COM/COMPANION/BRATTON-WORK-AND-ORGANIZATIONAL-BEHAVIOUR3/ FOR EXAMPLES OF TEAMWORKING IN THE EUROPEAN UNION AND THE USA.

Work teams and management theory

The theoretical interest in work groups or teams draws upon human relations, sociotechnical and Japanese perspectives on organizational design (Benders and Van Hootegem, 1999; Bratton, 1992; Procter and Mueller, 2000). Pioneering work on human relations by Roethlisberger and Dickson (1939), Mayo (1946), Maslow (1954) and McGregor (1960) focused top managers' attention on the importance of social relations within work groups.

The collaborative research by Roethlisberger, an industrial psychologist from Harvard University, and Dickson, a manager at the Western Electric plant, involved studying the job performance of two groups of front-line workers doing identical work but in separate rooms. Each work group's productivity was carefully monitored. One work group – the study group – experienced ergonomic changes including increasing the intensity of the lighting in the workshop. The study group's productivity increased. The other work group – the control group – experienced no changes in lighting. However, to the astonishment of the researchers, its productivity also increased. Even more mystifying to the researchers was that when the level of light intensity was lowered for the study group, the results showed that output continued to go up. After repeated experiments over many years, the researchers began to make connections between social interaction and job performance. In 1939, Roethlisberger and Dickson wrote:

> The study of the bank wiremen showed that their behaviour at work could not be understood without considering the informal organization of the group and the relation of this informal organization to the total social organization of the company. The work activities of the group, together with their satisfactions and dissatisfactions, had to be viewed as manifestations of a complex pattern of interrelations. (Roethlisberger and Dickson, 1939: 551–2)

After the Second World War, the work of Maslow and McGregor helped US human relations advocates to clarify their perspective, with its focus on the interrelations between workers and the quality of the employment relationship.

stop...

Think about your experience of working in a group. Do Roethlisberger and Dickson's findings resonate with any aspect of your own view on group working? Why?

...and reflect

systems theory: a set of theories based on the assumption that social entities, such as work organizations, can be viewed as if they were self-regulating bodies exploiting resources from their environment (inputs) and transforming the resources (exchanging and processing) to provide goods and services (outputs) in order to survive

In Europe, much of the early research on work teams was conducted within the framework of sociotechnical **systems theory**. This theory developed from work in 1951 on autonomous work teams in the British coal-mining industry under the supervision of Trist and Bamforth. These researchers proposed that 'responsible autonomy' should be granted to primary work groups, and that group members should learn more than one role, so that an interchangeability of tasks would be possible within the group. The flexibility would permit the completion of sub-whole units. The studies showed that the labour process in mining could be better understood in terms of two systems: the technical system – including machinery and equipment – and the social system, including the social relations and interactions among the miners.

Later advocates of the sociotechnical systems approach to organizational design argued that work teams provide a work regime for achieving the 'best match' between technical and social considerations or 'systems'. The term 'best match' is used to describe the relationship between the social and technological systems of the organization, where each is sensitive to the demands of the other (Yeatts and Hyten, 1998).

job enrichment: employees are given more responsibility for scheduling, coordinating and planning their own work

job rotation: the practice of moving employees from one job to another

job enlargement: increasing the number of tasks employees perform in their jobs

job characteristics model: a job design model that relates the motivational properties of jobs to the specific personal and organizational consequences of those properties

Attempts to implement the sociotechnical systems approach have included work redesign to 'enrich' jobs. The concept of '**job enrichment**' refers to a number of different processes of **rotating, enlarging** and aggregating tasks. It increases the range of tasks, skills and control that workers have over the way they work, either individually or in teams. Job enrichment theory, also known as **job characteristics** theory, was given theoretical prominence by the work of Turner and Lawrence (1965) and Hackman and Oldham (1980). As a counter to the thinking underlying Taylorism and Fordism, the job enrichment model has been influential in the design of work teams. It suggests a casual relationship between five core job characteristics and the worker's psychological state. If this relationship is positive, it leads in turn to positive outcomes. The five core job characteristics contained in the model are defined as:

1 *skill variety* – the degree to which the job requires a variety of different activities in carrying out the work, requiring the use of a number of the worker's skills and talents
2 *task identity* – the degree to which the job requires the completion of a whole and identifiable piece of work
3 *task significance* – the degree to which the job has a substantial impact on the lives or work of other people
4 *autonomy* – the degree to which the job provides substantial freedom, independence and discretion to the worker in scheduling the work and in determining the procedures to be used in carrying it out
5 *feedback* – the degree to which the worker possesses information on the actual results of her or his performance.

The more that a job possesses the five core job characteristics, the greater the motivating potential of the job (Figure 10.8).

The model also recognizes the importance of learning to achieve motivation and outcome goals. Workers' work-related learning is implicitly linked to the existence of 'moderators' – knowledge and skills, the strength of growth needs and context satisfaction – that are contained in the model. The presence of moderators is used to explain why jobs that are theoretically high in motivating potential will not automatically generate high levels of motivation and satisfaction for all workers.

The argument goes that an employee with a low 'growth need' is less likely to experience a positive outcome when her or his work is 'enriched'. Thus, the neo-human relations approach to job design in general, and the job characteristic model

stop...

What do you think of this job characteristics model? Think about any jobs you have had. Can you use this model to assess the 'quality' of the work you were paid for? What is missing from the model?

...and reflect

in particular, emphasizes the fulfilment of social or relatedness needs by recomposing fragmented jobs. In certain circumstances, self-managed teams could provide an alternative to individual job enrichment.

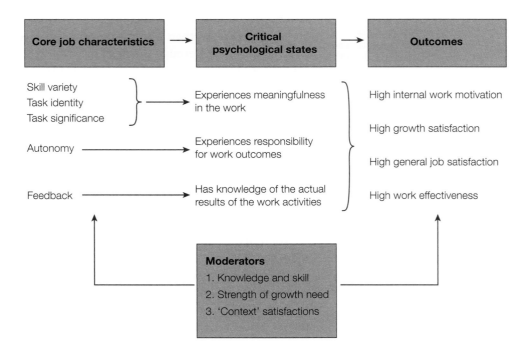

Figure 10.8 Oldham and Hackman's job characteristics model
Source: Fig 4.6, p. 90 in J. RICHARD HACKMAN & GREG R. OLDHAM, WORK REDESIGN, 1st Edition, © 1980. Printed and Electronically reproduced by permission of Pearson Education, Inc., Upper Saddle River, New Jersey

The quality of work and work-related learning in small SMWTs rests on five principles of 'good' job design:

- The first principle is *wholeness*. The scope of the job is such that it includes all the tasks to complete a product or process.
- The second principle involves individual and group *learning and development*. Opportunities exist to engage in a variety of fulfilling and meaningful tasks, allowing team members to learn a range of skills within a community of practice, and facilitating job flexibility (Hoeve and Nieuwenhuis, 2006).
- The third principle relates to *governance and self-regulation*. With the focus on product differentiation and the rise of knowledge-based economies, the imperatives of work do not permit managers to master all the challenges. As a result, they must allow team and project members to assume responsibility for the pace of work, problem solving and quality control.
- The fourth principle involves occupational *wellness and safety*. Work is designed to maintain the safety and wellness of team members and to support a good work–life balance (Lowe, 2000).
- Finally, the fifth principle is *social interaction*. The job design permits interaction, cooperation and reflexivity among team members.

Drawing upon the work of Klein (1994), the principles of 'good' job design are achieved by management interventions in the technical, governance and sociocultural dimensions of work (Figure 10.9).

The horizontal axis in Figure 10.9 represents the functional or technical tasks that are required to produce the product or service. Group working involves combining a number of tasks on the horizontal axis to increase the cycle times and create more complete and hence more meaningful jobs. The technical dimension is then regarded as the central purpose of work teams and is concerned with the range of tasks undertaken by its members, as well as with multiskilling and functional flexibility. The vertical axis represents the governance aspects of the labour process and shows the extent of workers' autonomy on the job. The third axis, the diagonal, represents the sociocultural aspects of work, one of which is the social interaction that takes place in work groups. The sociocultural dimension is perhaps the most interesting as far as organizational behaviour is concerned, since it represents the behaviour or 'normative' considerations – what ought to happen – that are needed to secure an effective team performance. This dimension of group work recognizes that employees' compliance and cooperation depend upon the complex interplay of social interactions in the group. It should be noted that, in a five-member team, there are 10 relationships (see Figure 10.3).

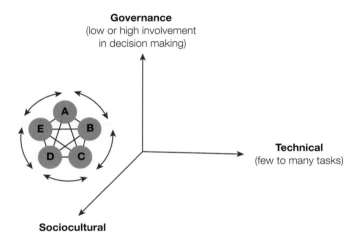

Figure 10.9 The three dimensions of group work: technical, governance and sociocultural

The SMWT represents an *ideal-type* work regime because it restores the craft paradigm by enlarging tasks on the horizontal axis and by giving members greater autonomy over how the work is accomplished on the vertical axis: a reversal of Taylorism. The movement along the diagonal axis represents the implications of group working in terms of group norms, group cohesion and organizational culture. The three dimensions of work organization in Figure 10.9 help to illustrate the point that top managers make strategic choices regarding how the work is designed, and alternative work structures have an impact on social behaviour and organizational culture.

IN THE EBOOK ACCESS THE **CRITICAL INSIGHT** ON 'THE LINK BETWEEN TEAMWORK, PERFORMANCE AND STRESS'.

Work teams: ending bureaucracy and extending employee empowerment?

Whereas groups as social entities go back thousands of years, management interest in work teams is much more recent. From early experiments in sociotechnical job design techniques in the 1970s, teams became the hallmark of postmodern work organizations in the 1990s. Teamwork has been popularized by mainstream organizational behaviour theorists and management consultants as a panacea for curing inflexible work systems and allegedly inefficient bureaucratic structures, and for enhancing employees' higher order 'growth' and 'relatedness' needs by job enrichment and empowerment.

Motivated by the prospect of connecting the synergy of work teams with corporate goals, managers have focused on teams to help improve organizational performance. In Sweden, the most celebrated example of work teams was introduced at the new Volvo car plant in Uddevalla in 1987. It was reported that the new assembly line avoided the classic problems associated with Fordism (*Business Week*, 1989). However, in 1992 Volvo closed its Uddevalla factory. For many organizational behaviour researchers, the Swedish plant had become an icon for a European, human-centred and productive organization, and its closure suggested that Taylorist and neo-Taylorist solutions still dominated management thinking in the automobile industry (Cressey, 1993).

In critical accounts of teamworking, in which group practices are connected to the class power relations in which they are embedded, there is considerable debate over whether or not these regimes constitute a significant departure from Western-style 'high-autonomy' work teams (Elger and Smith, 1994). Some argue that the difference lies in the fact that teamwork utilizes a control orientation that depends upon 'self-control'. Others persuasively argue that self-managed teams create a culture that enhances management control via self-regulation. This insight into group dynamics focuses on the socialization and organization culture, and on the behaviour deemed necessary to make teams work effectively (Thompson and Wallace, 1996).

The discussion on different group and team concepts highlights the array of definitions, and the need for commentators to define work groups carefully if comparisons are to be made. As mentioned earlier, the reason that so many organizations have 're-engineered' work processes around teams is that managers are looking for improvements in productivity resulting from the positive synergy associated with teams. Thus, the perceived connections between the way work is designed and organizational performance need to be appreciated to understand the current wave of corporate interest in teams.

In standard accounts of teamwork, such regimes do not necessarily lead to improved organizational performance. People must learn to work in team-based structures: clearly a lesson from sociotechnical theory, which acknowledges the importance of the dialectic relationship between the technical and social aspects of work. In critical accounts of teams, there is deep scepticism. Teams do not eradicate the three chronic capitalist antagonisms that centre on issues of managerial control: producing goods and services for a global market, which creates uncertainty and pressure to control costs; designing work structures and employee relations systems that maximize shareholder interests; and managerial top-down control over employees' behaviour, in contrast to employee autonomy.

Contrary to the management rhetoric, work teams involve elaborate ICT systems that are developed to support a control-oriented management philosophy (Yeatts and Hyten, 1998). This observation illustrates the work of critical scholars who tend to be interested in understanding the power relations in team design. For example, one study found that while team members had increased their autonomy in performing their work and had additional responsibilities, managers had actually increased their control over value-added activities through a computerized production system. This control-oriented approach can be given the name 'computer-controlled autonomy' (Bratton, 1992). Another study offered a scathing account of teamworking in white-collar work, arguing 'that workers experience forms of team organization as being no less coercive than classically understood Taylorism' (Baldry et al., 1998: 168–9).

Paradox in team-based work systems

How are we to interpret the effects of group membership on employees' behaviour? As with the other aspects of organizational behaviour we cover in this text, it depends on the author's approach to the subject. For some, team synergy can be a panacea to bureaucratic ills: 'Teams foster a sense of dignity, self-worth, and a greater commitment to achieving the performance that makes an organization competitive' (Manz and Sims, 1993: 10). More critical sociological analysis serves as an antidote to the mainstream assumptions that teamwork is inherently favourable. Critical analysis highlights the tensions between management's aim to control and direct employees and work activities to ensure performance targets are met and, simultaneously, the need to harness the skill and cooperation of team members in achieving those targets (Noon and Blyton, 2013). These competing pressures lead to contradictions resulting in outcomes for employers and employees that are not entirely positive.

As an empirical reality, for employers, working in self-directed teams was shown to have no significant effect on employees' commitment to the organization, whereas, for employees, it was associated with higher work-related stress (Danford et al., 2008). For others, teamwork, far from being 'empowering', actually intensifies management control over workers by cultivating a form of self-management through constant peer and self-monitoring (Thompson and McHugh, 2009). This critical perspective focuses on, among other things, the effect of team ideology and behaviour on the working lives of workers. Whereas the managerialist approach found in most mainstream organizational behaviour texts focuses on the technical and the empowering dimensions of teams and team efficacy, a feature of a critical approach is a focus on the normative dimension of groups and teams, the 'tyranny' arising from teamwork and paradoxes in team-based work structures.

A paradox involves ambiguity and contradiction, and both are evident in work group design. A central pillar of teamwork involves combining a number of tasks on the horizontal axis. This has led many traditional scholars to argue that SMWTs reverse Tayloristic deskilling tendencies by enhancing workers' skills. It is suggested that SMWTs exemplify the re-emergence of the craft model (Piore and Sabel, 1984). Critical organizational theorists, however, have challenged the popular logic that SMWTs lead to a more highly skilled workforce. Detractors argue that although they apparently give limited empowerment to workers, they do not necessarily reverse the general 'deskilling' trend, but generate new forms of control that assist management in extracting higher productivity from workers via work intensification as the range of horizontal and vertical tasks expands (Sayer, 1986; Turnbull, 1986; Willmott, 1995).

Those subscribing to this critique almost invariably draw parallels with Taylorism and Fordism. A number of accounts stress that, with the assistance of ICT, re-engineering work into teams is an 'up-dating of Taylor's crusade against custom and practice in which the silicon chip plays an equivalent role in [re-engineering] to that performed by the stop watch in Scientific Management' (Thompson, 1989: 96). In other words, it unwittingly provides a disguised form of intensified managerial control over the labour process. Others offer more optimistic analyses, in which the outcomes of teamworking are less deterministic. Whether work teams result in the 'upskilling' or 'deskilling' is contingent upon, among other things, batch size, managerial choice and negotiation (Bratton, 1992).

Critical organizational theorists have illustrated the paradox in another way. The behavioural dimension of the teamwork model emphasizes worker empowerment

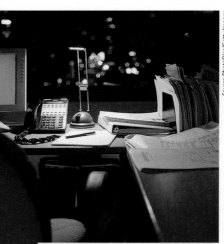

Source: PhotoDisc/Getty Images

plate 35 Team members can perceive a moral obligation to increase their level of effort on a job, and 'put in a full day' (or more) because of peer group pressure, or 'clan control', thereby unwittingly creating a control culture system.

stop...

Is there a general trend in upskilling associated with team work? Compared with blue-collar workers, are professionals and white collar workers more likely to experience upskilling? Hint: Go to Chapter 16 for a more detailed review of the deskilling/upskilling debate.

...and reflect

while simultaneously increasing management's control over the labour process. This is achieved using both 'hard' technology (such as computers) and 'social' technology (such as group norms). When decision making is devolved to the team, members begin to think and act like managers, and they internalize company values. In this way, teamwork influences the attitude and behaviour of the team's members by creating a work culture that reproduces the conditions of employees' own subordination. In other words, team members perceive a moral obligation to increase their level of effort on the job, and 'put in a full day' because of peer group pressure or 'clan control', thereby unintentionally creating a control culture system. Critical studies have found team members' discipline to be more punitive than that of managers: 'Team members are tougher on fellow workers than management is' (Wells, 1993: 75). In their account of team learning processes, Kasl and colleagues unwittingly provide further evidence of the control culture generated by work teams (Kasl et al., 1997). When one particular work team 'failed', some team members left the company, while others worked on 'disheartened'. Moreover:

> The team became the laughing stock of the whole company and the people who weren't involved in it at all, the people who worked on a different floor, would walk right in and say, 'How's logistics, ha ha ha?' They heard about it, it was like this big disaster. (Kasl et al., 1997: 238)

IN THE EBOOK ACCESS THE **OB IN FOCUS** BOX ON 'FEW EMPLOYEES HAVE A 'GOOD' JOB'.

There is another paradox. The managerial literature views teamwork as organizational synergy unifying people and thus developing members' capacities through dialogue and learning. Critical reflection in the workplace learning literature presumes that if team members can just detect their dysfunctional or inefficient practices, they will be free to find more creative and efficient ways of doing, and thus improve their performance in the workplace. One mainstream assumption is that all members of the work team are equal. Recent empirical research on multi-professional teamwork in the health sector, however, contends that, rather than unifying health professions, teamwork produces unintended divisive effects (Finn, 2008). It is argued that power relations and the language used by the health professionals both reflect and reproduce structural inequality between surgeons, anaesthetists and nurses within the team. In reality, where teamworking is characterized by social structures of inequality and clinical power – for example, surgeons and anaesthetists over nurses – critical reflection and dialogue, and thus the mobilization of alternative practices, are suppressed.

The discourse on work teams illustrates competing interpretations. On the one hand, the thinking and prescriptions in mainstream accounts tend to focus on the technical and the 'growth need' dimension of team-based work configurations, as well as the links between group processes and group performance. On the other hand, critical evaluations of teamwork focus on paradoxes and the effect of team ideology and behaviour on workers. Thus, teamwork arguably resembles Morgan's 'psychic prison' in the sense that peer pressure and self-surveillance are the norm, and this more accurately resembles reality than the optimistic notion of the learning-empowering SMWT. In his book *Images of Organizations* (2006), Morgan explains that the notion of organizations as psychic prisons is a metaphor that connects the idea that organizations are a psychic phenomenon, in the sense that they are ultimately constructed and sustained by conscious and unconscious processes, with the belief that people can actually become imprisoned or confined by the ideas, thoughts and actions to which these processes give rise.

Chapter summary

- In this chapter, we have examined the background, nature and behavioural implications of work groups. We have suggested that the current wave of interest in work teams, often located within a cluster of other employment practices constituting what is called a 'high-performance workplace', is linked to lean forms of work organizations and the perceived shortcomings of large bureaucratic organizational structures.

- The chapter has emphasized that understanding group processes, such as groupthink, group leadership, informal group learning and intragroup conflict, is imperative for the successful management of the HPW system.

- Management tries to persuade workers of the need to work beyond their contract for the 'common' good and to engage in self-regulatory norms. The SMWT is said to be upskilling and empowering workers.

- However, we have also gone beyond management rhetoric, and have presented arguments and evidence to suggest that self-managed teams shift the focus away from the hierarchy, from directive and bureaucratic control processes, to a culture of self-control mechanisms.

- The discussion has emphasized that orthodox and critical accounts of teamworking provide very different views of this form of work organization and employment relations. Both perspectives, however, conceptualize teamworking as influencing individual behaviour and contributing to improved organizational performance. While both approaches make employee autonomy central to their analyses, each conceptualizes team membership as having a different influence. Additionally, autonomy is theorized as leading to different outcomes (such as growth need versus self-regulation) in each perspective.

Chapter review questions

1 How useful are group development models for understanding group or team behaviour?
2 What effect, if any, do you expect workforce diversity to have on group processes and outcomes?
3 Explain how the size of the work group might affect group dynamics and performance?
4 'SMWT are simply attempts by managers to control individ-

uals at work by mobilizing group processes.' Do you agree or disagree? Discuss.
5 Students often complain about doing group projects. Why? Relate your answer to group processes and the critique of SMWT.
6 What is meant by 'groupthink', and how important is it in deciding group performance?

Further reading

Barker, J. R. (1999) *The Discipline of Teamwork: Participation and Concertive Control*, London: Sage.

Baron, R. S. and Kerr, N. L. (2003) *Group Process, Group Decision, Group Action*, Buckingham: Open University Press.

Behfar, K., Peterson, R., Mannix, E. and Trochim, W. (2008) 'The critical role of conflict resolution in teams: a closer look at the links between conflict type, conflict management strategies, and team outcomes', *Journal of Applied Psychology*, 93(1), pp. 170–88.

Belbin, R. M. (2010) *Team Roles at Work* (2nd edn), London: Butterworth/Heinemann.

Buyl, T., Boone, C. and Hendriks, W. (2014) 'Top management team members' decision influence and cooperative behaviour: an empirical study in the information technology industry', *British Journal of Management*, 25, pp. 285–304.

Cordery, J. (2002) 'Team working', pp. 326–50 in P. Warr (ed.), *Psychology of Work*, London: Penguin.

Danford, A., Richardson, M., Stewart, P., Tailby, S. and Upchurch, M. (2008) 'Partnership, high performance work systems and quality of working life', *New Technology, Work and Employment*, 23(3), pp. 151–66.

Dixon, K. and Panteli, N. (2010) 'From virtual teams to vituality in teams', *Human Relations*, 63(8), pp. 1177–97.

Forsyth, D. R. (2010) *Group Dynamics* (5th edn), Wadsworth: Cengage Learning.

Mintzberg, H. (2009) 'Rebuiliding campanies as communities', *Harvard Business Review*, 78(7/8), pp. 140–3.

Procter, S. and Mueller, F. (eds) (2000) *Teamworking*, Basingstoke: Palgrave Macmillan.

Sewell, G. (1998) 'The discipline of teams: the control of team-based industrial work through electronic and peer surveillance', *Administrative Science Quarterly*, 43, pp. 406–69.

Sinclair, A. (1992) 'The tyranny of a team ideology', *Organization Studies,* 13(4), pp. 611–26.

Taggar, S. and Ellis, R. (2007) 'The role of leaders in shaping formal team norms', *Leadership Quarterly*, 18, pp. 105–20.

van Dick, R., van Knippenburg, D., Hagele, S., Guillaume, Y. R. F. and Brodbeck, F. (2008) 'Group diversity and group identification: the moderating role of diversity beliefs', *Human Relations*, 61(10), pp. 1463–92.

Xenikou, A. and Furnham, A. (2013) *Group Dynamics and Organizational Culture*, Basingstoke: Palgrave Macmillan.

IN THE EBOOK ACCESS **WEB BASED ASSIGNMENTS** TO APPLY YOUR LEARNING.

Chapter case study: Building cars in Brazil

The setting

Founded in the earlier part of the twentieth century, the Cable Motor Company was a traditional, North American automobile manufacturer. They used Fordist management techniques and traditional assembly line production, and worked with a highly unionized workforce. By the mid-1980s, with their sales slumping, the company made the decision to purchase an obsolete automotive assembly plant in Brazil. The company quickly proceeded to upgrade the plant, resulting in a very large, modern, single-storey building of approximately 1.4 million square feet with four major manufacturing centres: stamping, body, paint and final assembly. The plan was to adopt the use of cooperative work teams, which had been used by Swedish car manufacturers such as Saab and Volvo, and to implement the Japanese lean production system originally created by Toyota and later adapted by Mazda.

The company spared no expense in planning for the workforce that would fit the plant's new approach to job design. Extensive pre-employment screening and selection techniques were used to recruit the 1200 people needed for the production run. Unlike the minimalist training normally provided under the Ford system, the company provided intensive classroom time and continuous on-the-job training for employees on the subject of SMWTs. Group decision making, integral to team success, was a strong focus.

The company found that the union representing the workers, the National Union of Cable Motor Company Workers, had little influence in the new Brazilian plant. This resulted in a much quicker implementation of the flexible production system. Production shifts of about 100 persons were scheduled with workers performing operations individually and in self-directed two-, three- or four-person teams. Any team member could pull a car off the line to check a quality issue. In such a case, a group walk-around decided whether a car needed 'finessing'.

CEO John Miner was impressed with the initial look of the new production system. 'Minimal supervision and a self-directed workforce are what we strive to maintain and encourage,' he remarked. 'We will not get bogged down in traditional thinking, processes or paperwork. All workers are encouraged to be free-thinking and to get creative.'

The problem

The selection of the team leaders was conducted by the senior management group. Maria Lopez, a 30-year-old clerical worker, was moved from the administration office to head up one of the teams. Shortly afterwards, production manager Clive Richards began to notice that the production cycle times of Maria's team were increasing. He also noticed conflicts within her group. Clive decided to approach one of Maria's team members, Juan Fernandez, who had formerly worked in a team at another car company's assembly plant in Brazil. 'We can't work with Maria as our team leader,' Juan said. 'The team finds it hard because she is a woman. You have to remove her.'

While Clive struggled to decide what to do with Maria, other problems emerged. Employees were arriving to work late on a consistent basis. City buses, the main source of transportation for the plant workers, ran late if they ran at all. This was beginning to impact the continual on-the-job training as it required workers to arrive at work on time. Other employees were hesitant to do quality checks on their own work, saying that it would create the impression that the supervisors did not trust them.

Clive decided to meet with the CEO to let him know about the increasing issues so that action could be taken before the problems got worse. John was concerned when he heard what was happening at the new plant as he had just returned from a meeting where there were preliminary discussions on opening another in a different Brazilian location. 'I need you to do a presentation for the Board of Directors,' John said to Clive. 'We have to show what we've learned from this experience and how we can move forward.'

The task

Prepare a short presentation, incorporating the answers to the following questions:

- How did Brazilian culture or work ideology contribute to the problems the company was experiencing with its use of teams?
- In what alternative way could the team leader have been chosen which might have been more acceptable to the team members?

- Should the conflicts in Maria's group only be viewed as a negative development?

Ask yourself:

- Why do you think the use of teams could weaken a union's influence or power in the workplace?

Further reading

Bouville, G. and Alis, D. (2014) 'The effects of lean organizational practices on employees' attitudes and workers' health: evidence from France', *International Journal of Human Resource Management*, 25(21), pp. 3016–37.

Franz, T. (2012) *Group Dynamics and Team Interventions*, London: Wiley.

Katz, H. C., Lee, W. and Lee, J. (2004) *The New Structure of Labour Relations*, New York: Cornell University Press.

Proctor, S., Fulop, L., Linstead, S., Mueller, F. and Sewell, G. (2009) 'Managing teams', pp. 539–73 in S. Linstead, L. Fulop and S. Lilley (eds), *Management and Organization: A Critical Text* (2nd edn), Basingstoke: Palgrave Macmillan.

Note: Cable Motor Company is a fictitious company, but the background material for the case is derived from Muller et al. (1998). Some circumstances of the case organization have been altered. This case study was written by Lori Rilkoff, Human Resources Director, City of Kamloops, BC, Canada.

IN THE EBOOK ACCESS AN **OB IN FILM** BOX THAT USES *TWELVE ANGRY MEN* (1957) TO ILLUSTRATE CONCEPTS OF GROUP POWER AND INFLUENCE AND TO ACCESS **AN INTERACTIVE QUIZ** TO TEST YOUR UNDERSTANDING.

chapter 11
Communication

Key concepts

- 4S model of speech making
- Aristotle's model of rhetoric
- channels of communication
- coding
- communication climate
- decoding
- emotional intelligence
- exchange model of communication
- feedback
- Generation Y
- grapevine
- impression management
- non-verbal communication
- social networking sites
- transmission model of communication

Chapter outline

- Introduction
- The nature of organizational communication
- Perspectives on communication
- Communication and management
- Channels of communication
- Leadership, persuasion and communication
- Communication and cultural diversity
- Gender and communication: 'She said, he said'
- Communication and paradox
- Summary and end-of-chapter features
- Chapter case study: Cancelling Casual Friday at Sydney's CLD Bank

Chapter learning outcomes

After completing this chapter, you should be able to:
1 Discuss the importance of communication in the workplace
2 Discuss alternative perspectives on managing diversity in the organization
3 Explain the communication process, including non-verbal communication
4 Understand the use of communication in the leadership process
5 Understand the relationships between culture, gender and communication
6 Appreciate the existence of paradox in communication processes in the workplace

introduction

Human beings are communicating creatures, but the language we use is not simply a means of communicating ideas. Rhetorical theorists are aware that language is a powerful force for getting people to do things, and cultural theorists emphasize that we define ourselves through our various communicative connections. Whether it's through face-to-face storytelling or sending messages to friends using Facebook or Twitter, language is central to understanding our identity. People express themselves to each other in symbolic form, and through verbal and non-verbal communication they create and shape relationships. Through communication we are comforted and feel empathy from others; through communication we are hurt, abused and trivialized by others. Language, the means by which we speak to and hear others, has been widely theorized as the very embodiment of an embedded society. In understanding why women's voices are being muted in the public spheres, it is necessary to recognize how attitudes and prejudices have been 'hardwired through culture over more than two millennia from Homer to Twitter' (Mary Beard, quoted in Davis, 2014). In the workplace, language is powerful in moving people to action, which emphasizes its persuasive force. Executive managers use rhetoric as a means of shaping and controlling members' behaviour, for changing the organization's culture and, in the post-2008 global financial crisis era, often to communicate the prospect of downsizing, organizational change or budget cuts. So how do women and men communicate at work? Are there distinctively 'feminine' and 'masculine' ways of interacting in organizations? Understanding these processes of **dialogue** and communication are core skills for managers and non-managers alike.

dialogue: a process of conversation among team members in which they learn about each other's mental models and assumptions, and eventually form a common model for thinking within the team

The exchange of information and the transmission of meaning are the very essence of formal work organizations. Information about the organization's products and services, its external competitors and its people is essential to management, workers, shareholders and customers. The string of accounting scandals that rocked the US dot-com business community in the summer of 2002 and the 2013–14 disclosure of a mass surveillance of Internet and phone traffic by Britain's security agency, GCHQ, and the US National Security Agency (Borger, 2013), illustrate how information that is communicated (or not communicated) helps to define a certain type of behaviour that we expect from the organizations we deal with. Communication in formal work organizations, however, is a more complex process than simply the disclosure of information.

This chapter examines different approaches to studying communication: functionalist, interpretivist and critical. It describes the functions and directions of communications in the workplace. It also explores the communication implications of culture, gender and diversity in the workplace, as well as the importance of persuasion in the communication process.

The nature of organizational communication

communication: the process by which information is transmitted and understood between two or more people

language: a system of symbols that expresses ideas and enables people to think and communicate with one another

symbolic interactionism: the sociological approach that views society as the sum of the interactions of individuals and groups

According to the behavioural perspective on **communication**, it is a symbolic process in which individuals exchange perceptions and ultimately build a knowledge bank for themselves and for others, for the purpose of shaping future actions (Byers, 1997). **Language** allows for the possibility of meaningful social interaction and shapes the self – that part of an individual's identity composed of self-image and self-awareness. It is also closely connected to power, and it shapes, and is shaped by, gender relations in organizations and the wider society (Holmes, 2006; Mumby, 2013). As we discussed in Chapter 3, **symbolic interactionism**, which originates from the work of the American philosopher George Herbert Mead, is concerned with how language enables individuals to become self-conscious beings, aware of their own individuality.

The key element in this process is the symbol, something that represents something else. For example, the words that people use to refer to objects are in fact symbols that represent what we mean. The word 'cup' is the symbol we use to describe a receptacle that we use in Western society to drink coffee or tea from. Non-verbal messages or forms of communication – such as hand signs, nods of the head or eye contact with others – can substitute for words. The use of symbols in social encounters both outside and inside the organization necessarily involves other people interpreting what they mean.

However, language is ambiguous and changes over time, and non-verbal symbols too can signify a multiplicity of meanings and ideas at any point in time. The phrases 'fat chance' and 'slim chance' might seem to be opposites, but they have the same meaning in English-speaking North America. Non-verbal symbols can signify different things depending on where they are used. For example, a thumbs-up sign is a gesture of approval in Britain, but in Ghana it is an insult. An open palm is an insulting gesture in Greece, while in West Africa it means you have five fathers, which is akin to calling someone a bastard (Rogin et al., 2009).

Language has become important for the sociological exploration of contemporary societies. It is associated, for example, with power and gender relations. In this context, it is argued that writing is an ideological act in the process of gender redefinition (Calas and Smircich, 1996; Holmes, 2006; Howells, 1987). The interplay of power and language comes through clearly in how people use masculine words to signify greater force, significance or value. For instance, the positive word 'seminal', meaning ground-breaking, is derived from the word 'semen' or 'male seed'. The positive adjective 'virtuous', meaning morally worthy, is derived from the Latin word *vir*, meaning man. By contrast, the disparaging adjective 'hysterical' comes from the Greek word *hystera*, meaning uterus or womb (Macionis et al., 2012).

Language plays a crucial role in establishing the status and power of a profession, particularly for high-status, knowledge-based occupations such as law and medicine (Hodson and Sullivan, 2012). A monopoly of esoteric knowledge is the essence or 'hallmark' of a profession: it marks out its members as 'privilege-knowing subjects' (and often seems to imply white male experience and a white male standpoint). The work of Erving Goffman (1967) demonstrates the importance of language and power in physician–patient relationships, particularly when a patient is obliged to enter hospital for medical treatment. Through the work of the historian and philosopher Michel Foucault, the relationship between language and knowledge has been turned 180 degrees. Far from language symbolizing original creative thought, Foucault argued that language as a social construct actually dictates the thoughts individuals have: 'Languages do not represent our meaning so much as construct them for us' (Bilton et al., 2002: 509).

From a managerialist standpoint, 'effective' communications is one means by which managers 'get things done', for example by articulating a vision, informing workers of organizational rules, and giving feedback in face-to-face interviews. In this sense, it should be self-evident that the process of management, as shown diagrammatically in Figure 1.6, depends critically on communication between managers and non-managers. Not surprisingly, therefore, management texts emphasize the importance of open, clear and precise communication. They also emphasize that managers cannot afford to underestimate the complex interconnections that can result in unanticipated face-to-face encounters. When managers fail to think interconnectedly or in 'circles', or are insensitive to 'gendered talk', they get into trouble (Holmes, 2006; Weick, K. 1979).

The nature of the communication process established in the organization reflects the management style, degree of employee participation, culture and efficiency of the workplace. It is suggested that 'improving the communication of senior executives, especially the CEO, may be the most cost-effective way to improve employees' satisfaction with communication in their organizations' (Gray and Robertson, 2005: 26).

stop...

Do you see language as a reflection of power in society?

...and reflect

Theorists have implied that the two constructs of 'communication' and 'organization' are equivalent (Smith, 1993; Taylor, 1995). Thus, all organizational models contain implicit notions about communication theories, and all communication theories, in turn, provide important insights into managing the employment relationship (Putnam et al., 1999). From a critical standpoint, organizational communication is an important tool for shaping and controlling various aspects of workers' behaviour in the workplace. It is a means of gaining commitment to the organization's goals, a means of conveying the organization's disciplinary practices, and ultimately a means of making workers more governable (Mumby, 2013; Townley, 1994).

stop...

Look again at Figure 1.3, which shows the management process. Why is communication so important to the management process and leadership?

...and reflect

Perspectives on communication

When reading about organizational communication, it is important to be alert to the different perspectives that authors and researchers select. In exploring the various approaches, we should remember that, at their core, each perspective is motivated by the problems associated with coordinating multiple work activities and managing large numbers of people in specific work settings (Mumby, 2013). We will consider three major perspectives for understanding organizational communications: the functionalist, interpretivist and critical approaches.

Functionalist approach

functionalist perspective: the sociological approach that views society as a stable, orderly system

The **functionalist** or mechanistic approach is the dominant perspective in management studies and sees communication as intended or unintended action. The work organization is viewed as an entity, and different communication acts are variables that shape and determine the operations of that entity (Neher, 1997). Communication occurs as a chain, the weakest link of which determines the effectiveness of the communication as a whole. Messages are concrete 'things' with properties that can be measured. Communication can be broken down into smaller and smaller units (known as message bits). The functionalist approach views communication as a metaphorical pipeline that transmits information between a sender and a receiver. Organizational members have three basic methods of transmitting information, as shown in Figure 11.1.

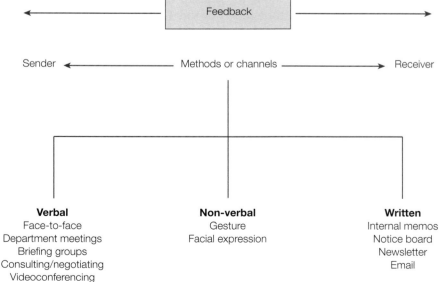

Figure 11.1 Organizational communication as action
Source: Bratton and Gold (2012). Used with permission

Verbal communication ranges from a casual conversation between two employees to a formal speech by a managing director. In face-to-face meetings, the meaning of the information being conveyed by the sender can be reinforced through gesture or facial expressions – referred to as non-verbal communication. Written communication ranges from a casual note to a co-worker to an annual report. Facebook, Twitter and other social media systems, videoconferencing and webcams have revolutionized written and verbal communication in organizations. Functionalists categorize behaviours or messages in terms of accomplishing goals and objectives.

Mainstream authors suggest that aspects of organizational communications include mechanistic, interpretive-symbolic and systems-interaction processes (Field and House, 1995). Another approach recognizes that the function of communication is to control, motivate and inform workers, and to enable them to release emotional expression. A communication style that recognizes the importance of emotional competencies is an important dimension of emotional intelligence (Goleman, 1996; see also Chapter 5). Thus, it is argued, the life-blood of the organization is communication: information is carried to all parts of the organization so that decisions and actions may be taken.

More critical authors – such as Putnam and his colleagues (1999) – identify seven clusters of metaphors or perspectives used in organizational communication theories – conduit, lens, linkage, performance, symbol, voice and discourse – which correspond to the theoretical approaches used in this chapter. They look at how the organizational context affects communication, and at how communication shapes the organizational context. By privileging communication as the producer of organizations, and examining the metaphors used in the organizational communication literature, they show that 'metaphors reveal alternative ways of thinking about the origin and nature of organizing, its processes, and the constructs that form its ontological roots' (Putnam et al., 1999: 126).

Early organizational communication theories included classical, or scientific, management and bureaucracy. The predominant metaphor applied to these organizations was the machine. Organizations were viewed as the primary vehicle through which lives were rationalized, 'planned, articulated, scientized, made more efficient and orderly, and managed by experts' (J. Scott, quoted in Eisenberg and Goodall, 1997: 57). The pipeline or chain images were absorbed into the conduit and lens metaphor clusters identified by Putnam and his co-workers. Communication was seen as the linear transmission of information. It was treated as a variable that influenced individual and organizational performance. The dominant interest was in the skills that make individuals more effective communicators, or in the factors that characterize a system-wide effectiveness of communication. Workers were viewed as a passive audience incapable of responding, interpreting, arguing or countering this form of control. Mainstream literature uses the words 'conduit', 'channel' and 'media' in descriptions of organizational communication (see, for example, McShane and Von Glinow, 2012). The lens metaphor provides a different slant on the transmission of information; the assumption here is that information is incomplete and is open to misinterpretation.

When a message is transmitted, the likelihood that the information will be converted, simplified, reduced or summarized increases if the senders and receivers have different cultural backgrounds and goals. The inevitability of misconception challenges traditional notions of accuracy, clarity and the effectiveness of communication by introducing meaning and interpretation into the message's transmission. One research domain that adopts a lens metaphor is **media richness**. Media richness theorists contend that managers will be more effective if they choose a communication medium that matches the ambiguity of their task (Daft and Huber, 1987). Lean and rich media diagrams can be found in mainstream texts. Grint char-

stop...

Looking at Figure 11.1, consider what barriers to communication exist in organizations.

...and reflect

media richness: refers to the number of channels of contact afforded by a communication medium; so, for example, face-to-face interaction would be at the high end of media richness, and a memorandum would fall at the low end of media richness

acterizes the functionalist approach, or the transmission model, in concrete terms: the 'language, technologies' are simply channels for telling somebody something. The manager chooses the most appropriate channel of communication to convey the information, accomplish goals and improve efficiency (Grint, 2000).

Interpretivist approach

interpretivism: the view held in many qualitative studies that reality comes from shared meaning among the people in that environment

The **interpretivist** approach is a reaction against the functionalist perspective (Neher, 1997). It attempts to understand human communication as something *in* the work organization, rather than something that *manages* the organization. Interpretivists argue that human beings do not behave as predictably as is suggested by the functionalist school. Thus, we may be able to predict that most people, or some people in the workplace, will react to a certain message in a certain way, but we cannot make the prediction for all workers. Some employees will do one thing and some another when presented with identical information. Interpretivist scholars argue that, because people are so complex in their behaviours and exhibit choice in responding to stimuli, functionalist explanations of organizational behaviour are inappropriate. The organism metaphor is associated with this approach. It is applied to a system of mutually connected and dependent parts constituted to share a common life (Morgan, 1980).

culture: the knowledge, language, values, customs and material objects that are passed from person to person and from one generation to the next in a human group or society

Communication is the transference and understanding of meaning. Most communication models convey this as a linear process (although they assume that both the sender and the receiver have an active role), but we need to be aware that the construction of meaning is affected by the skill, attitude and knowledge of the participants, and also by the sociocultural context in which the communication takes place. The creation of shared meanings is the basis of the interpretive-symbolic perspective. These shared meanings create the organization's **culture**, and can also serve to create and shape social reality. An organization's culture is partially created by the shared talk of its members. Organizational members capture complex experiences that are combinations of sense, emotion, reason and imagination, using narration and storytelling to impart meaning.

Cultural factors are strong influences on the interpretive process. The definition and meaning of culture has been contested more than any other concept in the social sciences. Raymond Williams, the father of 'cultural studies', suggests that it has three core meanings:

- a general process of intellectual, spiritual and aesthetic development
- a meaning that relates to the works and practices of intellectual and artistic activity
- a meaning that refers to a particular way of life, whether of people, a period or a group (Yuval-Davis, 1997).

The prominent sociologist Anthony Giddens claims that the last of these is the definition used by sociologists. He claims that way of life is composed of the values the members of a given group share, the norms that reflect or embody those values, either prescribing a given type of behaviour or forbidding it, and the material goods they create (Giddens and Sutton, 2013), which may describe a work culture. An important part of work culture is the social interaction involved in the interpretation of narratives, rites and rituals. These symbolic 'shared meanings' serve to socialize newcomers, solve problems and impart organizational values and beliefs. Rites such as award ceremonies, retirement dinners and new member orientations are elaborate dramatic activities that consolidate cultural expressions into one event. Rituals such as handshakes, coffee breaks, gift giving and staff meetings are the norms and behaviours that embody the rites. The interpretive approach to organizational communication seeks to make sense of organizational members' actions as part of the social constructions of individuals that have become shared. These symbols are more than manifestations of an organization's culture: they are the means through which organizing is accomplished.

Politicians and corporate leaders use metaphors as a rhetorical device to justify apparently any government programme or policy, or organizational strategy or goal. Take, for example, the phrase 'the global race'. The UK Coalition government tell us Britain needs to 'win' it, 'succeed' in it, 'compete' in it or 'get fit for' it. The phrase 'global race' appeared in British national newspapers 17 times in October, 38 times in November and 65 times in December 2013. British Prime Minister David Cameron invoked the 'the global race' in his New Year message that year and throughout 2013 in set-piece speeches to journalists and business leaders to justify tighter immigration controls, shorter school holidays, looser planning laws, reforming the European Union and investing in the high-speed HS2 rail project, for example (Beckett, 2013a). Although hardly the most subtle of rhetorical devices, the phrase 'the global race' is beginning to embed itself in modern British politics and management.

In work organizations, metaphors have been used to understand organizational behaviour. As a particular linguistic expression, metaphors can link abstract social constructs to concrete things, and, as in the world of politics, they can be used to legitimize managers' actions, set goals and guide managers and non-managers' behaviour in the workplace (Putnam et al., 1999). Metaphors help theory building by enabling us to examine images at different levels of analysis. A theory is metaphorical if it suggests, through language, enlightening comparisons between organizational communication and other processes. For example, scientific management theory compares organizations with machines. The predominant metaphor used during the Summit of the Americas in Quebec was the family of nations. Images of family and teams, the latter utilizing the language of sports, recur frequently in mainstream management texts on organizational design. In the Western tradition, metaphor has the privilege of revealing unexpected truth. As Aristotle put it, 'Midway between the unintelligible and the commonplace, it is metaphor which most produces knowledge' (Ashcroft et al., 1989: 151). Similarly, others believe that metaphors inform action, shape organizational practices or overcome resistance to organizational change (Alvesson and Billing, 1997; Hayes, 2014; Jabri, 2012; Morgan, 2006; Riley, 1983).

Many workplaces are pervaded by game and military metaphors, as well as metaphors of friends, family and home (Filipczak, 1996; Riley, 1983). Accordingly, 'A metaphor works through invoking a concept originating from another field or level than the one that is being understood. The former modifies the latter and forms a specific image or gestalt' (Alvesson and Billing, 1997: 112). The knowledge of theories about organizational communications enables us to participate in a particular **discourse community**, which in this case is made up of individuals who share an interest in organizations and communication. To join in this ongoing conversation, as communication theorist Kenneth Burke describes it, we need to be aware of the previous and present conversations. Theories enhance our ability to understand and explain a variety of practical issues, such as where the idea of organization originated and what motivates people to work. Theories can show how communication and efficiency are linked. Because organizational communication theories are dynamic, we should view each theory as a participant in a larger,

plate 36 Rituals such as handshakes, coffee breaks, gift giving and staff meetings are the norms and behaviours that embody the rites.

Source: Getty Images

discourse community: a way of talking about and conceptualizing an issue, presented through ideas and concepts, spoken or written, within a social group or community (such as lawyers or physicians)

ongoing discourse. One theory should not be given prominence over another; rather, we should recognize its origins, bias and relationship to other theories.

Critical approach

All large work organizations consist of complex webs of interconnected communication processes, the integration of which determines the success or failure of the organization (Mumby, 2013). The critical approach to studying organizational communications seeks to expose the often hidden but pervasive power that post-industrial organizations have over individuals, while also challenging the assumed superiority of unfettered market capitalism. Whereas the functionalist approach is

Source: PhotoDisc/Getty Images

Information overload

There is wide agreement among those who study organizations that while information may flow downwards, many factors inhibit the flow of information in the other direction. Typically, and with justification, managers feel frustrated because they lack knowledge of what is going on among front-line workers, complaining that they do not have a clear picture of work processes and the factors that influence productivity and quality. As a result, their ability to manage is compromised.

Pressure to obtain accurate information about the processes that produce (or fail to produce) the desired outputs has become especially intense in public, state-supported institutions such as schools, where calls for accountability and cost-effectiveness have led to the introduction of 'performance indicators'. It has been argued that performance indicators, often in the form of standardized test results, will help managers to identify under-performing schools, teachers and students. Those who support this position believe that large amounts of performance data will give administrators the tools they need to better manage the education system. Many also believe that the benefits of this innovation in communication will be widespread: additional resources will be allocated to ensure that everyone will be able to meet specified performance standards.

This approach to improving communication and organizational effectiveness sounds good in theory. But is it working? Jennifer O'Day (2007: 441) sounds a note of caution:

> Teachers and schools are constantly being bombarded by information and by demands to do something about that information – requests from parents, notices from the central office or federal and state departments, publishing companies, external advocates and programs, community groups, counselors, etc. In many schools, teachers' and students' work is subject to continual interruption as others try to thrust new information on them. What's worse, much of the information is irrelevant to the improvement of instruction and learning. It merely distracts attention and resources from what is supposed to be the main work of school personnel and students. Sifting through the morass to find what is likely to lead to improvement requires time, resources, and knowledge that school personnel may not

possess. Unable to make productive choices, some teachers and schools move chaotically from one demand or source of information to another, with insufficient focus and time to learn.

O'Day's account raises two key issues for those who seek to improve communication in complex organizations such as schools. The first concerns the need to start with an appreciation of the various challenges that confront teachers in the average working day. Research indicates that many teachers report being squeezed for time. As a result, they find it difficult to meet the learning needs of struggling students. Without time (and in some instances, additional professional training), the information generated by standardized tests will provide few usable insights into how the needs of individual students might be met. In such circumstances, teachers may respond very negatively to the introduction of performance indicators, viewing them as an instrument of managerial power, and nothing more.

The second issue concerns the characteristics of teachers' knowledge, including the information teachers already possess about student learning and the various factors that influence it. As a result of their experience working with students on a day-to-day basis, teachers acquire a rich storehouse of information about how best to teach in a particular content area, the difficulties students face in learning that content, and what is needed to enhance the progress of particular students. Teachers need opportunities to formalize, test and share this knowledge. Improvements in teaching and learning are more likely to occur when the production and mobilization of new information is a collaborative process in which teachers are recognized as active partners who work with administrators and formally trained researchers.

> **Stop!** How can information about the factors influencing quality performance at work be produced and communicated in ways that engage rather than alienate workers? To what other sectors might these findings be relevant?

Sources and further information

Krasas Rogers, J. (2001) 'There's no substitute: the politics of time transfer in the teaching profession', *Work and Occupations*, 28(1), pp. 64–90.

O'Day, J. (2007) 'Complexity, accountability, and school improvement', pp. 437–69 in A. Sadovnik (ed.), *Sociology of Education: A Critical Reader*, London: Routledge.

Thrupp, M. and Hursh, D. (2006) 'The limits of managerialist school reform: the case of target-setting in England and the USA', pp. 642–51 in H. Lauder, P. Brown, J.-A. Dillabough and A. H. Halsey (eds), *Education, Globalization and Social Change*, Oxford: Oxford University Press.

Note: This feature was written by David MacLennan, Assistant Professor, Thompson Rivers University, Canada.

concerned with making the organization more efficient, the critical theorist is more concerned with examining organizational communication, such as myths, metaphors and stories, as a source of power. Critical theorists also try to understand why organizational practices that maintain strong controls over workers are considered legitimate, and so are not resisted (Eisenberg and Goodall, 1997). Critical scholars of organizational communications therefore focus on the theme of management control, defined as:

> The dynamic communication process through which organizational stakeholders … struggle to maximize their stake in an organization. (Mumby, 2013: 4)

Organizational communication is thus studied in terms of hidden exercises of power and managerial influence. The metaphors of voice and discourse enable us to analyse the questions of who can speak, when and in what way. We need to consider communication as the expression or suppression of the voices of the organization's members. Morgan identifies a number of metaphors used to convey the perspectives of critical theorists (Morgan, 1980). We will consider the metaphors of culture, political system, language game and text/discourse in the next few pages.

Discourse analysis, inspired by Gramsci and Foucault, is a useful way of theorizing culture. Rather than seeing culture as something static and real that is common to all members of a nation or ethnic group, discourse analysis sees it as 'social processes operating in contested terrains in which different voices become more or less hegemonic in their offered interpretations of the world' (Yuval-Davis, 1997: 40). Organizational culture is a set of meanings, ideas and symbols that are shared by members of a collective and have evolved over time. Talking about culture, then, means 'talking about the importance for people of symbolism – rituals, myths, stories, and legends – and about the interpretation of events, ideas, and experiences that are influenced and shaped by the groups within which they live' (Alvesson and Billing, 1997: 104).

The critical theorists Alvesson and Billing (1997) argue that culture facilitates social life, but also includes elements of constraint and conservatism. It tends to freeze social reality in order to subordinate people to dominating ideas, beliefs and assumptions that are taken for granted. Wittgenstein's metaphor of a language game suggests that organizational activity is a game of words, thoughts and actions (Morgan, 1980). As individuals engage with their worlds, through specific codes and practices (using both verbal and non-verbal language), organizational realities arise as rule-governed symbolic structures. Language creates the organizational concepts that define the culture of an organization and give form to notions of control, delegation and rationality. Meetings, or 'technologies of power', are an example of the social reality created and controlled by management, which endorse and encourage certain understandings and feelings that reflect managerial interests and perspectives (Alvesson, 1996).

empirical approach: research that attempts to answer questions through a systematic collection and analysis of data

Alvesson's (1996) **empirical research** suggests that the meeting is one element of the ongoing creation and re-creation of the organization. Management of meaning is part of everyday leadership. Attention is placed on some things and not on others, and language is carefully chosen. One example of a simple, but powerful, word choice is the familiar 'them and us' concept being superseded by the use of 'we' and 'you'. During meetings, the phrase 'We did as you said' is frequently used. 'We' in this context is top management, and 'you' the collective workforce. This counteracts the idea that power is directed from the top downwards. It suggests that decisions are anchored in the workforce, and that top management is carrying out the wishes of the collective. 'We' is used to suggest a common identity among those present at the meeting; they are encouraged to consider themselves as part of the same unit, with common interests and objectives. As Frost puts it, 'Communication structures, channels, networks, and rules are avenues of power ... Thus the communication medium is never neutral' (Alvesson and Billing, 1997: 68).

Critical theory draws attention to the political and exploitative aspects of organizational life. This perspective seeks to expose the 'order' that interpretive theory seeks to understand, and functionalist theory to enhance, as superficial. Critical theorists suggest that, like other aspects of organizational life, the organizational communication process is complicated by organizational characteristics such as hierarchy and power relations, and by the fact that individual managers and non-managers have idiosyncrasies, abilities and biases. They argue that organizational communication is central to the other processes of power, leadership and decision making. Organizational communication involves more than providing employees with information about their employment and wider issues relating to the organization in which they work. It is as complex as human behaviour itself.

According to this perspective, every human act, both conscious and unconscious, contains information that is then interpreted by a receiver. The three notions associated with communications – behaviour, meaning and context – are synthesized in this definition of organizational communication: 'Both behaviours and symbols, generated either intentionally or unintentionally, occurring between and among people who assign meaning to them, within an organizational setting' (Byers, 1997: 4).

In modern organizations, symbolic power is particularly noticeable compared with technical and bureaucratic means of control. The management of meaning is regarded as symbolic action. The creation of a managerially biased social reality reduces the number of available variations in the way things can be perceived, when the possibilities of describing, understanding and evaluating workplace conditions and objectives are being negotiated:

> Generally dominance is manifested not in significant political acts but rather in the day-to-day, taken for granted nature of organizational life. Examples include privilege car parking allocation and separate spaces for eating and working. As such, the exercise of power and domination exists at a routine level, further protecting certain interests and allowing the order or organizational life to go largely unquestioned by its members. (Alvesson and Billing, 1997: 66)

Consequently, dominance is exercised chiefly by ensuring that the current reality in the organization is regarded as natural, rational, self-evident, problem-free, sensible and so on. Therefore, the power aspect is of crucial importance in organizational communication. Communication provides the means through which power can be exercised, developed, maintained and enhanced.

Communication and management

Now we have seen something of the different *perspectives* for studying organizational communications, it should not surprise us to find that the *function* of organizational communications is contested. Traditional approaches to organizational communication identify at least two functions of communication: to exchange information and to bring about change. Figure 11.1 illustrated the first function of communication, the process by which information is exchanged between a sender and a receiver. This function of organizational communication can be seen in studies of managers and their work. One classic study found that managers spend 80 per cent of their contact time on activities devoted exclusively to the transmission of information (Mintzberg, 1973). The second function of communication is to help those who manage the organization to bring about change, by persuading others to adopt a different work regime and/or behaviour.

Channels of communication

formal channels: a communication process that follows an organization's chain of command

informal channels: a communication process that follows unofficial means of communication, sometimes called 'the grapevine', usually based on social relations in which employees talk about work

genre: a term to describe the different kinds of writing and reading in the workplace, including reports, letters and memoranda

Communication theorists refer to **formal and informal channels** of communication in a work organization, both of which managers and employees use in order to exchange information. The three basic communication media – written, verbal and non-verbal – can be used in either of these types of channel. Formal channels are established by the organization and transmit messages relevant to job-related activities, using for example memos, voicemail, email and meetings. Informal channels, such as personal or social messages, contribute to the culture and social reality of an organization. Among those who have studied and researched these differences is Mikhail Bakhtin, a Russian literary and cultural critic. He was interested in language in actual use, the 'utterance', or primary speech genres. From these, the more complex 'secondary' genres of writing are derived.

In the workplace (as elsewhere), **genre** is the word used to indicate the different kinds of writing and reading that are required to complete the communication loop and ensure that efficient action is taken. Empirical studies of workplace writing reveal the complex social, cultural and institutional factors at play in the production of specific trends of writing (Freedman and Medway, 1994a). Freedman and Medway point to the interaction and interpersonal dynamics that are part of creating texts in an organization. The features of the text are often 'conventionalized by tacit agreement – the lore of the tribe' (Freedman and Medway, 1994b: 148). Written mission statements highlighting company 'green values', for example, can function as the social glue that helps an organization to establish its own culture. The interpersonal dynamics that surround and support the creation of texts in an organization reflect the levels of relative power, influence and access to information.

plate 37 Face-to-face communication might be more effective than sending an email.

Source: Getty Images

The verbal and non-verbal aspects of communication are inextricably linked. Even a verbal message on a computer-generated voice telephone voicemail system has a 'gender' and 'ethnicity' and so has a non-verbal aspect. Verbal communication ranges from a casual conversation between employees to the company president's speech transmitted to branch offices throughout the country. Face-to-face interaction is the most effective form of verbal communication when the sender wants to persuade or motivate the receiver. Research has found that face-to-face talk is preferred because it provides for the maximum amount of information to be transmitted during a communication episode. That is, it offers multiple information cues (through words, postures, facial expression and gestures), as well as the personal touch of 'being there'. Non-verbal cues may be organized into several categories: the environment, personal space, postures, gestures, facial expressions, eye behaviour, and tone and pitch of voice (Field and House, 1995).

Face-to-face interaction is considered to be the richest medium on the communication channel continuum. Recent research on face-to-face conversations confirms that individuals engage in these interactions to affirm themselves and express their relation to others. Conversations promote and share human knowledge (Mengis and Eppler, 2008). This approach is most suitable for non-routine messages, whereas routine messages use the poorest media: flyers, bulletins or general reports. Marshall McLuhan's popular phrase 'The medium is the message' refers to the idea that the sender's choice of communication channel transmits meaning beyond the message content. The symbolic meaning of choosing one medium over another may vary from one manager to another. For example, some people might see the use of email as a sign of professionalism and/or efficiency, while others might view it as impersonal and inappropriate. A research report by Neilson Online identifies social network sites as eclipsing email. Carmi Levy, technology analyst and journalist, concludes that email is yesterday's messaging platform. The social networking site Facebook, with 1.23 billion users in 2014, shows that the website can be vital for business as well as personal use.

IN THE EBOOK ACCESS THE OB IN FCOUS BOX ON 'THE $2-MILLION COMMA'.

One example of managerial insensitivity is the announcement on television that Canadian Airlines was shutting down: employees learned of their fate by listening to the national news. We must be sensitive to the meta-message, the larger message within which the smaller message is contained. The symbolic meaning of the selected communication medium should clarify rather than contradict the meaning found in the message content. Another example of a poor choice of medium is a memo sent to workers at the Women's Television Channel by their new employers. The first paragraph welcomed them to the company; the final paragraph informed them they would shortly receive dismissal notices.

The direction of communication

In formal organizations, communication flows downwards, upwards and horizontally (Figure 11.2). Vertical communications are the formal mechanisms established to disseminate information that involves the coordination of subordinates' work activities.

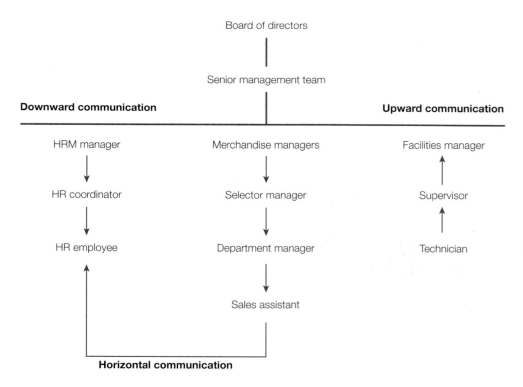

Figure 11.2 Downward, upward and horizontal communications in a retail store. HR, human resources; HRM, human resource management

Downward communication includes management directives, electronic newsletters, emails, telephone hotlines and corporate DVD programmes. In 1997, a North American survey of 2039 respondents in six industrial and service categories explored the state of communication in Canadian businesses. The discrepancy between senior managers' perception of how well they communicated with employees (61 per cent thought they did well) and the non-managerial employees' opinion of effective communication in the workplace (22 per cent thought the managers did well) highlights the difference between mainstream organizational behaviour prescriptions and reality (Robbins and Langton, 2001). A global survey of the International Association of Business Communicators highlighted the need for organizations to make significant changes in communication in order to connect with employees, in particular those of Generation Y (born between 1982 and 2000). Respondents, it was reported, wanted the opportunity to give feedback, collaborate and actively contribute to their organization. In the words of one precocious Generation Y participant, 'Most organizations do not give a chance for the younger generations to communicate effectively. You find now that younger generations have lots of ideas – really brilliant ideas actually. If management can find a way to tap the knowledge that is brought in by these young generations, it would bring a very big impact to the organization' (Reynolds et al., 2008).

VISIT THE *ONLINE RESOURCE CENTRE* AT HTTPS://HE.PALGRAVE.COM/COMPANION/BRATTON-WORK-AND-ORGANIZATIONAL-BEHAVIOUR3/ FOR MORE INFORMATION ON HOW MANAGERS COMMUNICATE IN THE WORKPLACE.

Upward communication in the workplace is underdeveloped in most forms, but employee surveys, reports from self-managed teams and various employee involvement arrangements are forms of upward communication.

Lateral communications among people at the same level in the organization are useful for increasing the coordination between individuals and departments.

grapevine: an unstructured and informal communication network founded on social relationships rather than organizational charts or job descriptions

The informal communication network, known as the **grapevine**, is formed and maintained by social relationships. Communication can flow across all levels and boundaries, and can use any or all of the channels available. The grapevine operates outside the usual bounds of the organization, and is also the main source of organizational narratives and other symbols of the organization's culture.

Leadership, persuasion and communication

As mentioned above, the second major function of communication is to bring about change, and hence communication is said to be one of the most critical skills for organizational leaders (Bratton et al., 2005). Leadership is defined as a process that brings about movement or change, and involves persuasion. Persuasive communication changes followers' behaviour when they accept the information; the information becomes part of their structure of beliefs about the workplace, and as a result it changes their opinions about reality. This is an integral element in the leadership process, and in turn in the creation of the culture of an organization, which serves to create a homogenous group who share ways of knowing, and interpret a range of symbolic activities in the same way.

The manager, or leader, should be aware, as a persuader, of the elements that can influence acceptance. Leadership theorists have emphasized the role of communication in developing an appropriate corporate culture and encouraging the acceptance of change among organizational members:

> Corporate culture ideas, meanings and norms [bring] about homogeneity and predictability in understanding, thinking and valuing among people. This is vital for the efficient functioning of complex large-scale

organizations. The need for smooth communication and the reduction of uncertainty and, relatedly, the importance attached to knowing the rules of the game, means a strong pressure towards conformity. (Alvesson and Billing, 1997: 107)

Exercising leadership depends on the use of verbal and non-verbal language, both words and behaviour, and communication style is linked to the notion of **rhetoric** (Witherspoon, 1997). Rhetoric, from the Greek word *rhetor* (speaker in the assembly), is the art of using speech to persuade. This involves the ability to motivate colleagues to take action rather than just accept arguments. Recent interest in the study of rhetoric by managers indicates an awareness of the importance of communication to leadership (Grint, 2001). Since almost 75 per cent of a manager's time is ostensibly involved in conversation, we may assume that most management is secured through talk, and therefore that most leadership is too (Stewart, 1967).

What kinds of conversation do managers have? It has been suggested that social order at any level (from family life through hospital discipline to international relations) is unthinkable without **negotiations**. In other words, order itself is better conceptualized as 'negotiated order', in so far as some form of negotiation is always critical to organizations. Barack Obama's 'A More Perfect Union' campaign speech made in March 2008 is considered to be one of his finest. He identified the contrasting experiences of races, recognized the underlying resentments of each, but was able to present himself as a unifying agent. The ability to change the opinions of those who disagree with you is the measure of a great rhetorician. Managers, and those aspiring to be organizational leaders, need to develop this skill.

Research into emotional intelligence in organizations concluded that effective leaders possess this quality to a high degree (Goleman, 1998). Empathy is the most easily recognized dimension of emotional intelligence, and is an important component of leadership for at least three reasons: the increasing use of teams, the rapid pace of globalization, and the growing need to retain talent. The social skill of managing leader–follower relationships is also closely linked to the powers of persuasion. Persuasiveness can be viewed as a social skill that is a component of emotional intelligence. Black contends that effective managerial communication involves taking responsibility for and ownership of the content (the message), ensuring recipients' understanding of the message, and knowing the organization's position on difficult issues and its rationale for decisions. To be competent, the leader-manager needs to create the right impact on her or his audience (Black, 1996).

Keith Grint (2001), a prominent researcher and writer in leadership, adopts classical rhetoric as his model to describe persuasive communication. People's ethos – which includes their perceived expertise on the topic, their credentials and their experience – contributes to their ability to persuade. Their expertise in how they speak also greatly influences listeners. This concerns issues such as speaking confidently and relatively quickly, using some technical language, and avoiding pauses ('erm' or 'uh') and hedges ('you know' and 'I guess'). Establishing trustworthiness and respect enables a communicator to be more effective. If listeners perceive that the communicator will not benefit personally from the proposal he or she is putting forward, and the communicator acknowledges that the opposing position has one or two positive elements, this helps to convince listeners of the reasonableness of the argument.

rhetoric: the management of symbols (such as a language) in order to encourage and coordinate social action. 'Rhetorical sensitivity' is the tendency for a speaker to adapt her or his messages to audiences to allow for the level of knowledge, ability level, mood or beliefs of the listener

negotiation: occurs whenever two or more conflicting parties attempt to resolve their divergent goals by redefining the terms of their interdependence

Source: Nick Tutton

plate 38 Organizations send employees to indoor climbing centres where they learn to solve communication problems and work as a team.

The message content is of course a critical feature of persuasive communication. If the speaker expects the audience to be resistant to the message, he or she must first present viewpoints that validate the audience's viewpoint, before presenting his or her own position. If the issue is highly emotive, a good alternative is the Rogerian structure of presenting arguments (Coe, 1990). This is appropriate if the leader wants to avoid threatening those who hold opposing views, since 'Rogerian persuasion basically aims at achieving consensus around a correct position. The objective is truth, not victory' (Coe, 1990: 397). Both classical and Rogerian rhetoric rely on emotional and logical appeals, which form Aristotle's three criteria of persuasiveness, as shown in Figure 11.3.

In organizational communication, it is often difficult to separate personal character and emotional appeal. Logical proof is seldom as effective as Aristotle maintains. This does not mean that appeals to rationality – to the 'truth' and to the 'facts' – are irrelevant. Far from it, they are crucial elements of persuasion, but they are not in and of themselves sufficient to persuade others on each and every occasion. This is blatantly clear when scientific 'experts' disagree on the 'facts', such as in the case of genetically modified foods or global warming. Effective communication involves the '4S' model, that is, a combination of speech (content), speaker, situation (context) and spectators (audience) (Figure 11.4) and also the active roles of individuals and groups who socially shape the contents and contexts, rather than merely responding to them (Grint, 2001). We must consider the rhetorical context of the communication process as including the social and collective forms of organization (that is, the culture) that generate persuasive interpretations of the message (Figure 11.4).

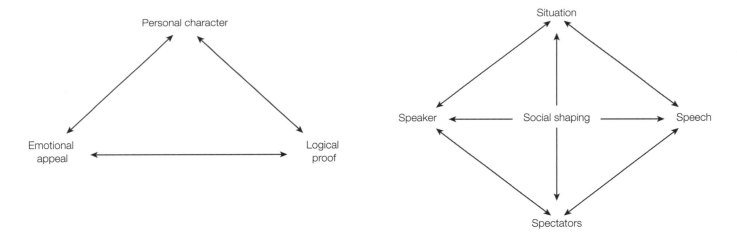

Figure 11.3 Aristotle's model of rhetoric

Source: *The Arts of Leadership*, Grint (2001) Fig. 9.1 p. 367. Used by permission of Oxford University Press

Figure 11.4 The immutable 4S model of speech making

The rhetorical context of meetings designed to convey information, which was studied by Alvesson (1996), reveals the techniques of power and discipline that are used in effective managerial communication. The seemingly neutral conveying of information and use of language can reinforce asymmetrical power relations and contribute to the disciplinary function, which is so central to management and to many other manifestations of organizational culture. Symbolically charged activities, events and words condense important ideas and assumptions, and convey them forcefully to the audience. Using 'we' and 'you' in this specific situation may have considerable rhetorical appeal. Managers are therefore agents of power, creating or reproducing shared meanings, ideas and values through acts of communication, which suspend social reality, or at least counteract an open, questioning approach to how it should be negotiated. The importance of communication is further discussed in Chapter 18 on managing change.

Communication and cultural diversity

With the globalization of markets, and an increase in mergers and acquisitions, the workplace is seeing greater interaction and communication among peoples of different cultures and experiences (Guirdham, 2011; Kidd et al., 2001). The multicultural nature of organizations is an indisputable thriving reality and, more now than ever before, people interact with others – people whose demographic profile is different from their own (Guirdham, 2011: 4). It can be argued that the way in which businesses manage cross-cultural communication between colleagues will determine their economic survival and competitiveness in the global marketplace. Managers who have a systematic understanding of the cultural and organizational dynamics of cross-cultural communication will enhance organizational effectiveness and performance. Managers and researchers need to guard against ethnocentrism, the tendency to judge other cultures by the standards of one's own.

VISIT THE *ONLINE RESOURCE CENTRE* AT HTTPS://HE.PALGRAVE.COM/COMPANION/BRATTON-WORK-AND-ORGANIZATIONAL-BEHAVIOUR3/ FOR FURTHER DETAILS ON THE IMPORTANCE OF BEING SENSITIVE TO DIFFERENT COMMUNICATION PRACTICES WHEN TRAVELLING ABROAD OR WORKING IN GLOBAL CORPORATIONS.

Diversity in organizations

Narrow definitions of diversity emphasize race, ethnicity and gender. As we discussed in Chapter 9, intersectional analysis starts from the premise that individuals live in multiple, layered identities derived from social relations and history (Bagilhole, 2009). Broader definitions of diversity tend to focus on issues of 'racism, sexism, heterosexism, classism, ableism, and other forms of discrimination at the individual, identity group, and system levels' (Nkomo and Cox, 1999: 88). Essentially, scholars are referring to 'diversity in identities' based on social and demographic groups: 'A mixture of people with different group identities within the same social system' (Nkomo and Cox, 1999: 88).

So the concept of identity is at the core of understanding diversity in organizations. This has implications for effective communication in the workplace. Studies of work teams reveal that people's identification with subgroups (*micro-identities* in the organizational context) takes precedence over their identification with the organization as a whole (their *macro-identity*). The ability of people to work together in teams composed of members from different group identities may be hampered by the consequences of group identification (Nkomo and Cox, 1999).

The interpersonal communications model discussed earlier in this chapter (see Figure 11.1) ignores different cultures and how culture impacts on the communication process (Tan, 1998). Critics of this linear communication model argue that people communicate differently because of their culture, their gender and how they have learned to perceive the world. Cultures differ in both their verbal and their non-verbal communications. A culturally diverse workforce has the potential to improve organizational effectiveness. It can provide improved decision making, creativity and innovation, and marketing knowledge to different types of consumer, all of which benefits the global organization. Employees must overcome their reluctance to communicate with co-workers from other cultural groups.

Cultural identity and history also shape language. This observation was illustrated by an incident involving the actor Benedict Cumberbatch. Interviewed on a

US television channel, the British actor used the word 'coloured' to describe black actors. Harker (2015: 30) observed that those criticizing the actor should take a step back because 'it wasn't so long ago that "coloured" was a perfectly respectful and polite term'. However, the term 'coloured', he suggests, makes a negative acknowledgement of people's skin tone and has links to racial segregation in apartheid South Africa and to the British colonialist era, and to the 'second-class status with which "coloured people" will always be associated' (p. 30). In culturally diverse societies, the Cumberbatch incident highlights the need, both outside and inside the workplace, for correct language that is accurate and does not cause offence.

A Canadian study of cultural diversity in Toronto's major hotels found that language barriers made it difficult for managers to give non-English-speaking employees meaningful feedback to help them improve their jobs (McShane and von Glinow, 2012). Even when people speak the same language, interpreting voice intonation can be problematic. In some cultures, the tone changes depending on the context, such as home, a social situation or work. Using a personal, informal style in a situation where a more formal style is expected affects the meta-meaning behind the message.

There was considerable research on racio-ethnicity and gender following the passing of equal opportunities and antidiscrimination legislation in the USA and Britain in the late 1960s and early 1970s. Taken as a whole, these studies suggest that black individuals and women face discrimination in terms of both access to and their treatment in organizations. However, it is important to note that assimilation theory underlies the questions studied and the solutions that are proposed. The successful integration of racial minorities and white women into organizations requires their loss of identity: they must adapt to the norms and behaviours of the dominant group.

The theory and research are dominated by dichotomous thinking about identity, that is, thinking that divides people into two opposed groups, such as black versus white, Anglo versus Latino, or male versus female. Oppositional thinking implies not only that there is a difference, but also that there is a hierarchy in which one group is superior to the other, the dominant group obtaining its privilege by suppressing the other group. In much of the research on diversity in organizations, the legitimacy and basic values of the organization are not questioned. Organizations are regarded as fundamentally sound and neutral sites. However, we argue that it is essential for attention to be paid to what sustains and maintains the pattern of power relations in organizations. Communication plays an essential role in the establishment and maintenance of these power relations.

Discourse theory and analysis, referred to above, also covers the study of all types of written text and spoken interaction (both formal and informal), with particular attention to the functions served by language. It asks how certain sorts of talk and writing can accomplish particular goals, such as exclusions, scapegoating or justifications. It is important to study the language we use to talk about diversity in identities because, as one researcher points out, 'Language is so structured to mirror power relations that often we can see no other way of being, and it structures ideology so that it is difficult to speak both in and against it' (Parker, 1992: 100).

IN THE EBOOK ACCESS THE **CRITICAL INSIGHT** ON 'LANGUAGE IN THE CONSTRUCTION OF SELF'.

In the globalized marketplace, international communication across political or national borders is an integral part of business negotiations. Success can depend on the implicit and explicit nature of the communication process (both verbal and non-verbal). The informational context and the degree of background data that has to be transmitted vary from culture to culture.

high-context culture: a culturally sanctioned style of communication that assumes high levels of shared knowledge and so uses very concise, sometimes obscure, speech

low-context culture: a culturally sanctioned style of communication that assumes low levels of shared knowledge and so uses verbally explicit speech

The anthropologist E. T. Hall developed a useful system for understanding the communication implications of culture (Hall, 1976). He classified cultures on a scale that ranges from '**high context**' to '**low context**'. (These are also sometimes described as individualistic [low-context] and collectivist [high-context] cultures.) In low-context societies, people are less able to agree or solve disputes without resorting to written contracts or litigation than they are in high-context ones. Explicit written and verbal messages are the norm in, for example, the USA, Canada, Scandinavia, Germany and Switzerland. High-context cultures emphasize collaboration and personal relationships as important aspects of doing business. Informal and unwritten contracts are the norm, together with the non-verbal language that surrounds the explicit message. This happens for example in Korea, China, Japan and Arab countries.

These two types of culture also differ in their patterns of time usage. Low-context cultures are characterized by monochronic time patterns. This is a linear and compartmentalized view of time. These cultures value quick responses and a direct approach to the issue, without the use of much background information. High-context cultures tend to work with polychronic time, which is more contextually based and flexible. Oral and written communication is less direct and more circular in nature. Discussion in business meetings may go off at tangents; the direct approach, to refocus on the agenda, can be considered rude. In resolving conflicts in cross-cultural communications, all parties involved must not only know about their own culture, but also demonstrate a willingness to accept differences in other cultures.

IN THE EBOOK ACCESS THE **OB IN FOCUS** BOX ON 'HUMOUR IN THE WORKPLACE'.

A variety of gestures are used only in certain cultures, or their meaning changes between cultures. In Canada and the UK, for example, nodding the head up and down signals 'yes' and shaking it back and forth means 'no'. In Bulgaria, parts of Greece, Turkey, Iran and Bengal, it is the reverse. The gesture where the thumb and forefinger form a simple circle means 'OK' or 'everything is fine' in Canada, the UK and the USA, but in France it means zero or worthless, and in Japan it is the signal for money. In many other countries, it is considered a sexually rude gesture (Field and House, 1995). Canadians are taught to maintain eye contact with the speaker to show interest and respect, yet this is considered rude to some Asian and Middle Eastern people, who are taught to show respect by looking down when a supervisor or older person is talking to them.

Gender and communication: 'She said, he said'

Just as culture affects interpretation, so research has demonstrated that gender plays a role in influencing what is considered to be the appropriate communication medium. Gender, however, is a constantly evolving concept, and through social interaction not only does gender influence communication, but communication also constitutes gender (DeFrancisco and Palczewski, 2014). The work of Tannen (1990, 2001) examines the conversational styles of women and men in the workplace – how they're the same, how they're different – and how the language of everyday conversation works – or fails to work – to create and maintain relationships in the family. There appear to be important differences between the conversational styles of men and women, which can be summarized in terms of 'report' and 'rapport', respectively (Robbins and Langton, 2001).

The desire to create a favourable impression on others is a basic survival impulse in organizations. Andrew DuBrin (2011) examines this theme through the concept of 'impression management', which he defines as 'the process by which people control the impression others form of them' (p. 1). Impression management can hide deficiencies, but the concept is relevant here because it helps us to contrast the communication tactics adopted by women and men. DuBrin has summarized the alleged differences in communication styles used by men and women (Table 11.1).

Table 11.1 Selective communicating styles used by men and women

Men	Women
Use conversation primarily to preserve independence and status by demonstrating knowledge and skill	Use talk to build rapport, listen carefully, be supportive
More direct, seek to build a positive impression by being decisive	Emphasize politeness, say 'Sorry', even when unnecessary
Talk a lot in meetings, create positive impression by being dominant	Speak less than men in meetings, create positive impression by nodding and being reflective
Adopt an intimidating stance when facing differences, to 'win' argument	Adopt a conciliatory stance when confronting differences, to maintain relationships

Source: DuBrin (2011: 49–50)

These contrasting conversation styles are only stereotypes, that is, generalizations about the behaviour of women and men, but they may also be useful for judging gender behaviours. DuBrin's work resonates with Judy Wajcman's research, which contrasted the qualities that women [and men] bring to management. Adjectives used to describe the male style include 'directive', 'decisive' and 'aggressive'. In contrast, adjectives used to describe the female style are 'collaborative', 'cooperative', 'caring' (1998: 66). However, Wajcman also acknowledges the difficulties of conducting research in this area because all managers 'use the language of the human resource management model' (1998: 71). A plausible explanation of why men and women use different conversation styles is that men *typically* see conversation as a tool: they use it to exchange information, accomplish a task, offer advice or defend or advance their status and position. For many men, conversations are primarily a means to preserve independence. On the other hand, it is suggested that, stereotypically, women talk in order to nurture, support and empathize. Women speak and hear a language of cooperation, connection and intimacy.

Research suggests that effective communicators, both women and men, adjust to the situation and use a variety of talk strategies in the workplace. Janet Holmes (2006) for example, observes:

> Effective communicators ... typically draw from a very wide and varied discursive repertoire, ranging from normatively 'feminine' to normatively 'masculine' ways of talking, and ... they skilfully select their discursive strategies in response to the particular interactional context. (Holmes, 2006: 1)

There is also evidence that female managers can mitigate the negative effects of being in a 'masculine' role by being able to perceive the non-verbal emotions of their subordinates. In addition, male managers who were emotionally perceptive garnered more employee satisfaction (Byron, 2008).

plate 39 Non-verbal messages can be a very powerful mode of conveying meaning.

Source: Getty Images

Studies have also indicated that female managers use an open communication style that centres on cooperation and request when dealing with personnel problems. However, male managers use their position in the organization's chain of command to resolve the problem. Interestingly, they tend to use their position of power when dealing with female employees, whereas when dealing with male employees they use communication strategies.

From a managerial perspective, gender issues play a part in the better utilization of human resources. An awareness of sex discrimination and conservative gender patterns enables the recruiting, keeping, placing, training and promoting of labour to be carried out in a more rational way. Embracing and welcoming diversity, and validating the viewpoints of women and men, may facilitate organizational learning and creativity. It is argued that managers need to address organizational cultures, structures and practices in terms of gender. We have used the term 'diverse' to convey cultural and gender differences between colleagues in a company, and cognitive and relational differences between Eastern and Western cultures. However, diversity is itself a contested term.

Communication and paradox

Contradictions and paradoxes are found everywhere in the organizational communication literature. The case studies on employee involvement arrangements in worksites reveal tensions in communication and employee empowerment practices. The term 'paradox' comes from the Greek words *para* and *dokein,* and means to reconcile two apparently conflicting views (Krippendorff, 1985). Four main types of paradox are apparent in management practices to improve organizational performance: structure, agency, identity and power (Stohl and Cheney, 2001).

Although work teams are intended to enhance productivity by empowering workers to make decisions, senior management make the 'really important decisions', for example on investment in new technology. In other words, workers can participate in learning, innovating and voicing their opinions using only the channels established by the organization.

The idea of agency refers to an individual's sense of being, and a feeling that she or he can or does make a difference (Giddens, 1984). A conflict may arise if self-managed work teams rely on the active subordination of team members to the will of the team. Members must retain their creative individuality while accepting 'our way'. Consequently, workers may become ambivalent and hesitant about participating in such a regime.

The paradox of identity addresses issues of boundaries, space and the divide between the in-group and the out-group. The paradox involves commitment to the group, embracing learning, discussion, diversity and difference. However, 'commitment is expected to equal agreement' (Stohl and Cheney, 2001: 380). Voicing an alternative view is seen as lack of commitment. The workers must comply with organizational priorities.

The paradox of power centres on issues of leadership, access to resources, opportunities for an alternative voice and the shaping of employee behaviour. It is argued that managers must meet the challenge of nurturing creativity and innovation in an atmosphere of 'Be an independent thinker, just as I have commanded you.'

The area of organizational communications is part of the broader field of organizational behaviour studies. In this chapter, we have explored a body of literature that many standard organizational behaviour texts have previously neglected. The nature of communication and the links between communication, power and decision making suggest that metaphors, cultural diversity, gender and rhetorical adroitness deserve greater attention in management theory and practice.

Chapter summary

- We have explained that the nature of the communication process established in the organization reflects the management style, degree of employee participation, culture and efficiency of the workplace. A knowledge of theories clarifies our understanding of organizational communications and enables us to explain a variety of practical issues, such as where the idea of the organization originated and what motivates people to work.

- It is important not to give one theory prominence over another. The three major perspectives for understanding organizational communications – functionalist, interpretivist and critical – allow us to comprehend the central role that communications has in the management process. The metaphors used to describe the perspectives – for example, organizations as machines and learning organizations – enhance our ability to view communications as not just being about the transmission and exchange of information in the context of organizational efficiency, but rather as being central to the other processes of power, leadership and decision making.

- We have emphasized that individuals engage with their world through specific codes and practices (verbal, non-verbal and written language). Language creates the organizational concepts that define the culture of an organization and give form to notions of control, delegation and rationality. Meetings are an example of the management of meaning. The choice of media, interaction and personal dynamics is part of the creation of texts within an organization, which in turn contributes to the establishment of its culture.

- The material reviewed in this chapter illustrates that managers are aware of the importance of persuasive communication in their role as negotiators. The growth of teams, globalization and the need to retain employees require managers to acquire expertise as accomplished presenters of rational arguments. A knowledge of the rhetorical context of the communication process enables the manager to create a managerially biased social reality.

- The chapter went on to explain how an understanding of the cultural and organizational dynamics of cross-cultural communications will enhance organizational effectiveness and business performance. E. T. Hall provides a useful system for understanding the communication implications of culture, both verbal and non-verbal.

- Research has revealed differences between the conversational styles of men and women. As managers, women try to develop *rapport* with colleagues, whereas men often *report* information or problems. It is important to embrace and welcome diversity in the organization to facilitate creativity and encourage the learning community. However, there are paradoxes tied up with the concepts of individual, micro- and macro-identities, and these might inhibit full participation in the organization. Although workers might apparently be encouraged to be creative, the organization typically places limitations on where, how and when they can speak.

IN THE EBOOK ACCESS **WEB BASED ASSIGNMENTS** TO APPLY YOUR LEARNING.

Chapter review questions

1 Explain the difference between a transmission model of communication and an exchange model.
2 If communication is so central to the management process, why do managers often fail to communicate effectively to others in the organization?
3 To what extent does electronic transmission affect communications?

4 What kind of communication skills should managers concentrate on?
5 How important is the context in explaining the success or failure of particular forms and styles of communication?
6 What is non-verbal communication, what part does it play in organizational settings, and does it vary between cultures?
7 In a social media world, is face-to-face communication important in a modern organization? Why?

Further reading

Baier, K. (2008) 'Diversity dialogue', *Communication World*, September–October, pp. 40–1.

Coupland, C., Brown, A. D., Daniels, K. and Humphreys, M. (2008) 'Saying it with feeling: analysing speakable emotions', *Human Relations*, 61(3), pp. 327–53.

DeFrancisco, V. P. and Palczewski, C. H. (2014) *Gender in Communication: A Critical Introduction* (2nd edn), Thousand Oaks, CA: Sage.

Eisenberg, E. M. and Goodall, H. L. (2007) *Organizational Communication: Balancing Creativity and Constraint* (5th edn), New York: St Martin's Press.

Goodley, S. (2012) 'HBOS executives "threatened" colleagues who questioned risk-taking', *The Guardian*, October 30. Available at: www.theguardian.com/business/2012/oct/30/hbos-whistle blower-threats-risk-taking (accessed February 10, 2015).

Guirdham, M. (2011) *Communicating Across Cultures at Work* (3rd edn), Basingstoke: Palgrave Macmillan.

Holmes, J. (2006) *Gendered Talk at Work*, Oxford: Blackwell.

Martin, J. and Nakayama, T. (2007) *Intercultural Communication in Contexts* (4th edn), Mountain View, CA: Mayfield.

Morgan, G. (1980) 'Paradigms, metaphors, and puzzle solving in organization theory', *Administrative Science Quarterly*, 25, pp. 605–22.

Mumby, D. K. (2013) *Organizational Communication: A Critical Approach*, Thousand Oaks, CA: Sage.

Reynolds, L., Campbell Bush, E. and Geist, R. (2008) 'The Gen Y imperative', *Communication World*, March–April, pp. 19–22.

Rosethorn, H. and Frem, A. (2010) *Harnessing the Power of Employee Communication*, London: CIPD.

Chapter case study: Cancelling Casual Friday at Sydney's CLD Bank

The setting

Banks are currently facing extremely difficult political and economic conditions. Following the 2008 global financial crisis, David Viniar, Goldman Sachs's chief financial officer, said that market conditions remained 'dangerous'. Most venerable banks have only survived by huge government bail-outs. Government interventions, however, draw criticism from politicians about how they do business. They question a business model that relies on rewarding top performers handsomely. Other criticisms focus on high-risk behaviour and on whether US and European banks should have so much invested in Asian banks. With so many people losing their life savings and pensions, bank executives have been the targets in the populist backlash too. Stones thrown through the windows of Fred Goodwin, former CEO of the Royal Bank of Scotland, in Edinburgh, UK, are an example of public anger and vilification.

Recent trends have shown, in the first quarter of 2014, improved revenue for banks, but the longer-term outlook remains fragile. In 2006, banks made an average return on equity of 17 per cent. To return to double digits, banks will have to cut costs by well over $100 million for every $100 billion of assets they hold.

The problem

The head office of CLD Bank, one of the largest banking and financial services organizations in the world, is located in London, UK. The bank's global network comprises around 8900 branches in 72 countries in Europe, the Asia-Pacific region, the Americas, the Middle East and Africa. The bank brands itself as 'the world's caring bank'. In Australia, the CLD Bank Group offers a full range of financial services through a network of 34 branches. CLD Bank's employee policies aim to attract and motivate talented people who have the drive and enthusiasm to find innovative ideas to fulfil the needs of the bank's customers. CLD Bank's values include placing great importance on respecting each other and embracing ideas, cultures and abilities.

Ian Green is the branch manager at CLD Bank located on George Street, Sydney, Australia, having been transferred from a branch in London, UK. He came to the branch just 3 months ago with a dynamic reputation based on efficiency and 'getting things done'.

At the regular team leaders' meeting, chaired by Ian Green, Jenny Gibson mentioned the upcoming Halloween festivities and the recent tradition for bank employees to wear costumes and offer candies to customers. This practice, and what is known as 'Casual Fridays', when staff members are permitted to wear jeans and casual apparel, although not as widely celebrated in Australia as it is in North America, is popular among the largely young employees at the branch. Both practices were introduced by the previous manager, a Canadian, 5 years ago.

Ian Green, however, said both practices were inappropriate and unprofessional. Several team leaders spoke out in favour of the practice and said how popular the tradition had become. After a short discussion, Ian said he appreciated their input but, 'There is a widely held perception that banks have become too cavalier, and the wearing of casual clothes doesn't help to counter that view,' he said. Hence he would be sending out a memo cancelling the practice. Two days later, the following memo was sent to each team leader for comment before it was due to be distributed to every branch employee:

DRAFT

DATE: October 15, 2014
TO: All Staff Members
FROM: Ian Green, Branch Manager
SUBJECT: CANCEL CASUAL FRIDAY AND HALLOWEEN

I am sorry to inform you that CLD Bank can no longer condone the continuation of 'Casual Friday'. Beginning November 1, ALL staff will dress in a professional manner every working day.

Also it has been decided that the Halloween festivities, for example wearing costumes and eating candies, will no longer happen at the end of the month.

In these troubled times, it is important for us all to remember that we need to conduct ourselves in a professional manner at all times.

When Jenny Gibson received a copy of the memo, she discussed it with another team leader whom she could trust: 'I don't think Ian is aware how important Casual Friday and the "Mischief Night" office party are to team morale,' she said. 'Ian would certainly benefit if he developed his humour skills,' added her colleague. 'I'm going to see him tomorrow to try to persuade him to change his mind,' said Jenny Gibson.

The task

Read the OB in Focus entitled Humour in the Workplace, which can be found at www.palgrave.com/bratton-ob. Working individually or in groups, prepare some notes that Jenny Gibson could use for her meeting with Ian Green, and address the following questions:

- What is the value of humour in the workplace?
- If Jenny fails to convince Ian not to cancel Casual Friday, can you suggest any improvements to the memo that need to be made before it is distributed to the staff?

Sources and further information

Crawford, C. B. (1994) 'Theory and implications regarding the utilization of strategic humor by leaders', *Journal of Leadership Studies*, 1, pp. 53–68.

Hayes, J. (2014) 'Communicating change', pp. 212–32 in *The Theory and Practice of Change Management*, Basingstoke: Palgrave Macmillan.

Romero, E. and Pescosolido, A. (2008) 'Humor and group effectiveness', *Human Relations*, 61(3), pp. 395–418.

www.halloween-australia.com for comments on Halloween in Australia.

Note: The case study is fictitious and was written by Carolyn Forshaw, formerly of Thompson Rivers University, Canada.

IN THE EBOOK ACCESS AN **OB IN FILM** BOX THAT USES *BABEL* (2005) TO ILLUSTRATE THE NATURE, CAUSES AND REPERCUSSIONS OF MISCOMMUNICATION AND TO ACCESS **AN INTERACTIVE QUIZ** TO TEST YOUR UNDERSTANDING.

chapter 12
Leadership

Key concepts

- behaviour perspective
- charismatic leadership
- contingency perspective
- distributed leadership
- glass ceiling
- integrative approach
- leadership
- management
- primal leadership
- shared leadership
- substitutes for leadership
- trait perspective
- transactional leadership
- transformational leadership

Chapter outline

- Introduction
- The nature of organizational leadership
- Leadership versus management
- Traditional leadership theories
- Contemporary leadership theories
- Power, gender and cross-cultural issues
- Evaluating leadership: is leadership important?
- Summary and end-of-chapter features
- Chapter case study: Hitting the glass ceiling at Hotoke, Japan

Chapter learning outcomes

After completing this chapter, you should be able to:
1 Explain the meaning of leadership and how it differs from management
2 Explain the different perspectives on studying organizational leadership
3 Explain whether effective leadership has positive performance outcomes

introduction

Great leaders ignite passion and inspire us to bring about change. Nelson Mandela, who died while we were writing this new edition, was, in every sense of its meaning, a leader. As a politician, he was, wrote Andrew Rawnsley (2013), 'the personification of the struggle against apartheid who inspired millions to take up his people's cause as their own, the father of his nation, a global icon, a conscience for the world, a legend in his own lifetime'. Leadership in work organizations is associated with vision and change too – but management with something less. For more than three decades, mainstream management literature had shown a preference for, and an interest in, 'leadership' that reflected a desire to move away from the 'command-and-control' systems and style associated with management. In 2004, when the Royal Bank of Scotland's Chief Executive Officer, Sir Fred Goodwin, was knighted 'for services to banking', it was fashionable to elevate leadership over management. Stripped of his knighthood in 2012, Fred Goodwin once revelled in his nickname 'Fred the Shred', which referred to his leadership role in cost cutting and job purges. More recently, revelations about the behaviour of former Co-operative Bank chairman, the Reverend Paul Flowers, has added to the public intolerance and disapproving perception of corporate leaders. Now, it seems, leadership is out, and management is in.

Source: © A-Shropshire-Lad

plate 40 Great leaders such as Nelson Mandela ignite passion and inspire us to bring about change.

leadership: influencing, motivating and enabling others to contribute towards the effectiveness and success of the organizations of which they are members

Giving evidence to members of the British Parliament Treasury Select Committee in February 2009, Fred Goodwin gave a 'profound and unqualified apology' for all the distress caused by the banking and financial crisis. Other former British bank executives, including Andy Hornby, CEO of HBOS, Dennis Stevenson, chairman of HBOS, and Tom McKillop, chairman of the Royal Bank of Scotland, also gave public apologies. Similar acts of atonement occurred when US banking executives gave evidence to the Senate Committee. When asked what went wrong, Goodwin said, 'The dilemma has always been it's a highly competitive landscape and many of the practices have come from the United States' (Farrell, 2009). In mid-2013, Paul Flowers quit his £132,000-a-year job as the bank disclosed a £1.5 billion capital shortfall. Questioned about the bank's conduct by the Treasury Select Committee chairman, Andrew Tyrie, Flowers did not know even 'very basic' details of the bank's finances, which raised questions about his level of competence as a 'leader'. Amid the age of austerity and falling living standards, the incompetence, reckless behaviour and perceived excesses of recent years have brought corporate leadership under the public microscope. This has led to some arguing that corporate leaders are no longer highly regarded or viewed as wise, neutral stewards of the UK economy (Stewart, 2015b).

How did the Royal Bank of Scotland and other European and US bank leaders not see the crisis coming? Laid-off workers in the banking sector know to their cost that poor leadership has consequences. So do the thousands of retirees and shareholders who lost their savings, pensions and investments when the Royal Bank of Scotland recorded losses of £28 billion, the biggest in UK corporate history, in February 2009. The scale of the British and US banking crisis and the reckless behaviour of its top leadership may surpass that of the US company Enron, which collapsed in May 2006, as the most analysed case study of leadership failure in corporate history.

The public atonement by bankers and utilities executives may be good political theatre, but recent corporate events emphasize that **leadership** and 'managership' is more than a rhetorical issue. British, Irish, Icelandic and US bankers did everything that leaders should do: exhibit vision, innovate and take risks. Their behaviour created what one British writer described as the 'buccaneer culture' of trading and banking (Kay, 2009). Tracing the start of the downward slide in the reputation of corporate leaders back to the 'naked capitalism' of the 1990s, John Cridland, director of Britain's employers' group the Confederation of British Industry, said that each leader must now 'act as the champion of consumers if [business] is to begin the generation-long process of rebuilding a reputation battered by failures' (Elliott, 2013b).

The past limitations of 'managership' now seem like virtues, with rigidity recast as 'meticulous processing', and risk aversion as prudence. Over the last century, there has been a plethora of research and scholarship devoted to 'leadership' and 'leaders'. Much of the debate is framed by a familiar conception of the subject: the effective leader is a hero possessing a variety of traits or attributes, competencies and charismatic powers that enable him or her (mostly it is a him) to bring about transformative effects (Wood and Case, 2006).

Not surprisingly, a key question asked by researchers and practitioners alike is 'What makes an effective leader?' Some suggest that one factor is the charisma and ability of an individual to inspire others to fulfil the visions and goals of the organization. Others emphasize that the leadership of an organization is shared, a collective phenomenon rather than a singular one: every leader needs competent followers, and good followers also perform leadership roles when needed (Lussier and Achua, 2015). Others suggest that organizations have had too much leadership and might need better management (Mintzberg, 2004). Still others posit that effective leadership is about embedding values and principles in the organization so that followers can respond rapidly and confidently to new situations (Moody-Stuart, 2014). More critical writers suggest that leadership behaviours are associated with the different levels of 'masculine' or 'feminine' values held by their followers (Mustafa and Lines, 2014). Leadership studies potentially offer a variety of explanations, including personal attributes, situational or contingencies and the role of co-workers or followers.

This chapter examines the different ways in which academics have defined organizational leadership, and the difference between leadership and management. We explain the different perspectives on understanding leadership, and conclude by assessing the evidence on whether 'good' leadership can improve organizational performance.

The nature of organizational leadership

Leadership has been studied since the emergence of civilization. The first serious attempt to develop a theory of leadership can be found in Plato's *The Republic*, 2000 years ago (Grint, 1997). In contemporary literature, leadership has acquired extraordinary importance to work organizations concerned with developing a 'strong' culture and building high-performance work systems. Over the last decade, voluminous articles on leadership have been published in English-language management journals. Originally made over 50 years ago, Burns' (1978: 259) observation that 'the concept of leadership eludes us or turns up in another form to taunt us again with its slipperiness and complexity' seems equally true today. The vast amount of contemporary scholarship has not resulted in a consensus on the substantive phenomenon itself, and the jury is still out on the effectiveness of leadership.

VISIT THE *ONLINE RESOURCE CENTRE* AT HTTPS://HE.PALGRAVE.COM/COMPANION/BRATTON-WORK-AND-ORGANIZATIONAL-BEHAVIOUR3/ TO READ MORE ON ORGANIZATIONAL LEADERSHIP.

Most authors begin by acknowledging the complexity and ambiguity of the concept of leadership. Part of the problem is that the word itself carries unrelated connotations that create ambiguity. This is because terms such as 'authority', 'management' and 'supervision' are used to describe similar phenomena. Indeed, the overlap between leadership and management is a common theme among practitioners and academics alike, and the terms are often used interchangeably. While we can define leadership and management as being two distinct roles, it is stating the obvious to observe that they can potentially coexist in the same individual. A manager is a person who has a formal title and authority, whereas a leader is a person who has the ability and opportunity to influence others and may be either a manager or non-manager. A follower is a person who is being influenced by a leader and may be a manager or non-manager (Lussier and Achua, 2015). As leadership theorist Gary Yukl rightly suggests, 'a person can be a leader without being a manager and a person can be a manager without leading' (2013: 6).

Leadership as a concept permeates the theory and practice of management. It has been conceptualized as a matter of personality, as particular behaviour, as a matter of contingency, as a position, as the focus of shared influence processes, and as combinations of these variables. Kouzes and Posner note, 'The best leaders are simply the best learners' (2012: 38). They 'teach, coach, and guide others to align their actions with the shared values of the organization' (p. 90). For Allio (2013), the primary role of leaders is to develop a culture that enables followers to coalesce around the shared purpose of the organization.

Most popular definitions of organizational leadership reflect the assumption that it involves a process whereby an individual exerts an influence upon others in an organizational context. For example, House et al. (1999: 184) define leadership as:

> The ability of an individual to influence, motivate and enable others to contribute toward the effectiveness and success of the organization.

The notion of influence and process is central to Gary Yukl's (2013: 23) definition:

> Leadership is the process of influencing others to understand and agree about what needs to be done and how to do it, and the process of facilitating individual and collective efforts to accomplish shared objectives.

Yukl's definition, while emphasizing many aspects of 'people skills', tends to focus on the dynamics and surface features of leadership as a process of social influence. The various definitions have, however, not produced a consensus about the concept. As Grint (2005: 17) observes, the disagreement falls into four domains as leadership is conceptualized as *person*, *result*, *position* and *process*. This chapter focuses upon the last of these, the notion that leadership is a process, but also we explore *what process* of leadership might be viable and whether it can reside in individuals and groups within the organization.

More critical accounts of leadership tend to focus on the hierarchical forms to which it gives rise: power relationships and gender dominance. Here, leadership is viewed broadly as a dialectical process, in which an individual persuades others to do something they would not otherwise do. Leadership is socially constructed through complex social interactions between leaders and followers in a specific context, and is equated with power. Figure 12.1 depicts leadership as a relational phenomenon, which resides in the context, and implies that a leader affects and is affected by other employees or followers and the situation in which she or he operates. The context refers to anything from global economic and political forces to the specific way a task is designed. It is not only constantly changing, but also shapes the other two parts of the leadership equation (see also Figure 1.3).

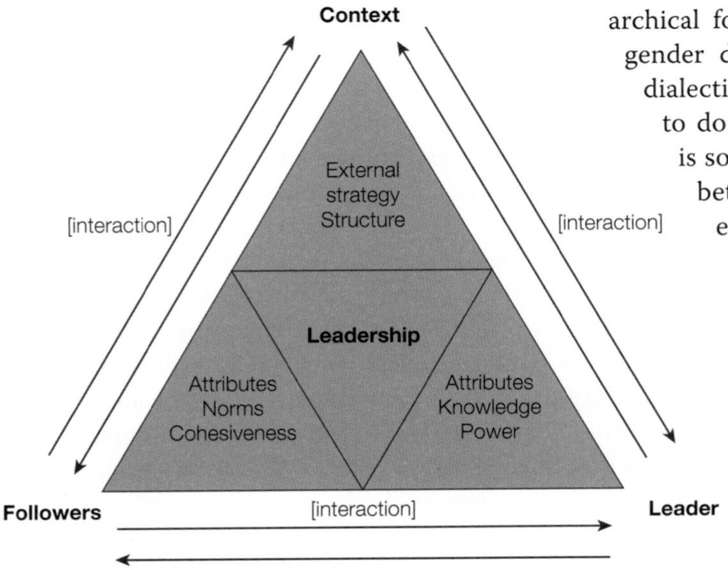

stop...

Think about a position you have held in a voluntary organization or a work organization. To what extent were you a leader? And to what extent were you a follower?

...and reflect

Figure 12.1 Leadership as a process

Leadership versus management

In this text, the terms manager and leader are not used interchangeably. So, what exactly is the difference between management and leadership? We can grasp the difference between management and leadership by examining the various roles carried out by managers. A role in an organizational setting is an expected set of activities or behaviours stemming from the position. Classical management theorists define the role of management in terms of planning, organizing, commanding, coordinating and controlling (see Chapter 1). Although this offers an idealized image of management, it emphasizes that leading is a subset of the roles performed by managers. Jeff Gold and his colleagues suggest that 'leadership is about direction and *pulling together towards a common goal*' and that management is about implementing those plans and managing the resources to execute them effectively and efficiently (2013: 261, emphasis added). Keith Grint offers a less functional definition of the two concepts: 'management is the equivalent of *déjà vu* (seen this before), whereas leadership is the equivalent of *vu jàdé* (never seen before)' (2005: 15).

Table 12.1 illustrates the mainstream consensus on the distinction between management and leadership. Management is more associated with words like status quo, consistency, order and efficiency, whereas leadership is associated with words such as vision, strategy, communications and change.

Table 12.1 Distinguishing leadership from managership

Managership	Leadership
1 Engages in day-to-day activities Maintains and allocates resources	Formulates long-term objectives for reforming the system Plans strategy and tactics
2. Exhibits supervisory behaviour Acts to make others maintain standard job behaviour	Exhibits leading behaviour Acts to bring about changes in others that are congruent with long-term objectives
3. Administers subsystems within organizations	Innovates for the entire organization
4. Asks how and when to engage in standard practice	Asks when and why to change standard practice
5. Acts within established organizational culture	Creates vision and meaning for the organization and strives to transform organizational culture
6. Uses transactional influence Induces compliance in manifest behaviour using rewards, sanctions and formal authority	Uses transformational influence Induces a change in work values, attitudes and behaviour using personal examples and expertise
7. Relies on control strategies to get things done by subordinates	Uses empowering strategies to make followers internalize work-related values
8. Supports the status quo and stabilizes the organization	Challenges the status quo and creates change

Source: Table 1.1 from Conger, J. A. and Kanungo, R. N. (1998) Charismatic Leadership in Organizations, Thousand Oaks, CA: Sage.

For Conger and Kanungo (1998), leaders challenge the status quo, engage in creative visioning for the future of the organization, and promote appropriate changes in followers' work values, attitudes and behaviours by using empowering strategies and tactics.

Some leadership theorists insist that leadership is fundamentally an interpersonal process, involving **dyadic** relationships (that is, relationships between two parties) and communications with followers. Others make the distinction by asserting that management is not a value-laden activity, whereas leadership is. One writer put it like this: 'What is important for the emerging age is that leaders have a foundation, an examined core of beliefs and values, that guides them during times of paradox, ambiguity, and chaotic change' (Apps, 1994: 36). Another suggestion is that managers 'do things right', whereas leaders 'do the right thing'. Grint suggests that managership might focus on solving complex but essentially 'Tame problems in a linear fashion: applying what worked the last time', whereas leadership is essentially about facing 'Wicked problems that are literally "unmanageable"' (2005: 9).

dyad: a group consisting of two members

globalization & organization misbehaviour

Source: DigitalVision/Punchstock

The 'global race' and the China Price

Leaders often tell stories to set the tone of an organization and create impetus. For example, a company might be a plucky underdog whose employees must work harder than everyone else. Or a leader might paint a picture of The Once and Future King – inspiring workers to pursue former greatness. While highly motivational, such narratives can curtail clear-headed thinking about just what exactly a return to Camelot might mean.

For example, consider the latest justification for grinding British wages and intensifying work: the notion of a 'global race'. In short, if British workers do not set aside their alleged sense of entitlement and put their noses to the grindstone, workers in foreign countries will out-compete British industry – taking away British jobs and prosperity. Britain, the Tories tell us, needs to 'win' it, 'succeed' in it, and get 'to the top' in it; 'compete' in it, 'thrive in' it, and be 'strong' in it; 'fight' in it; or merely, 'equip' itself for it and 'get fit for' it. If Britain fails to do some or all of these things, it will 'sink', 'lose', 'fall behind', be left in 'the slow lane' or let 'others take over' (Beckett, 2013b).

Britain's opponents? The rising economies of Asia and South America such as China, India and Brazil. And the prize?:

> [This] is vaguely and promiscuously defined: 'jobs', 'wealth', 'growth', 'trade', 'talent', 'technology', 'skills', 'capital', 'competitiveness', 'big ideas', 'influence', 'innovation', 'investment', 'investment opportunities', 'recovery'. (Beckett, 2013b)

As intended, the global race is galvanizing: everyone must pull together to protect the Empire, just like when former Prime Minister Margaret Thatcher went to war with Argentina over the Falklands in 1982. But step back from the hoopla and flag-waving for a moment and ask yourself, 'Who benefits?' Most of the effort will be made by the workers (who must work harder and make do with less), and most of the benefit will accrue to the wealthy.

In fact, the global race is just a different angle on economic globalization – the intensifying cross-border movement of goods that pressurizes employers to reduce the cost of production in order to retain market share. The rapid industrialization of China and the retail juggernaut of cheap Chinese goods is one example of economic globalization. Yet, as documented in *The China Price*, the 'boon' of low-cost Chinese goods comes at a significant cost to both Chinese workers and the environment (Harney, 2008).

Of course, the 'global race' does not just occur in far-off countries. Workers from the developing world increasingly go to the European Union to work, creating a secondary labour market with low wages and terrible working conditions. Consider Italy's burgeoning and Dickensian textile factories:

As many as 50,000 Chinese live and work in [Prato, Italy], making clothes bearing the prized 'Made in Italy' label which sets them apart from garments produced in China itself, even at the lower end of the fashion business.

Up to two thirds of the Chinese in Prato are illegal immigrants, according to local authorities. About 90 percent of the Chinese factories – virtually all of which are rented out to Chinese entrepreneurs by Italians who own the buildings – break the law in various ways, says Aldo Milone, the city councillor in charge of security.

This includes using fabric smuggled from China, evading taxes and grossly violating health and labour regulations. This month a fire, which prosecutors suspect was set off by an electric stove, killed seven workers as they slept in cardboard cubicles at a workshop. (Aloisi, 2013)

The paradox of a secondary labour market like the one mentioned above is that it both subsidizes the primary labour market (in this case, by cheapening the cost of necessities) and undermines the primary labour market (by providing a cheaper pool of workers). Over time, wages and working conditions in the primary labour market will deteriorate. Who, then, will be left to purchase the goods produced? And will citizens continue to support an economic system that provides them with a grim future as wage slaves?

The pressure to perpetually cheapen costs – whether through outsourcing and capital substitution in an individual firm or through national reductions in social protections and programmes – is often called 'the race to the bottom'. Of course, that slogan is a tougher sell than the cheery 'global race'. Setting aside this chummy, collegiate repackaging, the real question is whether extolling the virtues of the 'global race' is a desirable approach to corporate and political leadership.

> **Stop!** Who benefits when workers buy into the 'global race' narrative? Is trying to sell workers a plan that lowers their wages and worsens their working conditions an example of good leadership? And why would political leaders advance a narrative that contains within it the potential for electoral peril?

Sources and further research

Aloisi, S. (2013) 'Insight – Italy's Chinese garment workshops boom as workers suffer', Reuters, December 30. Available at: http://uk.reuters.com/article/2013/12/30/uk-italy-sweatshop-insight-idUKBRE9BS04A20131230 (accessed February 16, 2015).

Beckett, A. (2013b) 'What is the "global race"?' *The Guardian*, September 22. Available at: www.theguardian.com/politics/2013/sep/22/what-is-global-race-conservatives-ed-miliband (accessed February 16, 2015).

Harney, A. (2008) *The China Price: The True Cost of Chinese Competitive Advantage*, New York: Penguin.

Note: This feature was written by Bob Barnetson, Associate Professor of Labour Relations, Athabasca University, Canada.

For others, management is concerned with a set of transactional exchanges – 'you do this work for that reward' – whereas leadership is concerned with the reciprocal influence process that constitutes the 'psychological contract' (see Chapter 1).

There is a consensus in the practitioner literature that organizational members can and do embody both management and leadership roles. Adair (2006), for example, has distinguished three levels of leadership undertaken by individuals in

stop...

Recall an organization where you have worked, or perhaps a social club you have been a part of. To what extent were you a leader and a follower? Did the managers or organizers exhibit managerial or leadership behaviours? Explain your answer. Do you believe that managers and leaders reflect fundamentally different personality types?

...and reflect

complex organizations: strategic, operational and team. The behaviours associated with strategic leadership are visioning, communicating and empowering. The individual(s) engaged in operational leadership focus on day-to-day activities and have a major influence on reinforcing the organizational culture. The individual playing the role of team or front-line leader focuses on the specific timely outcomes to be accomplished by her or his immediate followers. According to prominent leadership writer John Kotter, the 'engine that drives change' is leadership, and if a purely 'managerial mindset' is adopted, useful change in organizations via restructuring, re-strategizing or re-engineering will inevitably fail, regardless of the quality of the followers involved (2012).

Links to management — David McGuire

David McGuire is Reader in Human Resource Development (HRD) at Edinburgh Napier University, Scotland. He has significant experience in teaching at undergraduate and postgraduate levels in the areas of HRD, managing diversity and leadership, and is Deputy Programme Director of MBA programmes. To date, he has published two textbooks, and over 30 articles in journals including the *European Journal of Training and Development, Advances in Developing Human Resources, Human Resource Development Review* and *Human Resource Development Quarterly*. David serves as Associate Editor of *Advances in Developing Human Resources* and also sits on the Editorial Boards of three leading HRD journals. He has been the recipient of a number of prestigious research awards including a Scottish Crucible award, a Fulbright Scholar award, a Government of Ireland scholarship and a number of Emerald Literati awards.

In the ebook click on the play button to watch David talking about leadership, and then answer the following question:

- What are the differences between leaders and managers?

Traditional leadership theories

Leadership as a field of study has produced an inordinate amount of literature, concerned with both what leaders *should* do and what leaders *actually* do. The former involves theories *for* leaders, while the latter involves theories *of* leadership. Theories for leaders are primarily normative, directed at providing '*how to*' prescriptions for improving leadership effectiveness. Theories of leadership, on the other hand, are primarily analytical, directed at a better understanding of leadership processes and at explaining *why* they vary across time and space.

Leadership theories are typically classified according to the types of variable emphasized in a theory or empirical study. We have divided the theories into two broad categories: classical and contemporary. Table 12.2 depicts this theorizing of leadership around traits, behaviours, contingencies, competencies and leader–follower relations. But we should note that modern is not necessarily better.

Table 12.2 Traditional and contemporary leadership perspectives

Classical perspectives	Modern perspectives
Trait theories For example, Stogdill (1974)	*Charismatic/transformational theories* For example, Bass (1985), Avolio and Bass (2005, 2006)
Behaviour theories For example, Lewin et al. (1939), Blake and Mouton (1978)	*Distributed/shared/superleadership theories* For example, Goleman et al. (2002), Manz and Sims (1989), Raelin (2003)
Contingency theories For example, Fiedler (1964), House (1971), Hersey and Blanchard (1969), Kerr and Jermier (1978)	*Competency theories* For example, Oram (1998)
	Leadership-as-practice For example, Carroll et al. (2008), Raelin (2011)

plate 41 Early research on organizational leadership focused on the notion that successful entrepreneurs like Sir Richard Branson possess superior qualities or attributes compared with the traits possessed by non-leaders.

stop...

What do you think makes an effective leader? List three leaders you know about who are alive today, and write down the special attributes you believe each of these people possesses. Compare your list of special qualities with that of your peers, and see whether you can agree on a 'master list' for an effective leader.

...and reflect

Trait perspective: the search for 'giants'

Early research on leadership focused on the notion that individuals who occupy leadership positions possess superior qualities or attributes compared with the traits possessed by non-leaders. The so-called 'great man' theories therefore focused on identifying the innate qualities possessed by influential leaders among European monarchs, military generals or politicians. The subject matter for these studies was drawn from the corporate elite; little interest was shown in identifying the traits of distinguished labour leaders. The focus was also androcentric, often ignoring influential women: 'great man' rather than 'great person' theories.

But in 1974, American researcher Ralf Stogdill found that leadership is based on complex groupings of traits and social interactions rather than on a single trait or a small cluster of traits (Stogdill, 1974). These data showed that leaders tend to be endowed with a large supply of positive physical characteristics such as stamina. Socioeconomic factors were also important variables. In terms of 'class position', few corporate leaders had fathers who were manual wage earners. Leadership was also found to be positively related to intelligence and fluency in speech. Task-related characteristics included such attributes as the desire to excel. Social attributes, such as the ability to exhibit tact and diplomacy, are another cluster of traits that 'successful' leaders appear to possess. Stogdill used these selective clusters of traits to differentiate leaders from followers, and effective from ineffective leaders. He concluded that specific 'patterns of traits' appear to interact in a complex way to give an advantage to an individual seeking a leadership position. The trait approach to studying leadership still flourishes. For example, it has been asserted that 'it is unequivocally clear that leaders are not like other people' (Kirkpatrick and Locke, 1991: 59). Eight major traits (including energy, internal locus of control, self-confidence, emotional maturity, integrity, power motivation, achievement orientation and a low need for affiliation) are positively related to leadership effectiveness (Yukl, 2013).

Evaluating the trait approach

The trait perspective has attracted several criticisms. First, the research has largely neglected the context within which the leaders find themselves. Second, it celebrates 'inequality' between the leader and others, and does not recognize the importance of followership in the leadership process (Harter et al., 2006). Third, the research is culturally determined: Asian and Anglo-American scholars, for example, might not agree on what counts as a positive leadership trait. In spite of globalization, major cultural differences exist within as well as between regions. In Asia alone, people speak at least seven different major languages and believe in a wide range of different religions, ranging from Buddhism and Hinduism to Islam and Christianity. Personal characteristics that appear as 'positives' in Anglo-American research might score negatively in other cultures (Granrose, 2001).

The behaviour perspective

Whereas trait theories emphasize the personal characteristics of leaders, behaviour leadership theorists focus on leaders' behaviour – that is, they move away from the notion that leaders are born, towards the investigation of what leaders *do*, and in particular how they behave towards followers. In the 1940s, two classic US research programmes at the University of Michigan and Ohio State University pioneered early research. Working independently, the researchers developed two similar analytical frameworks for followers' assessments of their leaders' behaviour, which were distilled into two core dimensions: a concern to accomplish the *task* and a concern for *people*.

IN THE EBOOK ACCESS THE **OB IN FOCUS** BOX ON RICHARD BRANSON.

task behaviour: focuses on the degree to which a leader emphasizes the importance of assigning followers to tasks and maintaining standards – in other words, 'getting things done' – as opposed to behaviours that nurture supportive relationships

relationship behaviour: focuses on leaders' activities that show concern for followers, look after subordinates' welfare and nurture supportive relationships with followers, as opposed to behaviours that concentrate on completing tasks

initiating: part of a behavioural theory of leadership that describes the degree to which a leader defines and structures her or his own role and the roles of followers towards attaining the group's assigned goals

consideration: the extent to which a leader is likely to nurture job relationships and encourage mutual trust and respect between the leader and his or her subordinates

The first dimension to consider, **task behaviour**, describes the extent to which the leader emphasizes productivity targets or the accomplishment of goals. These behaviours are also called 'production-centred' and task-oriented' leadership styles. The second, **relationship behaviour**, describes the extent to which the leader is concerned about his or her followers as people: their needs, development and problems. Around these two core dimensions, three studies have provided the foundations for behavioural theories of leadership.

At the University of Michigan, researchers differentiated *production-oriented* and *employee-oriented* managers. The former were characterized by detailed work routines and close supervision, and subordinates were viewed as a factor of production – as a means for getting the work done. The latter gave special attention to subordinates' personal needs, valued their individuality and generally approached subordinates with a strong human relations emphasis. With respect to effectiveness, the Michigan researchers found that employee-oriented leadership behaviours were associated with higher work group performance and higher satisfaction among group members (Kahn and Katz, 1960).

The Ohio State University studies suggested that two important dimensions underlie leader behaviours: an *initiating structure* and *consideration*. The first of these, an **initiating** structure, refers to the extent to which managers are likely to define and structure their own roles and those of their subordinates, and to establish clear patterns of communication towards completing formal tasks and goals. In contrast, **consideration** refers to the extent to which a leader is likely to nurture job relationships and encourage mutual trust and respect between the leader and his or her subordinates. The Ohio State researchers argued that a high 'initiating structure' was associated with greater effectiveness, higher employee absenteeism, higher turnover rates and a higher number of grievances. High 'consideration', on the other hand, was associated with higher subordinate satisfaction.

The Ohio State researchers regarded the initiating structure and consideration as being two independent dimensions. Thus, managers' behaviour was flexible and could be changed as the situation warranted. Leaders could score highly on the initiating dimension and not on the consideration dimension, but equally they could score high on both or low on both. The high grievance levels declined when the manager was rated high on both initiating structure and consideration. The Ohio State results were interpreted as indicating that the most effective leader would score high on both dimensions, and that leadership could derive from individuals holding no formal position in the organization (Grint, 1997). Subsequent research has tended to confirm the Michigan and Ohio State University results (Vecchio et al., 1996).

Robert Blake and Jane Mouton's highly influential Managerial Grid, later renamed Leadership Grid, is based on an extended version of the production-oriented and employee-oriented theme found in the Michigan and Ohio State studies (Blake and Mouton, 1978). The Leadership Grid was designed for leadership training by allowing trainees to assess their current levels of task-oriented and people-oriented leadership styles. Not surprisingly, it has been noted that these two core dimensions of leadership styles parallel McGregor's Theories X and Y,

Source: Getty Images

plate 42 Army NCOs (junior officers) exemplify individuals who are high in initiating structure. In training, they give orders and structure recruits' activities throughout the day. An emphasis on task accomplishment takes precedence over the recruits' personal needs.

respectively (see Chapter 6). The later version of the grid, by Blake and McCanse (1991), identifies five basic combinations of concern for production and concern for people, using a nine-point scale, where 9 shows a high concern for people and 1 shows a low concern (Figure 12.2).

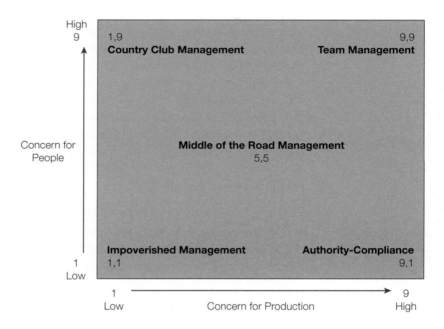

Figure 12.2 The Leadership Grid™

From Blake, Robert R. and McCanse, Anne Adams (1991) *Leadership Dilemmas – Grid Solutions* (Formerly the Managerial Grid by Robert R. Blake and Jane S. Mouton), Houston: Gulf Publishing Company, p. 29. Copyright 1991 by Scientific Methods, Inc. Reproduced by permission of the owners

stop...

Go back to Chapter 6 on motivation and look-up Theories X and Y. In what way is production orientation reminiscent of Theory X, and employee orientation reminiscent of Theory Y? Using the X and Y classification, how would you rate 'team management'?

...and reflect

The styles are the authority-compliance style (scoring 9,1), country-club management (scoring 1,9), impoverished management (scoring 1,1), middle-of-the-road management (scoring 5,5) and team management (scoring 9,9). The Leadership Grid model advocated the team management style, which suited the popular human relations theory that high levels of performance and job satisfaction could be mutually achieved.

Evaluating the behavioural approach

The Leadership Grid approach has been tested many times, but mixed results have generated criticisms of behavioural-style research. First, it has not adequately demonstrated how leaders' behaviours are associated with performance outcomes. The relationship between production and relationship behaviours and performance outcomes is tenuous. It is also argued that the behaviour approach, like the trait approach, looks for simple answers to complex questions (Yukl, 2013). Furthermore, behavioural taxonomies suggest that the most effective leadership style is the so-called 'high–high' style: that is, high production and high people-oriented behaviour. Yet extensive research in Anglo-American countries has found only limited support for the universal proposition that 'high–high' leaders are more effective. Researchers have concluded that there is no 'one best way' to lead; rather, it is believed that the effectiveness of a given leadership style depends on situational factors.

The contingency perspective

Contingency leadership theories are based on the idea that the most effective leadership style depends upon the leader, the followers and the situation. In other words, whether a set of traits or behaviours will result in leadership success is contingent, that is, will depend, upon the situational variables, including the characteristics of co-employees, the external and internal environments, and the nature of the work performed. The assumption is that different trait patterns (or behaviour patterns) will be effective in different situations, and that the same trait pattern (or behaviour pattern) is not optimal in all situations.

Most contingency leadership theories assume that effective leaders must be flexible and able to adapt their behaviours and styles to match the situation. This challenges the notion of 'one best way' to manage or lead. For example, British Prime Minister Winston Churchill, having exhibited inspiring leadership throughout the Second World War, was defeated in the July 1945 general election. Thus, it is suggested that Churchill's wartime leadership qualities no longer fitted the new contextual situation. Fiedler's contingency theory, Evans and House's path–goal theory, Hersey and Blanchard's 'situational leadership' model, and Kerr and Jermier's substitutes for leadership theory are four examples of leadership theories that diagnose contextual factors.

Fiedler's leadership contingency theory

Fiedler's contingency model: suggests that leader effectiveness depends on whether the person's natural leadership style is appropriately matched to the situation

Fiedler's contingency theory is the oldest and one of the most widely known contingency models of leadership (Fiedler, 1964). It proposes that the fit between the leader's need for structure and the favourableness of the leader's situation determines the team's effectiveness in accomplishing its work. This theory assumes that leaders are either task oriented or relationship oriented, and that leaders cannot change their orientations. Task-oriented leaders are focused on accomplishing tasks and getting work done. Relationship-oriented leaders are focused on developing good, comfortable interpersonal relationships. The effectiveness of both types of leader depends on the favourableness of the situation. The theory classifies the favourableness of the leader's situation according to the leader's leader–follower relations, the structure of the task and the leader's position power.

In later work, Fiedler (1970) classifies leaders using the Least Preferred Co-worker (LPC) scale. The LPC scale is an instrument to measure a manager's leadership style. Respondents are asked to think about the person with whom they can work least well (the LPC). Next, respondents are asked to describe this person using adjectives such as pleasant versus unpleasant, and inefficient versus efficient. Fiedler argues that leaders who describe their LPC in positive terms (that is, pleasant, efficient, cheerful and so on) are classified as high-LPC, or relationship-oriented, leaders. Those who describe their LPC in negative terms (that is, unpleasant, inefficient, gloomy and so on) are classified as low-LPC, or task-oriented, leaders. The LPC score is a controversial element in contingency theory because of measurement biases and low measurement reliability (McMahon, 1972; Peters et al., 1985).

Fiedler's model is based on the assumption that the situation determining the leadership style depends on three interrelated factors: (1) *leader–member relations*, which reflects the extent to which the leader has the support, respect and trust of her or his subordinates; (2) *task structure*, the amount of structure contained within the tasks performed by the work group, ranging from highly structured and detailed to low structure; and (3) *position power*, the degree to which the leader has the capacity to exercise formal authority through rewards or punishments to obtain compliance from the subordinates. Based on these three dimensions, the situation is either 'favourable' or 'unfavourable' for the leader.

Fiedler's contingency model is shown in Figure 12.3. The row labelled 'Situation' shows that there are eight different leadership situations. Each situation represents a unique mix of leader–member relations, task structure and position power. Situations I, II and III represent the most favourable or high-control situations,

stop...

To what extent are contingency theories of leadership bound by culture?

...and reflect

where there is little need for relationship-oriented action since leader–member relations are already good. Situations VII and VIII, on the other hand, represent the most unfavourable or low-control situations – here, the relationship-oriented leader may give insufficient attention to task-related problems. Figure 12.3 shows that task-oriented leaders are hypothesized to realize good group performance at these extremes, under favourable (high-control) and unfavourable (low-control) situations. The model also shows that in situations IV and V, in the centre, where the situation is moderately favourable (moderate control), the relationship-oriented leader achieves good group performance.

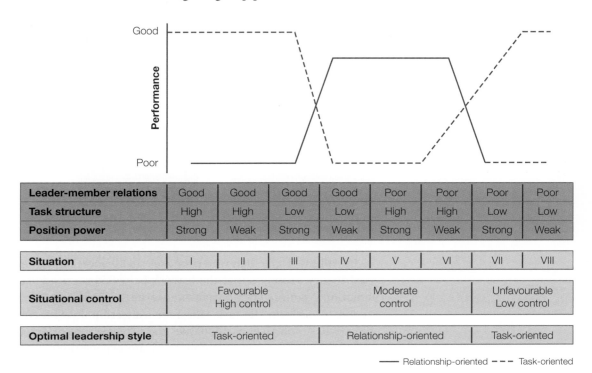

Leader-member relations	Good	Good	Good	Good	Poor	Poor	Poor	Poor
Task structure	High	High	Low	Low	High	High	Low	Low
Position power	Strong	Weak	Strong	Weak	Strong	Weak	Strong	Weak

Situation	I	II	III	IV	V	VI	VII	VIII

Situational control	Favourable High control			Moderate control			Unfavourable Low control	

Optimal leadership style	Task-oriented			Relationship-oriented			Task-oriented	

—— Relationship-oriented − − − Task-oriented

Figure 12.3 A representation of Fiedler's contingency model of leadership
Source: Adapted from Fiedler (1974), p. 71

What happens when a leader is in a moderately favourable or unfavourable situation? Fiedler (1965) argued that leader orientation is difficult, if not impossible, to change, so he recommends that leaders must learn to influence the leadership situation in order to create a match between their leadership style and the amount of situational control. Thus, a moderately favourable situation could be altered to be being more favourable and a better fit for the task-motivated leader. Similarly, the highly unfavourable situation could be changed to one that is moderately favourable, and a better fit for the relationship-motivated leader.

Evaluating Fiedler's model

There is considerable debate about the validity of Fiedler's model, and research suggests that the model has been better supported in laboratory studies than in field studies (Peters et al., 1985). Such criticism has prompted others to examine the contingency nature of leadership (Schriesheim and Kerr, 1977), which we discuss next.

Path–goal theory

path–goal leadership theory: a contingency theory of leadership based on the expectancy theory of motivation, which relates several leadership styles to specific employee and situational contingencies

Robert House's (1971) **path–goal theory of leadership**, which draws upon the expectancy theory of motivation, hypothesizes that leaders can by their actions affect the motivation, job satisfaction and performance of their work group members. In the expectancy theory of motivation, the linkages between effort and performance, and between performance and valued rewards, are critical to employee motivation. Chapter 6 explores this notion further in relation to the motivation of employees. In path–goal theory, the main task of the leader is to smooth the follower's path to the goal. The leader uses the most appropriate of four leader behavioural styles to help followers clarify the paths that will lead them to their work and personal goals, as shown in Figure 12.4.

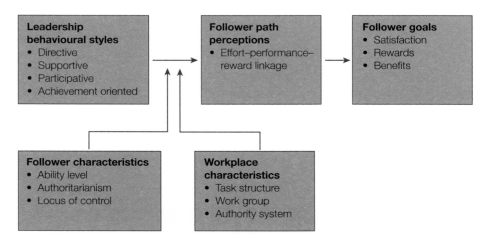

Figure 12.4 The path–goal model

In contrast to Fiedler, who proposes that leaders have one dominant style, path–goal theory proposes that the leader's behaviours are adjusted to complement the situational contingency variables in order to influence job satisfaction and motivation to perform the task. The four leadership styles identified in the model are directive, supportive, participative and achievement oriented. The *directive style* is used when the leader must communicate expectations, schedule work and maintain performance standards. The *supportive style* is used when the leader needs to express concern for followers and create a climate that demonstrates support. The *participative style* is used when the leader wants to share decision-making authority with the followers. The *achievement-oriented style* is used when the leader must set challenging goals for followers, expect very high levels of performance and show strong confidence in the followers.

The contingency variables in path–goal theory are the characteristics of the work environment (situation) and those of the followers. Research has focused on matching leaders' behaviours to followers' characteristics and environmental characteristics. For example, when tasks are ambiguous, directive leader behaviour is appropriate. When the environment is stressful, supportive leadership is appropriate. When followers are ready to be empowered, participative leadership is appropriate. When followers have high achievement orientations, achievement-oriented leadership is appropriate. These are just a few examples of the links between leaders' behaviour and contingency variables. The leader selects the leader behavioural style that helps followers to achieve their goals. Leaders can use several different styles, and can diagnose the situation and apply the appropriate style.

Evaluating path–goal theory

The research support for path–goal theory is mixed (Wofford and Liska, 1993) There is support for some of the model's predictions, for example the link between directive behaviour on the part of the leader and the job satisfaction of low-ability subordinates, and supportive leadership is shown to be related to subordinates' satisfaction across situations. We can conclude that the full path–goal model has not yet been sufficiently tested (Yukl, 2013).

Situational leadership theory

The situational leadership model, which was developed by Paul Hersey and Kenneth Blanchard (1969; Hersey et al., 1977), suggests that the leader's behaviour should be adjusted to the maturity level of the followers. The model employs two dimensions of leader behaviour as used in the Ohio State studies (Figure 12.2): one dimension is task or production oriented, and the other is relationship or people oriented. Followers' maturity is categorized into four different levels, 'unable and unwilling', 'unable and willing', 'able but unwilling' and 'able and willing'. Their maturity is determined by the ability and willingness or confidence of the followers to accept responsibility for completing their work. Followers who are unable and unwilling are the least mature, and those who are both able and willing are the most mature.

The four styles of leader behaviour associated with each level of follower maturity are telling, selling, participating and delegating. According to Hersey and Blanchard's situational leadership model, a leader should use a *telling style* of leadership with immature followers who are unable and unwilling to take responsibility for completing their work. This style is characterized by high concern with the task and strong initiating structure behaviour, coupled with low concern with relationships and little consideration for behaviour. The telling style of leadership corresponds to the 'Authority-Compliance' style shown in the bottom-right quadrant in Figure 12.2. For Warren Bennis (1985), an effective leader has to be able to communicate meaning to ensure that followers are inspired and support the organization's goals. This important characteristic of an effective leader is reflected in Hersey and Blanchard's model. As followers mature to the second level, the leader should use a *selling style*, in which there is high concern with both the task and relationships. This style of leadership matches 'Team Management' found in the top-right quadrant in Figure 12.2. The *telling* and *selling* styles both tend to be *leader directed*.

Followers who are able but unwilling are the next most mature, and require a *participating style* from the leader. This style is characterized by a high concern with relationships and a low concern with the task. A *participating style* corresponds to the 'Country Club' style in the top-left quadrant in Figure 12.2. Finally, the most mature followers are ones who are both able and willing, and these require a *delegating style* of leadership. The leader employing this style of leadership shows a low concern with both the task and relationships, because the followers accept responsibility. A *delegating style* of leadership corresponds to the 'Impoverished Management' style in the bottom-left quadrant in Figure 12.2. Both the *participating* and the *delegating* style tend to be *follower directed*. According to Hersey and Blanchard's situational model, therefore, leadership style is depicted as following an inverted U-shape changing to match followers' levels of ability and maturity.

IN THE EBOOK ACCESS THE **CRITICAL INSIGHT** ON THE HERSEY AND BLANCHARD MODEL OF SITUATIONAL LEADERSHIP.

Evaluating situational leadership theory

One key limitation of the situational leadership model is the absence of central hypotheses that could be tested, which would make it a more valid, reliable theory of leadership. Some partial tests of the model have indicated support, but others have found no support at all (Blank et al., 1990; Vecchio, 1987). However, the theory has intuitive appeal and is widely used for training and development in corporations. In addition, the theory focuses attention on followers as important participants in, if not determinants of, the leadership process.

Substitutes for leadership

The mainstream leadership theories we have examined so far all assume that formal leadership is necessary, whatever the circumstances. Kerr and Jermier (1978) challenge this basic premise. They contend that there are a variety of situational variables that can substitute for, neutralize or enhance the effects of formal leadership. These situational variables are referred to as substitutes for leadership. Table 12.3 shows representative examples of these variables. Ability, experience and knowledge can serve as follower characteristics; a highly structured and routine job can serve as a job characteristic; and a bureaucracy with explicit directives, formalized areas of responsibility and an inflexible application of rules and procedures can serve as an organizational characteristic.

Table 12.3 Substitutes for leadership

Characteristic	Affect on leadership	
	Task-oriented behaviour is unnecessary	Relationship-oriented behaviour is unnecessary
Of the follower		
1. Ability, experience, knowledge	O	
2. Professional orientation	O	O
3. Indifference to organizational rewards	O	O
Of the job		
4. Highly structured and routine	O	
5. Provides own feedback on performance	O	
6. Intrinsically satisfying		O
Of the organization		
7. Formalization/inflexibility	O	
8. Cohesive work groups/teams	O	O
9. Rewards not controlled by leader	O	O
10. Spatial distance between leader/followers	O	O

Source: Organizational Behaviour and Human Performance, Vol. 22, Kerr, S. and Jermier, J. M., 'Substitutes for leadership: their meaning and measurement,' pp. 375–403, Copyright Academic Press, Copyright Elsevier (1978)

A *leadership substitute*, Kerr and Jermier propose, can make a leader's behaviour unnecessary. For example, task-centred behaviour is less relevant for the experienced and well-trained employees who are often found in self-managed work teams or in professional occupations. These employees are more likely to be guided by their own initiatives or by their immediate peers, thereby replacing task-motivated behaviour. A similar prediction can be made for a highly structured job, in this instance the 'McDonaldization' approach noted in Chapter 2 to designing workers' roles based on fragmented tasks and repetitive work routines, including worker–customer interaction. The theory predicts situations when any type of leadership is negated. This situation is referred to as a *leadership neutralizer*. For example, when rewards are not within the leader's control, or if there is a spatial distance between the leaders and the work group, behaviour may negate these behaviours, but they are still necessary. Although the list of characteristics is not all-inclusive, it shows that there are more substitutes for task-oriented leadership than for relationship-oriented leadership. Theory suggests that managers should be attentive to the potential substitutes because they impact directly on intrinsic and extrinsic motivators (see Chapter 6).

Evaluating substitutes for leadership theory

The research results on the substitutes for leadership approach have been mixed. One study did find that combined attentiveness to leader behaviours and substitute variables significantly explained employees' work attitudes and behaviours (Posakoff et al., 1996). The theory assumes that the individual manager has the power and the discretion to change the situational variables. It also assumes that leadership is replaced by alternatives, but such variables may coexist alongside leadership (Howell and Dorfman, 1981).

Contemporary leadership theories

Transformational leadership

Most of the leadership theories we have discussed so far in this chapter were developed at a time when Fordism was the dominant production paradigm in Western capitalism. Yet from the beginning, Fordism based on mass production and consumption was plagued by economic and social problems. The model became inextricably associated with deskilled workers, standardized products, hierarchical managerial structures and conflict between labour and management.

In the 1970s, Fordism entered a crisis. Among the many solutions adopted to solve the crisis was post-Fordism. This new industrial model involved reversing the Tayloristic principles surrounding the design and managerial control of work (see Chapter 2). The diagnosis was that US and European organizations had too much management. Thus, new theories of leadership to enhance innovation and mobilize employees' underused intelligence and knowledge found expression in Piore and Sabel's (1984) concept of 'flexible specialization', the notion of the 'holistic assembly line' and Japanese cellular production (Bratton, 1992). In this new competitive, global context, leaders were to be separated into two types: the *transactional* and the *transformational* (Burns, 1978).

The essence of classical leadership is concerned with an exchange or transaction. Leaders motivate their subordinates by clarifying the role and task requirements. There are three defining features of *transactional leadership* according to Avolio et al. (1999). Specifically, the transactional leader (1) clarifies expectations and establishes the rewards for meeting these expectations; (2) monitors subordinates' behaviour, anticipates problems and takes corrective actions before the behaviour creates serious difficulties; and (3) waits until the behaviour has created problems before taking action. The transactional leader, first, uses contingent rewards and recognition to motivate employees towards an established goal or purpose, and second, exerts corrective and possible punishment when subordinates do not reach their performance expectations. At best, these leadership behaviours result in employee performance that meets expectations.

Transactional leadership is typically contrasted with *charismatic leadership* and *transformational leadership*. The Oxford Dictionary defines *charisma* as (1) 'the ability to inspire followers with devotion and enthusiasm', and (2) 'a divinely conferred power or talent'. By virtue of the leader's defining personal attributes, **charismatic leadership** creates respect for and trust in the leader. Whereas transactional leadership focuses on interpersonal exchanges, charismatic leadership emphasizes the symbolic and expressive aspects of the leader's behaviour. That is, it emphasizes the visionary and inspirational messages that appeal to followers' values and elicit self-sacrifice. Leaders who can do all these things and also produce profound social change, inspire others to transcend their own self-interests and have an astonishing effect on followers are said to be charismatic leaders. Winston Churchill, Martin Luther King, Nelson Mandela and, to some, Barack Obama are examples of charismatic leaders in politics. In addition, Richard Branson, previously mentioned, and Lee Iacocca of Chrysler are the most cited examples of charismatic Anglo-American business leaders. But charisma is something that followers perceive: like beauty, it lies in the eyes of the beholder (Grint, 2005).

charismatic leadership: a leadership style that emphasizes symbolic leader behaviour, visionary and inspirational messages, an appeal to values and self-sacrifice

Source: Shutterstock

plate 43 Barack Obama's communicative powers have been described as 'absolutely masterful' and, to some, speak to his charisma as a leader.

stop...

Can you think of people who illustrate charismatic leadership? Do you think that charismatic leadership was the answer to the economic and financial woes of the post-2008 era? Are there any 'risks' associated with following a charismatic leader?

...and reflect

The German sociologist Max Weber was the original writer on charismatic leadership. His contribution to charismatic leadership theory lies in his analysis of authority relations (see Chapter 3). Weber argued that people comply with a leader's demands based on three forms of authority: traditional, rational-legal and charismatic. In the case of charismatic authority, people obey because of the extraordinary endowments of charismatics, the 'bearers of specific gifts of body and mind' (1978: 1112). For Weber, charismatic leadership emerged only during periods of social crisis. At such 'moments of distress', the charismatic leader 'seizes the task for which he [sic] is destined and demands that others obey and follow him by virtue of his mission' (p. 1112). Although Weber's work relates primarily to religious phenomena, the idea that social crises can act as catalysts for change developed into a theory. In the 1980s, the US economist Milton Friedman wrote the highly influential statement: 'Only a crisis – actual or perceived – produces real change' (1982: ix). This became known as 'the crisis hypothesis'.

In the 1980s, at the beginning of the ascendancy of neo-liberalism and in response to the crisis in modern manufacturing industry, a model of leadership emerged from a recognition of the sparseness of charisma among industrial leaders that centred on the strategic influence of senior managers. Transformational leadership is a 'weaker' version of charisma (Grint, 2005), as defined by Weber, and is more far more modest in its goals – changing or transforming organizations, not nation states. Transformational leadership is sometimes identified separately from charismatic leadership in the literature, but the two formulations do not in fact differ. Transformational leadership is a weaker variant in which charisma is an 'important attribute' of leaders who serve in the change agent or transformational role (Bass, 1985).

The essence of *transformational* leadership relates to issues surrounding the processes of learning, creativity and transformative change (discussed in Chapter 18) (Bass and Riggio, 2006). In contrast to transactional leadership, Avolio et al. (1999) observed that transformational leadership has four dimensions. Specifically, the transformational leader (1) behaves in venerable ways that cause subordinates to identify with her or him by displaying conviction, taking stands and appealing to others on an emotional level; (2) communicates optimism about future goal attainment, provides meaning to the task at hand and challenges subordinates with high standards; (3) stimulates and encourages creativity in her or his subordinates by challenging assumptions, taking risks and soliciting subordinates' ideas; and (4) acts as a coach or mentor to the others, listens to subordinates' concerns and attends to each subordinate's needs. In general, transformational leadership is more likely to emerge in times of distress and change, whereas transactional leadership is more likely to be observed in a well-ordered society (Bass, 1985).

VISIT THE *ONLINE RESOURCE CENTRE* AT HTTPS://HE.PALGRAVE.COM/COMPANION/BRATTON-WORK-AND-ORGANIZATIONAL-BEHAVIOUR3/ TO READ MORE ON THE ROLE OF LEADERSHIP IN BRINGING ABOUT ORGANIZATIONAL CHANGE.

Figure 12.5 presents a summary of three sets of leader behaviour that are key to realizing organizational change. The first set of transformational leader behaviours involves responding to signals from the environment indicating that change is needed (stage I). The crisis event must be perceived and responded to by the leader. The second set of leader behaviours involves creating a vision that a critical mass of followers will accept as a realistic, credible and desirable change for the organization (stage II). The third set of leader behaviours involves three key elements: the transformational leader sets high performance expectations and standards, publicly communicates confidence in followers' ability to meet these high performance expectations, and acts as a role model for the desired new values, beliefs and behaviours that are needed to realize the new vision (stage III). These leader behaviours establish 'new realities, actions, and practices [that] must be shared so that changes become institutionalized' (Tichy and Devanna, 1990: 31).

According to Goleman (1996), traditional authoritarian leadership styles are outmoded and leadership is the 'art of persuading people to work towards a common goal' (p. 149). Goleman also emphasizes the importance of leaders possessing competencies related to emotional intelligence (EI). He writes:

> Imagine the benefits for work of being skilled in the basic emotional competences – being attuned to the feelings of those we deal with, being able to handle disagreements so they do not escalate, having the ability to get into the flow states while doing our work. (1996: 149)

Contemporary theories of transformative leadership seem to have gone full circle back to personal traits such as EI. Emotional competencies help to facilitate change by 'persuading people to work toward a common goal' (Goleman, 1996: 149).

Evaluating transformational leadership theory

Empirical research has found support for transformational leaders with charisma. Evidence indicates that transformational leadership can enhance employees' motivation and performance, as well as their levels of satisfaction and organizational measures of effectiveness (Conger and Kanungo, 1998). And those 'strong' transformational leaders are also likely to be strong transactional leaders; in other words, they are good 'all-rounders'. Empirical research suggests that the positive effects of transformative leadership are not universal but may differ between different employee groups. For example, Top et al.'s (2015) study of private and public healthcare workers reported a significant difference between the groups in terms of their perceptions of transformational leadership, which resulted in a significant difference in terms of the predictors of organizational commitment. Some detractors insist that the most consistently successful organizations are led by individuals with an unorthodox combination of attributes, skills or abilities that falls outside the usual transformational leadership paradigm (Collins, 2002). The research evidence underscores the importance of management development: individuals can be trained to be more transformational.

Distributed leadership

Transformational leadership theory focuses on extraordinary individuals at the top echelons of the organization; its premise is employees' lack of vision and creativity. Distributed or shared leadership theories propose that gifted leaders empower their subordinates by acting as a teacher or coach rather than an 'all-knowing' commandant. The rationale for this growing distributed leadership and employee engagement lies in the perception of its importance for predicting positive performances and the quality of decisions at work. This approach resonates with the work of Peter Senge, who insists that, in creative organizations, 'leaders are designers, stewards, and *teachers*' (1990: 340, emphasis added). Sarti's (2014) research that examined the relationship between participative leadership and employee engagement found that 'individual participation in decision making may have a positive impact on personal satisfaction' and in turn performance (p. 212).

Leadership has traditionally been associated with power and an organizational hierarchy. Underpinning the distributed approach to leadership is the notion that leaders can actually have more power and control if they share power with others in the organization. Distributed leadership theory

stop...

To what extent do the three sets of transformational leader behaviour resemble Kurt Lewin's (1951) model of change that are discussed in Chapter 18?

...and reflect

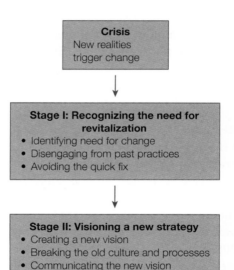

Figure 12.5 Transformational leadership
Source: Adapted from Tichy and Devanna (1990), p. 29

shifts the focus from hierarchy to heterarchy. The idea is that leadership is 'distributed' or 'shared' throughout an organization rather than residing in idiosyncratic individual leaders. Goleman et al. (2002: 14) attempts to contrast the distributed or 'leaderful' organization with the traditional hierarchical model by suggesting that leadership resides 'not solely in the individual at the top, but in every person at entry level who in one way or another, acts as a leader'. Harris and Spillane (2008), applying the theory to educational institutions, characterize distributed leadership as an interactive collaborative process:

> A distributed model of leadership focuses upon the interactions, rather than the actions, of those in formal and informal leadership roles. It is primarily concerned with *leadership practice* and how leadership influences organizational and instructional improvement. A distributed perspective on leadership acknowledges the work of all individuals who contribute to leadership practice, whether or not they are formally designated or defined as leaders. (p. 31)

In the practitioner literature, the concept of the high-performance workplace is heralded as a new management model in which the employment relationship is characterized by more socially consensual practices and leadership styles. In this context, distributed leadership involves sharing power with team members, and developing team leadership takes on a heightened importance (Manz and Sims, 1989). The distribution leadership model is also suggestive of substitutes for leadership theory. Finally, distributed leadership is associated with post-bureaucratic organizational designs, such as the 'boundaryless' forms (see Chapter 15), which necessitate lateral, fluid decision-making processes.

Evaluating distributed or shared leadership

Research has shown that distributed, shared or superleadership has the potential to reduce indirect costs (fewer managers) and free up time for top executives to engage in strategic behaviours (Bratton, 1992). As in the case of substitutes for leadership, distributed leadership is therefore likely to attract interest and further enquiry from practitioners and researchers. Precisely how distributed leadership and collective responsibility for leadership action is implemented across an organization is, however, not without its challenges, not least because of cultural issues (see Chapter 17). Gold et al. note that the practices to provide distributed leadership are 'still not very well understood' (2013: 277). Spillane (2005) observes that distributed leadership does not mean that leadership is 'delegated', where unwanted tasks are passed down to others. Grint notes that distributed leadership is both a philosophy and a process. More ominously, perhaps, while distributed leadership appears to be potentially 'progressive', he warns that the distribution of responsibility and leadership are the 'means by which profoundly undemocratic and illiberal organizations can distribute risk and confound those seeking their elimination' (2005: 144).

Competencies and primal leadership

The concept of leadership competency has become ubiquitous in the field of management development. The theory uses a taxonomy (a classification) of either standards of performance or criterion-related behaviours, which are referred to as 'competence' and '**competencies**'. The difference in spelling is noteworthy. We may define competence as 'the abilities to perform within an occupational area to a standard required in employment' (Gold et al., 2013: 135). A manager or other employee is said to be 'competent' if the output of her or his work meets written standards as specified by performance criteria and evidence-based.

competencies: the abilities, values, personality traits and other characteristics of people that lead to a superior performance

Source: Image Source

Irresponsible bank leaders and the credit crunch

The global financial crisis began with a run on the British bank Northern Rock in September 2007. In 2008, there was a succession of state bail-outs and collapses including the investment banks Bear Stearns, Lehman Brothers and Merrill Lynch. The American mortgage institutions Fannie Mae and Freddie Mac were nationalized, and the US government took a 79.9 per cent share of the insurer AIG when it needed to be bailed out. In September 2008 Lloyds Bank bought HBOS in what was called a merger in order to bail it out. The Icelandic banking system collapsed on 6 October, and 'During the weekend 11–12 October the British banking system teetered on the point of collapse' (Lanchester, 2010: 29). Eventually Lloyds-HBOS was part-nationalized by the British government along with RBS. The crisis also affected banks and insurance companies in various European countries, costing tax payers many billions of dollars, pounds and euros.

Lanchester (2010) offers, for the non-specialist, a scathing and comprehensible explanation of why the banks were allowed to run out of control. Following the collapse of the Soviet system, capitalism and the hegemony of free markets held sway, he says, providing an opportunity for bankers to amass huge amounts of wealth (Lanchester 2010: 12). One major contributor to the credit crunch was the ideology of deregulation and the belief among politicians that laissez-faire capitalism could regulate itself, which led many bankers to believe that they could write their own rules (Lanchester, 2010: 156).

This political and financial culture allowed greed and endorsed the lack of regulation. One aspect of this was the role of huge bonuses: '[bankers'] pay emphasized and encouraged the benefits of taking risks while removing any of the consequences when things went wrong' (Lanchester, 2010: 178). The banks were too big to be allowed to fail and had to be bailed out by governments.

Lanchester also blames the banks for a miscalculation of risk (2010: 178). Too many mortgages were given to families in the US with personal debt who would struggle to repay their loans, and this exacerbated the situation when the bubble burst and house prices fell by 20 per cent. New financial instruments, known as CDOs (collateralized debt obligations), enabled banks to pass on risky debts to other banks, thus globalizing these bad financial assets on a massive scale.

Lanchester's analysis of the credit crunch is multilayered, involving a 'climate (the post-Cold War victory party of free-market capitalism), a problem (the sub-prime mortgages), a mistake (the mathematical models of risk) and a failure, that of the regulators.' Lanchester endorses President Obama's characterization of bank leadership as 'irresponsible' (2010: 177). In their pursuit of profit and expansion, some bank leaders forgot about the value of caution and prudence and embraced 'reckless and destructive risk taking' (Kerr and Robinson, 2011: 158).

> **Stop!** Was it a failure of leadership or poor management tools that caused the historical financial crisis over 2007–09? What do you think needs to be done to prevent the next financial crisis?

Sources and further information

Kerr, R. and Robinson, S. (2011) 'Leadership as an elite field: Scottish banking leaders and the crisis of 2007–2009', *Leadership*, 7(2), pp. 151–73.

Lanchester, J. (2010) *Whoops! Why Everyone Owes Everyone and No One Can Pay*, London: Penguin.

Note: This feature was written by David Denham, Honorary Research Fellow in Sociology, Wolverhampton University, UK.

Competency, on the other hand, focuses on behaviour at work, and is concerned with the abilities of a manager that enable her or him to achieve a superior performance (Gold et al., 2013). The Chartered Institute of Personnel and Development defines competency as:

> The behaviours that employees must have, or must acquire, to input into a situation in order to achieve high levels of performance. (2008: 1)

For Armstrong (2002), there are three core aspects of competence: the input – knowledge, social and technical skills, and personal attributes; the process – the behaviour required to convert the input into an output; and the output – the outcomes that are achieved. The concepts of competence or competency are concerned not only with the inputs and process aspects, but also with the outcomes of people's or, in the context of leadership, followers' behaviours.

A competency model, when applied to leadership, tends to identify a set of desired values, skills and personal attributes, behaviours that organizational members feel their leaders need in order to be effective and to successfully meet current and future specified outcomes. Thus, a competency model is very reminiscent of early behavioural leadership theories. Studies in the UK underscore the importance of competency frameworks in management and leadership development programmes (Oram, 1998). One criticism of the general competency approach to leadership, however, is that it gives insufficient attention to the value of emotion (Bolden and Gosling, 2006).

Daniel Goleman and his colleagues (2013) offer a variant of the competency model that focuses on EI. In a well-documented exposition, they contend that highly effective leaders typically exhibit a critical mass of strength in terms of EI competencies. Goleman et al. argue that there are 19 EI competencies that are the vehicle of *primal leadership* (see Table 5.2). In their model, they divide these into four domains – self-awareness, self-management, social awareness and relationship management. For example, an EI domain would be relationship management, and a competency in that domain would be building bonds and relationships. The importance of this EI competency can be illustrated by French-American artist Louise Bourgeois' (1911–2010) sculpture *The Spider and the Mother*, which highlights the spider's tenacity for weaving and repairing her web – or, metaphorically, personal relationships. The competencies associated with 'building bonds' are highly relevant to leadership in a 'boundaryless' organization (see Chapter 15). According to Sotarauta (2005), leaders engaged in regional development activities must influence the actions and decisions of other leaders outside their own organizational authority, and to be effective they therefore have to exhibit networking competencies in order to cultivate and nurture a web of relationships.

The primal leadership model builds on connections to neurology. In a nutshell, people respond to their leaders positively when emotionally intelligent leaders 'drive resonance'. The root of the word 'resonance' comes from the Latin word '*resonare*', to sound again. The *Oxford English Dictionary* gives its modern meaning as, 'the reinforcement or prolongation of sound by reflection or synchronous vibration'. EI helps leaders to create resonance, which is a reservoir of human positivity that brings out the best in followers when their 'emotional centers are in synch in a positive way' (Goleman et al., 2013: 33). According to Goleman et al.:

> Underpinning that proposition is a theory of performance, one that surfaces the links between the neurology of the four fundamentals of emotional intelligence and the EI competencies that build on those fundamentals. These EI competencies are in turn the building blocks of the modes of leadership that prime resonance in a group. (2013: 38)

Although Goleman et al. insist that there is no 'fixed' formula for superior leadership, effective leaders should demonstrate a critical mass of strength in at least one competence from each of the four core areas of EI.

It is important to note that Goleman et al. do not suggest reviving the discredited claim that successful leadership resides in a single charismatic leader. Moreover, research shows that EI competencies can be *learned*, and that cross-cultural differences are 'insignificant', indicating that leadership capabilities that drive resonance can be assessed anywhere the organization operates.

Evaluating the competency approach

The competencies identified to promote an individual to a leadership role may be more likely to be exhibited by a particular gender or ethnic group. Applying Erving Goffman's 'dramaturgical' approach – the idea that everyday life is a theatrical stage – another criticism is the distinction between actual and perceived competence. If an individual cultivates the correct 'office front', it may enable a relatively incompetent individual to be perceived by co-workers as competent (Price and Garland, 1981).

stop...

Do these generalized competencies that Goleman and his colleagues have identified offer any new insights into what constitutes effective leadership? Why do you think cultural differences were found to be insignificant?

...and reflect

Leadership-as-practice

A limitation of the competency approach to leadership is that it gives insufficient attention to the value of 'reflexivity'. The leadership-as-practice perspective is another contemporary leadership model that attempts to dethrone traditional leadership paradigms, and, it is claimed, recognizes the value of reflexivity and emotion. Leadership-as-practice is concerned about *where*, *how* and *why* leadership activity is being organized and accomplished, rather than having the traditional focus on who is offering visions for others to follow. The focus is on social interactions and behavioural change within organizations. Specifically, the leadership-as-practice model focuses on the everyday *practice* of leadership, including its relational, moral and emotional aspects, rather than its rational and technical ones (Carroll et al., 2008). A practice is a cooperative effort among participants who choose through their own rules to achieve a distinctive outcome. According to Raelin (2011), the primary advantage of leadership-as-practice is that managers and others are better able to understand and reflect on their own actions, and are consequently better able to reconstruct their activity in light of their reflections and on behalf of their mutual interests. Leadership-as-practice is often depicted as a shared process that has collaborative tendencies. As such, the model is not value-free in respect of the nature of employee participation and is identified with the norms of the democratic tradition (Raelin, 2011: 196).

Evaluating the leadership-as-practice approach

Although the leadership-as-practice model does give greater attention to the value of 'reflexivity', the approach also has its shortcomings. For example, attempts to characterize leadership as a repertoire of practices may suffer from overplaying influence and agreement instead of divergence, unresolved conflicts and power relationships (Raelin, 2011).

Power, gender and cross-cultural issues

As we discussed in earlier chapters, critical organizational theorists are highly sceptical about the assumptions and motives upon which traditional accounts of management are based. The mainstream leadership literature assumes consensus in the workplace, namely that socially consensual leadership increases employee commitment, and that leaders actually influence organizational performance. Critical analysts emphasize that leadership is intrinsically rooted in power. The assumption made in the mainstream leadership literature is that if leaders can persuade their followers to act, the leaders appear to be powerful. The new popular rhetoric on leadership envisages the shifting from the old 'command and control' style of leading to 'shared leadership'. Thus, it is argued that, in the so-called knowledge economy, much of leadership is paradoxical: leaders gain more power by giving it away.

Power is related to leadership because it is part of the influence process. But what is power, where does it come from, and what do we know about the relationship between leaders and power? Some scholars interested in **power–influence theories** seek to explain leadership effectiveness in terms of the amount and type of power possessed by a leader, and how the leader exercises that power. One major issue addressed by scholars is the way in which power is 'acquired' and 'lost' by various individuals in the workplace. Team-based organizational designs and notions of power sharing through participative leadership styles have generated an interest in power–influence research.

Others scholars have emphasized the primacy of language and discourse in understanding power. According to this perspective, power is not a commodity

power–influence approach: an approach that examines processes of influence between leaders and followers, and explains leadership effectiveness in terms of the amount and type of power possessed by an organizational leader and how that power is exercised

possessed by leaders, but operates through discourses, which produce knowledge, and through disciplinary techniques that define and constrain the identities of both followers and leaders. Michel Foucault's work on power-knowledge, which suggests that followers are deeply enmeshed in their own subordination, is prominent in this approach to power–influence (Foucault, 1977). Chapter 14 provides further discussion on the traditional and contemporary approaches to power in the organization, and their relationship to work behaviour.

plate 44 Some argue that powerful economic and organizational imperatives do not permit opportunities for female managers to put into practice a 'feminist' style of leadership.

Source: SCOREGolf

Since the early 1990s, the topic of gender has entered the leadership literature, and has generated much research and questioning on, among other things, whether women lead differently from men. Mainstream analysts argue that women managers have a more interactive style, which includes more people-oriented, knowledge-sharing and participative leadership. Feminist leadership characteristics that have been identified include consensus building, shared power and the promotion of diversity.

Critical analysts have focused on the way in which jobs, occupations and organizations are themselves gendered, arguing that the processes and practices of gendering within the organization consolidate men's power in the workplace, and marginalize and exclude women from management positions. This is popularly referred to as the 'glass ceiling'. As we have already noted, numerous writers have pointed out that most leadership models are based on male behaviour.

Does gender make a difference? Do women managers have more people-oriented and participative leadership styles? Whereas some observers have proposed that stereotypically feminine characteristics, such as warmth, caring and **empathy**, allow women to succeed in organizational leadership roles because they are associated with a 'transformative' leadership style (Rosener, 1990), sociologists analysing from a critical perspective have argued that the belief that women are 'naturally' more consensual could be 'the expression of a relative lack of power rather than a characteristic of womanhood per se' (Wajcman, 1998: 165). Data on practising managers suggest that workers tend to perceive female managers as having an 'inclusive' and 'soft' leadership style, and male managers as having a 'controlling' and 'hard' style. Some feminists argue that women leaders in organizations have the interactional leadership style needed to encourage and nurture workers' commitment to organizational goals.

Sociological studies focus our attention on familiar antagonisms and imperatives, which avoid the tedious piety about female managers being inclusive and cooperative while male managers are competitive and controlling. Managers of both genders are competitive, and male managers are just as capable of being inclusive as women. The choice between different leadership styles is usually dictated by the situation and by economic and organizational imperatives. As Judy Wajcman compellingly argues:

> The literature on women's management style … has been concerned with the issue of whether women manage in the same way as men or have a distinct style of their own … We are asked to celebrate an idealized femininity as demonstrated by women's greater caring, intuitive qualities. The

stop...

Go back to Chapter 3 and read the section on feminist theory. How would you apply feminist approaches to leadership? To what extent does the majority male culture of organizations shape gender relations in the workplace?

...and reflect

empathy: a person's ability to understand and be sensitive to the feelings, thoughts and situations of others

trouble is that the qualities, characteristics and culture ascribed to women originate from the historical subordination of women … in practice, senior women managers manage in much the same way as senior men within the same specific context. This is because styles of management are shaped more by organizational imperatives than by the sex or personal style of specific individuals. (1998: 258–9)

Thus, the organizational dynamics and culture might not provide opportunities for female managers to put into practice a 'feminist' style of leadership, but might instead compel them to 'manage like men'.

Evaluating leadership: is leadership important?

Do leaders actually influence organizational performance? To begin to answer this question, we need a sense of the methodological challenges of measuring the leadership–performance link.

Numerous studies have found this area of research wanting in terms of theory, research methodology and the identification of leadership attributes and behaviours to be used when establishing a causal relationship with performance outcomes (Wright and Gardner, 2003). Theoretically, no consensus exists regarding what constitutes 'leadership', and thus what aspects of leadership should be selected and isolated. What types of performance variable should be measured? What variables are commonly used, including employee job satisfaction, productivity, customer satisfaction and market share? Any analysis is of course very much dependent on, among other things, the perspective that is used (Gaertner and Ramnarayan, 1983), the leadership attributes and performance variables selected to measure the leadership–performance relationship (Matsuo, 2012; Purcell and Kinnie, 2008) and the effect of societal culture on perceptions of what exactly constitutes effective leadership (Brodbeck et al., 2000; Den Hartog et al., 1997; Hofstede, 2001; Weiner and Mahoney, 1981; Zammuto, 1982). These problems echo the challenges of measuring the HRM–performance relationship (Purcell and Kinnie, 2008).

VISIT THE *ONLINE RESOURCE CENTRE* AT HTTPS://HE.PALGRAVE.COM/COMPANION/BRATTON-WORK-AND-ORGANIZATIONAL-BEHAVIOUR3/ FOR FURTHER INFORMATION AND RESEARCH ON EVALUATING THE LEADERSHIP–PERFORMANCE RELATIONSHIP.

In terms of performance variables, shareholders may evaluate the organization's performance solely in terms of financial outcomes such as profits and share values. For example, one study found that 44 per cent of the profitability of the organizations studied was accounted for by changing the leader (Weiner and Mahoney, 1981). Employees may, however, judge the organization's performance in terms of a healthy and safe workplace, while community groups may focus on compliance with environmental regulations.

The argument that leaders influence alternative performance outcomes, such as group dynamics, innovation and workplace learning, seems plausible and is made by numerous writers. Zohar and Tenne-Gazit (2008), for example, have reported that leadership is associated with positive effects on group members' shared perceptions of an organization's practices and the types of behaviour that are rewarded. Another study by Jansen et al. (2009) found that transformational leadership had a positive effect on exploratory innovation (pursuing new knowledge and developing products and services), but had no significant effect on exploitative innovation (building on existing knowledge resources and extending existing products and services); transactional leadership, however, had a positive effect on exploitative innovation but a negative effect on exploratory innovation. Nemanich and Vera

(2009) found that, in team-based environments, transformational leadership had a positive effect on a learning culture characterized by an openness to diverse opinions and participation in decision making, as well as encouraging employees to engage in creative processes. Based upon survey data, Matsuo (2012) found that attributes of transformative leadership facilitated reflective practice in leading employee learning, which, the author argues, may be a central characteristic of transformative leadership.

Even though situational leadership theories suggest that the leader's behaviour should be adjusted to meet the demands of situational variables, research examining the influence of organizational culture as a key moderator of the leadership–performance relationship has been neglected (Xenikou and Furnham, 2013: 143). The hypothesis is that organizational culture might be the 'filter' through which other important variables such as leadership influence organizational performance (Lim, 1995). Ogbonna and Harris (2000) have demonstrated that, within a culture of employee engagement, participative and supportive leadership had positive effects on performance by stimulating innovation.

Although there seem to be attributes of a leader that are universally endorsed as contributing positively to performance, cross-cultural research has explored the effect of societal culture on perceptions of effective leadership (Xenikou and Furnham, 2013). So, for example, in organizations that operate in feminine cultures (for example, Nordic countries) leaders are effective if they are characterized as being inclusive and less visible, and if they place a high value on consensus. On the other hand, effective leaders in masculine cultures such as the USA and Britain are dynamic, competitive and decisive. The existence of culturally contingent attributes of effective leadership has been empirically supported (see, for example, Brodbeck et al., 2000; Den Hartog et al., 1997). These results reinforce the findings that leadership has a fundamental role in shaping and guiding the cultural characteristics of the organization (Berson et al., 2008).

The counterargument is that leadership is of little consequence – that the forces the leader is subjected to are more influential (Pfeffer and Salancik, 1977). A dramatic example is the 2001 collapse of the North American airline industry, without any change in leadership, following the September 11 attack on the World Trade Center in New York. In some sectors, 'the leader is insignificant' hypothesis can be made following the global recession caused by the US and UK financial crisis of 2008/09. An adequate analysis of that crisis requires that we identify not only the reckless behaviour of the bankers, but also the social contexts that endorsed the merits of a 'light touch' regulation of the banking sector. Furthermore, as we have discussed, it is argued that leaders have limited discretion in their strategic behaviours, and ineffective leaders can be substituted by synergistic work teams and information technology (Howell et al., 1990).

Evaluating organizational leadership presents tough methodological challenges for researchers. The research on leadership outcomes calls for the disclosure of commercially sensitive information on performance indicators, which many managers are unwilling or unable to provide to an independent researcher. The researcher has to isolate the relevant variables. For instance, even if an apparently causal relationship between leadership and market share is discovered, can it be assumed that nothing else has changed in the meantime? Exchange rates can significantly affect market share, and factors like this make it difficult to assess the effectiveness of leadership with complete confidence. In addition, the selection of appropriate criteria depends on the objectives and values of the person making the evaluation (Yukl, 2013). Moreover, the effect of societal culture on the perceptions of what constitutes effective leadership broadens the research domain (Brodbeck et al., 2000). There is broad agreement, therefore, that it is difficult to evaluate the leader–performance relationship, as there are so many alternative measures of performance and it is uncertain which criterion is most relevant.

We started this section by asking the question, 'Do leaders actually influence organizational performance?' Arguably, in the last quarter of the twentieth century, when neo-liberalism dominated management and political thinking, there was popular enthusiasm for the transformative outcomes attributed to the perceived charismatic leader. In the post-2008 global financial crisis era, however, enthusiasm for the popular 'heroic' theories of leadership waned in the throes of a prolonged economic recession – the longest since 1929 – spectacular banking failures and corporate misbehaviour. Indeed, researchers have shown the 'dark side' of charismatic leadership, and some are scathing of the adulatory focus on so-called visionary leaders (Khurana, 2002).

We need a model of leadership that explicitly seeks to address social inequality, and produce a 'better' society, by rethinking and reinventing leadership (Western, 2013: 3), perhaps a leadership model that recognizes that the basis of ethical leadership is human dignity and social justice (Morrison, 2015), and that celebrates mutual equality between the actors and the active visible hand of government – for a stronger regulation of global capitalism. Challenging the traditional notion of leadership, Keith Grint argues that critical to successful leadership:

> Is not a list of innate skills and competences, or how much charisma you have, or whether you have a vision or a strategy for achieving that vision, but whether you have *a capacity to learn from your followers*. And that learning approach is inevitably embedded in a relational model of leadership. (2005: 105, emphasis added)

When organizational leadership is conceptualized not as a position, but as a complex social process involving leaders and others within specific contexts, an adequate understanding of leadership requires a study of the behaviours and attributes not only of leaders, but also of relevant others and groups, as well as of how societal and organizational contexts affect the social dynamics of leadership. Finally, when there is a greater awareness of climate change, we need to understand the interconnectedness of leadership, workplace learning, innovation and sustainable low-carbon workplaces.

stop...

The search for causal links between leadership and business performance has influenced debate for decades. Do you think researchers have generated sufficiently robust evidence of a leadership–performance linkage? Hint: in terms of methodology, is there a consensus on how leadership performance and organizational performance are to be measured?

...and reflect

Chapter summary

- Leadership is a dialectical process in which an individual persuades others to do something they would not otherwise do. It is a result of the interaction between the leader and followers in a specific context, and is equated with power.

- Leadership is not the same as management. Management is associated with functions such as planning, organizing, controlling and efficiency, whereas leadership is associated with vision making and significant change. Management processes produce a degree of order and consistency in work behaviour. Leadership processes produce significant change or movement.

- We observed that leadership theories are typically classified according to the types of variable emphasized in a theory or empirical study. We reviewed the major perspectives of leadership, including the trait, behaviour, contingency, transformational, shared and competency approaches. We showed how the systematic research on leadership has evolved from a narrow focus on the leader's traits to a multidimensional model of leadership, which looks at the exercise of leadership as a complex reciprocal process affected by the interaction between the leader, the followers and the opportunities and constraints afforded by the external and internal contexts in which they find themselves.

- We have examined contemporary leadership theories including distribution leadership, leadership competencies and leadership-as-practice. The effects of societal cultures and organizational cultures on leadership performance have also been examined. There is empirical evidence supporting the theory that organizational culture might be a filter through which leadership influences organizational performance outcomes.

- We have drawn attention to issues of power and gender, as well as to the limitations of individualistically oriented charismatic and transformative leadership models.

- In the context of twenty-first century corporate greed, irresponsibility, scandals and a single-minded focus on shareholder value, there is the danger that once people over-align themselves with a company, and invest excessive faith in the wisdom of its leaders, they are liable to lose their original sense of identity, tolerate ethical lapses they would have previously deplored, find a new and possibly corrosive value system taking root, and leave themselves vulnerable to manipulation by the leaders of the organization, to whom they have mistakenly entrusted many of their vital interests (Tourish and Vatcha, 2005).

IN THE EBOOK ACCESS **WEB BASED ASSIGNMENTS** TO APPLY YOUR LEARNING.

Chapter review questions

1 Are management and leadership diametrically opposed?
2 What are the main differences between classical and modern theories of leadership?
3 In the context of recent corporate and banking failures, does the use of unethical methods negate the claim to be a leader?

4 What contribution do critical analysts make to our understanding of organizational leadership?
5 After reading this chapter, do you believe that leaders are born or made?
6 How do managers and leaders make a difference to organizational performance?

Further reading

Alvesson, M. and Willmott, H. C. (1996) *Making Sense of Management*, London: Sage.

Bolden, R. and Gosling, J. (2006) 'Leadership competencies: time to change the tune?', *Leadership*, 2(2), p. 160.

Carroll, B., Levy, L. and Richmond, D. (2008) 'Leadership as practice: challenging the competency paradigm', *Leadership*, 4(4), pp. 363–79.

Goleman, D., Boyatzis, R. and McKee, A. (2013) *Primal Leadership* (10th anniv. edn), Boston, MA: Harvard Business Review Press.

Haslam, S. A., Reicher, S. D. and Platow, M. J. (2010) *The New Psychology of Leadership: Identity, Influence and Power*, New York: Psychology Press.

Herold, D., Fedor, D., Caldwell, S. and Liu, Y. (2008) 'The effects of transformational and change leadership on employees' commitment to change: a multilevel study', *Journal of Applied Psychology*, 93(2), pp. 346–57.

Jackson, B. and Parry, K. (2011) *A Very Short, Fairly Interesting and Reasonably Cheap Book about Studying Leadership* (2nd edn), London: Sage.

Kouzes, J. and Posner, B. (2012) *The Leadership Challenge: How to Make Extraordinary Things Happen in Organizations* (5th edn), San Francisco, CA: Jossey-Bass.

Lussier, R. N. and Achua, C. F. (2015) *Leadership: Theory, Application, and Skill Development*, Boston, MA: Cengage Learning.

Mustafa, G. and Lines, R. (2014) 'Influence of leadership on job satisfaction: the moderating effects of follower individual-level masculinity-femininity values', *Journal of Leadership*, 7(4), pp. 23–39.

Raelin, J. (2011) 'From leadership-as-practice to leaderful practice', *Leadership*, 7(2), pp. 195–211.

Sarti, D. (2014) 'Leadership styles to engage employees: evidence from human service organizations in Italy', *Journal of Workplace Learning*, 26(3/4), pp. 202–16.

Schnurr, S. (2008) 'Surviving in a man's world with a sense of humour: an analysis of women leaders' use of humour at work', *Leadership*, 4(3), pp. 299–319.

Sundgren, M. and Styhre, A. (2006) 'Leadership as de-paradoxification: leading new drug development work at three pharmaceutical companies', *Leadership*, 2(1), pp. 31–51.

Thomson, P. and Lloyd, T. (2011) *Women and the New Business Leadership*, Basingstoke: Palgrave Macmillan.

Western, S. (2013) *Leadership: A Critical Text*, London: Sage.

Zhu, W., He, H., Treviño, L. K., , M. M. and Wang, W. (2015) 'Ethical leadership and follower voice and performance: the role of follower identifications and entity morality beliefs', *Leadership Quarterly*, doi:10.1016/j.leaqua.2015.01.004.

Chapter case study: Hitting the glass ceiling at Hotoke, Japan

The setting

Women have long held subservient roles in Japanese society, and Japan's 1986 law barring sex discrimination in the workplace did little to stem societal perceptions on traditional gender divisions of labour. It established a social obligation not to discriminate, but does not impose penalties on those who breach the law. In 2004, only 2.7 per cent of division chiefs at Japanese companies with 100 employees or more were women. Japan's lack of external support for families, including daycare options, makes it difficult for married women to continue working once they start a family. Company expectations for workers to put in long days at the office and attend social events in the evenings also creates stress for women, who are typically responsible for the bulk of domestic responsibilities in the home. It is therefore not surprising that many Japanese women view having a long-term career and a life as a wife and mother as simply incompatible.

The problem

Hotoke is an international, well-established company based in Japan, where it has led the industry in producing a variety of information technology and security products, digital devices and parts, and power and industrial services for over half a century. This includes home electronics, audio/visual equipment, PCs, mobile phones and lifestyle services. The company also conducts advanced, wide-ranging research in fields ranging from parts and materials development to hardware, software and services, resulting in world-leading research achievements.

Shigeru Takahasi oversees the electronics business segment of the business. In recent years, it had become increasingly difficult to recruit for key positions within his division, and with the company's ageing workforce, Shigeru knew this problem would only become worse. When one of his lower level managers became ill and had to leave the company, Shigeru decided to look at employees in the non-management pool to see who might be a viable candidate.

Shigeru's first response was to look among the male workers as they made up the overwhelming majority of employees in the electronics area, but one female worker, 26-year-old Hirose Takako, caught his eye. Unlike most of the female employees who held university degrees in the humanities, education or the social sciences, Hirose had studied engineering. She had been with the company since she had graduated, and although she was an obviously intelligent woman, she was still working in an assistant's role similar to that of the other female employees. She had been provided with only minimal training since her arrival.

Shigeru knew that he would face a challenge from upper level management in recommending Hirose for the management vacancy. After all, there had never been a female manager in the entire history of the company. Shigeru felt the time was right to move in that direction. After preparing the background material, Shigeru made a presentation to the Board of Directors.

As expected, the Board was not initially impressed with the idea. 'We cannot promote women and give them more responsible jobs,' one Director remarked. 'She will be likely to quit to get married. We cannot invest in someone who will be leaving soon. We expect a lifetime commitment.' Another complained that female workers were not able to execute plans and lacked the socialization skills to be part of management.

Shigeru was persistent. 'We must become more diverse in our promotion process. It will help us to solve our demographic issue and to become more innovative.' After some persuasion and several meetings later, the Board agreed to provide Hirose with a trial period as the company's first female manager.

It did not take long for Shigeru to become disappointed. Although she was cooperative and demonstrated a consensus style of decision making, valued by the Japanese management, Hirose clearly lacked confidence and appeared uncomfortable at the thought of being the company's first female manager. She disliked socializing in the male-oriented bars with the other managers in the evenings. Hirose quit shortly after her promotion, telling Shigeru that she was stressed with the idea of being a role model for other women and was not willing to forego marriage and motherhood in exchange for such challenges. Shortly after Hirose's resignation, Shigeru's supervisor asked him to prepare a report on what the company, and Shigeru, had learned from the experience.

The task

Prepare a short report, including answers to the following questions:

- How do the trait and gender perspectives help to explain why Hirose may or may not have been the right choice for the management job?
- How did the company's culture, which reflects that of Japanese society as a whole, contribute to how Hirose reacted?
- What could the organization have done to help prepare Hirose and the company itself for her new role?

Essential reading

Adler, N. and Izraeli, D. (eds) (1994) *Competitive Frontiers: Women Managers in a Global Economy*, Cambridge: Blackwell.

Imamura, A. (ed.) (1996) *Re-imaging Japanese Women*, Berkeley, CA: University of California Press.

Shimada, H. and Rebick, M. (2005) *The Japanese Employment System: Adapting To a New Economic Environment*, Oxford: Oxford University Press.

Tanaka, Y. (1995) *Contemporary Portraits of Japanese Women*, Connecticut: Praeger.

Woods, G. (2005) 'Japan's diversity problem: women command too few posts', *Wall Street Journal*, October 24.

Note: This case study was written by Lori Rilkoff, Human Resources Director, City of Kamloops, BC, Canada.

IN THE EBOOK ACCESS AN **OB IN FILM** BOX THAT USES *MASTER AND COMMANDER* (2004) TO ILLUSTRATE KEY CONCEPTS AROUND LEADERSHIP AND TO ACCESS **AN INTERACTIVE QUIZ** TO TEST YOUR UNDERSTANDING.

chapter 13

chapter 13
Decision making, ethics and social responsibility

Key concepts

- bounded rationality
- brainstorming
- computer-mediated brainstorming
- corporate crime
- corporate social responsibility
- Delphi technique
- democratic leadership
- employee voice
- escalation of commitment
- ethics in decision making
- nominal group technique
- programmable and non-programmable decisions

Chapter outline

- Introduction
- The nature of decision making
- The rhetoric of decision making
- The realities of decision making
- Power, gender and decision making
- Employee voice in decision making
- Ethics and corporate social responsibility
- Developing decision-making skills
- Summary and end-of-chapter features
- Chapter case study: Ethical decision making at Primark

Chapter learning outcomes

After completing this chapter, you should be able to:

1 Define organizational decision making
2 Explain the process behind the rational model of decision making
3 Compare and contrast the rational model with how managers actually make decisions
4 Explain how power and gender dimensions affect the rational model of decision making
5 Describe the benefits of employee involvement in decision making
6 Explain the meanings of ethics and business ethics
7 Discuss the nature of corporate social responsibility
8 Discuss structured group interventions to improve the group process and the quality of group decisions

introduction

The 2014 BBC2 television programme *Horizon: How You Really Make Decisions* illustrated that most of the decisions we make every day – up to 10,000 of them – are not rational, logical and thought through, but are fast and intuitive. In addition, we sometimes make decisions predicated on unconnected decisions we have made in the past. The *Horizon* programme also identified something called confirmation bias, which means we search for information that supports what we believe. While it would seem a miracle that anyone ever makes a good decision in everyday life, it would be reasonable to assume that the decisions taken in corporate and organizational life are much more rational, logical and evidence-based. Yet when profit comes into the equation, decision making can be worse. Loss aversion (think of the 2008 banking crisis), an over-reliance on intuition, too much credence given to the notion that past practices will continue in the future, and ethical issues, all feature in organizational decision making. Take, for example, the catastrophic event involving the space shuttle *Columbia*. In technical terms, it was a piece of foam about the size of a laptop computer that caused the disintegration on re-entry into Earth's atmosphere of the space craft in February 2003. However, a scathing US government report concluded that the root cause of the fatal crash was managerial myopia and the culture of the US National Aeronautics and Space Administration (NASA). Individuals in NASA made decisions affecting *Columbia*. Senior managers determined NASA's goals, mission schedules and budget. Middle-level managers also made decisions impacting on *Columbia*'s mission: they determined production schedules and the design and safety of the space shuttle, and decided to reduce the involvement of NASA's workforce and instead increasingly rely on outside contractors. NASA's engineers 'found themselves in the unusual position of having to prove that the situation was *unsafe* – a reversal of the usual requirement to prove that a situation *is safe*', the report states (Anonymous, *The Globe and Mail*, 2003).

plate 45 A US government report concluded that a contributing cause of *Columbia*'s fatal crash was the culture of decision making at NASA.

The decisions made by managers, especially the major, far-reaching decisions, are of critical importance to workers, communities and other stakeholders. Of course, making decisions is not the sole prerogative of management. Non-managerial employees at NASA, for example, also made decisions that affected their work and the safety of the *Columbia* shuttle. The more obvious of these decisions might have included whether to comply with a request made by a manager, knowing that safety standards were being compromised. Although there may be employee involvement and participation (EIP), decisions can be viewed as being primarily concerned with the allocation and exercise of power in organizations (Miller et al., 1999). The study of decision making is therefore crucial to understanding why organizations come to be what they are and how people behave in them.

The work conducted at NASA is frequently used to illustrate the highest levels of cognitive ability, reflected in the popular comment 'This isn't rocket science.' So how could so many smart people who *do* engage in rocket science make a series of such bad decisions? We shall find out in this chapter. First, however, we define decision making and present a decision-making model that characterizes the process as a rational act. As we work through this model, we will be especially concerned with exploring the neoclassical economic assumption that managers act rationally towards a common purpose, and with the practical limitations of managerial rationality.

The limits of managerial rationality are perhaps best illustrated by recent decision making in the finance sector. Explaining why no one foresaw the timing, extent and severity of the 2008 global economic recession, a group of eminent economists tell of irrational factors such as the 'psychology of denial', the 'feel-good factor' and 'wishful thinking combined with hubris' (Stewart, 2009). Profit goals and stakeholder interests overlap with environmental and human rights issues, and fall under the notion of corporate social responsibility (CSR). Unsurprisingly, from the G20 summit to the workplace, business ethics and CSR have attracted more attention from practitioners, academics and politicians. Indeed, some academics observe that 'corporate social responsibility has increasingly become a social norm' (Shen and Benson, 2014: 17). The CSR perspective acknowledges that private and public organizations have not only economic responsibilities, but also legal and ethical responsibilities (Morrison, 2015). Ethical responsibilities entail making decisions that potentially conflict with economic goals. This chapter closes therefore with a look at ethics in decision making and CSR before examining some techniques to improve decision making. The purpose of the chapter is to situate decision making in the context of managerial rationales, opportunities, constraints and power.

The nature of decision making

decision making: a conscious process of making choices between one or more alternatives with the intention of moving towards some desired state of affairs

Decision making is the conscious process of making choices from among several alternatives with the intention of moving towards some desired course of action (March, 1997; Miller et al., 1999; Shull et al., 1970). Four things are noteworthy about this definition. First, decision making involves making a *choice* between several alternatives for action: for instance, NASA's engineers can choose to have a spacecraft carry more or less inventory, can decide to use different materials or can decide to rely on external contractors to make and assemble a spacecraft's components. Second, decision making is a *process* that involves more than simply the final choice from among the alternatives – if a NASA manager decides to outsource work, we want to know how this decision was reached. Third, the 'action' mentioned in the definition typically involves some commitment of *resources*, such as money, personnel or time. The *Columbia* shuttle project required a substantial resource commitment. Finally, the notion of 'choice' underscores the role of power. Critical workplace scholars take it as self-evident that decision making can only be understood in the context of power relations. As others have observed, 'decision making may be seen more accurately as a game of power in which competing interest groups vie with each other for the control of scarce resources' (Miller et al., 1999: 45–6).

Decision making is possibly the most important function of management. Ever since Fayol's (1949) seminal work, which identified management as a series of rational activities related to planning, organizing, directing and controlling, it has been appreciated that managerial behaviour involves decision making. This perspective on management assumes that managers act rationally as they continually strive to enhance the efficiency and competitive position of the organization. The control perspective of management also proceeds from the general assumption that managers act rationally, which, according to this school, involves making decisions designed to maximize control of the labour process and the level of 'surplus' extracted from workers.

stop...

Before reading on, think about your own work experience or your knowledge of work organizations. Can you think of a group or an individual decision that has led to success or failure?

...and reflect

Table 13.1 shows that organizational decision making can be studied at different levels: individual, group and organizational. Each level centres on its own set of assumptions and theoretical approach, and on its own key issues. However, the levels are interconnected, each one influencing and being affected by the other two.

Table 13.1 Levels of organizational decision-making behaviour

Level of analysis	Theoretical approaches	Key issues
Organizational	Theories of organizational power, politics, conflict and decision making	Effects of power, politics and conflict
Group	Group conformity, group dynamics, group size and networks	Effects of group dynamics, individuals' perceptions and behaviours
Individual	Information-processing theory Cognitive psychology	Information overload Personal biases

The rhetoric of decision making

The rhetoric and debate about organizational decision making draws heavily on what is referred to as the 'rational' economic model of decision making. This model has its roots in neoclassical economic theory. Managers continually strive to find the right mix of factor inputs (such as raw materials, machinery and labour) to enable them to minimize the per unit production costs and maximize their profits. The rational economic model underscores the importance of managerial decision making on issues of resource allocation, efficiency and labour productivity. The model is primarily normative, providing a guide on how managerial decision making ought to be done. It is shown in Figure 13.1.

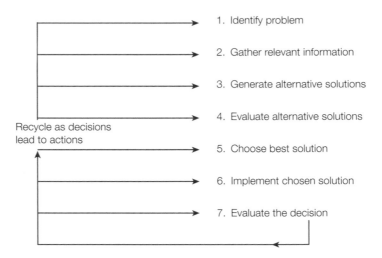

1. Identify problem

2. Gather relevant information

3. Generate alternative solutions

4. Evaluate alternative solutions

Recycle as decisions
lead to actions

5. Choose best solution

6. Implement chosen solution

7. Evaluate the decision

Figure 13.1 A rational decision-making model

The first step in the rational model of decision making is to identify a problem or recognize an opportunity. A *problem* is the deviation between the current and the desired situation – the gap between 'what is' and 'what ought to be'. An *opportunity* is a deviation between current expectations and a potentially better situation, which had not previously been expected. In other words, decision makers realize that alternative decisions may produce outcomes beyond current expectations or goals.

The second step is to gather all the relevant information related to the problem or opportunity, and the third step is to generate a list of possible solutions. This typically involves searching for off-the-shelf or ready-made solutions, such as practices that have been effective elsewhere in similar situations. Step four is to evaluate each alternative solution. In a purely rational process, this involves decision makers identifying all factors against which the alternatives are judged, assigning weights reflecting the importance of those factors, rating each alternative on those factors, and then calculating each alternative's total value from the ratings and factor weights.

Step five involves choosing the best solution based on the systematic rating exercise, and in step six the chosen solution is implemented. The final step in the rational decision-making model involves evaluating the decision to see whether the solution has narrowed the gap between 'what is' and 'what ought to be'. Ideally, these seven steps are informed by relevant and objective feedback in the form of a feedback loop.

Programmable and non-programmable decisions

Decision makers make myriad decisions every day. In his seminal text, Herbert Simon (1977) observed that different types of decisions can be processed in different ways. Some decisions follow pre-established rules that give employees guidance on *what* to do, *how* to do it and *when* to do it, often using computer technology. These are routine decisions, which tend to be familiar, repetitive and made by less senior employees. For example, the reordering of stock items that have fallen below a certain level on a supermarket shelf falls into this category of decisions. Simon classified these types of decisions as *programmable decisions*, which are 'repetitive and routine, to the extent that a definite procedure has been worked out for handling them so that they don't have to be treated from scratch each time they occur' (Simon, 1977: 46). Modern organizations engage in a form of programmable decision making much of the time.

In contrast, some decisions involve multiple variables, have major repercussions causing a redefinition of the organization and therefore need to be processed in a different way. An example of this type of decision includes an investment in energy-saving technology or a totally new product or service, or a decision to relocate or close an office. These are *strategic decisions*, which are unfamiliar, complex and usually authorized by the most senior managers. Simon classified these types of decisions as *non-programmable decisions* 'to the extent that they are novel, unstructured and unusually consequential' (Simon, 1977: 46). Another way to put this is that a strategic or non-programmable decision is the equivalent of '*vu jàdé*' (never before sanctioned).

risk: a situation in which decision makers have a high knowledge of alternatives, know the probability and can calculate the costs and assess the benefits of each alternative

Decisions in organizations also differ in terms of their degree of **risk**. Routine programmable decisions typically involve low levels of risk, while non-programmable decisions tend to be associated with high levels of risk. As a means of creating sustainable workplaces, there is a great deal of attraction in considering organizational learning as crucial to determining whether a decision lends itself to being programmable (Smith, 2012). Non-programmable decisions might involve a certain degree of 'advocacy' for lower level managers and other employees who can challenge assumptions and practices around the agency of senior management (Arrowsmith and Parker, 2013; see 'Employee voice in decision making'). A two-dimensional classification used to describe the differences between programmable and non-programmable types of decisions is summarized in Table 13.2.

Table 13.2 Programmable and non-programmable types of decisions

	Programmable	**Non-programmable**
Type of decision	Routine	Strategic
Problem	Well defined	Poorly defined
Risk	Low	High
Consequences	Minor	Major
Level	Lower level employee	Senior executives
Involvement (EIP)	Individual	Group
Time frame	Short	Long

The programmable and non-programmable typology involves a continuum, with only the extremes representing the two distinct polar types (Pomerol and Adam, 2004). The dimensions of decision making discussed so far, routine or strategic, have parallels with types of organizational change – 'third order', 'second order' and 'first order', which we examine in Chapter 18.

Assumptions of the rational economic decision-making model

Assumptions inevitably enter analyses of decision making. Take, for example, the identification of problems: this first step in the decision-making process makes assumptions about rationality. In the case of NASA's managerial decisions, one might ask, 'Why outsource work in the first place?' Perhaps, in order to ensure that safety standards are not compromised, NASA's engineers could manufacture and assemble the shuttle's components on site under rigorous supervision. Or why assume that outside contractors can meet safety standards and remain within budget? Perhaps the criterion for the decision is not simply to choose the low-cost option.

Multiple criteria might be to balance the cost of the component, the demonstrable safety results and the time taken to deliver the component. In order to be rational, NASA's decision makers would have to assign weights to each of these three criteria. These weights would indicate how important each criterion was compared with the others, and, given these weights, a new optimal production operation could be chosen. Although the decision to rely on outside contractors, for example, appears to fit the rational model, assumptions have been built into the solution.

Criterion weights are assumptions because they are based on the values and preferences of the decision maker. The point we are making here is that even decisions made using the rational model have assumptions built into them. These assumptions deal with the way the problem is identified and the way objectives are defined. The designers of the rational decision-making model hold a cluster of assumptions about human tendencies when it comes to decision making in the workplace. Let us briefly review some of those assumptions:

- *Problem clarity* – the problem is clear and unambiguous. The decision maker is assumed to have complete information regarding the situation surrounding the decision.
- *Known options* – It is assumed that the decision maker can identify all the relevant criteria and list all the viable alternatives. In addition, the decision maker is aware of all the possible consequences of each alternative.
- *Clear preferences* – rationality assumes that the criteria and alternatives can be ranked and weighted to reflect their importance.
- *Constant preferences* – it is assumed that the specific criteria for the decision are constant, and that the weights assigned to them are stable over time.
- *Maximum pay-off* – the rational decision maker will choose the alternative that yields the highest efficiency or return on factor inputs.
- *No time or cost constraints* – the rational decision maker can obtain full information about the criteria and the alternatives because it is assumed that there are no time or cost constraints.

> **stop...**
>
> Examine your own choice of which college or university you would attend. To what extent did your decision follow the rational decision-making approach?
>
> **...and reflect**

The realities of decision making

> All inferences from experience are effects of custom, not of reasoning.
> (David Hume, 1758/2007: 32)

The rational model is a rhetoric used by managers at the very top of an organizational bureaucracy, and it reinforces managers' claim to knowledge and competence. It is now widely recognized that the normative model of decision making is rarely realized either fully or extensively in practice. Contemporary cognitive research has attempted to explain why individuals, groups and organizations fail to follow the rational model. We shall discuss major impediments to rational decision making that operate at the individual, group and organizational levels.

At the individual level

Individual rationality is constrained by at least four factors: information-processing failure, perceptual biases, intuition and emotion, and escalation of commitment.

Information-processing failures

Individual managers do not make wholly rational decisions because they may not acquire sufficient information to make a 'perfect' decision, or they may have too much information, and this prevents them from making a good decision. Individuals may make bad or non-rational decisions because of incomplete information. Herbert Simon (1957, 1977) called this **bounded rationality**. The bounds

bounded rationality: processing limited and imperfect information and satisficing (see below) rather than maximizing when choosing between alternatives

intuition: the ability to know when a problem or opportunity exists and to select the best course of action without conscious reasoning

information overload: a situation in which the receiver becomes overwhelmed by the information that needs to be processed. It may be caused by the *quantity* of the information to be processed, the speed at which the information presents itself or the *complexity* of the information to be processed

satisficing: selecting a solution that is satisfactory, or 'good enough', rather than optimal or 'the best'

of rationality often force managers to make decisions based on **intuition**, or what is commonly called their 'gut feeling'. Although intuitive decisions may be seen as non-rational because they do not follow the model, it can be argued that hunches or guesses can be an effective way to decide as the subconscious brain may be providing the conscious brain with information (Levine, 1990).

Although incomplete or imperfect information can be a barrier to rational decision making, too much information can also prevent optimal decisions. **Information overload** is the reception of more information than is necessary to make effective decisions. Rather than improving decision making, information overload can lead to errors, omissions, delays and cutting corners. Managers facing information overload often attempt to use all the information at hand, and then get confused and permit irrelevant or low-quality information to influence their decisions.

For example, you may experience information overload when writing an essay. To impress your lecturer, you attempt to incorporate too many viewpoints and too many references into the paper, and this results in a disjointed, confusing and low-quality essay. So the lesson here is that more information does not necessarily lead to optimal decisions.

Managers may also choose the first alternative that does the job, or meets the requirements of the problem to a satisfactory degree, rather than the 'best' alternative. Simon called this behaviour **satisficing** – selecting an alternative that is satisfactory rather than optimal. Satisficing occurs because of information overload. It is not possible to identify all the feasible alternatives, and information about the alternatives is imperfect.

Even if individuals have all the relevant information, they cannot possibly think through all the alternatives and the outcomes of those alternatives as prescribed by the rational model because they lack the cognitive capacity (Cohen et al., 1972). This is not because they are dim-witted, but rather because managers typically have limited time in which to make decisions, and some decisions simply do not lend themselves to purely rational 'scientific' calculation. Complex managerial decisions usually involve both measurable and non-measurable, or qualitative, considerations. Consequently, managers normally look at only a few alternatives and only some of the main outcomes of those alternatives.

Students of decision process theory essentially argue that decisions are made and actions taken depending on the individuals who happen to be involved and the alternatives they happen to identify. For example, there are scores of MBA programmes to choose from and dozens of modules to consider, yet people typically evaluate only a few MBA offerings and the main features of each programme of studies. In summary, although relevant and timely information improves decisions, managers often obtain less or more information than is necessary for adequate decision making.

Perceptual biases

Along with processing information and evaluating quantitative and qualitative considerations, individuals make imperfect decisions because of flawed perceptions. As we learned in Chapter 5, selective interest mechanisms cause relevant information to be unconsciously filtered out. Moreover, managers, workers and others with vested interests try to influence people's perceptions so that it is more or less likely that a situation will be perceived as an opportunity or challenge.

Another perceptual problem, also noted in Chapter 5, is that people see opportunities or challenges through their mental models. These working models of reality help individuals to make sense of their world, but they also perpetuate assumptions that obscure new realities. Table 13.3 presents a list of these individual biases in decision making. For example, people judge actions that are more vivid in their memory, they fail to pay sufficient attention to the skewed effects of sample size when evaluating the importance of data, and they tend to be overconfident about the accuracy of their judgement when addressing moderately to extremely difficult problems.

Table 13.3 Individual biases in decision making

Perceptual bias	Description
Ease of recall	Individuals judge events that are more easily recalled from memory to be more numerous than events of equal frequency whose instances are less easily recalled
Insensitivity to sample size	Individuals frequently fail to appreciate the role of sample size in evaluating the accuracy of sample information
Overconfidence	Individuals tend to be overconfident about the accuracy of their judgement when they answer moderately to extremely difficult questions
Method of memory search	Individuals are biased in their assessment of the frequency of events based upon the way their memory structure affects the search process
Illusory correlation	Individuals tend to overestimate the probability of two events co-occurring when their memory recall finds that the two events have occurred together in the past
Hindsight	After finding out whether or not an event has occurred, individuals tend to overestimate the degree to which they would have predicted the event without the benefit of hindsight
Regression to the mean	Individuals fail to note the statistical fact that extreme events tend to regress to the mean on subsequent trials

Intuition and emotion

As shown by the 2014 BBC2 *Horizon* programme described at the start of this chapter, people often make decisions based on their intuition. This is usually called making a decision by 'gut instinct'. Many managers will tell you that they pay attention to their intuition or hunches when making decisions. Intuition is the ability to know when an opportunity or problem exists and to select the best course of action without conscious reasoning. These intuitions are, however, rarely the sole factor in the decision-making process. Individuals quite often analyse the available information, and then turn to their intuition to complete the process.

Intuitive decisions may be seen as non-rational because they do not follow the rational model, but research evidence suggests that intuition can play a role in strategic decision making (Brockmann and Anthony, 1998; Leonard and Sensiper, 1998; Lieberman, 2000). More than 80 per cent of organizational knowledge – information that has been edited, put into context and analysed in a way that makes it meaningful to decision makers – is implicit and difficult to quantify or even describe accurately (Stamps, 1999). It is suggested that intuition is the channel through which individuals use their implicit or tacit knowledge. Tacit knowledge is the wisdom learned from life experience, observation and insight, which is not clearly understood and is therefore impossible to transfer to others.

To grasp the significance of tacit knowledge in decision making, try to describe the physical characteristics of, for example, a good friend who buys antiques for a living. Now try to describe the methods your friend would use to make purchase decisions at an auction. The former involves explicit knowledge, while the latter involves your tacit knowledge of your friend. At an auction, your friend's behaviour appears to be instinctual, but it is based on her or his past experience, what she or he has heard and read, and the state of the market for a particular antique. Thus, intuition allows individuals to draw on a vast reservoir of knowledge, experience and process discoveries.

The neoclassical rational model neglects to factor into the process the effects of emotions on individual decision making (Ashkanasy et al., 2002). Emotions may shape decision making. Although we know that the rational dimension of the brain processes information about the various alternatives (imperfectly, because of cognitive capacity and time limits, as we have just learned), the emotional dimension more rapidly creates emotional markers that attract individuals to some alternatives and cause them to be repelled by others.

Take the three primary emotions of fear, hope and pleasure, for example. The first two are closely associated with the notion of confidence, which, it is argued, is the defining factor in how people address the challenges they face (Moisi, 2009). Fear is the absence of confidence. If our work life is dominated by fear, we are apprehensive about the present and expect the future to become increasingly unstable. By contrast, hope is an expression of confidence. And pleasure is the feeling of satisfaction or gratification. We can summarize the potential effects of these three emotions on decision making with three formulas: fear is 'Oh, my God, the economy is so bad, how can I safeguard my job?'; hope is 'I want to do it, I can do it, and I will do it'; and pleasure is 'Wow, it may be risky, but it's a great deal.' Let us consider the notion we discussed in Chapter 5, that the emotional bias in our schema to maximize pleasure feelings lies at the heart of irrational impulsive decision making. If we extend this to the banking crisis that began in 2008, banking executives were driven by the pleasurable feelings of 'easy reward' and ignored the long-term risks (House of Commons Treasury Committee, 2009).

Some research suggests that people's general disposition or mood can support or obstruct the decision-making process. Specifically, individuals tend to evaluate alternatives more accurately when they are in a negative or neutral mood, whereas they tend to engage in more perceptual biases when they are in a positive mood. This suggests that we need to be aware that decision making and logical analysis are affected by human emotion.

Escalation of commitment

escalation of commitment: the tendency to allocate more resources to a failing course of action or to repeat an apparently bad decision

The fourth factor that limits individual rationality in decision making is **escalation of commitment** to a losing course of action. Although it is clear why an individual would become more committed to a decision whose outcomes are positive, why does commitment sometimes increase when the outcomes are negative? For example, a project manager reviewing a lack of progress and a financial planner examining declining share prices might increase their commitment to their initial decision.

The objective characteristics of a project will be important in determining continued commitment to a decision (Ross and Staw, 1993; Staw and Ross, 1989). For example, large early losses or major setbacks can cause a project to be abandoned, while small losses or minor setbacks can be tolerated. However, as small losses become larger, the total loss accumulates, until so much is committed that an individual will tolerate future risk to try to avoid the certain loss. If the individual decision maker determines that early losses are the result of a temporary problem and that further investment is likely to ensure a good return, commitment to the project is likely to increase.

Psychological and political factors can also cause an individual to escalate his or her commitment to a decision. Despite large losses, individuals can tend to become more committed to a course of action when their decision is explicit and unambiguous, irrevocable, made publicly, made repeatedly and/or personally important.

stop...

Can you think of examples in which a CEO, politician or military commander showed escalated commitment to a bad decision? Have you ever done this yourself?

...and reflect

At the group level

As we discussed in Chapter 10, although teams and groups tend to make better decisions and produce better forecasts (Harford, 2014) than individuals working alone, research on group decision making has shown that groups often inhibit open-minded thinking. Groups tend to polarize group members' initial preferences, and group dynamics might sometimes also lead to more cautious decisions

would be a better term – to promote necessary change' (Mintzberg, 1989: 250). The political perspective, however, has been criticized for failing to give sufficient attention to 'power struggles' in the workplace (Willmott, 1989).

The decision process and political theories offer alternative insights into the nature of managerial decision making on a day-to-day basis. Rather than viewing decisions as a series of linear and rational steps, these schools of thought see managerial decision making as a cycle involving enactment, reflection on experience, reframing of meaning and re-enactment under conditions of competition, ambiguity and uncertainty, often subject to the 'invisible hand' of internal politicking. Not surprisingly, organizational decision making may appear complex, variable, inconsistent and often contradictory. However, it would be a mistake to believe that managerial decision making really is chaotic and irrational. Under the surface, it might be more rational in substance than it is in form (Godard, 2005b). Senior managers are generally able to use their power to impose rationality. It is also true that the management process takes place in an environment of capitalist employment relations, where it is overarched by powerful organizational and market imperatives. These permit few substantial irrational decisions that would threaten the organization's standing or competitive position.

Power, gender and decision making

Critical approaches to studying organizational decision making require an analysis of decision-making behaviour within a *social* context, that is, the relation of decisions to the social relations and wider societal structures in which non-programmable decisions are embedded. This involves recognizing that the process embodies the distribution of 'power' and the ordering of 'gender' in organizations. Power is an omnipresent phenomenon of organizational life. Such claims, then, suggest that power is the key factor in explaining how decisions are made. In Herbert Simon's conceptualization, 'bounded rationality' is the result of human constraints and, as such, arguably underscores the role of power in setting those constraints (Miller et al., 1999: 45). When managers exercise a constraint on the behaviour of others, they enact power (see Chapter 14).

Some writers have long considered that the rational decision-making model also underplays the effects of gender, which suggests that its underlying character is a male-related phenomenon and not inclusive of all employees. Legitimate power is allocated to positions of authority in the organizational hierarchy. Historically, this 'rational-legal' power, which gives access to the decision-making process, has, in the majority of organizations, privileged male managers. Indeed, Wajcman (1998: 54) has suggested that gender power pervades perceptions of authority. From this follows the argument that gender power relegates women to subordinate decision-making roles.

Source: © iStockphoto.com/Feverpitched

plate 47 A wise Latina woman and a white man: how might their judgements differ?

One example of this kind of power play is illustrated by the case of Judge Sonia Sotomayor. According to Verma (2009), President Barack Obama's nominee to the US Supreme Court represented an acknowledgement that 'A judge may and will make a difference in our judging. I would hope that a wise Latina woman with the richness of her experiences would more often than not reach a better conclusion than a white man who hasn't lived that life'. The notion of a separation between the public and private spheres is itself a social construction, because it traditionally privileges men's rather than women's life experience (Wajcman, 1998). As others suggest, the social context – how legitimate power is allocated in organizations, collective norms and gendered assumptions about workers and managers – frames 'sense making' or problem definition, and is generally neglected in orthodox treatments of decision making (Martin, 2000).

As we saw in Chapter 11, there are important differences between the conversational styles of men and women. For women who have been promoted into senior positions, gender could create communication barriers in the decision-making process because, as some academics have argued, women have a 'different voice'.

The difference thesis contends that men see conversation as a tool – to exchange information, accomplish a task or preserve power – while women see conversation as a way to nurture, support and empathize, and that female managers use a more open communication style than typical male managers when dealing with people issues (see Chapter 12). Radical feminists might argue that the collective and systematic oppression of women by men results in different moral values. Women construct and value knowledge in ways that are relational, and oriented more towards sustaining relationships than achieving autonomy and power. Adopting this view of women – the notion that they have a different voice and a more holistic view of reality – suggests that the decision-making process will be strongly influenced by the gender balance of the decision makers (see, for example, Gilligan, 1982).

Employee voice in decision making

employee involvement: the degree to which employees influence how their work is organized and carried out

'Employee voice' or '**employee involvement** and participation' is entrenched in contemporary people management theory. Employee voice and EIP are terms used to describe employment practices that are designed to allow employees some input into decision making and how their organizations are run. The meaningful pursuit of employee voice systems involves an approach predicated on recognising the limits of individual decision making, and an emphasis on the articulation of workers' voice (Arrowsmith and Parker, 2013; Macey and Schneider, 2008; Marchington and Kynighou, 2012). It is most often associated with theories of post-bureaucratic organizational structures, work teams and 'diffuse' or 'empowered' styles of managerial leadership. EIP refers to the degree to which subordinates influence how their work is organized and performed. Meaningful decision making requires that workers are able to exert some influence over their work and the conditions under which they work.

EIP initiatives suggest a commonality of interest between workers and management. Managerially driven EIP initiatives can only be understood in their historical and sociological context. Employers tend to pursue EIP practices to improve employees' cooperation and enhance productivity, and for their rhetorical appeal for change. More than any area of human resource management, EIP demonstrates the tension at the core of the employment relationship over whether workers are just resources to be utilized or assets to be developed and engaged in decision-making processes (Boxall and Purcell, 2011; Marchington and Kynighou, 2012). The emergence and take-up of EIP practices is clearly linked to changes in work organization and tends to be faddish in character (Kersley et al., 2005; Marchington, 2008; Ramsay, 1991).

There are two broad types of EIP system: direct and indirect. *Direct involvement* refers to those forms of participation where individual workers are involved in the decision-making processes that affect their everyday work routines, albeit often in a very limited way. Examples of direct EIP include briefing groups, quality circles, problem-solving teams and self-managed teams (see Chapter 10 for a discussion on work groups). At the lowest level, involvement involves asking workers for information. They might not even know what the problem is and do not make recommendations. At a moderate level of direct involvement, workers are told about the problem and asked to provide recommendations to the decision maker. At the highest level of direct involvement, the decision-making process is handed over to the workers. They identify the problem, choose the best alternative and implement their choice.

Indirect involvement refers to those forms of worker participation where representatives or delegates of the main body of workers participate in the strategic decision-making process. Examples of indirect participation include joint consultation committees, European Works Councils and 'worker directors'. All these forms are associated with the broader notion of **industrial democracy**. Some European Union countries require workers' involvement at both the worksite and corporate levels through a process of co-determination. In Germany and Nordic countries, for instance, employee representatives sit on supervisory boards, making decisions about executive salaries and recommendations on the company's strategic goals. At the same time, employers must consult with employee representation committees regarding matters of new technology, employment staffing and work and human resource processes.

Advantages of employee involvement and participation

The support for EIP needs to be viewed within the context of changing business and associated employment strategies, where the purpose of the latter is to secure employees' support for high-performance work systems (Bratton and Gold, 2012). EIP directly supports management's goals. In many respects, workers are the barometer of the organization. When operations or machines fail to meet performance standards, workers are usually the first to know. Thus, EIP ensures that problems are quickly identified and corrected.

EIP also supports management's goals indirectly through commitment (Marchington, 2001; Marchington and Kynighou, 2012). The general premise is that increasing workers' involvement in decision making will strengthen organizational citizenship. That is, involving people in decision making potentially increases their commitment to the organization's goals, and that will in turn result in enhanced performance. Surveys of managers have shown that EIP is typically initiated by management, with the objective of enhancing workers' commitment to organizational goals (Benders, 2005; Delbridge and Whitfield, 2001). The involvement–commitment cycle is shown in Figure 13.2, and is the reverse of the vicious cycle of control first that is discussed by Clegg and Dunkerley (1980).

industrial democracy: a broad term used to describe a range of programmes, processes and social institutions designed to provide greater EIP and influence in the decision-making process, and to exchange ideas on how to improve working conditions and product and service quality in the workplace

> *stop...*
>
> What do you think of the assumptions underpinning the involvement–commitment cycle? Can the growth of EIP be explained by employers' 'needs', or are there other forces determining this employee relations practice?
>
> *...and reflect*

IN THE EBOOK ACCESS THE **OB IN FOCUS** BOX 'TEAMS MAKE BETTER DECISIONS THAN INDIVIDUALS' AND VISIT THE ONLINE RESOURCE CENTRE ON HTTPS://HE.PALGRAVE.COM/COMPANION/BRATTON-WORK-AND-ORGANIZATIONAL-BEHAVIOUR3/ FOR MORE EXAMPLES OF COMPANIES INTRODUCING EIP PRACTICES.

The benefits of EIP also find expression in popular literature on the 'democratic' leader. For example, Goleman and his colleagues assert that 'The democratic style builds on a triad of emotional intelligence abilities: teamwork and collaboration, conflict management, and influence ... [Moreover,] Without the ability to attune to a wide range of people, a leader will be more prone to miscues' (2013: 69). Although management theorists consider that effective leaders are 'superb listeners' and advocate EIP, there seems to be a mismatch between theory and practice. In the UK, survey data indicate that, alongside a decline in trade union membership and collective bargaining (see Chapter 9), indirect EIP became less extensive in the period between 1980 and 2004 (Kersley et al., 2005). Equally revealing about the zenith of neo-liberal globalization – arguably the 1990s – is the growing proportion of workers who reported dissatisfaction with the amount of input they had over workplace decisions (Kelly, 2006).

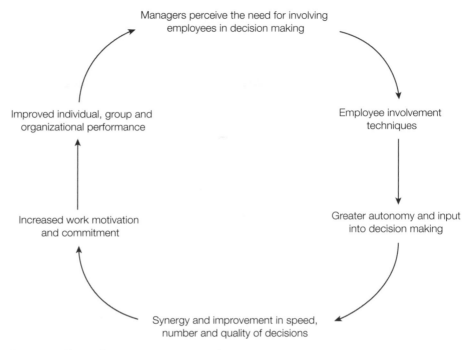

Figure 13.2 The involvement–commitment cycle

Management theorists (for example, Verma and Taras, 2005) have put forward three main reasons for senior management to introduce EIP schemes: moral, economic and behavioural. A variety of effects can then be seen:

- First, EIP is derived from an ethical, political and moral base. The argument is that, in a democratic society, workers should be involved in the decision-making process when the outcomes of those decisions impact on their lives. EIP presents a socially acceptable management style and projects 'a socially responsible stance' (Marchington and Wilding, 1983: 32).
- Second, EIP, according to the 'model of excellence' school in North America, improves the quality of decision making and productivity. Groups or communities of practice bring more input and diversity of views into the decision process. The evidence indicates that a group, team or community of practice will usually generate higher quality decisions (Goleman et al., 2013).
- Decisions made collectively tend to lead to increased acceptance of a solution. Members who participated in making a decision are more likely to support the decision and encourage others to accept it too. Research on the link between EIP and a firm's performance suggests that giving employees a 'voice' on a range of organizational decisions yields benefits for both the organization and the workforce (Heller et al., 1998).
- Furthermore, EIP potentially reduces employee misbehaviour: by accepting EIP interventions, 'Employers hope that participative mechanisms will create a greater coincidence of interests between employers and employees, thereby increasing trust, reducing the potential for conflict, and increasing the potential for an effective mutual influence process' (Beer et al., 1984: 53). As critics point out, EIP practices can be used to 'educate' and 'reconstitute' the individual as a more malleable and productive employee (Legge, 2005).

Ethics and corporate social responsibility

So far, we have considered individual, group and organizational decision making, but have given little consideration to whether that decision making is ethical or unethical. Ethics and CSR are increasingly important due to high-profile cases of unethical and, in some cases, criminal, managerial behaviour. High-profile cases include Martha Stewart of Martha Stewart Inc., Fausto Tonna at Parmalat, Conrad Black of Hollinger International, Bernard Madoff of Madoff Investment Securities and former chair of NASDAQ Stock Market, Tom Hayes of Citigroup and UBS, and Jonathan Mathew, Peter Johnson and Stylianos Contogoulas of Barclays Bank, charged with alleged conspiracy to manipulate interbank interest rates (Bowers, 2014).

At a corporate level, the British pharmaceutical company GlaxoSmithKline was embroiled in bribery scandals in China, Iraq and Poland, which, if proved, would breach the UK's Bribery Act and the US Foreign Corrupt Practices Act (Neate, 2014). More recently, leaked files from HSBC's Swiss bank exposed serious unlawful misbehaviour and wrongdoing, including corruption and money laundering (Leigh et al., 2015). The 'HSBC files' go to the heart of the ethical discourse surrounding individual values and the application of ethical principles in the decision-making process in the many different contexts in which organizations operate.

Public criticism about white-collar crime caused a member of the Toronto Stock Exchange's Committee on Corporate Governance to state:

> It is important, both to the corporate community and to society in general, that business achieve a higher degree of credibility. To do this, business must put its own house in order, starting with fundamental ethics and corporate governance issues and flowing on to responding more actively and publicly to the concerns of our society. (Brown, quoted in Carroll, 2004: 34–5)

In 2015, public criticism of HSBC also prompted the following response:

> This affair exposes shocking evidence of unlawful behaviour by an arm of one of Britain's biggest banks ... And underlying it all is a disturbing moral ambiguity to the whole question of paying tax that appears to be widespread in Whitehall, in government and among some rich donors to all parties ... It corrupts public attitudes to the common good. (Editorial, *The Guardian*, 2015, p. 32)

These white-collar crimes and the collective recognition that egregious and unethical behaviour has calamitous consequences, from a loss of jobs (Royal Bank of Scotland and AIG) to a loss of savings and retirement funds (Enron and Madoff) and government bail-outs (US and European banks), leads to an increasing public distrust of corporations. In the post-2009 global financial crisis era, collective anger over unethical and high-risk behaviour focused public attention on the need for business institutions to define their standards of ethical behaviour, as well as on the need for new CSR strategies and, moreover, greater government regulation. This section, therefore, follows naturally from the discussion of decision making. In it, we shall define business ethics and examine the nature of CSR.

IN THE EBOOK ACCESS THE **CRITICAL INSIGHT** ON 'ETHICS AND DECISION MAKING'.

Business ethics

ethics: the study of moral principles or values that determine whether actions are right or wrong, and outcomes are good or bad

Ethics is, according to the *Oxford Dictionary*, 'a set of moral principles'. Business ethics relates to a set of moral principles and values that govern the behaviour and decisions of individuals or groups. In essence, it involves values about right and wrong. In a globalized economy, Morrison (2015) provides a compelling case for seeking and establishing ethical guideposts in organizational decision making across national boundaries: 'ethical questions are central to how the business sees its role in the world. They concern who we are and what we should be doing' (p. 4),

globalization & organization misbehaviour

Source: Brand X Pictures

FIFA 2022: bribery versus exploitation

The 2022 FIFA (Fédération Internationale de Football Association) World Cup was awarded to Qatar in 2010, and preparations have been underway ever since. Yet the situation is being dogged by concerns that the rights of the migrant workers who are building the facilities are being trampled underfoot. The report entitled *The Case Against Qatar* has revealed that, at the current rate, 4000 workers will have died before a ball has even been kicked in the 2022 World Cup. At least 1200 Indian and Nepalese workers have already died since the £138 billion project began, compared with 60 during the entire construction of the Sochi complex for the 2014 Winter Olympics. According to the report, other problems include:

> salty water being provided to workers in camps for cooking and washing; employers demanding deposits of US$275 are paid by workers before they are allowed to leave for holidays; over 2500 Indonesian maids a year fleeing from abusive sponsors; and workers in squalid accommodation at the Al Wakrah Stadium. (Pitts, 2014)

FIFA has been reluctant to accept any responsibility for the treatment of workers in host countries. Theo Zwanzinger, Germany's representative on the FIFA executive board, admitted that conditions for migrant workers in Qatar were 'absolutely unacceptable' and that their human rights were being infringed, but verified that there could be no going back on decisions already taken. 'This feudal system existed [in Qatar] before the World Cup,' Zwanzinger said. 'What do you expect of a football organisation? FIFA is not the lawmaker in Qatar' (Pitts, 2014).

This reluctance to intervene may reflect the alleged bribery of soccer officials to award the tournament to Qatar in the first place (Vick, 2014). FIFA was more willing to criticize 2014 host Brazil, where only seven workers died (Associated Press, 2014). Yet FIFA also indicates that European political and economic interests influenced the awarding of the World Cup to Qatar:

> 'Yes, there was definitely direct political influence,' FIFA president Sepp Blatter told German weekly Die Zeit, the AFP reported. 'European leaders recommended to its voting members to opt for Qatar, because of major economic interests in the country'. (Waldron, 2013)

So what are these interests?

> New countries offer new frontiers for foreign investors and FIFA, primarily because they almost always demand the construction of lavish new stadiums and other related construction projects. Foreign investors have reaped

> huge profits by diving into Brazilian construction firms, for instance, and the design, consulting, and construction of Qatar's stadiums is being done mostly by international firms. …

> Those benefits are large: while Brazil is spending between $20 billion and $30 billion on its World Cup, Qatar is planning to spend 10 times that. (Waldron, 2013)

The FIFA situation in Qatar identifies some of the complex power relationships that exist in global capitalism. Countries, corporations and private bodies frequently act in concert to maximize the potential for investors (generally the most wealthy members of society) to maximize their returns. This cooperation runs contrary to the official discourse that continues to champion the free market and competition. For example, the bribery allegations surrounding the 2022 World Cup triggered condemnation from the British government and the suggestion that the bidding process be reopened (McTague, 2014).

The 2022 World Cup is an interesting study in contrasts. There is outrage and embarrassment over one group of rich people bribing another group of rich people to the disadvantage of even more rich people. Yet far fewer ripples are being generated by the fact that relatively powerless migrant workers from the global South must trade their rights – and, in more than a thousand cases, their lives – for an opportunity to earn exploitative wages in terrible working conditions.

> **Stop!** Why is FIFA unwilling to intervene in Qatari labour relations? Why do you think a rigged bidding process generates more outrage than the deaths of thousands of workers?

Sources and further research

Associated Press (2014) 'FIFA president critical of Brazil World Cup organizers after worker fatalities', April 3. Available at: www.cbc.ca/sports/soccer/fifa-president-critical-of-brazil-world-cup-organizers-after-worker-fatalities-1.2597546 (accessed February 16, 2015).

McTague, T. (2014) 'Prospect of 2022 England World Cup grows as pressure mounts on FIFA to strip Qatar of competition over corruption allegations', *Daily Mail*, June 2. Available at: www.dailymail.co.uk/news/article-2646190/Prospect-2022-England-World-Cup-grows-pressure-mounts-Fifa-strip-Qatar-competition-amid-corruption-allegations.html (accessed February 16, 2015).

Pitts, J. (2014) 'World Cup 2014: FIFA to help improve workers' rights in Qatar', *The Independent*, March 24. Available at: www.independent.co.uk/news/world/middle-east/world-cup-2014-fifa-to-help-improve-workers-rights-in-qatar-9208402.html (accessed February 16, 2015).

Vick, K. (2014) 'Qatar bribery allegations loom over the 2022 World Cup', *Time*, June 5. Available at: http://time.com/2822288/qatar-world-cup-bribery/ (accessed February 16, 2015).

Waldron, T. (2013) 'FIFA president admits political, economic interests drive Qatar World Cup selection', *Think Progress*, September 18. Available at: http://thinkprogress.org/sports/2013/09/18/2641651/fifa-president-tune-admits-european-economic-interests-drove-qatar-world-cup-selection/ (accessed February 16, 2015).

Note: This feature was written by Bob Barnetson, Associate Professor of Labour Relations, Athabasca University, Canada.

covering a range of business-related issues (Figure 13.3). Any set of ethical principles does not emerge in a vacuum but reflects the cultural values and norms of society. For example, bribing officials for contracts is regarded as bad in Western cultures but is much more commonplace around Africa. In the UK and the USA, for example, following the 2010 Bribery Act and the US Foreign Corrupt Practices

Figure 13.3 Ethical issues in business

Act, it is an offence to offer or receive bribes. *Ethical dilemmas* arise when two or more values conflict, for example when a pharmaceutical company has to meet profit targets but the process involves testing a new drug on animals.

In the past, business ethics consisted mainly of legally driven, compliance-based codes that guided workplace behaviour when making decisions on the improper use of the organization's resources or on conflicts of interest. In an ever more globalized economy, an increasing number of companies are undergoing 'a program of moral reform' (Carroll, 2004: 35) that involves crafting value-based ethical policies that are compatible with cross-global operations. The objective is to help employees make informed decisions when faced with new ethical situations. Studies assert a relationship between ethical behaviour and greater well-being, and a common belief that unethical behaviour is inclined to diminish well-being (Giacalone et al., 2015). Since 2008, because of the actions of the bankers, the importance of business ethics has been highlighted and has come under great public scrutiny. It is argued that their unethical behaviour, allowing senior bankers to take high risks, contributed to the global financial crisis (Archer, 2010; Martin, 2014). Senior executive Stephan Hester's diagnosis of the Royal Bank of Scotland in the 2000s sheds light on bankers' unethical behaviour: 'We financed ourselves in an unstable way, ... we were too leveraged, ... risk controls were poor, management process was a bit dysfunctional, and we were driven too much by profit expansion' (Martin, 2014: 296).

The ethical dimension of *employment* policies and practices relates to employee selection (for example, the avoidance of discrimination), rewards (such as the notion of fairness), training (for instance, equal opportunities), health and safety (for example, a full disclosure of chemicals used in the workplace, including any harmful long-term effects) and the protection of whistleblowers (Winstanley and Woodall, 2000). The ethical issues affecting *consumers* relate to how the marketing mix is applied to consumers, including, for example, product safety and testing, price fixing, respect for privacy, the false labelling of products and misleading advertising (Jobber, 2012). The ethical dimension of *environmental* issues, for instance carbon emissions, conservation and wasteful packaging, is a classic illustration of an ethical dilemma. For example, petroleum companies extracting 'dirty oil' from the oil sands in Alberta, Canada, satisfy shareholders' returns in preference to reducing carbon emissions and pollution.

Political issues refer to the lobbying of politicians to pass or not pass legislation that will impact adversely on business interests. They also relate to the politics of globalization. This includes the ability of global corporations to shape or circumvent national laws and local interests. Therefore, the ability of large multinational corporations to exert significant power in their host countries is an ethical concern. Multinational corporations face the twin pressures of cost reductions and differentiation to satisfy local markets – that is to say, there is on the one hand a pressure to cut costs by homogenizing goods, and on the other, a pressure to provide products that are uniquely tailored to suit specific markets (Bartlett and Ghoshal, 1989). Under such competitive conditions, the system of business regulations in host countries becomes an important factor in deciding where global corporations operate. Unsurprisingly, governments in developing countries increasingly face pressure to weaken their regulations for employment (for example, workplace safety), products (such as automobile exhaust emissions and clinical trials) and ecological controls to attract overseas investment. In her book *No Logo*, Naomi Klein (2000) offers a scathing criticism of global companies that exploit the world's poor. In particular, she identifies two key ethical concerns: unfair trading practices and the lack of human rights.

The ethical issues affecting corporate *governance* relate to issues associated with what some sociologists call *corporate crime*. Studies show that corporate crime is not confined to a few 'bad apples', but is pervasive and widespread. In addition to violations linked to employment, marketing and the environment, violations also occur in financial practices (for example, corporate tax avoidance or illegal bribes to secure contracts) and administrative practices (for example, non-compliance with national laws) (Slapper and Tombs, 1999).

VISIT THE *ONLINE RESOURCE CENTRE* AT HTTPS://HE.PALGRAVE.COM/COMPANION/BRATTON-WORK-AND-ORGANIZATIONAL-BEHAVIOUR3/ FOR FURTHER INFORMATION ON THE TOP 100 US CORPORATE CRIMINALS.

Corporate social responsibility

Although The Body Shop, famous for its 'ethical' manufacturing and retailing operations, is a well-known contemporary company adopting an ethical approach to business, there is evidence – more than 20 years after the disastrous oil spillage by *Exxon Valdez* of March 24, 1989 – that CSR is now a priority: it is a concept whose time has come (Moon, 2002; Shen and Benson, 2014; Yakabuski, 2008). CSR involves organizations taking an ethical stance that supports social and ecological issues (Johnson et al., 2008: 189). Underscoring CSR and forging its implementation is the ethical principle that managers should be accountable for how their decisions and behaviour might affect local communities, society and the planet as a whole.

Source: © iStockphoto.com/esolla

plate 48 The ethical dimension of environmental issues – for instance, carbon emissions, conservation and wasteful packaging – is a classic illustration of an ethical dilemma. For example, do these apples really need to be shrink-wrapped? What pressures on companies might have led to the overpackaging of foodstuffs? Do advertising campaigns such as 'A low carbon diet = locally produced' suggest that this trend might be changing?

CSR is not new. From the British Industrial Revolution (around 1780–1830) onwards, companies such as Cadbury and Rowntree adopted progressive employment standards and provided housing for their workers. Some employers established model villages to house their workforce. Cadbury established Bournville, Lever Brothers instituted Port Sunlight, and one of the earliest metropolis villages was at Saltaire, around the textile mills of Titus Salt near Bradford. These actions by early factory owners are often referred to as paternalistic management, as they are based on the premodern assumption that employers have a responsibility to look after the welfare of their employees (Godard, 2005b). Many of these early progressive employers were influenced by their Quaker beliefs.

CSR is based on the *stakeholder theory* of the firm, which contends that organizations should be managed not purely in the interests of maximizing shareholders' returns, but additionally in the interests of a range of groups or stakeholders who also have a legitimate interest in the organization, such as employees, customers, the local community, suppliers and environment and society in general (Donaldson and Preston, 1995). The core premise is that the organization has an obligation to other various groups in society to whom the company is responsible. The concept of CSR is problematic because, as we explained in Chapter 1, it is people, not organizations, who make decisions and engage in unethical behaviour. In the same vein, unarguably only *people*, and not inanimate objects such as organizations, can be responsible for human actions.

Some of the worst examples of corporate social *irresponsibility* have occurred in developing economies. In Bhopal, India, for example, a chemical plant owned by the US global company Union Carbide engaged in chemical production under conditions that would have been illegal in the USA. On December 3, 1984, the plant experienced a major leak. Within hours, 3000 people were dead, 15,000 more dying in the aftermath, and 200,000 were seriously injured; half a million individuals still carry special health cards. Eventually, the organization paid out just $470 million in compensation (Saul, 2005).

stop...

In the last decade, the Indian government deregulated the telecommunications industry, including changes to employment regulations, in order to increase foreign investment in call centres. Is it socially responsible when corporations encourage host countries to deregulate employment or health and safety standards? (See Maitra and Jasjit, 2005.)

...and reflect

CSR has been characterized as a multi-layered concept with four interrelated responsibilities: economic, legal, ethical and philanthropic (Carroll and Buchholtz, 2012). According to this model, the raison d'être of organizations is to produce goods and services for profit or within budget. Organizations must pursue their economic responsibilities within the legal and regulatory framework. Ethical responsibility means that organizations should operate in a manner consistent with the dominant values of society. Philanthropic responsibility extends CSR beyond legal compliance to actively promoting good in the community through collaborative projects related to education, employability and economic renewal, or being a good 'corporate citizen'. There is some evidence to suggest that an ethical approach to business will improve the organization's financial performance and contribute to employees' job satisfaction (Koh and Boo, 2001; Wilson, 1997).

VISIT THE *ONLINE RESOURCE CENTRE* AT HTTPS://HE.PALGRAVE.COM/COMPANION/BRATTON-WORK-AND-ORGANIZATIONAL-BEHAVIOUR3/ FOR MORE INFORMATION ON CSR.

Research evidence suggests that ethical behaviour and CSR are a function of *both* the individual's values and the context in which the decision-making process occurs. Figure 13.4 offers a model to account for ethical or unethical decision-making behaviour, drawing on the work of Trevino (1986), Carroll (2004) and Bratton et al. (2005).

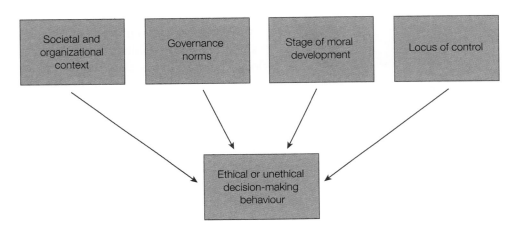

Figure 13.4 Determinants of ethical behaviour in work organizations

The *societal and organizational context* refers to an individual's perception of societal and organizational expectations. Does society or the organization encourage and support ethical behaviour by rewarding it, or discourage unethical behaviour by punishing it? Public policy statements, codes of ethics, financial performance expectations, appraisal methods that evaluate means as well as ends, visible recognition and promotion for employees who display high ethical behaviour, and visible punishment for those who act unethically, are all examples of societal and organizational context that are likely to promote high ethical decision making.

Commenting on the public backlash against US corporate leaders accused and convicted of engaging in fraudulent accounting practices, one of us elsewhere noted:

> Simply focusing on [individual] traits such as honesty and integrity inappropriately separates the leader from the followers and the context. Those corporate leaders … who engaged in criminal or highly unethical practices … did so largely because of profound changes in the context. In the late 1990s, shareholder-value-driven capitalism emphasized stock appreciation, the use of stock options to compensate leaders, and the attainment of short-term financial targets, which produced a culture of avarice. (Bratton et al., 2005: 323)

Governance norms focus on democratic decision making that is intended to encourage a free and full discussion in order to stimulate the mutual informal learning that can occur under conditions of social symmetry rather than hierarchy (Carroll, 2004). Stages of moral development estimate an individual's capacity to judge what is the 'morally right thing to do'. The higher a person's moral development, the less dependent she or he is on external influences, and hence the more she or he will be predisposed to behave ethically. Leadership theorists have emphasized the importance and centrality of the moral dimension of managerial leadership. Leaders who do not act ethically do not demonstrate true leadership, and this stresses that leaders must ultimately be judged on the basis of a system of values, and not just in terms of the instrumental value of profit. Thus, the conflicts and contradictions of leadership can only be resolved when leaders establish an ethical set of standards on which to base all their decisions and actions (Gardner, 1990; Kouzes and Posner, 2012).

Organizational decision makers who lack a strong moral commitment are much less likely to behave unethically and make unethical decisions if they are constrained by a societal and organizational context that disapproves of such behaviours. Conversely, very honourable employees can be corrupted by an organizational context that 'turns a blind eye' to, permits or encourages unethical behaviour. Much of the empirical research suggests a need for human resource policies and practices that scaffold and nurture ethical behaviour. Shen and Benson's research, for example, suggests that underpinning an effective CSR programme is the adoption of what they call 'socially responsible' human resource management, which is 'CSR directed toward the employees' (2014: 17). Sociologists use the term **socialization** to refer to the lifelong social experience by which individuals develop their human potential and learn moral standards.

Employees with an internal *locus of control* (that is, those who believe they are responsible for what takes place and for the outcomes of their decisions and actions) are more likely to rely on their own internal standards of right or wrong to guide their actions. Those with an external locus of control (who believe that what happens to them in life is due to chance or luck) are less likely to take responsibility for the consequences of their actions, and are more likely to rely on external influences. Stages of moral development and loci of control can change as we interact with different agents of socialization: family, school, our peer group and the mass media.

The concept of CSR has, however, its detractors. For some, the investment by oil and gas companies in alternative energy fuels and the greening of products is a public relations or marketing ploy, and consumers are deliberately misled into believing that they are helping the planet by buying 'green products'. For sceptics of CSR, the idea of good corporate citizenship in an era of largely unfettered global capitalism is a voluntary or self-regulatory response to public concerns that is still too marginal to make a real difference to irresponsible unethical behaviour. For critics, a real change to egregious managerial behaviour will only occur through a greater regulation of markets and business. If the proposals agreed at the 2009 G20 summit in London and the 2014 European Union-wide banking regulations were to be effective in reforming global and European financial architectures, these might have profound consequences for organizational decision making and CSR strategies.

socialization: the lifelong process of social interaction through which individuals acquire a self-identity and the physical, mental and social skills needed for survival in society

Developing decision-making skills

We have learned that the neoclassical rational model of decision making neglects to factor into the process the effects of culture, gender and race, and tends to give little consideration to social factors, such as how social norms and expectations frame problem definition, and the decision-making process. We have also learned that groups potentially make higher quality decisions than individuals in certain situations, but that group polarization can also lead to conformity and poor decisions. What can be done to improve the decision-making process and its outcomes? Training and work-based learning can improve group decision making and, moreover, can help to avoid the 'pitfalls' of group decision making (Xenikou and Furnham, 2013).

Researchers have identified various techniques to minimize the biases and errors that we have identified in this chapter. These structured group interventions have been designed to improve group processes and the quality of group decision making in a timely manner, and to encourage individuals to become engaged in critical and creative thinking. Five techniques help to improve decision making: brainstorming, the nominal group technique, the stepladder technique, computer-mediated brainstorming and the Delphi technique.

Brainstorming

brainstorming: a freewheeling, face-to-face meeting where team members generate as many ideas as possible, piggy-back on the ideas of others, and avoid evaluating anyone's ideas during the idea-generating stage

divergent thinking: involves reframing a problem in a unique way and generating different approaches to the issue

Brainstorming is a group technique to encourage creative thinking and alternatives to problems. It focuses on the generation of ideas and options, rather than on their evaluation. If decision makers engage in brainstorming, it is assumed that they can feed off each other's ideas and be stimulated to offer more **divergent** and creative ideas.

To be effective, brainstorming requires group members to abide by four rules:

- *Speak freely.* Individuals are encouraged to suggest 'off-the-wall' or wacky ideas. Group members should believe that no idea is considered too unusual or extreme to be voiced.
- *Multiple ideas.* It is assumed that groups generate better ideas and solutions when they generate multiple ideas. Brainstorming is based on the belief that creative thinking occurs after orthodox ideas have been examined and rejected.
- *No criticism.* Group members are more likely to break out of traditional practices and thinking and voice their crazy ideas if other group members are not permitted to ridicule or criticize them.
- *Build on the new ideas.* Group members are encouraged to synthesize, combine or 'piggy-back' on the new ideas presented. It is assumed that building on new ideas encourages the synergy of group processes.

The face-to-face brainstorming process might generate fewer ideas than individuals working alone, and thereby not fulfil its full creative potential, if the group is dominated by an outspoken member or if its members suffer from inhibition (Madsen and Finger, 1978).

Nominal group technique

The nominal group technique is a variation of the traditional brainstorming method that attempts to unite individual creative thinking with group dynamics. The technique curbs discussion during the decision-making process, hence the term nominal, as the group does not act together at this stage. Decision makers are all physically present, as in a traditional face-to-face brainstorming session, but they operate independently. In theory, this is how it works:

1. A problem or question is presented to the group.
2. Each member independently writes down her or his ideas to solve the problem.
3. Each member in turn describes one idea to the group. This process is repeated until all the ideas have been presented and recorded.
4. Members discuss and evaluate each idea.
5. Each member independently ranks the ideas presented. The idea or solution with the highest ranking determines the final decision.

'Smoke and mirrors accounting': do multinational corporations such as Google exploit weak tax laws?

Margaret Hodge MP, the chairwoman of the House of Commons Public Accounts Committee, has been critical of Google because in 2012 it paid only £11.6 million to the Treasury despite generating £3.4 billion of business in the UK (Press Association, 2013a; Rankin et al., 2013; Syal, 2013). MPs on the committee described Google's complex tax structure as 'deeply unconvincing'.

The US-based firm has its European headquarters in Dublin, where corporation tax is half that of the UK, to minimize its tax liabilities. The company claims that all its sales in Britain are booked in Ireland, and that the UK operation, headquartered in London, merely drums up business for the company. In 2012, Google's operation in Ireland handled €15.5 billion generated in Europe, the Middle East and Africa but only paid €15.9 million to the Irish exchequer.

Google is able to minimize the amount of tax it pays on the billions earned outside the USA through its complex tax arrangements. The revenue from sales booked in Ireland is then channelled to a subsidiary in the tax haven of Bermuda. Google is able to reduce its tax liabilities still further by charging 'administrative expenses' including a royalty fee that the European operation pays for the use of its brand. In 2012, this device enabled Google to reduce its tax exposure in Ireland by charging '€10.9 bn in "administrative expenses", reducing a gross profit of €11bn to a profit of €52m' (Rankin et al., 2013).

The view that Google in the UK did not conclude deals and make sales was challenged by Barney Jones, an ex-employee who felt morally driven to respond to Google's claims concerning its activities. He submitted evidence to the Public Accounts Committee that included details of contracts, invoices and correspondence between Google and its customers in Britain. In subsequent hearings of the Public Accounts Committee, Google Vice President Matt Brittin reiterated that British Google staff marketed their business 'but insisted that they did not handle the actual transactions' (Press Association, 2013a).

'A Google spokesman said it was only right the majority of its tax should be paid in the US, and argued the company made a significant contribution to the UK through investment and jobs' (Rankin et al., 2013). Google's complex tax arrangements are not illegal and this was recognized by the Public Accounts Committee. Nevertheless, it believed that the company benefits from using resources provided by the British tax payer, such as an educated workforce and infrastructure, so it should pay its fair share of corporation tax.

There are two possible views regarding Google's avoidance of corporation tax. A legalistic one is that tax laws allow the strategies described above so companies can benefit from weak legislation. Hodge took a moral stance and accused Brittin of 'devious, calculated and, in my view, unethical behaviour in deliberately manipulating the reality of your business in order to avoid paying your fair share of tax to the common good' (Press Association, 2013a). Hodge also criticized HM Revenue and Customs for failing to challenge the tax arrangements of multinational companies.

> **Stop!** Do you that think companies are entitled to use what Hodge called 'smoke and mirrors accounting' to exploit loopholes in weak laws? How can it be argued that Google's avoidance of corporation tax, although legal, is unethical? Carry out an Internet search on the payment of corporation tax in the UK by other multinational companies such as eBay and Amazon. Do you think you will find similar issues to those described relating to Google?

Sources and further information

Press Association (2013a) 'Google branded devious over tax arrangements', *The Guardian*, May 16.

Rankin, J., O'Carroll, L. and Monaghan, A. (2013) 'Google paid £11.6m in UK corporation tax last year', *The Guardian*, September 30. Available at: www.theguardian.com/technology/2013/sep/30/google-paid-uk-corporation-tax (accessed May 10, 2014).

Syal, R. (2013) 'Google whistleblower says he was motivated by Christian beliefs', *The Guardian*, June 13. Available at: www.theguardian.com/technology/2013/jun/12/google-tax-whistleblower-christian-beliefs (accessed May 10, 2014).

Note: This feature was written by David Denham, Honorary Research Fellow in Sociology, University of Wolverhampton, UK.

The advantage of the nominal technique is that it allows decision makers to meet formally but does not restrict individual input, as the traditional face-to-face brainstorming meeting potentially does.

Stepladder technique

This newer structured group decision-making technique begins with a discussion with a randomly selected dyad regardless of how many members are in the group. These two initial group members discuss the relevant information, assumptions and ideas. After a period of time, a new member is then added to form a triad. The new member has a specified period of time to present information and ideas individually to the original dyad, and this is then followed by a group discussion. New members are added one at a time in the same manner until all the members have joined the group and presented their ideas, and the group has discussed them. The complete group makes a final decision at the end of the process. The stepladder technique has a number of advantages, including allowing shy members to speak who would otherwise be reluctant to contribute in a full group situation, avoiding domination by an extrovert member and eliminating some social pressure from the majority to conform. Research has demonstrated that the stepladder technique is effective at improving group decision making, although Winquist and Franz's (2008) study had difficulty replicating the positive outcomes.

Computer-mediated brainstorming

Computer-mediated brainstorming permits decision makers to share ideas while minimizing many of the problems in group dynamics that were described earlier. An online facilitator begins the process by posting a problem or question. Members then post their answers or ideas on their computer terminal. All the group's ideas are posted anonymously and randomly on the computer screens. Members individually rank or vote electronically on the ideas or solutions presented. Typically, face-to-face discussion follows the computer-mediated process.

Research suggests that computer-mediated brainstorming generates more ideas than traditional face-to-face brainstorming, and that the participants are more confident and motivated to participate in the decision-making process than they are in other group structures (Dennis and Valacich, 1999). Computer-mediated brainstorming groups tend to be more egalitarian than face-to-face groups: that is, gender and status barriers tend to be broken down, and participation is more evenly distributed among men and women members than in face-to-face meetings.

The Delphi technique

Delphi technique: a structured team decision-making process of systematically pooling the collective knowledge of experts on a particular subject to make decisions, predict the future or identify opposing views

The **Delphi technique** methodically collates the collective knowledge of experts on a particular subject to scan the environment, predict the future, make decisions or identify opposing views. Its name derives from the future-telling ability of the famous Greek Delphic oracle. Delphi participants do not meet face to face – they may be located in different parts of the country or world, and may not know each other's identity. As with the computer-mediated brainstorming process, decision makers do not know who 'owns' the ideas or possible solutions. The Delphi method relies solely on a nominal group, and participants – usually experts in a relevant field – do not engage in face-to-face interaction.

Typically, Delphi group members submit ideas or possible solutions to the facilitator in response to a series of questionnaires. The respondents' replies are then compiled and returned to the group for a second round of comments. This process may be repeated a couple more times until consensus or dis-consensus emerges. It should be emphasized that the 'experts' taking part do not actually make a final decision: they provide expert advice and information for the organization's decision makers.

The advantage of the Delphi technique is that the process pools a large number of expert judgements while avoiding the problems of conformity and polarization that can occur in interacting groups. A disadvantage of the method is the rather lengthy time frame involved, and its effectiveness depends on the respondents' interest in the problem and commitment to the organization.

As we can see, decision making is a complex phenomenon because it involves dealing with technical matters and power struggles. The five processes reviewed can help employees to deal with the technical challenges and minimize human biases and errors. But decision making is central to innovation and organizational change and relations in the workplace. In this sense, it is at the heart of relationships of class and gender domination. The neoclassical rational model of decision making is associated with bureaucratic managerial structures, as well as with a vision of managers as omnipresent and omnipotent. The extent to which organizations can be designed with decentralized decision-making processes is examined in Chapter 15.

Chapter summary

- When the owners of the TV company CHUM Ltd decided to sell their company to Bell Globemedia of Canada, 281 people became redundant. Peter Murdoch, media vice-president of the Communications Energy and Paperworks Union, which represents employees in CHUM newsrooms, said 'It's absolutely a sense of betrayal. It's a sense of bewilderment.' From a different angle, CHUM chief executive Jay Switzer, commenting on the sale, said 'This is a challenged sector and we have some work to do' (Robertson, 2006). Such decisions by top managers impact on people on an almost daily basis in the corporate world.

- Decision making, the conscious process of making choices from among several alternatives to achieve a desired course of action, is said to be perhaps the most important management function. We have explained that decision making is central to managers' ability to alter the organization's activities and influence employees' behaviour, and is at the heart of relationships of class and gender domination. Decision making is a complex phenomenon because it involves technical problems and power struggles.

- We have explained that the dynamics of organizations create a need for decision making. Decisions can be viewed as being primarily concerned with the allocation of resources and the exercise of power. The neoclassical rational model of decision making has eight steps: identify the problem, define the objectives to be met, make a decision of who to involve in the solution and how to make the decision, generate alternatives, evaluate those alternatives, make a choice from among the alternatives, implement the choice, and follow up on the results of the decision. As decisions lead to actions and the discovery of new problems, another cycle of the rational model is begun.

- In reality, decision makers must suffer from bounded rationality. They do not have free and easy access to information, and the human mind has limited information-processing capacity and is susceptible to a variety of cognitive biases. In addition, time constraints and political considerations can outweigh the anticipated economic gain. Decision making may be seen as a power struggle in which competing interest groups vie with each other for the control of scarce resources. The concept of power in organizations is discussed more fully in Chapter 14.

- The neoclassical rational model neglects to factor into the process the effects of gender on individual and group decision making. Nor does it consider social factors, such as how social norms and expectations frame sense making or problem definition and the decision-making process. We have reviewed some of the literature which suggests that women construct and value knowledge in ways that are relational and oriented more towards sustaining relationships than achieving autonomy and power. The notion that women have a different voice and take a more holistic view of reality suggests that the gender balance of the decision maker's influences decision-making processes.

- Groups can make higher-quality decisions than individuals, but they might also experience groupthink and make decisions that are more risky or conservative than those of individuals. Research has demonstrated that groups do not necessarily make better quality decisions.

- Society, as well as organizations, is increasingly concerned about unethical behaviour and its consequences, from loss of jobs to loss of savings and retirement funds, and from government bail-outs to an increasingly collective distrust of corporations. Business ethics is about conducting business in an ethical manner and generating revenue with integrity. One response to the public concern about unethical behaviour has been to develop codes of conduct so that individual decision makers with different moral standards and bases of moral judgement will have a consistent basis for their decisions.

- 'Corporate social responsibility' refers to the ethical principle that an organization should be accountable for how its behaviour affects local communities, society and the planet. Violations, for example, of health and safety regulations and environmental pollution affect large numbers of people in developed and developing economies; such managerial behaviour has been referred by some criminologists to as 'corporate crime'.

- We have also addressed a number of structured group techniques designed to improve group processes and the quality of group decisions: brainstorming, the nominal group technique, the stepladder technique, computer-mediated brainstorming and the Delphi technique.

- Finally, decision making traditionally remains associated with a 'command and control' vision of management, as well as a vision of managers as being omnipresent and omnipotent. Decision making in the organization can be improved by using the four group processes described above.

IN THE EBOOK ACCESS **WEB BASED ASSIGNMENTS** TO APPLY YOUR LEARNING.

Chapter review questions

1 'For the most part, individual decision making in organizations is an irrational process.' Do you agree or disagree? Discuss.
2 What factors do you think differentiate good decision makers from poor ones? Relate your answer to the eight-step rational decision-making model.
3 If group decisions consistently achieve better quality outcomes than those achieved by individuals, how did the phrase 'a camel is a horse designed by a committee' become so popular and ingrained in our culture?

4 Are unethical decisions more a function of the individual decision maker or the decision maker's work environment? Explain.
5 To what extent do you believe managerial practices to be unethical, and how might unethical behaviour be restricted?
6 What are the arguments for and against CSR?

Further reading

Arrowsmith, J. and Parker, J. (2013) 'The meaning of "employee engagement" for the values and roles of the HRM function', *The International Journal of Human Resource Management*, 23(16), pp. 3336–54.

Bazerman, M. and Moore, D. (2012) *Judgement in Managerial Decision Making* (8th edn), New York: Wiley.

Beard, A. and Hornik, R. (2011) 'It's hard to be good', *Harvard Business Review*, 89(11), pp. 85–96.

Bondy, K. and Starkey, K. (2014) 'The dilemmas of internationalization: corporate social responsibility in multinational corporations', *British Journal of Management*, 25, pp. 4–22.

Derry, R. (1989) 'An empirical study of moral reasoning among managers', *Journal of Business Ethics*, 8(11), pp. 855–62.

Forte, A. (2004) 'Antecedents of managers' moral reasoning', *Journal of Business Ethics*, 51(4), pp. 315–47.

Fulop, L. et al. (2009) 'Decision making in organizations', pp. 667–708 in S. Linstead, L. Fulop and S. Lilley (eds), *Management and Organization: A Critical Text* (2nd edn), Basingstoke: Palgrave Macmillan.

Giacalone, R. A., Jurkiewicz, C. L. and Deckop, J. R. (2008) 'On ethics and social responsibility: the impact of materialism, postmaterialism, and hope', *Human Relations*, 61(4), pp. 483–514.

Giacalone, R.A., Jurkiewicz, C. L. and Promislo, M. (2015) 'Ethics and well-being: the paradoxical implications of individual differences in ethical orientation', *Journal of Business Ethics*, doi: 10.1007/S10551-015-2558-8.

Maclagan, P. (1998) Management and Morality, London: Sage.

Marchington, M. and Kynighou, A. (2012) The dynamics of employee involvement and participation during turbulent times', *International Journal of Human Resource Management*, 23(16), pp. 3336–54.

Morrison, J. (2015) *Business Ethics*, London: Palgrave.

Munby, D. K. and Putnam, L. L. (1992) 'The politics of emotion: a feminist reading of bounded rationality', *Academy of Management Review*, 17, pp. 465–86.

Nutt, P. (2002) *Why Decisions Fail*, San Francisco, CA: Berrett-Koehler.

Ryan, L. V. (1994) 'Ethics codes in British companies', *Business Ethics*, 3(1), pp. 54–64.

Sagie, A. and Aycan, Z. (2003) 'A cross-cultural analysis of participative decision-making in organizations', *Human Relations*, 56(4), pp. 453–73.

Shen, J. and Benson, J. (2014) 'When CSR is a social norm: how socially responsible human resource management affects employee work behavior', *Journal of Management*, 20(10), pp. 1–24.

Winquist, J. and Franz, T. (2008) 'Does the stepladder technique improve group decision-making? A series of failed replications', *Group Dynamics: Theory, Research and Practice*, 12(4), pp. 255–67.

Chapter case study: Ethical decision making at Primark

The setting

Over the last 15 years, the competitive UK retail clothing industry has seen discount chains increase their share of the $51 billion market. Such chains as Matalan, Peacocks and Primark Stores offer brands that are demanded by an increasingly value-focused consumer. Although continued growth in the market will come from the success of these retailers, it is expected that depressed demand and the prevalence of discounters will result in only a modest expansion in the next few years.

As UK clothing suppliers show lower productivity than their leading European competitors, the opportunities for low-cost foreign clothing suppliers to provide to these discount chains have increased. This has resulted in imports making up an estimated two-thirds of the value of the UK clothing market. Traditional sources, primarily Hong Kong and India, are now facing competition from countries such as Morocco and Romania.

Primark is one of the largest discount chains, with 250 stores in the UK, Ireland and Europe. It employs more than 30,000 people, and ranks as Great Britain's second largest clothing retailer by volume and the leading retailer in value clothing. It is expanding more rapidly than any other British retailer. Its primary customer

base is those under 35 years old who are fashion-conscious and want high-quality clothing at reasonable prices.

Primark prides itself on being a member of the Ethical Trading Initiative, which is an alliance of companies, trade unions and non-profit organizations that aims to promote respect for the rights of people in factories and farms worldwide. Primark's commitment to monitoring and improving the working conditions of its 400 suppliers is reflected in its Code of Conduct, which stipulates, among other standards, that the suppliers must pay living wages and ensure that working hours are not excessive.

Using internal Ethical Trade Managers and third-party auditors, the company conducts over 300 audits of their suppliers every year. All potential new suppliers are audited prior to commencing work with Primark, and must meet the company's ethical standards in order to be added to their supply chain. Primark continually reviews its auditing methodologies to improve its ability to identify non-compliance with these standards by its suppliers. Training is offered to suppliers to help them deal with any issues that are found.

The problem

In early 2009, an undercover investigation by the BBC revealed that workers in a Manchester factory owned by a supplier to Primark were on duty for up to 12 hours a day, earning only £3.50 an hour. Some workers were employed illegally and were working in poor conditions.

As the BBC had previously revealed that Primark contractors in India had employed children in slum workshops, Primark took these new allegations seriously. Auditors and senior Primark personnel immediately commenced an investigation of the supplier. The results of the audit were not positive; some findings included inaccurate records of rates of pay, fabricated payslips understating the hours worked, excessive working hours and cash payments made to employees. During the investigation, Primark agreed to remove all references to the Ethical Trade Initiative from 140 of its store fronts.

A Primark representative remarked: 'There are no excuses.

We are absolutely committed to ensuring that the factories who sell to us treat their workers fairly and equitably.' On its website, Primark stated that the supplier had to improve if they were to remain in Primark's supply chain. Primark also made the commitment to help the supplier improve its employment and management practices.

The task

On your own, or in a small group, discuss the following:

- Is it realistic for Primark to control the ethical practices of all its suppliers? If not, why?
- How could Primark's management evaluation and reward systems be used as encouragement?

- As a possible member of Primark's target customer base, what decision would you make about purchasing their products in light of the revelations by the BBC? What role, if any, do ethics play in that decision?

Essential reading

Ferrell, O. C, Fraedrich, J. and Ferrell, L. (2015) *Business Ethics: Ethical Decision Making and Cases* (10th edn), Stamford, CT: Cengage Learning.

For more information on the UK retail clothing industry, visit www.fashionunited.co.uk/facts-and-figures-in-the-uk-fashion-industry and www.britishfashioncouncil.co.uk/.

To learn about the Ethical Trading Initiative, go to www.ethical-trade.org.

Note: This case study was written by Lori Rilkoff, Human Resources Director, City of Kamloops, BC, Canada.

IN THE EBOOK ACCESS AN **OB IN FILM** BOX THAT USES *APOLLO 13* (1995) TO ILLUSTRATE DECISION-MAKING PROCESSES AT WORK AND TO ACCESS **AN INTERACTIVE QUIZ** TO TEST YOUR UNDERSTANDING.

chapter 14
Power, politics and conflict

Chapter learning outcomes

After completing this chapter, you should be able to:

1 Recognize and explain key debates concerning the concept of power in the context of the organizational behaviour field
2 Understand and explain the following key concepts: systems of power, authority, influence and hegemony
3 Compare and contrast major macro-theoretical approaches to the concept of power in the writings of Mann, Foucault, Lukes, Weber and Gramsci
4 Distinguish between unorganized and organized conflict, and between functional and dysfunctional conflict
5 Explain some well-known approaches to conflict resolution
6 Discuss possible implications of theories and research for workplace practice

introduction

In the field of physics, 'power' is defined as a quantity expressing the rate at which energy is transformed into work. In fact, thermodynamic laws see energy as flowing only in one direction. In addition, power is active, while the concept of 'resistance', of power being blocked or slowed down, is passive. We begin with these points for a reason. Simply put, some of these basic principles appear to be remarkably persistent in many common-sense views about the notion of 'power' in the corporate world, what it is and how it works. As the environmental and political activist George Monbiot (2014) points out, corporate power has shifted decisively: to places in which we, as citizens and employees, have no voice or vote. Special advisers, 'spin doctors' and advisory committees swollen with lobbyists forge domestic policies, while a hollowed-out state withdraws its own authority to regulate and direct. Simultaneously, international bureaucrats and corporate executives are filling the democratic vacuum at the heart of global governance. Sometimes corporations use their power well. They reduce carbon emissions or pollution or invest in more sustainable ways of adding value. Sometimes, it seems, the corporate elite of chief executives and vice-presidents, the 'supermanagers' to use Thomas Piketty's (2014) term, exercise their power to pay lobbyists to form laws that suit their corporate interests (Jones, 2014) or thwart government regulations such as the compulsory labelling of fat, salt and sugar on food, lobbying against minimum pricing on alcohol, and opposing banking regulations and controls.

Bakan (2004) makes an incisive case that corporate power and interests trump parliamentary accountability and society's interests. The draft text of the Trade in Services Agreement (TISA) disclosed by WikiLeaks in 2013 is a good example of this. TISA would, among other measures, prohibit a greater regulation of financial services and assist the increase in data flow across borders. For the corporation, global markets, not the 'plebiscite of the ballot box', should dictate economic policy, or, as the Italian economist Mario Monti put it: 'Those who govern must not allow themselves to be completely bound by parliamentarians' (Žižek, 2014: 25). According to Žižek, although it severely limits the space for decision making by elected politicians, TISA has been negotiated in secret. In a scathing account of corporate power, George Monbiot observes that TISA could expose Britain to cases like El Salvador's, where an Australian corporation is suing the South American government because it refused permission for a gold mine that could potentially poison the local supply of drinking water (Monbiot, 2014). The TISA draft affirms Bakan's premise that the corporation is a possessor of 'great power', which 'it wields over people and societies' (2004: 2).

In 2013, the use of corporate power was demonstrated at the Grangemouth petrochemical plant in Scotland (see The Reality of Work feature for this chapter). There, the workers had to capitulate to all of the employer's demands – a promise not to strike, a 3-year wage freeze, zero bonuses and the end of final-salary pensions – to avoid the company, INEOS, closing the plant. What was described as 'one of the worst industrial relations disasters of modern times' (MacWhirter, 2013b) demonstrates, if nothing else, that the exercise of power is not an abstract concept, but can have real repercussions for the lives of people within and outside the organization. At their worst, global corporations use their power to reshape politics in their own interests (Monbiot, 2014). In the preceding chapters, we pointed out how growing evidence of income inequality has ignited arguments about power, and how power influences, if not determines, the decision-making process. Indeed, decision making was described as a 'game of power' in which different organizational groups compete with each other for the control of scarce resources.

This chapter further examines the issue of power in work organizations. It provides an introduction to a range of thinking and research in order to help provide tools with which to expand readers' understanding. As some recent researchers have commented, 'Changes in power almost invariably lead to changes in behavior' (Sivanathan et al., 2008: 135).

Throughout, however, we explicitly reject the common-sense view of power. We argue that power is not simply something the powerful have and the powerless lack. Power, to borrow from the late French philosopher Michel Foucault, is not possessed – it is exercised. In addition, power does not simply limit what people do (that is, as Foucault also says, it does not simply 'say no'), but rather it is productive too (it also says 'yes' to certain behaviours). Across the work of the many intellectuals we discuss in this chapter, some look at macro-phenomena such as politics, society and history, and some look at micro-phenomena such as workplace practice and concerns about 'democratic deficit' (Casey, 2014). Still other academics focus on the many elements in between and the connections between the two. What is clear is that the most astute understandings of power see it as being, at its heart, relational or interactive in nature.

Although it is most often a charge levelled at the work of others, it has been fairly common in recent organizational behaviour writing to note that power as a concept is underdeveloped in this literature. In fact, it has been noted in the editorial introduction to a special journal issue devoted to the concept of power that very little has been written by behavioural analysts on the topic (Austin, 2002). There are some important indications that this trend may, however, be changing. Nevertheless, it runs like a thread throughout the chapter that, building on what has just been established, power is not an individual phenomenon. Despite the fact that the figure of the 'powerful person' appears in all our lives, there is in fact no individual who creates, constitutes or sustains 'power' as such.

Imagine, for example, the power of a police officer, a judge, a professor or a CEO. What are all the 'things' – the history, the traditions, the institutions, the distribution of resources, the socially granted authority and so on – that are necessarily in place to create this seemingly individual embodiment of 'power'? Take away the vastly networked, social, material, historical, cultural and ideological dimensions of the phenomenon, and what we find is that the person's 'power' virtually disappears. Imagine the power of a plumber (for example, when you have a flooded bathroom) or a secretary (for example, when their manager needs some important documents in an emergency). Here too, the power that these individuals may appear to embody, upon closer examination, rests on the particular situation as much as on any individual possession of power per se.

The point here is that while individuals may embody a variety of traits that seem to constitute and legitimize their 'power', we must not confuse individual traits with power as such, because where changes occur across the many dimensions of power – the cultural, the organizational, the political or the situational – the meaning of these traits can be radically transformed. Indeed, it is important also to remember that the exercise of power is often more contested, more conflictual, than is sometimes evident at first glance.

This book adopts a critical approach to organizational behaviour. In this sense, we include in our coverage of power an analysis of the concepts that slow power down – 'resistance' and conflict. How far and in what ways do employees contest or resist their employment situation? Conflicts are likely to concern disagreements over the core dimensions of the employment relationship. On the reward side, there is frequently conflict over workers' pay, and on the effort side, the exercise of power is often contested over changes to work routines. Conflict can lead to lower performance, project failure and even violence. In the early twenty-first century, researchers have developed a significant understanding of organizations as arenas of dissenting behaviour, resistance and conflict.

We begin, as we usually must, with the matter of definitions and related but distinct terms. Indeed, a sizeable proportion of this chapter must grapple directly with these matters of definition. After examining different forms of employee

Source: Getty

stop...

Before reading further, think about your definition of the term 'power'. Do you hold any of the 'common-sense' views on power discussed here? As you carry on reading, remember that a good definition of power should offer you the capacity to see the areas through which it might be questioned, challenged or altered where warranted.

...and reflect

plate 49 Imagine the power of a plumber (for example, when your boiler is broken and you have no heating or hot water in winter), a firefighter (for example, when your house is on fire), or a secretary (for example, when their manager needs some important documents in an emergency). The power that these individuals may appear to embody, upon closer examination, rests on the particular situation as much as on any individual possession of power per se.

resistance, the chapter concludes with a review of some well-known approaches to conflict resolution.

The nature of power

power: a term defined in multiple ways, involving cultural values, authority, influence and coercion as well as control over the distribution of symbolic and material resources. At its broadest, power is defined as a social system that imparts patterned meaning

Post-Hawthorne observational research and the 'discovery' that informal cultures affected and often restricted employee performance denoted the genesis of organizational theory studies of power (Clegg and Dunkerley, 1980: 433). Mainstream theories of '**power**' in organizations have located the bases of power in specific socially sanctioned 'resources' that a worker may control, or be in some relationship with, such that they enable 'power' to be 'exercised'. An example of this perspective is Robert Dahl's (1957) model, which conceptualizes social power by the phrase 'power over' versus 'power to', and which produced his much-quoted phrase, 'A has power over B to the extent that he can get B to do something that B would not otherwise do' (Dahl, 1957: 202–3).

Power 'over', whether individually or collectively, refers to the control of one agent over others, and power 'to' is the capacity to realize ends. Critical workplace scholars have tended to focus on 'power over', concentrating on its oppressiveness and injustice. However, Hearn (2012) argues that 'power over' and 'power to' are 'inextricably bound together … it is the increase in power over, in ever more extensive and complex forms of hierarchic social organization, which has yielded massive increases in our power to' (p. 7).

Closely related to this conceptualization of social power is a definition by French and Raven (1960) in which an *a priori* list of 'power resources' is formed. This explanation of social power likewise focuses on the potential ability of one individual to influence another within a certain social context. This theory assumes that the particular 'resource' possessed by the worker that has a utility in one situation will also have that usefulness in all situations. It also assumes perfect knowledge on the part of all concerned to be able to judge correctly the utility of the all resources in all situations (Clegg and Dunkerley, 1980). In fact, French and Raven went on to develop five bases of power, the most important of which, first suggested by Warren (1968), are those related to systemic reward and coercion.

Our goal in this chapter is to incorporate such statements into a more comprehensive understanding of power, and then test the current analyses of power in work organizations in relation to this new understanding. In doing this, we might add to Dahl's basic definition to relate it directly to the paid workplace: power is the ability to say no to certain behaviours, to say yes to others, and to shape how something should be done. And, building further on this, we can add that it is equally essential to know as much as possible about what 'B would otherwise do' (Ailon, 2006). Ailon's article offers a summary of the six ways in which 'what B would otherwise do' are typically understood by organizational researchers, arguing that there is an important difference between what are referred to as 'political' versus 'Foucauldian' approaches to power in organizations.

This is, of course, inseparable from many of the other issues addressed in the text, including equity and diversity, the organization of labour processes, the selection of technologies, the technical and social divisions of labour, and the accountability and reporting structures and pacing that shape, or rather influence, 'power' in organizations. Corporate economic power can be linked to political power, either directly, when corporations become enmeshed in government policy making, or more indirectly, by influence on government ministers. In his insightful critique of the British corporate elite, Owen Jones observes, 'Corporate giants bully and harangue civil servants' (2014: 219). Thus, politics and power theory is a close relative of ethical theories (Morrison, 2015).

authority: the power granted by some form of either active or passive consent that bestows legitimacy

It is vital that we recognize that, to complicate matters further, the concept of 'power' is often confused with the relatively distinct questions of 'influence' and '**authority**'. We see this, in fact, in the definitions of both Dahl (1957) and French and Raven (1960). The goal of our definition here is to recognize that authority is closely related to, but analytically distinct from, the concept of power. Authority, as it is defined in the social science literature, also tends to have a complex relational dimension but can be said to involve power granted by some form of active or passive consent – whether the consent is linked to specific individuals, groups or institutions – which bestows on it some level of legitimacy. Those readers who have seen Steve McQueen's 2013 film *12 Years a Slave* might like to read Genovese's (1972) fascinating treatment of this notion of coercion, consent and legitimacy applied to the analysis of the American system of slavery.

Some theorists use these words in ways that show a considerable overlap. As the German sociologist Max Weber's work represents the classic analysis of bureaucracy, his treatment of 'types of authority' rather than 'power' is frequently cited as the source of the neglect of power in organizational behaviour. The treatment of 'power' as 'authority' can be traced to the early translation of Weber's concept of *Herrschaft*. American sociologists translated this to mean institutionalized 'authority' (Clegg and Dunkerley, 1980). This definition of the topic became the basis for orthodox studies of power, in which power was seen to relate to authority, as a phenomenon developed informally rather than formally in the organization. The 'formal/informal' distinction thus becomes the focus where 'authority is the *potentiality* to influence based on a position, whereas power is the actual ability to influence based on a number of factors including organizational position' in the hierarchy (p. 435, emphasis added).

legitimacy: a term describing agreement with the rights and responsibilities associated with a position, social values, a system and so on

The issue of **legitimacy** opens up a range of important questions, which we discuss more directly below. Legitimacy depends on one's perspective in communities, organizations, institutions and the world (as a worldview). What is legitimate for some may not be legitimate for others, and this can and does change over time, and according to situations.

Even here, in these conceptually humble beginnings, we see that our rejection of individual models of power in favour of relational ones holds firm. In order to move further beyond conventional discussions of power, we can look beyond organization-based literature to some of the most general, macro approaches.

Traditionally, the field of social theory has understood the concept of power in broad macro terms. Indeed, there is a noticeable preoccupation with how the state, the Church, electoral politics, the military, and sometimes corporations and economic systems, may or may not be involved in systems of power. One of the key writers in this area is Michael Mann. His *Sources of Social Power* (1986) is considered a key text in these theoretical discussions, and builds from a detailed study of ancient Rome and world religions. The 'sources of social power' are determined to be ideological, military, political and economic. Indeed, Mann goes on to say that the object of this type of social power approach should be the development of an analysis of 'multiple overlapping and intersecting socio-spatial networks of power' (1986: 1).

Source: Digital Vision/Getty Images

Plate 50 Giddens' central thesis focuses on societal surveillance and the role of the state. Do you think GCHQ's illegal entry into the data of Facebook and Google validates Giddens' argument?

Social power, in this approach, is diffuse and what we might call 'infrastructural'. It can be understood, according to Mann, by taking into account a specific set of universal relations or dynamics: universalism–particularism, equality–hierarchy, cosmopolitanism–uniformity, decentralization–centralization and civilization–militarism. Each of these is concerned with the dynamic between control and diffuse freedoms and, when applied to his four sources of social power, produces a way of thinking about power that has been influential in social theory as well as history.

Mann's type of approach more or less rejects the explanation of power as simply a form of 'institutionalization' (which we discuss in relation to Weber below), but another key example that is influential in the mainstream social theory tradition is the work of Anthony Giddens (1985). His work on the 'central problems of social theory' seeks to provide an overarching approach while avoiding what he sees as the pitfalls of many broad social theories of power (from schools of social theory such as Marxism, phenomenology and structural-functionalism). His theory of **structuration** is intended to demonstrate the complex interrelations of human freedom (or agency) and determination (or structure), and emphasizes that, in the modern world, there has been a fundamental shift based on the enormous growth in the resources (what he refers to as 'containers') of power. Central to Giddens' (1985) thesis are societal surveillance, capitalist enterprise, industrial production and a centralized control over the 'means of violence' by the state (Figure 14.1). This prescient observation on the activities of the state resonates today in the light of the surveillance revelations by Edward Snowden published by *The Guardian* and *Washington Post* newspapers. Among the disclosures in 2013 were the 'mass dragnet' of the private phone records of millions of American and British citizens held by the US National Security Agency and its UK counterpart GCHQ (Pilkington, 2014).

It is important to the theory of structuration that these sources of power are not 'out there', but are rather the result of specific forms of human interaction mixed with 'authority' and a distribution of 'resources', which together shape and control time and space. This is important, in part, because of its lack of what we would call 'closure'. That is, power is always an open, historical question: things can and do change.

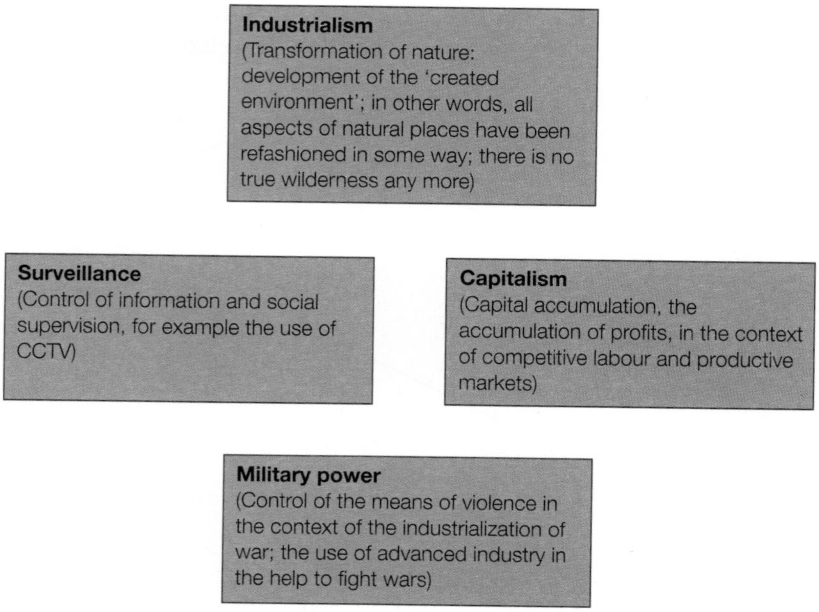

structuration: a concept focusing on balancing the dichotomies of agency, or human freedom, and social organization, or structures where individual choices are seen as partially constrained but nonetheless remain choices

Industrialism
(Transformation of nature: development of the 'created environment'; in other words, all aspects of natural places have been refashioned in some way; there is no true wilderness any more)

Surveillance
(Control of information and social supervision, for example the use of CCTV)

Capitalism
(Capital accumulation, the accumulation of profits, in the context of competitive labour and productive markets)

Military power
(Control of the means of violence in the context of the industrialization of war; the use of advanced industry in the help to fight wars)

Figure 14.1 Giddens' model of power

Source: Inspired by Giddens (1985)

ideology: a term with multiple uses, but in particular referring to perceptions of reality as distorted by class interests, and the ideas, legal arrangements and culture that arise from class relations (a term taken from Marx)

Although we do not review it here, it is worth noting the meta-theory of the German sociologist and philosopher Jürgen Habermas. He describes **ideology** as structure of communication (in his theory of communicative action) that has been systematically distorted by power in such a way as to mostly exclude the realm of daily human activity (what Habermas calls the 'lifeworld') when its activity does not align with dominant institutions and their unique interests and needs. Such domination comes to penetrate individuals' lifeworld, personal identity and inner mental experience – on the same level of analysis dealt with by Giddens' approach to human interaction – leading to their further domination by social systems.

Finally, we should note that, for Giddens, all individuals 'have power', but this power is influenced and constrained by the distribution of different types of resource. In this model, there are 'allocative resources', which refer to control over physical things such as money or property, and there are also 'authoritative resources', which involve control over people's practices. For example, a business owner has the allocative resources of her capital, as well as authoritative resources granted by our legal institutions to set her workplace up in the way she feels most appropriate.

This can lead us to a deeper discussion of the relations between power and authority. Having influenced researchers including Mann, Giddens and Habermas, Max Weber's work on the basic types of authority is closely linked to, although not the same as, the theories of power we have outlined. That is, Weber's theory of authority can be much more closely related to individuals, despite the fact that, ultimately, his approach too is a relational one. Authority necessarily involves others who grant this authority or legitimacy through complex systems of power.

Weber outlines three types of authority:

- *Charismatic authority* refers to leaders who are able to exercise power based on their personal traits.
- *Traditional authority* is dependent on a historical trajectory of past authority.
- *Rational authority*. Weber is most widely known for his analysis of this in his writing on bureaucracy. Here, authority rests on a specific system of laws or rules that establish a hierarchy in, for example, a public or private sector work organization.

Weber's perspective on authority is echoed in the work of Wrong (1979), who lays out a basic model of the relations between influence and power (Figure 14.2).

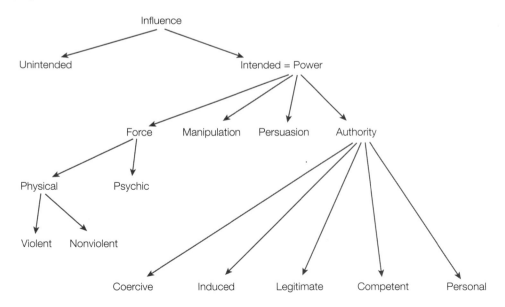

Figure 14.2 Wrong on influence and power

Source: Wrong (1979), p. 24

Another key body of writing on the concept of power is Steven Lukes' *Power: A Radical View* (1974). Lukes' theory is partially summarized in Figure 14.3. Lukes understands power and authority with the notion of 'bringing about consequences' not unlike, for instance, the way a teacher might seek to encourage students to complete their reading assignments prior to lectures. Part of this type of analysis is the recognition that obtaining compliance can require a multifaceted effort. It can be secured by the use of force or by people choosing to surrender to (or be led by) others. In fact, each is usually involved, as we shall see in our later discussion of Gramsci. When people choose to accept the will of others as legitimate, we can, according to Lukes, describe the relationship as one of authority. Some of the studies of behaviour in organizations that we discuss in the following section of this chapter appear to draw on this type of approach.

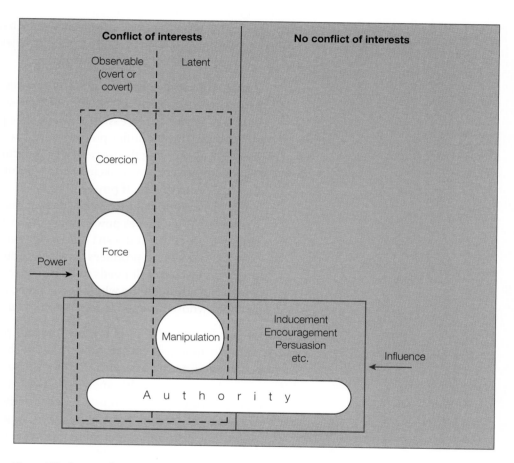

Figure 14.3 Steven Lukes' vision of power

Equally important to Lukes' explanation are the conditions of a **conflict of interest**. The identification of structural and idiosyncratic conflicts of interest is a key challenge for the organizational behaviour literature. Where, for example, is conflict just a matter of fine-tuning existing organizational structures and simply rooted in the contingencies and unpredictability of everyday life, and where might conflict be so deeply rooted in a structure that to challenge it is to simultaneously challenge the very nature of the organization itself? As Figure 14.3 shows, where such structural conflicts of interest do not exist, Lukes uses the word 'influence'. Where structural conflicts of interest exist, he uses the word 'power'. Both planned decision-making (overt and covert varieties) and latent (or unintended) uses of power play a role in Lukes' model, while issues of authority, not unlike those outlined by Weber, operate in contexts of both non-conflict and conflict of interest.

Additional definitions of power to consider

Up to this point, we have looked at what can be called traditional social theory approaches to power. They help us think outside common-sense views. There are, however, still other perspectives to consider. One of these is found in the work of Michel Foucault, another key thinker in the field of social theory. His work in, among many other texts, *Discipline and Punish* (*1977*) and *Power/Knowledge* (1980), although oriented by a stated interest in the 'micro-politics' of power and preoccupied with individual identity or 'subjectivity', is in the end a very broad macro theory as well. In this way, Foucault, like Giddens, is interested in breaking down the distinction between individuals and society, or 'agency' and 'structure'. Unlike Lukes, however, Foucault's definitions of power make it even clearer that there is a double edge to power. It prevents some behaviours while at the same time positively encouraging others, both at the broadest political and historical levels and at the deepest level of individual identity:

> it seems to me now that the notion of repression is quite inadequate for capturing what is precisely the productive aspect of power. In defining the effects of power as repression, one adopts a purely juridical conception of such power, one identifies power with a law which says no, power is taken above all as carrying the force of a prohibition. Now I believe that this is a wholly negative, narrow, skeletal conception of power, one which has been curiously widespread. If power were never anything but repressive, if it never did anything but to say no, do you really think one would be brought to obey it? What makes power hold good, what makes it accepted, is simply the fact that it doesn't only weigh on us as a force that says 'no', but that it traverses and produces things, it induces pleasure, forms knowledge, produces discourse. It needs to be considered as a productive network which runs through the whole social body, much more than a negative instance whose function is repression. (Foucault, 1980: 119)

For Foucault, power is all-pervasive. Indeed, power constitutes what we know as a society, including, of course, how we think about work organizations. Power is everywhere: 'there are no "margins" for those who break with the system' (Foucault, 1980: 141). Thus, in Foucault's analysis, power is discussed in terms of the many ways through which it is exercised – 'economies of power', 'regimes of power', 'networks of power', 'technologies of power' (Crane et al., 2008).

An important distinction that some researchers make here, however, concerns the difference between Foucauldian approaches to power and what are often referred to as political theories of organizational power:

> Foucaultians claimed that the two are characterized by an all-encompassing inseparability. Political theorists claimed that politics are everywhere: people always seek ways to fulfil their parochial interests, always want to impose upon others that which they would otherwise do despite legitimate power structures and at times in contrast to them. Foucaultians claimed that *power* is everywhere: what people see as their interests as well as the strategies they devise for achieving these interests are determined by existing power structures or discursive practices and to a considerable extent serve to reinforce them. (Ailon, 2006: 783)

For a key example of the political approach to power in organizations, see Astley and Sachdeva (1984).

Thus, although there are significant overlaps between Foucauldian and political approaches to power, an important distinction should be recognized. One tool for

hegemony: a conception of power that includes both conflict as well as consent and leadership by generating a particular worldview or 'common sense' on relevant and appropriate action

this recognition is hegemony. **Hegemony** is a key term in critical political theory that involves the complexity and mixture of consensus and conflict, and hence power relations in a broad sense. It derives from the Greek, where it originally referred to a leader or ruler (*egemon*), but was taken up in the English language in the nineteenth century and has come to describe a very nuanced form of sociopolitical predominance. It describes control that is both direct and indirect, and rests on the notion of a whole way of seeing the world, a 'normal reality' or 'common sense'.

Specifically, the term 'hegemony' can express two types of power relations. The first describes a group's *domination* over other groups, and the second describes a group's *leadership*. The concept represents a whole body of practices as well as expectations, assignment of energies and ordinary understandings of the world in terms of meanings and values. In essence, the concept expresses the relationships of leadership and domination that produce a general sense of coordinated reality for most people. However, it is a concept that lends itself to a wider discussion than Foucault's thesis encourages. Power is seen as all-pervasive in the sense that there can also be something called 'counter-hegemony'. Counter-hegemony is composed

the reality of work

Source: Brand X

Conflict at work: Grangemouth oil refinery

In October 2013, a dispute concerning the use of company facilities by a shop steward (union representative) for local Labour Party activity escalated into the closure of two plants and a humiliating defeat for the trade union Unite. In response to the suspension of their shop steward, Unite called for a vote for industrial action and further negotiations. The next day, Ineos, the Swiss-based owner of the company Grangemouth oil refinery, which produces 85 per cent of Scotland's petrol, locked the workers out and closed the refinery.

The company had wanted to make pension cuts for a long time and had demanded an end to workers' final-salary pensions, a wage freeze, a 3-year suspension of bonuses, the end of full-time union conveners on site and no strikes for 3 years. The union urged members to reject these demands and to support it in continued negotiations, but the company bypassed the union and sent out a letter to all 1350 workers giving them 5 days to accept or reject the company's offer of an alternative pension scheme (with enhanced employer contributions) and a transitional payment of up to £15,000. Ineos stated that within 2 days more than 250 workers had accepted the new terms and conditions, but when the deadline arrived half of the union members had rejected the proposals.

The following day, Ineos's majority owner, Swiss-based billionaire Jim Ratcliffe, ordered the closure of the neighbouring petrochemical plant that the company also owned, putting another 800 jobs at risk. Faced with the sudden closure of both plants, the union accepted all the owners' demands. This was a strike of capital, the refusal of business to invest in a particular sector of the economy, with the threat of permanent closure of the plants. Ineos was in a strong position as the Scottish and British governments were unwilling to nationalize the plants in order to maintain jobs. The employers contacted the workforce

directly, bypassing the union, and when a third of the oil refinery workers accepted the employer's offer in return for a new pension scheme, the union's support was undermined. A solution to the industrial dispute through union–employer negotiations and collective bargaining was weakened by individuals' decisions to protect their jobs and family income in the context of austerity and job insecurity.

The success of Ineos may encourage other UK employers to emulate such aggressive management. The UK's industrial relations is based on a conflict model that engenders insecurity, low pay and inferior individual and collective employment rights compared with other European countries. In the case of Grangemouth, 85 per cent of Scotland's fuel supply was in the hands of one tax exile based in Switzerland. Duffy et al. (2013) point out that the UK ranks a measly 26th out of 27 in a measure of industrial democracy. They show how employers, employees and trade unions in Denmark, Germany and elsewhere in Europe cooperate in company management in ways that make a strike of capital like the one at Grangemouth impossible.

> **Stop!** Imagine you are an employee facing the closure of your workplace if you do not accept a reduction in the terms and conditions of your employment. If you were offered a financial inducement, would you return to work under the less attractive conditions, or would you be prepared to accept the union's advice to strike in the hope that the company would return to negotiations?

Sources and further information

Duffy, J., Gall, G. and Mather, J. (2013) 'Working together: a vision for industrial democracy in a Common Weal economy.' The Jimmy Reid Foundation. Available at http://reidfoundation.org/portfolio/working-together/ (accessed April 26, 2014).

Farrell, S. (2013) 'Union climbdown gives hope to Grangemouth', *The Guardian*, October 25.

Milmo, D. and Godley, S. (2013) 'Grangemouth "faces permanent closure"', *The Guardian*, October 21.

Seymour, R. (2013) 'How Ineos humiliated Unite in Grangemouth', *The Guardian*, November 9.

Note: This feature was written by David Denham, Honorary Research Fellow in Sociology, Wolverhampton University, UK.

of and expresses competing ways of seeing the world and behaving, although this behaviour can at times be clandestine and underdeveloped.

The term 'hegemony' is now most closely associated with the writings of an early twentieth-century Italian Marxist, Antonio Gramsci (1971). Raymond Williams (1983), one of the earliest English-speaking writers on Gramsci's work, explains the importance of the concept of hegemony, in most general terms, as:

> The idea of hegemony ... is especially important in societies in which elec-toral politics and public opinion are significant factors, and in which social practice is seen to depend on consent to certain dominant ideas which in fact express the needs of a dominant class. (p. 145)

In earlier work of 1960, Williams observes how Gramsci asserted that hegemony is the 'normal form of control', and that state coercion and violence only become the norm at times of political crisis (J. Williams, cited by Clegg and Dunkerley, 1980: 492).

Gramsci used a historical analysis of specific periods of French and Italian society in order to refer to a system of alliances within a 'hegemonic bloc' of interests. A bloc necessarily contains significant competing interests, but it is unified on some core principles. This bloc was dependent on what Gramsci (1971) referred to as the 'powerful system of fortresses and earthworks' of civil society, including the multitude of social, economic, cultural, organizational, group and corresponding ideologies among which there is significant room for compromise (although only on non-hegemonic terrain). As Williams notes, however, much influential work on counter-hegemonic practices has ignored contemporary scenes of consensus and conflict, including work organization. This is not without its problems (Williams, 1977).

An important contribution to our general understanding of power, and in turn of power as it relates to work organizations and behaviour, comes from the notion of emergent forms of practice that lie in some form of opposition to a dominant or hegemonic bloc in the sense that Gramsci and Williams described. First, the notion provides a basic framework for understanding the character of alternative (resist-ant) practices in opposition to a complex of dominant presumptions. An entire sub-school of industrial sociology/organizational studies literature has specifically addressed the issue of resistance (Roscigno and Hodson, 2004). Building from this notion, we can see that organizational behaviour emerging from non-dominant (that is, workers' rather than managers') standpoints need not strictly reproduce a particular hegemonic order. It can at times run tangentially to it, and possibly even in direct opposition to it. In both cases, it represents an active, living process in which alternatives struggle against incorporation.

IN THE EBOOK ACCESS THE **CRITICAL INSIGHT** ON GRAMSCI'S NOTION OF A 'HEGEMONIC' BLOC'.

In less abstract terms, we are talking about people's behaviour that is rooted in processes that align with the basic assumptions and structures of the organization, have little to do with these dominant assumptions, or in some cases actively resist the major premises upon which the organization is based. This type of resist-ance can be ongoing and persistent, or it can be more likely to be seen in certain conflictual situations such as in union-organized workplaces during collective bargaining, or within a specific department of an organization that is experiencing organizational change (see Chapter 18). To put this in the language of social class, we are talking about organizational behaviour that can easily be incorporated into capitalism, is somehow outside this logic or opposes capitalism in some way, either persistently or idiosyncratically (and everything in between).

Micro-interaction and theories of power

These macro theories of power set the context for a consideration of theories of power in local, everyday interaction or behaviour. Analyses of micro-interaction form another distinct set of theories on power. For example, we can ask what Nietzsche's '**will to power**' (a term that defines social interaction as an ongoing contest between people constantly striving to exercise power over others) might mean in terms of behaviour in organizations. Is the 'will to power' a generalized (overt or covert) phenomenon, as Nietzsche's work suggests, or are there other central motivations in people's lives?

The work of another famous micro-sociologist, Erving Goffman, is also relevant in this context. His analysis of 'contests' as a major frame of social interaction offers a fascinating exploration of how people think and negotiate order in their daily interactions. Another concept that has similarities to this comes from the school of sociology called **game theory**. This is popular among economists and economic sociologists for its apparent pragmatism.

This school of thought, which focuses on the notion of contests or games, invites us to understand individual actors as acting in a way that they believe will provide the best outcome for them, given their objectives, resources and circumstances as they see them. Its focus is on voluntary actions and inter-actor exchange, and it encompasses both conflictual contests and cooperative games. It begins from the rather traditional economic assumption that individuals act to maximize their utility (that is, to do as well as is possible in the circumstances).

We can also consider micro-interactions through the work of discourse analyst Robin Tolmach Lakoff, which is discussed by Krippendorff (1995). How might 'power' be evident in this simple, everyday exchange?:

> Man: Wanna go to the movies?
> Woman: Oh, I don't know. Do you?

Krippendorf correctly points out that this is one example of a very common, gendered 'language game' that allows us to explore a host of possibilities. The male makes a proposal. The female has several options in response, including (among a vast array of others) ignoring, accepting, counterproposing and clarifying. Her different options (including the response she gives above) allow us to consider the system of power in operation at the micro level. For example, a counterproposal might signal some sort of equal power relation; a stern rejection might signal an unequal power relation; a deferral (as in her response above) might signal another form of unequal power relation; and of course any and all of the possibilities might be part of a clever, expanded set of negotiations that defy simplistic categorization.

Ailon's (2006) work can, in turn, be used to understand the option potentially open to this woman in terms of Dahl's traditional definition of power, which we used to begin this chapter. In this exchange, of course, the word 'power' is never used. The point here is that we can quite easily, even in this smallest of examples, draw into our analysis the concept of power. We can also see how it can include a whole infrastructure of, for example, gender relations.

Finally, returning to the work of Erving Goffman (1959) for a moment, micro-power can also be understood as part of people's 'presentation of self in everyday life'. It is echoed in the work of a range of others such as Finkelstein (1995), who writes extensively on how people's physical appearance or self-presentation involves a whole range of broader 'macro-forces' or systems of power. (See also the work of Marks (2008), which we reviewed in our case study at the end of Chapter 8.)

---

will to power: the notion that people are inherently driven to develop and expand power and control in their environments

game theory: a social theory premised on the notion that people do what is best for themselves given their resources and circumstances, as in some form of a competitive game

stop...

The example of going to the movies can readily be extended to a work context. How might you go about a micro-analysis of the following exchange?

Woman: Tell me how to fix this Xerox machine.

Man: Oh, don't you worry about this, honey. Leave it to me.

Now continue the exchange, taking account of the distinct backdrops of power and/or gender relations.

...and reflect

Source: © iStockphoto.com/MachineHeadz

plate 51 The micro-management of appearances has been understood for some time to be a vital component of how 'power' operates. The distinctive wig and black robe give barristers an air of distance and authority.

stop...

Can the management of appearances hold the balance between success and failure in organizations? How does power in organizations work in terms of a dress code? What ideological values are represented in such codes? Rubenstein (2001) discusses *Dress Codes: Meaning and Messages in American Culture*. What further details does it give you about the relationship between appearance and power?

...and reflect

In a particularly striking section of her book, Finkelstein gives an example of a Jewish prisoner in a Nazi concentration camp. His memoirs show him taking incredible pains to keep himself 'respectable' in appearance. As the prisoner notes, his captors' general beliefs about his 'respectability' could in fact hold the balance between life and death: 'He needed no more than his spruce suit and his emaciated and shaven face in the midst of the flock of his sordid and slovenly colleagues to stand out and thereby receive benefits from his captors' (Finkelstein, 1995: 136). This is an extreme example, but the point is that the micro-management of appearances has been understood for some time to be a vital component of how 'power' operates. It provides a mechanism of sorting, in Finkelstein's terms of 'social passport and credential', for how people can participate in the systems of power they are presented with.

VISIT THE *ONLINE RESOURCE CENTRE* AT HTTPS://HE.PALGRAVE.COM/COMPANION/BRATTON-WORK-AND-ORGANIZATIONAL-BEHAVIOUR3/ FOR A LINK TO AN INTERACTIVE WEBSITE DEALING WITH ADDITIONAL PERSPECTIVES ON POWER THAT WILL FURTHER ENHANCE YOUR UNDERSTANDING OF IDEAS IN THIS CHAPTER.

Power, conflict and resistance in organizations

Power in organizations is often revealed in different forms of conflict (for example, group and intragroup conflict; see Chapter 10) and resistance. Richard Sennett's (2012) 'social triangle' concept – authority, mutual respect and cooperation – remind us that people are different from other 'resources' because their cooperation and commitment always have to be won and sustained by management. Importantly, employees have the capacity to resist management's decisions and actions and to engage in strikes, sabotage, non-cooperation or absenteeism. Thus, any discussion of power has to acknowledge that social relations in the workplace are inevitably characterized by structured power, cooperation and conflict. In this section, we examine different forms of organizational conflict, and how workplace theorists have analysed the power struggles in organizations.

Industrial or workplace conflict refers to all expressions of dissatisfaction within the employment relationship, especially those pertaining to the effort–reward bargain (Scott and Marshall, 2009). Workplace conflict is an interactive process manifested in incompatibility, disagreement or dissonance within or between parties (Rahim, 2001). Observational research has identified many different kinds of conflict and resistance at work. Industrial sociologists have divided these into two classifications: informal and formal. *Informal conflict* is not based on any recognizable organization and results from an actual or perceived breach of the employment contract, or from a threat to an employee's dignity. Jan Karlsson (2012) goes as far as to argue that the defence of one's dignity at work is the 'main mechanism behind employee resistance' (p. 15).

Formal conflict, on the other hand, describes organized expressions of discontent that are articulated through an elected or appointed worker representative, such as a trade union or a member of the company's grievance committee. In his seminal text, *Strikes* (1989b), Richard Hyman, a labour relations theorist, labelled industrial conflict as 'unorganized' and 'organized', with the involvement of individuals or trade unions, respectively. For Hyman, *unorganized conflict* occurs when an individual employee responds to dissatisfaction by, for instance, exiting the organization, being absent or sabotaging a computer. When a group of workers engage in planned action, for example, a stoppage of work or a strike, a boycott of working overtime or occupation of the employer's premises to change the source of the dissatisfaction, Hyman calls this *organized conflict*. The economic and political contexts (see Figure 1.3) either enhance or weaken trade union bargaining power. Where a union's bargaining power is weak, because of high unemployment or restrictive employment laws, for instance, organized conflict is less likely (Farnham, 2015). Thus, organized conflict is closely related to theories of bargaining power.

There has been much debate concerning whether or not conflict is detrimental or beneficial. It seems intuitively plausible that conflict within organizations is always harmful (De Dreu, 2008). But, counterintuitively, conflict can be a catalyst for beneficial change. Tjosvold (2008), for example, has argued that conflict can lead to improvements by employees sharing their experience and knowledge to generate creative ideas.

Contrasting perspectives on conflict

There are different perspectives on the nature of conflict. Alan Fox's (1966) classic contribution distinguished four different approaches or frames of reference for studying conflict: unitarist, pluralist, radical and interactionist. The *unitarist perspective* views organizations as harmonious, cooperative entities and assumes a commonality of interests between an organization's managers, the other employees and, by implication, the owners. It explains observable conflict in psychological terms – personality clash – or as something that 'trouble makers' cause (Ackroyd and Thompson, 1999).

The *pluralist perspective* on conflict considers the organization as a microcosm of society, as a collection of many separate groups, each of which have their own legitimate interests. The indeterminacy of the employment relationship leads to uncertainty, insecurity and different perceptions of reality. In this context, workplace conflict is inevitable, indeed endemic. All parties recognize the need for negotiation and compromise to enable the organization to function. The occurrence of conflict provides a mechanism to 'regulate' the employment relation.

The *radical perspective* on conflict is rooted in a Marxist analysis of the capitalist employment relationship (see Chapter 3). It holds that the logic of capital accumulation – profit maximization – necessitates that managers relentlessly minimize costs, including labour costs, and maximize control of the manufacturing or service process. The radical perspective views the workplace as an arena of conflict between managers (as agents of capital) and other employees. Thus, conflict is intrinsic to the capitalist employment relationship. In contrast to other perspectives, however, radical theorists consider that managers can only mitigate, and not prevent, the occurrence of conflict by using people management practices.

A more recent view of conflict is the *interactionist perspective*, which believes that conflict is not only inevitable, but can also release positive energy, which is necessary for effective performance. Indeed, it is suggested that some managers deliberately 'engineer' conflict to counter 'groupthink' and encourage reflexivity, self-criticism and change (Xenikou and Furnham, 2013). However, in order for conflict to yield positive results, it has to be of the appropriate kind. Thus, the organizational theorists Robbins and Judge (2013) distinguish between 'functional' and 'dysfunctional' conflict. Whereas functional conflict supports the goals of the work group or organization and improves performance, dysfunctional conflict has the opposite effect. The notion that functional conflict is necessary for effective performance, and that a certain level of conflict should be encouraged depending on the situation, is referred to as the contingency model of conflict (Hatch and Cunliffe, 2012).

VISIT THE *ONLINE RESOURCE CENTRE* AT HTTPS://HE.PALGRAVE.COM/COMPANION/BRATTON-WORK-AND-ORGANIZATIONAL-BEHAVIOUR3/ FOR DETAILS OF A FACTSHEET ON INDUSTRIAL CONFLICT FROM THE CHARTERED INSTITUTE OF PERSONNEL AND DEVELOPMENT.

Misbehaviour in the workplace

A recent development in the study of conflict is the focus on organizational 'misbehaviour'. Current newspaper reports and research confirm what we all know: that people cheat, steal and commit acts of fraud at work. But we also know that senior executives, bankers and elected politicians cheat their companies or the tax payer. We should note too that the Internet has opened up limitless opportunities for criminal and deviant behaviour (Capeller, 2001). Organizational misbehaviour has also provoked individuals, often referred to as whistleblowers, to expose misconduct, for example corruption, health violations or a direct threat to the public interest. The often reported travails of whistleblowers emphasize that the conceptualization of organizational misbehaviour is relational, and is also often conceptually related to organizational power (Smith, 2015).

In an insightful and provocative study of organizational misbehaviour, Karlsson (2012) explores this area through the narrative of misbehaviour, the generic term for cheating, stealing, fraud, bullying, swearing, sabotage, abusive management and resistance behaviours directed upwards within the power hierarchy. McCabe's (2014) study demonstrates the complexity of disentangling different forms of misbehaviour. McCabe's study of banking employees reveals that they engaged in contradictory behaviours combining elements of both resistance – 'making out' – and consent – 'making do' – that are difficult to unravel. The former 'works against the grain of corporate intentions' because it aims to create space and autonomy, whereas 'making do' works with management intentions (p. 68). An early study by Ackroyd and Thompson defined organizational misbehaviour as 'anything you do at work you are not supposed to do' (1999: 2).

Karlsson adds another dimension to the concept by defining organizational misbehaviour as:

> Anything you are, do and think at work which you are not supposed to be, do and think. (2012: 156)

The subtle addition of the verbs 'are' and 'think' denotes the importance of self 'identity'. According to Karlsson, these cognitive processes recognize the effort that organizations put into 'indoctrinating' their employees' thinking and identities through corporate culture (see Chapter 17). That management are 'trying to change your personality' (McKinlay and Taylor, 1998: 179) and 'get inside your head' (Ezzamel et al., 2004: 289) demonstrates a conflict between corporate culture and identity. And it is this apparent clash that is embodied in Karlsson's broader concept of misbehaviour.

Karlsson's main finding is that, in order to understand misbehaviour, managers need to be cognisant of the 'rules' that help junior managers and other employees to 'keep their dignity' at work (2012: 178). The post-2008 austerity era is likely to be characterized by low levels of unionization, distributive bargaining and precarious, 'flexible' employment contracts, alongside conspicuous 'aristocratic' executive pay. Insofar as these developments will be mirrored by ever more ways to intensify work, managers and other employees may well need to find new coping strategies, and employee 'misbehaviour' is likely to remain a significant feature of organizational life (Collinson and Ackroyd, 2006).

Strikes, resistance and power

Planned organizational change can give rise to resistance and overt forms of conflict in almost any organization, and can involve any groups of its workers, even those not traditionally associated with collective trade union action. The strike is probably the most well-known form of conflict in organizations. Through the 1990s and into the new millennium, the number of strikes by workers in industrialized countries has tended to decline (Collins and Terry, 2010). In the UK, the number of days lost to strikes in recent years has been at its lowest since the Great Depression of the 1930s (Bratton and Gold, 2012: 399). What are we to make of this? Should we conclude that the power struggles in organizations have been reduced, giving way to greater consensus? Not according to some researchers (Aligisakis, 1997; Collinson, 1994; Smith and Morton, 2006). Labour law regulates union organization, unions' recognition by employers, collective bargaining and the manifestations of collective workplace conflict. Reviewing labour law under different UK governments since 1997, the study by Smith and Morton (2006) concludes that employers' power has become more 'entrenched'. They also contend that, to strengthen workers' power, legislation is needed to establish 'a statutory right of trade unions to have access to, and assembly at, the workplace' (p. 414).

Collinson's (1994) work is worth looking at in detail for its discussion of power in organizations. It represents an important type of research that has linked past discussions from industrial sociology and labour process theory to more contemporary concerns about individuals, identity and meaning under what are sometimes referred to as 'postmodern' conditions of globalization and the (apparently) 'new' knowledge or information economy. Collinson argues that despite the decline of organized workplace disputes, the power struggle continues to rage on in diffuse and pervasive forms. This is not simply either domination or resistance in organizations; instead, domination and resistance exemplify power. In this context, power is to be found in situations of apparent consent and domination as well as where there is resistance. Collinson maintains that labour process theory has made a distinctive contribution to the analysis of work by highlighting the 'irreducible interrelationship between employee resistance and managerial control … Emphasizing the extensive power asymmetries in contemporary organizations' (1994: 25). He goes on to claim that the founding preoccupations of traditional labour process theory with scientific management and Taylorism are still relevant, as is the classic critique offered in the work of Harry Braverman (see also the discussion of Braverman's, 1974, work in Chapters 2 and 16).

Collinson's specific contribution, however, emerges from his assessment that knowledge and information are key aspects of power. He draws on the work of Foucault, on writers who make use of Mann's work on power (see Clegg, 1989) and on the 'game metaphor' (Burawoy, 1979), but goes on to say that, despite the seemingly uneven distribution of access to organizational knowledge and information, other forms of knowledge (that is, technical and production-based knowledge) are available to workers. These alternative resources can be mobilized through a wide variety of strategies, and this variety in turn accounts for the very uneven and variegated results of power struggles in organizations.

The first of the two main strategies Collinson outlines is 'resistance by distance', in which workers restrict information from management. This is referred to as a type of 'escape attempt', and a denial of involvement or interest in work processes. The second strategy, 'resistance through persistence', involves efforts to extract information from management. In a sense, this involves voluntarily increasing involvement and interest in work processes. Of course, management in this framework tries to use the opposite strategies of extracting and restricting information, respectively, and this results in a complex spiral of control resistance, greater efforts at control and so on, or rather a series of strategies and counterstrategies.

Finally, Collinson emphasizes the role played by both management and workers' personal identities, or we might say social background, which significantly shapes which strategy is used. He qualifies his conclusions, which depend heavily on the exact context, but in general concludes that 'resistance through persistence' turns out to be a more effective strategy. However, as he notes, neither strategy constitutes a deep challenge to the structure of power (that is, management rights) in organizations.

globalization & organization misbehaviour

Source: PhotoDisc

Dead Bangladeshi workers: are corporations really responsible?

Have a quick look through your closet. The chances are good that workers in Bangladesh made at least some of your clothing. Working in a clothing factory is often the only way for these workers – especially Bangladeshi women – to make a living. Yet it is also extremely unpleasant and hazardous work. The 2013 collapse of a factory in Savar killed more than 1100 workers when vibrations from a generator brought illegally built upper floors down on top of the workshop below (Miller, 2012):

> Pakhi Begum … tried to stay at home on the day of the collapse amid concerns over the cracks in the wall of the building, but her manager threatened to dock her an entire month's pay. So she went to work. 'When it happened, it was very fast … a huge hole opened up in the floor and I fell into it. A concrete beam was across my legs so I couldn't move. I was screaming and praying,' Begum said.

> … After 36 hours, rescuers reached her … 'I was talking to them. I told the rescuers to cut [off] my legs. They refused. We argued. I was telling them to do it … The anaesthetics did not work properly so I screamed. He said: 'Don't scream or I can't work.' So I didn't scream when they cut again,' she recalled. (Burke, 2013)

The Savar deaths, while many and terrible, are not unusual. For example, an October 2013 fire in a Gazipur textile factory that made materials for Kmart and Just Jeans clothes was one of five such disasters in a 12-month period that killed over 1200 workers. The Gazipur fire was preceded by government warnings in which: 'government inspectors just a week before the blaze warned that the building was 'dangerous to human life'' (Doherty and Whyte, 2014).

So why do Bangladeshi factory owners expose their workers to such conditions? An important factor is the cost pressure exerted by corporations in the developed world. For example, Primark bought clothes made in Rana Plaza in Danka, Bangladesh. That factory collapsed in early 2013 (Kuenssberg, 2014a).

> Bangladeshi High Commissioner to London, Mohamed Mijarul Quaye, told one reporter that '(buyers) go round these manufacturers and they negotiate every cent of it … I believe this haggling on every cent has a negative impact on the terms of employment and on work conditions – that is decidedly the fact'. (Kuenssberg, 2014b)

Reeling from revelations of child labour and Dickensian working conditions, corporations have made various efforts to self-regulate. Yet corporate social responsibility codes have clearly not resulted in safer workplaces or better lives for many of the world's poorest workers. Indeed, some political scientists suggest that corporate social responsibility is more about corporations maintaining moral legitimacy by appearing to care, than

it is about actually upholding any meaningful ethical standards (Shamir, 2011).

More recently, some business leaders and academics have begun arguing that sweatshops are, on balance, good for workers:

> [While] 77 percent of Bangladeshis live on less than $2 a day – the international poverty standard – and 43 percent live on less than $1.25 a day, workers at the much-demonized Bangladeshi 'sweatshops' average more than $2 a day. Granted, that's not a lot. But it's more than they would earn elsewhere … Unfortunately, if U.S. companies abandon these factories, hundreds of thousands of garment workers could lose their jobs and be thrust into worse alternatives. (Powell, 2013)

Powell's argument assumes, of course, that the only alternative to unsafe working conditions is closing the factories. The notion of mandating better standards globally (which would take the cost of improvements out of competition) is absent from his analysis.

So why doesn't the government intervene? Well, poor working conditions are generally cheap working conditions. And Bangladesh's $20 billion garment industry generates 80 per cent of the country's export earnings and employs more than 4 million people. Tampering with the industry's formula for success (which includes low wages and hazardous working conditions) is hardly in the government's interests.

> **Stop!** What does the long string of workers' deaths say about the effectiveness of corporate social responsibility in the garment supply chain? Why would corporations create seemingly ineffective codes of conduct? Is the mutilation and death of Bangladeshi workers likely to change your purchasing habits?

Sources and further research

Burke, J. (2013) 'Bangladesh factory collapse leaves trail of shattered lives', *The Guardian*, June 6. Available at: http://nickjordan.ca/wp-content/uploads/2014/01/1.2-Bangladesh-factory-The-Guardian.pdf (accessed February 19, 2015).

Doherty, B. and Whyte, S. (2014) 'Bangladesh garment factory warned of danger before fatal fire', *The Age*, January 5. Available at: www.theage.com.au/world/bangladesh-garment-factory-warned-of-danger-before-fatal-fire-20140104-30ay9.html (accessed February 19, 2015).

Keunssberg, L. (2014a) 'Primark: taking responsibility over Dhaka', ITV, March 3. Available at: www.itv.com/news/2013-04-29/primark-taking-responsibility-over-dhaka/ (accessed February 19, 2015).

Keunssberg, L. (2014b) 'Western companies "should share blame" for Bangaldesh factory conditions', ITV, March 3. Available at: www.itv.com/news/2013-04-30/western-companies-should-share-blame-for-bangladesh-factory-conditions/ (accessed February 19, 2015).

Miller, D. (2012) *Last Nightshift in Savar*, Pembroke: McNidder & Grace.

Parvenn, S. (2014) 'Rana Plaza factory collapse survivors struggle one year on', April 23. Available at: www.bbc.com/news/world-asia-27107860 (accessed February 28, 2015).

Powell, N. (2013) 'Sweatshops in Bangladesh improve the lives of their workers, a boost economic growth', *Forbes*, May 2. Available at: www.forbes.com/sites/realspin/2013/05/02/sweatshops-in-bangladesh-improve-the-lives-of-their-workers-and-boost-growth/ (accessed February 19, 2015).

Shamir, R. (2011) 'Socially responsible private regulation: world culture or world-capitalism?', *Law and Society Review*, 45(2), pp. 313–36.

Note: This feature was written by Bob Barnetson, Associate Professor of Labour Relations, Athabasca University, Canada.

The key point for this section of the chapter is that, although power is often revealed in overt forms of conflict and resistance (such as strikes), both subtle and alternative forms of resistance can also be identified. You should be able to understand this better in the light of the various conceptual frameworks we explored earlier in the chapter.

Even the existence of consensus can be used to support the claim that work organizations are in many ways constituted by power relations. Drawing on Collinson as well as Kondo (1990), we can note that effective resistance requires elements of conformity to a rival power source. Collinson sees this as discursive and knowledge based, but we would suggest that this concept can easily be extended to include well-functioning communities of workers: bargaining units, neighbourhoods, social movements or occupational groupings. This brings us back in a sense to Giddens' claim that 'everyone has power', but that it is expressed in different ways depending on the (allocative and authoritative) resources. There is the power of enforcing democracies, forcing people to learn, and ultimately the power to remake existing power relations into something better.

Although there is not exactly a flood of interest in power issues in most of the recent empirical research outlined in the main organizational behaviour journals, these nevertheless reveal a significant consideration of issues of power. Studies in this area deal with a variety of topics, such as practical governance and managerial practices in work organizations. Often, although not exclusively, there is a particular interest in organizational change initiatives. Below (and in Chapter 18) we explore some key findings of the most recent studies that touch on important issues in the field. The aim is to balance our earlier conceptual discussion with some more concrete findings.

In a provocative study of relations between supervisors and their subordinates, Elangovan and Xie (1999) explore the results and perceptions of supervisory 'power'. Even this brief introductory line reveals that they conceive power in a way that is partially, not absolutely, at odds with the relational perspective we have developed here. The focus is on employees and supervisors, which is obviously a relational issue, but Elangovan and Xie tend to see power largely as something a supervisor has, rather than as a dimension of the social system (on the macro or micro level). A relational perspective, on the other hand, would highlight how power is systemic, put into effect or reproduced by all individuals subjected to the system, and not, for example, simply traceable to the characteristics of a particular supervisor. Nevertheless, Elangovan and Xie offer some important findings on how power is *experienced* by the individuals who are subject to it.

Among the important issues in workplaces today are motivation, on the one hand, and stress and people's individual and collective responses to it, on the other. Elangovan and Xie have found that people's backgrounds play an important role in their behaviour. For example, they focus on the issue of 'self-esteem'. This is seen as a product of nurture as opposed to nature: that is, it is inextricably linked to people's lives inside the workplace, as well as to their lives outside work, and indeed developmentally before they ever began to work. Broader theories of power also see these expansive connections as important. Elangovan and Xie conclude that those with low self-esteem show signs of higher motivation and lower stress as their perceptions of supervisory power increase. Importantly, those with high self-esteem actually show lower motivation and increased stress when they give a higher score to the perceived power of their supervisor.

This has important implications for the types of individual that the typical work organization appears to favour. Elangovan and Xie go on to explore the concept of 'locus of control', which we discussed earlier in the chapter, looking at workers with internal or external orientations (see also the discussion of this issue in Chapter 4). Those with an internal orientation were seen to respond to different types of power, authority and influence (the authors tending to see these as equivalent). Their motivation levels dropped in relation to the perceived rewards and the levels of coercive power that they associated with their supervisors. Those with a predominantly external locus of control had lower stress levels when they gave higher assessments of expert power to their supervisors.

Broadly similar dynamics to those analysed by Elangovan and Xie are also seen in two other important recent studies. Overbeck and Park (2006) and Raghubir and Valenzuela (2006) explore the relationship between positional power and the strategic use of 'social in/attention' in different work team contexts. Like Elangovan and Xie, these two sets of researchers make some important observations, particularly about how managerial decision making takes place. However, the way in which they frame 'power' in organizational behaviour as involving an individual/positional use of resources tends to downplay the broader systemic nature of power as something that is exercised.

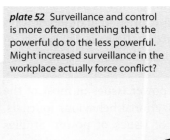

plate 52 Surveillance and control is more often something that the powerful do to the less powerful. Might increased surveillance in the workplace actually force conflict?

Source: Brand X Pictures

Collinson's (1994) approach to resistance can be applied to these findings. For example, the changing levels of motivation and stress can be interpreted as representing a form of resistance. This might be turned inwards in the form of stress or a loss of psychological commitment to the organization, but it is still apparent. Both motivation and stress are, of course, also the roots of more outward resistance, which could lead to expression in the form of political action (say, becoming more active in an employee association or union), industrial action or, at its most individualist level, sabotage or simply resigning from the organization.

Self-esteem is seen to be an important variable, but how does it come to be established? Mann's (2012) goal of identifying 'overlapping socio-spatial networks of power' might offer us some help in this context. Likewise, the work of Richard Sennett provides an accessible exploration of how deep wounds to self-esteem are inflicted in the form of 'hidden injuries' (Sennett and Cobb, 1972) and a 'corrosion of character' (Sennett, 1998). These writers help to show how visible symptoms have ideological, social and even political roots. To what degree could Giddens' interest in exploring the power of 'surveillance' be brought to play when looking at how stress develops in relation to perceived power issues? Might increased surveillance in the workplace actually force conflict inwards to produce these effects?

If surveillance and control are more often something that the powerful do to the less powerful, it makes some sense to highlight briefly the study of the choice, contingencies and organizational politics that are involved when those with less power respond. The last of these factors is particular difficult to study, although it is widely recognized. As Morgan and Kristensen (2006) note, organizations can be seen as highly complex configurations of ongoing micro-political power conflicts at different levels, in which strategizing social actors/groups inside and outside the firm interact with each other and create temporary balances of power that shape how formal organizational relationships and processes actually work in practice.

In such complex organizational settings, what does the research tell us about how low-power actors, groups or units respond? According to a recent study by Bouquet and Birkinshaw (2008), 'low-power actors' gain influence in either or both of two ways:

- by adopting creative strategies to effectively challenge the status quo in an organization (or their position within the status quo of an organization)
- by engaging in political gaming within their organization to push their agendas through existing circuits of power.

The first method refers to strategies such as attempting to build one's profile in a company, building relationships with supervisors or managers within the existing power structure of an organization, taking the initiative or, more radically, challenging the way in which business is done and breaking with established norms by working around the standard practices. The second method, **political gaming**, refers to recognizing and acting on and through existing factions, coalitions and cliques that make up any organization – in other words, engaging in intentional acts of influence to enhance or protect oneself, one's group or one's department.

Ultimately, however, there is a limited set of options for employees to exercise in organizations. One way of understanding these choices is through what has been referred to as the issue of exit and voice. Research exploring these types of choice has long been a subject of debate in industrial sociology, and it may be useful here to read the work of Ailon (2006) in relation to the classic '**exit or voice**' choice, since these are only two of the options available to employees when conflict arises. We have already touch on this earlier in the chapter, and it is dealt with in the organizational behaviour tradition by the researchers Mayes and Ganster (1988). In a rich and detailed look at the responses of public service workers to questions posed in questionnaires and interviews, these authors detail the relationship between 'voice' (or 'political action') and 'exit' behaviours on the one hand, and job stress on the other. Importantly, this analysis builds from observations that can be roughly aligned with Collinson's model of alternative, countervailing sources of power.

In Mayes and Ganster's (1988) terms, the countervailing source lies outside the bounds of the employee's formal, legitimate role in the organization. For these authors, what is at the heart of the matter is the fit between the employee and the environment. They note that when employees sense 'ambiguity' in their role in the organization, this is an immobilizing factor: it prevents their achieving 'voice' via political action in the workplace. This sense of ambiguity is found, Mayes and Ganster add, despite high levels of organizational commitment.

How can we understand variables such as worker–organization 'fit' and 'commitment' in relation to our opening set of theoretical discussions? Certainly, Foucault's and Gramsci's discussion of domination and consent as two sides of the same 'power coin' is useful here. Commitment, for example, is the side of power that Foucault speaks of when he describes 'induce[ing] pleasure, form[ing] knowledge, produce[ing] discourse. It needs to be considered as a productive network' (Foucault, 1980: 119). That is, commitment is what comes out when power works in a positive and productive way.

We could also tentatively link this to Lukes' (1974) distinction between power in the context of 'conflicts of interest', which may or may not be apparent. When conflicts of interest are evident, power is reflected as coercion, force and manipulation, whereas when they are not, it is expressed as inducement and encouragement. It is not hard to see that stress, resistance, exit and voice flow from the former a good deal more often than they do from the latter.

One of the most fascinating and recent sets of exchanges on the matter of 'power' in the organizational behaviour tradition is to be found in a 1982 special issue of the *Journal of Organizational Behavior Management*. At the centre of the debate is the work of Sonia Goltz and Amy Hietapelto (2002), and the question of resistance to organizational change. Goltz and Hietapelto's operant and strategic contingency models of power are based on the behavioural approach, as the concept of 'operant'

---

political gaming: a common practice in organizations, which has proven challenging to research, that involves recognition and organizational action based on existing factions, coalitions and cliques that make up any organization in order to engage in intentional acts of influence to enhance or protect oneself or one's group or department

exit and voice: a concept referring to the basic choice that defines an important part of employees' experience at work: they can either exit (leave) or exercise their 'voice' (have a say) in how the workplace is run

stop...

Looking at Figure 14.4, how can
we use the knowledge of how
individuals think as negotiators to
improve the resolution of workplace
conflict? What are the limits of this,
a theory that is primarily a cognitive
view of conflict?

...and reflect

of conflict management has been criticized for privileging a cognitive approach,
while neglecting the central role of affective or emotional reactions in conflict situations (Xenikou and Furnham, 2013: 60).

Negotiating strategies

A common way to manage organized workplace conflict is to engage in negotiations or bargaining. We can define this as a process that occurs between two or
more parties, with each party having its own goals and needs, but with each seeking
to establish common ground in order to reach an agreement to resolve a conflict
or settle a matter of mutual concern. Walton and McKersie's (1965) classic contribution to this area of research distinguished between 'distributive' negotiating
strategies and 'integrative' negotiating strategies.

Distributive bargaining aims to divide up a fixed amount of valued resources –
cutting up a 'pie' is a commonly used metaphor – thereby creating a 'win–lose'
solution. It therefore operates under zero-sum conditions. Distributive bargaining
takes place between negotiating teams from trade unions and management. In the
labour relations literature, this is called collective bargaining, and it decides on
the making, interpretation and administration of employment rules, as well as the
application of statutory controls that affect the employment relationship.

Integrative bargaining aims to create a 'win–win' situation; this type of negotiating is sometimes called mutual gains bargaining. An agreement between the
unions and management that increased both productivity (lowering costs) and
wages would be an example of integrated bargaining because the size of the 'pie'
would be increased.

Several points are worth noting about distributive and integrative bargaining.
First, both types of bargaining represent a form of workplace democracy (Bratton
and Gold, 2012). Second, the parties negotiating the final agreement also enforce it.
Unlike, for example, in Canada and the USA, the British system of union–management bargaining is most noted for its absence of legal enforcement. Third, in the
UK, survey data reveal a precipitous decline, alongside trade union membership,
in both distributive and integrative bargaining over the last three decades. By 2011,
only 6 per cent of private sector workplaces bargained over pay for any of their
employees. In public sector workplaces, the figure was 44 per cent, down from 66
per cent in 2004 (van Wanrooy et al., 2013: 22).

stop...

Politicians talk about a 'cost of
living' crisis in Britain. Recall the
discussion about inequality in
Chapter 8. To what extent has the
decline in distributive and integrative
bargaining contributed to the growth
of income inequality in the UK?

...and reflect

Third-party intervention in conflict resolution

In workplaces with or without a trade union presence, a common way to manage
conflict is to make use of third-party intervention, which can involve the third party
adopting the role of a mediator or arbitrator (Giebels and Janssen, 2005). External
consultants, professionals, for example from the UK Advisory, Conciliation and
Arbitration Service (ACAS), or managers outside the subunit experiencing the
conflict can play the role of these third parties.

ACAS defines *mediation* as a process that involves a neutral third party bringing
the two sides together with the aim of reaching a mutual agreement. The mediator
controls the meetings between the disputing parties, as well as the negotiating
process, but allows the parties to make their own decisions. Mediation can be especially effective when used in the initial phase of any disagreement, before conflict
escalates in the organization.

Arbitration is a process whereby management or an employer and trade union
in dispute agree to hand over to an independent third party the responsibility for
deciding how their differences should be settled (Lowry, 1990: 60). The role of the
arbitrator is different from the role of the mediator in that the former is asked to

Source: © tacojim

Plate 53 The strike is probably the most well-known form of conflict in organizations. There are different styles or strategies that characterize the behaviour of the parties engaged in resolving conflicts like these.

make a decision on a dispute. The two sides present evidence to an arbitrator, who then makes a decision that they have agreed in advance to abide by. In this way, it can be seen as a confidential alternative to a tribunal or court of law. As with mediation and conciliation, arbitration is voluntary.

Conciliation is a process that involves a trusted third party acting as an informal communication link between the parties. A conciliator can also engage in fact finding and help with interpreting language.

In summary, the extant literature suggests that there are different styles or strategies that characterize the behaviour of the parties engaged in conflict resolution. In general, if time permits, collaboration emerges as the most effective style for handling conflict in the workplace. Negotiations and third-party intervention are regarded as other conflict management styles (Xenikou and Furnham, 2013).

VISIT THE *ONLINE RESOURCE CENTRE* AT HTTPS://HE.PALGRAVE.COM/COMPANION/BRATTON-WORK-AND-ORGANIZATIONAL-BEHAVIOUR3/ FOR MORE INFORMATION ON THE PROCESS OF MEDIATION.

Chapter summary

- In this chapter, we began with broad theory to provide a basis for a better appreciation of grounded research at the level of the work organization. Common-sense views of power were outlined to explore the half-truths contained in them. Power appears to us to be 'embodied' in individuals, as something they possess and exert. However, macro theories of power show that there are many deep social roots or 'sources' of power systems, including the influences of ideology, military, politics and economics. Gramsci and Foucault outlined perhaps the most extensive theories of power, noting that it is anywhere and everywhere, because it constitutes the very way we talk and think about ourselves, as well as our organizational surroundings. Importantly, these two authors argue that power is a coin with two sides: on the one, consent, accommodation and domination; on the other, lack of commitment, stress, resistance, political action and 'voice'.

- This knowledge was then applied to a critical look at key examples of research on work organizations. Collinson is a representative example of the new social analysis of organization, which links old industrial sociology with labour process theory and the contemporary analysis of meaning and identity in the workplace. We then explored some key examples of organizational behaviour research that deal directly with the concept of 'power'. The field of organizational behaviour has hardly seen a flood of research on the topic of 'power', and when it does consider this, it usually adds the prefix 'perceived', further limiting the strength of its analysis. Nevertheless, some fascinating and provocative findings and debates were detailed.

- Clearly, not all power, authority and influence is bad. Good parenting, teaching, policing, political advocacy and, in a certain sense management, can be understood as positive influences. The question of legitimacy, which in turn evokes questions of larger political and economic systems, comes into play as we recognize that there are two main justifications for disobedience to authority. One occurs when a subject is commanded to do something outside the legitimate range of the commanding authority, and the other is when the history of acquiring the commanding authority is no longer considered to be legitimate or acceptable.

- These types of challenge to authority, building from the Gramscian and possibly the Foucauldian models above, start with recognizing people's complicity in the taken-for-granted nature of systems of power, or rather hegemonic blocs of assumptions. Challengers dare to articulate these taken-for-granted assumptions in order to engage in a rational analysis of legitimacy. What some refer to as a crisis in organizational commitment or loyalty may be the thin edge of this kind of wedge. Underlying it are frequently the types of challenge to the status quo or political gaming, for example. That is, it represents the removal of blind obedience, an erosion of the 'other side' of the power coin, that of consent and complicity. Managers as well as workers (and students of organizational behaviour!) have a right to think through and question the sources of legitimacy. Mahatma Gandhi, Martin Luther King and others operated on the principle of removal of consent, which for our purposes relates directly to a broad, social perspective on power.

- Politics and power involves conflict – between individuals and employee groups. This chapter distinguished between organized and disorganized, and functional and dysfunctional, conflict in the workplace. We explained four different perspectives or frames of reference on conflict before reviewing some common conflict resolution styles, including distributive and integrative bargaining, mediation and arbitration.

IN THE EBOOK ACCESS **WEB BASED ASSIGNMENTS** TO APPLY YOUR LEARNING.

Chapter review questions

1 What is the substance of the different social theoretic models of Mann, Giddens, Foucault, Weber, Lukes and Gramsci?
2 What is the difference between power and authority?
3 What is the relationship between power and resistance?
4 What is meant by the phrases 'power is relational' and 'power is not possessed, it is exercised'?
5 What are the strengths and weaknesses of the current conceptualizations of 'power' in organizational behaviour research?

6 What is meant by 'functional' conflict? Explain how conflict can benefit a work group or organization.
7 How can workplace conflict be managed? Based on either your university or your work experience, give an example of a situation in which one conflict resolution technique would be most appropriate, and why?
8 What can improve your effectiveness in conflict resolution?

Further reading

Ackroyd, S. and Thompson, P. (1999) *Organizational Misbehaviour*, London: Sage.

Casey, C. (2014) 'We the people at work: propositions for revitalizing industrial democracy through the use of Étienn Balibar's concepts', *Work, Employment and Society*, 28(3), pp. 469–80.

Clegg, S. (1989) *Frameworks of Power*, London: Sage.

Collinson, D. and Ackroyd, S. (2006) 'Resistance, misbehaviour, and dissent', pp. 305–26 in S. Ackroyd, R. Batt, P. Thompson and P. Tolbert (eds), *The Oxford Handbook of Work and Organization*, Oxford: OUP.

Foucault, M. (1980) *Power/Knowledge* (ed. C. Gordon), New York: Pantheon.

French, J. R. P. and Raven, B. H. (1959) 'The bases of social power', pp. 150–67 in D. Cartwright (ed.), *Studies of Social Power*, Ann Arbor, MI: Institute for Social Research.

Hearn, J. (2012) *Theorizing Power*, Basingstoke: Palgrave Macmillan.

Karlsson, J. (2012) *Organizational Misbehaviour in the Workplace*, Basingstoke: Palgrave Macmillan.

Lukes, S. (1974) *Power: A Radical View*, Basingstoke: Macmillan.

McCabe, D. (2014) 'Making out and making do: how employees resist and make organizational change work thorough consent in a UK bank', *New Technology, Work and Employment*, 29(1), pp. 57–71.

Pfeffer, J. (2010) *Power: Why Some People Have It – and Others Don't*, New York: Harper Business.

Sennett, R. (1980) *Authority*, London: Faber & Faber.

Weiss, J. and Hughes, J. (2005) 'Want collaboration', *Harvard Business Review*, 83(3), pp. 93–101.

Chapter case study: Aiming for a paperless world

The setting

In their book, *The Myth of the Paperless Office*, authors Abigail Sellen and Richard Harper note that office paper use makes up 30–40 per cent of total paper consumption in the USA and Britain, with the average American worker using an estimated 10,000 sheets of paper every year. Although it was originally believed that the use of computers would decrease the reliance on paper, the implementation of networked access to the Internet and company intranets typically results in more documents being printed. The introduction of an email system alone can cause a 40 per cent increase in paper use.

Despite this, organizations have increasingly striven to become 'paperless' in the hope of not only reducing the costs directly associated with paper, but also achieving greater efficiency, 'moving forward' and motivating change. However, Sellen and Harper caution that concentrating on a goal to eliminate paper can prevent organizations from identifying organizational work practices and value systems that really should be the focus of change.

The problem

FACTS Inc., a medium-sized accounting firm located in Paris, had gone through tremendous changes in the past year: a merger with another company, a new CEO and lay-offs caused by a decline in the local economy. Many of those affected by the lay-offs had been with FACTS for most of their career, and their abrupt departure caused fear and distrust among the employees who had remained. Absenteeism due to stress leave suddenly became commonplace. Staff morale had only been worsened by the announcement at a recent shareholder meeting that several senior executives would be receiving large bonuses at the end of that fiscal year.

At that same meeting, the company's new CEO, Adrien Webster, introduced himself to the audience as an 'environmental champion'. Downplaying the bonuses, he instead focused the meeting on the 'green' strategies he intended to implement during his first year with the company, proclaiming that 'accounting firms are the "watchdog" of the business world and we need to set an example by demonstrating environmentally friendly practices'. He laid out a corporate programme targeted at saving energy and conserving resources, with an initial focus on eliminating paper use. FACTS, he said, would be a paperless organization within 2 years.

The first step was to establish a paperless task force, which would identify key areas of the business and key processes involving the most paper use. When a call to the workforce failed to recruit volunteers, the CEO simply assigned management employees to the task force. Foremost on the task force's agenda was the implementation of an electronic records retention system to reduce paper usage, followed by the roll-out of a new corporate policy allowing only double-sided printing for company documents. Photocopiers and printers were adjusted to default to this setting.

Such policies and attempts to implement the new 'green' initiatives were quickly met with cynicism and scepticism on the part of the workers. Jokes about the next policy mandating 'paperless toilets' began to circulate throughout the offices. Returning to work after a holiday weekend, several managers found their office floors covered in hundreds of documents, with single-sided printing, produced by photocopiers that had been left to run continuously until depleted of paper.

Adrien Webster, shocked at the workplace response, quickly assembled his management team for an urgent meeting to review why the new corporate programme had failed to gain acceptance by the employees.

The task

Reflect on Collinson's research regarding power in the workplace. As a manager at the review meeting, consider how you would answer the following questions:

- How might the rise in staff absenteeism have been an indication of how the workers would react to the new 'green' strategies?
- How did the workers' technical knowledge assist them in using a 'resistance by distance' strategy in dealing with the 'paperless policy'?

Essential reading

Ackroyd, S. and Thompson, P. (1999) *Organizational Misbehaviour*, London: Sage.

Powell, J. (2010) *The New Machiavelli: How to Wield Power in the Modern World*, London: Bodley Head.

Sellen, A. and Harper, R. (2002) *The Myth of the Paperless Office*, Massachusetts: Massachusetts Institute of Technology.

Thompson, P. and McHugh, D. (2009) 'Power in organisations,' Chapter 9 in *Work Organisations: A Critical Approach* (4th edn), London: Palgrave Macmillan.

Note: This case study was written by Lori Rilkoff, Human Resources Director, City of Kamloops, BC, Canada.

IN THE EBOOK ACCESS AN **OB IN FILM BOX** THAT USE *MILK* (2008) TO ILLUSTRATE ISSUES OF POWER, AUTHORITY AND CONFLICT IN THE POLITICAL ENVIRONMENT AND TO ACCESS **AN INTERACTIVE QUIZ** TO TEST YOUR UNDERSTANDING.

part 4
Organizational design and change

In this final part of the book we shift our focus once again, this time to explore how organizational design, technology, culture and planned change influence social relations and the behaviour of people in organizations.

In Chapter 15, we explain that organizational structure refers to the formal division of labour and the formal pattern of relationships that coordinate and control organizational activities. Several theoretical frameworks are examined around the notions of the bureaucratic and post-bureaucratic.

In Chapter 16, we suggest that students need to think of technology as a social phenomenon by recognizing both consent and conflict within processes of adoption. We aim to stimulate a variety of questions, but perhaps more importantly, students should after reading this chapter be better able to understand, evaluate and affect the current landscape and trajectory of new technology.

In Chapter 17, we explore the nature of organizational culture, which we define as a pattern of shared basic assumptions, beliefs, values, artefacts, stories and behaviours, and we discuss how the concept has become closely associated with the notion of postmodern organizations and contemporary management theory.

In Chapter 18, we describe organizational change as a structured process in which an organization shifts from its current state to some specific desired future state in order to improve its effectiveness. Managing organizational change is the process of planning and executing change in such a way as to minimize individual and organizational resistance, while at the same time maximizing employee cooperation. The chapter explores processes of creativity and innovation before looking at organizational development approaches to continuous change.

Organizational design and change

chapter 15
Structure

Chapter learning outcomes

After studying this chapter, you should be able to:
1. Identify and define the concepts underlying organizational structure and design
2. Understand the meaning and significance of complexity, formalization and centralization
3. Explain the relationships between strategy, size, technology and capitalist development, and the different forms of organizational design
4. Describe the difference between classical and modern thinking on organizational design
5. Describe some of the emerging contemporary forms of organizational design and identify their potential impact on workplace behaviour
6. Explain and illustrate the basis of criticism of managerial thinking about organizational design with reference to power, gender and sexuality

introduction

In his influential book *Beyond Reengineering* (1997), Michael Hammer cited the Ford Motor Company as an exemplar of how a few American corporations had restructured and transformed 'beyond recognition' their old ways of doing things in order to meet the challenges of global competition. However, in February 2009, Ford chairman and CEO Bill Ford and other CEOs from General Motors and Chrysler publicly explained to the US Senate banking committee why they needed US$17 billion of emergency financial infusion to prevent bankruptcy. By March 2009, US President Barack Obama had rejected the restructuring plans submitted by General Motors and Chrysler, while demanding the resignation of General Motors' CEO, Rick Wagoner, as part of the government's offer to help General Motors to accelerate and deepen their restructuring plans. Since 2008, the quest for agile organizational structures and low-cost processes has also encouraged a restructuring of big corporations through merger and acquisition activity. For example, in 2014 the US pharmaceutical goliath Pfizer attempted significant restructuring by taking over UK-based AstraZeneca (Ward, 2014).

Since the 2008 global financial crisis, corporate bail-outs and the restructuring of a multitude of companies such as Fiat, Renault, Volvo, Opel and Marks & Spencer have been reported. And these restructuring initiatives have not been unique to the manufacturing sector. Accelerated by dysfunctional financial markets and deteriorating global trade, venerable financial firms such as American International Group, Fannie Mae, Freddie Mac, Citigroup, Bank of America, Northern Rock, Bradford and Bingley, Royal Bank of Scotland HBOS and Cooperative Bank have been bailed out, restructured or nationalized.

The form and structure that an organization adopts can have far-ranging effects on work and organizational behaviour. It affects, for example, the scope of autonomy, decision making, research and development, the opportunity to access career progression ladders and so on (Storey and Nyathi, 2015). Restructuring an organization can entail a significant decrease in the resources that a company allocates to process activities or product markets in which it has previously engaged, or involves a reallocation of resources to new geographical locations (Lazonick, 2006; Ward, 2014). A plethora of studies have analysed such 'downsizing' as part of a process of 'outsourcing' many of the functions that were originally assigned to permanent employees. Restructuring has been wrapped in the mantra of flexibility, lean and mean, and competitiveness (see, for example, Baumol et al., 2003; Delbridge, 1998; Hales, 2002; Innes and Littler, 2004; Tyler and Wilkinson, 2007). These studies emphasize that 'corporate anorexia' can fundamentally change how work is performed as well as reshape employment relations. Thus, the study of organizational structure and design is essential for a deeper understanding of work and behaviour in the workplace. In the twentieth century, an array of design choices evolved – 'functional', 'hierarchical', 'matrix' or 'lean', for example. What is the purpose of organizational form and structure? What exactly are senior managers 'restructuring'? What determines organizational design? What is the right relationship between the centre of a company and its periphery? How does the psychological contract between the worker and the employer change after restructuring? And how does organizational design and redesign modify behaviour?

> **stop...**
> Think about an organization where you have worked or studied. Can you identify a set of characteristics that help to describe its structure?
> **...and reflect**

IN THE EBOOK ACCESS THE **OB IN FOCUS** BOX ON 'CORPORATE RESTRUCTURING AND THE CAR INDUSTRY'.

The answer to these questions is the focus of this chapter. We begin by explaining the nature and purpose of organizational form and structure. To help with our analysis of different organizational forms, we offer a conceptual framework of the various types of organizational reconfiguring. We then move on to examine some

formal organization: a highly structured group formed for the purpose of completing certain tasks or achieving specific goals

traditional **formal organizational** designs: functional, product/service, divisional and matrix. New organizational designs that have allegedly supplanted the traditional forms are also examined. We conclude this chapter with a discussion on the links between gender, sexuality and organizational design.

The nature of organizational structure

As we briefly discussed in Chapter 1, organizations are created to produce goods or services and to pursue dominant goals that individuals acting alone cannot achieve. According to Peter Drucker (1997), the purpose of the work organization 'is to get the work done'. Organizations are purposive systems, and their design and form serve three main purposes: to help identify and disseminate the collective aims of the organization; to regulate the flow of resources into and out of the organization; and to identify and govern the duties, rights, functions and roles of the members of the organization (Aldrich, 1999). As such, from this perspective, the choice of an organization's structure can be seen as an important although often unacknowledged aspect of strategic management (Storey and Nyathi, 2015).

organizational structure: the formal reporting relationships, groups, departments and systems of the organization

organizational design: the process of creating and modifying organizational structures

However, **organizational structure** is not easy to define because it is not a physical reality, but rather a conceptual one. Let us begin to explain the concept in this way. To accomplish its strategic goals, an organization typically has to do two things: divide the work to be done among its members, and then coordinate the work. Organizational structure refers to the formal division of work and the formal configuration of relationships that coordinate and control the organizational activities. **Organizational design** is the planning and implementation of a structural configuration of roles and modes of operation. Arguably, theories of organizational structure are a product of modernity, because they are largely based on Weber's notions of rationality and bureaucratic specialization (see Chapter 2).

Thus, work is divided horizontally into distinct tasks that need to be done, into either jobs, subunits or departments. This horizontal division of labour is associated with specialization on the part of the workforce. The vertical division of labour is concerned with apportioning authority for planning, decision making, monitoring and controlling: who will tell whom what to do? For example, in a small restaurant, the horizontal divisions might be divided into three main work activities: preparing the food, service and running the bar. A vertical division of labour would describe the coordinating and directing work of the head chef, the restaurant supervisor and the head bar tender, all of whom report to the restaurant manager.

Source: Image Source/Michael Gross

plate 54 In a small restaurant, the horizontal divisions might take the form of three main work activities: preparing the food, service and running the bar. A vertical division of labour would describe the coordinating and directing work of the head chef, the restaurant supervisor and the head bar tender, all of whom report to the restaurant manager.

This small business has a simple structure. However, the structure could become more complex as more people were hired and as coordination and control became more difficult. As the business expanded and its management became more complicated, the manager might not have enough time to deal with the accounts and the hiring and training of new staff. To solve these problems, the restaurant manager might hire an accountant and a human resource manager, which would increase the vertical division of labour. The growth of an organization might therefore lead to a greater degree of **specialization** of its workforce.

specialization: the allocation of work tasks to categories of employee or groups. Also known as division of labour

Alternatively, the restaurant manager might create work teams and allow the team members to coordinate their work activities and hire and train their own members. This limited 'empowerment' of the workers would then free up time for the head chef, the restaurant supervisor and the head bar tender to handle the accounts for their departments.

Specialization occurs when people focus their effort on a particular skill, task, customer or territorial area. Our simple example of the restaurant illustrates two important points: managers have choices over how to divide labour, and different organizational configurations impact on people's work experience. For instance, if teams were introduced, additional tasks would have to be learnt and the pace of work might intensify.

organizational chart: a diagram showing the grouping of activities and people within a formal organization to achieve the goals of the organization efficiently

An **organizational chart** graphically shows the various parts of the structure as boxes, and the coordination and control by lines that connect the boxes. This system is used in Figure 15.1 to demonstrate the simple structure of the restaurant just described, and is used in the sample organizational charts that follow. Organizational design refers to the process of creating a structure that best fits a strategy, technology and environment. For example, Ford Motor Company has created a structure on a product basis, with separate divisions for specific models. So why do managers redesign structures? Management designs new structures in order to reduce costs, to respond to changing customer buying patterns or business boundaries, to reset priorities, to shift people and align capabilities, to shift perceptions of service among users, or to 'shake things up' (Gadiesh and Olivet, 1997).

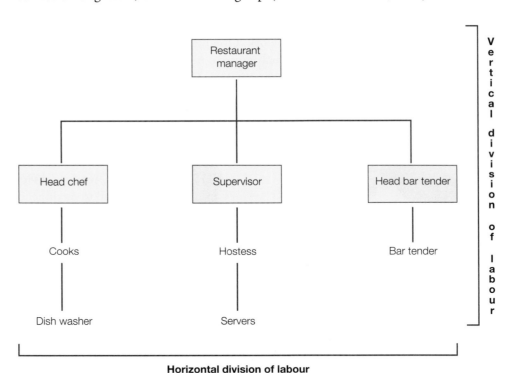

Figure 15.1 An example of a simple organizational structure

Why is organizational structure important? From a managerial perspective, structure may make the task of managing employees more complex, bringing into play the questions of efficiency and consistency that are likely to arise more often when different groups report directly to departmental managers, rather than to a single owner or manager in an organization employing relatively few people. Structure therefore defines lines of responsibility and authority. In terms of organizational performance, a 'good' structure is not a panacea, but it is very important, argues management guru Peter Drucker: 'Good organizational structure does not by itself produce good performance ... But a poor organization structure makes

informal structure: a term used to describe the aspect of organizational life in which participants' day-to-day activities and interactions ignore, bypass or do not correspond with the official rules and procedures of the bureaucracy

stop...

Think about an organization where you or someone you know well has worked. Can you identify a management practice that was designed to encourage one behaviour but also resulted in another behaviour that impacted on the activity?

...and reflect

good performance impossible, no matter how good the individual managers may be' (1954/1993: 4). A poor structure can also foster an *informal structure*, with negative outcomes.

The structure of an organization also affects the ability of workers to learn, be creative, innovate and participate in decision making (Galbraith, 1996). Other related effects of different designs are changes to job security and job satisfaction, and to perceptions about expectations and obligations. Redesigning the organizational structure will therefore affect the intangible 'psychological contract' that each individual worker has (see also Chapters 2 and 5). Each individual employee will have different perceptions of his or her psychological contract, even when the structure within which he or she works is identical. There will therefore be no universal notion of mutual expectations and obligations (Herriot, 1998). Redesign changes also impact on social relations and organizational governance. All this serves to remind us that organizational success and failure depend on the behaviour of people, who work within the formal structure and who mould and imprint their personality into their work activities.

Dimensions of structure

A variety of dimensions can be used to conceptualize organizational structure. There is a disagreement among theorists over what makes up the term 'structure', but a relatively recent way of thinking about organizations and structure is as 'discursive metaphors'. Advocates of this approach suggest that organizations are 'texts', created through discourses, which have symbolic meaning for managers and workers. These meanings are open to multiple readings even when particular meanings become sufficiently privileged and concrete. Here, we take a more orthodox approach to examining how researchers have analysed structure, before discussing how it affects organizational behaviour (Clegg et al., 1999). While we acknowledge the elastic definitions and various labels attached to organizational phenomena, here we examine three aspects: complexity, formalization and centralization.

Complexity

complexity: the intricate departmental and interpersonal relationships that exist within a work organization

Complexity is the degree of differentiation in an organization. Complexity measures the degree of division of tasks, levels of hierarchy and geographical locations of work units in the organization. The more tasks are divided among individuals, the more the organization is *horizontally complex*. The most visible evidence of horizontal complexity in an organization is specialization and departmentalization.

Specialization refers to the particular grouping of activities performed by an employee. Division of labour – for example, accounting activities – creates groups of specialists (in this case, accountants). The way in which specialists are grouped is referred to as *departmentalization*. As the vertical chain of command lengthens, more formal layers of authority are inserted between top management and front-line workers. In such circumstances, the organization becomes more *vertically complex*. Therefore, vertical complexity refers to the depth of the organization's hierarchy: the number of levels between senior management and the workers. Organizations with the same number of workers need not have the same degree of vertical complexity. Organizations can be 'flat', with few layers of hierarchy, or 'tall', with many levels of management between the top CEO and the front-line employees (Figure 15.2).

VISIT THE *ONLINE RESOURCE CENTRE* AT HTTPS://HE.PALGRAVE.COM/COMPANION/BRATTON-WORK-AND-ORGANIZATIONAL-BEHAVIOUR3/ FOR AN EXAMPLE OF TEAM-BASED ORGANIZATIONAL DESIGN AT SHELL.

During the last decade, organizations have moved towards flatter configurations by eliminating whole levels of middle managers and generally 'doing more with

span of control: the number of people directly reporting to the next level in the organizational hierarchy

less'. This form of restructuring, commonly called downsizing, increases the **span of control** for the managers who remain. The span of control defines the number of subordinates that a single manager or administrator can supervise effectively. If this span is narrow, managers have few subordinates reporting to them. If it is wide, managers are responsible for many subordinates. The larger the span, the less potential there is for control by direct supervision. When work tasks are routine, the control of subordinates through technology and output performance substitutes for direct supervision. At lower operational levels, it is not unusual to have spans of control of up to 20 individuals. In the managerial ranks, work is less routine, and spans of control tend to be smaller. Thus, the complexity of the task often dictates the span of control.

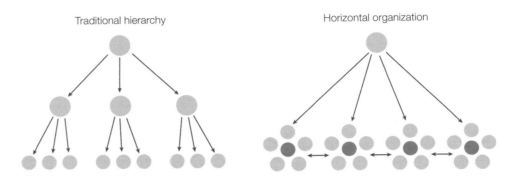

Figure 15.2 A tall organization structure versus a flat (team-based) structure

Vertical complexity can also affect managerial behaviour by impacting on other factors such as communication networks and manager–worker dynamics. For example, a wide span of control makes it more difficult for a manager to hold face-to-face meetings.

An organization can perform the same work activities in geographically separate locations, a fact emphasized by globalization. The existence of multiple workplaces increases complexity. *Spatial complexity* refers to the degree to which the organization's operations and core workforce are geographically dispersed. As spatial complexity increases, managers face coordination, control and communication challenges relating to their subordinates (Hamel and Prahalad, 1994).

Formalization

formalization: the degree to which organizations standardize behaviour through rules, procedures, formal training and related mechanisms

Formalization is the second core dimension of organizational structure, and describes the degree of standardization of work and jobs in the organization. It refers to the extent to which work is defined and controlled by rules. The more rules there are about what is to be done, when it is to be done and how it should be done, the more an organization is formalized. Where formalization is low, employees are given freedom to exercise discretion in their work. The degree of formalization can vary widely within and among organizations.

The extent of formalization typically varies with the nature of the work performed and the size of the organization (Daft et al., 2010). The most complex and creative paid work is amenable to low degrees of formalization. Formalization also tends to be inversely related to the hierarchical level in the organization. Individuals lower in the organization are engaged in activities that are relatively simple and repetitive, and therefore these people are most likely to work in a highly formalized environment. But although formalization regulates workers' behaviour, it can also impose constraints on managers and subordinates. In a unionized workplace, for instance, contract rules negotiated by union and management can constrain managers' ability to mobilize the skills, creativity, commitment and values of their subordinates (Champy, 1996).

Centralization

centralization: the degree to which formal decision authority is held by a small group of people, typically those at the top of the organizational hierarchy

Centralization, the third core dimension of organizational structure, refers to the degree to which decision making is concentrated at a single point in the organization. In essence, it addresses the question, who makes the decisions in the organization? A decentralized organization is one in which senior managers solicit input from members when making key decisions. The more input members provide or the more autonomy they are given to make decisions, the more decentralized the organization.

The degree of centralization affects workers' ability to make decisions, levels of motivation and the manager–subordinate interface. An ongoing challenge for managers is to balance the degree of centralization necessary to achieve control on the one hand, and to gain commitment through participation and work-related learning on the other.

Typologies of organizational structure

mechanistic organization: an organizational structure with a narrow span of control and high degrees of formalization and centralization

organic organization: an organizational structure with a wide span of control, little formalization and decentralized decision making

The three core dimensions of formal organizational structure – complexity, formalization and centralization – can be combined into a number of different types or models. Two popular descriptive models have received much attention: the mechanistic model and the organic model (Burns and Stalker, 1966).

The **mechanistic organization** has been characterized as a machine. It has high complexity, high formalization and high centralization. A mechanistic organization resembles a bureaucracy. It is characterized by highly specialized tasks that tend to be rigidly defined, a hierarchical authority and control structure, and communications that primarily take the form of edicts and decisions issued by managers to subordinates. Communication typically flows vertically from the top down.

The **organic organization** is the antithesis of the mechanistic organization. Organic organizations are characterized by being low in complexity, formality and centralization. An organic organization is said to be flexible and informally coordinated, and managers use participative decision-making behaviours. Communication is both horizontal (across different departments) and vertical (down and up the hierarchy), depending on where the information resides.

> **stop...**
>
> Can you identify organizations that have organic features and organizations that display mechanistic features?
>
> **...and reflect**

Determinants of organizational structure

competitive advantage: the ability of a work organization to add more value for its customers and shareholders than its rivals, and thus gain a position of advantage in the marketplace

The underlying rationale for mechanistic and organic organizations is, according to conventional organizational theory, explained by the choice of competitive strategy. The mechanistic organization strives for **competitive advantage** by maximizing efficiency and productivity, whereas an organic organization's competitive strategy is based on maximum adaptability and flexibility. Thus, structural characteristics concern contextual factors within the organization and affect the management process. So far, although we have examined a number of core organizational design concepts, we have not provided much insight into why organizational structures vary so much, or into the forces behind corporate restructuring. The purpose of this section is to discuss theories of organizational design in terms of their relevance for understanding current restructuring endeavours.

Early management theorists put forward universalistic theories of organizational structure: that is, the 'one size fits all' principle applied to organizations. Over the last 30 years, organizational analysts have modified the classical approach by suggesting that organizational structure is contingent on a variety of variables or contextual factors. The contingency approach to organizational design takes the view that there is no 'one best' universal structure, and emphasizes the need for flexibility. The significant contingency variables are strategy, size, technology and environment.

VISIT THE *ONLINE RESOURCE CENTRE* AT HTTPS://HE.PALGRAVE.COM/COMPANION/BRATTON-WORK-AND-ORGANIZATIONAL-BEHAVIOUR3/ FOR MORE INFORMATION ON CONTINGENCY THEORY.

Strategy and structure

As we discussed in Chapter 1, strategy can be viewed as a pattern of activity over time to achieve performance goals. The classical position that 'structure follows strategy' assumes that managers choose the structure they have: 'A new strategy required a new or at least refashioned structure' (Chandler, 1962: 15). This hypothesis is represented in Figure 15.3.

For example, if top management chooses to compete through product and service innovation and high quality – a differentiation strategy – then managers need to adopt an organic or horizontal organizational structure. A cost-leadership strategy, on the other hand, requires products or services to be standardized with minimum costs. A mechanistic, functional structure with more formalization and centralization is most appropriate with this strategy, so that managers can closely control the quality and costs.

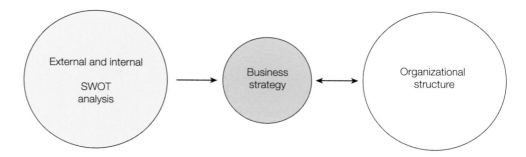

Figure 15.3 The strategy–structure thesis

A counterthesis sees strategy as being related less directly to organizational design. In this view, 'strategy follows structure' (Keats and Hitt, 1988). The design of the organization is the context in which top managers form the business strategy. Thus, the existing organizational configuration affects top managers' perceptions of internal strengths, weaknesses, threats and opportunities (SWOT) outside the organization, and helps to shape a strategy.

Empirical research offers support for both views of strategy affecting the design of an organization; this is illustrated in Figure 15.3 by a two-headed arrow between structure and strategy. This recognizes that the link between strategy and structure is affected by other contingency factors, such as size, technology and environment.

In her book *No Logo*, globalization critic Naomi Klein (2000) provides a more controversial account of the link between corporate strategy – a focus on 'branding' and the relocation of manufacturing capacity from the core capitalist economy to the periphery, where wage levels are low – and multifaceted structures spanning national frontiers:

> The astronomical growth in the wealth and cultural influence of multinational corporations over the last fifteen years can arguably be traced back to a single, seemingly innocuous idea developed by management theorists in the mid-1980s, that successful corporations must primarily produce brands, as opposed to products ... The very process of producing – running one's own factories, being responsible for the tens of thousands

of full-time, permanent employees – began to look less like the route to success and more like a clunky liability.

> At around this time a new kind of corporation began to rival the traditional all-American manufacturers for market share; these were the Nikes and Microsoft, and later, the Tommy Hilfigers and Intels ... What these companies produced primarily were not things, they said, but images of their brands. Their real work lay not in manufacturing but in marketing. This formula, needless to say, has proved enormously profitable, and its success has companies competing in a race towards weightlessness: whoever owns the least, has the fewest employees on the payroll and produces the most powerful images, as opposed to products, wins the race. (Klein, 2000: 4)

Of course, as globalization theorists have observed, the notion of 'weightlessness' is only feasible because of the developments in transportation, namely containerization and the Internet.

Size and structure

Most studies define organizational size as the total number of employees, and researchers suggest that larger organizations have different structures from smaller organizations. As organizations increase in size, they tend to develop more written rules and procedures, and division of labour becomes more specialized. A number of theorists have argued that size is an important factor affecting organizational design (see, for example, Child, 1972). It seems credible that there is a positive relationship between size and the degree of formalization, specialization and centralization.

Critics of the size imperative have countered that neither formalization nor complexity can be inferred from organizational size. An equally valid alternative interpretation of early empirical data is that size is the result, not the cause, of structure (Aldrich, 1972). The key point here is that there are obvious structural differences between large and small organizations, but a statistically significant relationship between size and structural dimensions does not imply causation. For example, technology influences structure, which in turn determines size.

Technology and structure

Technological change, especially information technology (see Chapter 16) is quintessentially a defining feature of the 'knowledge economy', and is also another important contingency variable explaining organizational structure. Researchers have adopted either a restrictive or an expansive definition of technology, and the early research on technology suggests a positive relationship between the type of technology and the organizational structure (Woodward, 1965).

The 'technology–structure' thesis has sought to analyse technology as an independent explanatory variable. The British academic Joan Woodward, for example, classified production technology into three main categories for analysis: unit production (as in a tailor's shop), mass production (as in an automotive plant) and continuous process production (like that of a pulp mill). Charles Perrow (1986) classified four types of technology: routine, engineering, craft and non-routine. Routine technologies have few deviations and are associated with easy-to-analyse problems (pulp and paper mills or chemical plants, for example, belong to this category). Engineering technologies have a large number of exceptions, but can be managed in a systematic manner (as with the construction of bridges). Craft technologies deal with relatively difficult problems with a limited set of deviations (such as in hand-crafted furniture making). Non-routine technologies are characterized by many exceptions and difficult-to-analyse problems (as with research and development).

Source: © Royalty-Free/Corbis

Fordism for doctors?

For those who study occupational change, the professions represent an interesting case. 'Professional' occupations span a broad range of areas – from established occupations such as doctor or lawyer, to so-called 'semi-professional' occupations such as teacher or social worker. What makes the professions unique is that they appear to have resisted many of the trends that have changed the face of work in the twentieth century. Although specialized, the professional worker is not alienated. He or she enjoys considerable discretion over how work is done, the settings in which it is done and the ways in which it is evaluated. Traditionally, professional workers have maintained control over their work processes, despite efforts by managers and consumers to challenge that control.

The world of professional work has undergone significant change in the last two decades. Professional authority has been contested, and there have been efforts to subordinate professional authority to managerial authority. Some of the more dramatic instances of this kind of challenge have occurred in Britain's National Health Service (NHS). Referring to specific moments in this process of reform, David Hunter (1994), a Professor at the Nuffield Institute for Health, offers the following analysis:

> Much of the impetus beyond the 1989 reform proposals … can be seen as an attempt to secure a shift in the balance of power between doctors and managers in favour of the latter. They seek to achieve such a shift in the context of advocating improved efficiency in the use of resources and in the provision of services. Much of the management problem in the NHS has centered on the notion of undermanagement in respect of the medical side of the service. Getting a grip on the freedom enjoyed by clinicians and holding them to account for expenditure they incur is seen as the last unmanaged frontier in the NHS. (p. 6)

As Hunter suggests, the rationale behind this attempt to limit the professional power of doctors was efficiency. But what is the larger historical context of this managerial initiative? Richard Sennett argues that the rationale for reform of this kind can be traced back to Henry Ford's views on how work should be organized. In Sennett's view, 'Fordism' entails a particular perspective on the division of labour: 'each worker does one task, measured as precisely as possible by time-and-motion studies; output is measured in terms of targets that are … entirely quantitative' (Sennett, 2008: 47). Sennett goes on to suggest how Fordism has shaped reforms in the NHS: 'Fordism monitors the time doctors and nurses spend with each patient; a medical treatment system based on dealing with auto parts, it tends to treat cancerous livers or broken backs rather than patients in the round' (p. 47).

How effective has this approach been to managing the clinical world of healthcare? Hunter maintains that while the power of doctors was constrained in some ways, doctors continued to exert considerable influence over how health and disease should be understood, and consequently on how the work of producing health and preventing illness should be organized. Moreover, as Sennett notes, 'doctors create paper fictions' to circumvent the practice guidelines imposed by managers in the NHS: 'Doctors in the NHS often assign a patient a disease in order to justify the time spent exploring a puzzling body' (p. 49).

The challenge of how to organize and manage professional work remains a central issue in the field of organizational design. We have yet to answer the question of what might constitute the optimal balance between professional and managerial power. Perhaps the best way to approach this question is to attempt to envision a situation where shared power enhances productivity and quality in the provision of healthcare.

Stop! Taking the doctor as an example, where would you position the threshold beyond which too much managerial power might erode productivity and decrease the quality of patient care? Provide some concrete examples to illustrate how a sharing of power between professionals (including allied professionals, such as nurses) and managers will enhance the overall effectiveness of the NHS and national health systems more generally. Can you identify the major source of managerial authority in a system like that of the USA where private corporations play a key role in the delivery of healthcare? Consider how these issues may apply to other professions, such as law and teaching.

Sources and further information

Freidson, E. (1998) *Professionalism Reborn*, Chicago: University of Chicago Press.

Hunter, D. (1994) 'From tribalism to corporatism: the managerial challenge to medical dominance', pp. 1–22 in J. Gabe, D. Kelleher and G. Williams (eds), *Challenging Medicine*, London: Routledge.

Sennett, R. (2008) *The Craftsman*, New Haven, CT: Yale University Press.

Note: This feature was written by David MacLennan, Assistant Professor, Thompson Rivers University, Canada.

The research found evidence of different types of technology being associated with different organizational designs. Non-routine technology, for instance, is positively associated with high complexity. So as the work becomes more customized, the span of control narrows. Studies also suggest that routine technology is positively related to formalization. Routine technologies allow leaders to implement rules and regulations because the work is well understood by their followers. It has been proposed that routine technology might lead to centralized decision making and control systems if formalization is low. Within this theoretical framework, it is suggested that technology mediates mechanical and integrated forms of management control, which are incorporated into the technology itself. Thus, employees' performance is subject to control by technology rather than by direct human supervision.

Joan Woodward died in 1971, but her thesis that technology is a crucial contingency influenced the American sociologist Howard Aldrich. For Aldrich (2002), as for Woodward, the technology in use in the organization had high priority in accounting for the degree of organizational structure. Both structure and technology are multidimensional concepts, and it is not realistic to relate technology to structure in any simple manner. In addition, all the technological paradigms have their strengths and weaknesses. Conceptualizing technology by degrees of 'routineness' leads to a generalizable conclusion that technology will shape structure in terms of size, complexity and formalization. The strategic choice discourse also suggests that it is managerial behaviour at critical points in the process of organizational change – possibly in negotiation with trade unions – that is critical in reshaping managerial processes and outcomes, including organizational structure.

Environment and structure

> **environment:** refers to the broad economic, political, legal and social forces, such as a nation's business system, that are present in the minds of the organization's members and may influence their decision making and constrain their strategic choices

The **environment** is everything outside the organization's boundary. The case for the environmental imperative argues that organizations are embedded in society, and therefore that a multitude of economic, political, social and legal factors will affect organizational design decisions. The attack on the World Trade Center on September 11, 2001 and the global financial crisis of 2008 are two catastrophes outside organizations that resulted in major restructuring within many airlines and banks.

An early study by Burns and Stalker (1966) proposed an environment–structure thesis. In essence, their study of UK firms distinguished five different kinds of environment, ranging from 'stable' to 'least predictable', and two divergent patterns of managerial behaviour and organizational structure – the organic and the mechanistic configurations. They suggested that both types of structural regime represented a 'rational' form of organization that could be created and sustained according to the external conditions facing the organization. For instance, uncertainty in the environment might cause top managers to restructure in order to be more responsive to the changing marketplace.

An organization's environment can also range from *munificent* to *hostile*. Organizations located in a hostile environment face more competition, an adversarial union–management relationship and a scarcity of resources.

stop...

Can you think of any developments in the UK or Europe that have changed organizational design?

...and reflect

These four distinct dimensions of environments shape structure. The more dynamic the environment, the more 'organic' the structure, and the more complex the environment, the more 'decentralized' the structure (Mintzberg, 1992). The explosive growth of e-commerce, for example, has created a dynamic complex environment for much of the retail book and clothing industry, and is therefore spawning highly flexible network structures. Despite the criticisms of contingency theory, it has provided insights into understanding the complex situational variables that help to shape organizational structure.

Globalization and structure

Our aim in this chapter is to offer a multidimensional understanding of organizational structure and restructuring. Existing organizational behaviour texts tend to be more narrowly focused, and give limited, if any, coverage to the causation and consequences of global capitalism.

> **globalization:** when an organization extends its activities to other parts of the world, actively participates in other markets and competes against organizations located in other countries

As a field of study, the term **globalization** is controversial, as are its alleged effects. Clearly, a detailed study of globalization is beyond the scope of this chapter, but to ground the arguments on organizational structure we need to at least acknowledge the interplay of continuity, restructuring and the diversity of experiences of globalization. For example, to what extent have emerging transnational corporations (TNCs), such as Acer (Taiwan), Samsung (Korea) and Tata (India), emulated the patterns established by Western TNCs with regard to the way they structure themselves and the way they control their overseas operations (Storey and Nyathi, 2015)? This contemporary debate on the organizational structures of multinational corporations from the emerging economies echoes earlier research and debate around Japanese management in the 1980s (see Chapter 10).

For some, globalization involves the spread of transplanetary connections between people (Scholte, 2005). For others, it revolves primarily around two main phenomena. The first is the emergence of a sophisticated system of global supply interconnections driven by global financing, innovations in ICT and the readiness of TNCs to outsource production (Friedli et al., 2014). The distinguishing feature of a 'global factory' is the organization of the production system on a transnational basis (Williams et al., 2013: 127). That is, the division of labour extends across national borders sometimes on a worldwide scale. Second is the notion of global culture, which focuses on the spread of particular patterns of consumption and the ideology of consumerism at a global level (Sklair, 2002).

The more radical globalization literature helps us to locate the main driver of organizational design and restructuring in the dialectical development of global capitalism. This argument is based on the theory that organizational restructuring occurs because of contradictions within systems (Hoogvelt, 2001). This approach, which has occupied an immense space in Marxist literature, searches for inherent tendencies in the global capitalist system that create tension and bring about their own conflicts, until such a system can no longer maintain itself without far-reaching structural adjustments. Thus, the particular model through which business organizations 'make their profits' characterizes every phase of capitalist expansion. In the Marxist literature, this is referred to as 'accumulation'.

> **stop...**
>
> Can you think of any risks associated with operating a 'global factory' with a long supply chain? Hint: Think of the 2013 horsemeat scandal in Europe.
>
> **...and reflect**

VISIT THE *ONLINE RESOURCE CENTRE* AT HTTPS://HE.PALGRAVE.COM/COMPANION/BRATTON-WORK-AND-ORGANIZATIONAL-BEHAVIOUR3/ FOR INFORMATION ON AN ORGANIZATION THAT MONITORS AND CRITIQUES GLOBAL CAPITALISM.

To apply accumulation theory to the various restructuring initiatives shown later in the chapter in Figure 15.5, profit maximization was achieved in the first half of the twentieth century through the use of bureaucracies modelled on Fordist-style production and employment relations. The whole point about bureaucratic Fordism as a profitable undertaking is that it achieves economies of scale: the system produces standardized products at relatively low unit costs.

However, as we explained in Chapter 2, the downside to Taylorism and Fordism is that the success of the operation depends on an expanding market for the same standard product, and mass production cannot readily adjust to changing consumer tastes. The offer to consumers of 'Any colour of car provided it's black' is less compelling when the market is saturated with black cars and competitors are offering a choice of colours. It is perhaps not surprising that, in order to maintain profitability, an early response of employers to the catalogue of problems associated with bureaucratic Fordism was to decentralize and transplant assembly-line systems from core capitalist countries (such as Germany) to the periphery (for example, to Mexico), where wage levels were very low. The systematic contradiction of Fordism and corporate imperatives created divisionalized structures, including strategic business units, as manufacturing was relocated to the newly industrialized economies of South-East Asia, Brazil and Mexico.

In recent years, market changes have compelled further restructuring and downsizing towards 'horizontal' or 'lean' organizations. As two US management theorists write, 'American companies were weighted down with cumbersome organizational charts and many layers of management' (Orsburn and Moran, 2000: xiii). Critical accounts of organizational restructuring also describe the associated changes in social relations: non-standard or precarious employment, and a new 'international division of labour' in which a small number of newly industrialized economies participate in the global dispersal of manufacturing by TNCs.

Feminist scholars have highlighted the exploitative and patriarchal nature of the new international division of labour. The critics of global capitalism argue that, as the dominance of the capitalist global system spreads and deepens, it simultaneously sows the seeds of organizational restructuring by providing resources, forms of organizational capacity and an ideological rationale (Sklair, 2002).

VISIT THE *ONLINE RESOURCE CENTRE* AT HTTPS://HE.PALGRAVE.COM/COMPANION/BRATTON-WORK-AND-ORGANIZATIONAL-BEHAVIOUR3/ FOR INFORMATION ON THE RELATIVE SIZE OF TNCS BY REVENUE.

Figure 15.4 is an adaptation of Figure 1.3 and offers a synthesis of current thinking. It suggests that organizational structure is influenced by business strategy, size, technology, environment and the economics of global capitalism. It is also influenced by internal situational variables, such as culture, managerial and worker behaviour, and the strategic choices available to dominant organizational decision makers. The end results include increased profits for corporations and a new international division of labour.

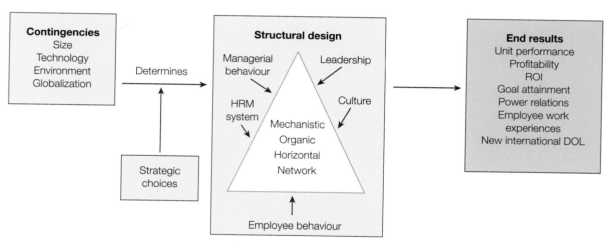

Figure 15.4 Determinants of organizational structure and end results. DOL, division of labour; HRM, human resource management; ROI, return on investment

Organizational redesign: a conceptual framework

Although organizational structure and redesign are widely assumed to influence behaviour in the workplace, most treatments of the subject in standard organizational textbooks give scant attention to the complex interplay of organizational structure, management strategies, politics and culture, and changes in global capitalist development. To help in analysing the interplay between the different dimensions that appear to have been critical in recent organizational restructuring, we have drawn upon the work of Mabey and his colleagues (Mabey et al., 1998) and constructed a conceptual framework using four interconnected dimensions. Each of these is shown in Figure 15.5.

On the bottom horizontal axis is the dimension of capitalist global development over the last century, from national economies to a global scale. On the right vertical axis is the dimension of competitive strategy, covering the spectrum from low cost to differentiation. On the left vertical axis is the dimension of formalization, showing the contrast between high/directive and low/autonomous, and on the horizontal axis at the top of the figure is the dimension relating to decision making, which contrasts the centralized and decentralized modes.

At the risk of oversimplification, some alternative structural designs are shown for illustrative purposes. In the first half of the twentieth century, at the lower left of Figure 15.5, the bureaucratic form is located to suggest a low-cost, mass-production competitive strategy, a high degree of formalization and direction, and a centralized decision-making mode. Ascending and moving to the right in the figure, from about the 1960s, we see the development of divisionalized configurations, to the development of strategic business units and then networks and virtual organizations.

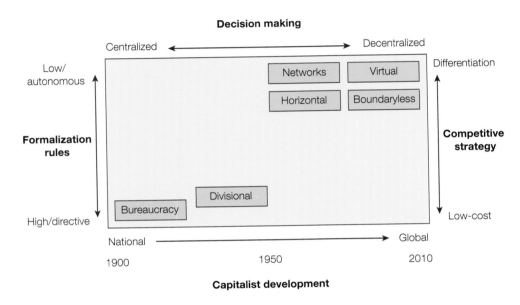

Figure 15.5 Types of organizational restructuring
Source: Adapted from Mabey et al. (1998), p. 235

In addition to the changes in conventional structural boundaries, organizations have recently undertaken other types of restructuring involving new commercial relationships. Manufacturing companies have **outsourced** the production of some parts – note the influence of just-in-time systems – and services (such as payroll, training and benefits handling), and in the public sector so-called non-core activities (such as laundry, catering and cleaning) have been privatized.

This framework is useful in illustrating the different organizational forms and design options facing top managers, when considered in relation to the core dimensions of formal organizational structure and in relation to each other. The argument of this book is that if we are to understand contemporary workplaces and explain what is happening in them, we need to locate restructuring initiatives in a multidimensional framework that includes capitalist global development. While we believe that the actions of TNCs and the international division of labour are intimately interconnected with organizational design and restructuring, the inclusion in the framework of capitalist global development does not suggest any inevitable linear progression (Scholte, 2005). We must remember that millions of people still work in 'sweatshops' and bureaucratic organizations – the 'global factory' with the division of labour extending across national borders on a worldwide scale (Williams et al., 2013) – in developed and emerging economies, and these traditional modes of organizing work exist alongside 'new' horizontal and process-based forms and 'frame-breaking' boundaryless organizations.

The next two sections review the traditional and contemporary types of organizational structure shown in Figure 15.5.

outsourcing: contracting with external providers to supply the organization with the products or back-office data processes that were previously supplied internally

Traditional designs: bureaucracy

In Henry Mintzberg's (1992) *Structure in Fives: Designing Effective Organizations*, he suggests that any work organization has five core parts, which vary in size and importance (Figure 15.6). The three line roles are senior management (the strategic apex), middle management (the middle line) and the production (operating, technical) core. The production core consists of those who do the work of the organization, making its products or servicing its customers. The two staff roles are technical support (technological structure) and clerical support (support staff). The model suggests that, given these five different parts, organizations can adopt a wide variety of structural configurations, depending on which part is in control.

At its simplest, work organizations must perform four essential functions to survive and grow in a capitalist economy:

1 A product or a service must be developed that has value.
2 The product must be manufactured or the service rendered by employees who rely on paid work as their only or major source of income.
3 The product or service must be marketed and made available to those who are to use it.
4 Financial resources are needed in order to develop, create and distribute the product or service provided.

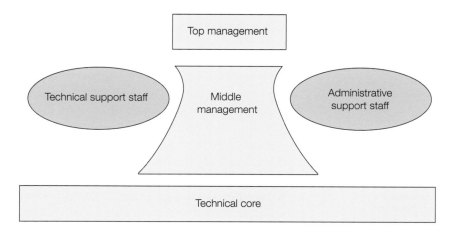

Figure 15.6 Five basic elements of an organizational structure

These 'task' functions are the basic activities of the organization, and are undertaken within each of Mintzberg's five basic elements: developing (support), manufacturing the product or providing the service (technostructure and operating core), marketing the product and service (support) and financing the organization (strategic apex and support).

The process of developing, manufacturing the product or providing the service and marketing it in a capitalist economy also results in a number of organizational imperatives (an imperative being something that dictates something else) that centre on issues of control. For those who sit at the strategic apex and for middle-line managers, producing for a market creates pressures to control costs and control uncertainties. Organizations that compete in the marketplace typically face two types of competitive pressure: pressure for cost reductions and pressure to be responsive to changing customer tastes.

Responding to pressures for cost reductions means that managers must try to minimize unit costs by, for example, producing a standardized product and achieving economies of scale. On the other hand, responding to pressures to be respon-

Source: © iStockphoto.com/plumchutney

plate 55 Government organizations are typically bureaucratic. They have numerous rules and procedures that white-collar workers must follow, and decision making lies mainly with high-ranking bureaucrats. This photo shows part of the parliament building in Wellington, New Zealand.

functional configuration: an organizational structure that organizes employees around specific knowledge or other resources

sive to customers requires that managers differentiate the firm's product offering in an effort to accommodate differences in consumers' tastes and preferences. These two types of competitive pressure are even more intense in the global marketplace (Hill and Jones, 2012).

In addition, the indeterminacy of employees' job performance creates pressures to render individual behaviour predictable and manageable. The control imperatives inherent in capitalist production and employee relations create a need for other managerial behaviour that is supportive of the organization's operating functions, including human resource management, industrial relations and public relations. Together, the pressures arising from 'task' functions and 'control' functions shape the formal organizational structure as a hierarchy, in which decision making is top-down, with subunits or departments, and with managers hired to control employees' behaviour.

In the industrial technology era, the organizational dynamics just described caused managers to adopt one of four common structural configurations. They could structure the organization by:

- function
- product/service
- division
- function and product (a matrix).

No formulas exist to guide the choices for organizational structure, and each structure has its advantages and disadvantages. The guiding principle is that although there is no one 'right' organizational structure, the right structure for top managers is the one that offers the most advantages and the fewest limitations, or, to put it another way, the one that 'makes their profits'.

Several newer contemporary forms of organizational design have evolved over the last two decades and are well established in the organizational discourse. These new designs focus on processes or work teams, or the electronic connection of widely dispersed locations and people to form an extended 'virtual' organization. Understanding the strengths and limitations of each structural design helps us to understand what informs design choices, as well as the interplay between different structural configurations and organizational behaviour.

A **functional configuration** is one in which managers and subordinates are grouped around certain important and continuing functions. For example, in an engineering company, all the design engineers and planners might be grouped together in one department, and all the marketing specialists grouped together in another (Figure 15.7). In a functionally designed organization, the functional department managers hold most of the authority and power. Key advantages of functional organizations include the development of technical expertise and economies of scale: this is the classic bureaucratic structure. Disadvantages can include the encouragement of narrow perspectives in functional groups, alienation and demotivation, and a poor coordination of interdepartmental activities.

A product or service design arrangement is one in which managers and subordinates are grouped together by the product or service they deliver to the customer. For example, at Volvo Motors there is a car division, a truck division and so on (as schematized in Figure 15.8). Another example is a hospital where a medical team and support workers are grouped together in different departments or units dealing with particular treatments, such as maternity, orthopaedic surgery and emergencies.

The advantages of product or service structures include an increased coordination of functional departments, improvements in decision making and the location of accountability for production and profit. Disadvantages of product or service structures can include a loss of economies of scale, the duplication of scarce resources and the discouragement of cooperation between divisions.

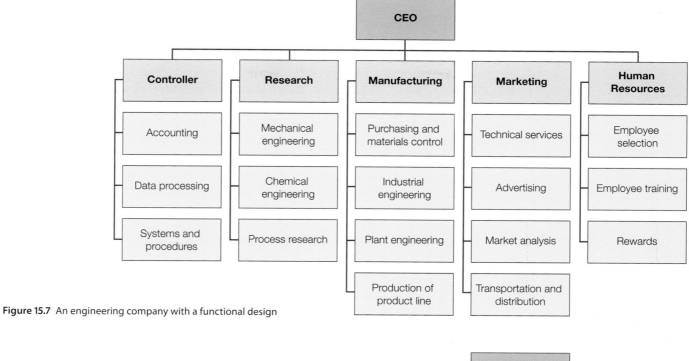

Figure 15.7 An engineering company with a functional design

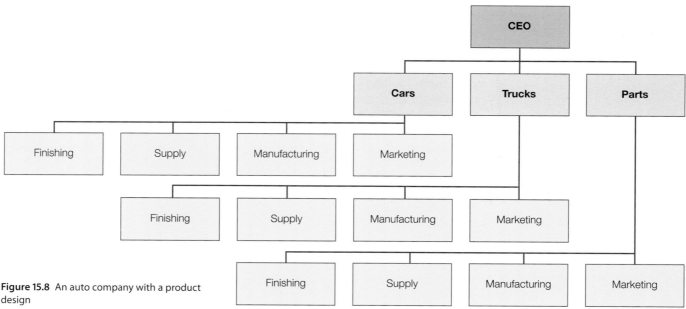

Figure 15.8 An auto company with a product design

divisional structure: an organizational structure that groups employees around geographical areas, clients or outputs

strategic business unit: a term to describe corporate development that divides the corporation's operations into strategic business units, which allows comparisons between units. According to advocates, corporate managers are better able to determine whether they need to change the mix of businesses in their portfolio

A **divisional structural** arrangement uses decentralization as its basic approach. The decentralized divisions can group employees together in one of three ways: by the products or services on which they work, by the sets of customers they serve, or by the geographical locations in which they operate. In the 1980s, these divisional structures developed into **strategic business units**, often with 20 levels of management between the corporate CEO and the front-line employees in the business units.

The Body Shop uses a divisional structure based on its major operating regions around the world. The company's products are sold in different markets in different parts of the globe. This is based on the premise that marketing the Body Shop's products in Canada is different from marketing skin and hair products in the UK or the Asian region.

Figure 15.9 shows one possible conception of a multidivisional corporation with strategic business units, built around core products and core competencies. Organizations often evolve from a functional design to a divisional arrangement. As the external environment changes and becomes more complex and uncertain, management might find that it must diversify its operations to remain competitive (Hill and Jones, 2012; Jacoby, 2005). Divisional organizational design emphasizes autonomy in divisional managers' decision making.

There are several advantages associated with a divisional configuration. It improves decision making by allowing many decisions to be delegated to divisional managers, who are generally more knowledgeable about local markets. Divisional managers are more accountable for their decisions. In many divisional organizations, units are 'profit centres', and divisional managers are evaluated on the overall performance of their unit.

The disadvantages of a divisional structure come partly from its decentralized activities. Economies of scale are lost because many task functions of the organization, such as marketing, and control functions, such as accounting and human resource management, are duplicated in each division. Specialists in one division may not be able or willing to share information with similar specialists in other divisions. Thus, the autonomy given to each division to pursue its own performance goals becomes an obstacle to achieving the overall corporate goals. As a consequence, warn Hamel and Prahalad (1994) in *Competing for the Future*, 'corporate' strategy is little more than 'an amalgamation of individual business unit plans' and managerial strategic behaviour tends to be parochial, focusing only on existing business units (p. 309). From a worker's perspective, the outcome can be catastrophic: the relocation to another geographical location means the loss of a job as the firm's products or services are relocated to typically low-wage economies or outsourced and, in the case of public corporations, privatized.

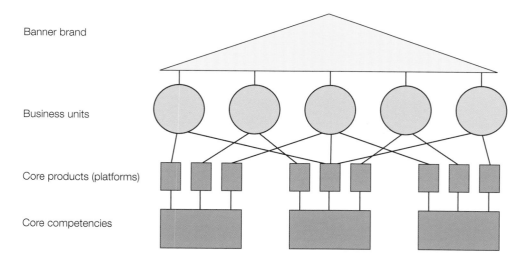

Banner brand

Business units

Core products (platforms)

Core competencies

Figure 15.9 Divisional organizational structure based on strategic business units
Source: Hamel and Prahalad (1994), p. 279

matrix structure: a type of departmentalization that overlays a divisionalized structure (typically a project team) with a functional structure

In the **matrix structure**, both functional specialities and the product or service orientation are maintained, and there are functional managers and product managers. Functional managers are responsible for the selection, training and development of technically competent workers in their functional area. Product managers, on the other hand, are responsible for coordinating the activities of workers from different functional areas who are working on the same product or service to customers. In a matrix design, employees report to two managers rather than to one (Figure 15.10).

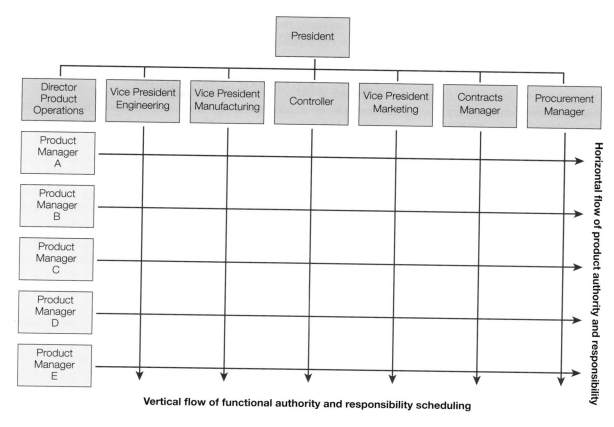

Figure 15.10 An engineering company with a matrix design

VISIT THE *ONLINE RESOURCE CENTRE* AT HTTPS://HE.PALGRAVE.COM/COMPANION/BRATTON-WORK-AND-ORGANIZATIONAL-BEHAVIOUR3/ FOR AN EXAMPLE OF A MATRIX STRUCTURE.

Emerging designs: post-bureaucracy

From the 1980s, accelerated changes in global capitalism exposed the limits of bureaucracy, which led to new post-bureaucratic designs. These developments attracted the attention of sociologists and management scholars, producing a plethora of descriptors in the literature, including the flexible firm (Atkinson, 1984), the cellular firm (Bratton, 1992), the adhocracy configuration (Mintzberg, 1992), the postmodern organization (Hassard and Parker, 1993), the individualized corporation (Ghoshal and Bartlett, 1997), the re-engineered corporation (Hammer and Champy, 1993), the boundaryless organization (Ashkenas et al., 2002) and the virtual (Goldman et al., 1995) and networked (Powell, 2003) organizations. All these post-bureaucratic architectural forms are conceived as substituting a hierarchical model of structure and achieving higher levels of labour flexibility, while conceding limited empowerment to workers (Felstead and Jewson, 1999). The centrepiece of social relations in the post-bureaucratic organization is a short-term contract that systematically makes employees more insecure (Standing, 2011), coupled with a 'new pay' paradigm linking individual or group performance to rewards (Corby et al., 2009; Pulignano and Stewart, 2006). Four leading-edge post-bureaucratic organization forms, which we examine here, are shown in Figure 15.5: horizontal, boundaryless, virtual and network.

Horizontal organizations

horizontal or 'lean' structure: an integrated system of manufacturing, originally developed by Toyota in Japan. The emphasis is on flexibility and teamwork

In a **horizontal structure**, work activities are centred around teams that complete a whole process. Decentralization shifts decisions to teams, and gives limited

Adopting this type of organizational design requires each of the four boundaries to be appropriately flexible and permeable so that information, creative ideas and internal and external resources can flow freely up or down, in and out and across the organization. The aim is to have sufficient permeability to allow the organization to quickly and creatively adapt to changes in the environment. The boundaryless organization still retains its boundaries 'but all the boundaries are more permeable, allowing greater fluidity of movement through the organization' (Ashkenas et al., 2002: 3).

This architectural form involves senior managers renouncing 'command and control' leadership in favour of practices that empower their subordinates. Leaders, observe Ashkenas et al. (2002: xix), need 'to shift from having the right answers to asking the right questions'. Importantly, the model involves developing four leadership capabilities to encourage and nurture appropriate permeability. Capabilities refer to a leader's ability to integrate, build and reconfigure internal and external resources and capabilities to address rapid changes in the environment (Teece et al., 1997). The possession of these capabilities helps an organization to achieve creative forms of competitive advantage. The model shows four dynamic capabilities: information, shared, development and network:

- *Information* capability refers to the ability to foster access to information across all boundaries, and to help people to interpret and use the information.
- *Shared* capability describes the capacity to share power with team members, to learn from followers and to foster team leadership in order to make independent decisions about actions and the allocation of resources.
- *Development* capability is the capacity to foster and nurture individual and group work-related learning through mentoring and coaching, for example, and to assimilate and apply new knowledge and creative ideas to product, process or service innovations.
- *Network* capability describes the ability to forge trust, mutual dependency, loyalty and horizontal cooperation among customers, suppliers and other stakeholders, to mutual benefit (Sotarauta et al., 2012). It also means finding ways to share common risks and costs, and to work with competing organizations, to underpin innovation and business success (Nowak and Highfield, 2011).

The boundaryless organization is associated with radical changes in the organization of production, including how teams are put together and the use of outsourcing to emerging economies where labour is considerably cheaper. Sophisticated communication technology (the Internet) and the rise of the 'BRIC' economies have also facilitated the development of other types of structure including virtual and network, which we consider next.

Virtual organizations

In the age of the Internet, it is not unsurprising that the 'virtual' organization has captured the attention of organizational analysts. The **virtual organization** is a temporary or permanent arrangement of otherwise independent companies or individuals, with a lead firm, which produce a product or service by sharing costs and core competencies. **Core competencies** are knowledge and expertise bases that reside in the organization (Hamel and Prahalad, 1994). This ever-changing constellation of organizations is connected not through formal rules, but rather through virtual networks. The Internet, the World Wide Web and information technology connect members of the virtual organization wherever they are in the world. Typically, data are transferred electronically around the virtual network, and separate competency sets work on the data either sequentially or in parallel (Davidow and Malone, 1992). Several factors have driven organizations to adopt virtual modes of

virtual organization: an organization composed of people who are connected by video-teleconferences, the Internet and computer-aided design systems, and who may rarely, if ever, meet face to face

core competency: the underlying core characteristics of an organization's workforce that result in effective performance and give a competitive advantage to the firm

organizing: an increased requirement for flexibility and global learning, reducing market uncertainty, managing joint production, a high-tech base and the perceived need to manage cultural diversity (Ferlie and Pettigrew, 1998).

Network organizations

network structure: a set of strategic alliances that an organization creates with suppliers, distributors and manufacturers to produce and market a product. Members of the network work together on a long-term basis to find new ways to improve efficiency and increase the quality of their products

Corporate global network connections have figured as a pervasive, major aspect of organizational life in the twenty-first century (Scholte, 2005). A **network structure** or organization is a constellation of several independent organizations or communities of people, usually linked on a large project basis, such as aerospace alliances between specialist engineering firms. The firms or groups in the network have a more formal and long-term commercial relationship than in a virtual organization (Rocket and Short, 1991). Hierarchy is sacrificed in order to speed decision making, and vertical integration is supplanted by horizontal integration across group boundaries. Each group in the network focuses on a set of competencies. This structure enables each community of people to be flexible and responsive to changes (Davidow and Malone, 1992).

Networks, argues Castells, have had a transformational effect on structures (Castells, 2000b). Examples of network structures exist at Cisco Systems, Dell Computers and Mozilla Corporation. Perhaps the best-known company using a network structure is Amazon.com, a virtual bookstore with no inventory, online ordering and electronic links to its customers. Cisco Systems, another exemplar, produces 80 per cent of the world's Internet hardware using a global network of employees and suppliers using web-based technology.

IN THE EBOOK ACCESS THE **CRITICAL INSIGHT** ENTITLED 'BUSINESS WITHOUT ORGANIZATIONS' IN WHICH CLAY SHIRKY ARGUES THAT INTERNET TECHNOLOGIES MAKE IT INCREASINGLY EASY TO CREATE CONSTELLATIONS OF NETWORKED PROJECT GROUPS (SHIRKY, 2008).

A network structure has neither a corporate head office nor an organizational chart. Mitchell Baker, the CEO of Mozilla Corporation, developer of the Firefox web browser, for example, describes her role not as head of the organization but as 'the coordinator and motivator of a group effort' (M. Baker, quoted in Hunt, 2009). Bartlett and Ghoshal (1989) describe an integrated global network structure with, for example, a firm in France receiving flows of components from across the globe. The concept of an integrated networked structure emphasizes the shift from inflexible to permeable structures and processes, accompanied by significant flows of components, resources, information and people. Unilever is an example of a networked company that has pursued a transnational strategy, with 17 different and largely decentralized detergent plants in Europe alone.

The network structure offers organizations access to wider markets, lower production costs and the potential to respond quickly to new product and service developments and markets. The weakness of the network arrangement is that associates have little direct control over the functions carried out by other members of the network. The number of independent members in the network creates a high-dependency relationship between each company within it. This requires new behaviours and a high trust in the network's members. Managers and knowledge workers need to radically modify their behaviours as strategic planning, for example, is no longer an independent activity, but a process needing coordination, information sharing and global learning (Bartlett and Ghoshal, 1989).

New post-bureaucratic design models are associated with the outsourcing principle. *Outsourcing* describes a practice in which the organization contracts with another company to supply it with either a component(s) for its final product (for example, car wheels) or with a management process (for example, recruitment, payroll, legal services or security) that it would previously have undertaken itself.

The practice of outsourcing used in new organizational forms has seen the development of hollow and modular organizational structures (Anand and Daft, 2007).

The outsourcing of the non-core processes or services that are not critical to organizational performance gives rise to the *hollow organization* structure. Its conceptual roots can be traced to the 1980s, with the removal of previously state-provided services – utilities, water and regulatory agencies – 'hollowing out' the state, reducing public sector workers and physical assets, hence the name. In private organizations, the outsourcing of previously internally provided processes or service hollows out the organization. For example, specialist suppliers provide components for automobile manufacturers or security for public events or supermarkets. This enables the parent organization to concentrate on its core competencies, such as research, design and marketing. Nike, the sports equipment company, for example, concentrates on its 'branding' strategy, rather than on manufacturing, which it outsources to low-wage economies – a case of organizational structure following business strategy (see Klein, 2000).

---

globalization & organization misbehaviour

Source: Brand X Pictures

Gender equality in times of economic transition: women workers in Russia

The late twentieth century brought significant changes to the world of work in Eastern Europe and the former Soviet Union. The fall of Communist state governments was accompanied by a massive restructuring of national and local economies, and of the social lives of the workers who populated these institutions. While old-order policies and practices were pushed aside in favour of open markets, social and cultural attitudes about gender endured, often extending into the offices and boardrooms of organizations trying to navigate this massive capitalist shift.

By the late 1990s, the new Russian economy was starting to look up, buoyed by successes in high-tech and natural resource sectors. Russian women, in particular, made strides in the new economy, creating successful businesses catering to the burgeoning Russian consumer culture. Two decades after this transition, scholars and journalists are turning a critical eye to how gendered experiences of work in post-Soviet Russia continue to be affected by enduring cultural attitudes about women in Russian society.

According to Russian *Vogue* magazine editor Alyona Doletskaya, although career opportunities for women in Russia have changed significantly over the past few decades, women workers continue to overpopulate sectors such as fashion, service and public relations (Weir, 2005). Furthermore, women's salaries are substantially lower than those of their male counterparts. Weir writes, 'A recent survey of living standards ... suggested that of the poorest 15 percent of Russians, 68 percent are women. Many of the poor are well-educated women who find their skills unrewarded in the new economic order.'

The contemporary experiences of Russian women in the workforce can be linked to the Soviet era, when women were often relegated to undesirable, low-wage work, a pattern that reflected the state's support for, and reproduction of, wider cultural attitudes on gender roles. Today, although the transition to a free market economy has resulted in access to new types of work for Russian women workers, enduring cultural attitudes towards gender roles continue to affect women's abilities to participate fully in the new Russian economy. This period of economic, political and social transition in Russia provides us with an opportunity to consider how cultural attitudes about gender can span major systemic changes, influencing local people's experience of such transitions. It also raises questions about how, over time, the new economic and political orders in Russia will affect local constructions of gender.

Stop! Using gender as an example, consider the often-entwined relationships between cultural beliefs and economic and governance systems. How do local attitudes towards gender influence government and economic policy and practice? How do governments and economies influence the local constructions of the 'glass ceiling'? What kinds of societal attitude and practice related to gender extend into the workplaces where you live? Who should be responsible for regulating gender roles and gender equity in the workplace? How should 'gender equality' be defined? Are there different organizational approaches to achieving equity? In times of political and economic upheaval, support for social conservatism can surge. How might this claim be used to explain – or dispute – the experiences of Russian women workers described here?

Sources and further information

Ashwin, S. (2005) *Adapting to Russia's New Labour Market: Gender and Employment Strategy*, New York: Routledge.

Brainerd, E. (1998) 'Winners and losers in Russia's economic transition', *American Economic Review*, 88(5), pp. 94–115.

McGregor, C. (2003) 'Getting beyond the glass ceiling', *Moscow Times*, February 10. Available at: www.themoscowtimes.com/business/article/getting-beyond-the-glass-ceiling/235514.html (accessed February 20, 2015).

Weir, F. (2005) 'For Moscow's businesswomen, a powerful new role', *Christian Science Monitor*. Available at: www.csmonitor.com/2005/0308/p07s01-woeu.html (accessed October 2, 2009).

Note: This feature was written by Gretchen Fox, Cultural Anthropologist and Impact Assessment Analyst, Fox Cultural Research, Canada.

The increasing readiness of corporations to outsource production and the development of global supply interconnections (Friedli et al., 2014) have also created *modular* organization structures. The difference between the modular and the hollow organization is that a modular structure outsources the production of significant *parts* of the total final product. The underlying principle of a modular design is to break products down into self-contained modules or sections, outsourcing product modules to external contractors and then assembling all the completed modules (Anand and Daft, 2007). The example most often used is the manufacture of civilian and military aircraft. The assembly of Europe's Airbus A380, for example, is the final stage in a long and complex global supply chain. This consists of external contractors manufacturing modules for the aircraft including the fuselage, wings and engines from plants inside and outside the European Union.

Although the boundaryless network or hollow organizational structure may have been the favoured paradigm of the 1990s, the 2008 global financial crisis caused firms to reassess the efficacy of lean global spanning models. As *The Economist* reported, before the global financial crisis, management wisdom was to make companies as lean as possible, expanding just-in-time supplier networks around the globe and outsourcing all but core competencies, lubricated by cheap credit. In September 2008, the abrupt closure of the overnight commercial paper market meant that most companies needed to accumulate cash to pay their employees and suppliers. Thus, 'ultra-lean supply chains no longer look like a brilliant idea when you have to find cash to keep a supplier afloat that cannot get even basic trade credit' (Anonymous, *Economist*, 2008, p. 17) – a case perhaps of a 'just-in-time' being substituted for a 'just-in-case' network.

More sceptical analysts have found the 'dark side' of new organizational forms. A characteristic signature of post-bureaucratic architectural forms is the exploitation of the less powerful by the more powerful members. Buttressing this assertion is evidence that employees experience 'uncertainty, ambiguity and frustration' in their attempts to enact their professional roles within this organizational form (Currie et al., 2008). Countering the academic hype around 'post-bureaucratic' organizations is a recent study by Pulignano and Stewart (2006). Analysing primarily qualitative data from global automotive companies, they persuasively argue that new employment arrangements have, paradoxically, revitalized Weber's typology of bureaucracy. According to the researchers, new employee performance-related incentives have generated behavioural rules that reinforce bureaucratic control at Fiat, Volkswagen and Renault: 'Thus, intriguingly, the use of bureaucratic control emerges as the main element of labour control in this type of workplace' (Pulignano and Stewart, 2006: 104). Arguably, the binary bureaucratic/post-bureaucratic view of organizational design is a somewhat misleading analytical paradigm. In reality, new organizational structures are likely to be hybrids, new forms coexisting alongside some old enduring elements of bureaucracy (Dunford et al., 2007).

Structural redesign and organizational behaviour

The downsizing and restructuring to create 'lean and mean' high-performance workplaces hit employees across the globe with cataclysmic force in the global economic recession that emerged in 2008–09. By definition, downsizing and restructuring affect both high and poor performers. Employees are therefore usually correct in predicting job losses, extensive changes in the way they perform their work, work intensification, skill changes and changes in employee relations (see Figure 2.3).

It is well documented that relocating operations to another city or country or outsourcing and privatizing a service in a public sector organization can have major

Sources and further information

Navickas, V. (2007) 'The reasons and consequences of changes in organizational structures of tourism companies', *Economics and Management*, 12, pp. 809–13.

Ogaard, T., Marnburg, E. and Larsen, S. (2008) 'Perceptions of organizational structure in the hospitality industry: consequences for commitment, job satisfaction and perceived performance', *Tourism Management*, 29(4), pp. 661–71.

Tribe, J. (1997) *Corporate Strategy for Tourism*, London: International Thomson Business Press.

For more information on Australia's tourism industry and the challenges it faces, go to www.tourism.australia.com/home.aspx.

Note: This case study was written by Lori Rilkoff, Human Resources Director, City of Kamloops, BC, Canada.

IN THE EBOOK ACCESS AN **OB IN FILM** BOX THAT USES *THE CORPORATION* (2003) TO REVEAL STRUCTURAL CONTRADICTIONS AND BEHIND-THE-SCENES TENSIONS IN THE WORKPLACE AND TO ACCESS **AN INTERACTIVE QUIZ** TO TEST YOUR UNDERSTANDING.

ᅠ

chapter 16
Technology

Key concepts

- deskilling
- disruptive technology
- labour process
- Luddite revolt
- material technology
- post-industrialism
- smartphones
- social technology
- sustaining technology
- technological determinism
- technology
- technology agreement
- upskilling

Chapter outline

- Introduction
- The nature of technology
- Critical debates on technology: the deskilling thesis
- Historical and philosophical contexts of ICT
- The social shaping of ICT
- Summary and end-of-chapter features
- Chapter case study: Technological change at the Observer–Herald newspaper

Chapter learning outcomes

After completing this chapter, you should be able to:

1. Understand the distinction between sustaining and disruptive technologies, and explain current trends in the relationship between technology and work organizations
2. Compare and contrast major theoretical perspectives on technology, including the labour process theory and the deskilling/upskilling debates
3. Understand and explain technology agreements, different forms of technological thought and the Luddite revolt
4. Discuss the possible implications of theories and research on technology for workplace practice

introduction

Technology has been the engine of modernity (Brey, 2003). The emergence of the industrial society was made possible by innovations in manufacturing technology. In the late twentieth century, the emergence of an information society was also largely the product of innovations in information and communications technology (ICT). Modernity is shaped by technology, and technology is a creation of modernity. Whether it is our everyday dependence on the Internet and iPhones or our daily use of washing machines and smart televisions, technologies are and continue to be an integral part of the architecture of modern life. In the workplace, technologies have created new products and services and are now reliably doing things that would have sounded implausible only a few years ago. According to Gavin Kelly (2014), by 2020 Amazon promises that electronic drones will be delivering books to our doorsteps, Rolls-Royce predicts that unmanned robo-ships will sail the oceans, and Nissan pledges the driverless automobile. Just as significant, and related, is the spectre of robot technology and microcomputer technologies undermining the economic security of not just skilled and unskilled workers, but also previously protected areas of professional work such as accountancy, law and medicine. Thus, any assessment of technology's impact on the employment is replete with paradox. Thus, technology has the potential to enhance skills, autonomy and individual freedom, yet it can make jobs and skills obsolete and provide a close intrusive monitoring of what we do and say (Martin, 2015). Thus, technology is deeply implicated in organizational life; it transforms the nature of work, and shapes and reshapes behaviour in the workplace.

The conventional wisdom that dominates government think-tanks and bodies such as the Organisation for Economic Co-operation and Development is that economic growth and success are dependent on an ever-increasing investment in new technology, its application and its diffusion (Castells, 1996; Patel, 2002; Reich, 1991). This thinking represents a type of orthodoxy that is rarely challenged. For these bodies, despite global warming caused by human action, there is little debate on the sustainability of a growth model that is 'hardwired to wriggle out of paying social and environmental costs' (Patel, 2009: 48) and predicated on 'more and more, bigger and bigger', creating a tension between global capitalism and nature (O'Conner, 1998). In this chapter, we shall look at the many different, competing theories of technology that are often left out of most work-based and government policy-based discussions.

The challenge of this chapter is to explore the relevance of this orthodoxy for a critical understanding of organizational behaviour. We can, and should, begin this in a simple way by asking how 'technology' itself is defined and understood. What are the presumptions made about the relationship between developments in technology, work design, organizational behaviour and the use of technology? Hidden in the answers to such questions, we argue, are important possibilities for understanding a topic that has become all but taken for granted – a sure recipe for arriving at a destination that is not of our own collective choosing.

In this chapter, we include a discussion not often seen in organizational behaviour textbooks, which points to the broad work-based policy and practice surrounding technology. Public policy and programmes are examined with reference to the European Union (EU). We look at important types of policy and practice at the level of the organization, with a focus on, first, the effect of scholarship on the practice of technological innovation and its use in the labour process, and second, **technology agreements** between employers and trade unions. There is an emphasis on what is known in the sociology of work field as the deskilling/upskilling debate, and what it can teach us about organizational behaviour.

We begin, however, with a brief discussion of the key concepts, main literature and central ideologies of technological thought. Taken together, this review sets the stage for critical and creative thinking about the relationship between technology, work and organizational behaviour.

stop...

Before reading on, think about how you define 'technology', based on how you have seen it applied in workplaces or educational institutions. Notions of conflict and consensus will be important in this chapter. From your experience, is technological change at work or university associated with conflict, consensus or both?

...and reflect

technology agreements: agreements with legal standing that set in place rules for negotiation over the selection, adoption and implementation of technologies

The nature of technology

Technology is a term that is used rather loosely in everyday discourse to mean machines, computers and robots. However, defining technology so narrowly neglects the effects on the labour process of changes in the social organization of production, for example flexible specialization (see Chapter 2). An operational definition is needed to evaluate the interrelations between technology, social relations and patterns of work, and organizational behaviour. When sociologists use the term 'technology', they can be referring to a physical device (for example, a computer or iPhone), a technique or a human skill (for example, a computer program), a social arrangement (for example, work teams) or some combination (or all) of these.

Over 40 years ago, Alan Fox (1974) made a distinction between material technology and social technology. *Material technology* is the physical device that can be 'seen, touched and heard'. *Social technology* is the human processing arrangements that 'seek to order the behaviour and relationships of people' (p. 13). Social technology includes job classifications and boundaries, payment systems, decision-making procedures, appraisal procedures and other workplace rules, which seek 'to govern what work is done, how it is done, and the relationships that prevail between those doing it' (p. 1). In the context of workplace organizations, we define **technology** as the means by which an organization transforms resources, including information, into products or services, and the social organization of work, which takes such forms as work teams, governance rules and procedures, communications and payment systems. The current new technologies that are of most interest to sociologists fall under the category of ICT, based upon microelectronics, the application of which is said to be transforming the organization of work.

technology: the means by which an organization transforms resources, including information, into products or services, and the social organization of work, which takes such forms as work teams, governance rules and procedures, communications and payment systems

Classic post-Second World War researchers examined the relationship between technology and organizational structure, work design, employment and society at large. For example, Joan Woodward (1965) studied the relationship between production technology and the organizational structure of firms, testing also for the possible roles of authority, control, division of labour and communications within the firm. She found that the type of organization corresponded to the (product or service) production technologies that it used. Other researchers of this period added additional insights into the relationship between technology and organizational forms, stressing not simply the correlation between the two, but also causative relationships – that is, the 'why' and 'how' of the relationship (Perrow, 1970; Thompson, J. D., 1967).

This classic research undertaken by Joan Woodward (1965), for example, has been criticized for its explicit determinist hypothesis. *Technology determinism* is the view that technology is the prime driver or determinant of developments in organizations, employment or even society itself. For example, computer numerically controlled machinery 'deskills' craft workers. Such views regard technology as the *independent variable*, the factor whose effects are to be studied. Craft skills or organizational structures become the *dependent variables* that are all but the inevitable outcome of technology. This relationship is shown in Figure 16.1.

It follows from the technological determinism viewpoint that the key challenge for understanding work and organizational design and behaviour is to comprehend how a technology (physical or social) impacts, either positively or negatively, upon

plate 57 New technology can eliminate jobs. For instance, workers can be replaced by industrial robots welding car bodies on a mass-production assembly line.

Source: PhotoDisc

individuals, groups and organizations. Technological determinism contains a partial truth: that technology matters to work and organizations (MacKenzie and Wajcman, 1999). But the key analytical limitations of this simple cause-and-effect approach are, first, the inconsistency in establishing the direction of causation, and second, the mediating effects of other key variables, not least human action, economics and politics, and, notably, the state. This means that a simple linear cause-and-effect technological determinant is not an adequate theory of organizational behaviour.

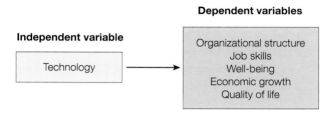

Figure 16.1 Technology as an independent variable in organizational and social change analysis

post-industrial economy: an economy that is based on the provision of services rather than goods

In the 1970s, there emerged an influential series of arguments – which are, nevertheless, contestable – that organizational structures, organizational behaviour and technology were combining to form '**post-industrial**', 'knowledge' and/ or 'information' economies, which were significantly different from the styles and structure of work that had been seen up to that point. Promoted by a variety of influential researchers, for example, Bell (1973) in the USA, Porter (1971) in Canada, Touraine (1971) in France and Richta (1969) in Eastern Europe, this school of thought is still with us today. It trumpets the collapse of workplace drudgery and the replacement of low-skill job roles by '**knowledge workers**', 'information workers' or 'symbolic analysts', all with an emphasis on the use of computerized technology. Even more recently, others have taken up the torch to perpetuate the tradition (see, for example, Reich, 1991).

knowledge worker: a worker who depends on her or his skills, knowledge and judgement, established through additional training and/or schooling

The current argument of these gurus of the 'perpetually coming but never arriving good times' is, in brief, that technology with informating properties – that is, the capacity to provide relevant information and generate analytically based knowledge – encourages the development of computer, social and analytical skills, and hence contributes both to the emergence of new occupations (such as software developer) and to worker empowerment. Although consumers of electronics may in their non-work lives tend to see ICT as expanding their capabilities in and access to information and services, it is vital to note that, in the paid workplace, ICT often has additional effects that are less likely to be positive. It may, for example, alter management–employee relations by encouraging decentralized activities and new forms of all-embracing 'panoptic' managerial surveillance and control (see Chapter 2).

Among some writers, there is an assumption that new forms of technology will lead to new organizational structures and designs, for example the 'boundaryless' firm (see Chapter 15), new products and new jobs. From a strategic management perspective, Christensen (2013), for example, observes that it is important to make the distinction between 'sustaining' and 'disruptive' technologies. Sustaining technologies have in common that they improve the performance of established products or processes. Disruptive technologies, on the other hand, create products that are typically cheaper, simpler, smaller and, frequently, more convenient to use (Christensen, 2013). The electronics that build automated telephone exchanges are an example of sustaining technology, whereas silicon chip technology, which produced microcomputers and mobile phones, is an example of disruptive technology. Sustaining technologies are associated with 'transitional' organizational change, whereas disruptive technologies often involve 'transformational' change (see Chapter 18). Some writers on the topic are particularly fascinated by the prospect of greater 'outsourcing', which is made easier since new technologies reduce the transaction costs that are associated with contracting. This places a downward pressure on wages and employee control, but is said to encourage innovation.

Technology, job designs, the form and structure of organizations and human agency are therefore linked narratives. Mainstream accounts, however, tend to ignore the messy work through which real technological or economic change emerges in society. In sum, both people's everyday experience of using new technology in their non-work lives and the hyper-Utopian views of those advocating technology in the workplace conspire to minimize the conflictual dimensions of change and overplay the consensual or rather mechanistic dimension: the view that change is simply an anonymous, faceless force of nature.

As the old adage goes, we cannot know where we are going unless we know where we have been. In this sense, economic and social history teaches us that the claims of links between technology, productivity and the emergence of apparently 'new' phases in the economy are not as straightforward as they may seem, and a healthy scepticism is, in our view, an important response for students and scholars of organizational behaviour in this topic area.

The key technologies of modernism that are said to have defined the first, second and third industrial revolutions – that is, steam, electricity and microcomputers – have seen fascinating and complex pathways to application in the workplace (Devine, 1983; Gospel, 1991; Hughes, 1983; Lipsey et al., 1998; Noble, 1984). Among these 'general-purpose technologies', electricity, ICT and in particular steam clearly emerged, not out of some inventor's mind as much as from the push and pull of the forces of political and economic struggle. The details of the emergence and diffusion or transfer of general-purpose technologies provide important clues to the actual nature of technology as a phenomenon. Is technology a 'thing', or is it a social process? Lazonick seems to suggest the latter in his discussion of the meaning of 'technological transfer':

> Insofar as the utilization of technology requires complementary human inputs with specific cognitive capabilities and behavioural responses, the transferred technology will have to be developed in the new national environment before it can be utilized there. As a result, when 'transferred' technology is ultimately developed so that it can be productively utilized in a new national environment, it is in effect a new technology. (1993: 194)

configurations: defines technology as the combination of social and technical factors. Configurations are a complex mix of standardized and locally customized elements that are highly specific to an organization

The type of description that Lazonick provides is aligned with Fleck's (1993) notion of **configurations** (as opposed to 'technologies' as such). Configurations are defined as complex mixes of standardized and locally customized elements that are highly specific to an organization. In fact, those who have been most insightful in considering the very nature of technology have defined the term quite broadly to reflect this broad set of considerations. These scholars tend to produce statements that are at first glance simple, but at a second glance can be seen to be deeply informed. Technology is not this or that tool, artefact or machine, and neither is it a general-purpose technology such as steam, electricity or ICT. Rather, it is 'the way we do things around here' (Franklin, 1990), the 'organization of resources' (Hacker, 1991; Mumford, 1964), 'society made durable' (Latour, 2000) and so on. Students of work, technology and society gain the potential for valuable leadership when they break the bonds of conventional wisdom to explore its terms critically. In this chapter, we suggest that we must approach technology and organizational behaviour as a thoroughly social phenomenon.

However, the question remains, what kind of social phenomenon are we talking about? We have already mentioned that steam, electricity and ICT all emerged

Source: Image Source

Computers and work

In her major study of the role of computers in the workplace, Shoshana Zuboff (1988) reviews the complex relations between technological innovation and work. She argues that it would be a mistake to view the process or impact of technological change as being predetermined. Patterns of technological change are shaped by political factors. Those who introduce new technologies into the workplace must make choices. What happens at work depends, in part, on the choices they make.

Of particular interest to Zuboff is the question of how the computerization of the workplace will influence the foundations of managerial authority. She suggests that the foundations of managerial authority were traditionally connected to management's knowledge of work processes. Due to a knowledge gap (favouring managers), it was believed that management had a right and responsibility to control the workers. According to Zuboff, the introduction of computers into the workplace has the potential to change this relationship between management and workers. One can imagine several possibilities, but one thing is certain: if the knowledge gap changed as a result of computerization – for example, if it were to shrink – this would have important implications for managerial authority.

What makes Zuboff's study so engaging is that she enables readers to view these issues through the eyes of the workers and managers at the pulping plants where she conducted her research. Some workers expressed concern that computerization had caused them to lose some of the sensory knowledge (sights, smells and sounds) they had used to run the plant effectively. Other workers expressed concern that they were not receiving the kind of training that would enable them to make decisions at the newly computerized plant:

> The technology lets us know a lot, but we need to know more. As a manager, you should teach everybody what you know – keep passing the knowledge on. But they do not give us the knowledge to think for ourselves. I think it is because it would do away with their jobs, or they would look stupid if we had the knowledge. (p. 278)

One of the managers Zuboff interviewed had this to say about his responsibility for 'passing the knowledge on':

> I am not willing to break things down real simply to explain something to the operators. I won't give up my terms that I learned as an engineer. The concepts are hard to understand. I am not here to teach those concepts. I went to college to learn these things, and so it proves I have a right to tell people what to do. (p. 281)

Zuboff is careful to make the case that the impact of computers at work is difficult to predict. She presents us with multiple scenarios, some that depict an almost Utopian future for workers and some that depict a darker outcome. Here is her optimistic account of the computerized workplace of the future:

> Organizational leaders recognize the new forms of skill and knowledge needed to truly exploit the potential of an intelligent technology. They direct their resources towards creating a work force that can exercise critical judgement as it manages the surrounding machine systems. Work becomes more abstract as it depends upon understanding and manipulating information. This marks the beginning of new forms of mastery and provides an opportunity to imbue jobs with more comprehensive meaning. A new array of work tasks offer unprecedented opportunities for a wide range of employees to add value to products and services. (p. 6)

Stop! It is possible that both the worker and the manager described above have valid points. Write a dialogue for a conversation that might take place between this worker and this manager at an informal meeting convened by senior management. Does Zuboff's optimistic scenario 'ring true' for you? In your experience, has the computerization of work increased or diminished workers' autonomy and the quality of working life?

Sources and further information

McLoughlin, I. and Clark, J. (1994) *Technological Change at Work*, Philadelphia: Open University Press.

Zuboff, S. (1988) *In the Age of the Smart Machine: The Future of Work and Power*, New York: Basic Books.

Note: This feature was written by Peter Sawchuk, Professor, University of Toronto, Canada.

from the push and pull of economic and political power. It is, moreover, a contested terrain, or, as Feenberg (1991, p. 14) says, 'technology is a scene of struggle ... a parliament of things'. Historically, as now, the intersection of work, learning and technological change has occasioned conflict: from the Luddite revolts in early nineteenth-century England to the countless more recent industrial conflicts caused by the imposition of technological change. More recently, this has involved the transformation of occupations including engineering (Jones, 1988), textile work (Lazonick, 1979), postal work (Louli and Bickerton, 1995), computer programming (Kraft, 1977) and – one of the more frequently documented occupations – printing (Bain, 1998; Wallace and Kalleberg, 1982; Zimbalist, 1979). Wallace and Kalleberg (1982), working in the US context, summarize it like this:

We have argued that while technology is the proximate cause of this transformation, the underlying and fundamental sources for these changes are found in historically developed social relations of production ... The stated goal of automation in printing, as in other industries, is the rationalization of the labor process: the streamlining of production and elimination of costly sources of human error ... However, efficiency is not a value-neutral goal in capitalist economies. (pp. 321–2)

Thus, it is the core point of departure in this chapter that our conceptions of technology and work must be conditioned by an impulse to 'de-reify' and to move beyond mere appearances.

Critical debates on technology: the deskilling thesis

We have explored the conceptual, historical and philosophical context of technology, and have also emphasized that the relationship between ICT, work and organizational structure is not one-directional, as has been portrayed in Figure 16.1. With this in mind, in this section we examine one of the most influential books concerned with the study of technology and work: Harry Braverman's (1974) *Labor and Monopoly Capital*. His thesis is that technology inevitably deskills workers as employers invest in new technologies to increase profits or remain competitive. Although his thesis has been criticized for analyzing technology as an independent explanatory variable, his contribution to the study of work cannot be overestimated (Noon et al., 2013). To recap a section in Chapter 3, Braverman conceptualizes managers as controlling agents. Their impulse to control labour is the key to understanding social relations, and leads managers to find new ways of reducing the discretion exercised by workers in performing their jobs in order to maximize efficiency and profitability. This, according to Braverman, leads managers to pursue systematic strategies of deskilling the workforce.

Workplace skills

Skill and knowledge development in the workplace have regularly been associated with the introduction of new technology. The term 'skill' is not easy to define. Skills include such diverse activities as rock climbing, driving, welding, word processing and operating a machine tool. Psychological scholarship has suggested that skills are inherent in the individual. The focus is on the learning of skills, that is, behaviours, through formal or informal learning (see Chapter 7), in which goal accomplishment depends on the levels of declarative knowledge (knowledge about a task) and procedural knowledge (knowledge of how to do a task) that are needed to perform to a satisfactory level (Gattiker, 1990).

The sociological analysis of skill concentrates on the organization or job and suggests that an occupational skill is a multidimensional concept involving complex cognitive, interpersonal and manipulative activities, discretion and social, including gender and discrimination, factors. Skill can take several forms:

- Skill can refer to complex competencies that are developed within a particular set of social relations in the workplace and are objective competencies.
- Skill can refer to the degree of autonomy and discretion involved in a job.
- Skill can refer to conventional definitions of occupational status (Beechey, 1983: 63–4).
- Skill can be seen as a product of 'social exclusion' in the workplace that succeeds in enhancing the relative strengths of certain (for example, male) employee groups (Penn, 1983).

● Skill can be 'generic' and applicable in diverse work situations, and some skills can be 'specific' and used in a particular context (Felstead et al., 2002).

In this section, we draw material from Mike Noon and his colleagues' (2013) exposition to examine the debate on organizational and technological **deskilling**.

Organizational deskilling

deskilling: a reduction in the proficiency needed to perform a specific job, which leads to a corresponding reduction in the wages paid for that job

Organizational deskilling is embedded in Tayloristic and Fordistic principles. As we discussed in Chapter 2, Tayloristic work regimes involve the separation of the mental (conception) and manual (execution) components of work. The more challenging and interesting mental tasks are transferred to technical and managerial employees, while the less challenging and mundane manual work remains with the workers on the factory floor. The economic effects of the division of labour were identified first by Adam Smith over 200 years ago, and were further developed by Marx in Volume 1 of *Capital*, but it was Harry Braverman's work that highlighted the contemporary relevance of the principle. He wrote:

> The separation of mental work from manual work reduces, at any given level of production, the need for workers engaged directly in production, since it divests them of time-consuming mental functions and assigns these functions elsewhere … A necessary consequence of the separation of conception and execution is that the labor process is now divided between separate sites and separate bodies of workers. In one location, the physical processes of production are executed. In another are concentrated the design, planning, calculation and record keeping. The preconception of the process before it is set in motion, the visualization of each worker's activities before they have actually begun, the definition of each function … all of these aspects of production have been removed from the shop floor to the management office. The physical processes of production are now carried out more or less blindly, not only by workers who perform them, but often by lower ranks of supervisory employees as well. The production units operate like a hand, watched, corrected, and controlled by a distant brain. (Braverman, 1974: 124–5)

Thus, appropriating knowledge from the workforce and relocating it in managerial functions removed discretion from the workers and enhanced management's control over the **labour process**.

labour process: the process whereby labour is applied to materials and technology to produce goods and services for the marketplace. The term is typically applied to the distinctive labour processes of capitalism

Technological deskilling

For Braverman and other advocates of the deskilling thesis, technological deskilling occurs when new technologies are used to further transfer workers' discretion and autonomy from the factory floor to the office (Glenn and Feldberg, 1979; Noble, 1979; Shaiken et al., 1986; Zimbalist, 1979). That is, key decisions about *what* and *how* work is performed are transferred from manual to clerical or managerial employee groups, which have a displacement effect on some direct labour.

Marx's analysis of nineteenth-century machinery has strongly influenced twentieth-century studies of technology (Bratton and Denham, 2014). Examining the impact of 'new' technology, Marx observed:

> Along with the tool, the skill of the workman in handling it passes over to the machine. The capabilities of the tool [machinery] are emancipated from the restraints that are inseparable from human labour-power. Thereby … in the place of the hierarchy of specialised workmen that characterises manufacture, there steps, in the automatic factory, a tendency to equalise and reduce to one and the same level every kind of work that has

to be done by the minders of the machines; in the place of the artificially produced differentiations of the detail workmen, step the natural differences of age and sex. (1887/1970: 420)

In seeking control, managers often dispense with the very employee capacities that today's managerial theories claim are so vital:

> The focus on the labour process points also to the irremediable necessity of a coercive system of control and surveillance, leading to a critical perspective towards the role of 'management'. Of crucial importance, such a focus also helps deflate the ideology of 'technology' as a neutral, autonomous and irresistible force. (Hyman, 1982: 93)

Braverman focuses on 'new' technology, new that is, at the time he was writing and before the invention of the microchip, introduced under the paradigms of craft production: numerical control machine tools. Prior to numerical control technology, apprentice-trained craft machine operators would use their own discretion to set and operate the machines. Numerical control technology only left the machinists with the simple tasks of loading and switching the machines on and off, allowing the separation of task conception (design and planning) from task execution (doing). In other words, numerical control technology is used to subordinate craft workers by decreasing their level of skill and enhancing management control. Braverman, mirroring Marx's observations, writes:

> In reality, machinery embraces a host of possibilities, many of which are systematically thwarted, rather than developed, by capital. An automatic system of machinery opens up the possibility of the true control over a highly productive factory by a relatively small corps of workers, providing these workers attain the level of mastery over the machinery offered by engineering knowledge, and providing they then share out among themselves the routines of the operation, from the most technically advanced to the most routine. This tendency to socialize labor, ... this promise, ... is frustrated by the capitalist effort to reconstitute and even deepen the division of labor in all its worst aspects, despite the fact that this division of labour becomes more archaic with every passing day ... The 'progress' of capitalism seems only to deepen the gulf between worker and machine and to subordinate the worker ever more decisively to the yoke of the machine. ... The chief advantage of the industrial assembly line is the control it affords over the pace of labor, and as such it is supremely useful to owners and managers whose interests are at loggerheads with those of their workers. (1974: 230–2)

Braverman's general deskilling thesis has attracted numerous criticisms (see, for example, Friedman, 1977; Littler and Salaman, 1984), and a number of empirically based studies of ICT refute it (for example, Jones, 1983; Wilkinson, 1983). Still other writers have defended Braverman (Thompson, 1989; Zimbalist, 1979). Furthermore, some studies contain evidence that is supportive of Braverman's work (Cooley, 1980; Noble, 1979; Thompson, 1981). Indeed, the refutation of Braverman became a major academic preoccupation in the 1980s (Hyman and Streeck, 1988). A more detailed discussion on these issues can be found in Knights and Willmott (1990), Tinker (2002) and Thompson (1989).

An early criticism related to Braverman's treatment of management behaviour suggested that it is one-dimensional, inadequate and vulgar (Bratton, 1992). Braverman, it is argued, assumes that management is a monolithic, unambiguous phenomenon whose actions are programmed by the overriding objective of

Source: © iStockphoto.com/4774344sean

plate 58 It has been suggested that call centres are a typical creation of a neo-liberal age, in which labour has been intensified and the rate of exploitation increased. They are sometimes described as 'electronic sweatshops'.

controlling labour (Knights and Willmott, 1986b; Whipp and Clark, 1986) and exaggerate the unity and rationality of management (Child, 1985; Hyman, 1988). Whipp and Clark challenge the notion of a monolithic management when they argue: 'It is just as likely that intra-management contests will cause fracturing as any which are generated from the frontier of control between management and labour' (1986: 213).

Moreover, the assumption that issues of labour control, rather than, for example, finance, investment and marketing, are *the* central concern of management is highly doubtful (Kelly, 1985; Purcell, 1989). Thus, as Kelly contends, managing the labour process is not an end in itself, but a means to achieve efficiency and profit: 'It is not simply the *extraction* of labour value in the labour process which is problematic for capital, but the *realisation* of that surplus through the sale of commodities in markets' (1985, p. 32). Beechey (1983) offers a feminist critique, arguing that Braverman's analysis follows that of Marx: it is gender-blind. For example, Braverman's concept of skill fails to explore gender dimensions and the social construction of 'gendered jobs' (see Noon et al., 2013: 123 for a discussion on skill in 'context').

VISIT THE *ONLINE RESOURCE CENTRE* AT HTTPS://HE.PALGRAVE.COM/COMPANION/BRATTON-WORK-AND-ORGANIZATIONAL-BEHAVIOUR3/ FOR FURTHER INFORMATION ON THE DESKILLING DEBATE.

Burawoy (1979) has argued that Braverman's work does not explore the extent to which workers may develop an informal subculture through which they consent to their own subordination. In practice, the management of labour tends to be a combination of consent and cooperation and economic coercion. Bratton (1992) carried out a relevant piece of research in this area, which is an important counterpoint to Braverman's work. His collection of case studies provides evidence of work teams creating conditions for their own subordination. Individual team members felt that they had a moral obligation to 'put a full day in'. As one team member explained:

> A person who under the old scheme might go away for an hour, now he thinks twice: Are they going to think they are carrying me because I've been away? … Because you are a close-knit community in the cell system. You get remarks: Where have you been all morning? That sort of thing, and it gradually works its way in psychologically. (Bratton, 1992: 186)

The informal culture can act as a powerful means of self-regulation and provide alternative means of control for management. Post-Braverman studies do not negate Braverman's thesis but, rather, suggest that he underestimates the complexity and diversity of management objectives and behaviour.

Braverman's classic form of deskilling still occurs widely, as you will know if you or your friends have worked in, for example, a fast-food outlet, but the introduction of new forms of ICT has redefined the deskilling process for a small number of occupational groups (Burris, 1999; Rothman, 2000). The classic separation of mental (task conception) and manual (task execution) has evolved into something more complex, although it remains difficult to argue that it is fundamentally distinct from the classic deskilling dynamics. In other words, in some organizations and among certain occupational groups, we now see a more nuanced form of the division between mental and manual labour. As mentioned above, reports also suggest that ICT is threatening highly skilled knowledge-based professions in architecture, law and medicine. Eventually, 'the robot will end up doing the surgeries on its own', it is reported (Meltzer, 2014: 11). Hosts of workers are now being asked to use the tools provided for them in creative and responsive ways, but in contexts and with goals that are pre-established and beyond their control. Cavazotte's et al. (2014) study of the impact of smartphones in law firms identified classic control issues that were traditionally associated with manual workers. They observed that while smartphones increased accessibility and a sense of autonomy and flexibility, the technology also 'helped to intensify the organization's hold on employees outside of working hours, reaching into new settings, time slots and social contexts' (p. 85).

We can of course see this predicted by classical social theorists such as Marx: he noted that the capitalist labour process can – although it does not necessarily seek to – eliminate the mental capacities of labour in order to appropriate and control work outcomes. For contemporary commentators such as Tinker (2002), the abiding value of Braverman's thesis is that 'It debunks academic dogma of management, popular nostrums about skill upgrading via education' (p. 274).

The upskilling debate

The deskilling thesis has its roots in Marx's economic theory of relative surplus value (profit maximization) and economic crises (profit loss) (Noon et al., 2013). In contrast, the **upskilling** thesis is rooted in Schultz's (1961) human capital theory that high investment in education and training is the key to economic growth in a post-industrial capitalist society (Spencer and Kelly, 2013). The arguments that high productivity and economic development hinge on investments in education and training were also individualized: 'If workers wanted good jobs and to avoid unemployment they had to "invest" in their own education and learning (this was no longer primarily a state responsibility)' (Spencer and Kelly, 2013: 11).

Those associated with the 'upskilling' thesis claim that increased technology leads to more, not less, skill on the part of the workers. This approach largely presumes that advances in technology require a more educated, better trained workforce in order to match the demands of increasingly complex work routines (Blauner, 1964). Proponents also presume that ICT requires advanced skills (Archibugi and Lundvall, 2001; Reich, 1991). Piore and Sabel's (1984) concept of **flexible specialization** supports the upskilling thesis. The shift from mass production (Fordism) to flexible specialization – 'the second industrial divide' – required a reversal of Fordistic principles and a return to craft-based knowledge, creativity and work-related learning, according to Piore and Sabel.

flexible specialization: a competitive strategy whereby a company invests in multipurpose equipment and employs and trains its workforce to be multiskilled, in order to adjust quickly to a fast-changing business environment

Links to management — Alison Jones

Alison works with small and medium-sized enterprises and entrepreneurs to make them stand out from the competition and grow their businesses, clarifying strategy and creating effective content marketing, including print and ebooks. She also provides executive coaching and consulting services to the traditional publishing sector.

After an MA in English Language and Literature from Edinburgh University and an MBA from the Open University, Alison pioneered digital publishing over a 22-year career in publishing, most recently as Director of Innovation Strategy with Palgrave Macmillan. She set up Alison Jones Business Services and the Practical Inspiration Publishing imprint in 2014 to establish a new model: position, or brand, publishing. She is an associate lecturer with Oxford Brookes University, teaching on their MA in Publishing, and an affiliate lecturer with the University of Falmouth.

In the ebook click on the play button to watch Alison talking about technology in the workplace, and then answer the following question:

- What technological advancements have changed the way people work?

However, many of those who have looked closely at skill and learning practice associated with technological change in the workplace have questioned this assumption (Gee et al., 1996; Hyman, 1991). Poster (2002), for example, suggests that levels of learning may be reduced in some ways by the introduction of ICT, and that, either way, accurate assessments of performance and skill change remain elusive. Important empirical analyses in North America seem to support Poster's claim, with some suggesting that there may in fact be a surplus of computer literacy: that is, there are inadequate real opportunities for workers to apply their skills at work (Livingstone, 1999; Lowe, 2000). By all estimates, North American workplaces are not alone in this paradoxical situation of, on the one hand, the relatively widespread availability of ICT, and on the other, apparent barriers to its effective diffusion, implementation, learning and use.

Thus, it is a core point of departure in this chapter that our conception of technology must be conditioned by an impulse to 'de-reify', that is to move beyond mere appearances and offer a counternarrative, one that sees technology as an elaborate historical process and to some extent legitimizes dominant interest groups.

IN THE EBOOK ACCESS THE **CRITICAL INSIGHT** ON 'THE PURPOSE AND OUTCOMES OF TECHNOLOGY'.

Historical and philosophical contexts of ICT

According to Theodore Roszak (1994), the word 'computer' entered the North American public vocabulary in the 1950s, at a time when the most advanced models were still room-sized beasts that burned enough electricity to present a serious cooling problem. Building on the principle of ICT, work and organizational behaviour as a conflictual social phenomenon, it is important to note that, as with the emergence of steam and electricity, historical scholarship has demonstrated that computers were not simply 'discovered' in the conventional sense of the term. Instead, ICT was brought into being by specific historical and political economic processes: by politics, policy and practice.

Noble (1984) provides the definitive analysis, noting that contemporary ICT emerged through a series of concerted and contested activities by which companies like General Electric, AT&T and IBM, relying upon private control over public funds for what could be called the 'university–industrial–military' complex of the post-Second World War era in the USA, developed specific forms of computer technology. These included numerical control, computerized numerical control, automated robotics and now advanced ICT including the Internet. Importantly, Noble makes it clear that, in fact, alternatives to computerized numerical control could have been just as efficiently developed, and that strategic choices revolved around issues of power and control over the organization of production.

Luddites: a group of textile workers, led by Ned Ludd in early nineteenth-century England, who systematically smashed new workplace technologies because they directly undermined their working knowledge and economic interests as workers

Just as the **Luddites** of nineteenth-century Britain were in favour of technologies that supplemented rather than displaced human skills (Sale, 1995), the key alternative during the early history of computers was 'record/playback' technology. This system was actively ignored largely because, as Noble puts it, 'to the software engineer, this places far too many cards in the hands of the lowly machinist' (1984: 190). Such matters, in fact, raise invaluable questions that are still applicable today as technological design continues to make presumptions about who should control what, and what features and purposes ICT should entail.

Although this historical background is important, it is equally essential – if we are to understand the intersection of ICT, work and organizational behaviour as a contested as well as a consensual social phenomenon – to have a basic understanding of the competing ideologies or philosophical approaches that are informing the development and use of ICT. As Williams and Edge remark, 'these debates are not merely "academic": they relate to policy claims and objectives' (Williams and Edge, 1996: 2). We can categorize the different approaches into four basic categories:

instrumental/technocratic, substantive, constructivist and what Feenberg (1991) refers to as a 'critical theory' of technology.

Instrumentalist or technocratic approaches tend to be the source of either positive or neutral characterizations of ICT in the workplace. This is the dominant approach in government, business and mainstream policy sciences. Here the transfer of technology is inhibited only by cost, what works in one context can be expected to work equally well in another, and 'the only rational stance is an unreserved commitment to its employment' (Feenberg, 1991: 6). More discussions of the origins of this approach can be found in the work of a variety of leading sociologists of the immediate and later post-Second World War era, who wrote at length on the issues of technology and industrial progression (Bell, 1973; Kerr, 1962). More often than not under this approach, technology comes to take on a kind of autonomous, creative and deterministic role (and thus it makes sense that *Time* magazine can designate a computer as the 'person of the year'). This autonomous casting in turn gives rise to exaggerated tales of the emergence of 'knowledge workers' and 'symbolic analysts' (Naisbitt, 1982).

A contrasting approach to technocratic thought is said to be the **substantive approach**, represented best by the writings of Jacques Ellul (1964) and Martin Heidegger (1977). In a type of mirror image, however, this approach also attributes an autonomous force to technology, although it sees it as a 'cultural system' that orients the world as an 'object of control'. This approach tends to see the future as dark (for instance, 'Only God can save us now', says Heidegger), and argues that a return to simplicity or primitivism offers the only viable alternative.

Standing in many ways separate from either of these approaches is the **constructivist approach**, exemplified (differently) by the likes of Latour (2000), Callon (1992) and Suchman (1987). Such works emphasize how technology is rooted in human interaction and the local activation or use of technologies by human beings. The meaning and effects of technology are determined in their use by actors, and not necessarily in any prior way by designers. Among all the approaches to ICT, it is the constructivist approach that most clearly articulates how users implement and appropriate ICT, sometimes in keeping with the intentions of the designers and those who contracted them, sometimes not. Others have echoed the importance of this approach for technological development, emphasizing how design, implementation, use (and redesign) are interrelated, and opening up new ground in conventional understandings of 'choice' in the course of technological development (Rip et al., 1995; Suchman, 2002).

Finally, there is the **critical approach**. Its roots are largely in the Frankfurt School of critical social theory (Feenberg, 1991), although a variety of work such as that of Lewis Mumford (1964) has relevant connections to this approach as well. In general, the approach rejects the presumptions of both the technocratic and the substantive approach, charting a course, as Feenberg says, between resignation and Utopian visions of efficiency. To the degree that the approach is defined by its reference to issues of *power*, it might overlap with certain elements of the constructivist approach. Some constructivist researchers (see, for example, Latour, 2000) overtly declare that there are inherent political dimensions to technological development. However, central to the critical approach is what Feenberg calls the 'democratic advance': that is, the democratic participation of citizens in establishing both the goals and the means for the development, implementation and diffusion of technology.

Echoing this concern in terms of policy analysis, Gartner and Wagner (1996) have carried out careful case studies in Europe and drawn attention to the difficulties faced by design efforts situated in 'fragmented cultures'. Mumford's (1964)

---

instrumentalist or technocratic approach: approaches to technology that are uncritical of its broader social, political and economic significance, viewing technologies as autonomous and positive

substantive approach: an approach that tends to see technologies as producing negative social and political effects

constructivist approach: an approach to technology that tends not to focus on social or political influences, but instead sees technologies as defined strictly by how they are put to use

critical approach: an approach to technology that tends to focus on how the social and political effects are produced through contestation and negotiation

pan-historic discussions also emphasize what he calls 'authoritarian and democratic technics'. By 'authoritarian technics' he means a development that is 'system-centred, immensely powerful and yet unstable due to its centralization of control'. Indeed, he goes on to say that 'if democracy did not exist, we would have to invent it' (p. 21) if we were to deal effectively with the technologies of the modern era.

We suggest that these four basic approaches to technological thought will be useful for analysing policy and practice, providing us with a type of philosophical compass. In other words, they orient us to the more general directions and purposes that all too often remain hidden beneath the surface of the legislation, policy, programmes and practice that expresses them.

---

globalization & organization misbehaviour

Source: Getty

Predictable deaths at Lac-Mégantic: technology, organizational behaviour and the profit imperative

The interaction between technology and money often shapes organizational behaviour in ways that reach far beyond a firm's structure and work processes. For example, one July night in 2013, a runaway train carrying crude oil exploded in the small Canadian town of Lac-Mégantic, destroying the high street and killing 47 people.

> Steeve Roy, 41, escaped with his two-year-old son from his third-floor apartment by a laneway behind his building. Roy said he was asleep but that it wasn't the derailment that woke him up.
>
> 'I heard people screaming and the shattering of glass … I heard people yelling: "Save yourself" and then there was silence.'
>
> Roy said he jumped out of bed, opened a window and saw a big wall of fire.
>
> 'I took my son and left by the laneway outside toward city hall, after that, things started exploding.' (Blatchford, 2013)

A factor contributing to the explosion was the use of DOT-111 rail tankers – tanker cars known to puncture or leak during crashes – to transport flammable liquids (Seglins, 2014). While the problems with DOT-111 rail cars have been known for years, approximately 50,000 cars still require upgrading to address inadequate construction.

The companies that lease the cars to rail-lines are reluctant to spend the $1 billion that is necessary to retrofit them properly. Railway companies, while publicly supporting retrofitting, continue to use the older DOT-111 cars to ship crude oil due to rising demand. For example, in the USA, crude oil shipments rose from 9500 tanker-car loads in 2008 to 434,000 in 2013 (Tumulty, 2014).

So what explains the willingness of rail companies to use equipment known to have defects that can cause catastrophic outcomes? One line of explanation is that firms in capitalist economies are responsive to the profit imperative. This results in a tendency to monetize risk and assess it on a cost–benefit

basis. Lac-Mégantic-like explosions, while catastrophic and costly, are rare, and whatever liability that will arise from them will be spread across many actors (including insurers) and over a significant amount of time. In a cost–benefit analysis, one (or more) Lac-Mégantics is simply an acceptable cost of doing business.

Many rail company executives will probably take offence at being labelled amoral calculators. And, to be fair, it is doubtful that any individual is so hard-hearted as not to be moved by the devastation wrought on the citizens of Lac-Mégantic. Yet the rail companies knowingly engaged (and continue to engage) in a dangerous practice, the outcome of which could be reasonably predicted.

Indeed, this kind of corporate killing is hardly new or unique. There are dozens and dozens of examples of corporations knowingly acting in ways that have endangered lives in order to reap often massive profit. The use of asbestos, benzene, lead and radium long after their hazardous natures was known jump to mind. Perhaps the best example is the continued production of cigarettes. In many cases, companies intentionally hid or falsified evidence that could have saved lives – often while government regulators turned a blind eye (Michaels, 2008). The contest between what behaviours technology enables and what behaviours organizations engage in is a poorly explored – but very important – aspect of organizational behaviour.

> **Stop!** Why do organizations sometimes act as amoral calculators? What does this suggest about the efficacy regulatory strategies that focus on educating organizations and the leaders about their obligations? What would trigger different organizational behaviour in an amoral calculator?

Sources and further research

Blatchford, A. (2013) 'Lac-Megantic explosions, fire: 5 deaths confirmed, about 40 considered missing', *Huffington Post*, July 7. Available at: www.huffingtonpost.ca/2013/07/07/lac-megantic-explosions-fire_n_3556584.html?utm_hp_ref=lac-megantic-explosion (accessed February 23, 2015).

Michaels, D. (2008) *Doubt is Their Product: How Industry's Assault on Science Threatens Your Health*, New York: Oxford University Press.

Seglins, D. (2014) 'Crude shipments, tanker punctures top agenda at rail talks', CBC, January 13. Available at: www.cbc.ca/news/canada/crude-oil-shipments-tanker-punctures-top-of-agenda-at-rail-talks-1.2491949 (accessed February 23, 2015).

Tumulty, B. (2014) 'Feds plan new rail oil tanker safety standards', *Poughkeepsie Journal*, April 26. Available at: www.poughkeepsiejournal.com/story/news/local/new-york/2014/04/26/crude-oil-train-transport-rules/8227751/ (accessed February 23, 2015).

Note: This feature was written by Bob Barnetson, Associate Professor of Labour Relations, Athabasca University, Canada.

The social shaping of ICT

If we commit to understanding the intersection between ICT, work and organizational behaviour as a broad, conflictual social phenomenon, we are in essence seeking to understand a process of social change. Social relations in the workplace affect technological change through the way in which they shape how work is organized. But work organizations are far from the only institutions that influence technological change and innovation. Since the beginning of modernity, state institutions – for example, the military, the police and intelligence agencies – have sponsored and shaped the technology that has emerged, how it is applied, and where. The crucial role of the state in research and development (R&D) is most evident in the sponsoring of military technology, electronics and nuclear power (MacKenzie and Wajcman, 1999).

R&D is central to the efforts of the state, as well as being carried out by corporations on a national scale by the core countries of global capitalism (Archibugi and Lundvall, 2001), although there is a considerable variation in the degree and focus that countries bring to it (see Mani, 2002, for a comparison of government sponsorship in developed and developing countries). When it comes to the relationship between direct and indirect involvement in the development of technology, we see that Northern European governments are often the most directly involved, with other European governments such as France and Germany (as well as non-European countries such as Japan) being moderately involved, and the governments of countries such as the UK, the USA, Southern Europe, Australia and Canada being least directly involved on a regulatory basis.

With regard to non-military technology, the most 'interventionist' government responses are to be found in countries such as Norway and Sweden, where issues from ICT research and application, as well as labour relations more broadly, are shaped by a commitment to 'co-determination' on the part of employers and employees alike. In general, however, the power of national or international governmental bodies to use regulation to influence the introduction and application of ICT in actual work processes and workplaces is quite limited. In the USA, for example, while Carnoy et al. (1993) have noted that the structures, policies and practices of labour relations are moving to the centre of the debate on the design and adaptation of new technologies, the most common model of employer–employee negotiation and ICT adoption is adversarial and antagonistic.

We can, however, briefly note that a parallel system of private sector policy and (corporate-based) governance has blossomed. For example, there has been a growing number of international agreements between large corporations about various forms of the development and application of ICT. According to Archibugi and Coco (2000), international company-to-company technological development agreements doubled between the periods 1981–86 and 1993–98. In particular, strategic technology partnerships (for R&D) between Europe and the USA spiked in the 10 years to 2006. These partnerships may also involve collaborations with public research institutions and universities, which play an increasingly important role in the international dissemination of knowledge and ICT development.

Although this layer of ICT and work policy is important, a solid grasp of the range of governmental legislation, policy and programmes in this area remains the most relevant for our discussion here. To review these, we look at several selected examples involving different member states in the EU.

Western Europe

One of the most comprehensive sets of studies of ICT, work and organizational change was conducted in Western Europe in the early 1990s. It was entitled Partic-

---

stop...

A major challenge for management is to engage employees' full capacities to learn, be creative, etc. What would it take to develop employee and trade union participation among management, that is, a 'social' approach to technological change?

...and reflect

ipation in Technological Change and was undertaken by the European Foundation for the Improvement of Living and Working Conditions. Based on 64 case studies and a large (7326 participants) survey, the study showed that technological change was dependent on national industrial relations regimes as well as, in broader terms, the 'historical and cultural factors' associated with particular nations and sectors. In keeping with our discussion, two key factors for success were shown to be unionization and workers' skill levels.

Links to management — Tony McGrory

Recently retired and free to participate in management, career development and alumni mentoring, Tony has spent 34 years in human resource and functional managerial roles spanning leadership and development, managing change and core talent, negotiation skills in sales and commerce, Six Sigma and a real estate portfolio in a major multinational company. Tony's broad background permits effective liaison, networking and communication with managers and organizations seeking guidance and experience in aligning project activities that match their strategy and deliver their corporate business objectives.

In the ebook click on the play button to watch Tony talking about social media, and then answer the following question:

- In what ways can social media technology affect work and the behaviour of people in the workplace?

The EU is a key example of how international government policy and programmes are created and carried out, and provides important information on the current status of the intersection between ICT, work and organizational behaviour in advanced capitalism. In general terms, this model of policy development contrasts starkly with the decentralized model seen in the USA. EU policies in the area of technology and training revolve around the principle that the circulation of knowledge is as important as a common currency. To put it more starkly, 'economic growth, employment and welfare in the old continent are strictly associated with its capability to generate and diffuse new technologies' (Archibugi and Coco, 2000: 1).

As a student of organizational behaviour, you should explore the outputs of such bodies to gain a sense of where practice, research and policy are headed. Perhaps as important as the centralized organization of ICT-related policy, however, is the willingness and ability of the EU to carry out combined R&D, training and implementation research programmes that link corporations, research institutions and governmental resources.

The most relevant example in this regard, according to Cressey and Di Martino (1991), is the European Commission's information technology programme entitled European Strategic Programme of Research and Development in Information Technologies (ESPRIT). ESPRIT represents an international example of an attempt at the policy/programme level to organize R&D- and ICT-based innovation, as well as work and learning outcomes, to respond to the needs of the workplace. Its outcomes have, however, remained partially ambiguous from a critical viewpoint. This is in part because of the phenomenon that Gartner and Wagner (1996: 203) describe as narrow forms of 'agenda setting':

> What is politically and ethically legitimate and desirable cannot be simply solved by establishing participatory structures. The kind of close partnership between designers and users at which, for example situated design, aspires is not a sufficient answer to the core question of what makes a 'good system'. Our case analysis points at the importance of understanding agenda setting. Each arena has its own set of legitimate agenda, from questions of user interface design to quality of working life and privacy issues.

The ESPRIT programme and the associated European Commission policies on which it was built were largely democratic, but at the same time its agenda was largely predefined along technocratic lines. On the point of learning and ICT use, for example, its motive was tied mostly, although not exclusively, to serving markets and relatively narrow interests of profitability, rather than to more broad issues of quality of working life, sustainability, equity and so forth.

Nordic nations

In Northern Europe, however, there is a different tradition at the intersection between ICT, work and organizational behaviour. Again, Gartner and Wagner's work is instructive. Their (1996) study looked closely at the role of formal national legislative frameworks, such as the Norwegian Work Environment Act (NWEA), which detail the relations between the various industrial partners and the norms of work, technological development and ICT use. The NWEA defines participation in work-related areas associated with ICT systems (among other things), and suggests a much deeper form of participation in policy formation.

Specifically, the 1970s was a watershed decade for progressive policy and legislation related to ICT design and implementation and work in Northern Europe. The Norwegians put the NWEA into place in 1977, giving workers formal participation in 'company assemblies' and the right to appoint trade union representatives in the area of technological change. Co-determination procedures were established, and a system of penalties was set in place.

Similarly, in the late 1970s, Sweden enacted a series of 'work democracy' regulations including the establishment of a legal framework for labour representatives on company boards, disclosure acts and other items under the Work Environment Act of 1978. This set of acts, described by some as the most important reform in Swedish society since the universal right to vote, also included the Joint Regulation Act of 1977, which guaranteed co-determination specifically around issues of the design and use of new technology. While management did retain certain rights of ownership, articles in these acts stipulated that employers must negotiate with local unions before making any major changes to work processes, that workers can initiate such negotiations as well, and that all parties have the rights to relevant documentation (financial and technical).

Significantly, in Sweden, these legislative and policy frameworks were complemented by specific research programmes on ICT development, namely DEMOS and UTOPIA (Ehn, 1988), which had as their central goal the investigation of how technical design could respond to this radical new legislative environment. Also complementing these legislative frameworks were innovative experiments in user-based design: Scandinavia's UTOPIA programme (Bjerknes et al., 1987) as well as the Effective Technical and Human Implementation of Computer-based Systems (ETHICS) programme (Beirne and Ramsay, 1992). As a result, the network of policies, programmes and legislation was particularly thick with ideas and potential.

The conclusions from this exciting period in Northern Europe were that local participants must be deeply involved in the process, but also that **participatory design** is necessary but not sufficient for genuinely progressive socioeconomic outcomes surrounding the design, implementation, learning and use of technology (Poster, 2002).

Trade unions and ICT

Since the late 1970s, trade unions throughout Western Europe have sought to confront and shape the technological change that has resulted from ICT (Bratton, 1992). The research body of the European trade union movement, the European Trade Union Institute, published a report in 1979, *The Impact of Microelectronics*

> ## stop...
>
> Gartner and Wagner (1996) argue that, today, machines take precedence over people in the workplace. Do you think this is true? Why or why not? Reading the original article may help.
>
> *...and reflect*

participatory design: an approach to the design and implementation of technologies that is premised on user participation

on Employment in Western Europe in the 1980s, which examined the effects on the quantity and quality of paid work and the trade union response. The British Trades Union Congress (TUC) affirmed its commitment to ICT while controlling undesirable employment consequences through negotiating 'technology agreements'. A TUC policy statement declared:

> Technological change and the microelectronic revolution are a challenge, but also an opportunity. There is the challenge ... of the loss of many more jobs. Equally, there is the realization that new technologies also offer great opportunities ... increasing the competitiveness of British industry ... [and] *the quality of working life*. (TUC, 1979: 7, quoted in Bratton, 1992: 61, emphasis added)

It also became apparent that as union membership drastically fell throughout the 1980s and 90s, and Thatcher's Conservative government introduced restrictive trade union laws, trade unions were not able to adequately negotiate technological change. Unlike Germany and the Nordic countries, union engagement and cooperation in the UK was regarded as an anathema because it interfered with labour 'flexibility'. Trade unions in Britain lacked the resources, organizational structure and negotiating power to shape technological change.

In the Nordic countries, the trade unions were more successful in negotiating technology agreements. This is perhaps not surprising given the context of the Nordic tradition in politics for a preference for compromise and negotiation, and to have a 'social contract' – the complex web of relations linking governments with citizens, and people with each other, including relationships between employers and workers (Rhodes, 1998). It also helps to have high levels of unionization and workplace engagement, and to have some of the lowest income gaps between management and shop-floor workers. Technology agreements, often although not exclusively seen in unionized firms, establish a form of co-determination over issues of ICT adoption and use. In some ways, these agreements mirror on a smaller scale the kinds of national legislative framework seen in Norway and Sweden. However, they have appeared in a much wider range of countries.

John Wilson has a PhD in educational psychology and worked in teacher education and training in Scotland before becoming Foundation Professor of Education at Victoria University, Australia in 1992. He worked in human resource development in the education and training sectors in several countries including Bangladesh, Botswana, Canada, Laos and Thailand. In 2014, he was Asian Development Bank consultant on a project planning assistance in secondary education for the government of Kyrgyzstan.

In the ebook click on the play button to watch John talking about employee resistance, and then answer the following question:

- Why do employees resist technology, and what are the most common reactions reflecting this resistance?

Although technology agreements are not as common now as when they were first introduced in the 1970s and 80s, the basic technology agreement remains an important form of workplace-based policy concerning the adoption and effective use of ICT. In the early days of their emergence, according to some writers (Evans, 1983; Small and Yasin, 2000), these agreements typically included two basic components. First, there were 'procedural' elements, which included broad statements on the need for new technologies and, arguably more importantly, agreements on the timely disclosure of information by employers. These were to include the likely effects of the changes and to set out options. The options often included procedures for the development of joint union–management committees and change-monitoring practices, the establishment of worker technology representatives, and arrangements for union and management to draw on outside experts or consultants. Unions were occasionally given powers of veto if management clearly violated the agreed procedures. A second component of technology agreements was what are called 'substantive' elements: specific statements on how various issues should be handled. The aspects covered included job security, retraining and adjustments, methods of sharing economic benefits, health and safety, and surveillance issues.

Small and Yasin (2000) have noted the varied effects that technology agreements have on practice in the workplace, and also note the importance of the related social relations infrastructure in an organization. (Basically, they emphasize the importance of unionization.) Although many factors affect the overall success of technology agreements, and the methodology for evaluating a link between a technology agreement and performance is problematic, evidence suggests that they tend to lead to better organizational performance, a broader and more productive labour process, and a collective learning feedback loop that leads to a better choice and implementation of new technologies.

Learning shapes technology

Technological change can be usefully studied as a process of 'learning', at the individual, and group or organizational levels. To understand the force of this argument, it is necessary to recognize that innovation does not largely stem from a 'great inventor', but is a matter of the incremental modification of existing technology (Hughes, 1989), which involves learning and creative thinking (see Chapter 18 for a discussion on the process of innovation). We therefore benefit by looking at work-related learning, whether it is formal training or learning that is undertaken informally in everyday participation in the labour process, as a phenomenon that sits above, gives meaning to, reacts upon and in turn affects policy regarding technology. Furthermore, invaluable as the deskilling/upskilling debate is for our understanding, it cannot help but gloss over the actual behavioural processes that surround technological change and organizational development. Looking at the role of knowledge development and learning helps us to understand the 'how' of successful ICT adoption in the workplace.

Lam (2002) provides a good comparative international analysis of how institutions, legislation and policy in different countries (looking at Japan, the UK, the USA and Denmark) support or inhibit innovation in and the adoption of ICT. At the centre of this analysis is the concept of 'tacit knowledge', rooted in the relationships of discretionary communities of practice (which can be established either within an organization or more widely across a specific occupational group). A host of detailed empirical studies of exactly how ICT and learning practice relate is provided by Luff et al. (2000). Each of these studies shows that ICT is not merely 'adopted' by a workplace, but rather is *activated* and in some sense *reconfigured* by users in the course of (learning) practice.

Livingstone and Sawchuk (2004) and Sawchuk (2006) carried out a particularly relevant piece of work in this area. Their collection of case studies provides an important complement to organizational behaviour scholarship, as well as the sociology of work and deskilling/upskilling debates. It is based on a comparative examination of workplaces across five sectors in the Canadian economy (auto assembly, garments, light

Plate 59 Early labour process theorists' posit that technology can be used to subordinate workers by decreasing their level of skill and enhancing management control by enabling the separation of planning (thinking) from execution (doing).

Source: © iStockphoto.com/darrenwise

manufacturing, chemicals and public service), and draws on in-depth 'learning life-history' interviews. These case studies demonstrate, among other things, how the adoption of ICT is shaped by the labour relations climate and the dynamics of a specific sector, as well as by the struggle of workers for greater participation in the labour process. The analysis also makes it clear that issues of race, gender and age (see Chapter 8), as well as occupational type, are significant indicators of the development of skill and knowledge. Overall in the work of Livingstone and Sawchuk, we see computer literacy skills among workers that far exceed the actual needs of their organization. In the post-2008 global financial crisis era, we have seen the UK economy trapped in a cycle of low value-added, low-skills, coupled with low wages and low security of employment (Gold et al., 2013). Thus, as we saw in the context of previous sections, important assumptions that inform mainstream, technocratic approaches to policy surrounding ICT, work and learning are questioned.

Figure 16.2 The social shaping of technology

To summarize, technology as an isolated physical device, tool or machine is an abstraction; in reality, it is an elaborate historical process, which mirrors society and to some extent legitimizes dominant interest groups. As such, it is a social and highly conflictual phenomenon. The perspective of the social shaping of technology is an important corrective to notions of technological determinism. This perspective views technologies as outcomes of complex technical, economic, political and cultural processes. The relationship between ICT, organizations and society is not one of a simple one-directional cause and effect, but rather a cycle of social processes, as depicted in Figure 16.2.

As MacKenzie and Wajcman (1999: 5) observe, in adopting a technology, society or an organization 'may be opting for far more – economically, politically, even culturally, as well as technically – than appears at first sight'. The social shaping of technology and other matters addressed in this chapter raise points that are now, more than ever, important to consider in a critical and careful manner. For what purposes and to whom should technology be directed? How is control over technological design, implementation and diffusion established, and for whom? What is technology's actual effect on performance, skill and the quality of life in the workplace? As we noted at the beginning of this chapter, taking a 'common-sense' view of technology that overlooks the many political, economic and even philosophical choices it entails will probably not result in an arrival at destinations that we collectively choose.

VISIT THE *ONLINE RESOURCE CENTRE* AT HTTPS://HE.PALGRAVE.COM/COMPANION/BRATTON-WORK-AND-ORGANIZATIONAL-BEHAVIOUR3/ TO READ MCKENZIE AND WAJCMAN'S INTRODUCTORY PAPER ON THE SOCIAL SHAPING OF TECHNOLOGY.

Chapter summary

- This chapter has examined the nature of technology and the role that technologies play in organizations and society. The aim has been to selectively present theoretical frameworks that provide a way to examine both mainstream and critical perspectives on technology. We also noted how a common-sense view of technology overlooks the many political, economic and even philosophical choices.

- We have also noted the influence of technological determinism, and the chapter reviewed the influential work of Harry Braverman and the 'deskilling' debate, examining both organizational and technological deskilling. We also selectively examined European and North American criticisms of Braverman's work.

- The chapter explained that comparative international analyses of concepts and theoretical debates, as well as policies and programmes, provide an important basis for understanding how technology is related to work and organizational behaviour. We introduced the concept of the social shaping of technology and proposed a broad, multilevel approach to understanding ICT. We suggested that technology should be thought of as a social phenomenon, recognizing both consent and conflict in processes of adoption. In reviewing these areas, we are aided by a general understanding of the ideologies of technological thought.

- This chapter has posed a variety of questions related to technology and its impact on organizational: What stories about technology are dominant, and why? What implications does technology have for human behaviour, society and ecosystems? To what extent and in what ways does democracy influence what technology we end up with? What do different stories about technologies obscure, hide or ignore? A variety of answers to these and other questions should begin to emerge, but, perhaps more importantly, you should be in a better position to understand, evaluate and perhaps even affect the current landscape and direction of ICT, work and related issues. This chapter aims to provoke such discussions.

IN THE EBOOK ACCESS **WEB BASED ASSIGNMENTS** TO APPLY YOUR LEARNING.

Chapter review questions

1 What is the substance of the claims by authors since the Second World War, such as Woodward, Bell, Blauner and others, regarding technology and changes to society?
2 What are the four key modes of technological thought?
3 Explain the deskilling and upskilling debate in the context of technological change.
4 How do different nations compare in their approach to technological development and work-based adoption?

5 How can organizational behaviour research benefit from broad understandings of international policy regarding technological development and workplace change?
6 How is the use of technology in our non-work lives different from and/or the same as the use of technology in our paid work lives, and what definitions of technology covered in this chapter help us to explain these potential differences?

Further reading

Beirne, M. and Ramsay, H. (eds) (1992) *Information Technology and Workplace Democracy*, London: Routledge & Kegan Paul.

Boreham, P., Parker, R., Thompson, P. and Hall, R. (2007) *New Technology @ Work*, London: Routledge.

Cavazotte, F., Heloisa, L. and Villadsen, K. (2014) 'Corporate smart phone: professionals' conscious engagement in escalating work connectivity', *New Technology, Work and Employment*, 29(1), pp. 72–87.

Dutton, W. (ed.) (1996) *Information and Communication Technologies: Visions and Realities*, Oxford: Oxford University Press.

Ellis, V. and Taylor, P. (2006) '"You don't know what you've got till it's gone": recontextualising the origins, development and impact of the call centre', *New Technology, Work and Employment*, 21(2), pp. 107–22.

Gee, J., Hull, G. and Lankshear, C. (1996) *The New Work Order: Behind the Language of the New Capitalism*, Boulder, CO: Westview.

Granter, E. (2008) 'A dream of ease: situating the future of work and leisure', *Futures*, 40(9), pp. 803–11.

Gratton, L. (2011) *The Shift: The Future of Work Is Already Here*, London: Collins.

MacKenzie, D. and Wajcman, J. (eds) (1999) *The Social Shaping of Technology* (2nd edn), Milton Keynes: Open University Press.

Noon, M., Blyton, P. and Morrell, K. (2013) *The Realities of Work*, London: Palgrave (see pp. 110–37).

Perlow, L. A. (2012) *Sleeping with Your Smartphone: How to Break the 24/7 Habit and Change the Way You Work*, Boston, MA: Harvard Business Review Press.

Thomson, R. (ed.) (1993) *Learning and Technological Change*, New York: St Martin's Press.

Zersan, J. and Carnes, A. (eds) (1991) *Questioning Technology: Tool, Toy or Tyrant*, Philadelphia, PA: New Society.

Chapter case study: Technological change at the Observer–Herald newspaper

The setting

The setting for this case study is London, UK, in 1980. The Observer–Herald newspaper had been around for over a half a century, and printing workers there, as elsewhere, had been regarded as master craftworkers, building their skill, knowledge and judgement through distinctive apprenticeships. Over the years, they had earned high wages, exercised considerable control over their work environments, and by and large been indispensable to the production process. Relations between the printers and management at the newspaper were good. Each respected the other, and each viewed the product (one of the leading daily newspapers in the country) with a good deal of pride.

But the 1970s had seen growing unemployment. Industry all over Britain had seen the introduction on the shop floor of new automated computer technologies. Computers were being touted in manufacturing and even in office work as the way of the future. Workers all over feared for their jobs and their future. Printing industry trade journals too had for several years been talking about technological change. New 'computerized' presses were said to be able to save companies thousands of hours of labour.

The problem

James Armstrong, a master printer at the Observer–Herald, had had decades of experience in the detailed work of typesetting the text of the newspaper. However, on a cool spring evening, James arrived at work to face a new challenge. Along with the other printers, he had been called to a meeting, at which he learned that the newspaper would be introducing new computer-based typesetting technology. He felt a stone in his stomach. His ideas about his work were being transformed.

'Together, we've got over a hundred and fifty of years of knowledge,' James said to the manager. 'Do you really think a machine can replace that?'

Craig Withnall, the production manager, had known James and the rest of the print workers for a long time. He looked sympathetically toward them and then turned to James. 'I know what you're saying, Jim. But if the company didn't think it would work, they wouldn't be doing this. You'll all have a job here, rest assured. It will just be different. You'll have to learn some new things, that's all.'

The task

- After reviewing the suggested readings below along with this chapter, what do you think will change in terms of skill level, control and sense of the job for James and his fellow printers?
- What is gained and lost in technological change initiatives of this kind? Are there ways in which you can see the company building on the years of knowledge and experience of workers like James, or is the replacement of such skills and knowledge simply inevitable?
- Drawing upon the insights of this case, can you identify the replacement of skills and knowledge in professional occupations in the twenty-first century?

Sources of further information

Gordon, D. (1976) 'Capitalist efficiency and socialist efficiency', *Monthly Review*, 28, pp. 19–39.

Wallace, M. and Kalleberg, A. (1982) 'Industrial transformation and the decline of craft: the decomposition of skill in the printing industry, 1931–1978', *American Sociological Review*, 47, pp. 307–24.

Visit web.mit.edu/~shaslang/www/WGS/BrayGT.pdf for a pdf on information on technology and gender.

Note: This case study was written by Peter Sawchuk, Professor, University of Toronto, Canada.

IN THE EBOOK ACCESS AN **OB IN FILM** BOX THAT USES JACQUES TATI'S (1967) CLASSIC *PLAYTIME* TO EXPLORE TECHNOLOGY AND ITS EFFECTS ON PEOPLE AND TO ACCESS **AN INTERACTIVE QUIZ** TO TEST YOUR UNDERSTANDING.

chapter 17
Culture

introduction

In 2013, Robert Francis QC, charged with answering the question of why hundreds of patients had died needlessly at the Mid Staffordshire hospital, identified a culprit: the culture of England's National Health Service (NHS). According to his report, the culture focused 'on doing the system's business – not that of the patients'. The wife of one patient described how her husband had been treated with 'coldness, resentment, indifference and contempt' on his hospital deathbed. It is argued Francis's report has increased the 'climate of fear' pervading the NHS (Toynbee, 2015). In another situation and faced with a dip in profits, Ryanair's chief executive Michael O'Leary announced that the airline was making changes, as O'Leary put it, to 'Stop unnecessarily p***ing people off'. There would be a 'new, cuddly Ryanair'. In the wake of public anger over exorbitant bonus payments to bank executives, it was reported in 2014 that, for the Co-operative Bank, the 'challenge is to marry Co-op values with a new and better functioning business model'. And in the same sector, following the revelations that HSBC's Swiss subsidiary had helped its clients to avoid tax, the Financial Conduct Authority affirmed the importance of 'firms operating with the *right culture* across all of their operations' (Mason and Treanor, 2015, emphasis added).

organizational culture: the basic pattern of shared assumptions, values and beliefs governing the way employees in an organization think about and act on problems and opportunities

These illustrative cases relating to some of Britain's biggest organizations have brought to the fore the importance of culture for organizational practices and performance. Indeed, the culture dimension is central to all aspects of organizational behaviour (Alvesson, 2013). The way things are done in a hospital trust is an example of **organizational culture**, as is predatory sexual harassment, or espousing the value of ethical investment, or a belief that university students are not 'customers'. Redesigning complex organizations to create new hierarchical structures and subunits (see Chapter 15), as well as installing new technology (see Chapter 16), sets the context within which people interact and work. However, the ways in which organizational actors and customers *experience* these formal structures of organizational charts and technology is shaped by the social and psychological scaffolding that governs what they believe, what they value and what they see as legitimate (Schneider, 2000). These informal structures at work that shape or even determine the customary ways of doing things can be thought of as the organizational 'culture'.

The concept of organizational culture has been around for over six decades and has become a pivotal concept in organizational studies over the last two decades. Implicitly, its importance in the mainstream literature is an acknowledgement of the imperfections of formal arrangements and practices, and, as such, culture has been cast in the role of transforming the workplace to unlock the 'holy grail' of individual and collective employee commitment, and to achieve extraordinary performance (Ashkanasy et al., 2002).

Cultural change has historical roots in *paternalistic management practices*, which are partly based on the premodern assumption that employers have a moral responsibility to look after the welfare of their workers. Always a minority phenomenon, well-known examples of companies with paternalistic cultures include Cadbury, Pilkington, Rowntree and Marks & Spencer in the UK, and IBM in the USA (Ackers and Black, 1991). As a contemporary strategy for managing people, the concept of organizational culture became prominent in North American literature in the 1980s, in response to a particular interpretation of the perceived competitive advantages of Japanese 'ways of doing'. Japanese management scholarship led to a recognition that national and organizational culture mattered (Ouchi, 1981; Wicken, 1987).

In globalized post-industrial capitalism, it has become common parlance that competitive advantage or superior services stem from mobilizing the creativity of employees and from managing cultural factors to create 'organizational ambidexterity', a metaphor describing organizations' ability to both explore new compe-

Source: Image Source

plate 60 Ryanair decided to make changes to its organizational culture in order to become 'more cuddly' and offer better customer service.

tencies and exploit existing competencies in the workplace. The introduction of cultural ambidexterity requires a fundamental change of 'management mentality', that is, from top-down leadership to bottom-up employee engagement and learning (Wang and Rafiq, 2014: 71).

This chapter begins with a brief discussion of national culture before examining the concept of organizational culture: what it is, how it manifests itself within the organization, and its importance for understanding organizational behaviour, employee development and employee performance. We look at the three levels of organizational culture and notions of dominant culture, cultural diversity, subcultures and countercultures. We examine mainstream and critical theoretical perspectives on organizational culture, and evidence of the culture–performance link, and finally consider whether managers can change the culture of their organization.

National culture and culture dimensions

culture: the knowledge, language, values, customs and material objects that are passed from person to person and from one generation to the next in a human group or society

The word '**culture**' originates from the Latin *cultura*, meaning cult or worship. Cult members believe in specific ways of doing things, and thus develop a culture, which safeguards those beliefs. Partly because of its historical development, but mainly because of its use in several distinct intellectual disciplines, Raymond Williams believes culture to be one of the several most complicated words in the English language (Williams, 1983). The complexity of its modern usage can be appreciated when, in everyday speech, we refer to painting, music, ballet or the opera as 'high culture', and activities such as football, rock music and Hollywood film-going as 'popular culture' or 'mass culture'. When anthropologists and sociologists use the term, it includes all such social activities, but far more than is implied in everyday conversation.

Within the discipline of sociology, culture and socialization are key theoretical concepts. The concept of culture is perhaps easier to grasp by a description than a definition. For example, suppose a young female student from Iran has joined your university class. It is immediately evident that her culture is different from yours: you can see it in her clothing. Although she will be at least bilingual, you can hear it in her language, and in class discussions you may hear her express different beliefs and values about the world. All these behaviours and social traits are indicative of culture. Anthropologists have produced scholarship that describes culture as comprising three levels: inner patterns of thought and perception; deep-level verbalization (for example, the syntax in language) of which a native speaker is seldom aware; and visible patterns of behaviour, which are also culturally determined.

Cultural variations among human beings are linked to different types of society. You might think of culture as a societal tapestry of woven threads that makes each society unique, or as a national characteristic – English as opposed to Indian or Chinese, for example. Alternatively, you might think of culture as multlayered, like an onion (see Figure 17.1).

To understand a culture, you have to unpeel it layer by layer. On the outer layer are the surface manifestations of culture, also called 'observable culture', such as the Georgian architecture of the feted New Town in Edinburgh, a monument of imperial wealth. Buildings, museums and public transport, visible physical objects, are expressions of deeper, invisible values in society. Culture therefore includes the physical objects or **artefacts** that are passed on from one generation to the next, as well as the complex social heritage of symbols, values, patterned ways

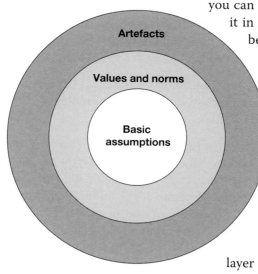

Figure 17.1 A model of national culture

artefacts: the observable symbols and signs of an organization's culture

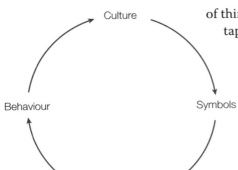

Figure 17.2 The influence of culture on human behaviour and behaviour on culture

Source: From ADLER. *International Dimensions of Organizational Behavior*, 5E. © 2008 South-Western, a part of Cengage Learning, Inc. Reproduced by permission. www.cengage.com/permissions

of thinking, feeling and learned behaviours shared by a people. This complex social tapestry is shown in Figure 17.2 (Giddens and Sutton, 2013).

Individuals and groups in a human society express culture and its normative qualities through symbols; these are ideas that convey meaning, such as language and mathematical signs. Symbols allow people to classify experiences, and to learn and to generalize from them. These symbols in turn determine the values individuals hold about the world around them. Values are a fluid set of concepts that can change over time and can be both unconsciously and consciously held. For example, over the last 50 years, 'British values ... have shifted from Protestantism, racism and the stiff upper lip to multicultural tolerance and emotional self-revelation' (Pittock, 2014: 16). These values in turn shape the form of human behaviour that is considered most appropriate and effective in different social situations. Values permeate political discourses. For example, it is argued that the growing divergence in social and economic values between Scotland and England gave rise to the nationalism of the 1980s and influenced debate in the 2014 Referendum on Scottish devolution (McCrone, 2001; MacWhirter, 2013a). *Mores* (the Latin word for 'customs', pronounced MOR-ays) are *norms* that specify social requirements. For example, if a woman walks down the street in Tehran without a head-cover, she is violating the mores of that society. People are usually punished when they violate norms. The strongest norms are *taboos*. When a person violates a taboo, for example incest, it causes revulsion in most communities, and the punishment is severe.

VISIT THE *ONLINE RESOURCE CENTRE* AT HTTPS://HE.PALGRAVE.COM/COMPANION/BRATTON-WORK-AND-ORGANIZATIONAL-BEHAVIOUR3/ FOR FURTHER INFORMATION ON CULTURE AND LEADERSHIP AND A DESCRIPTION OF ORGANIZATIONAL CULTURE.

mores: norms that are widely observed and have great moral significance

taboos: mores so strong their violation is considered to be extremely offensive, unmentionable and even criminal

socialization: the lifelong process of social interaction through which individuals acquire a self-identity and the physical, mental and social skills needed for survival in society

This social inheritance, or social ecosystem, of any society is called culture. The notion that this social inheritance is *learned* by each generation is captured by Hofstede's (2010) definition of culture: 'it is the collective programming of the mind'. One of Britain's leading cultural theorists, the late Stuart Hall (1932–2014), offers a complex conceptual prism to explain the temporal enigma of multicultural European modernity. For Hall, Western culture can only be understood in the context of European colonialism, twentieth-century post-colonialism and the global economic development, consciousness and humanity of late modernity. Such a position emphasizes that culture is not static, but malleable, in the making:

> Culture is not a matter of ontology, of being, but of becoming ... [it] is not just a voyage of rediscovery, a return journey. It is not an 'archaeology'. Culture is a production. (Hall, 2005: 556)

The process by which each generation, or other new members of society, are 'programmed' or learn the culture of their society – the process by which they acquire their social traits and learn the behaviour and ways of thought – is called **socialization**.

Shared values and behaviour, although socially embedded, often change over time and generations. During the last 200 years, the period of modernity, both Western and Eastern societies have witnessed tremendous social changes caused by industrialization and the secularization of thought, which has changed values, beliefs and patterns of behaviour. Thus, the continually changing patterns of individual and collective behaviour eventually influence the society's culture, and the cycle begins again. Anthropologists suggest that a national culture has five defining features: it is learned, cumulative, transmitted, shared and a product of human interaction (Ravelli, 2000). These five defining aspects of national culture are important in understanding the complexity of culture generally and how people maintain their social uniqueness over time.

Source: Donald Maclellan/Getty Images

Plate 61 The sociologist and cultural theorist, Stuart Hall, observed that national culture is not a matter of being, but of becoming.

plate 62 In many Muslim countries, if a woman walks down the street without a head-cover, she is violating that society's mores.

Source: Digital Vision/Nick White

Many scholars have written about the variation in cultural traits between Western and Eastern societies. Perhaps the best known in the field of management is Geert Hofstede's (2001) research, which measured national culture in terms of values, rituals, heroes and symbols in 64 countries. The manifestations of culture are portrayed by Hofstede, in a similar way to the layers of culture already described, as the layers of an onion, indicating that values represent the deepest (closest to the centre) and symbols the most superficial manifestations of culture, with heroes and rituals in between. Hofstede's data, based on one global corporation, IBM, initially identified four independent dimensions of national cultural differences:

1 *power distance* – the extent to which the less powerful accept that power is distributed unequally (see Chapter 14)
2 *individualism* versus *collectivism* – the degree to which members of society are integrated into communities
3 *masculinity* versus *femininity* – the general acceptance of sex-biased values and the sexual division of labour
4 *uncertainty avoidance* – which refers to society's tolerance for ambiguity and uncertainty; this ultimately deals with the search for truth.

The cross-cultural management literature examines the implications of different national cultures for managing people at work. For example, in Maslow's hierarchy (see Chapter 6), self-actualization is seen as the supreme human need. Drawing on Hofstede's cultural analysis, however, this assumption presupposes an *individualist* culture in which the ties between individuals are loose and everyone is expected to look after themselves and their immediate family. In the West, assertiveness has been much advocated as a way for women to communicate, but communication scholars point out that the effectiveness of this means of communicating is culture related (see Chapter 11).

VISIT THE *ONLINE RESOURCE CENTRE* AT HTTPS://HE.PALGRAVE.COM/COMPANION/BRATTON-WORK-AND-ORGANIZATIONAL-BEHAVIOUR3/ FOR FURTHER INFORMATION ON HOFSTEDE'S WORK AND FOR A CRITIQUE OF HOFSTEDE'S METHODOLOGY AND CORE ASSUMPTIONS.

The work of Geert Hofstede and his core assumption that countries have a singular national culture has attracted considerable criticism. The empirical basis for his assertion that a national population shares a singular culture is based on a statistical averaging of the quantitative data – the survey responses from IBM's employees. An average of personal values claiming to measure the values of a national culture is about as meaningful as an average of personal income. As has been well established elsewhere, in the same way that there is a wide variance in personal income in any population, so there is wide dispersion in the personal values of that population (McSweeney, 2002).

Among the developed countries in the global economy, few are likely to exhibit a single cultural orientation, and they are more likely to have a plural orientation with hyphenated identities such as African-American, Chinese-Canadian, Anglo-Indian and so on. The empirical evidence at the centre of Hofstede's claims is problematic, and the term 'national culture' is misleading. Nonetheless, deep cultural undercurrents structure human behaviour in subtle but highly regular ways, and managers and other employees carry their cultural heritage and ethnicity to the workplace (Adler and Gundersen, 2008). Research on the relationships of national cultures, based mainly on values, to organizational cultures are, however, 'loose ones' (Hofstede et al., 2010). Horwitz and Budhwar (2015) emphasize the need for a more pluralistic and critical perspective on the culture–organization interface. They argue that management theory is, in many ways, impoverished because too many management scholars have tended to focus on the wholesale adoption of Anglo-American management practices. In such areas as cross-cultural management, they suggest that scholars would benefit from considering post-colonial theory (Said, 1978/1995), which provides 'a critical perspective on cultural interaction on [organizational] power dynamics' (Horwitz and Budhwar, 2015: 44). Sociological and anthropological research demonstrates that cultural diversity is a global fact of human life. In the face of such plurality, will this diversity be reflected at work?

Understanding organizational culture

Organizations are embedded within national cultures and, according to Hofstede (2001), the national environment partly shapes the cultures of organizations, but national cultures and organizational cultures are not identical. The notion of organizational culture is a complex concept because it lends itself to very different uses. In the literature, the terms 'corporate culture', 'organizational culture' and 'organizational climate' are common. The distinction between corporate culture and organizational culture is that the former is devised and transmitted down to the subordinates by management executives as part of a strategy of mobilizing employee commitment, and emphasizes actors as 'culture-takers'. Organizational culture, on the other hand, is learned and shared among the organization's members. It is a product of members' creativity and emphasizes actors as 'culture-makers' (Linstead and Grafton-Small, 1992).

organizational climate: describes the dimensions of the organization that can be measured with relative precision, such as its structure and leadership

Schneider (2000) notes that 'organizational climate' is the 'elder child' in cultural scholarship, and some culture researchers use the terms 'culture' and 'climate' interchangeably. Others refer to the disagreements over whether the two concepts are distinguishable constructs as 'paradigm wars' (Payne, 2000). Organizational culture and **organizational climate** are two complementary constructs, but they reveal overlapping nuances in the social and psychological life of complex organizations. The former tends to take a sociological approach, using qualitative methodology derived from anthropology, to examine symbolic and cultural forms of organizations. Climate researchers, however, attempt to measure individuals' perceptions of autonomy, leadership, growth or whatever, and the meaning they assign to them, using quantitative methods derived from the nomothetic traditions of organizational psychology. The distinction between culture research and climate research lies in the different methodological traditions, what they consider to be significantly meaningful and their agendas. The sociologist Martin Parker argues that the psychological treatment of culture largely reflects 'a neo-human relations agenda' (2000b: 132). (For a discussion on epistemological and ontological issues, see Chapter 1, and for an introduction to the human relations movement, see Chapter 3.)

VISIT THE *ONLINE RESOURCE CENTRE* AT HTTPS://HE.PALGRAVE.COM/COMPANION/BRATTON-WORK-AND-ORGANIZATIONAL-BEHAVIOUR3/ TO FIND OUT MORE ABOUT THE DIFFERENCES BETWEEN ORGANIZATIONAL CLIMATE AND ORGANIZATIONAL CULTURE.

Writers have offered various definitions of organizational culture (Table 17.1), and a synthesis of these definitions captures most of its essential elements. It is about the importance of the shared values, beliefs and language that shape and perpetuate organizational reality, so that employees behave predictably to achieve the organization's goals.

To help us understand organizational culture, we need to examine its parts, even though any organizational culture is greater than the sum of these parts. Drawing on the work of Edgar Schein (2010), Figure 17.3 shows three fundamental levels of organizational culture: artefacts, values and basic assumptions. Again, using

Table 17.1 Some definitions of organizational culture

Social or normative glue that holds an organization together … The values or social ideals and the beliefs that organization members come to share. These values or patterns of beliefs are manifested by symbolic devices, such as myths, stories, legends and specialized language. (Smircich, 1983: 34)
Talking about organizational culture seems to mean talking about the importance for people of symbolism – of rituals, myths, stories and legends – and about the interpretation of events, ideas, and experiences that are influenced and shaped by the groups within which they live. (Frost et al., 1985: 17)
The shared beliefs and values guiding the thinking and behavioral styles of members. (Cooke and Rousseau, 1988: 245)
Culture is 'how things are done around here'. It is what is typical of the organization, the habits, prevailing attitudes and grown-up pattern of accepted and expected behaviour. (Drennan, 1992: 3)
For me values are less central and less useful than meanings and symbolism in cultural analysis … Culture is not primarily 'inside' people's heads, but somewhere 'between' the heads of a group of people where symbols and meanings are publicly expressed, for example in work group interactions, in board meetings but also in material objects. Culture then is central in governing the understanding of behaviour, social events, institutions and processes. Culture is the setting in which these phenomena become comprehensible and meaningful. (Alvesson, 2002: 3–4)

the onion metaphor, these three dimensions of organizational culture could be imagined as the layers of an onion, with artefacts representing the less abstract superficial, and basic assumptions representing the deepest, manifestations of organizational culture, with values lying in between. But here we can also use an alternative image, the iceberg (Figure 17.3). The uppermost sub-triangle might be viewed as the 'tip of an iceberg' representing observable parts of organizational culture, which are embedded in shared values, basic assumptions and beliefs that are invisible to the human eye (signified by the part of the iceberg below sea level). Each level of culture influences another level.

The first (uppermost) level shown in Figure 17.3 comprises visible culture, the *artefacts* and material objects such as buildings, technology, art and uniforms that the organization 'uses' to express its culture. For example, when a company uses only email for internal communication, the cultural message is that ICT is a highly valued resource. Displaying art on the office walls signals to members and visitors

stop...

Looking at Table 17.1, does it seem like your university might have a culture? How does this differ within and between the different faculties, schools or departments within the university?

...and reflect

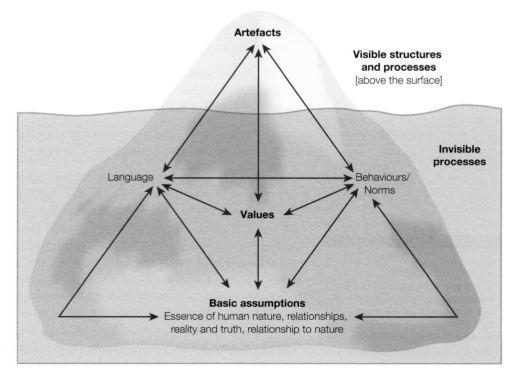

Figure 17.3 The three levels of organizational culture

Source: PhotoDisc

plate 63 Rituals are collective routines that 'dramatize' the organization's culture. For example, the office party can be viewed as a ritual for integrating new members into the organization. Ceremonies are planned and represent more formal social artefacts than rituals, for example the 'call to the bar' ceremony for graduating lawyers.

rituals: the programmed routines of daily organizational life that dramatize the organization's culture

ceremonies: planned events that represent more formal social artefacts than rituals

that creating a stimulating cultural context in which employees can explore ideas and aesthetics is highly valued (Harding, 2003). Other examples are the wearing of a professorial gown in universities and the judge's wig in British law courts.

The visible culture also includes *language*. How managers describe other employees is an example of using symbols to convey meaning to each other. For example, Wal-Mart refers to its employees as 'associates', and at Disneyland they are known as 'cast members'. Social *behaviour* is another aspect of observable organizational culture and includes **rituals** and **ceremonies**. Formal rituals and celebrations are collective routines that 'dramatize' the organization's culture. For example, the office party can be viewed as a ritual for integrating new members into the organization. Planned ceremonies represent more formal social artefacts than rituals, for example the 'call to the bar' ceremony for graduating lawyers.

The second level of organizational culture comprises shared work-related *values*, which are not visible, but which we recognize as an influence on patterns of observable behaviour at work. For example, in healthcare, standard medical practice is influenced by a belief in evidence or a commitment to patient-centred care. In many universities, practice is influenced by the espoused value of 'We are a teaching-centred institution.' Espoused values related to employment possess six characteristics:

1 They involve moral or ethical statements of 'rightness'.
2 They pertain to desirable modes of behaviour at a given point in time.
3 They directly influence employees' behaviour and experiences, and act as significant moderators of behaviour.
4 They are typically associated with strategic goals and address questions like 'What are we doing?' and 'Why are we doing this?'
5 They guide the selection and evaluation of members.
6 They may vary in respect to male/female, demographic and cultural differences (Warr, 2008), for example a belief that women in the armed forces should not engage in combat roles.

The term 'shared' in cultural analysis implies that organizational members are a whole. Each member has been exposed to a set of dominant values, although not every member may internalize and endorse them.

VISIT THE *ONLINE RESOURCE CENTRE* AT HTTPS://HE.PALGRAVE.COM/COMPANION/BRATTON-WORK-AND-ORGANIZATIONAL-BEHAVIOUR3/ FOR FURTHER INFORMATION ON EDGAR SCHEIN.

stop...

Think about your own university or college. As a student, do you expect a student-centred focus? Are teaching and support staff helpful? Do teaching staff focus primarily on teaching or on research? Try to answer in terms of observable artefacts, shared values and basic assumptions.

...and reflect

The third level of organizational culture relates to *basic assumptions*, which are invisible, unconscious, taken for granted, difficult to access and highly resistant to change. These are the implicit and unspoken assumptions that underpin everyday choices and shape how members perceive, think and emotionally react to social events. For example, in healthcare, assumptions about the relative roles of doctors and nurses, about patients' rights or about the sources of ill-health are purported to underpin everyday decisions and actions (Davies, 2002). The basic assumptions/ beliefs about human nature, human relationships, people's relationship to nature and how the world works form the base from which employees, who as social beings enter the workplace with life histories and experiences, build their values of how the world *should* be. As Schein (2010) observes, the occupations that govern work practices, for example, in the arenas of the NHS and universities, are themselves cultures with learned and shared values and tacit assumptions that shape behaviour. Thus, we know that doctors and academics strongly value autonomy, and practices are often contested to maintain control and authority over knowledge domains (Swan et al., 2002). In terms of influencing change, this makes certain kinds of reform in the NHS or universities more difficult.

Perspectives on organizational culture

As we discussed in Chapter 1, social scientists adopt different perspectives on the study of workplace behaviour. The genealogy of the different perspectives on organizational culture is rooted in classical sociological theory. The work of Durkheim and Weber is representative of the canonical literature on understanding behaviour in organizations as a social and cultural phenomenon. Here, for example, Weber stresses that individuals behave 'not out of obedience, but either because the environment approves of the conduct and disapproves of its opposite, or merely as a result of unreflective habituation to a regularity of life that has *engraved itself as a custom*' (Weber, 1922/1968: 312, emphasis added). From the 1950s, influential management writers, such as Peter Drucker, have stressed the importance of *integrity* of character and *values* in the practice of management.

Contemporary culture analysis can essentially be divided into what by now should be two familiar schools of thought: managerialist and critical. The managerialist-oriented perspective on the topic is functionalist, in that theorists in this school stress the value of culture from the premise that it can play a role in building organizational consensus, building harmony and improving performance. Organizational culture is viewed as a *variable* – an attribute that an organization possesses or '*has*', and as such can be produced by senior managers (Smircich, 1983). The critical-oriented school, on the other hand, focuses on describing and critically explaining cultural processes – how culture emerges through day-to-day social interaction, power relations, the shaping of communities of practice, emotion and norms of workplace behaviour. Viewed through a sociologist's lens, culture is something that a work organization '*is*' and emphasizes the symbolic, conscious and subjective aspects of the workplace, the role of culture in strengthening management control over employees, and the interrelationships between organizational cultures *inside* and social inequalities *outside* the workplace.

The managerialist (functionalist) perspective on organizational culture

functional theory: a sociological perspective emphasizing that human action is governed by relatively stable structures

The **functionalist** perspective is based on the assumption that the organization is a stable, orderly system that serves specific functions. Organizational culture, in terms of attitudes, beliefs, values and norms, is generated and managed according to organizational goals and needs. Cultural analysis from a functionalist perspective is based on the theoretical insights of Emile Durkheim, whose sociological studies focus on the integrative and social stabilizing ability of culture.

Neo-management theorists primarily understand organizational culture as a unifying phenomenon in which cultural processes can create organizational stability and consensus, focusing on how culture can be managed and disseminated downwards by senior management. Thus, mainstream theorists are said, in Martin's words, to follow an '*integration*' perspective. In this sense, management-inspired cultural processes and interventions attempt to mitigate the many forms of the ever-present conflict that arise from managing the labour process. This approach focuses on building a culture that binds members together around the same core values, beliefs and norms, which are considered to be prerequisites for achieving strategic goals. For integration or functionalism theorists, culture is conceptualized as organization-wide 'agreement with values' espoused by senior management

Source: Brand X Pictures

Bullying as a management strategy

Although 83 per cent of UK organizations have anti-bullying policies, at least one-third of workers report being bullied (Tehrani, 2005), with managers perpetrating the majority of workplace bullying in the UK (Beal and Hoel, 2011). Mainstream organizational behaviour research tends to consider the costs of bullying to the employer. For example, workplace bullying in Australia is thought to cost between $6 and $13 billion a year. This includes lost productivity, litigation, turnover and health costs (Friedland, 2014).

But if bullying is so expensive, why do employers allow it to continue? An intriguing hypothesis is that it actually provides a significant benefit to employers:

> bullying may be seen as a tool of management control, one which can sit alongside other control methods and approaches and can supplement them, though in developed economies it may be seen as the big stick often held in reserve. (Beale and Hoel, 2011: 10)

The notion that an organization may condone (or even require) bullying sits uneasily with much of conventional management theory, which implicitly casts organizations as rule abiding and benevolent. Yet history demonstrates that employers have used whatever means are necessary to convert workers' potential to do work into actual work.

Recently, a number of jurisdictions, including Sweden, France, Norway, Denmark and the Netherlands, as well as Australia, have enacted rules to regulate bullying. New South Wales enacted laws on January 1, 2014 to allow bullied workers to complain about their employers. Current anti-bullying laws better protect regional workers in New South Wales, who were 'nearly at breaking point', and some of whom were suicidal, the Australian Workers Union said (Begley, 2014).

The discussion of suicide is not simply union hyperbole. In February 2014, two managers in Sweden were convicted of driving a co-worker to suicide by bullying him at work. Both were handed suspended sentences, with one manager being fined

50,000 kronor ($7,700) and the other 23,000 kronor ($3,500). The case stemmed from the death of Lars Persson, who committed suicide in 2010 at the age of 53, bringing an abrupt and unexpected end to his nearly three-decade career as a social worker employed by Krokom municipality (*The Local*, 2014). A few years later, 300 shipyard workers in Canada walked off the job after a co-worker committed suicide in late 2013 – allegedly after being bullied by management (Devet, 2013).

Although workplace bullying is not new, the recent spate of anti-bullying legislation is. It is interesting that employers have long been prohibited by governments from subjecting workers to physical hazards, yet only recently have governments been prepared to recognize psychological hazards, such as workplace bullying. This suggests that workplace hazards are, to some degree, socially constructed. As norms – including organizational culture – shift, so too do behaviours that are considered valid and invalid.

> **Stop!** Have you ever experienced or witnessed bullying in the workplace, at school or in a social club? What do you believe motivated the bullying? And how did it affect the victim? Did the employer or other authority figure intervene effectively? Why or why not?

Sources and further information
Beale, D. and Hoel, H. (2011) 'Workplace bullying and the employment relationship: exploring questions of prevention, control and context', *Work, Employment and Society*, 25(1), pp. 5–18.
Begley, R. (2014) 'New laws a boost for the bullied, says union', *Daily Liberal*, January 8. Available at: www.dailyliberal.com.au/story/2009784/new-laws-a-boost-for-the-bullied-says-union/ (accessed February 24, 2015).
Devet, R. (2013) 'Irving Shipyard workers walk off the job after co-worker's suicide', Halifax Media Group, November 28. Available at: http://halifax.mediacoop.ca/story/irving-shipyard-workers-walk-job-after-co-workers/20090 (accessed February 24, 2015).
Friedland, H. (2014) 'Billion dollar bullying problem', *Brisbane Times*, June 3. Available at: www.brisbanetimes.com.au/small-business/managing/billion-dollar-bullying-problem-20140603-39fcv.html (accessed February 24, 2015).
Tehrani, N. (2005) *Bullying at Work: Beyond Policies to a Culture of Respect*. London: Chartered Institute of Personnel and Development.
The Local (2014) '"Bully" bosses convicted for co-worker's suicide', *The Local*, February 19. www.thelocal.se/20140219/bully-bosses-convicted-for-co-workers-suicide (accessed February 24, 2015).

Note: This feature was written by Bob Barnetson, Associate Professor of Labour Relations, Athabasca University, Canada.

(Martin and Frost, 1996). The notion of 'cultural engineering' – creating the 'right' kind of culture to align with strategic goals – is seen as a 'lever' for fostering commitment and loyalty in the workforce.

Searching for excellence and innovation

A cluster of functionalist writers put forward ideas about causality by attempting to demonstrate positive linkages between the 'right' corporate culture and performance (Deal and Kennedy, 1982; Ouchi, 1981; Peters and Waterman, 1982). Within this genre, Peters and Waterman's influential pop-management book *In Search of Excellence* is probably the best well-known example of the 'has' school. These gurus view culture as an elixir that binds together specific human qualities and skills that lead to organizational excellence and success. They write:

What our framework has really done is to remind the world of professional managers that 'soft is hard.' It has enabled us to say, in effect, 'All that stuff you have been dismissing for so long as the intractable, irrational, intuitive, informal organization *can* be managed ... you [are] foolish to ignore it.' (Peters and Waterman, 1982: 11)

What constitutes the 'right culture' for excellence is a matter of debate. A popular approach in functionalism is *contingency* theory (see Chapter 12). Based on the belief that senior managers need to consider a range of different external and internal variables when deciding what kind of culture best fits their particular organization, Deal and Kennedy (1982) and Handy (1993) identify a fourfold typology of culture in which the choice of each culture depends on an assessment of organizational situations. Contingencies that have been identified as important include level of risk, the size and design of the organization, ownership and governance, market preference, technology, national culture and the need for innovation.

For functionalist theorists, leaders can create 'strong' corporate cultures. Leadership studies consider change as a situation-driven contingency that moderates the effectiveness of certain leadership styles. It is suggested that transformational leadership is especially effective in shaping and guiding organizations towards innovation-oriented cultures. Thus, in Rosabeth Moss Kanter's *The Change Masters*, she notes that employees:

> find their stability and security not in specific organizational arrangements but in the *culture* and direction of the organization. It requires that they feel *integrated with the whole* rather than identified with the particular territory of the moment, since that is changeable. (Kanter, 1982, emphasis added)

In turn, the 'right' culture is counterposed to bureaucratic cultures. In Hammer and Champy's *Reengineering the Corporation*, the authors contend that 'the reigning values and beliefs in an organization must support the performance of its design process' (Hammer and Champy, 1993: 81). Similarly, in Champy's (1996) *Reengineering Management*, it is posited that 'values are our moral navigational devices', and that for real change to occur, leaders need 'cultural warriors' at every level of the organization to communicate new values to their peers (p. 79).

Whereas modern management gurus like Ouchi, Peters and Waterman, Deal and Kennedy, and Hammer and Champy focus on values that foster 'strong cultures', Handy and Kanter are more sensitive to the complexities and problematic aspects of culture (Table 17.2).

Table 17.2 Typologies of organizational culture

Deal and Kennedy's ideal types	Handy's ideal types
Process culture This type is concerned with ensuring that members follow uniform procedures, and is associated with low-risk hierarchical organizations; for example, hospitals	*Role culture* This type is mechanistic and highly formalized, abounds with rules, and is dominated by authority and the hierarchical structure; for example, utility services
Work hard/play hard culture This type is team- and customer-focused and stresses 'fun' at work; for example, Google	*Person culture* This type centres around 'star' performers who are loosely attached to the organization; for example, barristers, surgeons and architects
Bet-your-company culture This type characterizes high-investment, long-term, highly technical members; for example, the NASA space agency	*Power culture* This type exhibits a single power source, with centralized policy and decision making; for example, a family-owned, family-operated company
Macho culture This type is characterized by fast decision making and high risk; for example, traders in merchant banks	*Task culture* This type is organic, informal and product and project-based, the opposite of role culture; for example, firms of management consultants

Subcultures and countercultures

As is the case with anthropological studies of national cultures, contingency literature draws attention to cultural heterogeneity. Martin (1992) refers to such studies as the 'differentiated' perspective. A large complex organization, for example British Airways, might have one dominant culture expressing senior management's core values, but they also have sets of *subcultures* typically defined by professional occupations, spatial separation and departmental designations. These work groups might share a distinctive set of values, beliefs and norms that differ in some significant way from that of the organization's dominant values and philosophy. The concept of cultural heterogeneity has been applied to distinctions ranging from professional identities associated with engineers, artists, healthcare practitioners, researchers and ethnic- and religion-based groups, to small reservoirs of employees presumed to be marginalized from the larger organization as a result of distinctive work paradigms or the particular demands of the occupation. A subculture emerges to bind members working intensely together, as a means of coping with common frustrations concerning the demands of emotional labour, or as a way to preserve their distinctive identity (Bolton, 2005).

In the context of healthcare organizations, a recent study revealed that 'complex multiple cultural values are often hierarchical and are commonly interpreted in ways that ascribe differentiated, fragmented and collective meaning' (Morgan and Ogbonna, 2008: 61). For example, healthcare professionals may collectively interpret the espoused value of providing the 'best possible care' for their patients. But professional groups will perform the delivered 'care' differently, each with distinctive interpretations of what 'best care' means. For doctors, it may mean eradicating the cause of illness, whereas for occupational therapists it may mean helping patients to achieve greater mobility and improved quality of life (Fitzgerald and Teal, 2004). In contrast, a macho and highly aggressive subculture might exist among male manual workers doing repetitive, mundane work or among abattoir workers slaughtering animals (Ackroyd and Crowdy, 1990; Collinson, 1988). The analyses of subcultures reveal a wide variation in values, norms and assumptions both within and across subcultures, which might cause conflict – but this is a normal part of organizational life.

A sociologically informed analysis of culture acknowledges the existence of *countercultures* in organizations. As others have observed, these create their own form of organizational reality through a subculture that actively opposes the dominant values and norms (Jones et al., 2004). For example, a change in status of an education institution, from a college to a university for example, may produce countercultures: a particular teaching faculty may strongly reject university values on research and a 'publish-or-perish' culture. In the private sector, mergers and acquisitions may produce countercultures. There may be a 'clash of corporate cultures' when the values, beliefs and norms held by the members of an acquired organization are inconsistent with those of the acquiring organization. The debate surrounding the existence of subcultures and countercultures emphasizes the complexities and interwoven character of organizational culture, and avoids an overly static and monolithic picture of everyday organizational life.

Critical perspectives on organizational culture

Although all critical theorists share a similar view on the role of culture – that values and norms are deeply embedded but can change over time – they typically see organizational culture through somewhat different lenses as they are guided by different theoretical perspectives in their research. What do these critical perspectives tell us about organizational culture? In contrast to the mainstream functionalist

stop...

Does a complex organization like the England's NHS have subcultures? What are the management implications if core subcultures exist?

...and reflect

perspective that understands culture as something that an organization '*has*', critical perspectives proceed, as we saw earlier in the chapter, from the root-metaphor idea that the organization '*is*' a culture. Therefore, critical-oriented perspectives promote a view of organizations as manifestations of human consciousness, as a source of power and as a socializing and controlling force, and are studied in terms of their networks of symbols and shared meanings. Moreover, advocates of the 'is' view of culture are likely to play down the culture–performance outcomes in favour of a more general understanding and reflection as the major emphasis of cultural studies (Alvesson, 2013). Here, we look at three critical-oriented perspectives: the symbolic-interactionist, the conflict and the feminist. These perspectives will serve as alternative lenses through which to see organizational culture.

The symbolic-interactionist perspective

symbolic interactionism: the sociological approach that views society as the sum of the interactions of individuals and groups

The **symbolic-interactionist** approach, using a micro-level analysis, understands organizational culture as the sum of all its members' interactions (see Chapter 3). In this school of thought, culture plays the role of a vehicle for shared meaning (hence 'symbolic'), and is produced by workers and managers in face-to-face encounters (hence 'interactionist') as they go about their everyday workplace activities. Culture is constructed by organizational actors and reproduced by the networks of symbols and meanings that workers and managers share, and that make shared social behaviour possible. The analysis of organizational culture can therefore occur through studying observable artefacts, language, action and the beliefs and values of organizational members.

In the realm of shared *artefacts*, displayed mission statements, framed photographs of individuals and ceremonies, technology, paintings and sculptures are all manifestations of culture. Space is an element of culture. For example, if senior management has allocated privileged parking within the organization's boundary while others park outside in the street, the cultural message is that hierarchy and status are highly valued by the organization. Symbolic interactionists explore how *language* and emotion are used to communicate effectively in order to make social action possible. Shared stories, myths and legends serve to construct a common ground for understanding social behaviour. For example, an account of a dramatic event in the past history of the company serves to create a shared meaning of how workers are expected to handle problems in the present. Also scrutinized is shared social *action*. Rites commonly found in the workplace are those of acceptance (for example, an invitation to the office party), of recognition (for example, the employee of the month award), of conflict (for example, a disciplinary hearing) and of severance (for example, dismissal to emphasize unacceptable behaviour).

Source: © iStockphoto.com/JoePitz

plate 64 If senior management has allocated privileged parking within the organization's boundary while others park outside in the street, the cultural message is that hierarchy and status are highly valued by the organization.

Symbolic interactionists also examine shared *beliefs* and *values*. Beliefs are the dominant assumptions of the organization concerning the society and how it works, while values contain an 'ought to' implicit in them. In organizational talk, the assertion of 'values' is omnipresent, either of legislative provisions not always heeded (for example, antidiscrimination laws) or of espoused values not adequately funded. Groups in the organization will clothe their proposals around 'values' rhetoric to elevate these demands over more pedestrian ones, for example diverting resources from one department to another – from production to employee training – because a core 'value' is continuous work-related learning. This approach to cultural analysis highlights how members produce and reproduce the culture of an organization through day-to-day social interaction. However, symbolic interactionism tends to underemphasize how larger social structures cause disagreement on meanings.

The conflict perspective

conflict perspective: the sociological approach that views groups in society as engaged in a continuous power struggle for the control of scarce resources

Conflict perspectives are based on the assumption that conflict is a basic feature of organizational life as members seek to control scarce resources (Edwards, 1990). Unlike the integration perspective, critical theorists insist on treating conflict as a central concept in exploring how values, beliefs and norms develop to sustain the power and control of senior management. The conflict perspective sets out to develop an understanding of organizational culture by situating it in the context of capitalist relations of domination and control.

As early conflict theorist Karl Marx emphasized, ideas are the cultural constructs of a society's most powerful social elite (see Chapter 3). The creation of ideas is directly interwoven with work-related activity and the material interaction of people, the language of real organizational life. As Marx put it, 'The production of ideas, conceptions, of consciousness is, to begin with, immediately involved in the material activity and the material interaction of men [sic], the language of real life' (Marx and Engels, 1845/1978). Many conflict theorists agree with Marx's assertion

ideology: a term with multiple uses, but in particular referring to perceptions of reality as distorted by class interests, and the ideas, legal arrangements and culture that arise from class relations (a term taken from Marx)

that social elites use **ideology**, a non-material element of culture, to shape the thoughts and actions of members of other social classes – the common idea, for example, that an unfettered market can best decide society's economic priorities because 'Governments cannot pick winners' or 'What's good for Ford is good for America'. Public discourse often supports these views, since no other alternatives are debated or offered.

Conflict views on culture emphasize perpetual tension, conflict and resistance between different groups in the organization. This emphasis on a structured antagonism between 'capital' and 'labour', and concomitantly on managerial control, focuses on motive – the 'who' of power and the 'how' of employee commitment. It tends to dismiss conceptualizing organizational culture as the 'organization's personality' or as an overarching catch-all to describe 'the way we do things around here'. Instead, the focus is on how corporate culture attempts to generate *real*, as opposed to hollow, employee commitment and self-control by mobilizing values, beliefs and emotions. The study by Ray (1986) is an example of cultural control as an employment strategy:

> The top management team aims to have individuals possess direct ties to the values and goals of the dominant elites in order to activate the emotion and sentiment which might lead to devotion, loyalty and commitment to the company. (p. 294)

For Ray (1986), control by corporate culture did not rely on direct supervision, but primarily on 'soft' controls such as the acceptance of invisible espoused values and peer enforcement. It was the 'last frontier', in that a 'strong' corporate culture had enabled top management to generate employee emotion and commitment, at the same time internalizing control by fusing individual with corporate identity. Extant studies provide evidence that attempts to 'manage' culture frequently degenerate into the enforcement of espoused behaviours (Ogbonna and Harris, 1998), Shared social activities outside the organization's space and time, such as weekend 'retreats' or social events for employees' families, expand cultural controls by integrating both manual staff and managerial employees, and developing a sense of community or 'family' through what Thompson and McHugh describe as a form of 'compulsory sociability' (Thompson and McHugh, 2009: 203).

Source: Brand X Pictures

'Farmers' wives' working at Wal-Mart

Why is the idea of culture so important to the understanding of organizational behaviour? One reason is because it encourages us to move beyond narrowly individualistic accounts of what happens in organizations. To recognize the importance of culture in organizations is to recognize that there is a 'supra-individual' level of reality – shared values, for example – that influences what people in organizations do.

It makes sense to think about the ways in which cultural values influence behaviour, but we should never lose sight of the fact that people vary in the ways they respond to cultural values and the extent to which they care about those values. Sociologist Margaret Archer develops this point in a series of monographs on the complex interactions between structural factors such as culture and another set of factors she groups under the heading 'agency' (the human capacity to act in, and on, the world). Given the powers and preferences that individuals bring to any given situation, they have the capacity to respond in various ways to different cultural values and different forms of cultural conditioning. We must take these variations into account when we develop cultural explanations of organizational behaviour.

Take the case of Wal-Mart, widely recognized as one of the most successful companies in the world. Critics have argued that Wal-Mart's success has come at the expense of some of its employees. A review of several major studies of Wal-Mart describes the 'harshness' of Wal-Mart's working conditions (compared with similar companies, such as Costco) and suggests that some Wal-Mart employees 'have … been subjected to relentless harassment' (Head, 2004: 4). Women are particularly likely to experience harassment at Wal-Mart, and the reviewer, Simon Head, refers to evidence from 'the Dukes case, a class-action lawsuit brought in 2001 by six female employees and named for one of the six, Betty Dukes' (p. 4).

Head goes on to offer the following cultural explanation of the problematic features of the Wal-Mart approach to management:

> Sex discrimination at Wal-Mart has a long history. Bethany Moreton, a doctoral candidate in history at Yale, has stressed the importance of Wal-Mart's origins in the rural, small-town culture of the Ozarks, where Wal-Mart's corporate headquarters at Bentonville, Arkansas, is still located. In the early years some of the women who worked at Wal-Mart

were the wives of local Ozark farmers, and the women's earnings were a meagre supplement to their husbands'. The women in the Dukes case say that some of their store managers still often think of them as resembling those farmers' wives. Ramona Scott, a Dukes case petitioner who worked for Wal-Mart in the 1990s, was told by her store manager that 'men are here to make a career and women aren't. Retail is for housewives who just need to earn extra money'. (pp. 4–5)

This review of research on Wal-Mart contains a factual claim: the reviewer notes that some studies have discovered instances of harassment and discrimination at Wal-Mart. The review also makes reference to an explanatory claim: some researchers who study Wal-Mart have used a cultural explanation to account for documented cases of harassment and discrimination. In this context, the cultural explanation – the specific reference to rural, small-town culture – may seem persuasive.

However, bearing in mind Archer's more nuanced approach to culture, it is worth questioning whether all, or even most, managers at Wal-Mart see female employees as farmers' wives and therefore as deserving of the second-class status such a characterization supposedly entails. Perhaps this is typical only of male managers in certain geographical regions and would not be found, for instance, among female managers in Alaska.

Consider another possibility: perhaps many managers do not see women this way but are 'forced' to treat their employees harshly for other reasons. For example, earlier in the review, Simon Head notes that Wal-Mart typically fails to provide managers with the budgets they need 'to staff their stores at adequate levels' (Head, 2004: 3). Perhaps the harsh treatment of employees is more the result of pragmatic managers seeking to keep their jobs than it is the result of the managers' internalization of rural, small-town values.

To conclude, the idea of culture provides a valuable perspective on organizational behaviour, but we must be careful not to portray people as 'cultural dopes' whose behaviour is wholly determined by the cultural values to which they have been exposed.

> **Stop!** Develop a cultural explanation of organizational behaviour, but be sure that your explanation recognizes the agency of the people whose behaviour you are explaining.

Sources and further information

Archer, M. (2000) *Being Human: The Problem of Agency*, Cambridge: Cambridge University Press.

Head, S. (2004) 'Inside the Leviathan', *New York Review of Books*, 51(20), pp. 1–8.

Note: This feature was written by David MacLennan, Assistant Professor, Thompson Rivers University, Canada.

Around this thesis has developed a body of literature which argues that cultural control overlaps and exists alongside, rather than replaces, more traditional forms of management control strategies, such as bureaucracy (see Chapter 15), new technology (see Chapter 16) and human resource management (HRM) practices (see Chapter 9). Weberian internal bureaucratic control focuses on rules, internal labour market structures and reporting hierarchies. Computer-based technology can be used for the surveillance of employees by recording their attendance, output or productivity and time logged after hours as measures

sexual desire or innuendo than about control and male domination. Studies of the gendering of organizations emphasize that gender, sexuality and sexual harassment make an overwhelming difference to the reality of organizational life for women (Hearn et al., 1989; Mills and Tancred, 1992). Gender analysis questions research findings and analysis that segregates studies of organizational culture from those of gender divisions in the labour market, patriarchal systems, the processes of male institutionalized power, workplace inequality and 'dual-role' work–family issues.

Observing Indian culture in 2009, journalist Stephanie Nolen illustrates the interrelation of a patriarchal system, sexuality and gendered work organizations. She describes the culture shock for a Western woman moving to work in India like this:

> I am reminded more incessantly of the sexism here. It started when I signed our lease, and had to provide either my father's name or my husband's. I've had to adjust to the fact that every repair person, shopkeeper and many potential staff members utterly ignore anything I say to them, waiting for the voice of authority, my male partner, to tell them what they really ought to do. (Nolen, 2009: A13)

National culture, with its societal value system and norms of behaviour, and organizational culture are deeply intertwined in a **dialectical** relationship: each is fashioned and refashioned by the other. In an important way, by including the gender–sexuality paradigm in the study of the organizational culture, feminist writers have pushed the boundaries of organizational behaviour by examining the people who are deemed to be the 'recipients' of organizational culture. As sociologist Judy Wajcman (1998) observes in her insightful study, the individual, work groups and the modern organization are not gender neutral. Indeed, more controversially perhaps, she presents a powerful argument for gender-inclusive cultural theories if we accept her main premise that 'gender is woven into the very fabric of bureaucratic hierarchy and authority relations' (Wajcman, 1998: 47). The feminist perspective shares with the differentiation approach concerns with inequality and redressing discriminatory workplace practices.

Each of the four major ways of thinking about organizational culture we have examined involves different assumptions. As a result, each perspective leads us to ask different research questions and to view the realities of organizational life differently. Table 17.3 reviews the four perspectives in terms of three characteristics: (1) their primary level of analysis; (2) the primary concern of the theorists associated with each; and (3) how each understands the nature of organizations. These major perspectives can be used as a theoretical compass for navigating through the myriad competing views found in the organizational culture literature.

dialectic: refers to the movement of history through the transcendence of internal contradictions that in turn produce new contradictions, themselves requiring solutions

stop...

Looking at Table 17.3, what are the key differences between the 'has' perspective and the 'is' perspective on organizational culture? Which of these perspectives do you consider most useful for understanding the nature of organizations and shared behaviour, and why?

...and reflect

Table 17.3 The major perspectives on organizational culture

Perspective	Analysis level	Primary concern	Nature of organizations
Functionalist	Macro level	Maximizing efficiency/loyalty	A system comprising interrelated parts/groups that work together with no inherent conflict. Power is not important. Culture is something that an organization 'has'
Symbolic-interactionist	Micro level	How culture is learned/equity	Organizational culture is constructed and reproduced by symbols and shared meanings in interaction with members. Culture is a metaphor for the organization. It is something that an organization 'is'
Conflict	Macro level	Elimination of power imbalances	The organization is characterized by economic/power inequality/conflict over scarce resources. Culture is fragmented in complex and conflicting ways. It is something that an organization 'is'
Feminist	Macro level *and* micro level	Elimination of sexual inequality	The organization is characterized by pervasive sexuality/power inequality/sexual discrimination. Culture is fragmented, something that an organization 'is'

Managing cultures

Much management 'integrationist' theory identifies a robust corporate culture as an important factor in promoting work motivation. Proponents advocate that senior managers abandon bureaucratic 'command and control' regimes for a 'strong' corporate culture to win the commitment of their workers, much like a magnet will realign a chaotic collection of iron filings into a discernible pattern. A strong culture can help to activate latent employment-related values, which workers possess but have lain dormant or discouraged. In this narrative, corporate culture functions as the ultimate form of management control: self-control consistent with management expectations. Thus, developing a 'strong' culture in which members develop a fierce loyalty to the company is seen as central to modern management for its potential to close the 'gap' in the employment relationship and thereby release workers' creative capacity (Kirkpatrick and Locke, 1996).

As discussed in Chapter 5, it is considered central to 'soft' HRM practices to manage the *psychological contract*, to change the employment relationship from a binary, hierarchical, low-trust and low-commitment relation to a participatory, high-trust and high-commitment one, and to capture, manage and control emotion in the organization (Bolton, 2005). Drawing on concepts from the sociologist Erving Goffman from the 1950s and 60s, work that draws analogies between the interactions among individuals and what goes on in drama, a robust corporate culture provides normative and behaviour 'scripts' for employees when management seeks to capture and manage emotional labour and introduce new initiatives, such as high-performance work systems and team-total quality control (Thompson and Findley, 1994).

Ways of managing culture

Cultural theorists and managers alike have tried to identify effective ways to change manifestations of organizational culture: visible *artefacts*, including language and shared behaviour, and work *values*, which are invisible but can be espoused. This section reviews strategies of planned culture change in three ways:

- reframing social networks of symbols and meanings through artefacts, language, rituals and ceremonies
- initiating new HRM practices to change behaviours and norms
- introducing leadership processes that aim to create the motivation to change behaviour, with a particular emphasis on their symbolic content.

All three strategies implicitly adhere to Kurt Lewin's (1951) three-stage model of planned change, which involves 'unfreezing' present inappropriate behaviours, 'changing' to new behaviour patterns and positive reinforcement to 'refreeze' the desired changes (see Chapter 18).

Reframing of social networks and meanings

The reframing of social networks of symbols and meanings to strengthen commitment to the organization and espoused work-related values is manifested through changes in physical artefacts ranging from displaying a framed copy of the organization's new mission statement, and redesigning departments to create 'open-plan' office spaces or work teams with greater autonomy and new work uniforms, to establishing a research and development centre to emphasize the importance of research and innovation. Many organizations have reframed their shared symbols and meanings by changing their language to promote the customers' values and quality. Stories and storytelling are pervasive in culture management. Stories often contain, explicitly and implicitly, arguments for and against work-related values;

Source: Digital Vision

plate 66 Some universities reinforce a 'research culture' where promotion and pay are tied to research productivity rather than teaching students.

commodification: in Marxist theory, the production of goods and services (commodities) for exchange in the marketplace, as opposed to the direct consumption of commodities

they help members to locate work experiences and to develop new insights, which in turn promote sense making or sense giving and new ways of behaving (Jabri, 2012; Taylor et al., 2002). Notable examples of language and narrative strategies to achieve cultural change are British Airways 'Putting People First' and Hewlett Packard's 'HP Way'. Others include the 'corporate' university, where students are increasingly conceptualized as 'clients' and professors as 'service providers' who must 'brand' their institutions and sell their 'products' to 'clients', as do car and beer manufacturers (Gingras, 2009).

Rituals aim to change behaviour. For example, the 3M Corporation has its own version of a Nobel Prize for innovative employees. The general gist of this change strategy is that, properly introduced, the reframing of cultural artefacts is seen to be potentially very effective in disconfirming the appropriateness of employees' present behaviours, providing employees with new behavioural models and affirming new ways of doing things. The reframing of social networks of symbols and shared meanings to influence an organization's culture is nevertheless problematic when employees' knowledge activities and analyses (largely hidden to managers) judge that there is a mismatch between management-espoused rhetoric and management's actions (Whiteley et al., 2013).

Human resource management practices to change culture

The values that employees bring into the workplace may be identified through the selection process, and it is also posited that a particular culture can be created by a galaxy of HRM practices that select, retrain, reward or replace employees. Human resources selection techniques are an important means of 'knowing' and managing a culture change (Townley, 1994). Personality- and competency-based tests are the psychological calculation of suitability that enables managers to find the 'best person' for the new culture. Changing the culture requires employees to formally and informally learn, accept and identify with espoused values (Whiteley et al., 2013). This includes a process of socialization, through which employees learn the symbols and meanings and the shared practices: 'The fact that organizational cultures are composed of practices rather than values makes them somewhat manageable: they can be *managed* by changing the practices' (Hofstede, 1998b: 240, emphasis added).

The performance appraisal system is a systematic HRM mechanism that is used to classify and rank employees hierarchically according to how well they have integrated the newly defined set of beliefs, values and actions into their normal ways of doing things. The new espoused work values are incorporated into appraisal systems to allow employees to be compared with each other, to render them 'known' and to reinforce the desired change. The reinforcement effect is further secured when appraisals are linked to performance-related rewards. For example, given the general **commodification** of education, new contracts in university education reinforce a 'research culture' when promotion and pay are tied to research productivity rather than teaching. Such HRM initiatives help with 'cultural doping' so that employees exhibit new behaviours and attitudes (Alvesson and Willmott, 1996). Thus, a metaphorical 'glue' bonds employees and encourages each to internalize the organization's culture because it fulfils their need for social affiliation and identity.

Leading cultural change

The role of leadership in generating employees' support for cultural change is rooted in the leadership and management learning literature (see, for example, Bass and Riggio, 2006; Filstad, 2014; Schein, 2010). Cathrine Filstad's (2014) findings highlight, for example, that leaders and managers need to engage on two fronts: (1) formal and informal communication with their employees, and (2) interpretations and expectations of how to change work practice in order to develop their own sense making and help others at all levels in their own sense making processes. There are sociologically informed writers who recognize that cultures can be changed to match strategic goals. In contrast to the crudely prescriptive functional approach, Morgan, for example, cautiously argues that:

> Managers can influence the evolution of culture by being aware of the symbolic consequences of their actions and by attempting to foster desired values. But they can never control culture in the sense that many management writers advocate ... An understanding of organizations as cultures ... [does] not always provide the easy recipe for solving managerial problems that many managers and management writers hope for. (2006: 152)

In Chapter 18 we examine in detail different strategies for implementing successful cultural change that meets 'complexity with complexity' (Bate, 1995).

Is managing culture desirable?

Assuming that senior managers are able to transform organizational cultures, is this necessarily desirable? If the central premise of the 'has' theory is that ideas within a social work group are homogeneous, unified and uncontested, a strong culture can be a double-edged sword. It can give members an organizational identity, facilitate collective commitment, provide social stability and influence behaviour without the need for bureaucratic controls. If fundamental changes are needed, however, a strong corporate culture can actually be an impediment to creative thinking, to informal learning, creativity and innovation, and to change, and may thus undermine organizational excellence and success. The learning-creativity paradigm as a decisive source of competitive advantage is based upon spontaneity, irrational and idiosyncratic rather than conventional ideas and solutions, risk taking and rule breaking; it celebrates the creative potential of deviant thinking and action (Bratton and Garrett-Petts, 2008).

The much-vaunted 'learning organizations' in contemporary managerial lexicon meet the learning goals only if learners engage in critical reflection and open dialogue activities that may be considered deviant in organizations attempting to create cultural homogeneity (Fenwick, 1998). The current managerial and political infatuation with Richard Florida's concept of 'creative economy' must be squared with the complexities of managing the 'inherent tensions' between learning-creativity and control (DeFillippi et al., 2007). Furthermore, a strong corporate culture can undermine effective decision making because it encourages the phenomenon of group conformity or groupthink (see Chapter 10). Thus, although prescriptive literature presents organizational culture as a variable that can be manipulated at will to produce ideal types of coherence and integration to 'fit' new corporate aims, reservations exist on the appropriateness of such a strategy.

Evaluating cultural change strategies

Much cultural analysis is framed within a culture–performance relationship in which a 'strong' culture increases commitment, great loyalty to the organization and better all-round performance. Despite the fact that the culture–performance link has been studied from a multitude of different angles, demonstrating a causal relationship between a strong corporate culture and business performance has proven problematic (Sackmann, 2012). To say that culture and performance are correlated requires the measurement of particular attributes of one variable against particular attributes of the other. In addition, correlation in itself does not constitute a causal relationship between the two variables, although this is one criterion of causality. The methodology for ensuring high internal validity would ideally permit a calculation of how different cultures – 'weak' versus 'strong' – affect organizational performance while controlling the other factors that might influence those performance outcomes. The data must demonstrate the extent to which a stable group of employees have internalized the new 'ways of doing' and value demands, and the extent of the successful socialization of new members into these values, compared with a particular set of performance variables over a period of time.

These measurement challenges underscore the importance of the statistical concepts of **reliability** and **validity**, which raise questions concerning the appropriateness of 'culture change' and performance measures. For example, there is the challenge of isolating the external variables. Exchange rates can, for instance, significantly affect the financial bottom line, which makes it difficult to measure accurately the impact of a culture change. To be confident about the culture–performance link, we need credible evidence and a theory about how much of the variance can be explained by the culture factor. Otherwise, as two researchers have admitted, 'We cannot be sure of the extent to which the companies we studied were actually successful in creating that commitment or whether that commitment contributed to their success. All we can say is that the managers in question reported that their efforts … produced a significant improvement' (Martin and Nichols, 1987: ix).

The arguments around lack of rigor in research methodology have been well rehearsed (Anthony, 1994; Bratton and Gold, 2012; Ogbonna and Wilkinson, 1990; Sackmann, 2012). A small sample size, the exclusion of unfavourable data and citing corporate leaders as incontrovertible evidence of a culture–performance linkage is evidence of allegedly deficient research. When CEOs project an image of the organization via their espoused values to the outside world (for example, the researcher), the image and the values may be inconsistent with what they truly value – referred to as enacted values – and what internal stakeholders experience. In this respect, given the dynamics between employee insiders and community outsiders, incongruence between the corporate culture (or image) projected outwards and what is fed back into the organization is likely to breed cynicism, because the openly espoused values do not match the values and norms of the organization (Herrbach and Mignonac, 2004).

In addition, it must be kept in mind that individuals within the same workplace will not necessarily internalize the culture of their workplace in the same way, and predictions of a 'strong culture' creating commitment and motivating one employee do not necessarily work for all employees. Reviewing the extant studies, Sackmann (2012) concludes that even though a direct link between a strong corporate culture and good performance can be observed, 'the link may not always be direct' (p. 213), and that the culture–performance relationship needs further systematic research. Thus, the evidence for a positive culture–performance link is tenuous. Indeed, it is so deficient that some have argued that it should not be dignified with serious attention (Willmott, 1993).

The most sceptical detractors argue that organizational culture *as a whole* cannot be 'created, discovered or destroyed by the whims of management' (Meek, 1992: 209). Organizational culture is embedded in potent informal shared interactions and norms. Hugh Willmott (1993) – a deflater of the 'balloons of academic beliefs' – argues that resistance to strong cultures, or what he calls 'corporate culturalism', is found among powerful professional groups with considerable autonomy over how they perform their work. For example, a study found that a strategy for cultural change that focused on the 'bottom line' and expected engineers to 'sell their services to clients' caused many to resist and threaten resignation (Schein, 2004). Resistance to strategies for cultural change has also occurred in universities,

reliability: in sociological research, the extent to which a study or research instrument yields consistent results

validity: in sociological research, the extent to which a study or research instrument accurately measures what it is supposed to measure

healthcare and the BBC in the UK. This concept of 'misbehaviour' (see, for example, Karlsson, 2012) emphasizes that acts of resistance to new cultural demands can be less overt, less familiar and barely observable to the 'outsider'. And in what Sharon Bolton (2005) describes as 'small spaces of resistance', employees' misbehaviour is changing from the familiar acts of soldiering and absenteeism towards more subtle acts of resistance that are far more difficult for managers to manage.

Not surprisingly therefore, the critical school tend to be highly sceptical about claims of managing cultures and the causal links between culture and performance, regarding such claims as naive, unethical and questionable. Moreover, a strong corporate culture does little to alter the nature of the employment relationship, at least not in any meaningful way. The preoccupation with culture may obscure enduring structural antagonism and conflict. It does nothing to obviate the need for top management to try to reduce labour costs, to intensify the pressure of work and, sometimes, to render employees redundant (Edwards, 1990).

The binary conflict of interest between capital and labour that exists within a 'negotiated order' of mutual cooperation and combinations of values and norms suggests that the significance of organizational culture cannot be grasped unless it is related to structures of power within a context of market exigencies. In other words, culture can never be wholly managed, argue detractors, because it emerges from complex processes involving how employees construct their sense of identity in ways that are beyond management's control. Erving Goffman captures the scope for misbehaviour as well as indifference to values and the efficacy of culture change strategies:

> We find that participants decline in some way to accept the official view of what they should be putting into and getting out of the organization ... Where enthusiasm is expected, there will be apathy, where loyalty, there will be disaffection; where attendance, absenteeism; where robustness, some kind of illness; where deeds are to be done, varieties of inactivity ... Wherever worlds are laid on, under-lives develop. (Goffman, 1961: 267)

These arguments stress that people's work values are shaped by outside variables such as class, gender, race/ethnicity, disability and profession or trade union. At the very best, culture change interventions are only successful at the observable behavioural level rather than the subconscious level (Ogbonna, 1992).

Finally, adding to the complexity of managing culture is the omnipresent Internet. It has, for example, been argued that the Internet adds both new operational capacities and a 'space dimension' that affects organizational culture in new ways (Ogbonna and Harris, 2006).

IN THE EBOOK ACCESS THE **CRITICAL INSIGHT** ON 'THE CHALLANGES OF MEASURING ORGANIZATIONAL CULTURE'.

Chapter summary

- In this chapter, we have explored the nature of organizational culture – a unique configuration of shared artefacts, common language and meanings and values that influence ways of doing things in the workplace. The culture of an organization influences what employees should think, believe or value in this social discourse.

- The belief that organizational culture can be produced and managed has become closely associated with organizational redesign and management theories related to people management , the management of emotional labour and transformational leadership.

- Three fundamental levels of organizational culture comprise visible artefacts (buildings, technology, language and norms), underpinned by values, which are invisible, and basic assumptions, which are also invisible, unconscious and resistant to change.

- We explained that culture analysis can be divided into two schools of thought: managerialist and critical. The managerialist perspective is functionalist in that it stresses that culture can play a role in building consensus and harmony, and emphasizes how culture can improve performance. It views organizational culture as a *variable*: it is something that an organization '*has*' and, as such, can be produced and managed.

- The prescriptive literature tends to present too uniform a view of organizational culture. Alternative approaches point out the existence of *subcultures* and *counterculture*. These concepts are important if we believe that organizations consist of individuals and work groups with multiple sets of values and beliefs.

- The critical perspective focuses on a sociological concern to describe and critically explain cultural processes, how culture emerges through social interaction, power relations, social inequalities, influencing communities of practice, emotion and norms of individual and group behaviour. Viewed through a sociologist's lens, culture is something that a work organization '*is*'.

- The critical literature emphasizes the symbolic and subjective aspects of the workplace, the use of corporate culture as a soft control to strengthen management's position, and the relationships between social inequalities and patriarchal systems *outside*, and work socialization and behaviour *inside*, the workplace.

- We have discussed how national culture and organizational culture are deeply intertwined, each influencing the other and with the latter embedded in society. Gender refers to culturally specific patterns of human behaviour and is culturally learned or determined. Unarguably therefore, gender is a central facet of organizational analysis. Yet standard accounts of organizational culture have tended to neglect how gender, patriarchy and sexuality in society and in workplaces influence the dynamics of organizational culture.

- This chapter described a model for culture change. We emphasized that managers must be aware of the complexities of cultures. Finally, we discussed the problem of a strong corporate culture undermining decision making because it may encourage conformity or groupthink.

IN THE EBOOK ACCESS **WEB BASED ASSIGNMENTS** TO APPLY YOUR LEARNING.

Chapter review questions

1 What is meant by organizational culture, and how does it relate to national culture?
2 What are the three levels of culture, and how do they operate?
3 Review the 'mainstream' and 'critical' perspectives on organizational culture described in this chapter. Discuss the perspectives that you and other students find appealing and plausible. Explain your reasons.
4 What mainstream interventions have been used for changing

or reinforcing organizational culture? What are the strengths and weaknesses of each?
5 What impact do cultural values and expectations about gender have upon the design and operation of organizations, and how, in turn, does this impact on gender?
6 To what extent, if at all, do notions of masculinity and femininity reinforce or challenge traditional notions of organizational culture?

Further reading

Aaltio, I. and Mills, A. J. (2002) *Gender, Identity and the Culture of Organizations*, Routledge: London.

Alvesson, M. (2013) *Understanding Organizational Culture* (2nd edn), London: Sage.

Anthony, P. D. (1994) *Managing Culture*, Milton Keynes: Open University Press.

Dennison, D. R. (1996) 'What is the difference between organizational culture and organizational climate? A native's point of view on a decade of paradigm wars', *Academy of Management Review*, 21, pp. 619–54.

Edwards, D. (2011) *I'm Feeling Lucky: The Confessions of Google Employee Number 59*, London: Allen Lane.

Ehrhart, M. G., Schneider, B. and Macey, W. (2014) *Organizational Climate and Culture*, New York: Routledge.

Kramer, M. (2010) *Organizational Socialization*, Cambridge: Polity Press.

Martin, J. (2002) *Organizational Culture: Mapping the Terrain*, Thousand Oaks, CA: Sage.

McSweeney, B. (2002) 'Hofstede's model of national cultural differences and their consequences: a triumph of faith – a failure of analysis', *Human Relations*, 55(1), pp. 89–118.

Ogbonna, E. and Harris, L. (2006) 'Organizational culture in an age of the Internet: an exploratory case study', *New Technology, Work and Employment*, 21(2), pp. 162–75.

Parker, M. (2000) *Organizational Culture and Identity*, London: Sage.

Schein, E. (2010) *Organizational Culture and Leadership* (4th edn), San Francisco, CA: Jossey-Bass.

Taras, V. Steel, P. and Kirkman, B. (2011) 'Three decades of research

on national culture in the workplace: do the differences still make a difference?', *Organizational Dynamics*, 40(3), pp. 89–198.

Wang, C. L. and Rafiq, M. (2014) 'Ambidextrous organizational culture, contextual ambidexterity and new product innovation: a comparative study of UK and Chinese high-tech firms', *British Journal of Management*, 25, pp. 58–76.

Willmott, H. (1993) 'Strength is ignorance, slavery is freedom: managing culture in modern organizations', *Journal of Management Studies*, 30(5), pp. 515–52.

Chapter case study: Changing the University of Daventry's culture

The setting

The UK higher education sector generally is facing uncertainty about a continuing national demand for higher education as the level of unemployment, caused by the global economic recession, is increasing. Other challenges facing higher education are changes to student fee regimes, changing political agendas and public funding, as well as the unpredictable demand from international students. The increase in student fees has sharpened students' focus on the value they receive from their universities. Combined with an increase in the number of new universities

entering the sector, and at least a short-term reduction in the number of student applications, this will increase the pressure on universities to make their programmes and services more attractive to students while maintaining their academic standards. Globalization has created a booming market in higher education, and, aided by new technologies and the dissolution of national market borders, international partnerships have developed to create 'super' universities with overwhelming competitive advantages over individual locally or regionally focused institutions.

The problem

Located in central England, the University of Daventry, created from the amalgamation of Daventry College and Daventry Institute of the Arts, gained university status in 2009. Student numbers have grown steadily in the past few years, and it recruited to meet its target level for the first time in 2007/08. The headcount is 8500 full- and part-time students. The University's core activity is helping students to succeed. The vast majority of students attend the University to improve their career prospects or to change career. Daventry offers programmes across a comprehensive range of disciplines. Historically, it has been strong in business studies, but more recently technology, health studies and the creative programmes have experienced significant growth. Daventry has always attracted a high proportion of mature students, and its geographical location, discipline mix and entrance policies have made it attractive and accessible to a diverse student population drawn from larger cities such as Coventry, Leicester, Bedford and Peterborough. Mature students account for 50 per cent of full-time undergraduates, and international students account for 9 per cent of the student population.

The University of Daventry must reduce its dependence on undergraduate students funded by the Higher Education Funding Council for England, and create a more diverse portfolio of income streams without putting its core activity at risk. The University's strategic plan is to deliver high-quality, innovative, flexible programmes both on and off the campus. It also aims to work closely with employers, schools, colleges and agencies in the region to offer excellence in research, scholarship and knowledge transfer, which will shape and support cultural and economic development in support of a sustainable agenda.

The University of Daventry has a number of identifiable strengths: a significant proportion of teaching staff with professional qualifications and experience in addition to their teaching qualifications; an increasing number of programmes with professional accreditation, with recognition by over 30 professional bodies; and a high student satisfaction rate and reputation for excellent student support. The University also recognizes some

weaknesses, including a low proportion of teaching staff engaged in research, a poor track record in attracting students with high qualifications upon entry, and a low number of departments with strong working partnerships with relevant professional employers. In setting a course to achieve its new strategic vision, the University has established five strategic goals: (1) helping all career-motivated students to achieve their career aspirations; (2) consistently delivering academic excellence; (3) building the University's track record in applied research and innovation; (4) developing the capacity to generate income; and (5) contributing to the cultural and economic prosperity of the region.

The Ad Hoc Joint Committee established by the University's Board of Governors, which consisted of representatives from the teaching staff, deans, students' union and human resources, and was chaired by the President, Heather Gannon, was mandated to develop an action plan to build the University's track record in research (Goal 3). At the first meeting, James Duncan, the Human Resource Manager for University of Daventry, presented data on external research funding and research-based activities gleaned from the websites of six medium-sized universities. In closing his presentation, he remarked that although Daventry's teaching staff were highly committed to teaching, few engaged in research, and this was unlikely to change any time soon because 'There is no incentive to do so,' he said.

Bill Warren from the Department of Management forcefully countered, 'Teaching staff don't have time to do research', going on to say that 'The strength of the University lies in the quality of our teaching, not research.' Dr Michael Peters, from the Department of Applied Sciences, then responded to this by saying, 'High-quality teaching and research go together. If the University is to attract and retain students with high qualifications on entry, they must have the opportunity to become involved in research with their professors. When our teaching staff and their undergraduate students learn with each other and from each other, the result is powerful.'

A perceptive contribution came from the mature undergraduate student representative, Alex Boxall: 'Students are worried that if teachers are promoted on the books they write, they will be less interested in teaching.' Dr Margaret Cinel, Dean of Social Sciences and recently recruited from a large 'research-intensive' university, added that, compared with her previous institution, few of the teaching staff discussed research: 'This is a teaching institution, and if we are to achieve the strategic goals, we have to change the culture,' she said.

The President, Heather Gannon, summed up the contributions from around the table. Finally, following extended discussion, it was agreed that Dr Margaret Cinel, Dr Michael McLennan, Bill Warren, Alex Boxall and Mr James Duncan would draft a discussion paper for the next meeting on what could be done to change the culture at the University of Daventry.

The task

Workings in a small group, and role playing the five members of the subcommittee, prepare a report for the Ad Hoc Joint Committee drawing on the material from this chapter and addressing the following:

- What change interventions can senior administrators introduce in order to create a culture at the University of Daventry that is more aligned with the new strategic vision?
- What role, if any, should members of the Ad Hoc Joint Committee play in the culture change programme?

Sources and further Information

Edwards, D. (2011) *I'm Feeling Lucky: The Confessions of Google Employee Number 59*, London: Allen Lane.

Levin, J. S. (2003) 'Organizational paradigm shift and university colleges in British Columbia', *Higher Education*, 46, pp. 447–67.

Tam, P. (2007) Publish-or-perish culture at universities harms public good: scholar. *The Ottawa Citizen*. Available at: www.canada.com/ottawacitizen/news/story.html?id=6afef267-bb4d-4d06-a9f1-2078efe4416e (accessed March 2, 2015).

Willmott, H. (1993) 'Strength in ignorance, slavery is freedom: managing culture in modern organizations', *Journal of Management Studies*, 30(4), pp. 515–52.

Note: This case study was written by the author, John Bratton. Although the case draws upon material from UK and Canadian universities, the names of Daventry University and the individuals in the case study are fictitious.

VISIT THE *ONLINE RESOURCE CENTRE* AT HTTPS://HE.PALGRAVE.COM/COMPANION/BRATTON-WORK-AND-ORGANIZATIONAL-BEHAVIOUR3/ FOR A RANGE OF MATERIALS TO HELP YOU EXPLORE FURTHER AND REVISE CONCEPTS IN THIS CHAPTER.

chapter 18
Change

Chapter learning outcomes

After completing this chapter, you should be able to:

1 Understand the nature of organizational change and the importance of effective change management
2 Identify the main drivers of organizational change
3 Explain the sources of individual and organizational resistance to change and approaches to overcoming it
4 Understand the advantages and limitations of change management strategies
5 Explain the nature of organizational learning and development, and their connections to change strategies
6 Explain how the concepts of power, knowledge and insecurity can be an issue in the analysis of the relationship between human behaviour and organizational change

introduction

In 1988, Rose Forgrove, a company near Leeds, England, that engineers automatic packaging machinery for the food, drinks and pharmaceutical industries, was at the forefront of team-based production. At the time, it was considered avant-garde. The essence of the Rose Forgrove project was that the employees would be organized into work teams, technically called cellular technology, and undertake self-inspection of their work, known as total quality management. In addition, to avoid waste, teams were to make the parts and machinery only to order – just-in-time production. In cooperation with the trade unions, the management redesigned jobs so that team members became multiskilled and made most of the decisions that had previously been made by supervisors. The transformation of Rose Forgrove was written up as an example of Japanese management in Britain (Bratton, 1992). In 2001 the company was taken over and production transferred to Nottingham. Today, Rose Forgrove is a member of the Barry-Wehmiller group of companies, which is headquartered in South Carolina, USA. As part of the Barry-Wehmiller group, Rose Forgrove claims that its employees are empowered so that they can apply and develop their talents and feel a genuine sense of fulfilment. This example focuses on manufacturing, but knowledge workers are, of course, not immune from organizational change. In November 2011, the executive management at Macmillan, the publisher of this book,

announced to the workforce at a company meeting the closure of its Basingstoke and Oxford offices and the transfer of work to a new central 'campus' in London throughout 2013 and 2014. The essence of the Macmillan change project was to bring all the different parts of the company together in new, open-plan buildings in order to make communication between these parts more efficient and easier, and to foster innovation and creativity. Employees based at the Basingstoke and Oxford offices were offered financial support to help with the transfer to London.

Although different in scale and scope, Rose Forgrove and Macmillan illustrate several key issues and behaviour problems that confront organizational change efforts. First, and foremost, change has an enormous impact on how employees experience paid work, how work is designed, how employees are managed and how successful their organization is in achieving its goals. Change also puts a spotlight on employee voice. Planned change needs cooperation and emphasizes the need for responsive (ongoing) communication and consultation with employees who are affected by the process. The change often means that employees need to learn new skill sets, and it can also be extremely stressful. In addition, managers, as well as other change agents, have to be wholly committed and must exercise leadership.

This chapter is about organizational change. We begin by explaining the meaning of planned change, and then go on to review the structural forces that drive organizations to implement change. This is followed by a discussion of why people and organizations often resist change. We then move to management change strategies. We examine mainstream models of planned change and various processes to encourage and facilitate ongoing organizational learning and change.

The nature of organizational change

Since the beginning of modernity two centuries ago, social scientists have amassed a wealth of concepts and theories dealing with social change. Prompted by the need to explain the tsunami of change that swept across Europe in the mid-nineteenth century, efforts to understand the nature of social change have led social theorists to propose various theories of change. August Comte (1798–1857) offered a theory of change that was based on the development of human knowledge. Herbert Spencer's (1820–1903) theory of evolutionary change focused on population growth. Karl Marx's theory of social change was predicated on the underlying assumption that change is a continuing process arising from falling profits and the conflict between social classes, and that people can influence change through social action. This intellectual legacy continues to influence contemporary theories of social change.

Modern theories of change are, however, more complex. Change is often ubiquitous, uneven and partial; it may be regressive or destructive, or confused by 'cultural lag'. The cultural lag phenomenon is observed where there is a mismatch between the culture and developments in technology (Bell, 1973), for example using social media to tweet about legal proceedings or witnesses during a court trial. According to Sztompka (1993: 4), modern theories of change all contain three attributes: (1) difference, (2) at different temporal moments, and (3) between states of the same system. Scott and Marshall (2009: 72) offer the following definition of social change: 'a structured process in which it may be possible to identify a specific direction or tendency'.

In an age of global capitalism, we are all aware that society is facing new and unprecedented challenges, largely of our own making, and we have to cope with ongoing change. In turn, organizations of all kinds face a dynamic environment, and to survive in the long term, they must change and adapt to their environments. Over the last two decades, the pace and amount of significant, often traumatic, change in organizations has grown enormously (Kotter, 2012). In this section, we want to clarify what we mean by organizational change, identify different types of change and consider who is responsible for bringing about change in an organization.

'Change or lose the global race!' is the shared parlance of today's politicians and corporate leaders. But organizations change continuously, each and every day. The ongoing change that occurs in organizations is, for the most part, unplanned and unreported. The shorter, more traceable food supply chains at Tesco, Morrisons and Sainsbury's supermarkets after the 'horse-meat scandal' in the UK in 2013 provide an example of unplanned change. Far less common is significant planned change affecting the entire organization. By 'significant' we mean a fundamental overhaul of 'how things are done' in the organization. The introduction of work teams at Rose Forgrove is an example of planned change activities directed at responding to changes in the environment. Since an organization's success or failure is essentially due to the things that its managers and non-managers do or fail to do, planned change has two essential goals. First, it seeks to change employees'

transitional change: incremental change involving a planned and consistent movement from the current to the desired state

Plate 67 The ongoing change that occurs in organizations is generally unplanned and unreported. Less common is significant planned change that affects the entire organization. Shorter transparent food supply chains at UK supermarkets after the 'horse-meat scandal' of 2013 are an example of unplanned change.

Source: Brand X Pictures

behaviour. Second, it seeks to improve its competitive advantage or public services, as well as its ability to adapt to changes in its environment. The following definition seeks to capture the essence of the process:

> Organizational change is a structured process in which an organization shifts from its current state to some specific desired future state to improve the effectiveness of the organization.

Change management theorists have attempted to classify change into types (Jabri, 2012). Beckhard and Harris (1987) describe change in terms of 'transitional' versus 'transformational'. **Transitional change** utilizes existing capabilities and resources in the organization in order to manage an incremental movement from the current state to a new desired state through planned interventions in structures, processes and behaviours. Transformational change, in contrast, represents a radical shift in the way change is introduced and managed.

Transformational change questions the prevailing assumptions and values that are associated with the existing state, and involves modification of the mission and changes to the structure, systems, technology and culture that are driven from the top down. Weick and Quinn (1999) describe types of organizational change in terms of 'continuous' versus 'episodic'. A continuous change refers to alterations that are ongoing, evolving and cumulative. An episodic change occurs in distinct periods of time – for example, after ground-breaking technological change – and is therefore infrequent, discontinuous and intentional. Episodic change is often radical. Burke (2014) uses the terms 'evolutionary' and 'revolutionary' to describe the two types of change. An *evolutionary* change is gradual and, for the most part, unplanned by top management. A *revolutionary* type of change involves a significant change to the organization's mission statement, strategy, structure, leadership and culture. The distinction between different types of change is largely relative. The focus here is on goal-oriented, planned, **transformative change**. The reason for this focus is that the 'basics' of managing change among managers and leaders are said to be 'very poorly understood' (Kotter, 2012: 3).

transformative change: large-scale change involving radical and fundamental new ways of thinking and doing

Ways of thinking about organizational change

When theorizing about the change process, Jabri (2012: 8) emphasizes the need to use the dynamic verb 'changing' rather than the noun 'change' because the former better captures the notion of a continuous movement. In Chapter 17, the iceberg metaphor was used to characterize organizational culture. In a similar way, the metaphor of a river has been used to describe the fast-flowing state of change in organizations (Jabri, 2012). Imagine white-water rafting down a raging river in the Canadian Rockies that is made up of permanent white-water rapids, unseen rocks and calm eddies. To complicate things, the 10-metre raft is crewed by a small group of people who have never travelled the river before, and at intervals some crew members leave and others are added. Change is a natural state, and managing the raft is a continual activity.

Source: Getty

Plate 68 The river metaphor emphasizes the dynamic, unpredictable and unceasingly changing nature of the organization, as such change is an organization's permanent natural state.

Change management theories encompass a very broad range of organizational phenomena, including large-scale and small-scale changes, in the long term and short term, from the level of the multinational corporation (MNC) to the level of a work unit. Drawing on the concepts of 'hierarchy of corporate strategy', it helps to think of organizational change in terms of magnitude (Levy, 1986; Purcell, 1989).

Planned *'first-order'* change is concerned with infrequent, large-scale, long-term, multidimensional, multilevel, discontinuous, transformational change. Corporate restructuring in the form of downsizing, divestiture, relocation, bankruptcy and mergers and acquisitions (M&As) entails large-scale change. Restructuring involves a significant reduction in the resources that an organization allocates to research and development (R&D) activities, product markets or geographical locations in which it has previously engaged (Lazonick, 2006). During the spring of 2014, corporate restructuring was a major theme in the UK news media when US pharmaceutical giant Pfizer made a hostile £63 billion offer for the British-Swedish corporation AstraZeneca (Parker and Ward, 2014). The case illustrated an increasing trend towards the globalization of R&D and the contraction or 'hollowing out' of manufacturing by major industrial corporations in advanced Western economies (Milne, 2014). The 'ownerless corporation' of the new economy seeking to maximize share price and short-term profits (Hutton, 2014) is seen as the antithesis of the organizations spawned in the old economy, focused on long-term investment and innovation, that are the subject of organizational behaviour and change management theory (as shown in the Globalization and Organizational Misbehaviour feature).

Corporate strategy is closely tied to first-order change. First-order change constitutes a paradigm shift in thinking, doing, problem solving and organizational culture. Chief Executive Moya Greene is introducing first-order change at the UK's Royal Mail. Since privatizing the Royal Mail in 2013, she has been pursuing, among other things, radical changes in letter and parcel delivery processes to improve the Royal Mail's efficiency. In contrast, planned *'second-order'* change is continuous, is evolving and implies no fundamental shifts in the assumptions that employees hold about how the organization can improve its effectiveness. It may, however, involve changing the organization's definition of success, establishing new priorities or targets to change employees' behaviour, and appointing or promoting people to the senior management team. The introduction of low-carbon emission targets at Network Rail, Scotland, is an example of second-order change.

Processes classified as '*third-order*' change involve improving the present state through planned small-scale interventions using largely existing resources and capabilities. In some cases, it involves organizational changes driven from the bottom up (see, for example, Maimone and Sinclair, 2014). Examples include reallocating existing resources, a change in job design or an improvement in the unit's work schedule, knowledge creation and quality control. First-order, transformational change is far more challenging to implement than third-order change as it is more costly and time-consuming and affects a larger number of people in more significant ways. Second-order and third-order change often have unintended consequences or a 'domino effect'. The need for change in job design in a subunit or department might highlight the need for a change elsewhere in strategy, structure or technology as well as behaviour. The magnitude of organizational changes 'reflects the complexity of the situation and its dynamic' (Jabri, 2012: 18).

> ### stop...
>
> Before reading on, consider your own experience of organizational change. It could be in your school or part-time job, or the experience of a family member. What specific emotion and behaviour did you or others exhibit during the change process?
>
> *...and reflect*

The forces driving organizational change

Although it has become a cliché to say that 'change is constant', history reminds us that change has been a constant feature of modernity. However, taking a cue from Saul (2005), the historic truth about organizational change is that we cannot understand it if we accept what produced the need for it as an inevitable force rather the product of societal change. Karl Polanyi's book, *The Great Transformation* (1949), is about how the transformation caused by industrialization and the European Enlightenment changed not only entrepreneurial activity, but also, over time, society, by significantly altering us as individuals, our patterns of behaviour, our cultural values and how we see society and our place within it. Organizations are embedded in society (Maurice and Sorge, 2000) and are designed and developed on the assumption of continuity, to continue surviving and to last. The external environment is, however, volatile and the external forces driving organizational change are discontinuous and not interdependent, linear, homeostatic or highly predictable (Burke, 2014). Organizations encounter many external and internal forces that act as stimulants or triggers for change. Theorizing the organization as being 'embedded' in society offers an understanding of the external forces that signal the need for change largely by analysing the STEPLE – Social, Technological, Economic, Political, Legal and Ecological – context. The external forces for change were introduced in Chapter 1 and shown in Figure 1.3. What we present in this section is clearly not a complete picture. The discussion of the external and internal forces shown in Figure 18.1 has therefore, for reasons of space and to avoid repetition, to be minimal.

External forces for change

In a number of places in this book, we have identified external macro-forces that may trigger change. The macro-environment is highly complex and constantly changing, which requires STEPLE analysis (Frynas and Mellahi, 2011). In terms of the elements of STEPLE, Chapter 8 examined *social* and demographic changes affecting the nature of the European workforce. One key demographic trend identified in that discussion focused on workforce diversity and the dynamics of gender, race/ethnicity and management. Other demographic and social variables – an ageing population, attitudes toward obesity, attitudes towards organic food, work–life balance – suggest changes to which organizations have to adjust. The expansion of dual-income families and single-person households, for instance, has increased the demand for online grocery shopping, a social trend that is highly relevant to supermarkets. In 2014, it was reported that supermarket Morrisons' shrinking share of the market was due to its tardiness in introducing online shopping.

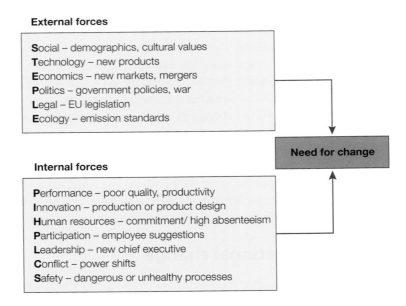

Figure 18.1 External and internal drivers of change

As outlined in Chapter 16, organizations are changed by the intended or unintended consequences of *technology* applied to production processes and/or product or service design. For instance, computer technology has transformed the way in which work and organizations are designed. In addition, the sophisticated 'smart' mobile phone has not only transformed personal communications, but also offers new ways to shop and carry out bank transactions.

Economics is a decisive force for change. We discussed the importance of globalization when we started our journey through this text. Joseph Stiglitz (2006) sees globalization as transforming every part of society and makes a compelling case to make it work by 'thinking and acting more globally' (p. 278). As European MNCs forge new markets and alliances with their suppliers, this spurs further changes. Heightened global competition from 'BRIC' and 'MINT' low-wage economies also means that organizations need to respond both to traditional competitors, domestic and foreign, and to small, entrepreneurial set-up firms with innovative products or services.

Alongside globalization, European and world *geopolitics* has undergone monumental change over the last 30 years. A few examples make the point here: the implosion of the Soviet Union, the reunification of Germany, the end of apartheid in South Africa, the eastward expansion of the European Union and the growing influence of the 'Green' movement. Government legislation or policy can produce organizational change too, for example changes to business policy such as the privatization of state-owned assets (for example, UK railways, gas and electricity services, and the Royal Mail) or, in the banking sector, the proposed market-share rules to encourage competition (Wintour, 2014). Social theorists acknowledge the role that political ideology plays in social change. Cliché has it that we live in a post-ideological age (Sandbrook, 2009), but ideology continues to run deep through the business and economic policies of Western governments. In the second half of the twentieth century, the ideologies of 'socialism' and 'social democracy' were designed to protect people against the vagaries of the market. Today, the ideology of neo-liberalist 'reform' means dismantling employee protections in a bid to reduce labour costs (Panitch, 2014). The ebbs and flows of the European political economy demand that every organization rethink its business or operations, and make significant changes in response to new political realities.

UK and European Union (EU) laws form the basis of *legal* pressures triggering change. Immigration controls, currently a major political issue in England, that occur across the EU impact on an organization's ability to hire new employees. Clearly, legal pressures and *ecological* changes are connected – as shown by the Waste (Scotland) Regulations in 2014 to encourage recycling, regulations to curb carbon emissions, the abolition of fossil fuel rebates that impacts on the biosphere when transport companies switch from diesel to eco-friendly electric buses (Wild, 2014), and organizations' investments in office insulation to save fuel and streamline energy usage (Jenkin, 2014). Legal changes can also bring about change by compelling organizations to operate within the biosphere's thresholds (Simms, 2014).

globalization & organization misbehaviour

Source: © Royalty-Free/Corbis

Pfizer's bid for AstraZeneca

MNCs such as Pfizer are the most public face of globalization. In the 1990s, the introduction of a single European currency created a wave of M&A activity in the European Union (Thun, 2011). The restructuring of an MNC through an M&A usually entails large-scale transformational change. A cross-border merger is a deal that combines two corporations from different countries to establish a new legal entity. A cross-border acquisition, on the other hand, is the acquisition of a local company's assets by a foreign MNC (Frynas and Mellahi, 2011).

There are three types of M&A: (1) *horizontal*, which involves two competing companies in the same industry; (2) *vertical*, which involves a merger between the organizations in the supply chain; and (3) *conglomerate*, which is a merger of two organizations from two unrelated industries (Frynas and Mellahi, 2011). The US pharmaceutical giant Pfizer's £63 billion bid for the British-Swedish corporation AstraZeneca is an example of a horizontal M&A. As Wood (2014: 17) observes:

> The controversial takeover of AstraZeneca by US drugs group Pfizer is to be investigated by MPs, who are being urged to take evidence from their chiefs amid fears the £63bn transaction could threaten the future health of the UK's science base. There are also concerns that Pfizer's main motivation is to use the deal to move its tax domicile to the UK, where the corporation tax rate is falling to 20% in 2015 compared with a US rate of up to 40%. Pfizer boss Ian Read told analysts the deal was an opportunity to 'get our tax rate down'. Analysts say Pfizer wants to get its hands on AstraZeneca's pipeline of new drugs.

The reported motives behind the merger resonate with Hopkins' (1999) thesis that M&As occur for strategic and economic motives, which include the desire to achieve economies of scale by joining together R&D facilities and eliminating duplicate resources (Frynas and Mellahi, 2011).

Mainstream research identifies risks associated with the M&A

strategy. Critical workplace scholars, on the other hand, identify consequences associated with M&As. In terms of the former, risk is associated with the misbehaviour of managers in the acquired organization. Managers may not, for example, internalize the new organizational culture, which will result in a weaker degree of managers' commitment to the new entity. In terms of the latter, for managers and workers alike, the economic consequences of M&As can be catastrophic, resulting in job loss. Other negative consequences may include major changes in autonomy and power structure. Wood (2014: 17) notes: 'AstraZeneca … employs 6,700 people in the UK. Three years ago Pfizer closed its world-renowned research laboratory in Sandwich, Kent, which triggered more than 1,500 job losses.' Marlano Mazzucato (2014: 42) also highlights the negative impact on society of the proposed mega-merger:

> Just like the banks, big pharma socialises the risk, but privatises rewards. The few drugs that are coming out would not have emerged without taxpayer-funded research. Yet the taxpayer then pays twice: first for the research then for the high prices, justified by the supposedly high risk that big pharma is taking on.

Stop! Imagine you are a middle manager at AstraZeneca facing the takeover by Pfizer. What consequences would there be following this M&A activity? Is there a gender or age difference in terms of such consequences? What would this tell you about the degree of alignment between your own interests and your employer's interests?

Sources and further information

Frynas, J. G. and Mellahi, K. (2011) *Global Strategic Management* (2nd edn), Oxford: Oxford University Press.

Hopkins, H. D. (1999) 'Cross-border mergers and acquisitions: global regional perspectives', *Journal of International Management*, 5, pp. 207–39.

Mazzucato, M. (2013) *The Entrepreneurial State: Debunking Private vs. Public Sector Myths*, London: Anthem.

Mazzucato, M. (2014) 'Big pharma relies on public money but shirks its obligations to society', *The Observer*, May 11, p. 42.

Thun, E. (2011) 'The globalization of production', pp. 283–304 in J. Ravenhill (ed.), *Global Political Economy* (4th edn), Oxford: Oxford University Press.

Wood, Z. (2014) 'Pfizer's bid for AstraZeneca under scrutiny', *The Guardian*, May 6, p. 17.

Note: This feature was written by the author, John Bratton.

Organizations not only react to external forces for change, but also try to anticipate and shape those forces in their own interests. Indeed, it is argued that real global power resides in MNCs such as Apple, BP, Google, Microsoft, HSBC and Goldman Sachs. Through their power, global corporations are able to challenge green levies, block restrictive business regulations and sidestep the EU rules to restrict bankers' executive bonuses in the face of hostile public opinion (Murden, 2014). Through SWOT (Strengths, Weaknesses, Opportunities and Threats) analysis, organizations and leaders generate knowledge to enable them to be proactive as well. Organizations are embedded in dynamic socioeconomic contexts, and therefore the major challenge for management is to develop the capacity to adapt as the contexts, challenges and opportunities change. Indeed, it is argued that the power of prime ministers and presidents has diminished in a global world. In order to anticipate the threats and opportunities, organizations need to focus not only on 'best practice', but also on 'next practice' to cope with new scenarios (Mohrman and Lawler, 2012: 42). Organizations also try to change their environment and reduce the inherent vulnerability caused by global capitalism by maximizing the benefits of both large-scale and decentralized supply chains. Large organizations in the twenty-first century have emerged as 'lean and mean' (Bakan, 2004).

That organizations seek to shape external forces is illustrated by the 'Wal-Mart effect' – the ways in which the world's largest retail store has changed other companies, local communities and people's everyday life around the world (Fishman, 2007). Describing the Wal-Mart effect, Fishman writes:

> It reaches deep inside the operations of the companies that supply it and changes not only what they sell, but also changes how those products are packaged and presented, what the lives of the factory workers who make the products are like – it even sometimes changes the countries where those factories are located. (2007: 5)

Although the 'Wal-Mart effect' will vary considerably across sectors, it is pertinent to note that for those small and medium-sized enterprises supplying the large organizations, uncertainty is inherent in disconnected and decentralized economies (Beynon et al., 2002; Thompson, 2003). Addressing the global challenge stemming from weak growth and rising inequality, Elliott and Treanor (2014) quote Klaus Schwab, founder and chairman of the World Economic Forum, to capture the turbulent condition of early twenty-first-century capitalism:

> Economic growth patterns, the geopolitical landscape, the social contract that binds people together, and our plant's ecosystem are all undergoing radical, simultaneous transformations, generating anxiety and, in many places, turmoil. (Elliott and Treanor, 2014)

VISIT THE *ONLINE RESOURCE CENTRE* AT HTTPS://HE.PALGRAVE.COM/COMPANION/BRATTON-WORK-AND-ORGANIZATIONAL-BEHAVIOUR3/ FOR FURTHER INFORMATION ON THE WAL-MART EFFECT.

Internal forces for change

A myriad of internal micro-forces drive change within the organization. The sources of structural internal triggers fall into four categories, as shown in Figure 1.3: people, structure, work and technology. In turn, these can be divided broadly into those that stem from employee behaviour and those originating, either intentionally or as a result of unintended consequences, from management behaviour and decisions. *Human resource* problems such as high recorded levels of absenteeism and turnover causing unusually high recruitment and training costs and, less obviously, low job satisfaction and employee commitment represent two clusters of triggers of change. Organizations might respond to these human resources problems by changing recruitment and selection processes, and the rewards system (Chapter 9), and by redesigning employees' work. Other people-related forces can manifest themselves in quantifiable ways, such as below-par *performance* standards – low productivity or poor quality – increased levels of work-related *accidents* or stress, and overt interpersonal *conflict* between managers and non-managers, or between departments or units within the organization (see Chapter 14).

Management behaviour and decision making are obvious forces for change, many examples of which are discussed in the preceding chapters. Inappropriate *leadership* behaviour is one such force for change. For instance, employees' role conflict may require leaders to provide a narrative to justify the change. Mainstream organizational change theorists emphasize that a narrative is important because it can capture vision, aspirations and diverse voices (Jabri, 2012). Moreover, insufficient communication between leaders (Chapter 11) and other managers or employees, as well as structural reorganization (Chapter 15), are additional internal forces for change. Positive change is initiated by *innovation*. Whether related to organizational processes or products or services, all innovations begin with creative ideas produced by people and then implemented using resources within organizations (Amabile et al., 1996). Other positive change stems from employees' *participation* in decision making (see Chapter 13), workplace learning (Chapter 7) and creativity-enhancement techniques and **organizational development**, processes that are examined later in this chapter.

We can be helped to understand the key driving forces behind the tendency towards constant organizational change by theorizing the organization as being 'embedded' in the context of a political economy with complex interorganizational relationships on the one hand, and competitive imperatives and the management of human resources on the other. In *The Communist Manifesto*, capitalism's most strident critics, Karl Marx and Friedrich Engels, captured the idea of continuous change: 'Constant revolutionizing of production, uninterrupted disturbance of all social conditions, ever lasting uncertainty ... all new-formed ones become antiquated before they can ossify. All that is solid melts into the air' (Marx and Engels, 1848/1967: 223). For Marx, the logic of capitalism, the accumulation of profit, demanded ceaseless change.

Joseph Schumpeter's (1954) concept of 'creative destruction', derived from the work of Marx, is a theory of economic innovation and the business cycle, which captures the idea that capitalism is characterized by constant change. The process of creative destruction results in the constant 'remaking' of new products/services and skills/occupations and, concurrently, the annihilation and 'unmaking' of old products/services and skills/occupations under capitalism on a global scale. Historically, organizational change has been driven by various strategies designed to lower labour costs and increase managerial control. Two key strategies stand out here. First is the 'technology fix', or the introduction of labour-saving technologies and the redesign of the production process (for example, teamworking). The other is the 'spatial fix', or the geographical relocation of business operation to low-wage economies, such as Bangladesh (Silver, 2014). As we discussed in Chapter 3, the major contribution to a critical analysis of work and organizational change has been Harry Braverman's *Labor and Monopoly Capital* (1974). Braverman and post-Braverman (Thompson and Harley, 2008) labour process theory is predicated on the assumption that macro- *and* microstructural forces cause organizational change – division of labour, new technology, work teams, outsourcing – and that these modifications of the labour process are designed to increase or shift control from workers to management to reduce operating costs.

innovation: the adoption of any process, thinking, product or service that is new to a particular organization or subsystem

organizational development: in this, change agents use the principles and practices of behavioural science to assist the change effort in order to increase employee and organizational effectiveness

stop...

Take a moment to re-read Marx's analysis of workplace change in Chapter 3. Is his analysis of the internal dynamics of capitalist production relevant today?

...and reflect

stop...

What external and internal forces for change have impacted on your university?

...and reflect

Thus, there are powerful external socioeconomic forces and organizational imperatives that dictate management goals and trigger change. Evidence suggests that, in a decentralized and uncoordinated economy with long supply chains, UK managers have less control of events and fewer levers to pull (Beynon et al., 2002). The forces driving change can cause destruction – workplace closure and job loss – but they can also cause innovation and job creation (Burke, 2014). It is the potential for destruction that often causes change to be resisted by employees.

Resistance to change

As Schumpeter's concept of creative destruction suggests, although there might be positive outcomes, change is also associated with negative outcomes for employees and managers alike, and resistance at both the individual and the organizational level is a common phenomenon. A decade before the major corporate restructuring and deindustrialization of UK industry, Alvin Toffler wrote about social change in *Future Shock* (1970), defining 'future shock' in terms of a personal perception of 'too much change in too short a period of time' (p. 27). Schneider and Goldwasser (1998: 42) also explored the psychological dimension and introduced the 'classic change curve'. This takes the shape of a peak showing high expectations, followed in the middle by a 'valley of despair' before a climb upwards to another peak depicting an improved, optimistic psychological state. Schneider and Goldwasser's analysis reaffirms critical studies that organizational change most often means economic loss and emotional pain. As John Kotter (2012) has observed, recent change has been accompanied by negative psychological emotion:

> Major change efforts have helped some organizations adapt significantly to shifting conditions … But in too many situations the improvements have been disappointing and the carnage has been appalling, with wasted resources and *burned-out*, *scared*, or *frustrated* employees. (p. 4, emphasis added)

All mainstream theories of organizational change acknowledge the likelihood of resistance to change. It has been estimated that at least two-thirds of organizational change efforts do not result in their intended aims, nor do they foster sustained change (Choi and Ruona, 2011), and the most cited reason why change efforts fail is employees' resistance to change (Hendrickson and Gray, 2012). Resistance to organizational change refers to the inability or unwillingness to accept changes that are perceived to be threatening or may bring negative outcomes for the individual.

Resistance can take many forms and can be overt or covert, and immediate or deferred. It is easier for change leaders to deal with resistance when it is overt and immediate, for example when change is introduced and employees quickly respond by voicing their complaints, resigning or threatening to withdraw their cooperation or labour. It is more difficult when resistance is covert or deferred. Covert resistance efforts are, by definition, less visible and more subtle, and they involve acts that combine elements of covert resistance and consent (McCabe, 2014). For example, loss of commitment and loyalty to the organization, loss of motivation, an increased number of errors, increased absenteeism or even sabotage may occur. Deferred misbehaviour, for instance, obscures the connection between the source of the resistance and the reaction to it. A change may produce what appears to be only a minimal reaction at the time it is initiated, but employees' reactions to the change can build up and so that resistance surfaces weeks or months later; the resistance has simply been accumulated and deferred. In reality, the sources of resistance often intertwine, but for analytical purposes, we can categorize them by individual and organizational sources (Table 18.1).

stop...

Make a list of what you think are the likely reasons for (1) workers' resistance to change, and (2) managers' resistance to organizational change.

...and reflect

Table 18.1 Sources of individual and organizational resistance to change

Individual resistance	Organizational resistance
Economics	Organizational culture
Security	Structural inertia
Habit	Existing contracts or agreements
Selective perception	Established resource allocations
Loss of freedom or inconvenience	Loss of expertise
Fear of the unknown	Threats to power relationships

Individual resistance

Individual sources of resistance to organizational change reside in basic human needs and characteristics such as personality, perception, values and motivation. There are six common reasons why individual employees may resist change.

Economic

Wages or salary have traditionally been the centrepiece of economic rewards for work, and for over 90 per cent of the UK working population pay is their sole source of income. Unsurprisingly, therefore, employees are likely to resist change that is perceived as threatening their job or lowering, either directly or indirectly, their employment income. Perceived changes in occupational skills or established work routines also can provoke economic fears if employees believe that they will be unable to perform the new tasks to their previous standard, especially when pay is related to performance.

Security

People with a high need for security are likely to resist change because it threatens their feelings of employment security. Gross inequality has deformed American and UK capitalism, creating an 'Age of Insecurity'. Insecure jobs, high levels of unemployment and high personal debt generate anxiety and fear. Too often, this can also come with a cost to dignity and well-being: bullying can become the norm when employees are fearful of losing their job because of workplace changes. When, for example, in early 2014, the Royal Bank of Scotland announced that it planned to undertake 'significant' downsizing, many employees feared that their jobs were in jeopardy. As discussed in Chapter 5, these changes may create altered perceptions about the permanence of employment and a recognition that the exchange of 'loyalty for security' has been superseded (Hendry and Jenkins, 1997: 39).

Habit

Life is complex, and to cope with this complexity, people tend to rely on habits or 'auto-pilot' responses. In the workplace, individuals find a sense of comfort and security in well-established procedures. Past 'tried and tested' work habits may serve as a guide for decision making. When confronted with change, this tendency to respond in programmable ways becomes a source of resistance. Thus, a proposal to relocate to a new open-plan office or changes to well-established work routines may well be resisted by some people because they wish to retain established and comfortable ways of working.

Selective perception

As explored in Chapter 5, individuals shape their world around them through processes of perception. People's interpretation of stimuli presents a unique image of the 'real' world. Once they have created this world and a sense of *self-identity*, it resists change. For example, front-line nursing staff may have a stereotyped view of administration as untrustworthy and ignore the arguments explaining the beneficial outcomes of change. Employees may seek to defend a sense of self-identity (for example, as a 'manager' or as a 'professional') and oppose change.

Inconvenience or loss of freedom

If the change is perceived to cause inconvenience, reduce freedom of action or result in decreased autonomy or empowerment, employees are more likely to resist.

Fear of the unknown

Major change substitutes uncertainty for the known. Change that confronts employees with the unknown tends to cause anxiety and can be a source of resistance. The transfer of Macmillan's operation from Basingstoke to the London office is typically such an experience. Employees based at the Basingstoke office understand how things work, but on relocation they face a whole new and uncertain system. They have substituted the known for the unknown and the anxiety that goes with it. Anxiety of the unknown may, therefore, become a source of resistance to change.

VISIT THE *ONLINE RESOURCE CENTRE* AT HTTPS://HE.PALGRAVE.COM/COMPANION/BRATTON-WORK-AND-ORGANIZATIONAL-BEHAVIOUR3/ FOR FURTHER EXAMPLES OF WORKER RESISTANCE TO CHANGE.

Organizational resistance

Although organizations have to be flexible and adapt to changes in the socio-economic environment, they are by their very nature conservative, with a small 'c'. Management tend to feel comfortable operating within the structure, policies and procedures that have been developed over time to meet a range of exigencies and organizational imperatives. Again, there are six common reasons why organizations may resist change.

Organizational culture

Recall from the previous chapter that the organization '*is*' a culture. Complex multiple cultural values and norms that shape an organization are deeply embedded and, although not set in stone, they may not be easy to modify. The functionalist-oriented perspective of culture in terms of 'ways of doing things around here' has an important effect on internal processes and employees' behaviour. A culture may result in a lack of flexibility for, or acceptance of, change. In addition, the concept of cultural heterogeneity, which may result in distinctive work paradigms, highlights potential sources of resistance.

Structural inertia

Closely related to organizational culture, structural inertia refers to built-in management mechanisms designed to achieve organizational goals and create stability. For example, the recruitment and selection process systematically selects certain people to 'fit' into the organization. Orientation, training and other socialization techniques reinforce specific role requirements and skills. Pay systems reward certain modes of employee behaviour. In large-scale bureaucratic organizations, formalization produces job descriptions and rules for managers and other employees to follow. When confronting forces for change, this structural inertia acts as a counterbalance to sustain stability and predictability. Recall that Taylorism promotes the division of work, narrow definitions of assigned duties and responsibilities, and top-down reporting structures; these management techniques can be a major obstacle to change. The more bureaucratic and 'mechanistic' the organizational structure, the more likely it is that managers and other employees will be reluctant to change.

Existing contracts or agreements

Organizations have commercial contracts or agreements with other parties, such as suppliers or customers, government agencies and trade unions. These contracts and agreements can limit managerial behaviour and become a source of resistance, for example if there is a collective agreement with a union that limits the opportunity to change working practices or introduce certain new technology.

Established resource allocations

Change often requires additional investment in, or a redistribution of resources to, other areas of the organization. Technology, space, structure and people may not be easily altered. For example, a manufacturer may find it difficult to change to a team-based approach because it cannot afford the cost of a new purpose-built factory. Those departments and managers who control sizable resources often see the redistribution of assets as a threat because the change may mean a reduction in their budgets or a downsizing of their unit. Those departments and managers with a vested interest in the status quo therefore often feel threatened by change and are more likely to be a source of resistance to innovation and change.

Expertise

Planned change, especially transformational change, may threaten the expertise of professional and specialized groups. The outsourcing of the human resource management (HRM) department's work, such as payroll or training, is an example of a change that may be strongly resisted by human resources professionals or payroll or training specialists in the organization, because outsourcing these functions is a threat to the specialized skills held by those in human resource departments.

Power relationships

Change may be perceived as a threat to long-established power relationships within the organization. For example, the introduction of self-managed work teams is the kind of change that may be resisted by supervisors and line managers because they see this as empowering non-managerial staff and undermining their power. The redistribution of decision-making authority within the organization can undermine power relationships and may act as a catalyst of resistance to planned change.

IN THE EBOOK ACCESS THE **CRITICAL INSIGHT** ON 'RESISTANCE TO CHANGE'.

Organizational change strategies

The propensity to resist planned change at either the individual or the organizational level is the reason why management theorists and practitioners develop strategies to manage change. Managing organizational change is the process of planning and executing change in the workplace in such a way as to minimize individual and organizational resistance, while at the same time maximizing employees' cooperation and the effectiveness of the change process.

change agent: the activities of an individual(s) that are directed towards accomplishing a change

Managing change is the responsibility of **change agents**. Change agents can be managers or non-managers, employees of the organization or external professional consultants. Management consultants can offer a more objective perspective than inside managers can. They are also more willing to initiate first-order changes, partly because they do not have to experience the repercussions. Consultants are, however, at a disadvantage in that they often do not have any insider understanding of the organization's history, operating procedures and key staff. But whether change agents emerge from inside the organization or are hired outsiders, they must have the capability to reframe assumptions about the organization and the environment in which it operates, and be able to articulate clearly the desired image of the desired future state. Leadership, rather than management, is more likely to emerge in situations involving rapid, major or catastrophic change in the environment and organizational crisis involving privatization, major downsizing or closure (Jabri, 2012; Kotter, 2012). Transformational change is closely tied to transformational leadership (see Chapter 12).

This section presents an overview of the work of Kurt Lewin (1951) and John Kotter (2012), with an emphasis on **force-field analysis** and the related process of action research. *Force-field analysis* involves employees working individually or in groups to engage in problem solving in an effort to understand the magnitude, direction and significance, both positive and negative, of the forces that are triggering a change. *Action research* is an iterative process that involves treating workplace problems as inseparable elements when exploring a change situation (Jabri, 2012).

> **force-field analysis:** an approach drawing on the physical (material) forces of nature, with the premise that, in any organizational setting, there are forces that push for change and forces that resist or act against change

Lewin's three-stage model

The behaviour process that is observed in Lewin's three-stage model of planned change involves *unfreezing* the present situation, *movement* to a new state and *refreezing* the new state to make it enduring. Force-field analysis is based on the concept of electromagnetic forces: in an organizational setting, there are forces (or 'charges') that push for change and forces that pull against change.

Figure 18.2 shows a diagrammatic representation of force-field analysis. Specifically, the three steps of unfreezing, movement and refreezing are shown against time on the horizontal axis. The step-by-step processes connect the present with the desired state, as represented by the diagonal line. The upward-pointing arrows represent the driving forces for change, and the downward-pointing arrows depict the opposing or resisting behavioural forces. To move from the status quo to the desired state, that is, to overcome the pressures of individual, group and organizational resistance, it is necessary to unfreeze the situation. This is achieved in one of three ways. The *driving forces*, which direct behaviour away from the status quo, can be increased. The *resisting forces*, which obstruct movement from the existing state, can be reduced. A third option is to combine the first two approaches. Let us now briefly explain the three stages of change.

The *unfreezing* stage is central to managing change. The focus here is to create the motivation to unfreeze the prevailing situation – thawing frozen rules, hierarchies and 'ways of doing'. It is concerned with challenging the prevailing state of balance and encouraging individuals to replace present values and behaviours with those desired by the change agent. Management can begin the unfreezing process through a dialogue that aims to help with disconfirming the benefits or usefulness of existing systems, procedures and behaviours (Ford and Ford, 1995; Jabri, 2012). Management could use positive incentives to encourage employees to accept the change. For example, in the Macmillan example, management might subsidize travel or moving expenses or accommodation to allow employees to relocate to London. Management might also consider unfreezing a prevailing situation by removing the restraining forces. Employees could, for example, be counselled individually so that each employee's concerns and fears could be heard and specifically clarified. If resistance is high, management may have to resort to both increasing the attractiveness of and reducing resistance to the alternative if the unfreezing stage is to be accomplished.

The purpose of the *movement* stage is to change the balance between the driving and the resisting forces. This entails modifying behaviours and attitudes within the organization to achieve the desired change. Change will involve both formal and informal workplace learning. Thus, at this stage management must provide employees with new information and behaviour models to help them learn new skills, procedures, concepts or ways of thinking and understanding. Human resource development professionals recommend that management should convey the idea that change is a continuous learning process rather than a one-off event. This resonates with the idea of seeing the 'organization as a system of learning' (Gold et al., 2013: 239).

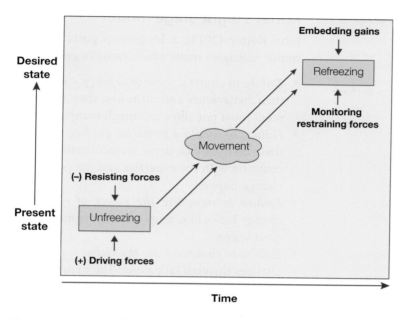

Figure 18.2 Lewin's three-stage force-field model

Finally, there is *refreezing*: Once the change has been implemented and the desired state has been achieved, the new situation needs to be entrenched to ensure there are no backward steps preventing the change from becoming successful. For Lewin, the refreezing phase is necessary or the change will be short lived because behaviours frequently revert to their original state. The objective of refreezing is to embed and stabilize the new situation by balancing the driving and restraining forces. This is accomplished by positive reinforcement once employees have exhibited the new and desirable types of behaviours and attitudes (for example, by a permanent upward adjustment of pay or promotion, or by individual feedback), by additional coaching and formal learning or by revising the formal rules and regulations governing behaviour to reinforce the new situation.

Lewin's third stage has, however, received criticism. In fast-paced, rapidly changing organizations, it is argued that there is an extraordinary disconnection between the theory of 'refreezing' and the realities of organizations actually undergoing change. Kanter et al. (1992: 10) describe the Lewinian 'refreezing' concept as 'quaintly linear and static', and, moreover, it is likely to constrain the change process and undermine the idea of continuous learning (Vaili, 1996). To emphasize the notion of continuous change, Jabri (2012: 102) adopts the notion of 'ice-topping' to denote an ephemeral act, rather than Lewinian 'refreezing' per se.

Kurt Lewin's force-field model of the 'forces for' and 'forces against' that are at work in social interaction is predicated on a number of assumptions (Schein, 1980). The first is that people are the hub of all organizational change. The core assumptions are that nothing changes – structure, technology or work process – unless people change their behaviour and attitudes. Second, change will not occur unless there is motivation to change. Third, resistance to change occurs even when the goals appear to be highly beneficial to individuals and the organization. Fourth,

stop...

Construct a force-field diagram for change at your university or a personal work-related change that you have experienced. How useful is the model in helping you understand and implement the change?

...and reflect

change involves learning new skill sets, behaviours, attitudes and practices. Next, the continuity of the change effort requires positive reinforcement to consolidate the new types of behaviour and practice. Finally, change involves communicating with employees. A communications strategy and employees' involvement in change decisions is highly desirable to help organizational members see the logic of a change and work to construct the newly desired state (Jabri, 2012).

Kotter's eight-stage model

John Kotter (2012), a leadership guru, identifies the most common errors that senior managers make which cause organizational change efforts to fail:

- *Failure to create a sense of urgency* – if employees do not see the need to change their behaviours and attitudes, they will not be motivated to change. Management must not allow too much complacency.
- *Failure to create a powerful guiding coalition* – one or two people acting on their own cannot drive transformational change. Management must create a coalition with the expertise and the power – the 'movers and shakers' – to make change happen.
- *Failure to recognize the power of vision* – without demonstrations of what change looks like, employees' imagination fails. Transformative change needs a clear vision.
- *Failure to communicate the vision* – nothing changes without talk, and nothing changes through talk alone. The management team must, in words and actions, repeatedly communicate the vision to the workforce.
- *Failure to remove the obstacles that block the vision* – organizational structures, job designs, reward and appraisal systems and key individuals can block efforts to implement the new vision. The management team must confront and remove the obstacles.
- *Failure to plan for and create short-term wins* – real transformation takes time, and the momentum can be lost if there are no interim achievements and successes to celebrate. Management should therefore create and reward short-term accomplishments.
- *Declaring victory too soon* – the change effort is still incomplete when the improvements are appearing. Management must not 'declare victory' prematurely before the new behaviours and processes have been embedded in the organization.
- *Failure to anchor the changes in the organizational culture* – unless the new behaviours are 'rooted' in social norms and shared values, they may be subject to degradation. As people leave and new talent joins the organization, the successors must champion the benefits of their predecessors.

In order to overcome these change errors, Kotter suggests a sequential planning process, working systematically through eight stages, and not skipping or rushing any of them. Each of the stages is associated with one of the common errors identified above. Kotter's eight steps subsume Lewin's three-stage model of change. The first four stages represent Lewin's 'unfreezing' stage, the next three represent the 'movement' stage, and the final stage represents the 'refreezing' process. Kotter's research underscores the fact that successful transformational change goes through all eight stages and in the sequence shown in Table 18.2.

Kotter emphasizes that establishing a *sense of urgency* among the workforce is crucial to gaining the necessary cooperation, whatever the nature or size of the organization. The motivation to 'unfreeze' may be provided by 'visible crises', which can be 'enormously helpful in catching people's attention and pushing up urgency levels' (Kotter, 2012: 45). Canadian writer Naomi Klein also reminds us that a sense of urgency for change can occur through what she calls 'shock therapy' as well as adroit leadership (Klein, 2007). A *coalition* of cross-functional, cross-level teams of change agents with credibility, skills, reputations and formal authority is needed for successful change.

Table 18.2 Kotter's and Lewin's sequential change models

Kotter's (2012) eight-stage model	Lewin's (1951) three-stage model
1. Establish a sense of urgency 2. Create the guiding coalition 3. Develop a vision and strategy 4. Communicate the change vision	Unfreezing
5. Empower broad-based action 6. Generate short-term wins 7. Consolidate gains and produce more change	Movement
8. Anchor new approaches in the culture	Refreezing

By *vision*, Kotter means creating a picture of the future with some explicit or implicit narrative on why employees should strive to create that future. Leaders should create a vision that is clear and uplifting to guide the change process. They also need to *communicate* the change vision by developing a communication strategy that consistently communicates the vision and new strategic plan in order to persuade followers of the need to change. Leaders should *empower* a broad base of employees to take action by eliminating barriers to change, and should encourage the learning of new behaviours, skills (technical and social) and attitudes that are aligned with the vision. The guiding coalition should generate *short-term wins* that help to provide credibility, resources and momentum to the overall change effort. As change cascades through the organization, effective change leaders *consolidate gains* and maintain momentum to create further change so that regression to status quo can be avoided. The new behaviour, practices and norms need to be *anchored* in the culture to prevent the 'old' culture reasserting itself.

Numerous studies give support to Kotter's model. With regard to the topic of vision, for example, Maurer (2009) draws attention to the role of an organization's vision in generating a compelling case for change. Jabri (2012) highlights the importance of 'storytelling' and sharing narratives about achievements to help a vision gain traction among the workforce: 'Stories tell what has happened, how it has happened and what has been learned as a result' (p. 16). As a communication tool, by providing images of behaviours or their associated processes, metaphors help to contrast and compare the present situation with the desired end state (Tsoukas and Chia, 2002). The movement process will be enhanced if change leaders create a climate of trust and keep their promises that the change effort will generate enhanced status or security (Chreim, 2006).

Kotter's top-down, orchestrated change model underscores the importance of leadership rather than managing change (also see Chapter 12). The driving force behind the organizational change process is 'leadership, leadership, and still more leadership' (Kotter, 2012: 31). Kotter's step-by-step process attempts transformational change through an empiricist-rational strategy, that is, with the view that individuals will make rational choices if they are provided with the 'correct' information. Change, however, does not always follow a step-by-step linear process. It can be messy, passing through periods of regression to the status quo (Weick, 2000). Other studies have highlighted problems with managing change in the turbulent times of the post-2008 crisis. Meaney and Wilson (2009) argue that Kotter's guidelines still apply in a recession, but that to enhance the readiness for change, it is important to balance the positive and negative messages, and not to communicate only bad news. In a recession, persuading employees of the need to change the status quo may be more straightforward. A high level of unemployment can, either directly or indirectly, act as coercion, that is, the direct threat of redundancy can 'persuade' those who are resisting to accept change (Bratton, 1992). Thompson (2003) has noted that, in a downturn, employers may not, however, be able to keep their promises to the workforce that beneficial outcomes will result from change.

Another problem is '*initiative decay*', where the benefits of a change are lost as the organization moves on to deal with new priorities. Alongside this problem is '*initiative fatigue*', when employees become weary of constant demands to do things differently, work better or work smarter. Whether an economy is in or out of a recession, therefore, there is growing concern with how to *sustain* the changes that are already in place (Buchanan et al., 2006). As highlighted by Bruch and Menges (2010), constant demands for fast-paced change can lead to organizational burn-out. For example, research suggests that market-based reforms and fast-paced change in England's NHS can result in negative outcomes for healthcare professionals, including low job satisfaction, demotivation, a high turnover of staff and a deterioration in physical and mental well-being (West and Dawson, 2012).

Source: © Royalty-Free/Corbis

Stress and change in the UK's National Health Service

Following a period of turmoil and change that lasted several years, the Health and Social Care Act 2012 introduced the most far-reaching reforms that the National Health Service (NHS) in England has experienced. These changes include the involvement of general practitioners in the commissioning of resources, for instance hospital services, and the opening up of services to external competition.

In the wake of these reforms, surveys of staff were undertaken by the NHS in England, the Royal College of Nursing and the union Unison, and revealed key sources of employee stress that included feeling 'overworked, dis-empowered and unappreciated' (Cornwell, 2014). Unison's survey of 5000 staff working across the NHS documented that only 31 per cent of staff believed there were enough people employed in their workplace to guarantee dignified and compassionate patient care (Campbell, 2013). A poll of 2000 nurses in the English NHS and the private sector found that 'more than half had been made unwell by stress in the last year. Four in five nurses said that they had gone to work despite feeling unwell.' Nurses criticized punitive sickness policies that pressurized them to go to work even when they were ill, and 23 per cent reported being bullied by their managers (Press Association, 2013b). A staff survey found that 40 per cent said they would not recommend the hospital or clinic where they worked to their family, and over 66 per cent thought that their place of work was understaffed (Ramesh, 2012).

At the other end of the spectrum, in their study on NHS performance, West and Dawson introduce a psychological orientation of 'engagement', which they describe as a 'positive, fulfilling, work-related state of mind characterized by vigour, dedication and absorption' (2012: 6). Engagement, in their view, also includes influence in wider decision making and advocacy, 'the extent to which employees would recommend their orga-

nization as a place to work or receive treatment' (p. 8). Engagement can be seen as one end of a continuum of psychological states with burn-out comprising 'cynicism (an indifference or distant attitude to work), exhaustion (a depletion or draining of emotional resources) and inefficacy (a lack of satisfaction with expectations)' (p.9) at the other.

West and Dawson believe that organizations can provide environments that stimulate the production of engagement through day-to-day individual support from line managers, appraisal and work teams. Recent survey data supported the thesis that well-structured development performance appraisals and team-working were antecedents to engagement. Additional data from their study on the NHS showed positive outcomes such as lower levels of staff absenteeism, turnover and patient satisfaction in those NHS trusts with high levels of engagement. Engaged staff were less likely to feel pressured to come to work when they were unwell. 'Employees who reported higher engagement were more likely to rate their own health and wellbeing more highly' (p. 17). Overall, when staff experience good quality management they can 'fulfil their calling of providing outstanding professional care for patients' (p. 20).

> **Stop!** West and Dawson refer to 'good' quality line management that is constructive and helps people to do their jobs and to feel valuable to the organization. Can you think of any other strategies that might contribute to staff engagement and fulfilment at work?

Sources and further information
Campbell, D. (2013) 'NHS staffing levels risk another Mid Staffordshire-style scandal-report', *The Guardian*, April 18.
Cornwell, J. (2014) 'Empowered and engaged NHS staff will provide better care', *The Guardian*, January 15.
Press Association (2013b) 'Stress on nurses putting patients at risk, warns RCN', *The Guardian*, September 20.
Ramesh, R. (2012) 'NHS staff survey: 40% would not recommend health service to family', *The Guardian*, March 20.
West, M. A. and Dawson, J. F. (2012) *Employee Engagement and NHS Performance*, London: King's Fund.

Note: This feature was written by David Denham, Honorary Research Fellow in Sociology, Wolverhampton University, UK.

Action research and action learning

Both Lewin (1951) and Kotter (2012) provide us with useful theories and methods for conceptualizing the management of change. According to Jabri (2012), Lewin pioneered *action research* as a methodology driven by the principle of 'no research without action; no action without research' (p. 111) Action research aims to solve organizational problems. The process of action research refers to a change process based on the collaborative 'research' of data on a perceived 'problem' and then the selection of a change 'action' based on the analysis of the findings. Its importance lies in the 'collaboration' between the change agent and knowledgeable employees close to the issues or problems. Its legitimacy lies in providing a systematic methodology for managing planned change. Action research consists of three major steps: data gathering, analysis of the data, and feedback and evaluation. The change agent and group start the process by *gathering* information about problems and concerns from members of the organization. This is followed by *analysis*, asking such questions as, what patterns do these problems seem to take? The third step in the process, *feedback and evaluation*, involves sharing with employees what has been found in the first two stages. Then, with the help of the change agent, the change group develop actions plans to correct the problems that have been identified.

Action research begins where force-field analysis ends. That is, once forces have been construed as issues or 'problems', an attempt is made to intervene in solving the problem by linking 'research' – understanding the identifiable problem – to 'action' – change. It is this linkage of 'theory' (understanding) and 'practice' (change) that empowers the movement. Bryant (1979) noted the dual benefits of action research to the organization. First, it finds and implements solutions to problems. Second, resistance to change is reduced because action research engages employees in the process of change.

VISIT THE *ONLINE RESOURCE CENTRE* AT HTTPS://HE.PALGRAVE.COM/COMPANION/BRATTON-WORK-AND-ORGANIZATIONAL-BEHAVIOUR3/ FOR FURTHER INFORMATION ON ACTION RESEARCH.

The problem-centric model highlights the role of learning in the workplace in general, and *action learning* in particular. For Kotter (2012), the older, traditional top-down approach to organizational change is 'nearly oblivious to the power and the potential of lifelong learning' (p. 176). The process of action learning involves leaders and stakeholders forming a small group (called a set) who agree to help each other work on 'individually owned problems', through the use of 'rich' questions and dialogue, in a 'challenging yet supportive way' in order to make decisions concerning the problem that will be reported back to the set (Gold et al., 2013: 276). By participating in enquiry, reporting what has been learnt and taking action beyond the set to other employees can help an organization to solve complex problems and deal with innovation and change (Claxton et al., 2009; Pedler, 2008).

The related notion of *participative enquiry*, which involves identifying and building on 'good practice' rather than problems, means that employees are 'learning through others' (Marshall and Reason, 2007: 373). And through 'reflexive practice', leaders, managers and other change agents can help the organization's members to learn from each other (Cunliffe, 2004). With its emphasis on talking, learning and action beyond the set, such an intervention treats employees as change agents, rather than the recipients of change (Marshall and Reason, 2007). Critical approaches to action learning and participative enquiry highlight the tensions and power dynamics that arise from such interactions (Bratton, 2001; Trehan and Pedler, 2009).

stop...

What contribution, if any, do action research and action learning have to making Kotter's and Lewin's sequential change models more successful?

...and reflect

Contingency and engagement models

In other chapters, we identified studies that compare and contrast different managerial behaviours depending on individual employee considerations, for instance employees' 'ability and maturity' (Hersey and Blanchard, 1969), as well as variations in the size, organizational culture, competitive pressures and skill levels of individuals and groups (Edwards, 1979; Thompson and McHugh, 2009). For example, Friedman (1977) observed different styles of managing highly skilled employees and professionals compared with less skilled employees. The dominant mode of managerial behaviour encouraged (or at least tolerated) employees' autonomy and participation in change decisions.

The variations in managerial behaviour in managing change are not random but are linked to the formation of particular strategies, which are often a response to perceived changes in the internal or external environment. We know that different behaviours and interventions reflect two management logics. The first of these is the logic of direct, process-based control, in which the focus is on efficiency and cost containment. The timescale available for strategic change can be an important variable in the cost equation. The second is the logic of indirect behavioural outcomes, in which the focus is on change leaders engaging employees' intellectual capital, commitment and cooperation throughout the change process. The level or scale of change, from 'third-order' to 'first-order', can be an important factor in retaining employees' commitment and cooperation. In relation to context, if the timescale and scale of change are important in generating radically different change problems that demand significantly variable styles of change management, it may be better practice to use a contingency-based approach, rather than a 'one-size-fits-all' approach, to implementing the change (Fiedler, 1997; Stace and Dunphy, 2001).

Early research underscores the value of employees' participation in successful organizational change. Coch and French (1948), for example, observed that it was not the employees per se but whether they were included in or excluded from participating in change processes that affected their acceptance of or resistance to change. Similarly, Landy and Conte (2013) observed that successful change interventions tend to be participative, encouraging the total engagement of all parties. As we discussed in Chapter 13, employee involvement and participation became prominent in the 'high-commitment work system' literature and is most often associated 'shared' or 'distributed' styles of managerial leadership. Although scholars generally recommend involving employees in order to enlist their cooperation in the change process, recent survey data covering UK workplaces in the shadow of the recession show that managers have since 2008 actually narrowed the range of options over which employees are consulted on workplace issues (van Wanrooy et al. 2013). These findings do not bode well for advocates of employee involvement and participation.

VISIT THE *ONLINE RESOURCE CENTRE* AT HTTPS://HE.PALGRAVE.COM/COMPANION/BRATTON-WORK-AND-ORGANIZATIONAL-BEHAVIOUR3/ FOR FURTHER INFORMATION ON EMPLOYEE ENGAGEMENT.

Organizations tend to pursue employee involvement and participation practices partly to retain employees' cooperation, and partly for their rhetorical appeal for change (Harley et al., 2005), especially if the employees involved provide high-skilled customer services or have a high level of responsibility for product quality. The notion of *path dependency* – that doing things in a particular way yields positive returns – is important in understanding management choices about how to manage change, especially at a time of crisis (Marchington and Kynighou, 2012). Employee involvement and participation can offer creative managers the opportunities to generate higher levels of employee engagement. Although it is not without controversy, the notion of employee engagement is a 'desirable condition' and connotes 'involvement, commitment, passion, enthusiasm, focused effort, and energy'; it therefore contains both attitudinal and behavioural elements (Macey and Schneider, 2008: 4). The antecedents of such attitudes and behaviours are located in the organizational culture in which the employees work, and the benefits include reducing resistance to change.

Planned transformative change necessitates an employee 'voice' and employees' engagement (Macey and Schneider, 2008; Marchington and Kynighou, 2012). For example, Keller et al. (2010) observe that high levels of employee engagement and collaboration make transformational change more successful. It seems self-evident that major change is more likely to be successful if managers and other stakeholders totally engage in organizational change. Although the context cannot explain everything, the literature suggests that change agents have to be sensitive to and give consideration to situational contingencies, such as the scale of change, the urgency and the provision for employees' engagement. Urgency is concerned with the speed with which change needs to proceed. For example, a situation of high employee engagement coupled with pressures for fast change (see strategy 4 in Figure 18.3) may warrant intervention that is driven from the top down. On the other hand, forcing top-down change under conditions of low urgency is more likely to result in outcomes such as increased levels of passive compliance (Jabri, 2012).

This form of reasoning implies a typology of managerial behaviours to manage change. By using conceptual frameworks or typologies, we are able to compare and contrast different configurations of management activities and further develop and test theories. The change model shown in Figure 18.3 draws upon contingency models of leadership (Fiedler, 1997) and organizational change (Stace and Dunphy, 2001). When the scale of change – from minor operational to major transformative – is plotted against employee engagement, it generates a typology of four change strategies. The four situational contingencies can be summarized as: (1) directive-operational, (2) engagement-continuous, (3) authoritarian-transformative, and (4) participative-transformative.

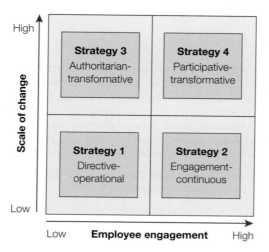

Figure 18.3 A typology of change management activities

Strategy 1 is *directive-operational*. This traditional 'command and control' style involves the use of formal authority in reaching decisions about organizational change. It tends to be the dominant mode when 'third-order' or minor operational adjustments are required, when time is limited or where key interested individuals and groups with little power oppose the change.

Strategy 2 is *engagement-continuous.* This style of management behaviour nurtures employee participation and engagement in key decisions. It is used when the organization needs 'third-order' and 'second-order' adjustment to address external drivers of change, where time is available, and where key stakeholders engage in continuous informal learning, for example through action research or action learning, and support change.

Strategy 3 is *authoritarian-transformative.* This senior management style unilaterally imposes top-down transformative change on the organization. It tends to be used when significant organizational changes are necessary, where there is no support for strategic change among key groups, but when it is necessary because of a crisis or threat to the organization's survival. The change tactic of coercion – the application of direct threats to the resisters – can be part of this strategy. For example, in 2013 senior management at INEOS threatened to close the oil refinery at Grangemouth, Scotland, unless the workforce acquiesced to major changes in their employment conditions (see The Reality of Work feature in Chapter 14 on power).

Strategy 4 is *participative-transformative.* Although this style is associated with employee involvement, participation and learning, it involves change that is driven from the top down to address changing environmental conditions when there is limited time for employee participation, but where there is a culture of cooperation and mutual trust, and support for transformative change. The change tactic of negotiation – overcoming potential resistance by exchanging something of value for agreeing to the changes – may be necessary in a union environment when resistance comes from a group of employees with high-value skills. What is substantially covered in the literature is that transformative change requires engagement, learning, knowledge sharing and dialogue across and within social activities in the organization. Dialogue – people interacting and thinking together to collectively find a solution to a problem – is central to the participative-transformative model. In dialogic interaction, employees affected by change 'come together and arrive at an understanding based on both reflection and action driven by the sharing of experiences' (Jabri, 2012: 173).

Recently retired and free to participate in management, career development and alumni mentoring, Tony has spent 34 years in human resource and functional managerial roles spanning leadership and development, managing change and core talent, negotiation skills in sales and commerce, Six Sigma and a real estate portfolio in a major multinational company. Tony's broad background permits effective liaison, networking and communication with managers and organizations seeking guidance and experience in aligning project activities that match their strategy and deliver their corporate business objectives.

In the ebook click on the play button to watch Tony talking about organizational culture, and then answer the following questions:

- Can an organization's culture affect its receptivity to transformative change?

- What other factors facilitate transformative change? What factors can inhibit it?

Interventions managed around strategies 3 and 4 deal with planned transformative change. Both change approaches are guided by what are called 'Theory E' assumptions about the purpose of and the means for change. For Beer and Nohria (2000), Theory E refers to economic value. In strategies 3 and 4, transformative change is driven from the top downwards and is planned, with the purpose of the change being to meet economic imperatives. In contrast, the strategy 2 approach is guided by 'Theory O' of change, which is based on internal capability. Its focus is the development of a high-commitment culture that is flexible and open to change, and this is achieved through an individual or group and is closely identified with organizational learning (Senge, 1990; see also Chapter 7). Beer and Nohria argue that both theories have validity, depending on the situation. Theory E is more able to capture the attention of stakeholders, to focus change on a single direction and to bring radical change fast, and is appropriate in times of crisis. In Theory O, change is more sensitive to contingencies, and is more likely to be effective and supported; however, it may also expose irreconcilable differences in interests, it may be slow to implement and it can be insufficiently visionary.

Innovation and organizational development

Some authors have observed that a large number of organizations compete by continuously changing their structure, technology and processes (see, for example, Hammer, 1997). For instance, companies such as Apple and Vodafone are constantly introducing newer features into their products or services. The ability to make changes that are permanent, evolving, cumulative and often ground breaking is seen as a core competence based on the notion of 'market-driving' rather than 'market-driven' innovation and change (Jacobs and Heracleous, 2005: 338). Jabri (2012: 102) notes that 'continuous change and changing would need to be construed as a facet of the life of people and organizations'. It is twenty-first-century global capitalism that has drawn renewed attention in recent years to the concept of the learning organization (Senge, 1990; see also Chapter 7). The complexity and rapid pace of change has also made organizational leaders keenly aware that employees' creativity can substantially contribute to an organization's innovation, effectiveness and survival (Amabile et al., 1996; Bratton et al., 2004; Maimone and Sinclair, 2014; Shalley et al., 2004). The multiperspective study by Maimone and Sinclair (2014), for example, provides insight into the cultural and individual characteristics of bottom-up organizational change, with a focus on creativity and knowledge creation.

Most theorists have defined *creativity* as the act of using one's knowledge to come up with novel ideas that are potentially useful to the organization (Shalley et al., 2004). These ideas can relate to organizational products, services, practices or processes. Ideas are considered novel if they are unique relative to other ideas that are currently available in the organization. Employee creativity forms the central premise of the 'core competence' thesis, which suggests that organizations need to build and manage their intellectual human capital (Hamel and Prahalad, 1994). As Figure 18.4 shows, knowledge and creativity provide the human energy for innovation. The cycle puts a premium on the managerial activities and organizational conditions that nurture creativity at work and on the management of information, knowledge and experiences, or what is referred to as 'knowledge management' (Mayo, 1998).

Shalley et al. (2004: 934) note that it is important to distinguish between creativity and innovation. Whereas creativity refers to a novel, potentially useful idea, not all the ideas produced are adopted. Definitions vary, but the term *innovation* is usually defined to mean novel ideas that are effectively implemented in the organization. Peter Drucker asserts that innovation is 'the act that endows resources with a new capacity to create wealth' (1985: 28). It is more of a process rather than being the outcome of geniuses: 'innovation is ... the whole process of taking a bright idea into successful implementation and use' (Bessant, 2003: 3). The 'bright idea' can be applied to developing a totally new product or service, or to improving an existing product, process or service. Once

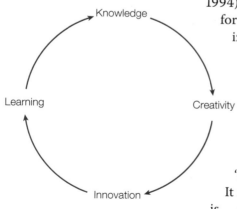

Figure 18.4 The learning, knowledge, creativity and innovation cycle

Plate 69 Creativity refers to a novel, potentially useful idea, but not all ideas are adopted. Innovation is more of a process than the outcome of geniuses, and refers to ideas that are effectively implemented in the organization. It the act of taking a bright idea that endows resources with a new capacity to create wealth.

Source: © IStockphoto.com/Robert Churchill

stop...

Identify (a) three sustaining innovations and (b) three disruptive innovations that have affected you in recent years. Were these innovations beneficial?

...and reflect

a novel idea has been developed, 'idea champions' actively promote the idea, build support for it, overcome resistance and ensure that the innovation is implemented. So innovation is a particular kind of change. All innovations involve change, but not all changes necessarily involve novel ideas or lead to significant improvements. As we noted in Chapter 7, workers can use their creativity in the service of their organization to remedy the dysfunctional aspects of the system or improve the product or service. However, they can also use their creativity to undermine the organization's rules in order to protect their dignity in and at work (Bolton, 2007; Karlsson, 2012).

Innovation

Innovation is best conceptualized as a spectrum of human activities. Bessant (2003) distinguishes between incremental innovations and breakthrough innovations. *Incremental innovations* improve existing products, services and processes: a more efficient vacuum cleaner, motorcar or mobile phone, for example. Incremental innovations enable organizations to 'do things better'. Over time, and in cumulative form, the effect of incremental innovations can be significant. *Breakthrough innovations* enable organizations to 'do things different'. Breakthrough innovations are the kind reported in the media and introduce wholly new products and services, such as the iPhone or magnetic resonance imaging or social networking websites such as Facebook. Christensen et al. (2000) classify this spectrum of activity as 'sustaining' and 'disruptive' innovations.

Bessant (2003) observes that most organizational innovation follows a pattern of occasional breakthrough (for example, Research in Motion's BlackBerry) followed by long periods of cumulative improvement (for example, Apple's iPhone). The US 3M Corporation, for instance, which many organizations aspire to match, has built a reputation as one of the most innovative organizations in the world. Porter and Ketels (2003) observe that innovation has a 'cultural' dimension. Comparing the UK and the USA, for example, they argue that UK managers have a low propensity to innovate, due to underinvestment in both human capital and new technology. Mazzucato's (2013) *The Entrepreneurial State: Debunking Private vs. Public Sector Myths* offers an alternative narrative on corporate innovation, and challenges the popular idea that the state cannot 'pick winners' and is incapable of innovation and entrepreneurial risk taking.

Organizational development

The *organizational development* approach to innovation and change is based on the premise that high-quality human capital matters. As the late Steve Jobs (1955–2011), inventor and CEO of Apple Inc, observed, 'Innovation has nothing to do with how many R&D dollars you have … It's about the people you have, how you're led, and how much you get it' (cited by Bessant, 2003: 6). In the quest for high performance, organizational development is an all-encompassing strategic approach to change that aims to develop agile structures, processes and people. Its theoretical roots are to be found in Kurt Lewin's work on the T-group in organizations (Burns, 2004). The term 'organizational development' refers to a cluster of planned interventions, managed from the top, using social and behavioural science knowledge and humanistic-democratic values to address change at an organization-wide level.

The organizational development paradigm is value loaded. Partly rooted in humanistic psychology, organizational development change agents value meaningful work and human growth over boring work and social alienation, self-control over management control, cooperation over conflict, and participative management over dictatorial management. Change agents with this motivation hold concepts such as power, authority, control and coercion in relatively low esteem. Dignity *in* and *at* work lie at the heart of the employment relationship (Bolton, 2007), which forms the bedrock for an effective and healthy organization. Organizational development is viewed as part of a 'bureaucracy-busting' agenda, a management strategy for leveraging employees' creative ideas and innovations. Robbins and Judge (2013) have identified the underlying values in most organizational development interventions:

stop...

Analyse how organizational development techniques help to enhance support for organizational change.

...and reflect

- *Respect* – employees should be treated with dignity and respect.
- *Trust* – healthy organizations are characterized by trust, authenticity and a supportive climate.
- *Power equalization* – effective organizations do not emphasize hierarchical control.
- *Confrontation* – organizational problems should not be ignored but should be openly confronted.
- *Participation* – employees affected by change will be more committed to its success when they are involved in the decisions surrounding the change.

Common interventions based in organizational development have been discussed in depth elsewhere in this book. Six popular organizational development interventions that change agents might consider using are shown in Table 18.3.

Table 18.3 Popular organizational development interventions

Intervention	Description	Application
Action research	The group analyses the problem; the results are used to design improvements	To address known problems
Action learning	The 'set' help each other to work on individually owned problems in a supportive way	To solve problems through rich questions and dialogue
Sensitivity training	This is a method for changing behaviour through unstructured group interaction	To develop social skills and emotional intelligence
Employee surveys	Feedback is used to identify actions to make improvements	To gather evidence on perceptions and solve communication and other problems
Process consultation	An outside consultant facilitates problem-solving sessions	To perceive, understand and act upon process incidents
Team building	This uses high-interaction team activities to identify team roles and increase openness and trust	To help team members understand their roles and improve team effectiveness

There is evidence-based support for using organizational development interventions to make fundamental and long-term improvements. The research suggests that a configuration and complementary bundles of organizational development practices give rise to positive outcomes for management. This resonates with research on the HRM–performance relationship. Ichniowski et al. (1996), for example, observe that there are no one or two 'magic bullets' that are *the* work practices that will improve both individuals' capabilities and commitment and organizational effectiveness. Instead, the most effective approach is the systematic application of a *bundle* of organizational development practices that change *whole systems* as well as the cultural human capital in the organization. Organizational development practices have been found to improve employees' morale and commitment to the changes, and to increase employee flexibility (Warrick, 1984). Reviewing over 100 studies, the meta-analysis carried out by Neuman et al. (1989) found that multifaceted organizational development practices, rather than just a single technique, were more effective in changing human behaviour.

The eclectic nature of organizational development interventions and the abundance of conflicting definitions inevitably mean that the theory and practice of organizational development have received criticism (Garrow, 2009). The idea behind the organizational development model is that it can produce continuous change because it enables organizations to deliver agile structures, processes and people on the basis of socially consensual management practices. A consensus is developed through a combination of organizational development practices including action learning, team building and employee engagement mechanisms. In this regard, it typically means that organizational development focuses on 'soft HRM' values rather than top-down 'hard HRM' (Bratton and Gold, 2012). Internal organizational development champions, located within the HRM function, may not have a presence around the 'strategic table' and may lack contact and influence with senior executives (Burke, 2014). According to Porras and Bradford (2004) organizational development has tried to impose its own humanistic values instead of working with organizations' own values. The organizational development approach to change can, as a result, be undermined if it is perceived as a new management 'fad' as managers search for 'new fixes' and solutions to facilitate change (Bunker et al., 2004). In her review, Garrow (2009: 15) concludes that organizational development has a strong legacy, but there is a 'need for both a whole system approach and one that is underpinned by values whether these are the original human relations values or more general organizational values that inspire employees'.

Paradox in change management

Mainstream literature sees organizational change as a rational response to unpredictable and uncontrollable external forces for change. Atzeni (2014) observes that critical social thinkers have long argued that constant change is an endemic feature of capitalism that is best captured by Marx and Engels' classic phrase 'All that is solid melts into air.' In addition, critics of capitalism have noted that ideas on ideology are highly relevant as a means of analysing the proactive behaviour of the corporate elite (Bratton and Denham, 2014). Arguably, organizations try to shape the turbulent external environment by lobbying politicians and funding research (for example, debunking climate change science) to counter ideas that challenge their interests. In the post-2008 global financial crisis epoch, for example, the richest 0.1 per cent corporate earners have lobbied senior European politicians to ensure that their businesses are not hampered by 'wealth-destroying' regulation, that state intervention is kept to a minimum and that taxes remain low. As Chakrabortty (2013) observes, lobbying politicians takes on a global dimension when it occurs at the annual World Economic Forum held at Davos, Switzerland. The Forum's notional purpose is to allow corporate executives, bankers and heads of state to mull openly over the future of the global capitalist economy. However, its real business takes place in private sessions with corporate peers and 'amenable politicians', and the price of the entry tickets to these sessions starts at around £98,000 (Chakrabortty, 2013: S5). The 'Davos effect' provides a context for the argument that 'The bigger the share of income the rich enjoy … the more power they have to enact policies in their own interests – and the more they do so' (McQuaig and Brooks, 2011: 226).

Mainstream management thinkers tend to view organizational change as a linear process from one organizational state to another, and assume that the outcome of change is always positive for both organizations and employees. Mainstream accounts fail to understand why change is often resented and resisted by managers and other employees. By and large, they assume that resistance occurs only when the rationale for change is not communicated effectively. Critical workplace scholars argue that a movement from one state to another is fraught with tension and contradiction. As we have emphasized throughout this book, understanding organizational behaviour, including organizational change, will allude us until and unless we understand capitalism's inherent contradictions. A conventional critique of orthodox change strategies is that it neglects power inequalities and structural conflict between employer and employees. Organizational change invariably threatens the status quo and therefore inherently implies political activity and power (see Chapter 14).

Although mainstream literature tends to focus on the power relations effects on managers high up in the organization, workers low in the organization, especially those employed on precarious zero-hours contracts, have a lot to lose from change. In this regard, Bolton and Houlihan (2009) provide insightful empirical accounts, many with a gender dimension, that probe the degree to which the rhetoric of change management is matching the reality. For example, changes in power relations increase the vulnerability of non-unionized workers, with 'women's harassment by men a frequent feature' (p. 71). It is not so much that the effects of globalization and neo-liberalism per se shape the experience of work (Sennett, 2004), but that the consequences for daily life, 'the constant movement of managers and organizational forms leads to the disablement of human relating in the workplace leaving so many workers without a sense of *witness* in their work, creating a systemic sense of perceived lack of fair play' (Bolton and Houlihan, 2009: 16, emphasis in original). The power dynamics within the organization will, to a large degree, determine the pace and scale of change. If workers perceive that new organizational forms or processes will have a negative effect, the change will be a source of resistance. Critical thinkers have focused on the concept of creative destruction with particular emphasis on the potential for destruction – jobs, conditions of employment, skills, status – that often causes organizational change to be resisted by employees. The effects of the post-2008 global financial crisis era on employment and working conditions have brought to the fore the role of workers in resisting or finding alternatives to a changed, exploitative context (Atzeni, 2014).

> **stop...**
>
> What does it mean to say that constant change 'leads to the disablement of human relating in the workplace'?
>
> **...and reflect**

Chapter summary

- In this final chapter, we have covered a wide range of issues that have built upon topics covered in earlier chapters. Organizational change refers to a structured process in which an organization shifts from its current state to some specific desired future state to improve the effectiveness of the organization. Theorists have classified change into different types: transitional versus transformational, continuous versus episodic, evolutionary versus revolutionary. Whereas transitional change utilizes existing capabilities and resources in the organization, transformational change represents a radical shift in that it questions the prevailing assumptions and values associated with the existing state, and involves major modification to the mission and changes to the organization's structure, systems, technology and culture.

- An organization's external and internal environment act as a stimulant or trigger for change. Theorizing the organization as being embedded in society helps us to understand the external forces that signal the need for change largely by analysing the STEPLE – Social, Technological, Economic, Political, Legal and Ecological – context. A myriad of internal forces drive change within the organization. These internal triggers include people, structure, work and technology.

- Mainstream thinkers emphasize the positive outcomes, but change is often associated with negative outcomes, and resistance at both the individual and the organizational level is a common phenomenon. Individual sources of resistance reside in basic human needs and characteristics such as personality, perception, values and motivation. Six common reasons why individuals resist change are economics, security, habit, selective perception, inconvenience and fear of the unknown. Organizations, by their very nature, are conservative. Six common reasons why organizations resist change are culture, structural inertia, existing contracts and agreements, established resource allocations, expertise and power relations.

- The propensity to resist planned change is why strategies to manage change need to be developed. Managing organizational change is the process of planning and executing change in the workplace in such a way as to minimize individual and organizational resistance while at the same time maximizing employees' cooperation and the effectiveness of the change process. The work of Kurt Lewin and John Kotter and force-field analysis were examined. Contingency change strategies acknowledge the importance of the timescale and scale of change in generating different challenges that demand significantly different styles of change management. The chapter introduced a typology of four change strategies: directive-operational, engagement-continuous, authoritarian-transformative and participative-transformative.

- The chapter noted that there are both advantages and limitations of participative methods of change management. Participative mechanisms can nurture creative thinking and increase employees' commitment to change, but this process is time-consuming. A rapid and major organizational transformation may be more successful when it is implemented using a dictatorial managerial style.

- Employees' creativity can substantially contribute to organizational innovation, effectiveness and survival. Creativity refers to the act of using an individual's knowledge to come up with novel ideas that are potentially useful to the organization. We said that innovation is best conceptualized as a spectrum of human activities. We distinguished between incremental innovations and breakthrough innovations. Incremental innovations improve existing products, services and processes; they enable organizations to 'do things better'. Breakthrough innovations enable organizations to 'do things different'.

- Organizational development approaches change based on the premise that the quality of human capital matters. In the quest for high performance, organizational development is an all-encompassing strategic approach to change that aims to develop agile structures, processes and people. The analysis offered here emphasized that the concept of organizational development is value loaded. It is rooted in humanistic psychology and values meaningful work and human growth over boring work and social alienation, self-control over management control, cooperation over conflict, and participative management over dictatorial management. Finally, we noted that the eclectic nature of organizational development and the abundance of conflicting definitions inevitably mean that organizational development has come under criticism.

IN THE EBOOK ACCESS **WEB BASED ASSIGNMENTS** TO APPLY YOUR LEARNING.

Chapter review questions

1 What is the main difference between transitional and transformative change?

2 What are the main sources of resistance to organizational change, and how should resistance be managed?

3 In your judgement, which of the theoretical approaches outlined in this chapter best helps us to understand the role of change agents?

4 Organizations are advised to change constantly in order to compete to survive. What dangers come with this advice?

5 What is the difference between creativity and innovation? What are the main types of innovation, and how can an organization develop a climate that encourages employee creativity?

6 What contribution do critical organizational theorists make to our understanding of planned organizational change?

Further reading

Benn, S., Dunphy, D. and Griffiths, A. (2014) *Organizational Change for Corporate Sustainability* (3rd edn), London: Routledge.

Burke, W. W. (2014) *Organization Change: Theory and Practice*, Thousand Oaks, CA: Sage.

Burns, B. (2004) 'Kurt Lewin and complexity theories: back to the future?', *Journal of Change Management*, 4(4), pp. 309–25.

Cameron, E. and Green, M. (2012) *Making Sense of Change Management: A Complete Guide to the Models, Tools and Techniques of Organizational Change* (3rd edn), London: Kogan Page.

Cheung-Judge, Mee-Yan and Holbeche, L. (2011) *Organization Development: A Practitioner's Guide for OD and HR*, London: Kogan Page.

Garrow, V. (2009) *OD: Past, Present and Future*, Brighton: Institute for Employment Studies. Available at: www.employment-studies.co.uk/pdflibrary/wp22.pdf.

Hendry, C. and Jenkins, R. (1997) 'Psychological contracts and new deals', *Human Resource Management Journal*, 7(1), pp. 38–44.

Jabri, M. (2012) *Managing Organizational Change*, Basingstoke: Palgrave Macmillan.

Maimone, F. and Sinclair, M. (2014) 'Dancing in the dark: creativity, knowledge creation and (emergent) organizational change', *Journal of Organizational Change*, 27(2), pp. 344–61.

McCabe, D. (2014) 'Making out and making do: how employees resist and make organizational change work thorough consent in a UK bank', *New Technology, Work and Employment*, 29(1), pp. 57–71.

Chapter case study: Resistance at RIC Health Services

The setting

RIC Health Services (RICHS) is a small to medium-sized enterprise operating as a supplier of sophisticated health and laboratory equipment to hospital and health research centres. RICHS's relationship with its customers is based around a high-trust, high-quality, 24/7 maintenance service. The company employs 70 staff consisting of technicians, office staff, managers and drivers, in two locations in Scotland – Glasgow and Edinburgh.

RICHS puts particular emphasis on environmental education through staff training and induction. New staff receive a half-day induction on sustainability during which they watch films including *An Inconvenient Truth*. In addition, monthly departmental meetings feature a 'green slot' that shows films with a message about environmental sustainability. RICHS also runs an internship programme, which has been a key source of new ideas for green initiatives.

The company has gone through two reorganizations in the past 3 years. Initially, its structure changed from a functional to a matrix form. However, managers complained that the matrix structure confused the authority and responsibility relationships. Facing competitive pressures and reductions in health capital equipment budgets since 2008, RICHS's senior management has to find ways of reducing operating costs.

The problem

At a recent meeting of the senior management team, it was decided to close the Edinburgh site and centralize all the company's operations in Glasgow. Because the lease on the building was due to expire, the relocation would take place within 6 months. The move would allow the Glasgow office to be redesigned as 'open plan', which would create savings by reducing energy costs, and the number of office staff would be cut by 5 per cent. There were to be no compulsory redundancies as it was anticipated that senior staff would retire rather than relocate. The number of front-line technicians would remain the same. To reduce operating costs, the company also plans to introduce a number of 'green' initiatives, including the following:

- *Recycling and waste reduction initiatives* – practical uses of 'nudge economics', such as putting lids on waste bins but not on recycling bins, which makes recycling easier. They will also provide recycling services to their customers.
- *Transport initiatives* – company drivers will be provided with training in fuel-efficient driving, and a bonus of around £50 twice a year will be offered to fuel-efficient drivers. The company will also introduce home working, and the entire sales team will work from home, only attending the office for monthly staff meetings. Home working will be facilitated by cloud computing.

Prior to the scheduled monthly meeting at the Edinburgh office, Eilidh James did not believe the rumours. But now that the rumours had been confirmed, she was annoyed. 'I can't believe it. We've only just got over the last reorganization,' she said. 'Now they tell me I have to relocate to Glasgow'.

Eilidh was not alone in her anger. The technicians attending the meeting were just as concerned with the prospect of relocating. 'The extra travel costs is a wage cut', said Fraser Thompson, an instrument technician. The other technicians attending nodded in agreement. Maura Phillips, a sales rep, liked the idea of working from home but didn't speak out.

Management's aim is to decrease the company's carbon footprint by one-third and deliver 50 per cent more services per tonne of carbon by 2020. To be successful, however, the relocation and the proposed green initiatives need to be fully supported by all RICHS's staff.

The task

With this information in mind, prepare a report or a presentation, either individually or in a group, addressing the following:

- What type of change is being attempted at RICHS?
- With reference to the material in this chapter, explain Eilidh's and Fraser's resistance.

- Identify any unintended consequences that might emerge as a result of the change, and that might have knock-on effects on the company.
- Choose a change strategy for what is happening at RICHS. Is a directive-operational approach appropriate, or an engagement-continuous one? Or what about the authoritarian-trans-formative or the participative-transformative approach? Justify your recommendation by identifying the benefits and disadvantages of the four options.
- Discuss what, if anything, you would have done differently if you had been a member of the senior management team.

Sources and further information

Plank, R. (2011) 'Green behaviour: barriers, facilitators and the role of attributions', in D. Bartlett (ed.), *Going Green: The Psychology of Sustainability in the Workplace*, Leicester: British Psychological Society.

Simpson, A. (2011) 'Winning the persuasion game', *Green Futures Magazine*, May.

Note: This case study was written by the author, John Bratton.

VISIT THE *ONLINE RESOURCE CENTRE* AT HTTPS://HE.PALGRAVE.COM/COMPANION/BRATTON-WORK-AND-ORGANIZATIONAL-BEHAVIOUR3/ FOR A RANGE OF MATERIALS TO HELP YOU EXPLORE FURTHER AND REVISE CONCEPTS IN THIS CHAPTER.

Glossary

A

activity theory: a view of adult learning that envisions learning as a social process whereby individual and group agency and learning occurs through interlocking human activity systems shaped by social norms and a community of practice

agency: often used as a substitute for 'action', but with a wider meaning in sociology. Here, it emphasizes the undetermined nature of human action, as opposed to the alleged determinism of structural theories. This wider meaning highlights the psychological and socially constructed make-up of the actor, and the capacity for voluntary action

alienation: a feeling of powerlessness and estrangement from other people and from oneself

andragogy: the processes associated with the organization and practice of teaching adults; more specifically, various kinds of interaction in facilitating learning situations

anomie: a state condition in which social control becomes ineffective as a result of the loss of shared values and sense of purpose in society

appropriation: the process through which, in capitalist workplaces, a proportion of the value produced in work activities – above investment in raw materials, equipment, health benefits, facilities and so on – is retained under the private control of owners, ownership groups and/or investors. A more critical perception of this process sees it as an 'exploitation' of the organization's collective activities for private use

artefacts: the observable symbols and signs of an organization's culture

authority: the power granted by some form of either active or passive consent that bestows legitimacy

B

bottom-up processing: perception led predominantly by gathering external sensory data and then working out what they mean

bounded rationality: processing limited and imperfect information and satisficing (see the text) rather than maximizing when choosing between alternatives

bourgeoisie (or capitalist class): Karl Marx's term for the class comprising those who own and control the means of production

brainstorming: a freewheeling, face-to-face meeting where team members generate as many ideas as possible, piggy-back on the ideas of others, and avoid evaluating anyone's ideas during the idea-generating stage

bureaucracy: an organizational model characterized by a hierarchy of authority, a clear division of labour, explicit rules and procedures, and an impersonal approach to personnel matters

bureaucratization: a tendency towards a formal organization with a hierarchy of authority, a clear division of labour and an emphasis on written rules

business process re-engineering: a radical change of business processes by applying information technology to integrate operations, and maximizing their value-added content

C

capitalism: an economic system characterized by private ownership of the means of production, from which personal profits can be derived through market competition and without government intervention

capitalist modernity: a term used to refer to the period in the history of social relations dating roughly from the 1780s that is characterized by the constant revolutionizing of production and culture

causal attribution: the explanations an individual chooses to use, which are either internal (about the person) or external (about the situation), and either stable or transitory

centralization: the degree to which formal decision authority is held by a small group of people, typically those at the top of the organizational hierarchy

ceremonies: planned events that represent more formal social artefacts than rituals

change agent: the activities of an individual(s) that are directed towards accomplishing a change.

charismatic leadership: a leadership style that emphasizes symbolic leader behaviour, visionary and inspirational messages, an appeal to values and self-sacrifice

class conflict: a term for the struggle between the capitalist class and the working class

class consciousness: Karl Marx's term for the awareness of a common identity based on a person's position in the means of production

classical conditioning: a view of 'instrumental' learning whose adherents assert that the reinforcement is non-contingent on the animal's behaviour, that is, it is delivered without regard to the animal's behaviour. By contrast, in instrumental conditioning, the delivery of the reinforcement is contingent – dependent – on what the animal does

cohesiveness: refers to all the positive and negative forces or social pressures that cause individuals to maintain their membership in specific groups

commodification: in Marxist theory, the production of goods and services (commodities) for exchange in the marketplace, as opposed to the direct consumption of commodities

communication: the process by which information is transmitted and understood between two or more people

communities of practice: informal groups bound together by shared expertise and a passion for a particular activity or interest

competencies: the abilities, values, personality traits and other characteristics of people that lead to a superior performance

competitive advantage: the ability of a work organization to add more value for its customers and shareholders than its rivals, and thus gain a position of advantage in the marketplace

complexity: the intricate departmental and interpersonal relationships that exist within a work organization

configurations: defines technology as the combination of social and technical factors. Configurations are a complex mix of standardized and locally customized elements that are highly specific to an organization

conflict: the process in which one party perceives that its interests are being opposed or negatively affected by another party

conflict of interest: a condition in which the needs of one party (such as an individual or group) run counter to the needs of another

conflict perspective: the sociological approach that views groups in society as engaged in a continuous power struggle for the control of scarce resources

consideration: the extent to which a leader is likely to nurture job relationships and encourage mutual trust and respect between the leader and his or her subordinates

constructionism: the view that researchers actively construct reality on the basis of their understandings, which are mainly the result of a shared culture. It contrasts with realism (see below)

constructionist model: maintains that feelings are socially constructed and do not apply to inner states, but are cultural meanings given to emotions

constructivist approach: an approach to technology that tends not to focus on social or political influences, but instead sees technologies as defined strictly by how they are put to use

contradictions: contradictions are said to occur within social systems when the various principles that underlie these social arrangements conflict with each other

control: the collection and analysis of information about all aspects of the work organization and the use of comparisons that are either historical and/or based on benchmarking against another business unit

core competency: the underlying core characteristics of an organization's workforce that result in effective performance and give a competitive advantage to the firm

corporate social responsibility: an organization's moral obligation to its stakeholders

corporation: a large-scale organization that has legal powers (such as the ability to enter into contracts and buy and sell property) separate from its individual owner or owners

co-variation model: Kelley's model that uses information about the co-occurrence of a person, a behaviour and potential causes to work out an explanation

creativity: the capacity to develop an original product, service or idea that makes a socially recognized contribution

critical approach: an approach to technology that tends to focus on how the social and political effects are produced through contestation and negotiation

critical realism: a realist epistemology which asserts that the study of human behaviour should be concerned with identifying the structures that generate that behaviour in order to change it

cultural relativism: the appreciation that all cultures have intrinsic worth and should be judged and understood on their own terms

culture: the knowledge, language, values, customs and material objects that are passed from person to person and from one generation to the next in a human group or society

D

decision making: a conscious process of making choices between one or more alternatives with the intention of moving towards some desired state of affairs

deductive approach: research in which the investigator begins with a theory and then collects information and data to test the theory

deindustrialization: a term to describe the decline of the manufacturing sector of the economy

Delphi technique: a structured team decision-making process of systematically pooling the collective knowledge of experts on a particular subject to make decisions, predict the future or identify opposing views

deskilling: a reduction in the proficiency needed to perform a specific job, which leads to a corresponding reduction in the wages paid for that job

dialectic: refers to the movement of history through the transcendence of internal contradictions that in turn produce new contradictions, themselves requiring solutions

dialogue: a process of conversation among team members in which they learn about each other's mental models and assumptions, and eventually form a common model for thinking within the team

discourse: a way of talking about and conceptualizing an issue, presented through concepts, ideas and vocabulary that recur in texts

discourse community: a way of talking about and conceptualizing an issue, presented through ideas and concepts, spoken or written, within a social group or community (such as lawyers or physicians)

distributive justice: justice based on the principle of fairness of outcomes

divergent thinking: involves reframing a problem in a unique way and generating different approaches to the issue

divisional structure: an organizational structure that groups employees around geographical areas, clients or outputs

division of labour: the allocation of work tasks to various groups or categories of employee

dyad: a group consisting of two members

E

effort-performance (E→P) expectancy: the individual's perceived probability that his or her effort will result in a particular level of performance

ego: according to Sigmund Freud, the rational, reality-oriented component of personality that imposes restrictions on the innate pleasure-seeking drives of the id

emotional intelligence: the personal faculty of knowing and managing one's own emotions, perceiving and understanding emotions in others and handling relationships

emotional labour: the effort, planning and control needed to express organizationally desired emotions during interpersonal transactions

empathy: a person's ability to understand and be sensitive to the feelings, thoughts and situations of others

empirical approach: research that attempts to answer questions through a systematic collection and analysis of data

empiricism: an approach to the study of social reality suggesting that only knowledge gained through experience and the senses is acceptable

employee involvement: the degree to which employees influence how their work is organized and carried out

employment equity: a strategy to eliminate the effects of discrimination and to make employment opportunities available to groups who have been excluded

empowerment: a psychological concept in which people experience more self-determination, meaning, competence and impact regarding their role in the organization

environment: refers to the broad economic, political, legal and social forces, such as a nation's business system, that are present in the minds of the organization's members and may influence their decision making and constrain their strategic choices

epistemology: a theory of knowledge particularly used to refer to a standpoint on what should pass as acceptable knowledge

equality: the state of being equal, especially in status, rights or opportunities

equity theory: the theory that explains how people develop perceptions of fairness in the distribution and exchange of resources

ERG theory: Alderfer's motivation theory suggests that more than one need may motivate simultaneously, and, contrary to Maslow's theory, that when a higher order need is obstructed, the desire to satisfy a lower need increases

escalation of commitment: the tendency to allocate more resources to a failing course of action or to repeat an apparently bad decision

ethics: the study of moral principles or values that determine whether actions are right or wrong, and outcomes are good or bad

ethnocentrism: the tendency to regard one's own culture and group as the standard, and thus superior, whereas all other groups are seen as inferior

exit and voice: a concept referring to the basic choice that defines an important part of employees' experience at work: they can either exit (leave) or exercise their 'voice' (have a say) in how the workplace is run

expectancy theory: a motivation theory based on the idea that work effort is directed toward behaviours that people believe will lead to desired outcomes

explicit knowledge: knowledge that is ordered and can be communicated between people

extrinsic motivator: a wide range of external outcomes or rewards to motivate employees, including bonuses or increases in pay

extrinsic rewards: a wide range of external outcomes or rewards to motivate employees

extroversion: a personality dimension that characterizes people who are outgoing, talkative, sociable and assertive

F

factor analysis: a statistical technique used for a large number of variables to explain the pattern of relationships in the data

factory system: a relatively large work unit that concentrated people and machines in one building, enabling the specialization of productive functions and, at the same time, a closer supervision of employees than did the pre-industrial putting-out system. Importantly, the factory system gave rise to the need for a new conception of time and organizational behaviour

false consensus effect: the tendency to overestimate the degree to which other people think and behave in the same way as we do

feedback: any information that people receive about the consequences of their behaviour

feminism: the belief that all people – both women and men – are equal, and that they should be valued equally and have equal rights

feminist perspective: the sociological approach that focuses on the significance of gender in understanding and explaining the inequalities that exist between men and women in the household, in the paid labour force, and in the realms of politics, law and culture

Fiedler's contingency model: suggests that leader effectiveness depends on whether the person's natural leadership style is appropriately matched to the situation

flexibility: action in response to global competition, including employees performing a number of tasks (functional flexibility), the employment of part-time and contract workers (numerical flexibility) and performance-related pay (reward flexibility)

flexible specialization: a competitive strategy whereby a company invests in multipurpose equipment and employs and trains its workforce to be multiskilled, in order to adjust quickly to a fast-changing business environment

force-field analysis: an approach drawing on the physical (material) forces of nature, with the premise that, in any organizational setting, there are forces that push for change and forces that resist or act against change

Fordism: a term used to describe mass production using assembly line technology that allowed for a greater division of labour and time and motion management, techniques pioneered by the American car manufacturer Henry Ford in the early twentieth century

formal channels: a communication process that follows an organization's chain of command

formalization: the degree to which organizations standardize behaviour through rules, procedures, formal training and related mechanisms

formal organization: a highly structured group formed for the purpose of completing certain tasks or achieving specific goals

functional configuration: an organizational structure that organizes employees around specific knowledge or other resources

functionalist perspective: the sociological approach that views society as a stable, orderly system

functional theory: a sociological perspective emphasizing that human action is governed by relatively stable structures

fundamental attribution error: the tendency to favour internal attributions for the behaviour of others but external ones to explain our own behaviour

G

game theory: a social theory premised on the notion that people do what is best for themselves given their resources and circumstances, as in some form of a competitive game

gender bias: behaviour that shows favouritism towards one gender over the other

gender identity: a person's perception of the self as female or male

gender role: attitudes, behaviour and activities that are socially defined as appropriate for each sex and are learned through the socialization process

gender socialization: the aspect of socialization that contains specific messages and practices concerning the nature of being female or male in a specific group or society

genre: a term to describe the different kinds of writing and reading in the workplace, including reports, letters and memoranda

Gestalt: a German word that means form or organization. Gestalt psychology emphasizes organizational processes in learning. The Gestalt slogan 'The whole is greater than the sum of the parts' draws attention to relationships between the parts

glass ceiling: the pattern of employment opportunities that disproportionately limits the achievement of top administrative posts by certain social groups

globalization: when an organization extends its activities to other parts of the world, actively participates in other markets, and competes against organizations located in other countries

goals: the immediate or ultimate objectives that employees are trying to accomplish from their work effort

goal setting: the process of motivating employees and clarifying their role perceptions by establishing performance objectives

grapevine: an unstructured and informal communication network founded on social relationships rather than organizational charts or job descriptions

group context: refers to anything from the specific task a work group is engaged in, to the broad environmental forces that are present in the minds of group members and may influence them

group dynamics: the systematic study of human behaviour in groups, including the nature of groups, group development, and the interrelations between individuals and groups, other groups and other elements of formal organizations

group norms: the unwritten rules and expectations that specify or shape appropriate human behaviour in a work group or team

group processes: refers to group members' actions, communications and decision making

group structure: a stable pattern of social interaction among work group members created by a role structure and group norms

groupthink: the tendency of highly cohesive groups to value consensus at the price of decision quality

growth needs: a person's needs for self-esteem through personal achievement, as well as for self-actualization

H

halo and horns effect: a perceptual error whereby our general impression of a person, usually based on one prominent characteristic, colours the perception of other characteristics of that person

hegemony: a conception of power that includes both conflict as well as consent and leadership by generating a particular worldview or 'common sense' on relevant and appropriate action; a term derived from Karl Marx's historical materialism and his theory of social classes. According to Marx, each ruling class leads and dominates over others, which includes the dissemination of ideas

high-context culture: a culturally sanctioned style of communication that assumes high levels of shared knowledge and so uses very concise, sometimes obscure, speech

high-performance working environment: describes efforts to manage employment relations and work operations using a set of distinctive 'better' human resource practices. These are intended to improve outcomes such as employee commitment, flexibility and cooperation, which in turn enhance the organization's competitive advantage

horizontal or 'lean' structure: an integrated system of manufacturing, originally developed by Toyota in Japan. The emphasis is on flexibility and teamwork

horizontal tensions: tensions and contradictions that emerge in terms of people's participation in group endeavours irrespective of hierarchical institutional relationships

HRM cycle: an analytical framework that diagrammatically connects human resource selection, appraisal, development and rewards to organizational performance

human relations: a school of management thought that emphasizes the importance of social processes in the organization

human rights: the conditions and treatment expected for all human beings

hypotheses: statements making empirically testable declarations that certain variables and their corresponding measures are related in a specific way proposed by theory

hypothesis: in research studies, a tentative statement of the relationship between two or more concepts or variables

I

id: Sigmund Freud's term for the component of personality that includes all of the individual's basic biological drives and needs that demand immediate gratification

ideal type: an abstract model that describes the recurring characteristics of some phenomenon

ideology: a term with multiple uses, but in particular referring to perceptions of reality as distorted by class interests, and the ideas, legal arrangements and culture that arise from class relations (a term taken from Marx)

idiographic approach: an approach to explanation in which we seek to explain the relationships among variables within a particular case or event; it contrasts with nomothetic analysis

impression management: the process of trying to control or influence the impressions of oneself that other people form

in-groups: groups to which someone perceives he or she belongs, which he or she accordingly evaluates favourably

individualism: the extent to which a person values independence and personal uniqueness

inductive approach: the researcher begins with data collection and observations and then data are used to develop theory

industrial democracy: a broad term used to describe a range of programmes, processes and social institutions designed to provide greater employee involvement and participation and influence in the decision-making process, and to exchange ideas on how to improve working conditions and product and service quality in the workplace

Industrial Revolution: the relatively rapid economic transformation that began in Britain in the 1780s. It involved a factory- and technology-driven shift from agriculture and small cottage-based manufacturing to manufacturing industries, and the consequences of that shift for virtually all human activities

informal channels: a communication process that follows unofficial means of communication, sometimes called 'the grapevine', usually based on social relations in which employees talk about work

informal group: two or more people who form a unifying relationship around personal rather than organizational goals

informal structure: a term used to describe the aspect of organizational life in which participants' day-to-day activities and interactions ignore, bypass or do not correspond with the official rules and procedures of the bureaucracy

information overload: a situation in which the receiver becomes overwhelmed by the information that needs to be processed. It may be caused by the quantity of the information to be processed, the speed at which the information presents itself or the complexity of the information to be processed

initiating: part of a behavioural theory of leadership that describes the degree to which a leader defines and structures her or his own role and the roles of followers towards attaining the group's assigned goals

innovation: the adoption of any process, thinking, product or service that is new to a particular organization or subsystem

instrumentalist or technocratic approach: approaches to technology that are uncritical of its broader social, political and economic significance, viewing technologies as autonomous and positive

instrumentality: a term associated with process theories of motivation that refers to an individual's perceived probability that good performance will result in valued outcomes or rewards, measured on a scale from 0 (no chance) to 1 (certainty)

intellectual capital: the sum of an organization's human capital, structural capital and relationship capital

interactionism: what people do when they are in one another's presence, for example in a work group or team

interactionist model: interprets emotions as an property that emerges from the interaction between the body and the environment

interpretivism: the view held in many qualitative studies that reality comes from shared meaning among people in that environment

intrinsic motivator: a wide range of motivation interventions in the workplace, from inner satisfaction after following some action (such as recognition by an employer or co-workers) to intrinsic pleasures derived from an activity (such as playing a musical instrument for pleasure)

intrinsic rewards: inner satisfaction following some action (such as recognition by an employer or co-workers) or intrinsic pleasures derived from an activity (such as playing a musical instrument for pleasure)

introversion: a personality dimension that characterizes people who are territorial and solitary

intuition: the ability to know when a problem or opportunity exists and to select the best course of action without conscious reasoning

J

job characteristics model: a job design model that relates the motivational properties of jobs to the specific personal and organizational consequences of those properties

job design: the process of assigning tasks to a job, including the interdependency of those tasks with other jobs

job enlargement: increasing the number of tasks employees perform in their jobs

job enrichment: employees are given more responsibility for scheduling, coordinating and planning their own work

job rotation: the practice of moving employees from one job to another

job satisfaction: a person's attitude regarding his or her job and work content

K

knowledge management: the capture of the individual's and group's tacit knowledge and learning, and its conversion into explicit knowledge so that it can be shared with, and built on by, others in the organization

knowledge work: paid work that is of an intellectual nature, is non-repetitive and results oriented, engages scientific and/or artistic knowledge, and demands continuous learning and creativity

knowledge worker: a worker who depends on her or his skills, knowledge and judgement, established through additional training and/or schooling

L

labour power: the potential gap between a worker's capacity or potential to work and their actual work

labour process: the process whereby labour is applied to materials and technology to produce goods and services that can be sold in the market as commodities. The term is typically applied to the distinctive labour processes of capitalism in which owners/managers design, control and monitor work tasks so as to maximize the extraction of surplus value from the workers' labour activity

language: a system of symbols that expresses ideas and enables people to think and communicate with one another

leadership: influencing, motivating and enabling others to contribute towards the effectiveness and success of the organizations of which they are members

learning: the process of the construction and ongoing reinforcement of new knowledge

learning contract: a learning plan that links an organization's competitive strategy with an individual's key learning objectives. It enumerates the learning and/or competencies that are expected to be demonstrated at some point in the future

learning cycle: a view of adult learning that emphasizes learning as a continuous process

learning organization: a metaphor representing an ideal of whole-organization learning on the part of all employees, and the use of learning to create value and transform the organization; an organization that facilitates its employees' learning as a strategy for continuous planned change

legitimacy: a term describing agreement with the rights and responsibilities associated with a position, social values, a system and so on

life chances: Weber's term for the extent to which people have access to important scarce resources such as food, clothing, shelter, education and employment

lifelong learning: the belief that adults should be encouraged, and given the opportunity, to learn either formally in education institutions or informally on or off the job

linguistic relativity: the theory that the language we speak has such a fundamental influence on the way we interpret the world that we think differently from those who speak a different language

locus of control: a personality trait referring to the extent to which people believe events are within their control

looking-glass self: Cooley's term for the way in which a person's sense of self is derived from the perceptions of others

low-context culture: a culturally sanctioned style of communication that assumes low levels of shared knowledge and so uses verbally explicit speech

Luddites: a group of textile workers, led by Ned Ludd in early nineteenth-century England, who systematically smashed new workplace technologies because they directly undermined their working knowledge and economic interests as workers

M

macrostructures: overarching patterns of social relations that lie outside and above a person's circle of intimates and acquaintances

management by objectives: a participative goal-setting process in which organizational objectives are cascaded down to work units and individual employees

matrix structure: a type of departmentalization that overlays a divisionalized structure (typically a project team) with a functional structure

McDonaldization (also known as 'McWork' or 'McJobs'): a term used to symbolize the new realities of corporate-driven globalization that engulf young people in the twenty-first century, including simple work patterns, electronic controls, low pay and part-time and temporary employment

means of production: an analytical construct that contains the forces of production and the relations of production, which, when combined, define the socioeconomic character of a society

mechanical solidarity: a term to describe the social cohesion that exists in pre-industrial societies, in which there is a minimal division of labour and people feel united by shared values and common social bonds

mechanistic organization: an organizational structure with a narrow span of control and high degrees of formalization and centralization

media richness: refers to the number of channels of contact afforded by a communication medium; so, for example, face-to-face interaction would be at the high end of media richness, and a memorandum would fall at the low end of media richness

microstructures: the patterns of relatively intimate social relations formed during face-to-face interaction

mores: norms that are widely observed and have great moral significance

motivation: the forces within a person that affect his or her direction, intensity and persistence of voluntary behaviour

Myers–Briggs Type Indicator: a personality test that measures personality traits

N

needs: deficiencies that energize or trigger behaviours to satisfy those needs

needs hierarchy theory: Maslow's motivation theory of five instinctive needs arranged in a hierarchy, whereby people are motivated to fulfil a higher need as a lower one becomes gratified

negative reinforcement: occurs when the removal or avoidance of a consequence increases or maintains the frequency or future probability of a behaviour

negotiation: occurs whenever two or more conflicting parties attempt to resolve their divergent goals by redefining the terms of their interdependence

neo-liberalism: a theory of political economics that proposes free markets (laissez-faire), free trade, deregulation, privatization, shrinkage of the state, a hollowing out of social provision and low taxes to advance the role of private enterprise in the economy

network structure: a set of strategic alliances that an organization creates with suppliers, distributors and manufacturers to produce and market a product. Members of the network work together on a long-term basis to find new ways to improve efficiency and increase the quality of their products

nomothetic approach: an approach to explanation in which we seek to identify relationships between variables across many cases

normative order: a concept most often found in functionalist theory. It is any system of social rules and shared expectations governing a particular social situation

O

objectification: Karl Marx's term to describe the action of human labour on resources to produce a commodity, which, under the control of the capitalist, remains divorced from and opposed to the direct producer

objectivism: an ontological position which asserts that the meaning of social phenomena has an existence independent of individuals; compare this with constructionism

occupation: a category of jobs that involve similar activities at different work sites

ontology: a theory of whether social entities such as organizations can and should be considered as objective entities with a reality external to the individuals who form part of them, or as social constructions built up from the perceptions and behaviour of these individuals

operant conditioning: a technique for associating a response or behaviour with a consequence

organic organization: an organizational structure with a wide span of control, little formalization and decentralized decision making

organic solidarity: a term for the social cohesion that exists in industrial (and perhaps post-industrial) societies, in which people perform very specialized tasks and feel united by their mutual dependence

organizational behaviour: the systematic study of formal organizations and of what people think, feel and do in and around organizations

organizational chart: a diagram showing the grouping of activities and people within a formal organization to achieve the goals of the organization efficiently

organizational climate: describes the dimensions of the organization that can be measured with relative precision, such as its structure and leadership

organizational commitment: the employee's emotional attachment to, identification with and involvement in a particular organization

organizational culture: the basic pattern of shared assumptions, values and beliefs governing the way employees in an organization think about and act on problems and opportunities

organizational design: the process of creating and modifying organizational structures

organizational development: in this, change agents use the principles and practices of behavioural science to assist the change effort in order to increase employee and organizational effectiveness

organizational learning: a metaphor representing an organizational culture in which learning is continuous and embedded in what and how employees work, and in the systems that connect the parts together

organizational structure: the formal reporting relationships, groups, departments and systems of the organization

out-groups: groups to which someone perceives he or she does not belong, which he or she accordingly evaluates unfavourably

outsourcing: contracting with external providers to supply the organization with the products or back-office data processes that were previously supplied internally

P

paradigm: a term used to describe a cluster of beliefs that dictates for researchers in a particular discipline what should be studied, how research should be conducted and how the results should be interpreted

participatory design: an approach to the design and implementation of technologies that is premised on user participation

path–goal leadership theory: a contingency theory of leadership based on the expectancy theory of motivation, which relates several leadership styles to specific employee and situational contingencies

patriarchy: a hierarchical system of social organization in which cultural, political and economic structures are controlled by men

perceived self-efficacy: a person's belief in his or her capacity to achieve something

perception: the process of selecting, organizing and interpreting information in order to make sense of the world around us

perceptual bias: an automatic tendency to attend to certain cues that do not necessarily support good judgements

perceptual set: describes what happens when we get stuck in a particular mode of perceiving and responding to things based on what has gone before

performance–outcome (P→O) expectancy: the perceived probability that a specific behaviour or performance level will lead to specific outcomes

personal identity: the ongoing process of self-development through which we construct a unique sense of ourselves and our relationship to the world around us

personality: a relatively enduring pattern of thinking, feeling and acting that characterizes a person's unique response to her or his environment

perspective: an overall approach to or viewpoint on some subject

phenomenological approach: a philosophy concerned with how researchers make sense of the world around them. Adherents to this theory believe that the social researcher must 'get inside people's heads' to understand how they perceive and interpret the world

political gaming: a common practice in organizations, which has proven challenging to research, that involves recognition and organizational action based on existing factions, coalitions and cliques that make up any organization in order to engage in intentional acts of influence to enhance or protect oneself or one's group or department

political theory model: an approach to understanding decision making whose adherents assert that formal organizations comprise groups that have separate interests, goals and values, and in which power and influence are needed in order to reach decisions

positive psychology: a branch of psychology that focuses on the positive, including positive state, strengths and happiness in an individual's personal or working life

positive reinforcement: occurs when the introduction of a consequence increases or maintains the frequency or future probability of a behaviour

positivism: a view held in quantitative research in which reality exists independently of the perceptions and interpretations of people; a belief that the world can best be understood through scientific enquiry

post-industrial economy: an economy that is based on the provision of services rather than goods

postmodernism: the sociological approach that attempts to explain social life in modern societies that are characterized by post-industrialization, consumerism and global communications

power: a term defined in multiple ways, involving cultural values, authority, influence and coercion as well as control over the distribution of symbolic and material resources. At its broadest, power is defined as a social system that imparts patterned meaning

power–influence approach: an approach that examines processes of influence between leaders and followers, and explains leadership effectiveness in terms of the amount and type of power possessed by an organizational leader and how that power is exercised

primacy effect: a perceptual error in which we quickly form an opinion of people based on the first information we receive about them

procedural justice: justice based on the principle of fairness of the procedures employed to achieve the outcomes

proletariat (or working class): Karl Marx's term for those who must sell their labour because they have no other means of earning a livelihood

putting-out system: a pre-industrial, home-based form of production in which the dispersed productive functions were coordinated by an entrepreneur

Q

qualitative research: refers to the gathering and sorting of information through a variety of techniques, including interviews, focus groups and observations, and inductive theorizing

quantitative research: refers to research methods that emphasize numerical precision and deductive theorizing

R

rationality: the process by which traditional methods of social organization, characterized by informality and spontaneity, are gradually replaced by efficiently administered formal rules and procedures – bureaucracy

realism: the idea that a reality exists out there independently of what and how researchers think about it. It contrasts with constructionism

recency effect: a perceptual error in which the most recent information dominates our perception of others

reflexive learning: a view of adult learning that emphasizes learning through self-reflection

relationship behaviour: focuses on leaders' activities that show concern for followers, look after subordinates' welfare and nurture supportive relationships with followers, as opposed to behaviours that concentrate on completing tasks

reliability: in sociological research, the extent to which a study or research instrument yields consistent results

rhetoric: the management of symbols (such as a language) in order to encourage and coordinate social action. 'Rhetorical sensitivity' is the tendency for a speaker to adapt her or his messages to audiences to allow for the level knowledge, ability level, mood or beliefs of the listener

risk: a situation in which decision makers have a high knowledge of alternatives, know the probability and can calculate the costs and assess the benefits of each alternative

rituals: the programmed routines of daily organizational life that dramatize the organization's culture

role: a set of behaviours that people are expected to perform because they hold certain positions in a team and organization

role ambiguity: uncertainty about job duties, performance expectations, levels of authority and other job conditions

role conflict: conflict that occurs when people face competing demands

role perceptions: a person's beliefs about what behaviours are appropriate or necessary in a particular situation, including the specific tasks that make up the job, their relative importance and the preferred behaviours to accomplish those tasks

S

satisficing: selecting a solution that is satisfactory, or 'good enough', rather than optimal or 'the best'

schema: a set of interrelated mental processes that enable us to make sense of something on the basis of limited information

scientific management: this involves systematically partitioning work into its smallest elements and standardizing tasks to achieve maximum efficiency

selective attention: the ability of someone to focus on only some of the sensory stimuli that are reaching them

self-actualization: a term associated with Maslow's theory of motivation, referring to the desire for personal fulfilment, to become everything that one is capable of becoming

self-efficacy: the beliefs people have about their ability to perform specific situational task(s) successfully

self-fulfilling prophecy: an expectation about a situation that of itself causes what is anticipated to actually happen

self-managed work teams: cross-functional work groups organized around work processes that complete an entire piece of work requiring several interdependent tasks, and that have substantial autonomy over the execution of those tasks

semiotics: the systematic study of the signs and symbols used in communications

sexual harassment: the unwelcome conduct of a sexual nature that detrimentally affects the work environment or leads to adverse job-related consequences for its victims

situated learning: an approach that views adult learning as a process of enculturation, in which people consciously and subconsciously construct new knowledge from the actions, processes, behaviour and context in which they find themselves

skill variety: the extent to which employees must use different skills and talents to perform tasks in their job

social capital: the value of relationships between people, embedded in network links that facilitate the trust and communication that are vital to overall organizational performance

social class: the relative location of a person or group within a larger society, based on wealth, power, prestige or other valued resources

social identity: the perception of a 'sameness' or 'belongingness' to a human collective with common values, goals or experiences

social identity theory: the theory concerned with how we categorize and understand the kind of person we are in relation to others

socialization: the lifelong process of social interaction through which individuals acquire a self-identity and the physical, mental and social skills needed for survival in society

social-learning theory: a theory stating that much learning occurs by observing others and then modelling the behaviours that lead to favourable outcomes, and avoiding the behaviours that lead to punishing consequences

social solidarity: the state of having shared beliefs and values among members of a social group, along with intense and frequent interaction among group members

social structure: the stable pattern of social relationships that exist within a particular group or society

society: a large social grouping that shares the same geographical territory and is subject to the same political authority and dominant cultural expectations

span of control: the number of people directly reporting to the next level in the organizational hierarchy

specialization: the allocation of work tasks to categories of employee or groups. Also known as division of labour

status: the social ranking of people; the position an individual occupies in society or in a social group or work organization

STEPLE analysis framework: This categorizes the external context into six main types: Social, Technological, Economic, Political, Legal and Ecological

stereotyping: the process of assigning traits to people based on their membership of a social category

sticky floor: the pattern of employment opportunities that disproportionately concentrates certain social groups at lower-level jobs

strategic business unit: a term to describe corporate development that divides the corporation's operations into strategic business units, which allows comparisons between units. According to advocates, corporate managers are better able to determine whether they need to change the mix of businesses in their portfolio

strategy: the long-term planning and decision-making activities undertaken by managers that are related to meeting organizational goals

structuration: a concept focusing on balancing the dichotomies of agency, or human freedom, and social organization, or structures where individual choices are seen as partially constrained but nonetheless remain choices

substantive approach: an approach that tends to see technologies as producing negative social and political effects

superego: Sigmund Freud's term for the human conscience, consisting of the moral and ethical aspects of personality

surplus value: the portion of the working day during which workers produce value that is appropriated by the capitalist

symbolic interactionism: the sociological approach that views society as the sum of the interactions of individuals and groups

systems theory: a set of theories based on the assumption that social entities, such as work organizations, can be viewed as if they were self-regulating bodies exploiting resources from their environment (inputs) and transforming the resources (exchanging and processing) to provide goods and services (outputs) in order to survive

T

taboos: mores so strong their violation is considered to be extremely offensive, unmentionable and even criminal

tacit knowledge: knowledge embedded in our actions and ways of thinking, and transmitted only through observation and experience

task behaviour: focuses on the degree to which a leader emphasizes the importance of assigning followers to tasks and maintaining standards – in other words, 'getting things done' – as opposed to behaviours that nurture supportive relationships

task identity: the degree to which a job requires the completion of a whole or an identifiable piece of work

task significance: the degree to which the job has a substantial impact on the organization and/or larger society

Taylorism: a process of determining the division of work into its smallest possible skill elements, and how the process of completing each task can be standardized to achieve maximum efficiency. Also referred to as scientific management

teams: groups of two or more people who interact and influence each other, are mutually accountable for achieving common objectives, and perceive themselves as a social entity within an organization

technology: the means by which an organization transforms resources, including information, into products or services, and the social organization of work, which takes such forms as work teams, governance rules and procedures, communications and payment systems; the means by which organizations transform inputs into outputs, or rather the mediation of human action. This includes mediation by tools and machines as well as rules, social convention, ideologies and discourses

technology agreements: agreements with legal standing that set in place rules for negotiation over the selection, adoption and implementation of technologies

the economy: the social institution that ensures the maintenance of society through the production, distribution and consumption of goods and services

top-down processing: perception led predominantly by existing knowledge and expectations rather than by external sensory data

trade union: an organization whose purpose is to represent the collective interest of workers

transformational learning: a view that adult learning involving self-reflection can lead to a transformation of consciousness, new visions and new courses of action

transformative change: large-scale change involving radical and fundamental new ways of thinking and doing

transitional change: incremental change involving a planned and consistent movement from the current to the desired state

U

UK Equality Act 2010: protects people against discrimination based on – age, disability, gender reassignment, race, religion or belief, sex, sexual orientation, marriage and civil partnership and pregnancy and maternity

urbanization: the process by which an increasing proportion of a population lives in cities rather than in rural areas

V

valence: the anticipated satisfaction or dissatisfaction that an individual feels towards an outcome

validity: in sociological research, the extent to which a study or research instrument accurately measures what it is supposed to measure

value: a collective idea about what is right or wrong, good or bad, and desirable or undesirable in a particular culture

values: stable, long-lasting beliefs about what is important in a variety of situations

Verstehen: a method of understanding human behaviour by situating it in the context of an individual's or actor's meaning

vertical tensions: tensions and contradictions that emerge in terms of hierarchical institutional relationships

virtual organization: an organization composed of people who are connected by video-teleconferences, the Internet and computer-aided design systems, and who may rarely, if ever, meet face to face

W

will to power: the notion that people are inherently driven to develop and expand power and control in their environments

work ethic: a set of values that stresses the importance of work to the identity and sense of worth of the individual, and encourages an attitude of diligence in the mind of the people

work group: two or more employees in face-to-face interaction, each aware of their positive interdependence as they endeavour to achieve mutual work-related goals

work–life balance: the interplay between working life, the family and the community, in terms of both time and space

work organization: a deliberately formed social group in which people, technology and resources are purposefully co-coordinated through formalized roles and relationships to achieve a division of labour designed to attain a set of objectives. It is also known as formal organization

work orientation: an attitude towards work that constitutes a broad disposition towards certain kinds of paid work

Bibliography

Ackers, P. (1992) 'Gendering organizational theory', in A. Mills and P. Tancred (eds.), *Gendering Organizational Analysis*, London: Sage.

Ackers, P. J. and Black, J. (1991) 'Paternalist capitalism: an organization in transition', in M. Cross and G. Payne (eds), *Work and the Enterprise Culture*, London: Falmer.

Ackroyd, S. and Crowdy, P. (1990) 'Can culture be managed? Working with raw material: the case of the English slaughtermen', *Personnel Review*, 19(5), pp. 3–13.

Ackroyd, S. and Thompson, P. (1999) *Organizational Misbehaviour*, London: Sage.

Adair, J. (2006) *Effective Leadership*, London: CIPD.

Adams, J. S. (1965) 'Inequality in social exchange', pp. 267–99 in L. Berkowitz (ed.), *Advances in Experimental Social Psychology*, New York: Academic Press.

Adler, N. J. and Gundersen, A. (2008) *International Dimensions of Organizational Behavior* (5th edn), Mason, OH: Cengage Learning.

Adler, S. and Weiss, H. (1988) 'Recent developments in the study of personality and organizational behavior', in C. Cooper and I. Robertson (eds), *International Review of Industrial and Organizational Psychology*, New York: John Wiley & Sons.

Agashae, Z. and Bratton, J. (2001) 'Leader-follower dynamics: developing a learning organization', *Journal of Workplace Learning*, 3(3), pp. 89–102.

Aidt, T. and Tzannatos, Z. (2003) *Unions and Collective Bargaining: Economic Effects in a Global Environment*, Washington, DC: World Bank.

Ailon, G. (2006) 'What B would otherwise do: a critique of conceptualizations of "power" in organizational theory', *Organization*, 13(6), pp. 771–800.

Alderfer, C. P. (1972) *Existence, Relatedness and Growth*, New York: Free Press.

Aldrich, H. (1972) 'Technology and organizational structure: a re-examination of the findings of the Aston Group', *Administrative Science Quarterly*, 17(1), pp. 26–43.

Aldrich, H. E. (1999) *Organizations Evolving*. London: Sage.

Aldrich, H. E. (2002) 'Technology and organizational structure: a reexamination of the findings of the findings of the Aston Group', pp. 344–66 in S. R. Clegg (ed.), *Central Currents in Organization Studies*, London: Sage.

Aligisakis, M. (1997) 'Labour disputes in Western Europe: typology and tendencies', *International Labour Review*, 136(1), pp. 73–94.

Allan, K. (2013) *Explorations in Classical Sociological Theory* (3rd edn), Thousand Oaks, CA: Sage.

Allen, B. P. (1995) 'Gender stereotypes are not accurate: a replication of Martin (1987) using diagnostic vs. self-report and behavioral criteria', *Sex Roles*, May, pp. 583–600.

Allen, K. (2014) 'Rise in Greek suicides linked to austerity', *The Guardian*, April 22, p. 24.

Allio, R. J. (2013) 'Leaders and leadership – many theories, but what advice is reliable?', *Strategy and Leadership*, 41(1), pp. 4–14.

Aloisi, S. (2013) 'Insight – Italy's Chinese garment workshops boom as workers suffer', Reuters, December 30. Available at: http://uk.reuters.com/article/2013/12/30/uk-italy-sweatshop-insight-idUKBRE9BS04A20131230 (accessed February 16th, 2015).

Alvesson, A. (2002) *Understanding Organizational Culture*, London: Sage.

Alvesson, A. (2013) *Understanding Organizational Culture* (2nd edn), London: Sage.

Alvesson, M. (1996) *Communication, Power and Organization*, New York: Walter de Gruyter.

Alvesson, M. and Billing, Y. D. (1997) *Understanding Gender in Organizations*, London: Sage.

Alvesson, M. and Billing, Y. D. (2009) *Understanding Gender and Organizations* (2nd edn), London: Sage.

Alvesson, M. and Willmott, H. (eds) (1992) *Critical Management Studies*, London: Sage.

Alvesson, M. and Willmott, H. (1996) *Making Sense of Management: A Critical Introduction*, London: Sage.

Amabile, T. M. (1996) *Creativity in Context*, Boulder, CO: Westview Press.

Amabile, T. M. and Kramer, S. J. (2007) 'Inner work life: understanding the subtext of business performance', *Harvard Business Review*, 85(5), pp. 72–83.

Amabile, T. M., Conti, R., Coon, H., Lazenby, J. and Herron, M. (1996) 'Assessing the work environment for creativity', *Academy of Management Journal*, 39, pp. 1154–84.

Ambrose, M., Seabright, M. and Schminke, M. (2002) 'Sabotage in the workplace: the role of organizational injustice', *Organizational Behaviour and Human Decision Processes*, 89(1), pp. 947–65.

Anand, N. and Daft, R. L. (2007) 'What is the right organization design?', *Organizational Dynamics*, 36(4), pp. 329–44.

Anderssen, E. (2009) 'Men open up like never before as recession takes its toll', *Globe and Mail*, April 1, p. A1.

Andrews, B., Karcz, S. and Rosenberg, B. (2008) 'Hooked on a feeling: emotional labor as an occupational hazard of the post-industrial age', *New Solutions: A Journal of Environmental and Occupational Health Policy*, 18(2), pp. 245–55.

Anonymous (2003) 'Managerial myopia attacked', *Globe and Mail*, August 27, p. A10.

Anonymous (2008) 'All you need is cash', *Economist*, November 22, p. 17.

Anonymous (2014) 'Sacked mother receives 27,000 compensation', *The Herald*, 6 June, p. 7.

Anthony, A. (2014) 'The class war is back again and haunting the politicians', *The Observer*, November 30, pp. 34–5.

Antonacopoulou, E. P. (2010) 'Making the business school more "critical": reflexive critique based on phronesis as a foundation for impact', *British Journal of Management*, 21, pp. S6–25.

Antony, P. A. (1994) *Managing Culture*, Milton Keynes: Oxford University Press.

Apps, J. (1994) *Leadership for the Emerging Age*, San Francisco: Jossey-Bass.

Aquino, K. and Douglas, S. (2003) 'Identity threat and antisocial behavior in organizations: the moderating effects of individual differences, aggressive modeling, and hierarchical status', *Organizational Behavior and Human Decision Processes*, 90(1), pp. 195–208.

Archer, M. (2010) 'Business ethics', *The Times*, May 18, p. 1.

Archibugi, D. and Coco, A. (2000) *The Globalisation of Technology and the European Innovation System*, Rome: Italian National Research Council.

Archibugi, D. and Lundvall, B. (eds) (2001) *The Globalising Learning Economy*, Oxford: Oxford University Press.

Argyris, N. and Schön, D.A. (1978) *Organizational Learning: A Theory of Action Perspective*, Reading, MA: Addison-Wesley.

Armstrong, M. (2002) *Employee Reward* (3rd edn), London: CIPD.

Armstrong, P. (1989) 'Limits and possibilities for HRM in an age of management accountancy', pp. 154–66 in J. Storey (ed.), *New Perspectives on Human Resource Management*, London: Routledge.

Arnolds, C. and Boshoff, C. (2002) 'Compensation, esteem valence and job performance: an empirical assessment of Alderfer's ERG theory', *International Journal of Human Resource Management*, 13(4), pp. 697–719.

Arrowsmith, J. and Marginson, P. (2011) 'Variable pay and collective bargaining in British retail banking', *British Journal of Industrial Relations*, 49(1), pp. 54–79.

Arrowsmith, J. and Parker, J. (2013) The meaning of 'employee engagement' for the values and roles of the HRM function', *International Journal of Human Resource Management*, 23(16), pp. 3336–54.

Arrowsmith, J., Nicholaisen, H., Bechter, B. and Nonell, R. (2010) 'The management of variable pay in European banks', *International Journal of Human Resource Management*, 21(15), pp. 2716–40.

Arshad, R. and Sparrow, P. (2010) 'Downsizing and survivor reactions in Malaysia: modelling antecedents and outcomes of psychological contract violations', *International Journal of Human Resource Management*, 21(11), pp. 1793–815.

Arunachalam, V., Pei, B. K. W. and Steinbart, P. J. (2002) 'Impression management with graphs: effects on choices', *Journal of Information Systems*, 16, 183–202.

Asch, S. E. (1951) 'Effects of group pressure upon modification and distortion of judgements', in H. Guetzkow (ed.), *Groups, Leadership and Men*, New York: Carnegie Press.

Ashcroft, B., Griffiths, G. and Tiffin, H. (1989) *The Empire Writes Back*, London: Routledge.

Ashcroft, K. and Allen, B. (2003) 'The radical foundation of organizational communication,' *Communication Theory*, 13, pp. 5–38.

Ashforth, B. E. and Humphrey, R. H. (1995) 'Emotion in the workplace: a reappraisal', *Human Relations*, 48(2), 97–125.

Ashkanasy, N., Zerbe, W. J. and Hartel, C. E. (2002) *Managing Emotions in the Workplace*, Armonk, NY: M. E. Sharpe.

Ashkenas, R., Ulrich, D., Jick, T. and Kerr, S. (2002) *The Boundaryless Organization*, San Francisco: Jossey-Bass.

Associated Press (2014) 'FIFA president critical of Brazil World Cup organizers after worker fatalities', April 3. Available at: www.cbc.ca/sports/soccer/fifa-president-critical-of-brazil-world-cup-organizersafter-worker-fatalities-1.2597546 (accessed February 16, 2015).

Astley, W. and Sachdeva, P. (1984) 'Structural sources of intraorganizational power: a theoretical synthesis', *Academy of Management Review*, 9(1), pp. 104–13.

Atkinson, C. (2008) 'An exploration of small firm psychological contracts', *Work, Employment and Society*, 22(3), pp. 447–65.

Atkinson, J. (1984) 'Manpower strategies for flexible organizations', *Personnel Management*, August, pp. 14–25.

Attneave, F. (1971) 'Multistability in perception', in R. Held and W. Richards (eds), *Recent Progress in Perception*, San Francisco: W. H. Freeman.

Atzeni, M. (ed.) (2014) *Workers and Labour in a Globalised Capitalism*, Basingstoke: Palgrave Macmillan.

Austin, J. (2002) 'Editorial', *Journal of Organizational Behavior Management*, 22(3), pp. 1–2.

Avolio, B. J. and Bass, B. M. (2005) 'Multifactor leadership questionnaire feedback report'. Available at www.destinysdoorcoaching.com/MLQ_Sample_11-05.pdf.

Avolio, B. J. and Bass, B. M. (2006) *Multifactor Leadership Questionnaire* (3rd edn), Menlo Park, CA: Mind Garden.

Avolio, B. J., Bass, B. M. and Jung, D. I. (1999) 'Re-examining the components of transformational and transactional leadership using the multifactor leadership questionnaire', *Journal of Occupational and Organizational Psychology*, 72(4), pp. 441–62.

Bagilhole, B. (2009) *Understanding Equal Opportunities and Diversity: The Social Differentiations and Intersections of Inequality*, Bristol: Policy Press.

Bain, G. (1998) 'The 1986–87 News International dispute: was the workers defeat inevitable?', *Historical Studies in Industrial Relations*, (5), Spring, pp. 73–105.

Bakan, J. (2004) *The Corporation*, London: Penguin.

Bakir, C. (2013) *Bank Behaviour and Resilience*, Basingstoke: Palgrave Macmillan.

Baldamus, W. (1961) *Efficiency and Effort*, London: Tavistock.

Baldry, C., Bain, P. and Taylor, P. (1998) '"Bright satanic offices": intensification, control and team Taylorism', pp. 163–83 in P. Thompson and C. Warhurst (eds), *Workplaces of the Future*, Basingstoke: Macmillan.

Baldry, C., Bain, P., Taylor, P. et al. (2007) *The Meaning of Work in the New Economy*, Basingstoke: Palgrave Macmillan.

Ball, G., Trevino, L. and Sims, H. (1993) 'Justice and organizational punishment: attitudinal outcomes of disciplinary events', *Social Justice Research*, 6, pp. 39–67.

Bamber, D. and Castka, P. (2006) 'Personality, organizational orientations and self-reported learning outcomes', *Journal of Workplace Learning*, 18(1&2), pp. 73–92.

Bandura, A. (1977) *Social Learning Theory*, Englewood Cliffs, NJ: Prentice Hall.

Bandura, A. (1978) 'The self system in reciprocal determinism', *American Psychologist*, 33, pp. 344–58.

Bandura, A. (1997) *Self-efficacy: The Exercise of Control*, New York: Freeman.

Banker, R. D., Field, J. M., Schroeder, R. D. and Sinha, K. K. (1996) 'Impact of work teams on manufacturing performance: a longitudinal field study', *Academy of Management Journal*, 39(4), pp. 86–90.

Bao, X. (1991) *Holding up More than Half the Sky: Chinese Women Garment Workers in New York City, 1948–1992*, Urbana/Chicago: University of Illinois Press.

Bao, X. (2002) 'Sweatshops in Sunset Park: a variation of the late 20th century Chinese garment shops in New York City', *International Labor and Working-Class History*, 61, pp. 69–90.

Baptista, M. (2010) 'CEO compensation and firm performance in France', Unpublished MSc thesis, HEC, Paris.

Barclay, J. (2001) 'Improving selection interviews with structure: organisations' use of "behavioural" interviews', *Personnel Review*, 30(1), pp. 81–101.

Bargh, J. A., Lombardi, W. J. and Higgins, E. T. (1988) 'Automaticity of chronically accessible constructs in person × situation effects on person perception: it's just a matter of time', *Journal of Personality and Social Psychology*, 55, pp. 599–605.

Barnes, C. (1996) 'What next? Disability, the 1995 Disability Discrimination Act and the Campaign for Disabled Peoples' Rights', National Bureau for Disabled Students Annual Conference, March 2, Leeds, UK.

Barsalou, L. (2008) 'Grounded cognition', *Annual Review of Psychology*, 59, pp. 617–45.

Bartlett, C. A. and Ghoshal, S. (1989) *Managing across Borders: The Transnational Solution*, London: Random House.

Bass, B. M. (1985) *Leadership and Performance Beyond Expectations*, New York: Free Press.

Bass, B. M. and Riggio, R. E. (2006) *Transformational Leadership*, Mahwah, NJ: Erlbaum.

Bate, P. (1995) *Strategies for Cultural Change*, Oxford: Butterworth-Heinemann.

Baumol, J. W., Blinder, S. A. and Wolff, N. E. (2003) *Downsizing in America*, New York: Russell Sage Foundation Press.

BBC (2005) 'Gold mine sparks battle in Peru'. Available at: http://news.bbc.co.uk/1/hi/uk_politics/4600009.stm (accessed March 20, 2015), cited by J. Foley and P. Ramand, *Yes: The Radical Case for Scottish Independence*, London: Pluto Press, p. 27.

BBC (2013) 'Swiss vote no to capping bosses' pay at 12 times lowest paid', November 24. Available at: www.bbc.co.uk/news/business-25076879 (accessed February 3, 2015).

Beale, D. and Hoel, H. (2011) 'Workplace bullying and the employment relationship: exploring questions of prevention, control and context', *Work, Employment and Society*, 25(1), pp. 5–18.

Beattie, V. and Jones, M. J. (2000) 'Impression management: the case of inter-country financial graphs', *Journal of International Accounting, Auditing and Taxation*, 9, pp. 159–83.

Bebchuk, L. and Grinstein, Y. (2005) *The Growth of Executive Pay*. Working Paper No. 11443, Cambridge: National Bureau of Economic Research.

Becker, G. S. (2001) *Human Capital: A Theoretical and Empirical Analysis*, Chicago: University of Chicago Press.

Becker, H. S. (1984) 'Social class variations in the teacher-pupil ratio', in A. Hargreaves and P. Woods (eds), *Classrooms and Staff Rooms: The Sociology of Teachers and Teaching*, Milton Keynes: Open University Press.

Beckett, A. (2013a) 'On your marks, get set…', *The Guardian*, September 23, pp. S9–11.

Beckett, A. (2013b) 'What is the "global race"?' *The Guardian*, September 22. Available at: www.theguardian.com/politics/2013/sep/22/what-is-global-race-conservatives-ed-miliband (accessed February 16, 2015).

Beckett, D. and Hager, P. (2002) *Life, Work and Learning: Practice in Postmodernity*, London: Routledge.

Beckhard, R. and Harris, R. (1987) *Organizational Transitions: Managing Complex Change*, Reading, MA: Addison Wesley.

Beechey, V. (1983) 'The sexual division of labour and the labour process: a critical assessment of Braverman', in S. Wood (ed.), *The Degradation of Work? Skill, Deskilling and the Labour Process*, London: Hutchinson.

Beer, M. and Nohria, N. (2000) 'Cracking the code of change', *Harvard Business Review*, May–June, pp. 133–41.

Beer, M., Spector, B., Lawrence, P. R., Quin Mills, D. and Walton, R. E. (1984) *Managing Human Assets*, New York: Free Press.

Begley, R. (2014) 'New laws a boost for the bullied, says union', *Daily Liberal*, January 8. Available at: www.dailyliberal.com.au/story/2009784/new-laws-a-boost-for-the-bullied-says-union/ (accessed February 24, 2015).

Behfar, K., Peterson, R., Mannix, E. and Trochim, W. (2008) 'The critical role of conflict resolution in teams: a closer look at the links between conflict type, conflict management strategies, and team outcomes', *Journal of Applied Psychology*, 93(1), pp. 170–88.

Beirne, M. and Ramsay, H. (eds) (1992) *Information Technology and Workplace Democracy*, London: Routledge & Kegan Paul.

Belenky, M. F., Clinchy, B. M., Goldberger, N. R. and Tarule, J. (1986) *Women's Ways of Knowing: The Development of Self, Voice, and Mind*, New York: Basic Books.

Bell, D. (1973) *The Coming of the Post-Industrial Society*, New York: Basic Books.

Benabou, R. and Tirole, J. (2003) 'Intrinsic and extrinsic motivation', *Review of Economic Studies*, 70(3), pp. 489–520.

Benders, J. (2005) 'Team working: a tale of partial participation', pp. 55–74 in D. Knights, P. Thompson, C. Smith and H. Willmott (eds), *Participation and Democracy at Work*, Basingstoke: Palgrave Macmillan.

Benders, J. and Van Hootegem, G. (1999) 'Teams and their context: moving team discussion beyond existing dichotomies', *Journal of Management Studies*, 36(5), pp. 609–28.

Bendix, R. (1956) *Work and Authority in Industry*, New York: John Wiley & Sons.

Benn, S., Dunphy, D. and Griffiths, A. (2014) *Organizational Change for Corporate Sustainability* (3rd edn), London: Routledge.

Bennis, W. G. (1985) *Leaders: Strategies for Taking Charge*, New York: Harper & Row.

Berg, M. (1988) 'Women's work, mechanization and early industrialization', in R. E. Pahl (ed.), *On Work*, Oxford: Blackwell.

Berger, P. (1966) *Invitation to Sociology*, New York: Anchor Books.

Bernstein, B. (1971) *Class Codes and Control*, Volume 1, London: Routledge & Kegan Paul.

Bernstein, D. A. (2015) *Psychology: Foundations and Frontiers* (10th edn), New York: Cengage.

Bernstein, D. A., Clarke-Stewart, A., Penner, L., Roy, E. and Wickens, C. (2000) *Psychology* (5th edn), New York: Houghton Mifflin.

Berson, Y., Oreg, S. and Dvir, T. (2008) 'CEO values, organizational culture and firm outcomes', *Journal of Organizational Behavior*, 29, pp. 615–33.

Bertua, C., Anderson, N. and Salgado, J. (2005) 'The predictive validity of cognitive ability tests: a UK meta-analysis', *Journal of Occupational and Organizational Psychology*, 78, pp. 387–409.

Bessant, J. (2003) *High-Involvement Innovation*, Chichester: John Wiley & Sons.

Beyer, J. and Trice, M. (1987) 'How an organization's rites reveal its culture', *Organization Dynamics*, 15(4), pp. 4–24.

Beynon, H. (1984) *Working for Ford*, Harmondsworth: Penguin.

Beynon H., Grimshaw D, Rubery, J. and Ward, K. (2002) *Managing Employment Change: The New Realities of Work*, London: Oxford University Press.

Bhaskar, R. (1989) *Reclaiming Reality*, London: Verso.

Bielby, W. (2000) 'Minimizing workplace gender and racial bias', *Contemporary Sociology*, 29, pp. 120–9.

Billett, S. (2001) *Learning in the Workplace: Strategies for Effective Practice*, Sydney Allen & Unwin.

Billett, S. and Choy, S. (2013) 'Learning through work: emerging perspectives and new challenges', *Journal of Workplace Learning*, 25(4), pp. 264–76.

Bilton, T., Bonnett, K., Jones, R. and Lawson, T. (2002) *Introductory Sociology*, Basingstoke: Palgrave Macmillan.

Bisom-Rapp, S. and Sargeant, M. (2014) 'It's complicated: age, gender and life-time discrimination against working women: the US and the UK as examples', *Elder Law Journal*, 22(1), pp. 1–110.

Bjerknes, G., Ehn, P. and Kyng M. (eds) (1987) *Computers and Democracy: A Scandinavian Challenge*, Aldershot: Avebury.

Black, O. (1996) 'Addressing the issue of good communication', *People Management* (online). Available at: http://proquest.umi.com.

Blair, T. (1999) 'UK Politics', BBC (online), September 28.

Blake , R. and Mouton, J. (1978) *The New Management Grid*, Houston, TX: Gulf.

Blake, R. and McCanse, A. A. (1991) *Leadership Dilemmas – Grid Solutions*, Houston, TX: Gulf.

Blank, W., Weitzel, J. R. and Green, S. G. (1990) 'A test of situational leadership theory', *Personnel Psychology*, 43, pp. 579–97.

Blatchford, A. (2013) 'Lac-Megantic explosions, fire: 5 deaths confirmed, about 40 considered missing', *Huffington Post*, July 7. Available at: www.huffingtonpost.ca/2013/07/07/lac-megantic-explosions-fire_n_3556584.html?utm_hp_ref=lac-megantic-explosion (accessed February 23, 2015).

Blauner, R. (1964) *Alienation and Freedom: The Factory Worker and his Industry*, Chicago: University of Chicago Press.

Blinder, A. (1990) *Paying for Productivity*, Washington, DC: Brooking Institute.

Bloom, R. (2004) 'Children think before they speak', *Nature*, 430, pp. 410–11.

Boffey, D. (2015) 'Firms are offered interns on half the minimum wage', *The Observer*, January 18, p. 16.

Boghossian, P. (2006) *Fear of Knowledge: Against Relativism and Constructivism*, Oxford: Oxford University Press.

Boje, D. M., Gephart, R. and Thatchenkery, P. (eds) (1996) *Postmodern Management and Organization Theory*, Thousand Oaks, CA: Sage.

Bolden, R. and Gosling, J. (2006) 'Leadership competencies: time to change the tune?', *Leadership*, 2(2), p. 160.

Bolton, S. C. (2005) *Emotion Management in the Workplace*, Basingstoke: Palgrave Macmillan.

Bolton, S. C. (ed.) (2007) *Dimensions of Dignity at Work*, Amsterdam: Elsevier.

Bolton, S. C. and Houlihan, M. (eds) (2007) *Searching for the Human in Human Resource Management*, Basingstoke: Palgrave Macmillan.

Bolton, S. C. and Houlihan, M. (eds) (2009) *Work Matters: Critical Reflections on Contemporary Work*, Basingstoke: Palgrave Macmillan.

Bonney, N. (2005) 'Overworked Britains?: part-time work and work–life balance', *Work, Employment and Society*, 19(2), pp. 391–401.

Borger, J. (2013) Union of spies: Europe's league of surveillance', *The Guardian*, November 2, p. 1.

Bosseley, S. (1999) 'Gentlemen prefer blonde stereotypes', *The Guardian*, April 10, p. 34.

Bouchard, P. (1998) 'Training and work: some myths about human capital theory', pp. 128–39 in S. M. Scott, B. Spencer and A. M. Thomas (eds), *Learning for Life: Canadian Readings in Adult Education*, Toronto: Thompson Educational.

Boud, D. and Garrick, J. (eds) (1999) *Understanding Learning at Work*, London: Routledge.

Bouquet, C. and Birkinshaw, J. (2008) 'Managing power in the multinational corporation: how low-power actors gain influence', *Journal of Management*, 34(3), pp. 477–508.

Bowen, D. E. and Ostroff, C. (2004) 'Understanding HRM–firm performance linkages: the role of the 'strength' of the HRM system', *Academy of Management Review*, 29(2), pp. 203–21.

Bowers, S. (2014) 'Ex-Barclays trio charged over Libor allegations', *The Guardian*, February 18, p. 28.

Boxall, P. F. (1992) 'Strategic human resource management: beginnings of a new theoretical sophistication?', *Human Resource Management Journal*, 2(3), pp. 60–79.

Boxall, P. and Macky, K. (2009) 'Research and theory on high-performance work systems: progressing the high-involvement stream', *Human Resource Management Journal*, 19(1), pp. 3–23.

Boxall, P. and Purcell, J. (2011) *Strategy and Human Resource Management*, Basingstoke: Palgrave Macmillan.

Boxall, P., Purcell, J. and Wright, P. (eds) (2008a) *The Oxford Handbook of Human Resource Management*, Oxford: Oxford University Press.

Boxall, P., Purcell, J. and Wright, P. (2008b) 'Human resource management: scope, analysis, and significance', pp. 1–16 in P. Boxall, J. Purcell and J. Wright (eds.), *The Oxford Handbook of Human Resource Management*, Oxford: Oxford University Press.

Boyce, T. (2002) 'The power is in parsimony: commentary on Goltz's operant analysis of power interpretation of resistance to change', *Journal of Organizational Behavior Management*, 22(3), pp. 23–7.

Bradley, H. (1986) 'Technological change, management strategies, and the development of gender-based job segregation in the labour process', pp. 54–73 in D. Knights and H. Willmott (eds), *Gender and the Labour Process*, Aldershot: Gower.

Branden, N. (1998) *Self-esteem at Work: How Confident People Make Powerful Companies*, San Francisco: Jossey-Bass.

Bratton, A. and Bratton, J. (2015) 'Green human resource management', pp. 275–95 in Robertson, J. and Barling, J. (eds), *The Psychology of Green Organizations*, New York: Oxford University Press.

Bratton, J. (1992) *Japanization at Work*, Basingstoke: Macmillan.

Bratton, J. (2001) Why workers are reluctant learners: the case of the Canadian pulp and paper industry, *Journal of Workplace Learning*, 13(7/8), pp. 333–43.

Bratton, J. (2005) 'Work redesign and learning at work: a win-win game?', pp. 101–129 in E. Poikela (ed.), *Osaaminen ja kokemus*, Tampere, Finland: Tampere University Press.

Bratton, J. and Denham, D. (2014) *Capitalism and Classical Social Theory* (2nd edn), Toronto: University of Toronto Press.

Bratton, J. A. and Garrett-Petts, W. (2008) 'Art in the workplace: innovation and culture-based economic development in small cities', pp. 85–98 in D. W. Livingstone, K. Mirchandani and P. Sawchuk (eds), *The Future of Lifelong Learning and Work*, Rotterdam: Sense Publishing.

Bratton, J. and Gold, J. (2003) *Human Resource Management: Theory and Practice* (3rd edn), Basingstoke: Palgrave Macmillan.

Bratton, J. and Gold, J. (2012) *Human Resource Management: Theory and Practice* (5th edn), Basingstoke: Palgrave Macmillan.

Bratton, J. and Gold, J. (2015) 'Towards critical human resource management education (CHRME): a sociological imagination approach', *Work, Employment and Society*, doi: 10.1177/0950017014545266.

Bratton, J., Helms Mills, J., Pyrch, T. and Sawchuk, P. (2004) *Workplace Learning: A Critical Introduction*, Toronto: Garamond.

Bratton, J., Grint, K. and Nelson, D. (2005) *Organizational Leadership*, Mason, OH: Thomson-South-Western.

Braverman, H. (1974) *Labor and Monopoly Capitalism: The Degradation of Work in the Twentieth Century*, New York: Monthly Review Press.

Bregn, K. (2013) 'Detrimental effects of performance-related pay in the public sector? On the need for a broader theoretical perspective', *Public Organization Review*, 13(1), 21–35.

Brewer, M. (2008) *Globe and Mail*, November 11, p. B1.

Brewis, J. and Linstead, S. (2000) *Sex, Work and Sex Work: Eroticizing Organization*, London: Routledge.

Brey, P. (2003). 'Theorizing technology and modernity', pp. 33–71 in T. Misa, P. Brey and A. Feenberg (eds), *Modernity and Technology*, Cambridge, MA: MIT Press.

Brief, A., Dietz, J., Cohen, R., Pugh, S. D. and Vaslow, J. (2000) 'Just doing business: modern racism and obedience to authority as explanations for employment discrimination', *Organizational Behavior and Human Decision Processes*, 81(1), pp. 72–97.

Broad, D. and Hunter, G. (2010) 'Work, welfare, and the new economy: the commodification of everything', pp. 21–42 in N. Pupo and and M. Thomas (eds), *Interrogating the New Economy: Restructuring Work in the 21st century*, Toronto: University of Toronto.

Brockmann, E. N. and Anthony, W. P. (1998) 'The influence of tacit knowledge and collective mind on strategic planning', *Journal of Managerial Issues*, 10(Spring), pp. 204–22.

Brodbeck, F. C., Frese, M., Akerblom, S., Audia, G. and Bakacsi, G. (2000) 'Cultural variation of leadership prototypes across 22 European countries', *Journal of Occupational and Organizational Psychology*, 73, pp. 1–29.

Bronfenbrenner, K. (2003) 'Organizing women: the nature and process of union organizing efforts among US women workers since the mid-1990s', paper presented at the Cornell ILR Conference on Women and Unions, Ithaca, NY, November.

Brooks, A. and Watkins, K. E. (1994) 'The emerging power of action inquiry technologies', *New Directions for Adult and Continuing Education*, 63, pp. 131–43.

Brooks, E. (2002) 'The ideal sweatshop? Gender and transnational protest', *International Labor and Working-Class History*, 61, pp. 91–111.

Brown, D. (1987) 'The status of Holland's theory of career choice', *Career Development Journal*, September, pp. 13–23.

Brown, J. S., Collins, A. and Duguid, S. (1989) 'Situated cognition and the culture of learning', *Educational Researcher*, 18(1), pp. 32–42.

Brown, R. K. (1988) 'The employment relationship in sociological theory', pp. 33–66 in D. Gallie (ed.), *Employment in Britain*, Oxford: Blackwell.

Brown, R. K. (1992) *Understanding Industrial Organizations*, London: Routledge.

Brown, S. P., Westbrook, R. A. and Challagalla, G. (2005) 'Good cope, bad cope: adaptive and maladaptive coping strategies following a critical negative work event', *Journal of Applied Psychology*, 90, pp. 792–8.

Brown, W. (2010) 'Negotiation and collective bargaining', pp. 253–74 in T. Colling and M. Terry (eds.), *Industrial Relations: Theory and Practice* (3rd edn), Chichester: John Wiley & Sons.

Bruch, H. and Menges, J. (2010) 'The acceleration trap', *Harvard Business Review*, pp. 80–6.

Bruyere, S. (2000) *Disability Employment Policies and Practices in Private and Federal Sector Organizations*, Ithaca, NY: Cornell University, School of Industrial and Labor Relations, Program on Employment and Disability.

Bryant, D. (1979) 'The psychology of resistance to change', *Management Services*, 3, pp. 10–11.

Bryman, A. (2012) *Social Research Methods* (4th edn), Oxford: Oxford University Press.

Bryson, V. (2003) *Feminist Political Theory* (2nd edn), Basingstoke: Palgrave Macmillan.

Buchanan, D. (2000) 'An eager and enduring embrace: the ongoing rediscovery of teamworking as a management idea', in S. Procter and F. Mueller (eds), *Teamworking*, Basingstoke: Palgrave Macmillan.

Buchanan, D. A., Fitzgerald, L. and Ketley, D. (eds) (2006) *The Sustainability and Spread of Organizational Change: Modernizing Healthcare*, London: Routledge.

Budd, J. W. (2004) *Employment with a Human Face: Balancing Efficiency, Equity, and Voice*, New York: Cornell University Press.

Bunker, B., Alban, B. and Lewick, R. (2004) 'Ideas in currency and organizational development practice: has the well gone dry?', *Journal of Applied Behavioural Science*, 40(4), pp. 403–22.

Burawoy, M. (1979) *Manufacturing Consent*, Chicago: University of Chicago Press.

Burchill, F. (2014) *Labour Relations* (4th edn), Basingstoke: Palgrave Macmillan.

Burke, B., Geronimo, J., Martin, D., Thomas, B. and Wall, C. (2003) *Education for Changing Unions*, Toronto: Between the Lines Press.

Burke, J. (2013) 'Bangladesh factory collapse leaves trail of shattered lives', *The Guardian*, June 6. Available at: http://nickjordan.ca/wp-content/uploads/2014/01/1.2-Bangladesh-factory-The-Guardian.pdf (accessed February 19, 2015).

Burke, W. W. (2004) 'Internal organization development practitioners: where do they belong?', *Journal of Applied Behavioural Science*, 40(4), pp. 423–31.

Burke, W. W. (2014) *Organization Change: Theory and Practice*, Thousand Oaks, CA: Sage.

Burkeman, O. (2015) 'The I in mind', *The Guardian*, January 21, pp. 25–7.

Burns, B. (2004) 'Kurt Lewin and complexity theories: back to the future?', *Journal of Change Management*, 4(4), pp. 309–25.

Burns, J. M. (1978) *Leadership*, New York: Harper & Row.

Burns, T. and Stalker, G. M. (1961) *The Management of Innovation*, London: Tavistock.

Burns, T. and Stalker, G. M. (1966) *The Management of Innovation* (2nd edn), London: Tavistock.

Burrell, G. and Morgan, G. (1979) *Sociological Paradigms and Organizational Analysis*, London: Heinemann.

Burris, B. (1999) 'Braverman, Taylorism and technocracy', in M. Wardell, T. Steiger and P. Meiksins (eds), *Rethinking the Labor Process*, New York: SUNY.

Business Week (1989) 'Volvo's radical new assembly plant: "the death of the assembly line"?', *Business Week*, August 28.

Buyl, T., Boone, C. and Hendriks, W. (2014) 'Top management team members' decision influence and cooperative behaviour: an empirical study in the information technology industry', *British Journal of Management*, 25, pp. 285–304.

Byers, P. Y. (ed.) (1997) *Organizational Communication: Theory and Behaviour*, Boston, MA: Allyn & Bacon.

Byron, K. (2008) 'Differential effects of male and female managers' non-verbal emotional skills on employees' ratings', *Journal of Management Psychology*, 23(2), pp. 118–34.

Caffarella, R. (1993) 'Self-directed learning', *New Directions for Adult and Continuing Education*, 57, pp. 25–35.

Calas, M. B. and Smircich, L. (1996) 'From the woman's point of view: feminist approaches to organization studies', pp. 212–51 in S. Clegg and C. Hardy (eds), *Studying Organization: Theory and Method*, Thousand Oaks, CA: Sage.

Caldwell, R. (2001) 'Champions, adaptors, consultants and synergists: the new change agents in HRM', *Human Resource Management Journal*, 11(3), pp. 39–52.

Callaghan, G. and Thompson, P. (2001) 'Edwards revisited: technical control and worker agency in callcentres', *Economic and Industrial Democracy*, 22, pp. 13–37.

Callon, M. (1992) 'The dynamics of techno-economic networks', pp. 72–102 in R. Coombs, P. Saviotti and V. Walsh (eds), *Technological Change and Company Strategy: Economic and Social Perspectives*, London: Harcourt Brace.

Campbell, D. (2013) 'NHS staffing levels risk another Mid Staffordshire-style scandal-report', *The Guardian*, April 18.

Campion, M. A., Papper, E. M. and Medsker, G. J. (1996) 'Relations between work team characteristics and effectiveness: a replication and extension', *Personnel Psychology*, 49, pp. 429–52.

Capeller, W. (2001) 'Not such a net net: some comments on virtual criminality', *Social and Legal Studies*, 10, pp. 229–49.

Card, D., Lemieux, T., and Riddell, W. C. (2003a). 'Unions and the wage structure', pp. 246–92 in J. T. Addison and C. Schnabel (eds), *International Handbook of Trade Unions*, Cheltenham: Edward Elgar.

Card, D., Lemieux, T. and Riddell, C. (2003b) *Unionization and Wage Inequality: A Comparative Study of the US, the UK and Canada*. NBER Working Paper No. 9473. Available at: www.nber.org/papers/w9473.

Carlson, N., Buskist, W., Enzle, M. and Heth, C. (2005) *Psychology* (3rd edn), Toronto: Pearson Education.

Carnoy, M., Pollack, S. and Wong, P. L. (1993) *Labour Institutions and Technological Change: A Framework for Analysis and a Review of the Literature*, Stanford University/International Labour Organization.

Carroll, A. B. and Buchholtz, A. K. (2012) *Business and Society: Ethics and Stakeholder Management*, Mason, OH: South-Western.

Carroll, B., Levy, L. and Richmond, D. (2008) 'Leadership as practice: challenging the competency paradigm', *Leadership*, 4(4), pp. 363–79.

Carroll, W. K. (2004) *Corporate Power in a Globalizing World: A Study of Elite Social Organization*, Don Mills, ON: Oxford University Press.

Carter, B., Danford, A., Howcroft, D., Richardson, H., Smith, A. and Taylor, P. (2011) 'All they lack is a chain: lean and the new performance management in the British Civil Service', *New Technology Work and Employment*, 26(2), pp. 83–97.

Caruth, D. and Handlogten, G. (2001) *Managing Compensation: A Handbook for the Perplexed*, Westport, CT: Quorum.

Casey, C. (2014) 'We the people at work: propositions for revitalizing industrial democracy through the use of Étienn Balibar's concepts', *Work, Employment and Society*, 28(3), pp. 469–80.

Castells, M. (1996) *The Rise of the Network Society*, Volume 1, Oxford: Blackwell.

Castells, M. (2000a) 'Information technology and global capitalism', pp. 52–74 in W. Hutton and A. Giddens (eds), *On the Edge: Living with Global Capitalism*, London: Cape.

Castells, M. (2000b) *The Information Age: Economy, Society and Culture*, Volume 1: *The Rise of Network Society* (2nd edn), London: Blackwell.

Cattell, R. B. (1965). *The Scientific Analysis of Personality*, Baltimore: Penguin.

Cattell, R. B. and Kline, P. (1977). *The Scientific Analysis of Personality and Motivation*, New York: Academic Press.

Cavazotte, F., Lemos, A. H. and Villadsen, K. (2014) 'Corporate smart phone: professionals' conscious engagement in escalating work connectivity', *New Technology, Work and Employment*, 29(1), pp. 72–87.

Chafetz, J. (1988) *Feminist Sociology: An Overview of Contemporary Theories*, Itasca, IL: Peacock.

Chakrabortty, A. (2013) 'In an Alpine hamlet in Switzerland, where the rich plot to get even richer', *The Guardian*, January 22, p. S5.

Chakrabortty, A. (2014a) 'The right need to tackle the wealth gap but can they even see the goal?', *The Guardian*, June 9, p. G5.

Chakrabortty, A. (2014b) 'The Tories should be defending union rights: capitalism depends on them', *The Guardian*, July 7.

Chakrabortty, A. (2014c) 'Unions need more rights: capitalism depends on it', *The Guardian*, July 8, p. 30.

Chakrabortty, A. (2015) 'Ghost jobs, half lives. How shadow workers "get by" in today's Britain', *The Guardian*, January 20, p. 33.

Chambel, M. J. and Fortuna, R. (2015) 'Wage reduction of Portuguese civil servants and their attitudes: the psychological contract perspective', *International Journal of Human Resource*, doi: 10.1080/09585192.2015.1004099.

Chamberlain, L. J., Crowley, M., Tope, D. and Hodson, R. (2008) 'Sexual harassment in organizational context', *Work and Occupations*, 35(3), pp. 262–95.

Champy, J. (1996) *Reengineering Management*, New York: HarperCollins.

Chance, P. (2009) *Learning and Behavior* (6th edn), Belmont, CA: Wadsworth.

Chandler, A. (1962) *Strategy and Structure*, Cambridge, MA: MIT Press.

Charmaz, K. (2005) 'Grounded theory: objectivist and constructivist methods', pp. 509–35 in N. Denzin and Y. Lincoln (eds), *Handbook of Qualitative Research* (2nd edn), Thousand Oaks, CA: Sage.

Chartered Institute of Personnel and Development (2000) *People Implications of Mergers and Acquisitions, Joint Ventures and Divestments: Survey Report*, London: CIPD.

Chartered Institute of Personnel and Development (2007) *Diversity in Business,* London: CIPD.

Chartered Institute of Personnel and Development (2008) 'Competency and competency frameworks factsheet'. Available at: www.cipd.co.uk/subjects/perfmangmt/competnces/comptfrmwk.htm (accessed March 12, 2015).

Chartered Institute of Personnel and Development (2009) *Performance Management in Action*, London: CIPD.

Chartered Institute of Personnel and Development (2010) *Opening Up Talent for Business Success*, London: CIPD.

Chartered Management Institute (2008) *Implementing a Diversity Management Programme*, London: CMI.

Child, I. L. (1968) 'Personality in culture', in E. F. Borgatta and W. W. Lambert (eds), *Handbook of Personality Theory and Research*, Chicago: Rand McNally.

Child, J. (1972) 'Organizational structure, environment and performance: the role of strategic choice', *Sociology*, 6(1), pp. 331–50.

Child, J. (1985) 'Managerial strategies, new technology, and the labour process', in D. Knights, H. Willmott and D. Collinson (eds), *Job Redesign Critical Perspectives on the Labour Process*, Aldershot: Gower.

Choi, J. N. (2007) 'Group composition and employee creative behaviour in a Korean electronics company: distinct effects of relational demography and group diversity', *Journal of Occupational and Organizational Psychology*, 80, pp. 213–34.

Choi, M., and Ruona, W. (2011) 'Individual readiness for organizational change and its implications for human resource and organization development', *Human Resource Development Review*, 10(1), pp. 46–73.

Chowdhry, A. (2013) 'India-US diplomatic row puts spotlight on globes domestic workers'. Available at: www.theglobeandmail.com/news/world/india-us-diplomat-row-puts-spotlight-on-globes-domestic-workers/article16069305/ (accessed December 13, 2014).

Chreim, S. (2006) 'Postscript to change: survivors' retrospective views of organizational changes', *Personnel Review*, 35(3), pp. 315–35.

Christensen, C. M. (2013) *The Innovator's Dilemma: When New Technologies Cause Great Firms to Fail*, Boston, MA: Harvard Business Review Press.

Christensen, C. M., Bohmer, R. and Kenagy, J. (2000) 'Will disruptive innovations cure health care?', *Harvard Business Review*, 78(5), pp. 102–12.

Christiansen, C. H. and Townsend, E. A. (2004) *Introduction to Occupation: The Art and Science of Living*, Upper Saddle River, NJ: Prentice Hall.

Clark, T. (2014) 'Truth: the first casualty in the war on poverty', *The Guardian*, July 3, p. 30.

Clarke, J. and Koonce, R. (1995) 'Engaging organizational survivors', *Training and Development*, 49(8), pp. 22–30.

Clarke, M. C. (1993) 'Transformational learning', pp. 47–56 in S. Merriam (ed.), *An Update on Adult Learning Theory*, San Francisco: Jossey-Bass.

Clarkson, L. A. (1971) *The Pre-Industrial Economy of England, 1500–1750*, London: Batsford.

Claxton, J., Gold, J., Edwards, C. and Coope, G. (2009) 'Relevant and timely learning for busy leaders', *Action Learning Research and Practice*, 6(1), pp. 63–70.

Clegg, S. (1989) *Frameworks of Power*, London: Sage.

Clegg, S. and Dunkerley, D. (1980) *Organization, Class and Control*, London: Routledge & Kegan Paul.

Clegg, S. and Hardy, C. (1999) *Studying Organization: Theory and Method*, Thousand Oaks, CA: Sage.

Clegg, S., Hardy, C. and Nord, W. (eds) (1999) *Managing Organizations: Current Issues*, Thousand Oaks, CA: Sage.

Clegg, S. R., Hardy, C., Lawrence, T. and Nord, W. R. (eds.) (2006) *The Sage Handbook of Organization Studies* (2nd edn), London: Sage.

Coch, L. and French, J. R. P. (1948) 'Overcoming resistance to change', *Human Relations*, 1, pp. 512–32.

Cockburn, C. (1983) *Brothers: Male Domination and Technological Change*, London: Pluto.

Cockburn, C. (1991) *In the Way of Women: Men's Resistance to Sex Equality in Organizations*, Basingstoke: Palgrave Macmillan.

Coe, R. M. (1990) *Process, Form, and Substance: A Rhetoric for Advanced Writers* (2nd edn), Upper Saddle River, NJ: Prentice Hall.

Cohen, M. D., March, J. G. and Olsen, P. (1972) 'A garage can model of organizational choice', *Administrative Science Quarterly*, 17, pp. 1–25.

Cohen, S. G. and Bailey, D. E. (1997) 'What makes teams work: group effectiveness research from the shop floor to the executive suite', *Journal of Management*, 23, pp. 239–90.

Cohen-Charash, Y. and Spector, P. (2001) 'The role of justice in organizations:

a meta-analysis', *Organizational Behavior and Human Decision Processes*, 86(2), pp. 278–321.

Colarelli, S., Spranger, J. and Hechanova, M. (2006) 'Women, power, and sex composition in small groups: an evolutionary perspective', *Journal of Organizational Behaviour*, 27(2), pp. 163–84.

Cole, M. S., Walter, F. and Bruch, H. (2008) 'Affective mechanisms linking dysfunctional behavior to performance in work teams: a moderated mediation study', *Journal of Applied Psychology*, 93(5), pp. 945–58.

Coleman, A. M. (2009) *Oxford Dictionary of Psychology*, Oxford: OUP.

Collins, J. (2002) 'Level 5 leadership', cited by Grint, K. (2005) *Leadership: Limits and Possibilities*, Basingstoke: Palgrave Macmillan, p. 222.

Collins, M. (1991) *Adult Education as a Vocation: A Critical Role for the Adult Educator*, London: Routledge.

Collins, T. and Terry, M. (2010) *Industrial Relations: Theory and Practice* (3rd edn), Chichester: John Wiley & Sons.

Collinson, D. (1994) 'Strategies of resistance: power, knowledge and subjectivity in the workplace', pp. 25–68 in J. Jermier, D. Knights and W. Nord (eds), *Resistance and Power in Organizations*, New York: Routledge.

Collinson, D. and Ackroyd, S. (2006) 'Resistance, misbehaviour, and dissent', pp. 305–26 in S. Ackroyd, R. Batt, P. Thompson and P. Tolbert (eds), *The Oxford Handbook of Work and Organization*, Oxford: OUP.

Collinson, D. L. (1988) '"Engineering humour": masculinity, joking and conflict in shop-floor relations', *Organization Studies*, 9(2), pp. 181–99.

Collinson, P. (2014) 'Refillable tanks fuel printer revolution', *The Guardian*, October 2, p. 25.

Colquitt, J. A., Conlon, D. E., Wesson, M. J., Porter, C. O. L. H. and Ng, K. Y. (2001) 'Justice at the millennium: a meta-analytic review of 25 years of organizational justice research', *Journal of Applied Psychology*, 86(3), pp. 425–45.

Colquitt, J., Scott, B., Judge,T. and Shaw, J. (2006) 'Justice and personality: using integrative theories to derive moderators of justice effects', *Organizational Behaviour and Human Decision Processes*, 100(1), pp. 110–27.

Confederation of British Industry/Trades Union Congress (2008) *Talent not Tokenism*, CBI/TUC: London.

Conger, J. A. and Kanungo, R. N. (1998) *Charismatic Leadership in Organizations*, Thousand Oaks, CA: Sage.

Conley, J. J. (1984) 'The hierarchy of consistency: a review and model of longitudinal findings on adult differences in intelligence and self-opinion', *Personality and Individual Differences*, 5, pp. 11–25.

Cook, M. (1994) *Personnel Selection and Productivity*, Chichester: John Wiley & Sons.

Cook, M. (2013) *Levels of Personality* (3rd edn), Cambridge: Cambridge University Press.

Cooke, F. L. (2000) *Human Resource Strategy to Improve Organisational Performance: A Route for British Firms?* Working Paper No. 9. Economic and Social Research Council Future of Work Programme, Swindon: ESRC.

Cooke, R. A. and Rousseau, D. M. (1988) 'Behavioural norms and expectations: a quantitative approach to the assessment of organizational culture', *Group and Organization Studies*, 13, pp. 245–73.

Cooley, C. H. (1902), *Human Nature and the Social Order*, New York: Charles Scriber.

Cooley, M. (1980) *Architect or Bee?,* Slough: Hogarth Press.

Cooper, C. (2010) *Individual Differences and Personality* (3rd edn), London: Hodder Education.

Coopey, J. (1996) 'Crucial gaps in the learning organization', in K. Starkey (ed.), *How Organizations Learn*, London: International Thomson Business Press.

Corby, S., Palmer, S. and Lindop, E. (eds) (2009) *Rethinking Reward*, Basingstoke: Palgrave Macmillan.

Cornwell, J. (2014) 'Empowered and engaged NHS staff will provide better care', *The Guardian*, January 15.

Courier-Mail (2014) 'It's clearly time to tighten net on disability support pension scheme. Courier-Mail', January 14. Available at: www.couriermail. com.au/news/opinion/editorial-its-clearly-time-to-tighten-net-on-disability-support-pension-scheme/story-fnihsr9v-1226801005873 (accessed January 21, 2015).

Covert, B. (2014) 'Enough mansplaining the "boy crisis" – sexism still holds back women at work', *The Guardian*, May 20. Available at: www. theguardian.com/commentisfree/2014/may/20/boy-crisis-sexism-women-at-work (accessed January 23, 2015).

Cowling, A. and Walters, M. (1990) 'Manpower planning – where are we today?', *Personnel Review*, 19(3), pp. 3–8.

Cox, T. H. and Finley, J. A. (1995) 'An analysis of work specialization and organization level as dimensions of workforce diversity', pp. 62–88 in M. M. Chemers, S. Oskamp and M. A. Costanzo (eds), *Diversity in Organizations*, Thousand Oaks, CA: Sage.

Craft, M. and Craft, A. (1983) 'The participation of ethnic minorities in further and higher education', *Educational Researcher*, 259(1), pp. 45–51.

Craig, J. and Yetton, P. (1993) 'Business process redesigns critique of *Process Innovation* by Thomas Davenport as a case study in the literature', *Australian Journal of Management*, 17(2), pp. 285–306.

Crane, A., Knights, D. and Starkey, K. (2008) 'The conditions of our freedom: Foucault, organization, and ethics', *Business Ethics Quarterly*, 18(3), pp. 299–320.

Cressey, P. (1993) 'Kalmar and Uddevalla: the demise of Volvo as a European icon', *New Technology, Work and Employment*, 8(2), pp. 88–96.

Cressey, P. and Di Martino, V. (1991) *Agreement and Innovation: The International Dimension of Technological Change*, New York: Prentice Hall.

Cropanzano, R. and Greenberg, J. (1997) 'Progress in organizational justice: tunneling through the maze', pp. 317–72 in C. L. Cooper and I. T. Robertson (eds), *International Review of Industrial and Organizational Psychology*, New York: John Wiley & Sons.

Crow, G. (2005) *The Art of Sociological Argument*, Basingstoke: Palgrave Macmillan.

Cullen, D. (1994) 'Feminism, management and self-actualization', *Gender, Work and Organization*, 1(3), pp. 127–37.

Cunliffe, A. L. (2004) 'On becoming a critically reflexive practitioner', *Journal of Management Education*, 28(4), pp. 407–26.

Currie, G., Finn, R. and Martin, G. (2008) 'Accounting for the "dark side" of new organizational forms: the case of healthcare professionals', *Human Relations*, 61(4), pp. 539–64.

Currie, G., Knights, D. and Starkey, K. (2010) `Introduction: a post-crisis critical reflection on business schools', *British Journal of Management*, 21, pp. S1–5.

Curson, J. A. (2006) 'Crystal-ball gazing: planning the medical workforce', *British Journal of Hospital Medicine*, 67(8), pp. 1141–7.

Curson, J. A., Dell, M. E., Wilson, R. A., Boswell, D. L. and Baldauf, B. (2010) 'Who does workplace planning well?', *International Journal of Health Care Quality Assurance*, 23(1), pp. 110–19.

Curtiss, S. (1977) *Genie: A Psycholinguistic Study of a Modern-day 'Wild Child'*, New York: Academic Press.

Daft, R. L. and Huber, G. P. (1987) 'How organizations learn: a communication framework', *Research in the Sociology of Organizations*, 5, pp. 1–36.

Daft, R., Murphy, J., and Willmott, H. (2010) *Organization Theory and Design*, London: Cengage.

Dahl, R. A. (1957) 'On the concept of power', *Behavioral Science*, 2, pp. 201–15.

Dalen, L. H., Stanton, N. A. and Roberts, A. D. (2001) 'Faking personality questionnaires in personal selection', *Journal of Management Development*, 20(8), pp. 729–41.

Dalton, M. (1959) *Men Who Manage*, New York: McGraw-Hill.

Dalton, M. and Wilson, M. (2000) 'The relationship of the five-factor model of personality to job performance for a group of Middle Eastern expatriate managers', *Journal of Cross-Culture Psychology*, March, pp. 250–8.

Danford, A., Richardson, M., Stewart, P., Tailby, S. and Upchurch, M. (2008) 'Partnership, high performance work systems and quality of working life', *New Technology, Work and Employment*, 23(3), pp. 151–66.

Daniel, W. W. (1973) 'Understanding employee behaviour in its context', in J. Child (ed.), *Man and Organization*, London: Allen & Unwin.

Daniels, K. (2000) 'Measures of five aspects of affective well-being at work', *Human Relations*, 53, pp. 275–94.

Datta, D., Guthrie, J., Basuil, D. and Pandey, A. (2010) 'Causes and effects of employee downsizing: a review and synthesis', *Journal of Management*, 36(1), pp. 281–348.

Davidow, W. H. and Malone, M. A. (1992) *The Virtual Corporation: Structuring and Revitalizing the Corporation for the 21ˢᵗ Century*, New York: HarperCollins.

Davidson, M. and Burke, R. (2011) *Women in Management Worldwide: Progress and Prospects*, Aldershot: Gower Publishing.

Davies, C. and Butler, S. (2014) 'Supermarket staff could win millions in equal pay case', *The Guardian*, April 11, p. 37.

Davies, H. T. O. (2002) 'Understanding organizational culture in reforming the National Health Service', *Journal of the Royal Society of Medicine*, 95(3), pp. 140–2.

Davis, C. (2002) '"Shape or fight?": New York's black longshoremen, 1945–1961', *International Labor and Working-Class History*, 62, pp. 143–63.

Davis, C. (2014) 'Abused, trolled, trivialised: from Twitter to TV women's voices are being muted', *The Guardian*, February 15, p. 3.

Davis, K. (1940) 'Extreme social isolation of a child', *American Journal of Sociology*, 45(4), pp. 554–65.

Dawber, A. (2010) 'We're all in it together? Company bosses enjoy £500, 000 pay increases', *The Independent*, August 11, p. 6.

De Cieri, H., Holmes, B., Abbot, J. and Pettit, T. (2002) *Work/Life Balance Strategies: Progress and Problems in Australian Organizations*. Working Paper No. 58/02. Melbourne: Department of Management, Monash University.

De Dreu, C. and Van de Vliert, E. (eds) (1997) *Using Conflict in Organizations*, London: Sage.

De Dreu, C. K. W. (2008) 'The virtue and vice of workplace conflict: food for (pessimistic) thought', *Journal of Organizational Behaviour*, 29(1), pp. 5–18.

Deal, T. E. and Kennedy, A. A. (1982) *Organization Cultures: The Rites and Rituals of Organizational Life*, Reading, MA: Addison-Wesley.

Deetz, S. (1998) 'Discursive formations, strategized subordination and self-surveillance', pp. 151–72 in A. Kinlay and K. Starkey (eds), *Foucault, Management and Organization Theory*, London: Sage.

DeFillippi, R., Grabher, G. and Jones, C. (2007) 'Introduction to paradoxes of creativity: managerial and organizational challenges in the cultural economy', *Journal of Organizational Behavior*, 28, pp. 511–21.

DeFrancisco, V. P. and Palczewski, C. H. (2014) *Gender in Communication: A Critical Introduction* (2nd edn), Thousand Oaks, CA: Sage.

Delbridge, R. (1998) *Life on the Line in Contemporary Manufacturing*, Oxford: Oxford University Press.

Delbridge, R. and T. Keenoy, T. (2010) 'Beyond managerialism?', *International Journal of Human Resource Management*, 21(6), pp. 799–817.

Delbridge, R. and Whitfield, K. (2001) 'Employee perceptions of job influence and organizational participation', *Industrial Relations*, 40(3), pp. 472–89.

Den Hartog, D., Koopman, P., Thierry, H., Wilderom, C., Maczynski, J., and Jarmuz, S. (1997) 'Dutch and Polish perceptions of leadership and culture: the GLOBE project', *European Journal of Work and Organizational Psychology*, 6, pp. 387–413.

Dennis, A. R. and Valacich, J. S. (1999) 'Electronic brainstorming: illusions and patterns of productivity', *Information Systems Research*, 10(2), pp. 375–7.

Despres, C. and Hiltrop, J.-M. (1995) 'Human resource management in the knowledge age: current practice and perspectives on the future', *Employee Relations*, 17(1), pp. 9–23.

Devet, R. (2013) 'Irving Shipyard workers walk off the job after co-worker's suicide', Halifax Media Group, November 28. Available at: http://halifax.mediacoop.ca/story/irving-shipyard-workers-walk-job-after-co-workers/20090 (accessed February 24, 2015).

Devine, W. (1983) 'From shafts to wires: historical perspective on electrification', *Journal of Economic History*, 43, pp. 347–72.

Dickens, L. (1994) 'Wasted resources? Equal opportunities in employment', in K. Sisson (ed.), *Personnel Managements Comprehensive Guide to Theory and Practice in Britain*, Oxford: Blackwell.

Dickens, L. (1998) 'What HRM means for gender equality', *Human Resource Management Journal*, 8(1), pp. 23–45.

Dickerson, P. (2012) *Social Psychology Traditional and Critical Perspectives*, Harlow: Pearson.

Dobb, M. (1963) *Studies in the Development of Capitalism*, London: Routledge.

Dochy, F. J. (2012) *Theories of Learning for the Workplace: Building Blocks for Training and Professional Development Programmes*, London: Routledge.

Dodd, V. (2012) 'Metropolitan Police "buried" report in 2004 warning of race scandal', *The Guardian*, April 6, p. 1.

Doherty, B. and Whyte, S. (2014) 'Bangladesh garment factory warned of danger before fatal fire', *The Age*, January 5. Available at: www.theage.com.au/world/bangladesh-garment-factory-warned-of-danger-before-fatal-fire-20140104-30ay9.html (accessed February 19, 2015).

Dombrowski, K. (2002) 'Bill Budd, choker-setter: native culture and Indian work in the Southeast Alaska timber industry', *International Labor and Working-Class History*, 62, pp. 121–42.

Donaldson, T. and Preston, L. E. (1995) 'The stakeholder theory of the corporation: concepts, evidence and implications', *Academy of Management Review*, 20(1), pp. 15–19.

Dorling, D. (2014) *Inequality and the 1%*, London: Verso.

Dörnyei, Z. and Ushioda, E. (2013) *Teaching and Researching Motivation* (2nd edn), Abingdon, Oxon: Routledge.

Dougherty, D. (1999) 'Organizing for innovation', in S. Clegg, C. Hardy and W. Nord (eds), *Managing Organizations: Current Issues*, Thousand Oaks, CA: Sage.

Douglas, J., Ross, J. and Simpson, H. (1968) *All Our Future*, London: Peter Davies.

Doward, J. and Bissett, G. (2014) 'Pay squeeze worst since Victorian age, study finds', *The Observer*, October 12, p. 6.

Downey, S. N., van der Werff, L., Thomas, K. M., and Plaut, V. (2015), 'The role of diversity practices and inclusion in promoting trust and employee engagement', *Journal of Applied Social Psychology*, 45(1), pp. 35–44.

Drennan, D. (1992) *Transforming Company Culture*, London: McGraw-Hill.

Driver, M. (2002) 'Learning and leadership in organizations', *Management Learning*, 33(1), pp. 99–126.

Drucker, P. (1954/1993) *The Practice of Management*, New York: Harper Collins.

Drucker, P. F. (1985) *Innovation and Entrepreneurship Practices and Principles*, New York: Harper & Row.

Drucker, P. F. (1997) 'Toward the new organization', pp. 1–5 in F. Hesselbein, M. Goldsmith and R. Beckhard (eds), *The Organization of the Future*, San Francisco: Jossey-Bass.

Du Bois, W. E. B. (1903/1994) *The Souls of Black Folk*, New York: Dover.

DuBrin, A. J. (2011) *Impression Management in the Workplace*, New York: Routledge.

Duffy, J., Gall, G. and Mather, J. (2013) 'Working together: a vision for industrial democracy in a Common Weal economy', Jimmy Reid Foundation. Available at http://reidfoundation.org/portfolio/working-together/ (accessed March 20, 2105).

du Gay, P. and Salaman, G. (1992) 'The cult(ure) of the customer', *Journal of Management Studies*, 29(5), pp. 615–33.

Dundon, T., Dobbins, T., Cullinane, N., Hickland, E. and Donaghey, J. (2014) 'Employer occupation of regulatory space of the Employee Information and Consultation (I&C) Directive in liberal market economies', *Work, Employment and Society* (28), pp. 21–39.

Dunford, R., Palmer, I., Benveniste, J. and Crawford, J. (2007) 'Coexistence of "old" and "new" organizational practices: transitory phenomenon or enduring feature?', *Asia Pacific Journal of Human Resources*, 45(1), pp. 24–43.

Dunlop, P. D. and Lee, K. (2004) 'Workplace deviance, organizational citizenship behavior, and business unit performance: the bad apples do spoil the whole barrel', *Journal of Organizational Behavior*, 25, pp. 67–80.

Durkheim, E. (1893/1997) *The Division of Labor in Society*, New York: Free Press.

Earley, P. C. and Gibson, C. B. (2002) *Multinational Work Teams: A New Perspective*, Mahwah, NJ: Lawrence Erlbaum Associates.

Easterby-Smith, M., Thorpe, R. and Lowe, A. (1991) *Management Research: An Introduction*, London: Sage.

Editorial (2015) *The Guardian*, February 13, p. 32.

Edwards, E. P. and Sengupta, S. (2010) 'Industrial relations and economic performance', pp. 378–97 in T. Colling and M. Terry (eds.) *Industrial relations: Theory and Practice* (3rd edn). Chichester: John Wiley & Sons.

Edwards, P. (2003) *Industrial Relations: Theory and Practice* (2nd edn), Oxford: Blackwell.

Edwards, P. K. (1990) 'Understanding conflict in the labour process: the logic and autonomy of struggle', pp. 125–52 in D. Knights and H. Willmott (eds), *Labour Process Theory*, Basingstoke: Macmillan.

Edwards, R. (1979) *Contested Terrain: The Transformation of the Workplace in the Twentieth Century*, London: Heinemann.

Ehn, P. (1988) *Work-Oriented Design of Computer Artifacts*, Stockholm: Arbetslivscentrum.

Eisenberg, E. M. and Goodall, H. L. (1997) *Organizational Communication: Balancing Creativity and Constraint*, New York: St Martin's Press.

Elangovan, A. R. and Xie, J. L. (1999) 'Effects of perceived power of supervisor on subordinate stress and motivation: the moderating role of subordinate characteristics', *Journal of Organizational Behavior*, 20(3), pp. 359–74.

Elger, T. and Smith, C. (eds) (1994) *Global Japanization?*, London: Routledge.

Elkes, N. (2013) 'NEC sale on cards as council's equal pay bill hits £1bn: city's "crown jewels" will have to be sold to repay massive claims following workers' legal action', *Birmingham Post*, November 14, p. 5. Available at: http://search.proquest.com/uknews/docview/1457105708/14338E169C5711F6E53/16... (accessed January 27, 2014).

Elliott, L. (2013a) 'Britain falls behind best developing countries as gender gap stays static', *The Guardian*, October 25, p. 34.

Elliott, L. (2013b) 'CBI boss: business must rebuild reputation', *The Guardian*, November 1, p. 42.

Elliott, L. and Treanor, J. (2014) 'Davos faces up to weak growth and rising inequality', *The Observer*, January 19, p. 44.

Elliott, L. and Treanor, J. (2015) Bank of England's disarray in the face of financial crisis revealed', *The Guardian*, January 7, p. 27.

Ellul, J. (1964) *The Technological Society*, New York: Vintage.

Emery, F. E. and Thorsrud, E. (1976) *Democracy at Work*, Leiden: Martinus Nijhoff.

Engeström, Y. (1994) *Training for Change: New Approaches to Instruction and Learning*, Geneva: International Labour Office.

Esland, G. and Salaman, G. (1980) *The Politics of Work and Occupations*, Milton Keynes: Open University Press.

European Commission (2013) 'Women on boards – factsheet 2. Gender equality in the Member States'. Available at: http://ec.europa.eu/justice/gender-equality/files/womenonboards/factsheet-general-2_en.pdf (accessed January 23, 2015).

European Trade Union Confederation (2009) 'Factsheet: Working Time Directive'. Available at: www.etuc.org/a/504 (accessed November 2, 2009).

Evans, J. (1983) 'Negotiating technological change', pp. 152–68 in H. J. Otway and M. Pletu (eds), *New Office Technology: Human and Organizational Aspects*, London: Frances Pinter.

Eysenck, H. (1973) *The Inequality of Man*, London: Temple Smith.

Eysenck, H. J. (1970) *The Structure of Human Personality* (3rd edn), London: Methuen.

Eysenck, M. W. (2009) *Fundamentals of Psychology*, Hove: Psychology Press.

Eysenck, M. W. and Keane, M. T. (2005) *Cognitive Psychology: A Student's Handbook* (5th edn), Hove: Lawrence Erlbaum.

Ezzamel, M., Willmot, H. and Worthington, F. (2004) 'Accounting and management-labour relations: the politics of production in the factory with a problem', *Accounting, Organizations and Society*, 29(3–4), pp. 269–302.

Fairholm, G. W. (1996) 'Spiritual leadership: fulfilling whole-self needs at work', *Leadership and Organizational Development*, 17(5), pp. 11–17.

Falkenberg, L. and Boland, L. (1997) 'Eliminating the barriers to employment equity in the Canadian workplace', *Journal of Business Ethics*, 16(9), pp. 963–75.

Farmer, H. S. (1997) *Diversity and Women's Career Development: From Adolescence to Adulthood*, Thousand Oaks, CA: Sage.

Farnham, D. (2015) *The Changing Face of Employment Relations*. London: Palgrave.

Farrell, S. (2009) 'Bonfire of the bankers'. Available at www.independent.co.uk/news/business/analysis-and-features/treasury-select-committee-bonfire-of-the-bankers-1606332.html (accessed October 11, 2009).

Fayol, H. (1949) *General and Industrial Management*, London: Pitman.

Federation of Small Businesses (2014) 'Small business statistics'. Available at: www.fsb.org.uk/stats (accessed December 2014).

Federici, S. (2014) 'The reproduction of labour power in the global economy and the unfinished feminist revolution', pp. 85–107 in M. Atzeni (ed.), *Workers and Labour in a Globalised Capitalism*, Basingstoke: Palgrave Macmillan.

Feenberg, A. (1991) *Critical Theory of Technology*, New York: Oxford University Press.

Feldman, D. C. (1984) 'The development and enforcement of group norms', *Academy of Management Review*, 1, pp. 47–53.

Feldman, D. C., Leana, C. R. and Bolino, M. C. (2002) 'Underemployment and relative deprivation among re-employed executives', *Journal of Occupational and Organizational Psychology*, 75(4), pp. 453–88.

Felstead, A. and Jewson, N. (eds) (1999) *Global Trends in Flexible Labour*, Basingstoke: Palgrave Macmillan.

Felstead, A., Gallie, D. and Green, F. (2002) *Work Skills in Britain: 1986–2001*, London: HMSO.

Fenwick, T. (1998) 'Questioning the concept of the learning organization', pp. 140–52 in S. Scott, B. Spencer and A. Thomas (eds), *Learning for Life*, Toronto: Thompson Educational.

Ferlie, E. and Pettigrew, A. (1998) 'Managing through networks', pp. 200–22 in C. Mabey, G. Salaman and J. Storey (eds), *Strategic Human Resource Management: A Reader*, London: Sage.

Fernie, S., Metcalfe, D. and Woodland, S. (1994) 'Does human resource management boost employee management relations?', London School of Economics CEP Working Paper No. 546, London: LSE.

Fiedler, F. E. (1964) *A Theory of Leader Effectiveness*, New York: McGraw-Hill.

Fiedler, F. E. (1965) 'Engineering the job to fit the manager', *Harvard Business Review*, 43, pp. 115–22.

Fiedler, F. E. (1970) 'Leadership experience and leader performance: another hypothesis shot to hell', *Organizational Behaviour and Human Performance*, 5, pp. 1–14.

Fiedler, F. E. (1974) 'The contingency model – new directions for leadership utilization', *Journal of Contemporary Business*, 3(Autumn), p. 71.

Fiedler, F. (1997) 'Situational control and a dynamic theory of leadership', in K. Grint (ed.), *Leadership: Classical, Contemporary and Critical Approaches*, Oxford: Oxford University Press.

Field, R. and House, R. (1995) *Human Behaviour in Organizations: A Canadian Perspective*, Ontario: Prentice Hall.

Filipczak, P. (1996) 'The soul of the hog', *Training*, 33(February), pp. 38–42.

Filstad, C. (2014) The politics of sensemaking and sensegiving at work, *Journal of Workplace Learning*, 26(1), pp. 3–21.

Fincham, F., Stanley, S. and Beach, S. (2007) 'Transformative processes in marriage: an analysis of emerging trends', *Journal of Marriage and the Family*, 69, pp. 275–92.

Fineman, S. (2003) *Understanding Emotion at Work*, London: Sage.

Finkelstein, J. (1995) *The Fashioned Self*, Cambridge: Polity Press.

Finn, R. (2008) 'The language of teamwork: reproducing professional divisions in the operating theatre', *Human Relations* 61(1), pp. 103–30.

Fishman, C. (2007) *Wal-Mart Effect*, New York: Penguin.

Fiske, S. T. and Taylor, S. E. (1991) *Social Cognition* (2nd edn), New York: McGraw Hill.

Fitzgerald, J. A. and Teal, A. (2004) 'Health reform and occupational subcultures: the changing roles of professional identities', *Contemporary Nurse*, 16(1/2), pp. 9–19.

Flavelle, D. (2014) 'Skills shortage top concern, employers say', *Toronto Star*, June 2. Available at: www.thestar.com/business/2014/01/21/skills_shortage_top_concern_employers_say.html (accessed January 20, 2015).

Fleck, J. (1993) 'Configurations: crystallizing contingency', *International Journal of Human Factors in Manufacturing*, 3(1), pp. 15–36.

Florida, R. (2002) *The Rise of the Creative Class*, New York: Basic Books.

Foley, G. (2001) *Strategic Learning: Understanding and Facilitating Organizational Change*, Sydney: Centre for Popular Education.

Folger, R. and Cropanzano, R. (1998) *Organizational Justice and Human Resource Management*, Thousand Oaks, CA: Sage.

Fombrun, C. J., Tichy, N. M. and Devanna, M. A. (eds) (1984) *Strategic Human Resource Management*, New York: John Wiley & Sons.

Ford, J. D. and Ford, L. W. (1995) 'The role of conversations in producing intentional change in organizations', *Academy of Management Review*, 20(3), pp. 541–70.

Foucault, M. (1977) *Discipline and Punish: The Birth of the Prison*, New York: Pantheon.

Foucault, M. (1979) *The History of Sexuality*, Harmondsworth: Penguin.

Foucault, M. (1980) *Power/Knowledge* (ed. C. Gordon), New York: Pantheon.

Fox, A. (1966) *Industrial Sociology and Industrial Relations*, London: HMSO.

Fox, A. (1971) *The Sociology of Work in Industry*, London: Collier Macmillan.

Fox, A. (1974) *Beyond Contract, Power, and Trust Relations*, London: Faber & Faber.

FRA (2014) *Violence against Women: An EU-wide Survey*, Luxembourg: European Union Agency for Fundamental Rights.

Franklin, U. (1990) *The Real World of Technology*, Toronto: CBC Enterprises.

Freedland, J. (2014) 'This is the choice we offer the hungry: dignity or food', *The Guardian*, February 22, p. 33.

Freedman, A. and Medway, P. (eds) (1994a) *Genre and the New Rhetoric*, London: Taylor & Francis.

Freedman, A. and Medway, P. (eds) (1994b) *Learning and Teaching Genre*, Portsmouth, NH: Heinemann.

Freire, P. (1972) *Pedagogy of the Oppressed*, New York: Herder & Herder.

French, J. P. R. Jr and Raven, B. (1960) 'The bases of social power', pp. 607–23 in D. Cartwright and A. Zander (eds), *Group Dynamics*, New York: Harper & Row.

Frese, M. (1982) 'Occupational socialization and psychological development: an underemphasized research perspective in industrial psychology', *Journal of Occupational Psychology*, 55, pp. 209–24.

Friedland, H. (2014) 'Billion dollar bullying problem', *Brisbane Times*, June 3. Available at: www.brisbanetimes.com.au/small-business/managing/billion-dollar-bullying-problem-20140603-39fcv.html (accessed February 24, 2015).

Friedli, T., Mundt, A., and Thomas, S. (2014) *Strategic Management of Global Manufacturing Networks*, London: Springer.

Friedman, A. (1977) *Industry and Labor: Class Struggle at Work and Monopoly Capitalism*, London: Macmillan.

Friedman, M. (1982) *Capitalism and Freedom*, Chicago: Chicago University Press.

Frisby, D. (1981) *Sociological Impressionism: A Reassessment of Georg Simmel's Social Theory*, London: Heinemann.

Frost, P. J. , Moore, L., Louis, M., Lundberg, C. and Martin, J. (1985) *Organizational Culture*, Newbury Park, CA: Sage.

Frynas, J. G. and Mellahi, K. (2011) *Global Strategic Management* (2nd edn), Oxford: Oxford University Press.

Fuller, A. and Unwin, L. (1998) 'Reconceptualising apprenticeship: exploring the relationship between work and learning', *Journal of Vocational Education and Training*, 50(2), pp. 153–71.

Fulop, L. and Linstead, S. (2009) 'Motivation and meaning', pp. 411–72 in S. Linstead, L. Fulop and S. Lilley, *Management and Organization: A Critical Text* (2nd edn), Basingstoke: Palgrave Macmillan.

Furness, V. (2008) 'Impact of economic downturn on the psychological contract between employer and employee'. Available at: www.employeebenefits.co.uk/item/7912/23/307/3 (accessed February 27, 2009).

Furnham, A. (2004) Performance management systems. *European Business Journal*, 16(2), pp. 83–94.

Furnham, A. F. (1997) 'Vocational preference and P-O fit', in J. Arnold (ed.), 'The psychology of careers in organizations', *International Review of Industrial and Organizational Psychology*, 12, pp. 1–37.

Gadiesh, O. and Olivet, S. (1997) 'Designing for implementability', pp. 53–78 in F. Hesselbein, M. Goldsmith and R. Beckhard (eds) *The Organization of the Future*, San Francisco: Jossey-Bass.

Gaertner, G. H. and Ramnarayan, S. (1983) 'Organizational effectiveness: an alternative perspective', *Academy of Management Review*, 8, pp. 97–107.

Gagne, R. M. and Medsker, K. L. (1996) *The Conditions of Learning*, Fort Worth, TX: Harcourt Brace.

Galabuzi, G.-E. (2006) *Canada's Economic Apartheid: The Social Exclusion of Racialized Groups in the New Century*, Toronto: Canadian Scholars' Press.

Galbraith, J. R. (1996) 'Designing the innovative organization', pp. 156–81 in K. Starkey (ed.), *How Organizations Learn*, London: International Thomson Business Press.

Gardner, J. W. (1990) *On Leadership*, New York: Free Press.

Garrow, V. (2009) *OD: Past, Present and Future*, Brighton: Institute for Employment Studies. Available at: www.employment-studies.co.uk/pdflibrary/wp22.pdf.

Gartner, J. and Wagner, I. (1996) 'Mapping actors and agendas: political frameworks of systems design and participation', *Human–Computer Interaction*, 11, pp. 187–214.

Gates, W., with Myhrvold, N. and Rinearson, P. (1996) *The Road Ahead*, New York: Penguin.

Gattiker, U. E. (1990) *Technology Management in Organizations*, London: Sage.

Gee, J., Hull, G. and Lankshear, C. (1996) *The New Work Order: Behind the Language of the New Capitalism*, Boulder, CO: Westview.

Geller, E. S. (2002) 'Leadership to overcome resistance to change: it takes more than consequence control', *Journal of Organizational Behavior Management*, 22(3), pp. 29–49.

Genovese, E. (1972) *Roll Jordan Roll: The World the Slaves Made*, New York: Vintage Books.

George, C. S. (1972) *The History of Management Thought* (2nd edn), Englewood Cliffs, NJ: Prentice-Hall.

Gerhart, B. (2008) 'Modelling HRM and performance linkages', pp. 552–80 in P. Boxall, J. Purcell and P. Wright (eds), *The Oxford Handbook of Human Resource Management*, New York: Oxford University Press.

Gersick, C. J. (1988) 'Time and transition in workteams: towards a new model of group development', *Academy of Management Journal*, 31, pp. 47–53.

Gherardi, S. (1994) 'The gender we think, the gender we do in our everyday organizational lives', *Human Relations*, 47(6), pp. 591–606.

Ghose, A. K., Majid, N. and Ernst, C. (2008) *The Global Employment Challenge*, Geneva: International Labour Organization.

Ghoshal, S. and Bartlett, C. A. (1997) *The Individualized Corporation: A Fundamentally New Approach to Management: Great Companies Are Defined by Purpose, Process, and People*, New York: HarperBusiness.

Giacalone, R. A. Jurkiewicz, C. L. and Promislo, M. (2015) 'Ethics and well-being: the paradoxical implications of individual differences in ethical orientation', *Journal of Business Ethics*, doi: 10.1007/S10551-015-2558-8.

Giberson, T. R., Resick, C. and Dickson, M. (2005) 'Embedding leader characteristics: an examination of homogeneity of personality and values in organizations', *Journal of Applied Psychology*, 90(5), pp. 1002–10.

Gibson, C. B. and Zellmer-Bruhn, M. E. (2001) 'Metaphors and meaning: an intercultural analysis of the concept of teamwork', *Administrative Science Quarterly*, 46(2), pp. 274–303.

Giddens, A. (1984) *The Constitution of Society*, Cambridge: Polity Press.

Giddens, A. (1985) *A Contemporary Critique of Historical Materialism*, Volume 2: *The Nation State and Violence*, Cambridge: Polity Press.

Giddens, A. (1990) *The Consequences of Modernity*. Cambridge: Polity Press.

Giddens, A. (1991) *Modernity and Self-Identity*, Palo Alto, CA: Stanford University Press.

Giddens, A. (2009) *Sociology* (6th edn), Cambridge: Polity Press.

Giddens, A. and Sutton, P. (2013) *Sociology* (7th edn), Cambridge: Polity Press.

Giebels, E. and Janssen, O. (2005) 'Conflict stress and reduced well-being at work: the buffering effect of third-party help', *European Journal of Work and Organizational Psychology*, 14, pp. 137–55.

Gillies, M. (2009) 'Losing your job, losing your identity', *Globe and Mail*, April 22, p. C1.

Gilligan, C. (1982) *In a Different Voice*, Cambridge, MA: Harvard University Press.

Gilliland, S. W. and Chan, D. (2001) 'Justice in organizations: theory, methods and applications', in N. Anderson, D. Ones, H. K. Sinangil and C. Viswesveran (eds), *Handbook of Industrial, Work and Organizational Psychology*, Volume 2: *Organizational Psychology*, London: Sage.

Gingras, Y. (2009) 'Marketing can corrupt universities', *University Affairs*, February, p. 39.

Gladwell, M. (2005) *Blink: The Power of Thinking Without Thinking*, Harmondsworth: Penguin.

Glenn, E. and Feldberg, R. (1979) 'Proletarianizing clerical work: technology and organizational control in the office', pp. 51–72 in A. Zimbalist (ed.), *Case Studies on the Labor Process*, New York: Monthly Review Press.

Glomb, T., Richmann, W., Hulin, C. and Drasgow, R. (1997) 'Ambient sexual harassment: an integrated model of antecedents and consequences', *Organizational Behavior and Human Decision Processes*, 71(3), pp. 309–28.

Godard, J. (2005a) 'Contemporary management practices', pp. 112–48 in *Industrial Relations, the Economy and Society* (3rd edn), Concord: Captus.

Godard, J. (2005b) *Industrial Relations: The Economy and Society* (3rd edn), Concord, ON: Captus Press.

Goffman, E. (1959) *The Presentation of Self in Everyday Life*, New York: Anchor.

Goffman, E. (1961) *Asylums*, London: Penguin, quoted in S. Bolton (2005), *Emotion Management in the Workplace*, Basingstoke: Palgrave Macmillan, p. 267.

Goffman, E. (1967) *Interaction Ritual: Essays on Face to Face Behavior*, New York: Anchor.

Gold, J., Holden, R., Stewart, J., Iles, P. and Beardwell, J. (eds) (2013) *Human Resource Development: Theory and Practice* (2nd edn), Basingstoke: Palgrave Macmillan.

Goldberg, L. R. (1990) 'An alternative "description of personality": the Big-Five factor structure', *Journal of Personality and Social Psychology*, 59, pp. 1216–29.

Goldman, S. L., Nagel, R. N. and Preiss, K. (1995) *Agile Competition and Virtual Organizations: Strategies for Enriching the Customer*, New York: Van Nostrand Reinhold.

Goldthorpe, J. H., Lockwood, D., Bechhofer, F. and Platt, J. (1968) *The Affluent Worker: Industrial Attitudes and Behaviour*, Cambridge: Cambridge University Press.

Goleman, D. (1996) *Emotional Intelligence*, London: Bloomsbury.

Goleman, D. (1998) 'What makes a leader?', *Harvard Business Review*, November–December, pp. 93–102.

Goleman, D., Boyatzis, R. and McKee, A. (2002) *Primal Leadership: Realizing the Power of Emotional Intelligence*. Boston, MA: Harvard Business School Press.

Goleman, D., Boyatzis, R. and McKee, A. (2013) *Primal Leadership: Unleashing the Power of Emotional Intelligence* (10th anniversary edn), Boston, MA: Harvard Business School Press.

Goltz, S. and Hietapelto, A. (2002) 'Using the operant and strategic contingencies models of power to understand resistance to change', *Journal of Organizational Behavior Management*, 22(3), pp. 3–22.

Goodley, S. (2014) 'Government warned it may miss target for women in FTSE 100 boardrooms', *The Guardian*, March 26. Available at: www.theguardian.com/business/2014/mar/26/government-warned-may-miss-target-on-women-in-ftse-100-boardrooms (accessed January 23, 2015).

Gordon, J. R. and Whelan, K .S. (1998) 'Successful professional women in midlife: how organizations can more effectively understand and respond to the challenges', *Academy of Management Executive*, 12(1), pp. 8–27.

Gorz, A. (1982) *Farewell to the Working Class*, London: Pluto.

Gospel, H. (ed.) (1991) *Industrial Training and Technological Innovation: A Comparative and Historical Perspective*, London: Routledge & Kegan Paul.

Graeber, D. (2014) 'Savage capitalism is back – but tinkering will not tame it,' *The Guardian*, May 31, p. 35.

Gramsci, A. (1971) *Selections from the Prison Notebooks*, London: Lawrence & Wishart.

Granrose, C. S. (2001) 'The challenge of Confucius: the generalizability of North America career assumptions', in J. Kidd, X. Li and F.-J. Richter (eds), *Maximizing Human Intelligence Deployment in Asian Business: The Sixth Generation Project*, Basingstoke: Palgrave Macmillan.

Gray, R. and Robertson, L. (2005) 'Effective communication starts at the top', *Communication World*, 22(July), p. 4.

Green, F. (2004) 'Why has work effort become more intense?', *Industrial Relations*, 43, pp. 709–41.

Greenhaus, J. H. (1987) *Career Management*, Chicago: Dryden.

Greenhaus, J. H. (2008), 'Innovations in the study of the work–family interface: introduction to the Special Section', *Journal of Occupational and Organizational Psychology*, 81, pp. 343–8.

Grey, C. (2005) *A Very Short, Fairly Interesting and Reasonably Cheap Book about Studying Organizations*, London: Sage.

Grey, C. (2013) *A Very Short, Fairly Interesting and Reasonably Cheap Book about Studying Organizations* (3rd edn), London: Sage.

Griffin, E. (2013) *Liberty's Dawn: A People's History of the Industrial Revolution*, Yale, CT: Yale University Press.

Grimshaw, D. and Rubery, J. (2010) 'Pay and working time: shifting contours of the employment relationship', pp. 347–77, in T. Colling and M. Terry (eds), *Industrial Relations Theory and Practice* (3rd edn), Chichester: John Wiley & Sons.

Grint, K. (1995) 'The culture of management and the management of culture', pp. 162–88 in *Management: A Sociological Introduction*, Cambridge: Polity Press.

Grint, K. (ed.) (1997) *Leadership*, Oxford: Oxford University Press.

Grint, K. (1998) *The Sociology of Work* (2nd edn), Cambridge: Polity Press.

Grint, K. (2000) *The Arts of Leadership*, Oxford: Oxford University Press.

Grint, K. (2001) 'Martin Luther King's "Dream Speech": the rhetoric of social leadership', pp. 359–408 in *The Arts of Leadership*, New York: Oxford University Press.

Grint, K. (2005) *Leadership: Limits and Possibilities*, Basingstoke: Palgrave Macmillan.

Grint, K. and Willcocks, L. (1995) 'Business process re-engineering in theory and practice: business paradise regained?', *New Technology, Work and Employment*, 10(2), pp. 99–108.

Guardian, The (2013) 'Gender pay gap stands at 15%', *The Guardian*, November 7. Available at: www.theguardian.com/money/2013/nov/07/gender-pay-gap-official-figures-disparity (accessed January 23, 2015).

Guest, D. E. (1997) 'Human resource management and performances review and research agenda', *International Journal of Human Resource Management*, 8(3), pp. 263–76.

Guest, D. E. and Conway, N. (2002) 'Communicating the psychological contract: an employer perspective', *Human Resource Management Journal*, 12(2), pp. 22–38.

Guidice, R. M., Thompson, Thompson Heames, J. and Wang, S. (2009), 'The indirect relationship between organizational-level knowledge worker turnover and innovation', *Learning Organization*, 16(2), pp. 143–67.

Guirdham, M. (2011) *Communicating Across Cultures at Work* (3rd edn), Basingstoke: Palgrave Macmillan.

Guthrie, J. P. (2008) 'Remuneration: pay effects on work', pp. 344–63 in P. Boxall, J. Purcell and P. Wright (eds), *The Oxford Handbook of Human Resource Management*, Oxford: Oxford University Press.

Haart, E. G. O.-de, Carey, D. P. and Milne, A. B. (1999) 'More thoughts on perceiving and grasping the Müller–Lyer illusion', *Neuropsychologica*, 37, pp. 1437–44.

Hacker, S. (1991) *Doing it the Hard Way: Investigations of Gender and Technology*, Winchester, MA: Unwin Hyman.

Hackman, H. R. (1986) 'The psychology of self-management in organizations', pp. 89–136 in M. S. Pallack and R. O. Perloff (eds), *Psychology and Work: Productivity, Change and Employment*, Washington, DC: American Psychological Association.

Hackman, J. and Oldham, G. (1980) *Work Redesign*, Reading, MA: Addison-Wesley.

Ha-Joon Chang (2013) 'We need to focus on the quality of our life at work', *The Guardian*, December 23, p. 26.

Hales, C. (1986) 'What do managers do? A critical review of the evidence', *Journal of Management Studies*, 23, pp. 88–115.

Hales, C. (2002) 'Bureacracy-lite and continuities in management work', *British Journal of Management*, 13(1), pp. 51–66.

Hall, E. T. (1976) *Beyond Culture*, New York: Doubleday.

Hall, S. (1995) 'Negotiating Caribbean identities', *New Left Review*, January 1, pp. 3–14.

Hall, S. (2005) 'Thinking diaspora: home thoughts from abroad', pp. 543–560 in G. Desai and S. Nair (eds), *Postcolonialisms: An Anthology of Cultural Theory and Criticism*, New Brunswick, NJ: Rutgers University Press.

Hamel, G. and Prahalad, C. K. (1994) *Competing for the Future*, Boston, MA: Harvard Business School Press.

Hammer, M. (1997) *Beyond Reengineering*, New York: HarperBusiness.

Hammer, M. and Champy, J. (1993) *Reengineering the Corporation: A Manifesto for Business Revolution*, New York: HarperBusiness.

Handel, G. E. (2006) *Childhood Socialization* (2nd edn), Berlin: De Gruyter.

Handy, C. (1985) *Understanding Organizations*, London: Penguin.

Handy, C. (1993) *Understanding Organizations* (4th edn), London: Penguin.

Hanson, J. (2003) 'Fighting for the union label: the women's garment industry and the ILGWU in Pennsylvania', *Oral History Review*, 30(1), pp. 143–58.

Hardill, L. and Green, A. (2003) 'Remote working – altering the spatial contours of work and home in the new economy', *New Technology, Work and Employment*, 18(3), pp. 212–22.

Harding, K. (2003) 'Working with art', *Globe and Mail*, August 20, p. C1.

Hardy, C. and Clegg, S. R. (1999) 'Some dare call it power', pp. 368–87 in S. R. Clegg and C. Hardy (eds), *Studying Organization: Theory and Methods*, London: Sage.

Harford, T. (2014) 'How to see into the future', *Financial Times Weekend Magazine*, pp. 15–19.

Harker, J. (2015) 'Cumberbatch got it wrong, but we can cut him some slack', *The Guardian*, January 28, p. 30.

Harley, B., Hyman, J. and Thompson, P. (2005) *Participation and Democracy at Work*, Basingstoke: Palgrave Macmillan.

Harney, A. (2008) *The China Price: The True Cost of Chinese Competitive Advantage*, New York: Penguin.

Harrel, A. M. and Strahl, M. J. (1981) 'A behavioral decision theory approach to measuring McClelland's trichotomy of needs', *Journal of Applied Psychology*, 66, pp. 242–7.

Harris, A. and Spillane, J. (2008) 'Distributed leadership through the looking glass', *British Educational Leadership, Management and Administration Society*, 22(1), pp. 31–4.

Harter, N., Ziolkowski, F. and Wyatt, S. (2006) 'Leadership and inequality', *Leadership*, 2(3), pp. 275–93.

Haslam, S. A. (2001) *Psychology in Organizations: The Social Identity Approach*, London: Sage.

Haslam, S. A. (2004) *Psychology in Organizations: The Social Identity Approach* (2nd edn), London: Sage.

Hassard, J. and Parker, M. (1993) *Postmodernism and Organizations*, London: Sage.

Hassard, J. and Parker, M. (eds) (2000) *Postmodernism and Organizations* (2nd edn), London: Sage.

Hatch, A. and Cunliffe, A. (2012) *Organization Theory: Modern, Symbolic and Postmodern Perspectives* (3rd edn), Oxford: Oxford University Press.

Hayes, E. and Flannery, D. D. (2000) *Women as Learners: The Significance of Gender in Adult Learning*, San Francisco: Jossey-Bass.

Hayes, J. (2014) *The Theory and Practice of Change Management*, Basingstoke: Palgrave Macmillan.

Head, S. (2004) 'Inside the Leviathan', *New York Review of Books*, 51(20), pp. 1–8.

Healy, G., Hansen, L. L. and Ledwith, S. (2006) 'Editorial: still uncovering gender in industrial relations', *Industrial Relations Journal*, 37(4), pp. 290–8.

Hearn, J. (2012) *Theorizing Power*, Basingstoke: Palgrave Macmillan.

Hearn, J., Sheppard, D. L., Tancred-Sheriff, P. and Burrell, G. (eds) (1989) *The Sexuality of Organization*, London: Sage.

Heery, E. (2000) 'The new pay: risk and representation at work', pp. 172–188 in D. Winstanley and J. Woodall (eds.), *Ethical Issues in Contemporary Human Resource Management*, Basingstoke: Palgrave Macmillan.

Heidegger, M. (1977) *The Question Concerning Technology*, New York: Harper & Row.

Heller, F., Pusic, E., Strauss, G. and Wilpert, B. (1998) *Organizational Participation: Myth and Reality*, Oxford: Oxford University Press.

Helm, T. (2013) 'More than 5 million now paid less than living wage', *The Observer*, November 3, p. 8.

Helm Mills, J. C. and Mills, A. (2000) 'Rules, sensemaking, formative contexts, and discourse in the gendering of organizational culture', pp. 55–70 in N. M. Ashkanasy, C. P. M. Wilderom and M. F. Peterson (eds), *Handbook of Organizational Culture and Climate*, Thousand Oaks, CA: Sage.

Hendrickson, S. and Gray, E. J. (2012) 'Legitimizing resistance to organizational change: a social work social justice perspective', *International Journal of Humanities and Social Science*, 2(5), pp. 50–9.

Hendry, C. and Jenkins, R. (1997), 'Psychological contracts and new deals', *Human Resource Management Journal*, 7(1), pp. 38–44.

Hendry, C. and Pettigrew, A. (1990) 'Human resource management: an agenda for the 1990s', *International Journal of Human Resource Management*, 1(1), pp. 17–44.

Herod, A., Rainnie, A. and McGrath-Champ, S. (2007) 'Working space: why incorporating the geographical is central to theorizing work and employment practices', *Work, Employment and Society*, 21(2), pp. 247–64.

Herrbach, O. and Mignonac, K. (2004) 'How organizational image affects employee attitudes', *Human Resource Management Journal*, 14(4), pp. 76–88.

Herriot, P. (1998) 'The role of human resource management in building a new proposition', pp. 106–16 in P. Sparrow and M. Marchington (eds), *Human Resource Management: A New Agenda*, London: Financial Times Management.

Herriot, P., Hirsh, W. and Reilly, P. (1998) *Trust and Transition: Managing Today's Employment Relationship*, Chichester: John Wiley & Sons.

Hersey, P. and Blanchard, K. H. (1969) 'Life cycle theory of leadership', *Training and Development Journal*, 23, pp. 26–34.

Hersey, P., Blanchard, K. H. and Johnson, D. (1977) *Management of Organizational Behavior: Utilizing Human Resources* (3rd edn), Upper Saddle River, NJ: Prentice Hall.

Hertog, J. F. and Tolner, T. (1998) 'Groups and teams', pp. 62–71 in M. Poole and M. Watner (eds), *The Handbook of Human Resource Management*, London: International Thomson Business Press.

Hertz, N. (2002) *The Silent Takeover: Global Capitalism and the Death of Democracy*, London: Arrow.

Herzberg, F. (2003) 'One more time: how do you motivate employees?', *Harvard Business Review*, 81(1), pp. 87–96.

Herzberg, F., Mansner, B. and Snyderman, B. (1959) *The Motivation to Work* (2nd edn), New York: John Wiley & Sons.

Hewitt, J. P. and Shulman, D. (2011) *Self and Society* (11th edn), Boston, MA: Pearson Education.

Highhouse, S. (2001) 'Judgment and decision-making research: relevance to industrial and organizational psychology', in N. Anderson, D. Ones, H. K. Sinangil and C. Viswesveran (eds), *Handbook of Industrial Work and Organizational Psychology*, Volume 2: *Organizational Psychology*, London: Sage.

Hill, C. and Jones, G. (2012) *Strategic Management Theory* (10th edn), Andover: Cengage.

Hinojosa, A. S., Walker, H. and Tyge Payne, G. (2015) 'Prerecruitment organizational perceptions and recruitment website information processing', *International Journal of Human Resource Management*, doi: 10.1080/09585192.2014.1003081.

Hinton, J. (1973) *The First Shop Stewards Movement*, London: Allen & Unwin.

Hirsch, B. and MacPherson, D. (2003) *Union Membership and Earnings Data Book: Compilations from the Current Population Survey*, Washington, DC: Bureau of National Affairs.

Hobsbawm, E. (1968) *Industry and Empire*, London: Weidenfeld & Nicolson.

Hobsbawm, E. (1994) *Age of Extremes*, London: Abacus.

Hobsbawm, E. (1997) *On History*, London: Weidenfeld & Nicolson.

Hochschild, A. (1983) *The Managed Heart: Commercialization of Human Feeling*, Berkeley, CA: University of California Press.

Hochschild, A. (2003) *The Second Shift*, New York: Penguin.

Hodgkinson, G. (1997) 'Cognitive inertia in a turbulent market: the case of UK residential estate agents', *Journal of Management Studies*, 34, pp. 921–45.

Hodson, R. (1999) 'Management citizenship behavior: a new concept and an empirical test', *Social Problems*, 46(3), pp. 460–78.

Hodson, R. and Sullivan, T. A. (2012) *The Social Organization of Work* (5th edn), Belmont, CA: Wadsworth/Thomson Learning.

Hoel, H. and Beale, D. (2006) 'Workplace bullying, psychological perspectives and industrial relations: towards a contextualized and interdisciplinary approach', *British Journal of Industrial Relations*, 44(2), pp. 239–62.

Hoeve, A. and Nieuwenhuis, L. (2006) 'Learning routines in innovation processes', *Journal of Workplace Learning*, 18(3), pp. 171–85.

Hofstede, G. (1998a) *Masculinity and Femininity: The Taboo Dimension of National Cultures*, Thousand Oaks, CA: Sage.

Hofstede, G. (1998b) 'Organization culture', pp. 237–55 in M. Poole and M. Warner (eds), *The Handbook of Human Resource Management*, London: International Thomson Business Press.

Hofstede, G. (2001) *Culture's Consequences: Comparing Values, Behaviors, Institutions, and Organizations across Nations*, Thousand Oaks, CA: Sage.

Hofstede, G., Hofstede, G. J. and Minkov, M. (2010) *Cultures and Organizations: Software of the Mind* (3rd edn), New York: McGraw-Hill.

Hogg, M. and Terry, D. J. (2000) 'Social identity and self-categorization processes in organizational contexts', *Academy of Management Review*, 25, pp. 121–40.

Hogg, M. A. and Vaughan, G. M. (2004) *Social Psychology: An Introduction* (4th edn), Hemel Hempstead: Prentice Hall.

Holland, D., Lachicotte, W. Jr, Skinner, D. and Cain, C. (1998) *Identity and Agency in Cultural Worlds*, Cambridge, MA: Harvard University Press.

Holland, J. L. (1985) *Making Vocational Choices: A Theory of Vocational Personalities and Work Environments* (2nd edn), Englewood Cliffs, NJ: Prentice Hall.

Holmes, J. (2006) *Gendered Talk at Work*, Oxford: Blackwell.

Holt, N., Bremmer, A., Sutherland, E., Vliek, M. L. W., Passer, M., and Smith, R. (2012) *Psychology: Science of the Mind and Behaviour*, Maidenhead: McGraw-Hill.

Hollway, W. (1991) *Work Psychology and Organizational Behaviour*, London: Sage.

Hoogvelt, A. (2001) *Globalization and the Postcolonial World* (2nd edn), Basingstoke: Palgrave Macmillan.

Hope, S. and Figiel, J. (2012) *Intern Culture: A Literature Review of Internship Reports, Guidelines and Toolkits from 2009–11*, London: Artquest.

Höpfl, H. (1992) 'The challenge of change: the theory and practice of organizational transformation', presented to the Employment Research Unit Annual Conference, Cardiff Business School, September, quoted in P. Thompson and D. McHugh (2009), *Work and Organisations*, Basingstoke: Palgrave Macmillan, p. 205.

Hopkins, H. D. (1999) 'Cross-border mergers and acquisitions: global regional perspectives', *Journal of International Management*, 5, pp. 207–39.

Hoque, K. (1999) 'Human resource management and performance in the UK hotel industry', *British Journal of Industrial Relations*, 37(3), pp. 419–43.

Horwitz, F. M., Chan Feng Heng and Quazi, H. A. (2003) 'Finders, keepers? Attracting, motivating and retaining knowledge workers', *Human Resource Management Journal*, 13(4), pp. 23–44.

Horwitz, P. and Budhwar, P. (eds) (2015) *Handbook of Human Resource Management in Emerging Markets*, Cheltenham: Edward Elgar.

House, R. T. (1971) 'A path goal theory of leader effectiveness', *Administrative Science Quarterly*, 16, pp. 321–38.

House, R. J., Hanges, P. J., Ruiz-Quintanilla, S. A. et al. (1999) 'Cultural influences on leadership and organizations: Project GLOBE', pp. 171–233 in W. H. Mobley, M. J. Gessner, and V. Arnold (eds.), *Advances in Global Leadership*, Stamford, CT: JAI Press.

House of Commons (2009) 'Treasury – Ninth Report, banking Crisis: reforming corporate governance and pay in the City', May. Available at: www.publications.parliament.uk/pa/cm200809/cmselect/cmtreasy/519/51902.htm.

House of Commons (2013) 'The role of Jobcentre Plus in the reformed welfare system', *Work and Pensions Committee*. Available at: www.publications.parliament.uk/pa/cm201314/cmcelect/cmworpen/479/47909... (accessed March 24, 2014).

House of Commons Treasury Committee (2009) *Banking Crisis: Dealing with the Failure of the UK Banks*, London: Stationery Office.

Houtenville, A. J. (2003) *Disability Statistics in the United States*, Ithaca, NY: Cornell University Rehabilitation Research and Training Center.

Howell, J. P. and Dorfman, P. W. (1981) 'Substitutes for leadership: test of a construct', *Academy of Management Journal*, 24, pp. 714–28.

Howell, J. P., Bowen, D., Dorfman, P., Kerr, S. and Podsakoff, P. (1990)

'Substitutes for leadership: effective alternatives to ineffective leadership', *Organizational Dynamics*, 19, pp. 21–38.

Howells, C. A. (1987) *Private and Fictional Words*, London: Methuen.

Hughes, F. (1983) *Networks of Power*, Baltimore, MD: Johns Hopkins University Press.

Hughes, T. P. (1989). *American Genesis: A Century of Invention and Technological Enthusiasm, 1870–1970*, New York: Penguin.

Human Rights Watch (2014) 'UK: Migrant domestic workers face serious abuse'. Available at: www.hrw.org/print/news/2014/03/31/uk-migrant-domestic-workers-face-serious-abuse?dm_i=LF4%2C2BRLI%2C86UIIE%2C8G06K%2C1 (accessed December 13, 2014).

Hume, D. (1758/2007) *An Enquiry Concerning Human Understanding*, Oxford: Oxford University Press.

Hung, D. (1999) 'Activity, apprenticeship and epistemological appropriation: implications from the writings of...', *Educational Psychologist*, 34(4), pp. 193–205.

Hunt, K. (2009) 'The chaos theory of organization', *Report on Business*, March, p. 18.

Hunter, D. (1994) 'From tribalism to corporatism: the managerial challenge to medical dominance', pp. 1–22 in J. Gabe, D. Kelleher and G. Williams (eds), *Challenging Medicine*, London: Routledge.

Hurley-Hanson, A. and Giannantonio, C. (2008) 'Human resource information systems in crisis', paper presented at Academy of Strategic Management Conference, Tunica.

Hutchinson, S., Purcell, J. and Kinnie, N. (2000) 'Evolving high commitment management and the experience of the RAC call centre', *Human Resource Management Journal*, 10(1), pp. 63–78.

Hutton, W. (2014) 'It's easy to moan about bonuses, but just how do we fix banks?', *The Observer*, April 27, p. 42.

Hyman, R. (1982) 'What ever happened to industrial sociology?', in D. Dunkerley and G. Salaman (eds), *The International Yearbook of Organisation Studies 1981*, London: Routledge & Kegan Paul.

Hyman, R. (1988) 'Flexible specialization: miracle or myth', in R. Hyman and W. Streeck (eds), *New Technology and Industrial Relations*, Oxford: Blackwell.

Hyman, R. (1989a) *The Political Economy of Industrial Relations*, Basingstoke: Macmillan.

Hyman, R. (1989b) *Strikes*, London: Macmillan Press.

Hyman, R. (1991) 'Plus ça change? The theory of production and the production of theory', pp. 259–83 in A. Pollert (ed.), *Farewell to Flexibility?*, Oxford: Blackwell.

Hyman, R. and Streeck, W. (eds) (1988) *New Technology and Industrial Relations*, Oxford: Blackwell.

Ichniowski, C., Kochan, T., Levine, D., Olson, C. and Strauss, G. (1996) 'What works at work: overview and assessment', *Industrial Relations*, 35(3), pp. 299–333.

Industry Weekly (2013) '75% company tax on high salaries approved by French Court', December 30. Available at: www.industryweek.com/finance/75-company-tax-high-salaries-approved-french-court (accessed February 3, 2015).

Innes, P. and Littler, C. (2004) 'A decade of downsizing: understanding the contours of change in Australia, 1990–99', *Asia Pacific Journal of Human Resources*, 42(2), pp. 229–42.

Irish Times (2014) 'Know your rights as a temporary worker in Australia'. Available at: www.irishtimes.com/blogs/generationemigration/2014/02/05/know-your-rights-as-a-temporary-worker-in-australia/.

Jabri, M. (2012) *Managing Organizational Change*, Basingstoke: Palgrave Macmillan.

Jacobs, C. and Heracleous, L. (2005) 'Answers for questions to come: reflective dialogue as an enabler of strategic innovation', *Journal of Organization Change Management*, 18(4), pp. 338–52.

Jacobs, E. (2008) 'Redundancy and a depression', *Financial Times*, August 19. Available at: www.journalisted.com/article?id=763449 (accessed December 14, 2014).

Jacoby, S. M. (2005) *The Embedded Corporation: Corporate Governance and Employment Relations in Japan and the United States*, Princeton, NJ: Princeton University Press.

Jaffee, D. (2001) *Organization Theory: Tension and Change*, Boston, MA: McGraw-Hill.

Janis, I. L. (1972) *Victims of Groupthink*, Boston, MA: Houghton Mifflin.

Jansen J. P., Vera D. and Crossan M. (2009) 'Strategic leadership for exploration and exploitation: the moderating role of environmental dynamism', *Leadership Quarterly* 20(1), pp. 5–18.

Jarvis, P. (1985) *The Sociology of Adult and Continuing Education*, London: Routledge.

Jarvis, P. (ed.) (1991) *Twentieth Century Thinkers in Adult Education*, London: Routledge.

Jenkin, M. (2014) 'Small businesses strive to be lean and green', *The Guardian*, January 9, p. 30.

Jenkins, J. (2008) 'Pressurised partnership: a case of perishable compromise in contested terrain', *New Technology, Work and Employment*, 23(3), pp. 167–80.

Jenkins, R. (2008) *Social Identity*, London: Routledge.

Jensen, M. C., Brant-Zawadzki, M. N., Obuchowski, N., Modic, M. T., Malkasian, D. and Ross, J. S. (1994) 'Magnetic resonance imaging of the lumbar spine in people without back pain', *New England Journal of Medicine*, 331, pp. 69–73.

Jewson, N. and Mason, D. (1986) 'The theory and practice of equal opportunities policies: liberal and radical approaches', *Sociological Review*, 34(2), pp. 307–34.

Jobber, D. (2012) *Principles and Practice of Marketing* (7th edn), London: McGraw-Hill.

Johnson, D. W. and Johnson, F. P. (2014) *Joining Together: Group Theory and Group Skills* (11th edn), Maidenhead: McGraw-Hill.

Johnson, G., Scholes, K. and Whittington, R. (2008) *Exploring Corporate Strategy: Text and Cases* (8th edn), Harlow, UK: Financial Times Prentice Hall.

Johnson, R., Selenta, C. and Lord, R. (2006) 'When organizational justice and the self-concept meet: consequences for the organization its members', *Organizational Behaviour and Human Decision Processes*, 99(2), pp. 175–201.

Jones, B. (1983) 'Destruction or redistribution of engineering skills: the case of numerical control', pp. 179–200 in S. Wood (ed.), *The Degradation of Work? Skill, Deskilling and the Labour Process*, London: Hutchinson.

Jones, B. (1988) 'Work and flexible automation in Britain: a review of developments and possibilities', *Work, Employment and Society*, 2(4), pp. 451–86.

Jones, O. (2014) *The Establishment, And How They Get Away with It*, London: Allen Lane.

Jones, R., Lasky, B., Russell-Gale, H. and LeFevre, M. (2004) 'Leadership and the development of dominant and countercultures: a narcissistic perspective', *Leadership and Organization Development Journal*, 25(1/2), pp. 214–33.

Jones, T. (1993) *Britain's Ethnic Minorities*, London: Policy Studies Institute.

Josselson, R. (1987) *Finding Herself: Pathways to Identity Development in Women*, San Francisco, CA: Jossey-Bass.

Jrvensivu, A. and Koski, P. (2012) 'Combating learning', *Journal of Workplace Learning*, 24(1), pp. 5–18.

Judd, C. M. and Park, B. (1993) 'Definition and assessment of accuracy in social stereotypes', *Psychological Review*, January, p. 110.

Judge, T. A. and Cable, D. M. (2004) 'The effect of physical height on workplace success and income: preliminary test of a theoretical model', *Journal of Applied Psychology*, 89, 428–41.

Judge, T., LePine, J. and Rich, B. (2006) 'Loving yourself abundantly: relationship of the narcissistic personality to self- and other perceptions of workplace deviance, leadership and task and contextual performance', *Journal of Applied Psychology*, 91(4), pp. 762–76.

Kahn, R. L. and Katz, D. (1960) 'Leadership practices in relation to productivity and morale', in D. Cartwright and A. Zander (eds), *Group Dynamics: Research and Theory*, Elmsford, NY: Paterson.

Kalayann (2014) 'Still enslaved: the migrant domestic workers who are trapped by the immigration rules'. Available at: www.kalayaan.org.uk/documents/tied%20visa%202014.pdf (accessed December 13, 2014).

Kanter, R. (1990) 'Motivation theory in industrial and organizational psychology', pp. 75–170 in M. D. Dunnette and L. Hough (eds), *Handbook of Industrial and Organizational Psychology*, Palo Alto, CA: Consulting Psychology Press.

Kanter, R. M. (1982) *The Change Masters*, New York: Simon & Schuster.

Kanter, R. M., Stein, B. and Jick, T. (1992) *The Challenge of Organizational Change: How Companies Experience It and Leaders Guide It*, New York: Free Press.

Kanungo, R. and Mendonca, M. (1997) *Compensation: Effective Reward Management*, Toronto: Butterworth.

Kaplan, R. and Norton, D. (2000) *The Strategy-focused Organization: How Balanced Scorecard Companies Thrive in the New Business Environment.* Boston, MA: Harvard Business School Press.

Karlsson, J. C. (2012) *Organizational Misbehaviour in the Workplace*, Basingstoke: Palgrave Macmillan.

Kasl, E., Marsick, V. and Dechant, K. (1997) 'Teams as learners', *Journal of Applied Behavioral Science*, 33(2), pp. 227–46.

Katzenbach, J. R. and Smith, D. (2005) *The Wisdom of Teams*, New York: HarperBusiness.

Kay, J. (2009) Quoted in 'Praise for the steady', Editorial, *Globe and Mail*, February 13, p. A14.

Keats, B. W. and Hitt, M. (1988) 'A causal model of linkages among environmental dimensions, macro organizational characteristics, and performance', *Academy of Management Journal*, September, pp. 570–98.

Keller, S., Meaney, M. and Pung, C. (2010) *What Successful Transformations Share*, Chicago: McKinsey.

Kelley, H. H. (1973) 'The process of causal attribution', *American Psychologist*, 28, pp. 107–28.

Kellner, D. (1992) 'Popular culture and the construction of postmodern identities', pp. 141–77 in S. Lash and J. Friedman (eds), *Modernity and Identity*, Oxford: Blackwell.

Kelly, G. (2014) 'The robots are coming: will they bring wealth or a divided society?', *The Observer*, January 5, pp. 24–5.

Kelly, J. (1985) 'Management's redesign of work: labour process, labour markets and product markets', in D. Knights, H. Willmott and D. Collinson (eds), *Job Redesign: Critical Perspectives on the Labour Process*, Aldershot: Gower.

Kelly, J. (2005) 'Industrial relations approaches to the employment relationship', pp. 48–64 in J. A.-M. Coyle-Shapiro, L. M. Shore, M. S. Taylor and L. E. Tetrick (eds), *The Employment Relationship*, Oxford: Oxford University Press.

Kelly, J. (2006) 'Labor movements and mobilization', pp. 283–304 in S. Ackroyd, R. Batt, P. Thompson and P. S. Tolbert (eds), *The Oxford Handbook of Work and Organization*, New York: Oxford University Press.

Kelly, R. and Barsade, S. G. (2001) 'Mood and emotions in small groups and work teams', *Organizational Behavior and Human Decision Processes*, 86(1), pp. 99–130.

Kepes, S., Delery, J. and Gupta, N. (2009) 'Contingencies in the effects of pay range on organizational effectiveness', *Personnel Psychology*, 62, pp. 497–531.

Kerr, C. (1962) *Industrialism and Industrial Man*, London: Heinemann.

Kerr, R. and Robinson, S. (2011) 'Leadership as an elite field: Scottish banking leaders and the crisis of 2007–2009', *Leadership*, 7(2), pp. 151–73.

Kerr, S. and Jermier, J. M. (1978) 'Substitutes for leadership: their meaning and measurement,' *Organizational Behaviour and Human Performance*, 22, pp. 375–403.

Kersley, B., Alpin, C, Forth, J. et al. (2005) *Inside the Workplace: First Findings from the 2004 Workplace Employment Relations Survey (WERS 2004)*, London: Department of Trade and Industry.

Kersley, B., Alpin, C., Forth, J. et al. (2006) *Inside the Workplace: Findings from the 2004 Workplace Employment Relations Survey*, London: Routledge.

Keunssberg, L. (2014a) 'Primark: taking responsibility over Dhaka', ITV, March 3. Available at: www.itv.com/news/2013-04-29/primark-taking-responsibility-over-dhaka/ (accessed February 19, 2015).

Keunssberg, L. (2014b) 'Western companies "should share blame" for Bangaldesh factory conditions', ITV, March 3. Available at: www.itv.com/news/2013-04-30/western-companies-should-share-blame-for-bangladesh-factory-conditions/ (accessed February 19, 2015).

Khurana, R. (2002) 'The curse of the superstar CEO', *Harvard Business Review*, 80(9), pp. 60–6.

Kidd, J., Xue, L. and Richter, F.-J. (2001) *Maximizing Human Intelligence Deployment in Asian Business*, Basingstoke: Palgrave Macmillan.

Kim, J. (2002) 'Taking note of the new gender earnings gap: a study of the 1990's economic expansion in the US labor market', *Journal of American Academy of Business*, 2(1), pp. 80–5.

Kimmel, M. (2004) *The Gendered Society* (2nd edn), New York: Oxford University Press.

King, O. (2012) 'Yes, race does matter', *The Guardian*, December 22, p. 36.

Kirkpatrick, S. A. and Locke, E. A. (1991) 'Leadership: do traits matter?', *Executive*, 5, pp. 48–60.

Kirkpatrick, S. A. and Locke, E. A. (1996) 'Direct and indirect effects of three core charismatic leadership components on performance and attitudes', *Journal of Applied Psychology*, 81(1), pp. 36–51.

Kirton, G. and Greene, A. M. (2000) *The Dynamics of Managing Diversity*, London: Butterworth-Heinemann.

Kitchin, R., Shirlow, P. and Shuttleworth, I. (1998) 'On the margins: disabled people's experience of employment in Donegal, West Ireland', *Disability and Society*, 13(5), pp. 785–807.

Klein, H. J. (1989) 'An integrated control theory model of work motivation', *Academy of Management Review*, 14, pp. 150–72.

Klein, J. (1994) 'Maintaining expertise in multi-skilled teams', *Advances in Interdisciplinary Studies of Work Teams*, 1, pp. 145–65.

Klein, N. (2000) *No Logo*, London: Flamingo.

Klein, N. (2007) *The Shock Doctrine: The Rise of Disaster Capitalism*, Toronto: Alfred Knopf.

Kline, T. (1999) *Remaking Teams*, San Francisco: Jossey-Bass.

Knights, D. and Willmott, H. (eds) (1986a) *Gender and the Labour Process*, Aldershot: Gower.

Knights, D. and Willmott, H. (1986b) *Managing the Labour Process*, Basingstoke: Palgrave Macmillan.

Knights, D. and Willmott, H. (1990) *Labour Process Theory*, Basingstoke: Palgrave Macmillan.

Knights, D. and Willmott, H. (1992) 'Conceptualizing leadership processes: a study of senior managers in a finance services company', *Journal of Management Studies*, 29(6), pp. 761–82.

Knowles, M. (1973) *The Adult Learner: A Neglected Species*, Houston, TX: Gulf.

Knowles, M. (1975) *Self-Directed Learning*, New York: Associated Press.

Knowles, M. (1980) *The Modern Practice of Adult Education: From Pedagogy to Andragogy* (2nd edn), New York: Cambridge Books.

Knox, A. (2010) '"Lost in translation": an analysis of temporary work agency employment in hotels', *Work, Employment and Society*', 24(3), pp. 449–67.

Knox, S. and Freeman, C. (2006) 'Measuring and managing employer brand image in the service industry', *Journal of Marketing Management*, 22(7–8), pp. 695–717.

Kochan, T. A. and Osterman, P. (1994) *The Mutual Gains Enterprise*, Boston, MA: Harvard Business School Press.

Koh, H. C. and Boo, E. H. (2001) 'The link between organizational ethics and job satisfaction: a study of managers in Singapore', *Journal of Business Ethics*, 29(4), pp. 309–24.

Kolb, D. (1984) *Experiential Learning: Experience as the Source of Learning and Development*, Englewood Cliffs, NJ: Prentice Hall.

Kondo, D. (1990) *Crafting Selves: Power, Discourse and Identity in a Japanese Factory*, Chicago: University of Chicago Press.

Kooij-de Bode, H. J. M., Hanneke J. M., van Knippenberg, D. and van Ginkel, W. P. (2008) 'Ethnic diversity and distributed information in group decision making: the importance of information elaboration', *Group Dynamics: Theory, Research and Practice*, 12(4), pp. 307–20.

Koring, P. (2004) 'Iraq war based on "flawed" reports', *Globe and Mail*, p. A11.

Kornelakis, A. (2014) 'Liberalization, flexibility and industrial relations institutions: evidence from Italian and Greek banking', *Work, Employment and Society*, (28), pp. 40–57.

Kotter, J. (2012) *Leading Change*, Boston, MA: Harvard Business School Press.

Kouzes, J. and Posner, B. (2012) *The Leadership Challenge: How to Make Extraordinary Things Happen in Organizations* (5th edn), San Francisco, CA: Jossey-Bass.

Kraft, P. (1977) *Programmers and Managers: The Routinisation of Computer Programming in the United States*, New York: Springer-Verlag.

Kray, L., Galinsky, A. and Thompson, L. (2002) 'Reversing the gender gap in negotiations: an exploration of stereotype regeneration', *Organizational Behavior and Human Decision Processes*, 87(2), pp. 386–409.

Krippendorff, K. (1985) 'On the ethics of constructing communications', ICA presidential address, Honolulu, Hawaii, quoted in E. M. Eisenberg and H. L. Goodall (2004), *Organizational Communication: Balancing Creativity and Constraint* (4th edn), New York: St Martin's Press, p. 26.

Krippendorff, K. (1995) 'Undoing power', *Critical Studies in Mass Communication*, 12(2), pp. 101–32.

Kvande, E. (2009) 'Work–life balance for fathers in globalized knowledge work. Some insights from the Norwegian context', *Gender, Work and Organization*, 16(1), pp. 58–72.

Kwarteng, K., Patel, P., Raab, D., Skidmore, C., and Truss, E. (2012) *Britannia Unchained: Global Lessons for Growth and Prosperity*, Basingstoke: Palgrave Macmillan.

Lakshmi, R. (2014) 'Indian rights groups say Khobragade case shows callousness toward domestic workers', *Washington Post*. Available at: www.washingtonpost.com/world/indian-rights-groups-say-khobragade-case-shows-callousness-toward-domestic-workers/2014/01/12/8ecb9f88-7ba9-11e3-97d3-b9925ce2c57b_story.html (accessed December 13, 2014).

Lanchester, J. (2010) *Whoops! Why Everyone Owes Everyone and No One Can Pay*, London: Penguin.

Landes, D. S. (1969) *The Unbound Prometheus*, Cambridge: Cambridge University Press.

Landy, F. and Conte, J. (2013) *Work in the 21st Century*. New York: McGraw-Hill.

Lapavitsas, C. (2011) *Profiting Without Producing: How Finance Exploits Us All*, London: Verso.

Lapavitsas, C. (2013) 'Finance's hold on daily life must be broken', *The Guardian*, January 2.

Lash, S and Urry, J. (1987) *The End of Organized Capitalism*, Cambridge: Polity Press.

Latham, G. P. and Locke, E. A. (1990) *A Theory of Goal Setting and Task Performance*, Englewood Cliffs, NJ: Prentice-Hall.

Latham, M. (2014) 'The age gap', *Sunday Herald*, June 15, p. 38.

Latour, B. (2000) 'Technology is society made durable', pp. 41–53 in K. Grint (ed.), *Work and Society: A Reader*, Cambridge: Polity Press.

Lave, J. (1993) 'The practice of learning', in S. Chaiklin (ed.), *Understanding the Practice: Perspectives on Activity and Context*, Cambridge: Cambridge University Press.

Lave, J. and Wenger, E. (1991) *Situated Learning: Legitimate Peripheral Participation*, Cambridge: Cambridge University Press.

Lawler, E. E. (1971) *Pay and Organizational Effectiveness*, New York: McGraw-Hill.

Lawler, E. E. (1973) *Motivation in Work Organizations*, Monterey, CA: Brooks-Cole.

Lawrence, P. R. and Lorsch, J. W. (1967) *Organisation and Environment: Managing Differentiation and Integration*, Cambridge, MA: Harvard University Press.

Lazarus, R. S. (1991) *Emotion and Adaptation*, New York: Oxford University Press.

Lazonick, W. (1979) 'Industrial relations and technical change: the case of the self-acting mule', *Cambridge Journal of Economics*, 3, pp. 231–62.

Lazonick, W. (1993) 'Learning and the dynamics of international competitive advantage', pp. 172–97 in R. Thomson (ed.), *Learning and Technological Change*, New York: St Martin's Press.

Lazonick, W. (2006) 'Corporate restructuring', pp. 577–601 in S. Ackroyd, R. Batt, P. Thompson and P. S. Tolbert (eds), *The Oxford Handbook of Work and Organization*, Oxford: Oxford University Press.

Leadbetter, R. (2014) 'Who do we think we are?', *Sunday Herald*, April 27, p. 8–9.

Ledwith, S. and Colgan, F. (eds.) (1996) *Women in Organizations: Challenging Gender Politics*, Basingstoke: Palgrave Macmillan.

Lee, S. and Klein, H. (2002) 'Relationships between conscientiousness, self-efficacy, self-description, and learning over time', *Journal of Applied Psychology*, 87(6), pp. 1175–82.

Legge, K. (2005) *Human Resource Management: Rhetorics and Realities* (2nd edn), Basingstoke: Palgrave Macmillan.

Lehrer, J. (2009) *The Decisive Moment: How the Brain Makes up its Mind*, Edinburgh: Canongate.

Lei, D., Slocum, J. W. and Pitts, R. A. (1999) 'Designing organizations for competitive advantage: the power of unlearning and learning', *Organizational Dynamics*, Winter, pp. 24–38.

Leigh, D., Ball, J., Garside, J. and Pegg, D. (2015) 'HSBC files', *The Guardian*, February 13, pp. 1, 4–5.

Leonard, D. and Sensiper, S. (1998) 'The role of tacit knowledge in group innovation', *California Management Review*, 40(Spring), pp. 112–32.

Leonard, N. H., Beauvais, L. L. and Scholl, R. W. (1999) 'Work motivation: the incorporation of self-concept-based processes', *Human Relations*, 52(8), pp. 969–98.

Leontiev, A. N. (1978) *Activity, Consciousness, and Personality*, Englewood Cliffs, NJ: Prentice Hall.

Leontiev, A. (1981) *Problems of the Development of the Mind*, Moscow: Progress Publishers.

LePine, J., Hollenbeck, J., Ilgen, D. and Colquitt, J. (2002) 'Gender composition, situational strength, and team decision-making accuracy: a criterion decomposition approach', *Organizational Behavior and Human Decision Processes*, 88(1), pp. 445–75.

Leslie, L. M. (2014) 'A status-based multi-level model of ethnic diversity and work performance', *Journal of Management*, 20(1), pp. 1–29.

Lester, S. W., Turnley, W. H., Bloodgood, J. M. and Bolino, M. (2002) 'Not seeing eye to eye: differences in supervisor and subordinate perceptions of and attributions for psychological contract breach', *Journal of Organizational Behavior*, 23, pp. 39–56.

Levashina, J. and Campion, M. A. (2006) 'A model of faking likelihood in the employment interview', *International Journal of Selection and Assessment*, 14, pp. 229–316.

Levine, S. B. (1990) 'Understanding industrial relations in modern Japan', *Industrial and Labor Relations Review*, 43(2), pp. 326–7.

Levy, A. (1986) 'Second-order planned change: definitions and conceptualization', *Organizational Dynamics*, 15(1), pp. 5–17.

Lewin, K. (1951) *Field Theory in Social Sciences: Selected Theoretical Papers*, London: Tavistock.

Lewin, K., Lippitt, R. and White, R. K. (1939) 'Patterns of aggressive behaviour in experimentally created social climates', *Journal of Social Psychology*, 10, pp. 271–99.

Lieberman, M. D. (2000) 'Intuition: a social cognitive neuroscience approach', *Psychological Bulletin*, 126, pp. 109–37.

Lim, B. (1995) 'Examining the organizational and organizational performance link', *Leadership and Organizational Development Journal*, 16, pp. 16–21.

Linden, M. V. (1995) *Racism and the Labour Market: Historical Studies*, New York: Bern.

Linstead, S. and Grafton-Small, R. (1992) 'On reading organizational culture', *Organization Studies*, 13(3), pp. 331–55.

Lipsey, R. G., Bekar, C. and Carlaw, K. (1998) 'What requires explanation?', in E. Helpman (ed.), *General Purpose Technologies and Economic Growth*, Cambridge, MA: MIT Press.

Littler, C. R. (1982) *The Development of the Labour Process in Capitalist Societies*, London: Heinemann.

Littler, C. R. and Salaman, G. (1984) *Class at Work: The Design, Allocation and Control of Jobs*, London: Batsford.

Livingstone, D. (1999) *The Education Jobs Gap*, Toronto: Garamond.

Livingstone, D. and Sawchuk, P. (2004) *Hidden Knowledge: Organized Labour in the Information Age*, Toronto: Garamond/Washington, DC: Rowman & Littlefield.

Livingstone, D. and Scholtz, A. (2007) 'Contradictions of labour processes and workers' use of skills in advanced capitalist economies', pp. 131–62 in V. Shalla and W. Clement (eds), *Work in Tumultuous Times: Critical Perspectives*, Montreal: McGill-Queens University.

Locke, E. A. (1968) 'Towards a theory of task motivation and incentives', *Organization Behavior and Human Performance*, 3, pp. 152–89.

Locke, E. A. (ed.) (2003) *Postmodernism and Management: Pros, Cons and the Alternatives*, Amsterdam: Elsevier.

Locke, E. A., Feren, D. B., McCaleb, V., Shaw, K. and Denny, A. (1980) 'The relative effectiveness of four methods of motivating employee performance', pp. 363–83 in K. D. Duncan, M. Gruneberg and D. Wallis (eds), *Changes in Working Life*, London: John Wiley & Sons.

Long, R. J. (2000) 'Employee profit sharing: consequences and moderators', *Relations Industrielles/Industrial Relations*, 55(3), pp. 477–504.

Lopez, J. (2003) *Society and its Metaphors: Language, Social Theory and Social Structure*, London: Continuum.

Loprest, P. and Maag, E. (2001) *Barriers and Supports for Work among Adults with Disabilities: Results from the NHIS-D*, Washington, DC: Urban Institute.

Louli, C. and Bickerton, G. (1995) 'Decades of change, decades of struggle: postal workers and technological change', pp. 216–32 in C. Schenk and K. Anderson (eds), *Re-Shaping Work: Union Responses to Technological Change*, Toronto: Our Times.

Lowe, G. (2000) *The Quality of Work: A People-centred Agenda*, New York: Oxford University Press.

Lowry, P. (1990) *Employment Disputes and the Third Party*, Basingstoke: Macmillan.

Luff, P., Hindmarsh, J. and Heath, C. (2000) *Workplace Studies: Recovering Work Practice and Informing System Design*, New York: Cambridge University Press.

Lukes, S. (1974) *Power: A Radical View*, Basingstoke: Macmillan.

Lussier, R. N. and Achua, C. F. (2015) *Leadership: Theory, Application, and Skill Development*, Boston, MA: Cengage Learning.

Mabey, C., Salaman, G. and Storey, J. (1998) *Human Resource Management: A Strategic Introduction* (2nd edn), Oxford: Blackwell.

Macdonald, C. L. and Sirianni, C. (1996) 'The service society and the changing experience of work', in C. L. Macdonald and C. Sirianni (eds), *Working in the Service Society*, Philadelphia: Temple University Press.

Macey, W. H. and Schneider, B. (2008) 'The meaning of employee engagement', *Industrial and Organizational Psychology*, 1, pp. 3–30.

MacGillivray, E., Fineman, M. and Golden, D. (2003) 'Roundup of employment related news', *Journal of Organizational Excellence*, 22(3), pp. 83–102.

Macintosh, R. and Maclean, D. (2014) *Strategic Management: Strategists at Work*, London: Palgrave.

Macionis, J. J., Jansson, S. M. and Benoit, C. M. (2012) *Society: The Basics* (5th edn), Toronto: Pearson.

MacKenzie, D. and Wajcman, J. (eds) (1999) *The Social Shaping of Technology*, Buckingham: Open University Press.

Macrae, C. N., Bodenhausen, G. V., Milne, A. B. and Jetten, J. (1994) 'Employee involvement management practices, work stress and depression in employees of a human services residential care facility', *Human Relations*, 54(8), pp. 1065–92.

MacWhirter, I. (2013a) *Road to Referendum*, Edinburgh: Cargo.

MacWhirter, I. (2013b) 'Labour Party and Scotland will pay price for the Grangemouth industrial relations disaster', *Sunday Herald*, October 27, p. 17.

Madsen, D. B. and Finger, J. R. (1978) 'Comparison of a written feedback procedure, group brainstorming, and individual brainstorming', *Journal of Applied Psychology*, 63(1), pp. 120–3.

Maimone, F. and Sinclair, M. (2014) 'Dancing in the dark: creativity, knowledge creation and (emergent) organizational change', *Journal of Organizational Change*, 27(2), pp. 344–61.

Maitra, M. and Jasjit, S. (2005) 'Corruption and corporate social responsibility', in *Proceedings of the 47th Meeting of International Business*, Quebec, July 9–12.

Makin, K. (2009) 'Lawyer-moms aim to change law firms' punishing work culture', *Globe and Mail*, April 11, p. 4.

Malm, S., Reilly, J., Deegan, G., Bates, D., Thornhill, T and Gayle, D. (2014) '"I was not intoxicated": Ralph Lauren's niece insists she was real victim of air rage incident as she blames rude flight attendant', *Daily Mail*, January 14. Available at: www.dailymail.co.uk/news/article-2539092/I-not-intoxicated-Ralph-Laurens-niece-insists-real-victim-air-rage-incident-blames-rude-flight-attendant.html (accessed January 21, 2015).

Malott, R. (2002) 'Power in organizations', *Journal of Organizational Behavior Management*, 22(3), pp. 51–60.

Mandel, E. and Novack, G. (1970) *The Marxist Theory of Alienation*, New York: Pathfinder.

Mani, S. (2002) *Government, Innovation and Technology Policy: An International Comparative Analysis*, Cheltenham: Edward Elgar.

Mann, M. (1986) *The Sources of Social Power*, Cambridge: Cambridge University Press.

Mann, M. (2012) *The Sources of Social Power* (2nd edn), Cambridge: Cambridge University Press.

Manz, C. C. and Sims H. P. Jr. (1989) *Superleadership: Leading Others to Lead Themselves*, New York: Berkley Books.

Manz, C. C. and Sims, H. P. Jr (1993). *Business Without Bosses*, New York: John Wiley & Sons.

March, J. G. (1997) 'Understanding how decisions happen in organizations', pp. 9–32 in Z. Shapira (ed.), *Organizational Decision Making*, New York: Cambridge University Press.

Marchington, M. (2001) 'Employee involvement', pp. 232–52 in J. Storey (ed.), *Human Resource Management: A Critical Text*, London: Thomson Learning.

Marchington, M. (2008) 'Employee voice systems', pp. 231–50 in P. Boxall, J. Purcell and P. Wright (eds), *The Oxford Handbook of Human Resource Management*, Oxford: Oxford University Press.

Marchington, M. and Kynighou, A. (2012) 'The dynamics of employee involvement and participation during turbulent times', *International Journal of Human Resource Management*, 23(16), pp. 3336–54.

Marchington, M. and Wilding, R. (1983) 'Employee involvement in action?', *Personnel Management*, pp. 73–83.

Marglin, S. (1974) 'What do bosses do? The origins and functions of hierarchy in capitalist production', *Review of Radical Political Economy*, 6, pp. 60–112.

Marglin, S. (1982) 'What do bosses do?: the origins and functions of hierarchy in capitalist production', in A. Giddens and D. Held (eds), *Classes, Power and Conflict*, Basingstoke: Macmillan.

Marks, M. (2008) 'Looking different, acting different: struggles for equality within the South African Police Service', *Public Administration*, 86(3), pp. 643–58.

Marshall, J. and Reason, P. (2007) 'Quality in research as "taking an attitude of inquiry"', *Management Research News*, 30(5), pp. 368–80.

Marsick, V. and Watkins, K. (1990) *Informal and Incidental Learning in the Workplace*, London: Routledge.

Martin, A. (2015) 'My mobile phone, the portable paradox', *The Guardian*, January 3, p. 35.

Martin, G. N., Carlson, N. and Buskist, W. (2013) *Psychology* (5th edn), Harlow: Pearson Education.

Martin, I. (2014) *Making It Happen*, London: Simon & Schuster.

Martin, J. (1992) *Culture in Organizations: Three Perspectives*, New York: Oxford University Press.

Martin, J. (2000) 'Hidden gendered assumptions in mainstream organizational theory and research', *Journal of Management Inquiry*, 9(2), pp. 207–16.

Martin, J. and Frost, P. (1996) 'The organizational cultural war games: a struggle for intellectual dominance', pp. 599–621 in S. R. Clegg, C. Hardy and W. Nord (eds), *Handbook of Organization Studies*, London: Sage.

Martin, P. and Nichols, D. (1987) *Creating a Committed Workforce*, London: Institute of Personnel Management.

Marx, K. (1867/1970) *Capital: A Critique of Political Economy*, Volume 1, London: Lawrence & Wishart.

Marx, K. (1887/1970) *Capital, Volume One*, London: Lawrence & Wishart.

Marx, K. (with Friedrich Engels) (1845/1978) 'The German ideology', p. 154 in R. Tucker (ed.), *The Marx–Engels Reader* (2nd edn), New York: Norton.

Marx, K. and Engels, F. (1848/1967) *The Communist Manifesto*, London: Penguin.

Maslow, A. H. (1954) *Motivation and Personality*, New York: Harper.

Maslow, A. H. (1964) *Religions, Values, and Peak-Experiences*, New York: Viking.

Mason, R. and Treanor, J. (2015) 'City regulator puts spotlight on HSBC after tax evasion scandal', *The Guardian*, February 17, p. 21.

Masterson, S., Lewis, K., Goldman, B. and Taylor, M. (2000) 'Integrating justice and social exchange: the differing effects of fair procedures and treatment on work relationships', *Academy of Management Journal*, 43, pp. 738–48.

Mathias, P. (1969) *The First Industrial Nation*, London: Methuen.

Matsuo, M. (2012) 'Leadership of learning and reflective practice: an exploratory study of nursing managers', *Management Learning*, 43(5), pp. 609–23.

Matthews, P. (1999) 'Workplace learning: developing a holistic model', *Learning Organization*, 6, pp. 18–29.

Maurer, R. (2009) 'What's happening these days with change?', *Journal for Quality and Participation*, 32(2), pp. 37–8.

Maurice, M. and Sorge, A. (2000) *Embedding Organizations*, Amsterdam: John Benjamins.

Mayes, B. and Ganster, D. (1988) 'Exit and voice: a test of hypotheses based on the fight/flight response to job stress', *Journal of Organizational Behavior*, 9(3), pp. 99–117.

Mayo, A. (1998) 'Memory bankers', *People Management*, January 22, pp. 34–8.

Mayo, E. (1946) *The Human Problems of an Industrial Civilization*, New York: Macmillan.

Mazzucato, M. (2013) *The Entrepreneurial State: Debunking Private vs. Public Sector Myths*, London: Anthem Press.

Mazzucato, M. (2014) 'Big pharma relies on public money but shirks its obligations to society', *The Observer*, May 11, p. 42.

McAlpine, R. (2014) *Common Weal: Practical Idealism for Scotland*, Glasgow: Jimmy Reid Foundation.

McCabe, D. (2014) 'Making out and making do: how employees resist and make organizational change work thorough consent in a UK bank', *New Technology, Work and Employment*, 29(1), pp. 57–71.

McClelland, D. (1961) *The Achieving Society*, Princeton, NJ: Van Nostrand.

McClelland, D. C. and Burnham, D. H. (1976) 'Power is the great motivator', *Harvard Business Review*, March–April, pp. 100–10.

McCormick, K. (2007) 'Sociologists and "the Japanese model": a passing enthusiasm?', *Work, Employment and Society*, 21(4), pp. 751–71.

McCrae, R. R. and Costa, P. T. (1995) 'Toward a new generation of personality theories: theoretical contexts for the five-factor model', pp. 51–87 in J. S. Wiggins (ed.), *The Five-Factor Model of Personality: Theoretical Perspectives*, New York: Guilford Press.

McCrone, D. (2001) *Understanding Scotland: The Sociology of a Nation*, London: Routledge.

McFarlin, D. and Sweeney, P. (1992) 'Distributive and procedural justice as predictors of satisfaction with personal and organizational outcomes', *Academy of Management Journal*, 35, pp. 626–37.

McGregor, D. (1957/1970), 'The human side of enterprise', pp. 306–19 in V. H. Vroom and E. Deci (eds), *Management and Motivation*, London: Penguin. McGregor, Douglas.

McGregor, D. (1960) *The Human Side of Enterprise*, New York: McGraw-Hill.

McKenzie, H. (2014) *All in a Day's Work? CEO Pay in Canada*, Ottawa: Canadian Centre for Policy Alternatives.

McKinlay, A. and Taylor, P. (1998) 'Through the looking glass: Foucault and the politics of production', pp. 173–90 In A. McKinlay and K. Starkey (eds), *Foucault, Management and Organization Theory from Panopticon to technologies of Self*, London: Sage.

McLaughlin, H., Uggen, C. and Blackstone, A. (2009) 'A longitudinal analysis of gender, power and sexual harassment in young adulthood', presented at the American Sociological Association's 104th annual meeting, August 8, quoted in *Globe and Mail*, August 11, 2009, pp. L1, L3.

McLeod, J. and Yates, L. (2008) 'Class and the middle: schooling, subjectivity, and social formation', in L. Weis (ed.), *The Way Class Works: Readings on School, Family, and the Economy*, New York: Routledge.

McMahon, J. T. (1972) 'The contingency theory: logic and method revisited', *Personnel Psychology*, 25, pp. 697–710.

McNamara, M., Bohle, P. and Quinlain, M. (2011) 'Precarious employment, working hours, work-life-conflict and health in hotel work', *Applied Ergonomics*, 42, pp. 225–32.

McQuaig, L. and Brooks, N. (2011) *The Trouble with Billionaires*, Toronto: Penguin.

McShane, S. L. and Von Glinow, M. A. (2012) *Organizational Behavior* (6th edn), Boston, MA: McGraw-Hill.

McTague, T. (2014) 'Prospect of 2022 England World Cup grows as pressure mounts on FIFA to strip Qatar of competition over corruption allegations', *Daily Mail*, June 2. Available at: www.dailymail.co.uk/news/article-2646190/Prospect-2022-England-World-Cup-grows-pressure-mounts-Fifa-strip-Qatar-competition-amid-corruption-allegations.html (accessed February 16, 2015).

Mead, G. H. (1934) *Mind, Self and Society*, Chicago: University of Chicago Press.

Meaney, M. and Wilson, S. (2009) 'Change in recession', *People Management*, 15(10), p. 62.

Meek, V. L. (1992) 'Organizational culture: origins and weaknesses', pp. 192–212 in G. Salaman (ed.), *Human Resources Strategies*, London: Sage.

Meltzer, T. (2014) 'Computers say go', *The Guardian*, June 16, p. 11.

Mencl, J. and Lester, S. W. (2014) 'More alike than different: what generations value and how the values affect employee workplace perceptions', *Journal of Leadership and Organizational Studies*, doi: 10.1177/1548051814529825.

Mengis, J. and Eppler, M. J. (2008) 'Understanding and managing conversations from knowledge perspective: an analysis of the roles and rules of face-to-face conversations in organizations', *Organizational Studies*, 29(10), pp. 1287–13.

Merriam, S. (ed.) (1993) *An Update on Adult Learning Theory*, San Francisco: Jossey-Bass.

Merzel, C. (2000). 'Gender differences in health care access indicators in an urban, low-income community', *American Journal of Public Health*, 90(6), pp. 909–16.

Metso, S. and Kianto, A. (2014) 'Vocational students' perspectives on professional skills workplace learning', *Journal of Workplace Learning*, 26(2), pp. 128–48.

Meyerson, D. E. and Fletcher, J. K. (2000) 'A modest manifesto for shattering the glass ceiling', *Harvard Business Review*, 78(1), pp. 127–37.

Mezirow, J. D. (1981) 'A critical theory of adult education', *Adult Education Quarterly*, 32(1), pp. 3–24.

Mezirow, J. D. (1990) *Fostering Critical Reflection in Adulthood: A Guide to Transformative and Emancipatory Learning*, San Francisco: Jossey-Bass.

Mezirow, J. (1991) *Transformative Dimensions of Adult Learning*, San Francisco: Jossey-Bass.

Michaels, D. (2008) *Doubt is Their Product: How Industry's Assault on Science Threatens Your Health*, New York: Oxford University Press.

Milgram, S. (1973) *Obedience and Authority*, London: Tavistock.

Miller, D. (2014) *Last Nightshift in Savar*, Pembroke: McNidder & Grace.

Miller, N. and Brewer, M. B. (eds) (1984) *Groups in Contact: The Psychology of Desegregation*, New York: Academic Press.

Miller, S. J., Hickson, D. and Wilson, S. D. (1999) 'Decision-making in organizations', pp. 43–62 in S. R. Clegg, C. Hardy and W. Nord (eds), *Managing Organizations: Current Issues*, London: Sage.

Millett, K. (1985) *Sexual Politics*, London: Virago.

Mills, A. (1995) 'Managing subjectivity, silencing diversity: organizational imagery in the airline industry: the case of British Airways', *Organization*, 2(2), pp. 243–69.

Mills, A. and Tancred, P. (eds) (1992) *Gendering Organizational Analysis*, Newbury Park, CA: Sage.

Mills, A., Simmons, A. and Helms Mills, J. (2005) *Reading Organizational Theory* (3rd edn), Toronto: Garamond.

Milne, S. (2014) 'Big pharma needs a public stake, not a praying mantis', *The Guardian*, May 8, p. 33.

Milne, S. (2015) 'The Davos oligarchs are right to fear the world they're made', *The Guardian*, January 22, p. 32.

Milner, A. (1999) *Class*, London: Sage.

Mintzberg, H. (1973) *The Nature of Managerial Work*, New York: Harper & Row.

Mintzberg, H. (1989) *Mintzberg on Management*, New York: Free Press.

Mintzberg, H. (1992) *Structure in Fives: Designing Effective Organizations*, Englewood Cliffs, NJ: Prentice Hall.

Mintzberg, H. (2004) 'Enough leadership', *Harvard Business Review*, 82(11), p. 22.

Mintzberg, H. (2009) 'Rebuilding companies as communities', *Harvard Business Review*, 78(7/8), pp. 140–3.

Mintzberg, H., Ahlstrand, B. and Lampel, J. (1998) *Strategy Safari: A Guided Tour Through the Wilds of Strategic Management*, New York: Free Press.

Mishra, R. C., Dasen, P. R. and Niraula, S. (2003) 'Ecology, language, and performance on spatial cognitive tasks', *International Journal of Psychology*, 38, pp. 366–83.

Mishra, R. K. and Jhunjhunwala, S. (2013) *Diversity and the Effective Corporate Board*, Amsterdam: Elsevier.

Modood, T. (2007). *Multiculturalism: A Civic Idea*, Cambridge: Polity Press.

Modood, T., Berthoud, R., Lakey, J. et al. (1997) *Ethnic Minorities in Britain: Diversity and Disadvantage*, London: Policy Studies Institute.

Mohrman, S. A. and Lawler, E. E. (2012) 'Generating knowledge that drives change', *Academy of Management Perspectives*, 26(1), pp. 41–51.

Moisi, D. (2009) *The Geopolitics of Emotion: How Cultures of Fear, Humiliation, and Hope are Reshaping the World*, New York: Doubleday.

Monaghan, A. and Inman, P. (2014) 'Manufacturing stalls as global conflict and sluggish eurozone hit economies', *The Guardian*, October 2, p. 24.

Monbiot, G. (2014) 'Our bullying corporations are the new enemy within', *The Guardian*, October 8, p. 33.

Montague, R. (2007) 'Neuroeconomics: a view from neuroscience', *Functional Neurology*, 22, pp. 760–67.

Moody-Stuart, M. (2014) *Responsible Leadership*, Sheffield: Greenleaf Publishing.

Moon, H., Kamdar, D., Mayer, D. and Takeuchi, R. (2008), 'Me or we? The role of personality and justice as other-centered antecedents to innovative citizenship behaviors within organizations', *Journal of Applied Psychology*, 93(1), pp. 84–94.

Moon, J. (2002) 'Corporate social responsibility: an overview', in C. Hartley (ed.), *The International Directory of Corporate Philanthropy*, London: Europa Books.

Morgan, G. (1980) 'Paradigms, metaphors, and puzzle solving in organization theory', *Administrative Science Quarterly*, 25, pp. 605–22.

Morgan, G. (2006) *Images of Organization* (4th rev. edn), Thousand Oaks, CA: Sage.

Morgan, G. (2014) 'Rising to the challenge of Canada's skills shortage', *Globe and Mail*, April 6. Available at: www.theglobeandmail.com/report-on-business/economy/rising-to-the-challenge-of-canadas-skills-shortage/article17850271/ (accessed January 20, 2015).

Morgan, G. and Kristensen, P. (2006) 'The contested space of multinationals: varieties of institutionalism, varieties of capitalism', *Human Relations*, 59(11), pp. 1467–90.

Morgan, P. I. and Ogbonna, E. (2008) 'Subcultural dynamics in transformation: a multi-perspective study in health care professionals', *Human Relations*, 61(1), pp. 39–65.

Morris, M. W. and Peng, K. P. (1994) 'Culture and cause: American and Chinese attributions for social and physical events', *Journal of Personality and Social Psychology*, 67, pp. 949–71.

Morris, N. (2014) 'World's 85 richest people have as much as poorest 3.5 billion: Oxfam warns Davos of "pernicious impact" of the widening wealth

Pritchard, R. D. and Ashwood, E. L. (2008) *Managing Motivation*, New York: Routledge.

Probert, B. (1999) 'Gendered workers and gendered work', pp. 98–116 in D. Boud and J. Garrick (eds), *Understanding Learning at Work*, London: Routledge.

Procter, S. and Mueller, F. (2000) *Teamworking*, Basingstoke: Palgrave Macmillan.

Proctor, S., Fulop, L., Linstead, S., Mueller, F. and Sewell, G. (2009) 'Managing teams', pp. 539–73 in S. Linstead, L. Fulop and S. Lilley (eds), *Management and Organization: A Critical Text* (2nd edn), Basingstoke: Palgrave Macmillan.

Pugh, D. S. and Hickson, D.J. (1996) *Writers on Organizations*, London: Penguin Business.

Pulignano, V. and Stewart, P. (2006) 'Bureaucracy transcended? New patterns of employment regulation and labour control in the international automotive industry', *New Technology, Work and Employment*, 21(2), pp. 90–106.

Pun, K. F. and White, A. S. (2005) 'A performance measurement paradigm for integrating strategy formulation: a review of systems and frameworks', *International Journal of Management Reviews*, 7(1), pp. 49–71.

Purcell, J. (1989) 'The impact of corporate strategy on human resource management', pp. 67–91 in J. Storey (ed.), *New Perspectives on Human Resource Management*, London: Routledge.

Purcell, J. and Kinnie, N. (2008) 'HRM and business performance', pp. 533–51 in P. Boxall, J. Purcell and P. Wright (eds), *The Oxford Handbook of Human Resource Management*, New York: Oxford University Press.

Purcell, J., Kinnie, N., Hutchinson, S., Rayton, B. and Swart, J. (2003) *Understanding the People and Performance Link: Unlocking the Black Box*, London: CIPD.

Purcell, J., Purcell, K., and Tailby, S. (2004) 'Temporary work agencies: here today, gone tomorrow?', *British Journal of Industrial Relations*, 42(4), pp. 705–25.

Purcell, J., Hutchinson, S. Kinnie, N., Swart, J. and Rayton, B. (2009) *People Management and Performance*, London: Routledge.

Putnam, L. L., Philips, N. and Chapman, P. (1999) 'Metaphors of communication and organization', pp. 125–47 in S. Clegg, C. Hardy and W. Nord (eds), *Managing Organizations. Current Issues*, Thousand Oaks, CA: Sage.

Radaelli, G., Guerci, M., Cirella, S. and Shani, A. B. (2014) 'Intervention research as management research in practice: learning from a case in the fashion design industry', *British Journal of Management*, 25, pp. 335–51.

Raelin, J. A. (2003) *Creating Leaderful Organizations*, San Francisco, CA: Berrett-Koehler.

Raelin, J. A. (2011) 'From leadership-as-practice to leaderful practice', *Leadership*, 7(2), pp. 195–211.

Raghubir, P. and Valenzuela, A. (2006) 'Centers-of-inattention: position biases in decision-making', *Organizational Behaviour and Human Decision Processes*, 99(1), pp. 66–80.

Rahim, M. A. (2001) *Managing Conflict in Organizations*, Westport, CT: Quorum Books.

Ramachandran, V. S. and Rogers-Ramachandran, D. (2005) 'How blind are we?', *Scientific American Mind*, 16(2), pp. 95–6.

Ramesh, R. (2012) 'NHS staff survey: 40% would not recommend health service to family', *The Guardian*, March 20.

Ramsay, H. (1991) 'Reinventing the wheel: a review of the development and performance of employee involvement', *Human Resource Management Journal*, 1, pp. 1–22.

Rankin, J., O'Carroll, L. and Monaghan, A. (2013) 'Google paid £11.6m in UK corporation tax last year', *The Guardian*, September 30. Available at: www.theguardian.com/technology/2013/sep/30/google-paid-uk-corporation-tax (accessed May 10, 2014).

Rasminsky, L. (2001) 'Hire an artist, it's good for business', *Globe and Mail*, July 14, p. A13.

Ravelli, B. (2000) 'Culture', pp. 39–61 in M. Kanwar and D. Swenson (eds), *Canadian Sociology* (3rd edn), Dubuque, IA: Kendall-Hunt.

Rawls, J. (1971) *A Theory of Justice*, Cambridge, MA: Harvard University Press.

Rawnsley, A. (2013) 'A shining lesson that politics can be a tremendous force for good', *The Observer*, December 8, p. 39.

Ray, C. A. (1986) 'Corporate culture: the last frontier of control?', *Journal of Management Studies*, 23(3), pp. 287–97.

Ray, L. J. (1999) *Theorizing Classical Sociology*, Buckingham: Open University Press.

Redelmeier, D. A. and Tibshirani, R. J. (1997) 'Association between cellular-telephone calls and motor vehicle collisions', *New England Journal of Medicine*, 336, pp. 453–8.

Reed, L. (2003) 'Paternalism may excuse disability discrimination: when may an employer refuse to employ a disabled individual due to concerns for the individual's safety?', *Business and Society Review*, 108(3), pp. 417–24.

Reich, R. (1991) *The Work of Nations: Preparing Ourselves for 21st Century Capitalism*, New York: Knopf/London: Simon & Schuster.

Reskin, B. and Padavic, I. (1994) *Women and Men at Work*, Thousand Oaks, CA: Sage.

Reynolds, L., Campbell Bush, E. and Geist, R. (2008) 'The Gen Y imperative', *Communication World*, March–April, pp. 19–22.

Rhodes, M. (1998) *Defending the Social Contract*, London: Routledge.

Richta, R. (1969) *Civilization at the Crossroads*, White Plains, NY: International Arts and Science Press.

Rifkin, J. (1996) *The End of Work*, New York: Tarcher/Putnam.

Riley, P. (1983) 'A structurationist account of political cultures', *Administrative Science Quarterly*, 28, pp. 414–37.

Rinehart, J. W. (2006) *The Tyranny of Work: Alienation and the Labour Process* (4th edn), Scarborough, ON: Nelson Thomson.

Rip, A., Misa, T. and Schot, J. (eds) (1995) *Managing Technology in Society: The Approach of Constructive Technology Assessment*, London: Pinter.

Ritzer, G. (2010) *Classical Sociological Theory* (5th edn), New York: McGraw-Hill.

Ritzer, G. (2012) *The McDonaldization of Society* (20th anniversary edn), Thousand Oaks, CA: Pine Forge Press.

Robbins, S. and Judge, T. (2013) *Essentials of Organizational Behavior* (15th edn), New Jersey: Pearson/Prentice Hall.

Robbins, S. P. (1990) *Organization Theory: Structure, Design, and Applications* (3rd edn), Englewood Cliffs, NJ: Prentice-Hall.

Robbins, S. P. and Langton, N. (2001) *Organizational Behaviour: Concepts, Controversies, Applications* (2nd edn), Toronto: Prentice-Hall.

Roberson, Q. (2006) 'Justice in teams: the activation of role and sensemaking in the emergence of justice climates', *Organizational Behaviour and Human Decision Processes*, 100(2), pp. 177–92.

Robertson, G. (2006) 'Layoffs come as a deal is unveiled', *Globe and Mail*, July 13, p. A6.

Robertson, I. T., Baron, H., Gibbons, P., MacIver, R. and Nyfield, G. (2000) 'Conscientiousness and managerial performance', *Journal of Occupational and Organizational Psychology*, 73(2), pp. 171–81.

Robinson, V. (1990) 'Roots of mobility', *Ethnic and Racial Studies*, 13(2), pp. 274–86.

Robinson-Easley, C. A. (2014) *Beyond Diversity and International Management*, London: Palgrave.

Rocket, J. F. and Short, J. E. (1991) 'The networked organization and the management of interdependence', in M. S. Scott Morton (ed.), *The Corporation of the 1990s: Information Technology and Organizational Transformation*, Oxford: Oxford University Press.

Roddick, A. (1991) *Body and Soul*, New York: Crown.

Roethlisberger, F. J. and Dickson, W. J. (1939) *Management and the Worker*, Cambridge, MA: Harvard University Press.

Rogers, C. R. (1961) *On Becoming a Person*, Boston, MA: Houghton Mifflin.

Rogers, C. R. (1983) *Freedom to Learn for the 80s*, Columbus, OH: Merrill.

Rogin, P. Rhodes, K. and Guffey, M. (2009) *Business Communication: Process and Product* (5th edn), Scarborough, ON: Thomson Nelson.

Rogoff, B. (1984) 'Introduction: thinking and learning in social context', pp. 1–8 in B. Rogoff and J. Lave (eds), *Everyday Cognition: Its Development in Social Context*, Cambridge, MA: Harvard University Press.

Rogoff, B. (1990) *Apprenticeship in Thinking: Cognitive Development in Social Context*, Oxford: Oxford University Press.

Rogoff, B. (1995) 'Observing sociocultural activity on three planes: participatory appropriation, guided participation, and apprenticeship', pp. 139–63 in J. V. Wertsch, P. del Rio and A. Alvarez (eds), *Sociocultural Studies of Mind*, Cambridge: Cambridge University Press.

Romero, E. and Pescosolido, A. (2008) 'Humor and group effectiveness', *Human Relations*, 61(3), pp. 395–418.

Roscigno, V. and Hodson, R. (2004) 'The organizational and social foundations of worker resistance', *American Sociological Review*, 69(1), pp. 14–39.

Rose, M. (1988) *Industrial Behaviour*, London: Penguin.

Rose, N. (1990) *Governing the Soul: The Shaping of the Private Self*, London: Routledge.

Rosener, J. (1990) 'Ways women lead', *Harvard Business Review*, December, pp. 199–225.

Rosenfeld, P., Giacalone, R. and Riordan, C. A. (2002) *Impression Management: Building and Enhancing Reputation at Work*, London: Thomson Learning.

Ross, J. and Staw, B (1993) 'Organization escalation and exit: lessons from the Shoreham nuclear power plant', *Academy of Management Journal*, 36, pp. 701–32.

Roszak, T. (1994) *The Cult of Information: A Neo-Luddite Treatise on High Tech, Artificial Intelligence and the True Art of Thinking*, Berkeley, CA: University of California Press.

Roth, E. M. and Woods, O D. (1988) 'Aiding human performance. I: Cognitive analysis', *Le Travail Humain*, 51, pp. 39–64.

Rothman, H. K. (2000) 'What has work become?', *Journal of Labor Research*, 21(3), pp. 379–92.

Rotter, J. B. (1966) 'Generalized expectations for internal versus external control of reinforcement', *Psychological Monographs*, 80(1), pp. 1–28.

Rousseau, D. M. (1995) *Psychological Contracts in Organisations: Understanding Written and Unwritten Agreements*, Thousand Oaks, CA: Sage.

Rousseau, D. M. and Ho, V. T. (2000) 'Psychological contract issues in compensation', pp. 273–310 in S. L. Rynes and B. Gerhart (eds), *Compensation in Organizations: Current Research and Practice*, San Francisco: Jossey-Bass.

Rowbotham, S. (1973) *Woman's Consciousness, Man's World*, London: Penguin.

Rowley, J. (1998) 'Creating a learning organization in higher education', *Industrial and Commercial Training*, 30(1), pp. 16–19.

Rowlingson, K. and Connor, S. (2011) 'The "Deserving" Rich? Inequality, morality and social policy', *Journal of Social Policy*, 40(3), pp. 437–52.

Rubenstein, H. (2003) *Women and Leadership: Review of Recent Studies*, Washington, DC: Growth Strategies.

Rubenstein, R. (2001) *Dress Codes: Meaning and Messages in American Culture* (2nd edn), Boulder, CO: Westview Press.

Rubery, J. (2006) 'Labour markets and flexibility', pp. 31–51 in S. Ackroyd, R. Batt, P. Thompson and P. Tolbert (eds), *The Oxford Handbook of Work and Organization*, New York: Oxford University Press.

Ruble, T. H. and Thomas, K. (1976) 'Support for a two-dimensional model of conflict behaviour', *Organizational Behaviour and Human Performance*, 16(1), pp. 143–55.

Russell, H. (2013), 'Are you planning to have kids?', *The Guardian*, February 5, p. S13.

Russell, N. and Gregory, R. (2005) 'Making the undoable doable: Milgram, the Holocaust, and modern government', *American Review of Public Administration*, 35(4), pp. 327–49.

Ryan, R. M. (2007) 'Motivation and emotion: a new look and approach for two reemerging fields', *Motivation and Emotion*, 31, pp. 1–3.

Ryan, R. M. and Deci, E. L. (2000) 'Self-determination theory and the facilitation of intrinsic motivation, social development, and well-being', *American Psychologist*, 55(1), pp. 68–78.

Rymer, R. (1994) *Genie*, New York: Harper Perennial.

Sackmann, S. A. (2012) 'Culture and performance', pp. 188–224 in N. M. Ashanasy, C. P. M. Wilderom and M. F. Peterson (eds), *Handbook of Organizational Culture and Climate* (2nd edn), Thousand Oaks, CA: Sage.

Said, E. (1978/1995) *Orientalism*. London: Penguin.

Sainsbury, D. (2013) *Progressive Capitalism: How to Achieve Economic Growth, Liberty and Social Justice*, London: Biteback Publishing.

Salaman, G. (1979) *Work Organizations: Resistance and Control*, London: Longman.

Salaman, G. (1981) *Class and the Corporation*, London: Fontana.

Salaman, G. (2007) Managers' knowledge and the management of change, pp. 137– 58 in J. Storey (ed.), *Human Resource Management: A Critical Text* (3rd edn), London: Thomson.

Sale, K. (1995) *Rebels Against the Future: The Luddites and their War on the Industrial Revolution – Lessons for the Computer Age*, London: Addison Wesley.

Salgado, J. F. (1997) 'The five factor model of personality and job performance in the European Community', *Journal of Applied Psychology*, 82, pp. 30–43.

Salmon, J. (2013) 'Top business leader' pay packets rise by 10%: bosses of top companies now enjoy £4.3million in pay and perks', *Daily Mail Online*, June 10. Available at: www.dailymail.co.uk/news/article-2338697/ Top-business-leaders-pay-packets-rise-10--Bosses-companies-enjoy-4-3million-pay-perks.html (accessed Febuary 3, 2015).

Sandbrook, D. (2009) 'The death of ideas', *New Statesman*, August 6. Available at: www.newstatesman.com/plitics/2009/08/ideas-ideological-politics-age.

Sarti, D. (2014) 'Leadership styles to engage employees: evidence from human service organizations in Italy', *Journal of Workplace Learning*, 26(3/4), pp. 202–16.

Saul, J. R. (2005) *The Collapse of Globalism*, Toronto: Viking.

Saunders, M. N. K. and Thornhill, A. (2006) 'Forced employment contract change and the psychological contract', *Employee Relations*, 28(5), pp. 449–67.

Sawchuk, P. H. (2006) '"Use-value" and the re-thinking of skills, learning and the labour process', *Journal of Industrial Relations*, 48(5), pp. 589–613.

Sawchuk, P. H. (2008) 'Theories and methods for research on informal learning and work: towards cross-fertilization', *Studies in Continuing Education*, 30(1), pp. 1–16.

Sawyer, J., Houlette, M. and Yeagley, E. (2006) 'Decision performance and diversity structure: comparing faultlines in convergent, crosscut, and racially homogenous groups', *Organizational Behaviour and Human Decision Processes*, 99(1), pp. 1–15.

Sayer, A. (1986) 'New developments in manufacturing: the just-in-time system', *Capital and Class*, 30, pp. 43–72.

Sayer, A. (2000) *Realism and Social Science*, London: Sage.

Sayer, D. (1991) *Capitalism and Modernity*, London: Routledge.

Schein, E. (2010) *Organizational Culture and Leadership* (4th edn), San Francisco, CA: Jossey-Bass.

Schein, E. H. (1996) 'Culture: the missing concept in organization studies', *Administrative Science Quarterly*, 41, pp. 229–40.

Schein, E. H. (1980) *Organizational Psychology* (3rd edn), Englewood Cliffe, NJ: Prentice Hall.

Schein, E. H. (2004) *Organizational Culture and Leadership* (3rd edn), San Francisco, CA: Jossey Bass.

Schein, V. E. (1973) 'The relationship between sex role stereotypes and requisite management characteristics', *Journal of Applied Psychology*, 57, pp. 95–100.

Schein, V. E. (1975) 'The relationship between sex role stereotypes and requisite management characteristics among female managers', *Journal of Applied Psychology*, 60, pp. 340–4.

Schein, V. E., Mueller, R., Lituchy, T. and Liu, J. (1996) 'Think manager – think male: a global phenomenon?', *Journal of Organizational Behavior*, January, 33–41.

Schneider, B. (2000) 'The psychological life of organizations', pp. xvii–xxi in N. M. Ashanasy, C. P. M. Wilderom and M. F. Peterson (eds), *Handbook of Organizational Culture and Climate*, Thousand Oaks, CA: Sage.

Schneider, D. M. and Goldwasser, C. (1998) 'Be a model leader of change', *Management Review*, 87(3), pp. 41–5.

Schneider, R. (2001) 'Variety performance', *People Management*, 7(9), pp. 26–31.

Scholte, J. A. (2005) *Globalization: A Critical Introduction*, Basingstoke: Palgrave Macmillan.

Schriesheim, C. A. and Kerr, S. (1977) 'R.I.P. LPC: a response to Fiedler', pp. 51–6 in J. G. Hunt and L. L. Larson (eds), *Leadership: The Cutting Edge*, Carbondale, IL: Southern Illinois University Press.

Schultz, T. W. (1961) 'Investment in human capital', in M. Blaug (ed.), *Economics of Education*, London: Penguin.

Schumpeter, J. A. (1954) *Capitalism, Socialism and Democracy* (4th edn), New York: Allen & Unwin.

Schwandt, T. A. (1994) 'Constructivist, interpretivist approaches to human inquiry', pp. 118–37 in N. K. Denzin and Y. Lincoln (eds), *Handbook of Qualitative Research*, Thousand Oaks, CA: Sage.

Scott, J. and Marshall, G. (2009) *Oxford Dictionary of Sociology*, Oxford: OUP.

Scott, S. M. (1998) 'Philosophies in action', pp. 98–106 in S. M. Scott, B. Spencer and A. Thomas (eds), *Learning for Life*, Toronto: Thompson Educational.

Seabright, P. (2012), *The War of the Sexes: How Conflict and Cooperation Have Shaped Men and Women from Prehistory to the Present*, Princeton, NJ: Princeton University Press.

Seglins, D. (2014) 'Crude shipments, tanker punctures top agenda at rail talks', CBC, January 13. Available at: www.cbc.ca/news/canada/crude-oil-shipments-tanker-punctures-top-of-agenda-at-rail-talks-1.2491949 (accessed February 23, 2015).

Seligman, M. E. P. (1991) *Learned Optimism*, New York: Knopf.

Senge, P. M. (1990) *The Fifth Discipline*, New York: Currency/Doubleday.

Sennett, R. (1998) *The Corrosion of Character*, New York: Norton.

Sennett, R. (2004) *Respect: The Formation of Character in an Age of Inequality*. London: Penguin.

Sennett, R. (2008) *The Craftsman*, New Haven, CT: Yale University Press.

Sennett, R. (2012) 'The social triangle: how social relations become embittered at work', pp. 148–178, in *Together*, New Haven, CT: Yale University Press.

Sennett, R. and Cobb, J. (1972) *Hidden Injuries of Class*, New York: Anchor.

Sewell, G. (1998) 'The discipline of teams: the control of team-based industrial work through electronic and peer surveillance', *Administrative Science Quarterly*, 43, pp. 406–69.

Sewell, G. and Wilkinson, B. (1992) 'Empowerment or emasculation? Shopfloor surveillance in a total quality organization', in P. Blyton and P. Turnbull (eds), *Reassessing HRM*, London: Sage.

Shaiken, H., Herzenberg, S. and Kuhn, S. (1986) 'The work process under more flexible production', *Industrial Relations*, 25, pp. 167–83.

Shalley, C. E., Ehou, J. and Oldham, G. R. (2004) 'The effects of personal and contextual characteristics on creativity: where should we go from here?', *Journal of Management*, 30(6), pp. 933–58.

Shamir, R. (2011) 'Socially responsible private regulation: world culture or world-capitalism?', *Law and Society Review*, 45(2), pp. 313–36.

Shang, X. (2000) 'Bridging the gap between planned and market economies: employment policies for people with disabilities in two Chinese cities', *Disability and Society*, 15(1), pp. 135–56.

Shen, J. and Benson, J. (2014) 'When CSR is a social norm: how socially responsible human resource management affects employee work behavior', *Journal of Management*, 20(10), pp. 1–24.

Sheridan, A. (1980) *Michel Foucault: The Will to Power*, London: Tavistock.

Sherif, M., Harvey, O. J., White, B. J., Hood, W. R. and Sherif, C. W. (1961) *Intergroup Conflict and Cooperation*, Norman, OK: Oklahoma Book Exchange.

Shirky, C. (2008) *Here Comes Everybody: The Power of Organizing Without Organizations*, New York: Penguin.

Shull, F. A., Delbecq, A. L. and Cummings, L. (1970) *Organizational Decision Making*, New York: McGraw-Hill.

Siebert, S. and Wilson, F. (2013) 'All work and no pay: consequences of unpaid work in creative industries', *Work, Employment and Society*, 27(4), pp. 711–21.

Siegrist, M., Cvetkovich, G. and Gutscher, H. (2002) 'Risk preference predictions and gender stereotypes', *Organizational Behavior and Human Decision Processes*, 87(1), pp. 91–102.

Silver, B. (2014) 'Theorizing the working class in twenty-first-century global capitalism', pp. 46–69 in M. Atzeni (ed.), *Workers and Labour in a Globalised Capitalism*, Basingstoke: Palgrave Macmillan.

Silverman, D. (1970) *The Theory of Organizations*, London: Heinemann.

Silvestor, J., Wyatt, M. and Randell, R. (2014) 'Political personality, Machiavellianism, and political skill as predictors of performance', *Occupational and Organizational Psychology*, 87, pp. 258–79.

Simmel, G. (1900/2004) *The Philosophy of Money* (trans. T. Bottomore and D. Frisby, ed. D. Frisby), London: Routledge.

Simms, A. (2014) 'Knowing our limits is the only way to run the economy', *The Observer*, 5 January, p. 38.

Simon, H. A. (1957) *Administrative Behaviour*, New York: Macmillan.

Simon, H. A. (1977), *The New Science of Management Decision* (3rd edn), Englewood Cliffs, NJ: Prentice-Hall.

Simons, D. J. and Chabris, C. F. (1999) 'Gorillas in our midst: sustained inattentional blindness for dynamic events', *Perception*, 28, pp. 1059–74.

Simons, D. J. and Levin, D. T. (1998) 'Failures to detect changes to people in a real-world interaction', *Psychonomic Bulletin and Review*, 5, pp. 644–9.

Sinclair, A. (1992) 'The tyranny of a team ideology', *Organization Studies*, 13(4), pp. 611–26.

Singh, V. (2002) *Managing Diversity for Strategic Advantage*, London: Council for Excellence in Management and Leadership.

Singh, V., Kumra, S. and Vinnicombe, S. (2002) 'Gender and impression management: playing the promotion game', *Journal of Business Ethics*, 37, pp. 77–89.

Sivanathan, N., Pillutla, M. and Murnighan, J. K. (2008) 'Power gained, power lost', *Organizational Behavior and Human Decision Processes*, 105, pp. 135–46.

Skinner, B. F. (1954) 'The science of learning and the art of teaching', *Harvard Educational Review*, 24, pp. 86–97.

Sklair, L. (2002) *Globalization: Capitalism and its Alternatives*, Oxford: Oxford University Press.

Slapper, G. and Tombs, S. (1999) *Corporate Crime*, Essex: Longman.

Slaughter, J. E. and Zicker, M. J. (2006) 'A new look at the role of insiders in the newcomer socialization process', *Group and Organization Management*, 31(2), pp. 264–90.

Small, M. and Yasin, M. (2000) 'Human factors in the adoption and performance of advanced manufacturing technology in unionized firms', *Industrial Management and Data Systems*, 100(8–9), pp. 389–401.

Smircich, L. (1983) 'Concepts of culture and organizational analysis', *Administrative Science Quarterly*, 28, pp. 33–58.

Smith, A. (1776/1982) *The Wealth of Nations*, Harmondsworth: Penguin.

Smith, A. (2015) 'Whistleblowers outside the NHS deserve support too', *The Guardian*, 13 February, p. 38.

Smith, J. W. and Calasanti, T. (2005) 'The influences of gender, race and ethnicity on workplace experiences of institutions and social isolation: an exploratory study of university faculty', *Sociological Spectrum*, 25(3), pp. 307–34.

Smith, P. and Morton, G. (2006) 'Nine years of New Labour: neo-liberalism and workers' rights', *British Journal of Industrial Relations*, 44(3), pp. 401–20.

Smith, P. A. (2012) 'The importance of organizational learning for organizational sustainability', *Learning Organization*, 19(1), pp. 4–10.

Smith, R. C. (1993) 'Images of organizational communication: root metaphors of the organization–communication relation', paper presented at the International Communication Association Conference, Washington, DC.

Smooth, W. G. (2010) 'Intersectionalities of race and gender and leadership', pp. 31–40 in K. O'Conner (ed.), *Gender and Women's Leadership: A Reference Handbook*, Volume 1, London: Sage.

Smyth, P. (2008) 'Closing the gap? The role of wage, welfare and industry policy in promoting social inclusion', *Journal of Industrial Relations*, 50(4), pp. 647–63.

Soares, A. (2003) 'Tears at work: gender, interaction, and emotional labour', *Just Labour*, 2, pp. 36–44.

Society for Disability Studies (1993) See www.disstudies.org.

Somers, M. J. (2001) 'Thinking differently: assessing nonlinearities in the relationship between work attitudes and job performance using a Bayesian neutral network', *Journal of Occupational and Organizational Psychology*, 74(1), pp. 47–62.

Sotarauta, M. (2005) 'Shared leadership and dynamic capabilities in regional development', pp. 53–72 in I. Sagan, I. and H. Halkier (eds.), *Regionalism Contested: Institution, Society and Governance*, Urban and Regional Planning and Development Series, Cornwall: Ashgate.

Sotarauto, M., Horlings, L., and Liddle, J. (eds.) (2012) *Leadership and Change in Sustainable Regional Development*, London: Routledge.

Spencer, B. (1998) *The Purposes of Adult Education: A Guide for Students*, Toronto: Thompson.

Spencer, B. (2001) 'Changing questions of workplace learning researchers', pp. 31–40 in T. Fenwick (ed.), *Socio-cultural Perspectives on Learning through Work*, San Francisco, CA: Jossey-Bass.

Spencer, B. and Kelly, J. (2013) *Work and Learning: An Introduction*, Toronto: Thompson Education.

Spillane, J. (2005) 'Distributed leadership', *Educational Forum*, 69, pp. 143–50.

Stace, D. and Dunphy, D. (2001) *Beyond the Boundaries: Leading and Recreating the Successful Enterprise*, Sydney: McGraw-Hill.

Stamps, D. (1999) 'Is knowledge management a fad?', *Training*, 36(3), pp. 36–42.

Standing, G. (2011) *The Precariat: The New Dangerous Class*, London: Bloomsbury.

Stanford, J. (2013) 'Canada's sluggish labour market and the myth of the skills shortage', *Academic Matters: The Journal of Higher Education*, November. Available at: www.academicmatters.ca/2013/11/canadas-sluggish-labour-market-and-the-myth-of-the-skills-shortage/#sthash.Ym5HvUfe.dpuf (accessed January 20, 2015).

Stanworth, M. (1981) *Gender and Schooling*, London: Hutchinson.

Stavrou, E. T., Parry E. and Anderson D. (2015) 'Nonstandard work arrangements and configurations of firm and societal systems', *International Journal of Human Resource Management*, doi: 10.1080/09585192.2014.992456.

Staw, B. and Ross, J. (1989) 'Understanding behavior in escalation situations', *Science*, 246, pp. 216–20.

Steele, C. M., Spencer, S. J. and Aronson, J. (2003) 'Contending with group image: the psychology of stereotype threat and social identity threat', pp. 102–15 in M. P. Zanna (ed.), *Advances in Experimental Social Psychology*, San Diego, CA: Academic Press.

Stewart, H. (2009) 'Economists tell Queen how they failed to see the recession coming', *Observer*, July 26, pp. 1, 5.

Stewart, H. (2015a) 'The great wages crash', *The Guardian*, January 30, p. 1.

Stewart, H. (2015b) 'After the Blair years, party has a tough fight to win over big business', *The Guardian*, February 7, p. 7.

Stewart, P. and Danford, A. (2008) 'Editorial: Union strategies and worker engagement with new forms of work and employment', *New Technology, Work and Employment*, 23(3), pp. 146–50.

Stewart, R. (1967) *Managers and their Jobs*, Basingstoke: Macmillan.

Stiglitz, J. (2013) *The Price of Inequality*, London: Penguin.

Stiglitz, J. E. (2006) *Making Globalization Work*, New York: Norton.

Stogdill, R. M. (1974) *Handbook of Leadership: A Survey of Theory and Research*, New York: Free Press.

Stohl, C. and Cheney, G. (2001) 'Participatory processes/paradoxical practices', *Management Communication Quarterly*, 14(3), pp. 349–407.

Storey, J. (1992) *Developments in the Management of Human Resources*, Oxford: Blackwell.

Storey, J. (1995) 'Human resource management: still marching on or marching out?', pp. 3–32 in J. Storey (ed.), *Human Resource Management: A Critical Text*, London: Routledge.

Storey, J. and Nyathi, N. (2015) 'Strategies and structures of MNCs from emerging economies', pp. 68–95 in F. Horwitz and P. Budhwar (eds), *Handbook of Human Resource Management in Emerging Markets*, Cheltenham: Edward Elgar.

Strayer, D. L. and Johnston, W. A. (2001) 'Driven to distraction: dual-task studies of simulated driving and conversing on a cellular telephone', *Psychological Science*, 12(6), pp. 462–6.

Stuart, A. (2014) 'Cinema catching up', *The Guardian*, June 13, p. 38.

Sturges, J. and Guest, D. (2004) 'Working to live or living to work: work/life balance and organizational commitment amongst graduates', *Human Resources Management Journal*, 14(4), pp. 5–20.

Su, R. (2014) 'New Zealand migrant workers complain of exploitation; law proposed to make worker abuse a crime', *International Business Times*. Available at: http://au.ibtimes.com/articles/533030/20140106/new-zealand-christchurch-filipino-migrant-workers-worker.htm (accessed November 25, 2014).

Suchman, L. (1987) *Plans and Situated Action: The Problem of Human–Computer Communication*, New York: Cambridge University Press.

Suchman, L. (2002) 'Practice-based design of information systems: notes from the hyperdeveloped world', *Information Society*, 18, pp. 139–44.

Sundgren, M. and Styhre, A. (2006) 'Leadership as de-paradoxification: leading new drug development work at three pharmaceutical companies', *Leadership*, 2(1), pp. 31–51.

Sveiby, K. E. (1997) *The New Organizational Wealth: Managing and Measuring Organizational Wealth*, San Francisco, CA: Berrett-Koehler.

Swan, J., Scarbrough, H., and Robertson, M. (2002) The construction of 'communities of practice' in the management of innovation, *Management Learning*, 33(4), pp. 477–96.

Syal, R. (2013) 'Google whistleblower says he was motivated by Christian beliefs', *The Guardian*, June 13. Available at: www.theguardian.com/technology/2013/jun/12/google-tax-whistleblower-christian-beliefs (accessed May 10, 2014).

Sydie, R. A. (1994) *Natural Women, Cultured Men*, Vancouver: UBC Press.

Sztompka, P. (1993) *The Sociology of Social Change*, Blackwell, Oxford.

Taggar, S. and Ellis, R. (2007) 'The role of leaders in shaping formal team norms', *Leadership Quarterly*, 18, pp. 105–20.

Tajfel, H. and Turner, J. C. (1979) 'An integrative theory of intergroup conflict', in W. G. Austin and S. Worchel (eds), *The Social Psychology of Intergroup Relations*, Monterey, CA: Brooks/Cole.

Tan, J.-S. (1998) 'Communication, cross cultural', in M. Poole and M. Warner (eds), *International Encyclopaedia of Business and Management*, London: Thomson.

Tannen, D. (1990) *You Just Don't Understand: Women and Men in Conversation*, New York: Ballantine Books.

Tannen, D. (2001) *I Only Say This Because I Love You*, New York: Ballantine Books.

Tatli, A., Mulholland, G., Ozbilgin, M. and Worman, D. (2007) *Managing Diversity in Practice: Supporting Business Goals*, London: CIPD.

Taylor, J. R. (1995) 'Shifting from a heteronomous to an autonomous world view of organizational communication: communication theory on the cusp', *Communication Theory*, 5(1), pp. 1–35.

Taylor, M. S. and Tekleab, A. G. (2004) 'Taking stock of psychological contract research: assessing progress, addressing troublesome issues, and setting research priorities', in J. A.-M. Coyle-Shapiro, L. M. Shore, M. S. Taylor and L. E. Tetrick (eds), *The Employment Relationship: Examining Psychological and Contextual Perspectives*, Oxford: Oxford University Press.

Taylor, S. S., Fisher, D. and Dufresne, R. (2002) 'The aesthetics of management storytelling', *Management Learning*, 33(3), pp. 313–30.

Teece, D. J., Pisano, G. and Shuen, A. (1997) Dynamic capabilities and strategic management, *Strategic Management Journal*, 18(7), pp. 509–33.

Tehrani, N. (2005) *Bullying at Work: Beyond Policies to a Culture of Respect*, London: Chartered Institute of Personnel and Development.

Tennant, M. (1997) *Psychology and Adult Learning* (2nd edn), London: Routledge.

Tetlock, P. (1983) 'Accountability and complexity of thought', *Journal of Personality and Social Psychology*, 45, pp. 74–83.

Tharenou, P. (1997) 'Determinants of participation in training and development', *Journal of Organizational Behavior*, 4, pp. 15–28.

Thomas, K. (1999) 'Introduction', pp. xiii–xxiii in K. Thomas (ed.), *The Oxford Book of Work*, Oxford: Oxford University Press.

Thomas, K. W. (1992) 'Conflict and negotiation processes in organizations', pp. 651–717 in M. D. Dunnette and L. M. Hough (eds), *Handbook of Industrial and Organizational Psychology*, Palo Alto, CA: Consulting Psychologists Press.

Thompson, D. (2013) 'What's behind the huge (and growing) CEO-worker pay gap?', April 30. Available at: www.theatlantic.com/business/archive/2013/04/whats-behind-the-huge-and-growing-ceo-worker-pay-gap/275435/ (accessed Febuary 3, 2015).

Thompson, E. P. (1963) *The Making of the English Working Class*, London: Penguin.

Thompson, E. P. (1967) 'Time, work and discipline, and industrial capitalism', *Past and Present*, 38, pp. 56–97.

Thompson, J. A. (2005) 'Proactive personality and job performance: a social perspective', *Journal of Applied Psychology*, 90(5), pp. 1011–17.

Thompson, J. D. (1967) *Organizations in Action*, New York: McGraw-Hill.

Thompson, P. (1981) 'Class, work and the labour process in Marxism and sociology: a survey and evaluation', Unpublished PhD thesis, Liverpool University.

Thompson, P. (1989) *The Nature of Work* (2nd edn), London: Macmillan.

Thompson, P. (1993) 'Fatal distraction: postmodernism and organizational theory', in J. Hassard and M. Parker (eds), *Postmodernism and Organizations*, London: Sage.

Thompson, P. (2003) 'Disconnected capitalism: or why employers can't keep their side of the bargain', *Work, Employment and Society*, 17(2), pp. 359–78.

Thompson, P. and Findley, T. (1994) 'Changing the people: social engineering in the contemporary workplace', in A. Sayer and L. Ray (eds), *Culture and Economy after the Cultural Turn*, London: Sage.

Thompson, P. and Harley B. (2008) 'HRM and the worker: labour process perspectives', pp. 147–65 in P. Boxall, J. Purcell and P. Wright (eds), *The Oxford Handbook of Human Resource Management*, Oxford: Oxford University Press.

Thompson, P. and McHugh, D. (2002) *Work Organisations* (3rd edn), Basingstoke: Palgrave Macmillan.

Thompson, P. and McHugh, D. (2009) *Work Organisations: A Critical Approach* (4th edn), Basingstoke: Palgrave Macmillan.

Thompson, P. and Wallace, T. (1996) 'Redesigning production through teamworking', *International Journal of Operations and Production Management*, 16(2), pp. 103–18.

Thompson, W. R. (1999) 'Diversity among managers translates into profitability', *HR Magazine*, April, p. 10.

Thorndike, E. L. (1913) *The Psychology of Learning*, New York: Teachers' College.

Thornton, R. and Lunt, N. (1997) *Employment Policies for Disabled People in Eighteen Countries: A Review*, York: University of York Policy Research Unit.

Thun, E. (2011) 'The globalization of production', pp. 283–304 in J. Ravenhill (ed.), *Global Political Economy* (4th edn), Oxford: Oxford University Press.

Tichy, N. and Sherman, S. (1993) *Control Your Destiny or Someone Else Will*, New York: Doubleday.

Tichy, N. M. and Devanna, M. A. (1990) *The Transformational Leader* (updated edn), New York: John Wiley & Sons.

Tinker, T. (2002) 'Spectres of Marx and Braverman in the twilight of postmodernist labour process research', *Work, Employment and Society*, 16(2), pp. 251–81.

Tisdell, E. (1993) 'Feminism and adult learning: power, pedagogy and praxis', pp. 91–103 in S. Merriam (ed.), *An Update on Adult Learning Theory*, San Francisco, CA: Jossey-Bass.

Tjosvold, D. (2008) 'The conflict-positive organization: it depends on us', *Journal of Organizational Behaviour*, 29(1), pp. 19–28.

Toffler, A. (1970) *Future Shock*, London: Random House.

Tong, R. P. (1998) *Feminist Thought* (2nd edn), Boulder, CO: Westview Press.

Top, M., Akdere, M. and Tarcan, M. (2015) 'Examining transformational leadership, job satisfaction, organizational commitment and organizational trust in Turkish hospitals: public servants versus private sector employees', *International Journal of Human Resource Management*, 26(9), pp. 1259–82.

Touraine, A. (1971) *The Post-Industrial Society: Tomorrow's Social History: Classes, Conflicts and Culture in the Programmed Society*, New York: Random House.

Tourish, D. and Vatcha, N. (2005) 'Charismatic leadership and corporate cultism at Enron: the elimination of dissent, the promotion of conformity and organizational collapse', *Leadership*, 1(4), pp. 455–80.

Townley, B. (1994) *Reframing Human Resource Management: Power, Ethics and the Subject of Work*, London: Sage.

Toynbee, P. (2015) 'Who dares confront Jeremy Hunt, NHS bully-in-chief', *The Guardian*, February 17, p. 31.

Treanor, J. (2013) 'It's so unfair: why £4m a year just isn't enough for a banker', *The Guardian*, November 12, p. 1.

Treanor, J. (2014a) 'Barclays condemned over £2.4bn bonuses', *The Guardian*, February 11, p. 19. Available at: www.theguardian.com/business/2014/feb/11/barclays-hikes-bonuses-profits-slide (accessed March 25, 2014).

Treanor, J. (2014b) 'Osborne under pressure as bonuses surge to £35m at bailed-out banks', *The Guardian*, March 7. Available at: www.theguardian.com/business/2014/mar/07/bailed-banks-rbs-lloyds-management-team-bosses-bonus-payouts-35m/ (accessed March 20, 2015).

Treanor, J. and Farrell, S. (2014) 'London's super-rich dominate as UK leads G7 economies for inequality', *The Guardian*, October 15, p. 8.

Trehan, K. and Pedler, M. (2009) 'Animating critical action learning: process-based leadership and management development', *Action Learning: Research and Practice*, 6(1), pp. 35–49.

Trevino, L. K. (1986) 'Ethical decision making in organizations: a person-situation interactionist model', *Academy of Management Review*, July 11, pp. 601–17.

Tsoukas, H. and Chia, R. (2002) 'On organizational becoming: rethinking organizational change', *Organization Science*, 13, pp. 567–82.

Tubbs, M. E. (1986) 'Goal-setting: a meta-analytic examination of the empirical evidence', *Journal of Applied Psychology*, 71, pp. 474–83.

Tucker, K. H. (2002) *Classical Social Theory*, Oxford: Blackwell.

Tuckman, B. and Jensen, M. (1977) 'Stages of small group development revisited', *Group and Organization Management*, 2, pp. 419–27.

Tumulty, B. (2014) 'Feds plan new rail oil tanker safety standards', *Poughkeepsie Journal*, April 26. Available at: www.poughkeepsiejournal.com/story/news/local/new-york/2014/04/26/crude-oil-train-transport-rules/8227751/ (accessed February 23, 2015).

Turnbull, P. (1986) 'The Japanisation of British industrial relations at Lucas', *Industrial Relations Journal*, 17(3), pp. 193–206.

Turner, A. N. and Lawrence, P. R. (1965) *Industrial Jobs and the Worker*, Boston, MA: Harvard University, Graduate School of Business Administration.

Turner, H. A. (1962) *Trade Union Growth, Structure and Policy: A Comparative Study of the Cotton Unions*, London: Allen & Unwin.

Turner, J. H. (2009) 'The sociology of emotions: basic theoretical arguments', *Emotion Review*, 1(4), pp. 340–54.

Tyler, M. and Wilkinson, A. (2007) 'The tyranny of corporate slenderness: "corporate anorexia" as a metaphor for our age', *Work, Employment and Society*, 21(3), pp. 537–49.

Tyler, T. (1990) *Why People Obey the Law: Procedural Justice, Legitimacy and Compliance*, New Haven, CT: Yale University Press.

Tynjälä, P. (2008) 'Perspectives into learning at the workplace', *Educational Research Review*, 3(2), pp. 130–54.

Ulrich, L. and Trumbo, D. (1965) 'The selection interview since 1949', *Psychological Bulletin*, 63, pp. 100–16.

United Nations (2007) *The Employment Imperative: Report on the World Social Situation 2007*, New York: United Nations Department of Economic and Social Affairs.

US Bureau of Labor Statistics (2002) 'Employment and earnings'. Available at: www.bls.gov/cps/home.htm.

Vaili, P. B. (1996) *Learning as a Way of Being*, San Francisco, CA: Jossey-Bass.

Vallas, S. (1999) 'Re-thinking post-Fordism: the meaning of workplace flexibility', *Sociological Theory*, 17(1), pp. 68–85.

Vallerand, R. J. (1997) 'Toward a hierarchical model of intrinsic and extrinsic motivation', *Advances in Experimental Social Psychology*, 29, pp. 271–360.

VandenHeuvel, A. and Wooden, M. (1997) 'Participation of non-English-speaking-background immigrants in work-related training', *Ethnic and Racial Studies*, 20(4), pp. 830–48.

Vandercammen, L., Hofman, J. and Theuns, P. (2014) 'The mediating role of affect in the relationship between need satisfaction and autonomous motivation', *Journal of Occupational and Organizational Psychology*, 87, pp. 62–79.

Van de Vliert, E., Van Yperen, N. W. and Thierry, H. (2008) 'Are wages more important for employees in poorer countries with harsher climates?', *Journal of Organizational Behavior*, 29, pp. 79–94.

van Dick, R., van Knippenburg, D., Hagele, S., Guillaume, Y. R. F. and Brodbeck, F. (2008) 'Group diversity and group identification: the moderating role of diversity beliefs', *Human Relations*, 61(10), pp. 1463–92.

Van Ruysseveldt, J. and Van Dijke, M. (2011) 'When are workload and workplace opportunities related in a curvilinear manner? The moderating role of autonomy', *Journal of Vocational Behavior*, 79(2), pp. 470–83.

Van Wanrooy, B., Bewley, H., Bryson, A. et al. (2013) *The 2011 Workplace Employment Relations Study (First Findings)*, London: ESRC/ACAS/NIESR/Department of Business, Innovation and Skills. Available at: https://www.gov.uk/government/uploads/system/uploads/attachment_data/file/210103/13-1010-WERS-first-findings-report-third-edition-may-2013.pdf (accessed March 20, 2015).

Varela, O. E., Burke, M. J. and Landis, R. S. (2008) 'A model of emergence and dysfunctional effects of emotional conflicts in groups', *Group Dynamics: Theory, Research and Practice*, 12(2), pp. 112–26.

Vecchio, R. P. (1987) 'Situational leadership theory: an examination of a prescriptive theory', *Journal of Applied Psychology*, 72, pp. 444–51.

Vecchio, R. P., Hearn, G. and Southey, G. (1996) *Organizational Behaviour*, Sydney: Harcourt Brace.

Verma, A. and Taras, D. (2005) 'Managing the high-involvement workplace', pp. 134–73 in M. Gunderson, A. Ponak and D. Taras (eds), *Union–Management Relations in Canada* (5th edn), Toronto: Addison Wesley.

Verma, S. (2009) 'From the Bronx to the top court in the land: the American dream comes true', *Globe and Mail*, May 27, p. A11.

Verstegen, R. L. and Rutherford, M. A. (2000) 'Mary Parker Follett: individualist or collectivist? Or both?', *Journal of Management History*, 5, pp. 207–23.

Vick, K. (2014) 'Qatar bribery allegations loom over the 2022 World Cup', *Time*, June 5. Available at: http://time.com/2822288/qatar-world-cup-bribery/ (accessed February 16, 2015).

Vosko, L. (2000) *Temporary Work: The Gendered Rise of a Precarious Employment Relationship*, Toronto: University of Toronto Press.

Vosko, L. (2006) 'Precarious employment: towards an improved understanding of labour market insecurity', in L. Vosko (ed.), *Precarious Employment: Understanding Labour Market Insecurity in Canada*, Montreal: McGill-Queen's University Press.

Vroom, V. H. (1964) *Work and Motivation*, New York: John Wiley & Sons.

Vygotsky, L. (1978) *Mind in Society: The Development of Higher Psychological Processes*, Cambridge, MA: Harvard University Press.

Wajcman, J. (1998) *Managing Like a Man: Women and Men in Corporate Management*, Cambridge, MA: Polity Press/Penn State University Press.

Waldron, T. (2013) 'FIFA president admits political, economic interests drive Qatar World Cup selection', *Think Progress*, September 18. Available at: http://thinkprogress.org/sports/2013/09/18/2641651/fifa-president-tune-admits-european-economic-interests-drove-qatar-world-cup-selection/ (accessed February 16, 2015).

Walker, J. T. (1996) *The Psychology of Learning*, Englewood Cliffs, NJ: Prentice Hall.

Wallace, M. and Kalleberg, A. (1982) 'Industrial transformation and the decline of craft: the decomposition of skill in the printing industry, 1931–1978', *American Sociological Review*, 47, pp. 307–24.

Walters, A., Stuhlmacher, A. and Meyer, L. (1998) 'Gender and negotiator competitiveness: a meta-analysis', *Organizational Behavior and Human Decision Processes*, 76(1), pp. 1–29.

Walton, R. (1985) 'From control to commitment in the workplace', *Harvard Business Review*, March/April, pp. 77–84.

Walton, R. E. and McKersie, R. B. (1965) *A Behavioral Theory of Labor Relations*, New York: McGraw-Hill.

Wang, C. L. and Rafiq, M. (2014) 'Ambidextrous organizational culture, contextual ambidexterity and new product innovation: a comparative study of UK and Chinese high-tech firms', *British Journal of Management*, 25, pp. 58–76.

Wapshott, N. (2011) *Keynes and Hayek: The Clash That Defined Modern Economics*, New York: Norton.

Ward, A. (2014) 'How Pfizer snatched defeat from victory', *Financial Times*, May 24/25, p. 15.

Ward, L. (1998) 'Ethnic minorities pessimistic over race relations', *Guardian*, September 10.

Warhurst, C. and Nickson, D. (2007), 'A new labour aristocracy? Aesthetic labour and routine interactive service', *Work, Employment and Society*, 21(4), pp. 785–98.

Warhurst, C., Eikhof, D. R. and Haunschild, A. (2008) *Work Less, Live More?*, Basingstoke: Palgrave Macmillan.

Warr, P. (2008) 'Work values: some demographic and cultural correlates', *Journal of Occupational and Organizational Psychology*, 81, pp. 751–75.

Warr, P. B. (ed.) (2002) *Psychology at Work* (5th edn), London: Penguin.

Warren, D. I. (1968) 'Power, visibility, and conformity in formal organizations', *American Sociological Review*, 6, pp. 951–70.

Warrick, D. D. (1984) *Managing Organizational Change and Development*, New York: Science Research.

Watkins, K. E. and Cervero, R. M. (2000) 'Organizations as contexts for learning: a case study in certified public accountancy', *Journal of Workplace Learning*, 12(5), pp. 187–94.

Watkins, K. and Marsick, V. (1993) *Sculpting the Learning Organization*, San Francisco, CA: Jossey-Bass.

Watson, D. and Clark, L. A. (1994) 'The PANAS-X: Manual for positive and negative affect schedule', Unpublished manuscript, University of Iowa, quoted by Eysenck, M. W. (2009) *Fundamentals of Psychology*, Hove: Psychology Press, p. 77.

Watson, T. (1986) *Management, Organization and Employment Strategy*, London: Routledge.

Watson, T. J. (2010) 'Critical social science, pragmatism and the realities of HRM', *International Journal of Human Resource Management Studies*, 21(6), pp. 915–31.

Watts, J. H. (2007) 'Porn, pride and pessimism: experiences of women working in professional construction roles', *Work, Employment and Society*, 21(2), pp. 299–316.

Weber, M. (1905/2002) *The Protestant Ethic and the 'Spirit' of Capitalism*, London: Penguin.

Weber, M. (1922/1968) *Economy and Society*, Los Angeles: University of California Press.

Weber, M. (1927/2003) *General Economic History*, New York: Dover.

Weber, M. (1949) *The Methodology of the Social Sciences* (trans. E. Shils and H. Finch), Glencoe, IL: Free Press.

Weber, M. (1978) *Economy and Society*, New York: Bedminster.

Weick, C. E. (1979) 'Cognitive processes in organizations', in B. W. Staw (ed.), *Research in Organizational Behaviour*, Greenwich, CT: JA Press, quoted in J. Hayes (2014) *The Theory and Practice of Change Management*, Basingstoke: Palgrave Macmillan, pp. 504–5.

Weick, K. (1979) *The Social Psychology of Organizing* (2nd edn), New York: McGraw-Hill.

Weick, K. (2000) 'Emergent change as a universal in organizations', in M. Beer and N. Nohria (eds.), *Breaking the Code of Change*, Boston, MA: Harvard Business School Press.

Weick, K. and Quinn, R. E. (1999) 'Organizational change and development', *Annual Review of Psychology*, 50, pp. 361–86.

Weick, K. E. (1995) *Sensemaking in Organizations*, London: Sage.

Weick, K. E. (2001) *Making Sense of the Organization*, Oxford: Blackwell.

Weiner, N. and Mahoney, T. A. (1981) 'A model of corporate performance as a function of environment, organization and leadership influences', *Academy of Management Journal*, 24, pp. 453–70.

Weir, F. (2005) 'For Moscow's businesswomen, a powerful new role', *Christian Science Monitor*. Available at: www.csmonitor.com/2005/0308/p07s01-woeu.html (accessed October 2, 2009).

Wells, D. (1993) 'Are strong unions compatible with the new model of human resource management?', *Relations Industrielles/Industrial Relations*, 48(1), pp. 56–84.

Wenger, E. (1998) *Cultivating Communities of Practice*, New York: Cambridge University Press.

Wenger, E. (2000) 'Communities of practice and social learning systems', *Organization*, 7(2), pp. 225–46.

Wenger, E., McDermott, R. and Snyder, W. (2002) *Cultivating Communities of Practice*, Boston, MA: Harvard Business School Press.

West, M. A. and Dawson, J. F. (2012) *Employee Engagement and NHS Performance*, London: King's Fund.

Western, S. (2013) *Leadership: A Critical Text*, London: Sage.

Whipp, R. and Clark, P. (1986) *Innovation and the Auto Industry*, London: Francis Pinter.

Whiteley, A., Price, C. and Palmer, R. (2013) 'Corporate culture change: adaptive culture structuration and negotiated practice', *Journal of Workplace Learning*, 25(7), pp. 476–98.

Wicken, P. (1987) *The Road to Nissan*, London: Macmillan.

Wiener, N. (1954) *The Human Use of Human Beings: Cybernetics and Society*, New York: Avon.

Wild, J. (2014) 'Electric buses steal march on diesel', *Financial Times*, January 9, p. 19.

Wilk, S. and Cappelli, P. (2003) 'Understanding the determinants of employer use of selection methods', *Personnel Psychology*, 57, pp. 103–24.

Wilkinson, B. (1983) *The Shopfloor Politics of New Technology*, London: Heinemann.

Wilkinson, R. and Pickett, K. (2010) *The Spirit Level: Why Equality is Better for Everyone*, London: Penguin.

Williams, R. (1977) *Marxism and Literature*, Oxford: Oxford University Press.

Williams, R. (1983) *Key Words* (rev. edn), New York: Oxford University Press.

Williams, R. and Edge, D. (1996) 'The social shaping of technology', *Research Policy*, 25, pp. 856–99.

Williams, S., Bradley, H., Devadason, R., and Erickson, M. (2013) *Globalization and Work*, Cambridge: Polity Press.

Williamson, M. (2015) 'Union fears over major North Sea pay cuts', *The Herald*, January 2. Available at: www.heraldscotland.com/news/home-news/union-fears-over-major-north-sea-pay-cuts.1420110167 (accessed January 2, 2015).

Willmott, H. (1989) 'Images and ideals of managerial work', *Journal of Management Studies*, 21(3), pp. 349–68.

Willmott, H. (1993) 'Strength in ignorance, slavery is freedom: managing culture in modern organizations', *Journal of Management Studies*, 30(4), pp. 515–52.

Willmott, H. (1995) 'The odd couple?: re-engineering business processes: managing human relations', *New/Technology, Work and Employment*, 10(2), pp. 89–98.

Wilson, A. (1997) 'Business and its social responsibility', in P. W. F. Davies (ed.), *Current Issues in Business Ethics*, London: Routledge.

Wilson, A. L. (1993) 'The promise of situated cognition', pp. 71–9 in S. Merriam (ed.), *An Update on Adult Learning Theory*, No. 57, San Francisco, CA: Jossey-Bass.

Wilson, F. M. (1992) 'Language, power and technology', *Human Relations*, 45(9), pp. 883–904.

Wilson, F. M. (2003) *Organizational Behaviour and Gender*, Aldershot: Ashgate.

Winquist, J. and Franz, T. (2008) 'Does the stepladder technique improve group decision making? A series of failed replications', *Group Dynamics: Theory, Research and Practice*, 12(4), pp. 255–67.

Winstanley, D. and Woodall, J. (eds) (2000) *Ethical Issues in Contemporary Human Resource Management*, Basingstoke: Palgrave Macmillan.

Wintour, P. (2014) 'Miliband vows to fix 'broken' British banks', *The Guardian*, January 17, p. 4.

Witherspoon, P. D. (1997) *Communicating Leadership: An Organizational Perspective*, Needham Heights, MA: Allyn & Bacon.

Witz, A. (1986) 'Patriarchy and the labour market: occupational control strategies and the medical division of labour', in D. Knights and H. Willmott (eds), *Gender and the Labour Process*, Aldershot: Gower.

Witzel, M. (2012) *A History of Management Thought*, Abingdon, Oxon: Routledge.

Wofford, J. C. and Liska, L. Z. (1993) 'Path–goal theories of leaderships meta-analysis', *Journal of Management*, 19, pp. 858–76.

Womack, J., Jones, D. and Roos, D. (1990) *The Machine that Changed the World*, New York: Rawson Associates.

Wood, D. J., Bruner, J. and Ross, G. (1976) 'The role of tutoring in problem solving', *Journal of Child Psychology and Psychiatry*, 17, pp. 89–100.

Wood, M. and Case, P. (2006) 'Leadership refrains – again, again and again', *Leadership*, 1(2), pp. 139–45.

Wood, S. (ed.) (1982) *The Transformation of Work?*, London: Unwin Hyman.

Wood, Z. (2014) 'Pfizer's bid for AstraZeneca under scrutiny', *The Guardian*, May 6, p. 17.

Woodruffe, C. (2001) 'Promotional intelligence', *People Management*, January 11, pp. 26–9.

Woodward, J. (1958) *Management and Technology*. Problems of Progress in Industry No. 5, London: HMSO.

Woodward, J. (1965) *Industrial Organizations: Theory and Practice*, London: Oxford University Press.

Wright, E. O. (1997) *Class Counts: Comparative Studies in Class Analysis*, Cambridge: Cambridge University Press.

Wright, L. (2014) 'Labour, skills shortage in Canada? Budget watchdog says no', *Saskatoon Star-Phoenix*, March 25. Available at: www.thestar.com/business/2014/03/25/labour_skills_shortage_in_canada_budget_watchdog_says_no.html (accessed January 20, 2015).

Wright, P. and Gardner, T. (2003) 'The human resource-firm performance relationship: methodological and theoretical challenges', in D. Holman, T. Wall, C. Clegg, P. Sparrow, and A. Howard (eds.), *The New Workplace: A Guide to the Human Impact of Modern Work Practices*, London: John Wiley & Sons.

Wright Mills, C. (1959/2000) *The Sociological Imagination* (40th anniversary edn), New York: Oxford University Press.

Wrong, D. H. (1979) *Power: Its Forms, Bases, and Uses*, Oxford: Wiley-Blackwell.

Xenikou, A. and Furnham, A. (2013) *Group Dynamics and Organizational Culture*, Basingstoke: Palgrave Macmillan.

Yakabuski, K. (2008) 'The kindness of corporations', *Report on Business*, July–August, pp. 66–71.

Yeatts, D. E. and Hyten, C. (1998) *High-performing Self-managed Work Teams*, Thousand Oaks, CA: Sage.

Yoder, J. (2002) 'Context matters: understanding tokenism processes and their impact on women's work', *Psychology of Women Quarterly*, 26(1), pp. 1–8.

Yoder, J. and Berendsen, L. (2001) '"Outsider within" the firehouse: African American and white women firefighters', *Psychology of Women Quarterly*, 25(1), pp. 27–36.

Young, R. A. and Chen, C. P. (1999) 'Annual review: practice and research in career counselling and development – 1998', *Career Development Quarterly*, December, p. 98.

Yukl, G. (2013) *Leadership in Organizations* (8th edn), Harlow: Pearson Education.

Yuval-Davis, N. (1997) *Cultural Reproductions and Gender Relations: Gender and Nation*, London: Sage.

Zammuto, R. F. (1982) *Assessing Organizational Effectiveness*, Albany, NY: State University of New York Press.

Zimbalist, A. (ed.) (1979) *Case Studies on the Labor Process*, New York: Monthly Review Press.

Zimbardo, P. (2008) BBC *Hardtalk* interview, April 22, 2008.

Žižek, S. (2014) 'Rule by brute market force', *The Guardian*, July 14, p. 25.

Zohar, D. and Tenne-Gazit, O. (2008) 'Transformational leadership and group interaction as climate antecedents: a social network analysis', *Journal of Applied Psychology*, 93(4), pp. 744–57.

Zuboff, S. (1988) *In the Age of the Smart Machine: The Future of Work and Power*, New York: Basic Books.

Zweig, J. (2008) *Your Money and Your Brain*, New York: Simon Schuster.

Index of personal names

Subject index